A Companion to the
Confessions of St. Augustine

PETER LANG
New York • Washington, D.C./Baltimore • Bern
Frankfurt am Main • Berlin • Brussels • Vienna • Oxford

John M. Quinn, OSA

A Companion to the
Confessions of St. Augustine

PETER LANG
New York • Washington, D.C./Baltimore • Bern
Frankfurt am Main • Berlin • Brussels • Vienna • Oxford

Library of Congress Cataloging-in-Publication Data

Quinn, John M.
A companion to the confessions of St. Augustine / John M. Quinn.
p. cm.
Includes bibliographical references and index.
1. Augustine, Saint, Bishop of Hippo. Confessions.
2. Christian saints—Algeria—Hippo (Extinct city) —Biography. I. Title.
BR65.A62 Q56   270.2'092—dc21   2002013061
ISBN 0-8204-2406-4

Die Deutsche Bibliothek-CIP-Einheitsaufnahme

Quinn, John M.:
A companion to the confessions of St. Augustine / John M. Quinn, OSA.
–New York; Washington, D.C./Baltimore; Bern;
Frankfurt am Main; Berlin; Brussels; Vienna; Oxford: Lang.
ISBN 0-8204-2406-4

Cover design by Dutton & Sherman Design

The paper in this book meets the guidelines for permanence and durability
of the Committee on Production Guidelines for Book Longevity
of the Council of Library Resources.

© 2002 Peter Lang Publishing, Inc., New York
275 Seventh Avenue, 28th Floor, New York, NY 10001
www.peterlangusa.com

Printed in the United States of America

In Memory
of
My Mother and Father

Contents

Preface

Some years ago during a trip to Italy with fellow Augustinians I was struck by the enthusiasm of one of our Italian guides, an Augustinian seminarian, when he commented that he had read from start to finish the *Confessions* no less than five times. Apparently what had fired and firmed his zeal was the pronounced spiritual character of the work in which the soul colloquying with God lends its ears to the Lord's direct and indirect responses. Spirituality is undoubtedly one main reason why the *Confessions* has enjoyed, scholars show, an enduring, indeed a perennial appeal throughout sixteen centuries, from the High Middle Ages to the Renaissance and the sixteenth-century Spanish mystics and Bossuet in the seventeenth century, then with a literary accent in the nineteenth century, with interest still unflagging throughout the twentieth century and into the present as well. Yet it is not diminishing the devotional motif to also focus on an exegesis that probes key ingredients in each section. The pages the reader holds in his hands modestly ambition to furnish such an analysis. Surely other works have addressed various problems in the *Confessions*, but, as far as I know, none has ventured a roughly point-by-point commentary on all chapters. Hence the title: a *Companion*, an intellectual partner enabling one to make headway through the underbrush as well as the more open pathways of Augustine's masterpiece.

Since the field of Augustinian scholarship is immense and literature on the *Confessions* vast, no one can take a single step forward in the study of Augustine without dependence on predecessors, whose insights are gratefully recognized in the notes within. In particular, I wish to express thanks to colleagues in the Augustinian Historical Institute, Karl Gersbach, OSA, Joseph C. Schnaubelt, OSA, and Professor Frederick Van Fleteren. I am grateful to John E. Bresnahan, OSA, for his support. I owe a special debt of gratitude to Sister Mary Clark, RSCJ, for her thorough, constructive-critical appraisal of the manuscript. A word of appreciation is due also to deceased confreres, Robert Russell, OSA, and John Gavigan, OSA, whose scholarly accomplishments have served as a model.

The dedication to my mother and father is proffered in the spirit of Augustine's own farewell to his parents at the close of Book 9: to "my parents in this transient light and my brethren under you, Father, in our mother the Catholic Church, my fellow citizens in the eternal Jerusalem for which your pilgrim people sigh from their departure until their return."

Abbreviations

Works of Augustine

AC	*De agone christiano*
AdC	*De adulterinis conjugiis*
AO	*De anima et ejus origine*
Bap	*De baptismo*
BJ	*De bono conjugali*
Bonvid	*De bono viduitatis*
BV	*De beata vita*
CA	*Contra Academicos*
C Adim	*Contra Adimantum*
CALP	*Contra litteras Petiliani Donatistae*
C Cresc	*Contra Cresconium*
CD	*De civitate Dei*
CDEP	*Contra duas epistulas Pelagii*
C Don	*Contra Donatum*
CE	*De consensu Evangelistarum*
CEF	*Contra Epistulam quam vocant Fundamenti*
CF	*Contra Faustum Manichaeum*
CG	*De correptione et gratia*
CJ	*Contra Julianum*
CJOI	*Contra Julianum opus imperfectum*
C Max	*Contra Maximum*
Cont	*De continentia*
CR	*De catechizandis rudibus*
C s arr	*Contra sermonem Arrianorum*
C Sec	*Contra Secundinem*
Dial	*De dialectica*
DA	*De duabus animabus contra Manichaeos*
DC	*De doctrina christiana*
DP	*De dono perseverantiae*
DQ	*De diversis quaestionibus LXXXIII*
E	*Epistulae*
EJ	*In epistulam Johannis ad Parthos*
EN	*Enchiridion*
ExR	*Expositio quarundam propositionum ex Epistola ad Romanos*
Fel	*Contra Felicem*

Fort	*Contra Fortunatum*
FQNV	*De fide rerum quae non videntur*
FS	*De fide et symbolo*
GC	*De gratia Christi*
GCM	*De Genesi contra Manichaeos*
GI	*De Genesi ad litteram liber imperfectus*
GL	*De Genesi ad litteram*
GLA	*De gratia et libero arbitrio*
H	*De haeresibus*
Imm	*De immortalitate animae*
J	*In Johannis Evangelium tractatus*
LA	*De libero arbitrio*
M	*De musica*
Mag	*De magistro*
ME	*De moribus ecclesiae catholicae*
MM	*De moribus Manichaeorum*
NB	*De natura boni contra Manichaeos*
NC	*De nuptiis et concupiscentia*
NG	*De natura et gratia*
O	*De ordine*
OM	*De opere monachorum*
Oros	*Ad Orosium contra Priscillianistas et Origenistas*
P	*Enarrationes in Psalmos*
Parm	*Contra Epistulam Parmeniani*
PJ	*De perfectione justitiae hominis*
PMR	*De peccatorum meritis et remissione*
PS	*De praedestinatione sanctorum*
QA	*De quantitate animae*
QH	*Quaestiones in Heptateuchum*
QS	*De diversis quaestionibus VII ad Simplicianum*
R	*Retractationes*
S	*Sermones*
SDM	*De sermone Domini in monte*
SL	*De spiritu et littera*
Sol	*Soliloquia*
SV	*De sancta virginitate*
Sym ad cat	*De symbolo ad catechumenos*
T	*De Trinitate*
UB	*De unico baptismo*
UC	*De utilitate credendi*

| UJ | *De utilitate jejunii* |
| VR | *De vera religione* |

Confessiones is cited only numerically according to book, chapter, and section.

Other Abbreviations

AE	*Augustine through the Ages An Encyclopedia*
AL	*Augustinus-Lexikon*
AM	*Augustinus Magister*
AS	*Augustinian Studies*
Atti	*Congresso internazionale su s. Agostino nel XVI Centenario della conversione (Roma, 1986), Atti (Roma, 1987)*
AUG	*Augustinianum*
AUG(L)	*Augustiniana*
AUGS	*Augustinus*
BA	*Bibliothèque Augustinienne*
CAH	*Die Confessiones des Augustinus von Hippo*
CC	*Corpus Christianorum*
CollAug	*Collectanea Augustiniana*
CSEL	*Corpus Scriptorum Ecclesiasticorum Latinorum*
DG	*Doxagraphi Graeci*
DTC	*Dictionnaire de Théologie Catholique*
GM	*Giornale di Metafisica*
LASAP	*Lectio Augustini-Settimana Agostiniana Pavese*
ML	*Migne, Patrologia Latina*
NS	*New Scholasticism*
OCD	*Oxford Classical Dictionary*
RA	*Recherches Augustiniennes*
REA	*Revue des Études Augustiniennes*

Significant Works

Brown	P. Brown, *Augustine of Hippo*
Bonner	G. Bonner, *St. Augustine of Hippo: Life and Controversies*
Courcelle	P. Courcelle, *Recherches sur les Confessions de saint Augustin*

Coyle	J.K. Coyle, *St. Augustine's De Moribus Ecclesiae Catholicae*
D	J. O'Donnell, *Augustine Confessions*
G-M	J. Gibb and W. Montgomery, *The Confessions of Augustine*
HC	H. Chadwick, *St. Augustine Confessions*
James	W. James, *The Principles of Psychology*
Marrou	H.-I. Marrou, *Saint Augustin et la fin de la culture antique*
O'D	G. O'Daly, *Augustine's Philosophy of Mind*
O'Meara	J. O'Meara, *The Young Augustine*
Pope	H. Pope, *St. Augustine of Hippo*
Pontet	M. Pontet, *L'éxegèse de saint Augustin prédicateur*
Starnes	C. Starnes, *Augustine's Conversion*
TeSelle	E. TeSelle, *Augustine the Theologian*
Van der Meer	F. Van der Meer, *Augustine the Bishop*
V	Possidio, *Vita di S. Agostino*

Principal Dates

Events Recorded in the *Confessions*

354   Born November 13, in Thagaste, Numidia Proconsularis, son of Patricius and Monica.

361   Pupil in Thagaste

c.367-9   Studies in Madauros.

369-0   Year of idleness at home

c.370-1   Death of Patricius.

370   Autumn, student in Carthage.

372-3   Birth of his son Adeodatus. Reads Cicero's *Hortensius*. Becomes a Manichean hearer.

374   Conducts school at Thagaste.

376   Autumn, returns to Carthage, opens a school.

375   Death of friend

380-1   *De pulchro et apto*, first published work.

382-3   Doubts concerning Manicheism.

383   Summer, voyage to Rome.

383   Autumn, opens school of rhetoric in Rome. Struggles with skepticism.

384   Professor of rhetoric in Milan. First Influence of St. Ambrose.

385   Second period of St. Ambrose's influence.

386   May, June, reads the books of the Platonists.

386   August, moral conversion in garden in Milan.

386   Resigns chair of rhetoric.

386-7   Sojourn at Cassiaciacum.

387   April 24, Holy Saturday, baptized, together with Adeodatus, at Milan.

387   Autumn, death of Monica at Ostia.

Later Events

388   Returns to Africa.

389-90   Death of Adeodatus at Thagaste.

391   Ordained priest at Hippo.

395   Ordained bishop, assistant to Valerius, Bishop of Hippo.

Introduction

The *Confessions* is generally esteemed a literary, spiritual, and philosophico-theological classic. Unlike some others hailed as masterworks, it continues to appeal to a considerable audience, especially to Christians, for most of whom it is essentially the story of the conversion of Augustine, a transition from darkness to light, from sin to grace, from the exterior to the interior self. Hence the title, which conveys a twofold meaning, first, praise of God, then, confession of sins. In brief, the *Confessions* praises God for the healing of sins confessed.[1] Like most classics indited by outstanding minds, it does not deliver all its secrets in one effortless cover-to-cover sitting. While intrinsically pellucid, its interpretation is hardly uncumbered by difficulties. Overall unity remains a nagging question. Again, it is an autobiography distinct from modern kin. Moreover, only when conjoined with ideationally affiliated texts does this masterpiece yield more sense. Finally, historicity, though its battles lie largely in the past, merits a word or two.

Composed, it is generally held between 397-401,[2] the work no doubt exhibits a broad unity. According to the greater majority of scholars, Books 1-9, the account of conversion, form a first part, Book 10, a present examen of conscience, a second part, and Book 11-3, an exegesis of Genesis 1, a third part.[3] The first part is ordinarily subdivided: Books 1-4 deal with moral failings and intellectual mistakes; Book 5 records the beginning of disenchantment with Manicheism; Books 7 and 8 retail intellectual and moral conversion.[4] Problems arise, however, in trying to integrate Books 11-3 with the first ten. One initially promising approach bases itself on the three ways of knowing time: memory, intuition, and expectation (11.29.39). The first part, Books 1-9, concerned with Augustine's past, corresponds to memory; the second part, Book 10, which meditates on his current spiritual condition, coincides with intuition or attention to the present; the third part, Book 11-3, focused on Genesis, jibes with the expectation of the future or the eternal life to come.[5] Unhappily, this neat tri-parallelism breaks down at its third stage. Though Book 11 analyzes the meaning of eternity and Book 13 ends with reflections on the eternal Sabbath without evening, the exegesis of Genesis 1.1-31 cannot serve as an explicit or implicit expectation of the world to come. Some detect a trinitarian structure, Books 1-9 directed to the Father, Book 10 to the Son, and Books 11-3 to the Spirit.[6] However, evidence for such a division seems less than compelling. Some scholars locate unity in the notion of confession itself. For H. Böhmer, confession includes admission of sin and praise, with broader significations including confession of faith and narration. J. Ratzinger accents doing the truth and coming to the light (10.1.1), with recognition of human sinfulness in the perspective of divine sovereignty. According to G. Pfligersdorfer, confession of knowledge is quite important; it runs through Book 11-3 and, in particular, from 10.10.8.38 to 10.39.64. All of these distinctions, however broadly helpful, fail to specify how confession is operating in Books 11-3.[7] For another opinion, the first nine books highlight redemption, Book 10 dwells on sanctification, and Books 11-3 focus on creative activity.[8] It is, however, not easy to see why creation should follow upon the other two divine actions. Apparently somewhat more attractive is the view that after Books 1-9 recount Augustine's life, Book 10 examines his moral condition, and Books 11-3 expose his theological stance.[9] Yet Genesis 1.1-31 is a contracted framework for delineating a theological outlook; so the unanswered question remains: why does this portion of Genesis serve as a format for such exposition? One striking interpretation with historical roots claims that the work is a Christian protreptic.[10] As is well known, Aristotle, Cicero (in *Hortensius*, which significantly influenced Augustine, 3.4.7-8), and Iamblichus, among others, authored a protreptic, which is an exhortation to a new and higher plane of thought or way of life. The *Confessions* aims at exciting hearts to know and love the God who is *magnus dominus*, "the great Lord"(1.1.1). The protreptic deals with the life (Books 1-9), wisdom (Book 10), and Scripture (Book 11-3). Along with the other parts, the life does function as an instrument of protreptic strategy. However, the relation is actually the other way around. The protreptical aspect serves as an instrument in the exposition of the life. In general, the protreptic factor is one but not the main element; it is simply not the principal theme or leitmotif. Again, other suggestions for unity are too general or vague. According to one scholar, the unifying theme is the profound awareness of the presence of God in man.[11] For another savant, the sovereign unity of the *Confessions* consists simply in confession itself.[12] Still another scholar maintains that the work emphasizes speaking with God,[13] while leaving unresolved the problem of selecting Genesis for such prayerful conversation. According to another scholar, the unifying notion is the beautiful.[14] A notably different tack is taken by G. Knauer, who regards the Psalms as conjunctive points that hook up certain chapters and books. Ps 21.27, e.g., at the start of the work (1.1.1) is repeated at the end of Book 10 (10.43.70).[15] However, some of the linkages (such as that between Book 10 and through Psalm 102.3) seem superficial. While the pattern of the work is indicated by certain Psalms, an indication is far from a strict proof.[16] Leaving aside the Knauer hypothesis, we may conclude that none of the views advanced bridge the apparent hiatus between the prior ten and the last three books.

Thus despite multiple and varied solutions the cognitive discontinuity between the last and the earlier books stays unresolved.[17] As other masterpieces such as *The Trinity* and *The City of God* attest, Augustine was sensitive to the need of a recognizable overall unity. Perhaps because the *Confessions* is more of an informal exposition than a treatise, it boasts at best an informal unity, one that writers of late antiquity rated adequate. In this type of work a broad directive idea instead of rigorous development of closely knit notions furnished sufficient unity.[18] It was with this sort of unity that Augustine was satisfied since his *Retractationes* or *Reconsiderations* poses no difficulties on this score.[19] Yet the specific unity that he may have considered unproblematic still escapes the contemporary reader.

An autobiography in the sense that it narrates events of boyhood, puberty, and young manhood, the *Confessions* departs from contemporary counterparts in that it is selective in its reporting of persons and events, skipping items ordinarily not neglected in the common run of autobiographies. Only elsewhere (BV 1.6) are we informed that the date of his birth is November 13, 354. Geographical data also are generally scanty, though he twice mentions (2.3.5; 4.7.12) his hometown Thagaste (now named Souk-Ahras), which belonged to the North African province of Numidia (part of what is now eastern Algeria). We told nothing of the height and other physical characteristics of Patricius and Monica and are left in the dark also about the physical features and voice registers of his friends Alypius and Nebridius. Significantly, as with other individuals, only their moral and spiritual qualities are singled out for attention. In other words, the work is principally a spiritual and intellectual autobiography.[20] It is intellectual: almost from the opening pages it poses the question of the immanence of God. After Book 2 grapples with the apparently purely evil vandalizing of a neighboring pear orchard, Book 3 ponders the meaning of morality in the face of Manichean confusions. Overwhelming grief over the tragic death of a friend in Book 4 leads him to conclude that, in the perspective of unceasing process, friendships cannot endure. Against Manichean rationalism Book 6 forges the link between natural and supernatural faith that provides grounds for reasonable belief. Book 7 recounts how he came to know God not as a Manichean material deity but as truly spiritual, the highest good reconcilable with evil, which is not, as Manichees contend, a positive reality but a privation. The discovery of the nature of God and the authentic meaning of evil is a culminating point, an intellectual breakthrough that opens the door to assent to the redeeming Christ. In Books 10 and 11, outside narrative proper, Augustine analyzes memory and defines time.

Yet the *Confessions* is also a spiritual autobiography, and predominantly so. Its spiritual character may sometimes be somewhat overlooked by scholars eager to dissect and sub-dissect various conceptual strands. Indeed the intellectual thrust is ancillary to its spiritual core. Thus the *Confessions* has been called a dialogue with God,[21] one long prayer to the most high, a much more intricately textured extension of the earlier *Soliloquies.* Hence the story of his conversion is a tale of divine providence highlighting three major themes. First, the Lord is a God of mercy, responding to Augustine's radical misery that is sin. Second, it is mercy constantly operative his whole life long, in every incident, every event, every significant person who crosses his path. Third, this divine action works "in wonderful and hidden ways"(4.4.7; 5.6.10; 7.21.27), especially by drawing good out of evil, by employing the very depths of desolation of the prodigal son to vault him to the embrace of the Father. This spiritual quest reaches its climax in the striking conversion scene in a garden of Milan in 386. As already intimated, a spirit of prayer suffuses the entire work. At various junctures prior to a new phase of inquiry, Augustine invokes the power and light of the all-good Father in what are not perfunctory gestures of routine piety: at every turn he is actually beseeching the Lord for fresh assistance.

The method of exposition adopts to some extent an approach indirectly suggested by E. TeSelle: "The *Confessions* should be read sentence by sentence in the original guided by a detailed commentary" that captures "all its resonances".[22] While the pages that follow by and large attempt to supply what approximates a sentence-by-sentence commentary, they understandably cannot catch all the resonances in every sentence. Constraints of time and talent compel the commentary to fall distant from the exhaustive rendering that TeSelle ideally envisages. To thoroughly carry out what TeSelle's proposal implies, a commentator would have to be equipped with an encyclopedic mastery of all the aspects of Augustine's wide-ranging thought. Since it is well-nigh impossible to furnish a scholarly nuance for every sentence, I have, while simply presenting an adequate sketch of issues raised, concentrated on unpacking Augustine's analysis. Along with always spiritualizing, he is always intelligizing, always reasoning, always arguing, always pursuing the what and why of matter under investigation. Some years back a North American Thomist steeped in Aquinas humbly confided to a student, "Some day we will find out what St. Thomas is saying." Analogously, this commentary tries to find out in modest fashion what Augustine is driving at by laying bare filaments of reasoned discourse in a work that is, broadly speaking, a series of arguments from start to finish. When strict argumentation occurs, the type of argument, whether that of evidence, self-evidence, or syllogistic reasoning, is frequently specified. Since a commentary in which not every line is given an express scholarly gloss runs the risk, it may seem, of lapsing into mere paraphrase, nearly every line scanned, is, as far as possible, in some fashion clarified; in many instances companion lines are elucidated by correlated texts.

This is not to say that all the issues broached are resolved beyond all doubt. The exact makeup of the *libri Platonicorum* seems out of precise reach. In the opinion of some savants, the import of the ostensibly mystical flights in Books 7, 9 and 10 may only be hypothetically ventured. Again, the seemingly paradoxical character of forgetfulness in Book 10 seems hard to set down exactly. There are of course matters of lesser moment in which only plausible conjecture instead of exact determination can be suggested, such as why Augustine leaves both his concubine and his friend of Book 4 nameless.

Explication of the *Confessions* has been facilitated by reference to other works. The *Sermons* and the *Enarrations on the Psalms,* which relate in a condensed fashion many of the doctrinal themes,[23] have been especially helpful in expositing Augustine's hundreds of quotations from the Psalms. Except where textual considerations strongly indicate otherwise, texts later than the *Confessions* have also been counted on to throw light on passages. This accords with the judgment of scholars who believe that, in the light of the continuity of Augustine's ideas, later works, cautiously used, may fruitfully gloss earlier texts.[24] Cajetan, the celebrated Thomistic commentator, was at times indicted for investing his commentaries with a too refined subtlety, which occasioned the observation in simple Latin, *Si vis intelligere Cajetanum, lege Thomam.* Along like lines we may say, " If you want to understand Augustine, read Augustine." Augustine is best understood through Augustine, or, as I have phrased it in conversations with colleagues over the years, Augustine has no better commentator than Augustine.

Augustine's Conversion, C. Starnes' scholarly commentary, also lays strong stress on Augustine's argumentation. However, along with opting not to reflect on the last four books, his less detailed version contains treatments of some themes that I cannot wholly agree with. While minutely poring over the text, J. O'Donnell's *Augustine Confessions,* a most impressive three volumes (including a new critical text), tends to be, as some reviewers have pointed out, mainly philological in tenor. Sparse analytical discussion, e.g., is given the inquiry into the definition of time prominent in Book 11. More recently there has been published *Die Confessiones des Augustinus von Hippo,* edited by N. Fischer and C. Mayer, a distinguished work of German erudition jointly authored by thirteen savants, each of whom examines one book. Most of the contributors, however, only selectively study their particular areas. As our presentation indicates, we have profited from all of these commentaries, each in its own way valuable.[25]

Notice, to the dismay of some admirers Augustine does explicitly repeat certain points, especially some complex matters in Book 12. This suggests that his reading was geared not only to experts in Scriptural exegesis but also to spirituals with the requisite intelligence. Correspondingly, may I mention, this commentary is not directed to specialists alone but also to generalists who are educated Christians. Moreover, though so styled that parts of it can be studied independently, for maximum understanding it would seem desirable to first consult the text to which the commentary is keyed.

It seems appropriate also to touch on the question of historicity. For roughly 1500 years after its composition no doubts were raised about this crux. Then late in the nineteenth and the early twentieth century, G. Boissier, A. Harnack, L. Gourdon, and W. Thimme[26] severally claimed that Augustine's conversion was actually a turn to Neoplatonism with a Christian veneer. Later this thesis was defended with seeming scholarly thoroughness by P. Alfaric, in whose opinion Augustine, a pure Platonist at the time of his conversion, assented to Christianity only because Catholic doctrine conformed to authentic Platonism; only some time later did he assign priority to Christian doctrine.[27] If Augustine had died after writing *De animae quantitate*, he would have been classified as a convinced Neoplatonist more or less tinctured with Christianity.[28] However, meticulous study of early works proved contra Alfaric that Augustine was converted morally as well as intellectually (in regard to basic doctrine) not to Neoplatonism but to the Gospel, the disciple of Plotinus largely yielding primacy to the follower of Christ. BV 4.35 presents the trinity as the font of full happiness, achieved by Christian faith, hope and love. According to CA 3.20.43, he will never depart from the authority of Christ, in line with whose injunction prayer of petition is employed (CA 2.1.1-2). A companion dialogue recommends petitionary prayer, absent from Plotinus (O 1.15.29; 2.20.52) while the trinity is also recognized (O 2.5.16). The *Soliloquies* continues emphasis on prayer, now in all its forms, adoration, supplication, self-donation to God (Sol 1.1.5).[29] In short, more careful scrutiny of the Cassiciacum texts shows that the God of Augustine, unlike the One of Plotinus, can be invoked in prayer. A personal God and a beneficent creator of all things, he is truly a triune God who reveals himself most fully in the incarnate Word, adherence to whom basically depends on faith. Eleven steps in Augustine's conversion related in the *Confessions* are, furthermore, condensed in BV 1.4 and CA 1.2.5.[30] Thus at Cassiciacum Augustine was substantially a genuine Christian, but he did not become fully developed at one bound; further growth would occur after his ordination.

Catholic critics of Alfaric demonstrated that the pre-ordination Augustine was authentically Christian: essential Christianity obtained in a purportedly Neoplatonic or philosophical environment. Then in 1950 the remarkable research of P. Courcelle established that

Neoplatonism was prevalent in a Christian setting.[31] In the Christian milieu of Milan imbued with Neoplatonic ideas Ambrose, Simplicianus, and others endorsed a partial harmony of Christian and Neoplatonic views, at times applying Neoplatonic concepts as instruments for expounding Christian doctrine. Thus was a final nail driven into the coffin of Alfaric's already apparently defunct thesis. Oddly, Alfaric's critique of the *Confessions* as not objective was itself not strictly objective. Implicit in his strictures was his own subjective baggage, in particular, the rationalist assumption derivative from the Enlightenment that reason and faith are fundamentally antagonistic rather than, as Augustine held and as Catholic tradition has always maintained, complementary. This rationalist construct that underlay his bifurcation of the post-conversion Augustine into an at-once convinced Neoplatonist and superficial Catholic distorted the consistency of his thought from 386 to 391. Indeed it is but one extreme example of the sort of subjective invention that is still being forced on the *Confessions*. One lesson seems plain: apparently impeccable scholarly explications of the text can, because of one-sidedness, suppress countervailing evidence that ensures the whole truth.[32] Like some others, Alfaric's reconstruction led not to a fresh instruction about but a deconstruction of Augustine's authentic posture.

Many Latinists have remarked on the beauty of Augustine's prose. This "grand virtuoso of language" displayed "a passionate delight in words" along with "an amazing variety of style."[33] The words which he valued as "choice and precious vessels"(1.16.26) are always deployed in the service of the truth (DC 4.26.61).[34] In many places his affective and poetic vocabulary is colored by Biblical and Christian expressions and allusions. Because of a protreptic strain the text moves and excites the spirit. Dependence on the Bible and, in particular, the Psalms opened up horizons on God and man of which Plotinus had not the slightest clue.[35] Occasional disjointedness and dissonances occur because the work is not strictly didactic but the outpouring of a soul seeking God.[36] Other than occasional mention of irony, paradox and oxymoron, we have avoided comments on the various figures of speech and other literary-rhetorical devices that abound in the *Confessions*. Similarly, save in a few instances, we have not emphasized Augustine's lyricism, an ongoing prose-poetry, which has elicited the judgment, perhaps somewhat exaggerated, that he is "the greatest poet of Christian antiquity."[37] Another omission may be noted. For the most part we have steered clear of the dense and tricky thickets of *Quellenforschung*, ordinarily sources are marginally introduced only in the service of exposition of the text. Moreover, usually we have not cited the Scriptural texts indicated by Augustine since these are given in nearly all editions of the *Confessions*. Again, because based on Latin translations derivative from the Septuagint, Augustine 's numbering of the Psalms varies from that now current in most English translations. While Psalms 1-9 and 149-50 have identical numbering in both St. Augustine's and contemporary versions, in the case of Psalms 10 to 148 it is necessary to add one to jibe with the equivalent text in current English Bibles.[38] Augustine's Psalm 22, e.g., is the same as the well-known twenty-third Psalm.

The text used is that of M. Skutella, as reprinted in BA 13-4. That used for *Sermones* and *Enarrationes in Psalmos* is found in *Opere di Sant' Agostino*, an Italian edition that largely reproduces *Corpus Christianorum*. Citations from *The City of God* are also taken from *Corpus Christianorum*. References to other works substantially rely on the Maurist edition, compared, where appropriate, with *Corpus Scriptorum Ecclesiasticorum Latinorum*.

In appraising the *Confessions* toward the end of his life (R 2.6.1), Augustine remarked that it was intended to deeply move the mind to praise of God. Not only in writing but also afterward in reading it, he himself experienced an identical profound feeling. In addition, he noted, his *Confessions* blessed many of his Catholic brethren with similar intellectual and affective fruit. It would not seem presumptuous then to hope that this *Companion* may help readers enjoy, if not a transforming inner growth, at least some measure of satisfaction of spirit.

NOTES

1. The term has also a third but secondary signification, in the latter books it means profession of faith (13.12.13). Bonner, 49-50. The occasion for writing remains a subject of discussion and dispute. According to one view, favored by Courcelle, 29-32, the work was initiated in response to a request by Paulinus of Nola, for a short biography of Alypius, which was eventually incorporated in the *Confessions* as 6.7.20. However, there is no evidence that Augustine wrote such a biography. In his survey D 2.360-2 raises doubts about the Paulinus hypothesis. For M. Wundt and others, the work served as an apologia to counter Donatist calumnies. But the texts relevant to this hypothesis are dated around 401, toward the finis of the composition of the work. Others, such as P. de Labriolle and M. Zepf, trace the origin of the work to QS 1.1.11, the treatise sent to Simplicianus in which Augustine roots all good will in grace: the *Confessions* is a massive testimonial to this central truth. However, the *Confessions* does contain much more than a witness to grace. Admission of guilt, praise, thanksgiving, murmurings and outbursts of loving prayer run through it. See Solignac's shrewd comments, BA 13, 26-36.

2. According to most commentators, the work was probably begun toward the end of 397. It was completed by 401 since GL 2.9.22, which was started in 401, refers to 13.15.16 (though in the opinion of F. Van Fleteren, it was most probably finished prior to this date). Hence it seems safe to say that it was composed between 397-401. As regards the division of parts, Books 1-9 were completed as a unit. There may have been an interlude between Books 1-9 and the composition of the remainder. However, contrary to some scholarly claims, Book 10 was not a later redaction tacked on as a kind of appendix after the rest of the work was completed. Throughout the work for precise reasons not altogether clear to us an Augustine in midcourse was moved to produce his many-faceted soliloquy with the God of his heart (6.1.1). See especially Solignac, BA 13,25-6, also E. Feldmann, "Das literarisches Genus and das Gesamtkonzept des Confessiones", CAH, 25, and F. Van Fleteren, "Confessiones," AE 222-8.

3. While today texts in the *Confessions* are ordinarily identified by book, chapter, and paragraph, medieval manuscripts carried only divisions into thirteen books, with chapter numbers originating in early printed editions of the later fifteenth and sixteenth centuries. Not until 1679 did the Maurists introduce paragraph numbers. HC xxvi.

4. Solignac, BA 13,26.

5. P. Landsberg, "La conversion de saint Augustin," Supplément à La Vie Spirituelle, 1936, 31-56. This view was endorsed by J.M. Le Blond, *Les conversions de saint* Augustin, Paris, 1950. Both are cited in BA 13, 14.

6. Starnes, xiv-xv.

7. See H. Böhmer, "Die Lobpreisungen des Augustinus", *Studien zur Kircheigeschichte*, 11,14,16. E. Feldmann, "Confessiones", AL I. 1144, J. Ratzinger, "Originalität und Ünderliefrung in Augustins Begriff der 'confessio'", REA 3 (1957), 385-92. Feldmann, 1144. G. Pfligersdorfer,

"Augustins 'Confessiones'" und die Arten der Confessio," in G. Pfligersdorfer, *Augustino Praeceptori*, 65-71. See Feldmann, 1144-5.

8.   K. Grotz, *Die Einheit der Confessiones. Warum bringt Augustinus in letzen Büchern Seiner Confessiones eine Auslegung der Genesis?*, 104-49. Feldmann, 1147.

9.   G-M 332. Feldmann, 1148.

10. Feldmann, 1168-77.

11. F. Cayré, "Le sens et l'unité des Confessions," *L'Anne théologique augustinienne*, 13 (1953), 13-32, cited in BA 13, 19.

12. Landsberg, loc. cit. in n. 5 above.

13. R. Herzog, "Non in sua voce, Augustins Gesprach mit Gott in den Confessiones—Voraussetzungen and Folgen," 223, 232-33. Feldmann, 1148-9.

14. K. Steinhauer, "The Literary Unity of the Confessions," in J. McWilliam (ed.), *Augustine: Rhetor to Theologian*, 15-20.

15. G. Knauer, *Psalmenzitäte in Augustins Konfessionen.* Feldmann, 1149.

16. Solignac, BA 13, 22, n. 1. Feldmann, 1149.

17. Feldmann, 1143-50, lists over twenty unsatisfactory solutions.

18. Solignac, BA 13, 25.

19. Giving no hint of a rupture between earlier and later books, Augustine tersely writes: "Books 1 to 10 concern myself; the other three deal with Holy Scriptures"(R 2.6.1).

20. This characterization was first used in an earlier article, J.M. Quinn, "Anti-Manichean and Other Moral Precisions in *Confessions* 3.7.12.–9.17", AS 19 (1988), 165.

21. G. Bouissou, BA 13, 223.

22. TeSelle, 190.

23. W. Schumacher, *Spiritus and Spiritualis: A Study in the Sermons of Saint Augustine*, 11: "Practically everything which he treats in his didactic and controversial works also appears in his sermons, in an intensely practical manner." Sermons is taken broadly to include not only sermons in the usual sense but also expositions of the Psalms and tractates on the Gospel and the first epistle of St. John.

24. In "Research Techniques in Augustine Studies," AS 1 (1970), 281, J. O'Meara observes, "It is undeniable that a later text can illuminate one that is earlier and obscure." According to G. Madec "Diagramme augustinien," AUG 25 (August, 1985), 92, a later text can be used in conjunction with earlier texts, this in accord with the position of E. Gilson, *The Christian Philosophy of Saint Augustine*, 363-4, n. 49, that the psychological development of Augustine's views did not affect the constancy of his chief philosophico-theological ideas that always remained stable from the time of his conversion.

25. M. Pellegrino's *Le Confessioni di Sant Agostino* is more doctrinally systematic than O'Donnell, but its account of Book 10 is rather abbreviated and the discussion of the last three books somewhat skimpy. Also worth mentioning is the commentary of P. de Luis, which omits the last three books: *Las Confesiones de San Agustin Commentadas* (Libros 1-10).

26. See BA 13, 56-8, for details on these scholars.

27. P. Alfaric, *L'évolution intellectuelle de saint Augustin*, 1, 380-1.

28. Alfaric, 527.
29. Basing her analyses and conclusions on scholars of the caliber of C. Boyer, M.P. Garvey, in *Augustine: Christian or Neo-Platonist?*, 67-112, throws adequate light on the undeniable Christian ideas of Augustine in the early dialogues. In addition, she calls attention to the Christian content in works up to his priestly ordination in 391; 118-209. For further discussion see Solignac, BA 13, 55-84. In the opinion of Starnes, 277-85, Courcelle's clinching thesis, which he accepts, raises fresh questions. While hailing Alfaric as brilliant, one renowned scholar puts down Sr. Garvey as naive. This dismissive gesture toward a work that is fundamentally satisfactory glides over the incontrovertible fact that in the essentials of historicity, to put it simply, she got it right whereas he got it wrong. Indeed evidence continues to mount in support of the traditional account. According to N. Cipriani, "Marius Victorinus," AE 533-5, Augustine drew upon Victorinus for concepts concerning the trinity and for an understanding of St. Paul. Such research further exposes the shallow character of Alfaric's misguided interpretation. Also somewhat relevant here is the fact that in 1775 A. Lavoisier undermined the phlogiston theory by proving that burning is fundamentally a process of oxidation. Today no scientific historian praises the brilliance of the proponents of this deservedly discarded theory. Correspondingly, one would expect that late-antiquity scholars would consider Alfaric's radically flawed reading of Augustine no less lamentable because it is robed in apparently brilliant (actually grossly misleading) scholarly apparatus.
30. BA 13, 65-72.
31. Courcelle, 93-138, argues that Augustine discovered Christian Neoplatonism in the sermons of Ambrose, who was not a philosopher per se but whose Scriptural expositions were interthreaded with Neoplatonic ideas. In 168-74 he traces the influence of Simplicianus, a Christian Neoplatonist, on the correlation of the *Enneads* with the Prologue of John's Gospel. BA 14, 529-36, perceptively comments on the Milan circle in whose blend of Christianity and Neoplatonism Augustine first encountered a doctrinally sophisticated Catholicism.
32. Alfaric reached his questionable rationalist misreading in a scholarly climate that generally favored such rationalist-inspired miconstruals of Catholic figures, some of which survive to this day. The deprecatory term dunce was deliberately derived from Duns Scotus (1255/6-1308), to denigrate this topnotch thinker and all he stands for. Worse, still lingering on, even among professionals, is the Columbus myth which holds that Columbus believed that the earth was flat– an utterly false assertion invented to disparage the Church as an engine of darkness. Again, Galileo (1564-1642), the father of modern science, has long been an object of rationalist misinterpretation, this contrary to historical evidence. Moreover, a generally anti-religious current influenced many academic circles in the late nineteenth and early twentieth century, as noted by R. Allers, *The Successful Error*, 225. More specifically, modernism was gradually making its impact on Catholicism. As Solignac, BA 13, 58, remarks, Alfaric endorsed the essentials of modernism, according to which Catholic dogmas had to be brought in line with newly emerging concepts in modern

science. In effect, modernism demanded that doctrines of faith be adjudicated before the bar of reason, there to be modified or simply discarded. Such a theological outlook inclined Alfaric to contend that Augustine at Cassiciacum was a convinced rationalist of the Plotinian stripe, so that only later under the pressure of his priestly status did Augustine feel the need to acknowledge faith. This interpretation was of course baseless because anachronistic, reading back into Augustine the rationalist/modernist schema of the early twentieth century.

33. C. Mohrmann, "Saint Augustin écrivain" *Études sur le latin des chrétiens* 2 (1961), 247-75. Quoted in Feldmann, 1181.

34. G. Boissou, "Le Style des Confessions", BA 13, 207-8.

35. Feldmann, 1181-2.

36. Boissou, 231-2. For expert reflections on style see Pellegrino, 125-213. In the preface to his translation, *The Confessions of St. Augustine*, 8-9, E. Blaiklock faults Augustine for verbosity and other lapses from the beauty of classical Latin.

37. Van der Meer, 567; quoted in J. O'Meara, "Augustine's *Confessions*: Elements of Fiction," in *Studies in Augustine and Eriugena*, 48.

38. HC xxvi.

Book One
Infancy and Childhood

Chapter 1: Praise and Invocation in Faith

1. This opening chapter compactly states the theme that will resound throughout: God magnificent in his power and infinite in his wisdom deserves to be praised for goodness and mercy to man, or human being, the creature oriented to his creator; man given especially to the radical sin of pride; yet man, because remade later in faith and love, who yearns to praise God. Man is a portion of God's created universe; unable to comprehend or fully grasp the greatness and wisdom of God, he nevertheless desires to praise God (P 144.5). Not a small part, man occupies the middle rung in the universe.[1] Rational in soul, he is mortal in body: his earthly existence is a dying life and a living death (1.6.7); very simply, he is physically destined to die. He carries his mortality about as sign and effect of his sinful condition. Through the primary sin of Adam sin entered the world and, through sin, death: death is the price paid for sin (S 144.4). Mortality is the penalty for the pride that underlay Adam's disobedience (CD 14.13).

Still, man, Augustine in particular, wants to praise God because this portion of creation has been recreated in love won by the incarnate God (1.1.1). Indeed through the stimulus of God praise becomes a delight. Augustine basically relies on Scripture to praise God, in whose words God praises himself so as to make himself lovable (P 144.1). In loving God, Augustine shares more in the divine good he loves; in praising God, he delights even more in the possession of the

God he loves (P 144.1). God spurs man to praise him because "you have made us for yourself and our heart is restless until it rests in you." Here heart signifies the spiritual "I" (10.3.4), the whole spiritual self including understanding and conscience.[2] These celebrated words, perhaps the most quoted in the work of Augustine, mean that the interior man is oriented to God as his terminal place or lasting home of rest, ordained to end in the divine beginning. This orientation is principally supernatural rather than natural.[3] While attracted by the transcendental true and good, man as a natural part of creation cannot aspire to God himself. His *pondus* or weight is directed upward to God, by the fire or love of the Spirit (13.9.10) that bestows grace. Restlessness here fundamentally denotes lack of fulfillment, movement that has not yet reached its goal; only secondarily does it connote lack of satisfaction. Rest is achieved when a thing reaches its proper place. In a supernatural context God is man's proper place (P 30 [S.3].8). Restlessness has two basic senses. First, a sinner is restless because his desires are disordered, appointing first place to lower things and the lowest place to the highest good that is God. The love of God rights the sinner's desires through virtues implanted in the soul. The virtuous man is also restless, this in a second sense. Though virtue issues in satisfaction, the person of virtue is not wholly fulfilled; one still tends upward to one's ultimate end that is lasting peace (T 11.6.10). Only in the eternal Sabbath with morning but without evening (13.36.51) will the yearning soul achieve terminal rest, everlasting peace in God that participates in the rest that is God himself (13.37.52).

Next, as he does throughout, Augustine prays for the light of understanding, in this instance for illumination concerning two questions, both quickly resolved. (i) Which is prior, invocation, i.e., prayer, or praise? (ii) Which is prior, knowledge or invocation? (i) Augustine apparently solves the first problem implicitly. Prayer precedes praise; seekers of benefactions concretely know God as the giver of all gifts and so are led to praise him. (ii) Prior to prayer is knowledge in the primary sense. An individual ignorant of the true God cannot call upon him. At this juncture Augustine very probably has in mind the Manichean deity that is a blasphemous caricature of the true God (7.2.3). When his error was his God (4.7.12), any beseeching of this pseudo-God was valueless; a nonexistent illusion was powerless to answer prayers, and indeed was to be abominated rather than worshiped.[4] From prayer in a second sense stems richer spiritual understanding; persevering invocation is the precursor of growth in knowledge of God. Here, however, Augustine does not address the second-order priority of prayer to deeper knowledge. Paul holds that an individual comes to know God (in the primary sense) by faith which is aroused by preaching (Rom 10.14). Thus the order within spiritual acts becomes clear: preaching elicits faith; faith-knowledge grounds prayer; finally, prayer precedes praise. When individuals pray for the riches of God, they find him; relatively filled with his wealth, those who seek God praise him for his goodness (P 21[En.2].27).[5]

Augustine begs that God will renew his spirit of prayer or invocation, increasing his faith so that he can call on the Lord more fervently as he recalls how he first received faith through preaching. The faith that is the fount of his prayer was given by the Father, who infused it into his soul some eleven years back, around 386, through Jesus, the one mediator between God and man (10.43.68). Jesus is not the preacher. Rather, the messengers of the word of God are preachers who, guided by his light, ignite and sustain faith in believers. The particular instrument whose preaching elicited faith in Augustine was Ambrose, whose exegetical sermons opened his eyes to the spiritual sense of Scripture (6.4.6) and who catechized and baptized Augustine in 387 (9.6.14).[6]

The first chapter broadly encapsulates the autobiographical (mainly Books 1-9) and reflective passages to follow. Augustine's life is the quest of a heart unquiet because stumbling about in an inner blindness, exchanging one form of darkness for another no less wounding. Through his intellectual and moral conversion Augustine achieved some of the rest that envelops the spirit in the light of God. These were channeled into his soul through the divine humanity of Jesus that is the way to the Father, the Word made flesh disclosing his word to him through human agencies. Augustine's story is the cry of misery for mercy: a confession of sins. His story is a hymn singing the mercy of God using his wisdom and power to heal him with divine love: a confession of praise.

Chapter 2: How Can God Be Present in him and he in God?

2. *Invocare*, which usually signifies "to invoke" or "to pray," has a twofold import: it means both to call upon God and to call God to or

into oneself.[7] When Augustine calls upon God, he is calling God to come into him. God is not simply a remote, overtopping impersonal force, fearsome but devoid of love. For Augustine, he is "my God", a personal God of love and consolation, with whom he communes as friend to friend.[8]

It may seem paradoxical to pray that God will come into him. The middle portion of creation that is man (7.7.11) cannot contain the limitless Lord who made heaven and earth. Indeed heaven and earth, of which Augustine is a part, is not grand enough to encompass the Lord God. Still, whatever exists cannot exist without God; God is in all things created. Hence in spite of apparent paradox God has to be in things created. Moreover, a second problem arises: if God is in all things created, why does Augustine pray that God come into him? Plainly God cannot, need not, come into a heart where he is already necessarily present. Augustine is not a fugitive from God who has fled to hell,[9] i.e., the nether world, but even if he were there, he would not escape the God who is everywhere present, even in the underworld. From another perspective, a third difficulty poses itself: how can Augustine call upon God to enter into him when he is already in God, from, by, and in whom all things exist. If he is already in God as in a kind of place so that he shares the same place with God, there is no new place to which God can come. If too God is already there, if one is in God, God cannot come into one anew. Or, Augustine conjectures, perhaps he is intended to somehow travel to be where God is in order that God can come into him. Since God is said to fill heaven and earth, there may be some special place beyond the universe to which he can voyage so that he can coherently speak of God's coming into him.

Chapter 3: God Wholly Present Everywhere

3. The God who fills heaven and earth is either contained by things or contains them. The first hypothesis compromises the spiritual infinity of God. A God contained by creatures would have to be conceived as an enormous material thing overflowing heaven and earth, perhaps depositing the surplus of his being in a place oddly beyond heaven and earth (7.1.1). More importantly, were God contained by things, he would be made less than God, a material thing subject to things beneath him. The truth of the matter is the

other way around: rather than being contained by or dependent on things, a spiritual God contains the creatures he fills, sustaining their existence and action. Because he is spiritual, God does not fill things in a material way. He is not fixed in place by them as water filling vessels is held in place by the vessels. When the vessels fall to pieces, the water spills out, losing its place. But God is not so destabilized; the shattering of the vessels does not send him flowing forth. God pours forth his Spirit on men in a spiritual manner, i.e., unlike a material fluid dropping from heaven to earth: his Spirit through Christ raises up men fallen through Adam (P 145.17). The outflow of his Spirit does not make him like creatures but makes creatures like himself by lifting them up to himself. Similarly, once the vessels are broken, water is scattered about. But shattering vessels does not scatter the unchangeable God, who, rather than being dispersed, gathers together the fragments of the broken vessels that are human hearts, repairing and making them one again as sharers in the One that is himself (11.29.39). So one is God that his whole self fills all things; his one spiritual self is present as a whole, wholly present, in all things.

Next, Augustine clarifies the mode of this total presence: it cannot be partitive. Various things do not contain various parts of God; otherwise the whole self of God would not be present in each of the various things. Nor do all things simultaneously contain the same part of God; not the whole but only a part of God would be present in all things. Nor is God proportionally distributed according to the different dimensions, some larger, some smaller, of the things in which he is present; again, his presence would not be whole in each thing but divided, each part accommodated to the size of the creature in which he was present. The view that God has in himself larger and smaller parts does not save the totality of his presence; if his parts are intrinsically larger and smaller, he still cannot be totally present in various larger and smaller things. God's presence, like his being, is spiritual. He is *ubique totus*, everywhere wholly present; his whole reality is present in all the things he contains.[10] God is wholly everywhere because he is purely spiritual, as Augustine happily discovered while becoming undeceived about Manichean falsehoods concerning the Church. If God were a body, he would be wholly in one whole place but not whole in each part of the place (T 6.6.8). As spiritual, he is not delimited by any one place; he is *ubique*, in every place (5.2.2). He is not present quantitatively, part by part; he is *totus*, his whole self present everywhere (E 187.5.17). Simply put, if God were in place, he would not be God (P 74.9). Conversely, if he is truly God, he is not in place. In other words, no one thing in which he is wholly present can wholly contain him. He is wholly present in a sparrow, but the wholeness of his presence is not exhausted in that single containment. If he were material and finite, his whole present in a sparrow would forbid his being wholly present elsewhere (7.1.2). But his presence is not quantitative but spiritual and, as spiritual, not limited to any one place. Indeed he does not dwell in place as such. He is not contained or held in place by the sparrow's body; rather, he contains and upholds the sparrow by his presence. No one thing can exhaust his total presence because without his presence no one thing would actually continue to be. It is not the sparrow's body that gives location to God's presence; rather, God's presence gives location to the sparrow. God cannot be circumscribed by a being that he sustains; he is illimitable in being and therefore ubiquitous throughout creation.

This explication of the divine presence implicitly settles difficulties raised in the foregoing chapter. God is not a material being infinitely diffused through space (as Augustine mistakenly thought during his Manichean period; 7.1.1-2) but a supremely spiritual entity that pervades and contains all things in an immaterial manner. While God is totally independent of things, creatures depend on him, requiring the support which the presence of his being and action lends. God's intrinsic action is creative; it constitutes things in existence by governing or containing things. The presence of God in things lays emphasis on the source of divine sustenance: things are in God as effect is traced to its cause. On the other hand, reference to God's presence in his creatures accents the terminus of his activity: he is in things as a cause bears on its effect. Hence though Augustine is in God (the source of his being), he can, without contradiction, call upon God to be in him (the terminus of divine power). Since God contains things in a purely spiritual fashion, God cannot come to Augustine from some locus beyond heaven and earth.[11] Moreover, Augustine can entreat God to enter into him even though he would not exist if God were not already in him. In the line of nature God is present in all men, indeed all things, but in the line of grace he indwells only in certain human souls by faith and love, and more intimately in some than others (E 187.5.16-7). So in later passages an Augustine thrashing through dense thickets bewails his ignorance of the divine presence: while God was within him, he was outside, chasing poisonous bagatelles; while God was present everywhere, Augustine was absent from him. Thus by the prayer of faith and love he can call the God of grace to enter more into him without contravening the fact that all along God is present within him in the line of nature.

Chapter 4: Praise of God in his Attributes

4. Assuming the existence of God, which he will later explicitly prove (7.17.23), Augustine inquires into what God is. His God is the Lord God, the master and ruler whom to serve is to reign (P 17.32); the Lord of Lords, without peer; the God of Gods: only he is truly God. Not an infinite luminous body, as Augustine misconceived him in the years of Manichean captivity (7.1.2), he is a spiritual being, than which none greater, better, and more excellent can be conceived (DC 1.7.7); the one and only true God, the God of Christian faith and sound reason.[12]

These attributes evoking praise are not uttered ·at random but divide into four classes. First, he hails the unsurpassable inner being of God. God is super-being, the highest possible; best possible; super-powerful, indeed super-omnipotent.[13] A second focus deals with attributes bearing on creatures, which are grouped in pairs that look contradictory but are really complementary. God is most merciful, most loving toward the miserable, seeking to liberate them from their misery; yet he is, without incongruity, most just, requiring submission of all creatures to ordinances of his providence and exacting retribution for violation of his laws. In his transcendence he is most hidden, in his immanence most present. He is, in R. Otto's well-known phrase, *numen fascinans et tremendum*, at once enchanting the heart and arousing reverential fear; most beautiful, most one and harmonious in himself, yet most formidable, inwardly armored to vanquish every foe. Because entirely immutable, God is apparently easier to grasp than a shifting entity, but since his being as supreme is remote from us, he is incomprehensible (S 117.3.5).[14] Continuing in this vein, Augustine points up the relative opposition, distinct from strict contrariety, between the transcendent creator and his immanent executive power at work in creatures. Unchangeable in himself, he changes all things; he administratively moves creatures to change.

Ageless, he never becomes new and never grows old. Never new, he makes all things new; a changeless wisdom causes creatures to change, i.e., become different (P 138.8). In this context innovation intimates renovation, the formation of the new man through grace (S 212.1). While never aging, God brings the unwitting proud low by reducing them to spiritual decrepitude that afflicts the self immersed in sin. The proud man falsely imitates God in his divine exaltation (2.6.13), acting as if he were God or Godlike on his own (P 33[S.2].5). Instead of being ageless like God, the proud man becomes aged, bent over by his downward-tending sin (P 57.10). Indeed every soul trapped in sin is spiritually old: old age is the life of sin (ME 19.36. CF 24.2). God leads the proud to old age in the sense that he ordains feebleness as the inevitable outcome of sin. The proud "do not know this," for they are afflicted with spiritual blindness (1.18.29), so far from divine light that, unable to distinguish good from evil, they delusively rate themselves spiritually sound when, in fact, their spiritual gait is slow and fitful.[15]

God is incessantly active; were he to suspend his action, the universe would collapse into nothingness. Still, he is ever at rest, always enjoying the beatitude that consists of possession of his own supreme good (GL 4.16.17); and his governance directs all rational beings to the all-satisfying rest that is endless sharing in his rest (GL 4.16.17). All-sufficient in himself and needing nothing from creatures, he gathers things in not because he depends on them but because they depend on him: he organizes the universe toward the ends he appoints. Conserving things in existence, he governs them by his power; he protects them, arranging circumstances conducive to continuance in existence; he nourishes them, furnishing sustenance for growth to various phases; he leads them to perfection, which is completion of being according to their specific pattern of existence, as in the growth of oak from acorn. He pursues the good of creatures not for his but for their good since, resting in himself, he needs no other good than himself. When he makes provision for the flourishing of creatures, they rather than he profit, he gaining nothing because he lacks nothing.

Third, various Scriptural attributes are explicitly or implicitly ascribed to God only in an apparently metaphorical sense; detached from human imperfections, they may be literally predicated of him. God's love for man (Jer 31.3) is without physical passion, containing no emotional fire. He is jealous (Ex 20.5) yet exempt from care and anxiety. His repentance (Gn 6.7) is not associated with passional sorrow. He becomes angry (Ps 2.12) but never forfeits tranquillity; his anger involves no turbulence of emotion but simply signifies the vigor of his just retribution.[16] Stripped of anthropomorphic associations, his repentance and anger express the initiation of changes in his works while his plan stays unchanged.

Fourth, he contrasts the activity of the divine artisan with the actions and aims of human workers. Unlike the earthly herdsman, the Lord who is our shepherd recovers what he finds but has never lost; souls desert him, not he them; they lose him, not he them. He is never in want but rejoices in his gains; his changeless joy is reflected in the joys of redeemed men. Unlike some businessmen, he exacts interest without becoming covetous; men are bound to give their creator due compensation of worship. Works of supererogation, acts of out-of-the-ordinary virtue, are paid to God, seemingly putting him in debt to his human servants; only seemingly, because created goods descend from God: there is nothing, whether property or person or virtue, whether gold or grace, that does not directly or indirectly belong to the Lord, the owner of all things (7.9.15). In contrast to human entrepreneurs, he pays back debts not owed; out of his generosity he obliges himself, as it were, to answer prayers conforming to conditions appointed (5.9.17). He writes off debts while suffering no loss; in his infinite mercy he forgives sins whose dismissal deprives him not one whit of the wealth of his goodness.[17]

Words fail Augustine as he tries to describe his amazing Lord. Yet distress would disturb him and others if, holding their tongues, they neglected to proclaim the beauties of God because the loquacious are effectively dumb. Because God is transcendent, no human thought can adequately enclose him in finite meshes. We can speak and think of God; we think of God more truly than we speak of him, but he exists more truly, i.e., immutably and infinitely, than we think of him (T 7.4.7). We can say everything of God but nothing worthy of God: in terms of his infinite being or goodness our everything amounts to nothing (GCM 1.8.14. J 113.5). Hence "What can anyone say about [God] when he says anything about [God]"? God is inaccessible in his concrete being, in his actually living infinity. Anyone who pretends to comprehend God is not comprehending God (S 117.3.5). Yet God is understandable or partially intelligible; the mind can veridically aver,

God is super-good and immutable (1.4.4). Indeed man is made to praise God, the very praise begetting joy (1.1.1). If man does not praise God, he fails in his vocation and thereby brings down trouble on his head. Moreover, if Christians, who alone know the true God, do not proclaim him in his attributes, then no one will magnify his name. Woe betide Christians who say nothing about God since even the verbally gifted say nothing about God. Christians must never stop trying to utter the unutterable in analysis certainly, but especially in prayer and praise. If the word-fluent are, as it were, wordless, if the verbally gifted cannot say enough about God, those less verbally talented surely cannot say enough, yet they must go on expressing the inexpressible as far their powers permit. At certain junctures when the most soaring descriptions of God's perfections cannot do justice to the sublimity of divine life, doing God more honor than speech is respectful silence (C Adim 11), which prompts adoration; and at times the accompanying awe over the super-wonder may evoke jubilation, wordless accents of praise (P 102.8).

However, the last line may admit of another interpretation: woe to Christians, who failing to praise God, say nothing about God because the loquacious, failing to know the true God, say nothing about God. The term *loquaces* may allude to Manichees, to whom it is specifically applied three times (3.6.10; 5.7.12; 7.2.3). Significantly, 7.2.3 uses the very same words as 1.4.4 to characterize them: *loquaces mutos,* gabblers who are effectively speechless, whose torrent of words is, because false, conceptually meaningless. The Manichees volubly spoke nonsense about a triune God who was the fantastic creation of undisciplined imagination (3.6.10). If Christians do not speak of the true God, he will not be accorded the verbal homage his majesty deserves since the doctrinal falsity of conceptually dumb Manichees signified nothing. Although not all *loquaces* or rhetoricians were Manichees (8.5.10) and not all Manichees were *loquaces,* Augustine's immediate proselytizers were probably fellow rhetors who were Manicheans. For all their loquaciousness, a besetting professional vice, rhetoricians by and large managed to communicate some nonreligious truth; they were not conceptually dumb. Augustine's proselytizing colleagues, however, are so characterized because their incessant chattering conveyed no genuine religious truth. Interestingly also, in a later work he labels himself loquacious and, by implication, intellectually mute when, as a Manichee, he boldly attacked Catholicism: "with a very furious loquacity I used to lay waste" the Catholic faith (DP 20.53).

Chapter 5: Prayer for Closer Divine Union through Mercy

5. He beseeches grace to rest in him (1.1.1), his heart so intoxicated by divine love that he becomes oblivious to all his own sins, past and present, and, in a spiritual euphoria, clings to God as his very own all-precious good.[18] What is God for him? Mercy: so he asks for divine mercy to speak the truth about himself. What is he for God? Misery needing mercy to hallow him. Why does God command him to love God, threatening him with distress if he fails in that love? Because only through love that enlarges the spirit to commune with the divine can the restless heart be healed. What God means for man is mercy; what man means for God is a share in his mercy. Thus though Augustine is only one among myriads, his failure in love is no light affliction since, if not reversed, it seals his doom in darkness without end. Besides, he is maximally important to God because God cares for and loves him as if he were the only man in existence (3.11.19). Feeling pangs of spiritual sadness, he asks the merciful God to disclose what he means to Augustine. God's response lies in his holy word (P 34.3): he is Augustine's salvation, the donor of grace, through whose justice he can live righteously (P 34.5). Begging God not to hide his face, for otherwise he will drop into the pit of sin (P 142.13), he prays, "Let me die lest I die, so that I may see your face."[19] The somewhat enigmatic words, "Let me die lest I die," mean: let me be transformed lest I be eternally damned. Let me die: let me die to the old self and be spiritually resurrected with Christ to a new life. Lest I die: lest I suffer damnation that is the second or eternal death following upon the first or temporal death of the body (S 23.1.2). So that I may see your face: dying to self and rising with Christ in this life ensure eternal life whose happiness essentially consists in seeing God face to face, a direct intuition ordinarily not attainable on this side (S 231.3). Since Augustine was baptized in 387, at the time of dictating his memoirs in 397 he was presumably in the state of grace: his prayer then implores continuance in godly living that is dying to self.

6. The house that is his soul, too cramped for divine entrance, requires charity to make it spacious enough for divine occupancy.

Here Augustine seems to be exaggerating; because in 397 God does dwell within his episcopal heart, he is longing for further expansion through charity won by prayer (S 69.1) that will widen divine indwelling. His inward habitation, no longer lying in the wreckage of sin, needs mercy for further rebuilding along godly lines. Having confessed past transgressions, he asks to be purified from minor faults and sinful tendencies still lingering within. Further, he pleads to be cleansed from hidden cupidities or secret stains, and to be spared from being gulled by evil persuasions of contemporaries (P 18[En.1].14; [En.2].13). His confession is a sign not of a shallow nominal belief but of genuine faith exercised in love. His belief is the cause of his speaking; conversely, his speaking is the sign of true, i.e., mature, faith (P 115.2). He confesses his past injustices not against God but against himself: "It is I who sinned; neither fate nor the stars nor God, the maker of the stars, is guilty; I am guilty" (P 31 [E.1].5;[En.2].16). Thus God forgave him because his confession was a sincere self-accusation from the heart, which did not question the judgment of the God who can neither deceive nor be deceived. Unlike the pronounced iniquity of those committed to evil, broadly liars because not in God's truth, who delight in deception and self-deception (P 2[En.1].12;[En.2].21), his "iniquity", which involves no grave sins, no longer entangles him in self-deception and self-exculpation. He does not dispute the infallible judgment of the truth, before whose all-seeing gaze lie exposed all past grievous sins and present lesser failings. As he retraces past and present, his conscience accuses his inner self of numerous sins. Not fully chaste or holy, unable to presume on his own justice, his heart is compelled to cry out for mercy. If God minutely records his sins, he cannot claim to be righteous in God's eyes, cannot pretend to overcome his injustices by his own justice. So he begs once more to be ransomed by mercy that tempers rigorous justice (P 129.2).

The *Confessions*, recall, is in a certain respect a dialogue with God. The foregoing introductory portion summarily states the nature of the God with whom Augustine is dealing. God is the being to whom he is wholly oriented (1.1), a spiritual being present wholly everywhere (2.2-3.3), absolutely supreme yet in contact with man (4.4), from whom Augustine implores more power and light (5.5-6). Then follows the autobiography proper, which divides into two parts. The first part (6.7-7.12) reflects on the origin and psychology of infancy. The second part (8.13-20.31) concerns Augustine's boyhood, his first actual speaking, his triumphs in schooling, along with his problems with schooling that rated skill in grasping literary views, however immoral, superior to moral rectitude.

Chapter 6: God's Gifts in Infancy

7. Nevertheless, despite a shameful past that the pages ahead will retail, despite present sinful tendencies, though dust (earth) and ashes, he makes bold to colloquy with the God who is mercy. "Earth" stands for flesh given to earthy desires, or simply a son of the earth who is a sinner (P 2.7;11.7;48[S.1].3). "Ashes" symbolizes the humility exemplified by repentant Job who said, "I am dust and ashes" (P 147.24) A mere man, outlook narrowed by stingy justice, would deride him as a hypocrite in the light of his past wickedness. Indeed God might have scorned him when he was previously mired in iniquity, repelling him as an enemy for whom the wrath of hell is stored up on the day of reckoning (P 36[S.2].2). Happily, divine pity liberated him from enchainment by sin.

First, he wonders where he came from, touching on the vexing question of the origin of the soul, some of whose possible answers he will consider shortly (1.6.9). The human existence into which he entered is characterized as a dying life and a living death. Existence is a dying life in the sense that through ceaseless change one stage of life ends or dies. In 397 Augustine's infancy is long dead and in 385, at the age of 31, his *adulescentia* or youth died as his *juventus* or early manhood began (7.1.1). The stages of life are stages of death; the emergence of a new phase tolls the death knell of its predecessor (P 65.67). The span of man may also be portrayed as a living death. In terms of his mutable body each human being is inexorably determined to die. From the very first moment up to the outer limit that is death, human existence is a life-toward-death, a life-in-death (CD 13.10).[20] Here notice, moral time is touched on, to be further explored in 11.29.39 and Book 11's Excursus on the kinds of time. Augustine is not sure precisely how his soul was joined to his body, but he is certain that God was with him from the beginning of his earthly existence. His entrance into this death-in-life and life-in-death, a condition death-ridden because aboriginally sin-ridden, was attended by the consolations of God's mercy, affording comfort and alleviation of suffering in the process of gestation and birth. In other words, God in his mercy ordained that his mother be blessed with an uneventful pregnancy and a successful delivery of a healthy, normal child, details of which he then had no cognizance and therefore could have no memory, data he believed true, facts concerning which his parents Patricius and Monica had informed him.[21] The primary cause of his being was God, whose power under his mercy formed him in the line of time through his parents, the instruments in his conception, and through Monica, in whose maternal nest he was formed into a human embryo and readied for birth (CJ 6.43).

Thus God continued his support after birth, furnishing him the consolations of breast milk, so designated in the broad sense because the milk relieved his hunger pains. As God used his parents to conceive and Monica to prenatally carry him, so the Lord employed Monica and his nurses to feed him, as causes real yet subordinate to his directive agency. The milk in their bodies was not voluntarily caused by Monica or his nurses but was effected in them by a law of nature implanted by God. Similarly, God fed him with natural milk through his mother and his nurses acting as secondary causes. The milk was dispensed according to God's prescribed pattern and in accord with the prodigality of divine creation. Put otherwise, it was God who worked intrinsically in the mother and nurses, sustaining the inner natures that supplies the milk. Foods other than milk as well as medicines were furnished extrinsically by servants and others (GL 8.25.46). Thus God operating intrinsically in mother and nurses produced the milk, which was received from them but not through them. Notice, the distinction, intrinsic/extrinsic, differs from the distinction, creation/governance (1.10.16).

No miser, God is super-generous in the abundance and variety of the structures and activities of things throughout the universe; an organization and wealth remarkable even at the lowest level. The reference to order in the least portions of the universe implicitly repudiates the opinion that the lower region of the world, including earth, is indeterminate through and through, subject to the lawless play of chance (P 148.10.GL 5.21.42). It also carries the claim, here generally expressed, that the tiniest animals, such as gnats and worms, are marvelously equipped with delicate organs that illustrate divine design and bounty (P 148.10). Ordaining a balance between demand and supply, God caused Augustine to desire no more than necessary, i.e, no more than divinely appointed, and similarly caused the nursing women to want to give only what God planned. The use of *dabas* indicates that God was giving both the good that is milk and the goodwill of the nurses providing the milk. Their desire to feed Augustine was well-ordered in that they realized that in God's plan their breasts were formed precisely to produce milk. Their milk flowed originally from the secret springs of divine action at work throughout the universe; milk and nursing came secondarily through them, not primarily from them. It was the supreme good from whom all finite goods derive, who was the ultimate source of these goods. God was his salvation in every respect, securing natural as well as supernatural (1.5.5) welfare. Later Augustine recognized that all goods flow from the all-good God, who bespoke his existence loudly and clearly through the very gifts bestowed on Augustine within and without. The gifts within were goods of the mind, of man's interior and superior self, such as truth and goodness that come down from and lead back to the truth and goodness that is God (E 140.3); the gifts without were external and inferior goods, intended to serve the higher goods (E 140.4). Yet in the first days of infancy Augustine's as yet undeveloped mind and will had no inkling of or option concerning these diverse goods. He only knew how to quasi-instinctively drink in milk at the breast like other infants, drawing infantile happiness from sensory delights, while avoiding bodily pain, whose presence he signaled by crying for attention (E 140.3). Early infant life turned on the pleasure-pain axis. There was nothing else; only pleasurable goods and painful nongoods dominated his primitive existence to the exclusion of awareness and capability of choice of goods within and without.

8. As he grew, the infant Augustine began to smile and laugh, first while sleeping, then while awake. This he learned not by immediate inspection but by inference from later personal observation of infants. Gradually, through further development baby Augustine vaguely perceived his surroundings and the individuals, especially his mother, peopling it. Rudimentary speech mechanisms prevented precise communication of wants within to elders without, who of course were not endowed with a sixth sense that could read his mind. Speechless, he had to resort to flinging his limbs about and uttering unintelligible

sounds, intentionally expressed but "not like the truth," i.e., incapable of precisely signifying the objects intended, signs grossly inferior to words in clarity. When adults failed to cater to what his little heart desired, either because they had no idea of what he wanted or because satisfaction of his immediate wants, they feared, might do him harm, he became angry, avenging himself by indulging in the emotional, nondenotative signal of crying; ironically so, for in a disorderly but nonsinful way he was demanding that free individuals to whom he was subject should function as his personal slaves. These insights he gleaned from later empirical scrutiny of infants. With apparent paradox infants who knew nothing taught him more about his infancy than nurses who knew something about his infant behavior.

9. Consonant with the dying-life theme (1.7.7), he describes his infancy as long dead. Yet he is alive because upheld by the God always alive and so deathless that none of his life admits of stages of death. God is eternal, existing before the beginning of the ages, i.e., prior to the creation of time, existing before anything could be called before, i.e., in terms of time. In God, lord or owner of all things because he is their creator, unpassingly stand the causes of all things passing and the unchangeable reasons of all things changing; in him live the eternal reasons of all things without reason and in time.[22] Groping for light on a perplexing problem he never resolved—the origin of the soul, he wonders, was there a period that, once dead, was succeeded by his now dead infancy? Was the prior period the time of his gestation about which he had learned some scientific data and received experiential information (probably from his mother and concubine along with observation of pregnant women)? Or if his soul was in existence even before the span in which Monica carried him, what was the location, if any, of such a conjectural pre-earthly state? Even granted such a state, was his true self actually there? His inquiry is empirically stymied since none of the usual channels of data, parents, the reports of others, his own memory, afford the slightest clue.[23] In his frustration attendant upon irresolution, he asks whether God smiles at his childish fumbling, on the supposition that the Lord is pleased only by clear-cut certitudes. The answer is plain: God is not amused by his searching, nor does he want Augustine to praise him for only what he certainly knows. He has already praised God in the mystery of his transcendence and immanence (1.4.4), and shortly

(1.6.10) he will deem it preferable to find God while remaining unsure about the relation between eternity and time rather than not find God while being sure about the eternity-time linkage.

10. Without a doubt he existed and was alive during infancy, at the close of which he groped for conventional signs to transmit his interior meanings to those outside; otherwise put, toward the end of babyhood he made his first faltering attempts at uttering words. Unlike a twentieth-century pragmatist, he is not implicatively compelled to construct himself, a special, i.e., rational, sort of animal. His being and life issue from his creator, in whom the highest being and highest life are one and the same. Strictly, God does not have being and life; he is his being and life; otherwise he would be prey to imperfection and change (CD 12.2). Because highest, God is unchangeable (T 15.13); he is eternal, inwardly unaffected and immeasurable by time; hence today does not come to an end in him: his life is not divided into days. Yet from another angle, today does come to an end in him, as controlled by his eternity; for God contains all things (1.2.2; 3.3), including these days. The years of God do not come and go; he lives on in a single ever-present today that is eternal. All of Augustine's yesterdays and those of his forebears were in God's present, the state of his eternity. God assigned them their measures, their modes of being with fixed limits of duration, in accord with their relative existence. All tomorrows will be similarly contained by that today. Past, present, and future things and events are measured by the all-at-once eternal present of the God changeless in being and without duration. All things to come will be made in the light of his everlasting today, just as all things now bygone in his supertemporal vision were fashioned in his supertemporal present.[24] A little one, or carnal Christian, who, unable to properly conceive eternity, is baffled by the nexus between the today of eternity and the successive todays of time, should exult in his lack of understanding, delighting in, while not understanding, the meaning of eternity as the Israelites of old rejoiced in, without understanding, the God-given manna in the desert (P 94.13). He should rejoice that his bare belief, faith without understanding, enables him to find, to be united with, the one true God. It is better to find God by not finding him than not to find God by finding him.[25] This rhetorical paradox may bear more than one interpretation. It may mean that it is better for a Christian of simple faith to believe in God while failing to understand his eternal mode

rather than to conceive of an eternal backdrop to time while somehow losing hold of the living God. Or the sense may be this: it is better to lovingly accept, without understanding, God in his mysterious eternity than to know his eternity as regards time with learning so proudful that it stifles moral-spiritual union with God. A third meaning seems more probable: a devout Christian who simply believes in God does not find or understand the eternal God in this life, but his life of not finding, of simple faith that works through charity, wins in the next life a more perfect understanding or finding of God. Though he is nonplused, helpless to answer the question, "What is this?", i.e., "What is eternity?",his faith fructifies in moral satisfaction. Love-filled faith without understanding here below is preferable to finding God here while not finding him hereafter.

Earlier Augustine held that men of faith trained in the liberal arts could rise to a genuine intellectual vision of God in this life inaccessible to unlettered fellow Christians (O 2.9.26) After 395 he discarded the possibility of an earthly intellectual vision of God. For most, only in the life to come would learned as well as unlearned fully possess God; though it was not impossible that some of the educated could reach a limited adherence to a high understanding of God. According to R 1.10.1, the sixth book of M deals with the passage of the mind from mutable to immutable numbers that reside in immutable truth; the invisible things of God are known by starting from perception of things made. Spiritual men with analytical skills can attain some understanding of God in this life until they grasp him more certainly and happily in the life to come. Analytically gifted nonbelievers who lack faith in Christ achieve understanding of God in this life but, because they repudiate faith, undergo eternal death in spite of all their knowledge. In addition to spirituals who reach understanding and carnals, individuals of simple faith alone,[26] there would seem to be a distinct class comprising Christians advanced in virtue, borne toward God with the highest charity (M 1.1.1). Yet while cleaving to God and his revealed truths by sovereign love, they do not mount to understanding in the line of cognition. Like the carnals, they find God (in the next life) by not finding (not understanding) him (in this life).

Chapter 7: Sins of Infancy

11. The authority of Jb 14.4 (Septuagint), "For in your sight no one

is free of sin, not even the infant who has spent only a single day on earth," underlies reflection on sins of his infancy. The imputation of moral faults to babies may seem at first glance strangely aberrant, for clearly infants are incapable of the sound judgment betokening responsibility. More attentive reading shows, however, that Augustine is taking sin in a broad acceptation that does not include responsibility; neither custom nor reason, he explicitly remarks, judges infants blameworthy for what is reproachable in adults. Deliberation and informed choice are necessary conditions of sin in the strict sense (S 251.2.2).[27] Objectionable behavior in infants is loosely named sinful for two reasons: their actions are principally the effects of original sin, indices of the legacy of a fallen race (S 175.1); their behavior harbors germs of sin that will flower out in their adult years. Moral disorder makes its appearance in infancy not substantively but seminally. Singled out are analogously sinful actions such as irately striking aides; only analogically bad, to be sure, but nonetheless unacceptable, for, in growing up, individuals strive to eradicate such offensive actions. Misbehavior of infants is tolerated not because it is not misguided but because it generally fades away with development.

Ascription of sin, broadly taken, to infants is meaningful in the context of all-pervasive, persistent moral evil. Contemporary culture tends to reduce moral evil to nonmoral categories; so sometimes monsters of iniquity like Hitler and Stalin are simplistically labeled sick personalities in need of psychiatric therapy. The salient truth attested by all history that even brilliant educated men can be and have been ruthless exposes this theory as illusory. Moral evil essentially originates not in an abnormal mind but in a twisted will, deliberately bent out of shape by self-interest and pride. The classic Christian doctrine of original sin accounts for worldwide, pertinacious evil: the human race was stricken with a primordial calamity, the first sin of Adam. Because of the solidarity of humankind, every newborn child comes forth affected by traces of original sin, i.e., the loss of original righteousness. "Every man who is born is born as Adam" (P 132.10); an Adam *redivivus*, he inherits the legacy of wounded humanity. It is then not surprising but predictable that an infant, albeit not morally responsible, will betray tendencies to wrongdoing, which are retrospectively rooted in Adam and prospectively serve as incipient roots of moral faults strictly taken. Moreover, discipline dispensed by mothers and nurses to unruly youngsters indicates that misbehaving infants are involved in some sort of broadly understood misbehavior.[28] Many practical experts in childbearing, i.e., mothers who have actually raised a number of children, are convinced that it may be somewhat late, even at the age of two, to set down moral guidelines for infant behavior. Again, childish misconduct, prolonged into adulthood, seems abhorrent; if such later misbehavior is reprehensible, the earlier misconduct must be in some way inordinate, i.e., broadly classifiable as sinful, however unblameworthy, action.

12. Augustine returns, now with stress on the structure of the body, to the motif of order as the signature of the divine artist, mentioned earlier (1.6.10). God equipped his body with senses, fitted it with members, adorned it with beauty and proportion, built into it vital drives, all aimed at his integrity and protection. Through the alerting of the exterior senses by the interior sense, the organism becomes aware of what is useful and harmful to its continuance, thus assuring its self-preservation (LA 2.5.12). If God made nothing other than the human organism, he would still deserve the highest praise, for only his power and goodness can create.[29] Everything fashioned by him is marked by measure, species or form, and order.[30] As all-good, God is absolutely one or the supreme measure, is super-form, and is perfectly ordered in his oneness. As one, he produces unity or measure in creatures; as measured, a thing is set off from others as one such being. As supreme form, he fashions all forms, assigning each thing a specific makeup. As resting in himself, God is not ordered to anything but is the source of the directedness of creatures, ordaining all to their appointed ends. Rounding off description of his infancy is the epistemological comment that his account, howbeit lacking strict scientific certitude, is solidly probable, indeed most probable, the outcome of human faith based on the word of trustworthy elders, along with reasonable inferences concerning his infancy supported by observation of other babies. In any case, he was conceived in iniquity, i.e., his sinful condition replicated Adam's; because of the bequest of original sin this was hardly a time of sinless innocence (P 50.10).

Chapter 8: Learning to Speak

13. He passed from infancy to young childhood, the earliest stage of

boyhood, a period of life extending roughly to the age of sixteen.[31] In the perspective of the past-present-future schema, he advanced toward boyhood. But from another angle, the future succeeds to the present that has become past: in this sense boyhood came to him. From the standpoint of physical origin, he moved from infancy to boyhood; from the standpoint of psychologically viewed term, boyhood came or happened to him, displacing infancy.[32] His infancy was not an entity in a spatial sense; he cannot specify the place where its movement ended. Nevertheless, it ceased to exist; it was a transient, accidental phase, a time of his life destined, like all temporal segments, to come and go. The dividing-line between infancy and early boyhood is the appearance of speech. According to Latin etymology, an infant is an *in-fans*, a nonspeaker, while a boy is a *fans*, one who actually talks. When his elders associated a sounded word with its object by pointing to it, he passively retained the word and its referent in memory; next, he began to actively employ the word with regard to its proper object. Afterward, reflecting upon the memorial data of emerging speech and contrasting its acquisition with formal schooling, he discerned how he, like others past infancy, first learned to speak. His learning was informal; he did not procure language by a fixed program of instruction, as was to occur later in primary school. Previously (1.6.8) the underdevelopment of speech mechanisms compelled him to express desires in nonverbal signs like emotional cries or crude sounds, inadequate indicators of his needs. By degrees he grasped and began to use the names of things, conventional signs conveyed by "natural words", a sort of natural language, i.e., movements of the body such as smiles, grimaces, glances, and various intonations of the voice.[33] These few sentences apparently set down the essentials of a realistic theory of the acquisition of language. (i) The newly learned word he fastened in his memory, the storehouse of ideas; a word is a conventional sign signifying the meaning or idea of a thing (Mag 4.9). (ii) Gradually, through repeated hearing of the word in various sentences, he saw the connection between the vocable and the idea of a certain object. (iii) He started with the names of things, not with more complex modes of speech like phrases and sentences. (iv) Though his learning was not purely pragmatic or nontheoretical, he accumulated a small fund of words in practical situations befitting the mind of a child; certain objects were to be sought and possessed (mother and father, toys, food), others to be rejected or avoided (harmful animals, fire, knives). (v) Not conversant with any conventional tongue, he mastered his first words through the body language or pointing of elders correlated with their articulated sounds; linguistic activity sprouted in a community. It seems impossible for children to start talking apart from the influence of others. No child or group of children can invent a language on his or their own. (vi) His mouth and lips slowly became accustomed to shaping the basic vocables, a feat, experiments attest, that chimpanzees, apparently the most perceptive of apes, when constantly exposed to like sounds, do not, because they cannot, accomplish.[34]

Thus did Augustine journey from childish babbling to articulate sounds, enabling him to understand and make himself understood, thereby gaining admission into a society that is a linguistic world, a community bonded by verbal communication. Notice, here authority refers not to the doctrinal sort (as distinguished from reason; UC 11.25) but to societal governance whereby parents rule the household (CD 19.14). In spite of his initial social commerce, the society into which he was thrust would prove to be one of storm and stress, in which the harshness of adults and his own waywardness would rain down griefs.

Chapter 9: Primary School and its Troubles

14. Shortly before his seventh birthday (361) Augustine was enrolled in a primary school in Thagaste, his home town, where he would spend the next four years absorbing the basics of reading, writing, and arithmetic. Indispensable though it was for his mind, the first years of schooling inflicted tribulations of spirit and body, along with resentment at being fooled and made a fool of by adult attitudes. The only rule for right living was obedience to teachers who promoted unright goals. Assiduous study leading to skill in the linguistic arts would ensure worldly success, consisting of "bubble reputation," honor due to high social status and wealth, the prestige and riches that were really false because temporal and fleeting. Oddly, though denied any idea of the real value of learning, he was beaten if sluggish in learning. As an apologia for this systemized severity, his elders fell back on tradition: literati and rhetoricians of the past had run the same gauntlet. But for Augustine, the

continuance of the inhuman discipline, rather than increasing zeal for fruits of learning, multiplied the sorrows to which Adam's stock is heir. Observing how others (probably, in particular, his mother Monica) prayed in need, he vaguely thought of God as a Great Someone to whom, though not sensorially accessible, he could gain sure access in anguish; in search of protection from beating, Augustine called on God, a refuge to whom he repaired for hope of liberation (P 17.3; 93.27). So he broke the knots binding his tongue; apparently in his first spontaneous personal prayer he, however little, begged with no little fervor for strength from his Refuge to whom he repaired for liberation (P 17.3; 93.27). The thrashings did not stop; yet God was answering his pleas not to satisfy Augustine's unwisdom but to achieve the divine plan of wisdom. God was allowing him to walk trying paths toward the shaping of his character for eternal life (P 21.3; 21[En.2]4; 53.5). These punishments wrung no sympathy from adults; rather, the young lad was stung when he observed that, incredibly, even his parents, who sought only his best, joked about his plight.

15. Imagine an individual so closely united to God that, while dismissing as trivial various instruments of torture, loves relatives and friends who are terrified by the prospect of being savaged by racks and hooks. His posture is morally paradoxical; though he is insensitive to torture, love of fellow men does not make him sensitive to those who shrink from torture. His parents' attitude was correspondingly incongruous; they were wholly insensitive to his torments but deeply affectionate toward their prized son who was brutalized by teachers behaving as quasi-torturers. In other words, the beatings he underwent in school seemed at core no less frightening than the tortures that anguished the martyrs; yet to his bruised bewilderment parents who would never laugh at martyrs' agonies made fun of their own son's suffering. At first blush this analogy seems overdrawn; the cruelty endured by schoolboys pales in comparison with the unspeakable pain wrought by the stretching of limbs and tearing off chunks of flesh; still, in the constricted world of the child routine beatings can really be felt as a horrific enormity. Again, Augustine may have been a sensitive child, with a low threshold of tolerance for physical pain and psychological abuse. Furthermore, the beatings were unremitting; day by day, hour by hour, the punishments went on. Perhaps the unrestrained scope

accorded such ferocity, casually unleashed with not the least fear of
reproval but with the hearty endorsement of parents, spurred the
punitive gusto of instructors like Augustine's to the verge of sadism,
manifest not only in rapping of hands with a ferule but with canings
and floggings as well. Perhaps also his teacher was mystified by the
inability of a boy of Augustine's outstanding talents to become
proficient in Greek and, in line with a crude educational psychology,
reasoned that only pitiless beatings could rouse the lout out of his
contumacious refusal to learn. Close to seven decades later, in 426,
the agony this pedagogical savagery induced still burned in the aging
prelate's memory. As he looked back in loathing on those horrors, he
mused: were he given the option, he would prefer to die rather than
be forced to relive his boyhood with its relentless cruelty from
masters whose brutalities were merrily ratified by his parents (CD
21.14).

   Admittedly, he was not faultless; he was lax in his studies, a defect
perhaps more reproachable in an intellect of his acumen and
retentiveness (a mind he modestly ranks as above-average, one not
deficient in memory and intelligence). Some punishment was
warranted but surely not unabated pummelings from mean masters.
He detects a triple irony in punishment unjust not only in its purpose
but in its harsh measures. (i) He was punished for playing when adults
were doing essentially the same thing, their amusements cleverly
disguised under the label of business. Sadly, no one was perceptive
enough to pity the children for being routinely beaten; or the adults
for being blindly hypocritical; or both for being entangled in a web
of injustice. (ii) In short, he was punished for play that impeded
schooling so that schooling might prepare him for more unbecoming
play. *Bonus rerum arbiter* may savor of a mild sarcasm since a skilled
educator can hardly be a fully capable judge of these matters if he
sanctions the continual beating of his pupils. (iii) Those adept in the
arts to be learned were no more immune to sins than boys wasting
their time in games. When bested by a colleague in a dispute over
some piddling academic point, his merciless preceptor was more
eaten up by anger and envy than Augustine when outplayed in a
game of ball.[35]

   Inevitably schooling with a lopsided stress on rhetoric shaped him
into a narrow literary humanist. Yet he was not afforded the leisure
for study available to a scholar of our day who may without

compunction consume twenty years in formal education; supposing that he started teaching rhetoric in 374, Augustine enjoyed at most twelve, perhaps only eleven, years devoted to formal learning. Such a shortened time-frame left little or no room for science. Still, his writings evidence, as the years went on, he delved into doxographical material and various manuals to reach a commendable level of understanding of disparate philosophical positions and a sound, if not wholly professional, knowledge of the sciences and mathematics (3.3.4) of his era. Apparently he gained a broad acquaintance with the history of philosophy through a study of Cornelius Celsus' *Opiniones omnium philosophorum.* Finally, a providential encounter with certain Neoplatonic writings opened his eyes to a systematic metaphysics of spiritual realities with a hierarchical view of the universe (7.9.13). The autodidact largely overcame the limitations that cramped the student. His success in expanding his horizons would seem due, first of all, to an intellect of versatile super-acuity enabling him to seize key ideas and relationships in diverse sectors of knowledge. Marvelously complementing his wide-ranging mind was a physique blessed with unflagging energy. Because tireless, he could read voraciously and conquer new territories of learning while maintaining a busy workaday schedule as a teacher.[36]

Chapter 10: Love of Shows

16. In confessing school-life delinquencies, Augustine carefully distinguishes between God as creator and governor. God creates all natural things as good, but he does not cause moral evil. Rather than directly producing sin (to hold that God does so is morally insane and blasphemous), God allows it, channeling it by his wisdom and power for the ultimate good of the universe (EN 3.11). Not causatively but permissively is moral evil included in the universal plan of God's sovereign justice. Significantly too, Augustine says, in honest self-examination, "I sinned."[37] Refusing to wear the mask of injured innocence, he does not castigate parents and teachers for his own misdoings. Unlike some moderns whose self-actualization is a masked egoism, he does not posture as a Victim whining about his wretched upbringing under malign elders as the crucial reason for his deficiencies. Searching self-knowledge that yields unsoftened self-accusation enlarges the heart for divine forgiveness (P 7.19). Though

parents and teachers held up before his eyes tawdry goals of
education, he does not pretend that he disobeyed them for noble
motives. He scanted school work because of the pleasure of games,
the fascination of stories and legends, and eye-struck curiosity[38]
toward public shows.[39] This last point intimates an additional irony,
perhaps more morally paradoxical than its three kin (1.9.15). Those
who subsidized spectacles were worthies of wealth and repute, after
whom their offspring, parents hoped, would one day model their
careers. In other words, parents lauded beatings dealt to their
children to stop their indulgence in shows subversive of study, in
order that subsequently their sons might underwrite productions for
the indulgence of adults.

Here he briefly broaches the knotty problem of evil that
preoccupied him his whole life long. During his student days he
puzzled over the question of the source of evil (LA 1.2.6), a specious
solution to which trapped him in the strange sect of the Manichees for
nearly a decade (UC 1.2). A complex Christian resolution may be
reduced to four points. (i) God creates all finite things, but he does not
create but only permits moral evil, which is a disorder of the will or
a privation of proper willing (7.16.22) in the fallen angels and men.
Evil is not a created thing; not positive but negative, it is a deordination in a created will. Not God but angels and men are the
originators of moral evil (CD 11.17). (ii) Though not the creator of
evil, God ordains evil to appointed ends. While defying God, no
sinner escapes the divine order of justice. Punishment is the means
God uses to correct the disorder that is sin; a sinner, because of his
evil, is always thrust down to a lower level. The devil, e.g., now
occupies a lower station in the universe (P 7.19.CD 11.17). (iii) God
brings good out of evil. As creatures use good things in an evil way,
so God uses evil wills in a good way (CD 11.17). God used the devil,
the agent of Christ's death, and Judas, Satan's instrument, to effect the
crucifixion of his Son that won salvation for mankind (S 301.6). (iv)
Only an infinitely good and omnipotent God can permit moral evil.
As all-good, God orders evil to good and, as all-powerful, he can draw
good out of evil (EN 3.11). Hence in spite of evil the universe is
wonderfully well-ordered because evil is assigned its place in a
superbly organized universe (GL 3.24.36). If a painter dexterously
inserts a dark color to make his painting beautiful, surely no one is
bold enough to assert that the divine artist cannot assign a proper

place to a sinner in a beautiful universe (S 301.5.4).

Chapter 11: Baptism Deferred

17. Straightway after birth, when he became a catechumen, a candidate for baptism, his forehead was anointed with the sign of the cross and his tongue touched with blessed salt, the sacramental which spiritually seasons the soul, i.e., helps preserve it from the corruption of sin.[40] Monica instructed him in the basics of the Christian faith: Christ was the savior of humankind, the Lord who clothed himself in the lowly garb of human flesh in order to lead men to eternal life; the descent of a humble God compensated for the proud ascent of fallen man.[41]

When stricken with a an abdominal ailment so critical that he seemed on the brink of death,he pleaded, in deep faith[42] for baptism from his mother in the flesh and the Church, spiritual mother of every Christian.[43] Monica's heart of chaste faith was distressed since his salvation was hanging in the balance; here chastity signifies purity of intention that loves God for himself (P 55.17; 72.32.33).[44] In travail to give him birth to eternal life more lovingly than she had labored to give him temporal birth, she quickly arranged for the first sacrament of initiation.[45] However, after his illness suddenly vanished, baptism was once again deferred. Utilizing a dubious accommodation of the Lord's dictum, "Of him to whom much is given much will be required" (Lk 12.48), Christians of Monica's milieu reasoned that it was more salutary to delay baptism till after adolescence; in the eyes of God lapses of a soul graced with baptism are more malicious and therefore more liable to smooth the slide to final perdition. Nevertheless, he grew up in a home of faith, in which everyone but his father Patricius was a Christian. Through head of the household, his father ceded in matters of religion to the concretely higher status earned by Monica's fervor, making not the slightest effort to rear his son as a nonbeliever. Monica besought the heavenly Father that he would act as Augustine's surrogate father, her prayer to the Father and obedience to Augustine's father eventually winning the conversion of Patricius (9.9.22), who, however, even then did not serve as spiritual father. Superior in virtue, Patricius' wife was inferior in the marital covenant, ordinarily submitting to her husband. Yet in the paramount issue of Christian faith she set aside the *patria potestas* or earthly father's power and instead obeyed the heavenly Father's command to seek first the kingdom of God.

18. The apparent good of deferral turned out to be real evil. Yet the question may be raised whether postponement helps restrain the lower inclinations or affords freer rein for sin. Doubt soon fades in observing what is generally recognized by men insouciant about moral standards; postponement is bound to reap fruits not of the spirit but of the flesh. An unbaptized individual can be less inhibited in pouncing on the illusory good that is indulgence of his passions. Thus the policy of delaying baptism seems morally absurd; it is tantamount to advising a wounded man, because not yet cured, to gladly expose himself to worse wounds. Early reception would have scattered the darkness of ignorance (13.12.13) and shielded him against assaults of evil (13.20.26). Lamentably, without this sacramental retaining wall he was to be swamped by huge waves of temptation during and after adolescence. Though dreading pitfalls that lay ahead, Monica still put off his baptism. Well-intentioned, she unquestioningly complied with misguided custom; invincibly ignorant, she was absolved of wrongdoing (LA 3.18.52. R 1.15.3). She deemed it less risky to let temptations buffet the clay, i.e., the natural self of her son, rather than the image, i.e., his soul newly patterned after the Son, perfect image of the Father (T 7.6.12); the baptized incur greater guilt and severer punishment for sin that gravely defaces the restored image of God engraved at baptism.[46]

Chapter 12: God Brings Good out of Evil

19. In permitting evil to draw good from it (1.10.16), God does not allow evil to defeat his order; he ordains the punishment of the sinner. Indeed each sin has its own built-in penalty, disorder sown within being the sanction for disorder executed without; a law of living Augustine verified in his schooling, out of which good was extracted despite his wrong motives and those of teachers. His boyhood, while not as precarious as adolescence, was not without its moral dangers. Repelled by the dull drilling, he hated the pressure applied to make him learn; the upshot was that good was done to him rather than he himself doing good. Forced to learn, he deserved no moral credit for the good that ensued. A voluntary act is a movement of the soul to retain or obtain something, which is made without compulsion (DA

10.14) whereas coercion renders an act involuntary and therefore incapable of merit (E 102.4.26). Again, though his instructors compelled him to feed upon goods of the mind, their teaching was vitiated since the goals proposed were immoral. Any profit was bestowed by the all-good God employing for his good end worldly teachers as instruments, whose bad end rendered their good or indifferent action evil (3.12.18. S 54.2.3). His compulsory learning would delusorily "satiate his insatiable cravings" for wealth that is spiritual penury.

Gratitude for germination of educational fruit was due the Lord alone, who, reversing the enterprise of evil men who make evil use of good creatures, uses evil men for good ends (S 301.5.4). In his infinite caring (P 98.3; 103 [S.4].10; 145.14) God controlled all the particulars of his schooling for the morally best. From the unwisdom of those driving the lad to learn, divine wisdom trained Augustine's mind in fundamentals that, properly exploited, would later enrich Catholic doctrine. Yet the divine plan was executed in accord with the universal moral pattern: sin works in the soul an intrinsic penalty. Through repetition sin solidifies into a habit, which hardens into an ironclad necessity, the sinner becoming the slave of his sin (8.5.10). The individual vaunting his freedom to do as he pleases is shackled by his passions; aspiring to be master of his fate, he is degraded to a puppet of tyrannous impulses (2.2.2). The sinner turning his back on the rules for reaching infinite good is delivered over to the empire of materially infinite appetites.

Chapter 13: Primary School Studies More Certain Than those in Secondary School

20. After finishing four years in primary school, probably in 365, when he was nearly eleven years old, Augustine was sent to Madauros, 18.6 miles (thirty kilometers) south of Thagaste, to spend four years in a so-called grammar, actually a secondary, school, where he was to concentrate on Latin grammar and literature, poring over writings of lights like Virgil, Cicero, Terence, Sallust, and Seneca. Explications of the texts tended to be precious and fastidious about etymological and grammatical minutiae, with too skimpy a focus on the aesthetic qualities of the excerpts. The tipping of the balance toward a pedantic virtuosity exercised over trivialities

notwithstanding, the young student's mental horizons must have remarkably widened as he was caught up in the play of verbal rhythms and ideas and entered imaginatively into the farflung worlds of fine poets and essayists.

In spite of his linguistic propensities Augustine detested Greek. Exactly why Greek repelled him, he was never able to adequately explain. One of the reasons for his disgust was the disproportionate drilling to the neglect of other language-learning techniques (1.14.23). Equally burdensome as his struggles with Greek was primary school training in elementary Latin. Now, while composing his autobiography, he realized that his embittered reaction as a young boy to these first studies was injudicious because he was formulating judgments in the perspective of unredeemed nature rather than that of grace. His displeasure was grounded in sin; unbaptized, vain i.e., missing the vantage point of truth, he made value judgments according to the emptiness and mendacity of a worldly outlook. He was flesh and spirit, going and not returning; going; far away from God, oppressed by the weight of lower things; not returning: a prodigal son, he had not yet heeded the secret second call bidding him to come back to the Father (P 77.24). In short, since, as ungraced, he could not descry moral essentials of the two stages of education, he despised primary schooling and was enthralled by secondary schooling. Now from the standpoint of grace, as he looks back on the enthusiasms of callow youth, he rates his taxing primary school studies spiritually superior to their secondary school counterparts. Though more dull-looking, they were more certain, blessedly free of the illusions and moral errors polluting classical literature.

21. The juxtaposition of coldness toward his own misery and compassion for Dido was morally incoherent. Moved by the death of Dido caused by love of Aeneas, he was unmoved by his own spiritual death caused by the lack of love of the Lord. He abandoned the God who is light, bread, and power of his mind; the light through which his mind grasps what is true; the bread of truth upon which his interior mouth feeds; the power wedded to his mind, fecundating his thinking with the seed of truth. Severed from the truth, he embraced darkness, fed on stones, and became spiritually sterile. His infidelity was fornication; a fornicator proves unfaithful by rejecting chaste love and running after lower goods apart from and against God (P 72.33). So lauded was he for playing the wanton (P 39.26) that he would have

been socially ashamed if his behavior had not been morally shameful. In identifying with the Dido whose suicide caused the extreme, i.e., the end of her life, he followed the more extreme course of opting for the "extremes," the lowest things created. He became, morally speaking, earth, the dregs of the universe, because love, in carrying the lover by wayward desire to the earthly, makes him earth (EN 2.14). Had these tales been denied him, he would have felt grief over not being able to read what elicited misguided grief that induced moral grief. Study of the Aeneas-Dido scenario of immorality was madness, irrational in the light of faith and reason, oddly hailed as more valuable than the morally higher skills of reading and writing.

22. According to Augustine's theory of knowledge, intellectual judgments are assessed as sound by the inner standard of truth, which derives from the light of God who is eternal truth (Mag 11.38). Through the truth of God within, he ascertains that moral follies, however beautifully crafted, are not superior to elementary skills.[17] His first schooling was best because fundamental. Far better would it have been to blot out of memory literary fictions than to forget the hard facts of reading and writing. His secondary school classroom was a shop curtained off from the noise and curiosity-seekers among passers-by. The curtains of his schoolroom were as misleading as those that covered a pagan temple. Rather than providing honor to a false god, temple curtains covered the false teaching it symbolized. So the curtains over his classroom did not represent the honor of the instruction therein but camouflaged its misguided teaching. No longer subservient to former teachers, he will not be bothered by strictures they may level against his confession of evil ways related to bad literature; reprobation of evil and espousal of good now anoint him with inner peace. These he puts down as peddlers of academic wares concerned not about truth or moral value but only about profiting from the purveyance of literary commodities. First, elementary school learning is factually superior to literature. While the more learned teachers admit that Aeneas never really set foot on Carthage, all agree on the spelling of Aeneas according to the conventional signs of Latin:[48] socio-linguistic fact is true, literary fiction false. Second, the loss to memory of literary fables would be much less damaging than the oblivion of reading and writing. Wipe out data garnered in elementary school, and the superstructure of higher learning crumbles to bits. Still, in the ignorance of boyhood he

contemned the useful and was enamored of inane studies. Accorded only a pinched appreciation of his special capacities, a gifted child like Augustine naturally loathed a system pitched to the lowest common denominator while his lively imagination was enchanted by spectacles recounted in the *Aeneid* and other classics. Yet the substance of the disgustingly presented three R's was solid fact, and the delightful literature no more than the puff of mere myth.

It would be a mistake to write off these comments on the relative subordination of literature as tainted with Philistinism. He is assaying his literary studies in a moral-religious frame of reference, within which aesthetic value is situated beneath moral and religious aims. Granted, literature does present a certain virtually real action, but it remains a world of fiction, which, not properly envisaged and participated in, can unfortunately serve as a romantic flight from stern moral fact. Moreover, the basics of arithmetic are more worthwhile than the charms of Virgil's poetry. Albeit repellent-seeming because of crude educational methods, $7+3=10$ is analytically superior to the exciting description of the cunningly devised wooden horse and the haunting account of the appearance of the wraith of Creusa. However trite, $7+3=10$ is indubitably true, which, needing no empirical proof, remains timelessly so (6.4.6). Yet, it bears repeating, the poetic dimension is not barren of cognitive value; not a set of subrational or sheerly emotional effusions, it does communicate meanings, to be appraised not only by literary canons but primarily according to moral-religious standards.

Chapter 14: Why he Failed to Learn Greek yet Learned Latin

23. If Latin literature enhanced his spirit, why then did he abominate the Greek that engagingly sang like tales? The poetic fictions of Homer, however charming to a Greek-speaking student, arrived before his eyes dressed in a foreign tongue.[49] Perhaps Greek pupils rated the beauties of Virgil as repugnant as he did the sweets of Homer. With obvious hyperbole he remembers that at first he did not retain a single word of Greek. His instructors were baffled by the inefficacy of their punishments to rouse him from his inertia; perhaps the young Augustine turned mulish under this subhuman duress, inwardly shoving back the harder the more he was outwardly pushed. Yet the theory and strategy his teachers utilized in teaching a foreign

language were topheavily visual and analytic. Practically no time was devoted to aural-oral exercises, as the Greek was learned by concentration on individual words apart from use in sentences and by endless recitation of declensions and conjugations. The teaching of a foreign language, he contends, should image the almost effortless acquisition of a language by young children. His ear and mind had gradually picked up words and sentences in the nonacademic setting that was conversation. Without exterior pressure but simply in virtue of interior urging, his mind conceived new meanings and gave birth to words signifying them. (*concepta* means thoughts that are produced or given birth in words, his own words signifying his own concepts); words absorbed by the informal aural-oral language technique practically applied by those with whom he talked. Hence, he infers, in learning a language, free curiosity is a more powerful than rigidly imposed rote learning founded in fear. However, curiosity can become eccentric, hunting for gratification in the abnormal (1.10.16; 10.35.55). It has to be reined in by laws, ultimately traceable in some way to God, modes of discipline exemplified in beatings administered by teachers' rods up to tortures undergone by martyrs. Notice, Augustine is not recommending that schoolboys undergo cruel punishment or martyrs suffer atrocities. Law as an instrument of coercion externally checks inclinations to wallow in immoral pleasures. Because of man's fallen condition the dream of perfect justice in human societies is no more than that – a dream and nothing more, dissipated by the counter-utopian experience of history witnessing to the inevitability of imperfect rulers who many times impose unjust laws. God does not directly will but permits unjust regulations, some approving harsh discipline of students, others condemning martyrs to wild beasts. As argued earlier (1.12.29), God allows these injustices only so as, by supernatural power, to reap good from them.

A qualifying remark seems in order on the sharp contrast between conditions of smooth assimilation of Latin and those of his meager learning of Greek. Free curiosity supplies a necessary but not a sufficient condition for mastery of a new tongue. The aural-oral method is de rigueur, but its application beyond early boyhood has to be adapted to the altered circumstances of later years. As a young child, Augustine had a lalling impulse, a propensity to spontaneously articulate sounds, that makes very young children natural-born language-learners; this plasticity enabled him to learn Latin much more easily than an adult garners a new language. Furthermore, according to linguistic experts, more than immersion in the fresh language is required. Along with vocabulary, the essentials of the grammar, including vocabulary, word order, declensions, and conjugations, have to be studied. Otherwise the learner is confined to passively repeating phrases and expressions he has memorized; without a grasp of the grammar he cannot actively fashion varying modes of expression. Candidates for diplomatic posts are trained by immersion in the new language, but such immersion is always correlated with a sound grounding in grammar; a key point in later aural-oral acquisition passed over in Augustine's perceptive but sketchy proposal for a more quasi-natural style of language-learning.

Chapter 15: Prayer for Perseverance

24. Confident that not his own but divine power will deliver him from every temptation (P 17.30) to the end, i.e., till his dying breath (P 37.10), he commits himself to his king, shepherd of his every step, and his God, changeless director of changing times (P 43.5), consecrating on the altar of his heart exercises in elementary school fundamentals and features of enduring worth in his secondary schooling. However, he cautions that Christian youth should not be, as he unhappily was, tempted by the immoralities of the classics; he suggests that morally harmless selections from the pagans be studied and, in addition, as a Christian literature grows, that the finest of its output be read, now with paradigms of virtue instead of exemplars of vice serving as concrete standards for a code of living.

In "you granted your discipline to me," the word "discipline" means reproof leading to correction, through which he had to be compelled to learn, all this subsumed under the laws of the God (1.14.23) who, controlling sins (1.10.16) and administering punishment, plucks good fruit from the evil tree (1.12.19).[50] It is not unlikely that at this point he may be punning a bit; discipline (correction) is disposed toward discipline (instruction) in boyhood subjects. The self-effacing remark that he "learned a number of useful words in these studies" tersely voices a tremendous debt of gratitude to the authors devoured. Learning more than a ready vocabulary, his prehensile intellect laid under tribute the whole of accessible Latin culture. Along with invaluable stylistic devices he appropriated moral and social concepts that would be worked into the framework of his world outlook. Thus, as later with Neoplatonic writings (7.9.15), he capitalized on the gold of the classics, converting their style and content into spiritual nuggets.[51]

Chapter 16: Danger of Immoral Literature

25. Vanity means pursuit of the passing things of time; what is vain lacks cohesiveness and solidity; it is unstable, and undependable. Unlike the true, which is fixed forever with its foundation in God, the vain comes and goes, flowing on without let-up (P 136.4.31; 143.4.11).[52] So Augustine portrays human custom that is embodied in his vain studies as a river resistlessly sweeping students along to unhappiness. On this side the river will never be dried up; men will be caught up in vanities till the end of time. The river rolls sons of Eve, individuals sullied with the effects of man's sinful condition, into the frightening sea symbolizing the world, the reign of evil apart from God. In the ancient world ships were not of the sturdiest; the lanteen sail developed by the Arabs had yet to come, and navigational instruments were lacking—the magnetic compass needle was not used till the twelfth century. As a consequence, travelers dreaded storms that could cause shipwreck, fear of which was proverbial among the Romans, even a tranquil sea carrying the potential for disaster: "Fear the sea even when calm" (S 105.8.11). Hence the sea is an apt figure for the world threatening to gobble up souls. Salty, bitter, heaving with waves, it is beset by storms (standing for surges of passion) that permit no human craft to survive; crippled by gales, a vessel is bound to be sucked into the deep (S 75.2;76.9.P 118 [S.26].9).[53] Only those borne on the wood of the Cross have some warranty for weathering the tempestuous sea and dropping anchor in the port that is the eternal homeland. So menacing is the sea that even those aboard the cruciform ship of Christ will be hard put to make it safe to shore (J 2.2. 4.P 103 [S.4]. 4.5).[54]

Exemplifying the river of evil is a scene in Terence's *Eunuch* that glorifies Jove as thunderer and adulterer.[55] Plainly he could not be both; if he had been a lower-order god controlling weather phenomena, he would have been without physical flesh and therefore incapable of sexual activity. The false thunder played the panderer to lend credence to, and so solicit, true adultery. His fictive production of thunder could not be duplicated, but, because a god, he functioned as a model of real adultery. Of course the begowned teachers of literature[56] who covertly endorsed Jupiter's adultery would have been offended if one of their colleagues had cited Cicero to the effect that, rather than attributing human qualities to gods, Homer would have done better to confer divine qualities on men.[57] But Homer did, in fact, assign divine qualities to wicked men, with the result that their crimes were admired as noble actions, mirroring the behavior not of the dross of humanity but of the elite on high. In one way Homer ascribed human qualities to the gods, but in a perverse sense he attributed divine qualities, the wicked habits of the gods, to men. The gods behaved like men, but (insofar as Jupiter and the wanton deities serve as paradigms) men behave like gods, ironically acting not like superhuman but subhuman beings.

26. This social pattern, called hellish because tending to bear its victims to hell, is backed by academic prestige and its stipends, teachers' salaries paid by municipalities publicized in the forum along with supplemental income consisting of students' fees.[58] Its allure lies in its promise to accouter students with the art of eloquence, persuasive presentation and lucid exposition of one's claims; skills that are sine qua non means to legal and political success.[59] Yet the sordidness of the graphic seduction episode does not make the words easier to learn; rather, the words that make the act look fetching prompt students to copy the vile action. Words themselves are not evil but simply bearers of thoughts good or evil, functioning as "choice and precious vessels." Unfortunately, into these cups was decanted wine adulterated with moral error by teachers become drunk, i.e., morally incoherent. Under threat of being beaten, students drank the wine like it or not, with no chance of appeal to a sober judge, i.e., a morally wise authority of equal academic weight. Swept along by tides of conformity, Augustine needed no one to pressure him to imbibe immoral literature; aesthetically elevated, he was morally debased by the mores of a decadent culture.

Chapter 17: Example of Vain Use of Talent

27. Still fresh in memory is a second triumph, in which he

squandered God-endued talents in highlighting the emotions of a false deity. As he practiced his exercise,[60] he inwardly winced at the prospect of a flogging as painful compensation for shoddy work. He had been assigned, as one of the prescribed weekly recitations, the task of inventing a prose paraphrase of the scene in the *Aeneid* in which Juno, wife of Jupiter and queen goddess, becomes enraged because she cannot stop Aeneas from sailing to Italy. With colorful and moving language he dramatically enacted the wrath and desolation of the frustrated goddess in a performance easily besting endeavors of schoolmates.[61] His declamation and the attendant praise, he now perceives, were smoke and wind, fugitive movements in and of the air. Symbolizing pride and its offshoot, vainglory, smoke raises itself up into heaven, but the more it increases, the more it decreases; as it spreads, it thins out, then vanishes (S 22.8; 36[S.2].12). Wind also stands for pride and its effects; unstable, it quickly passes and disappears (S 66.1; 67.5.9; 87.10.12). His true life, he realizes, unlike ever-varying vanity, is based on the truth that stays everlastingly the same (P 143.11). Far better would it have been if, instead of celebrating an unreal goddess, he had spent himself in praising the Lord, especially in the Psalms, where God, bidding men praise him in his own words, apportions a share in the divine perfections they praise (P 144.1). Then the inner strengths that are virtues, which divine praise fashions in the spirit, would have functioned as a kind of trellis protecting the tender vine that was his young heart. Had he lavished praise on the God who fortifies, his mind would not have been torn away from its trellis by the bibelots of earthly accomplishment and equally evanescent human laudation. Loosed from its support, his mind lay unguarded, an easy target of birds that represent the proudful;[62] who thrust their mouth into heaven, daring to usurp the place of God (P 8.13). Pride, frequently pictured as a swelling tumor, is here symbolized by an agent without, predacious birds that gorge on the young life of the spirit, with an essentially similar outcome: so consumed, the heart is dominated by pride. Moreover, indulgence in these vanities bespeaks a pride that effectively homages Satan and his myrmidons, for evil spirits batten not on the odor and smoke of material sacrifice but on the lies that are human errors (CF 20.22).[63] The devil and his demons, aping God, crave divine honor, worship only accidentally signified by incense and other externals, a cultus essentially centered on adoration of false gods and fealty to every strain of falsity (P 96.12).

Chapter 18: Concern for Laws of Grammar, Unconcern for Laws of God

28. However, not gods but men daily swept him up into vanities. There is no reason for puzzlement about why he became estranged from God: he patterned[64] his moral conduct after teachers who were living exemplars of literary excellence.[65] Sophisticated in letters, they were morally barbarous; scrupulous, one might say religious, in observing rhetorical canons, they were routinely callous in flouting moral standards. If, while relating some morally questionable personal actions, they slipped into a barbarism (usually a mispronunciation of a single word, such as *omo* instead of *homo*; 1.18.29) or a solecism (a fault usually pertaining to a meaning rather than vocalization as in *deserta sum* when *diserta sum* is required), they became abashed.[66] Yet, after retailing reprehensible immoral feats in impeccable cadences, they became puffed up with pride as their literary gifts were applauded.

In his eternal present God as longsuffering and merciful remains silent for a time, apportioning sunshine and rain to unjust and just alike, expending his pity to awaken the unrighteous to repentance by consolations and hardships. The tomorrows for repentance, however, are not endlessly available. God is also truth, in the glare of which sinners heedless of insistent divine calls will be judged according to the wrath they have stored up for themselves (P 102.16). The sinner is hurled into a abyss, a region of darkness reserved for the soul that pridefully despises God (P 35.10). On the other hand, the convert from slavery to freedom has a scorching thirst for God alone (P 62.5),longing to feast forever on his all-precious face (P 26.8; 41.5). During his tutelage under secondary school teachers, darkness of affection put Augustine far from the face, i.e., the presence, of God. The gap between the soul and God is not spatial but spiritual-psychological, a flight from and return to God worked essentially by movements of the heart. In abandoning his father and wasting his inheritance, the prodigal son symbolic of Augustine did not travel by horse, chariot, ship, or on foot, nor, like Daedalus and Icarus, did he fashion unreliable wings from feathers and wax (3.47; 3.6.1; 4.16.30). The bodily motions were merely exterior means used by interior movements of his disordered spirit. The physical distancing from home represented spiritual wandering from the Father; tender in love: he handed over to the younger son the inheritance standing for spiritual gifts; more tender in mercy: after his son had squandered his substance, the Father, unbelievably forgiving by human reckoning, hugged the wastrel, now in rags befitting a bum, then celebrated his renewed spiritual status.[67]

29. His teachers meticulously abided by conventional rules of grammar and eschewed barbarisms and solecisms in line with recognized usage, while grossly ignoring eternal rules laid down by God's covenant pledging salvation without end. If an educated man lapses into the vulgar North African custom of saying *omo* rather than *homo* (man),[68] his careless suppression of the "h" provokes more censure then if he breaks God's law of love by venting hatred against a fellow man. Hatred damages hater more than hated because hate corroding the heart disintegrates the spiritual tissues that are virtues. Yet the destruction wreaked by hatred goes uncensured among the cultivated despite the truth, evident to the morally perceptive, that the science of letters, i.e., grammar, is not as interior to or deeply seated within the mind as moral science or rules for right living inscribed on the conscience. Grammar is a practical science or art;[69] its basic rules or laws of language are notionally achieved, i.e., known within the mind without empirical proof(10.9.16). The primary precept of the natural law, "Do not do to another what you do not want done to yourself," is more interior because it governs the whole of human living, not simply exact, polished speech, and because its observance secures not limited professional success but happiness of the whole man. Here conscience denotes moral consciousness or man's general moral outlook;[70] the general moral law is written on conscience in the same sense that it is naturally implanted in man's moral being. It is an intrinsically given precept that is not constructed by men. Reflection may discover it and judicious analysis formulate it, but what is discovered and properly expressed is ingredient in his very makeup as a moral being.[71] The *aeterna pacta* differ from grammatical *pacta* on four scores: they are not the outcome of human consensus but are ordained by God; they are not conventional, the offspring of a particular culture, but natural, woven into moral consciousness; they are not modifiable but invariable; ordinarily their violation is a fault more serious than infringement of grammatical rules.

Through all, God patiently dwelling on the heights of his transcendent wisdom, operates through his general law of inner retribution prescribing that every inordinate affection be its own punishment (1.12.19). The ineluctable penalty of unlawful desire is spiritual blindness. Thus a lawyer ambitious to achieve a reputation for eloquence will not spare his adversary before judge and onlookers. Conscientious about not committing a barbarism like *inter omines* (the correct form of which is of course *inter homines*), he is conscienceless about the human life of his opponent, which in a capital case may be effectively destroyed through his hate-filled rhetoric. Ironically, some rhetorically gifted men sensitive to discourse legislated by rules of grammar are totally insensitive to basic laws of moral living; a terrible irony that is the inescapable upshot of disordered desire: rhetorically insightful, they are morally sightless.

Chapter 19: The Noninnocence of Boyhood

30. As a student, Augustine lay prone on the ground, his earthy desires making him morally one with things of earth he hankered after. A proportionally similar sinfulness and consequent spiritual obtuseness afflicted him even before he crossed the threshold into the rhetorical field. In the training ground of the arena that was the rhetorical profession,[72] he was already guilty of his teachers' anomalous pairing of literary refinement and moral coarseness; more in dread of committing a barbarism than of feeling envy of any fellow student who steered clear of such crudities. Since the outlook and, more importantly, the behavior of his teachers counted as his practical moral ideals, he regarded their praise as a sure sign that he was living honorably, i.e., doing what was academically respectable. His life was being determined not by the firm laws of God but by the ever-changing flux of custom. Darkling disorder in word and deed cast him far from the eyes of God, cutting him off from God's presence (1.18.28.P 30 [En.2.S.3].10). Words and deeds not regulated by the changeless rules of God, he was spun about in a whirlpool of shifting subjective opinions of teachers. An imagination as resourceful as his was never at a loss for a plausible alibi to explain away transgressions, and even when he suspected that his mendacity might be unmasked, he persisted in his strategy of hoodwinking, along with

slaves who accompanied him to and from school, teachers and parents. Chronic lying enabled him, under the pretense of engaging in legitimate activities, to indulge his love of boyhood games, a craving for public shows, and a restless urge to imitate plays, i.e., the passion to copy in his own life the aesthetically appealing but morally repellent misconduct of actors (1.16.25-6).[73] His artistic identification with leading actors carried with it a pseudo-ethical imprimatur for their immoral behavior, which he pined to translate into his own life. The desire was restless because, in fact, it was yet unfulfilled and, more significantly, because even its gratification, yielding only sham contentment, would leave him restive still. Furthermore, he pilfered food and wine from his parents' stock to glut a piggish appetite or to bribe peers to give their playthings to him. When outplayed in these games, he compensated by cheating, dominated by a drive to be always number one. He hypocritically upbraided others caught perpetrating the same trickery he felt no remorse about stooping to. When he, in turn, was detected breaking the rules, he faked a countenance of innocence and flew into a rage over what he deceitfully denounced as an instance of deception.

The ugly portrait of the twists and turns of boyhood malefactions impels him to burst out suddenly in skepticism toward, then rejection of, conventional wisdom that boyhood is a morally idyllic period of near-unsinfulness, warmed in the sunshine of early virtues. Though not exactly a juvenile delinquent or budding criminal, the boy of Augustine's past habitually committed sins without apparent remorse. These grim facts expose the notion of boyhood innocence as humbug; he tellingly lists, along with lying, cheating, and phony indignation, five or what are now termed capital sins: envy, sloth, gluttony, pride (the source of vainglory), and anger (while lust will flash its leering smile in the next book). It is intolerable sentimentalism to reduce youthful sins to moral naughts, i.e., to trivial psychological kinks or frolicsome misadventures without moral import, all absolved by a "Boys will be boys" stance.[74] Misdeeds of youth are real sins, not to be pooh-poohed as inconsequential but to be scrutinized as roots of adult enormities; a point corroborated by a pregnant maxim, "Sow an act and reap a habit: sow a habit and reap a character; sow a character and reap a destiny." Only an era still wrapped in the darkness of the Enlightenment obstinately clings to a denial of consequences, the inevitable linkage of moral cause and moral effect, the inexorable, one might say, pitiless, outworking of the law of habit for moral health or misery: "Nothing we ever do is, in strict scientific literalness, wiped out".[75] Pride, envy, gluttony, anger and sloth, abetted by lying and double-dealing, whose seeds are sown in youth, are essentially, albeit less intensively, the same sins tarnishing the adult world, in which individuals scheme and prevaricate, breaking the laws of governors and kings to amass money, estates, and slaves.[76] Moral personalities become hardened in vicious practice as youth develops into full maturity, with more severe penalties for adult offenses because these are crimes against the law. So Jesus could not have been commending childhood innocence when he bade his followers imitate the lowliness of children. Christian humility is represented not by a prettified picture of pseudo-faultless children but by their small stature, which, implying dependence on earthly father and mother, symbolizes the spirit of interior tininess of the disciple of Jesus surrendering himself to the Father.

The underscoring of the causal continuity between boyhood and maturity may help dissipate the doubts of some who may be perplexed by what at first glance looks like morbid preoccupation with miscues that resemble peccadillos rather than full-blown sins. Augustine is not obsessed with hyperbolically inflated self-flagellation but is tracing to childhood beginnings the configuration his moral personality was to take in years ahead. Long before Freud and without the deadly baggage of his pansexual and mechanistic psychology, the ancients were actually aware that the child is father to the man. The self-aggrandizing drives of Augustine the rhetorician were initially spawned in the schoolrooms and play areas of Thagaste and Madauros. Laying responsibility for his later moral self at his own door, while implicitly discounting the shallow evasion of moderns who tax a benighted father and/or domineering mother for distortions in his development, he realistically accounts for the later warping of the moral self as the outgrowth of the earlier weaving of his own choosing. He was morally palsied later because he had deliberately committed real sins, not just childish foibles, in his early years. The vices of manhood enacted in bolder relief and more lurid colors the malefactions of boyhood; his mature years were noninnocent because his boyhood days were noninnocent.

Chapter 20: Thanksgiving for Natural Gifts of Boyhood

31. Confession of sins largely cedes place to the confession that is praise as Book 1 ends by returning to the theme of its opening chapters. There he praised God for the beauty of his transcendent and immanent attributes; here he praises him for his goodness resplendent in the natural gifts of boyhood. God diffuses his goodness in the universe first as creator, then as ongoing providential director. Even had Augustine not survived boyhood, he would not have stinted gratitude to the all-good for the scalar phases of his own being, stages of increasing specific complexity and concretion: he had natural existence, possessed life, and was endowed with sensation. To God also goes gratitude for instilling a desire for self-preservation, an automatic tendency manifest in the self-love of beasts as well (DC 1.26.27); a concern for well-being stamped with the imprint of divine oneness from which Augustine's own unity derives.[77] Because God is absolutely one, Augustine is whole and complete. Beings flowing from the creative hand resemble the One, bearing within their makeup traces of his unity. The unities in creatures multiplied through the universe signalize the immanent presence of the One that is their sovereign maker.[78]

Moving to a higher level, that of sensory activity, he indicates the estimative office of the interior sense, which guards the integrity, i.e., the soundness and unimpaired functioning, of the exterior senses. As a vital tendency preserved his organism, so his interior sense monitored the health of his outer senses (LA 2.5.12).[79] Even in his boyhood, howbeit problems pondered were not weighty, his cognitive powers were operating at a still higher level as the intellect in its apprehension of truth sat in judgment on sensory deliverances. His quest for truth was facilitated by a capacious memory that stored away most of the data and conclusions learned or discovered. He became a cultivated public speaker, skilled in orchestrating the complexes of words that are the signs and expressive instruments of truth. On the affective side, youthful friends buoyed his spirit. In aspiring for proper goods of body, sense, and mind, he recoiled from their evil counterparts: pain along with its companion, sorrow, dejection, and ignorance; canings and floggings that horrified him; loneliness and depression owing to absence of friends; and the emptiness of mind that is nescience. These qualities excite wonder over their beauty, evoking praise of "my God." Collectively taken as features of his individual nature, all these gifts constitute his "I" ordained to the God who is "my good." Unhappily, his self pursued pleasures, honors, and truths not for but against God, making him the prey of evils opposite to the three goods pined for: sorrows, confusions, and errors. The sorrows arose from a disordered spirit, the disorder itself being a punishment (1.12.19). Confusions were the bad fruit of inward disorders centered in self-sufficiency; the higher he was exalted, the more forcefully he was thrown down to the ground (P 32.[En.2.S.2].24). He fell into errors, downplaying his sins while distraught by the slightest imperfections in grammar (1.18.29). The three contraries of those aberrations supremely exist in God, who is his sweetness, honor, and confidence. His sweetness: whereas the world sweet in name is bitter in fact, God fills with divine pleasure those who lovingly taste him (P 51.18). His honor: in glorifying God, the human spirit is glorified (P 144.1); man never rises higher in spiritual honor than when he drops to his knees in adoration. His confidence: his salvation resting not on his own strength (P 32[En.2.S.2].24), he relies on the promised power of the One. Because ingredients of his being, these goods, when brought to full fruition, ensure that his self will be with God, analogously present to God as God is present to him. This development is possible only because God is, more radically, the source of the existence of the self that is the focus of these goods: "...and I myself will be with you because the existence of my self is your gift." He will be with God because he is from God; companionship presupposes the originative gift of existence. Any obscurity hovering about these somewhat cryptic words vapors off when they are taken to impart, though less memorably, the gist of the heart's seeking rest in God (1.1.1). The blessing of natural existence preludes the blessing of supernatural existence, in which he will finally rest in or be with God, his place (P 30[S.3].8). Moreover, the coupling of natural existence with union with God may anticipate 13.21.46, according to which, as God is good because he exists, so Augustine is ontically good because he exists. But only through the Holy Spirit can he become morally good, particpating in the inner life of God. It is grace that links natural existence with being-with-God or intimate union here and hereafter. The context of the union between existence and the fulfilling goodness that is companionship with God is supernatural; commanding the drama of creation and providence is the leitmotif of Spirit-initiated love orienting natural existence to supernatural destiny, urging finite human beings upward to lasting rest in an ecstatic fusion with infinite good.

NOTES

1. It does not seem altogether accurate to translate, as some do, *aliqua portio*, "a particle (or: tiny portion) of your creation." Augustine is not speaking deprecatingly of man but remarking his status in the universe. Man is a creature with a rank and function determined by his creator. Specifically, in terms of his soul, man occupies a middle position between the purely corporeal and God. On the lowest rung is a body mutable in space and time. A middle position is held by the soul, immutable in space but mutable in time. The highest being is God who is immutable in both space and time (E 18). Man achieves happiness or overcomes restlessness by holding the lowest or bodily things in subjection to his spirit and by becoming fully converted to the highest being that is God. As explicitly pointed out later (7.7.11), in virtue of his soul, Augustine was superior to lower things, inferior to God: this was his proper mean, the middle region appointed for his salvation. In the realm of grace Augustine is to live perseveringly in accord with the image of God, and, by so thriving as a servant of God, make lower things his servants. His pre-conversion restlessness stemmed from a foredoomed attempt to find a place of rest in lower things. When man gives way to pride in his middle station, *superbire in medio* (E 18), God resists the proudful person by casting him down to lower things; in exchange for his honor that is likeness to God, he suffers the dishonor that is likeness to cattle (T 12.11.16). For further analysis of man's median position see Madec, "Diagramme augustinienne," AUG 25(August, 1985), especially 81-8.

2. As E. De La Peza, *El significado de "cor" en San Agustin*, carefully shows, the term *cor* is polyvalent, used with multiple significations. At times the word is identified with *animus* (8.10.24), *anima* (8.10.24), *mens* (SDM 2.3.14), cogitation (P 7.9), and conscience (P 100.4). On other occasions it is distinguished from *animus* (4.13.20) and *anima* (4.11.16). These diverse meanings are interrelated and may be tied together in one signification: *cor* is the total activity of the soul in its operational dynamism. As *mens*, it is the specific human operation; as *intellectus*, it grasps meaning; as conscience, it is aware of the moral value of its actions. It is also equated with the will (GLA 14.29) and with the spiritual "I" (*cor meum ubi ego sum quicumque sum*; 10.3.4), the whole self (S 34.4.7). Thus *cor* denotes the source of specific human activity accompanied by a moral orientation; Pieza, especially 71-94. In viewing the heart as equivalent to or the ground of intelligence and as the seat of moral personality or conscience, Augustine meshes with the Biblical sense that the heart is one with intelligence (Solomon asked for an understanding heart; 1K 3.9) and also the radix of character (Mk 7.21.2Cor 5.12); on the Biblical notion see J. McKenzie, *Dictionary of the Bible*, 343-4. Neither the Bible nor Augustine makes the distinction, originating in roughly the last four centuries, between head and heart, between mind as the subject of intelligence and the heart as the seat of affectivity. *Cor inquietum* would seem to mean the whole interior man that embraces the operational mind oriented toward its culminating spiritual place.See also A. Maxsein, "Philosophia cordis bei Augustinus," AM 1, 357-71;

"Das Herz in der Erkentnis bei dem hl. Augustinus," AUGUS 3 (1958), 323-30. In spite of the learned suggestion in BA 13,579, n. 2, Augustine's signification seems more dissimilar then akin to the meaning of Pascal, for whom the heart is distinct from mind or reason, as indicated in the famous line, "The heart has reasons that reason knows nothing of."

3. A median portion of creation comes to know and love God by supernatural faith and charity. Prayer grounded on faith beseeches goods, spiritual values especially, and in response man praises God. Such praise is not a matter of discharging a duty, of making recompense to God for his goodness; rather, God moves the heart to rejoice in praising him. As love of God issues in spiritual delight, so praise that is joined to love is accompanied by delight. As man is made to love and thereby enjoy God, so he is made to praise him and rejoice in the very praising. From another angle, God spurs man to rejoice in praising him because he is made for God; by praising God, he participates more in divine perfections; by praising God, he is more united with him and, less restless, possesses more interior rest insofar as he shares more in the rest that is God.

4. As G-M 2, n.8, suggests, worthlessness of prayer to a false God probably alludes to Augustine's fruitless invocation of a spatialized unreality fabricated from phantasms (3.6.10). After the death of his friend his grief-stricken heart was inconsolable because it could not be healed by a pseudo-God (4.7.12).

5. Faith is prior to invocation. Faith is the fount of prayer: without it prayer dries up and dies. (i) So we believe in order that we may pray. (ii) So we pray in order that the very faith by which we pray not fail. Faith issues in prayer; the prayer elicited, in turn, implores fresh strength for faith. The Lord says, "Watch and pray lest you enter into temptation." To fail the trial implies departure from faith; a point confirmed when the apostles ask the Lord, "Increase our faith", their faith being not yet perfect (S 115.1.1).

6. In the opinion of BA 13, 275, n.2, following Courcelle, 43, n.5, the preacher is not Ambrose but Jesus Christ. While dismissing as fanciful P. de Labriolle's identification of Ambrose as *praedicator*, Courcelle, 43, n. 5, introduces no evidence at all for alleging that "in reality Jesus Christ, the author of revelation," is the preacher Augustine had in mind. Even if we call Jesus Christ the author of revelation, it seems gratuitous to assert that "author of revelation" means one who exercises the ministry of preaching. As 11.2.2 and 13.15.18, along with other texts, testify, preachers are ministers of the word sent by God to broadcast the word of salvation revealed through Christ. Walking in the path blazed by Paul and the other apostles, they are agents of God and Christ. Christ is the head of his body, the Church that is a supernatural organism equipped with diverse organs or ministries, modes of service in the Spirit of Christ. Christ as head cannot be assigned the work of his members; since he operates through his ministers, he is plainly then not one of his own ministers. Ministry, which is given a number of senses, takes on a very specific meaning to designate a holder of ecclesiastical office, a Church authority such as priest or bishop (P 67.34). See J. Lienhard, "Ministry," AE 567-9.

7. For word play concerning *invocabo* see G-M 3, n. 5.

8.   In its principal declensional variants *Deus meus* is used, by F. Van Fleteren's reckoning, some 667 times in the *Confessions.*

9.   Hell or *infernus,* so named because under the earth, is the abode of the dead, a region with two separate provinces, one of the just prior to Christ's resurrection and ascension, the other of the wicked in the hell called Gehenna. GL 12.33.62; 34,66. R 2.24.2. J. Taylor (tr.), *The Literal Meaning of Genesis,* 2, 320, nn. 171-2.

10.   At the outset Augustine wrestles with and summarily unravels the knotty question of the omnipresence of God because its resolution was one key to repudiation of Manichean dogma leading to espousal of Catholic doctrine (7.10.16; 11.17). This short analysis assures himself and his readers that he is indeed praying to and dialoguing with the true God. Du Roy, 469, lists over twenty texts in which Augustine employs the *ubique totus* formula. Spanning nearly three decades, from 388 to 417, these evidence that the wholly-everywhere theme was a constant in Augustine's thinking about God. Though compactly stated, his view of divine omnipresence in the *Confessions* concurs in essentials with the more elaborate exposition propounded some twenty years later in E 187, to which Augustine himself assigned the unofficial title "Treatise on the Presence of God" (2.49). Since the early dialogues carry no mention of *ubique totus,* Du Roy, 470, questions whether Augustine attained at Cassiciacum the notion signified by the phrase. However, the simple fact that the problem of divine ubiquity does not arise during the early dialogues at Cassiciacum would seem to explain the absence of *ubique totus.* Indeed since the account in Book 7 of a nonspatial God is veridical, Augustine undoubtedly arrived at an understanding of divine omnipresence prior to Cassiciacum, a view that was couched in words similar to, if not identical with, those in the pregnant phrase, *ubique totus* (5.2.2).

11.   Creation establishes things in being while divine conservation maintains them in existence (GL 8.26.48). The omnipotent and all-sustaining (*omnitenens*) maker of the subsistence of every creature (GL 4.12.22), the Father goes on working in the sense that his providential operation is a continuation of creation (GL 4.12.23). God's conservation of the universe is also called his containment of things, a dependence on him that is doubly expressed; God is in them and they are in God: "Thus I would not exist, my God, I would not exist at all unless you were in me, or, rather, I would not exist unless I were in you" (1.2.2). God-in-him stresses the effect; he-in-God, the cause. At times Augustine seems to prefer the latter formula: all things are in God rather than he in all things (DQ 20). Providential action also includes administration of created things toward their proper ends and to the good of the whole universe. Thus God's providential operation manifests divine immanence: God is present in all creation because all are in him. In contrast to human crafts-manship or all subdivine activity, the operation of God is interior to created things. Once a carpenter makes a box, the box remains outside him, lying in another place; he is exterior to the box. But God is so inwardly present to the world he fashions that after its making he is still everywhere present in the world (J 2.10), so that without his ongoing containment the world would utterly disappear (GL 4.12.23). Notice, interiority of God to things or things to God is

in the line of action or cause-and-effect, not in line of substance; things "are not in God as in his substance" (GL 4.12.23). In terms of substance or *essentia* (being) God is not interior but superior to creation; ontically he utterly transcends them. However, this ontic distance underlies causal intimacy; it is because God is transcendent, utterly superior to things, that he is so interior to each created thing. Because he is ontically above all, he is operationally inward to all (3.11.19). See S. Grabowski, *All-Present God*, 124.

12. While Augustine never explicitly elaborated the triple predication of divine attributes according to causation, negation, and analogy, these three modes are discernible in the list of attributes. In the line of causation God is designated creator of all finite things. In a negative perspective, God is called unchangeable; of him is denied the mutability at the core of all creaturehood. Later he learned that God is nonmaterial or spiritual (7.10.26), nonspatial or everywhere whole (5.2.2), and nontemporal or eternal (11.13.16). In a certain sense God is better known negatively than affirmatively, better known by not knowing (O 2.16.44). Finally, in the analogical mode features that are traces of God in the finite order are predicated of him on the infinite plane. Since God is absolute existence, attributes are predicated of him eminently or to a superlative degree; hence he is named most good or super-good, most just or super-just, and most beautiful or super-beautiful (S 341.7). In "Die unbegreifliche Wirklichleit der menschlichen Sehnsuch nach Gott," CAH 82-4, K. Kienzler contends that in 1.4.4 God is portrayed in superlative terms, then as immutable, then again as ever-active while inwardly at rest, next as affective, finally as a stern but kind judge.

In a textually rich article, "God in between Affirmation and Negation according to Augustine," *Augustine Presbyter Factus Sum*, CollAug. 1993, 73-97, T. van Bavel, sensitively explores the range and depth of negative appreciation of God. Again and again Augustine emphasizes man's radical incapacity to fully grasp or comprehend God. Since the mind can lay hold of the meaning of God in some fashion, Augustine favors the aphairetic posture of Plato rather than the totally apophatic method of Plotinus, which is equivalent or reducible to ontic agnosticism concerning God. A circumspective word needs to be said about the distinction between comprehending and understanding God. Augustine does not claim, "If you understand God, it is not God you are understanding." Rather, because the mind does understand or grasp (*intelligit vel capit*) God in some measure, he holds, "If you comprehend God, it is not God you are comprehending," (S 117.3.5; so also in S 21.2 and S 52.16, nn. 60 and 62, 92). Certainly God is radically other, as van Bavel trenchantly argues, but he is minimally accessible to human understanding and, where this language seems to fall short, the wonders of his being evoke fervent praise. On the divine attributes see also Gilson, *The Christian Philosophy of Saint Augustine*, 217-8, 22-3, and D. Burt's rigorously developed, though deceptively simple, account in *Augustine's World*, 239-42. See also L. Ayres and M. Barnes, "God," AE 384-90, especially 384-7, with updated bibliography.

13. Augustine hails God as *omnipotentissime*, most omnipotent. As is well known, he had a penchant for the superlative, describing his unconscious friend as most

absent in mind and sense (4.4.8) and the watered-down wine as most tepid (6.2.2. G-M 87, n. 3). Designation of God as super-omnipotent, however, may not be simply rhetorical exaggeration. It would seem to be one particularly justifiable attempt to break out of linguistic restraints to utter the unutterable somewhat less inadequately. In speaking of the inexpressible, we can express in some way what we can adequately express in no way (T 5.12.2). Though perhaps questionable by analytic criteria, "super-omnipotent" strains to better express inexpressible divine power.

14.   The wisdom that is God is said to remain standing not in virtue of immobility but in virtue of immutability. God is not immobile, a predicate suggesting possible subjection to motion; rather, he is immutable, free of all variation in place and time (P 138.8).

15.   To be led in old age is to be humiliated by the breakdown of the spiritual organism. The proud man, whatever his outwardly impressive flourish of self-worship, is inwardly frail, in decline that portends the second or final death in sin. (AJ 9.5. G-M 5,n.1.)

16.   As knowledge and mercy are properly but analogously said of God, so anger and repentance are predicated of God properly rather than metaphorically. When we purge human knowledge of its mutable features, we achieve a notion of the absolutely certain knowledge of God. Similarly, in thinking away the emotional sympathy in human mercy, we reach a notion of divine mercy that is the tranquil goodness designed to free individuals from misery. Again, in subtracting passional storm from anger, the mind seizes the notion of the vigor of retribution that is part and parcel of divine justice (QS 2.2.3). Only spiritual or intellectually mature Christians can properly understand God as angry and repentant. Carnal individuals, unable to rise above sensory associations, tend to ascribe such attributes to God in an anthropomorphic fashion. They cannot delete from these notions corporal features that condition only human anger and repentance (P 26 [En.2].8). Interestingly, Thomas Aquinas does not ascribe anger to God by proper analogy. In his view, anger is a sensitive appetite that so entails matter that the matter cannot be abstracted from its concept. Since anger, unlike joy, always inescapably implies imperfection, predication of anger of God can only be made metaphorically. S. th. 1.19.11;20.1 ad.2.

17.   In the fourth category of divine attributes Augustine alludes to the key truth of his salvific doctrine that grace is all, an all that proceeds initially and consum-mately from the sovereign One. God is most just and most merciful in distributing divine life and ultimate beatitude, at times in mysterious ways that escape human comprehension. *Initial* salvation is never merited but depends absolutely on the mercy of God. Through divine generosity Saul the persecutor was transfigured into Paul the preacher (QS 1.2.22). To challenge such a conversion would be to set human envy against divine generosity (S.168.4.4). However, *terminal* salvation that is heavenly reward requires human cooperation with grace; the common denarius of eternal life is given to those who labor in the vineyard (S 87.4.6). God demands a return on his investment, not because he gains but because his servants reap spiritual profits: God is "greedy" for man's salvation (S 94). But since his never-failing grace assures

success of spiritual enterprises, God, in rewarding his servants, crowns his own gifts. "Thus if good merits are the gifts of God, God does not crown your merits as your merits but as his own goods" (GLA 6.15). As God is the Lord of all material possessions, allotting them as he wills according to his justice (7.9.15), so is he Lord of all graces or spiritual possessions, apportioned according to his super-justice and super-mercy. Later Augustine will underline the supremacy of divine grace in his conversion (9.1.1) and ongoing progress (10.29.40).

18.   Intoxication cripples normal sensory and rational consciousness; his dehumanized state deprives a drunkard of perception of his surroundings. Analogously, the wine of divine love frees the self from normal rational awareness; in his superhuman state a soul intoxicated with God becomes oblivious of his human condition and concerns. Alypius becomes subhumanly drunk on the savage pleasures of the gladiatorial spectacles (6.8.13) while Nebridius in the bosom of Abraham becomes divinely inebriated by drinking from the fount of supernal wisdom (9.3.6).

19.   *Moriar, ne moriar* has proved to be a kind of *pons asinorum*, an aporia for some scholars, a number of whom render it with minor variations in this wise: Let me die [physically], lest I die [spiritually, i.e., of the final death of sin]. Solignac notes that the line may be rendered as a subjunctive of supposition, "whether I die or do not die" (BA 13, 282-3,n.1). In *Vig. chr.*, 1956, 229, quoted in BA 13, 282-3, n. 1, G. Wijdeveld suggests an alternate textual reading: *moriarne? moriar ut eam videam*: "Shall I die? Indeed I shall die in order to see your face". Such scholarly interpretations, albeit plausibly argued, are misguided because they take for granted that Augustine is once more using the couplet of contrasting deaths, bodily death and eternal death (S 231.2). However, commenting on Col 3.1-3, he decisively settles the question by providing what is, in effect, his own gloss. "If we live well, we died and rose again. But the individual who has not died and risen again is now living evilly: let him die lest he die. What is the meaning of, 'Let him die lest he die?' Let him change lest he be condemned (Col 3.1-3). These are the words of the Apostle. To him who has not yet died, I say, he should die. To him who is still living evilly I say, he should change" (S 231.3). *Moriatur, ne moriatur* means "let him die to sin (or: let his old, sinful self die), lest he die eternally;" or, summarily, *mutetur ne damnetur*. In this new couplet death to or mortification of the old self in time forestalls death of the old self in irremediable sin in eternity. Death to sin is a transformation, a sharing in the life of the risen Christ; the Christian who perseveres to this new life of love will not suffer eternal death.

20.   In BA 35, 271,n.2, G. Bardy traces the living-death insight to Seneca, *Consol. ad Marciam*, 21.6: "From the moment that a man sees light he starts walking along the road to death." H.-I. Marrou, *Théologie de l'histoire*, 54, also sources this in Seneca, *Ep. ad Lucil.* 24.20: "Each day we live, we die; each day subtracts a slice of our life from us"; an observation that may also indicate that existence is a dying life.

21.   Not by empirical inspection but by firm natural faith did Augustine learn that Patricius and Monica were his parents (6.5.7). Occasionally a switch of babies at birth induces a mistaken faith. In December, 1978, Regina Twigg and

Barbara May gave birth to girls in a Wauchula, Florida hospital. However, Barbara's ailing child was somehow substituted for Regina's healthy daughter. After Arlena, the substituted child, died of a heart defect in 1988, genetic tests established that she could not have been Regina Twigg's child. Subsequent inquiry showed that Kimberly, the girl raised by the Mays, was the Twiggs' biological child. After lengthy legal disputes, Kimberly eventually returned to live with her biological parents. *Philadelphia Inquirer*, July 27, 1991, A3. More recently, genetic tests proved that Paula Johnson was the biological mother not of the girl she raised for three years but another child switched for hers in a Virginia hospital in 1995. *Philadelphia Inquirer*, August 1, 1998, A2. Genetic testing does not displace faith as practically primary in determination of parents but is employed secondarily, in comparatively rare cases, to confirm veridical faith or disconfirm erroneous faith.

22.   In God "there live the eternal reasons of all irrational and temporal things." This summary statement counterposes for rhetorical effect the eternal in God and the temporal in creatures, and the "rational" in God and the irrational in creatures. Other texts (13.3.4. GL 7.2.7.43) see God's creative power encompassing the rational as well as the irrational among his creatures.

23.   Augustine briefly broaches the vexing problem of the origin of the soul, which he first raises in LA 3.20.56-21.59. Four possibilities are considered, without resolution of the matter. (i) From the soul of Adam all other souls are derived (spiritual traducianism); (ii) each soul is created at the proper time of conception or birth (creationism); (iii) preexistent souls are sent by God to dwell in bodies; (iv) preexistent souls choose to dwell in bodies. In a later more closely argued account creationism is found wanting (GL 10.4.5), but he remains unable to determine whether either traducianism or a modified creationism (according to which souls are made in the primal creation, to be infused into singular bodies at the proper times; GL 7.24.35) is rationally preferable (GL 10.6.9-9.16). His thinking stayed inconclusive throughout the rest of his life, forcing him to confess that he did not know before and does not know the answer now (R 1.1.3). See O'Daly, 16-8, for a precise balanced account. By way of parenthesis we may remark that while holding that the fetus in the mother's womb was an unborn child, truly human, he never settled the question of when preborn life becomes specifically human, either at the conception, at the time it assumes a human figure, or at the time of quickening. QH 2.80. DG 56. AO 1.25. See O. Wermlinger, "Abortus," AL 1. 6-10. O'Daly, 19. J. Bauerschmidt, "Abortion," AE 1.

Augustine's vague references to a possible preexistence of the soul seem to lend credence to R. O'Connell's contention that Augustine, in his early works especially, espoused Plotinus' theory of the fall of the soul (see his *Saint Augustine's Early Theory of Man, A.D. 380-391*). According to C. Harrison, *Beauty and Revelation in the Thought of Saint Augustine*, 33,"...most scholars...now regard [his opinion] as having been satisfactorily refuted." As R. Russell argued in his review of O'Connell's works in *Thought* 44 (1969), 303-5, Augustine acknowledged his incertitude about the origin of the soul from LA to R. Even granted, not conceded, that a younger Augustine did embrace the Plotinian theory, it beggars belief that he never explicitly repudiated it in R. Moreover, investigation of some thirteen texts discloses that Augustine never unequivocally subscribed to the theory; O'Daly, "Did St. Augustine Ever Believe in the Soul's Pre-existence"?, AS 5 (1974), 227-35. Besides being devoid of any solid evidential support in key texts, O'Connell's claim may commit the fallacy of affirming the consequent in terms of the psychic disorders proceeding from the fall of the soul. Stated very compactly, his argument goes: if the soul of Augustinian man is fallen, it should be malordered; but it is afflicted with moral time, torn apart and scattered in multiplicity (11.29.39. O'Connell, *Saint Augustine's Confessions: The Odyssey of Soul,* 142-4); therefore the soul suffered a Plotinian fall. This line of reasoning is fallacious, logically identical with the line of argumentation: if this man has cancer, he will lose weight, experience a decline of appetite, and become listless; but he shows these symptoms; therefore he has cancer. One need not be an Aristotle to discern that the symptoms may very well arise from another cause. The formal invalidity is a sign of the material unsoundness of the reasoning. Correspondingly, another cause underlies moral disharmony and breakdown; on Augustine's showing, the massive fact of original sin that has wounded the race from the beginning is the reason why man is beset by moral time. Indeed the Adamite Fall made it unnecessary for Augustine, we may suggest, to invoke a Plotinian fall. Had he even seriously considered this fall, he would have dismissed it as a redundancy, a sort of bootless and ineffective moral tautology, an explanation that, not to instance other deficiencies, sins against the principle of natural and supernatural economy; a double fall is as indefensible as reliance on two saviors to redeem man from debilities consequent upon one primordial disaster. It would be ungenerous to let this occasion pass without noting that throughout his impressively styled exposition and defense of his controverted thesis Fr. O'Connell exhibited not only dialectical acumen but never swerved from a gentlemanly, urbane temper.

24. Dealing more systematically with eternity is 11.11.13-13.16, which argues that God as the Selfsame enjoys an eternity that transcends all times. Because changeless, his day is an immutable today, an eternal present, within which all times are created, contained, and measured. Other texts reiterate the theme that the temporal day (with its parts) is unceasingly ceasing: P 38.7; 76.8; 101 (S.2). 10.

25. With the possible exception of his opening chapter (1.1.1), Augustine employs our Lord's directive, *quaerite et invenietis,* and its correlative phrases (Mt 7.7) in reference to faith seeking understanding. The seeker is the believer; the finder, the one who achieves understanding of Christian doctrine in Scripture. The same parallel between belief and understanding and seeking and finding appears in 12.1.1; 23.32; 24.33, and 13.38.53. Knocking and having the door opened, a similar couplet from Mt 7.7, occurs by itself in at least six places (6.4.5; 11.18; 11.20. 11.2.3; 2.4.12.12.15), and in conjunction with seeking-finding in two other passages, 12.1.1 and 13.38.53.

26. In "L'humanité du Christ comme lac parvulorum et comme via dans la spiritualité de saint Augustin," AUG(L) 7(1957), 245-81, T. van Bavel

discerningly distinguishes two sorts of Christians. The first is the *parvulus*, the little one who feeds on the milk of Christ, not yet strong enough to be nourished by the solid food of doctrine. He is carnal in the sense that his religious thinking is ordinarily tied to images. In virtue of faith he believes that Christ died on the cross to redeem mankind, and while he believes in the triune God, he cannot understand or properly conceive the trinity. The second kind of Christian is the *intelligens*, who understands the truths of faith; he is a spiritual capable of grasping spiritual or nonmaterial entities. R. Teske, in "Spirituals and Spiritual Interpretation in Augustine," AS 15 (1984), 65-81, while refining the meaning of carnals and spirituals, traces the origin of the distinction to Augustine's encounter with Christian Neoplatonism, which opened the door to cognition of incorporeal beings. Notice, Augustine employs carnal in an analogous manner. The word signifies bodily activity, then by extension improper moral conduct, then again image-ridden thought. As signifying the corporeal, carnal is used four times: 9.10.24; 9.13.34; 13.17.21; 12.24.37. In the acceptation of improperly sensual outlook the word is found five times: 2.1.1; 4.15.25; 5.8.15; 6.16.26; 8.5.11. The term as adjective or noun meaning image-ridden thought occurs at least eight times: 6.3.4; 7.17.23; 12.17.24; 12.30.41; 13.12.13; 13.13.14; 13.18.23; 13.23.33.

27. In recent years misinterpretation has beclouded Augustine's nuanced attribution of the outward signs of original sin to infants. In the opinion of A. Sage, not till PMR (412-3) did Augustine elaborate a fully developed doctrine of original sin. The first stage of his thought restricted the consequences of original sin to the body; not the soul but the body alone suffered a disharmony. Aberrant infantile actions manifest *péché d'origine*, not original sin in the strict sense. However appealing because of its scholarly niceties, this interpretation fails to account for the plain reference to each man as a son of Adam (8.10.22), a protoparent who is the source of the bitter sea afflicting the race (13.20.28). Unfortunately, in his judicious critique of Sage, P. Rigby slips into an error at the opposite extreme, contending that the conduct of infants proves them guilty of personal sins, their actions reprehensible not simply as indicators of a state of sin but as actual sins. Rigby's contention that infants, though without knowledge, are nonetheless guilty is at odds with Augustine's position, unswervingly avowed over the years, that knowledge and will must be operative for the commission of personal sins, for which infants are not blameworthy. Explicitated, the reasoning in the *Confessions* runs: if an infant is responsible, he commits personal sins; if he commits such sins, he is blameworthy; yet the undeniable fact is, he is not blameworthy; therefore he cannot be charged with personal sins. Elsewhere Augustine affirms the traditional teaching that infants are not guilty of personal sins (*innocentes a propriis peccatis*; E 186.8.30), this in accord with John Chrysostom, who avers that they have no sins of their own (CJ 1.6.22). Yet since, in effect, every man is Adam (P 132.10), infants manifest their state of original sin by nonvoluntarily or subvoluntarily sinful actions, inexplicable unless they arise from some condition of disorder. See A. Sage, "Péché originel: naissance d'un dogme," REA 13 (1967), 11-48 and "Le péché originel dans la pensée de saint Augustin

de 412 à 430," REA 15 (1969), 75-112. P. Rigby, *Original Sin in Augustine's Confessions*. See R. DeSimone, "Modern Research on the Sources of Saint Augustine's Doctrine of Original Sin," AS 11 (1980), 205-27.

28. Their use of reason yet underdeveloped, very young children rely more on sense than reason. Hence it is that infants who are crying show a greater facility in sensorially distinguishing even the touch and the closeness of their nurses and will not tolerate the odor of unfamiliar persons (QA 28.54.) Since babies tend to put all and sundry objects into their mouths, nurses resort to various precautions to prevent contact with harmful entities like sharp knives and dirt-encrusted sticks.

29. God's proper power and goodness are manifest even in one section of the universe. If nothing but Augustine's body with its highly articulated sensorium existed, only God could have produced it, for creation requires omnipotence and directedness to the goods of bodily integrity.

30. According to Aristotle, each being of nature is constituted by material and formal causes and activated by efficient and final causes (*Phys.* 1.7-9, 189b30-192b6; 2.3-5, 194b18-197a35; 2.8-9,198b10-200b10). For Augustine, each thing in the universe is constituted and determined by three explanatory factors or ontic ingredients: measure, number, and weight; or, in another formulation, mode, form or species, and order. (i) Measure originally bespeaks quantity; measurement ascertains that a room is ten feet wide and twelve feet long. Thus measurement assigns a limit or definite size to an object. Since measure betokens limit (*modus*), measure and mode are used interchangeably. By extension measure or mode is predicated of the ontic structure of things. In a universe consisting of a plurality of substances, no substance is utterly diffuse; each substance is a definite thing, with a discernible ontic boundary. (ii) Number also has a quantitative sense; we count five fingers on a hand. By analogical transfer number gives form to things; number is said to signify form. Number or form designates the specific makeup of a thing that has mode; it is the species of an entity, the inner law of its being that bespeaks unity and harmony of its parts. (iii) Like its ontic co-ingredients, weight too has a primary quantitative signification. Whatever the units of measurements, lead is heavier than a stalk of wheat, water heavier than oil, and a stone heavier than air. Strictly speaking, in ancient physics a stone has a natural heaviness that bears it downward, and fire a natural lightness that carries it upward. Analogously, weight is taken to mean any natural tendency in a thing that bears it to its proper place. Weight then comes to signify order: by an inner weight or order a thing is ordained to act or move toward a certain goal (GL 4.3.7).

As omnipotent, God is creator of all measure, number, and weight or of all mode, form, and order. Not only does he fashion these ontic ingredients according to eternal reasons or exemplars, but each of these exists in an eminent or more excellent manner in God himself. Stripped of creaturely imperfections, measure, number, and weight properly exist in God. God is the supreme measure, the supreme number, the supreme order (or weight), these features being present in God in an immutable and eternal way (GCM 1.12.18). God is the measure without measure, the number without number, the weight

without weight (GL 4.4.8). God is absolute measure in virtue of which all other
measures exist. He is without measure; no outside agent measures or
determines him. So too is he absolute or infinite form, forming all others,
formed by no other. God is order or weight in a special sense: he is wholly at
rest in himself. God is not ordered to another good; rather, all other things are
ordered or weighted toward him. Moreover, it may be mentioned, the
arithmetical one is said to be the source of all measure in things; the one is the
measure of the measures that are numbers. Analogously, God as One is the
measure of all created measures; as utterly indivisible, he is the measure of
lesser measures that are undivided but multiple. See W. Roche, "Measure,
Number, and Weight in Saint Augustine," NS 15, (1941), 350-76. Also V.
Bourke, *Augustine's View of Reality*, 18-27, 31-2, 63-4, 63-75, 109. See also L.
Ayres, "Measure, Number, and Weight," AE 550-2.

31.   In common with ancient thinkers Augustine listed six ages of human life:
        infantia, pueritia, adulescentia, juventus, senior aetas (or *senior* [*aetas*]), and *senectus*
        (or *deterior aetas*) (GCM 1.23.35-40. VR 26.48). (1) Infancy (1.6.10) lasts
        ordinarily until around the age of two. It is a period of nourishment and rapid
        growth of the body, all of whose events are totally forgotten by the baby (VR
        26.48). *Primordia* and *infantia* seem to be roughly synonymous; the terms are
        assigned the same signification in GCM 1.23.35. Courcelle's suggestion, 43,
        that *primordia* refers to prenatal existence is not altogether accurate. (ii)
        Boyhood starts with the memory of words, which underlies actual speaking
        (VR 26.48) and runs from around the age of two till fifteen (1.8.13). (iii)
        Adulescentia, young manhood, begins at fifteen (2.1.1) with the appearance of
        puberty, the capacity to propagate offspring (2.2.2. VR 26.48), and is
        terminated at thirty. (iv) There follows *juventus*, manhood, the initial stage of
        mature adulthood, at thirty-one (7.1.1), when an individual performs the duties
        of his social station (VR 26.48). (v) *Juventus* is succeeded, probably around the
        age of forty or forty-five, by *senior aetas*, later manhood which is marked by
        some respite or quasi-retirement from burdens of *juventus* (VR 26.48). (vi)
        Senectus, old age, probably beginning in the fifties, is characterized by a
        lessening of physical energy and at times by a decline of mental powers.
        Courcelle suggests that at times *puer* is used somewhat loosely; Adeodatus,
        when fifteen or sixteen in 387, is still called *puer* (44, n.3); however, 9.6.14 states
        not that he was fifteen but nearly fifteen–hence still reckoned a *puer*. Yet
        apparently Augustine does employ the term less strictly when he refers to the
        sixteen-year-old Valentinian as *puer* (9.7.15). Courcelle 44,n.31.

32.   Ordinarily, Augustine considers time coming from the future through the
        present into the past (11.21.27. GL 2.14.29; 5.5.12. CD 12.16; 13.11). In a
        physical perspective, however, the time unit moves from what was past
        through the present to the future.

33.   Changes in countenance, like those evincing anger and sorrow, Augustine
        regards as natural signs (DC 2.1.1). These are designated, figuratively of course,
        natural words, natural signs that, in lieu of verbal communication, serve as
        surrogates of words. Reference to natural words apparently alludes to the Stoic
        position that all words are natural signs, a contention that he first partially

accepted while maintaining that some words have natural origins (*Dial* 6.3-5). Later he seems to have largely abandoned the Stoic claim (D. Jackson, "The Theory of Signs in St.Augustine's *De Doctrina Christiana*," in R. Markus [ed.] *Augustine: A Collection of Critical Essays*, 97); the only natural words among men are facial expressions that are natural but nonverbal.In the same volume see: R. Markus, "St. Augustine on Signs," 61-91.

34.   For a brief judicious survey of the meaning of human language and the means of its acquisition see S. Langer, *Philosophy in a New Key* [3rd ed.], 103-43.

35.   It may be appropriate at this point to comment briefly on the four stages of the Roman educational system through which Augustine passed. (i) The primary school in his hometown, which he entered near seven in 361, was presided over by a *primus magister* (1.13.20), a teacher first in time but lowest in rank. Instruction was elementary, drilling being the rule, with little left to imagination. Insistence on learning by rote, though excessive by contemporary standards, was necessary because printed books were nonexistent. Fixed impressions in memory had to do duty for what repeated consultations of textbooks furnish today. Such constant drilling Augustine judged odious (1.13.22); understandably so, since his intelligence was that of a budding mastermind quick to grasp, sure to retain. (ii) Augustine, when near eleven in 365, advanced to the secondary school in Thagaste, taught by a *grammaticus* in a shop curtained off from passerby (1.13.20). Along with meticulous dissection of the various parts of speech, a thorough explication from every angle analyzed principal passages from the *quadriga*, Virgil (poetry), Terence (drama), Sallust (history), and Ciero (oratory), including selections from other authors. (iii) Two years later, in 367, toward the age of thirteen, he traveled south to Madauros for studies that apparently constituted what might be called a kind of a basic training in rhetoric. There he pursued development in literary and rhetorical matters (2.3.5), in which more emphasis was laid on creative rendition of stock characters and situations (1.17.27). After two years in Madauros shortage of funds brought schooling to a halt: 369-370, his sixteenth year, was spent in idleness back in Thagaste (2.2.4). (iv) In 370 he migrated to Carthage, at whose quasi-university the shining star was Cicero, the study of a number of whose works constituted the core of the rhetorical program.

36.   For the Roman system of education see H.-I. Marrou, *A History of Education in Antiquity*, 265-91; BA 13, 659-61. For Augustine's later intellectual development see A. Solignac, "Doxographies et manuels dans la formation philosophique de saint Augustin," RA (1958), 113-48. BA 13, 83-112.

37.   An uncompromising moral realist, Augustine discerns that God cannot forgive him unless he frankly confesses that he has sinned. His sinning cannot be shifted onto fickle fortune or inevitable fate (whose concrete workings astrologers pretend to determine) or some alien nature or substance, rooted in the evil principle of the Manichees (P 7.19). His *peccabam* implicitly blocks access to the illusory escape routes from guilt laid down by the effective denial of personal responsibility for evil in astrological and Manichean theories.

38.   False curiosity is the desire to experience objects simply for the thrill of experiencing them. The curiosity that induces men to take pleasure in gazing at

sensorially repulsive objects like a mangled corpse also draws people to the excitements of the circus and gladiatorial combat (10.35.54-5). Even men of solid virtue were not immune to addiction to the circus and gladiatorial contests, during the latter of which the usually sober Alypius turned into a manic fan reveling in the bloodshed (6.7.12-8.13). Moreover, the expression, *eadem curiositate...per oculos emicante in spectaculis*, alludes to Augustine's theory of vision, according to which rays of light shine out or radiate (*emicant*) from the eyes to illuminate the visible object. QA 23.43.GL 1.16.31; 4.34.54; 7.13.20; 12.16.32. T 9.3:3. E 137.8. S 277.10. GL 4.34.54 speaks of the *radius emicans ex oculis nostris*, and, according to T 9.3.3, we see bodies because our eyes radiate light-rays, *radios qui per eos [oculos] emicant*).

39.   Spectacles or public shows is a general term embracing circus games, horse racing, gladiatorial combats, and theatrical plays. Only the wealthy could finance the considerable outlay for these enterprises. Hence such donors were held in high repute in their community, their largess earning them the secular nimbus of Men of Distinction.

40.   It was apparently not unusual for the catechumenate signs to be conferred more than once. CR 25.46-9. PMR 2.26.42. S 201A.8; 260 C.1. BA 13, 114.

41.   When drawing closer to full commitment to Catholicism, Augustine first espoused the false opinion of Photinus that Christ was not truly the Son of God but a man filled with unequalled divine wisdom (7.19.25). Yet twice in this passage he refers to Christ as God: "the humility of the Lord our God" descended to earth; and "baptism of your Christ, my God and Lord." Monica probably taught him that Christ was God in some vague sense. Perhaps later in Milan his fundamental belief in Christ's divinity was "hermeneuticized" or deconstructed, under the influence of "advanced" misled Catholics, into the theory that divine sonship reduces to the milder claim that God was in Christ. Again, he may be glossing his recall of the events with the wholly orthodox interpretation of the Catholic bishop of 397.

42.   Augustine was surely a Catholic Christian from the very beginning. He drank in the name of Christ with is mother's milk (3.4.8), and the Catholic religion was knitted into the marrow of his soul. But apparently he never received detailed instruction in the truths of the faith; perhaps Monica, who had no formal education, felt incapable of imparting such instruction. Again, it seems that his home was not marked by formal or informal prayer; only at school, to escape punishment, did he venture his first prayers for divine solace and protection (1.9.14). It seems reasonable to think that his acceptance of God's existence and divine providence, which he never doubted (6.5.7-8), started in his boyhood. The outline of the life of the Christ who came to save man from the consequences of human pride implies the existence and providence of God. The existence of an all-caring God is also betokened in the boy Augustine's belief in the salvific efficacy of baptism. On Augustine's initial Christian outlook see BA 13,114-5.

43.   "The whole Church is his [Christ's] mother because through the grace of God it gives birth to his members, i.e., his faithful" (SV 5.5). *Ecclesia mater* is adopted from prior ecclesiastical writers. P. Rinetti, "Sant' Agostino e l' *Ecclesia Mater*."

AM 2, 827-34. S. Grabowski, *The Church*, 27.

44. A person of chaste love loves God for his own sake, worshiping gratis him by whom he has been redeemed gratis. Husband and wife evidence chaste love when they love one another gratis. Similarly, the bonding of the soul with God is quasi-marital; God the true and truthful husband, makes the soul fruitful with offspring in the line of eternal life (P 55.17). Moreover, reward is not wanting to the chaste heart that loves God gratis, God himself being the reward of chaste love (P 72.32). Again, chaste love is the contrary of fornication of the spirit that is desertion of God for the service of earthly goods and the demons. The Christian of chaste love lacks nothing in loving God alone, he possesses all things in possessing the God through whom all things were made (P 72.33).

45. Monica is described, *sempiternam salutem [Augustini] carius parturiebat*: she was undergoing labor pains for Augustine's delivery into eternal salvation. Only much later did the delivery end in successful birth; the servant of God travailed (*parturivit*) in her body to enable Augustine to be born in temporal light, and travailed in her heart to enable him to be born to eternal light (9.8.17). Though the Latin spelling is Monnica (9.13.37), it seems preferable to retain the traditional English equivalent.

46. Putting off baptism was common not only in North Africa but throughout the Roman Empire. It is well known that Ambrose was still unbaptized prior to becoming bishop of Milan in 374. Some candidates were spiritually indifferent, others simply too lazy to bother about baptism. Most resorted to postponement as a handy excuse for ongoing casual disobedience of the commandments; freedom from baptism was tantamount to license in action. In effect, catechumens delayed baptism in the hope that toward the end of their days an auspicious baptism would wash them clean of all debris of the past (S 16A.6). During physical and civic disasters the dilatory panicked and hastily begged for baptism. An earthquake in Jerusalem prompted 7,000 baptisms, and a like calamity in Sitifi in Mauretania galvanized nearly 2,000 to be laved (S 19.6). Augustine continually took up the cudgels against the shallowness and grave peril of this easy-does-it short cut to last-minute salvation without sweat or tears (S 229.8-9). Van der Meer, 48-51.

47. Augustine speaks the truth that cries out (*clamet*) within his spirit, truth in whose light he dispassionately discriminates between solid learning and the error of literary fiction. However unappealing to sense, factual learning is preferable to literary pictures attractive to the fleshly self. The crying out of truth within overcomes the crying out without, the powerful opinion of the literary establishment.

48. Augustine shrewdly singles out the spelling of Aeneas as the outcome of conventional determination, to which literati conformed in his day. Thought occupies the primary place, then is signified by the sounded word, and finally is expressed by the written word (T 15.10.19). The spelling of words and, in particular, proper names tends to be the last to receive fixed specification. Scholars agree that Shakespeare was spelled in more than one way even by the great poet himself during his lifetime.

49. Ascertainment of the extent to which Augustine's thought was dependent on

Greek sources is the reason why scholars are concerned about of how much Greek he knew. It seems agreed that over the years he gradually progressed in his knowledge. For reasons he was never able to elucidate, his early performance in Greek was dismal (1.13.20;14.23). Apparently his schooling touched on only the barest elements of the language. In the opinion of Solignac, BA 13, 662, n.6, however, Augustine's estimate seems too self-disparaging; the Greek he garnered was roughly equivalent to the amount of Latin learned by an intelligent French student who graduates with a bachelor's degree in the classical program. In any case, through further study he was capable of revising with some competence parts of the Latin Bible in the light of the Septuagint. In 415-6, during the Pelagian controversy, he had no trouble checking the Latin translation of the Cappodocians and St. John Chrysostom against the original Greek. Finally, in 428 he translated directly from the Greek the *Anacephalaiosis*, a short version of Epiphanius' *Panarion*, which he used as chapters 1-7 of H, a rendering, however, not accomplished without tears (Marrou, 637). On the basis of Augustine's manifest reliance on or reference to Greek sources, Marrou, following S. Angus, concludes that "he had a limited working knowledge of Biblical Greek, a very slight working knowledge of patristic Greek, and apparently no knowledge of classical Greek;" Angus, *The Sources of the First Ten Books of St. Augustine's De Civitate Dei*, 276. Still, as Solignac, following P. Henry, *Plotin et l'Occident* 133-7, notes, it seems inadvisable to accept without qualification Augustine's self-deprecatory assessment of himself as not competent in Greek (T 3, *proemium*); his lack of competence may mean that he never achieved a mastery of Greek. Worth remarking is that the judgment of the Spanish-born American philosopher G. Santayana (1863-1952) of his own linguistic attainments was severe: "Latin and Greek, French, Italian and German, although I read them, were languages I never learned well" (6); "A General Confession," *The Philosophy of George Santayana*, 3-30. Because he never acquired full fluency, Santayana believed that he was not proficient in these tongues. Perhaps a somewhat similar scrutiny in the light of exacting criteria was operative in Augustine's low assessment of his grasp of Greek. For a thoughtful appraisal see Bonner, 394-5. Academics subconsciously inclined to cast a supercilious eye on Augustine's limitations in Greek might reflect on the intellectually cramping conditions of his working life as a cleric. A genius gifted not only with the visual but also the aural-oral apparatus for linguistic fluency, he would have experienced little trouble in mastering Greek under favorable circumstances. But his crushing work load as a bishop effectively denied him the leisure to concentrate on Greek. In 416 two episcopal councils directed that each week he be allotted five days of seclusion in which to make a more probing study of the Scripture. However, in fact, except for a short span, he was not accorded this intellectual-spiritual solitude (E 213.5). Although he was tireless, the demands on his schedule were so clamorous that he could spare only small slices of time, unsystematically seized upon, for improving his Greek. In short, periods for gaining advanced proficiency were just not available: this is probably one major reason why this outstanding linguist never attained overall fluency in

Greek commensurate with his prodigious verbal prowess.

50. According to T. van Bavel, "Discipline," AE 273-6, especially 223, *correptio*, reproof, is distinct from *correctio*, correction.

51. DC 2.40.60 sets this forth in more detail. "As the Egyptians possessed not only idols and heavy burdens...but also vessels and ornaments of gold and silver;...so all the teachings of the pagans contain not only superstitious views...but also liberal disciplines more adapted to use in pursuit of the truth and certain very useful moral precepts; in addition, there are found among them some true teachings, bearing on worship of the one true God." Along with Cyprian, Lactantius, Victorinus, Hilary, and countless others, Augustine expropriated the wealth of pagan thought. Moreover, in DC, especially, Book 2, Augustine elaborates a firmly textured program of Christian education that utilizes the liberal disciplines for the formation of laity as well as clergy; see E. Kevane, *Augustine the Educator*, 134-9, who bases himself on Marrou, 331-2, 383. Apparently the Cassiaciacum dialogues dealt with some of the elements of a schema of a school curriculum, presenting the broad outlines of a philosophical outlook in a Christian framework; see Kevane, 83-110, 362-9, who draws support from the authority of Marrou, 299-327, for whom the *exercitatio animi*, the training of the mind in the liberal arts, sets the stage for the *purgatio animae*, the moral purification of the soul. In fine, for Augustine, all that is precious in ancient thought is to be exploited for Christian intellectual maturation that disposes toward moral refinement, both oriented to the happiness which consists of the union of the mind with the truth that is God.

52. See I. Bochet, *Saint Augustin et le désir de Dieu*, 52-4, 140,n.1.

53. O. Perler, *Les voyages de saint Augustin*, 74-81.

54. By metonymy wood stands for the ship that is the Church piloted by Christ, which is fashioned from the wood of the Cross; BA 13,316, n. 1, and V. Bourke, *Confessions*, 25, n.68. Texts on the menacing character of the sea are examined in H. Rondet, "Le Symbolisme de la mer chez saint Augustin," AM 2, 691-701.

55. The relevant lines from Terence's *Eunuch*, occurring within 584-91, may be rendered in simple English verse: "Said he, O what an awesome, mighty god! / Heaven's temples tremble when booms his sovereign sound. / Shall I not copy this, I, a mere clod? / So did I imitate and pleasure found."

56. The *paenula* was a long sleeveless cloak, a kind of scholar's gown, worn by grammarians. According to G-M 25, n.10, Augustine may be speaking somewhat sarcastically; the outer garment of academic distinction conceals a lack of inner moral distinction.

57. This incisive remark is a slightly adapted quotation from *Tusc. disp.* 1.26.

58. From Vespasian on, emperors decreed that teachers be subsidized by state salaries, (the salaries were supplemented by student fees), the amount of which was probably displayed in the forum. G-M 26, n. 7.

59. *Eloquentia rebus persuadendis sententiisque explicandis*: some have translated, not altogether felicitously, the latter phrase, as "for (or: in) developing thoughts (or: opinions)." Here Augustine refers to the two main features of rhetoric: it is persuasive and explanatory or, simply, rhetoric is the persuasive exposition of claims. Rhetoric is the dialectical or analytical feature in eloquence necessary

for *sententiisque explicandis*, for a reasoned account of claims. Again, the distinction between *persuadendis* and *explicandis* may allude to the two sorts of declamation performed in the schools: *suasoriae*, which stressed dramatization of events; *controversiae*, which laid emphasis on rational analysis in presentation of a court case. In practice, outside an academic milieu both the persuasive and analytical were operative in every rhetorical assignment. See Marrou, *History of Education*, 202-3. See J. Campbell and M. McGuire, *The Confessions of St. Augustine*, 87, n. 212, resting on the authority of earlier classical scholars such as J. Duff, J. Sandy, A. Gwynn, and C. Baldwin. See Marrou, *History of Education*, 202-3.

60.   In an age of the slickly packaged TV sound-bite, we are apt to forget that oratory in the ancient world demanded long years of training. Augustine's declamation in the person of the distraught Juno, though only secondarily persuasive and emphatically dramatic, was an excellent propaedeutic to proficiency in oratory; he had to carefully plan his declamation, giving it a firm logical texture. After drawing up a scheme, an orator had to enflesh the skeleton in moving prose, marked by vivid imagery and affectively charged phrases. Though more persuasion than a declamation, the ordinary speech was a kind of dramatic presentation, in which an orator performed as an actor, moving his hearers with feelingful intensity. No doubt Augustine fully displayed these components in the well-articulated ideas delivered with panache in the address at the installation of Bauto as consul (January, 385) and the encomium to Emperor Valentinian II (November, 385; 8.7.17), both given at Milan in his post as official orator (5.12.23). More recent scholarship apparently raises doubts about the date of the Valentinian encomium. See Book 6, n.27 below.

61.   Today oratory is labeled public speaking, with most graduates acquiring their degrees without taking the subject. In late antiquity, however, oratory was not a marginal discipline but the acme to which other pursuits were subordinate. Concretely viewed, grammar, dialectic, and literature, including the study of Virgil and Cicero, were instruments to be applied to the shaping of the accomplished rhetor, who was more orator than writer. Hence whereas contemporary education stresses composition of a scholarly paper worked up in the library and delivered orally, if at all, in the seminar, ancient education aimed principally at readying, through countless hours of practice, a rhetorical piece, this recast again and again till raised to full orational life by polished diction, facial movements, and artlessly smooth body language.

62.   In GCM 1.23.40, birds, serpents, and beasts of the field symbolize respectively pride, curiosity, and carnal concupiscence. The pairings are slightly altered in P 8.13, where fish rather than serpents stand for curiosity while birds and beasts of the field continue to symbolize pride and lust of the eyes. The symbols are not invoked in the extended treatment of the threefold concupiscence in 10.30.41-41.66. Later the animal symbols reappear, again somewhat modified, in 13.21.30-1, in which serpents and beasts of the field symbolize curiosity and lust of the eyes, with pride figured by wild beasts. The birds of Gn 1.20 are deputed a new symbolic office, standing for the voices of divinely anointed

messengers of Christianity (13.20.26).

63. The connection between worship of idols and worship of demons is so close that they are virtually one and the same. Slaves of enormous pride, the devil and his minions hunger for worship as veritable gods, which wins from men public recognition of the divine honor they inwardly arrogate to themselves. So intense is this desire for worship that they become furious if sacrifice is not offered to them in the name of idolatry. P 26[En.2].19; 96.12. CD 2.10; 8.14,24.

64. Augustine learned the rules of rhetoric from his teachers but garnered expertise in eloquence mainly by close observation, leading to imitation, by prolonged practice, of the performances of his teachers (DC 4.1.5). Analogously, a matter he regrets, he assimilated practical rules of a misguided morality by copying examples of a pagan value system in the avowed outlook of his teachers, notably the prominent guideline that a minor grammatical miscue is always egregious and a grave moral lapse always negligible. In may be added that his earlier proposal of almost effortless learning of a second language at a post-infantile period supposes an environment in which elders speak the language correctly all the time (DC 4.1.5). Such conditions, however, are ideal. In an imperfect world of less than flawless speaking, boys cannot become adept in a language without mastering the rules of grammar.

65. The qualities of the fine rhetorician instanced—deft organization, logical development, a varied and commanding vocabulary, a forceful style—were very probably evinced by Augustine, in a manner remarkable for his years, in his prose enactment of Juno's distress (1.17.27). Adapted to his personal narrative, with its crisp, incisive, fast-paced *modus scribendi*, these literary-rhetorical characteristics bulk large in the *Confessions*. In passages of philosophical and theological import rhetorical refinement of course cedes place to dry, nonaffective prose proper to analysis. It would betray noetic imbalance to wax eloquent over $7 + 3 = 10$ as it would be to record Monica's last days with a quasi-mathematical abstractness drained of all emotional resonance.

66. A barbarism usually concerns mispronunciation of a single word, though it can occur in writing also. A solecism deals with a meaning as in the *disertus-desertus* disparallel and in instances where a singular term is employed to indicate a referent that is more than one individual, e.g., *hic meus est dies* rather than *hic noster est dies*. For definitions and illustrations from Latin authors see OCD, 225, 1786.

67. That the mind travels toward its goals by psychic movements rather than by means of locomotion is an insight not uncommon in Augustine. The particular images of physical movement which are rejected as vehicles for returning to the soul's homeland, are, as is well known, borrowed in part from *Enn.* 1.6.8. On the prodigal son see L. Ferrari, "The Theme of the Prodigal Son in Augustine's Confessions," RA 12 (1977), 105-18. See D 95-8.

68. According to G-M 30, n. 12, based on G. Boissier, *Roman Africa*, 207, the aspirate is missing in *hoc* in a Numidian inscription containing *Occ*, which perhaps suggests that the dropping of the aspirate in words like *homo* was not unusual in popular exchanges in North Africa. Apparently other barbarisms

were in colloquial circulation there. *Ossum* replaced *os*, a gaucherie that Augustine employed for homiletic advantage (P 138.20.DC 3.3.7). So also with the incorrect *fenerat* in place of *feneratur*, a lapse in propriety that served to ensure easier understanding (P. 36 [En.3].6). See Pope, 149.

69. For the ancient grammarian, grammar was an art; at times Augustine speaks of it as a science. As a liberal art, it could be referred to interchangeably as an art or science. Marrou, 10-2.

70. Differing from St. Paul who equates it with the outlook of faith, the overall Christian vision of the universe, Augustine views conscience in terms of moral awareness in the light of the New Testament that censures past transgressions and prescribes right actions in the making. It is an interior chamber (S 117.4) of knowledge (P 34.2.2) so recessed that only God can enter therein (P 54.9). Since *conspectus conscientiae* and *conspectus Dei* are identical (P 5.11), conscience may be designated the voice of God. In the whole of Augustine conscience occurs in some 200 citations, roughly one-half (105) from the Bible. See C. Mager, "Conscientia," AL 1. 1218-28, with extensive bibliography.

71. The meaning of the moral law will be discussed in more detail in 3.7.13-9.17 below.

72. As the expression, *ex eodem pulvere*, figuratively designates rhetoricians (1.16.25), so *huius haerenae* similarly signifies the rhetorical profession. The *palaestra* was the intellectual gymnasium preparatory to station as a professional rhetorician.

73. At first blush *imitandi ludicra inquietudine* may seem to indicate a restless passion for mimicking actual dramatic performance as well as the restless desire to imitate the immoral behavior dramatized. The ambiguity, however, is only apparent, for Augustine is summarily restating the fascinating lure to imitation of immoralities depicted in plays (1.16.25-6). As far as I know, Augustine never explicitly mentions copying various actors' styles. But if, as is probable, he did assimilate some of their dramatic techniques, he does not advert to this since he is mainly concerned with the powerful impact of the enticingly packaged immoral contents of plays.

74. Whether or not Augustine exaggerates the quality and quantity of the evil to which he surrendered in boyhood, there can be no doubt that *innocentia puerilis*, boyhood innocence or largely guilt-free early youth, is apparently a misconstrual of a youthful capacity for sometimes shocking evil. This misjudgment that apparently obtained among some of the ancients prevails more commandingly today because of the secular humanistic belief, one might say, blind faith, in the perfectibility of man, along with a recent tendency to worship of the young. Empirical data, however, undercut this opinion. In fact, children have a capacity for grave evil, not infrequently socially harmful. To quote only one empirical report among many, according to Jessica Collins, "Kids Hurting Kids for Sex," *Insight*, 8, n. 32 (August 10, 1992), 12-3, 37-8, appalling acts of sexual abuse have been increasingly perpetrated in recent years by juvenile offenders. Two seven-year-old boys in Indianapolis raped a first-grade female classmate on March 26, 1992. Across the U.S. the rate of arrest of males younger that twelve climbed 244 percent in roughly twenty-five years up to 1989. According to an FBI study, in 1990 534 individuals under fifteen were

arrested for rape. Interestingly, the impact of bad example is more widespread because modern technology such as graphic film and TV scenes has helped pervert youngsters' psyches. Contemporary civilization with its squalid endorsement of almost unlimited license seems sexually saturated to a point of decadence, rivaling in some measure the corruption of some pre-Christian cultures. In any event, it is clear that boyhood innocence is a myth of liberal humanism; the young are not exempt from a capacity for repulsive evil. Moreover, it would betray a naive slippage into the psychiatric fallacy concerning evil to label these child offenders mentally ill. Their minds are normal and sane; it is their wills that are debased under the influence of a corrupt society.

75. W. James, 1.127.

76. Viewed prospectively, childhood evils with their misguided superiors and playthings prefigure and essentially resemble the larger-scale evils of adulthood. Looked at retrospectively, the money and estates that preoccupy adults are ironically their playthings; in the light of eternal truth these are worth no more than childhood gewgaws of games. As Courcelle 50, notes, here following De Labriolle, *S. Augustin et Séneque, Rev. de Philol.*, 54 (1928), 47-9, the observation that money and estates are the games of adults may derive from Seneca. However, as BA 13, p.329, n.1, perceptively indicates, Augustine's point is the inverse of Seneca's comment. According to Augustine's text, children's games are as proportionally sinful as the delinquencies of adult malefactors. Nonetheless, the Senecan comment may be taken as implicit in Augustine: regarded retrospectively, the money and land for which adults cheat and lie involve the games of bigger boys.

77. As creative, God imparts in some measure his being and other communicable perfections to creatures. Adopting with some modification a crowning insight of Plotinus, Augustine maintains that God is the ineffable One, in whose unity each created thing proportionally shares. Subintellectual beings are stamped with a *vestigium* or trace of his unity; Augustine's body, his exterior, subrational self, bears only the trace of divine unity (T 11.1.1. CD 11.28). Because spiritual, man's mind has imprinted on it the image of God (6.3.4. GL 6.27.38). God's primary or essential perfection is existence as such. [*Deus*] *non aliquo modo est, sed est est*: God "is the Is" or simply existence itself(13.21.46); he is "the great Is" (P 101 [S.2].10). He is designated the Is because he is absolutely immutable (S 6.3.4). As unchangeable, the divine nature admits of no division within itself.

78. On Plotinus' theory, God is essentially the One (*Enn.* 5.1.5; 4.1), which is beyond being in the sense that it is supremely removed from all lower beings (*Enn.* 5.5.6). While it can be designated the Good (*Enn.* 5.5.10), attributes cannot be predicated of the One. Lower entities proceed from the One by emanation (*Enn.* 5.4.1. 4.8.6), by necessity rather than free choice since fresh volition would insert movement into its unchangeable unity (*Enn.* 5.1.6). Plotinius' view, however guardedly articulated, is not without its difficulties. In refusing to predicate being of God, he apparently lays himself open to the charge of a tendency to ontic agnosticism; we simply cannot say that God exists. Conversely, if lower things share in the unity of the One (*Enn.* 6.9.2),

why cannot they be said to share in a kind of super-being of the One? Moreover, except in his ascription of oneness to God, Plotinus fails to distinguish the human mode of knowledge of attributes and the mode of their existence in God. In our experience intellect and the self, insofar as understood, are ontically distinct while in God they are indivisibly united. His being is so totally one that being and attributes are existentially undifferentiated: he is what he has (T 15.13.CD 11.10). God is valuationally one as well as ontically one; his own beatitude, he rests in himself and indeed is his rest (GL 4.17.29). Man is called to imitate the valuational oneness of God by integrating his desires through focus on the eternal One. Prior to his moral conversion, Augustine turned away from the eternal One and, absorbed in the shifting manifold of temporal goods, his moral I was disintegrated (11.29.39). His reunification is the work of redeeming mercy that reassembles the scattered parts and fuses them into a graced whole that images and is oriented toward the One (2.1.1; 11.29.39).

79. Both animals and men are endowed with an interior sense (7.17.23), which functions similarly in both in the line of perception but varies in the line of estimation or sensory valuation. An animal perceives that it is not seeing; otherwise it would not open its eyes to focus on an object. If it perceives that it does not see, it must also perceive that it sees. It is the interior sense that mediates this perception: it perceives the very act of sensation of each of the five senses (LA 2.4.10). Furthermore, the animal interior sense exercises an estimative or evaluative role. Animals seek certain sensory objects as pleasant, though these objects are not necessarily sensorially appealing and, correspondingly, avoid other sensory objects as unpleasant, which seem valuationally neutral to the five bodily senses (LA 2.3.8). In other words, animals evince behavior that we call instinctive, activity that is uniformly patterned in each species. A sparrow constructs its nest in a specifically ordered way while its fellow birds build diversely designed nests proper to their species (VR 43.80). Lizards instinctively catch flies while various species of spiders instinctively weave specific webs to capture prey (10.25.57). Instinctive behavior does not spring from reason or from the exterior senses but is governed by the laws of nature within that are sensorially applied in animals through the interior sense (VR 42.79). In addition, higher animals learn from experience, which is deposited in memory, then recalled, as in the case of his dog recognizing Odysseus upon his return (QA 26.50). Through the interior sense functioning estimatively, a dog judges as attractive what he perceives as a concrete qualitative-quantitative whole. From the angle of perception, the work of the human interior sense duplicates that of animals. The interior sense perceives sense data delivered by the bodily senses (7.17.23) and also perceives the very acts of sensing; it senses not only the green but the seeing of the green. From the angle of estimation, it diverges from that of animals. No complete uniform behavior that we name instinctive is discernible in man; the startle response labeled instinctive by some psychologists is relatively simple. Man is not sensorily determined to build a specific dwelling but through reason constructs a variety of houses (VR 43.80). Besides perceiving their proper

objects, the external senses judge them according to aesthetic estimation or appreciation, insofar as they experience pleasure or displeasure from the gentleness or harshness of their objects (LA 2.5.12). Bright light, melodious song, fragrance of a flower, sweet honey, and a gentle hug evoke pleasure (10.6.8). The estimative thrust of the interior sense, however, is pragmatic rather that aesthetic; it aims at securing the soundness or integrity of the bodily senses, trying to keep them receptive to data with undiminished vigor, alerting the senses lest normal activity be impaired (LA 2.5.12). Light that is too bright can injure the eye, and sound of very intense vibrations can harm the ear (10.26.38). Disapproving of the unsoundness in any of the bodily senses, the interior sense directs the senses to remove obstacles or repair dysfunctional features. Correspondingly, trying to preserve normal functioning of the sense organs, it successfully leads them to their appointed sensory operations.

Aristotle was the originator or discoverer of this inner sense, which he significantly called *sensus communis* (*koiné aesthesis*) because it is not a proper sense but one that commonly focuses on the proper activities and sensory objects of the five external senses. Moreover, because it is causatively common, it can compare diverse proper objects, such as the white to the sweet. Entitatively, the five proper senses and the common sense are distinct; causally, they conjointly operate, with the common sense as the primary radix of sensation that applies the proper senses to the perception of organized sensory wholes (*De an.* 2.6, 418a7-25; 3.1-2, 427a16). Aristotle's theory became the common patrimony of later thinkers. On the perceptual side, Augustine's interior sense seems essentially akin, in somewhat less sophisticated form, to Aristotle's analysis. But his deputation of an estimative function to the animal and human interior sense is not found in Aristotle. The presiding and judicative functions of Augustine's interior sense seem related to the Stoic *hegemonikon.* Texts in the *Enn.* (1.1.7; 4.3.3, 4.2.6; 4.8.8) indicate that Plotinus adopted with some variations the Aristotelian common sense. Augustine departs from the available Stoic and Plotinian views, as he does from Aristotle's version, by assigning, along with the perceptual role, an estimative function to the interior sense. On Stoic and Plotinian views see O'Daly, 102-4.

Book Two
Sixteenth Year

After four years (365-9) at a more advanced school in Madauros, a shortage of funds forced on him a year of idleness at home. Evil tendencies first latent in childhood, then operative in a low key in boyhood, flowered out fully in adolescence. An Introduction (1.1) underlines his inner disorder. A first section (2.2-3.8) dwells on false loves on which he wasted his substance, in particular, sexual adventures toward which his developed physique disposed him. A second part (4.9-9.17) narrates his theft of pears, then probes the motivation for this. A conclusion (20.18), partly replicating the Introduction, reveals his soul as loathsome. Over two-thirds of this book is spent on elucidating what looks like a minor act of vandalism. The second part divides into three subparts. (1) The theft occurred at night (4.7). (ii) Though seemingly a case of doing evil simply for the sake of evil, the act had to be motivated by some good since evil is absolutely nothing (5.10). The essential reason for the stealing was a perverse imitation of God, specifically a parody of omnipotence (6. 12-4). (iii) The social pressure exerted by his accomplices was a necessary condition (8.16-9.17). Subparts (ii) and (iii) are demarcated by 7.15, wherein Augustine offers thanks for the sins God has forgiven him, along with those from which he has been providentially spared.[1]

Chapter 1: Why he Recalls Past Wickedness

1. He reviews past wallowings in the flesh not because he is still enthralled by them but in order to free himself from them so as to love and, concomitantly, praise God. He recalls his sins by love of God's merciful love, his own love being a response to the love God

showed first (EJ 7.9). Formerly he had committed his love to false loves, coveting illicit pleasures. More precisely, he now loved God's love focused on divine goodness that guarantees happiness to those who observe his commandments. Memory of his past induces bitterness that his confession, he hopes, will transmute into sweetness that is genuine, not counterfeit like that of lust, because issuing from the God who is all-sweetness. His recollection will evidence how divine sweetness organized his inner self, gathering into unity of spirit energies scattered in racing after diverse lesser goods. In turning away from God who is the One, he had torn apart his spiritual self, losing a shared unity (11.29.39), with the result that his soul had become as manifold as the many lower goods pursued. Right remembrance of disintegration spurs ongoing integration of spirit.

He was now fifteen years old, at the start of the span of adolescence that ran from fifteen to thirty (7.1.1). In 369-70, covered by shady leaves, symbolizing perverse pleasures, his soul was shrouded in darkness.[2] Deprived of life-giving light, his inward beauty or goodness wasted away, and his soul became a putrefying mass of corruption exuding a stench before God, for sin is spiritual death, the sinner a spiritual corpse (P 48 [S.2].2;70[S.2].3). Yet delusive self-satisfaction (10.39.64) made him appear comely to himself, and vainglory (10.37.60) preened himself to look pleasing to fellowmen.

Chapter 2: Lusts of Adolescence

2. With adolescence dawned a concentration on love, Augustine being so obsessed with it that he wanted only to love and be loved. But his experiences in love were not controlled by the measure of practical wisdom that delimits true friendship or love (2.2.3). Mists arising from swamps of fleshly desires and from the hot springs of youthful passions clouded his moral vision, blacking out the light of truth, so that his heart, i.e., conscience, could not draw the line between authentic love and its pseudo-copy that is lust. His passions precipitated him into the swirling vortex symbolizing the instability of the soul captured by vice. The retribution of God was woven into his sins, an inexorable consequence to which indulgence in passions blinded him. Enchained in his mortality, the outcome of the Fall, enslaved by his passions, he could not even hear the clanking of his chains, his deafness being an intrinsic punishment for his pride

(1.12.19). As the Father permitted Augustine, the prodigal son (1.18.28), to wander far from him, he became the puppet of his fornications, primarily sexual excesses; broadly, the term also extends to all sins by which he played the wanton (1.13.21). Morally depersonalized, all consistency of character destroyed, his inner self was spilled out on exterior goods; so hot were his false desires that the projection of self became a boiling current. In seeking exterior things, he abandoned the interior, making God distant (M 6.13.40). Thus through and throughout this dissipation God remained remote, a joy slow in coming, which Augustine would take years to possess (10.27.38). God said nothing, his silence only apparent due to Augustine's failure to listen. Meanwhile, as he careened wildly along paths of lust, the roaming prodigal son was sowing sterile seeds of sorrow; sterile because, unlike repentance, they would not fructify in virtue. Such fruitless seeds would leave his soul a wasteland (2.10.18) in which flourished only exalted abasement and agitated fatigue, an abjection due to the loftiness of pride and an exhaustion made pseudo-dynamic by restlessness of spirit.

3. The bright limits of friendship (2.2.2) are laid down by commandment and counsel, prescribed by marriage or available in a life of celibacy (SV 14.14). Marriage tempers the disorder of the passions and relieves its malaise, harnesses for right use the fugitive charms of what can be the grossest of temptations, and fixes the moral boundaries of sexual life. Had Augustine married (and this would not have been unusual for a North African in his sixteenth year), the waves of sexual cravings would have spent themselves on the shore of marriage; the desire for sexual union would have been amply gratified within the licit precincts of marriage. Thus his appetite would have been appeased even if he had not married simply for the sake of begetting children, one essential end of the marital state. The Lord, author and lawgiver of marriage, is the primary cause of the children conceived in marital union (J 9.2. CD 14.22). Offspring are called, by seeming paradox, "children of our death" rather than fruit of our life, to set in relief the truth that bonds of marriage splice human beings only in their mortal condition, to be superseded by marriage-free ties of love hereafter (NC 1.16.18). God's power at the service of his mercy gently touches married partners to blunt the thorns of toil and tears inevitable in the human condition. Whereas, as mentioned earlier, in their perversity bad men use good things for

bad ends, the good Lord uses persons' bad deeds for good ends (S 214.3); his all-powerfulness ennobles the depressed state of man and woman after the Fall. God's omnipotence is always at work in men by his presence even when in the line of grace their sins drive him away personally (E 187.5).

Celibacy, a life of chastity without sexual union, is another, a higher path that he chose after the inundation of divine light in the garden outside Milan in 386, seventeen years later (8.12.29); one he might have then elected had he listened more attentively to the voice of the Lord thundering in the clouds, in this case in 1 Cor 7.1,28,32-3. The Scriptures are depicted as clouds because from them God waters the souls of men; too his words sound loudly, with divine energy, from clouds of darkness which signifies the sometimes obscure allegories of prophets and apostles whose teachings shine the brighter through miracles (GCM 2.3.5. E 56.11.17). No more than Paul does he belittle marriage, which is a vocation to sanctity, graced with fidelity, children, and the sacrament (GL 9.7.12.CJ 9.7.11. GC 2.34.39.BC 24.32). Christian marriage is holy (SV 12.12), but because marriage is beset with special problems (S 351.3.5), because a spouse has to be more attentive to the needs of the partner, a life of consecrated virginity lived in charity is rich with the possibility of more love for others (S 132.3.3). Consecrated virginity is higher not because it requires forgoing what is evil but because it demands sacrificing a sacred good for a still higher good (SV 18.18.5. S 191.3.4). Had he heeded voices counseling celibacy, he would have become a spiritual eunuch, one unmarriageable for the glory of God and his kingdom, in this virginal state enjoying a richer happiness as he awaited the interior caresses of the divine beloved in a union of hearts (10.6.8).

4. Unhappily, Augustine bent his neck to the yoke of neither marriage nor celibacy; his sexual activity boiled over, i.e., passed the bounds of human decency. He chose to be swept along in the strong current of his passions, the flow again representing the fluctuating character of the flesh in contrast to the stability of habitual moral living (S 119.3). Throwing God aside, he threw aside all the legitimate restraints God ordains for sexual expression. His sexual excesses brought interior whippings consequent upon sins (1.12.19); unavoidable because God is always present in his creatures, interiorly administering rewards and allowing sanctions (P 91.4). In Augustine's story, as is the case in all divine retribution, God's ire is bedewed with

mercy. Divine pity made delights of the flesh disgusting, not to deny him pleasure but to point him toward greater pleasure in morally pure actions and things, unalloyed especially in the font of joy that is the Lord (S 117.5. P 48[S.2].5). Divine mercy brings good out of evil (1.12.19), using suffering to impart a lesson in godly wisdom, wounding only to heal the soul, and letting the body be killed, lest the soul die the death of sin and forfeit eternal life (1.5.5).

In wondering, "Where was I?," Augustine may allude to the bewilderment of a prodigal son feeling alienated in a foreign land. He intimates a disorientation in spiritual space that may evoke the image of an individual lost, stumbling in the semi-dark through a strange forest, or the picture of an urbanite suddenly set down in a trackless desert. So engrossed was he in the disorder of moral time (11.29.39) that he lost all track of his distance from his eternal home. Or he may be referring to temporal disorientation. The short span of a year appeared long because his multiple sexual excesses were of a sort that might have well spanned several years. In a self-imposed exile from the true pleasures of the Father's home, he was tyrannized by the moral insanity that was lust; a subjugation which he welcomed and to which he gladly surrendered body and soul. Unfortunately, his parents devoted hardly a thought to encouraging marriage as a means of delivering him from his ruinous lapse into lust. Their sole concern was that Augustine master the art of the spoken word, a skill that was the conventional road to social and economic success, intended in Augustine's case to qualify him to become a lawyer and perhaps eventually to be appointed to a secure position in the Roman government.

Chapter 3: A Year of Dangerous Idleness

5. After four years at Madauros, which lay 18.6 miles (29.9 kilometers) south of his hometown, funds had run out, and his father, Patricius, a burgher of Thagaste of modest means, wealthier in fatherly zeal for his son's schooling than in money and property,[3] had to postpone for a year Augustine's journey for higher studies to Carthage, located by one route 160.9 miles (259 kilometers) to the northeast.[4] Writing in the presence of God, doubly confessing him, confessing his sins and praising him, he aims at moving himself and his readers to ponder the misery of man beseeching the mercy of

God: out of the depths of wretchedness we must cry out to the Father (S 351.5.12). Even meditating now as a bishop, he can profit, in a spirit of compunction, from the lesson of divine mercy: a cry from the depths vaults a sinner to the heights.

Fellow townsmen lavished praise on Patricius who scrimped, even going beyond his income and resources, to assure his son's socio-economic advancement. Oddly, on the other hand, Patricius, while concerned about the culture of Augustine's mind, was uninterested in the Godward culture of his soul, caring not one whit whether Augustine resisted the cultivation of the God who is the teacher, the single true (as opposed to bogus), and good (as opposed to malevolent) sovereign husbandman of the field that is his heart or conscience. The soul possesses God, and God possesses the soul; its praise-enriched living faith ``cultivates" (expresses cult or worship to) him, and his love cultivates it (P 32[En.2.S.2].18).[5]

6. Augustine repudiated the love the divine farmer would expend on the field that was his heart. Rank vegetation or voluptuous desires running wild (2.1.1) swarmed over the growth of desirable plants, whose seeds were, in effect, sterile (2.2.2). Idleness during 369-70 provided opportunity for unchecked irresponsibility. The tireless adolescent prowled about hour after hour, seeking outlets for his large store of sexual energy, engaging in nocturnal sexual forays without thought of the morrow. During that year of release from study and work briars of lustful desires grew thick and wild over his head, this another allusion to the parable of the sower (Mt 13.22). The briars are a figure of all ungodly desires that choke the fledgling life of the spirit. The brambles are said to cover his head, here doing duty for the mind, because the head governs the other parts of the body as the soul governs the body (SDM 2.12.42). It serves as a metaphorical equivalent of the mind insofar as the mind has, loosely, its organic locus in the head. The hand of neither father nor mother was ready to uproot his flourishing lustful desires. On the contrary, his father seemed oblivious to all but the physical function of sex. Once after observing at the baths that Augustine was blossoming into a full-grown man, he expressed pleasure in the prospect of grandchildren in the near future.[6] His joy was the inherent delight of a quasi-drunkard, stupefied by false ambition, an inveterate imbiber of the wine that was a disordered will which ranked the base things of this world higher than their creator (S 9.2.1); so befuddled, he was

incapable of discriminating between moral and immoral sexual activity. Monica, on the other hand, was spiritually perceptive and chaste; the Holy Spirit was manifestly dwelling in her as in a temple, and the graced habitation that was her soul was sexually pure; she glorified God in her body. Unlike Patricius, who was only a recent catechumen, Monica was spiritually perspicacious and therefore became painfully aware of the pitfalls that lay ahead in the enticingly pagan atmosphere of Roman Africa for an energetic youth greedy for novel experiences. Although he was not yet baptized, i.e., not yet formally bound to conform to the Church's moral teaching, her motherly love wanted him to live in Christian purity; she dreaded that he might walk crooked ways, i.e., replicate the licentious style of pagans who take for granted or even applaud sexual immorality.

7. As briars of lust suffocating his spirit caused woe, at first blush no divine word seemed to enlighten him and heal malodorous sores. Yet, later reflection made clear, God did really speak to him insistently through his mother. Through Monica, he arrestingly says, God sang into his ears. Christian morality, when sung in the dulcet melody of Monica, must have seemed, at least initially, inviting. But the song of moral purity impinged on only his physical, not his spiritual, ears. Howbeit pleasant-sounding, the Christian law of purity made no existential impress on his heart; it would be a standard that he would usually breach rather than observe. The briars covering his head blocked the sound of Monica's voice from his spiritual ears; the head, representing the soul, possesses all five spiritual senses (P 29[En.2]2).[7] Monica anxiously counseled him in private, warning against fornication, illicit relations with a single woman, and begging him especially not to stoop to adultery, illicit relations with a married woman. This latter is twice wrong, violating not only chastity but sinning against the justice of the marriage contract—an adulterer double-crosses the innocent spouse. However melodiously garbed, her admonitions struck him as overcautious bleatings typical of the timorous half of the human race. A lusty youth heady with the ripening of sexual powers, he was ashamed to have anything to do with such enervating advice. Years later, he discerned, his mother's voice was the channel of God's wisdom; so in contemning her, he was actually despising the God speaking through her. The wanton son was far distant from his mother, the fervent handmaid of the Lord; briars thick about his head suppressed spiritual sight, so blinding him that

he felt degraded if he appeared less impure than his peers when they regaled him about their sexual conquests. The more debased their exploits, the haughtier was their swagger; the more vicious their conquests, the more vigorous their boasting. So a twofold pleasure lured him into sexual misbehavior: the satisfaction of the act itself and the plaudits of oversexed companions. In decent circles vice is deserving of censure, but in his sexually defiled environment Augustine ironically had to commit more and more impurities to escape reproof. So strong was the pressure to conform to a code of dishonor that when he heard his fellows glorying in triumphs he had not pulled off, he felt compelled to invent tales of his own equal or superior sexual feats; otherwise his compatriots would have looked down upon him as worse because better, as more rotten because purer.

8. Augustine adumbrates a theme that he will later expatiate on in his "great and arduous work" (CD, *Proem.*). The whole of humankind divides into two cities or nonpolitical commonwealths, the city of God and the earthly city, which are mystically, i.e., figuratively, named Jerusalem and Babylon. Noninstitutional and transhistorical, the city of God includes not only all human beings graced with charity but the good angels as well (CD 12.1). Its founder and father is God, its king is Jesus Christ, and the heavenly Jerusalem is the supernatural mother of its members. The earthly city embraces all evil men and the fallen angels, whose self-love impels them to finally reject the love of God (CD 14.28). Satan is its father and king, and all those prior to receiving charity have Babylon as their mother. Citizenship in Jerusalem, taken by faulty etymology to signify vision of peace, issues in the peace that is the tranquillity of order (CD 19.13). Allegiance to Babylon, called the city of confusion by verbal linkage to Babel, brings with it radical dissatisfaction, the untranquility of disorder (P 26[En.2].2; 61.6; 64.2).

Under the influence of dissolute companions he roved the streets of Babylon, the twistings and turnings of their stones long familiar as the native land of his soul. Rolling in the gutter, in the moral stupidity induced by lust, he imagined himself lying in the princely comfort of a bed of fragrant spices and costly ointments. Unlike the heavenly Father who uplifts his servants, the devil, his father according to the evil side of his spirit, ground him under his heel; the suggestions of the invisible and only lasting enemy of every man had betrayed him

(P 69.2). He had been fooled because love of pagan shows, admiration of lewd Roman literature, and thirst for the approval of associates made him easily seducible. "Being seduced" here primarily means being led along wrong paths; only secondarily does seduction have the sense of enticing an individual into loss of chastity. This diabolical seduction succeeded in fastening him more closely to, literally, the navel of the country of evil; he was pressed more tightly to the bosom, the very center, of the wicked city. In contrast to Babylon, his mother according to the evil side of the inner self, Monica is called the mother of his flesh. In her the Holy Spirit was building his temple; she had fled from the center of Babylon to the living faith of a citizen of Jerusalem. Still lingering on the outskirts of Babylon, she was somewhat tainted with worldly ambition, a strain of the love of the world characteristic of Babylon. The essential Jerusalem within, her supernatural center, came to the fore when she urged her son to remain chaste; and when, alarmed by the degradation into which his potential for waywardness might plunge him, she considered marriage as a recourse for appeasing his sexual appetite if his sexual drive could not be cut to the root, i.e., in the likely event that Augustine would not be capable of disciplining his sexual craving by a strictly chaste life outside marriage. But a peripheral Babylonian tincture surfaced when she dismissed the prospect of marriage because she feared that wife and family would thwart his higher studies at Carthage and, consequently, frustrate his chances for a higher status in society. In their anxiety over Augustine both parents misguidedly sought to underpin more his hope of future success in life than hope in a future life. This warped outlook had to be expected of a Patricius, slightly instructed in Christianity, who paying scarcely a passing thought to God and his ways, was doing his utmost to aid Augustine to pursue of vain things, i.e., fluid goods like success and honor. Monica, a bit surprisingly, also fell prey to worldliness, a small stain that was mitigated somewhat by her naive belief that the program of studies ahead would prove to be not a barrier but a stepping stone to Augustine's reaching God.

However conjectural his appraisal of his parents' characters, it is absolutely certain that at this time he abandoned all restraints, even the cautions of a milder hedonism, hurling himself into a life of dissipation that had inscribed within it a variety of punishments. A thick cloud shrouded his spirit in the darkness that is part of the wages of many-befouled lust, shutting out the beams radiating from the sunlight of divine truth. His iniquity burst forth from his fatness; he was sinning not out of need, as a poor man might steal, but out of sheer insatiable desire for more and more, as a billionaire might rob the near-destitute of their pennies. Not needing the sexual expression, he stuffed himself with sexual pleasures, nowhere drawing a line of limitation (P 72.12).

Chapter 4: Robbing a Pear Tree

9. As with every other sin, so with theft: for it is provided inescapable punishment, inwardly a crookedness of soul and, through habit, slavery to the sin (P 18[En.2].14. CJI 1.14); outwardly, for hardened thieves, loss of everlasting life. The divine law that proscribes stealing is the exterior and written double of a law written on the human heart, i.e., natural to the conscience, which may be obscured but can never be blotted out by depraved habits or corrupt cultures. The law forbidding stealing is recognized by every conscience and foundationally operative in every society. Thus not even a well-heeled thief will tolerate thieving by a poverty-stricken individual. Like nineteenth-century robber barons in the United States who countenanced no robbery of their goods, modern gangsters deal ruthlessly with crooks preying on their property. Since it springs from the eternal law, this natural precept against theft bears, within, sanctions against its violators. On one occasion Augustine apparently stole simply because he wanted to steal. He was not driven by economic necessity; he was neither destitute nor close to starving. He suffered from penury not of purse but of spirit; what he lacked was justice; indeed he felt a repugnance toward honesty. He was not compelled to steal out of an excess of wealth, which is impossible; a rich man is not driven by economic want to filch from his impoverished servant. Rather, because empty of justice, Augustine was full of injustice; he was driven by an excess of iniquity. Here he is implicitly adapting Ps 72.7, quoted at the end of the foregoing section: "My iniquity burst forth as from fatness." He stole neither out of leanness that is economic necessity nor out of fatness that is avaricious abundance but out of the fatness that is obesity of spirit, the overgrowth of malice in the soul (P 72.12). The fruit he stole was intrinsically worthless, substantially valueless; his father's vineyard

put at his disposal plenty of this fruit of a far better quality. Not hankering after the satisfaction of eating the fruit he stole, he wanted to simply enjoy the very act of stealing; seemingly all his pleasure lay in nothing but the sin itself.

In search of a fresh escapade, the band of roguish adolescents with whom Augustine associated raided a garden lying close to his family's vineyard, where they shook down, in the dead of the night, pears from one tree, not to feast on them, neither their color nor the taste being particularly appealing, but to sheerly relish the stealing itself.[8] While throwing most of them to the hogs, they did taste a few but only casually and incidentally, for they had no essential interest in the pears. They stole forbidden fruit not because it was fruit but simply and solely because it was forbidden. Not eating the stolen pears but the delicious taste of the stealing itself filled them with pleasure. Such was his conscience prostrate in the bottom of the abyss that was its dark night of evil. In a spirit of malevolence, hungering for evil gratis, he looked for no recompense but the evil itself. Detached from all self-interest, his intention seemed pure, perversely so, fastened on evil per se. Apparently the only motive for his malice was the malice itself. In treasuring not the relatively comely but the absolutely foul, in loving sheer moral evil, which is fatal to the life of the soul, he effectively committed spiritual suicide. Instead of loving the pears he stole, he loved the theft itself, the very sin destroying the life of his spirit. His soul hurled itself down from the divine firmament to its ruin, not groveling in shameful means to gain its end but seeking nothing but shame. The image evoked would seems to be this: an individual jauntily leaps from a cliff to be dashed to pieces on the rocks below. The firmament of God is his truth, solid and fixed in contrast to fleeting, figmentlike vanities of a strictly this-world view. It may mean also, in particular, his word revealed in Scripture (13.18.22). In any case, it symbolizes moral truth, the law God inscribes in hearts, the law his Spirit pens in his written word. By breaking the law against theft, Augustine broke his spirit; by jumping down from God's law, his inner frame was smashed at the base of the cliff. Spurning the law of the spirit, he flung his soul into the law of the flesh that spells doom of the spirit.[9]

Chapter 5: Every Sinner Seeks Some Good

However final its conclusion seems, Augustine's account of his motive in the stealing of the pears marks only the first stage of his inquiry. For according to his concept of evil (3.7.12), which he reached later with the help of Christian Neoplatonists (7.16.22), it is impossible to act sheerly for the sake of evil. Not something positive, evil is a lack and, in the case of moral evil, the privation of moral good. Evil is relatively being but absolutely nonbeing or nothing (CD 12.7). As in the line of being something cannot come from nothing, so in the line of conduct an action cannot be done for nothing, i.e., the privation that is sin. Hence in this and the following chapters Augustine is compelled to explore the question further, to track down the elusive good or goods ingredient in what at one level struck him as an act of unadulterated malice.

10. The opening part of this section approaches the goodness of created things from the angle of beauty. The good and the beautiful overlap insofar as both contain unity, form, and order, and evoke enjoyment. Delight in a beautiful object is contemplative and disengaged while the enjoyment of the good is practical and committed, the culmination of desire in possession. But as interwoven, beauty and goodness bespeak each other. A beautiful thing attracts the heart; it elicits desire. Conversely, the well-ordered patterns of action called virtues are beautiful. Thus because the beautiful and the good shade into one another, beautiful bodies, appealing social ranking, and attractive human life on earth and friendship are implicitly considered goods, objects of desire. Beautiful bodies like gold and silver please eye and mind by their appearance or outer form, and indeed all material things, rightly appreciated, are attractive and beautiful. Each body is beautiful insofar as its parts are congruent or similar to one another, with the congruence outwardly manifested by an appealing color. The parts of bodies are not only similar and coordinated but subordinated one to another; each body is then beautiful as an integrated whole, one thing formed of many parts. The lowly worm and the pesky flea, when carefully examined in their exquisitely articulated parts, are recognized as beautiful organisms (P 148.10). Bodily beauty reaches its peak in the matchlessly ordered human body (CD 22.24).[10]

Congruence and the beauty it constitutes are discernible in the material conditions of sensation. Following the Greek dictum that like is known by like, Augustine held that the physiological makeup of the sense organ resembled or corresponded to the medium transmitting its particular sensory object. The eyes contain light in sympathy with the physical light conveying the form of color.[11] So with the other senses: in the ears is a refined air, in the nostrils a mist or vapor, in the mouth a wetness, and in tactile areas an earthy material, each similar to the particular medium (with one exception: touch) transmitting its proper sensory object (M 6.5.10). Congruence, Augustine observes, is most marked in the line of touch. In effect, there is no external medium in tactile sensation; the hard or soft massy object presses directly against the skin of the hand. The physically unmediated contact is the closest possible, joining the organ of touch, whose dominant element is earth, to the body touched, whose dominant element is the same. So he singles out touch: "Congruence is strongest (or most pronounced) in the touch of flesh (or of the body with reference to a similar body touched)" whereas in the other sense organs, which require a medium, "there is a tempering of bodies properly adapted to these senses," the tempering being an attuning or assimilation of the physiological state of the sense organ to the proper medium of its object. The division of the physiological materials of the five sense organs is keyed to the four elements. The light of the eyes is related to fire, air is in the ears, water in the taste area, mist (the condensation of air) or vapor (the rarefaction of water) in the nostrils, and earth in the line of touch. The nobility of the elements is correlated with the clarity and objectivity of the senses. Thus fire, the noblest element, subserves sight, the clearest of the senses, while earth, the least noble element, is dominant in touch, the grossest sense, albeit the only sense needing no physical intermediary (M 6.5.10. GL 3.4.6).

Moving up the scale of beauty, Augustine next instances types of beauty in the sphere of human conduct. Even honor in this passing world can be fetching and good because of the just congruence between the actions performed and the esteem accorded an individual; beauty shines out of the glory bestowed on an outstanding ruler. The right exercise of authority, which is the power to rule in the body politic by commanding citizens through laws and other directives, inserts a due order into society, which, in this case, is a component of the beauty of the virtue of justice. However, he notes, with the cruelties of Roman political history in mind, power can be twisted into an instrument of injustice, a weapon for gratifying a ruler's thirst for revenge. Honor and power are splendid goods that retain their moral radiance so long as those achieving them do not wander away from the path of righteousness that is the law of the Lord. The life man lives here below is inviting, its appeal consisting in the proper measure of its beauty, i.e., consisting in the congruence of the features of the soul and the order stamped on its tendencies by the types of order that are the virtues. An individual's life is a thing of beauty when his life is, in Juvenal's phrase, *mens sana in corpore sano*,[12] the health being a moral soundness complemented by a reasonable health due to the order springing from physical nature and nurture. The soul rendered sound by the ordering of the virtues makes a fitting or judicious use of the goods of natures inferior to strictly human values. Hence the good life of man on earth manifests two features of beauty: in itself it has order; and it harmonizes with lower-order beauties that are lesser goods (4.14.21).

Indeed the whole of life lived here below, even that undistinguished by honor or political power, is prepossessing, moral-aesthetic charm consisting in the proper measure of its beauty, which lies in its ordered achievement of goods of the soul, principally those of the moral virtues and, in union with these, goods of the mind. Only the life that is controlled by the standard of virtue is beautiful. The good or beautiful life is one with an ordered love, a life of virtue-impregnated love, for virtue is defined as the order of love, the order imprinted on and directing love (CD 15.22). Justice, prudence, temperance, and fortitude each stamp a special order, reflecting a special measure or set of rules on human desires. Justice orders the body to the soul and the soul to God (CD 19.3). Against this background of moral order the goods of the mind evidence beauties with their proper delights. The understanding experiences satisfaction in discerning the order and interconnections in things. Even in minor matters (1.20.31) the grasp of truth is not devoid of its beauty and pleasures; indeed, the very exercise of the mind in a powerful memory and the fluent articulation of its ideas in organized discourse boasts a beauty all its own. Arts like rhetoric and poetry also adorn and beautify the human scene. The charm of human life springs not only from its own measure of beauty that consists of the complex of virtues governing soul and body but also from a suitable relationship with all things of lesser beauty. These lower-order beauties or goods are food, drink, clothing, money, and property, goods without which man cannot subsist, subordinated to the higher beauties and goods of body and soul whose proper order is furnished by the virtues (S 50.5.7. E 140.2.4). One of the most precious and consoling flowers of human life is friendship, which, wherever found, inside or outside the home, is beautiful because its bond makes souls effectively one. Congruence of parts makes a body one and therefore beautiful; so similarity of interests and principally resemblance in virtues knits souls as one in the harmony that is friendship (GI 16.59. CD 19.8). Sin intrudes when an individual yields to immoderate inclination, called immoderate because it lacks the proper measure stemming from virtue. Sin then is inordinate love of inferior goods in preference and in opposition to superior goods. Sin unmans man; gluttony degrades him to a sophisticated pig; drunkenness unreasons his reason. Friendship becomes poisonous, a sort of anti-friendship if it serves as a vehicle for social sin that would not have been perpetrated apart from the urge to conform (2.9.17). These lower goods unquestionably offer delights; food and property are satisfying, but, overindulged in or idolized, they are sources of disorder. Moreover, the pleasures lower goods harbor, however gratifying, cannot match the delights of God, super-delightful fount of all delights.

11. The upshot of the prior section is that sin is an inversion, turning upside down the right order of values, setting lower over higher, putting superior beneath inferior goods. This section applies this analysis to two cases of social sin,[13] one hypothetical, the other historical. As a rule, the motive for social sin is the disordered desire for lower goods. The answer to the question why someone committed a social sin ordinarily comes down to this: the malefactor was trying to gain or was afraid of losing some of these lower goods, which, appealing as they are, look mean when set over against higher goods that are literally happiness-causing, i.e., the goods of virtues. First, suppose a man commits murder. Inevitably we ask, why did he do it? Probably for one or more of several motives. Perhaps he fell in love with his victim's wife; perhaps he wanted the property or money that would ensure his own livelihood; perhaps he regarded his victim as a threat to his own life, property, or money; perhaps he was angry (2.6.13), his heart on fire with revenge for some injury suffered. In any event, there had to be some reason for the murder. It goes against the grain of normal moral thinking to hold that there was no reason for the murder other than the murder itself. No one believes that one

man kills another simply and solely for the pleasure of killing. Second, a like conclusion emerges from examination of the criminal career of Catiline (Lucius Sergius Catilina, 108? - 62 B.C.), depicted as the epitome of evil by Cicero, almost unrivaled in Roman literature as a rhetorician/man of letters, and a historian like Sallust, both of whose invective-loaded accounts of Catiline's unspeakable depravity Augustine accepted without question.[11] A number of disaffected elements in Roman society rallied around Catiline, and under his leadership revolted against the established order, an alliance of the old aristocracy and business class represented by Cicero. Early in 62 B.C. Catiline and his force of 3,000 were wiped out by the regular army in Etruria, north of Rome. According to Sallust, prior to his rebellion Catiline, whom Augustine characterizes as morally deranged and cruel, preyed on and killed innocent and guilty alike, apparently working his evil and cruelty gratuitously, sheerly for the sake of evil and cruelty. Apparently but not really, for, Sallust notes in addition, there was a purpose in what looked like aimless degradation and brutality: idleness, Catiline believed, would dull the quickness of his hand and the zeal of his spirit for crime; practice would lead him and his troops closer to the perfection of viciousness. His seemingly random, senseless wrongdoing was not actually without its point. By keeping supple his sinews for crime, Catiline strengthened himself for more ambitious crimes. Thoroughly skilled in the art of evil, he strove to seize Rome and, after overthrowing the old regime, make himself dictator. He resolved to lay hold of power, riches, and honors, and with these to disencumber himself of three burdens that beset him. Dictatorial fiat would dissipate fear of the established laws; plunder from the public treasury would do away with his poverty; fawning adulation that a victor earns would erase every vestige of his consciousness of social sins—that stigma on his actions would vanish with the disappearance of the old order. Hence not even Catiline, master criminal and personification of political evil, loved his sins per se; he did not commit social sins sheerly for the sake of social sins. These were not ends in themselves but means for achieving power, riches, and honors.

Chapter 6: Stealing the Pears a Perverse Imitation of Omnipotence

Analytically and inductively, it is now clear, it is impossible for anyone to perform an evil action for the sake of the evil alone. Analytically, because the object that human desire seeks can never be other than something good whereas evil consists of the lack of proper order in the goods sought. Inductively, because law officers and people in general deem it inconceivable that a murder be committed without a motive, a thirst for some good; because, in fact, the consummately malevolent Catiline wreaked his havoc in quest of political and financial prizes. It is unthinkable then that Augustine loved his theft as such, that he stole simply for the delight of stealing. Though he did not realize it at the time of the raid on the neighbor's orchard, his theft had to aim at or implicitly involve some good; his evil act had to be a violation of divinely appointed order. Precisely what was the good his evil action sought?

12. What was the beauty in his theft that drew his love? Surely the stealing itself could not be counted beautiful; as evil, it was without a glimmer of beauty. Since evil as evil is a privation, or absolutely nothing, he wonders whether it is anything at all or capable of being rhetorically addressed; evil is of course relatively real, i.e., in relation to the good it distorts. Surely too the pears stolen were good, for, as created by a God supremely beautiful and good, they share in his beauty and goodness. Still, he stole the pears not for the pears but for the stealing itself. That is why he chucked the pears, content to banquet on his wretchedness and to delight in evil as strictly enjoyable, not as a means or something useful but as an end in itself. He speaks of himself as *fruens*, indicating that his perversity was so pronounced that the evil in his action was sought as an absolute end. Goods divide into two classes: those to be used (*uti*) and those to be enjoyed (*frui*). In the most rigorous sense only God is an enjoyable good while, more broadly, the goods of the virtues as means to authentic happiness can be enjoyed (DC 1.4.4). In fact, he again recalls (2.4.9), he munched on some of the fruit, but the fruit itself was attractively neuter. What made biting into the pears delicious was the theft itself. Nothing in the pears as pears was tasty; it was the fact that they were stolen that made them succulent to his soul.

Continuing his inquiry, he asks: what lovely quality elicited his delight in his theft? It had to have some beauty, yet after a quick canvassing of the various beauties in the moral realm such as equity or justice (6.10.16) and prudence; then in mind, memory, and senses; then in vegetative life; then in stunningly arranged stars and in corruptible things of earth and sea; and even in the blemished strain ingredient in vices, he remains stymied, unable to identify the good or beauty latent in his nakedly evil theft. His stealing could not contain the loveliness of equity or practical wisdom, for it was palpably unjust and wise. Its beauty was not akin to that of the mind, which grasps incorporeal things and engages in matterless self-knowing (T 9.3.3) nor to that of memory, which in one sense is the bank in which are deposited the forms of bodies (10.9.16.T 11.3.6) nor to that of the senses, which exhibit a congruence of the dominant element in each sensory organ with the physical medium (2.5.10) while the fruit stolen were external, physical objects. No doubt the objects of his theft were a type of vegetative life, but the pears as pears conveyed no charm whatsoever. Since it was an action executed by mind and will, its attractiveness did not resemble the beauty of things of nature; not that of the stars fixed in their places, i.e., wheeling about with unalterable regularity; not that of the lower zone, whose individual land animals and fish unceasingly come to be and pass away as contingent parts contributing to the order and beauty of the universe (4.10.15). The beauty in his theft cannot even be likened to the defective and darksome vices that beguile the soul; defective, because the lower goods are desired in a disordered fashion; darksome, because the blotches dim their glow; beguiling, because material goods are vanities pretending to be morally authentic. Rich foods of the glutton and gold fondled by a miser are not without their allure, however inordinate, but not one scintilla of this tarnished brilliance gleamed in his stealing for stealing alone.

13. But not all possibilities are exhausted. In the overriding truth that man always remains the image of God Augustine discovers a basis for a broken, stained beauty in his act of pure stealing. Not merely a likeness of God, the spirit of man is an image, a likeness produced by the pattern it expresses (CD 22.4). Men are called to cleave to God's law of love, especially to love enemies and pray for persecutors, living as true sons of their heavenly Father, his authentic images (P 70[S.2].6). When men sin, they become unlike yet like God. Sinners who choose their own rather than God's way disfigure the image within through pride, uncharity, and injustice, becoming sons of disorder and darkness. But nonparadoxically such sins make them like God in a warped fashion. In declaring independence, a sinner acts as if he were God, as if he had no one ruling over him. A sinner

playing God relies solely on his own power, subject to no one, attributing to himself all that he is and does (P 70[S.2].6. T 10.5.7; 12.9.14). The supposititious self-sufficiency of a sinner perversely imitates the all-sufficiency of God.

(i) Pride heads the list because it is the primal sin in salvation history, the reason for the apostasy of Satan and his minions, the radix of the disobedience of Adam (S 123.1.1. P 1.4; 18 [En.2].15.). Historically, it is the first of human sins, the beginning of sin (Eccli 10.15). Structurally or according to its makeup, it is also the head and cause of all other sins (P 19.15). The pride that induced Adam to a self-centered imitation of God lies coiled at the heart of every spurious endeavor to become like God by purely human initiative. Affecting to be like the all-high, the self-exalted man who views himself as the sovereign reason for his own goodness glories in his own nimbus (P 144.1). (ii) Following upon pride are ambition and vainglory. Pride incites certain individuals to lord it over fellow men. Lust for power in the old Romans was harnessed to the service of ambition for reputation and renown, making them eager to valorously sacrifice all for the glory of their country that they identified with their own. Though this ruling passion helped Romans cultivate civic self-discipline, their quest of glory was partially egoistic and woven out of injustice; a transitory vainglory, in Seneca's eyes the greatest of vices,[15] that was nothing but smoke and wind, mimicking the highest honor due the God everlastingly glorious in his changeless being and mercy (CD 5.13, 17. J 10.6). (iii) Not all the Romans coupled desire for domination with love of glory; some disesteeming human esteem kept their hold on power by counting on cruelty to strike fear in their subjects. Roman history was blemished by a large number of cases of calculated savagery. Caligula reportedly had suspected subverters thrown to the beasts or sawed in two.[16] Nero murdered his mother Agrippina and his first wife Octavia and purged wholesale actual and alleged conspirators, including his mentor Seneca, three years before his own unlamented suicide (CD 5.19). Such ruthless exercise of power is only a shadowy reflection of the power of God which alone deserves the deepest reverential fear, power that no rival can usurp and no creaturely stratagem can undermine. In the face of wickedness, his power remains impregnable, for, as one with his changeless will, it orients all evil to his love and justice (S 214.3). (iv) Moreover, caresses of lechers solicit a like return of affection, but illicit love-making is a cheap, soiled image of the charity of God that woos the heart with inward intimacies far more exquisite than pleasures wrested from debauchery (10.27.38). The God whom the soul embraces in return is truth itself, beautiful with an unbounded goodness, luminous with infinite light that satisfies the soul's hunger for meaning. (v) Curiosity makes a pretense of being a zealous search for solid knowledge and therefore darkly imitates the universal and supreme knowledge of God. At times curiosity designates a legitimate search for knowledge; a free curiosity might have enabled Augustine to master Greek (1.14.23), and a curious skill of mind equipped astronomers to chart the courses of the stars (5.3.3. GL 2.10.23). Here, as occurs more frequently, (1.10.16), curiosity is assigned a pejorative sense, as a type of the concupiscence of the eyes that craves fresh acquaintance with things not in order to nourish the mind with factual and analytical truths but simply to indulge in pleasures that new experiences afford. The individual consumed with curiosity gears his knowing not to the object under inquiry but to the subject, his pleasure-seeking ego; he is interested not in learning things but in having a learning experience. Gaining additional facts is a way of amusing himself, and the items he meets are toys with which he entertains himself. So curiosity is titillated by the rare and novel, shocking sights like a mangled corpse, monstrosities in theaters, and feats of magic (10.35.54). This debased form of knowledge distortedly resembles divine knowledge that compasses all things because, as creator, God cognizes all that proceeds from himself with a knowledge that is the highest because one with his supreme existence (J 99.4. T 6.10.11).

(vi-vii) As curiosity cloaks itself in the robes of serious knowledge, so ignorance and stupidity are dressed as simplicity and innocence. Here he is directing a shaft at Manichean dogma and ethics. In its ignorance of the true nature of God Manichean doctrine maintained that the source of all good is a finite God called the Principle of Light, particles of whose light, after the invasion of his kingdom by forces of the Prince of Darkness, are scattered in things. From the theory that divine life as fragments of light is actually present in things issue the strange features of the Manichean moral code that Augustine puts down as stupidity. Strictly speaking, Manicheans were constrained to obey absurd, unlivable rules. They could not kill animals or plants lest they violate the divine life within, they were forbidden to plow fields for fear of injuring the life in the soil, and they could hardly walk on stones since these also were animated with the divine. As a Manichean, he accepted such nonsense, believing that a fig shed tears when it was plucked and that its mother, the fig tree itself, shed milk-like tears (3.10.18). So Manichees considèred themselves morally superior in simplicity and innocence—virtues through which we do no harm or injury to others—to Catholics who randomly trampled on the divine life hidden in things. The pseudo-simplicity and pseudo-innocence of Manichees spawn grotesque moral consequences. A Manichee is obliged to let a man starve to death rather than give him a morsel of food since plucking fruits of the earth is equivalent to killing them. In line with this strange logic of morality figs and the like are accorded higher moral rights than the human beings they are meant to serve (3.10.18). This simplicity in name only crookedly mirrors the supreme simplicity of God. God is absolutely simple, first of all, because, unlike the Manichean Principle of Light, he is not composed of substance and accident; he is nothing other than he has (E 169.2.7). Also he is supremely simple in a second sense: as nothing but changeless being, he is immutably good; in willing only goodness, he can do no harm to anything (E 169.2.7.CD 11.10). God is supremely innocent because, as absolutely impeccable, he cannot suffer the consequences of sins. An innocent being does no harm to others or to himself. Per contra, an individual, in deciding to harm others, harms himself. Hating his own soul, the lover of iniquity is his own enemy; the damage he does to others first damages himself; the harm he metes out to others recoils on himself (1.12.19).[17]

(viii) Sloth, which desires a sort of rest, is a limp simulacrum of the true rest that is found only in God. What sloth seeks is described as a quasi-rest because in creatures rest is strictly the terminus of striving and movement, both of which the do-nothing program of the lazy man eschews. At its best the rest that sloth affords is time-bound, quite short-lived; the refusal of a social parasite to contribute by work to the public welfare stamps a man as basically irresponsible; and out of its torpor comes the fruitlessness of a failed self. Rest in God, on the contrary, is authentic; it is sure and fixed, the authentic outcome of labor consecrated to the Lord, the fruit of striving graced with virtue immune to loss because one with divine rest that lasts forever. The rest of God that is God strictly means that God as all-good needs nothing outside himself.

(ix) Sensuality or luxuriousness in the broadest sense aims at
satisfying here and now desires for as much of food and drink, the
comforts of life, and sexual relations as possible. Unfortunately, as
valiant efforts of translators testify, a precise English equivalent for
luxuria, does not seem available, though sensuality may do as a close
approximation. Luxuriousness usually signifies sumptuous living and
in this sense adequately renders lines which speak of the *luxuria* of
Asia, illustrated by bronze beds and expensive coverlets invading
Rome after Scipio's conquest of Carthage (CD 3.21), but it cannot
cover the unrestrained sexuality of the Roman emperors. So too the
prodigal son, described in the Vulgate as living *luxoriose*, ran the
gamut of sensuality (Lk 15.14).[18] Exemplifying this pleasure-seeking is
the rich man described in Lk 12.16-20, whose only concern is to eat,
drink, and be merry, while building bigger barns for his crops.
Similarly sensual is the so-called Dives (Lk 16.19-31) who, clothed in
costly garments, wined and dined daily at a sumptuous banquet,
pitilessly oblivious to the near-starving, ulcer-ridden Lazarus
stretched outside his door. The self-indulgence of these New
Testament figures was far outstripped in quantity and scope by the
Roman emperors whose periodic raids on the public treasury funded
their hedonistic dissolution. Reaching the peak in profligacy as well
as cruelty was Nero, who in disguise raped young boys for the fun of
it, staged exotic banquets at stupendous expense, and was blatantly
homosexual in a way that shocked even loose-living pagans (CD
5.19). But the gratification of the most uninhibited sensuality is never
more than a fleeting copy of the fullness of joy in God, the abundance
of whose delights, unlike those of earth and time, is inexhaustible and
deathless; the honey of whose wisdom caused hearts of martyrs to
rejoice amid their torments (P 51.18; 118[S.22].7).

(x) In remarking that extravagance literally stretches out a shade,
Augustine once more employs an overgrowth of foliage to symbolize
vice (2.3.6). An excess of liberality partly covers over liberality, not
adding to but subtracting from the virtue, resulting in the defect called
prodigality. Drawing upon public coffers some felt were bottomless,
various Roman emperors squandered money in pseudo-humani-
tarian displays.[19] Wastefulness posing as a super-liberality is a dimmed
replica of the genuine super-liberality of God. Not out of necessity but
out of the infinite riches of his liberality God created a universe
everywhere sharing in his goodness: all are gifts of his infinite largess

(P 134.4).

(xi) Avarice seeks many possessions, too many; the much it wants to store away is overmuch. Greed is insatiable, its appetite infinite. Avarice is corrupt principally because it blocks out God, so that, even on the impossible hypothesis that one super-greedy Croesus could control all the goods in the universe, his holdings would amount to comparatively nothing. For, if a man does not have God, what does he have? And if a man has God, what does he not have? (S 311.18.15). In rejecting greed's feverish desire to possess all, an individual seeking first the kingdom of God possesses all. In turn, God possesses such a seeker so that he may possess God in an exchange in which God, free of avarice, makes no profit, possessing and being possessed for the profit of the person (P 34[S.1].12).

(xii) While pride is love of one's own excellence, its kin is the hatred of excellence in others that confers happiness (GL 11.14.18). Excellence, honor, power, love, studiousness, simplicity, innocence, inner peace, pleasure, liberality, a measure of wealth—anyone of these can arouse the envy that is tortured by the benisons of others. The envious man envies an individual of equal status, for he cannot suffer equals gladly; he envies inferiors for fear they may match his standing; he envies those of higher rank, for he is not on par with them (3.8.16. GL 11.14.18). Feeling diminished by the good fortune of others, envy litigates about excellence, stooping to a shyster-lawyerlike trickery to demean its targets (S 353.1.1). In tearing down others to inflate his excellence, the individual twisted by envy crookedly images God who needs nothing outside himself to make him more perfect. Magnificent in himself, God is supremely munificent in sharing his excellence with his earthly images.

(xiii) Anger, fear, and sadness, the last three instances of misimitation of God, involve misguided use of the passions. On Augustine's reckoning, the passions themselves are morally neutral (CD 14.9).[20] Deployed by a bad will, they bear evil fruit, but under the aegis of reason directed by good will, the passions become instruments of and ingredients of virtuous acts (CD 14.7). The Jews' hardness of heart caused sadness and anger in Jesus (Mk 3.5), who also wept before restoring Lazarus to life (Jn 11.35), and became sad as his death drew near (Lk 22.15). Good Christians become justly angry at the sight of fellow Christians praising God with their lips while denying him by their lives (P30[En.2 S.2].3). Probably more frequently, anger is unjustly applied. Then its uprush beclouds the mind (P 4.6), which lashes out at difficulties and, in relation to human beings, tries to undo real or fancied injustices (E 9.4). In short, it seeks vindication or revenge (S 58.7.8. CD 14.15), but, unfortunately, its desire for vengeance is inordinate.[21] Sinful wrath is a bespeckled image of divine anger. God is said to be angry only in a properly analogical sense, (1.4.4), for, contrary to Manichean misreadings of the Old Testament, he is bodiless and immutable; he has no eyes that can bulge nor emotions subject to turbulence (P 78.8). Not an upsurge of passion, his anger is the power by which he serenely bestows retribution, most just because he administers the whole of creation in both this and the next life (P 82.12). In his perfectly ordered plan of vindictive justice God acts as a Father lovingly correcting his children rather than as a judge ruthlessly punishing malefactors.

(xiv) Fear is affective withdrawal in the face of future and imminent evils, such as the loss of one's goods or the failure to obtain what one hopes for (DQ 33. P 87.15).[22] Dealing with a special type of fear, Augustine adds two additional notes; the fear is unusual and unexpected. Herod the Great, for example , was deeply disturbed by strange news conveyed by the Magi about a newborn king (Mt 2.31). Full of fear, he ordered the massacre of all male infants to ensure the liquidation of this potential usurper (S 200 1.2). In shrinking from evils menacing its well-being, carnal fear viciously images the absolute immunity of God to the incursion of all evils. So tranquil is God in goodness that we do not speak of him as fearful even in an analogical sense. Nothing out of the ordinary can perturb him since his universal order makes provision for the humanly unusual as well as routine occurrences. A sudden turn of events cannot trouble him, for he sees all history in one all-encompassing intuition. As unchangeable, he is unconquerable by any assault, the only firm rock of refuge for hearts imperiled by a tempestuous world (CD 11.21;12.17).

(xvi) Sadness is a sorrow that the soul undergoes when afflicted by evils it feared (CD 14.15). The soul feels a discord arising from the presence of evil things it finds repugnant. In other words, since evil is the lack of good, sadness pines over the loss of goods that formerly brought delight. The death of the dearest of friends plunged Augustine into an inordinate grief that wasted his spirit. Death blackened every place he set his eyes on, and in recollection their pleasant encounters turned into torture (4.4.9). In implicitly desiring to be protected from all losses, sinful sadness is a shadowy likeness of the immutable God who cannot be dispossessed of any good. Biblical language about God's repenting certain actions is properly analogical, for God cannot experience the weakness of human sorrow. Divine repentance signifies that God changes things in the light of his changeless foreknowledge, altering a situation according to the perpetual and peaceful judgment of his equity (CD 12.17 and 17.7).

Since an intellect of Augustine's genius was not wont to set down items slapdash, it would be surprising if there were no order in the representative but not exhaustive list of fifteen sins perversely imaging the features of God. The first twelve are disordered desires for goods while the last three bear on evils on the passional level. The goods wrongly pursued divide into goods internal to human life (sins one to eight) and external goods (sins nine to eleven), with envy (number twelve) playing a special role. Pride or self-deification ranks first, followed by the second worst sin, vainglory or self-praise. Third, continuance in power motivates the cruelties of tyrants. After cravings related to self and power comes impure love, following which are instanced three misshapen species of knowledge: curiosity and, coupled, ignorance and stupidity. Then follows sloth, which aims at a false form of the rest that is the consummatory point of knowledge and love, which is truth and the goodness found fully in God. Next are briefly mentioned in decreasing order of depravity sins dealing with external goods: extravagant living, prodigality, and greed. Envy concludes the list bearing on goods because it inordinately desires goods, internal or external, possessed by others. The final three sins arise from passions confronting evils. Anger, defined as the thirst for revenge (2.9.17), is the worst of these and is therefore noted first, with misdirected fear viewed as less malicious and irrational grief as least malicious.

14. Specifically, fornication is illicit sexual union between the unmarried; in this place, as in 1.13.21 and 2.2.2, it is taken in its broader acceptation for any sin, which is illicit love of things apart from and against God. Such general fornication moves outside the orbit of God's law; sinning individuals turn aside from God, preferring lower goods no longer pure but smudged with evil. Such fornication is both aversive of and adversive to God; sinners both abandon and stand up to him. In not seeking God, sinners perversely

seek God. Insofar as they contain any good, the very substitutes of God chosen against his law testify that God is the maker of every substance, howbeit wrongly sought. Their very repudiation of God an aberrant likeness of him, sinners proclaim that God is lord of heaven and earth. The link in the creator-creature chain that cannot be broken is the deformed trace of goodness, the disfigured semblance of the God of goodness, in every sin. In refusing to be like God, individuals commit sins that are distortedly like God.

If defiance of God viciously mirrors him in some way, then the stealing of the pears had to sketch with crooked lines some lineaments of God. Augustine took pleasure in breaking the moral law not by power but by deceit. Devoid of authority to justly appropriate the fruit in broad daylight, he shook down the pears under the cover of darkness. Unobserved in his looting, he went unpunished. He did as he pleased, but his liberty was lamed by evil. In his display of freedom he was ironically a captive, enchained by carnal desires. Exercising a sort of power over another's property, acting freely, suffering no apparent consequences—these traits exhibit a likeness to omnipotence. But the resemblance was tarnished because the power applied was unjust, the liberty deformed, the exemption from punishment only exterior. God is called omnipotent because he can do whatever he wills to do in his wisdom and goodness (S 214.4. CD 21.7). As almighty, he freely created all things out of nothing. In his infinite power he can suspend the laws of nature, these miracles not being against but beyond nature (CD 21.8). Under his eternal law he freely decrees that the rules for holy living will not be as demanding for the patriarchs in the Old Dispensation as they are for the followers of his Son in the New (3.7.13). As king of the universe, God can intervene at certain junctures to suspend certain moral precepts. As lord of life and death, he commanded Abraham in a test of faith to sacrifice Isaac (H 7.49.4). As possessor, because creator, of all things, God ordered the Israelites to despoil the Egyptians, a sacrilegious and wicked people who had pressed the Jews into forced labor (CF 22.71). In contradistinction to Augustine's seizure of the pears, God's was an authentic power directed toward his goodness. God acted with full freedom as regards laws that are means to ends appointed by his love and wisdom (Sym ad cat 1.2. S 213.2) whereas Augustine's liberty was slightly crippled, a spastic gesture of a spirit fettered in man's primary captivity, a halting movement in a state in which lower members war against the law of the spirit.

All-just, God cannot suffer retribution while Augustine's impunity was only illusory, for his soul was damaged by the intrinsic punishment commensurate with the sin itself. Thus in looting the neighboring orchard, Augustine, a mere mortal, acted as if he were God almighty. With a deceit one with self-deceit he pretended to have absolute dominion over the fruit. He destroyed the pears as if he were above the law, an omnipotent creator suspending certain laws. In his soulless vandalism he was the servant of Job 7.2 (old Latin) who ran away from his master to embrace a shadow, in this respect the same as Adam who, in abandoning God, became a split self covered for and with shame (AJ 67.2). On the vertical plane, in the line of transcendence, Augustine's theft as a caricature of omnipotence was performed for the sake of some good. On the horizontal plane, in the line of immanence, without direct reference to God, the stealing was void of all good. Executed simply and solely for the sake of evil, his action was nothing but putrefaction, malodorous with sheer malice. Since even evil deeds ordinarily bespeak a good pursued in disorderly fashion, his stealing divested of all immanent good was a monstrosity, an action unnatural and counter-natural, a grotesquerie of moral life. A deeply fatal misdeed, his theft solely for theft, taken on the level of immanence, could not elicit any pleasure, for evil as evil cannot yield the tiniest delight, which is the fruit of good alone. Was it possible, he wonders, to take pleasure in a forbidden action done only because it is forbidden? Analysis of the concept of evil answers no; evil as such cannot arouse the delight that arises only from the good. Yet his actual experience offers counterveiling testimony; without a doubt he did enjoy the gratuitous evil of his vandalism. How could he really enjoy what seems analytically impossible to enjoy? The paradox is resolved in his luminous delineation of every sin as a perverse imitation of God. Implicit in the pilfering of the pears was a nexus with good, indeed the supreme good; his stealing was a dark parody of omnipotence. The malevolent pleasure afforded by filching pears sprang from the warped goodness the act contained: he thrilled with delectation because he was dizzily posturing as God almighty.[23]

Chapter 7: Praise of God's Mercy for Preventing as well as Healing Sins

15. The vivid remembrance of his theft chagrins him (2.8.16), yet he is not overcome with dread of the divine judgment, for he has been bathed in healing light. What return shall he make to the Lord for the peace due to freedom from condemnation? Simply as a man, he would return evil for good in unhappy disparity with God who returns good for evil (P 115.4). But graced, he renders love and thanksgiving to God, voicing gratuitous confession (praise) in return for gratuitous mercy toward his gratuitous stealing. Freely he gives, for freely has he received mercy in the fire of the Holy Spirit (13.9.10) melting the ice, his wicked acts, that had turned his spirit into a patch of winter. Praise is also owed for sparing him from sins he did not commit. Stealing for the sake of stealing itself bespoke his illimitable potential for sin. If he could apparently relish evil for evil's sake, what was there to stop him from indulging his pleasure in evil in every sort of unspeakable crime? "Any sin any one man commits, any other man can commit once he cuts himself off from the ruler of the universe" (S 99.6). Without exaggeration he could have matched or topped the pride, vainglory, savagery, lust, and greed of Nero, Caligula, and other emperors. His passions unleashed, he would play the pig and brute, the rapist and the murderer, the seducer and the colossal hater, nothing inhuman and subhuman being alien to him (CD 22.22). The thinking and thanking heart renders praise for mercy that not only wipes the slate clean but keeps it unsullied.

Augustine's futile grappling with mutinous passions is the rueful story of the human race that inherited a stricken nature from Adam and Eve (P 70[S.2].1). The man who presumes on his own invincibility is soon toppled into sin. So spent do his energies become that without the divine assistance not only can he not vanquish his lower self but he is drained of stamina even to fight. Man can no more remake himself than he can make himself (P 45.14). Sincere pursuit of a rational moral temper, shrewd isolation of vice-engendering trends, noble desires, questing for serenity—all these and other ingredients compounded into a physic of human devising are not potent enough to cure diseases of the soul. Virtue maintained as well as virtue regained is owed to the ministration of the divine physician, who should be loved not less but more for his preventive care of moral health (P 45.14). The same mercy that restores to life those who have fallen keeps others steadfast in virtue. Hence, he urges, those who do not bear his scars should not hoot at him as they scan this report of sicknesses of which he has been freed, for the very doctor who healed him treated their souls in such a way that they did not fall ill or rather (since no man on the planet is without some minor ailment) they became less ill than he (S 156.2.2). Souls that stay consistently healthy, because divinely inoculated against illnesses, are ordinarily more fortified than their fellows who are afflicted with maladies, then cured (S 99.6). If more blessed, so much the more the immunized praise their saving Lord. Instead of loving Augustine less because of sins recounted, such specially graced individuals should love God the more for his preventive mercy which is usually more powerful than his remedial compassion.

Chapter 8: Social Pressure a Necessary Condition for his Theft

16. Fruit of his loose-living year away from school could only be evil; but what fruit could he gain from an action, taken immanently, whose sole motive was the stealing itself? He loved the stealing for the sake of stealing, this alone, nothing else. Playing on the word "nothing," he continues: no doubt true, for his action purposed by evil itself was nothing; evil is a privation, absolutely nothing of itself. So he was all the more unhappy; wretched in his sin, he was doubly wretched because his sin apparently brought no return of satisfaction. Yet, though essential, desire of evil for its own sake was not the only decisive factor in the stealing. Crucial also in the incitement to and performance of the theft was the influence of his companions. At first glance then it seems that he did not love anything but the stealing itself. But reflective pause brings him back to his first position: he sought nothing else than the stealing, for the evil companionship, considered precisely as evil, was nothing; devoid of good, deprived of value, its fruit could equal no more than zero. But this answer will not do; it is implausible because of the unforgettable fact that Augustine did take delight in his thieving. Where there is delight, there must be an object to be enjoyed. Thus his delectation arose not from nothing that is evil but from something good. Additional examen uncovers two goods in his action, one already discerned, the other emerging from its social aspect. If he had stolen the pears to enjoy them, he

would have committed the theft by himself to get all the pleasure he wanted. But, in fact, he did not do the thieving alone; he stole the pears under the pressure of adolescent associates. The social impact was mutual; like stones perhaps of the sort Latins called live pyrites, which are struck and rubbed against one another to kindle a spark;[24] they stimulated one another to set aflame the impulse to rob the pears. Without this social percussion that enkindles desire, Augustine would not have despoiled his neighbor's orchard. Throwing the pears to the pigs indicated that what he loved in the theft was not the pears but the theft itself (2.4.9). Here the social percussion sparking him and his accomplices shows that he found his pleasure not in the pears but in the very evil of the misdeed. So, he concludes, his evil action done for the sake of evil yielded two fruits, in which he took pleasure. The crippled liberty recklessly destroying another's property darkly imaged God's omnipotence, (2.6.14); this power perversely wielded was the primary and essential good delighted in. The social dimension was the sine qua non or necessary condition for the action; the companionship of fellow culprits, with its reciprocal social approval, was the secondary but indispensable good that supplied his desire with the fruition that is joy.

Chapter 9: Further Analysis of Social Influence

17. Without a doubt his deed was depraved, yet he wants to lay out specific features of the socially conditioned theft. Implied in "Who can understand sins?" is another short prayer for more light. The craving for lower goods that is sin, which shakes an individual loose from the solid firmament of virtue, changes the soul into water, merging it with the flux of vanities (P 74.6). It is as hard to understand sins as it is to see darkness. The habitual sinner is like a blindfolded individual unable even to see his blindfold. Still, Augustine, now plainly renewed, is aware of some darkness dulling analytical and moral perception.

With all the blind callousness of adolescents he and his companions laughed aloud as they imagined how the trick they were to play would leave the family that owned the orchard helplessly outraged. Significantly, he calls their laughter a kind of tickling of the mind, for an individual can never tickle himself to the point of laughter. Like tickling, their merriment over the plight of their victims was socially induced. Was this reciprocal tickling the reason why he experienced pleasure he could not have felt alone? Laughter often occurs in a particular social setting, its jokes and witticisms so suffused with local color that they often escape translation.[25] Laughter is infectious; it grows in volume and intensity as it spreads around a room. Even raconteurs, ordinarily unmoved by their punch lines, break out in laughter as the merriment rolls around them. While they plotted their theft, he and his confederates guffawed as they pictured the crestfallen reaction of the dumbfounded owners after the despoiling of the pear tree. Gales of laughter helped fuel their enthusiasm and stiffen their resolution to pull off the stealing. Yet the heightened pleasure that laughing induced could not account for his delight in the act, for, however commonly social, laughter does at times overcome people who are alone when something ridiculous strikes the mind or senses. The skeptic's contention, "Probability is the guide of life," is ludicrously absurd in the moral sphere, tantamount to "Anything goes," for on any vicious action, even Catiline's parricidal assault on the Roman republic, a probable face can be persuasively put (CA 3.16.36). The Manichean belief that when a fig is plucked, its mother tree sheds milky tears, is natural nonsense so incongruous, Augustine suggests, that it is laughable (3.10.18). Elsewhere he explicitly counts other pieces of Manichean fantasy ludicrous (O 3.17.46.CF 2.6); since the laughable is situated in the incongruous, he had to laugh at their doctrinal oddities. Since companions are not always needed to trigger laughter, the delight linked to laughter cannot be equated with the pleasure garnered in his thieving. He has laughed alone, but he could not have stolen the pears alone.

To clarify further the meaning of the theft, he reviews the key components of his state of mind: the pleasure in his theft stemmed not from what he stole but the fact that he stole; he would have garnered no pleasure if he had done it by himself, and therefore he would not have done it alone. Rising above the law by trampling on the rights of others thrilled him with a degenerate sense of power; but without the constraint of the gang he would not have wrought evil for evil's sake. It was an unfriendly friendship that excited this delight. Accepting the loose-knit creed and code of his clique, subordinating any repugnance to evil to the desires of the group, he felt pressured to cooperate in a practical joke that was actually a wicked scheme. It was a friendship essentially inimical to his moral personality, sapping the moral strengths that true bonding of hearts nourishes: with friends like these, he needed no enemies of his soul (CF 2.6).

The human heart is an abyss, an impenetrable depth (4.14.22); the secret intentions of the heart, what men interiorly do or not do, elude human scrutiny (P 41.13). Hence after discriminatingly investigating his socially instigated evil act done for evil, he is brought up short before the regions of the human heart that resist investigation. He cannot plumb the depths of his own heart as it was misled by the claims of loyalty due his friends(P 18[En.2].13). In strict observance of gang morality he flagrantly broke the moral law. Along with his companions, he was eager to inflict harm on others in an atmosphere supercharged with emotions expressive of group loyalty. Social homogeneity dictated the path he walked; he had to square his behavior with the standard, "Everybody is doing it." To assure the continuing acceptance of the group, he felt compelled to share in their raid on the pear tree. The fruit, the delight he experienced, was the glow of social approval merited by sharing in a joint action, manifesting the solidarity of his clique. Stamped with the imprimatur of the group, the stealing was performed with a clear social conscience, without the slightest shame. He and his fellow thieves would have felt ashamed only if they had not felt unashamed. Had he expressed genuine shame after the stealing, he would have been stung by social sanction; first, reprimanded, then snubbed, perhaps later isolated and ostracized. Moral shame, a sign of remorse, would have brought down on his head social shame for daring to call into question rigid conformity to the injunctions, however intrinsically evil, of the group mind. Shame, in betraying revulsion for the thievery, would have signaled disaffection from the group consensus and, by way of reaction, invited stern rebuke and perhaps ejection.

Chapter 10: Alienated from God, he Became a Wasteland

18. His soul was a mass of knots, so intertwisted as to appear beyond disentangling. Each human heart, is unfathomable (2.9.17), whose sin, a privation, is more elusive than a positive reality, with doing evil for evil's sake darker still; the imperious drives of his social self bafflingly overrode any sense of respect for others that his individual self harbored. However inexplicable, his sin was clearly loathsome. Earlier he basked in the commendation of shallow

friends; now he perceives himself, as he was in the eyes of God, rank and stinking (2.1.1). Quivering with revulsion, he no longer wants to fix his eyes on the hideous scene flashed on the screen of memory; more, so abominable is it that he finds even a quick look revolting.

Turning away from his disgusting sixteenth year, he now longs only for the light within whom are pure justice and innocence, the God who ordains all things toward his unalloyed goodness and cares for all without willing the least harm. He yearns to embrace his Lord; comely not with a counterfeit glamour but brilliant with the richest lights of divine love; enchanting not with a treacherous charm that seduces the flesh but all-lovely to lights or inner eyes purified by the holy fire of God.[26] He pines for a face-to-face vision of the truth, infinitely enjoyable with an insatiable satiety; satiety because in eternal union there will be no lack of delights; insatiable because there will be no end to the delectation consequent upon eternal contemplation of the insatiable truth that is God (S 362.28.29). He who is his own rest (2.6.13) dowers man with his grace here that he may give him his rest hereafter. This shared life with God will be immune to all the shocks that make social and individual peace here below fragile (P 127.16). Those endlessly replenished at the divine banquet enter into the joy of the Lord (9.10.25), drinking of the torrent of his delights, ecstatically delighted with the plenty of his heavenly home. In his sixteenth year of lust and thievery, however, Augustine was bereft of the idea of this vision of the highest good with its imperturbable peace and lasting joy. He flowed down from God, he literally says; departing from the divine firmament of moral truth, he was caught up in the flux of vanities; he lost moral consistency, becoming morally flaccid. Enthralled by moral fictions, he forsook the firmament of divine happiness (4.16.29): to become morally delinquent means to flow down after the fashion of a liquid from the solidity of the firmament of justice. Like the prodigal son, he wandered far from the stability of virtue that is the Father's house, not only drifting into but becoming a region of want, a wasteland. Deserting God, he became a desert (2.3.5). Forsaking unfailing plenty (9.10.24), he became an arid emptiness, not poor in spirit but spiritually bankrupt. Love of evil for evil's sake that was a nothing and seduction into thievery that was a nothing (2.8.16) estranged him from the God who is the plentitude of goodness, and turned him into a moral zero. Ironically, he gloried in conduct overbrimming with evil (2.1.1) that in his darkness he did not see left his insatiable appetite wholly unsatiated.

NOTES

1. The division that follows is based on Solignac, BA 13,333 ff.
2. In "Symbols of Sinfulness in Book II of Augustine's "Confessions"", AS 2(1971), 93-104, especially 93-6, L. Ferrari finds the roots of *silvescere* or running wild in the first part (chapters 1-39) of Isaiah. The metaphor of shade or its variants occurs in five other places (1.1; 6.12; 6.13; 6.14; 7.16) in Book 2.
3. In late antiquity free men were divided into *honestiores* and *humiliores.* The first class included senators on the top rung and decurions and veterans on the bottom rung while the second class consisted of the impoverished, who usually owned no land. See Agatha Mary, S.P.B., *The Rule of St. Augustine,* 71. Augustine's father was a decurion, a member of the Thagaste senate or *curia.* The decurions were generally a group from which municipal officials were drawn. Members took turns in supervising, under the imperial administration, activities such as collection of taxes. Though not wealthy, a decurion was expected to own some property. See P. Salway, *Roman Britain,* 463, 575-6. In 426 Augustine described himself as "a poor man born of poor parents" (S 356.13). He was then poor because he was living the common life in a monastic community. His parents had been relatively poor, neither utterly impoverished nor wealthy (HC 26, n.7), whose household also included some slaves (1.19.30). As part of his patrimony Augustine still legally possessed a few small fields, whose acreage was less than 1/20th of the property that as bishop he was officially in charge of in Hippo (E 126.6). See Perler, *Voyages,* 123-4, and Pellegrino, V, 48, n.5.
4. Perler, *Voyages,* 131.
5. The play on the words *disertus* (cultivated man) and *desertus* (deserter) escapes exact translation. Patricius' myopic concentration on shaping his son into a *disertus* was ensuring that he be a deserter of God.
6. Apparently this is the only passage in Augustine's writings which would seem to imply that, as the first from whom a grandchild would spring, he is the eldest child. HC 27, n. 8. One scholar offers the suggestion, without textual documentation, that his brother Navigius was older than Augustine.
7. The five spiritual senses are dealt with in 10.6.8 and 27.38.
8. Oliver Wendell Holmes remarked, "Rum thing to see a man making a mountain out of robbing a pear tree in his teens." Quoted in Brown, 172, n. 5; cited in Starnes, 37. Augustine's handling of the episode seemed to be a grossly overblown piece of pietistic rhetoric. Along similar lines B. Russell, in *A History of Western Philosophy,* 345, deems it odd that Augustine regarded the theft of the pears as "an act of almost incredible wickedness". His preoccupation with a minor adolescent prank was morbid, with its roots in an obsessive sense of sin. Russell's criticism, however, is clearly extravagant. For Augustine, the stealing is not unbelievably evil since 2.6.13 lists evils that are far more shocking: pride, lust for power, cruelty, and gross sensuality, among others. Augustine's piercing awareness of sin was in no way morbid. While laying bare the corruption eating away at the heart, he appeals to prayer for healing. In a perceptive article, "The Pear-Theft in Augustine's 'Confessions'," REA 16 (1970), 234-42,

L. Ferrari, in responding to Russell's comment, argues that for Augustine, who evinces a profound interest in trees (235), the episode draws its significance from the contrast between the Tree of Knowledge of Good and Evil, symbolized by the Pear-Tree, and the Tree of the Cross (i.e., of Life), symbolized by the Fig-Tree in the garden of Milan in 386 (241). Still, this suggestive analogy seems more conjectural than convincing. As our text below shows, Augustine's interest in the theft is piqued because it appears to be an instance of evil done solely for the sake of evil, which, on his reckoning, is psychologically and physically impossible. The stealing of the pears draws its primary goodness from imitation (actually perverse) of omnipotence (2.6.12-4) while social pressure of companions functions as a secondary good.

9. Some translations render the "your firmament" of the Latin as "your support" or "security in you." However, he does not pray, "You are my firmament (or tower of strength)," as he does elsewhere in commenting on Ps 70 (P 70 [S.2].5) but speaks of throwing himself down from "your firmament," i.e., the unvarying truth of God opposed to the turbulent currents of misleading human opinion rooted in or grouped under the heading of vanity.

10. K. Svoboda, *L'esthétique de saint Augustin et ses sources*, researches references to beauty, especially in the early works; see 46-7. According to R. O'Connell, *Art and the Christian Intelligence in St. Augustine*, Svoboda's study shows that beauty consists of the relation of the parts of the beautiful thing to one another and the entire object; a relation usually called equality, measure, and concord. The ontic foundation for the relation is number, which signifies the form of beauty in quasi-mathematical vesture (14-5). In *Beauty and Revelation in the Thought of Saint Augustine*, 22-4, Harrison substantially agrees with Svoboda and O'Connell, noting that unity is a key notion: "Unity is the form of all beauty" (E 18.2).

11. However odd-seeming to modern physiological psychology, the ray theory of vision was generally accepted after Plato (*Tim.* 67c-68a), though it is not embraced by Aristotle in *De an.* 2.7.418b and is repudiated in *De sens. et sensib.* 2.437b. See J. Beare, *Greek Theories of Elementary Cognition From Alcaemon to Aristotle*, 84, n. 1. The correlation between elements and senses derives from the Old Academy; this according to O'Daly, 82, n. 8. For other texts in Augustine endorsing the ray theory of vision see Book 1, n. 37, above.

12. *Sat.* 10.356.

13. According to DC 3.10.16, the two most general categories of sin are *flagitium*, a sin against one's own good, and *facinus*, a sin against the good of another, with *flagitium* prior and more basic. "Undisciplined desire that causes harm to one's own soul and body is called personal sin; but what causes harm to another is said to be social sin." The terms resist rendering into appropriate English; for better or worse, it seems acceptable to translate them as personal sin and social sin.

14. Sallust, *Bellum Catalinae*, 16. Cicero delivered four orations against the rebel whom he apparently tended to demonize.

15. Seneca, "On the Shortness of Human Life," cited in H. Deane, *The Political and Social Ideas of St. Augustine*, 268, n.53.

16. W. Durant, *Caesar and Christ*, 267. According to S. Dill, *Roman Society From Nero to Marcus Aurelius*, 86, emperors not uncommonly punished delators or informers from a prior regime.

17. In Augustine's eyes, simplicity as a moral virtue is roughly equivalent to innocence. In bidding his followers in Mt. 10.16 to be simple as doves, the Lord commands men not to injure any rational being. The dove symbolizes simplicity because it does no harm to any other animal, even the tiniest (QE 8).

18. *Luxuria* and its cognates are variously rendered in the translation of the Vulgate New Testament by gifted Latinist and wordsmith Ronald Knox. Lk 15.14: riotous living; Gal 5.19: luxury; Eph 5.18: [wine] (*in quo est luxuria*) which leads to ruin; Tit 1.6: reckless living; Jas 5.5: with luxuries; 1 Pet 4.3: incontinence; 1 Pet 4.4: debauch; 2 Pet 2.2: wanton creeds; 2 Pet 2.18: wanton appetite; Jude 4: life of wantonness.

19. Durant, *Caesar and Christ*, 267.

20. Adopting the Stoic position, channeled through Cicero, Augustine recognizes four emotions, joy, sorrow, fear, and anger. He was apparently not acquainted with the more nuanced classification of the passions, derived from Aristotle, which distinguishes between the concupiscible appetites, love, hate, joy, and sorrow, and the irascible appetites, daring, fear, hope, despair, and anger.

21. Thinkers of old, CD 14.15 tells us, defined anger as nothing else than a lust for revenge, "old" referring to Cicero, *Tusc. disp.* 3.5.1. According to E 9.4 and CD 14.15, derived from *Tusc. disp.*, 4.9.21, men get angry with inanimate objects, throwing down a stylus or breaking a pen that writes badly. Apparently even anger of this sort may harbor an irrational libido of vengeance, a shadow of the retribution that is based on the maxim, "Whatsoever does evil suffers evil."

22. Interestingly, on Augustine's reckoning, the fear of fear itself is psychologically impossible (DQ 33). Fearing fear, an individual would possess the subjective state of fear that he does not desire to possess. Notice, his insight bears on sensory or passional fear. It is surely possible to have without incoherence an intellectual or nonpassional fear of sensory fear.

23. VR 45.84 describes pride as the desire to be sole master of things, a desire that perversely imitates divine omnipotence. Interestingly, this broad sense of pride is echoed in C. Jung's characterization of man's prideful estimate of self as "his Godalmightiness" (cited in J. Whale, *Christian Doctrine*, p.45, n.1). Here, however, Augustine more clearly defines and distinguishes the concepts of pride and false imitation of omnipotence. Pride means self-deification or soverign self-exaltation (2.6.13). The seemingly senseless stealing of the pears specifically imitates, albeit wickedly, the almightiness of God (2.6.14).

24. R. Forbes, *Studies in Ancient Technology*, 8-9.

25. On humor in Augustine, see Pope, 169-82.

26. Reference to God's justice and innocence as *decora honestis luminibus* may be translated "lovely with noble lights" or "lovely to virtuous lights (eyes)." Most English translations favor the latter reading while a large majority of French, German, Italian, and Spanish versions prefer the former rendering. French: BA 13; German: H. Hefele (1928); Italian: C. Carena (1982); Spanish: C. Coscaya (1986); but A. Vega's well-known Spanish rendering (1946) uses the expression common in English translations.

Book Three
Sojourn in Carthage

After an introductory section portraying him caught up in love of love that was illicit, (1.1-2) he analyzes the allure of stage plays (2.2-4). Next he came upon Cicero's *Hortensius*, a protreptic that inflamed his desire for wisdom (4.7-8). After the coarse style of Scripture affronted him (5.9), he became trapped in Manicheism (6.10-1). Remembrance of this fatal encounter prompted a critique of the morally parochial stand of the Manichees, to which are added moral precisions (7.12-9.17). Monica is assured of her son's conversion by a dream (11.19), buttressed by a bishop's prophecy of his return to the faith (12.20).

Chapter 1: Pleasures and Pains of Illicit Love

1. Once his father Patricius had garnered enough funds from Romanianus, his principal benefactor, Augustine's year of errant idleness came to an end. Probably in the autumn of 370 he traveled roughly 160 miles northeast for further and final schooling at Carthage, a cosmopolitan seaport. A big city by any standard, the so-called Rome of Africa, a flourishing political, economic, and military center, was for Augustine principally a cultural center, in which he could, under the eyes of cultivated masters, become skilled in rhetoric, with Cicero as his chief model of eloquence. Unhappily, *Cartago* (Carthage) was a *sartago*, a cauldron boiling with illicit loves. According to Salvian, Africa and Carthage, in particular, were utterly depraved.[1] While other peoples had some redeeming virtues, the Africans were distinguished by none, excelling in all vices and outstripping themselves in impurity and blasphemy. Brothels did a

brisk business on nearly every street and crossroad. Homosexuals, transvestites, and quasi-transsexuals brazenly paraded their deviance. No doubt Carthage was not as unspeakably debauched as Salvian's jeremiad paints it; still, it was in some sense a Sin City, a metropolis so indulgent of casual sex and easy impurity of every strain that blatant sexual mimicry and gross obscenities were woven into the liturgy honoring the goddess called the Great Mother (CD 2.4). Thrown into this polluted environment, Augustine's heart was contaminated with its prevailing lust; not yet in love with anyone in particular, he fell in love with sensuous love, i.e., he was hot with desire for a lifestyle of erotic love. Translated literally, the obscure phrase that follows tells us, "By a deeper indigence I hated myself as less indigent." Here he is not reporting his state of mind in 370; rather, he is evaluating it from the spiritually purified perspective of the bishop of 397. From this coign of vantage, though the student of sixteen was bewitched by sensual love and panted after pleasures he hoped would profit his heart, he was, in fact, spiritually impoverished, and his love of the sensual, because misguided, involved a hatred of his true self. Thus this difficult line would seem to mean: because of his deeper spiritual impoverishment he hated (falsely loved) himself while he was less spiritually impoverished (and on the threshold of becoming more spiritually impoverished). First, a sinner's flight from God causes the more hidden or deeper indigence. Second, as a result, in deserting God, the source of true self-love, he hates or falsely loves himself. Third, not stabilized within, he is driven out of himself and divorced from his true or interior self, flinging himself downward into outer goods. Exteriorization of the self involves a lesser indigence, the loss of the interior self, the submission of the self to lower things. Valuationally he forfeits his interior self to what is below him; choosing the earthy, he becomes morally earthy.[2]

In love with love, he let his eyes rove about in search of an object of love, i.e., some consort to satisfy his ravenous sexual appetite. Contemptuous of chastity, he hated security, or freedom from care, opting for restlessness rather than inner peace, scorning any path that was not strewn with traps set by the Evil One (P 90 ([S.1].4.). Hating the riches of spiritual liberty, he loved entrapment. In a previous sentence "hate" signifies wrongful love of the false self; here it denotes vicious repudiation of the trap-free path of moral wisdom. His spiritual penury was the reason why he pursued this reckless course.

Within he was famished, deprived of God, the food of his interior self. Hungry of spirit without being aware of his hunger, he did not hunger after God. He had no desire at all for food that does not perish, not because his soul was sated (it was actually starved) but because in his emptiness his emaciated spirit was nauseated by spiritual food. As starving, his soul became ill and, in the absence of spiritual nutrients, broke out in sores. In this condition, instead of turning to healing resources within, his soul thrust itself outward, seeking remedy in exterior things, barren objects that, when seized, make the soul equally empty (S 96.2). He avidly tried to soothe the itching of the ulcers of his soul by rubbing them with sensuous things, i.e., carnal touches. As the following line makes clear, contact with sensible things means physical encounters with persons of the opposite sex; he could not have loved them humanly or been loved in return had they lacked a (rational) soul. Only a minded inamorata one in nature with and equal to him (unity and equality are required for even the friendship that is illicit love) could consciously exchange affection displayed in feelings and sensory activity. To be enjoyed instead of being sheerly endured, illicit love has to be not a purely physical but a human union. Put more concretely, contact with sensible things issues in the sweetness of loving and being loved and the more delicious sweetness that is the pleasure of sexual foreplay and union. This embrace of bodies was a false love, an illicit friendship, because the sexual pleasure given and received was relished against the will of the Father revealed in the love of Christ. Simply stated, it was fornication, an act not of true love but of lust. The filth of concupiscence polluted the spring of friendship; it was a union of bodies that broke the union of spirits with God. Not God-inspired but hellborn, his love was a lust that muddied the limpid waters of friendship. Inwardly vile, he was outwardly polished; his morals were foul, his academic manners impeccable. It was exorbitant vanity, i.e., abundant emptiness, that enabled him to be at once gross and refined. The movements of his heart were precipitous and impetuous: he cast himself headlong at love, yearning to be carried away by it, glad to be subjugated by his lower self (2.6.14). Even in this darkness the mercy of God was at work: indeed, God is, for Augustine, my mercy, personally bathing his wounds. God's mercy permissively visits afflictions on souls to draw them to his love, and, the more manifold the troubles, the more mighty his mercy (P 6.6.9; 68[S.2].1);

so mercy apportioned gall to be sprinkled on the sweets of sensual amours. Loved with piercing bodily love in his secret affairs, he reveled in sexual delights, but the bond of sexual union brought with it another bond, the painful chains of fleshly existence forged by his bad will (8.5.10). The flames of illicit love entrained scourging of his spirit. On fire with love, he was beaten by red-hot rods, instruments of torture used in trials of criminals, slaves in particular, to extract information.[3] At the tribunal not of human justice but of divine mercy this slave of sin was inwardly beaten by rods of jealousy, suspicion, fear, anger, and quarreling. Jealous of potential rivals for the affections of one or other transitory sexual partner; he became suspicious of his paramour, fearful that she might play him for a fool and, erupting at times in anger, he became embroiled in quarrels. So sorrows soured his pleasures, only faint images of the true happiness, however imperfect, begotten of the nuptial union of man and woman become one flesh in accord with the law and love of God.

Chapter 2: Love of Stage Plays

2. Augustine, still the impressionable youth, was enraptured by stage plays, which depicted his own miseries; superficially joyful, his life apart from God was inwardly sad, furnishing fresh fuel for his fire, here a symbol not of the ardor of divine love (4.12.19; 13.9.10) but of the burning of the passion of lust (2.2.2). While at the theater, Augustine witnessed acrobatic exhibitions, often obscene pantomiming, stories about the gods, and comedies as well as tragedies.[4] What excites his reflection is certain strains of incongruity in the popularity of tragic motifs. Viewers like to feel disconsolate over woeful theatrical events that they would not like to experience themselves. Theater-goers draw pleasure from psychic pain; in sorrow lies their joy. Spectators apparently make a spectacle out of themselves at these spectacles, their gladness in sadness savoring of a miserable lunacy; lunacy, because a theater-goer seeks delight in the contradictory of delight that is sorrow; miserable in the sense that the spectator's odd way of thinking becomes equivalent to the theatrical misery that stirs feelings of sorrow and pity. The unsound attitude is commensurate with an unsound subjection to the passions; and the less control his higher self exercises over emotions, the more he is moved by passions enacted in the plays.[5] Augustine interjects a

semantic point: misery is the condition in which a person is suffering, and mercy is the response of compassion for those who are suffering; in mercy (*misericordia*) the heart (*cor*) becomes miserable (*miserum*) or sorrowful over a plight befalling another (ME 27.53). The mercy or compassion elicited by the imaginary portrayals of the stage seems unreal, diverging from real compassion on two counts. First, the sorrow remains enclosed within the self; it is a subjective, a morally aloof aesthetic sadness that does not, as does genuine pity, inspire the viewer to relieve or remove the suffering. Second, the viewer lauds the cause of his fictively induced sorrows. The sadder he feels, the more he applauds the playwright. When he feels no aesthetic pain because the tragic events are poorly dramatized, he departs the theater disgusted; on the other hand, if he does experience the sadness art engenders, he stays, fascinated to the end. The truly compassionate person, however, is appalled by suffering and, rather than praising, at best tolerates the wellsprings of suffering.

3. However strange-seeming, men do actually love to be moved to tears and to undergo sorrow at the sight of suffering on the stage. On the other hand, it is no less indubitable that everyone prefers to value good things; this universally desired joy seems in paradoxical contrast to the sorrow that spectators of tragedies pursue. Perhaps, he suggests, a way out of the impasse lies in a distinction between feeling misery and feeling mercy. While no one covets misery, theater-goers delight in pitying another; a pity that would be impossible if there were no one to pity. Aficionados of shows want to feel sorrows only in a limited sense, only insofar as the sorrows registered are a factually necessary condition for the exercise of compassion. Theatrically depicted tragedies evoke sorrow; playgoers desire to feel sorrow not in itself but obliquely, i. e., only in connection with and derivation from the pleasure felt in being compassionate toward individuals with woes. As a type of love, compassion takes its rise from the stream of friendship. But the course of pity can take a wrong turn, rushing away from lofty moral standards into a torrent of boiling pitch, surge after surge torrid with passion. By misdirected choice an individual's expression of friendship, i.e., love, forfeits its heavenly calm; rather than being properly formed, it becomes deformed; no longer securely anchored in the firmament of devotion, it is devoured by drives of the flesh. But in no way does this mean that all compassion has to be shunned as intrinsically evil. There are times when men may

indirectly love sorrows, occasions when they legitimately exercise compassion. But it is sinful sources of sorrow and compassion that the soul is bade eschew through the overarching protection of the all-caring Father of our fathers, i.e., of all generations of the people of God.

Therefore at present he does not repudiate compassion, but when he haunted the theater in Carthage, his compassion was soiled by uncleanness. He took delight in illicit amours portrayed on the stage, and when events sundered the lovers, he experienced a sort of, i.e., an artistic, compassion for these tragic figures, whereby he was satisfied by not only their passionate encounters but their heart-rending separation as well. At present his vision is roughly the reverse of the illusion-ridden outlook of his Carthaginian days. He feels not joy but compassion, indeed greater compassion for an individual taking pleasure in illicit love-making; for such a misled individual he feels more pity than he does for an individual grieving over the deprivation of some harmful pleasure or the loss of some form of apparent happiness that is really unhappiness. This morally controlled compassion is the truer type of pity and, because nobler, contains no love of sorrow. An individual who feels sorrow over the sufferings of another deserves praise for his charity, yet, if his compassion is genuine, he would prefer that there were no sufferings at all to sorrow his heart. Only on the impossible hypothesis that a person was at once both good-willed and bad-willed could such a man gifted with sincere compassion desire that some people suffer in order that he might have objects on whom to lavish compassion. Hence the sorrow a compassionate man feels is praiseworthy, but it would be wrong to simply aim at feeling such sorrow since it would entail the malevolent desire that others be afflicted with misery. The heart of God, immutable and therefore invulnerable to, without being wounded by, sorrow, pours out mercy on souls he loves. Divine compassion, exempt from the passion of sorrow, is eminently purer as infinitely spiritual (free of matter) and more incorruptible (absolutely immune to change) than passions seated in a corruptible body. Quoting 2 Cor 2.16, Augustine suggests that no human being is capable of perfectly duplicating or comprehending sorrow-free divine compassion. In exercising compassion, men must feel sorrow while striving to avoid desiring to feel sorrow for its own sake.

Sections 2 and 3 contrast on four scores the theater-goer's feeling of pity with moral compassion. First, though absorbed in the events, a playgoer as a spectator contemplating dramatically enacted sufferings remains morally detached from the sorrows depicted. A morally compassionate person, on the other hand, is morally involved in the suffering of the individual whose anguish evokes pity. Consequently, and this marks a second difference, a playgoer is not moved to lend assistance to the victim of suffering while a truly compassionate man actually gives of himself to ease another's suffering. Third, the more grief he experiences, the more pleased is a viewer of plays while the opposite is the case in real-life compassion; the greater the grief, the more disconsolate a man of merciful heart becomes. Fourth, in the world of the theater sorrows are loved for the sake of art while in a Christian context of actual life sorrows cannot be loved save indirectly, i.e., only insofar as they excite mercy. In fact, it would be better if there were no sorrows to be compassionated and alleviated. But since every man must struggle through a valley of tears, sorrows are ineliminable; and misery is commended not for its own sake but only in view of the mercy it elicits.

4. After analyzing Christian compassion, he attends once more to his former play-loving state of mind. In his miserable condition he yearned to feel sadness, hunting for opportunities to be stabbed by psychic pain. His sadness was stirred by tribulations actors endure on the stage; the more copious the tears, the more splendid seemed the performance of the tragedian. A straying sheep who would not suffer the loving guidance of the divine shepherd, he was made to suffer from a disease of the soul, lust in particular. He delighted in sorrows that plays arouse, but only as a spectator of fictional scenes, not as a participant stung by the anguish of real events. Initially the sorrows grazed only the surface of his heart. Yet this initial scratching results in disease; the fingernails of sorrow scratched his spirit, making it inflamed, its sores puffy from a horrible pus. His was an existence mired in the sensual; grieving over fictive woes, he was content, howbeit steeped in spiritual misery.

Chapter 3: A Student at Carthage

5. His voracious mind was inflamed with false curiosity, which is not a zealous search for truth but a craving for novel experiences sheerly for their own sake(2.6.13). Stained in this instance with the

sacrilegious;[5] he enjoyed watching sacrilegious ceremonies, a perversion of authentic sacred rites, effectively equivalent to acts of idolatry(8.2.3-4). He seems to be alluding to fascination with impure pagan rites(3.1.1) witnessed in Carthage as a young man or "adolescent"(370-4 or 376-83). Repulsive spectacles were performed in veneration of the gods and goddesses. Especially homaged every year on March 27 was the Great Mother, Cybele or Berecynthia, mother of the gods. Obscene actions were performed and lewd airs sung as modes of worship, so shocking that actors and singers would be ashamed to execute them in the presence of their own mothers; ironically, the exalted mother of the gods was honored by deeds and words so depraved that their use would totally dishonor ordinary mothers(CD 2.4). Not an actual worshipper of idols, Augustine was not wholly passive; his curiosity linked him to, and tarred him with the brush of, idolatry. Because idolatry is effectively the cult of demons(P 96.11), his curiosity obliquely entangled him in the service of demons, called deceitful in the sense that unclean spirits dupe men and thereby receive adoration under the name of gods (CD 2.4). Men who cave in to lower concupiscences are delivered over to subjection to demons (P 77.20); the viciousness that is idolatry betrays even greater domination by demons (P 96.11). Though Augustine never adored idols, his intense curiosity countenancing sacrilegious acts indirectly enmeshed him in idolatry that beckoned demons to control his life (P 96.11). Instead of making the usual sacrifices to idols, he offered his evil deeds as a sacrifice to demons. A man of God, so dedicated to God that he dies to the world in order to live solely for God, is himself a living sacrifice (CD 10.6). Augustine's sacrifice to the demons was a caricature of this authentic sacrifice, turning him in some sense into a man of the devil.

After falling into the pit of infidelity, he was so reckless as to negotiate an impure union during the Sunday Mass of the catechumens (the service of the word alone). In a building consecrated to God he arranged a rendezvous that would desecrate a body destined to be a temple of the Spirit. It seems highly unlikely that, as some claim, he engaged in a gross sexual act. This encounter took place not in an isolated spot but "within the walls of the church", in the special section assigned to penitents or catechumens, during the liturgy itself; probably no more than a few surreptitious light touches were ventured. This occasion, others speculate, was his first meeting with his future concubine. In any event, he perverted an edifice of holy faith into a locus for planning unholy infidelity, which is fruit for death, so described because in sexual transaction the present pleasure is paltry but the loss grievous; a sinner hurtles into the abyss of death (P 58 [S.1]. 20). His sins were properly met with the lashes of divine retribution. Surely spiritual blindness was one punishment, and his will certainly became more debased, for evildoers suffer more than those on whom they inflict evil (5.8.14). On occasion he probably felt some stings of a true conscience; possibly at times his arrogance was rebuked by fellow students. Only mercy from above saved him from ultimate destruction, for he held his neck high, i.e. he was smugly self-confident, distant from God because he loved his own ways, those of the flesh rather than those of the spirit. Free he was but only with the sham-freedom of a fugitive, actually slavery to sin. Augustine is not conjuring the image of a runaway slave; quite the opposite: by running away from God, the soul became enslaved in passions, wandering famished because barren of God. A runaway slave in the empire, motivated by the prospect of capture and execution, might be able to hide for a time; a spiritual fugitive had nowhere to hide; he fled simply from God displeased (P 30 [En.2.S.1] 14; 94.2; 138.12), his flight no more than a pseudo-flight.

6. At this time he was pursuing studies labeled honorable that would fit him for arguing lawsuits in the forum, excellence in which required skill in the art of deception. The more dishonorable the lying, the more successful he would be in this discipline ironically called honorable. At its core the art of the rhetorician and lawyer-to-be was artifice; the more morally unworthy of honor an unscrupulous lawyer was, the more honor he received for cases he won. Cut off from divine light, articulate deceivers ensnarled in this web of moral irony were powerless to see their predicament. Unlike the physically blind whose plight makes them unhappy, the spiritually blind are so sealed off in darkness that they glory in their blindness; added to the penalty of blindness is the punishment of boasting of being happy while being really miserable (P 6.8; 68 [S.2].10). Already recognized as the brightest star, Augustine swelled with self-importance because of his polished mastery of the art of artifice: he was proud of being the blindest of all.

Yet withal there were borders beyond which he would not traffic in evil. For the most part he was a reserved student; a certain Vincentius, a fellow student and later a member of the Rogatists, a splinter sect within Donatism, corroborated Augustine's report of his decorous conduct (E 93.13.51). His behavior was light years distant from that of the gang of ruffians who gloried in the name of *eversores*, overturners or wreckers. Bearing this barbarous style as a badge of urbane sweetness and light, they probably carried out to perfection the unruly interruptions, upsetting pranks, and general disruptive rowdiness characteristic of Carthaginian students (5.8.14). Augustine lived among them with a kind of shameless shame; with shame, because outraged by their calculated roistering, he held himself aloof from their nastiness; with a certain shamelessness, because he associated with them and at times took pleasure in their company, which public reproof might forfeit. He shrank in horror from their hazing of neophytes, in which they sneered, perhaps with raunchy epithets,at the modest behavior and decent language of new students. Augustine advisedly characterizes their conduct as diabolical. Feasting, as do demons, on malevolent joys (CD 2.4), these human spirits of disorder betrayed a family likeness to demonic spirits of disorder, They were rightly named overturners, for, in turning things upside down, in their trickery of the innocent they were themselves perverted by the chicanery of secretly seducing spirits. Imitators of evil spirits, they were also their derided playthings; making fools of others, they were being ridiculed. Externally agents of disorder, they were internally victims of disorder. In spurning God's law by mocking fellow students, the overturners abjectly paid homage to demons (1.17.27). They already had their reward for contempt of God and man: contempt heaped on them by demons.

Chapter 4: *Hortensius*: A Call to Wisdom

The ugly antics of the overturners, however, formed only background noise that did not essentially distract him from dedication to learning. While untainted by their meanness, he was mentally incapable of distinguishing between flashy veneer and analytical depth. His rhetorically strong but philosophically weak mind would soon brush the Scriptures aside as coarse fare for only the simple-minded (3.5.9), and shortly thereafter commit him to a Manicheism full of fables. Intellectual immaturity launched him into the spiritually costliest misadventure of his life (3.6.10).

7. With his usual assiduity he concentrated on advanced works in eloquence, some of which, like Cicero's *De oratore*, exemplified as well as explicated oratorical skills, for a damnable and windy end; damnable, morally reprehensible, because he was hankering after lower goods; windy, proud or conceited. He was a rhetorician-in-the-making purposing to banquet on a spiritually empty *Lebenanschauung*, a career with a fine income and elevated social status accompanied by, as cause and effect, secularly blessed reputation. While making his way through the books assigned, he came upon Cicero's *Hortensius*,[6] a milestone that some designate, in a broad sense, the first and most general of his conversions.[7] Though executed with all the charm of Cicero's style, the work, whatever its analytical limitations, gripped Augustine because it was a protreptic, an exhortation to quest for a domain that capped but soared beyond and above rhetoric: philosophy, the realm of wisdom. Oddly, Augustine refers to Cicero not as the renowned Cicero but as a certain Cicero. This vague qualifier is surely not pejorative since he immediately notes that everyone admires Cicero's literary style. This apparently demeaning mode of expression may have been a way of deferring to some Christians' low regard for pagan writers. Perhaps he was resorting to a late Latin stylistic device whose full import still escapes us. A similar rhetorical tactic seems employed in the designation of St. Paul as *quidam servus tuus*, "a certain servant of yours [of God's]" (12.14.20), generally revered as the Apostle and hailed as great (13.26.40).[9] In any case, Augustine's first aspiration toward wisdom was awakened by Cicero, those tongue, i.e., rhetorical brilliance, won the applause of all but whose heart, i.e., mind, was not of the highest caliber, Plato far outstripping him in originality, analytical power, and height and surety of vision (CD 8.5).

8. The exhortation on the life of the sage not only excited his admiration but radically altered his whole heart-set, implicitly and potentially his whole way of living. A new horizon opened up, new possibilities for happiness stretched out before him; his entire outlook, theoretical and practical, was transformed. Whereas prior to his encounter with *Hortensius* he had pined for place, power, pelf, prominence, prestige, and their attendant status symbols, he now pointed his prayers, however desultory and infrequent, to God, through whom only after a long struggle in an infra-spiritual dark night that was his Manichean experience he was to discover

Catholicism, which would pacify his restless heart (T 14.1). So, like
the prodigal son, he began to rise so as to return to the Father (Lk
15.18-20).[10] This decisive turn, not a giant leap forward but only a first
yet significant step, occurred in his nineteenth year (373), two years
after his father's death (370/1).[11] His search was to continue for
thirteen more years before he fully embraced intellectual and moral
wisdom in the Catholic Church. At the time he providentially
became acquainted with *Hortensius*, his mother, with considerable
assistance from Romanianus, a wealthy patron and friend in Thagaste
(CA. 2.2.3), was funding his education in rhetoric. But what
captivated him in *Hortensius* was not its rhetorical brilliance but its
summons to a sapiential vocation. From *Hortensius* he gained no
breakthroughs in stylistic technique but a completely novel
perspective of seeing and living: the way of wisdom.

According to its Greek roots, philosophy means the love of
wisdom; Pythagoras is credited with coining the term.[12] The desire for
wisdom that suddenly came to white heat in his soul was implicitly a
burning longing to rise above all that is earthly and fling himself into
the arms of God, for wisdom contemplates supertemporals whose
source is God (T 12.14.22). As supreme truth and infinite goodness,
God is the ultimate object of wisdom seeking satisfaction of mind. In
loving wisdom, he was implicitly loving God, but at the time of his
first enthusiasm for philosophy he was in the dark about the divine
action in him; he did not realize that God used Cicero's protreptic to
philosophy to implant an intense yearning for himself above all other
things. Besides initiating a shift in perspective that liberated his mind
from the cramped horizon of rhetoric, *Hortensius*, in criticizing as well
as surveying philosophical stances past and current, alerted him to
the deceptiveness beneath the surface of many subtly argued
viewpoints. Every philosopher, he realized, labels his particular
outlook the true philosophy, the authentic wisdom superior to
competing views because its whole truth satisfies the mind as its
highest good fulfills all desires. Half-truths and downright sophisms
are advocated with such suasive charm that the untutored mind may
be lured into acquiescing in what are at bottom no more than
seductive fallacies. Cicero's critical recounting of dubious
philosophies echoes on the natural plane Paul's warning against false
systems of thought that stem not from divine revelation but from
human tradition, according to which human life is not governed by

divine providence but determined by the inexorably fixed interplay of material factors alone. The philosophy that is in accord with the elements of this world is materialistic, admitting no genuine spiritual realities or a higher intelligible world (CA 3.19.42) but explaining all events, human and nonhuman, within the agencies of the material cosmos. Against this materialistic position, notably that of the Stoics, Simplicianus will caution Augustine in 386 (8.2.3).[13] But in 373, when set on fire by *Hortensius,* he had not read Paul or any of the New Testament. Yet it would be a long time before Augustine concretely heeded Paul's admonition; for close to a decade he was to give credence to the human revelations of Mani's wildly imaginative materialism; and secondarily, for years he was to count on astrology which pretends, by reading the stars, to unknot the puzzles of day-to-day contingencies. Because at this juncture Paul was a closed book, he had no inkling that in Christ was the fullness of God, including all of divine wisdom. Cicero's work did kindle his first desire for wisdom; indeed the only thing that delighted him therein was its exhortation to pursue not the views of any particular philosophic school but wisdom itself. His hunt for wisdom was not a cool cerebral inquiry but a passionate quest of the whole self. So he loved wisdom as his highest good; he wanted to seek it, i.e., to clarify its meaning by definition and to determine its locus; he planned to specify the correct means for its attainment: by application of the proper means he would finally lay hold of it as an end achieved; lastly, he would firmly espouse it, i.e., his initial grasp would deepen and become more satisfying. Actually the road from desire to possession of the end proved painfully protracted; he had to endure a depressing march through a Manichean desert before, some twelve years, arriving at the verge of his moral conversion to Catholicism. Nearly destitute of philosophic discernment, Augustine was to define, mistakenly and tragically, wisdom in terms of Manichean dogma and morals, adopting a philosophy "according to the elements of this world" (Col 2.8), a through-and-through materialistic posture. At this moment what chilled his ardor for whatever fragments of wisdom were scattered through secular philosophies was the glaring absence of any reference to Christ. Though by and large ill-instructed in the Christian faith and only a fitful assister at its liturgy, Augustine, while still a child at the breast, had learned from Monica how to be pious in regard to Jesus, i.e., how to pray to him as savior, a reverence for

Christ that remained impressed on his memory. Thus no merely human ideas, no matter how many gleamings of truth they radiated, could utterly win his heart; devoid of Christ, they had to be void of the ultimate in light and healing. Only later did he understand that Christ is the personal wisdom of God (10.43.70;11.2.4.T 14.1); yet in his earliest groping he cloudily realized, because of the indelible traces of childhood piety, that any doctrine which assigned no room for Christ could not be true wisdom.

Chapter 5: The Apparently Inferior Character of Holy Scripture

9. Therefore he set his mind toward examining the Scriptures to discover their worth; *quales essent* is the third question to be asked about an object under investigation (10.10.17). The "therefore" betokens that he was seeking books containing wisdom; understandably he first opened the Scriptures, probably the Gospels, which, he had learned from Monica, recounted the words and works of Christ, texts which he had heard commented on in sermons during infrequent attendance at the service of the word. After his conversion he would reverence the Scriptures as a treasure trove of wisdom (S 60A.1), but his initial study or, perhaps more accurately, rapid perusal was a disaster, for he measured its value according to the extrinsic criterion of literary merit, turning the blind eye to its spiritual riches. From the vantage point of a learned Catholic bishop in 397, Augustine sees that two keys are necessary to unlock Scriptural treasures: faith, for which humility disposes the mind, and understanding, which explicates the data of faith. Faith is the introductory acceptance, understanding, the developed grasp of Scriptures.[14] Or, as he puts it negatively, the wealth of the Scriptures is neither disclosed to the proud nor laid bare to the "boyish" or mentally immature; the proud lack the humility that is a necessary condition for faith; the mentally immature have no acquaintance with liberal arts and other investigative devices to explain the Scriptures. The word of God is at first lowly, its inferior language calling for a lowliness enabling the mind to submit to its truth in faith; but as challenging depth of understanding, it is sublime, accessible not to casual inspection but only to protracted pondering. Veiled in mysteries, its truths are obscure (S 51.5. P 140.1), primarily because

they reveal the life and designs of a God who is ineffable, surpassing all complete understanding (S 52.16). To the eye of faith ripened to understanding are disclosed the things of God in the Bible. Scriptural language is largely simple or unadorned, but its contents, long meditated in prayer, stand out as majestic. Augustine was at once spiritually decrepit (1.4.4) and intellectually puerile, too proud to believe in the word of God, too mentally underdeveloped to understand Biblical insights.

He could not stoop down to enter into what seemed lowly, refusing to bend his neck, i.e., bow to its revelation in humble faith; therefore he could make no progress on the path of understanding that leads to wisdom. Later he would cherish the Scriptures for speaking of Christ in both Old and New Testament, the Jesus who is the way to the truth that in its fullness is one with wisdom (P 96.2). But as a rhetorician in the making, he was repelled because its prose fell appallingly shy of Ciceronian standards. Barren of stately periods and advanced techniques, the old Latin versions first employed by Augustine were marked by wooden, at times gauche turns of phrase, with very little rhythm or assonance. Augustine rated the contents of *Hortensius* more appealing than its style (3.4.8); but if superior style was not a sufficient condition, it remained at this stage a necessary condition for according approval. Proud of his dexterity in weaving arabesques of prose, he found the graceless writings of Scripture aesthetically repulsive, next-to-worthless in comparison with noble Ciceronian cadences. Without the illumination of faith, the diseased eyes of the soul are irritated even by sunlight (J 34.9.T 5.16.17.CD 22.2). Since pride blocked the way to faith, he could not penetrate the mysteries or hidden inner meanings of Scripture (CR 9.13), which are dug out by painstaking prayerful inquiry. First, humble faith of little ones assents to the word of God; then understanding is crescive: it increases as little ones grow in spiritual knowledge, gradually progressing to mental maturity. Some twelve years later the Lord will urge him along the path of crescive understanding: "I am the food of the great [the spiritually- intellectually mature]: grow and you will feed on me" (7.10.16). Augustine, however, disdained to become a little one (*parvulus*); literally, he refused to undignify himself to the level of the word of God valueless (*indigne*) in comparison with the value (*dignitati*) of Ciceronian prose. In the broad sense *parvulus* denotes every Christian who acknowledges Christ as his teacher and savior, whose grace empowers him to observe the commandments by faith working through charity (J 29.71). Even St. Paul, the light of the Gentiles who called himself the least of apostles, was a *parvulus* in this acceptation (P 18:8; 114.5; 118[S.27].3). In a more restricted sense *parvulus* signifies a little one, a beginner who believes but is unable to properly conceptualize the truth of the Bible; a *parvulus* is identical with a *carnalis* not yet grown into a *spiritualis* or person of understanding.[15] Actually spiritually-intellectually runty, no more than mentally immature, he overrated his mind as one of achieved intellectual stature. The maturity that made him complacent was bogus, mirroring in his imagination the bloated condition of his will. Instead of applying the "boyish" strategy of reason first and only, he should have docilely believed the word of God, then through prayerful study striven to understand it. His refusal to knock in prayer barred shut the door to understanding. His prideful reason rashly, i.e., unreasonably, endeavored to seek what only a mind of humble faith can find. At this time of his disenchantment with the Bible, he was at least nominally a *parvulus*, a catechumen, a tiny one still not fledged, who audaciously flew out of the nest of faith, plummeting to the earth, where the mercy of the Lord, after saving him from being trampled to death, raised him and deposited him again in the nest (S 51.5.6).

Chapter 6: Trapped in Manicheism

10. Significantly, this chapter also opens with *itaque*, therefore he spurned the Scriptures out of pride and intellectual puerility, the same two basic reasons for his succumbing to Manicheism.[16] It seems appropriate to first set down summarily some reasons why Manicheism attracted Augustine, explanatory factors more loosely indicated in relevant sections below. This religion of Iranian provenance with notable Christian lineaments appealed to Augustine's pride because it was portrayed as superior in three respects. (i) Acceptance of its teachings rested not on faith but on reason (BV 1.4). The Manichean view rationally accounted for man's moral plight, the means of redemption through higher illumination, and the cosmogony and cosmology of the universe that serve as the theater of redemption. (ii) Manicheism claimed to be a higher form of Christianity. Catholic Christians were only semi-Christians while Manicheism was the last word, the peak of redemptive doctrine and

morality. (iii) To justify this second point, Manichees savaged traditional Christianity, deriding the Old Testament and eliminating portions of the New (CF 8.1; 6.1; 32.1).[17] This exercise in animadversion afforded considerable satisfaction to Augustine's superiority complex; the iconoclasm implicit in unsparing criticism tends to buttress confidence in the value of one's acuity and *Weltanschauung*. Had Augustine possessed the proper philosophical apparatus, he might well have paused to scrutinize Manicheism for possible weaknesses. Unfortunately, during this period his analytical attainments were puerile, his philosophical aptitude retarded. Like a college freshman with no systematic outlook enabling him to refute the apparently convincing but radically flawed ratiocination of a crusading secular humanist professor, he could not mount a counter-attack against a seemingly suasive case that was riddled with incoherences. Abstractly aware of *Hortensus'* warning against the lure of false philosophies, he lacked the philosophic tools that would have equipped him to become concretely skeptical of Manichean criticism of his cradle Catholicism. His precipitous conversion to Manicheism (DA 1.1) betrayed analytical ineptitude more than infirmity of character. He impulsively transferred his religious commitment mainly because he felt overwhelmed by the seeming cogency of an all-encompassing system buttressed by a remorseless collateral critique of Catholic Christianity.

Psychological factors also probably played a dispositive part in his Manichean turn. Some of his converters were fellow rhetoricians, close friends (4.8.13) bonded by common interests in an affective rapport that inclined him to look benignly on their initially strange-sounding opinions. It does not seem unlikely that some of his proselytizers were ex-Catholics, who could personally witness to the fact that acquaintance with Mani's teachings had liberated them from the inconsistencies of traditional Christianity. These psychological influences formed the necessary condition, but Augustine's pride and puerility were the essential determinants of his shift, puerility proving to be the more decisive in the retention of his Manichean stance.

Intellectually naive, he buckled under to the high-pressure prosely-tizers, delirious with pride, thoroughly carnal, and loquacious. They were proud because in their purported rational path to enlightenment they bypassed the disposition of humility requisite for faith. He labels them mad because their world view consisted of a collection of intellectual and moral insanities;[18] of members of the sect was demanded assent to physical impossibilities (transportation of light from moon to sun), analytical absurdities (evil as a substance), and theological nonsense (God both infinite and material). Too they were extremely carnal; not that they were prisoners of lust or other species of disordered passion; rather, restricted to image-thinking, they could not conceive any being as other than material. Moreover, Augustine's seducers belonged to the intellectual milieu of Carthage, in particular to the rhetorical tribe, whose special badge was loquacity, excessive speaking in this case devoted to enthusiastic religious testimony. Their glib words were nooses of the devil, the father of lies and heresies; heretics follow the father of lies while those fully illumined listen to the Father of truth (J 8.44; 42.13). Their slick apologetics resembled birdlime, which, when smeared on stakes, held fast a bird unwarily perching thereon (UC1.2). Originally an Oriental religion, Manicheism was adaptively presented to Western minds as the outflowering of Christianity. All the letters of Mani, who claimed to be the last and greatest of the prophets, begin with the title, "Mani, Apostle of Jesus Christ" (CEF 5.6. CF 7.2; 13.7.); hence he proclaimed himself the Paraclete promised by Christ (5.5.8. Fel 1.9. H 46.38). Whatever its essential center, the Manicheism that attracted Augustine was offered as the summit of Christianity; a Christianity purged of errors and self-contradictions, most of these rooted in Hebraic muddlement and immorality. Almost wholly without critical faculty for testing religious claims, he was, like a dumb bird, entrapped, almost immediately enlisting in Manicheism. While real birdlime was composed of mistletoe berries or oak-sap, the more deadly stuff that captured Augustine was made from a mixture of syllables apparently denoting the holy trinity. To win over Christians, Manichean evangelizers stressed that they too worshipped one God as Father, Son, and Holy Spirit. But these names were sheer words, a combination of syllables that did not really signify the triune God. In their tenuously material Godhead the Father dwells in the primary, inaccessible or invisible light; the Son in secondary, visible light, as power in the sun and as wisdom in the moon; the Holy Spirit, the third majesty, in the entire circle of the atmosphere, his outpouring causing the earth to conceive and bear the suffering Jesus suspended from every tree or quasi-cross (CF 20.2). Astutely attuning their conversional pitch to Augustine's orthodox Christian background, the Manichees kept dinning the names of the three divine persons in his ears; names that were only linguistic noises, for their minds were empty of the truth about the triune God.

Indeed while entangled in fantastic untruths, smooth-talking Manichean apologists never stopped invoking intellectual piety to truth in all its nobility, suavely adjusting their message to Augustine's avid hunger for truth. In the Manicheans' repeated exaltation of truth, Augustine is probably alluding to their contention that, instead of forcing him to hew to the line laid down by Catholic authority, they would rely on nothing but pure reason to lead him to God and his salutary light. Divest yourself of these superstitions and myths that Catholic credulity burdens you with, they exhorted him, and follow the free path of strictly rational elucidation (UC 1.2). The way of faith was déclassé; all religious claims were to be adjudicated before the bar of reason alone. Later Augustine discovered that this rationalist posture was only a pose; Manicheism was, in fact, a belief system requiring credence in the incredible(6.5.2). So convincingly did the Manicheans emphasize truth that Augustine, we saw, right away joined their ranks; yet their system was error-infected from top to bottom, its propositions insupportable in physical philosophy as well as in theology. Their God was material, finite, incongruously embattled by forces of evil. Moreover, they propounded opinions about nature flatly contrary to observed fact: five good and five evil elements; (CF 2.3; 11.3; 20.9); an earth upheld by an Atlas-like figure (CF 20.9); buckets in heavens collecting particles of light for the Kingdom of Light (NB 44. E 55.4.6). Augustine mentions parenthetically that philosophers had demonstrated many truths concerning the created world (here "philosophers" means natural philosophers, whom we call scientists): astronomers accurately predicted solar and lunar eclipses, a fact at loggerheads with and destructive of Manichean tenets (5.3.3-4); even prior to conceiving God as spiritual, Augustine began his breakaway from the Manichees because of disparities between their views and scientific fact and theory (5.14.25). Mani's claim to be the Paraclete was indirectly discredited by disproof of his baseless physical theories by competent scientists (5.5.8).

Perhaps implicitly anticipating in part the celebrated line, "Late have I loved you"(10.27.38), Augustine wistfully remarks that he would have preferred to have bypassed knowledge of natural-philosophic truths if forgoing them would have carried him more swiftly to the love of his Father, the source of all beauty and all felicity, for the most unlettered individual in the world united to God has more happiness than the most cultured of savants separated from God (5.4.7). Rather than plod along the path of understanding, with its always-present risk of being diverted into error, he would have opted to find God by not finding him (1.6.10), by the high holiness of faith without understanding that marked the piety of advanced Christians like Monica (9.10.23-6), who fly on the wings of charity toward God above the laborious road of understanding (M 6. 1.1). Even then, on the brink of his descent into Manicheism, within the marrow of his soul, i.e., his innermost self, he was intensely longing for the truth, not simply for God as truth that throws light on the origin and meaning of man, the universe, and history, but especially for God as all-satisfying truth.

Over and over, his Manichean associates dilated on the truth, which was no more than a word barren of real referent, however iterated in conversation and accented in many large tomes, which included Mani's works along with disciples' compendia and commentaries. Unlike previous founders of religion, Mani, reportedly under divine inspiration, penned seven books that came to be revered as scriptural canon, no doubt constantly consulted in order to justify or clarify a doctrinal point. These works Augustine arrestingly calls *fercula* or dishes; a *ferculum* was the litter used during sacred rites to bear the images of gods.[19] Served on the Manicheans' symbolic *ferculum* were the sun and moon, which were accorded divine worship (in the Manichean teaching instilled in Augustine), the sun considered the residence of Christ the power of God, the moon regarded as the seat of Christ the wisdom of God (CF 22.2).[20] The sun and the moon are no doubt beautiful because reflecting the all-beautiful Father but ultimately unfulfilling for an Augustine hungering for the one true God. Shining celestial bodies, which change in place and time, are surpassed by spiritual beings such as angels, which change in time but not according to place (GL 8.20.39). Beyond these two planes, at the peak of a three-tiered order of reality (11.4.6. M 6.5.13. CD 8.6)[21] resides the Father of Lights in whom "there is no change or shadow of alteration," who admits not the slightest variation in place or time (GL 5.18.36. J 1.12). Possibly making an ironic allusion to Manichean dietary rules or to their "eucharist," their ceremonial offering of bread and fruit to the elect, Augustine recalls the dishes of splendid phantasms they served him; splendid because the sun and moon were pure luminaries in realms of richest grandeur lying far above a lightsome earth (NB 42). As the outcome of Manichean misrepresentations, they were phantasms, products of a bizarre religious imagination; phantasms, which are formed by productive imagination, are images of images. But *phantasiae* or veridical images, which issue from reproductive imagination, are impressed by actually perceived objects.[22] Properly understood, phantasms are not inevitable sources of error; from what he had heard of his grandfather, whom he never met, Augustine could fashion a vague phantasm (M 6. 11.32), and from his knowledge of Carthage he could construct an acceptable phantasm of the Alexandria he had never laid eyes upon (GL 12.6.15. T 8.6.9). However, phantasms become the foci of delusion when regarded as genuine images of actual things first conveyed by sense data. The radical error of Manicheism is the phantasmical fallacy, the confusion of sheerly imaginary inventions with structures in the external world (6.11.32). If there had been a live option, it would have been wiser or less reprehensible to homage the visible sun, which our eyes perceive as true, really there, than the fancies of wayward Manichean imagination, religious aberrations belying the evidence of the eyes and the findings of science. Authentic knowledge of physical things ordinarily originates in the senses, in particular, the eyes; men basically come to know the rising and setting of the sun and moon, along with other movements, through ocular observation. The inverse is the case with the Manichees, whose undisciplined imagination contrives a peculiar theory of sun and moon, a mythic fabrication that the mind imposes on the senses toward the warping of their data. Augustine was conned into believing that his soul was being nourished with God and his light when, in fact, Manichean victuals were spurious, without the savor of truth. Addressing God, he recalls, "You did not taste (*sapiebas*) in my mouth as you really are." Allusively intimating the connection between *sapire* (to taste) and *sapientia* (wisdom), Augustine may be averring: "You [presented as a false god, without wisdom] did not convey the savor of wisdom, which you actually are, to my [mental] mouth."[23] With no vibrant enthusiasm Augustine pledged fealty to unappetizing Manichean ideas, many of which tasted like sawdust. His soul ingesting these was not truly fed since they were devoid of spiritual nutrients, leaving his spirit not energized but enervated to the point of exhaustion.

The food men dream of is highly similar to food of waking life; yet because it is sheer image, and purely visual at that, the most sumptuous of dream-banquets provides no sustenance for the sleeping body. Locked in the sleep of the soul, worshipping idols of their imagination and misconceiving God as bodily, Manicheans were poles apart from the true God who is purely spiritual (P 72.4). The physical entities on earth or in the sky are more real than phantoms bodied forth from a riotous imagination. From the angle of cognitive clarity, the objects we observe are more certain, i.e., their actual physical aspects much more determinate and detailed, than imaginative representations. Images of the sun and moon are sketchy at best, retaining only the more striking features. Yet incomplete as they are, these images are more certain than the concoctions of Manichean revelation, for they are anchored in reality. Pictures in the Manichean fabulous cosmos, like the ships of light (NB 44.CF 20.6), look more majestic, and their God and his Kingdom of Light appear relatively infinite, but they remain mere fictions, the stuff of incoherent dreams of the soul, with no footing in fact. After feasting on such pseudo-food, his soul was starved; the fanciful dishes of the Manichees could supply no more vigor for the soul than the food of dreams can for the body.

The Manichean God was spatially infinite, a kind of religious sun diffused everywhere through things via particles of the divine light-substance. The physical sun and our image of it, albeit limited, are more real than the limitless Manichean deity, for, as Augustine later recognized, the true God is spiritually infinite (7.14.20; 13.11.12). It is this wholly matterless God whom he affectionately addresses as "my love," which woos his heart. In weakness he pines for God so that he may wax strong in his love; like Paul, when he is weak, he is strong (P 98.13; 118[S.13].3; P 118[S.20].1). Through the intensity of divine light he now sees, contrary to Manichean views that held him captive earlier, that God cannot be identified with anything visible or bodily. God is neither one with nor resides in any of the heavenly bodies, whether visible to the naked eye, such as the sun, or invisible, for every one of these has been produced by his creative power. However elevated, celestial entities are inferior to angels, spirits that occupy the top rung of creation. A still greater gulf lies between the creator who alone absolutely exists and the grotesqueries of the freewheeling Manichean mentality which can claim not a shred of real existence. Whereas fantasies simply do not exist, mental impressions received from real bodies such as trees and dogs are real and therefore more certain than the unrealities spawned by Manichean invention, and the bodies that images stand for and therefore depend on are more certain than their images. Yet, as just remarked, the being of God cannot be equated with that of bodies, however firm their hold on existence. Though a principle and cause of things, God is not the soul or life-principle of entities like horses and dogs, which, as causative, is superior to and more real than the bodies it causes. Rather, God is the life of souls, the ultimate living principle from which all souls, all life-principles, spring. Living by and of himself, God is life itself, unadulterated by imperfection or decay (T 6.10.11). In Augustine's perceptive analogy, God enlivens the life that is the soul as the soul gives life to living bodies. Sound in itself, the analogical nexus may become, if pressed too far, so unsound as to lead to pantheism. Confining the parallel within rational bounds is the disanalogous fact that the life that is God is creative and the life that is the soul is created. As absolute life infusing life into souls, God transcends his creatures; he is wholly other, in no way a part of the soul he quickens. Each soul, on the other hand, is an immanent part of the composite to which it communicates life.

11. Though God never stopped being the life of his life, God seemed far removed from him during his Manichean period. It was not God who absented himself; rather, Augustine, like the prodigal son, wandered afar from the Father. God remained operatively present, the life upholding his life, but Augustine's capitulation to Manicheism drove a moral gap between his soul and God, setting him affectively distant from the God always dynamically present. As a deserter of God, it was his unenviable lot to be volitionally absent from the God who is everywhere present. In the alien country of the Manichees his soul was forced to do without food; denied the opportunity to feed on the real husks of the swine, this prodigal son was famished, fed without being fed (3.6.10). Even literary fictions are more soul-nourishing than fraudulent Manichean myths. Verses, poems, or literary characters upbuild the soul more than Manichean errors like the five good elements, air, fire, wind, water, and light, outfitted in various disguises to be deployed as weapons in combating

the five evil elements, smoke, evil fire, evil wind, evil water, and darkness (CEF 28.31). While stories and legends of a folk or nation ordinarily suggest or illustrate truths, at least partially, Manichean constructs are utterly baseless, harboring not one whit of truth. Further, they not only famish but poison the soul. Affective separation from God is the death of the soul; in the moral line the soul dies once it abandons the God who is its life (P 70 [S.2].3). Out of verses and poems authored by pagans men can extract some of the soul-nourishing food that is truth. Unquestionably there was truth to be gathered from the sharp, if acidulous, portraits of decadent Roman social types that Juvenal's satires draw. The literary immortality that Horace envisaged for himself in the lines beginning with "I have built a monument more enduring than brass"[24] may carry intimations of a real immortality of the soul; and later Augustine reflects on the truth of Horace's description of a friend as one-half of his soul (4.6.11). To be sure, he did declaim Ovid's lines about Medea, who flew through the air in her dragon-chariot, but not for one moment did he think her as other than fictive. When he listened to others poetically dramatizing her exploits, he put no stock whatever in her actual existence. But, unhappily, he gave credence to Manichean fictions masquerading as facts. His spirit, aching in its toil to absorb mortal errors, was feverish with enthusiasm since his mind was infected with doctrines shot through with falsehoods. He was seeking God (the God of his heart to whom he now confesses his sins, who rained down mercy on him long before he was moved to sorrow for his wrongdoing), but, unfortunately, with a misguided spiritual program, he was depicting God in carnal fashion, putting him on the same plane with objects grasped by sensory perception. Yet God, he was to discover later, was a purely spiritual being (3.7.12), knowable only by the spiritual mind with which the creator set man above the beast (6.3.4). So he addresses God: "However, you were more inward than my inner self and higher than the highest of my self." God was, in fact, within, more inward than his innermost self because the dynamic divine presence continuously poured existence into his soul. God is present by immanent causation within every creature because he is higher than the highest point in human existence. Only because God is entitatively transcendent or wholly other in being from creatures, as noted earlier, is he able to be omnipresent, everywhere immanent, present by his causation in all he has made and upholds in existence.

His ruinous lapse into Manicheism is depicted as an encounter with the brazen-faced woman, the enigma of Solomon (Pr 9.17), i.e., an obscure allegory or parable (P 48[S.1] 5. T 15.9.15) in a book whose author, it was then mistakenly thought, was Solomon.[25] Destitute of prudence, she stood for folly or unwisdom; here prudence primarily denotes theoretical cognition, which peaks in wisdom that is the contemplation of truth (13.18.23. GCM 2.10.14), and secondarily practical reason that governs conduct. She symbolizes proud and curious Manichean teachers who lure potential adherents like Augustine; proud because they look down their noses on a vulgar faith that calls for humility as its prerequisite (3.6.10); curious because they are thinking not according to understanding but according to sense, in line with the Manichean curiosity that befogs the mind (GCM 1.23.40); a curiosity that turns inquirers into earth-eaters, whose sense-bound and time-bound outlook explains even higher beings in terms of causes grounded in matter (GCM 2.18.27). Spiritually and analytically deficient, Augustine was taken in by the boldness evinced in the claim to provide wisdom when the woman was actually the epitome of unwisdom. Possessing only one loaf of bread, she guaranteed hearers many loaves; totally ignorant, she unblushingly pledged to provide fullness of truth. She cunningly promised, along with secret bread, stolen waters. A coating of secrecy makes doctrines look fascinating and relishing; Manichean doctrines were abhorred by the Church. Stealing also represents the hearing of forbidden views. The fact that Manichean teachings are secret and stolen, i.e., prohibited, seasons them and, making them look delicious, fascinates unprayerful minds unaware that Manichean food and drink contain not knowledge and wisdom but ignorance and unwisdom (J 97.2) Manichean folly seduced Augustine because he dwelt out of doors, i.e., after the style of the exterior man, plying his mind with notions accessible to the eye of the flesh, reducing God and the human soul to the level of material objects. *Consuetudo carnalis*(7.17.23), habitual thinking according to the eye of the flesh or image-thinking, is a mindset found among Christians as well as Manichees. The Manichean sort was an egregious strain of carnal thinking. While carnal Christians believe in, without being competent to understand, spiritual realities, Manichees are uncompromising materialists who account for everything from highest to lowest by material elements and agencies. Moreover, he ruminated their views, which he had greedily devoured, i.e., hastily and uncritically assented to, with the consequence that his mind gradually assimilated their systematic outlook, until he became a largely committed Manichee. More precisely, he was seduced because of pride and curiosity that are the badge of the Manichean tribe. He fell among Manichees because he had fallen through pride from interior to exterior realities. The inner good of the soul is service of the God who enlivens its conscience; pride, however, sunders the soul from God, causing it to swell with arrogance, so that it flings itself into things exterior, removed from interior goods and the true God (M 6.13.40). Out of this prideful declension into exterior things arises curiosity. Tied to things outside its inner self, the soul employs a matter-bound mode of cognition, pursuing inquiry into spiritual realities with a fleshly eye (GCM 2.26.40).

Chapter 7: Ignorance of Spiritual Truths Reason for Manichean Conversion

12. Augustine became enwebbed in Manichean darkness because he had no knowledge of the other, the spiritual dimension, the true world of God and man, a realm including a spiritual God, a matterless mind, a nonmaterialistic meaning of evil, and the law of God, unchanging in itself but changing in its applications.[26] In his ignorance of the spiritual sphere, he was impelled by apparently telling reasons to accept the cramped outlook of purveyors of sophistries. In the three sections of this chapter he puts his finger on ignorance, impecunious knowledge of philosophy, as the radical reason why he found himself defenseless before Manicheans. In spite of first-rate acuity, his mind, bereft of all but the scantiest training in philosophical analysis, was a tyro in the handling of philosophical and religious issues. Except for the broad survey of opinions cursorily reviewed in *Hortensius* (3.4.7), he had hardly the slightest familiarity with strategies for conceiving God, the soul, and morality along spiritual lines. A philosophical novice, he was taken in by the glibly exposited but specious arguments of Manicheans, fools filling him with the folly of Solomon's obscure figure (3.6.11). Of Augustine's brilliance there cannot be the least doubt, but at this stage, unstocked with analytical instruments, he could only be doctrinally uncircum-

spective. Instead of testing Manichean assertions in a cool, dry light, he assented, we saw, to their tenets precipitously, only a few days after mulling over their startlingly novel world picture (DA 1.1. CEF 2.3). Perhaps because he vigorously grappled, to the point of being wearied with the problem of the origin of evil (LA 1.2.4), he rushed, with the impulsiveness of mental puerility (MM 8.11), to ratify an oversimplified dualistic explanation; as the sting of the scorpion attests, evil, he was told, is as positively real as the good, emanating from a Principle of Darkness opposed to the Principle of Light (MM 8.11). The Manicheans also pressed their case against the anthropomorphic God implied in the traditional Christian belief that man is made in the image and likeness of God. For if man is like God, then God is like man, ridiculously cut down to human size, a deity anomalously accoutered with hair, nose, fingernails, and interior and exterior organs and members (GCM 1.17.27). To undermine further the inspired character of the Old Testament, the Manicheans pilloried the patriarchs not as holy but as unholy, "dirty old men"(CF 22.3),[27] scandalous in their routine polygamy, murderous in their massacres of fellow men, and cruel in their sacrifice of animals to a pseudo-God, really a devil, gorging himself on animal blood (CF 21.5; 22.2, 5; 18.5. H 46.39). Undeft in handling philosophical questions, he could not thoroughly investigate the difficulties raised. He had no idea that, as he was to learn later, evil is not a positive reality but the privation of good, to the point of being nothing at all; of itself, over against the good, it is absolutely nothing, having only relative existence as the lack of good. At this point this illuminating insight escaped him because his sensory perception was restricted to bodies and his mental perception to images, in particular, to Manichean fancies dressed up as fact. Manichean materialism stifled any possibility of thinking of evil as the privation of good. The same constricted horizon blocked him from seeing God as spiritual. As a spirit, God has neither extension nor mass; there are no divine members whose length and breadth can be measured; nor can we ascribe mass to God because part of a mass is less than the whole, and, even supposing an infinite mass, one part of the mass as delimited by a certain place has to be less than the whole in its infinity (1.1.2). God is extensionless and massless; not present partitively, he is and acts wholly everywhere. As a spirit, unencumbered by hair and fingernails, indeed of all material parts, God, Augustine would come to understand, was totally and all at once present in his being and operation; he was absolutely ubiquitous. At this time also Augustine, knowing next to nothing about the nature of the human soul, had no precise concept of the soul as the principle that communicates life to the body. Nor did he know that the soul also was a spiritual substance, wholly present everywhere throughout the body it animates (CEF 16.20. E 166.2.4).[28] Unschooled in the authentic notion of a spirit, Augustine at this point of his allegiance to Manicheism failed to perceive that Genesis was right in stating, and Manicheism wrong in denying, that man is made in the image of God, not according to his physical makeup but according to his spirit or matter-free mind (GCM 1.17.28).

13. Philosophical naivete also barred him from grasping that an absolute but relatively applied moral code confutes Manichean censure of the behavior of Old Testament patriarchs as filthy (CF 22.1), which is expressed in the "natural law" (DQ 53.2) ineffaceably "written on the hearts of men" (2.4.9) or rational souls (DQ 53.2). This "interior" justice is "true" justice because it is absolute or unchanging. This natural law is a moral law, discovered by reason as the basic standard governing all moral conduct. Hence it is distinct from the law of nature, the law of self-preservation that is a subrational determination, one held in common with brute animals, whereby men automatically tend to safeguard bodily integrity (1.20.31. DC 1.26.27). The natural law flows from the eternal law, "the law of the highest quality of God omnipotent," a law enshrining a super-justice, a matchless morality. The rules of justice in the eternal law are first of all written in the book of light that is eternal truth. Therefrom they are transferred to the human heart, transcribed as the natural law; imprinted on the mind as the image on a ring is stamped on wax, with the original image remaining on the ring (T 14.15.21). "The eternal law is the divine reason or the will of God commanding the preservation of the natural order and forbidding transgression against it" (CF 22.27). As the well-known definition has it, order is "the assignment of equal and unequal things to their proper places" (CD 19.13). In general, observance of natural order bespeaks appointing superior status to superior objects and inferior status to inferiors. Beast is subordinate to man and, in man, body to soul; within the soul lower inclinations are to be subject to reason, and reason to God (CF 22.27). As the transcription of the eternal law in the human mind, the natural law is universal and unchangeable; it is

"everywhere and always" operative in the universe. In itself it does not differ from one place to another nor does it undergo change with the passage of time. Because universal and uniform, it determines the patterns of behavior or customs of certain places and times commensurate with local and temporal milieus. The basic precepts of the natural law mold and inform legitimate modes of conduct in various countries and periods. But the precepts are diversely applied according to the variables of diverse cultural situations. Though not in conformity with the later, perfect directive of Christ, the polygamy of Abraham, Isaac, and Jacob was morally unimpeachable. In acquiring several wives, they were obeying, albeit less perfectly, the divine injunction to increase and multiply, craving not gratification of passions but pursuing the conjugal good of offspring – a sound moral intention corroborated by the approval their first wives accorded the taking of other partners. In their morally inferior religio-cultural context they were not capable of observing monogamy (CF 22.30-1. S 51.15.25; 18.28). More precisely, polygamous marriage in those climes and times did not run counter to nature, custom, or law. It was not *contra naturam* and therefore not in conflict with the eternal law that prescribes the order of nature because the patriarchs assumed several wives not to multiply sexual pleasure but to procreate offspring. Their motives and actions subserved the primary good of marriage; polygamy was in harmony with the basic law of nature for marriage (CF 22.47). Besides, neither customs nor laws of the epoch banned the practice (CF 22.47). At the time Augustine wrote, however, Roman custom and law proscribed this type of marriage (CF 22.47), yet neither before nor after did polygamy transgress the law of nature.

Other actions of revered Old Testament figures are defensible in themselves or in the light of subsequent remorse. Moses slew a few idolatrous Israelites not out of brutality but out of love, to warn the vast majority of the final punishment in store for worshippers of demons (CF 22.70). No doubt David's adultery was reprehensible, yet his scandalous fall was outbalanced by his repentance, faith, humility, meekness, and holy fear (CF 22.46). Thus while living in a less elevated moral atmosphere, the patriarchs were indeed holy, fully deserving of the praise that poured from the lips of God himself. The Manicheans habitually fulminated against the patriarchs as iniquitous because they themselves were philosophically unlearned, ignorant of the universality of the moral code, i.e., locked in a severely constricted cultural horizon. They were casualties of cultural parochialism, the not uncommon social fallacy of partialism that erects the customs of a particular group into a paradigm for the whole of mankind's patterns of conduct throughout history. A truncated yardstick vitiated their round condemnation of the patriarchs. They shaped their judgments myopically, according to the day of man, according to the relative frame of reference of their present, not according to the day of God that is eternity (11.13.15), whose one identical law adaptively legislates for different cultural settings and changing modes of moral concretion.

Adaptive application of basic rules is not an ad hoc ruse crafted to wriggle out of an apologetic impasse but a commonly heeded motif in human society. The rule, "Wear your armor properly," enjoins that pieces of battle gear be fitted on the right members, the shin guard not on the head but on the shins, the helmet not on the foot but on the head. Moreover, the positive law, "Run your business at the proper times, "stipulates that on public holidays a shop be open in the morning but closed in the afternoon. Again, a well-organized household lives by the rule governing each member's duty, "Do your job for the good of the household." Particular functions vary; the servant who pours wine may not be allowed to carry and arrange dishes, a task that falls to another. The satisfaction of bodily needs, warrantable behind the stable, would be abhorrent at the dining table. It would be irrational to complain because pieces of armor are worn on appropriate parts of the body, to grumble because the law provides for the closing of shops at one time and not at another, and to wax wroth because duties are so apportioned in a household that no one can do anything his little heart desires as regards any task at any time in any part of the house. Unhappily, the Manicheans did not perceive that it was likewise unreasonable to become scandalized about the assignment of functions and tasks in God's ordering of the human community. Oddly, they became indignant because God allowed just men in one epoch actions disallowed in a later age, suitably adjusting the standards of the natural law rooted in eternal law to particular cultures and times. As with the human economy or household, so with the divine economy: ordinances are distributively laid down according to the shifting circumstances of time and place. Along with most thinkers in the mainstream of ancient ethical thought, Augustine would have been appalled were he accused of advocating moral relativism or cultural subjectivism. As we shall see in a bit more detail later, the basic principles of natural law are fixed and unchangeable; circumstances may accidentally alter but do not essentially determine the morality of actions. The fundamentals of morality do not fluctuate according to the eye of the beholder but are objectively etched in the conscience of every man. Not the core precepts of natural law but the times or cultural conditions are mutable and various, for the reason that time bespeaks novelty and diversity; as even a scanty knowledge of history witnesses, historical periods differ, sometimes radically. Because of cultural influences, the moral behavior of individuals in one historical time may concretely vary from that of people in a later historical time though both groups conform their conduct to one and the same rule of justice in the identical natural law.

This pattern of identical moral rule diversely applied in diverse circumstances is readily observable in the management of a household. The identical rule, "Do your job," applies diversely to the wine bearer and the custodian of the stables. One and the same injunction, "Perform your job on time," is properly observed if the meal is served, say, at noon, and violated if the meal is served an hour later. Again, one and the same directive, "Serve the meal," is correctly carried out in the dining room, but its execution is forbidden in the stable area. The household rules remain the same; only their circumstantial application as regards particular personal times and places admits of variation. Analogously, justice or the basic rules of justice in the natural law are not diverse and changeable. Not justice but the times that justice governs are variable and mutable simply because times as times are inevitably diverse. Here time does not mean psychological time (11.27.34-6) or physical time (12.8.8), each of which is detached from the events that it measures. The social time in the running of the household is quite different: it fuses with the events that it arranges in a time-frame. Social times differ because the events scheduled are different. The third hour or nine o'clock differs from the sixth hour or noon because 9:00 A.M. is the time for housecleaning and noon the time for the main meal. The times vary because the events they order vary. Similarly, historical time is fused with the cultural structure of the period that it dates. Historical times vary with shifting cultural motifs that hold sway, then yield sovereignty to succeeding cultural outlooks divergent in mores. Yet one and the same justice of the basically unchangeable natural law presides over human conduct as diversely exhibited in historical times or temporally diverse cultural modes. Regrettably, there are men, i.e., Manicheans, whose thinking is carnal or sense-bound. Because their experience is confined to only the pitiably brief span of individual life, because they cannot live long enough to sensorially observe various eras, they cannot harmonize the cultural causal factors operative among peoples of prior periods that they have not experienced with the cultural determinants at work in the (for them) present cultural situation in which they are immersed, the only period with which they are concretely acquainted. As sense-bound and time-bound, they have no sense-free knowledge of the natural justice that rules everywhere and always, among all peoples and through all historical times. Historically insensitive men like the Manicheans pronounce culturally biased judgments on the behavior patterns of peoples of prior eras. So culture-bound is their outlook, so insulated are they from transcultural values, and so wedded are they to personally experienced ways of acting that they are victimized by what has been called the dogmatism of experience, and therefore cannot fairly appreciate the cultural contents of periods other than their own. This foreshortening of perspective, a contraction of vision due to ignorance of the natural law and its flexible concretion, explains why Manicheans and others readily countenance differences of persons, stations, times, and places in the performance of duties in a household regulated by the one rule of proper organization yet incongruously find fault with the appointment by natural law, which transcribes eternal law, of diverse concrete practices jibing with diverse times and places. While granting it is right and necessary for a household to distributively apportion its ranks and tasks, they inconsistently deem it wrong for the divine economy to proportionally dictate diverse concrete moral patterns for different periods in sacred history.

14. When he cast his lot with the Manichees, Augustine was bereft of all conception of an identical but variously adaptable moral code. From every side evidence analogically pointing to distributively applied moral standards impinged on his mind, without making the slightest impression. He failed to seize the implications for a divinely proportional moral law staring him in the face in the diversely worn

pieces of armor, in the varied open and closing times of shops, and in the multi-functional activities of households managed according to one overriding rule. Furthermore, the declamation of poetry in his student days furnished additional signs of an immutable moral law: absolute rules of art determine the compositions of poems of various meters.

The parallel between the fixity-in-relativity of poetic art and morality, which may strike some as vague and forced, becomes clear and convincing in the light of Augustine's signification of art. Contrary to the modern notion of art, which tends to accentuate the expression of a creative idea in a sensuous medium, Augustine directed his attention primarily to the suprasensuous form or number, the basic principles that superintend artistic performance. While incarnated in movements or artworks of space and time, the art itself is situated not in but above space and time. So unalterable are these fundamental rules that, in line with the Roman rhetorical-literary tradition, Augustine considers *musica* or the poetic art a practical science, *scienta bene modulandi*, the science of skilful modulation. It is the science that measures or determines arrangement of intervals of time, i.e., the science of skilful control of variation of sounds; it is the know-how or art that regulates movements and intervals in rhythm and harmony (M 1.2.2).[29] Declamation, singing, and the playing of instruments, because immersed in the sensory, are rated artistically inferior. Not the polished declaimer or the accomplished singer or the gifted instrumentalist but the individual who completely understands the rules of music is the poetic artist in the highest sense (M 1.4. 6-9).[30] Because not under the dominion of time, the art of versifying possesses its constitutive rules *omnia simul*; all the essential components of the art exist all at once, in supratemporal fashion. The poetic feet and verses which spring from the art obviously occur in time, one succeeding the other. The changeless, timeless art itself is variously embodied in various temporalized verses, and its beauty shines forth in a lovely but fainter degree in actual poetry (VR 22.42). The most general rule that governs all poetry is this: equality and likeness must always be preferred to inequality and unlikeness. This primary rule branches out into two general rules, both invariable. First, feet of the same kind are to be combined with one another. Second, equality also obtains in the judicious conjoining of feet of a different sort that are of the same measure (M 2.9.16).

These few background comments, however slender, provide enough clues to substantiate Augustine's correlation of morality with art. If only he had garnered some measure of philosophic perceptiveness in his student days, he laments, he would have quickly discerned that declamation of poetry illumined and confirmed the essential absoluteness and applicative relativity of the moral law. He was not free to indiscriminately commingle various kinds of feet. He could not combine other feet with the pyrrhic, though he was permitted to artistically join the spondee, dactyl, and anapest (M 2.14.26). In heroic verse or dactylic hexameter he was free to substitute a spondee or dactyl but was required to end a verse in a spondee (though a trochee might also serve as a sixth foot) (M 5.4.5). Fidelity to fixed rules, nevertheless, does not doom poetry to a dead monotony. It is aesthetically senseless to insist on using, throughout, no more than one syllable or foot all the time in the recitation of a celebrated poem (VR 22.43). Thus the rules grounding the art of poetry are absolute, binding in basically the same way throughout the Roman world, commonly operative in Thagaste, Carthage, Rome, and Milan, changeless no matter what the passage of time. Yet these fundamental rules are adaptively applied. Under certain conditions there are 568 different meters; and apart from these conditions meters are innumerable (M 4.17.37).

While laying hold of the relatively universal scope of the rules of Latin poetry, he missed the unrestrictedly universal character of the eternal law, with whose precepts of righteousness principled men of every time and place comply. Its imperatives are more excellent than those of the art of poetry because they underpin virtue, the art of living rightly (CD 4.21; 19.3; 22.24), the moral know-how that lays down the path to happiness of the whole self for all men, nonpoets as well as poets. In addition, they are more sublime because, not merely limited to one culture and not destined to wane with its decline in time, they originate in the eternal heights, in the mind of God, and serve to elevate those obeying them, empowered by grace, into a share in the everlasting divine presence. Its directives are *omnia simul*; its fundamental scale of values stays invariant throughout history; of the one stock, all men everywhere are bound to observe the basic dictates of the law engraved on their hearts. This law, however, is relatively and distributively applied; it is flexibly and variously imposed on different cultures in different epochs. Augustine did not catch sight of the universal yet adaptable character of eternal law, he tells us, because he was blind, his vision snuffed out by pride, his mind clouded by mists of ignorance. So he put down the patriarchs' behavior as immoral; he was unable to see that their obedience to God was authentic, however geared to their culture-conditioned usages in what was for them the living present. With equal undiscernment he spurned the prophecies that God had revealed to them concerning the Messiah to come because he maintained, in consonance with Manichean dogma, that truths could no more be foretold by men cankered with vice than figs could spring from thistles (CF 12.1).

A few additional comments may serve to clarify further the notion of natural law by touching on the meaning of conscience and the enunciation and role of the primary moral precept. The eternal law is not the arbitrary fiat of a sheerly willful super-potentate or overtopping tyrant. It exists and evidences itself in the mind of man, pointing him to the good proper to his nature. The eternal law as relevant to and transmitted to man is the natural law, which, as noted earlier, is written on the human heart (2.4.9), i.e., which is not of human contriving but implanted by its author as a principle of operation. Hence the actions of everyone who has reached the use of moral reason are measured by this intrinsic norm (E 157.15). Even individuals purblind from cupidity act at least tenuously according to the natural law (SDM 2.9.32). Manicheans too are constrained to observe the basic natural precept of not doing to others what they would not do to themselves (CF 15.7). Only in a surreal scenario according to which men lived without the features characteristic of mankind could they function without the natural law (P 118 [S.25].4); this is an impossible hypothesis, for it conjectures a situation in which, after ceasing to be men, men continue to behave as men. Conscience testifies to the paramount status of this internal norm. Conscience, which Augustine never stops to define explicitly, seems to signify moral self-consciousness, which embraces reflection on moral imperatives, and an accompanying sensitivity that discriminates good from evil in concrete situations (S 12.4.4).[31] A good conscience begets good actions (S 37.9.10) and, as a consequence, the spirit breathes in the air of delight and peace (GL 12.34.65). A bad conscience, on the other hand, spawns bitterness, upset, tumult (S 37.9.10). Even individuals scorned as without conscience exhibit some awareness of the potency of moral maxims. If we may choose modern examples, the now disgraced former Communist leaders in Eastern Europe, however poisoned by loyalty to their immoral "morality" of lying and murder, from time to time did sincerely invoke justice; and gangsters are not wholly hardened against appealing in word and in deed to the directives of conscience (SDM 1.9.32; 2.4.9).

In rebutting Manichean denunciations of Catholicism, Augustine strives to show, and successfully, that natural law, the human transcript of unchangeable, eternal law is relatively applied. On the other hand, against others who contend that the moral law is the changeable product of particular societies, he probatively argues that running through the multiple contingent customs is the thread of a natural law that is absolute and necessary. Such misled ethicists are not wholly asleep, submerged in ignorance and error; they are, rather, somnolent, half-asleep proponents of a half-truth (DC 3.14.22). While right in observing that men part company in concrete modes of behavior, they are radically wrong in drawing from this sociological fact the conclusion that moral law is nothing more than regnant social convention in a particular setting.

Through all the multitudinous differences in mores one basic rule stands unaltered: "Do not do to another what you do not want done to yourself" (DC 3.14.22). No one can honestly aver that he wants his home robbed or burnt to the ground, or his children abused, or his spouse to cheat on him. Each individual, as a member of the human race, then must respect the right of others not to be so harmed (P 57.1).[32] This fundamental imperative is a moral constant at work in every society. Wherever one travels, whatever the social variation, seven plus three always equals ten; so, similarly, is this primary maxim always appealed to as the first rule of conduct all over the world, among primitive tribes no less than in advanced communities (LA 2.8.21). Thus the denial of natural law is unthinkable and unlivable; practically unthinkable because abandonment of natural law entails the tolerance of the intolerable (such as Joseph Stalin's murder, by one estimate, of sixty million Soviets in the twentieth century); unlivable because the norm of nature is ineradicable, all men, even the evil, relying on the natural law. Else there would be moral anarchy: as mentioned earlier, "Anything goes" would function as the "law" of lawlessness. Not even a thief suffers gladly the theft of his own goods (2.4.9) Nor, as remarked previously, did gangster states like the radically inhuman former Soviet Union neglect routine recourse to at least the principles of natural justice in the international forum (CD 4.4).[33] Too, once removed from the academic hothouse, professors defending situation ethics invariably seek anchorage in an absolute moral law. If someone dared to intimate that the situation of the thief justified the stealing of the professorial situationist's car, the argument would fall on the deaf ears of the enraged academic. Outside the classroom the sophistries of moral relativism are exposed as mere mouthings that the plain man, undebauched by unrealism, dismisses as morally inane and insane.[34]

The precept St. Augustine designates as primary, "Do not do to others what you do not want done to yourself," may bear in some measure a rough resemblance to St. Thomas' primary precept, "Do good and avoid evil."[35] In refraining from acts against justice such as robbery, adultery, and murder, a moral man is avoiding evil and, in properly valuing the rights of others to be accorded justice, doing good. This basic ordinance inscribed on the human heart is reiterated and reinforced by promulgation in the ten commandments (P 118[S.25].4). Through revelation justice flowers out into love; by faith man is bade, first, to love God totally with whole heart and soul and mind and, secondly, to love his neighbor as himself. Incorporated within Christian ethics and linked to Christian morality's two principal precepts (love of God and love of neighbor) (CD 19.14),[36] the primary precept of natural morality, when conscientiously lived out, ensures the suppression of all wrongdoing. Where there is love of God, there are no personal sins, and where there is love of neighbor, no social sins. No one with any sense wants to wreck his own home; as no one wants to be harmed by others, so he ought not to harm others (DC 3.14.22). In a Christian context a second precept, it may be noted, follows upon the first general precept: an individual should help any person he can (CD 19.14).[37] The Christian is commanded to help the body and soul of his neighbor; the body, by corporal works of mercy; the soul, by correction and restraint in terms of fear and by instruction in terms of love (ME 27.5-54;28.55-6).[38]

Chapter 8: Invariable Moral Precepts, Personal and Social Sins

15. While the Manicheans are mistaken in their straitened,

moralistic-parochial condemnation of the patriarchs, no less misguided are moral relativists who, taking the opposite tack, infer that, because customs are multifarious, there can be no changeless natural justice (DC 3.14.22). Against the Manichees Augustine furnishes warranty for a relative application of the primary dictates of eternal law in disparate cultural environments. Against relativists he vindicates the absolute, immutable character of basic precepts of the natural law. Moreover, while some moral imperatives may be changeably observed in varying cultural contexts, certain main positive and negative maxims are enjoined always and everywhere, with no significant adaptable alteration allowed. It is never wrong and always invariably right to love God with the whole of the self and love one's neighbor as oneself. The main moral virtues, prudence, justice, fortitude, and temperance are four forms of love of God; indeed every virtue is an order or pattern of love (ME 15.25). Love of neighbor is the outflow of and sign of love of God. These two commandments, which sum up the whole law and the prophets (12.18.27), noted in the preceding section, are the Christian outflowering of the primary natural precept, "Do not do to another what you do not want done to yourself," which is inexpungeably imbedded in the ethical outlook of every culture and nation. Similarly, in no time or place can the sins of Sodomites be tolerated or condoned. Abhorrent in themselves and deserving of sanction, they admit of no exception in special circumstances. Even on the unlikely supposition that men of all nations habitually indulged in homosexual activity with the approval of the majority of their peers, sodomy would remain no less perverted. The corrupt consensus of debased societies cannot veto the law of God forbidding sexual relations between individuals of the same sex. The man who defiles his nature with unnatural lust ruptures his common bond with God. In so polluting his body, he defaces his spirit, the image of God, meant to make human nature one with, and to bind him to, God.

Again, though custom and positive law are not as fixed as the primary precepts of the natural law, it is wrong for any citizen or alien in a commonwealth to defy established custom or law. True, a custom may wear a new face with the passage of the years. It was scandalous for ancient Romans to wear a long-sleeved tunic down to the ankles, but at the time Augustine was writing, the custom was reversed so that it was an offense not to be so clad if garbed in a tunic (DC 3.12.20).

Yet citizens and foreigners in a particular community must conform to its prevailing laws or thwart attainment of the chief human goods. A body politic is not a random, incidental collection of individuals but a well-organized association of human wills aspiring for an object commonly loved. In Augustine's later definition, it is "the association of a multitude not of animals but of rational beings that are joined together by a common agreement (*concordi communione*) concerning objects they love" (CD 19.24). The community is the outgrowth of their "concordant communion," i.e., their union of minds in pursuit of the common welfare of the group. They are fused into one by a *pactum*, a compact or conventional agreement of wills aiming at common interests. In virtue of this pact moral links are forged, binding members of the society together through recognition of mutual rights and duties.[39] The most general pact or agreement consists in obedience to the government. The government, the main political instrument, fashions laws that, along with customs, safeguard rights and institute duties which assure order and concord whose issue is peace. Observance of law and custom at once discloses and fortifies fidelity to the covenant that coalesces individuals into a civil unity. Each citizen or resident alien is a part whose compliance with law and custom ministers to the smooth functioning of the political whole. A part out of harmony with the whole Augustine stigmatizes as *turpis*, vile or foul. Since it is the whole that bestows beauty on members of the human body, a hand attractive as part of the body loses its beauty when severed from the body (GCM 1.21.32). But here Augustine is apparently referring to another type of anti-holistic deformity. A part is ugly when it clashes with the design of the whole. A black smear or a dog's head in place of a human countenance in a portrait; a gong cacophonously clanging at scattered intervals during a Beethoven symphony; turgid, ungrammatical, and gauchely metered doggerel in the middle of a lyric poem; an adobe facade for a Gothic cathedral—all these incongruous parts are intrinsically repugnant; they conflict with the pattern of the whole and jar artistic sensibilities. Analogously, a part of society that flouts settled social behavior clashes with the social whole; so the anomic individual is misshapen and loathsome. Augustine resorts to condemnatory language at this point because a body politic is in grave danger of breaking down if its members, dislocated from the whole, are allowed with impunity to routinely disregard its laws and fly in the face of longstanding customs. Systematic lawlessness that approximates a practical anarchism first disrupts, then shatters the legal machinery of the state, and threatens to tear asunder the political whole into warring, stomistic parts, each of the mob of despotic egos competing for its own selfish interests to the ruin of the commonwealth. Even as a nonChristian, Augustine bent his will to the demands of civil law in major matters such as marriage statutes. While he cohabited for around fifteen years with a woman whom apparently he deeply loved (6.15.25), he could consider her only his concubine, not his wife, for inferior social status barred, in the eyes of state and Church, a valid marriage. After their separation Augustine heeded the law by agreeing to wait two years before marrying a girl not yet of age, with whose parents Monica had arranged a future valid marriage (6.15.25).

Not only by civil obligation but also by religious duty are Christians bound to obey the laws of the ruler. False pride inclines a Christian to claim that his higher calling dispenses him from obedience to civil laws. The true Christian should pay proper honor to his ruler while faithfully paying taxes and carrying out other societal obligations. Ideally, he will submit to political authority not simply to avoid the wrath of the ruler embodied in civil penalties (such a low-level obedience may be simulated), but to act in accord with conscience directing that he obey with a genuine love of or respect for the ruler to whom he is subject by the ordinance of God. Since it is God who either directly ordains or simply permits the laws promulgated by rulers (CF 22.75), Christians who obey the ruler are effectively obeying God (Ex R 72, 74). Indeed the self-discipline and social good will of Christians translate into socio-political virtues, attesting that Christians are the more desirable of citizens in a state (E 137.5.20). Love of God expressed in love of neighbor does not only continually keep in mind but concretely demonstrates by solid moral conduct that for good men there is no limit to service and devotion to country (E 91.1). So overriding was Augustine's respect, even reverence, for political order that he insisted that Christians were bound to obey evil rulers, tyrants who in practice governed primarily, if not exclusively, for their own selfish ends rather than for the public interest. The hardships consequent upon grossly unjust rule are means that God employs to exercise his sons and daughters in patience, sparing not his fatherly correction to save his people from worse punishment (P 65.14). Even Nero, in whom *luxuria* and cruelty oddly reached their joint peak (CD 5.19), was accorded his power from God, and therefore had to be obeyed, for out of such heinous inquity God brings good for those who love him. The law of drawing good out of evil, which is operative through the history of the city of God, transforms temporal degradation and defeat inflicted by the city of man into growth and victory for his people (CD 18.5). Consistent with his profound respect for order flowing even only permissively from God, Augustine does not countenance rebellion or revolt against cruel tyrants (CD 5.19. BJ 14.16). However uninviting this doctrine may sound to the contemporary mind, it is not without its merits. *Sub specie aeternitatis* various emperors are dying men, men marked for earthly extinction (CD 4.5; 5.17), the weaknesses of whose reigns Christians endure during the short span of human life. Moreover, he was too much of a realist about the consequences of man's fallen condition to indulge in the utopian illusion that change always entrains growth rather than decline. Roman history plainly taught that an emperor was far from necessarily superior to his predecessor. Again, as a man of his time, Augustine had no concrete awareness of the technically efficient horrors of a modern totalitarian state such as Nazi Germany or the Soviet Union whose tyranny over the minds and bodies of its subjects, exercised through incessant propaganda backed up by quickly applied force and terror, achieved a scope and thoroughness impossible in prior less organized despotisms. Had Augustine been faced with the enormity of totalitarian states, he might have given fresh consideration to the moral desirability of rebellion under certain circumstances. While we may fault him for making no provision for revolution even in extreme cases, the judicious observation of C. Dawson may repay reflection: "Social and political revolution has become so common a feature of modern European life that we are apt to forget how rare such movements are in history."[40] Moreover, the tendency to laud nearly every revolutionary enterprise has blinded some modern thinkers to the truth that many major political revolutions have been disastrous. Worship of revolution in the name of a spurious freedom exacted the sacrifice of millions in Soviet Russia and Communist China alone.

To return to express explication of the text; as remarked earlier (2.6.14), God is all-powerful, able to do anything he wills according to his wisdom and love. (EN 95). Since all laws that are just well up from God's justice and mercy (LA 1.5.11-3. CD 19.21), since divine good as

the source of all created goods towers far above the public interest of
any particular commonwealth, God in his goodness is free to depart
from prevailing laws. To him belong the right and power to ordain
what has not been observed before, to restore laws that have been
embellished or become dead letters, and to make binding what
formerly had no force under law.[41] It would be anomalous to refuse to
God, the ruler of the universe, what we recognize as the right of an
earthly monarch. A king is invested with the authority to institute
laws without precedent. Hence obeying a new ordinance he enjoins
is not an anti-social act; rather, not obeying it betokens a breach of
community ties, for the consent of its members to obey the laws of the
king (or governmental leader) is fundamental and indispensable to
the continuing life of a body politic. A headless commonwealth is
practically impossible; without the authority of a ruler and the order
he prescribes a body politic cannot survive, let alone thrive.

On the other hand, unless citizens obey statutes their government
lays down, its authority is balked, and the value of its laws is near
zero, with no impact or import beyond the paper they are written on.
Correlative with the necessary authority of a governing power is the
necessary obedience of citizens to its dictates; missing such a
response, no laws are concretely effective. This collective response is
the most general or most sweeping pact of the society, i.e., the
common agreement or communal consent of citizens to comply with
the laws of their commonwealth. When deprived of such concord and
its corollary, practical obedience, the fabric of a body politic is bound
to break down. Correspondingly then, men are constrained to obey
without the slightest hesitation whatever God, the ruler of all creation,
commands. There are degrees of obedience; the measure and priority
of obedience depend on the relative rank of the official issuing a
directive. In Roman society the law of a proconsul overrides the
injunction of a magistrate, and, in turn, the ordinance of an emperor
supersedes the directive of a proconsul. The precept of God,
moreover, nullifies even laws laid down by the emperor since he is
omnipotent, the fount and author of all just laws. Thus an imperial
edict to worship idols, no matter how long and deeply woven in a
community, is voided by the law of God (S 62.8.13).[42]

16. Augustine reckons social and personal sins in violation of the
natural law, these being ultimately rooted in pride in which the
exiguous one of self fatuously pretends to surpass the One that is

God. The essential feature of social sins is doing harm to another by word or deed, by outrage or by injury. In accordance with Cicero, anger is defined as the desire for vengeance (2.9.17. CD 14.15.P 138.2.9).[43] An angry man relieves his inward pain by striking back at a malefactor; attacking his foe gains him vindication (2.5.11). Moreover, a robber waylays an unsuspecting traveler, very probably on a side road (CA 1.5.13), forcing him to hand over his possessions. Further, a person overwrought with fear may smite or vilify a rival menacing his status. Again, the man eaten up by envy may spread lies about a more prosperous colleague. Another strain of social sin occurs when a wealthy businessman becomes jealous of a competitor, apprehensive lest the other match his success, or grieved because he is already his equal. In addition, spectators of the gore of gladiatorial shows wallow in a befouled pleasure, as do in another fashion those who, like the overturners (3.3.6), guffaw at the misery they inflict on others by taunting them (3.8.16). All these social sins betray passions undisciplined by reason and faith. Anger arises from an aggressive tendency, and others from (here misguided) simple desires, analyzed, we saw, as four after the Stoics: love and joy in relation to good, fear and sorrow in relation to evil (10.14.22. CD 14.3,5).[44] Stealing stems from an inordinate love of temporal goods; calumny from anxiety spinning off from fear; jealousy from fear and sorrow; and captivation by gladiatorial shows, along with derision of others, from perverse joy. These constitute some, not all, of the capital or chief forms of wickedness directed at others, which ramify from a socially oriented triple concupiscence: the inordinate desire to gain the first place, an illicit urge to gratify the eye, and a proclivity to sensuality.[45]

Each social sin has its roots in one or two or all three of these evil inclinations. Delight in gladiatorial combat sprouts from curiosity, radically a lust of the eyes. Anger and its key ingredient, revenge, may be set ablaze by the will to dominate and a craving for luxurious living. Envy and jealousy may emanate from a desire for primacy and more opportunity for sensual pleasure. Stealing may aim to use ill-gotten goods to bribe one's way to the top position, to be enthralled by or even to fund gladiatorial spectacles that feed curiosity, and to give free rein to *luxuria*, which runs the gamut of sensual living (2.6.13). Thus does evil living break the ten commandments, the ten-stringed psaltery with which men are bade sing the new song of love (S 9.6). The first three commandments express love of God, the latter seven love of neighbor, all ten appointed by a God who, while in the line of being sovereign and most distant from men, is in the line of immanent causal influence and personal touch most intimately related to inner selves (3.6.11). But no sin, social or personal, can directly affect God. Personal faults, which kill the good in souls, cannot corrupt a Lord who is incorruptibly good. In contradistinction to the Manichean deity of Light, the true God cannot be injured nor can the precincts of his nature be invaded by social transgressions. According to the inexorable moral-causal law of consequences, determined by the justice of God, men who do evil do interior evil to themselves. Ineluctably inscribed in every sin is its intrinsic penalty; a fault primarily deforms the soul (1.12.19).

Man commits personal sins when he unmakes and misshapes his nature made by and modeled after God, as in pride, greed, and sloth; when he uses, beyond limits set by the measures of reason and faith, goods necessary for individual and social living, as in gluttony, drunkenness, and lust; and when he bemires himself in unnatural or counternatural acts such as sodomy. Further, man affixes guilt in his soul, thus victimizing himself, by personal sins specifically targeted toward God: he rages against the ways of God, cursing the Lord for evils that befall him, and blaspheming his name; and he kicks against the goad, i.e., arrogantly and recalcitrantly resists and rejects various spurs to reform of life, such as graces and lights, along with chastisement imposed by the merciful hand of God.

Moreover, man commits social sins by overstepping boundaries set by customs and laws of the community. Anti-social rugged individualists damage the public good; corrupt men insolently band together in self-serving private groups such as a clique of senators imposing oppressive taxes to fund more personal perquisites; or, more brazenly, they rupture social order as did the overturners (3.3.6) or try to subvert the state, as did Catiline's insurgents (2.5.11); or rob or even murder other Christians, as later would the roving gangs of Donatists called Circumcellions (E 88.8). Averting their gaze from the upset and destruction their anti-social behavior wreaked, they consulted nothing but their own self-satisfaction; they were concerned only with aggrandizing the dominion of the lordly self.

Men fall into these sins because they forsake God, the unfailing font of life, preferring death of soul to his life. Spurning the one true creator and ruler of the universe, each sinner delusively pictures himself as the sovereign reason for his own existence and goodness. All other forms of malice are rooted in pride, which is structurally as well as historically the beginning of sin (CD 12.6).[46] This self-exaltation is a *privata superbia*: a privatized part, a middle portion of creation (1.1.1), loves himself as a false one, a spurious surrogate of God who is the true One. In his self-idolatry the sinner apes God, making a show of being the creator and ruler of his own life – a posture that is imposture. Cast in the mold of the fallen angels, he does not seek God as the beatifying common good but pursues his own private good to the exclusion of God. He wants his way alone, ambitioning to personally appropriate his own good independently of and in defiance of divine help. Each sinner prefers the pomp of self-elevation to the sublimity of the eternal, empty self-deceit to fulfilling truth, and a fractious party spirit to a union of love (CD 12.1). Against God the evil heart raises "the horns of a false freedom," horns symbolizing the pride that renders the sinner's liberty bogus. As omnipotent, God can do whatever he wills and frame whatever laws he desires, neither capriciously nor tyrannically, but always in accord with his wisdom and goodness. Distortedly imaging God's liberty, a sinner exercises a fraudulent liberty that self-deceivingly imagines that man, outside and above the law of God, can fashion his own laws in contravention of God's law. Such freedom is a fake, indeed an illusion, because sinning entrains not an expansion but a contraction of the spirit; the bitter price exacted for a counterfeit freedom is slavery under the law of sin (P 18[S.2].4. CD 4.3). Furthermore, in loving his own good rather than God, who is the good of all, a sinner ventures a wild gamble: in his insatiable avarice for more and more of mostly fool's gold, which actually amounts to very little, he runs the risk of losing everything – the boundless good that is God.

Here avarice is given a broad or spiritual sense that makes it the rough equivalent or the inevitable concomitant of pride. Like pride, avarice is the "root of all evils" (1 Tim 6.10). The prideful or spiritually greedy individual, discontented with his status as a part, hankers after a good greater than the universe itself; but since nothing finite is more immense than the universe, his desire proves frustrating. He feels himself trapped in his cramped niche; his role as part becomes a cage against whose bars he futilely and pathetically beats his wings. The upshot is that instead of growing, he shrinks almost to the point of morally withering away. The fantasizing hunt

for what is more vast but unreachable warps as well as stunts him. A
self-proclaimed "God" cuts a pitiable figure; pining to be all and to
grab and get all, he reduces himself to a next-to-nothing whose
spiritual blindness may eventually cause him to lose the all of
salvation (GL 1.15.20. T 12.9).[47]

The way out of prideful sin is the unillusioned route laid out by
God: humble piety; a lowliness of spirit avowing absolute
dependence on the need of divine succor; a piety voiced in contrition
for sin and pleading for mercy. Divine love alone can burn away
chains of evil habit forged into iron necessity by pride and supposititious freedom. God's mercy alone can strike off fetters sinners fasten
on themselves by a sham liberty.

Chapter 9: Further Moral Precisions

17. Along with validating standards of right and wrong and
cataloguing misdeeds as social or personal sins, Augustine takes into
account concrete features of moral action such as the condition of the
agent, the intention, particular circumstances, and the "circumstance"
or special role of God in certain events.[48] Sins of the reformed newly
groping along the path of virtue, however blameworthy in the eyes of
the spiritually discerning and mature who measure performance in
the light of the strictest norms of moral fulfillment, merit praise,
nevertheless, in one significant sense. These are the faults of
individuals whose fresh resolve gives promise of a later harvest of
virtue. No matter how zealous the yearning, it is hard to eradicate
long-entrenched habits; the soul recently turned toward God may
occasionally slide back into ways of the old man, into excessive
drinking, a bit of thievery, even an adulterous affair. Yet the struggle
to build new habits is applauded; it is the young shoot that is a
harbinger of the full-grown wheat. Without a doubt the sins of the
reformed person are lapses, but they may be the failings of a saint in
the making. Again, though superficially looking like personal and
social sins, certain actions offend neither the divine nor the public
good. Abraham of old and Romanianus, a wealthy benefactor who
helped fund Augustine's schooling, might be heedlessly taxed for
greed when, in fact, they amassed holdings in accord with the private
property system of their epochs; indeed, as the Lord indicates,
Abraham was poor in spirit (P 85.3). Similarly, a malefactor severely

punished by legally constituted authority may bemoan his sentence as an act of vindictiveness when, in truth, the judge administering the penalty is a scrupulous interpreter of the law. Moreover, a good number of actions men disapprove of are laudable in the eyes of God while many acts applauded by men are condemned by God; for, an action is composed of not only its outward lineaments but also the intention of the agent and its particular circumstances, at times veiled from human inspection. Only God who reads the motives of the heart can perfectly see and weigh obscure factors; only God can descry the total situation; only God can comprehend the concrete intricacies within this subject in this action. Alypius, e.g., was at first arrested as a thief at the scene of an attempted burglary when he innocently picked up the hatchet of the thief who had fled (6.9.14). Throughout history, it seems worth adding, others, including the saintly, have sometimes been, humanly speaking, less fortunate in being branded malefactors or incompetents. St. Joan of Arc (1412-1431) was executed as a witch; St. Alphonsus Liguori (1696-1787) was expelled for a time from the congregation he launched; and St. Raphaela Mary (1850-1925), accused of being managerially gauche and mentally deranged, was deposed as superior general of the institute she founded, then banished to thirty-two years of oblivion. In less striking circumstances the inadequacies of individuals laboring heroically to carry out their duties while suffering from an undiagnosed heart condition or narcolepsy may be ascribed to malingering or sheer laziness. On the other hand, deeds that men esteem good or even exemplary may be vitiated by an ignoble motive. A man of opulence may tender a large donation to charity mainly in order to embellish his public image; a government official may appoint an assistant not because of his apparent capability but because of a secret bribe; vanity and self-seeking may hiddenly prompt a social reformer's activities; indeed "pride lurks even in our good works in order to destroy them" (NG 29.33).[49] Furthermore, God can suddenly intervene to command an unprecedented action contrary to usual social behavior, one going against the grain of received social patterns, generally with the reason for God's directive perhaps fuzzy at the time. God directed Abraham to slay his son Isaac (Gn. 22 1-18); he permitted the spoliation of Egypt by the Israelites (Ex 12. 35-6); under divine impulse the prophet Hosea married Gomer, an adulteress-harlot (Hos 1.2). These extraordinary actions were untainted by the least tincture of evil because they were ordered by the all-just God, upon service to whom hinges the full justice of any polity.

As regards Abraham, Augustine judiciously remarks that certain precepts of the natural law which occupy a middle ground (what realistic moralists today name secondary precepts) are alterable under certain conditions. The rule, "You shall not kill the innocent," must be understood not only according to the act itself (the object) but also according to the agent (the intention) and the authority for the action. If Abraham had intended to kill Isaac on his own initiative, we would recoil from him as revolting and morally insane. But because he submitted to the special command of God, his intended action was praiseworthy, and he himself acclaimed a paradigm of faith and obedience. In short, the crucial factor is the command of God. As master of life and death, God can directly or indirectly give or take away human life at any time determined by his loving wisdom. The precept, "You shall not kill," is immutable for human authority (to kill the innocent is against nature), but it is mutable for the authority of the God who is author of nature and sovereign of life (CF 22.83. QH 2.49.4).[50] The problem of the spoliation of the Egyptians is resolved along like lines. The rule forbidding expropriation of another's property was suspended in this special case. God ordered, or perhaps permitted, the Israelites to despoil the Egyptian as punishment for misusing their possessions to rebel against God by idolatry and to oppress the Israelites. He elected to employ the Israelites as his instruments of sanction. Again, the cardinal point is the authority of God: God is Lord of all possessions, man only the steward (J 6.25); as the supreme owner of all the goods of the earth (7.9.15), he can apportion them as he wills according to his wisdom (CF 22.71).[51] For Augustine, the difficulty of Hosea is more amenable to solution because Scripture itself is unchallengeably perspicuous concerning the source and purpose of God's directive. The meaning of the command is typical; Gomer stands for the Israelites, a faithless nation that has played the wanton in regard to God; and the names of her offspring symbolize God's temporary repudiation of his estranged people. Implied here also is the primary moral determinant, the authority of God. As the author of marriage, God is empowered to change in certain circumstances the law against marriage to an adulterer (CF 22.89). In brief then, as Lord of life and death, as sovereign owner of all the goods of the earth, and as institutor of marriage, God can, in his infinite justice, equitably decree that certain lives be taken and certain unusual marriages be entered into in exceptional circumstances. The recipients of such extraordinary injunctions are of course blessed with a special divine light enabling them to know infallibly, without the slightest possibility of self-deception, that it is indeed God who is ordering this departure from the standard of moral behavior. Blessed too are those gifted with faith who recognize that these Biblical commands are truly directives from God.

As mentioned earlier (3.7.14), the actions of the Old Testament servants of the Lord do more than square with what of God requires in their actual present situation; they also portend future events. "In the Old Testament the New is concealed; in the New Testament the Old is revealed" (S 160.6). Each and every event in the Old Testament harbors a hidden mystical meaning foretelling a future occurrence in the New Covenant. The ram that Abraham substituted for Isaac prefigured the Jesus whose hands and feet were dug by his enemies in the sacrifice that is to bring all nations under his kingship (S 2.7.8 CD 16.32). The spoliation of the Egyptians Augustine reads as a foretoken of the appropriation by Christians of the riches of pagan learning. Once prostituted to promote idolatry and to undergird the persecution of Christians, the gold and silver vessels and splendid apparel of profane erudition are to be converted to the service of the true God and the upbuilding of his Church (DC 2.40. 60-1). Hosea's union with the adulteress, as just noted, is through and through typical in meaning for the Old Testament. As Paul tells us (Rom 9.25-6), God's promise to make Israel once more his beloved foreshadows the union of God with the Gentiles called to be his people upon whom he lavishes mercy (CF 22.89).

In these five sections included in three chapters (3.7.13–9.17), Augustine offers illuminating comments on the moral makeup of man. First, under the spur of the Manichean disparagement of Old Testament patriarchs, he claims that God flexibly yet justly applied the eternal law to jibe with the circumstances of Old Testament periods. None of the actions of the patriarchs ran counter to the prescriptions of nature of the laws and customs of their day (3.7.13-4). Second, yet relative application of moral rules is not a slick rationale or sophisticated license for moral relativism. The primary moral precepts of the natural law implanted in the heart are immutable.

Man is always obliged not to harm another and, in Christian ethics, to love God and his neighbor as himself. A sin against nature like sodomy is intrinsically wrong, evil in all circumstances (3.8.15). Third, Augustine details certain chief social and personal sins that deviate from natural law. All other sins spring from a pride that assigns top priority to its own private good while turning its back on God, the common good (3.8.16). Fourth, he briefly distinguishes end, object, and circumstances. In terms of the supernatural "circumstance" of divine authority God can, in special situations, direct Abraham to kill Isaac, the Israelites to despoil the Egyptians, and Hosea to marry an adulteress (3.9.17). The account proffered in these three chapters falls short of constituting a mini-treatise on the essentials of morality. However nicely structured, it surely does not issue in an outlook as unified and systematic as other analytical ventures such as the treatise on psychological time (11.14.17-28.38). Yet in spite of lacunae, these reflections remain a signal, albeit tightly compressed and at times too cursory, piece of moral analysis whose penetration sheds light on knotty questions still mooted in lively fashion to this very day.

Chapter 10: Manichean Absurdities

18. But Augustine was not among those blessed in knowing that God had commanded certain adaptively applied moral precepts. Unhappily, as repeatedly stated before (3.7.14), he was ignorant, and, gulled through his ignorance by Manichean sophisms, heaped derision on leading Old Testament figures, despising their prophecies as bogus, ridiculing these holy men as adulterous and murderous (3.7.14). Ironically, he proclaimed himself ridiculous in the eyes of God through espousal of Manichean views that were nugatory, i.e., baseless and self-stultifying.[52] Ironically too, while criticizing in the name of reason what he deemed superstitious beliefs of Catholicism, he uncritically believed the irrational tenets of Manicheism. Bowled over by the superficially impressive Manichean critique of the Old Testament, he quickly committed himself to the Manichean way.[53] Only imperceptibly and gradually did he come around to accepting Manichean doctrines and moral views that were aberrant parodies of scientific truth.[54] The Manicheans were radical panpsychists.[55] insisting that all beings are alive and feel pain, because intermingled in their substance are particles of divine light. Plucking a fig causes

pain to the tree; the slight snapping sound is its groaning, and the drops that form at the point of breakage are the tears of its mother tree.[56] Such a belief is of course rejected by sober common sense and the organized common sense that is natural science; stones manifest none of the salient features of life, and plants give no evidence of consciousness; neither experiences pain nor suffers in any proper sense. Figs simply do not weep, and the contrary opinion is one strand of gross religious myth (CF 6.4). Again, the moral directive concerning the consumption of the fig was paradoxical. It was accounted sinful to pluck a fig or the like, but it was the duty of a Manichean auditor or hearer, the lowest grade, to feed a holy man, one of the elect,[57] with sacrilegiously garnered and prepared fruits and vegetables. After bestowing a ritual malediction on the donor, the elect formally cooperated in the sin of the auditor yet was regarded as saintly. Indeed the auditors were not merely less perfect but through-and-through sinful since their routine human activities did harm to the light-particles incarcerated in matter. Moreover, against all evidence Augustine believed that after ingesting and digesting the fruit,[58] the elect individual would release the trapped particles by groaning in prayer and by belching. The elect, it was contended, breathed forth angels, i.e., air and light (two of the five good elements);[59] further, they eructated particles of light, fragments of the very divine substance imbedded in the food consumed. Credulous Manichees overlooked the glaring incongruities implied: particles of the true (and therefore inviolable) God are incarnated in matter, the lowest substance; the supreme (and therefore independent) God depends on inferior beings; the holy elect do not escape bondage to matter; the Father of Greatness who redeems men from darkness has to be partitively redeemed. This last contention is blasphemous (blasphemy means branding good things evil; MM 11.20); the incorruptible God is depicted as corruptible. Liberated by the prayerful groans and anointed gastronomical ructations of the elect, divine light-particles ascended along the column of glory to the light-ships (moon and sun), whence they were borne back to the realm of light.[60]

The misconceptions that had the most high God imprisoned in lowly matter bred cruel, perhaps tragic, moral directives. Though plainly fruit is for man and not man for fruit, Manichean doctrine dictated that fruit be denied a starving beggar who was not a

Manichean; on their showing, such misguided mercy would be equivalent to condemning the morsel to a kind of capital punishment. Inserted in the body of a nonbeliever, the light-particles are made to agonize anew as part of the "suffering Jesus" who hangs from every tree. Particles of light enchained in a sinful body undergo suffering akin to crucifixion; they are part of the cross or crucifixion of light; these light-particles are the very members of God that have been captured by the forces of evil and bound within the darkness of matter (P 140.12). Entrance into the body of a sinner would pollute the light-particles and block their return to the Kingdom of Light; surely such bondage involving an attack on the divine within the particles was tantamount to capital punishment. The Manichean contention that eating of a fruit by a nonbelieving beggar is effectively murder flies in the face of reason. Unfortunately, in legitimating denial of food to the beggar, it may result in real murder. In the case of a starving person at the point of death, Manichees filled with pseudo-compassion for the tree and pear, in refusing to relieve real suffering, effectively murder the man (MM 16.53; 17.58).

Chapter 11: Monica's Dream of Augustine's Conversion

19. Augustine, however, was not to be doomed to lifelong captivity to Manichean fantasies. From on high God sent down his hand, which usually stands for divine power and here symbolizes the savior, the power of God enfleshed in Jesus his savior, to segregate him from heretics (P 143.14), to draw his soul from the pit of Manichean darkness, i.e., to spare him from Manichean untruths that could lead to the hell to come (P 85. 17-8). His deliverance was won by holy tears, these being frequently more appealing than words (E 130.10.20), and pleadings of his mother, the Lord's faithful servant, a tabernacle in which he dwelt (P 41.91), ever faithful in assenting to and fulfilling the promises of her God (P 32 [En 2.S.1]. 9). She wept more for Augustine than other mothers bereaved of their sons because eyes of faith saw that her son's soul was dead, i.e., its life of grace was withdrawn by God (CD 13.21). Here Augustine allusively links Monica to the widow of Naim (Lk 7.12-5) in a comparison later made explicit (6.1.1). Hyperbolically described, her tears were so copious that they drenched the ground wherever she prayed. The force of her entreaties was irresistible: God heard her, Augustine says

three times in a few lines, suggesting that divine clemency was obliged, so to speak, to hearken to the outpourings of her heart and eyes (3.12.22;5.9.17;6.1.1). Only her prayerful display of misery could account for the consolation of a vision she was accorded. So strong was her loathing of Manicheism that prior to this vision Monica had refused to have Augustine live in her home (during his period of ostracism Augustine probably stayed with Romanianus, his wealthy patron [CA 2.2.3]). She was revolted by the Manichees because they maligned God by conceiving him as subject to corruption and contamination, insultingly contending that a part of God would remain everlastingly befouled in the Kingdom of Darkness.[61] In her divinely inspired dream[62] Monica saw herself standing on a wooden rule of faith while there approached a dazzlingly handsome man smiling and radiating joy,[63] his bearing in sharp contrast to Monica's mournful visage. Since a heavenly visitant comes to tell rather than be told, any question put aims at teaching rather than learning from a recipient of a heaven-sent message; such was the case with Jesus inquiring about recent events in Jerusalem (Lk 24.17 ff.), with Jesus asking a question of the apostles (Jn 21.3), and the angel querying the apostles (Ac 1.11). In general, an instructor uses questioning as an exterior instrument to lead a learner to explicit cognition of basic truths known from the light within the interior self (Mag 12.40). Hence, in asking Monica, "Why are you so sad?," the celestial visitant aimed at bringing Monica to recognize the truth. In every instance, whether the truth consists of basic notions within the mind, to be made explicit by step-by-step questioning, or whether the truth is grasped by sensory observation, the teacher acts only as an extrinsic agent, whose strategy of questioning is the tool employed to bring the learner to personal appropriation of the truth. The grammar is wrong, the sense right: a learner "learns" himself. However, ordinarily in a heavenly visitation the recipient is not plied with questions so that, by consultation with the light within, he can dig out the basic notions virtual or latent in consciousness. Rather, the initial questioning opens the way to perception of the truth whether by senses or by the senses illuminated by faith. After asking the apostles if they had caught anything (the answer to which he knew), Jesus directed them to cast their net to the right side where they hauled in a huge catch of fish. In the cases of Jesus' encounter with the disciples on the road to Emmaus and the angel's dialogue with the disciples, questioning preceded a statement or statements about his passion and post-ascension return. Both verbal presentations were outwardly learned, then inwardly acknowledged by an act of supernatural faith through the illumination of the mind by the Spirit of the interior teacher who is Christ (Mag 11.38). The teaching of Monica is patterned after these latter instances: in brief, after the heavenly visitor first asked Monica the cause of her distress, a reason that he was already aware of, he disclosed the meaning of the wooden rule, thus evoking in Monica supernatural belief enunciated in the light of the Holy Spirit. To expand a bit, in asking Monica why she was sorrowfully weeping day after day, the not-of-this-world visitant elicited information to which he was already privy, bringing her to affirm the truth: she was brokenhearted over the death of Augustine's soul due to separation from God. Then the heavenly apparition gently urged her to expel all anxieties as she focused on the rule on which Augustine was standing beside her. His new position meant that one day her son would fully embrace the Catholic faith, believing God, i.e., assenting to the teachings of Christ, and believing in God, i.e., morally committed to his commandments, living, as the man of virtue does, by faith (P 32[En.2.S.1].9). The rule as wooden symbolizes the Lord who reigns, not with a rod of iron but with the scepter that is the rood of wood (P 95.2); the saving standard by which Christians concretely measure all doctrines and all patterns of living (J 1.16. CR 32).[64] Assured that the Lord's ears were pressed close to her heart, i.e., that one day Augustine would return to the faith of his mother, Monica's soul was becalmed; her all-loving and all-powerful Father was attentive to her least need. All-good and omnipotent, God cares for each as if each were all and for all as if all were but one. Unlimited in his goodness and power, God is able to concentrate all his love on any one person, as if that single microcosm were the whole macrocosm. Again, God cares for all as if all were but one; because infinite, his goodness and power are not scattered or watered down when applied to billions of individuals; with a singular, personal love the Father provides for the whole universe. This concern for each person is sharply opposed and markedly superior to the Epicurean outlook that denies providential interest in particular individuals. All the entrances and exits, the ups and downs, marriages and births and deaths, all the pain in the valley and all the pleasure on the mountaintop, all these events in the theater of life the gods view with Olympian aloofness and detachment, serenely uninterested and unaffected. For Augustine, the providence of God that extends to the lowest and tiniest things in the earthly region must encompass, for a greater reason, all men, including all of their actions (GL 5.22.43). The overall design of God assigns even sinners like Judas their proper place. God sees and cares for the collective order of individuals as if it were a single person, a quasi-organismic particular whole (S 125.5).[65]

Moreover, in praising God as both good and omnipotent, Augustine is implicitly repudiating the Epicurean contention that because of uneradicated evil in the world God cannot be both good and all-powerful.[66] According to this formidable objection, with which nontheists and proponents of a finite God have repeatedly confronted traditional theists down to modern times, God is either all-good or all-powerful but cannot be both at once. For if God is all-good, he wills that evil not exist, but the unrelenting course of evil plainly evidences that he lacks the power to exterminate it. On the other hand, if he is all-powerful, i.e., able to abolish all evil, the tragic pertinacity of evil proves that he is not all-good: he does not will the elimination of evil. The gods of Epicurus, however, were no more than finite, limited in goodness and partially handicapped in exercise of power. At best they could tolerate evil from afar in a disengaged way, unable to check its apparently resistless metastasis, let alone to uproot it from the hearts of men. On Augustine's reckoning, God is both all-good and all-powerful. So good and so powerful is he that he can permit evil to draw good or a greater good out of evil. As infinitely powerful, he miraculously causes evil to fructify into good. The full outworking of this law will not be manifested until the end of history, at the final judgment, when God's master-plan of justice and mercy in all its intricacies will be revealed to all. This vantage point of the transhistorical and eternal nullifies one argument against God's totally personalized providence, which runs; "If the gods cared for men, they would do good to good men and evil to evil men, which is not the case" (ND 3.32.79). Both good and evil individuals enjoy prosperity and suffer adversity in historical time, but not until the Grand Assize will God in his infinite justice and mercy apportion their proper deserts to good and evil men; the good such as the martyrs crowned with imperishable glory because of their dying for love of Christ at the hands of brutal executioners—out of the evils inflicted on the good God draws the greater good of eternal communion in his bosom.

20. As Monica's beseechings gained for her the consoling forecast of Augustine's conversion, so her unflagging prayer brought down divine illumination in her interpretation of the dream. Apprised of the vision, Augustine was first taken aback, then cocksurely rebutted her reading of the dream. The vision, he forcibly argued, foretold not his conversion to Catholicism but hers to Manicheism. To Augustine's chagrin, Monica, though the beneficiary of hardly a smattering of formal education, with no training in dialectical maneuvering, immediately parried his thrust and drove home a telling counter-thrust, rejoining: "You have it backwards. He did not say, 'Where he is, you are too.' Rather he said, 'Where you are, he is too.'" Monica's penetrating reply stamped a deeper impression on Augustine than the dream itself. In the past he had probably resorted to like dialectical tactics to throttle relatively uneducated discussants. But Monica was not to be checked by a shallowly plausible but utterly warped interpretation of the dream's point. Graced by light, she answered with the self-confidence one would expect of only a skilled disputant. Her subtlety and clarity astonished and disturbed Augustine. The rejoinder delivered with the facile spontaneity of an adept in debating lit up the import of her vision: she clearly showed that he had got the meaning back end to. For once the gifted speechifier was silent; so trenchant was the mother's answer that the son who was accustomed to skewering opponents surrendered by his silence. While Augustine licked his wounds, Monica experienced comfort in her present worry. But the hour of return was not to fall on the day after tomorrow. Monica's vision probably occurred late in 374, and Augustine did not start to break away decisively from Manicheism till nearly nine years later, around 382/3. Manichean untruths still engulfed his mind in thick darkness. In the course of his captivity he frequently tried to clamber out of the pit but, with every failed attempt to escape, sank deeper into the black hole. The religious strength of his widowed mother released the liberating power of the Father in his soul. She was chaste: pure in the sexual sense but also in intention as well, desiring God without the slightest tinge of self-interest (P 72.32); pious: consecrating all of self to God; sober: temperate in food and drink, even in her time of want, and discreet in word and measured in deed (QE 2.11). As Augustine's dramatic conversion was to witness, her entreaties entered into the presence of the Lord, i.e., God inclined his merciful ear to her beseechings (P 87.2). According to the

divine pledge, he could not but hear them; her indomitable hope was to fructify in the conversion she desired, and more (8.12.22). Because of his perverse resoluteness, for the time being God left Augustine to toss in Manichean darkness (P 34 [S.1].9). Unable to stand upright, he could only shift back and forth, lying prone in the mud, then supine, then once more prone, all the while shrouded in a pitch-black night of ignorance.

Chapter 12: A Reassuring Prophecy

21. The second divine emissary was not an apparition but a priest, more specifically, a Catholic bishop or priest of a higher rank in charge of a local church,[67] whose name eludes scholars. He was well-versed in Scripture, to the point of being an acceptable theologian; his early faith matured into understanding proper to spirituals. Monica begged him to dissipate her son's errors, for he was successful in recovering fallen-aways hospitable to instruction.[68] The bishop declined since Augustine was simply unteachable, a fierce advocate of Manicheism not because he really knew it to be true but because he desired it so (DA 9.12), concerned only about propagandizing for what he liked (10.23.34). Smugly obstinate, he bemused simple Catholic faithful with religious pettifoggery (4.15.26) and, while notching frequent easy victims in apologetic duels, seduced some friends into the Manichean camp (DA 9.11). Insufferably sure of himself, he would have turned a deaf ear to the bishop's teaching while his agile tongue would have repeatedly stabbed at apparently vulnerable flanks of Catholicism. Any present attempt to disabuse him would be idle. The bishop advised instead that she go on trusting that his reading would in time alert him to the incoherence of the sect, his own experience being proof of this strategy. Though a Catholic in his earliest years, as a small boy he had been handed over to the Manicheans by his mother who had been duped by their teachings; it was not uncommon for the sect to request hearers to donate a child for training in the sect.[69] After laboriously copying by hand nearly all their available books, principally, we may suppose, the seven sacred books of Mani, in time, without encountering a single dialectical demurrer, he discovered for himself how repulsive Manicheism was. His moving witness was not enough to satisfy the heavy-hearted Monica, who pleaded anew for the bishop to disabuse her son. Here

she was not lapsing from the discretion for which she is praised a few lines back (3.11.20); weeping out of an overflowing affection, more than most mothers she loved to have her son by her side (5.8.13). But the closeness sought was only secondarily physical, for spiritual nausea over Augustine's turn to this appalling heresy so overrode natural affection that she expelled him from her home, allowing him to return only after the heavenly visitant's assurance (3.11.19). Becoming understandably a trifle impatient because Monica apparently had not perceived that it would have been a waste of time to dialogue with a refractory know-it-all, the prelate quickly terminated their colloquy with a religious-literary gem: "As sure as you live, the son of such tears cannot perish." She took the bishop's discerning words as a message from heaven, as indeed they indirectly were, for his prophecy was fulfilled in the fact and route of Augustine's return to the Father. Though convinced by the primary theses of the Manichees, their solution to the problem of evil and their rejection of the Old Testament (3.7.12), in the back of his mind he always retained misgivings about the seeming bizarreries of their cosmogony like the ships of light; mountain-high obstacles that over the years prompted him to try to vault, but in vain, out of the ditch (3.11.20). It was personal reading and reflection that mainly snapped Manichean fetters. Deficiency in astronomy showed up Faustus, a leading Manichean bishop-spokesman, as an irrational advocate for shabbily unscientific doctrines (5.3.3-4). Later, Christian Neoplatonism resolved two primary issues, viewing God as wholly spiritual and defining evil as strictly a privation (7.9.13; 12.18). Engrossed listening that was a sort of aural reading of the sermons of Ambrose furnished a method of exegesis that vindicated the moral behavior of Old Testament figures (6.4.6). Indeed, as not even this foresighted bishop presaged, he would further imitate the bishop by becoming a bishop who would also undeceive the wayward and lead them back into the fold. Amazingly, as not even his confident mother dared hope (8.12.22), so learned in the books of the Lord would he become that future ages would hail him as the doctor of doctors, so luminous in his prodigious output that no bishop since has proved his equal in Christian wisdom.

NOTES

1. Salvian, *De gubernatione Dei*, 7.13-8.
2. Our construal of these vexing words largely derives from the analysis of Solignac, BA 13, 665-6. However, our explication parts company with his on the sense of *minus indigentem*, which he takes to mean "while he was less spiritually indigent yet on the threshold of becoming even more indigent." This lesser indigence, he holds, is, in fact, the same as the *secretior indigentia*, the more hidden indigence viewed from an objective standpoint. In other words, in his opinion the lesser indigence (with the potential to become greater objectively or exteriorly) exhibits the greater indigence of the subjective or interior sinful self.
3. HC 35, n.l.
4. O'Meara, 54.
5. His friend Alypius was also sucked into the whirlpool of the Carthaginian passion for spiritually enervating spectacles (6.7.11). The craze for the theater distorts the moral sense, poisoning the soul with pernicious as well as idle images. When the eyes of those who were disgorged from the amphitheater fell upon practical Christians crossing their paths, they were wont to remark to fellow theater-worshippers, "Look at those poor people. They simply do not know what they are missing" (P 147.8).
6. Similar language indicates that Augustine's *sacrilegam curiositatem* compactly distils the enamored witnessing of the obscene worship of the mother of the gods in Carthage; the huge crowd of spectators was allured by curiosity (*illecta curiositate*) enacted with the foulest moral turpitude (CD 2.4). In the *Confessions* sacrilege means the perversion of the sacred in demon-ridden idolatrous rites or false teaching. Victorinus participated in sacrilegious rites (8.2.3), the rites of demons (8.2.4); later Augustine detested all sacrilegious rites (10.35.56), a usage duplicated in S 293.5. Manichean doctrine is described as sacrilegious (4.16.3; 5.5.8; 5.10.20; 8.7.17), and Augustine's heart or conscience is termed sacrilegious because he espoused Manicheism (5.9.16). In later works sacrilege signifies the violation or profanation of sacred things. Judas was guilty not only of stealing but of sacrilege, for he stole from the purse that was the Lord's; comparably sacrilegious is theft by any Christian from the Church (J 50.10). Interestingly, Augustine does not call his sexual negotiation sacrilegious, though it apparently involved profanation of a sacred place.
7. In this dialogue of two books Cicero argues that philosophy is superior to the oratory defended by Hortensius. Only 103 fragments of the work survived, 16 occurring in Augustine. It is the main source of the principle (10.21.31), originating with Aristotle, that all men desire happiness. See W. Collinge, "Hortensius," AE 437. In particular dependence on Aristotle's *Protrepticus*, as Lactantius in *Divinae Institutiones* 3.16.9, observes, quoting Fr. 12, Hortensius' attack on philosophy is self-stultifying; to claim that philosophy is not necessary involves philosophizing since the job of the philosopher consists in disputation of what must be done or not done in this life. See M. Bettetini, "Augustinus in

Kartago: Gleich einem Roman," CAH 143, n. 42.

8. According to L. Ferrari, *The Conversions of Saint Augustine*, iv, the word conversion may be used to describe Augustine's encounter with *Hortensius*, his adoption of Manicheism, and his acceptance of Neoplatonism as well as his moral-religious conversion in Milan in 386.

9. For a brief inventory of the reasons suggested for *cujusdam Ciceronis* see BA 13, 667, n.12, which does not settle the question. The three opinions in our text are offered by Testard, 1.11-19; G-M 58, n.1; HC 38, n.10.

10. See L. Ferrari, "The Theme of the Prodigal Son in Augustine's *Confessions*," RA 12 (1977), 105-18.

11. Some may find it odd that Augustine simply records the fact of his father's death, without indicating his mortal illness, some details of the obsequies, and his own and Monica's sorrow at his passing. Since the *Confessions* is a spiritual-intellectual autobiography that ordinarily omits particulars not relevant to his conversion, only scanty information is provided about Patricius, who exercised little influence on his religious development. Not that Augustine was a vengeful son, empty of all filial piety. He remarks on his gratitude and a certain justifiable pride that neighbors praised his father for the financial sacrifices he exacted of himself to further the education of his promising son (2.3.5). Later, when noting that his father was subject to outbursts of wrath, he pointedly observes that his father's anger was balanced or perhaps outbalanced by his generous ways (9.9.19). A moving passage begs prayers for the release of his father's soul to eternal glory (9.13.34). Patricius is not given short shrift but is accorded less attention because he is overshadowed by Monica in the molding of Augustine's spiritual personality. To the never-say-die perseverance in prayers of this uneducated woman who was a spiritual genius, he owed his entrance into the supernatural. She was an apostle of love, a proselytizer of souls to be won for Christ. Her meekness overcame Patricius' wrath; her holy tolerance conquered his adultery by praying him into the Catholic faith (9.9.22). Her nearly single-minded zeal, especially between 371-86, bore her son anew into eternal life, capturing him for Christ (9.8.17). Patricius could work no parallel impact upon Augustine's soul. Prior to his entrance into the Catholic faith, he was at best a good pagan. After his baptism (9.9.22) he died in 370/1, in Augustine's seventeenth year, his brief life as a Catholic debarring him from leaving a profound spiritual impress on his son. In short, very little is said of Patricius because very little can be said of him in terms of input into Augustine's conversion.

12. Cicero, *Tusc. disp.* 3.5.8.

13. Col 2.8 distinguishes between true philosophy and philosophy tied to the elements of the world (MM 21.38.E 149.25, 30). For Augustine, under the tutelage of Simplicianus (8.2.3), true philosophy, preeminently Platonism, recognizes spiritual realities while the false brand is a traditional materialism such as Stoicism or Epicureanism. CA 3.19.42 contrasts the Stoic philosophy limited to the sensible world with the Platonic philosophy of the intelligible world. According to MM 21.38, the Manichean outlook, which reduces all existence to the material plane, is also a philosophy of the elements of the

world.

14. Augustine ordinarily has recourse to an older translation of Is 7.9 to underpin his linkage of faith and understanding: "If you do not believe, you shall not understand." He is also familiar with an alternative rendering: "If you do not believe, you shall not remain (*permanebis*)" (DC 2.12.17).

15. The growing Christian man passes from milk to solid food, while also consuming food in greater measure. This growth occurs by illuminated understanding because the very food of understanding is light (J 97.1). Gnosticism is excluded; there are no hidden chambers of secret knowledge. Both carnals and spirituals grasp the same truth according to their capacity (J 96.4; 98.2).

16. *Puer*, which means a boy up till fifteen, can also signify an older youth; Cicero, *De fin.* 1.2, 25, 12, where Octavian is called *puer egregius* at age nineteen. In addition, *puer* and its cognates are not uncommonly taken to designate an analytically retarded psychological state. Augustine was a *puer* in this sense when he misjudged the value of Scripture and was entrapped by Manicheism (3. 5.9–6.10). Apparently alluding to this lapse, he comments that a man left unsatisfied by Scripture becomes engrossed in fables: "Fables exert an attraction on souls that are puerile no matter what their physical age" (CF 12.27).

17. The fundamental text for understanding Manicheism is H.-C. Puech, *Le Manicheisme: son fondateur, sa doctrine* (Paris, 1949). For a truly excellent, wide-ranging, and thorough account of the sect see J.K. Coyle *Augustine's De moribus ecclesiae Catholicae*, 9-57, 144-240, whose bibliography is extensive. The best short, very lucid introduction to the intricacies of this religion is available in Bonner, 157-92, whose bibliographical comments are valuable. See the recent survey, J.K. Coyle, "Mani,Manicheism," AE 820-5, with an updated bibliography, among whose citations Coyle modestly declines to list his own earlier, rich analysis.

18. Recourse to the term insanity to describe extreme intellectual infirmity cannot be put down as an oddity of the rhetoric of late antiquity. In *A History of Western Philosophy*, 494, 718, 818, and 828, B. Russell decries the madness of extreme subjectivism in modern thought, an insanity especially virulent in G. Fichte.

19. BA 33,318, n.1.

20. Celestial objects like the sun and the moon, perceptible by the senses or eye of the flesh, are worshipped daily by the Manicheans who, while praying, turn toward the sun during the day and toward the moon at night (Fort 3. H 46.38). This cult rested on the belief that, loosely speaking, the sun visible to animals as well as men is Christ the Lord (J 34.4). More precisely, according to the Manicheans, the sun seems round but is triangular in the sense that its light shines through a triangular opening in heaven. What the Manicheans worship is strictly not the visible sun but a fictive ship of light (CF 20.6). More generally, the sun was worshipped as a particle of light in which God dwells (GCM 1.3.6). Some documents apparently show that some Manicheans believed that the sun and the moon represented the divine or were ways to the divine. Many filaments of Manichean teaching have come down to us blurred with

ambiguity, but it seems unquestionable that the creed in which Augustine was
indoctrinated considered sun and moon in some respect divine luminaries
deserving of worship, an expression that Faustus, a renowned Manichean
spokesman, seems to ratify. On his reckoning, the sun and moon resemble the
consecrated bread and wine of Christians; vessels of the substance of God,
which are properly accorded divine worship (CF 20.1-2). However, Faustus'
analogy is not entirely clear. He seems to be contending that sun and moon are
worshipped in the way that the bread and wine, which contain the Eucharist,
are worshipped by Catholics. This is, as Augustine explains, a misconstrual of
Catholic teaching (CF 20.13). Apparently the Manichean position on the
divinity of sun and moon was equivocally presented by various teachers. See
the excellent discussion in Coyle, 355-9.

21.   Bourke, *Augustine's View of Reality*, 33-4.
22.   The distinction between reproductive and productive imagination has become
a commonplace in modern psychology.
23.   *Sapire* in 3.6.10 does not connote *sapiens* or being wise, though Manichees are
apparently said to be perversely wise or sapient about earthly things (GM
2.26.40). In the usage of Augustine's contemporaries *sapire* had broken free
from its metaphorical roots so that it signified in a nonmetaphorical, analogical
fashion "to perceive by the mind"; similarly *visio veritatis* means intellectual
apprehension of truth. Though ordinarily we do not speak of savoring a fact or
truth, our culture does employ *sapire* in a nonfigurative sense in remarks such
as "His earlier political views savored of a policy more murderous than
Stalin's."
24.   *Odes* 3.3.
25.   See E. Peters, "Aenigma Salomonis: Manichean Anti-Genesis Polemic and the
Vitium Curiositatis in Confessions III. 6," AUG (L) 38 (1986), 48-64.
26.   Much of the discussion of chapters 5-7 is drawn from my article, "Anti-
Manichean and other Moral Precisions in *Confessions* 3.7.12–9.17," AS 19 (1988),
165-94.
27.   Brown, 50.
28.   Not only the human soul but the animal soul also is *tota ubique*, everywhere
present as a whole in the body it animates. Augustine also admits a life-
principle in plants, the lowest grade of soul (CD 7.23). Whereas the ubiquity of
the whole being of God is unlimited, the ubiquity of the soul is circumscribed
by the dimensions of its body (CEF 16.20. E 166.2.4).
29.   W. Jackson Knight, S*t. Augustine's De Musica: A Synopsis*, 11-3. In accord with the
Greeks, Cicero stressed that the knowledge of an art consists essentially of a
grasp of its first principles; *De orat.* 1.92,186-8. A. Gwynn, *Roman Education From
Cicero to Quintilian*,88-9.
30.   Marrou, 199-200. Actors, instrumentalists, and singers acquire mastery of their
techniques by sensory experience and memory utilized by their aptitude for
imitation; skills that can be exercised without any understanding of the
principles of their techniques (M 1.4.8).
31.   Conscience perceives the difference between good and evil, which is an office
deputed to prudence, yet Augustine never explicitly adverts to their

connection. According to ME 15.45, it is the job of prudence to draw the line between objects to be desired and those to be avoided; similarly in CD 19.4, prudence discerns between good and evil so that we may seek the one and avoid the other; but neither passage mentions or even alludes to the corresponding function of conscience; neither suggests in any way that prudence may be the core of conscience stamping right reason on desires. See E. Fortin, "The Political Implications of St. Augustine's Theory of Conscience," AS 1 (1970), 133-52.

32. In a passage from an earlier exploration of evil (LA 1.3.6) Evodius concludes that adultery is evil because he would not want to be so sexually betrayed by his wife. In general, he argues, anyone who does to another what he does not want done to himself does evil; this is a tentative formulation of what, on our reckoning, Augustine later holds to be the primary precept of morality. But at this juncture a younger Augustine counters with an example of what is now labeled spouse-swapping, the mutual exchange of spouses for adulterous satisfaction. Such spouse-exchange seems to nullify Evodius' general principle, for each husband willingly gives his wife to another, apparently without suffering harm. He does what he wants done to him. Clearly a wiser Augustine later abandoned this dialectical ploy despite its success against Evodius. But apparently he offered no direct, explicit retractation of this erroneous dismissal of the primary precept. As noted below, SDM 2.22.74 implicitly retracts his mistaken position. The case instanced in LA 1.3.6 is only seemingly exceptional; it does not upset the general norm, proposed by Evodius and later constantly recurred to by Augustine, because the primary imperative supposes some good will, a measure of conscientious willing of the good. The objective validity and universal scope of the primary maxim cannot be annulled by its wantonly subjective denial attempted by calculatedly hedonistic spouses. Augustine's comment in CD 14.8 seems to confirm the validity of our suggestion. "The most salutary and truest precept"–"Whatever you want men to do to you, do the same to them" (Mt 7.12)–presumes good will. Were no good will implied, the Golden Rule could be prostituted to a psuedo-rule of dross giving free rein to wallowing in sordid pleasure. In SDM 2.22.74, while discoursing on the Golden Rule (Mt 7.21, to which Lk 6.31 corresponds), Augustine makes the same point from another angle when he stresses that good will is properly implied in the injunction, "Do to other men whatever you will (*quaecumque vultis*) they do to you." Though unlike the Latin version accessible to Augustine (which differed from the Vulgate), the Greek text did not contain the word *bona* to make the verse read," *quaecumque vultis...bona*," there is no need to add *bona*, for *quaecumque vultis* is to be taken not in a conventional or random way but in the proper sense. *Voluntas* or will properly refers only to good actions, whereas from *cupiditas* or inordinate desire properly spew forth evil deeds.

Interestingly, in *Augustine* (1994), 196, J. Rist refers to "wife-swapping." May I remark that, as mentioned in n. 21, I used this or like terminology in an article published in 1988.

33. CD 4.4: *Remota itaque justitia quid sunt regna nisi latrocinia?* Once justice

disappears from a state, once a body politic is misruled by evil men for an evil end, Augustine shrewdly observes, the state becomes morally no different from a large gang of robbers; it is a gangster-state. For recent recourse to the gangster figure in regard to totalitarian regimes, see P. Johnson, *Modern Times*, 261,263, 356, 359, 360, 361.

34. Contemporary thinkers of various hues, it may be noted, have weighed and found wanting the claims of moral relativism, a view that oddly still remains in vogue in certain circles. In *On the Diversity of Morals*, M. Ginsberg, a theoretical sociologist of rationalist persuasion, convincingly establishes that fixed moral standards are universal; the diversity of their social embodiments is explainable by variations in concrete elements. B. Blanshard, a rationalist in the idealist tradition, in *Reason and Goodness*, elaborates a theory of invariable intrinsic values, while leveling strictures on the relativistically charged views of sociological subjectivism, instrumentalism, and emotivism. E. Vivas' *The Moral Life and Ethical Life*, the work of a humanist of religious orientation, casts a cold critical eye on the moral fraudulence of the relativistic evaluation of the good in modern naturalism. In *Deeds and Rules in Christian Ethics* the Protestant ethicist P. Ramsey lays bare the grave shortcomings of relativism, especially the morally self-stultifying method and content of situation ethics.

35. Aquinas, *S. th.* 1-2. 94.2.

36. Significantly, S 9.14 grounds the ten commandments in the two chief commandments, love of God and neighbor, and the latter two in the primary precept of the natural law. "For the ten commandments are reduced to these two commandments that we love God and neighbor (Mt 22.37-40), and these two commandments, in turn, are reduced to that one precept. Now the one precept is this: 'Do not do to others what you do not want done to yourself.' There in the two are contained the ten, there in the one are contained the two." In the perspective of Christian ethics, i.e., in the light of faith in God's love enfleshed in Christ, the two chief commandments spring from the natural soil of the primary precept. This citation, unearthed by that indefatigable researcher, A-M. La Bonnardière, appears in her "En marge de la 'Biblia Augustiniana'; une 'retractatio', REA, 10(1964), n. 4, 305-7, which came into my hands only after the foregoing comments were finished.

37. Augustine seems to root the precept of love of neighbor and its kin, the Golden Rule, in the primary precept. "If an individual does what is written, 'You shall love your neighbor as yourself' (Mt 22.29) and 'Whatever good things you want men to do to you, do also to them' (Mt 7.12), he has within and by himself the means of knowing well-doing because he ought not to do to another what he does not want done to himself" (P 51.10).

38. Nowhere, as far as I know, does Augustine codify in detail the precepts of natural law. Still, our interpretation, that "Do no harm to others" may be styled the primary natural precept, seems corroborated by Augustine's discussion in CD 19.14. After writing that love of God and neighbor are the two chief commandments of the Christian way of life, he sets down precepts subserving peace or ordered harmony, the first of which is, "Do no harm to others." In other words, the natural law is a means or instrument for achieving order or

peace; its most fundamental or primary injunction is, "Do not do to others what you do not want done to yourself." According to La Bonnardière, loc. cit., p. 305 (whose article I did not become acquainted with till my own views had been worked out), what we designate Augustine's primary precept does not precisely derive from Tb 4.16 but is "le precepte fondamentale de la loi naturelle." After consulting La Bonnardière, I came across the judicious reflection of H. Deane on the natural law, which underscores that what we style the primary precept is "the basic precept of the natural law," in *The Political and Social Ideas of St. Augustine*, 86-92, especially 86-7. Contrary to the opinion of some scholars, this maxim, because negatively formulated, cannot be identified with the affirmatively couched Golden Rule, "As you want men to do to you, so do you to them" (Lk 6.31) or, in the more common version, "Do to others as you would have them do to you." As W. Barclay points out in *The Gospel of Luke*, 79, what we name Augustine's primary precept was enunciated by the renowned Jewish rabbi Hillel, Philo, and, among pagans, by Isocrates, the Stoics, and Confucius. The Golden Rule originated with Christ alone. According to Augustine, the Golden Rule (though he does not employ this term) issues from the second commandment, to love one's neighbor as oneself; see CF 19.14 (see n. 32 above and its referent in the text), along with ME 27.42-54 and 28.55-6, and P 51.10 (see n. 32).

In "Augustine, Thomas Aquinas, and the Problem of Natural Law," *Mediaevalia* 4 (1978), 179-208, reprinted as Chapter 10 in *Classical Christianity and the Political Order*, 199-222, E. Fortin shrewdly points out Aquinas' modification of Augustine's natural law theory. Augustine specifies only two laws, eternal and natural; Aquinus differentiates four types, eternal, natural, human, and divine. Again, Thomas grants more scope to reason independent of revelation. Moreover, whereas Aquinas sees the commandments of the second table as equivalent to the natural law, Augustine hesitates to equate the two.

39. G. Combès, *La doctrine politique de saint Augustin*, 78.
40. C. Dawson, *Progress and Religion*, 203.
41. We have deferred to later consideration particular cases of divine intervention that suspends lower-level precepts of the natural law such as the command to Abraham to slay Isaac and the despoliation of Egyptian property.
42. In justifying God's right to introduce fresh measures of action by analogy with the right of a king to enact new laws, Augustine only skims the surface of a complex political philosophy that, touched on in many works, is principally expounded in *The City of God*. For balanced, though diverging, accounts of his political thought, see Combès and Deane. D. Burt's more recent *Friendship and Society* argues that the state in Augustine is a natural institution.. See E. Fortin's expert reflections in "The Political Thought of St. Augustine," in *History of Political Philosophy*, (ed.) L. Strauss and J. Cropsey, 176-205; reprinted as Chapter 1 in E. Fortin, *Classical Christianity and the Political Order*, 1-29. See also R. Dodaro, "Church and State," AE 176-84, especially 181-4.
43. The source of the definition is *Tusc. disp.* 3.5.11. On the connection of *libido* in the definition, *ulciscendi libido*, with the other shades of meaning see Bonner, 398-401.

44. This Stoic division of the passions was channeled to Augustine through Cicero; *Tusc. disp.* 3.11 24 and 4.4.10.

45. For a thorough discussion of the variant expressions of the triple concupiscence see Du Roy, 343-52. It seems necessary to append one clarifying remark to Du Roy's excellent research. Augustine uses "pride" analogously, chiefly in two related senses (i) Principally and primarily pride means self-exaltation, the pretension to live and act on one's own power apart from God (2.6.13 and 3.8.16. M 6.13.40. GCM 2.5.6. J 25.15-6. T 12.9.14. CD 12.1). Pride is the beginning of all sin in the history of mankind (Eccli 10.15) and it is first also according to the logic of morality, i.e., it is the primary radix, the cause, of all other sins (J 25.15 and T 12.9.14). Thus the three concupiscences in which various sins are rooted (3.8.16) are themselves rooted in pride. (ii) Pride is employed in an extended sense to refer to *ambitio saeculi* (10.31.41; 36.59. VR 3.4), worldly ambition or the hot pursuit of honors, or to *libido principandi*, the disordered desire to achieve first place (3.8.16). As the content of 3.8.16 indicates, this latter concupiscence or pride in the broad sense itself arises from pride in the primary sense, which is *privata superbia* that tries to play God by substituting its own minuscule good for the common good that is God.

46. In the opinion of W. Green, in *Initum Omnis Peccati Superbia*, 412-3, Augustine, encountering the Pelagian contention that every sin is one of pride, departs from his earlier view that pride accounts for all other sins and embraces, as a final position, the more guarded claim that some sins take their rise from ignorance and weakness. Pride continues as the beginning of every sin (Eccli 10.15) but only in the historical sense; it was the first sin committed by man (NG 29.33 and P 118 [S.9].1). However, closer scrutiny suggests that Augustine's qualification is a nuance that clarifies rather than alters his earlier stand. As J 25.16 plainly evidences, pride is also structurally the cause of all sins: *Caput omnium morborom superbia est, quia caput omnium peccatorum superbia est.* By purging the humor that causes ulcers, a physician wholly heals his patient; similarly, if pride were purged from the soul, all iniquity would vanish. Thus not every sin is proximately due to pride, but pride remains the remote, ultimate, primary radix of all sins. In short, some sins are immediately traceable to ignorance and weakness; others are rooted in the triple concupiscence; but the head, the ultimate source of all sins, is pride.

47. LA 3.17.48, a passage written earlier, defines avarice in the specific sense as immoderate desire of possessions, immoderate because it seeks more than is sufficient or necessary for the preservation of life. Viewed generally, avarice is identified with cupidity or a disordered will, which is the root of all evils (1 Tim 6.10). This interpretation of avarice in general jibes nicely with the underlying anti-Manichean thrust of LA that answers the question posed by the Manichees and long pondered by Augustine: *unde malum?* The source of moral evil is not agents of darkness, not substantially evil things, not an evil nature within man, but a perverted will, one that turns away from divine and stable goods and turns downward to changeable and uncertain goods (LA 1.16.35).

48. See the judicious comments of J. Harvey, *Moral Theology of the Confessions of St. Augustine*, 14-5.

49. See *Regula sancti patris nostri Augustini*, tr. R. Russell, 1.8.
50. Augustine's resolution of the Abraham-Isaac crux seems linguistically and analytically more deft than the more controverted solution proposed by S. Kierkegaard in *Fear and Trembling*, tr. W. Lowrie. This intense religious thinker hails Abraham as a "knight of faith" (86-8) who "believed by virtue of the absurd" (47), submitting to "a paradox" that transformed "a murder into a holy act" (64). However, Kierkegaard, careful examination shows, does not advocate an antinomian irrationalism; the absurd is what is beyond "all human reckoning" (47) or understanding, the murder is only seeming, and the paradox only apparent. Still, his overcharged rhetoric, with a predilection for shock effects, blunts the force of his argument, leaving him vulnerable to attacks mounted by rationalist critics. Apart from his loose language, Kierkegaard's conceptual tools seem partially defective. He does not evidence a refined grasp of eternal and natural law; his knowledge of moral law is cramped by Kantian and Hegelian categories. Moreover, he tends to exaggerate to the point of antithesis the differences between faith and reason. But Augustine, besides sticking to exact terms, sensitively situates the divine command within the framework of eternal and natural law. Too, while reverencing the grandeur of divine belief, he accords proper attention to the nuanced compatibility of faith and reason. Thus in his eyes Abraham's obedience does not in the least hint at or savor of the irrational or immoral. Abraham's yes to God is super-rational and super-moral, a heroic act illumined and empowered by divine light. On Kierkegaard see J. Collins, *The Mind of Kierkegaard*, 91-6, and R. Perkins (ed.), *Kierkegaard's Fear and Trembling: Critical Appraisals*.
51. Harvey, *Moral Theology of Confessions*, 13-4.
52. To bolster their claim to be full Christians, the maturation of the semi-Christianity of Catholics, Manichees advanced the audacious claim that whereas Pauline Christianity saw only darkly and in part (1 Cor 13.9, 12), Mani's Christianity views all things with perfect clarity and discloses the truth face to face. A more critical Augustine rejects this: dupes of Mani feed on the wind, i.e., are nourished by notions empty of truth, and bow down to idols of their own heart, false gods fabricated by footloose imagination (CF 15.5).
53. In the line of religious knowledge *pueri* and *senes* are grouped as *aetates* or stages of growth not by time or physiological age but by virtue and analytical discernment (MM 10.17). At the time Augustine fell into Manichean hands, he was an adolescent whose head was stuffed with puerile opinions (MM 10.16). Catholic teaching safeguards its members who have progressed beyond mental puerility into the "white hairs" of wisdom, which is in the line not of physiological time but mental maturity (MM 10.17). The Church nurses at its bosom those who are mere babes in doctrine so as to later raise them to doctrinal maturity (MM 10.17).
54. More than the common sense is required to detect the absurdities in Manichean tenets. Manicheans prey on the unlettered who are devoid of education in basic physical philosophy and are therefore unable to rise above image-thinking. Invisible objects are cleverly presented to the uneducated in the guise of visible things. Fortunately, many of those vulnerable to Manichean

deception resist their attack through healthy religious fear grounded in fundamental faith (MM 16.38). In 13.30.45, Augustine touches on the physical and metaphysical absurdities consequent upon the denial of creation.

55.   The theory of metempsychosis weighs down the Manichean conscience with guilt for multiple murders. Logically extended, this doctrine entails that souls formerly inhabiting human bodies are now encased in the bodies of horses, foxes, weasels, mice, locusts, bees, flies, lice, and bedbugs, the last three species being routinely exterminated every week or month (GL 7.9.12–11.17).

56.   According to Manicheism, there are three different Christs. "The first is the one whom the earth, conceiving by the power of the Holy Spirit, brings forth as suffering; this Christ is not only hanging from every tree but lies within every plant. The second Christ was crucified under Pontius Pilate. The third is the Christ divided between sun and moon" (CF 20.11). (i) The *Jesus patibilis* is the Jesus of light present in all trees and vegetables, and in virtue of this enclosure in matter is said to be on the cross or crucified (MM 17.54. P 140.12). (ii) The second Jesus, the "Son of Greatness," was only apparently crucified under Pilate. As divine, Christ's nature could not be commingled with and sullied by matter. In fact, Christ was neither born nor died (CF 30.6; 5.2.S 92.2.3; 83.1.). (iii) Jesus the splendor had a dual location; as the power of God, he dwelt in the sun and, as the wisdom of God, in the moon (CF 20.8). A fourth Jesus, the God incarnate proclaimed by Catholic Christians, is bogus, a sort of salvific charlatan; not a genuine savior but a serpent or devil incarnate was actually crucified (H 46.37). Notice, Jesus suffering in matter is rather saved than savior; he has to be "redeemed" from enslavement to matter (CF 2.5). The connection between the three Christs is entirely nominal; the name Christ is used equivocally by Manicheans.

57.   The Manichean church was hierarchally organized. Mani's successor was the principal *magister*, who exercised the highest authority, his closest advisors being twelve *magistri*, the number apparently modeled after the twelve apostles. Below the teachers were seventy-two bishops, a figure recalling the number of Christ's disciples. Next lower in rank were 360 priests. Below these were the unordained elect, with the auditors lowest in rank, both unlimited in number. Only elect could be ordained priests by bishops; bishops, in turn, were ordained by teachers (H 46.38). Faustus, whose scientific learning proved sadly deficient, was a bishop (5.3.3). Fortunatus, who was converted to Catholicism after debating Augustine, was a priest (Fort prol. R 1.15.1). Among the elect was the Felix, who, after being defeated in debate by Augustine, felt compelled to leave Hippo. Certain documents indicate that there were women auditors and women elect, but their roles, if any, in the religious activity remain vague. Coyle, 348-51. See also S. Lieu, *Manicheism*, 20-1.

58.   The assonance of Augustine's phrase, *dente et ventre*, "by tooth and stomach," is hard to convey in English. Even in translation the irony retains its bite: sheerly material activities, mastication and digestion, in the lower body effect the liberation of particles of God.

59.   According to the *Fibrist Al-alum* ("Catalog of the Sciences"), "the power of the Father of Greatness is the five angels, *viz.*, the air, the wind. the light, the water,

and the fire" (quoted in F. Burkitt, *Religion of the Manicheans*, 50). The *Fibrist* was finished in 987 by An-Nadim. The section on Manichaeism was translated and commented on by G. Flügel, *Mani, seine Lehre und seine Schriffen*, (Coyle, p.38 with n. 169). In addition to the Father of Greatness, there are large numbers of gods and angels (CF 15.5); in the Manichean kingdom angels dwell in happiness (CF 15.6); in addition to the supreme deity, the other lofty ruler is surrounded by his angels (CF 15.6).

60. Because mythical, largely woven by ingenious imagination, the Manichean system throughout crumbles to bits against the bedrock of observed and analyzed fact. Augustine has little trouble adducing additional incoherences in the tissue of fantasies that did dubious service as a Manichean philosophy of nature. It seems strange that trees endowed with a rational soul (MM 17.55) were not instructed by Manichean apostles of light (MM 17.56). Since it is quite probable that many trees are the present forms of existence of men whose insufficiency of virtue in a previous life caused them to fall to the arboreal plane, the elect should be hard at work every day cutting down trees so as to release these souls and to guide them to full salvation (MM 17.55). Moreover, trees, when struck, give no indication at all that they are suffering the least pain. Indeed when their branches are cut by pruning, they do not perish because of the wounds but flourish more fruitfully (MM 17.59). Finally, the elect are not rendered oddly inculpable by requiring auditors to commit the crime of plucking fruit for them; indirectly but really they cooperate in the crime committed against the fig tree (MM 17.57).

61. Besides, the Manichees were virtually demon-worshippers. In deflecting Faustus' charge that Christians were essentially akin to pagans (CF 20.3-4), Augustine counter-argued that the pagans were closer to the truth than the Manicheans since they worship real things while the Manicheans largely worship purely fictional entities (CF 20.5). In their false worship both pagans and Manicheans indirectly worship demons, in accord with the Apostle's words, "the sacrifices of the Gentiles are sacrificed to demons, not to God" (1 Cor 10.20).

62. P. Courcelle, *Les Confessions de saint Augustin dans la tradition littéraire*, 127-36, marshals evidence to show that autobiographical dreams or visions were not uncommon in African Christianity. But unlike the content of the dreams of Donatists, those of Monica were indubitably authentic since, consonant with Catholic doctrine and welling up from a deep life of prayer, their forecasts actually eventuated; they met the pragmatic (not pragmatistic) test, "By their fruits you shall know them," i.e., the fruits of the Spirit grow the more in the recipient of the visions. Significantly, Monica was gifted with the charism of discernment of spirits that empowered her to distinguish between dreams of divine origin and those arising from the human spirit (CG 12.23) See L. Ferrari, "The Dreams of Saint Monica in St. Augustine's *Confessions*," AS 10 (1979), 3-17, in particular, 6-7. Also, M. Dulaey, *La rêve dans la vie et la pensée de saint Augustin*.

63. The heavenly visitant is described as *iuvenem...arridentem*. While *iuvenis* is usually rendered "a young man", it seems well to keep in mind that the word

means a mature man, who has reached his thirtieth year (7.1.1). The context suggests that *arridens* does not signify laughing but smiling.

64.   L. Ferrari, "Monica on the Wooden Ruler," AS 6 (1975), 193-205, deftly and ingeniously but always with strong textual support, traces the ramifications of the *regula* and its wooden character as implying the wood of the cross of Christ the king. According to S. Poque, *Riv. stor. e lett. rel.* 30 (1984), 480-8, *regula* means a *chorobates*, which is a rule around ten feet long, a leveling instrument employed in the construction of aqueducts (D.2. 199, n. under *regula*). This is a useful suggestion possibly throwing fresh light on a key feature of Monica's dream, yet it seems far from decisive. In Augustine the term *regula* ordinarily signifies a measuring-rod or analogously a rule or standard of faith. Had he had recourse to this unusual sense, it seems reasonable to think that he would have clarified the term by a reference to *chorobates.* The comparison with 8.2.5, which provides the detail that Victorinus made his profession of faith *de loco eminentiore* is inapt since Augustine significantly adds the qualifying remark that a raised platform for profession of faith was a custom peculiar to Rome. As already mentioned, no qualifier is inserted in 3.11.19 to indicate a peculiar, highly specialized sense of *regula.* How, some may wonder, could Monica and Augustine stand on the usual rule? Figures in a dream are not ordinarily life-size; the smaller apparitions of the two could be easily envisaged standing on a somewhat expanded wooden ruler.

65.   The massive fact that is the tremendous mystery of providence caring for the single individual who was Augustine is one central theme that lends cohesion and texture to the seemingly odd web of circumstances which made up his pre-Christian groping for light and meaning; a web in which at times he appeared hopelessly entangled in the pull of wayward appetites. Yet God continuously hovered over him, directing him "by marvelous and hidden ways" (4.4.7; 5.7.10, 5.13; 7.21.27) through the hurly-burly of events and the darkness within the deeps of his spirit (BA 13, 185). Especially marvelous, basically really miraculous, was the fructification of good from evil. By his goodness and super-power, God caused smooth roads to emerge from rough tracks, straight paths from curved lanes; the way that is Christ from the false ways of the triple concupiscence; upright stance on the wooden rule of faith after supineness in Manichean materialism. God writes straight with crooked lines, goes the familiar Portuguese proverb; this providential subtheme of capitalizing on evil for the production of good runs through the first nine books of the *Confessions.* To choose only a few instances, God oriented the excessive punishments of early teachers to rein in trends towards self-assertiveness. God employed the errors of his teachers, who were driving him to learn, to work toward his advantage (1.12.9). Out of his heartless deception of Monica prior to sailing to Rome without her, the all-provident Father eventually drew the good of his conversion (5.8.15) principally through Ambrose, the Lord's chosen preacher of reassuring truth and love (1.1.1). Especially through his bitter experience in the barren wilderness or the Manichean night was Augustine's soul readied for the food and light of Catholic truth. Abjection in Manichean unwisdom disposed Augustine toward humility. In stumbling along the tortuous

Manichean path, his soul learned its fragility through constant downfalls, which opened it to dependence on God. As he was whirled about in Manichean multiplicity, he hungered the more for the One; the more wretched he was, the nearer God moved toward him (6.16.26). In the pit of Manicheism his self-sufficiency and vanity were broken to pieces; out of this fragmented self God formed Augustine into a lowly seeker of the truth that was to be actually attained through the humble mediator, Christ Jesus (7.18.24;21.27).

66.   This objection was first formulated in its essentials by the Greek philosopher Epicurus (c.340–271 B.C.). As recounted by the Christian apologist Lactantius (c.260–c.320), *De ira Dei*, ML 7.121A, Epicurus' repudiation of divine providence rests on an exhaustive four-part division of the ways in which God can conceivably confront and blot out evil. (i) God wills to get rid of evil but cannot. (ii) He can but will not remove evil. (iii) He neither will not nor cannot remove evil. In implying that God is weak and/or envious, these first three alternatives incongruously construe God along unGodlike lines. (iv) God both wills to and can get rid of evil. This fourth possibility, the only one that harmonizes with the divine nature, seems nullified by insuperable difficulties. (a) In a world cared for by a God good and powerful enough to forestall all evil, how did, how could, easily preventable evil arise? (b) Even granted that evil somehow unexplainably springs up in a universe controlled by a provident God, why does a God sufficiently good and powerful not exercise his will and power to immediately obliterate all evil? Within the constricted horizon of Epicurus' theology, which pictures gods as quasi-human in form and therefore finite, the objection against divine providence is indeed irresolvable. Hence, he concludes, the gods have to be detached from and unconcerned about human weal and woe. Augustine repels this powerful polemic by acutely perceiving that, precisely because he is God, i.e., unlimited in goodness and power, God can provide or make room for evil in the universe he creates and governs. Out of evil his infinite power miraculously harvests good planned by his infinite wisdom and flowing from his infinite goodness (EN 3.10-1). At present we cannot pinpoint the source or sources through which Augustine became acquainted with the gist of Epicurus' argument. Some scholars conjecture that the third book of Cicero's *De nat. deor*, now lost, may have transmitted Epicurus' gravamen to Augustine. Whatever the value of such speculation, it seems likely that fourth- and fifth-century Christian thinkers were commonly aware of and engaged in informal as well as formal exchanges (independently of explicit references to or reliance upon particular sources) concerning the kernel of Epicurus' attack against providence. In fine, the thorny issues Epicurus raised probably constituted a stock but no mean part of the problem of God that Christian theologians and apologists of Augustine's day had to wrestle with.

67.   A bishop is superior in status to an ordinary priest (E 82.3.33), given by special ordination the authority to govern his community as pastor and teacher (P 126.3; 183.2. E 209.3). Grabowski, *Church*, 105-6.

68.   The translations of P. de Labriolle and Tréhorel-Bouissou (BA 13,402), taking Monica as the subject of Augustine's parenthetical remark, render *faciebat enim*

hoc, quos forte idoneos invenisset: "For she used to make a like request when she met individuals capable of instructing her son."

69. According to the *Mani-Codex*, it was the practice of early Manichees to bring young children into the fold. See S. Lieu, *Manicheism in Mesopotamia and the Roman East*, 151.

Book Four

Manichee and Teacher
in Thagaste and Carthage

In addition to Manicheism, he was duped by astrology (3.4-6), allegience to which would last for another decade. Crushed by the loss of the closest friend of his youth (4.7-7.12), he probed the inescapability of death in a material world (10.15--11.17). He then scrutinized his motives in dedicating his first work (13.20) to a famous Roman orator (14.21-31). Happily, there fell into his hands Aristotle's *Categories* (16.28), which exposed a rough-stroke realistic picture of the universe. Yet, as he later perceived, because the academic is only a relative good, secular learning could not deliver him from Manichean darkness (16.29-31).

Chapter 1: This-Worldly and Manichean Delusions

1. Augustine spent nine years as a Manichee; from 373 to 382 he was a committed member of this pseudo-Christian sect. But as late as autumn, 384 (5.13.23), eleven years after his initiation, he was still a nominal adherent. For close to one-third of life up to young manhood he was a believer in and practitioner of Manichean creed, code, and cult. A not inconsiderable portion of Books 3-6 portrays him striving to break its manacles. His intellectual conversion (5.14. 24-5; 6.4.5-6; 7.2.3; 7.9.13-4; 7.10.16) was principally a Manichean deconversion. During the same period he taught liberal arts, first at Thagaste (4.4.7), then at Carthage (4.7.12). As professional teacher and ardent Manichee, he was led astray and led others astray; steeped in miscon-

ceptions, he industriously purveyed falsities to others while dominated by wayward desires, in particular, the triple concupiscence. As a rhetorician, he was charmed by misleading values, panting after higher social and political status, to be gained by all the clever techniques, including fabrication of lies, that he could deploy. Naturally he indoctrinated his students in like glittering ideals; under his tutelage they could become well-heeled, renowned, and influential. The phrase, "the arts that are called liberal," may carry a note of implied irony; liberal in name, they often turned out to be, in fact, illiberal or counter-liberal. As actually inculcated by teachers in servitude to inordinate appetites, the liberal disciplines, rather than freeing the mind, tended to become instruments for enslaving the spirit of the student.

Gulled by Manichees' astute apologetic for a higher, purely rational Christianity, he became a fervent proselytizer; the combination of zealotry, energy, and dialectical intricacy overwhelmed Catholic disputants, sweeping many into his new religion. Like a wolf pouncing on a flock of sheep, in his early Manichean years he "ravaged" the faith of Catholics "with a ferocious loquacity" (DA 9.11. DP 2.55). He attracted to the sect Romanianus (CA 1.1.3), Alypius, who was beguiled by Manichean asceticism (6.7.12), his unnamed friend (4.4.7), and Honoratus, a fellow student at Carthage (UC 1.2), among others, though he was never able to breach Monica's unshakable faith (3.11.20) or convince the critical Nebridius (7.2.3). On the basis of 9.3.6, which characterizes Nebridius as a Docetist, some have described him as a Manichee; however, while all Manichees were Docetists, not all Docetists were Manichees. A first-rate mind can make the most counter-evidential errors look appealing, waffling about glaring difficulties along with ignoring plain inconsistencies. In the modern world some philosophies with an apparently rigorous logical apparatus construct universes of discourse that match, in some respect, some of the Manichean incoherencies. Searchingly scrutinized, the foundations of the system of I. Kant (1724-1804) seem somewhat strange. As is well known, he maintained that space and time are forms of sensuous intuition and that causal patterns are basically mental frames imposed on the real. However, whereas the Kantian mind of each individual lays down the laws of nature in space and time, cosmogony and paleontology infer a universe shaping events prior to man and to all life. Again, it is extremely odd to imply that a man's body, brain, and psyche, all causally patterned, are, in effect, somehow basically manufactured by himself. Yet in spite of these and other insuperable paradoxes, Kant's extraordinary acumen was able to sway many thinkers. If Kant could overcome objections of fellow philosophers, it becomes understandable how a genius like Augustine could make a bizarre religious system look ideationally compelling.

He lived a kind of double life, the public acceptable, the private socially disapproved.[1] His dissemination of errors about the goals of living was open to social inspection. He functioned as a respectable rhetorician, schooling his students in a program of ideas and implied values not essentially divergent from that of colleagues. But his Manichean liaison had to be kept secret, for Manichean practices had been barred for decades; the latest law proscribing it had been enacted only four years prior to his conversion.[2] Governmental officials feared Manicheism as a potentially subversive influence on Roman mores; strict Manichean abjuration of marriage was considered socially destructive. The work and worship of Manichees were perforce carried on clandestinely, their conventicles concealed from the eyes of authorities. As a rhetorician, he was swollen with pride; as a Manichee, he was sunk in superstition; in both spheres the outcome was vanity or untruth, manifest in personal vacuity and moral fruitlessness. Along with companion Manichean sectaries, he hungered for empty fame and recognition to be garnered through the applause of audiences, winning prizes in poetry contests, and wearing a crown of grass which, as crown, symbolized victory but which, as grass, symbolized the quickly withering character of such triumphs.[3] He continued to indulge in undisciplined living by pursuing the superficial entertainment of stage shows and by giving free rein to sexual appetite. When he and fellow Manichees relied on Manichean practices for cleansing from pride, vanity, and lust, they were cruelly cheated; the path of purgation was fraudulent. As indicated above (3.10.18), the elect were believed to be divinely deputed to liberate, through their digestive processes, angels, that is, good elements like air and light, and gods, which were particles of the divine substance imprisoned in the darkness of fruits and vegetables. By separating the light from the dark factors in permissible food, the stomachs of Manichean holy men fashioned angels and gods. One principal responsibility of hearers, the class of the imperfect to which Augustine belonged, was to offer alms, namely, to prepare and serve proper fruits and vegetables (such as melons, grapes, and mushrooms) to the elect. This almsgiving brought deliverance in a twofold sense. First, the particles of light journeyed back to the domain of light, making one more advance in the campaign toward the eventual victory of the Kingdom of Light. Then, in accord with the Manichean doctrine of reincarnation, devotion to the elect helped guarantee hearers return to earth in the body of an elect and eventual entrance into the Kingdom of Light. The elect, considered, recall, saviors of God (P 140.12) were granted special reverence; not only from bishops, priests, and deacons, but also from the elect did kneeling hearers receive a blessing through the imposition of hands (E 236.2). Augustine's past transgressions may excite ridicule from the self-exalted because these have never passed through what Kant somewhere called the hell of self-knowledge; because they have never fallen into the pit of sin, which, sorrowed over, turns humiliation into humility. Sins repented for, in deflating the soul, become salubrious—healing brings the health of humility (CG 9.23-4). Confessing his shameful past, he confesses to, or praises, God for his mercy.

Adapting the words of Ps 26.6, he offers God a sacrifice of jubilation. As the psalmist goes round the tabernacles of the Lord, jubilating over the marvels of creation (P 26 [En. 2].13), so he goes round in memory past wanderings in darkness, jubilating over wonder upon wonder that in the line of recreation divine mercy has wrought in his spirit (P 88 [S.1].15-7). The sacrifice celebrated within is praise that causes his spirit to cleave more closely to God; and insofar as he has died to self to live for God, he himself is that sacrifice (CD 10.6). Taken strictly, jubilation, a species of praise, breaks forth in joyful sounds untranslatable in any human language (P 102.8). At times during his meditation Augustine may have cried out in ineffable accents of delight as he retraversed in contemplation the beauty of divine pity. Here, because he articulates his praise in a structured tongue, jubilation is employed in the broad sense to signify praise in general. Without God his merely natural light is blindness hurling him over the precipice to perdition; only with God is he assured energy for doing good moment to moment from the God who is pure goodness. He is absolutely dependent on the continuous nurture of God; like a tiny child nursing at the breast, he constantly feeds on life flowing from the divine bosom. Perhaps better put, while his Christian living is that of a suckling, still immature as regards understanding, he may become, in addition, a mature Christian, able to eat solid food, the incorruptible knowledge and charity with which God nurtures his sons and daughters (P 8.5). Whether a neophyte or a proficient, he requires at every moment divine nourishment, either milk or solid food, to stick to the narrow road of faith-filled love. Moreover, the lesson of inevitable self-wrought downfalls is written in every person's moral career. Any man, no matter how magnificently endowed, is no more than a human being. Thrown back on his own devices because he repulses divine support, a man,recall, has an infinite potential for evil; there is no sin, however horrifying, that he is not capable of committing, not once but again and again to the point of a perfection of corruption (S 99.6.6). Man who is *capax Dei* is also *capax peccati*; when he abjures union with God, there is no abyss of wickedness into which he cannot plummet. The irony of the mighty mocking him is that their strength is bogus; men relying solely on their own moral sinews are reeds shaken in the wind. The weak and indigent, denuded of the illusion that they are masters of their fates and captains of their souls, confess any evil they have done while they confess to, that is, praise, God for any good they have managed to accomplish.

Chapter 2: Teacher of Rhetoric, Concubinage, Rejection of Haruspex

2. The two features of nine-some years of his life, his rhetorical profession and his adhesion to Manicheism, are the points around which this chapter organizes three events, its treatment thematic rather than strictly chronological. He first speaks of his life as a teacher of rhetoric at Carthage (376). Next, he reports the start of his concubinage while a student at Carthage (370), an arrangement which, while prior to his becoming a Manichee, dovetailed nicely with Manichean disapproval of child-bearing. Third, refusal to avail himself of the services of a haruspex arose out of Manichean convictions, which ironically ensnared him in equally reprehensible sacrifices to demons. The sentence at the outset, "In those years I was teaching the art of rhetoric," is elliptical because for at least one year or, more probably, two years (c. 374-6), he taught grammar, not

rhetoric, at Thagaste. The ellipsis is defensible since he spent seven out of his nine years as a committed Manichee in teaching rhetoric, which he deprecates as a smooth salesmanship of words. Ironically, while schooling his charges in techniques that would conquer rivals, he himself was conquered by false desires for fame and honors. He wanted his students to be good in the conventional academic sense; talented, hardworking, eager to become adept in stratagems of rhetoric but not necessarily good in the strictly moral sense. Nor were they always good in terms of classroom discipline; later he left Carthage for Rome partly because his Carthaginian students were chronically disruptive, and at times unmanageable in class, turning instruction into daily anguish for teacher and serious students (5.8.14). Without trickery, i.e., candidly and diligently, he instilled in his students all the tools of trickery an accomplished rhetorician must command. Without deceit he armed budding rhetoricians with a sophisticated arsenal of deceit. He mitigated the injustice aimed at by warning them against making the right a capital wrong, i.e., trumping up evidence that would condemn the innocent to execution. But he encouraged his students to become expert in techniques to make the wrong look right, thus sparing the head of a criminal. As noted earlier, he is leveling strictures not against rhetoric but against its intellectual and moral abuse. In his day rhetoric, departing from the foundations of Plato and Aristotle, had loosened its moorings in theoretical and practical philosophy. No longer an instrument in the service of truth and justice, it had degenerated into a tool for masquerading the false as true and for helping malefactors evade due punishment. What he laments is not rhetoric as such but rhetoric as evilly exercised. Rhetoric that has gone astray from its proper office discredits true rhetoric; in this sorry state of rhetoric he justifiably pours contempt on rhetoric (witness the critique of sophists' rhetoric in Plato).[4]

God, distant because driven away by pride, watched him slipping on the treacherous path of moral emptiness, yet his loyalty to the moral precept of rhetoric insisted upon by Cicero[5] was one redeeming feature in his largely amoral teaching. Not once did he breach the moral rule that a rhetor must never manipulate evidence to secure the death sentence of a man he knows to be innocent, though he may defend a client he knows is guilty since in courtroom the prosecution carries the burden of proof.[6] This faith, which here means not belief but good faith in the sense of adherence to moral principle, was a spark of light gleaming through the near-suffocating smoke, the contrivances of calculated sophistry. To the best of his capacity he trained his students in one form of moral observance—a shining point, even though they learned from him by word and example to love vanity, to prize success as the highest good, and to cultivate lying, the suppression of truth and invention of falsehood, to shore up a questionable case.

In those years also, he was living with a woman. Actually their cohabitation started in 370/1, prior to his becoming a Manichee. It is not whitewashing the relationship to note that she was not a mistress, a paramour on the side, but a concubine, a kind of quasi-wife who was more than a common-law partner. Both Church and state recognized concubinage as a sort of de facto marriage that entailed no public scandal. Apparently his unnamed concubine was of such a lower class that it was impossible for her to be strictly his wife. Hence their relationship, which he says, was not lawful, was easily dissolved years later, without recourse to divorce (6.15.28). Nor was this an arrangement ambition dictated as a convenience for a period; he explicitly states that his decision to take a concubine was governed by passion for ongoing sexual satisfaction. His roving eye found the girl physically desirable; and then without circumspection, with moral discernment not vigilant but somnolent (MM 1.24.45), he precipitously started to cohabit with her. Yet love of some sort was enkindled, so that Augustine remained faithful, never once trysting with another, till they parted in Milan some fifteen years later. Their union was so intimate that Augustine speaks of her as "torn from [his] side"; his heart with which her heart was inwardly one was wounded, its blood gushing out (6.15.25). Omission of her name indicates not coldness but sensitivity to her need for anonymity. Were her name disclosed, she would have been the object of busybodies cruelly invading her privacy and disturbing her dedication to her new Christian commitment as a celibate (6.15.25). Nevertheless, the love that brought a measure of contentment to their relationship was far removed from the genuine love quickening Christian marriage. Whereas Christian marital union aims at procreating children, concubinage is inherently selfish. Every method is used to ensure that there will be no offspring, the partners seeking only their own sexual pleasure. But when the unwanted child, its conception contrary to the will of the partners, does unexpectedly come on the scene, its sweetness compels the couple to delight in him. So Augustine's first and only child was significantly named Adeodatus, literally gift of God, which in its Punic form, Iatanbaal, was common in North Africa. All that was good in him was due to the Father; only the sin that conceived him was attributable to his father (9.6.14). Adeodatus was an unsought-for boon, a beautiful accident, but an accident nonetheless. Concubinage not only does not welcome children; it deliberately shuns them. Hence he calls this association a compact or a deal of lustful or sheerly pleasure-pursuing love. No second child followed because Augustine's original determination to avoid children was reinforced by the anti-life Manichean moral teaching that considered child-bearing in marriage a graver sin than cohabitation. Manichean marriage was, in effect, a concubinage, rated superior to genuine marriage because child-bearing in the latter incarcerates the soul within darksome flesh (MM 2.18.66). The Manichees also recommended contraceptive procedures whereby he could successfully practice planned parenthood by planning how not to be a parent. He was advised to observe periodic abstinence and ordered, when necessary, to spill the God within the seed rather than enchain him in the carnal bondage of the womb (CF 22.30); a directive that proposes withdrawal as a means of birth control.[7] Thus though his was initially a pre-Manichean concubinage, Augustine learned by hard experience the superiority of selfless-oriented Christian marriage to its selfish Manichean counterpart, which, whatever its legal status, was no better than the concubinage that was a bargain of sexual gratification within one household.

3. On one occasion, when, while teaching in Carthage (376-83), he decided to enter a poetry contest, a haruspex, a diviner of events through the reading of animal entrails, promised to guarantee his victory if adequately compensated.[8] Augustine recoiled in horror at the proposal. He would spurn a crown of imperishable gold if it were won at the price of the life of even a single fly. He detested the rites of haruspices as filthy because they involved the killing of animals which, for Manichean doctrine, was murder (MM 12.54). These homicidal practices effectively leagued diviners with demons in the spread of the Kingdom of Darkness. Further, the slaughter of the animals was explicitly intended as supplication to demons. He was right in repudiating solicitation of demons as evil, but his reason was

wrong, based as it was on faulty Manichean tenets. He did not spurn the soothsayer's offer "out of your [God's] chastity" or pure love; God's chastity or holiness embraces the divine good alone while human chastity or holiness that loves God gratis (P 72.33) shares in divine chastity.[9] The chaste love that as a Manichee he lacked some twenty years before (c. 376) he now possesses as a Christian (c. 397); so he addresses the Lord, "God of my heart," the God of a heart that loves him, as its one and only spouse (P 72.32). He had no inkling of this love; he did not know how to love God because he did not really know God, conceiving him only as a huge corporeal being of light in his kingdom peopled by lightsome gods and angels, with sun and moon worshipped as either divine beings or divine shrines. So in hankering after these fantasies, he could not be espoused to the true God in pure love; rather, playing the wanton, he was a fornicator deserting true love, his heart frozen stiff in death (P 72.32). He could not love the true God because he was putting his faith in falsities; the wind or the spirit of love was denied him because he was feeding the winds, venting errors that made him food for unclean spirits (CS 26). Ironically, the Manichean superstition on the basis of which he had shrunk from assenting to the soothsayer's sacrifice implicitly involved sacrifice to demons. Thus to feed the winds through profession of religious errors is nothing other than to feed demons or offer them sacrifice; proud spirits do not wax mainly on the fragrance and smoke of animal sacrifice but on religious untruths. Such errors excite in them a perverse pleasure because, as totally committed to the lie, they enjoy hoodwinking fallible humans and too because, as apes of God, they crave such sacrifice as quasi-divine homage testifying to their own majesty (CF 20.22). A Manichee like Augustine, cocksure that he was thriving in light while actually buried in darkness, was also an object of demonic derision; in his own eyes standing right side up, he was actually positioned upside down. As with the overturners (3.3.6) but on another plane, he was mocked by primordial overturners who never stop straining to turn human lives topsy-turvy. As the unwitting cat's-paw of demonic malice, he was easily made sport of; thus Manichean beliefs that theoretically opposed demons practically aggrandized their power.

Chapter 3: The Lure of Astrology

4. The "therefore" at the outset indicates a line of reasoning;

because haruspices invoked demons, he had refused the services of a discerner of entrails, but because astrologers did not sacrifice to demons, his Manichean creed allowed him to consult readers of horoscopes. Manicheans not only tolerated but, though some disdained the astrological approach as childish in comparison with Manichean revelation, generally encouraged such consultation because of homage accorded the sun and moon and other planets.[10] Furthermore, their cosmogony contained a considerable number of astrological data. In one work Mani paired the signs of the zodiac with the five regions of the Kingdom of Darkness; an empirically baseless parallel that hardly qualified him as a professional astrologer.[11] For at least three centuries astrologers had been called mathematicians because their predictive art developed out of and resembled the science of astronomers, practical mathematicians who, quantitatively analyzing the movements of the stars, forecast eclipses and conjunctions of planets. But the applied mathematics that was astrology was a pseudo-science, and its adepts who claimed to scientifically foretell the determining influence of the stars on human conduct were scientific quacks whose mathematical ingenuity was at bottom sleight of hand. Christian piety condemns these claims as superstitious because they are at odds with the sinfulness of man and the sinlessness of God. Astrology reduces men to puppets of celestial bodies, and the astrologers from whom they seek advice sell them as slaves to stars implicitly considered false gods (DQ 14.1). Under the total control of heavenly "gods" men are relieved of all responsibility, and sin and guilt brushed off as unscientific illusions. But a Christian undeniably knows that he is a sinner, deeming it good to confess to God in a twofold sense, to praise him and to confess his sin as he asks for deliverance. Yet it would be an abuse of this forgiveness to take it as a carte blanche for further sinning. As after thirty-eight years the miraculously touched cripple rose and walked (JN 5.4), after thirty-two years the crippled Augustine, miraculously cured, began to leap and bound in faith and love; yet he had to go on corresponding with that grace to avoid toppling into pits more demon-ridden than those of his past. Astrologers virtually deal a deathblow to the whole program of inner healing. Eliminate responsibility, and you wipe out sin, thereby doing away with need for healing. An astrologer informs a client, "You did not sin; the heavenly bodies ineluctably determined you to sin. Not you but Venus is responsible for this adultery. The miserliness is the fault of Saturn. Mars is guilty of murder because it compelled you to kill this man"(P 61.23; 128.9). Astral determinism runs counter to the massive fact that Christianity fronts: man is a sinful creature, sometimes actually, always potentially, a breaker of moral law.

A second inconsequence is far worse. If the stars are proximately guilty, God, the ultimate cause of the stars because their creator and director, is primarily guilty. Astrology blasphemously turns the all-holy into the fountainhead of all sin, transmogrifying him into a fiend who perversely produces all the horrors of iniquity in the universe. Such a God is a wickedly absurd caricature of the true God (GL 2.17.35). The God revealed in Jesus is not a lustful miser, hands dripping with the blood of all those murdered throughout history. Rather, he is all-goodness, the wellspring of all justice, ordering all things smoothly. Thus Augustine's life is governed by a God whose power is the executive expression of his mercy, which draws good out of evil. God rains down mercy that gracefully accouters a person to do good that merits rewards (P 61.22); to each God equitably appoints merits or sanctions. Supremely sinless, he does not set his face frigidly against the sinner; his justice is at the service of his pity, which embraces in forgiveness the broken and humbled heart. The man of contrite heart[12] is angry with himself, sorry for the sins that he, not the stars, has committed; and humble, for the all-high lavishes compassion not on the self-centered but on the self-abased (P 74.2; 50.21).

Some twenty years before this 397 critique, astrology had gripped him because its scientific cachet had led to very broad acceptance. In the ancient world astrology was classified as a subspecies or an applied branch of astronomy. It seemed solidly grounded in natural science; it appeared to be an extension to the human domain of proven physico-mathematical knowledge. Over two hundred years before Augustine the *Almagest* of Ptolemy (90-168) mathematically explicated the retrograde movements of the planets, along with other apparently erratic phenomena, through a system of eccentrics and epicycles. Later his *Tetrabiblos* purported to demonstrate how human affairs can be explained by an analysis of celestial phenomena. His astronomical prestige thus lent respectability to the scientific credentials of astrology. According to Ptolemy, just as medicine furnishes diagnoses and prognoses about the body based on physiological findings, so astrology applies astronomical formulas to the inspection and prognostication of human events.[13] In his encounter with Augustine the physician Vindicianus (so named, 7.6.8) implied an analogy between medicine and astrology; grasping the scientific basis for medicine was harder than understanding the scientific grounds of the art of astrology.[14] Whether or not compared with the corpus of Hippocrates, treatises on astrology were mathematically complex and exacting. In the calculation of the significance of a birthday, much more than the determination of the star under whose aegis the birth occurred was required; the astrologer had to reckon, along with other factors, the quarter of heavens where the sun was positioned, the constellations connected with the dominant constellation, the four houses of the planets, and the twelve divisions of the zodiac.[15] Armed with such calculations, the accomplished astrologist could determine why two individuals both died at the age of 67 and could apparently explain the high and low points in various careers worked by beneficent and unfavorable stars.[16] Augustine was persuaded by the scientific-seeming expertise of authors of manuals and almanacs of astrology, who buttressed their case with intricate computations and numerous examples of successful readings and predictions (4.3.5).[17]

Moreover, belief in and recourse to astrology were widespread in the Roman empire. His fascination with astrology had to be conditioned by the fact that astrology nearly saturated the psychic landscape of the ancient world. High and low, the intellectual elite and the illiterate, scientists, philosophers, poets, rhetoricians, political figures, emperors, army commanders, artisans, and farmers trusted that competent astrologers would spell out plainly the propitious times for certain projects and affairs. Not only pagans cultivated it but religious believers, not excluding Christians, who, nominally believing that astrology involved superstition, refused to plant vines during a leap year or to take a business trip during an unpropitious month or to close a business deal on an unlucky day (P 61.23; E 55.2; EN 21. 79-80).[18]

When a client of astrologers, Augustine met Vindicianus, once a practitioner and now a disbeliever of astrology. A man of practical wisdom, whose delicate conscience conformed to strict moral norms, he was a highly competent physician, who served as chief physician of the court of Emperor Valentinian.[19] In 377, during his year as proconsul or governor of North Africa, he placed on Augustine's head a floral crown representing victory in a competition of self-composed dramatic verse. Not as healer but as proconsul did he crown Augustine; for even in his moment of wreathed triumph Augustine's head, symbolizing his mind, stàyed unhealed. Yet even now through a physician working not as a physician but friendly counselor was God beginning to act as physician of his fevered soul. Augustine's winning of first prize in poetry was an occasion that sparked a friendship with Vindicianus lasting through his year in office. The proconsul's speech did not scintillate with flashy metaphors or clever epigrams; but, while unadorned by literary bon mots, his vigorously stated views, capitalizing on long experience as physician and canny observer of men, invested his conversation with charm and weight. He urged Augustine to throw away the books of composers of horoscopes or *genethliaci*, nativity calculators or genethialogists (so termed earlier because they focused on days of birth whereas in Augustine's day they were commonly styled mathematicians; DC 2.21.32). Earlier Vindicianus had studied astrological literature with a view to making his living as a professional. His had not been a superficial learning; scientific propensity that later disposed him to a command of Hippocrates assured that he would have no trouble in fathoming astrological works. Yet after entering astrological practice, he learned to his dismay that astrological treatises were totally barren of scientific warranty. In attempting to map the horoscopes of clients, he noticed that there was no scientifically determinable hook-up between the behavior of the stars and the events in an individual's life. Any connection proffered was due to the lively imagination and the creative ingenuity of the astrologer, not to the regular courses of the stars. Astrological diagnoses and prognoses were mainly the outcome of sheer guesswork. So Vindicianus abandoned astrology for medicine since he could not scruple to make a living out of advising people in terms of a fraudulent science. A peddler of astrological wares is, in effect, a smooth-talking confidence man expoliting the folly of his clientele. A second, corollary pragmatic argument ratified that his disavowal was not an exercise in paper logic. His critique carried in its train renunciation of an achieved profession and financial loss. The cost to him in quitting astrology was all the more reason why Augustine should acquiesce in his anti-astrological brief. If Vindicianus, going against the professional and economic grain, could reject astrology, Augustine, facing no professional dislocation and financial insecurity, should be more readily able to drop astrology as baseless.

A major difficulty, however, deterred Augustine from disassociating himself from astrology. If, he objected, astrology is through-and-through false, how account for the many true predictions in astrology? Conversely, if astrologers frequently foretell future events, their art must have a reliable scientific basis. Apparently limited by his less-than-abundant philosophical resources, Vindicianus ascribed astrologers' successful predictions to chance, which is widely operative in nature.[20] As a being of nature, man, he implied, was frequently subject to chance. From time to time an individual looking for guidance will open at random the work of a poet and lay his finger on a passage that presages an event; so use of the Virgilian lots, dipping haphazardly into a book of the *Aeneid,* yielded foreknowledge of the accession of Hadrian as emperor.[21] Similarly but in a manner more spiritual than mechanical, chance is at the core of astrological foretelling. The forecasts that jibe with business or personal needs of clients are not the outcome of art; they arise from a fortunate intuition, a prompting of astrologers' minds by some higher power. Astrological predictions are many times on target because the predictors count on a sort of clairvoyance whose source men cannot specify. This explanation was clearly less than satisfactory. Chance events are rare, yet Vindicianus held that incidents of chance, which pervades nature, frequently occur. But chance, which is irregular, cannot be relatively widespread in nature; coincidences that often occur cease to be regarded as coincidental. Augustine had to be puzzled also by Vindicianus' invocation of a mysterious higher prompting that makes astrologers often foresighted. Out of respect for Vindicianus, after benignly forgoing reference to deficiencies in his explanation, he stresses the providential boon in this exchange. From Vindicianus, as an extrinsic agent, speaking through him as an intrinsic instrument, God provided for Augustine a key to the fatal flaws in astrology. As yet it was only a seminal clue sketchily scrawled in memory, which further inquiry would bring to full flower and fruit. Some years later (either in Carthage, 382-3, or in Milan, 385-6) Augustine perceived that successful astrological predictions were due to chance, but chance disengaged from its incoherent linkage with frequency (7.6.8).

Nebridius, first his pupil at Carthage and later a most cherished friend, also endeavored to undeceive Augustine.[22] Not only a young man of virtue, blessed with religious devotion along with a mind of a pronounced philosophic bent, Nebridius scorned astrology as rubbish, just one more coarse brand of worthless divination. However, Nebridius' dialectical salvos were unavailing. Augustine was still under the spell of the authority of writers of astrological works, specialists who listed case after case in which the dexterous application of astronomical data had consistently predicted contingent human events. He had not been presented with any contrary evidence or analysis that proved beyond reasonable doubt that astrologers formulated their prognostications by luck rather than by applied science. Unmoved by Vindicianus and Nebridius, Augustine remained swayed by astrological writers because these experts underlined the frequency of their predictions, which had to be attributed not to chance but to an art adroitly adapting regularly recurring scientific patterns to human events.[23]

Chapter 4: Death of a Friend

7. The scene shifts to an earlier period, the autumn of 374 and a prior place, his hometown, where he first started teaching in a curriculum limited to grammar, which, we saw, involved advanced study of language and an introduction to classical Latin authors. At this time he became the very close friend of a fellow Thagastan, left unnamed perhaps in order to forestall intrusion of the privacy of any of his relatives who might be still residing in Thagaste around 397. They had been classmates and playmates, but it was only now when they were flourishing as adolescents in the ancient sense (adolescence, recall, covered the period from fifteen to thirty; both were now in their twentieth year) that common interests initiated mutual sympathy that held them fast. Yet since they were not Christians, theirs was not a true friendship in the absolute sense; love that fuses hearts in true friendship has to come from the Holy Spirit (Rom 5.5). True friendship has to be through and in God; it is his gift of love that graces the souls of those who are friends. Yet, Augustine is quick to add, theirs was a real friendship in the relative sense, on the plane of nature rather than supernature; a friendship modeled after and substantially squaring with the Ciceronian ideal. He and his

friend shared common interests and pursuits; their minds were in
concord concerning religious and human matters; they were joined
by good will and affection; their relatively real friendship was
founded on virtue.[24] The very rarity of such intense mutual regard
shows that theirs was a solidly moral accord. Their religious outlooks
coincided because Augustine had succeeded in luring his friend into
Manicheism–not a strenuous task since from the age of fifteen on, the
young man had been a not-too-well-instructed and largely nonprac-
ticing Catholic. Yet in spite of their shared Manichean untruth they
were friends, each unable to exist without the other. His friend
banked on Augustine doctrinally; Augustine clung to him with
interior affection, his soul unable to live without him. God, however,
intervened to break the bonding; hardly more than a year later,
toward the end of 375, his young friend died. The Lord is at one and
the same time a God of retributive justice, who allows sins, to be
painful and a God of mercy, who administers justice to draw vagrant
souls to his heart. God attracted Augustine back to himself in ways
that were wonderful; his providence harvested spiritual fruits out of
the evil that was the death of his beloved friend. From his loss he
experientially learned that only those who are friends in God are
truly blessed (4.9.14). God detached him from a friendship that was
his sweetest delight as a way of readying for him the supernatural joy
of conversion in which he would possess and be possessed by the
God who is sweeter than any purely earthly pleasure (9.1.1).

8. All the praises due the Lord are beyond recounting (P 105.3),
ineffable even in the life of a single individual; the whole of man's
inner life is impenetrable by human reason (P 41.13). Profounder yet
is the abyss of divine judgments, whose incomprehensible mercy
worked out his salvific life through his friend's death, which, along
with the circumstances prior to it, was disquieting. After his friend
became critically ill, his family asked that he receive emergency
baptism (probably from a priest); a fairly common practice
permissible so long as there were reasonable signs of the right
intention, namely, belief in the basic truths of Christianity (Parm
2.13.29,30. Bap 7.53.102).[25] Augustine considered baptism by water a
meaningless ritual that conferred no new light on a worldly soul
(CDEP 2.2.3); infusion of water accompanied by a mumbled
invocation of a false trinity, empty of all redemptive value. Now he
was sure that the Manichean doctrine to which his friend's soul had

knowingly assented would not be erased by a profitless enactment unknowingly worked on his body. But exactly the opposite occurred. As soon as his friend rallied, Augustine began to make fun of the baptism as a fruitless rite imposed on him when he was senseless. Obviously, in the normal exercise of his powers his friend, as a good Manichee, would have declined baptism. But against Augustine's expectation, his friend had endorsed its reception. Instead of welcoming Augustine's ideas, as he had done so pliably in the past, he recoiled from the sarcasm, and castigated him as he were an enemy, leaving Augustine dumbfounded and upset; dumbfounded, because hitherto his friend had never doctrinally crossed swords with him; upset, because his friend's rapid change of mind clashed with Augustine's plan to reinforce his friend's Manichean allegiance. He decided to bide his time; once fully recovered, his friend would be putty in his hands. But God had other plans; his friend's relapse and death protected him from a possible relapse into the religious insanity of Augustine. Twice more did God's mercy cause evil to fructify in good: the death brought not only everlasting life to his friend but also to the later Augustine consolation that his friend now lived deathlessly in God.

9. Consolation, however, was years away; in the wake of his friend's death Augustine became in a sense desolation itself. His friend wrapped in a shroud, his heart was enshrouded in sorrow. With the snuffing out of life that was the life of his world, the whole world swarmed with death. Everywhere the grinning skull stared him in the face. Everything appealing became appalling; even the most attractive haunts disgusted him. His homeland, instead of joying him, tormented him, and his own home, the shrine of family happiness, now reviled him. Recollection of their sharings pressed his soul on the rack and tore it with hooks. Before, everything murmured of his friend and evoked love; now, eyes roaming everywhere in vain search of his friend, he detested all their usual spots of rendezvous. Overwhelmed by this first major crisis, sickened in spirit, drowned in grief, his normal affective life turned upside down, his still-acute mind fumbled for answers to his existential problematic. Affectively he was a huge enigma; moving inwardly, he wondered why he was swamped by sorrow. Manichean teachings robbed him of understanding in his terrible bereavement. Attempting to make the counsel of the psalmist, "Hope in God" (Ps 41. 6,12), his own would have been mere

mouthing of words. It was sensible not to heed such an imperative
because the Manichean deity to which Augustine paid homage was a
sheer nonentity, powerless to instill patience in a soul that was a
slough of despond and to guarantee security in the life to come (P
41.10-1). Indeed this most precious of friends whom he now mourned
was more real and more beneficial than Mani's crude parody of God;
his friend had really existed and given him the boon of friendship,
and after his death still lived on in memory. Hence at this time
Augustine's extreme anguish was accorded no relief. With his friend
rotting in the grave, he felt driven to near-despair, beyond the
assistance of God and man. Yet his bitterness was not without some
delight: weeping tasted sweet. He could not strictly pray the words of
the psalm, "And night is my light in my delights" (Ps 138.11), for it is
Christ, making the night shine as the day, who delights the heart. In
a Manichean night unlit by Christ's wisdom, he had only marginal
natural delights of his weeping that were the somewhat odd-looking
spin-off of his distress.

Chapter 5: The Problem of Sweetness in Weeping

10. Over twenty years later he remains perplexed by the strange
fact that weeping feels sweet to those sorrowing. He first raises the
point as a logical possibility, whether God, though omnipresent, is,
along Epicurean lines, totally absorbed in his own immutable bliss
and wholly unconcerned about human wretchedness. Is he
unchangeably happy in himself while leaving to their own devices
men wheeled about in woes? He had already answered this earlier:
God cares for each individual as if he were the only one in the world
(3.11.19), intimately providing for all human needs (6.5.7). If God's
ears were deaf, life would be without hope of healing. Perhaps, he
next muses, the sweetness arises because tears betoken hope that we
will garner what we are praying for. However, this was not the case
in his overwhelming bereavement: at no moment did he tearfully
pray for his friend's restoration to life; he had simply cried over the
loss. Thus the sweetness in sorrow could not spring from an attitude
akin to prayer hoping to be heard; the sweetness coexisted with the
sorrow, with no expression of hope or prayer. An alternative surfaces;
perhaps weeping that is intrinsically bitter becomes sweet only extrinsically, insofar as backing away in disgust from things once loved

affords pleasure. Sorrow is ordinarily elicited by what is directly painful, joy by what is directly pleasurable. Here, he suggests, the sweetness of joy is felt indirectly by withdrawal from what is painful. A patient feels relief when a doctor, without administering an anesthetic, lances a boil or drains a tumor. So tears, though bitter, are satisfying because they signalize a withdrawal from what is painful—the grim hollowness of life without the loved one. Tears are a means by which the spirit gainfully retreats from the sorrowful: they help negative the terrible pain of loss. This, it would seem, is Augustine's summary, never-to-be-repeated explanation of the succor in tears and the ensuing sweetness.[26]

Chapter 6: Disgusted with Living, Afraid of Dying

11. He hammers home the wretchedness underlying his grief by using "wretched" either as adjective (four times) or noun (twice) in consecutive sentences. His condition was miserable because he was enchained by a friendship that, as earthly, was bound to perish, with the result that when his friend died, his soul was torn to shreds. That misery was already there, rooted in his narrow earthbound outlook. As he wept, bitter tears afforded a sweet release (4.5.10), serving as a bed on which he could rest (9.12.33), bringing partial soothing of the agony of total separation. Still, he prized his life, unhappy as it was, as dearer than the friend whose loss of life made his own life miserable. Surely he wanted to climb the professional ladder, but he would not have elected to undergo the most radical change, death; he would rather part with his friend than his own life. Though admiring the mythical devotion of Orestes and Pylades who pledged to die together rather than suffer the worse lot of not living together, he was not inclined to die for, so as to be in company with, his friend. Indeed there surged up a diametrically opposite feeling hard to classify: at one and the same time he was disgusted with living yet afraid of dying. This initially paradoxical-seeming state of simultaneous recoil from both life and death is not unique. In *Manfred* Byron wrote, "We are fools of Time and Terror: Days / Steal on us, and steal from us; yet we live, / Loathing our life and dreading still to die…"[27] The apparent ambivalence is resolved in the grounding of both attitudes in love of his friend. So burning was his love that his friend's death made living insufferable; yet the more he loved his friend, the more

he hated death, as the most fearsome enemy poised to pounce on all humans.

His memory is soundly reporting, not melodramatizing, every detail, in the presence of his hope (P 70.7). The Father's mercy raised his eyes to understand that human love is transitory and death the gateway to life; an eternal perspective liberated him from time-tethered thinking. During this period he wondered how anyone could remain alive when his friend had died. If death had destroyed his friend whom his love had rendered indestructible, how could destructible humans continue to evade death? Even more riddlesome was the fact that he himself was still alive; as his friend's alter ego, he should have somehow perished through the extinction of his friend. How was he still alive if Horace's felicitous line, "A friend is one-half of one's soul," is true? How could life go on pulsating in his members if, in Ovid's observation (possibly originating with Aristotle), his soul and that of his friend had been as one soul in two bodies?[28] Life seemed a frightful enormity; he shrank from living as a half-being, a sort of fractured freak. Still, he was consumed by dread of death, perhaps because if he were to die, his profoundly loved friend would totally die; by fending off death, Augustine as the other half of his friend's soul was somehow keeping his dead friend alive,[29] if only partially so.[30]

Chapter 7: Grief Unassuaged, Return to Carthage

12. Living in the moral madness of a dream-world, he had failed to love a human being humanly, in the human condition in which death is inevitable. Once death shattered his utopian illusion, the dream of endless life on earth became a nightmare of death. Then bogged down in a second stupidity, he unrestrainedly threw himself into a grief that was excessive but at no point pathological. It was impossible calmly to take stock; there was no light at the end of the grief he had tunneled himself into. None of the usual sources of sensuous pleasure singly or collectively could serve as an analgesic; not even the higher pleasures of spirit that books and poems convey could palliate the torment. No consolation issued from even the light whose irradiation symbolizes the Father of light. His friend was gone forever: everything seemed void because he who was everything was void of life. He was unable to disenburden himself of his mass of misery

because a mythical God, destitute of meaning and therefore devoid of power, could not support his burden. The load of sorrow slipped through the blankness that was pseudo-divineness and once more fell back on him with all its force. He could not bear his inner environment, but he could not leave since his heart could not flee from his heart. He was holed up in grief; no change in outer place could fully free him from the inner abode of unhappiness that was his self. Nonetheless, he did take flight from his hometown, outward departure promising partial release from inward woe. Elsewhere, far away from sights and sounds that, arousing memory of his friend, lacerated his heart a thousandfold, his sorrowing eyes would not be painfully hunting for his friend. In 376 he left Thagaste to go, for a second time, to Carthage where his absent friend would not appear so near-palpably present.[31]

Chapter 8: Healing through Friendships

13. Time, which is properly a measure (11.26.33), is characterized as an agent of healing. Taking no vacation, it rolls through the senses not idly but productively, its passage working wonders in the soul, especially in this case the marvel of the partial curing of his agony of bereavement. This expresses one apparent linkage between time and change with which the ancients were familiar, whose present-day recognition is formulated in the adage, "Time heals all wounds." Strictly, time does not heal, for it is not an efficient cause but a measure of change; accidentally related to causes that initiate and sustain process, it is only equivocally designated an agent of healing. With the passage of time psychological factors come to the fore to quiet grief; family support, new interests, deeper friendships, and prayerful reflections on the meaning of time. Here he highlights the healing role of renewed friendships with Manichees in Carthage. In this instance time betters the man; in nearly all other cases in which Augustine fuses time with change time disintegrates the human personality (11.29.29). As day by day the sun revolved in its observable circuit, so day by day curative time revolved through his senses; the daily coming and going of time eased his tortured heart by implanting other hopes, i.e., expectations of satisfaction through meeting former friends, and other memories, i.e., recollections of pleasant get-togethers with friends. Gradually time the physician

reinvigorated his spirit by friendships (initiated during his first year or more as a Manichee in Carthage [373-4]) which mollified the inward ache. Reunion with Manichean brethren was a mixed blessing; remedial of the anguish over his loss but deleterious in that the solidarity solidified him the more in Manichean error. Underlying his terrible sadness was a terrible fallacy; affective imagination had vested a mortal with immortality. The more entrenched the illusion, the deeper the piercing of the sword of sorrow; so he wept fruitlessly, pouring himself out like water on sand. Until his Manichean deconversion he was to remain spiritually sterile, mechanically observing dead ordinances that ignited not a single spark of inner life. True, Manichean friends comforted him; unhappily with a love that encouraged him to love their bizarre substitute for the true God. Their theology was an intricately textured but monstrously warped tissue of untruth. His mind (*mens*, the highest part of the soul) had itching ears that craved opening up superior horizons. Flirtation with the novel soon triggered an adulterous affair with the Manichean big lie; a wrongly curious pursuer of the truth, he was seduced by the prostitute that is Manicheism, rubbing against, i.e., intimately fondling, untruth, with the result that outwardly alive, he lay inwardly dead in the Manichean charnel house. The unsatisfactory effects were ineradicable so long as he stayed a Manichee. If a Manichean friend died, he would lament his passing, but the severance of this friendship would not sunder ties to Manicheism. The death of a friend would bring grief; continued attachment to Manicheism induced greater grief. While earlier fantasizing about the immortality of his mortal friend submerged him in tidal waves of sorrow, the larger Manichean myth about God and salvation was fatal; his true spiritual life was slain.

The consequences of Manichean error he would suffer over the long haul, but in the short run friendships rekindled softened the tragic sense of loss. Enthrallment with friends loosed the thrall of sorrow. First, he and they did things together; they exchanged kindnesses, while bantering and seriously conversing together. Second, a remarkable harmony obtained. Occasional disagreements were settled without rancor, in the irenic spirit with which a man might resolve disputes with himself. These rare instances of dissension, handled with benignity, fostered rather than damaged rapport. Third, a spirit of equality reigned; each was, by turns, teacher of and learner from others. Apparently these friends had benefitted from like academic backgrounds, all discussing thoughtful books and engaging in high talk. Fourth, their encounters were not academic seminars but gatherings enlivened by morally controlled warmth in which every possible token of friendship was extended to express and repay love. Countless signs of fellow-feeling served as fuel to set spirits aflame, merging many souls and hearts into one soul and heart (P 78.2).[32] Close bonding among Manichees contributed in no small measure to Augustine's nearly-decade-long adherence to the sect. A unanimity of interests and affections tended to overbalance nagging doubts about doctrine. Spiritual infecundity and intellectual bafflement arising from Manichean incongruities were a large part of the price that he would have to pay in the years ahead for the pleasures of a family-like concord.

Chapter 9: Lost Friends Never Lost in God

14. Rating, like most of the ancients, friendship one of the highest of the virtues, he did not take the claims of friendship lightly. A failure to pay one's dues to a friend left the wrongdoer not casually indifferent but conscience-stricken: he had neglected to repay his friend's love (E 192.1). Men pay love to enemies but repay love only to friends (CDEP 1.1). Mutual sympathy goes on and on, not only repetitively but more intensely: love is repaid by love, and this repayment is matched by further love, and this second recompense receives its response in still further love, thus generating a virtuous circle of friendship. Exchanges of friendship are always uncompromisingly moral, sternly but pleasantly virtuous; all immoral or carnal use of the body is reprobated as loathsome. Friends, he explicitly says, should expect nothing of a physical or bodily sort but only moral signs of good will and chaste fondness. Unhappily, the more intimate a friendship, the more excruciating the death of a friend. To sparkling gladness there succeeds tenebrous sadness. Robbed of its most prized gem, life seems to be no longer worth living; the friend-deprived self is a living dead man, exteriorly alive but interiorly, valuationally, dead.

To forestall such stark grief he recommends the practice of a three-layered beatitude of friendship: blessed is the man who loves God, and loves his friend in God, and loves his enemy for the sake of

God. First, love of God enables him to love God by God because he is first loved by God (S 34.1.2; 2.3). Second, in the truest sort of friendship (4.4.7) the love of God welds hearts together, each loving God in the other. Loving God in one another, they love one another in God. Third, an enemy cannot be loved in God because his hostility repels such union. Since his inimical attitude blocks being loved for his own sake, he is loved for the sake of God, who commands men to love and forgive even enemies. In loving enemies, man, the image of God, best imitates the Father who makes the sun shine and the rain fall on just and unjust alike(P 94.2). A person living by this beatitude of love will never completely lose a friend in death, for at death a friend goes home to God, whose infinite love gathers all the dear departed to his everlasting bosom. Filling all things, God is dynamically present to all, always there, always caring, always sharing his love. The love of friend for friend does not die with death; it lives on, preserved as a treasure hidden with Christ in God (E 263.2). Death signals only temporary separation; a friend is not lost but sent ahead, one to whom the bereaved will be rejoined in an ever dearer union (E 92.1). Only the individual who abandons God loses him; yet even then he cannot absolutely escape omnipresence. Flight from God carries him from God well-pleased to God angry; in violating divine law, he calls down retribution within his own soul (1.12.19). An evil man becomes the slave of his vices (CD 4.4). The tyranny of twisted desires torments a spirit (LA 1.11.22) become the slave of vices (CD 4.4). Even minds of brilliance, however much they theoretically extol virtue, are reduced to puppets of lust, vanity, greed, and cruelty.[33] The law of God that orders all things to the highest degree (LA 1.6.15) is truth itself in the practical sense, from which proceed all penal laws (LA 1.6.14) and all rules for right living (LA 2.19.52). The existential truth by which all things are true, God is the truth not only to be abstractly contemplated but also to be concretely enjoyed as the highest good (LA 2.13.36-7). Subjected to the truth that is God, men are liberated from death that is sin. In union with this truth friends stay fully true friends, emancipated from sin and time's grief, suffused with the light of the law of love that guarantees never-to-be-lost friendship in God.

Chapter 10: Transience Necessary in Creatures

15. A soul riveted to goods apart from God is impaled by sorrows.

These creaturely goods are of course beautiful but, because outside God, i.e., not sought in line with his law of love, and outside the soul, i.e., inimical to its weal, they become sources of sorrow. Contrary to the Manichees, who denigrated the material world as evil, these things are beautiful; beautiful and existent, however, only because they derive beauty and being from the all-beautiful God (1.2.2). All are streaked with change and temporality; they come to be and pass away, coursing through a three-stage career toward fulfillment. First, they come to be; next, they grow, then reach full stature; finally, upon maturation ensue decline and demise. Not all grow old: in most species many individuals perish before reaching the adult stage; but all die: all things are inexorably programmed to expire. As a consequence, their ascent toward fullness compasses, within, descent toward death. The faster they rise to completeness, the faster they speed to extinction. This is their mode of being: as creatures, mutable; as material creatures, existing only by coming to be and passing away. As noted earlier (1.7.10), a mode, the limit of a thing's existence, sets the outer bounds of a thing's operation.[34] As inherently corruptible, material units may seem paltry, but, closer inspection discloses, God has appointed to them indispensable roles in the cosmic whole. Not isolated atoms operating in a higgledy-piggledy, they are parts of a universe, in whose scheme individuals have to cease to make room for succeeding generations. The past has yielded to those present, and the present, in turn, yields to future entities. A changeless material universe would remain only a frozen monolithic block, bereft of alternation of day and night, variety of seasons, and generation of novel individuals (E 138.1.2-5). Indeed in grumbling about the deficiencies of a cosmos of continuous change, men implicitly attest the value of passing away since the complaint can be fully expressed only if prior parts of the sentence cede place to later words (LA 3.15.42). Every sentence uttered, whose words are not pronounced all at once, witnesses to the beauty and worth of a universe whose parts do not exist all at once. The first line of the hymn, "God, the Creator of All Things" (9.12.32), bids the soul praise the creator of the many-splendored physical universe, with its magnificence fashioned from radically contingent parts; a whole formed from the fitness of lapsing parts that interlock with one another. Yet while lauding these wonders, his soul must not be fooled into training its gaze on corporeal goods to the exclusion of God. The soul thus enchanted becomes so glued to sensory goods that it cannot break free; wherever they go, it must slavishly follow, willy-nilly (VR 38.69). But as things of matter, they go where they were going, i.e., where they are determined to go: they are headed toward nonbeing. The soul in bondage to evanescent temporals is pulled apart by false desires chasing after fleeting goods (11.29.39). The desires are pestilential, making the soul feverish in its restlessness. The soul cannot obtain satisfaction in fluctuating goods whose unstopping passage has no stopping place of rest. So fragile are these fugitive goods that a spark of fire can quickly wipe them out (VR 38.69), and the bite of a malaria-bearing insect can wipe out their miserly possessor.

Not only do sensory goods bring no fulfillment; the bodily senses that originally mediate their presence cannot understand them. Sensory goods are here today, gone tomorrow; the granaries of yesterday are the charred ruins of today. The senses perceive only the sequence of passing events; the eye of the body cannot perceive what the eye of the mind sees, that the fire was the cause of the loss of property. Nor can sensory perception understand things that are right at hand, occurring here and now. The senses, perceiving only the glitter, texture, and weight of a gold coin, cannot grasp gold as a valuable object of exchange. Whereas the senses may observe one man handing a gold coin to another, only the mind can discern whether the coin is being offered as a bribe or a just payment. Like a dull or relatively retarded individual with small retentiveness and incapacity to count to ten, the bodily sense is slow, unable to obtain and retain as much as the mind. In other words, it is incapable of grasping the intelligible characters of things. The senses can distinguish a true from a false sphere but cannot understand a true sphere precisely as a sphere.[35] Animal sense perceives pleasure in a certain rhythm without understanding why the rhythm gives pleasure (M 6.9.23).[36] A songbird sings beautifully, without apprehending the structure that gives charm to its song (M 1.4.6).[37] A dog routinely recognizes its master by sensory cues reinforced by long perceptual association, yet its sensory apparatus cannot isolate his nature or relationship; it does not recognize its master as man or master (M 1.4.8).[38] Such then is the mode or limit of sheer sensory perception: restricted to sensory phenomena and their associational clustering, it cannot single out the what and why of material things and events it perceives. Hence it cannot understand change as change, as a passage from appointed beginning to appointed end; it cannot know the pattern of the birth and death of things. A horse gives birth to a colt without understanding birth as birth, as a fixed feature of natural becoming; in dying, a horse does not realize the meaning of death as death. Sense knowledge, its range severely contracted, cannot attain understanding of the whence and whither of change; nor can it apprehend in any way the role of temporal succession as an instrument of beauty in the variegated unfolding of the universe. God the Father is the supreme measure, according to which the measures or modes of all things are established (BV 4.34). In the line of principle truth proceeds from measure; in the line of sign truth manifests measure. So from the Father as measure proceeds the Son as truth; in the Word of God as truth, through whom things are created, all material beings hear the decree specifying their mode: this point is your beginning; this other, your terminus. One never-to-be-forgotten truth about material things is this: they are limited in duration. So ties of earthly friendship have to be cut by death; a hard but also a healing truth: through the illuminating love of God's countenance wounds of bereavement are by and large closed.

A few additional comments seem appropriate on the role of the bodily sense (*sensus carnis*), which is briefly broached in a compressed and somewhat elliptical fashion in this and the following chapter (4.11.17). In these places, as sometimes elsewhere (M 1.5.10), bodily sense does not signify the sense power in the strict sense but the sensory power working in conjunction with the mind in the formulation of the lowest level of intellectual judgments. We may roughly distinguish four sorts of judgment in Augustine, the first of which is strictly sensory, the other three intellectual. The first sort, the strictly sensory judgment, is evident, we saw, in animals; a bird sings and enjoys singing, albeit without grasping the nature of singing (M 1.4.6). Judgments superior to the sensory are either sensory-intellectual or strictly intellectual. The second kind of judgment, the lowest level of human knowledge, which is strongly dependent on the senses, achieves a vague cognition of objects as such. Ordinary sensory-intellectual knowledge routinely distinguishes a man from a tree but is unable to specify precisely what demarcates the nature of man from that of tree. Correspondingly, a musically untutored audience is capable of intellectually distinguishing harmonies from discordant music but cannot spell out precisely the nature of musical harmony (M 1.6.11). On the third level the mind achieves the laws of harmony in music and the poetry that is one of its branches. In an analogous vein, the mind comes to know the nature of man: he is a rational animal, a composite of body and soul (QA 25.47). On the fourth plane the mind reaches the immutable principles of art and science, which are strictly intellectual, above space and time (VR 30.56). As noted previously (3.7.14), in poetry, for example, the most general principle is that equality and likeness must be preferred to inequality and unlikeness (M 2.9.16).

These four levels of judgment are ascertainable in Augustine's analysis of the meaning of death initiated by the memory of his immoderate grief over the demise of his beloved friend. The first level, that of bodily sense taken strictly, is present only implicitly or in the background. A dog judges death in terms of purely sensory cues. Its companion or perhaps its mother lies before it inert, a mass of decaying flesh that emits an unpleasant odor. But while a dog does not apprehend death as such, the consciousness of death as such is certainly but vaguely attained by sense knowledge of the kind Augustine puts under the heading of bodily sense taken loosely, on the second level of judgment. Unreflective individuals know death as death but in a factual manner, as a dreadful datum of human existence—every human being will eventually die—without pondering in detail the what and why of death. Death unavoidably occurs—that must be admitted; but it is never analytically examined. Indeed without such probing, death and its consequences may not be properly faced. Augustine, deceiving himself into believing that his friendship would never cease, treated his friend as if he were not mortal (4.7.12) and, as a result, was immersed in unspeakable grief. On the third level the meaning of death is intelligized as a fixed pattern in the cosmos; each material thing moves from an appointed or lawlike starting point to a definite terminus. Beginning and end do not occur at random or by happenstance; the appearance and disappearance of material units are rigorously determined according to their modes; the course of material existence is shaped by natural necessity. On the top or fourth level, the mind clearly grasps, in the light of the whole, the relation of ceaseless material coming and going, of incessant emergence and extinction. One angle or corner studied in isolation from the whole building may look peculiar or misshapen, but in relation to the total structure it appears apt. Viewed in itself, the tendency to death may appear ugly, but taken in relation to the totality of the cosmos, it is rightly deemed beautiful because it meshes with the whole of the material universe. Remorseless change assures the plurality and variety that make the universe a diamond of countless gleaming facets. Equality and inequality in things result in a cosmic harmony analogous to the harmony attained by the rule-governed equality and inequality of measures in a poem: the universe is a cosmic poem (M 6.10.29).

In short, human knowledge too closely bound to the senses cannot seize the meaning of death because it regards it only partitively, as a brute fact unconnected with the general law or overall order in nature. This narrow cognition of death may lead to a faulty moral attitude toward death. Incapable of understanding death as lawlike, Augustine fell prey to the practical illusion that his friend would never suffer death (4.7.12), and, this dissipated, became one massive wound, all around nauseating him.

Chapter 11: The Healed Soul Sees Parts in the Whole and the Whole in God

16. In 4.11.16-7 and 4.12.18-9 Augustine, inspiring preacher as well as coolly analytical teacher, adopts the style of a sermonette to address readers more personally. The heart must resist vanity, for, feeding on empty objects, the heart becomes empty. Since the cacophony of exterior vanities drowns out all other sounds, the heart should shut the door against external din, so as to listen to the Word of God crying aloud with the fire of love (4.12.19), instructing it to go back once more into its interior region of imperturbable peace because the inner self is the temple of God who is all peace (S 53.7). While fleeting objects of time such as friends who die can forsake its love, the eternal God never fails to requite its love. Without, things vanish to make way for succeeding entities; so does transiency ensure that the lowest level that is the physical universe be constituted of all of its parts. Within, insulated from the racket of the world, the heart listens to the changeless Word speaking, where in its bosom (P 34 [S.2].5) the heart is bade erect an enduring home or temple. The soul now recognizes that it has been weighed down by deceits ingredient

in a fleshly outlook; on the occasion of his friend's passing away, a sensory picture of death fatigued Augustine to the point of exhaustion. This encounter with the Word that refreshes the error-battered and sin-diseased soul is not simply a theological reflection but a communion of hearts that is prayer (P 34[S.2].6), wherein not only is the mind illumined but the whole self recharged. When in this exchange the heart confides to the truth all the truth given by the truth, it gives the truth without giving it away. Interior wonders abound: putrid features flower; ills healed by the divine physician (P 102.5), the heart is once more youthfully robust. Its components freed from their earthward drive, the heart perdures unchanged in union with the ever-unchanging God.

17. Continuing to exhort his inner self to gain and retain a purified vision of the part in relation to the whole, Augustine counsels: rather than being betrayed by your carnal self, confined to sensory-intellectual cognition, make your fleshly side follow you in your conversion to strictly intellectual knowledge, in which you turn aright from outward to inward, from downward to upward: do not let sense-bound knowledge pervert you but convert it, along with yourself, to God. Particular intellectual-sensory cognition perceiving the part to the neglect of the whole can be misleading; it would be incorrect to call a man handsome simply because of his muscular arms or to rate a speech good simply because of well-controlled gestures. Analogously, it is wrong to weep over the death of a friend without subsuming death under the law of transiency-for-variety. Nonetheless, even considered in isolation from the whole, parts undoubtedly afford some delight; there is beauty in powerful limbs, and skilled recourse to gestures does elicit a measure of pleasure. Yet satisfaction in the part cannot match pleasure excited by the whole. Next, speaking hypothetically, Augustine muses: imagine yourself like Adam in the Garden of Eden prior to the Fall, with mind unclouded and will unlamed, with senses perfectly under the control of reason; there fleshly sense as intellectual-sensory perception, would be capable of comprehending the whole; there you would want present objects and events to pass so that you might rejoice in the vision of the whole.[39] Unfortunately, through the Fall this heightened intellectual-sensory perception was lost; an equitable diminution of noetic scope was punishment for the primordial sin. Yet, in the fallen state, with the sensory ambit severely restricted, we receive greater

pleasure in the whole than in the parts taken singly. In ordinary conversation we desire to hear the whole sentence or series of statements expressing consecutive thought. So with other objects whose parts course one after another to form a whole: the whole gives more enjoyment than the individual parts, as the whole poem is always more pleasing than one word or line (VR 22.42). Hence transience, once accepted, evidences its own beauty; but refusal to assent to the perishing character of things, so loving temporals as not to have them pass away, is as absurd as wanting to hear one and only one syllable of a poem constantly repeated (VR 22.43). Furthermore, as the beauty of verses of a poem which are not recited all at once embodies small traces of the beauty of the art of poetry whose rules unchangeably coexist all at once (VR 22.42), so the beauty of a universe whose change engenders variety manifests in a faint way the beauty of its maker, whose comeliness begets the highest joy, for he alone is absolutely invariable. He does not pass away, indeed he cannot perish because, unlike entities of the physical universe, he is not one individual of a species. God is imperishable because he is induplicable: there can be only one absolutely immutable entity. The statement, "...he does not pass away because no being succeeds him or takes his place," is a somewhat unusual formulation in Augustine, who ordinarily grounds divine deathlessness in immutability. Apparently he introduces this entailment to contrast God's unicity with individual diversity: material entities cease to exist so that individuals of the same type may come after them whereas God does not cease to exist because there is no other individual of the "species" God that can come after or replicate him.[40] However God's unicity is substantiated, the parts are to be seen and loved in the whole, and the physical universe seen and loved as oriented to the changeless One.[41]

Chapter 12: Exhortations to Love All in God through the Power of Christ

Two sermonettes iterate the theme of Chapters 9-11: stability and rest can be secured in the love of God alone, which is mediated by the healing life and death of Jesus.

18. All the beauties of the cosmos, along with accompanying pleasures, men in particular, especially those cherished in friendship, are to be loved in and through God. Falling under the sway of change,

they are guaranteed fixity only by dependence on the wholly immutable, severed from which they shrivel up. Only in God can they be truly loved; apart from him human love evaporates without a trace in the destruction of loved ones.

19. The second exhortation focuses on Christ's mediating mission, adumbrating 7.21.27 and 10.43.68. (i) Christ, man's life, came down to die so that man might live; by dying he put death to death. (ii) From his divine abode he came forth to be among men, first of all in the womb of the Virgin Mary, the bridal chamber wherein human nature was wedded to his divine nature. Deathless divinity espoused death-bound human flesh so that it would not stay forever subject to the reign of death. Specifically, the outcome of this marriage is the whole Christ forming one body with members of his Church (S 341.1.1), a union in which bridegroom and bride become two in one flesh (C Don 4.7). Humble in shedding his blood for the redemption of his bride (J 8.4), Christ as a giant sans pareil displayed incomparable strength (P 18[En.2].6). (iii) Gentle in mien, he asserted divine authority in words and deeds, his descent among men and his ascension to the Father proclaiming in stentorian tones: men are to return to him. (iv) Visibly gone at the ascension, he remains invisibly accessible within; leaving without ever leaving, no longer present to eyes, he is present in the heart. Because the Son pitched his tent among men to save sinners, the soul confesses: each soul should not shrink from the hard saying, "I am a sinner," trusting that Jesus the healer will free his soul of inner pus and poison (P 40.6). The obtuse and sluggish should hearken to the Son's words of truth and life: stop canonizing shadows of time as if they were imperishable goods of eternity, but believe that Jesus lives in his body that is his Church, promising to stay in and with us till the end of time. Thus even now through faith and love Christians can ascend and live with him (S 263 A.1). (v) But it is bootless to strive to scramble up to heaven on one's own power. The man who so rises is puffed up with pride (P 72.15) and, in effectively blaming God for his faults, places his mouth against heaven, defying God himself. The proper stages are descent, then ascent. Descent: after confessing themselves sinners, through grace all will ascend in spirit to the Father. Ascent: before, by going up in pride, all went down in sin; now by going down in humility, they will go up in faith and love. Only the grace of Jesus terminates the internal civil war in which flesh battles against spirit, closing wounds and

bringing interior peace to the heart in its ascension. Put otherwise, the valley of weeping is a winepress, through whose pressure the good become more holy, their tears being changed into a new wine for lovers of God (P 83. 10-1).[12]

Clamor, a cognate of *clamans*, used here three times, has a special signification. In the line of prayer the burning of charity is the clamor of the heart to God for assistance; the heart continually on fire with charity continues to cry out (P 37.14). Crying out, empowered by God's love, is the sign of divine love. Analogously, the crying out of the God-man in his work of redemption denotes his love for man. As the enfleshed revelation of the love of God, Christ continuously uttered his cry of love in every aspect of his life, in every breath of his body, in every beat of his heart, in every insight of his mind; in every word and work, in his death and resurrection, in his descent among the shades, in his ascension to the Father. He cries out in love to human beings so that they will cry out love in return, uniting their hearts to him as he in united to the Father. In the line of human knowing we analogously grasp the *clamor* of Christ through the human *clamor* of prayer; in the real order the *clamor* of Christ is primary, the cause of and model for the fire burning within the human *clamor* that is prayer.

Chapter 13: His First Work, *The Beautiful and the Fitting*

20. His ever-inquisitive mind discussed with Manichean friends the necessary connection between the lovable and the beautiful and the meaning of beauty. Perhaps it was the comeliness due to balanced proportion that moves us to love things. In reflecting on the beautiful, he discriminated between the beautiful and the fitting. Because they are whole or have integrity, bodies are beautiful. Other objects are becoming not in themselves but in relation to other things; such proportioned objects are better named fitting. The right part is fitting in reference to the whole; so the normal head is proportioned to the human body, and normal eyes, nose, and mouth properly shaped and sized in relation to the head. Again, a piece of apparel is fitting as regards the wearer; correctly designed shoes or gloves are fitting in regard to the feet or hands for which they have been fashioned. Conversely, it would be grossly unfitting for a soldier to wear his shin guard on his head or his helmet on his leg (3.7.13). This distinction

and its development abruptly welled up from the depths of his mind, from what is today called the subconscious. After mulling over the problem with friends and after intense personal pondering, he probably put the matter aside for a time. While he was preoccupied with other interests, the subconscious was busily at work; under ground complex lines were disentangled, and threads of reasoning knitted together. After a period of incubation the ideas suddenly surged up, full-formed and viable. Notice, the preparatory stage was not rumination, which, located in memory, fortifies recollection (10.14.22). Note again, while undoubtedly the pattern of his work and the very words clothing it upflowed spontaneously from his subconscious, prior to this upwelling Augustine, though a genius, had to intensely concentrate on the problem, aided by canvassing of friends' views for clarification and criticism. The conscious elaboration marked by testing somewhat shaky hypotheses necessarily preluded the gestation period within the subconscious.[43]

The Beautiful and the Fitting probably concerned types of beauty, bodily and nonbodily, with the nonbodily divided into two subtypes, the beauty of the soul and of God. Though Augustine does not recall whether his little treatise handled the tripartite division in two or three books, he cannot be faulted for such forgetfulness; the sketchy, confused presentation of themes in a work not distinguished for its veridical character inevitably left only the faintest imprints for recollection of its precise division and contents. Indeed he no longer possessed a copy of the work; unaccountably unremembered, there disappeared all copies of his earliest treatise. He wrote *De pulchro et apto* around 380 (4.15.27); intervening between it and the *Confessions* were about seventeen years, a span in which major shifts radically altered his religious outlook, vocation in the Church, station in society, lifestyle, and domicile. Moreover, since it was patently an error-laden, fumblingly articulated essay, it exerted practically no impact on more mature views. It was, in the current phrase, a quite forgettable work.

The work arguably contained three books:[44] the first focused on corporeal beauty (4.13.20; 15.24); the second considered the beauty of the soul (4.15.24); perhaps a third explored the similarity of man and God, with some exposition of divine beauty (4.15.26). Though at this time Augustine could not conceive of the rational soul and God as strictly spiritual, he did deem them ostensively nonbodily, inaccessible to ordinary sensory experience; he plainly speaks of corporeal beauty as distanced from that of the soul and God.[45]

Chapter 14: Dedicating the Work to Hierius

21. This first work was dedicated to Hierius, an outstanding Roman orator, whom Augustine had never met but to whom he felt attached because of his brilliant reputation; fame being fleeting, practically none of his works survive.[46] He was impressed by certain passages packed with literary gold, but his admiration was mainly sparked by glowing reports of the orator's gifts. Enthusiasts praised him to the skies because they were amazed by his linguistic prowess. A Syrian first remarkable for his Greek eloquence, this apparently natural-born linguist accomplished the rare feat of also mastering the Latin tongue. Not only an adept bilingual rhetorician, he was, in addition, proficient in the philosophy, including what we label science, of his day. As both rhetor and philosopher, he concretely enfleshed the Ciceronian model after which Augustine was working hard to pattern himself since coming upon *Hortensius.* Yet what motivated him to dedicate the volume to a man he did not personally know? Already furnished is the answer in germ, soon to be reaffirmed (4.14.22), later to be elaborated (4.14.23): his admiration was shaped by the opinion of others. How, he wonders, is love for a gifted individual communicated? Does the love of the praiser automatically trigger love in the heart of the listener? No; the process is not a sheer mechanical transmission since the listener may throw cold water on the burning admiration. Instead, the listener must subjectively appreciate the love; his heart must elect to be inflamed by a like love; the love of the listener is enkindled only if the praiser is authentically lauding the subject of his admiration.

22. In admiring Hierius, as he did others under the influence of peers, he was being guided by the defective compass of inherently fallible human judgment. Yet his love and praise of Hierius were notably different and far more serious than the love and praise he accorded other famous figures; these he admired with no desire to emulate while he aspired to imitate Hierius and be praised for similar accomplishments. Popularly acclaimed charioteers, fighters of wild animals, and actors excited his liking and praise for, respectively, keen coordination, disciplined daring, and dramatic talents of voice

and gesture. Though loving and praising such performances, he opts
not to share such fame, preferring to be despised rather than loved
like such performers. No matter how popular, charioteers, gladiators,
and actors were held in low repute.[47] So his admiration veers away
from sympathy that fathers imitation. Objectively, he highly regards
their excellence; subjectively, he would be abashed if he were
applauded for being a performer whose expertise he loves but whose
occupation he abhors. Still, the issue is not so clearly settled. The
human soul harbors manifold weights,[48] namely, loves tending
upward or downward (13.9.10), assorted likes and dislikes, not only
varied but also subtly competing and conflicting. While sharing a
common human nature, Augustine loved excellence in a public
performer from which he would recoil were it in himself. Some
suggest that his love-hate ambivalence is what is operative in a man
who admires a fine horse but who would rate it repugnant to be
turned into a horse even if this impossibility were possible. But this
analogy falters; the main disanalogous point is that a man and a horse
are not formed by a common nature. The reverse is the case with
Augustine and an actor or other performer: both enjoy fellowship in
human nature. So a difficulty arises: since they have an identical
nature, how can Augustine love in his fellow man what he himself
would loathe to be? This love-hate polarity, howbeit analyzable,
seems at another level a mystery. Indeed "man himself is a vast
deep," a grand abyss of mystery. We can evaluate the personality and
character of others by their words and actions, but the innermost core
of their thoughts and desires slips through the net of understanding.
Every man, even one spiritually advanced, is an abyss defying
explanation (P 41.13).[49] Nor do men totally understand themselves.
Unaware of his abyss of weakness, Peter shamelessly denied the
master whom he boasted he would die for (P 138.21). Man does not
existentially think as a precision-perfect logical machine but is pulled
here and there, with seeming paradox, by desires working at cross-
purposes. God alone is able to reckon the ideal 100,000 hairs of each
man's head. Yet this counting is more easily done than the tracing of
the tortuous and tangled gyrations of the heart. In their diversity and
opposition the desires of the psyche are humanly innumerable,
resisting total detailing and exhaustive concrete analysis. In loving
and hating one and the same characteristic in another, man is a
mystery; and a vast one because other polarities surge up from the

depths.

23. His admiration for Hierius was of a different kind because the celebrated Roman was a different sort of man, an orator-philosopher, a figure of eminence whose success and glory Augustine craved to duplicate. Moreover, his eyes opened to his own gifts, he was stimulated to walk along the same path and, if possible, to soar with the Roman rhetorician. But eagerness to mount to excellence was marred by pride; he wanted to enlarge his mind only as a means of puffing up his spirit. Further, while discovering himself in making Hierius his lodestar, he admired him for the wrong reason, choosing him as a model not by independent judgment but mainly because of the opinion of others. He was blown about by every wind, slavishly conforming his ideas to prevailing opinion. Nevertheless, secretly, in his inmost being, he was being directed by God. Ambition would spur him three years later to depart suddenly for Rome (5.8.14-5); and in 384 he would secure the coveted office of offical orator in Milan (5.13.23), where he was to encounter Ambrose, who would baptize him in the Catholic faith (6.3.3-4). After ordination (391) rhetorical proficiency and philosophical acumen would be providentially directed to the service of the truth; incidentally earning a worldwide renown down through the centuries, in the light of which the reputation of a hundred Hieriuses pales. Yet his professed admiration for Hierius's rhetorical endowments owed more to respect for the attitude of those lauding Hierius than for esteem for his qualities. If his praisers had been, instead, mordant critics, the flame of Augustine's enthusiasm would not have been lit, let alone burned brightly. In this changed scenario the man himself would have remained unaltered, his exceptional qualities modified not one whit; the decisive factor in the switch in appreciation would have been the posture, now cuttingly negative, of those appraising Hierius.

His was a miserable condition; having lost his hold on the solid firmament of truth, he had dropped into the pit of darkness, where, enervated, he lay prostrate, tossed about by the varying forces of dominant ideas. The literary establishment vented hurricane-force winds that propelled him upward like a puffball, then whipped him around, twisting him one way, then suddenly bending him in another direction. Not channels of the truth these but opinion-mongers, who, feigning to know without truly knowing, rashly disguise their false ideas as authentic truths (UC 11.25). Yanked here, then there, his distracted mind was helpless to perceive the truth right in front of his eyes. Had he looked inward and gazed upward, he would have seen the truth laid open by light shining within: to supreme beauty all beautiful below owes its beauty. Geared not to the truth within and above but to opinions without, he hungered for even a few scraps of commendation from Hierius. For a promising writer at the outset of his career it was a matter of much moment to win Hierius' recognition of his literary-rhetorical artistry. If his hero bestowed his benediction, he would be all the more fired to author kindred, more substantial works. However, if his idol voiced cold disapproval, his inner being would be left bleeding, for he valued not the beautiful as such for its own sake but the comments of leading makers and shapers of culture. Yet apart from his hunger for, if not resounding applause, at least a gracious nod from a master, Augustine drew satisfaction from continuing to meditate on the theme and subthemes of his first creation, mentally retouching phrases and tightening his analysis, so as to draw it nearer to the ideal perfection every author, fledgling or mature, secretly aspires his work to embody. Moreover, like the mother of a newborn, he delighted in caressing this fruit of his generative spirit, needing no one else to corroborate his admiration for his offspring. Again and again he fondled his first-born as a mother hugs her first newborn to her bosom. "Show me a lover, and he will know what I am talking about," Augustine said in appealing to experience as warranty for the magnetic force of goods loved (J 26.4). Analogously, one may suggest, show me a first-time author, and he will understand the affection Augustine lavished on this first child of what would prove to be an extraordinarily fecund progenitive potency.

Chapter 15: The Main Lines of *The Beautiful and the Fitting*

Two sections very briefly sketch the contents of his first work; the first book examines corporeal beauty (24); the second, beauty as regards the soul (24); the third, the beauty of the soul with reference to God (26). His summary report uncovers a number of egregious errors, even glaring contradictions, in his gauche inquiry into the beautiful. Unfortunately, at this time Augustine's concept of God was deficient. As a Manichee, he could not admit that God is the all-powerful spiritual being "who alone does marvelous things," who out of his goodness created out of nothing (P 135.4) and who, through his dynamic presence, goes on working in the activity of each and every agent (P 71.20).

24. Unable to understand that God is the supreme artist, whose art is the source of all the wondrous beauties in the universe, he could not understand that the pivotal factor in the tough question that he was tackling is the art of God.[50] The laws of beauty within whereby the mind judges beautiful things originate in the art of God; human art is modeled on divine art; so cosmic and spiritual beauty flow from divine beauty (LA 2.16.41-2). Missing the cardinal role of divine art, his analysis was doomed to go astray. The first book defined, then distinguished the beautiful and fitting in corporeal forms. The beautiful is what is beautiful in itself; it is the well-ordered wholeness of a body. The fitting is what is adapted to another thing; the human sensory organs are fitting—they are properly ordered to the whole human body. The second book apparently examined the beauty of the soul, a nonsensible entity insofar as it is not immediately observable by the senses. But false opinion, that is, the materialistic views of his Manichean circle, prevented him from discerning that the human soul is strictly nonsensible, absolutely spiritual. So tenacious was this misconception of his Manichean environment that he disavowed the very truth forcibly impressing itself upon his mental eyes. At every waking moment he was conscious, at least indirectly, of his soul or inner self, while during certain times of introspection he knew his mind as directly present. He could not directly know the intentions of others, manifest through actions; nor could he see his face except in a mirror; but his mind was immediately present in experience; and it was apprehended as something incorporeal, without need of sensory attributes for existence, without need of sensory signs for recognition. But under the pressure of his materialistic prejudice Augustine, blinded to the intellectually palpable fact of the mind's self-awareness, tried to describe the soul in terms of quantity and qualities. Since he could not perceive the mind exhibiting special lines, distinctive color, and a volume that grew at a certain rate, he concluded that he could not see the mind.[51] What was inwardly staring him in the face eluded him because Manichean materialism led him to believe that only entities with sensory or quasi-physical properties were thinkable or mentally seeable (T. 10.7.10; 9.12).

Unity is the source of lovable virtue, whose fruit is peace; division is the source of detestable vice, whose fruit is discord. In unity, he argued, are grounded the rational mind, the nature of truth, and the highest good. In division, he misguidedly thought, are rooted the substance (difficult to specify) of nonrational life and the nature of the greatest evil. Paradoxically alive is the supreme evil, Augustine implied, since all life should flow from God who is all-good. Apart from this, the supremely evil substance seems to have been conceived as an enormous beast, a monster pulsating in every fiber with vibrations of evil, nonrational in that it had only a brute mind devoid of reason; nonrational also in that, uncontrollable by reason, it was driven by an overpowering appetite for strife and destruction of anything good, thus underlying all the vices that pollute human existence. The principle of unity he called monad (literally one or a unit), a sexless mind; its asexual character signified that it was uncontaminated by evil, in accord with Manichean doctrine that sexual differentiation is produced not by God but by the evil one (Cont 9.23).[52] The principle of evil he named dyad (literally two or a couple). While the monad caused virtue and concord, the dyad in its multiplicity was the mainspring of vice, discord, and breakdown. In social sins its radical divisiveness issued in anger, the uncontrollable desire for revenge (2.9.17. CD 14.15) that results in social disruption and even vendetta violence. In personal sins it ignites unrestrained desire for things of the flesh. Unhappily, as he bluntly puts it, he simply did not know what he was talking about; uncritical acquiescence in the Manichees' notion that evil is as real as good denied him opportunity to learn that no substance as such is evil. The poverty of their thought also balked him from recognizing that the human mind itself is not the highest good.

While his self-critical deprecation put himself down as ignorant, the confusion and contradictions arose not from any penchant for illogicality but from resistance to rational interpretation of Manichean beliefs. His initial work, principally a reflection on the meaning and manifestations of beauty, apparently set out to apply philosophical instruments to analyze central Manichean doctrines. His primitive theological exercise in understanding what he believed came up short not because his conceptual acumen was defective but because Manichean dogmas were through-and-through irrational. The very endeavor to make them appear reasonable laid bare their counterfactual and absurd character. Incoherence is strikingly evident in the conception of the mind itself as the supreme good. It is hard to figure out what reasons he may have marshalled to justify this claim since he situated God above the human mind (4.15.25). Though an intellect of the highest order, Augustine, super-burdened by Manichean howlers, was driven into a quagmire of inconsistencies. At this point it becomes clearer why he never betrayed anxiety over the disappearance of his earliest work. Remembrance of its indefensible metaphysical theses, such as the positive reality of evil and the existence of a purely malign principle of evil, and its untenable foundational-ethical assertions such as the strange contention that the human mind is the supreme and unchangeable good, along with its internal incongruities, may have moved him, in later years, to intellectually shudder. Only reluctantly then, and in a spirit of humility, did he force himself to dredge up from memory the muddled tenets of a work that was nothing less than an analytical disaster.

25. In the sphere of being the rational soul rules the body (QA 13.22); in the sphere of conduct the rational mind is intended to rule the body. Its governance consists in imposing an order upon aggressive and pleasure-seeking inclinations, regulating them according to the rule that greater goods are to be preferred to lesser (LA 1.8.18).[53] When the mind loses control over aggressive emotions, the eruption of disorder that is social sin occurs; an angry man, perhaps vehemently, mounts an offensive against others. When the mind slackens its rein on pleasure-seeking passions, personal sins result; roués and drunkards revel in carnal delights. In addition, the governor may become ungoverned; the rational mind itself may become unhinged, vitiated by errors and false opinions. Whereas errors are untruths, propositions not in accord with reality, false opinions belong to a subspecies of error; the strictly opinionated man is obstinately steeped in his error, so convinced of the soundness of his misguided view that he freezes his face against any reasonable counter-evidence and counter-argument (UC 11.25). Augustine's first venture proposed that the mind itself is the essence of truth, that it is self-luminous (4.14.25), a claim that enveloped his mind in darkness. Later he came to know that the light whereby the mind builds virtue is only a borrowed light; not originating but participating in the truth, the mind is a lamp lit by light from a higher source: God illuminates

his darkness, i.e., incarceration in error and sin (P 17.29). In the theoretical sphere the mind knows truth through the light flowing from God who is light itself; in the line of action the rational mind illuminating the emotions furnishes lights that are the virtues, by which it partakes of divine light (LA 2.19.52).[54] The fullness of God's light we have all received, sharing in it speculatively and practically (CD 10.2); Christ, the interior teacher for knowledge of truths and for right actions, enlightens each and every individual (CJP.4.3.14); he is light and law, the unalterably fixed standard by which men are to measure all that is and all that ought to be (O 2.8.25).

26. However, in 380 he divorced himself from the light and life of God. Thirsting for the truth that suffers no shadow of alteration (3.6.10), he was repulsed because pride tyrannizing his soul (P 42.3) was so repelled by the font of life that his soul tasted death, the soul without God being a spiritual corpse (J 19.12). His self-exaltation was second to none in cognitive arrogance, for, in effect, he actually believed his soul equal to God. As a result of the war between the Kingdom of Light and the region of Darkness, Manichees held, good souls spun off from God as his emanations, to be mingled with matter or evil (MM 2.18.66). The identification of the soul's substance with that of God provoked a nettlesome problem. His soul was plainly mutable; else there was no accounting for his struggle to winnow the chaff from the grain of wisdom. If his soul was clearly changeable, was he not saddled with the apparently unpalatable corollary that God was mutable as well? An ignorant and arrogant Augustine did not back away one inch from this paradoxical implication. Rather than forgo the co-substantiality of his soul with God, he boldly insisted that God was indeed mutable. Throttled by this opinion, he was rebuffed by God, who turned aside his windy neck, the neck a symbol of his proudful thrusting of himself upward into divine estate (3.5.9; 7.7.11); like his brethren, he was windy, word-fluent and truth-desiccated. His Manichean materialism could only imagine spiritual realities in corporeal guise; the Father dwells in visible light, the Son in both sun and moon, and the Holy Spirit in the circle of the air (CF 20.7-8). He was flesh; recognizing only sensorily cognizable material entities, he was restricted to image-thinking. Hence he blamed the flesh, imagining that neither he nor his good soul but a bad soul within caused his sins (DA 1.1). A wandering spirit, driven by the weight of carnal custom deeper into darkness, he was a prodigal son

whose pride stonewalled any return inward to himself to beckon to the upward call of the Father (P 77.24). Pride held him captive among Manichean fictions such as a triangular sun that is a ship of light, a Primal Man warring with the five evil elements, and a world-upholder itself supported on the shoulders of a gigantic Atlas (CF 20.6,9); sheer inventions without existential ground in God, the self, or any body. He used to cross swords with God's little ones, many of them unlearned, who were to be his fellow citizens of the kingdom of God, the Church from which at that time he had unwittingly exiled himself. As with his Manichean compatriots, his argument was long on language, short on logic. He questioned Catholics to expose their incoherence: "How can you explain erring souls? If, as you suppose, God is errorless and he has made the soul in his very own image, why is the soul not errorless also?" Even as he pressed this objection, he felt uneasy, fearful that his Catholic adversaries might turn the tables on him by retorting that the error-proneness of man demands error in the Manichean God. He wanted to dodge the really unanswerable question: "How can you believe that God, who is truth itself, actually errs? But if your soul, which errs, is truly the substance of God, then the substance of God errs, indeed has to err" (Fort 11). Bullheadedly refusing to acknowledge that his soul was not, could not be, co-substantial with God, he went on insisting that the immutable substance of God was compelled to err in his own mutable soul co-substantial with God. He clung to the anomalous contention that the inherently immutable is necessarily mutable rather than concede that his plainly mutable self did wrong by its own free will and not by the inexorable determination of his evil soul. Such crude incongruities were the appropriate chastisement for his pride.

27. He wrote his first work while teaching in Carthage when he was about twenty-six or twenty-seven (380-1), some seven or eight years after reading *Hortensius* in his nineteenth year (3.4.7) awakened desire for wisdom. His meditations were designed to signal advance in wisdom, but the din of imaginary figments deafened his heart to the words of truth uttered within from above. He was straining, but at that time to no avail because of the noise of Manichean fictions, to hear the interior melody of the sweet truth who is God, savoring which required residence in the house of God, the Catholic Church. After his conversion his soul, withdrawn from earthly tumult, would be charmed by the song of the spirit that faintly anticipates the ravishing

song of the everlasting celebration (P 41.9). As he pondered leading ideas on the beautiful and fitting, he was yearning to stand, as did John the Baptist, and hear the Lord's precious words so as to rejoice in the voice of the divine spouse. John was humble, deeming his status beneath that of a slave; Augustine, however, was proud, thirsting for prestige and arrogant in his errors. While John longed for Christ to increase as he decreased, Augustine wanted to grow on his own. While John remained inward and went upward to hear the spouse's sweet melody, the racket of Manichean errors muffled the voice of the spouse, and swept him outward, with the affective weight of self-exaltation inevitably pulling him downward. Unlike John, who stood and heard the spouse, Augustine fell flat on his face, taking in nothing but false Manichean clamor (P 50.13). In contrast to the psalmist praising God for gladness clothing humbled bones, Augustine did not rejoice in God because the bones of his spirit were tumorous with pride (P 50.13).

Chapter 16: Learning Profitless without God and Virtue

"What shall it profit a man if he gains the whole world and suffers the loss of his soul?" (Mk 8.36). These words familiar to Christians in sermons on the last things are a constant background refrain in his remembrance of his relatively easy conquest of provinces of knowledge. "What did it profit me...?", which appears six times, at least once in each paragraph, lays emphasis on the paltry value of academic triumphs apart from knowledge of God and progress in moral virtue. Education in the arts and sciences makes a man only relatively good; without God, without virtue, he later saw, he could not be absolutely or morally good. Of course he prized learning, but with the cautious qualification that learning without virtue is spiritually worthless. These are not the pious yet irrelevant preachments of a bishop of late antiquity. The scientific brilliance of the German people in the first half of the twentieth century was similarly profitless under the heel of a brutal Nazi dictatorship. As the threat of a nuclear holocaust, which hovered over the world especially between 1950-1990, grimly reminds moderns, knowledge per se reaps no moral harvest. Knowledge without virtue not only stores up no treasures in heaven but, improperly applied, can be socially ruinous and remains potentially catastrophic. In the line of socio-historical time as well as from the standpoint of eternity, it is spiritually bankrupt for men to bestride the whole world of knowledge like a colossus while destitute of the moral virtue that harnesses science for the absolute good of man.

28. When he was nearly twenty, there came into his hands Aristotle's *Categories*, probably in a translation by Marius Victorinus.[55] Again chronologically backtracking, he moves backward six or seven years from his first work (380-2) to his first encounter with the foundations of a realistic philosophy (374). His teacher of rhetoric in Carthage and others reputed as learned extolled the work as so noble that it approximated the knowledge of the gods. To his surprise he found, when back in Thagaste teaching, that he was able, without consulting colleagues or commentaries, to master its contents.

The categories are the modes in which we think of things; they are also modes of being, aspects of the real world. Here Augustine apparently deals with them in the second sense, as features of reality outside the mind. The primary category is substance, such as a man. The other nine categories concern things in or dependent on substance, which are accidents of substance. Some are absolutely intrinsic, such as quantity (the figure of a man), and quality (his height). Relation is relatively intrinsic: it is the reference of one thing to another (Monica was Augustine's mother). Four accidents are extrinsically said of substance. "Where" indicates the place of a substance (he read the *Categories* in Thagaste). "When" covers the time of an event (he was born in 354). Posture or position refers to the disposition of the parts of a substance in place (later, when preaching, he usually sat while his congregation stood). State of possession is said of a man in terms of extrinsic things in which he is garbed (he is wearing a tunic and sandals). Finally, action and passion (being-acted-on) show the substance as agent (doing something, such as writing) or recipient of action (having something done to him, such as having a tumor lanced). Not only the objects he offers as examples but all entities in the universe can be subsumed under these ten genera. The classifiable beings are literally countless; an infinitely possible number can be situated in any one of the categories.

29. The *Categories* marked an immense intellectual gain, furnishing the outline of a solidly realistic world picture. Because of bondage in Manichean materialism, however, this firm hold on the general makeup of things proved at first spiritually unrewarding; more, it was

harmful because the apparently necessary treatment of God as a substance in which accidents are subjectified seemed to buttress the Manichean opinion that God, however exalted, is also only a material substance endowed with greatness and beauty as corporeal accidents. As he was to recognize later, God does not strictly have greatness and beauty. God as spiritual has to be understood transcategorically. He is not a substance that contains accidents that bespeak composition and change but is simply and immutably being itself that implicitly encompasses his attributes (CD 8.6. T 5.2.3). He is nonqualitatively good, nonquantitatively great, placelessly wholly everywhere, and immutably active (T 5.1.2). But a body is not identified with its greatness or beauty; should its magnitude shrink or its beauty fade, it remains the same body. In misapplying the categorical framework to God, Augustine misconstrued him as a body; the notions in the *Categories* were true, but his adaptation of them to God was false.

His misconceptions originated in the unscientific fictions of Mani, whose outcome was unhappiness, the inescapable penalty for obstinate commitment to Manichean untruths. These errors turned him away from the firmament that symbolizes inalterable truth and law, cleaving to which entrains sharing in the very beatitude of God. Sanction is built into the wrongdoing itself (1.12.19); wrong pleasures turn into whips inflicting rightful pain (P 7.16). So with Augustine: the malordered strivings of his Manichean-afflicted spirit reaped not fruits of the Spirit but thorns and thistles. Every sin carries thorns within it (P 102.17). Out of his pride sprang thorns of spiritual idiocy, an anthropomorphic notion of God and a faulty divinization of man. Again, his upwardly mobile bent induced gnawing anxiety (4.2.2); so tortured at times was he by thorns that his life verged on a living hell (P 102.17). Along with the thorns, the thistles stand for valueless vegetation, no better than a barren harvest of his Manichean years, which stifles the flowering of the truth within (GCM 2.20.30). Love infuses meaning into the daily grind of unremitting work; where there is love, there is no labor, or if there is labor, it becomes a labor of love (Bonvid 21.26). Augustine's ambition-ridden endeavors were drudging toil unrelieved by the balm of genuine love, shadowed over by meaninglessness and frustration.

Nevertheless, this temporary misuse was far outstripped by later philosophical and theological use of the predicaments. In putting at his disposal the instruments of a sketchy yet serviceable substantialist metaphysics, a conceptual framework of key motifs in Aristotelian realism, the *Categories* equipped him to coherently grasp nature, man, and God. Since God absolutely transcends the universe, substance said of him has to be purified of imperfections that would derogate from his immutability: God is substance or being itself, without accidents as such. Surely God is wise but only in the respect that he is his wisdom; so with other attributes: he does not have but is them (T 5.2.3). Moreover, in the sphere of theology Augustine the bishop will capitalize on the notion of relation to account for the three persons in one God. As substance, God is one; because of the relations within the Godhead, God is Father, Son, and Holy Spirit: each of the divine persons is a subsistent relation (T 7.6.12).

30. The enrichment of mind won from the liberal arts left him no less spiritually impoverished. Devouring all the available treatises in arts reserved for free men (as distinguished from the mechanical arts, which the ancient world commonly deputed to slaves), he was ironically still held in bondage to the vilest desires. The vices that shackled him were of the basest sort; a worshipper of a false god, and, worse than a pagan idolater, he blasphemed the one true God; he was swollen with pride and on fire with ambition and, though faithful in the arrangement, a tinge of lust stained his concubinage. In any event, as he read these works, some of them challenging, with a shock of delight he realized he could thoroughly understand them. The capture of truth carries a special pleasure; books joy the mind in opening up new continents of learning: undreamt-of kingdoms entranced his mind. Yet his fresh knowledge was not without ignorance; he did not know the whence and wherefore of the new truths; he had no idea why they were true and certain, no concept of the God who as immutable truth is the source of the truth and fixed content of the general rules of each and every art. Guilty of the aversion from God that is sin, he was akin to a man with his back to the light (symbolizing the illumination of God the truth), whose face (mind) views objects (the arts) in the light, without itself being illuminated. His mind was, in fact, illuminated by the light that is God; else he could not have known the meaning of the arts, most of whose basic principles are apprehended notionally, in an a priori fashion, independent of sensory experience (10.9.16). However, insofar as aversion from God made him unaware of the divine light that lit up the arts, his face (mind) was deprived of illumination. He

lists the arts in which he became professionally competent through schooling: the art of speaking (grammar and rhetoric), the art of reasoning (dialectic), the science dealing with the dimensions of figures (geometry), the science of orderly versification (music), the science of numbers (arithmetic).[56]

On his own he grasped the kernel of the arts with relative effortlessness, without the clarifying assistance of a teacher or without comparing notes with a colleague. He was able to become proficient in these disciplines because God had gifted him with one of the finest intellects of all time; a mind of superbly quick absorptive and firm retentive capacity, though perhaps not endowed with eidetic imagery and a photographic memory. Just as importantly, his mind was blessed with the topmost analytic acumen; not only could his intellect rapidly assimilate information, but it pierced to the meanings of ideas, their interconnections, and the overall systematic structure of various works. Here Augustine is not slipping into conceit; he is matter-of-factly recording the prowess of what was actually a supremely penetrating mind, whose perspicacity may have first become fully evident to him at this time. He speaks less emphatically of his mental talents earlier (1.20.31) when he was appreciated as one bright lad among other promising youngsters. Again, he praises not himself but God to whose generosity he owes his intellectual prowess. Yet estranged from God by defection to Manicheism, he could not lift up his mind as a sacrifice to God. A sacrifice, recall, is any action so done for God that we may join with him (CD 10.6). Since a true sacrifice requires the true God and the true religion, he could not make an oblation of his mind. Hence his genius worked not for happiness but toward spiritual harm and possible ruin. He considered his towering intellect as his share of the inheritance, wholly his own and no one else's, to be exploited to glorify himself and to gratify his appetites. Unlike the psalmist, he preserved his strength not for God but against and away from him. Trusting in God, the soul receives power; betrayed by presumption that is sham self-trust, the soul keeps its apparent strength (really weakness) apart from God (P 58[S.2].1). Abandoning the Father, Augustine forsook his home and, like the prodigal son, traveled to a far-off country, the region of unlikeness and ungodliness, where he squandered his substance or mind by consorting with carnal cupidities that were harlots of his soul.[57] In contradistinction to moral virtues, which always have to be well used, his prodigious intellect could be misused; sheer might of intellect is no more than an intermediary good, inferior to that of moral virtue. Instead of preventing morally offensive behavior, his mental endowment ensured that he would be more cunningly immoral (LA 2.18.50). The awesome quality of his mind, attested by his self-instruction, was confirmed when he tried to teach others what he had appropriated with such facility; even the most intelligent savant had to sweat to assimilate the material, so that he rated an instructee topnotch not because he learned fastest but because he was the least slow.

At this point a few more detailed remarks on Augustine's shift on the value of the liberal arts may be added (see 1.6.10). Prior to a searching study of Scripture after ordination in 391, Augustine maintained that erudition in the liberal arts, coupled with moral purification, was indispensable for acquiring happiness in this life. Fortified by the liberal arts and detachment from things sensory, the mind passes from corporeal entities to things incorporeal things (R 1.6), from the sensory world to God (M 6.1.1). Refined in the liberal disciplines, and purified by moral virtues, certain educated men, albeit few in number, are capable of rising to a certain vision of God in this life that is tantamount to an attainment of *beata vita* or happiness.(7.10.23). Specifically, the liberal disciplines rigorously train the mind, making it more capable of seizing the truth that involves the vision of God. This *exercitatio animi* justifies the protracted analysis of seemingly trivial points in various disciplines. The study of geometrical figures builds up the mind so that it can seize more subtle issues; without such training it might be repulsed by the stronger light of higher truths (QA 15.25). Intellectual calisthenics of detailed grammatical analysis prepares the mind to apprehend and indeed love the divine light whose vision begets happiness (Mag 8.21). Close scrutiny of minor matters in poetic meter in the first five books of *De musica* serves as a propaedeutic to help elevate the mind from the sensory order to the region of happiness free from care (M 6.1.1). Expertise in the liberal disciplines that entrains advance in acumen is preliminary to the various levels of moral purification; concentration on these grades disposes toward the highest stage, the very contemplation of truth that is God, in which some outstanding souls have apparently dwelt even in this life (QA 33.72-6).

Augustine made room for an exception to the necessary condition of the liberal arts; certain spiritually advanced Christians who "adhere to the one God and Lord of all things" without training in liberal disciplines fly to God by charity of the highest type (M 6.1.1); for example, Monica, who, in spite of a lack of liberal schooling, lived in the presence of God (O 2.17.45). After 391 further reflection turned the exception into a general case that canceled the stipulation of the necessity of liberal disciplines for happiness. There is no causal nexus between skill in liberal arts and holiness. A number of holy persons know nothing at all about liberal disciplines and, conversely, some who are proficient in liberal arts lag behind in holiness (R 1.3.2). The liberal arts are morally neutral; possessing no per se connection with moral virtue, they carry no guarantee of moral virtue; evil as well as good men could be, indeed were, expert in these disciplines. Distinguishing between what is morally good and what is relatively good, he realized that the good of arithmetic (or any liberal art) is not a pleasurable or useful good but an intrinsic good sought for its own sake, yet it is not good per se or morally good; it can be used by an administrator to embezzle money. Hence here and elsewhere (E 101.1.2) Augustine finds wanting a misguided theory that would assign a morally ennobling role to liberal disciplines. Pursued apart from moral standards, the liberal arts do not liberate the mind but help enchain it in concupiscences (4.16.30). Alienated from the divine truth that frees from sin, cognoscenti pore over poems packed with fables, applaud polished orations laced with falsehoods, and wrestle with the verbose subtleties of philosophies ignorant of God.

One generally excellent scholar seems shy of the mark when he indicts the *Confessions* for "a deep-seated hostility to the old cultural tradition."[58] Augustine was critical not of the measured use but of the improper use of the intrinsic goods of the liberal disciplines.[59] A younger Augustine was not the last to overrate the moral import of purely intellectual attainments. Progeny of the Enlightenment in the twentieth century have extolled the moral value of education per se, relying on learning as such, elementary or advanced, to heal the moral infirmities of individual and social man. J. Dewey (1859-1952), whose instrumentalism was enormously influential in the U.S.A. in the first-half of the twentieth century, tirelessly proclaimed in season and out of season the application of scientific method to problems as the key to social reorganization and redemption, even naively advocating the proper teaching of social psychology as the warranted means for inculcating the principal social virtues. But, as Augustine gradually perceived, excellence in the arts and sciences does not infallibly assure abolition of evil and triumph of the good. Knowledge as such cannot be counted on as an automatic agency of good and a defense against evil. Then as now, savants can become corrupt while the uneducated fly to spiritual heights on the wings of piety. In short, the liberal arts must be highly prized, but as such they do not contribute to moral upbuilding and spiritual fulfillment. Their riches are only relatively good; because open to misuse, they are neither virtues nor necessary conditions for virtues. Only moral virtues and spiritual virtues stemming from the love of God are absolutely good; these are inner moral-spiritual disciplines wrought in the soul by grace.

31. Unassisted command of the reigning disciplines, he underscores, reaped no spiritual fruit, for his sharp intellect had unquestioningly embraced the material God of Manicheism and a human soul consubstantial with God. His God was a fantastic body full of light, immense in a relative sense: the Kingdom of Light extending upward had no limits, but on its lowest side it was bounded by the Kingdom of Darkness (CEF 20.22–22.24).[60] Augustine's spiritual self was considered a particle of light, detached from the divine substance and trapped in the matter that composed his body. Thus he doubly blasphemed, conceiving God as a material substance and assigning his soul equality to God. Now in humility he is not ashamed to confess his sin because then in brazen pride he was not ashamed to profess his blasphemies before men and to play the blind barker (9.4.11), a dog among a pack of curs; dominated by custom, capable of only mindless resistance to Catholic truth (MM 1.18.33; 19, 34) and the true God (P 21 [En.1]. 17). While disentangling all the most complicated knots in the received sciences, he was hopelessly enmeshed in a maze of Manichean error crookedly knitted after the pattern of matter and man; God was misconceived as material and the soul reckoned consubstantial with him. On the other hand, deprivation of a superb mind inflicted no spiritual harm on the little ones of the Lord, who, like tiny birds, are lodged in the nest that is the Church where, free from Manichean darkness, they can fledge; fed by bracing doctrine, tiny ones are energized to spread their wings and perform works of mercy (P 83.7).

Begging for grace to hope under the shadow of God's wings that symbolize protection, he trusts not in material goods of the present but in spiritual goods to come, specifically the fulfillment of the mercy of God in heaven (P 35.12). True Christians have to huddle under God's sheltering wings; they are little ones to be borne by God their whole lives long.[61] Physically and psychologically they grow older and more mature with the passing of years, but spiritually, whatever their stature or human wisdom, they always remain tiny ones. In the economy of mercy aimed at disenthralling the fallen self, human strength is simply not enough; with God's oversight persons can become spiritually lofty so long as they stay content to be little ones even in old age (P 62.16).[62] Let them now return to him so as not to be overturned, i.e., not be tricked by demons (3.3.6).[63] Grace will assure fulfillment in this good, which, because one with God, shines free of all defect. No matter how long their soul's habitation is demolished, they will never find their house on high razed.

NOTES

1. Starnes, 107, n.3, translates *palam...occulte* as "publicly"..."privately." His work as a rhetorician was public, his Manichean life private.
2. Roman emperors in 372, 381, 382, 389, and 399 promulgated edicts proscribing Manicheism. Coyle, 29-30.
3. G-M 78, n. 8
4. In peddling his false goods, the sophist relies on the persuasive power of rhetoric to win over unwary listeners; *Soph.* 220 A5, 223 B7. Rhetoric is put at the service of sophistry; *Gorgias* 520B2 ff. See J. Wild, *Plato's Theory of Man*, 309 along with n. 160.
5. *De off.* 2.14.51.
6. M. Testard, *Saint Augustin et Cicéron*, 1. 44-5. HC 53, n.2. D 2.207.
7. Bonner, 183, n.3. On contraception see E. Clark, "Adam's Only Companion: Augustine and the Early Christian Debate on Marriage," RA 71 (1986), 147, nn. 56-9.
8. Haruspices were diviners who foretold the future by examining significant features of the vital organs of animals, such as livers and gallbladders. Roman haruspices also figured out the predictive import of *monstra*, i.e., strange births, and flashes of lightning. Distinct from soothsayers were augurs, who in Rome were officially deputed not to forecast future events but through the inspection of natural phenomena like the flight of birds to determine whether the gods favored a certain course of action. See J. O'Meara's commentary on his translation, *St. Augustine Against the Academics*, 173, nn. 43-4, some of whose data, as he notes, are drawn from C.O. Thulmin, "Haruspices," RE 7, 243-68, A.S. Pease, "Haruspices, " OCD, 405 ff., and H.J. Rose, "Augures," OCD, 120.
9. "He [God] makes us chaste as he himself is chaste" (EJ 4.2.9.). In his eternity God is absolutely holy and pure; through faith given by grace men become holy and purified. See BA 13, 410, n.1.
10. O'Meara, 95. Brown, 58.
11. S. Lieu, *Manicheism in the Later Roman Empire and Medieval China*, 141-2. So far as I know, Augustine never recognizes a per se connection between his espousal of Manicheism and his acceptance of astrology. Apparently recourse to astrology was so widespread that it cut across diverse religious and philosophical allegiances. Hence Augustine availed himself of astrology because of its seeming scientific cachet and not because of its secondary place in Manichean dogma. Again, the fact that professionals looked down on Mani's venture into astrology as an amateurish incursion without scientific grounding may have influenced Augustine to say little or nothing concerning a per se connection between Manicheism and astrology. Moreover, it is perhaps significant that he embraced, then discarded, astrology and Manicheism independently of each other; he experientially perceived only an incidental connection between the two. BV I.4 separates his endorsement of astrology from his deception by Manichees. First, the falling of the stars into the ocean led him into the error of astrology; only later in a different setting was he duped

by Manicheism. BV 4/1, 57, n. 12, reports the view of L. Alfonsi, "Sant'
Agostino *De beata vita* c. 4," *Riv. di Istruz, e di Filol. classica*, 36 (1958), 249 54.
Consistent with BV 1.4, nowhere in the *Confessions* does Augustine expressly
associate astrology with Manichean doctrines. Prior to becoming a practitioner,
he makes no mention of Manichean approval of astrology. Toward the end of
384 he severed even nominal ties to Manicheism by reaffirming his status as a
Catholic catechumen (5.14.25). But since it was not until 385/6 at the latest that
he finally rejected astrology as scientific imposture, we may infer that his
dismissal of astrology was not the upshot of his abandonment of Manicheism.
Elsewhere he discusses both astrology and Manicheism as views that effectively
deny personal responsibility and guilt. Believers in astrology blame their sins
on fate or the decree of the stars necessitating their actions. Manichees,
however, aver that human sin occurs because the nature of evil within them
prevails over the divine nature (Cont 5.14). Here also he does not expressly
relate Manicheism to astrology in a per se fashion. What they have in common
is their repudiation of personal guilt; but the reasons for this denial are specifically diverse, which suggests in this instance not an analogous resemblance but
only an equivocal connection.

12. The contrite of heart punish themselves and visit stern judgment on themselves
so that they can experience the mercy of God. Hearts crushed and laid low are
humbled, ready for healing (P 146.5-6). No need to select a choice animal from
the herd or purchase incense from far-off lands; a contrite heart is the sacrifice
that pleases the God who can make our heart clean only if we crush our
unclean heart (S 19.3).

13. O 2.15.42 notes the original physico-mathematical similarity of astronomy and
astrology. In defining and distinguishing celestial phenomena and linking them
in a systematic way, reason gives birth to astronomy, which provides a
powerful argument for religious minds, but, wrongly used, becomes a snare for
the curious whose minds are tricked by astronomical data warped by
astrological guesswork; this indicates that astrology is pseudo-science illicitly
begotten of astronomy.

14. J. Lindsay, *The Origins of Astrology* 347-8. For more details see J. Tester, *A History
of Western Astrology*, which, by the way, basing itself on O. Neugebauer and
others, claims that astrology did not originate with the Egyptians and
Babylonians but was a product of Hellenistic culture.

15. Van der Meer, 61.

16. Lindsay, *Origins*, 334.

17. Certain astrologers carried impressive credentials that made their claims
plausible. Albericius, a well-known astrologer in Carthage, whom Licentius
consulted at Augustine's suggestion, immediately disclosed to him the
whereabouts and owner of a lost spoon. He was also a sort of mind-reader able
to report exactly the verse that a student was thinking about (CA 1.6.17-8).
Nevertheless, Albericius, besides being debauched by loose living, missed the
target on many occasions (1.6.17;7.20). It should be mentioned that the
remarkable intuitions instanced were not the outcome of astrology; Albericius
consulted no charts. The text suggests that his successful exercise of divination

that was clairvoyance was inspired by demons (CA 1.7.20-1). However, according to B. Bruning, "De l'astrologie à la grâce", *Collectanea Augustiniana, Mélanges T. van Bavel,* 2.583, n. 21, relying on P. Courcelle, *Divinatio,* RAC, 3.1239, the whole of astrology may be considered a province of divination. See also n. 30, 584-5, which links astrology and the art of haruspices as parts of inductive mantic. Bruning, in addition, shrewdly highlights the role that *sors* plays in divine judgment. Both just and unjust have a lot, one of sanctity, the other of punishment. God saves the just by the *sors* of his will simply because he wills it; Bruning, 2.623, n. 156.

18. Van der Meer, 64-5.
19. BA 13, 413, n. 2.
20. Vindicianus ascribed accurate astrological prognostications to chance taken in the broad sense as dependent upon the influence of higher factors in the universe. According to BA 13, 416, n.1, this view apparently reflects a Neoplatonic outlook that recognizes a certain harmony of the universe with states of the soul, a point elaborated in *Enn.,* 4.4.32, 35,40, 41. According to CD 21.2, two factors account for the success of astrological predictions; primarily, astrologers achieve accurate judgments by the "instinct" or impulse of evil spirits; second, and less frequently, they hit on the truth by luck. See D 2.215.
21. G-M 84, n. 6.
22. Nebridius is described as *valde castus,* very pure of heart, chaste in conduct, and in some sense devoted to God, but in 377 he was still a pagan. Perhaps Augustine is depicting him unchronologically, as he lived after his conversion to Catholicism. Or perhaps he means that despite his pagan outlook Nebridius implicitly conformed his action to a stern moral code, an index of which is his ridiculing of every brand of divination; a chaste person is free of contamination by magical arts (CD 8.18). BA 13, 417, n.2.
23. Nothing in the contemporary world can match the extensive fascination of astrology among minds, learned and unlearned, in the ancient world. In bursting on the Western scene in the 1960s and 1970s, the Age of Aquarius brought with it new movements and sects proclaiming that their lore contained the open-sesame to happiness. Most of those have been falsely religious or ersatz-religious, such as transcendental meditation, Zen Buddhism, the Hare Krishna cult, and EST. Yet in the academic world some pseudo-sciences have flourished. Mathematical logic seems to be analytically groundless; its theory of material implication has simply nothing to do with scientific or even common-sense explication. As an instrument of science, mathematical logic is bankrupt—a pseudo-science; see Blanshard, *The Nature of Thought,* 2.372-81. On a lower plane, after its sterile implementation had cost millions of dollars, the so-called new mathematics that was foisted on the American educational system in the 1960s and 1970s was later discarded as pedagogically unworkable and analytically untenable; unworkable: average students lost ground in learning traditional mathematics; unteachable: a number is not a set; the null set is as self-contradictory as a house without parts. In recent years Freudian psychoanalysis has been increasingly discredited. Its pansexualism and crude metapsychology of ego, superego, and id have long come under fire. In

addition, it has been faulted for empirically unwarranted constructs like the Oedipus complex and its lack of scientific method; Freudian data are acquired by an anecdotal method that reports the clinician's findings without recourse to control and experimental groups. Moreover, according to A. Esterson, *Seductive Mirage*, along with other critics, the very data were radically flawed in case after case by the imposition on the patient of a priori inventions of Freud. Most, perhaps all, of his findings were specifically obtained by the continual intrusion of the analyst's artifacts. In spite of success among literati, it would seem that strictly Freudian psychoanalysis is by and large pseudo-science, perhaps, as P. Medawar charges, the most stupendous intellectual confidence trick of the twentieth century. Its currently shaky status is one main reason why we have paid no attention to psychoanalytic interpretations of the *Confessions*. Plainly the rise of modern science that demolished astrology's claim to scientific status has not done away with certain forms of pseudo-science, albeit much more restricted in their appeal.

24. Common interests; *De am.* 4.15. Affection: 6.20. Founded on virtue: 6.20. Nourished by virtue: 5.20.

25. Van der Meer, 351.

26. According to the study, M.Osterweis, F. Soloman, and M. Green, (eds.), *Bereavement*, 49, two phases characterize bereavement. First, immediately after death the bereaved feels "shock, numbness and a sense of disbelief." Second, after some months, according to B. Raphael (*The Anatomy of Bereavement*, Basic Books, 1983), cited in the above study, the bereaved finds "the absence of the dead person...everywhere palpable," while also feeling "as if the dead person had been torn out of his body." Augustine's reaction fundamentally jibes with these two phases. First, he experienced shock, intensified by the suddenness of the death. Again, he was almost disbelieving of the demise of a friend vibrant with life. However, though he portrays himself as cloaked in grief (4.5.10), he was not numbly cocooned from the reality of death but enveloped in the sense that the grief wrapped him totally round, like a second skin overlying his psyche, which functioned as a sort of a psychic atmosphere. Shocked not into insensitivity but into a super-sensitivity, in grief he lived and moved and had his affective being. B. Raphael's description of the second phase by and large catches Augustine's piercing awareness of the reminders of his departed friend.

27. Quoted in J. Choron, *Death and Modern Man*, 165.

28. Horace, *Odes* 1.3.8. Ovid, *Tristia* 4.4.72. Aristotle, *Nic. Eth.* 8.12 1161b18; 9.4 1166 a33. Pellegrino, 75, n.5 cites other texts sounding a similar note, such as Horace, *Odes* 2.17.5 ff. and Ovid, *Tristia* 1.2.4 ff. The per se link between oneness and friendship is remarked elsewhere: "What else do friends strive for than to be one? And the more they are one, the more they are friends" (O 2. 18.48).

29. R 2.6.2 criticizes this last observation as inept, "a superficial declamation rather than a serious confession," a shallow literary conceit rather than an instance of thoughtful confession. Its inaptness, he remarks, is mitigated somewhat by use of the qualifier "perhaps."

30. Drawing upon a passage quoted in Courcelle, *Les Confessions de saint Augustin dans la tradition littéraire*, 533, n.2, D 2.227 thoughtfully comments on a letter of

Nietzsche to F. Overbeck (*Nietzsche Briefwechsel: Kritische Gesamtaugabe*, 3.3.34) that ridicules Augustine's inflated rhetoric. Sneering at the description of the theft of pears as laughable, Nietzsche castigates the expression of oneness in spirit with his friend as a nauseous mendacity. Augustine's general stance is put down as a vulgarized Platonism, which betrays a slave-mentality repugnant to a sensitive spiritual aristocrat who has nothing but disdain for an ordinary plebeian outlook as he aims at a transvaluation of values toward the shaping of superman. Unfortunately, Nietzsche neglected to see that Augustine's rhetoric is usually under the constraints of and at the service of reason. The slip into rhetorical extravagance was one he himself later faulted (R 2.6.2), a piece of poetic license partly explicable by its status as a commonplace among classical authors like Horace and Ovid. Ironically, Nietzsche's rhetoric was not always impeccably rational. Here, as frequently elsewhere, he gives free rein to *argumentatio ad abusum*, substituting sarcasm for sober analysis. For all his gifts, he usually succumbed to the worst type of impassioned literary philosophy.

31. Augustine was driven not only by grief but by ambition to move from the professionally unpromising town of Thagaste to Carthage, the largest city in Africa that offered golden opportunity for advancement. With the moral and financial assistance of Romanianus, his patron, and without informing Monica, he arranged to migrate to Carthage to give his considerable talents a wider scope of exercise and a more real possibility of honor and fortune, the expenses of his change of venue being underwritten by Romanianus (CA 2.2.3).

32. See J. Lienhard, "Friendship, Friends," AE 322-3, with accompanying bibliography. In particular, M. McNamara, *Friends and Friendship for St. Augustine.*

33. In *Intellectuals* P. Johnson stresses the wide disparity between the pronounced moral delinquencies of secular intellectuals like Marx, B. Russell, and J.P. Sartre, among others, and their lofty programs.

34. W. Roche, "Measure, Number, and Weight in Saint Augustine," NS 15 (1941), 350-76.

35. R. Buckenmeyer, "The Meaning of *Judicium* and its Relation to Illumination in the Dialogues of St. Augustine," 1 AS(1970), 111.

36. Buckenmeyer, 100.

37. Pope, 235.

38. Pope, 231.

39. Unlike some of the Greek Fathers, Augustine did not think that the body of the first man was spiritualized, a prototype of the resurrected body (GL 6.23.24). Still, on his showing, knowledge of the sensory-intellectual sort prior to the Fall was sharper and more encompassing than such knowledge in our present state. The *Confessions* seems to be the only source touching on this matter; in any event, I have not been able to discover any parallel passages. On Augustine vis-a-vis certain Greek Fathers see G. Ladner, *The Idea of Reform* 153-7.

40. Obviously Augustine never held that God belonged to a species since he transcends all genera and species. The term, introduced here to elucidate the drift of his thinking, is put in inverted commas to indicate that it has no existential referent.

41. This passage emphasizing the majesty of the God-man depicts him as a super-giant overpowering obstacles and enemies and covering his earthly career with enormous strides. Elsewhere, however, Augustine limns the weakness of Jesus as the channel of the power recreating man. At the time he encountered the Samaritan woman, Jesus was weary from his journey. Jesus is both strong and weak; strong as the Word through whom all things were made, weak as the Word made flesh. "But do not be weak. Be strong in his weakness because what is weak as regards God is stronger than men" (J 15.6-7). The power of the divine nature shone through the weakness of the human nature, proving that Jesus is the instrument of divine strength. When human weakness is joined to that of Jesus, men become not weaker but stronger, for divine weakness is far stronger than the most colossal human strength.

42. Excerpts from the Latin are given in D 2.245.

43. See Blanshard, *Nature of Thought*, 2.166-211.

44. BA 13, 470-3.

45. Donald A. Cress, "Hierius and Augustine's Account of the Lost *De Pulcho et Apto*, "AS 7(1976), 153-63. Also Svoboda, *"L'esthéthique"* 10-6, 47. See the comments of D 2.246-8 on Augustine's view of beauty.

46. D 2.250

47. HC 66. n. 25.

48. *Pondus...est impetus quidam cujusque rei, velut conantis ad locum suum* (Weight is a certain force of any thing, as striving towards its proper place). A stone presses against your hand because it is seeking its proper place. Take your hand away and it falls to rest in its place. Weight then is that motion that is, as it were, spontaneous, which is without life and sensation. Water seeks its own place; it seeks to be ordered , because it is outside order for water to be above oil. Until it comes to its order, until it holds its proper place, its motion is restless" (P 29[En.2].10) (abridged). Reference to the weights of various loves (4.14.22) anticipates 13.9.10: "My love is my weight." As mentioned above (1.1.1), the famous text, "Our heart is restless. . ." (1.1.1), implies weight and its order to rest in God, its proper place, as a stone is ordered to rest on the earth, its proper place. "Until it comes to the place toward which it is ordered, until it attains its proper place, its movement is restless" (P 29[En.2].10). The movement of the heart ordained for God is restless till comes to rest in God, requiring fire from the Spirit to rise up to God, its proper place (13.9.10).

49. Latin text in D 2.252-3.

50. Divine art is the paradigm for all human art; in all his works God perfectly executes the beautiful and fitting. To each thing, no matter how inferior its species, he gives perfection or wholeness. Moreover, limbs and other parts are fittingly and harmoniously positioned for the good of the whole body. Again, things that are beautiful wholes in themselves are fittingly arranged, the inferior serving the superior species, for the good of the beauty of the whole dynamic universe that is an awesome edifice or, in terms of the dynamic, a grand song of ineffably rich harmony (CF 21.5-6). See O'Connell, *Art and the Christian Intelligence in St. Augustine*, 20-2, 47-9.

51. The reference is to the three dimensions: lines, colors, and volumes. For

Augustine, tridimensionality is a necessary feature of bodies (QA 3.4. GL 7.21.27). Hence during his Manichean years he applied corporeal criteria to knowledge of the soul; if visible in any way, the soul had to have three dimensions. Yet he did not thereby deny the existence of the soul; not directly apprehensible, its existence was inferred. After being emancipated from Manichean materialism, Augustine argued that the soul's very recognition of length or width as such showed that it has no dimensions; it is purely spiritual, with its own spiritual power (QA 14.23).

52. See T. Kato, "Melodia interior: sur le traité *De pulchro et apto*," REA 12 (1966), 229-40; 237. Following Alfaric and Kato, Starnes, 11, n. 80, argues that for two reasons the main influence in the shaping of *De pulcho et apto* was Manichean: a Manichean outlook rather than a Neo-Pythagorean stance dominated Augustine's mind at this time; and the features of the monad and dyad bespeak affectivity while the Pythagorean distinction focuses on the properties of numbers.

53. There are three sorts of goods: great goods, such as the moral virtues; intermediary goods, such as the powers of the soul like reason, memory, and will; and least goods, such as the forms of bodies (LA 2.18.48-19.53). Only great goods cannot be badly used; they are always and everywhere morally good, properly ordained to the divine good. Because the intermediary and least goods can be put to the service of evil ends, they are not per se morally good.

54. As several commentators have remarked Augustine's use of terms is not always governed by the most rigorous scientific precision. The *mens* or mind is the highest part of the soul (T 15.11). Sometimes the soul itself (*animus*) is identified with mind. Here Augustine employs rational mind to designate the spiritual source of light and direction for nonrational powers such as sensory perception and appetite (Imm. 25. DQ 46.2. CD 5.11). See G. O'Daly, "Anima, Animus," AL 1.316.

55. BA 33, 87-8, n.1. Not all are convinced that Marius Victorinus' translation came into Augustine's hands. P. Hadot, *Marius Victorinus. Recherches sur sa vie et ses oeuvres*, 182-8. Starnes, 111, n. 96.

56. As Marrou, 189-93 shows, Augustine includes eight disciplines in the cycle of sciences: grammar, dialectic, rhetoric; arithmetic, music, geometry, astronomy, and philosophy; O 2.4.13; 5.14; 12.35; 16.44; 18.47. QA 33.72. R 1.6. The *Confessions* notes the six arts acquired during his student years, a list that omits astronomy and philosophy. Astronomy is not mentioned because it is not notionally but empirically known: its principles are not known sheerly in the light of truth falling upon interior objects (4.16.30); indeed all the conclusions of this science are garnered by empirical investigation (R 1.8.2). Philosophy is not included because it is the crown of the liberal arts, which are the objective and subjective instruments preparatory toward and dispositive of philosophy. Objectively, the truths attained in arithmetic, dialectic, and grammar, when pondered, lead to philosophic propositions on the level of wisdom. Subjectively, the intricate, subtle handling of problems in the liberal arts constitutes an *exercitatio animi*, an austere drilling of the mind that builds up its thews to wrestle with and achieve a measure of the philosophy that is true

wisdom. For Augustine's *reductio artium ad philosophiam*, his strategy of ordering the arts to the service of philosophy, see Marrou, 277-98; for the training in the arts as exercises propaedeutic to skills in the precise treatment of philosophic concepts, Marrou, 299-327.

57. Initially the prodigal son is described only as wasting his substance in dissolute living; it is the elder son who accuses his wayward brother of throwing away money on harlots (Lk 15.30). Here as elsewhere (P 95.5) Augustine accepts this particular charge as accurate, recourse to prostitutes being implied in the general expression, "dissolute living."

58. H. Hagendahl, *Augustine and the Latin Classics* 715. In "Augustine's Classical Readings," *RA* 15 (1980), 144-75, J. O'Donnell supplements Hagendahl by endeavoring, with considerable success, to establish precisely when Augustine expressly consulted, read or re-read, a classical source. It seems unlikely, he holds, that as a bishop, Augustine spent much time in revisiting the classics when preparing ammunition for his counter-assault against the pagans in CD. He largely relied on memory of quotations, verified from time to time by comparison with the original texts. This prodigious memory confirms the fact that his mind and literary imagination were saturated with the classics when he was writing the *Confessions*, which contain relatively few direct quotations from classical authors.

59. See G. Bonner, "*Vera lux illa quae illuminat*: the Christian Humanism of St. Augustine," 1, reprinted as Ch. IV in *God's Decree and Man's Destiny*. See also D 2.269-78.

60. Coyle, 33.

61. While a bishop, Augustine self-effacingly describes himself not as a ruling official but as a common fellow citizen (4.15.26) of his brethren in the city that is the Church; not as a learned theological preacher but as a tiny one (4.16.31) sharing the simple faith of his flock, along with whom he was nourished and sustained by the word of truth that is the food of sound faith. When his preaching dispensed to them a portion of the word of God, it was food on which he himself first fed to keep alive in the Lord. Hence in his ministry of feeding the lambs he ranked himself not as the master of the household but simply as a fellow servant. S 339.4.

62. Commenting elsewhere on Is 46.4, Augustine says: "Your old age indeed grows white with the white hairs of wisdom, but it does not grow feeble with the effects of old age in the flesh. Here youth (*pueritia*) stands for humility. Let your old age be youthful and your youth be old-aged, i.e., your wisdom should not be with pride nor your humility without wisdom." (P 112.2)

63. Here Augustine plays on the nuances of verbs rooted in *vertere*, which are difficult to render in English in his exact sense. Because we have been "averted," we have become perverted; we are then to be "reverted" to God so that we may not be "everted" (overturned). See BA 13, 461, n. 64.

Book Five
Augustine Abandons Manicheism

This book begins a distinct part, Books 5-8, which narrate Augustine's gradual disenchantment with and abandonment of Manicheism, a step clearing the way for truths that will lead to his conversion. At this juncture the account becomes more detailed; while the first four books canvass roughly twenty-eight years, the following four chronicle only four years, the decisive period between 383-6.[1] Book 5 consists of three parts. Following an Introduction (1.1-2.2), is the record of his encounter with Faustus (3.3-7.13), which culminates in a doctrinal withdrawal from Manicheism. Secondly (8.14-12.22), he describes his voyage to and stay in Rome. Thirdly, from Rome he traveled as official orator to Milan, where he first providentially came in contact with Ambrose (13.23-14.25).

Chapter 1: A Sacrifice of Praise

1. To mark this turning point, Book 5 starts, as did Book 1, with a prayer stressing praise of God. The confession proffered by the hand that is his tongue is a sacrifice offered from a heart aglow in the Spirit (Rom 12.11); a sacrifice in general, recall, signifies any work performed toward union with God in holy fellowship (CD 10.6). The tongue of the soul is moved for precisely this: to praise the name of the Lord in words that substantially reiterate the third sentence of Book 1, "[God], you arouse man to delight in praising you" (1.1.1). Then he beseeches God to cleanse his bones, to renew his spiritual vigor, the bones standing for the soul's firmament, which is spiritual strength or fortitude (P 6.4). Purified, the bones pray, "Lord, who is like you?" God is transcendently unique, his immeasurable mercy

induplicable (P 34 [S.1].14). His penetration of the soul is also unmatchable; requiring no instruction from man, his all-seeing eye comprehends all in the depths of the soul. No heart, however tightly shut, can block his vision; no heart, however strong can fend off his touch of mercy or justice that dissolves the hardness. No one can escape the divine heat that purifies the soul of every impediment to divine union (P 50.23). So the soul on fire praises God in order to love him the more and, meditating on multiple mercies that again delivered it from darkness, is galvanized to praise God. Praise and love go round in a virtuous circle: praise issues in love, and confession of the mercy that is love oriented toward misery issues in praise.

The whole created universe never stops proclaiming praise of God. All spiritual beings, including the angels and here especially men, cry out their praise through hearts fastened on God. Even things below, which lack reason, never cease praising him through the voices of men discerning their beauty. When human beings ponder the magnificence of the universe and admire its beauty, they praise God in the universe. Each is a kind of priest of creation who lifts up the praise of mute stones and dumb animals to the most high (P 144.13). Through man all creation sings its song of praise. In the one voice of man acting as proxy for the countless voices of roses, worms, and dogs, the universe cries out its love and chants its praise of its maker. The spectacle of beauty and the praise it elicits rouses the soul from earthbound weariness. Freshly energized, its spirit focuses on and is nourished by the lovely things made; then rising higher, it trains the eyes of the inner self on the maker of these stupendous wonders. Resting in the arms of God, the soul gains more strength because coursing within is the force of the omnipotent One. It is praise that lifts up the soul from the lassitude of sin and earthly cares; the praising soul is released from its burdens and renewed in hope (P 145.2). God alone works these marvels; out of his goodness he created this dazzling universe; out of his mercy he heals the sin-stricken spirit so that, admiring things made and praising their maker, the soul can ascend to the divine bosom, there to feed on the very refreshment and lasting might of God (P 135.41).

Chapter 2: God Ever Present Awaits the Return of Strays

2. The iniquitous are troubled with inquietude; yet the divine eye

pierces through shadows in which they have ensnarled themselves. Ugly in themselves, sinners are, nevertheless, like a painting containing black spots to accord with its motif, the beauty of the universe as a whole; its sinful blotches fall in with the total design (CD 11.23). Unable to besmirch the divine plan, sinners are also incapable of harming God, who always remains innocent, immune from all evil since the evil harm only themselves (2.6.13). In no way can deformities of sinners deform God's kingdom, which from the majesty of the heavens, with its inalterable stars, to the clods of earth, is ever perfectly ordered, ever a whole with all parts properly integrated. Here Augustine is pointing up the disparity between the kingdom of the true God and the Manichean Kingdom of Light which is overrun by forces of the Prince of Darkness. In repudiating God, sinners hope to flee from his face, here a figure for his presence. Still, in moral isolation themselves, they cannot ensure insulation from the God who fills the whole world. Whether they fly to the ends of the world or the depths of the nether world, there is God present in his being and power (P 138.11). Not seeing God, they delusively imagine that he is not always seeing them. Spiritually blinded by wickedness, in their flight they unwittingly run up against him; while they ostensibly flee, God stays ever with them. Because they unjustly offend God, they are justly punished; wounded, they withdraw from his gentle touch. The source of their sorrow is ignorance of the truth that God is everywhere, intimately present even to the morally remote. Since the creator does not desert his creature as the creature deserts him, those who have strayed should turn back to discover the Lord within. There they will be moved to confession, begging forgiveness and praising him, weeping on his bosom after being liberated from the stony path of anguish born of self-seeking. Yet the restored spirit weeps the more and, supernaturally, rejoices in the tears; these are at once tears of sadness over past failings and of gladness over healing. Forgiveness and joy stream from God; no limited creature of flesh and blood can pardon sins and transmute them into wellsprings of joy. Only the Lord who made man can remake in him the divine image; only the infinitely merciful One can console aggrieved souls, drawing out stings and bathing wounds. The concluding sentences unmistakably evidence that the foregoing lines sketch his pitiable condition as a Manichee. He simply did not know that God was a pure spirit everywhere present; ignorant of his ubiquity, he blindly hurled himself against God's firmament of justice, falling headlong to the jagged rocks and wasteland below (2.4.9). Where was I, he asks, when I was searching for you? He was engrossed in things outside, blacking out the vision of God right in front of the inward man. After his conversion he prayed: "O God, let me know myself, let me know you" (Sol 2.1.1). The opposite occurred in the pre-conversion Augustine; by projecting himself outward, he lost concrete awareness of the inner self, thereby thwarting knowledge of God.

Chapter 3: Manichean Myth Refuted by Astronomy

3. Since Book 5 covers a period of two years, from autumn, 382, to autumn, 384, this section begins with the verb *proloquar*: "I will start by speaking of my twenty-ninth year," that is, close to the end of that year, the first principal event of which would be his encounter with Faustus (6.11-7.13)[2]. Later he will retail events of his thirtieth year, culminating in his traveling to Milan (5.13.23-14.25). In late autumn of 382, during his twenty-ninth year, he was struggling with difficulties concerning Manicheism. Co-believers directed him to Faustus,[3] one of the seventy-two Manichean bishops, reported to be a clear-sighted sage in both Manichean doctrine and secular sciences. He was, in fact, more eloquent and charming than sagacious and subtle, an artful talker whose suavity had imprisoned many gullible Christians in the Manichean cave. When nineteen, Augustine had spurned Holy Writ because of its unadorned style (3.5.9). Now intellectually more mature, while still attracted by fetching diction, he no longer equated style with meaning. What counted more was not the dish garnishing the content but solid truth nourishing the mind, food that Faustus, renowned among Manichees as a sort of mastermind, was reputed to furnish. Hailed as a man of encyclopedic learning, supposedly competent in all the higher domains of knowledge, and especially erudite in the liberal arts, Faustus probably resorted less to deduction and induction than to personalistic suasion. Affable, never lost for a word, he was ready to smooth the ruffled feathers and calm the turmoil of a vacillating co-religionist. Unhappily for Faustus, he was confronted by a mind not only more adept in rhetoric but also more dexterous in dialectic. "In the realm of the blind the one-eyed man is king": Faustus, who could reign

among analytically sightless Manichees, was easily dethroned by a mind with intellectual eyesight of the keenest; his honeyed tongue was powerless to dissolve Augustine's wide-ranging doubts. Augustine had assimilated many exact propositions of "the philosophers", actually scientists, in this case astronomers; in the West the terms philosophy and science were commonly used interchangeably well into the nineteenth century to designate a body of propositions both certain and explanatory[4]. Though not a working scientist, he was well versed in arithmetic and geometry, besides possessing an aptitude for spatial relations, so that he became proficient in the essentials of astronomy. Set over against astronomical rules, the vagaries of the Manicheans looked shoddy; the scientific picture seemed far more likely to be true. Not all scientists, gifted in their painstaking mensuration of the heavens, were able to discover the maker of heaven and earth. Not eminence of mind but lowliness of heart draws down divine blessings. God turns away from the self-exalted because their pride affronts him, even if they are top astronomers whose assiduous empirical investigation, facilitated by mathematical tools, enables them to compute the number of the stars, to identify the constellations, to measure with exactitude distances in celestial space, and to chart the course of the stars or planets (P.132.1; 33.19). Finite intelligence meets mystery here; if men try to mount to the all-high sheerly on their own, they are rebuffed as usurpers by a jealous God who brooks no self-deified human "gods" before him; but if they abase themselves, he comes down to them (P 33[S.2].23).

4. The fertile minds of astronomers uncovered many features of the celestial realm with so sure a grasp that they foretold, many years prior to the events, solar and lunar eclipses. These predictions were accurate down to the last detail, identifying not only the day but the very hour and specifying, in addition, whether the eclipse was to be total or partial. Astronomy was not an esoteric science, with its arcane formulas sequestered from all but a select scientific elite. Along with rigorous treatises, popular works on astronomy enjoyed circulation, supplemented by almanacs that set down techniques for calculating the positions of the planets and occurrences of eclipses (E 55.4.7). These physico-mathematical techniques were no doubt the rules in writing Augustine refers to here. As a later passage shows (5.3.6), Augustine himself, with the aid of an almanac, was favored with

sufficient numerical capacity to personally compute the year, month, day, and hour of future solar and lunar eclipses. Hence these sentences are not redundant; Augustine modestly indicates in the third person that he himself mathematically forecast eclipses. When the eclipses actually verified the predictions, individuals unfamiliar with astronomical literature were filled with wonder or puzzlement in the face of what they found baffling, ignorance being the mother of wonderment (13.21.30), and were stupefied as well by the almost-beyond-belief wizardry of the uncanny exactitude of the predictions.

Per contra, scientists experienced not puzzlement but a wonder-free certitude leavened with elation. Some of Augustine's acquaintances, upon receiving praise, lapsed into self-praise, irreligious pride causing them to lose the light of God. Scientifically sharp, they foresaw eclipses in the future; spiritually obtuse, they ironically failed to see the eclipse of the soul they were experiencing in the present. In a solar eclipse the moon blocks the light of the sun from the earth; the earth lies within the shadow of the moon. In a spiritual eclipse pride blocks the light of divine truth from illumining the soul; pride is the source of the darkness that shadows over the soul. While probing the origin of eclipses, these astronomers did not push an inquiry into the ultimate origin of the intelligence whereby they initiated their inquiry; pride stopped them from seeing that the eye of intelligence receives its light from the God who is truth (P 25.2,3). Even when they recognized that God had made the universe, they neglected to give back all of the self he had given them (S 34.7). They were meant to offer up all their scientific success, to slaughter in sacrifice all proclivities to self-elevation. Instead of dying to the world so as to live to God (CD 10.6), they lived for self and sacrificed the demands of God to the needs of self; instead of surrendering all to God, they became vulnerable to the lure of the triple concupiscence (EJ 2.13-4). In their pride they were raised on high, flying like birds of the air. False curiosity, resembling in its various manifestations fish of the sea traveling through the hidden paths of the abyss, is a passionate quest for trivial data of only transient value, to be swallowed up in the shifting currents of the sea of knowledge (P 8.13). Those riveted on maximum sensory pleasure are comparable to cattle wholly absorbed in gratifying bodily needs (P 8.13). Here Augustine is lamenting the state not of former Manichean colleagues but of nonManichean scientists. Unlike Manichees, the astronomers attained a scientific cognition of heavenly bodies, some knowing God as their maker; yet like Manichees, they paid fealty to the suzerainty of the triple concupiscence. Had these errant astronomers put to death their pride, curiosity, and sensuality, the jealousy of the God who is a consuming fire would have crowned their sacrifice in the flames of his love, turning the human sacrifice into a whole-burnt offering which, after reducing dead cares to ashes, remakes them in view of deathless life that blazes forth from the heart of the everlasting God.

5. These savants, while knowing the way the heaven goes, did not know the way to go to heaven; they were, in particular, ignorant of Christ, the mediator, the Word of God through whom all things were made, including the entities that scientists number, the scientists themselves, the senses that see numberable objects, and the mind that analytically numbers the stars. Men who cannot ordinarily count the grains of sand on the seashore or hairs on the head surely cannot fully understand the wisdom of the Word beyond human reckoning (P 146.11). Yet through his self-giving in the incarnation, the only begotten Son of God shares with men his wisdom, righteousness, and holiness. The King of kings was numbered among men, numbered in the Roman census (Mt 17.24-7), and paid a "number" of money, a tax, to an earthly monarch. In their arrogance these pagan scientists did not recognize the Christ, in union with whom men are bade to forgo the lofty perch of self and, ensouled with his humility, rise to his incarnate lowliness. These pagan savants fancied themselves as luminous as the stars, but, in fact, not anchored in the spiritual firmament (2.4.9), they plummeted earthward, clods shattered by pride, and, far from being enlightened, were spiritually imbecilic. No doubt they did track down truths about the cosmos, but they neglected to religiously seek truth itself, the architect of the universe. Their learned explorations did not discover God or, if they did admit his existence, they denied him adoration and gratitude. They diminished God either by confusing themselves with God or confusing the creator with creatures. Smug in their worldly learning, they accorded to themselves what is God's, imagining themselves to be creators of their gifts. Worse, they ascribed to God what was theirs, thrusting their falsities on the God who is truth itself, perverting the glory of the incorruptible God to the idolatrous image of a corruptible creature (Rom 1.21-5): man (symbolizing vanity and darkness), birds (symbolizing pride), four-footed beasts (symbolizing lust of the flesh),

and serpents (symbolizing curiosity, lust of the eyes). In more detail, in worshiping an idol, say Apollo, individuals turn the truth of God into a lie. Should they insist that they are actually worshiping the sun symbolized by Apollo, believers point out that then they are worshiping a creature rather than the creator (S 197.2. P 113[S.2].4).[5]

6. Yet in spite of their belief and practice, pagan astronomers channeled to Augustine theories proved true analytically and empirically; their calculations explained, i.e., charted and forecast, the positions of stars, and supplied quantitative reasons for the order of times or divisions of temporal periods: days and years are determined by solar movements, months by phases of the moon, and the changes of the seasons by the solstices. They also explained the appearances of stars like Mars, Venus, and Jupiter visible to the naked eye, which Augustine was able to observe in the night sky, their locations specified in astronomical handbooks. In comparison with this science based on mathematical analysis and verified in experience, Mani's effusions were scientifically insane, providing not one coherent explanation for solstices, equinoxes, and eclipses. For Mani, recall, the light liberated from the earth is gathered by buckets of the constellations and poured into the sun and moon; the moon waxes when it receives light from below, then wanes when it transmits particles of light to the sun (E 55.4.6). Eclipses occur when Primal Man veils his face to spare himself the disgust and sorrow produced by observing lightsome beings assaulted by the forces of Darkness (CF 18.7; 22.12).[6] According to Simplicius, a sixth-century pagan Neoplatonist, some Manichees adopted another literary explication. When the actions of evil archons incarcerated in creation generate disturbances and disorder, light particles within them send out a veil to shield them from vexation by these disturbances; this veil is what causes eclipses.[7] Yet though Manichees boldly appealed to reason rather than faith, Augustine was called upon to believe Mani's astronomical fantasies, totally at variance from what mathematical analysis and the witness of his eyes solidly informed him. However impious, pagan astronomers taught truth about nature while Mani and his disciples, however apparently pious, taught what looked like nonsense.

Interestingly, he terms astronomy a secular wisdom. As moral theory whereby a person lives rightly according to the rules of the virtues is a wisdom (LA 2.10.29), so astronomy that determines the rules that regulate the stars is a kind of wisdom of the cosmos, in particular, the celestial domain. The astronomer judges sensory experience by mathematical-physical rules, invariant relations quantitatively formulated and confirmed by empirical checking. His wisdom sees and foresees; explanatory insight into the positions of sun, moon, and earth underlies rational foresight of a solar eclipse.

Chapter 4: Piety as such Superior to Science as such

7. Science as such does not make a man pleasing to the Lord of truth, who is primarily served by piety, in which lies religious wisdom, a practical life of devotion in word and deed to the true God (T12.14.22). An astronomer who knows everything in his secular wisdom but nothing of God lacks fulfillment of spirit in the truth that is God. On the other hand, a scientific ignoramus who truly knows and loves God is fundamentally happy. Moreover, a Christian who is an accomplished scientist is not guaranteed greater happiness than his unscientific brother in religion. Not science as such but piety wins happiness; he earns inner peace as he worships God as the all-loving maker of all. A scientifically illiterate Christian, while ignorant of the exact dimensions of the tree of life, plucks its fruit for which he thanks its maker. However, a nonbelieving scientist who carefully measures the tree is not fed by it or its maker. His scientific precision is sterile, his spirit famished. In general, because lived-out faith conduces to serenity, the faithful Christian is superior to the pagan scientist. Scientifically impoverished, even knowing nothing of the constellation visible every night, whose stars are the brightest in the sky,[8] he is spiritually rich because in union with the creator of all the treasures of the universe. He spiritually possesses all the wealth of the world; he is richer in happiness than the astronomer who maps the heaven and numbers the stars, as well as the physicist who weighs the elements, analyzing the dynamics and proper location of fire, air, water, and earth, yet is totally unconcerned about God. The man of faith cleaves to the God who arranges all things according to measure (limited substance), number (form or specific makeup), and weight (order or natural tendency). Indeed, recall, God is the supreme measure, the uncreated form, the perfect peace or rest that terminates ordered movement (VR 11.21. NB 12. GL 4.4.8-10).

Chapter 5: Fallacies of Manicheism

8. Mani, who oddly did not perceive the preeminence of piety and its independence of science, foolishly inserted a cosmology and cosmogony into the center of his religious teaching. Without knowing science, an individual can achieve religious wisdom; conversely, a scientist can be totally ignorant of religious wisdom (5.3.4). Mani, who could have been a first-class scientist without a shred of piety, unfortunately believed that justification of his new religious outlook called for a novel version of the shaping and running of heaven and earth. The effrontery of his pseudo-science bared the fraudulence of his religious claims. It is spiritual emptiness for a scientist to profess knowledge to the exclusion of God while it is piety to confess God with heart, lips, and life. But Mani's vanity was egregious: his scientific picture itself was humbug; so his piety had to be cankered with errors. Astronomers' censures of his prolix misconstructions indirectly evidenced how shabby were his pronunciamentos in more arcane matters, i.e., in religious knowledge. Not exactly deficient in self-esteem, he strove to convince disciples that the Holy Spirit really dwelt, personally and with all his authority, within him. Thus in tackling astronomical questions, which do not essentially bear on religious doctrines, he exposed himself as a scientific mountebank; worse, he suffered from the sacrilegious delusion that all his teachings were stamped with a divine warranty because dictated by the Spirit incarnate within him.[9]

9. Mani's ignorance of science and his pseudo-scientific bizarreries were defensible in some respect, but his arrogance in identifying himself with the Holy Spirit himself was wholly inexcusable. If a fellow Christian vents baseless opinions about the movements of the stars, Augustine can listen patiently, deeming his blunders harmless so long as his misguided views on things created do not denigrate the creator. However, if this Christian, grossly lumping religion and science, thinks that his scientific views are strictly relevant to religious doctrine and, even when set straight, obstinately persists in pontificating on what he really knows nothing about, his conduct is sinful. Yet he remains pardonable if he is only a religious infant; Christian charity, like a loving mother, tolerates infantile infirmity, trusting that in time he will become immune to every buffeting from winds of false doctrine. Analogously, if he had been open to the truth, Mani's

scientific inadequacies might have been forgivable in part. However, his boast that he was the Holy Spirit himself was the most blasphemous of his errors. But the enormity of these preposterous pretensions became patent only later. In 382-3, when doubts began to shake his Manichean faith, Augustine was still striving to understand whether Mani's teachings could be squared with celestial phenomena. Even if Mani's ideas could hypothetically account for the stars in their courses, he was still confronted by the alternative explications of the received astronomical science of his day. Both the Manichean and scientific versions might be consistently reconciled with data observed, but they were irreconcilable with each other. Not yet firmly convinced that Manichean explanations of celestial occurrences were unsubstantiated, he remained suspended in doubt; either explanation might prove satisfactory. Apparently at this time he never explicitly attempted to break out of the impasse but, if pressed for a resolution, would have opted for Mani's stance, making a decisive act of natural faith in the authority of Mani because of his reputation as a holy man. For all their impressive skills, the pagan astronomers, repugnant in their idolatry, were more liable to be off the mark than an ascetical missionary of the Light wholly consecrated to the good. Mani's sanctity fixed a tentative seal of authenticity on his questionable cosmological teachings. At this point Augustine was applying the moral-religious test, "By their fruits you shall know them," (Mt 7.16) as a criterion superior to cognitive clarity and consistency. A life of holiness was incontestable proof of religious truth, however apparently garbled the doctrines professed. The heart that had been set afire by *Hortensius* (3.4.7) still burned to grasp a lived truth. The sanctity of the Manichean elect, their happiness-engendering truth, was one of the main reasons why he first became strongly attracted to the cult. This wisdom of life sustained his fidelity, inclining him to only slowly relinquish his loyalty in the teeth of doctrinal absurdities.

Chapter 6: Disappointment with Faustus

10. For nine years (373-82)[10] Augustine was a hearer[11] in the sect but, in fact, a nonhearer of the truth, a prodigal son wandering in a wasteland of myth. All this time he had been intensely looking forward to dialogue with bishop Faustus, reputedly a first-rate

theologian and extraordinary apologist. On occasion he had casually raised questions that his brethren felt helpless to resolve. All that would change, he was assured, when Faustus' acumen would solve the puzzles posed and, if necessary, unriddle more troublesome perplexities. Faustus finally did arrive in the summer of 382, having recently departed Rome, probably because of the stern edicts directed at Manichees by Theodosius in 381 and 382. Unhappily for the Manichees and much to Augustine's disappointment, Faustus' performance did not measure up to advance billing. He turned out to be a gracious gentleman whose smooth speaking was as becoming as his warm personality. But for all his bewitching polish he threw no more light on thorny questions than other Manichean compatriots. However comely its bearer and however exquisitely designed, an empty cup could not sate Augustine's thirst for the truth. Faustus' style was, to be sure, more graceful and his reasoning more eloquently expressed; but the cogency was mere appearance – arguments clothed in appealing garb are not necessarily sound. Wanting in critical judgment, Augustine's co-religionists counted Faustus prudent, practically judicious, and wise, skilled in theoretical analysis, since they were taken in by the glitter of his discourse. Augustine had also encountered another type, which judged dubious any argument clothed in appealing literary dress. Well-turned language, on this view, automatically invalidates an argument. Here Augustine probably had mainly in mind certain astronomers of his acquaintance, whose lean prose was bare of metaphor, and who were suspicious of language loaded with rhetorical flourishes that smacked of quack science. From God, the only teacher of truth in the absolute sense, (Mag 11.38; 12.40), he learned the true approach to evaluating statements. A proposition should not be judged true because elegantly enunciated nor false because gracelessly phrased. Conversely, a proposition is not necessarily true because awkwardly expressed nor necessarily false because finely arrayed. The wisdom that is truth and the folly that is untruth resemble edible and inedible foods. Both sorts of nutriment, one for the soul, the other for the body, can be tendered through the same means. Truth and falsity can wear either well-styled or shabby garments, and good and bad food can be served on ornate or crude platters.

11. He next calls attention in more detail to Faustus' analytical gaps. As a sensitive rhetorician, he could not help but be impressed by the

fire and force of Faustus' sparkling presentation. When an opportunity finally arose to ply Faustus with questions, he soon found to his dismay that Faustus' conceptual facility lagged behind verbal fluency. The defender of the Manichean faith displayed some command of grammar or elementary literature, a field in which his attainments were not above average; but his acquaintance with vast stretches of Latin literature was slender, for he had read only some of Cicero's orations, a handful of Seneca's works, and a smattering of poetry. The fact that Manichean treatises he studied were well written, along with daily practice of oratory in Latin, ensured his fluency. He was not at home in arithmetic and astronomy, areas crucial to analysis of stellar movements, calculations about which had provoked doubts about cosmologically based Manichean theories.

As a shrewd theoretical and practical psychologist, Augustine was hardly unaware that a treacherous memory can weave a layer or marginal section of nonfact into memorially recovered data. So once again he appeals to the infallible judge of his conscience to witness to the complete veracity of his memorial recording. God, before whose all-seeing eye his recollection lies wholly open, can verify that he has not falsified his narrative by inventing spurious facts or even by embroidering his report with self-flattering, fictive details. In the depth of his providence God arranged this meeting with Faustus so as to draw good out of an encounter with an evil man, awakening him to recognize errors that had long held him in bondage. Now he was turning toward, not away from, the presence of God; a start of deconversion from untruth, a significant step toward full conversion.

Chapter 7: Disenchantment with Manicheism Followed by Disaffection

12. Augustine was frustrated by the severely truncated learning of the vaunted Faustus, who was almost wholly untutored in mathematics and astronomy, with the result that he was hopelessly unprepared to ponder, let alone resolve, Augustine's problems. If Faustus had not been a Manichean, he might have been able to separate strictly religious doctrines from questionable scientific opinions; but this was not the case. So closely intertwined were Manichean religious and cosmological beliefs that if the cosmological foundation was blasted, the religious edifice tumbled down.

Unfortunately for Faustus, Manichean doctrines were chockablock with nonsensical myths concerning the shape of the heaven (not the sky) and the movements of sun, moon, and planets (called wandering stars by the ancients). Their theories were not even the stuff of scientific fiction, which consists of plausible narrative founded on scientific data, but sheerly unscientific fables, stories manufactured by undisciplined imagination rather than explorations of sober intellect. As instanced earlier, the sun and moon are pictured as ships carrying cargos of light-particles through the ocean of the heaven while Atlas upholds all eight earths and *Splenditens* supports all ten heavens. Augustine had hoped that Faustus would be able to validate one of two points: either to prove that the Manichean cosmology was preferable to the mathematically based astronomy; or, failing that, to show that the Manichean account was an equally acceptable alternative. When Augustine broached his difficulties, Faustus flatly demurred at engaging in disputation. Not ashamed to admit ignorance, he was commendably different from other Manichean discussants from whom Augustine had suffered, garrulous know-nothings, all mouth and no meaning, who, in feigning to overcome Augustine's ignorance, only paraded their own. Faustus did have a heart, i.e., he possessed an adequate mind, of neither superior nor mean capacity. Because darkened by Manichean untruth, he could not be right as regards God nor seek God for the sake of God (P 77.21). He was, however, not uncritical of his limitations; he was in some measure a man of principle, who made no bones about the fact he was scientifically unschooled. Further, he was discreet enough not to rush into argumentative ambushes with no escape route. Augustine generously comments that he rated the modesty of a Faustus willing to confess his lacks more attractive than the knowledge he had originally hoped to gain from him; a candor consistently evinced when quizzed about more knotty points.[12]

13. Faustus' shortcomings so aggrieved Augustine that he broke off study of Manichean writings[13], for if a man of such scholarly esteem had utterly failed, he could not realistically expect solutions from lesser lights. In spite of his huge disappointment, he was not personally repelled by Faustus; he graciously agreed to help expand Faustus' limited erudition. One ironic feature usually goes unremarked; the heralded teacher from whom Augustine had beseeched light sat as a learner at the feet of the uncelebrated disciple.

While undoubtedly a committed Manichee in belief and practice for nine years, apparently he had not given full assent to all the dogmas; he had entertained some doubts about the cosmological myths which, he had hoped, would be interpreted as symbols of deeper truths.[14] But the post-Faustus situation was radically different. At this point his Manichean allegiance lay in ruins, beyond restoration. However perturbed, Augustine did not straightway withdraw from the sect; he would bide his time until perhaps some sounder set of beliefs appeared on the horizon; a wise decision, for he might have precipitously embraced a world view worse than Manicheism.

He explicitly mentions a second ironic ingredient; through his meeting with a deadly snare (5.3.3) he was unsnared; it was the hand of God, always loving, that reaped good from evil. In union with and like God, Monica never abandoned Augustine as she offered herself as an oblation in his behalf, specifically spilling the blood of her heart, her inner self, as an internal sacrifice externalized in tears. As Jesus shed his heart's blood on the cross as a perfect sacrifice of propitiation (P 21.28; 64.6; 129, 3, 7), so Monica expended the blood of her spiritual self in reparation for her son. Her interior anguish went on without let-up, imitating her never-ceasing pursuit of God. Thus did God work Augustine's healing by near-miraculous guidance, employing Monica as his chief instrument in untrapping him from the trap that was Faustus. God directed him along every inch of the road to new life; otherwise his path would have continued winding down to destruction (P 36.15). The dispositive sacrifice of Monica's tears helped ready Augustine for recreation through the sacrifice of Jesus.

Chapter 8: Deceiving Monica, he Leaves for Rome

14. In this chapter and the next, Augustine unveils features of his psyche that repay inspection. Working above and within any human influences in his decision to depart for Rome was the silent but potent persuasion of God's mysterious mercy, always most intimately present (3.6.11). Inducements that friends put before his eyes, such as enhanced income and academic prestige, did not substantially motivate him. The overriding reason was the prospect of teaching students who were docile in the twofold sense of being tranquil and therefore teachable, their behavior controlled by the regulations of the Theodosian Code, according to which breaking classroom rules

was a civil offense punishable by the imperial government. They could not, with impunity, rush pell-mell into a school in which they were not enrolled. It was quite otherwise in Carthage where students reveled in bursting into a schoolroom and wrecking its order. No law could penalize the recklessness of this privileged group, whose outrageous behavior was shielded by custom. Yet their advantaged status actually made them more wretched. Uncorrected by the law of man, they were punished by the law of God. Outwardly escaping punishment by human law, inwardly they were smitten by eternal law with terrible retribution that was blindness to their actions; a persistent sinner tears out his own spiritual eyes. With great relief Augustine looked forward to emigrating to Rome, where he would no longer have to fear hooligans who trampled on his dignity. His was a sensitive spirit that could not withstand savage assaults on the inner citadel of his professional self. These last few lines seem unwittingly self-revelatory. Calm and self-contained, Augustine was not a man of steel, not tough enough to denounce young hoodlums. It is not improbable that other teachers faced down disrupters, adopting an aggressive adversarial response that he was constitutionally incapable of mustering. Again, apparently he was somewhat thin-skinned, favored but also burdened with too delicate a sensibility; other teachers probably brushed aside or tolerated passing affronts.

In this pivotal decision God was his solid secret support, his hereditary "portion in the land of the living" even in this life, with full inheritance to come in the life beyond (P 141.12), leading him to change his earthly domicile in view of an inward change, healing of his soul. From on high God was applying the spur that drove him away from Carthage, his direction to divine life initiated in time by men enamored of this death-ridden life (1.6.7). Deploying misguided men to guide Augustine to truth, God applied students' moral craziness to make him spiritually sound, and turned friends' exhortations to seize the main chance into means for spiritual riches. His infinite ingenuity governing both their and Augustine's warped ways set him firmly on the straight path. God was once again writing straight with crooked lines. Loathing a real unhappiness in Carthage, he hoped for an unreal happiness in Rome; a yearning out of which divine husbandry that transcends natural moral causation was inducing false happiness to fructify into true.

15. This section opens another window, not often remarked, on the

moral personality of Augustine, catching also an unusual feature of Monica's character. In hoodwinking his mother, Augustine disclosed a suave-salesman side with a beyond-the-ordinary power of invention and charm to make his lie credible. Beneath the urbanity lay a heart as hard as nails, which callously matched her motherly truth with filial mendacity. In coldly lying through his teeth, he repaid her love by rebuffing her as a nuisance. For her part, Monica was ordinarily the gentlest and most patient of women (9.9.19), but in this instance the fire of this most loving of mothers overbalanced her meekness, so that in her anguish she actually grabbed hold of her son and tried to restrain him, promising to relinquish her grip only if he agreed to go back with her or at least take her along with him. *Mulier pietate fortis* (6.1.1)[15] indeed, but now in an unsuspected vein; as first of all *mater fortis*, she reacted with physical vehemence uprising from the strength of her motherly heart. Moreover, it was this same heart that swept aside all doubts about the prevaricative strains in her son's story; she simply could not believe that the apple of her eye would brazenly deceive her.

The deeper reason why Augustine was traveling to Rome in the summer of 383 God alone knew, in whose plan for his conversion the road to Rome would open the road to Christ in Milan. So the Lord, mercifully forgiving his unconscionable deception, spared his soul from being lost through the death of his body at sea. As noted previously, ancients were understandably fearful of sea voyages; sudden storms easily engulfed the slight crafts, causing them to capsize. He was saved from drowning in the sea so that he might be saved in the waters of baptism less than four years later (9.6.14). The laving waters would evaporate the river of Monica's tears that daily soaked the earth. Betrayed by her son's sweet reasonableness, Monica consented to spend the night in prayer in a nearby oratory dedicated to St. Cyprian (c. 210-258), the most popular African martyr.[16] While she prayed that Augustine would not leave, that very night a favorable wind propelled the ship toward Italy. Though her prayers seemed in vain, in the depths of his wisdom God heard the essence of her prayer, not giving her what she was then praying for so as to give later what she always prayed for: Rome would lead to Ambrose and thence to Christ. Once she realized that Augustine had set sail, she was choked with grief, emitting groans to an apparently unresponsive God. Actually, once more he was causing good to emerge from evil, managing Augustine's false desires to obliterate those very desires: the new man in Milan would stifle the disordered impulses of the old; using Moncia's sorrow as a kind of scourge to purify her spirit of a yet too earthly affection for her son: self-giving, she had not yet totally surrendered herself and him to the will of the Father. Her weeping gave proof of the lot of "the remnant of Eve" destined to bear children in suffering. On the son of this daughter of Eve brought forth in pain life could be bestowed only through pain; spiritual mother, she had to travail at birth (9.8.17).

Chapter 9: Serious Illness at Rome

16. Upon arriving in Rome he fell seriously ill, his sickness a whip permitted by God to punish him for his sins. At that time he was sliding down the slippery slope to hell, his soul bludgeoned by blasphemy, self-pride, and envy (3.8.16). In addition to the bond of original sin deriving from Adam (LA 3.10.31; 20.55; 23.7), his soul was enchained by actual sins. His fetters could not be broken by Jesus because Christ's death on the cross, he believed, was sheer illusion. The Manichean Jesus of pure light could not become intermingled with flesh that was part of the realm of Darkness (CF 20.11). As mentioned earlier, the individual who died on the cross was vituperated as a spiritual impostor, actually a demon in disguise (CF 15.9. H 46.37). Denial of Christ's physical death was rooted in the spiritual death of his own soul. Because Christ's death on the cross seemed false, the spiritual death of his soul was true; conversely, because Christ's death was true, the life of his soul was false. Objectively, because he had no belief in the cross, his soul was dead; subjectively, because his soul was dead, he had no belief in the cross. As the fever heightened, his life started to ebb, and if the fever were not checked, he would undergo a double perdition, loss of bodily life and loss of soul-life. Through physically absent, Monica, by prayer, was spiritually present through the everywhere-present God hearkening to her with never-failing mercy. God's hand healed his body while his soul remained diseased by sacrilegious tenets.

As a young lad, in sickness he had begged for baptism (1.11.17), but after a near-decade as a Manichee, he could only disdain the rite, in his demented state condemning the very medicine prescribed by the divine physician. Yet the God whose ways he ridiculed pulled him back from the brink of a twofold death, one in time, the other in eternity. If he had succumbed to the fever while in grave sin, his mother's shock would have been unassuageable, her sorrow inconsolable. Words cannot describe the immense love her grieving heart bore the darling and dread of her life; the agonizing labor she long experienced in giving him spiritual birth far surpassed the protracted pangs she felt in his physical birth.

17. Could Augustine in this concrete situation have been lost? In the light of overriding divine sovereignty it might seem that God could have justly let him suffer perdition. On the other hand, his loss would seem to render Monica's efficacious prayers utterly sterile. To some who discount Augustine's God as intolerably super-rigorous, it may come as a surprise that he resolves the dialectical tension by arguing that God was bound to save Augustine, constrained by himself to answer love-pervaded prayer flowing from mountain-moving faith. Monica's prayer was an example, perhaps an exemplar, of human desire that binds omnipotence; to her, God was compelled to respond, "Thy will be done," because, in line with his economy, to God she never ceased crying out, "Thy will be done."

Augustine's death in body and consequent death in sin would have irreparably broken Monica's heart, signaling that her faith and love were feckless, her hope mocked. However retained in the divine mind, her constant prayer would have borne no fruit in the world of man. It would seem well-nigh impossible that an infinitely merciful God would turn a deaf ear to the entreaties of a woman who had fulfilled all the conditions for effective prayer. Abasing herself before the all-high, Monica was chaste, that is, holy, sober, totally self-disciplined. Nor was hers a dead faith but one that practiced spiritual and corporal works of mercy, frequently giving alms to needy brothers and sisters. She also served God's holy ones, the clergy;[17] not a day passed that she did not make an offering, supplying bread and wine for the Mass she daily attended. At both morning and evening services she was wrapped in prayer, not caught up in the gossip of old women; during a time when the Blessed Sacrament was not yet reserved in church, there was greater opportunity for casual chatter therein. She stormed heaven simply and solely for a one lofty spiritual good, the redemption of her son. A God whose plan is mercy could not repulse her; he had to do what she patiently prayed for because he had inspired her to pray so that she might harvest the fruit of her prayers. In fulfilling her desire, God was simply executing the plan he had fore-appointed. The God who moved Monica to furnish the means that were her prayers would undoubtedly assure the end. Since both means and end were parts of his design, he would only be defeating his own plan if he cold-shouldered her. Again, it is concretely impossible to think that God would have tricked Monica in the authentic vision promising Augustine's salvation. Confident that the God who is truth cannot deceive, she was spurred to go on in her prayer by the memory of this and other real visions. These were indelibly engraved in her heart of faith as promissory notes bearing the personal signature of God. In his everlasting mercy that forgives all debts the God who will have no one his debtor (1.4.8) makes himself the debtor of all by his promises. Thus God was bound to save Augustine only because his mercy bound himself. In summary, God obliged himself to heed Monica for four reasons: she was holy and self-giving; her prayer was unflagging, her charity constant; her prayer was fueled by the purest intention: she sought the Lord alone; God had favored her with visions, whose promises he was beholden himself to fulfill.

Chapter 10: Skepticism and Manichean Errors

18. So through the intercession of Monica, the handmaid, spiritual servant of the Lord (9.9.22), God healed Augustine's body so that in time he might heal his soul, his recuperation taking place in the home of an unnamed fellow auditor (possibly Constantius, later converted to Catholicism by Augustine), with whom he was residing.[18] He also mingled with other auditors and the ascetical elect, both described, perhaps half-sarcastically, as saints, apparently serene in light and love but really diseased by and carriers of pestilence (4.1.1).

One untruth he accepted from Western Manichees was the two-soul theory, according to which it was not he who was responsible for sin but an alien nature within: all good actions flow from the good soul, all evil from the evil soul (DA 1.1. H 46.38), which are also denominated natures, minds, or spirits (8.10.22. CJI 6.3).[19] This exemption from evil induced pride with pleasure; as wholly innocent, he was a special being enjoying a simon-pure status. Since he did not, because he could not, do wrong, he felt no need to repent. No matter how often he apparently sinned, he exculpated himself, by blaming the difficult-to-describe evil factor within. In fact, as he learned later (8.10.22), he was not a loosely knit combination of two disparate natures; rather, he was one being, a psychological whole rather than an aggregate of two opposing parts. Yet spiritually he was two; sin split his one soul into a moral diversity, pulled apart and down to lower objects (11.29.39). Moreover, his sin seemed beyond remedy; no sinner can be cured if convinced he is unsullied by sin. Further, his wickedness was execrable; one consequence of the two-souls theory was that he did not hold, as do Christians, that the invincible God vanquished his sin. On the Manichean view, the good soul was a part of God's substance; the sin of Augustine's bad soul inflicted defeat on his good soul and therefore on God: his sinning vanquished God. The opposite, however, is the truth. Sin is radicated in free will; in a sinner disposed to God's mercy the guilt is wiped out, the disfigured moral self reshaped by grace. The paradox is muted but plain: in the Manichean scheme the all-powerful God is conquered by sinful man, only one portion of creation (1.1.1). Still in the company of evildoers and hence barred from applying to himself Ps 140.3-4, his lips were deprived of a moral guard to stop him from speaking evil; instead of confessing sins, his lips were volubly professing a view that illusorily abolished his sin.

Though the intellectual tether of Manicheism had slackened, then worn threadbare, he still frequented the elect, mainly in order to distribute alms to members of the perfect stratum, in particular obtaining and cooking food, among other necessities, for these self-denying righteous ones. He could hardly keep up the appearance of being a bona fide Manichee without discharging this fundamental duty to the "liberators of light-particles from vegetables" (P 140.12), who, he came to see, were actually prisoners of darkness. For want of a better religion he decided, he repeats, to continue as a nominal adherent of a largely doctrinally demolished sect (5.7.13). The pathetic performance of Faustus having sapped zeal for Manichean thoughtways, his study of Manichean tenets became desultory, shortly to fade away entirely (5.14.25).

19. Since he had been existentially involved in the Manichean teaching and way of life, what was devastated was not just a philosophical position but his *Weltanschauung*, a cluster of attitudes embedded in the cultural complex that was Manicheism. As his inner being reeled under the blows that flattened his whole framework of

meaning and value, it does not seem psychologically inappropriate that he was moved to judge the Academics' stance inviting. Since his world picture had been reduced to rubble, it seemed reasonable to give a hearing to philosophers who insisted that certitude is a delusion. His ironclad certitudes had been dismantled; perhaps there was merit in the contention that no philosophy can achieve certitude. In addition, for a time he found suasive, if not coercive, some of their arguments for the skeptical route (CA 3.15.34). In tentatively concluding that the Academics, who held certain wisdom unattainable, were wiser than thinkers who ambitioned to chart the course to wisdom, Augustine was walking in the footsteps of the revered Cicero, who professed to be a skeptic of the Academic stripe;[20] incongruously, the author of the *Hortensius* that in 372/3 had launched Augustine on a quest of wisdom.

After by and large shedding fealty to Manicheism, he passed through a time of doubt, a phase of limited skepticism (5.14.25), during which, he experienced despair of finding any solid truth (R 1.1.1). Apparently he never unwaveringly subscribed to skeptical doctrine; he was never a continuous full-blown skeptic. When frequently but not always truth seemed simply beyond human reach, he was swirled about in a sea of doubt, helpless to arrive at any firm position incontestably identifiable with truth and certitude (5.14.25.UC 8.20). While at times he yielded to the spell of strict skepticism, on other occasions a robust confidence in the liveliness and penetration of the human mind asserted itself, urging him to trust that he would somehow be able to lay hold of truth. In other words, there surfaced healthy doubts about total doubting; he became wisely skeptical about an unwise sweeping skepticism. Contrary to the dogma of the Academics, he continued to recognize the real possibility of certitude. After a final critical assessment he regarded as certain, not merely probable, the untenability of Manichean claims (5.14.25). At the end of Book 5, when he renews his status as a Catholic catechumen, he is biding his time until *aliquid certi*, some certain doctrine, provides light for firm direction of thought and life (5.14.25), although defeat in the search for certitude still remains possible (UC 8.20).

Its presentation, like much of the *Confessions*, compressed, this section does not spell out the pros and cons of his approach to skepticism. It seems reasonable to hypothecate, I believe, that his grappling with skepticism at this point implicitly harbored the essentials of his brief later expounded in *Contra Academicos*. Conversely, this work explicitly articulates concepts that Augustine was working through in Rome. Thus the few paragraphs that follow, largely derived from this dialogue, substantially record his understanding and evaluation of the skeptics in the summer of 383. The founder and chief luminary of the New or Third Academy was Carneades (c.314-219), a thinker of unbelievable intellectual prowess who was reputedly conversant with every province of philosophy or science.[21] He argued that it is impossible to achieve a standard of truth enabling one to distinguish between true and false appearances. In other words, all things are doubtful, even the most manifest (T 14.19.26); all things are obscure and uncertain (CA 3.5.11. R 1.1.1). Nothing true can be apprehended by the mind, and no one thing can be certainly distinguished from something else. Bereft of clarity and distinctness in its notions, the mind is compelled to use *epoché*, a suspension of judgment. Nevertheless, even skeptics cannot remain mute; judgments have to be enunciated; still, every proposition is no more than probable (R 1.1.4). In the line of the practical also, the mind cannot discover certain rules for the direction of life (6.11.18), yet human action is not thereby paralyzed; probability can be taken as a sufficient guide of life (CA 2.5.12).

This dialogue rejects the Academics' posture as unthinkable and unlivable. It is strictly unthinkable because its basic claim that only the probable or truth-like is attainable implicitly carries an appeal to truth. It is senseless for an individual to state, "This young man resembles his father Romanianus," while acknowledging that he never set eyes on Romanianus. It is equally self-defeating for someone to maintain that he is aware of what resembles the truth while denying acquaintance with truth itself (CA 2.7.19). This animadversion does not turn on a mere semantic quibble that exploits the connection between *verisimilis* and *verum*. Reference to the probable as such implicitly invokes a standard of truth or certitude: the probable is what does not reach the factually or necessarily true.[22] Moreover, skepticism is broadly unthinkable in the sense that it runs counter to truths attained in the physical and dialectical spheres. In the line of the physical, the mind knows with surety that there is either one world or six worlds and that the normal operation of the senses is trustworthy. Here also it may be remarked, by the way, that

3 x 3 = 9, like all mathematical truths, is immutably certain (CA 3.11.21,25-6). Rules of dialectic, such as the principle of noncontradiction, are known with certitude (CA 3.13.29). Carneades' contention that laws of logical necessity do not bear on the physical world is true only in the formal sense in which logic may be said to prescind from all specifiable content. But taken applicatively or instrumentally, dialectic or logic, "the science of truth" (CA 3.13.29), refers to the physical world. "Either I am a man or a not a man" is a truth about the physical world that is an application of the law of noncontradiction. Stated otherwise, if the law of noncontradiction is not applicable to the real world, a human being cannot know whether he is a man or an ant (CA 3.10.22); or on the supposition that he knows that he is a man, he cannot aver that he is an ant at the same time and in the same respect. Moreover, if logical necessity does not basically mirror the physical world, then dialectic or logic is emptied of content and converted into a kind of game in which intellectuals fruitlessly disport themselves. Moreover, in the line of ethics probability as a guide of life fails to guarantee protection from misguided action (CA 3.15.34). Worse, falling back on the probable as an ultimate guide for conduct effectively entails a moral relativism, in which anything goes as long as its value is labeled probable. Not only easy adultery but murder, parricide, and every personal and social sin imaginable would be tolerated and condoned, and at times proposed as situationally obligatory. The skeptics' slack guideline of probability virtually canonizes immorality, even of the most monstrous type, thereby making life unlivable.[23]

These were some of the reasons, not explicitated in Book 5, why Augustine never uninterruptedly endorsed skepticism. However, he deployed its searching question-raising techniques as a strategy for stringently testing various propositions. Before all truth-claims he would methodically suspend judgment, refusing assent until he had conducted a most exacting inquiry. Prior to dismissing Manicheism, he subjected its views to the most meticulous examination. He also capitalized on skeptical strategy to withhold for a time unqualified assent to natural-philosophical, in particular, astronomical, conclusions (5.14.25), propositions that, he indicated earlier, unfailingly forecast the precise details of eclipses (5.3.4). The close of Book 5 depicts him venturing no assent and making no existential commitment until Spartan scrutiny validates the truth he hungers for or, on the other hand, reluctantly persuades him that his hunt for truth is a fool's errand (UC 8.20). Later, in listening to Ambrose, he practiced suspension of judgment so scrupulously that the prolonged doubt threatened to choke off truth and leave him vulnerable to error (6.4.6). Often, it is true, he was whirled about in the official uncertainty of skepticism. Yet his espousal of skepticism was never unvarying; a nonskeptical approach broke through in the total rejection of Manicheism and in the acknowledgment of the real possibility of positive certitude; further reflection pushed doctrinal skepticism to the vanishing point as he profited from his adapted or strategic skepticism.

During this period he understood skepticism in the popular or exoteric sense (5.14.25). Later he became aware of its esoteric dimension, according to which the Academics were actually secret followers of Plato's spiritualism who, admitting truth and certitude, contrived their skeptical front as a dialectical weapon for riddling the sense-based materialism of Zeno (CA 3.17.38; 18.41); their attack razed a philosophy resting on matter and sensory knowledge so as to raise anew the Platonic edifice.

While circumspectively silent about his inward withdrawal from Manicheism, Augustine did not hesitate to chide his host about excessive credulity as regards the bizarre tales that pack Manichean treatises. Intellectually alienated from Manichees, he remained socially attached. The esprit de corps of community that helped him absorb the shock of the sudden death of his friend (4.8.13) now ironically fortified him as he prepared to disengage himself from the sect. He simply could not feel happy without friends (6.16.26), even though this friendship was like a bond of many folds wrapped around his neck (DA 9.11). His ardor for defending the dubious doctrines of the sect had notably cooled, yet the pleasure of friendship made him at the moment less ready to search for the truth elsewhere. Interestingly, there were a good number of the sectaries in Rome, initially surprising since recent imperial decrees had banned membership under harsh penalties; probably the edicts were not thoroughly enforced. Abjuration of Manichean teaching, however, did not abate revulsion toward Catholicism. As mentioned above (3.7.12), he scorned as degrading the notion that man was made in the image of God since this entrained the fatal inference that God, like man, had nose, mouth, and other undivine members. Against this analogy that jammed God into the small dimensions of the human frame, Manichees argued that God was not narrowly circumscribed but infinite, widely diffused through space. God was wholly material, for at this stage in his mental development Augustine found it impossible to conceive of a spiritual substance. Since a substance without matter was no being at all, God had to be wholly material. Inability to conceive of a spiritual substance was the most formidable and nearly unique reason why he could not make a final break from every vestige of Manicheism.

20. He thought of evil as a natural substance, a dark and formless mass; dark as opposed to lightsome; formless as deprived of order and beauty. Substantial evil was viewed in two ways. (i) It was solid, a darksome earth (CEF 28.31); earth is the essence of all five evil natures. (ii) It was also as tenuous and rarefied as air, an ethereal stuff or malign mind gradually seeping through and polluting the earth. Since his materialism allowed him to consider mind a rarefied body, he had no trouble regarding evil as a mind.

Because God is good, he cannot create evil; hence the domain of evil has to be independent of and separate from the Kingdom of Light. Both realms are materially infinite, yet the good kingdom is larger than the evil; were the two equal in size, the Kingdom of Darkness would be incongruously made equal to the Kingdom of Light. The good kingdom stretches boundlessly to the north, east, and west, we saw, while the evil kingdom extends only to the south, with, however, one point of contact: the Kingdom of Darkness enters like a wedge into the Kingdom of Light (CEF 37.23; 21.23. CF 14.18-20).[24] From his radical materialism (5.10.19) springs this division of the universe into two kingdoms that, however rarefied, are basically material. Now, he indicates, a second or derivative error spawns other sacrilegious notions concerning God, evil, and the identity of Christ the savior. In his critical review of Manichean claims (5.10.19) Augustine raised, then disavowed once again, the possibility of a return to the Catholic faith, for, probed through the distorting lens of the Manichees' polemic, the Catholic explanation of God, evil, and Christ was pitifully inadequate. First, a God infinite on three sides, while limited only on the fourth or south side, is superior to a Catholic deity trimmed down to the dimensions of the human body; in this view man is like God only because God is like man (3.7.12). Second, the Manichean view that God did not create evil also attested greater exaltation of God. Catholic belief in a God who creates everything implies that God creates evil as well; a God who directly creates evil has to be unspeakably evil. This dismissal of creation hinges on the mistaken opinion that evil is a substance, indeed something bodily. Evil, recall, was taken to be a malign mind, a highly rarefied body, diffused through various segments of space. Third, the Catholic idea of an incarnate God is religiously repellent. Piety gives preference to the Jesus of Splendor who was evoked by the Father of Light from the luminous divine mass;[25] unlike the Jesus of Catholicism, he was not generated nor contaminated by the matter of a human body. Though the conception of the Catholic Jesus was supposedly virginal,[26] the Son of God was begrimed by flesh containing evil particles. Belief in a God become flesh, Augustine feared, entailed belief in a God irremediably defiled. The Manichean Christ, the Luminous One projected by the Father of Light, however, was not at all entangled in flesh. His idea of the Catholic Jesus, Augustine notes, was woven out of imaginings that were vain, mythical rather than veridical. Even if Christ had been conceived without sexual congress, the Luminous One would have still been chained in the darkness of the flesh, a state of utter degradation for the divine substance evoked in Christ, the Splendor of God.

A concluding parenthetical remark begs spirituals to smile indulgently on his peculiar opinions, especially on his inability to understand that God is totally without matter. However abhorrent they and he now deem them, he actually clung to these jejune theses even as he was inwardly splitting off from Manicheism.

Chapter 11: Continuing Difficulties with Scripture

21. During his stay at Carthage (374-83), when his own critical mind was casting about for a Christian counter-explanation to confute the Manichean attack on Scripture, he was fortunate to attend the conferences of Elpidius (a Catholic of whom we know nothing in detail), who usually worsted Manichees in argument by appealing to texts they could not deconstruct. Elpidius' critique of the Manichean critique even then began to pose doubts in his mind. Their rebuttal of Elpidius, which they dared not ventilate publicly, seemed lame. In private they retorted that the New Testament texts on which Elpidius depended had been corrupted by interpolations, borrowings from the

discredited Jewish Scripture. Their rejoinder Augustine judged suspect because they could not identify individuals liable for the corruption and, even more damaging, could not exhibit copies of the uncorrupted text. The charge of tampering seemed barren of factual support and even plausibility; it was a desperate ad hoc measure sprouting from wishful thinking, a purely gratuitous interpretation without foundation in objective fact.

However forceful-looking Manichean protests against Scripture, his dualistic materialism was principally responsible for the two dead weights of corporeal thinking (a material God and a substantial evil); only when the crushing masses were lifted would he be lifted up, gulping in great draughts of the pure air that is truth. Prosaically put, the conception of a spiritual being will mark a significant stage in his intellectual conversion (7.10.16), and recognition that moral evil is a privation of a good will basically solve the whence of evil (7.16.22).

Chapter 12: Dishonest Students at Rome

22. When word spread about the outstanding new instructor, students flocked under his wing. But felicity was unexpectedly fleeting. Not mindlessly fractious like their fellows in Carthage, his new charges had formed the economically unsettling habit of dodging payment of fees. When time for remuneration neared, they would transfer en bloc to another teacher.[27] In detesting his unscrupulous students, Augustine did not hate them with the perfect hate prescribed by Scripture. A perfect hater does not hate men (P 138.28). Positively stated, a perfect hater hates the sin but loves the sinner not as such but as potentially good, as redeemable. In Rome his hatred was ignited by what they did to him personally rather than by the harm they did to others. Souls that betray God play the wanton, committing spiritual fornication. Severing their troth of love with God (P 23.33), these dishonest students lusted after quickly vanishing fleshly gewgaws that, as lucre, stains the heart with filth. At the time of his writing (c. 397), Augustine does hate such students with a perfect hate, recoiling from their twisted ways, but loving them as capable of being reformed in God's love so that they reckon the truth learned more valuable than the fees, and God, fount of all truth, more precious than the truth of rhetoric. Far superior to currency that comes and goes, God is the superabundance of every lasting good.

Contrary to the cupidity of the spiritual harlotry of students, his bridegroom-love is most chaste and faithful; so his is the super-tranquility of super-ordered love. But Augustine, still short of perfect hate, hated students for sinning against him. Only after his conversion did he come to love them in the eyes of God, praying that they be remade through the Lord's remedial touch.

Chapter 13: A New Life in Milan

23. Word reached Symmachus, Prefect of Rome, that Milan, now the imperial seat, was searching for an official teacher of rhetoric, salaried by the empire, whose traveling expenses to Milan would be covered by imperial post. Augustine personally solicited Manichean friends to propose his name to Symmachus. His departure to the northern capital would signalize his ultimate rupture from the Manichees, though neither they nor he realized this; again, he adverts to the motif of providence: an unknowing Augustine was in the hands of an all-knowing God. The Manichees were drunk with vanities, errors which befuddled them, causing their religious speech to be analytically slurred. Symmachus, a rhetorician in his own right, selected Augustine after he displayed, despite his African accent (O 2.17.45), the requisite skill in a set speech. A double irony: a pagan appointed Augustine to a position through which he would be converted to the Catholicism that Symmachus had long combated; also Symmachus was facilitating the advent of one of the mightiest Christian foes of paganism. For Augustine Milan came to mean Ambrose (339-97), its bishop since 374, who enjoyed a worldwide reputation as an prominent Catholic leader and a deeply pious priest. His eloquence pointed Christians toward the fatness of divine wheat, to the Eucharist that is the living bread come down from heaven (P 4.9; 50.27). Sacramental life quickened souls with the gladness of divine oil, the luster of grace shining in their souls and faces (P 103.13). He also dispensed the divine wine of the Mass that soberly intoxicated the faithful (P 4.9);[28] the inebriation was supernatural, detaching the spirit from the earthly, raising its eyes to the heavenly (P 103.13). Unlike the stuporous false-religious intoxication of the Manichees, it was inebriation flowing from contact with the spirit of truth that lights up rather than darkens the soul. In contradistinction to physical drunkenness, in sober intoxication the believer retains full

possession of his senses after imbibing a modicum of consecrated wine that lifts up his heart to joys not of this world. God led him, all unknowingly, to Ambrose in 384 so that within three years Ambrose might lead him, now knowing, to God in baptism April 24, 387.

On Ambrose Augustine bestows the lofty Scriptural accolade: a man of God (1 K 17.24. 2 K 1.19), a servant of the Lord, from whose mouth comes the truth of God. Thus he accorded Augustine a fatherly welcome, with warmth and solicitude for his soul.[29] Though Augustine was a nonCatholic immigrant from faraway Africa, Ambrose greeted him with the cordiality and graciousness proper to a bishop, and with the friendly civility due a new public official who has just finished a physical journey, one, Augustine implies, who is still making a spiritual journey.[30] Augustine responded with reciprocal friendliness to the bishop's benignity, turning affectionately toward him not as a learned spiritual leader decanting religious truth (he had jettisoned all hope of gaining truth from the Catholic Church) but as a spiritual man who had befriended a stranger in the imperial city.[31] Still the master rhetorician, he faithfully attended Ambrose's homilies to determine whether his performance matched his reputation for eloquence. He drank in every word, but not to ingest spiritual truths, for he was totally indifferent to Catholic doctrine. Indeed he contemned it as an error-plagued amalgam of beliefs beneath inquiry and analysis, harboring gross blunders; creation implied that God produced evil, and the incarnation entailed that matter contaminate the divine substance. Much more erudite than Faustus, the Catholic bishop, while polished, did not command a style as winning as his Manichean counterpart. Yet, he recognized later, Ambrose's content was incomparably richer. Whereas Faustus stumbled along winding paths of gross errors, Ambrose's words carried healing for spirit and mind. At this time, however, spiritual health lay a long way distant from a sinner like himself; those far off do not seek the justice of God (P 118[S.30].3). Nevertheless, Augustine, still in darkness, was inching nearer to salvation. His current nonknowledge is the polar opposite of earlier ignorance (3.7.12,13); then notknowing trapped him in Manichean error while now it is gradually readying him for Catholic truth.

Chapter 14: The Allegorical Meaning of Scripture

24. At first Augustine was interested not in the what but in the how

of Ambrose's discourse, not in his doctrine but in his rhetoric.[32] Looked at from the coign of wisdom, concern for eloquence for its own sake was a kind of mandarin pastime, a dilettantism void of truth-value. Yet it was all he had retained in his present stance that called into question all certitude in religion. Strategically adapting the Academics' counsel of despair, he was exceedingly wary about ratifying any self-styled true way to God. Because the Manichean polemic against Catholicism seemed insurmountable, he had decided to simply set aside Catholic teaching and concentrate upon Ambrose's finely crafted sermons. But he soon found that he could not bifurcate content and rhetorical mode; concepts garbed in fetching language began to steal into his mind. Formerly he had deprecated the Catholic view as indefensible against assaults by Manichees who hammered away at Old Testament barbarities and discrepancies from the New Testament. Now, through generative ideas from Ambrose, Catholicism seemed intellectually respectable, its doctrine maintainable without offense to religious reason. Especially important was Ambrose's disentangling of thorny Old Testament passages, which he interpreted in accord with an accommodated reading of 2 Cor 3.6, "The letter kills, but the spirit gives life." In cleaving to the mere letter, Augustine was religiously slain; it turned out quite otherwise when the texts were read in a spiritual, that is, an allegorical fashion. Suddenly light flooded in; through the allegorical method a great majority of obscure passages glowed with fresh meaning. Thus did he disengage himself from despair that any tenable sense could be wrested from these refractory texts. At last, he saw, erstwhile Manichean colleagues who heaped sarcasm on the Old Testament could be effectively countered. But confutation of Manicheism was one thing, proof of Catholicism another. Impressive as was the force of arguments marshaled by Catholic apologists, they did not thereby demonstrate that Catholicism was positively true in every respect. The repulse of Manichean onslaughts on the Old Testament left his dualism unaffected; he still thought that God was fundamentally corporeal, and evil an independent substance uncreated by God (5.10.20). The cogency of a defense of Catholicism did not nullify the potency of his defense of dualism. The insight that Catholicism was not conquered did not ensure that it was automatically the undisputed conqueror or wholly true. True in its negative case against Manichean animadversions against the Bible, Catholicism was not necessarily true in its affirmative case for all of its intricate doctrine. In brief, Catholicism could not yet claim possession of the entire field; it had not yet overmastered the dualism that he still rated close to coercive.

25. Not a coolly uninvolved spectator of events, measuring the competing claims of various philosophies with Olympian detachment, Augustine was bending all his energies to descry impregnable arguments that would deal the deathblow to the Manichean outlook. But he could hit on no decisive refutation because he was still immured in a basic materialism. Admission of spiritual being would have at a single stroke uncluttered his mind of all the useless conceptual furniture of the Manichees. Still, his striving came to nothing; he simply could not frame the idea of the strictly spiritual. Nevertheless, point-by-point comparison with Manichean cosmology impelled him to embrace as more probable the opinions of the natural philosophers or scientists concerning the structure of the universe and the makeup of natural entities. Astronomers reliably forecast the right time and type of eclipses (5.3.4), and physical thinkers account for the changes in natural phenomena in terms of four apparently verifiable elements (5.4.7) rather than in virtue of the fantastic five good and evil elements of the Manichees.

Strategically following the Academics whose posture was popularly held to be skeptical but who, in fact, were Platonists using skepticism as a mask to undercut Stoic materialism (5.10.19), at this point he accorded natural philosophy not certitude but only high probability. In addition, he finally rejected Manicheism as empty of even a shred of probability. The views of natural scientists, though analytically satisfying, failed to win his unreserved allegiance, for they were all morally unattractive, offering no means for healing the soul. Not only did these natural thinkers make no room for the worship of the true God (5.3.5); they omitted Christ (5.3.5), whose name, Monica had taught him, was identified with salvation (3.4.8). Repeated reference to that name had ensnared him in Manicheism; total disregard of that name now kept him from committing himself to the natural philosophers. Still in his strategically skeptical phase, still cultivating a suspension of judgment, he was fluctuating, far from the port of certitude. In this uncertainty he judged it prudent to return, at least nominally, to his religious roots.

Book 5 records the final phases of Augustine's deconversion from

Manicheism. At the outset at least nominally a Manichee, at the end he totally emancipated himself from Manichean belief and practice. His gradual withdrawal may be set down in four stages. (i) The mathematical analysis and empirical data of astronomers posed grave hurdles for Manichean cosmology. Unable to resolve the clash of contentions, Augustine opted to stay loyal to Mani because of reverence for his holiness (5.8-9). (ii) After the disastrous encounter with the facile but less than wholly educated Faustus (6.10-7.13), he started to drift into a programmatic or strategic skepticism (10.19-20). (iii) Elpidius' earlier critique of Manichean attacks on Scripture (11.21) disposed him for Ambrose's allegorical exegesis that solved puzzles raised by Manichees (14.24). Moreover, their expurgated canon was dubious since they could not furnish original codices prior to interpolation (11.21). (iv) He retained the dualism of a material God and an independent material substance of evil but dropped the grotesque Manichean trappings. The highly probable natural philosophy of the scientists was morally inadequate and devoid of the name of Christ. So, still strategically doubting, he chose to stay a nominal catechumen in his parents' religion (14.25).[33] This decision was not the fruit of a renewal of faith but a pragmatic move; for the time being, it seemed discreet to rest secure in a Church to which he was bonded by family fidelity, making no further commitment until an indisputably certain truth captured his assent, its beams illumining the road to genuine happiness.

NOTES

1. Pellegrino, 78, who bases himself on G. Misch, *Geschichte der Autobiographie*, 1. 684, 3rd ed.

2. A. Mandouze, "Le Livre V des *Confessions* de Saint Augustin", LASAP Libri III-V, 43.

3. Faustus was an African raised in Milevis, who put his eloquence and nimbleness of mind to the propagation of Manichean error (CF 1.1). Apparently he tried to abandon all things earthly in the service of his creed (CF 5.1), though Augustine raises doubts about the extent of his asceticism (CF 5.5). About 385/6 he was banished to a small Mediterranean island, where he composed his defense of Manicheism, which Augustine critiques in CF (D 2.286), an apologia for Manicheism, argued with no mean dialectical skill. But in the sphere of liberal arts he was probably an autodidact, with huge lacunae in his learning and with no knowledge at all of astronomy, for which lacunae Augustine judged him wanting in their 382/3 tête-à-tête (5.6.10-1). For a more detailed account of Faustus see A. Mandouze, *Prosographie.*, 390-7.

4. The philosophers to whom Augustine refers would seem to be physical philosophers or natural scientists, in particular, astronomers. From the ancient world down to the nineteenth century philosophy and science signified the same general subject matter, a body of analytically certain propositions. Galileo called himself a geometrical philosopher, in our terminology a mathematical physicist, and Newton's masterpiece is entitled *Philosophiae naturalis principia mathematica*. In the first half of the nineteenth century some basic textbooks in physics were still named *Elements of Natural Philosophy*. Even to this day some universities in Great Britain boast chairs in natural philosophy occupied by prominent physicists.

5. E. TeSelle "Porphyry and Augustine", AS 5(1974), 113-21.

6. Starnes, 114.

7. *In Epict. Ench.* 27, p. 71, 44.72-15. Lieu, *Manicheism in Mesopotamia and the Roman East*, 171-2.

8. According to *De nat. deor.*, 2.41.105, "...every night we observe these brightest stars" that belong to the Great Bear; BV 1.4. After his misadventures in astrology and Manicheism and after skeptical fluctuations terminated in *terra firma*, Augustine writes: *Hic septentrionem cui me crederem didici*. In other words, after being gulled by the pseudo-sciences of astrology and Manicheism, in astronomy he gained some authentic science, an acquisition exemplified by observation of the Great Bear. The events are not related in chronological order; he was conversant with astronomy prior to disaffection from Manicheism and rejection of astrology (5.3.3-6).

9. It seems unquestionable that, on Augustine's view, Mani esteemed himself one in person with the Holy Spirit as the human nature of Jesus is one in person with the Son of God: Mani was the incarnate Holy Spirit (CF 13.17). In the opinion of J. Ries, "Saint Augustin et le Manichéisme à la lumière du Livre III des *Confessions*," LASAP, Libri III–V, 14, the dogma of Mani as Paraclete which

is stated in the *Kephalaia*, is, as a rule, expressed in prayers and hymns. One hymn sings of the Spirit (Mani) as the one who revealed the way to truth. According to Lieu, *Bull. Rylands*, 68 (1986), 444 (quoted in D 2.178), the Manichean *Psalmbooks* reference to Mani as the Paraclete in a Manichean trinity confirms Augustine's interpretation. However, F. Decret, *Aspects du Manichéisme dans l'Afrique romaine*, 294, thinks that the Manichean Felix takes Paraclete in a diluted sense: as the last apostle of Christ, Mani is the principal apostle in and through whom the Holy Spirit speaks. According to Lieu, *Manicheism in Mesopotamia*, 163-4, strictly, Mani was not the Paraclete. He was gifted with a *syzygos* (companion), the Light-Nous who was his divine twin or heavenly alter-ego. The Light-Nous was the Paraclete. Mani's disciples, blurring the distinction between the Light-Nous as Paraclete and divine twin, came to consider him the Paraclete. Since Manichean doctrine was complex and not all of its teachers wholly able theologians, it is not hard to conjecture how the confusion arose. Perhaps some Western Manichees resorted to the identification of Mani with the Paraclete as, in some measure, an apologetic adaptation of their views to Christian doctrine.

10.   There can be no doubt about the fact that Augustine maintained that he had been a Manichee for nine years; a point noted three times in the *Confessions*; 3.11.20; 4.1.1; 5.6.10. Three prior works mention this datum; MM 1.19.68; 2.18.34; UC 1.1.2; CEF 10.11. However, this enumeration struck Courcelle as odd since the time from 373/4 to 383/4 seemed to be obviously a span of ten years. In "Augustine's 'Nine Years' as a Manichee," AUG(L)25 (1975), 210-6, L. Ferrari judiciously accounts for the apparent miscalculation. During his final year as a Manichee Augustine was no more than a nominal adherent of the sect. Though he continued a friendly relationship with its members and perfunctorily carried out the duties of a hearer, he had inwardly discarded all commitment to Manichean beliefs; in spite of appearances, he was interiorly an ex-Manichee.

11.   As mentioned above, the hearers, as imperfect, were permitted to engage in activities strictly forbidden the perfect or the elect. They could cultivate fields, though such farm work entailed doing harm to the "Cross of Light"; Coyle, 197. Other differentiations were more notable. As noted previously, in the Manichean hierarchy the top officials were *magistri* or teachers; ranking above these was a thirteenth teacher, reverenced as Mani's successor and therefore the supreme authority. Below the teachers were seventy-two bishops, and below the bishops were an indefinite number of priests who were ordained by the bishops; assisting the bishops were deacons whose precise function remains obscure (H 46.16). See Coyle, 349-51, for Manichean documents corroborating Augustine's hierarchical order.

12.   Augustine commends Faustus' honesty as refreshingly admirable because, not unlike the intelligentsia of our day, some intellectuals of his acquaintance were probably a vain breed, touchy about their public image, ready to resort to dialectical acrobatics and even duplicity to circumvent criticism or exposure of ignorance. So transparently candid was Faustus in his self-knowledge that he could not only utter the hard saying, "I was wrong," but also the harder saying,

"I do not know."

13. Five of Mani's seven works were probably circulated in North Africa: the *Treasure, Pragmateia, The Great Gospel, Book of Mysteries,* and a collection of letters, We cannot determine whether Augustine read all five. If the *Pragmateia* is identified with the *Epistle Called Fundamental,* which Augustine incompletely criticized, then he certainly read at least two, for he quotes a passage from *Treasure* in NB 44 and Fel 2.5. See Coyle, 20-2. In any case, we cannot entertain the slightest doubt that Augustine's extraordinarily retentive mind mastered the minutiae as well as the essentials of Manichean doctrine. In his criticism of Secundinus he does not hesitate to claim, not by way of boasting but as matter of fact, that, if necessary, he can quote countless Manichean texts dealing with the two Kingdoms of Light and Darkness (C Sec 3). See D 2.303. J. Ries, a specialist in Manicheism, pays tribute to the breadth and accuracy of Augustine's knowledge of Manicheism. His "documentation on the doctrines of the sect is solid and abundant. He speaks from personal knowledge of the large number of their enormous books. Augustine did not say everything about Manicheism, but everything he did say came to him from Manichean sources." LSAP, Libri III-V, 25.

14. Corroborating this text, according to Courcelle, 275, is 8.2.17: *Et ieram per vias pravas superstitione sacrilega non quidem certus in ea.* Not entirely certain about all of Manichean teaching, he found it generally preferable to other positions, especially Catholicism, toward whose doctrines he was hostile rather than hospitable.

15. According to Pellegrino, 90, noted in BA 13, 515, n. 1, this "lapidary formula" captures Monica's character with remarkable truth and force.

16. According to Van der Meer, 477, three chapels honoring St. Cyprian were built in the vicinity of Carthage. Two lay outside the city proper; one was constructed at the site of his martyrdom, called *ad mensam Cypriani,* while the other, *in Mappalibus,* was erected over his grave. A third, an oratory, was located close to the harbor. It seems that Monica painfully renewed her confidence in God at this last site. In their translation with notes of Ps. 30-8, *St. Augustine on the Psalms,* 2, 377, n.1 on P 32 (S. 2), S. Hebgin and F. Corrigan reach, independently of Van der Meer, an identical conclusion, that it was in the third of the edifices dedicated to Cyprian, this "near the seashore," that Monica spent her period of prayer. For additional discussion and references see D 2. 309.

17. J. Campbell and M. McGuire, *The Confessions of St. Augustine,* 139, n.103.

18. In the French translation of Pellegrino, *Les Confessions de saint Augustin,* 133, n.5, a note supplied by H. Chirat holds that it was undoubtedly Constantius who gave lodging to Augustine in Rome as he did to so many other Manichees (CF 3.5). It seems at least likely that Constantius did play host to Augustine during his stay in Rome.

19. As propagated in the West, Manichean doctrine elaborated a theory of two souls or natures in man. However, it would seem that Manicheism outside the West did not invoke a two-souls theory but confined itself to speaking of the old and the new man warring against one another. See Coyle, 42, n. 185, with

references.

20. *Academica* 2.3.8.; 31.99. See M. Garvey's translation, with notes, of *Contra Academicos*, entitled *Against the Academicians*, 59, n. 11. Also well worth consulting for their scholarly approach are J. O'Meara's translation, *St. Augustine Against the Academics*, whose notes are excellent, and D. Kavanagh's translation, *Answer to the Skeptics*. See also O'Daly, 162-71. For an overview and appraisal of CA see B. Voss, "Academicis (DE-)," with updated bibliography, AL 1.45-51, and J. McWilliam, "Academicos Contra," AE 2-4.

21. *Academica* 1.12.46. Garvey, *Against the Academicians*, 79, n. 66

22. It seems relevant to note that total skepticism, however oddly alluring at times in the groves of academe, is a hothouse flower that never survives in the lived-out epistemology of the real world, which dismisses it as existentially and scientifically meaningless. Most working scientists in modern physics, the most advanced science, experience no trouble in distinguishing between the probable and the certain. The law of the lever is a fixed truth while the special and general theories of relativity are considered probable, still open to revision or complete overhaul. Moreover, experts in the applied science of forensic medicine routinely rely on DNA, the so-called genetic fingerprint, to identify a suspected criminal; an exact identification is as certain as or more certain than that obtained by demonstration *ad oculos* or videotape.

23. If hardly seems appropriate in this context to attempt anything near an exhaustive report of Augustine's polemic in CA. It should suffice to indicate a few of the main arguments in his critique. Moreover, since he directs most of his fire against the probable, which is Carneades' guideline, I have omitted consideration of Arcesilas' guideline, the reasonable. In AS 12, (1981), 89-113, D. Mosher, "The Argument of St. Augustine's *Contra Academicos*," essays an explanation of CA diverging from "the received interpretation." On his reckoning, the principal purpose of CA was not epistemological refutation of the Academics but validation of the view that the man of wisdom can probably attain wisdom, which, over against the Manichees, disposes toward rational grounding for the Christian faith. Along with J. Mourant, "Augustine and the Academics", RA 4 (1966), 67-96, he maintains that Augustine never passed through a skeptical phase. However, R 1.1.1, saying nothing at all about Mosher's alternative reading, simply states that he wrote CA to remove from his mind the skeptics' arguments. Again, at least three texts supply telling evidence for the opinion, accepted by the greater majority of commentators, that Augustine experienced a skeptical phase. E 1.3 speaks of despair of truth induced by the Academics. According to BV 1.4, skepticism was the helm that directed his thinking for a long time. Paralleling this is UC 8.20: often when truth seemed unattainable, his shifting thoughts were borne to the Academics' position. Mosher commendably cites these texts as objections; unfortunately, in my opinion, his counter-analysis of their meaning does not seem persuasive. On skepticism see M. Balter, "Academia," AL 1.40-6 and P. Carey, "Academics," AE 4-5, along with his "Skeptics, Skepticism" AE 802-3.

24. Starnes, 143, n. 159, notes that Cicero, in speaking of the skeptics' *epoché*, explains: *id est adsensionis retentio* (*Ac* 2.18.59), an expression mirrored in

Augustine's averral, *Tenebam cor meum ab omni adsensione* (6.4.6).

25. Bonner, 163.

26. Significantly, he was not said to be generated; Manichees abhorred the word generation because of it usually bespoke conception and birth of offspring in whom light-particles are imprisoned.

27. The Manichees denied the virgin birth: CEF 2.2.3. See D 2.317.

28. Customarily the fee was paid annually in a lump sum. HC 86, n. 20.

29. Possibly the phrase "sober intoxication" is deliberately borrowed from the sixth stanza of the hymn usually attributed to Ambrose, *Splendor paternae gloriae*: Christusque nobis sit cibus/ Potusque nobis sit fides,/ Laeti bibamus sobriam/ Ebrietatem spiritus. Though many scholars regard this hymn as authentically Ambrosian, some doubt that it originated with him. See M. Mara, "St. Ambrose of Milan,", *Patrology IV*, 178.

30. Ambrose bases a bishop's duty to be hospitable on 1 Tim 3.2, where Paul expressly states that one principal episcopal obligation is hospitality. A bishop should be available to those coming to see him, take the initiative in meeting them, and in a friendly spirit acquire information about their travels. Ambrose, *Abr.* 1.5.32. According to Augustine, a bishop should show an unfailing cordiality and kindness, a considerate hospitality, to those coming to his residence and also to travelers passing through his area en route elsewhere. S 355.2. Texts in D 2.323.

31. According to G.N. Knauer, "Peregrinatio animae", *Hermes*, 85 (1957), 226 (cited in BA 13, 507, n.1), *peregrinatio* has a dual meaning, signifying both Augustine's exterior trip to Milan while implying his interior spiritual journey eventually to Catholicism.

32. Because of the abundance of material available, only a short account of Ambrose would seem advisable here. According to M. Mara, "St. Ambrose of Milan," *Patrology IV*, 144-80, Ambrose was born at Trier probably in 339 or perhaps in 337, who, after education, including Greek, in Rome, rose to provincial governor of Aemilia-Liguria in 370. In 374, though still a catechumen, he was ordained bishop on December 7 or December 1. His twenty-three years as bishop were marked by a constant struggle to fend off and circumvent the incursions of Arianism. In general, he maintained cordial relations with the emperors, Valentinian I, Gratian, Valentinian II, and Theodosius. After Gratian had the pagan Altar of Victory removed from the Senate Forum in 382, Ambrose encouraged the Senate against its restoration. Following upon the massacre at Thessalonica led by Theodosius in the summer of 390, Ambrose required the emperor to perform public penance at Christmas, 390. Ambrose died in Milan on April 4, 397. Mara lists twenty exegetical works, six moral and ascetical works, eight dogmatic treatises, along with various sermons, letters and hymns. For Augustine he was *tuus praedicator* (1.1.1), the preacher providentially appointed to expound Scripture, initiating, then helping to complete, his intellectual conversion. Remarkably Ambrose was the first Catholic thinker of high intelligence and impressive erudition that Augustine encountered, adept at articulating Catholic doctrine in an advanced systematic fashion. Ambrose's discourses, while dissipating objections that had

befogged Augustine, persuasively threw light on the reasonable foundations of
a Catholicism essentially accepted on faith; the rapid spread of the Church was
apologetic proof of its divinely bestowed authority (6.11.19). Interestingly, as B.
Beyenka points out in "The Names of St. Ambrose in the Works of St.
Augustine", AS 5 (1974), 19-28, Augustine refers to Ambrose by name or
various titles no fewer than 408 times (19); ninety different expressions are
applied to the bishop of Milan (27). Because he regards Ambrose as "the
combatant against heretics" (CJ01 4.50), his critique of Pelagianism relies
heavily on Ambrose. Ambrose's name occurs fifty-eight times in *Contra
Julianum* and 181 times in *Contra Julianum opus imperfectum*, significant numbers
since Ambrose is named only 355 times in the whole of Augustine's corpus. His
dependence on Ambrose is indicated in his veneration of the bishop of Milan
as his father (E 147.23.25. CJ 1.3.10). Thus the *Confessions* that describes Monica
as his spiritual as well as his physical mother (9.8.17) suggests that Ambrose
became his spiritual father who begot in Augustine a thoroughly Catholic
mentality; he was the first to generate in him Catholic truth in a solid and
profound way. Books 6 and 7 will deal with crucial concepts in his new
religious development that were part of Ambrose's paternal legacy.

In "Ambrosius," AL I 270-85, especially 277-82, E. Dassmann reflects on the
theological influence of Ambrose. Though we can indicate, in general, the
connection between the two Latin doctors, we lack details on the central
themes. Both were imbued with a Christocentrism, stressing the humility and
subjection of Christ. Both meditated on the mystery of the Church that is born
in the hearts of the faithful after emerging from the wounded side of the savior.
In both, the sea symbolizes the world while the ship stands for the Church with
Peter as helmsman. In North Africa the struggle against Donatism tended to
nuance the meaning of the sacraments, the Eucharist in particular. As regards
Church and state, Ambrose formulated a basically positive view of the state,
which tolerated no interference of the state in ecclesiactical affairs, a position
that Augustine fundamentally recognizes in his treatment of the Roman
Empire. In the matter of grace, we lack a comprehensive study of the relations
between the two doctors. Both agree on the sin-ridden condition of man;
Augustine quotes one expression from Ambrose twenty-seven times. In
general, Ambrose serves as both a source and model of exegesis for Augustine,
especially in his sermons. Ambrose downplays the role of philosophy whereas
Augustine links the wisdom of *Hortensius* with the logos and Christ. A
difference in temperament along with very varying actual experience tends to
incline the two doctors to diverse views on the human condition, the world,
and history. Mara's bibliography is most extensive, Dassmann's thorough. See
also N. McLynn, "Ambrose of Milan," AE 17-9.

33.   Augustine's assertion that he opted to *remain* a catechumen in the Catholic
Church may seem vexing in view of the prominent fact that for nine years he
had dedicated his heart to Manicheism, in which he functioned as a hearer.
Monica's horror attested that he was an unabashed Manichee (3.11.19). Yet in
384 after ridding himself of Manichean baggage, he found one slender thread
tying him to religion: he was still a Catholic catechumen. On the supposition

that this statement is not just a *façon de parler*, he made the claim possibly because he had never been officially disenrolled from the catechumenate and because he had never *explicitly* avowed, "I am no longer a Catholic catechumen." Moreover, perhaps even during his Manichean period he felt some kinship, tenuous, however external, to the Church in which he had been raised by his dear parents (UC 8.20), continuing out of respect for them to consider himself a nominal Catholic catechumen while believing and practicing the Manichean religion. Such external attachments to ancestral faith are not unheard of in the history of thought. Never strictly a Catholic writer, G. Santayana (1863-1952) (see Book 1, n.48), basically a materialist, never relinquished reverence for Catholicism, the religion of his Spanish compatriots, though he thought it, as he did all other religions, empty of all truth-value, no more than a set of symbols that enriches the mythic-aesthetic imagination.

Book Six
Theoretical Indecisiveness, Moral Groping

The end of Manicheism was not the end but the beginning of the end of the pursuit of fullness of truth. The decision to remain a Catholic catechumen readied his heart for the sowing of supernatural faith that, initially rudimentary, was reducible to obedience to God speaking in the Scriptures. Only later, starting with Book 7, would he grow to a wholly formed faith.[1] After arriving in Milan (1.11) Monica deferred to Ambrose's prohibition of *refrigerium* (2.2). Ambrose's tutelage corrected the distorted Manichean interpretation of man as image of God (3.3-4), then led Augustine to recognize a spiritual sense of Scripture (4.5-6). Next came the insight that just as it is wise to rely on human faith, so it is reasonable to depend on divine faith (6.7) professed in the authority of the Catholic Church (6.8). A chance encounter with a beggar raised questions about the happiness Augustine was pursuing (6.9). Sections 7.11-10.16 offer a sketch of Alypius, followed by a brief description of Nebridius (10.17). After Alypius' addiction to gladiatorial shows was healed by divine power (8.13), false accusation of theft in Carthage taught him never to rush to judgment (9.14-5). Later his work as assessor displayed integrity that yielded to neither bribes nor threats (10.16). A small portrait depicts Nebridius as a serious seeker of the truth (10.17). Next, Augustine surveyed past opinions while remarking on his present state of mind (11.18-20). In a discussion of marital sex with Alypius Augustine cleverly justified his position(12.21-2). Meanwhile, Monica arranged for a legitimate marriage for her son (12.23). A plan for a quasi-intellectual community proved abortive because wives could not be integrated into the group (12.24). Sadly he had to separate from his beloved concubine (15.25). The Epicurean hypothesis was found wanting because its self-centeredness clashed with the self-giving central to friendship (16.26).

Chapter 1: Monica Arrives in Milan

1. Protected during infancy, boyhood, and adolescence (from fifteen to thirty), only close to the onset of youth (when thirty-one; 7.1.1) did Augustine elect to explicitly hope in God (P 70[S.1].7) He was now released from Manichean toils bedeviling adolescence (from nineteen to twenty-eight) but had still to unearth the truth about God and man. Apparently departed, God was secretly leading him, increasing present thirst to ensure future delight in the fount of life (P 9.20). With more wisdom than the beasts and the birds, which bade him to seek amid afflictions God himself rather than earthly goods from him, yet he was engulfed in unwisdom, formerly that of Manicheism, now intermittently that of doctrinal skepticism, along a slippery path of concupiscence of the flesh and pride of life (6.6.9. P 24.6). When he had been picturing God as ubiquitously diffused light, residing within was his intimate lover, always ready to commune with him as Spirit to spirit (10.27.38). Thrown into the depths of the sea, he was submerged under sins of mind (P 67.31), earlier Manichean fatuities, now a partially persistent corrosive doubt. As noted above (5.10.19) his temporary acceptance of doctrinal skepticism was not unvarying; from time to time renewed trust in the truth-orientation of mind dispelled the fog of total doubt. In addition, he adopted a programmatic skeptical style to dissect, then pulverize, insupportable truth-claims.

At that moment (spring, 385)[2] there disembarked Monica, *pietate fortis*,[3] a truly valiant women, a pillar of faith, hope, and love. When a heavy storm in the Mediterranean threatened to capsize the frail ship, Monica, in a reversal of roles, confidently reassured the sailors that the boat would reach shore, a vision or dream from God guaranteeing arrival in port of call. Though she found her son dangerously adrift on a sea of doubt (5.14.25), her strong faith would save him from despair of grasping the truth, piloting him to the port of God that is the Church. The good news of his disaffection from

Manicheism she received calmly since a dream informed that her spiritually deceased son would be borne to Jesus on the bier of her heart. She absolutely trusted that Jesus' words, "Young man, I say to you, arise," would restore life to her son (young in an extended sense of thirty-one upward). She placidly said that she believed in Christ, this with a living faith working through charity (S 162A.4), assured that the estranged Augustine would be living as a Catholic before she died, partial unshackling from falsehood presaging entrance into the whole truth. However, not temporizing one whit, she stepped up her campaign of intercession toward his total healing (P 7.10) and the banishing of darkness, his state of sin caused by blindness to truth (P 17.29). In accord with Ps. 30.3, she pleaded that God would hasten his deliverance; a human way of speaking, for a span of time long in human eyes is short in the eyes of God, for whom one hundred years seem like a point in time since both century and time-point come to an end (P 30 [En.2.S.1].8).[4]

She hung on every word of Ambrose, a preacher deputed to channel the waters of divine life; one of the select company so filled with the Spirit that in them springs up a fountain leaping up to eternal life (Jn 4.14. P 2.8).[5] Monica loved Ambrose as an angel; strictly, angel signifies a messenger sent to announce what God has ordered (P 103 [S.1]15), but, broadly, the term is extended to men. As the Galileans received Paul as an angel (S 37.19), so Monica reverenced Ambrose. More particularly, an angel is a spiritual person deputed to preach the Gospel (P 103 [S.2].4), who, when on fire, like Ambrose, enkindles the hearts of those to whom he preaches (P 103[S.2].4). Her love intensified when she learned that Ambrose's sound spiritual exegesis had dismembered Manichean objections against Scripture. As a consequence, Augustine, disabused of Manichean pseudo-certitudes, was still intellectually at sea, yet skepticism (5.14.25), an advance beyond Manicheism, gave promise, she thought, of being the sickness that would prelude his full healing. However, her not altogether sanguine spiritual discernment foresaw that other dangers lay ahead, analogous to the sudden reversal that physicians name the *accessio critica* or critical onset just prior to health, during which greater danger in the form of a higher fever occurs (whereas when recovery is comparatively remote, lesser illness is experienced).[6] After sorrowfully separating from his concubine, Augustine was so tyrannized by lust that he was driven to acquire a new mistress

(6.15.25). Then immediately before conversion, at a climacteric in his spiritual illness, he seemed to be totally subjugated by irresistible sexual passion (8.11.26).

Chapter 2: Monica Submits to Ambrose's Prohibition of an African Custom

2. In the *refrigerium* or refreshment, a North African practice considered an act of piety in honor of the dead, bread, wine, and meal were brought to the graves of deceased relatives and to the shrines of martyrs, where relatives would partake of food and drink. Originating as a tolerated adaptation of the pagan *parentalia*, this Christian custom, while laudable in intent, degenerated at times into revelry and intoxication. When told that Ambrose had forbidden the practice, Monica, to Augustine's astonishment, immediately became a critic of her formerly cherished custom rather than an objector to its removal, the piety whereby she honored the dead moving her to submit at once to Ambrose's directive. Lending occasion for unbecoming tipsiness, the observance also contained superstitious ties with heathen beliefs; at times wine was poured through an opening in the grave to refresh departed shades.[7] It was Monica's practice to honor the martyrs by giving food to the poor while offering at their shrines a heart full virtues. In particular, she shared in the Mass that sacramentally represents the Lord's death, a sacrifice victoriously imitated by martyrs; she banqueted on the Lord's body and blood under the appearances of bread and wine.

In astutely conjecturing that Monica would not have so readily dropped a custom highly prized in her homeland if some prelate other than Ambrose had prohibited it, Augustine is putting his finger on the concrete dimensions of feminine judgments, whose estimate of moral matters is often framed in personalistic terms. The bishop, in turn, was taken by Monica's total commitment; aglow in the Spirit (Rom 12.11), she spent hours in church and lavished mercy on her neighbors (5.9.16). Unable to restrain his admiration, Ambrose would often burst forth in praise of Monica's spiritual beauty when he encountered her son; congratulations that had a hollow ring, making Augustine sad as well as glad. Monica's fervor left him cold, for the beliefs and values she treasured seemed to him without reasonable grounds, dubious at best, delusive at worst; so he remained a truthless wanderer suspended in doubt. Since by criteria of his skeptical stage Catholic thoughtways fell lamentably distant from certitude, he could not be expected to conform his conduct to a discipline that unwarrantably professed to be the genuine route to surcease of restlessness.

Chapter 3: Further Light from Ambrose's Sermons

3. Significantly, he remarks, he did not pursue the avenue of prayer toward resolving difficulties. Instead of following the affective mode of Monica, he confined inquiry to the cold court of the mind, laboriously sifting through various hypotheses. Without fixed religious allegiance he could not converse with God; for a nominal Catholic, the acid solvent of doubt rendered Catholic claims wholly suspect.

Augustine respected the outward Ambrose as a justly esteemed figure of rank and status. Only his celibacy did he deem intolerable, understandably so, since nearly fifteen years of concubinage made it impossible for him to imagine himself deliberately renouncing sexual commerce (6.12.21-2). But about the inward Ambrose Augustine had not the slightest inkling. During the period described (385), he could not guess, let alone infer from experience, what Ambrose felt as a bishop. Only later, at the time of writing (397-401), would he concretely perceive the hope that raised a bishop's eyes heavenward, (10.1.1), the fierce fight to subdue temptations to vainglory (10.38.63) and the consolations that soothed him during his woes(10.40.65). Only later would he be, in particular, delighted by fresh strength nourishing hearts by the bread that is the word of God (P 36[S.3].5), on which the just man feeds day and night and also ruminates, retasting it with fresh satisfaction. In physical rumination, as in cattle, food is first deposited in the rumen, where it is broken down; then it is regurgitated, transferred to the mouth, there to be rechewed. In spiritual rumination food profitable for the mind is stored in the intestine of memory, from which it is transmitted to the mouth of thought, there to be mentally rechewed in fresh remembrance affording new pleasure (CF 6.67).[8] Correspondingly, the eyes that saw only the apparently fortunate son of Monica were closed to the interior Augustine tormented by a bleak materialism, vulnerable to grave perils such as possible lifelong submersion in the pit of

impurity. Augustine's problems were so spiny that they could not be
disposed of in a casual conversation, yet Ambrose could budget
neither time nor leisure for lengthy discussions. His flock constantly
besieged him not only for spiritual counsel but also for judgment on
quasi-legal matters. Like other bishops of his day, he was expected to
arbitrate disputes over land, cattle, and legacies; laid at his feet were
family troubles such as the unfaithful spouse and the delinquent son,
all these molehills accumulating into a mountainous burden.[9] The
brief period snatched from exhausting duties he hoarded for
nourishment of body or soul, this latter being spiritual rumination on
the word of God to savor and assimilate its import.

Departing from the practice of the age, Ambrose read not out loud
but silently[10] (reading out loud, which engages ear and mouth as well
as eye, facilitates easier retention). The reserved Augustine, when he
came upon him so reading, conjectured that it would be insensitive to
intrude upon Ambrose's concentration and rob him of the short
respite he could apportion to nurture of spirit, husbanded from the
clamor of others' concerns. Incredibly, Ambrose had no official
hours; anyone, unannounced, could enter at any time. (Here
Augustine for the first times introduces an editorial "we": *cum
adessemus*.) Perhaps he read silently lest an inquirer overhearing an
obscure passage beg for an elucidation that might eat up precious
time best saved for books. Another, perhaps paramount, reason
underlay his silence: it helped preserve his voice that became strained
through frequent preaching.

4. Ambrose was a holy oracle; an oracle is a divine utterance that
by extension designates the messenger conveying the
pronouncement; in his sermons Ambrose communicated the mind of
God. This high praise ranked him in some way with Moses, whose
books are "the oracles of the Holy Spirit" (12.15.22). As an angel of
God (6.1.11), a messenger appointed to impart the word of God, he
was in a related sense an oracle, a channel of divine illumination that
Augustine yearned to consult privately. The disorder in his appetites,
however, was so deepseated that none of his thorny problems could
be unsnarled in short order. What he might have learned from private
conferences was supplied in part by sermons in which, while
throwing Scriptural light on the meaning of life, shredded the
intricate mass of Manichean polemics decrying the Scriptures. In
particular, he was informed that the Manichean interpretation of Gn

1.26, which reveals that man is made in the image of God, was a crude distortion (6.4.5). Spirituals supernaturally born in Mother Church (SV 5.5) do not think that God is in any way bounded by a human body; educated Catholics clearly grasped that God is spiritual. Churchly infants (7.18.24), the simple faithful fed by the milk of the creed (J.98.5), believed without understanding that God is spiritual; given to image-thinking, they ascribed corporeal features to every entity. While now sure that, by Catholic reckoning, God is purely spiritual, he could not articulate the fuzziest suspicion of what a spiritual substance meant. He felt confounded also because he had been barking against not tenets but coarse misconceptions of Catholicism, engendered by carnal imaginings that invest all objects in material garb; his anti-Catholic mouthing is described as barking (4.16.31) since dogs bark not in the light of truth but under the pressure of earthbound custom (P 21[En.1].17); his Manichean outlook conditioned him to cast religious ideas in terms of matter alone. His attitude toward Catholicism was foolhardy and irreligious; foolhardy: instead of judiciously assaying Catholic claims, he simply trashed its doctrines; irreligious: he neglected to deal with sacred questions in the proper spirit of reverence (GCM 1.3.5.CF 33.7). Rashness and impiety were the subjective reasons why he languished so long in Manichean fatuities.

In his partisan smugness he never paused to inquire whether the God Catholics worshipped was purely spiritual; entitatively the highest but operatively close at hand; most hidden, infinitely distant from creatures, yet most immanent, most present, causally supporting all of creation (1.4.4). As pure spirit, he has no bodily parts, some larger, others smaller, but is *ubique totus*, present everywhere in all of his being; present in every place but limited to no one place (1.3.3). Man who is spread out in bodily space is made in the image of the God not circumscribed by a body or space; this implied difficulty would be dissolved once he understood that man in his spiritual component images a wholly spiritual God (7.10.16)

Chapter 4: Further Critique of Manicheism: Spiritual Sense of Scripture

5. Instead of knowing, prayerfully pursuing, the truth by querying educated Catholics about their understanding of image, he ridiculed

a straw man, according to which, if man was the divine image, God would be trammeled by a huge quasi-human configuration. Again, the more the problem of certitude troubled him, the more abashed he felt over his abject failure to subject to exhaustive examination flimsy noncertitudes he had naively propagated as if rock-solid certitudes. Later he would discount these as myths violating elementary rational canons, but in 385 he became certain that Manichean tenets were at best uncertain. Further, not yet certain that Catholic doctrines were true, he was at least certain that earlier strictures were wholly untenable. Embarrassed over his false charges, he was partly focused on the truth, pleased to learn that the Church to which he had been joined as an infant did not espouse infantile inanities (BV 1.4. UC 9.21), in particular, the absurdity that the creator was squeezed into the limited place of a quasi-human body. A God with a humanized figure could not be God; indeed any bounded God could not be God. Catholics, however, thought that God was wholly spiritual, unbounded by any body at all.

6. Earlier Augustine had inveighed against parts of the Old Testament as nonsensical and its patriarchs as shockingly immoral (3.7.12). Under the guidance of Ambrose, who invoked the text, "The letter kills but the spirit gives life" (5.4.5) as a rule of Biblical exegesis, he came to value the spiritual sense of God's word, a principle of interpretation in the light of which Scriptural teachings were not only admissible but religiously rich. Ambrose's spiritual insight removed the veil of mystery enveloping texts, disclosing their deeper spiritual meaning. Thus illuminated, the texts ceased to repel; yet freed from Manichean dissent, he could not yet muster Catholic assent. Still utilizing his strategic skepticism, scrupulously adhering to *epoché* or suspension of judgment (CA 2.5.12), with epistemic austerity he eschewed any step forward as a possible misstep. However, refusing all assent became more deadly than apparently precipitous assent. Intransigent hanging in suspense turned into a kind of self-hanging or intellectual suicide.[11]

Invoking mathematical certitude as a model for eliciting assent (CA 2.3.9), he wanted to be as absolutely sure of objects unseen, that is, neither directly nor indirectly accessible to the senses, as he was that $7+3=10$ (LA 2.12.34). This mathematical example is not used casually. Three stands for the trinity (S 105.4; 252.10). Seven represents creation; God worked for seven days and rested on the seventh (S 252.10). Creation is also symbolized by three plus four, three representing the psychic features, heart, soul, and mind (with the whole of which men are bade to love God), and four standing for the bodily elements (DC 2.16.23). Ten is the first articulation of number, including one and two (the principles of number) and three and four (the first odd and even numbers) (M 1.12.20-6).[12] But whether we choose 1+2+3+4=10 (CA 2.3.9), 3x3=9 (CA 3.11.25), or another example, every mathematical, in this case arithmetical, proposition unfailingly coerces the mind to assent to its undeniable truth. Such a judgment evinces a character so compelling that even uncompromising materialists of a much later era concur that mathematical "truths are so securely based that any doubt of them seems to amount to insanity."[13] Moreover, mathematical truths are universal and independent of sensory verification (LA 2.8.24). The expression, "mathematical lab", favored by some educational pragmatists, is an oxymoron; mathematical truths can be drilled into the mind, but they cannot be strictly tested in a laboratory. Suppose you drop seven small pebbles into a box, then add three more. If, after counting those in the box, you observe that there are not ten but eleven pebbles, are you going to conclude that you have experimentally found that 7+3=11? Obviously not; the eleventh pebble was the result of a change in material conditions: perhaps a pebble was already lying in the box before the ten were dropped in; perhaps one of the pebbles broke in two; perhaps the experimenter accidentally dropped in eleven rather than ten pebbles. Elementary education, it is true, relies on physical objects to inculcate truths, but these serve as instruments of a pedagogical technique adapted to children's capacities. Again, not only arithmetical whizzes but all normal individuals can work out sums in their minds. Hence at least basic mathematical truths are viewed by all as objectively and subjectively certain. Twentieth-century logical positivists committed to a dogmatic empiricism admitted that such truths are necessary, although they regarded pure mathematical propositions as empty of content, with mathematical reasoning reduced to a chain of tautologies. On the subjective side even young children can master the fundamentals of arithmetic: they are convinced that 2+2=4.

This standard of exact mathematical certitude is not subjectively achievable in other fields. A pagan who assents without possible demur to 7+3=10 might not assent to Augustine's proof for the existence of God or proofs for the reasonable credibility and credendity of Catholicism as coercively true. That an infinite God exists is objectively certain but, for many inquirers, far from subjectively certain. Since propositions in other provinces of knowledge do not possess the clarity and forcefulness of mathematical truths, their certitude, at least on the subjective side, approximates but does not equal mathematical certitude: theirs is at best a quasi-mathematical certitude. Moreover, ordinarily in other cognitive areas the standard of exact mathematical certitude is not objectively attainable as well. Mathematical objects are denuded of reference to sensible qualities; we think away the fingers in five fingers so as to think five. Nonmathematical objects are not apprehended with this stripped-down perspicuity. The meanings of common physical objects such as cause, motion, and time are objectively determinable but hardly with the clarity of $7+3=10$; they are notoriously difficult to define with precision (11.14.17). Hence we cannot specify their meanings with an exactitude equivalent to that which obtains in mathematics. Though his language proposing mathematical certitude as the standard for all certain knowledge apparently adumbrates the mathematicism of R. Descartes (1596-1650), Augustine never adhered to a rigid mathematicism.[14] As his employment of *epoché*, while at times extreme, was not doctrinally but strategically skeptical, so his designation of mathematical certitude as the ideal criterion was not a doctrine of mathematicism but a strategy, a policy for ensuring that prior to assent every proposition be determined, as far as possible, beyond doubt. To forestall error in every sphere of discourse, only propositions that are coercive are to be accorded assent.

Besides demanding quasi-mathematical certitude concerning sensorially imperceptible physical objects such as entities that lie so far up in the heavens as to be beyond reach of the senses (GL 5.18.36), he required a quasi-mathematical standard to win assent to the existence of spiritual beings like God and the human soul, neither of which he could initially conceive without bodily attributes. However, he could not attain certitude about metaphysico-religious truths by reason alone. Understanding flowing from faith is prior by excellence of knowledge, but faith is prior in time. Faith, the first step in healing, is a sort of temporal medicine that summons to health of soul not those who strictly know the truth but those who need to believe (VR 24.45).[15] Had he, under the hailstorm of Manichean criticism against faith, turned first to believe God's word, the purified gaze of his mental seeing would have been fastened on God's truth at least in some measure. Faith is the salve that so cures the diseased eyes of the mind that it may be open to the ever-abiding divine truth (J 18.1). The faith-cleansed heart (P 72.7) is oriented toward growth in knowledge that is understanding. "Unless you believe, you shall not understand" (Is 2.9. Septuagint); understanding is the higher mode of cognition, but its fruits are prepared for by faith (P 118 [S.18].3). In other words, God's ever-shining light was always there, but his mental eyes were clouded over by what might be described as ripe cataracts. Unhappily, he was like a man who, after being cauterized by a gauche physician, now disdains treatment from an expert doctor. Once burnt, twice shy; mutilated by a sham Manichean faith masquerading as reason, he shuddered at the prospect of being maimed once more. Since the wounds of his former false faith still festered, he spurned a new faith that would have closed his wounds, pushing away the super-skilful divine hand whose genuine medicines, word and sacraments, were at the moment curing spiritual diseases worldwide. Unfamiliar with the verifiable claim that this power was broadcast, against all odds, all over the world, he could not yet be cognizant of the universal scope of super-potent remedies.

Chapter 5: Human Faith Points to Divine Faith

7. From then on, while not embracing the Catholic position as true, he counted the Catholic version of faith and reason preferable to the Manichean because more measured and not guilty of making deceptive claims; more measured, because it used a noetic gold mean, properly nuancing the distinction between faith and reason; not misleading, because it did not pretend that all its doctrines were directly accessible to reason independent of and superior to bare faith. On Catholic reckoning, of truths that have to be believed, some, like the existence of God, are objectively demonstrable but not provable by all individuals; others, like the trinity and incarnation, lie beyond strict rational proof for all minds. Manichees, on the contrary were rash and fraudulent; cognitively indiscriminatory, because they lumped all religious statements as provable by reason, mocking Catholics as credulous; fraudulent, because theirs was not a genuine enterprise of reason but a pseudo-rationalism that actually proposed

not for reason but for belief a number of propositions, some the product of myth-making and others aberrations that were physically or metaphysically impossible. As mentioned earlier, the phantasmagoria of the battle between the two kingdoms and the theory of the five evil elements were fantastic while the theory of the transmission of light buckets to moon and sun, along with the preposterous account of eclipses, was physically impossible; and an incorruptible God vulnerable to invasion by the forces of darkness was metaphysically impossible.

Next, he gradually realized that divine faith may be reasonable since human faith that pervades and cements social relationships is strikingly reasonable. Divine light illumined the nexus between human and divine faith: human faith is eminently reasonable for gaining cognition of items not actually seen or proved; divine faith is analogously reasonable, given the grounds for credibility and credendity of claims for knowledge of higher entities and for religious bonding. Step by step he perceived that human life is permeated with human faith, which is the acceptance of something as true on the word of another. There were countless things he took as true apart from either inspection or demonstration. Some phenomena, such as historical occurrences, can be learned by faith alone. Because the past is strictly unrepeatable, historical events cannot be personally validated; oral traditions or documents convey their truth to nonobservers (FQNV 2.4). Geographical data, though objectively observable, are ordinarily accepted on faith; most do not have the income or leisure to travel to all far-off lands. Information or personal secrets confided by friends are taken on faith. Moreover, friendship is so rooted in faith that the very attempt to test a friendship presupposes belief in the friendship (FQNV 1.3). Again, without faith friendship withers away. In addition, such a lack of faith threatens the destruction of the mutual love essential to marriage; without faith spouse ceases to love spouse. Other items, which an individual may be objectively capable of personally verifying, are received on the word of experts. Diagnoses and prognoses of illnesses are believed on the authority of physicians, and other points of knowledge in various fields, because certified by experts, elicit faith. Without faith human society cannot function; at every turn men rely on the word of another. In particular, Augustine unshakably believed that Monica and Patricius were his parents: he could not have verified his own birth (1.6.7). It would have been callous of him to refuse reverence to his parents for the reason that he could not absolutely prove their parenthood (UC 12.26). In some instances, a weaker infant is substituted for the stronger baby, who, once stolen from his true parents, grows up believing that the deceiving couple are his true parents (UC 12.26).[16] In sum, since human faith is indispensable for knowing innumerable truths in human society, divine faith would seem reasonably required to know the more obscure truths of religion.[17] Too, as human faith is necessary to maintain the bonds of mutual love and social stability, divine faith is required to keep firm the bonds of piety in religion (FQNV 3.5).

So divine prompting persuaded without convincing him that not believers but nonbelievers are to be faulted. The near-universality of the spread of the Gospel, a phenomenon not explicable by mere human design and dynamics, inclined him to look favorably on the Scriptures. The appeal to the amazingly rapid expansion of the Church from a backwater of the Roman Empire to all parts of the world was a stock argument, whose potency was not diluted by continual employment by Catholic apologists, a line of reasoning forcibly impressed on his mind through colloquies with Catholics who worshipped in the Milan cathedral; indeed he may have become acquainted with the argument, it is not impermissible to suggest, when alluded to in one of Ambrose's no longer extant sermons. Later Augustine was to hail the swift spread of the Church as "a divine miracle" (FQNV, 4.7), usually described by apologists as of the moral order. An astounding effect cannot be explained by sheer human causation. Purely human efforts to propagate a movement centered on a crucified Jew, an unprestigious near-nobody, fall far shy of accounting for the diffusion of Christians throughout the world. The gap between ordinary cause and super-extraordinary effect is bridged by divine intervention: the rapid spread of Christianity is principally produced by God suspending and superseding the normal outworking of events.[18]

As yet not even a theological tyro, he wisely decided to pay no attention to the objection that he could not substantiate the claim that the books of the Bible were really inspired by the Spirit of the true and veracious God. Later a theologically mature Augustine maintained that God, by the power of the Holy Spirit, the finger of God, authors Scripture through human agents (P 8.7, 8). The justification for this contention lies in the divine origin of the Church. Miracles, physical and moral, and prophecies attest that the Catholica is the true Church of Christ. The Christ who worked physical miracles during his public life continues to work them through his Spirit especially in the early years of the Church (UC 16.34). As already noted, the rapid expansion of the Church throughout the world is a moral miracle, impossible of achievement by natural chains of social causation (UC 17.35). The fulfillment of the prophecies concerning the spread of Christianity and the emergence of properly triumphant *tempora Christiana* bespeak special overarching divine activity (UC 17.35)

Next, since the Church is the body of Christ, with Christ as its head (S. 341.9.11.P 36[En.3].4) and the Holy Spirit as its soul (J 27.6), the Spirit of Jesus operating within the Church empowers her leaders to stamp their imprimatur on certain books, canonizing them as Scriptural. The Church as the living extension of Jesus recognizes certain books as Spirit-inspired because these are the expression of her inner spiritual being.[19] The Church in her doctrine is the canon or standard by which the books are measured and validated; the teaching of the books has to accord with Church teaching. To put it negatively, *sola Scriptura*, one shibboleth of sixteenth-century reformers, is devoid of canonical status; it is found nowhere in the Scriptures; ironically, it is a human "tradition," an unScriptural invention of religious innovators. The simple verses used by some Christians to encapsule their faith are surely moving: "Jesus loves me. / This I know / Because the Bible / Tells me so." But unfortunately, the Bible is not self-authenticating: nowhere does it explicitly state that the Epistle to the Romans is divinely inspired; nowhere does it list the genuine epistles of the New Testament. Only through the Church whose Spirit authors the Scriptures through human instruments (DC 2.6.8) can Christians infallibly know which are the canonical Scriptures.

That is basically why Augustine uttered the well-known pronouncement: "I would not believe the Gospel if the authority of the Catholic Church had not so moved me" (CEF 5.6). As Bonner notes,[20] the context of this avowal is polemical, making the point that it is the Catholic Church, not Manichean authority, that determines the true Gospel. No doubt the setting for this recognition of Church authority was apologetic; still, the statement is not simply a piece of polemical strategy but is grounded in a theory of the Church that identifies it with the body of Christ which is the very life of Christ himself. In addition, the Scriptures function as a rule of authority for the Church; God has established the Scriptures as a firmament of authority (13.15.16). However, the Scriptures that enjoy supreme authority (E 54.6. CF 11.5) are interpreted within the framework of the Church; in practice, the working rule of faith is the belief and practice of the Church (J 106.2). Scriptures and the Church are not opposed but, along with the Fathers, harmoniously elucidate divine revelation. Taken conjointly, Scriptures and the Church in union with tradition constitute "a quasi-single principle of authority".[21] True, the Scriptures are the sublime authority in the Church (J 30.1), but it is no less true that the Scriptures are canonized by the Church as divine (CALP 1.20.39. CD 15.23). Out of its oneness with Christ, the Church can discern with divine eyes which books are canonical, which only apocryphal (DC 2.8.12). Once the Church has constituted the Scriptures as valid, she can appeal to their eminent authority as a rule of faith within the authority of the living Church. Christianity, it is implied, will always be a Bible Christianity because it is foremost a Churchly Christianity. The true Church is arguably a Bible Church in the sense that the Bible is a Churchly Bible. The Scriptures are Catholic Scriptures because the Catholic Church has identified them as her own, as the written offspring of her life made divine by Christ, her head, and the Spirit, her soul.

But proper understanding or ample theological elaboration of these matters lay years away. Now he had to believe most of all that God would not deceive men by causing apparently true but really false Scriptures to be spread worldwide in a manifestly divine manner. His acknowledgment of a veracious God was founded on two basic truths that all the dialectical sleight of hand and gross misrepresentations of Christianity in the sophistical objections of various philosophers, who contradicted one another,[22] could not dislodge from his mind: God exists (though he did not know his nature) and his providence governs all human affairs.[23]

8. His belief in the existence and providence of God, at times robust, on other occasions feeble, never essentially fluctuated, though he remained in the dark about the nature of God and the right moral path to reach God or, having backslid, to return. Human reason is not powerful enough to reach the full truth about God and man; God's

revelation of himself in Holy Writ is absolutely necessary. To lay hold of truths surpassing rational capacity, he had to go beyond reason, a move that was not a descent to the irrational but an ascent to the super-rational realm. It was reasonable not to rely on reason alone; it appeared reasonable to believe in God's revelation of himself in Jesus conveyed through the Scriptures. This faith was not merely rational—otherwise it could not go beyond reason; nor was it a blind existential leap in the dark in defiance of reason; it was a rationally grounded assent, one based on motives of or reasons for credibility. No one can rationally prove the central supernatural claims of Christianity; else faith would be swallowed up by reason. What can be proved is that it is reasonable to believe the claims of Christianity. The dissemination of Catholicism throughout the world was a phenomenon unexplainable by purely rational categories. Though its founder was a crucified criminal, in a few short centuries it became prominent in every part of the then-known world (FQNV 7.10). This unexampled upsurge in daunting circumstances had to be ascribed to the miraculous working of God that apparently testified to the truth of the Christian Church. He was now becoming disposed to believing that God, who can neither deceive nor be deceived, would have impressed his approval on the Scriptures by ordaining that they spread through every land only if he desired that the Scriptures elicit belief in him and point out the paths for reaching him. In short, God could not be God unless the Scriptures contained the truth about him; providence could not be providence unless the Scriptures spelled out the way to find him.

As he heard many vexing Scriptural passages expounded with lucid probability that defused Manichean charges of the absurdity of Catholicism, he started to notice too that the obscurity of the Bible betokened not incoherence but the profundity of rich mysteries. Remarkably, God's word appeals to learned and unlearned alike. Its plain language and unadorned style preserve the essential truths of salvation for all. It gathers little ones, religious infants, to its ample bosom and, as mother, nourishes them with the milk of faith (E 137.4.J 98.5,6).[24] On the other hand, Scripture contains depths upon depths of meaning, veins to be tapped by the understanding of the spiritual sons of the Church (6.3.4), schooled minds who are not academic dilettantes but zealous pursuers of lived truth. Unlike uneducated Catholics, they are not "light of heart"; to use a contemporary colloquialism, they are in some measure mental heavyweights, in comparison with whom their uneducated brethren might be styled lightweights (with all resonances of possible snobbery expunged). The spirituals are relatively few in number because many or most individuals lack the acumen, the time, or the sustained interest to concentrate on high-level matters of the mind. The unornamented style of Scripture draws all, but only a few, the spirituals, are intellectually endowed to reach God by narrow passages, that is, to decipher tough-to-grasp portions. In contrast to the broad bosom available to all, apertures by which the learned or spirituals attain God are constricted because paucity of talent, time, and/or energy reduces the opportunity to read Scripture with perspicacity. Few spirituals there are, but they would be scantier still if the towering authority of Scripture had not been divinely diffused all over the world, and if grace had not lured great multitudes to its motherly heart with its holy lowliness of language and style. In other words, because the Church to which the Scriptures lead men is so vast, the number of spirituals is much larger than would be found in a community ungraced by divine love and power.

He was not yet fully disposed by reason to utter the yes of divine faith to Catholic truth, the grounds of credibility seeming not certain but only probable. However, as he sighed or prayed for light, his divine pilot was slowly directing him to the port of truth. He was walking the broad highway of this world, which, if not escaped from, flings the soul into a pit of hell (P 8.13; 36 [S.1].9). Yet as he slogged along the path of self-love, dominated by lust of the flesh and pride of life, over him every single moment hovered mercy.

Chapter 6: Outer Happiness, Inner Unhappiness

9. The well-traveled road to perdition contained two of the three lanes of concupiscence;[25] he was lusting after not only marriage but honor and wealth. God is imagined as gently laughing at his passional subjection, for pursuit and partial possession of pleasures engendered one galling displeasure after another. Divine mercy embittered these goods so as to drill in that anything other than or unrelated to God could never yield unmixed delight. Before, his soul was gripped unto death by the birdlime of passion, which, sticking to the soul's wings, balks flight to God (S 311.4.4);[26] now he prays that God's love

embrace his soul with equal force unto life. Introduced earlier (3.5.10) to describe entanglement in Manichean errors, birdlime here symbolizes ensnarement in two of the triple concupiscence that effects spiritual death. Augustine experienced a strange unhappiness; according to his station, he had or soon would have nearly everything he had ambitioned, but he felt as if he had nothing. Utilizing his despondency from servitude to passions, the divine physician lanced his wound, inducing intense agony along with the release of the foul matter, a passing pain that would culminate in full healing: in roughly one year he would turn his back on honors, money, and marriage, to seek only the good of all goods without whose sustaining power no goods exist.

Probably in the fall of 385 Augustine, as official rhetor, was working on a panegyric in honor of Valentinian II.[27] In eulogizing the young emperor, he would not only resort to extravagances but manufacture thinly veiled untruths about his subject's slender accomplishments, hoping that sophisticated lying would earn him praise from influential figures who admired rhetorically adroit deception. This unestimable performance reflected the mendacious underside of a social order woven, to no small degree, out of a web of lies.

As he was psychologically hyperventilating from fever of ambition, a chance observation of a drunken beggar on a street in Milan sharpened awareness of his squalor. While with his wonted industry he was slaving to compose a declamation praising the little-praise-worthy monarch, the derelict, with practically no strain or pain, was reaping more earthly joy than his harried spirit. Moreover, the panhandler was relatively carefree while Augustine was ridden with anxieties. His impassioned chasing after worldly success seemed morally mad; the input of talent and energy was so huge, the output so meager. His pursuit of happiness turned into a doubly intolerable burden of unhappiness; the more he ran after honors, the more he staggered under the load imposed. Furthermore, the unvexed beggar had directly laid hold of some temporal happiness with a few coins cajoled from passers-by, the very thing that Augustine was still doggedly hunting for with mazy maneuvers of mental and social dexterity. Unquestionably the joy the beggar derived from transitory sensory goods was not authentic but actually misery. Yet the joy that Augustine's ambitions beckoned him toward was even more illusory because more deceptive; the prestige of high-ranking personages masks the folly of servitude to passing baubles. Undoubtedly too, the beggar's outer face was lighthearted while that of Augustine's was knitted in worry; the panhandler's inner face was free of care, content to live a lowly life while that Augustine's was on edge about the outcome of his panegyric. As he compared his lot with that of the beggar, Augustine found himself in a sort of paradox: though apparently more unhappy than the beggar, he would refuse, nevertheless, to change places with him. His decision was the product of a pragmatic saving of face rather than of moral truth; if consistent, he should have opted for the role that earned the most felicity with the least stress. Appeal to the importance of his learning was ineffectual because his scholarly status did not issue in true joy and because he was teaching others not to impart the truth but to garner fame. In servilely catering to the desires of others, he ironically humbled himself in worldly fashion in order to delusively exalt himself. Pursuit of self-glory begloomed him; inward groaning was the rod that God used to break his bones, to sap his misdirected psychic energy (bones stand for strength or courage [P 41.18]), disciplining the lower self to tear his soul away from the ungodly. His self-assurance was shaken: the genial beggar disclosed how idle were his vaulting ambitions; psychic pain taught him how fruitless are purely temporal goals. As he aspired for the heights, he was overwhelmed by a dejection bespeaking the bleak assessment of Qoheleth: "Vanity of vanities, and all is vanity" (Eccl 1.2). His laurels seemed already withered, his zest for new worlds to conquer almost snuffed out: on the verge of social triumph he tasted the ashes of defeat.

10. On the plane of carnal goods Augustine denies that the particular source of one's joy registers a significant difference. The beggar's wine and the fame Augustine hungered for are essentially the same and only accidentally different, for neither the beggar nor he sought spiritual goods. Indeed he was mired deeper in the flesh because hankering after glory drove him further away from the sovereign good. Moreover, both were drunkards. The beggar could sleep off his physical drunkenness, but Augustine's moral drunkenness, his blurred nonawareness of sound values, left him careening every day, continually inebriated by the psychic wine of desire for greater glory. Next, he explicitly qualifies his paradoxical-seeming remark of a few lines back: in a spiritual perspective a fine

distinction demarcates delights; joy that rests on rocklike faith and hope is immeasurably superior to joy that is sourced in treacherous carnal goods. Yet even on the fleshy level the beggar was happier, albeit accidentally so. The beggar was saturated in cheer (6.6.9), his countenance wreathed in a glad smile while Augustine was gnawed by anxieties. In addition, the bum's friendly greetings that exhibit a benevolence, which is a kind of social truth, gained him wine, a positive material good, while Augustine's refined lying as panegyrist would win him only a more diseased pride. Constant brooding over sorrows doubled his distress, provoking a mild existential despair. The prospect of some higher post made him so dispirited as to not even bestir himself. It seemed futile to try to seize some possible good fortune (6.11.18-9), for, like all else, it was begrimed by the ephemeral, one more vanity that disappeared as fast as it appeared.

Chapter 7: Alypius Healed of Passion for Circus

Suspending his ongoing narrative, he allocates six sections (7.11-10.16) to a sketch of Alypius' character,[28] which concludes with a cameo of Nebridius (10.17).

11. Born and reared in Augustine's native town, Alypius was blessed with well-to-do parents who ranked among its leading citizens. Understandably captivated by the magnitude of the mind of Augustine, at whose feet he sat in Thagaste and Carthage, he also esteemed Augustine's uprightness and kindness. Augustine, in return, admired him for his advanced virtue, a maturity rare in a younger person. Unfortunately, in Carthage, ostensibly a Sin City (2.1.1), he became the victim of a passion for the circus games, mainly the races of the charioteers (not the gladiatorial shows, these to come later). At the time (375/6) Augustine started teaching rhetoric in Carthage, a rift between Alypius' father and Augustine deterred him from enrolling in Augustine's classes. Because of the split Augustine could not advise him as friend nor counsel him as teacher concerning the threat his passion posed. To his surprise Alypius, not sharing his father's displeasure, occasionally dropped in to hear segments of Augustine's lectures.

12. The God who superintends each and all in creation, however, never for a moment forgot this man he had foreordained to be a bishop nourishing his flock with word and sacrament (Alypius would

serve as bishop of Thagaste from before 395 till after 427). Once when Alypius was present, to help throw light on a text Augustine was explicating, he drew a comparison with devotees of the circus games, deprecating with mordant humor fools hooked on this senseless addiction. Augustine had not inserted the point with Alypius in mind, but Alypius docilely applied the lesson to himself, under the impression that Augustine had designedly drawn the parallel to the stupidity of such fans. God used this witty gibe as hot coals to cauterize the spirit of Alypius. Burning coals, unlike those that are cold and dark, purify gold or change a man from death to life as in the transformation of Saul into Paul (P 139.14). From another angle, the hot coals burn to the ground the prior habitation or carnal lifestyle, enabling God to rear a new structure of virtue on the scorched ground; among those who are candidates for such transformation are those enamored of the circus or gladiatorial shows (P 19.4).[29] The central theme of the *Confessions* sounds anew: the man who does not reflect on the mercies of God should utter no praise of God; conversely, anyone like Augustine who does meditate on divine mercies has to sing the praises of God out of the depths of his very being. His divinely ordained comments bestirred Alypius to immediately pull himself out of the pit in which he had cheerfully hurled himself. A sort of gangrene had lodged in his spirit; his more vigorous temperance shook his spirit, so that all the decay of sordid desires dropped away like dead flesh: he never went to the games again.

Relenting, Alypius' father allowed him to follow Augustine's lectures: unhappily, as he progressed in rhetoric, he became entrapped, under Augustine's tutelage, in Manicheism, being especially enamored of the continence of the Manichean elect, which, in his ignorance of sound Christian asceticism, he took to be authentic when, in fact, it was an irrational chastity based on a detestation of the body as evil and a horror of reproduction (MM18.65. CF 30.6). Its superficial self-abnegation captured precious souls, innocents of good will and rudimentary virtue, who, like Alypius, aspired to a strict program of self-discipline but were unable to discriminate between the true and counterfeit article.

In the morally sane approach of the Catholic Church marriage is good because instituted and blessed by God for the procreation of the human race. The imperative, "Increase and multiply," is promulgated to humankind in general, not to each and every individual, so that the door is left open for renunciation of marriage for the sake of the kingdom of heaven. In other words, marriage is good, yet virginity is better insofar as the celibate forgoes the good of marital union by a vow that consecrates the self to God (ME 35.79. CF 30.6). Not prohibited, marriage remains a necessary good (ME 35.78); still, virginity is the higher state when it entails the sacrifice of this good for a greater love of God. Indeed if a marriage were not good, virginity or continence would not bespeak a sacrifice. Manicheism, however, counts marriage repulsive, spurning it as intrinsically evil. Strangely, while permitting sexual intercourse as such, Manichees condemn marriage because it is aimed at reproduction. Thus a Grand-Canyon-wide gap yawns between the Catholic recommendation of virginity or continence as the higher state and the Manichean prohibition of marriage as an institution for procreation that snares the divine in the darkness of the flesh (CF 30.6). As regards advanced asceticism, monks in the desert have especially outstripped Manichean ascetics. Hermits or anchorites live by themselves in remote areas, satisfied with bread and water, men of *summa castitas* and *summa continentia*, devoting themselves to continual colloquy with God, spending their days contemplating God's beauty in a manner hardly possible except for perfect Christians or saints (ME 31.65-6). Perhaps a rung down the ladder but still remarkable in their holiness are cenobitical religious in the desert who live austere lives in community, obeying a superior called father and subsisting on a simple diet that excludes meat and wine, so detached that they donate all surplus possessions to the needy. Communities of woman, similarly dedicated to chastity and poverty, also flourish in similar areas (ME 31.67-8). Moreover, practicing the same sort of austere chastity are communities of men and women in large cities like Milan and Rome, whose members are noticeably holy. Hence even cenobites far surpassed the Manichean elect in the loftiness of their genuine continence. Manichean asceticism that dispensed with divinely ordained marital union was also a vehicle for self-glorification, a means for purifying the elect so that they could release particles of divine light, making them not saved by God but saviors of God (P 140.12). Out of their viciously grounded self-denial arises a self-salvation so incongruous that to them might be adapted the characterization applied to Jansenist nuns of Port-Royal: they were pure as angels and proud as devils. Thus from more than one angle, Manichean continence was shadowy, shaded over with untruth (2.6.13,14), only a simulacrum of true virtue.[30]

Chapter 8: Alypius' Passion for Gladiatorial Contests

13. Under the spell of worldly ambition, pride of life in the extended sense (3.8.16;10.38.41), Alypius journeyed to Rome for studies preparing him for a career in law. In Carthage (6.7.12) he had conquered his craze for chariot races; in Rome prior to Augustine's arrival in 383,[31] he again capitulated to curiosity, this as regards gladiatorial fights. Both the ferocity of his passion and the way in which he was victimized defy belief. Bowing to the insistence of friends, he reluctantly entered the amphitheater, pledging to be present in body but absent in eyes and mind. His ears, however, remained open, and the frenzied roaring of the crowd over a fallen gladiator kindled the concupiscence of the eyes fascinated by the unusual and monstrous (10.35.55), prompting him to uncover his eyes. His bold resolution to stay in Olympian detachment above the fray instantly collapsed; morally he fell more wounded than the fallen swordsman who had ignited the shouting. He toppled because he had no real courage, only rash bravado; the stronger he felt on his own, the weaker he became. So he drank in the savagery in huge draughts till he became morally drunk, reeling with an uncontrollable curiosity. So unrestrained did his emotional intensity become that, surrendering his personal moral identity, he was swept up and became a faceless unit in the cheering crowd. Furiously roaring with the rest, he vanished as an individual, becoming an indistinguishable part swallowed up in a collective lump, a carbon copy of the unselfed others in the herd. Years later mercy shattered the fetters of this addiction, instilling also the precious admonition to trust not in his own but in God's power. The lesson imprinted was one he would never forget, especially as a bishop compassionating with an errant flock.

Chapter 9: Alypius Mistaken for a Thief

14. Sickening absorption in gladiatorial shows so seared Alypius' memory that the burning became a shame that led to healing. Another occurrence, earlier and of shorter duration, was also

memorially banked for future growth in virtue. While a student of
Augustine's in Carthage, he was wrongly charged with theft. God
permitted Alypius to suffer this ignominy for one reason: to sharpen
the prudence he would be called on to exercise as a great man, that
is, a Churchly personage, bishop of Thagaste and primate of his
province for over thirty-two years. The traumatic experience of being
unjustly denounced as a thief furnished astringent teaching in the
"college of hard knocks" that recommended circumspection in
rendering decisions as bishop. After a fellow student had failed to
break into a silversmiths' shop[32] and, in fleeing the scene, had
dropped his axe, Alypius, who was strolling by, had naively picked
up the offending tool, upon which he was apprehended by the shop's
employees; he was caught apparently *in flagrante delicto*.

15. Luckily, an architect with whom Alypius had become
acquainted at a senator's residence[33] intervened and led his captors to
the home of the real thief, where a slave boy identified the axe as his
master's and confirmed Alypius' version. In any event, God
providentially employed the architect's fortuitous appearance to
attest Alypius' innocence, of which God himself was the primary
witness. His chilling ordeal was an ongoing font of illumination for
him as an episcopal arbiter in the disputes commonly brought for
settlement. His narrow escape from being branded a robber and
consequently imprisoned and tortured induced him to be ever wary
about not rushing to judgment: a man plausibly accused may be
falsely convicted; wrong-seeming may be actually right; only
balanced inquiry, disentangling all the threads of a case, could spare
the innocent of miscarriage of justice.[34]

Chapter 10: Alypius' Honesty, the Friendship of Nebridius

16. So highly regarded was Alypius for his legal skills that he served
three times in Rome as an assessor, a lawyer attached to a magistrate
or provincial treasurer deficient in technical knowledge of the law. To
the astonishment of colleagues his continence of heart was so strong
that he steadfastly declined to take bribes, he himself being
astonished that reputedly moral men would rate gold more valuable
than justice. During his stint in Rome Alypius was assessor to the
Count of the Italian Treasury, who controlled government finance,
whose particular role was to collect "old cash-taxes" and, in general,

currency,[35] before reporting to the Count of Sacred or Imperial Largesse, the top financial official in the state.[36] As assessor to this key official, Alypius exhibited not only freedom from greed but also courage in the face of fearsome pressures. On one occasion he was approached by a powerful senator who was wheedling, as was his wont, special consideration amounting to circumvention of the law. Though the title had lost connection with political office, this senator still exerted solid clout—he was what is today dubbed "a political animal," a wily operator whose benefactions built a network of friends whose favors expect a return; a schemer who was not disinclined to make threats if oily persuasion proved unavailing. Nevertheless, in spite of the senator's influence and reputation, Alypius flatly turned down his request for special exemption. Next, the senator promised a handsome payoff, promptly rejected by Alypius. Finally, as a hard-nosed politician accustomed to getting his way at all costs, he had recourse to unspecified threats, but Alypius resolutely held his ground, not knuckling under and indeed scoffing at the intimidation. Observers could only marvel at the superb integrity of Alypius who neither cultivated this wheeler-dealer as a friend nor dreaded him as an enemy. All this powerful politician's weapons for helping or harming others were blunted by Alypius' massive strength of character. When directly solicited by the politician, the judge for whom Alypius functioned as assessor refused his appeal but not openly; out of fear of the redoubtable senator he shifted the blame for the turndown to Alypius, who indeed would have resigned had his superior caved in to the corrupt official.

For a while Alypius, a voracious reader of literature, gave in to a minor weakness when he ordered copyists hired by the state to duplicate codices or, loosely speaking, books at praetorian or palace prices—a practice usually countenanced as a legitimate perquisite. In the opinion of some,[37] he had copies of books transcribed at reduced rates; according to another reading,[38] at first he had works transcribed by official copyists and charged to the official budget or, more simply put, initially he complied with the prevailing custom of having copyists reproduce books for him "on company time." Nevertheless, after some soul-searching, a tender conscience moved him to choose the most just course; a sensitivity auguring well for his career as bishop, for fidelity in minor matters readies one to be exact in handling larger issues. Furthermore, steward of the goods of others, through grace he became master of the spiritual wealth that is virtue.[39]

17. Augustine sketches a few traits of Nebridius, another close associate.[40] A former student of Augustine's (who died around 390; 9.3.6), Nebridius had left his parents and family estate in the Carthage area simply to be by Augustine's side in their quest for existential truth and lived wisdom, the constituents of happiness. Like Augustine, Nebridius was gifted with an uncommon clarity and precision in probing thorny religio-philosophical questions. A very careful and penetrating searcher who totally concentrated on points, he had little patience with dilettantes who treated important problems in an offhand manner, as the grist of relaxed, after-hours conversation. He abhorred shallow spirits who preferred a short answer to a great difficulty (E 98.8). In his quest for truth and wisdom, he wavered, along with Augustine and Alypius, on the meaning of happiness. Since no one answer seemed analytically compelling and morally appealing, their exchanges were without decisive issue. Famished for the truth, they could only wait, hoping that God would somehow supply food, the truth and wisdom, to sate their starved minds, in due season, at the time foreordained by the Father; for Augustine and Alypius, finally in August, 386, when they were suddenly fed with the full light of conversion (8.12.29). Out of mercy, in order to lead them to all-satisfying truth, God allowed them to taste numbing frustrations in their worldly aspirations. Subjected to a kind of nonverbal instruction, they were stumbling about, unable to grasp the why and wherefore of their distress, an inky gloom engulfing their spirits. Though their searchings had not been stretched over years, the intensity of their probing and a feeling of semi-futility left the impression that they had been struggling for a long time, the minutes seemingly extended into hours, the hours inflated to months, the months distended to apparent years. In desperation they cried out, "How long is this anxious searching going to continue"?—an entreaty for resolution of their difficulties that anticipates the poignant plaint immediately prior to moral conversion in the garden (8.12.28).[41] In spite of their anguish they did not alter their worldly outlook or way of life since they were strictly applying the strategic canon of skepticism Augustine had adopted earlier: employ the most exacting criteria to determine what is unexceptionably certain. Up to this stage no one doctrinal position seemed true beyond a shadow of doubt; not a single ray of certitude could justify shifting to a different mode of

thinking and living.

Chapter 11: The Past Reviewed. Present Irresolution

Augustine pauses to review past opinions, slow progress, and present ambivalence.

18. Reflection triggers puzzlement over high expectations and low returns in pursuit of wisdom; the quest has been protracted, lasting well over a decade, spanning more than one-third of his life, more than 45% of his educable years, yet short of fruition. In 373 *Hortensius* had set him on fire for a life dedicated to wisdom alone. Now in 385, some eleven/twelve years later, to his sorrow he finds himself mired in the two lusts of the triple concupiscence, still hot after fleeting goods that enervate rather than energize his spirit. Naively imagining that the key to wisdom would soon be disclosed, he committed the not uncommon moral-psychological fallacy of identifying a desire for a general end with the choice of particular means, a blunder whose outcome is pithily caught in the popular saying, "The road to hell is paved with good intentions." He was without the self-discipline to unremittingly pursue the concrete means, not realizing that, as with science, there is no royal road to wisdom. The anguish of the years of groping belied puerile anticipation of easy conquest of wisdom. After the initial blaze of enthusiasm an often grim search lay ahead, as he now briefly recalls.

(i) Perhaps this naivete partly accounts for his impetuous conversion to Manicheism (DA 1.1). Later Faustus, far from answering everything, turned out to be capable of solving practically nothing (5.6.10). (ii) The "all-explainer" was succeeded by the ironically designated "mighty" Academics who, denying that the mind can grasp any certain knowledge about moral living, contend that only probability can serve as the guide to right conduct—a position at loggerheads with fact and logic. Still, the posture of doubt helped launch emancipation from Manichean falsities (5.14.25). (iii) Ultimately, he deliberately relied on the skeptical approach not as a world view counseling despair of truth but as a limited method that cautions against injudicious leaps to shaky conclusions, while urging critical inquiry with no a priori foreclosure of the real possibility of attaining certitude. (iv) Moreover, there was no reason for a retreat into despair. Persistent investigation showed not that the claims of the

Catholic Church were indubitable but that at least the Scriptures are not packed with nonsense. Various cruxes explicable by spiritual interpretation now looked reasonable, and passages under attack made sense. Under Ambrose's guidance he dismissed Manichean criticisms of Scriptures as caricatures; the charge of absurdity was negated by an alternative reading of many passages (5.14.24). (v) Without committing himself to Catholicism, he would continue as a nominal Catholic until he discovered truth so perspicuous that it squared with the most rigorous standards of certitude. (vi) Lamentably, the when and where of substantiating Catholicism remained stumbling blocks. The heavily scheduled Ambrose was not easily available for one-on-one consultation while Augustine himself had a tight program allowing hardly any time for study of the Catholic problem. In any event, whatever the pressures of work and social obligations, he needed to appoint top priority to the full healing of his sickly mind, especially since he now had a radically new perspective; his gravamen against the Church had arisen from gross distortions: the Church in no way embraced tenets laid at its door (6.4.5). In particular, spirituals repudiated as blasphemous the notion that God is circumscribed within a human body. Emboldened, because no longer duped by Manichean misrepresentations, he should, he felt, prayerfully reflect so as to let in more light on other possibly mischaracterized Catholic teachings. (vii) But practical obstacles and opportunities for social advancement applied the brakes to such single-mindedness.

19. (ix) However, more incisive inquiry perceives these worldly aspirations trained on transitory goods. He fronts two harsh facts: life is at bottom wretched, and his own death unavoidable. The unhappiness of even the most enriching temporal life and the real possibility of his own death bring him up short—success is hollow in comparison with acquisition of imperishable truth. *Mors certa, hora incerta*; death is absolutely certain, the hour uncertain (P 38.19). Suppose his life were suddenly snatched away: how much virtue would uplift, how much vice weigh down, his soul at the instant of death? More probably, he implies, in the world to come he will be called to account and punished for misdoings. It seems permissible to surmise that remotely Monica in spiritual aperçus and proximately Ambrose in his sermons urged the need to meditate on the ultimate destiny of the soul. Ambrosian sermons on the *Hexameron*, the *De*

Isaac, and the *De bono mortis*, which dealt with the spirituality and deathlessness of the soul and the afterlife, were probably preached in April and May, 386,[42] many months after Augustine raised the foregoing question of the final state of the soul. Still, since the last things are not uncommonly broached indirectly in Catholic sermons, it is not succumbing to unrealistic guesswork to suggest that Ambrose mentioned eschatological topics in other sermons no longer extant, which Augustine's all-absorptive mind retained. Yet, he wonders briefly, is the Epicurean hypothesis true? Does the destruction of all sensory life at death carry with it the dissolution of the soul as well? This remains to be examined (6.16.26), but he immediately backs away from a materialistic stance incompatible with the towering authority of Christianity and the providence of God—possibly an argument whose main lines were gleaned directly or indirectly from Ambrose's preaching. If the soul perishes with the death of the body, it would have been fruitless for God to have ordained the incalculable worldwide spread of the Gospel, which promises everlasting happiness after a troublous sojourn on earth. It would have been idle to work a moral miracle of world evangelization for men doomed to utter corruption of soul as well as body. A personal corollary follows: if man's spirit is truly immortal, it is stupid to go on racing after fulfillment in fragile trifles of this world. Spiritual procrastination being irrational, he should surrender himself to seeking God, the source of genuine happiness. (x) Unfortunately, he was hamstrung by infirmity of will. In spite of repeated affirmations of love of wisdom, he still looked longingly toward worldly goods, which promise a solid psychic sweetness not to be scanted. Well-placed friends should encounter no difficulty in landing him a third-level governorship.[43] Nor does marriage necessarily debar one from cultivation of wisdom; a number of outstanding men who rated marriage no hindrance to consecration to wisdom could well serve as models for smoothly wedding fidelity to a wife to fidelity to wisdom. Moderns for whom marriage does not appear per se antithetic to possession of wisdom may be reminded that, for Augustine and many of the ancients, total dedication to wisdom entrained detachment from worldly goods, including renunciation of a morally acceptable vocation like marriage. The sage of old would have no truck with worldly rank or social status, even forgoing a suitable marriage that augured reasonable happiness. Subconsciously, Augustine was inclining toward a complete conversion of self, a sacrifice of his entire being to God alone, to be granted from above in the garden in Milan (8.12.29-30).

20. After this synoptic review Augustine, taking stock of his present situation, found to his dismay that his heart was a light skiff tacking back and forth, buffeted by various winds of desire. Ordinarily decisive and strictly scheduled, he was letting never-stopping time slip by while he dragged his feet over abandonment to the Lord; yet his hesitation could not halt his daily dying, continuance in the death of the soul that is mortal sin. Inexorably destined for death, day by day he moved one step closer to the grave; it seems questionable that his daily dying here refers, save by tenuous allusion, to his life-in-death (1.6.7). Fervent aspiration toward his ambitioned end was not paralleled by assiduous application of prosaic means. Hungering for felicity, he shrank from seeking it in God's plan of abnegation and chastity. Concretely, his pursuit of happiness became a flight from it. In particular, he simply could not imagine himself as any other than miserable without the tender caresses of a caring wife. On mercy abundantly accessible for curing infirmities, he expended not a single thought, for he had never experienced an infusion of divine power conferring continence. Obtuse in spirit, he believed that continence could be won by self-mastery. Not only did Manichean teaching on asceticism not stress the uncovenanted gift of divine power, but it made hardly any mention of it. Sheer force of self raised the elect to elitehood; they were spiritual athletes, champions toughened by their program of ascetic calisthenics (P 140.12). Theory and practice taught nothing of the Scripture proclaiming that continence is God's gift (Wis 8.21).[44] Surely he would have won this precious virtue if his prayers had knocked on the divine heart with faith strong enough to abase self. At a later stage, as he pondered gratuitously liberating grace marvelously illustrated in his sudden healing in Milan in August, 386 (8.12.28-9), he would express the nexus between grace and obedience to divine commands in the now-celebrated formula, *Da quod iubes et iube quod vis* (10.29.40; 31.45): "Give what you command, and command what you will." Still bereft of unwavering faith in Christ the mediator, in 385 he could not hope for this sheer gift that would make and keep him continent.

Chapter 12: Discussion of Marriage

21. Largely immune to tugs of sexual desire, Alypius had slipped into sexual intercourse at about fifteen but, after repenting, had triumphed over the sexual drive with a self-control that excited the admiration, in the double sense of appreciation and perplexity, of an Augustine whose appetite for sex was almost as imperious as his hunger for food (6.3.3). When Alypius pointed up how inharmonious marriage would be with a life free of worries tied to getting and spending, Augustine deftly countered with examples of men whose love of a wife proved to be no obstacle to love of wisdom, illustrations that embodied paper logic since he was far from blending marriage with a life of wisdom—he dreaded loss of his sexual lifestyle. He resisted Alypius' healing advice, like a wounded man pushing away a physician's balm, or like a captive shoving aside the hand of a liberator. Through Augustine's cleverly honeyed rejoinder the serpent entered the garden of Alypius' purity.

22. In being bemused by the disparity between Augustine's analytical perspicacity and his seeming lack of practical intelligence, Alypius capitulated to the fallacy that theoretical intelligence almost automatically assures control of desires, an erroneous equation of intelligence with virtue, not uncommon, we have already remarked, in Western thought: various prominent thinkers have proclaimed that informed intelligence is the key to virtue. As the scientifically advanced but morally decadent twentieth century witnessed, intelligence, however necessary, is far from sufficient. Other ingredients, hard to specify in brief, are required, especially conscientiousness sprung from a character molded by good habits. Plainly Augustine was wanting in the resolve and virtues indispensable for mastering entrenched sexual proclivities.

To dispel Alypius's bafflement, Augustine suavely justified his apparently odd behavior with incisive dialectic force, by arguing that a gulf stretched between Alypius' casual, tawdry encounter and a settled life of disciplined sex during his own lengthy concubinage. Alypius' experience bore characteristics of what is today colloquially called a one-night stand, devoid of the slightest commitment because quickly over and done with. Hence while Alypius understandably now considers his short adventure misguided and hardly worth recollecting, he is wrong, Augustine argues, in paralleling his fleeting episode and Augustine's lifestyle. Whereas Alypius' encounter lasted less than a day, Augustine's concubinage had endured in fidelity for nearly fifteen years; whereas Alypius' action was furtive, Augustine's relationship was open and publicly respected; therefore their diverse experiences resisted facile comparison. Now, Augustine astutely continued, on the supposition that the state of concubinage were blessed with the lawful condition of marriage, there would be no reason whatsoever why Alypius should be perplexed by the fact that Augustine refused to contemn marriage: how could anyone be repulsed by a secularly revered state? Augustine's adroit marshaling of facts and analysis amounted to a persuasive equivalent of a Q.E.D. that disarmed Alypius, who for the first time began to feel the attraction of marriage not out of sexual desire but out of a hankering for the out-of-the-ordinary. What piqued his curiosity was the mysterious character of sex, so inviting for an Augustine apparently otherwise fulfilled, whereas, deprived of it, his existence became one ongoing punishment. In a kind of existential paradox Alypius who was free from bondage to sex wondered about the enticing features of Augustine's repellent slavery to sex. This novel approach was no less perilous than the wonted route, for wonder fueled by curiosity could well lead to experiment, unchecked experiment to habit, and habit, once fixed, to slavery to sex. In taking a spouse, he would, in effect, be choosing as spouse death of soul. Espousal in marriage would become the spiritually deadly espousal that is lust or enslavement to sex (Is 28.18).[45]

Chapter 13: A Marriage Arranged for Augustine

23. Meanwhile, the ever-practical Monica busied herself with concrete steps to arrange a Christian marriage valid in the eyes of state and Church, which would ready Augustine for a cleansing of his old self in baptism. Earlier her bumptiously Manichean son had stooped to sophistry to twist the import of Monica's vision topsy-turvy (3.11.19-20). Now, more impressed by her spiritual endowments (6.2.2) and more hospitable to Catholic claims (6.3.4), he asked her intercession for a vision indicating divine approval of the value of the marriage.[46] Impelled by a subconscious yearning for the success of the marriage, she painted a picture begotten of wishful thinking, its elements the outpourings of an overexercised imagination. So, minus

her usual confidence she reported the vision to Augustine in a deprecatory tone, for through grace she perceived that the vision was the upshot not of divine light but of desire-slanted illusion. Apparently she was gifted with discernment (1 Cor 12.10), one of what theologians today name the nine ministry gifts of the Spirit, empowering her to discriminate between genuine divine disclosure and sheerly human vision. She ascertained this difference by a sort of spiritual tasting, inexpressible by pedestrian reason. A divinely induced vision savored of the fruits of the Holy Spirit (Gal 5.22-3), such as love, joy, and peace, whereas a purely human dream was accompanied by coldness, displeasure, and vague disquiet. Nevertheless, Monica went on pressing for marriage with a bride-to-be, only ten, two years under the legal age, for whom, since she looked fetching, Augustine consented to wait.[47]

Chapter 14: A Project for a Community

24. The pressures of ordinary life with its multifarious concerns stimulated Augustine and his friends to propose the formation of a community that would afford ample leisure for study and scholarly interchange. About ten friends were to pool their resources in a common household. Romanianus, a fellow townsman who had helped subsidize his education in Carthage (3.1.1), emerged as the most enthusiastic proponent; to his voice weight was lent by the fact that his investment would be the largest in underwriting the new community.[48] Each year two magistrates or coordinators would manage material necessities such as purchase of food and care of clothing, leaving the rest free to concentrate on intellectual interests alone.[49] However, a crucial division arose over whether present or prospective wives of married members would be integrated into the community. Living in community without wives would effectively alienate the married men from their wives, much to the discontent of both spouses. Yet if the wives were given entrance, the original design would be significantly altered, to the dissatisfaction of the unmarried; presumably the women would not evidence a like intellectual bent. Splendid-looking on paper, the plan foundered on the unworkable character of an association of marital couples and bachelors.[50] So Augustine and his two confidants, held captive by two of the three concupiscences, went on conjuring fresh projects and mentally

exploring new avenues of happiness. Later, through light from on high, Augustine would strive to form a community of lay celibates at Thagaste, then a community of clerics at Hippo, in which all things would be possessed in common. The Christian model enshrining their ideal was not a Pythagorean brotherhood or the Platanopolis, a city of philosophers projected by Plotinus, or a Manichean quasi-monastery,[51] but the first Christian community in Jerusalem where the brethren marvelously shared all in common (Ac 4.32-5).[52] Then would the God who gives spiritual meat at the right time fill their souls with the blessings of true community life based on New Testament self-giving. Delaying, not denying, an answer to their imprecations, God would respond at the time appointed by his eternal counsel (P 144.19-20).[53]

Chapter 15: Adeodatus' Mother Returns to Africa

25. Monica's negotiation for a Christian marriage for Augustine implied that his concubine's lower social class barred, according to a constitution of Constantine, legitimate marriage. The arrangement also demanded that he part from the woman with whom he had lived for some fifteen years (371-86). Augustine does not disguise the pain and pathos of the parting. Against his emotional bias, under the dictate of duty, this loyal woman was torn from his side, leaving his lacerated heart bleeding. As a pledge of her undying love, she forswore all future marriage or liaison, and, though it wounded her motherly heart, she generously gave over Adeodatus, now fourteen, to Augustine.

However, the moving, quasi-tragic features of this scene do not warrant sentimentalizing it.[54] Neither Augustine nor Monica was snobbishly cold or cruel in the dismissal of his concubine. Because of her inferior social station, she simply could not hope to marry him. At that time also women did not expect, let alone campaign for, equality of rights with respect to marriage. Once Augustine decided upon a suitable marriage, he was compelled to separate from his beloved concubine.[55] A frightfully distressing situation indeed; but his conduct was in no way morally reprehensible: in justice he was obliged to leave his companion. Moreover, it was not unfeeling or harsh to omit mention of his concubine's name.[56] Disclosure might well have made her the target of curiosity-seekers in Carthage and if, as some surmise, she later took the veil, she was insulated from grosser invasions of privacy by pesky fellow Africans.

Meanwhile, as mentioned earlier (6.12.21), Augustine's sinning increased, especially indulgence in illicit sex. He could not even imitate, he ironically comments, the will power of a member of the reputably weaker sex. On the sexual prowl, helpless to stand a two-year hiatus without sexual pleasure, he took to himself a mistress, neither a wife nor a concubine, bringing him to realize that he would be enslaved to sex right into marriage itself. The psychological wound caused by rupture from his concubine failed to heal. Ordinarily in the physical order, as a fever dies down and pain becomes less intense, the prospect of full healing appears promising. But in certain instances the vanishing of pain is an illusory index of the onset of healing: "In a body a wound accompanied by pain is better than putrefaction without pain, which is specifically called corruption" (NB 20).[57] Somewhat similar was the case of Augustine's psychological laceration; after the initial fever and acute pain the wound suppurated. The ebbing of fever and earlier pain signaled not the threshold of healing but the presence of a kind of gangrene, along with fresh pain. So the waning of earlier pangs indicated that his chances for recuperation were not brighter but fainter. Gone were the fever and earlier pain, but the wound remained in a state of putrefaction. The fever was replaced by coldness of spirit; new pain was associated with the festering that made him more despairing than ever of the cure of the gaping laceration inflicted by the departure of his faithful concubine.

Chapter 16: Further Musings on the Meaning of Life

26. What especially restrained Augustine from a wilder plunge into sexual gratification was fear of death as hooked up with fear of judgment with its threat of inexorable retribution. Significantly, during the back-and-forth of exchanges, he constantly clung to this fear. The seeds may have been implanted as part of the Christian teaching gathered from Monica's informal instructions. Again, Manichees believed that at death hardened sinners are sentenced to a kind of hell as everlasting punishment.[58] Furthermore, final retribution in terms of justice would seem to be a corollary of the never-relinquished certitude, that God exists and that his providence

governs all human life (6.5.7). Finally, it would seem reasonable to infer that the motif of inescapable accountability in the life beyond was underscored in *De bono mortis* and kin sermons delivered by Ambrose. As he worried over the meaning of good and evil, including possible afterlife sanctions, he would have given the nod to Epicurus' philosophy of pleasure if answerability in a life to come could be nullified by a this-life immortality of body and soul devoted to a balanced intake of pleasures ensuring happiness. Epicurus labored to demolish two underpinnings of belief in an afterlife that torments the mind: the arbitrament of the gods and the imperishability of the soul. First, the gods are serenely indifferent to the hurly-burly of events below. Second, at death the body decomposes into atoms, and the soul, made up of fine atoms, also disintegrates (indeed the soul decomposes prior to bodily dissolution; S 150.6). No conscious life survives death since sensation, the only mode of cognition, depends upon body and soul, both of which dissolve at death. Release from fear of divine judgment of an immortal soul contributes to the atraraxy, absence of disquietude, which, along with the virtues, is a means to temporal happiness. However, because for Augustine, a providential God bound to pass judgment and souls surviving death are not illusions but credible realities, he deemed Epicurus' analysis untenable and morally unsatisfying. Still, he conjectured, with an alteration of conditions the Epicurean way might prove hypothetically admissible. On the supposition that man could enjoy an earthly immortality, with a life of increasing pleasure not subject to loss, Epicurus' program seemed irrefragable: everyone would be undoubtedly blissful in a deathless life of unending pleasure. Unfortunately, the hypothesis is clearly fictional, spun out of the counterfactual conditions that death is not inevitable and that human life is not beset by evils. Letting its dream-world deficiencies pass, Augustine puts his finger on its radical error, the contention that sensory pleasure alone, by fulfilling human aspirations, can make man genuinely happy. Far from guaranteeing happiness, the ruling assumption, the sensistic outlook, of his fictional hypothesis, underlay his gnawing anxiety. It was bitterly ironical that the key Epicurean motif of sensism that he was pondering as a source of happiness had him trapped in actual unhappiness. At the time he was evaluating this apparently appealing hypothesis, he was, in theory and practice, locked in a materialism narrowed down to sensory objects, which left only emptiness in the center of his soul. Buried under sensory goods, his cognition resembled that of an animal, blind to the intellectual light that illumines spiritual goods like moral goodness and moral beauty, which are sought primarily for their own sake, not simply for associated pleasures. Epicurus' goods are strictly accessible only to the eye of the body whereas these goods are seen within, by the eye of the soul; only the mind can interiorly perceive these intelligible objects. Further, the espousal of this pleasure-philosophy in the presence of friends was self-stultifying. While he discussed with his friends the merits of self-gratification through total immersion in pleasure, the existence of friendship, a supersensual good, ran counter to a life of pleasure that was purely sensory. Again, even if he were saturated with sensory pleasures, he could not be happy without friends for whom true friendship was a matter not of grabbing but of giving, in which not self-centeredness but the love of the other or authentic benevolence claims highest priority. Loving his friends, and they him, in terms of the inner spirit, not in terms of the carnal senses, he gave them his friendship gratis, for their sake, not with egoistic self-satisfaction but with self-oblivion. Self-giving in friendship being meaningless in an Epicurean context, the very fact that Augustine broached with true friends the attractiveness of the Epicurean stance testified to its essential unattractiveness. Because its ideal is the self-obssessed individual who exploits others for his own pleasure, it clashes with other-oriented genuine friendship.

Foeda, foul or sordid things, which preoccupied him while pondering the unrealistic hypothesis, are sheerly carnal pleasures, subhuman or animal, prized by Epicurus; foul in contrast to noble virtues of the spiritual realm. The term may also allude to the state of degradation to which Roman thinkers ordinarily consigned Epicurus. Although Epicurus never proposed pursuit of pleasure in a brutish manner, Roman intellectuals generally interpreted him as one who would prefer, in J.S. Mill's phrase, to be a pig satisfied than Socrates dissatisfied. Cicero strongly accents the predominant pleasure-motif in Epicurus,[59] and Horace addresses Epicurus as a leader or member of a herd of pigs.[60] In line with this tradition Augustine portrays Epicurus as a pig wallowing in the sty of the flesh (P 73.25). Earlier, possibly echoing Cicero's depiction of Epicureans as cattle, he disdainfully refers to the open stables in which Epicurean herds are lodged (CA 3.18.41).[61] Though Augustine, in common with the

Roman reading, mischaracterizes Epicurus as a proponent of crass indulgence in pleasure, his underlining of the paradoxical claims of Epicurus stands: an Epicurean interested only in his own self-satisfaction cannot, without self-refutation, praise or practice true friendship, which entails primary love of the friend for the friend's sake, thereby excluding cultivation of friends primarily for one's own pleasure.[62]

Treading paths made treacherous by untruths, especially by the root-falsity that man's mode of cognition and valuation is no higher than the sensory,[63] his quest for the truth from a purely sensory perspective fluctuated from one inadequate solution to another, with the give-and-take of dialogue finally fruitless.[63] His woe-begone spirit thrashed about, now lying on one side, now on the other, now supine, then prone, feeling only disquiet and bitterness, utterly without rest, for he had withdrawn from the God who is and gives rest (1.1.1).[64] Yet God, ever-faithful, was to liberate Augustine from error grounded in the sensism plaguing him with unhappiness and plant his feet firmly on the straight path of light and virtue, while consoling him with assurance of never-failing support: "Run [with divine energy], I will bear you up [I will empower you], and I will lead you to the goal [of truth] and, once you are there, I will go on bearing you up [empowering you with divine life]" (Is 46.4). Loosing him from all ties of temptation to the garden of Epicurus, God would bear him up in the garden of Milan (8.12.28-9), then later bear him up to shoulder all the grinding labors of the priestly vocation mapped out for him.

NOTES

1. J. Rodriguez, "El Libro VI de *Las Confesiones*," in LASAP, Libri VI-IX, 9-44, especially 35, 37-40.
2. BA 13, 141, n. 1.
3. As mentioned in Book 5, n. 14, Pellegrino, 90, underlines the exquisitely exact quality of this description of Monica. BA 13, 515, n.1.
4. See D 2.333.
5. See D 2.333.
6. HC 91, n.2.
7. Van der Meer, 500,
8. Text quoted in D 2.344.
9. Van der Meer, 259-61.
10. Reading out loud, an aural-visual exercise that was the accepted practice among the Greeks, continued to be the custom till Augustine's time – hence his surprise at Ambrose's reading in silence. See Marrou, *Hist. of Educ. in Antiquity*, 81, 154, 195, and 89. For other references see Courcelle, 155, n.2, who notes that Augustine and his friends read aloud to one another (4.8.13) and that, in instructing Faustus, he read aloud select passages (5.7.15). Apparently Augustine had his amanuensis read aloud letters written to him. For other perceptive comments see D 2.345, who remarks that Cassian recommended prayer in silence and that Ambrose is struck by the inward outcry of Anna (1 Sam 1.13) whose silent voice was heard by Jesus (*Exp. Ps.* 118.17.9).
11. Latinists concede that the word-play in this line defies precise rendering in English: ...*tenebam cor meum ab omni adsensione timens praecipitium et suspendio magis necabar....*
12. Ladner, *Idea of Reform*, 216.
13. F. Engels, *Herr Dühring's Revolution in Science*, 101-2.
14. In the seventeenth century Decartes advocated a total assimilation of all other branches of knowledge to the mathematical ideal of certitude. As his *Discourse on Method* put it, to be acceptable, thought had to possess "a certitude equal to that of the demonstrations of arithmetic and geometry." Success in applying algebra to geometry to achieve what we call analytic geometry encouraged him to propose a universal mathematics, whose object is not quantity alone but order and measure, as the one science embracing all other provinces of knowledge. See E. Gilson, *The Unity of Philosophical Experience*, 139-42. Augustine's erection of mathematics as the model for certitude, however, was more modest. Instead of integrating all cognition into a de-quantified universal mathematics, he set mathematical certitude as the rigorous standard to which all propositions must conform before being acknowledged as certain. In fact, as our text indicates later on, he never fullly carried out this austere program of certification; the spirituality of the soul and the definition of evil are truths achieved with a certitude that is not as unchallengeable as $7+3=10$.
15. Text quoted in D 2.352.
16. As mentioned in Book 1, n. 21, through DNA we can scientifically establish that

this man and this woman are the parents of a particular child. However, since the use of DNA is practically unobtainable by the vast majority of parents, human faith, in fact, attests that these individuals are the parents of this child.

17. J. Ramirez, "The Priority of Reason Over Faith in St. Augustine," AS 13(1982), 123-31.

18. Augustine was to descry the hand of God at work in the spread throughout the whole world of the Scriptures as authorized by and channeled through the Catholic Church. The worldwide diffusion of the divine word and the expansion of the one Church are inexplicable by merely human causes: God designed this authoritative route as a providential means of reaching him by faith (6.5.7). The rapid growth of the Church is a "mighty thing" that invests life with permanent meaning, affording assurance that human existence does not wholly die in the dissolution of the body. After his conversion Augustine further elaborated this apologetic thrust. See E. TeSelle, *Augustine's Strategy as an Apologist*, a short work remarkable for its balanced concision.

19. K. Adam, *The Christ of Faith*, 4-7.

20. Bonner, 229-31.

21. R. Eno, "Doctrinal Authority in Saint Augustine," AS 12(1981), 133-72, especially 136-45. In "Authority," AE 80-2, while continuing to indicate the preponderant role of the Church in interpreting Scripture, and the primacy of the Roman see, Eno remarks that at times African dealings with Rome were not unfailingly harmonious. He cautions that later controversies about the scope of Roman authority had yet to surface. In *Forma Petri–Petrus, Figura Ecclesiae*: "The Uses of Petrus", AUG(L), 41 (1991), *Mélanges T. J. van Bavel* 2, 659–76, Eno shows that Augustine's *figura* of the Church emphasized the Church's humility while the Roman model or *forma* highlighted the authority of the Church.

22. According to I. Kant, *Kritik der reinen Vernunft*, Vorred der zweiten Auflage, 27, metaphysics or philosophy is "*ein Kampfplatz*," a battlefield, an arena of incessantly conflicting views. Like its modern descendant, ancient philosophy was territory in which rival outlooks took up cudgels against one another. Philosophy consisting of divergent philosophers did not speak a single conceptual language but voiced a Babel of opinions. It was the product of Babylon, the city of confusion, the polity of untruths, in which philosophers unendingly manufactured opinions diverse from and adverse to one another. The Church, on the other hand, proposes one truth, a single consistent set of doctrines; CD 18.51.16.26. Lack of objectivity or intersubjectivity still bedevils contemporary philosophy, justifying the witty remark: if you took all the philosophers in the world and laid them end to end, they would never come to a conclusion.

23. At this point he confines divine governance to human events, with the extension to nonhuman events still implicit. Cicero, who denied a perfect providence, mentions all events, nonhuman as well. *De nat. deor.* 2.1.3.

24. The analogy of mother is variously employed. In 5.5.9 charity is said to be a mother. Wisdom is also designated a mother (J 98.6). Jesus is a mother supplying milk for infants (7.8.24). Scripture is a mother (6.5.8)

25. Starnes, 252-3, maintains that the triple concupiscence, "a perverted imitation

of the Trinity," is a dominant theme in the *Confessions.*

26. Quoted by D 2.356.

27. Relying on C. Lepelley, *Atti,* 1986, 1.109, D 2. 356-7 claims that the panegyric did not mark the tenth anniversary of Valentinian's reign, on November 22, 385 because the decennial celebration occurred in 384, "too soon after Augustine's arrival" in Milan. In any case, the panegyric which Augustine was preparing must be distinguished from the panegyric in honor of Bauto's inauguration as consul in January, 385 (CALP 3.25.30).

28. As mentioned in the Introduction, n. 1, Courcelle, 29-32, suggested that a request by Paulinus of Nola for a brief biography of Alypius was the occasion for composing the *Confessions.* After fulfilling the request, Augustine included his account of Alypius in his own autobiography. See BA 13,2, 27-8, and Starnes, 154. However, as the Introduction, n.1, indicates, there is no evidence whatsoever that Augustine composed such a biography.

29. These texts are cited in D 2.363-4.

30. On Christian asceticism see the perceptive remarks of Coyle, 205-7. On the possible sources of Augustine's information, 208-40.

31. When young, Augustine attended gladiatorial contests only occasionally; P 147.7. He laments the lot of gladiators who fight with a kind of despair, destined as they are to fall by an opponent's sword. Doomed to die, they wrench a certain satisfaction from their fighting before their own blood reddens the sands of the arena. No genuine glory is gained in an occupation shot through with cruelty. S 20.3.P 101 (S.1).10. See W. Weismann, "Ampitheatrum," AL 1.300-3.

32. According to D 2.367, a sort of primitive, small-scale mass-production obtained in silversmiths' shops (CD 7.4).

33. Some suggest that Alypius' connection with this senator weighed heavily in his favor. D 2.367.

34. D, 2.368 instances OM 29.37 to point up a bishop's difficulty in administering justice. Augustine would prefer to engage in manual labor upon which followed leisure for prayer rather than put up with trying to thread his way "through the troublesome perplexities of others' cases bearing on secular matters, to be settled by adjudication or brought to an abrupt end by judicial intervention."

35. D 2.365.

36. HC 103, n.13.

37. G-M 156, n.14.

38. BA 13,555, n.1.

39. Under Augustine's tutelage first of all in Thagaste in 374/6, Alypius followed Augustine to Milan, during which time through Augustine's persuasion he became a Manichee who was particularly impressed by the continence of the elect (6.7.12). In autumn, 384, he traveled north to Milan with Augustine, discarding Manicheism along with his master, his intellectual conversion to Catholicism somewhat delayed because he mistakenly ascribed to the Church an Apollinarist concept of Christ (7.19.25). He witnessed Augustine's conversion in the garden, and was himself converted to an ascetic style of life (8.12.29-30). At Cassiciacum he was present, at least in part, for the three dialogues, describing himself as a skilled discussant of mature power. A close

confidant of Augustine who characterized him as "a brother of my heart" (9.4.7), he was a member of the community at Thagaste (E 22.1.2), and after he was ordained bishop of Thagaste (before March 4, 395), prior to Augustine's elevation to the episcopate (May/June, 395), he was in charge of the monastery. When Paulinus of Nola requested the story of his conversion and ordination, Alypius asked Augustine to discharge this task. As mentioned in n. 28 above, some scholars hold the questionable opinion that the short narrative on Alypius in the *Confessions* was excerpted or adapted from the account Augustine composed at Alypius' bidding. Later Alypius played an active role in various councils that combated Donatism and Pelagianism. He died some time after 427-8. For a lengthier treatment and more detailed discussion of Alypius' later years, see Mandouze, *Prosog.*, 53-65, from which the bulk of the foregoing has been derived. See also the longer article in AL 1.246-67, with more extensive notes and bibliography, authored by E. Feldmann, A. Schindler, and O. Wermelinger. Also A. Fitzgerald, "Alypius," AE 16-7.

40. Nebridius, an intimate friend, whom Augustine first encountered in Carthage in 373 at the start of Augustine's Manichean period, wrestled along with Augustine and Alypius over the meaning of life in Milan in 386 (though he was not present during the conversion scene), and exchanged letters with Augustine (E 3-14, Nebridius being the writer of E 5,6, and 9). His death probably occurred before Augustine was ordained priest in 391. A serious thinker and conscientious researcher, gifted with remarkable dialectical facility, he exposed the fraudulence of divination (4.3.6) and proved that Manichean claims for the incorruptibility of their God were self-contradictory (7.2.3). After overcoming acquiescence in a sort of Docetism (9.3.6), he became a Catholic shortly after Augustine's baptism on April 24, 386. Socially reserved, he committed himself to a life of chastity after his return to his family estate at Carthage, where he helped convert the entire household to the faith (9.3.6). For further nuances along with complete references, see Mandouze, *Prosog.*, 224-6, upon which our short sketch depends. See also A. Fitzgerald, "Nebridius," AE 587-8.

41. See D 2.370 on this last point.

42. Courcelle, 123-4.

43. *Praesidatus* denoted the bottom level of governorships. *Consulares* governed around twenty-two provinces, *correctores*, three, while *praesides* ruled thirty-one. This rank was of course not the highest but the lowest of his ambitions; like any political figure, he was not exactly averse to vaulting higher. See D 2.374.

44. As A. Zumkeller, (*Augustine's Ideal of the Religious Life*, 254, 277, n. 451), indicates, 6.11.20 is the first place in which Augustine explicitly states that no one can be continent unless God gives him the power. Right down to the end of his days (DA 4.3) he insisted, with increasing force, especially against the Pelagians, that man can live continently only by the *donum Dei* that is uncovenanted grace. Those who arrogate their goodness to themselves are ignorant of the righteousness of God (E 140.83), displaying an imprudence comparable to that of the five foolish virgins. For this last reference see D 2.374-5, who notes that the *Da quod iubes* formula frequently occurs in anti-Pelagian texts.

45. In the judgment of Starnes, 166, n. 101, Augustine, by excruciating sexual temptations, and Alypius, by wonderment or perplexity concerning sex, were vexed by unchastity till their conversions.

46. See L. Ferrari, "The Dreams of Monica in Augustine's *Confessions*", AS 10(1979), 3-17. Also, M. Dulaey, *Le rêve dans la vie et la pensée de saint Augustin.*

47. According to Justinian, *Inst.* 1.10.22, for females the legal age for marriage is twelve. G-M 162, n.5.

48. Romanianus is remembered principally as the wealthy friend who was a benefactor of the young Augustine. Though probably not too much older, he paid for Augustine's higher studies in Carthage. Upon Augustine's return to Thagaste after joining the Manichees, when Monica refused to let him live at home (3.11.19). Romanianus, a relative of Alypius (Starnes, 139, n. 103), gave him lodging and encouragement in his own residence (CA 2.2.3). Under Augustine's influence Romanianus accepted Manicheism (CA 1.1.3). While in the court at Milan to settle business affairs, Romanianus enthusiastically concurred with Augustine's community project, agreeing not only to help underwrite the cost but also to become a member of the group. The pressure of business having compelled him to return to North Africa, he was not present with Augustine during the Cassiaciacum period (autumn, 386, to March 10, 387). Significantly, Augustine dedicated CA to him, with the hope that its polemic would free him from any lingering traces of skepticism. VR, penned two years later, was also dedicated to him (E 15.1) to disabuse him of Manichean misconceptions originally instilled by a younger and philosophically ignorant Augustine. As plausibly argued by A. Gabillon, "Romanianus, alias Cornelius," REA 24 (1978), 58-70, a Thagaste inscription "Cornelius Romanianus" indicates that Cornelius (the *nomen* of Romanianus) was the recipient of E 259 (408) that identifies Romanianus, now a Christian who had been baptized in danger of death, as the widower of a certain Cypriana, who unfortunately suffered relapse into sexual license. More details can be gathered from the account of Mandouze, *Prosog.*, 994-7, from which most of these data have been culled. See also A. Fitzgerald, "Romanianus," AE 730-1.

49. It does not seem possible to specify exactly what prior pattern of community Augustine drew upon as the model for his community of scholars. Because of his definitive disaffection from Manicheism, it seems certain that the Manichean conventicle at Rome in 383 did not serve as the concrete image of his projected community; in addition, the Manichean convent was not centered on the cultivation of learning. Despite the opinion of one prestigious scholar, it is doubtful that Augustine modeled his intellectual community after the Platonopolis of Plotinus, which is mentioned in Porphyry's *Life of Plotinus,* since it seems likely that this, along with the *libri Platonicorum* came into his hands some months later (7.9.13); on this see D 2.379-80. According to BA 13, 566-7, n.1, in dependence upon W. Theiler, Augustine may have gleaned some knowledge of Pythagorean communities, as described by Iamblichus (*De pyth. vit.* 30), through his reading of Varro's *Liber de philosophia.* As is well-known, Pythagoras (fl. 530 B.C.?) was the founder of a religious society, some of whose members committed themselves to the study of the arts and sciences, with

special emphasis upon mathematics and mathematically grounded sciences. While Augustine had great respect for Pythagoras, whom he hails as "the individual most renowned in that contemplative virtue of which Greece could boast" (CE 1.7.12; cited by D 2.380), it would seem that the connection between Pythagoras and Augustine's community stems not from solid evidence but only the speculation of scholars.

50.   A. Mandouze, *L'aventure de la raison et la grâce*, 193, n.1, suggests that the roughly ten potential members of the community included Augustine, Nebridius, Alypius, Romanianus, Verecundus, Adeodatus, Navigius (Augustine's brother; BV 1.6), Licentius, and Trygetius. The first four listed were certainly slated to be members, but the rest may be only doubtfully counted part of the pioneer group.

51.   BA 13, 566-7.

52.   *Rule* 1.4.

53.   G. Lawless, *Augustine of Hippo and His Monastic Rule*, 45-59, makes a strong case for the view that Augustine established a lay monastery in Thagaste in 388, after which, following ordination in 391, he founded in Hippo a similar community, the garden monastery for which he composed his *Rule*.

54.   O'Meara, 129, shrewdly remarks that it is anachronistic to assign equality of opportunity, not to speak of equality of rights, to all African women of Augustine's day.

55.   According to BA 13,677-79, n.22, at the time of Augustine's relationship with his concubine, in various regions of the West stable concubinage without a wife was regarded as legitimate, roughly equivalent to a de facto marriage, upon which no public obluquy was visited. However, it is not clear whether concubinage was considered the de facto duplicate of a de jure marriage under civil or religious law. Later Augustine urged the newly baptized not to imitate those who live in concubinage (S 221.4.4). He warns of the danger of a married man taking a concubine; the hour of death may suddenly strike, with the unpurified soul facing the stern judgment of God (S 224.3.3).

56.   In his work of historical fiction, *Celle qui fut aimée d'Augustin*, L. Bertrand assigns the name Modesta to Augustine's concubine, grippingly depicting their reunion in North Africa at the bedside of the dying Adeodatus. Later she is called Numida in D. Villemain, *L'Innommé de saint Augustin. Confessions de Numida*. See G. Madec, "Adeodatus," AL 1.88. More recently in *Saint Augustine* G.Wills gives her the name Una, flimsily based on the words, *unam habebam*, "I had one companion" (4.2.2).

57.   G-M 163, n.20.

58.   Coyle, 49-52.

59.   *De fin.* 1.12.40.

60.   *Ep.* 1.4.6.

61.   *De am.* 9.32.

62.   In "*Anima una et cor unum*. Friendship and Spiritual Unity in Augustine", *Recherches de théologie ancienne et médiévale*, 53 (1986), 40–92, J. McEvoy points out the roots of Cicero's *De am.*, evident in the passage. Later sections, especially 68 ff., deftly, indeed movingly, link Augustine's notion of friendship

with Christian love.

63. G-M 164,n.11, believes that Augustine's fictional Epicurean hypothesis may derive from *De fin.* 1.12.40. However, according to BA 13,572,n.1, the entire *doxa* of Epicurus with which Augustine is concerned is not found in *De fin.* or any Ciceronian text. The *Placita* of Aetius or the *Philosophumena* of Hippolytus, as transmitted through Celsus' *Opiniones omnium philosophorum*, was probably the source since the language of either closely approximates Augustine's description of Epicurus' basic tenets.

64. D 2.390 suggests that the restless tossing and turning symbolize spiritual insomnia.

Book Seven
Encounter With Neoplatonism: Intellectual Conversion

In Book 6 Augustine emancipated himself from distorted conceptions of Catholicism bequeathed by Manicheism. Ambrose's spiritual exegesis blunted the Manichees' polemic against Scripture (6.4.6); as understood by spirituals, that is, educated Catholics, God is a pure spirit, in no way crammed within the limits of a human body (6.3.4). Against the Manichean pretense of pure rationalism Augustine perceived the similarity between human and divine faith: as in human life, so in revealed religion it is reasonable, even necessary, to believe certain truths (6.5.7). Moreover, he intellectually sympathized with the authority of the Church and its Scriptures without giving full credence to Catholicism. Certain that Manicheism was uncertain, he was not yet certain that Catholicism was wholly true because he could not think of God as a spirit nor grasp the meaning of evil. The single principal barrier to his conversion was inability to conceive of God except as a huge body (5.10.19). The outset depicts him still incapable of thinking of God save as a vast material entity (1.2). After certitude that he enjoys a free will (3.5), and repudiation of astrology (6.8-9), contact with Neoplatonic writings caused the scales to fall from his eyes, enabling him to understand God as pure spirit (9.13-5). This insight led to the first ascent of his mind to God (10.16). Next, he realized that God alone absolutely exists, with other things limited to relative existence (11.17). Correspondingly, he saw, all lesser things are good because deriving their goodness from God (12.18). Subsequently, the same Milanese circle taught him that evil was not a substance but a sheer lack (16.22). He then ventured a second ascent to God yet was compelled to once again fall back from the heights (17.23). However resplendent, the Neoplatonic vista remained religiously unsatisfying. Christianity overcame the deficiency through Christ who trod the way of humility (18.24). Paul proved superior to the Platonists (21.27).

Chapter 1: God Viewed as Immutable but Materially Infinite

1. Now thirty-one (385/6), Augustine was in "youth" or manhood; "adolescence" or young manhood, which covered the fifteenth to the thirtieth year, was now dead. Recall, any change bringing the cessation of a state is termed death in the broad sense (C Max 2.12.2); earlier his infancy was dead (1.6.9), for human existence as death-in-life is a series of deaths (1.6.7). His now-defunct segment of life was a time of spiritual defeat, during which he was beguiled by the triple concupiscence, a period marred by a year of dissolute idleness (2.3.6-7), union with a concubine (4.2.2), and especially seduction by Manicheism (3.6.10). Physical growth was not accompanied by a development in truth but by its opposite, increasing defilement by vanity or untruth. This may savor of unwarranted breastbeating since his disaffection from Manichean profession and practice toward the end of his young manhood indicated that he had traveled some distance toward truth; however, contamination by vanity refers particularly to his claim that everything real had to be material. As the years rolled on, he became more, not less, convinced that every substance had to be accessible to the senses, at least indirectly (since God, the most tenuous and pervasive of realities, is not directly observable). Yet from the time *Hortensius* bestirred him to start to philosophize, he had always resisted the gross view that God bore a human shape (3.7.12). Coupled with disenthallment from Manichean misconstruals was liberation from uncritical acceptance of the erroneous charge that Catholics conceive of God as a super-gigantic man (6.4.5). Unable to think of God in the figure of a man, he was still unable to think of God as other than a strictly material substance.

It is hard for a finite mind to understand, even partially, the nature of God, whose mode of being is infinitely higher than human thought. The difficulty was increased for Augustine because his thinking was saddled with an unyielding materialistic bias. Only subsequent to his intellectual conversion would he apprehend God as the highest of beings; and because supreme (there cannot be two supremes), the one and only God, not a *primus inter pares* in a pantheon of gods; and because the sole supreme being, the true God, distinct from pseudo-divinities, in particular, the Manichean Father of Greatness. While yet incapable of correctly seizing the divine nature, he was sketchily catching some of its lineaments. The marrow of his spirit, the innermost region of his mind (P 65.20), believed that God was incorruptible, unable to undergo diminution of being; inviolable, immune from all harm (MM 12.25); and immutable, not subject to any change whatsoever, such as in time or space. At this stage he simply believed, accepted as true on the authority of others, without knowing the why and how of ascription of these perfections to God.[1] In a little while, he would put his finger on the why, the radical source of these attributes. God, he came to understand, is the supreme good, that being than which nothing better can be thought (MM 11.24. DC 1.7.7); if God were not incorruptible, he would not be the best of beings (7.4.6). Also, in the same context, God as incorruptible is implicitly inviolable, unable to be compelled to act contrary to his will because his will is equal to, not greater than, his power (7.4.6). Moreover, the ground of divine immutability is God's absolute existence: because God is *ipsum esse*, existence itself, he is unchangeable (7.11.17). Then the writings of the Platonists unmanacled him from matter-bound thinking, empowering him to grasp spiritual objects for the first time (7.10.16). Therewith he understood the how or mode of existence of the divine attributes: they are the spiritual perfections of a God who is infinite spirit (7.10.16).

Yet however unsure in this section about the rational ground and existential mode of the divine attributes, he possessed solid cognitive certitude, not mere belief, concerning the ontic status and dignity of these attributes. Intellectual insight saw as necessary the truth that by their intrinsic character the corruptible, violable, and mutable are inferior to the incorruptible, inviolable, and immutable. The truth that the incorruptible is superior to the corruptible, along with its kin truths, is a self-evident proposition, attained by direct comparison of subject and predicate, without reliance on a middle term. Whatever is incorruptible is superior to whatever is corruptible; whatever has most goodness because it cannot lose any is superior to whatever has less goodness, an entity that can and will lose some (7.4.6). So coercive were these self-evident truths that they survived the severe scrutiny of Augustine's strategy of exploratory skepticism.

Lack of clues here and elsewhere renders it impossible to ascertain on what source Augustine drew for belief that God was incorruptible and immutable. It does not appear unreasonable to suggest that belief in the predication of these attributes may rest on the authority of Ambrose, though he did not understand their ground or mode of existence.[2] Probably also Nebridius' acuity buttressed Ambrose's claims and, in addition, helped clarify the self-evidential superiority of the incorruptible to the corruptible.[3] In any case, whatever the source, he cognized, because compelled by the necessity of the terms, the superiority of the incorruptible to the corruptible, the necessary truth serving as a rational fundament, at least temporarily, for his belief that God is incorruptible. Shortly, further analysis would fashion the key to the whence or why, the rational ground, and the how, the mode of existence, of the attributes.

While trying to fasten on God as immaterial, his thinking was infested by a pack of images; specifically phantasms, not images with real referents but ideational fantasies relevant only to a material God; unclean insofar as they smacked of blasphemy. One moment pushed aside, the next moment they crowded back in, beclouding mental vision, like a swarm of gnats that, once brushed away, almost immediately fly back to blur eyesight. So forceful were the images (representing constitutive features of the physical world) that he was driven to think of God not as a human body but as an extra-large material entity spread out in space, either infused as a sustaining factor in the cosmos or diffused, beyond the cosmos, through space without end. Yet he did not detect the internal strains in his view; an incorruptible, inviolable, and immutable substance cannot, without contradiction, abide spatial extension. Nevertheless, he continued, however paradoxically, to believe that a God with such perfections is superior to a substance lacking them. As before (5.10.19), he was the captive of the conviction that existence was, indeed had to be, coextensive with material existence. A nonmaterial thing was unthinkable, as self-refuting as an actually existing absolute nothing. But a relative nothing that is a physical vacuum, which results from the particular evacuation of a body composed of earth, water, air, or celestial matter, is thinkable, at least initially, because the hypothetical void is a special case surrounded by matter similar to the body evacuated. The space suppositionally occupied by the vacuum would not be a mathematical but a physical space, a particular physical region emptied of a particular body, simple or complex. Aristotle's *Phys.* 4.213a12-217b27, the first systematic inquiry into the possibility of a physical vacuum of the sort mentioned by Augustine, may have impacted on the discussion of the question of a void in doxographical literature on natural philosophy. Yet it seems more plausible to conjecture that the *spatiosum nihil* which Augustine finds initially acceptable is the void, lying, according to Stoics, outside the material universe.[4] The void is a member of a class called incorporeal, included in which are time, space, and meanings, states said to subsist rather than exist.[5] Only material things exist; what is absolutely nothing of course does not exist; the void, as subsisting outside the universe, is relatively nothing, a space in which no matter exists.

This plausible Stoic source for a nothing that is emptiness of space lends credence to the suggestion that Augustine's view of God here is connected with the Stoic contention that God infused or inspirited the material universe, an account which Augustine may have gathered from Varro. The Stoics, however, did not consider God infinitely extended, spread out beyond the material universe.[6] In addition, for the Stoics, God, because one with a changing universe, is not immutable.[7] Although he parted company with the Manichees, the notion of divine diffusion through infinite space may partially derive, purified of its mythology, from the Manichean position that the divine substance is diffused through infinite space (CEF 43.49).[8]

2. He was coarse of heart, not affectively crude but analytically gross. If he had understood that his soul is spiritual, he would not have remained the prisoner of materialism. In truth, his soul had no size, no shape, no local movement, but his materialism blocked awareness of extensionless consciousness. As his physical eyes fixed attention on material objects alone, so his mental eyes fastened on images of material objects alone. Yet he was able to sense and form images of material objects only because his spiritual power was active in perceiving the sense-objects and fashioning their images. The soul, he reasoned only later, is incorporeal because its cognitive operations exhibit immaterial features. First, it is not bound by the law that corporeal images must seem small if bodies reflecting them are small. Whereas the face reflected in a tiny mirror looks small because the

mirror is small, the soul can know cities of no mean size. Were it corporeal, it would be powerless to represent cities on a large scale (QA 3. 8-9). Second, the eye of the soul can detach objects from their concrete setting. While even the slenderest strand of a spider's web is three-dimensional, human mentation can focus on length alone, thinking away the other two dimensions. It may even mentally isolate a point; the one-dimensional and nondimensional do not exist as such in the physical order, apart from dimensional associates. In attending to a line and a point, apart from their physical environs, in de-concretizing these objects, the soul knows material objects in an immaterial mode (QA 6.10). Third, self-consciousness evidences incorporeality. In physical movement one part of an extended body acts on another part. In reflection the whole soul knows the whole of its activity in a nonextended or indivisible manner. Operating as an indivisible whole, the soul acts incorporeally (GL 7.21.28). True, the soul has no bulk, no presence in space at all, yet because rational and therefore spiritual, it possesses an immaterial magnitude whereby it towers over the other beings, great not by size but by cognitive power that makes it superior to all other entities in the physical universe (QA 14.24. NB 3). If the soul's activity did not stem from a nature of a high degree (NB 3. CD 11.15), it could not have formed the images. That nonmaterial activity was necessary to fashion images of material things confuted his thoroughgoing materialism, but he was unblissfully ignorant of the deadly irony. So he conceived the God who was life of his life, the infinite spirit quickening his spirit that enlivened his body, as remarkably material but material nonetheless. The greatest of beings, everywhere operative throughout all space, God permeates every particle of matter, and outside the cosmos he is everywhere present in all the infinite space beyond. In one respect earth and heaven contain him, but, strictly, he is operatively superior to them: boundless in himself, he bounds all things. God is fully present in things like light in the atmosphere. The light penetrates the air without slicing it into segments, wholly filling the atmosphere. Analogously, God undisruptively penetrates each and every part of the cosmos both intrinsically and extrinsically. From God intrinsically flows a pneuma, literally spirit, a quasi-vital force that constitutes each and every thing: God "in-spirits" or pneumaticizes each thing. The inspiration is hidden because the pneuma is quasi-metaphysical, not accessible to the senses, and thus distinguishable from the physiological pneuma linking the brain with senses and limbs (GL 7.19.25),[9] which is empirically determinable. Extrinsically, God directs each thing to its proper end and all things to the order of the universe. Hence the immutable God, though essentially material, somehow creates all things and is omnipresent, creatively everywhere by constitutive power, providentially everywhere by administrative power.[10]

In this phase Augustine's conception of God is an unstable commingling of Christian and Stoic elements. The main Christian ingredient is the recognition of God as creator, possibly owed to Ambrose. As creator, God is transcendent in a certain respect, present in all in the universe and present also outside the universe. Concomitant with creative power is administrative power that superintends the entire universe. This nascent Christian view, however, is set in a Stoic frame of reference. A God no less essentially material then the universe is posited as superior because his substance consists of matter so exceedingly fine that it can interpenetrate, and thereby be present in, grosser bodies. Light is so thin that it can penetrate air without decomposing it; much thinner still is the pneuma of divine agency, so tenuous that it is invisible, lying beyond empirical inspection.[11]

This accommodation of Christian to Stoic notions of God was not a solidly warranted theory but a sort of a makeshift hypothesis, an unwieldy compromise of conflicting features. It was beset by paradox: a God with material properties could not possess the attributes of immutability and ubiquity; a truly ubiquitous God is immutably present everywhere the same. But a partially Stoic God, while purportedly constant in magnitude, is not wholly everywhere but partially present in one thing, partially in another; an elephant contains more of him than does a sparrow. Nor is he everywhere the same; he is differently present in elephant and sparrow. The lack of uniformity of presence entails a mutability fatal to divineness: he becomes different from one thing to the next. Only some months later would divine light dissipate incoherences that hobbled this garbled account.

Chapter 2: Nebridius' Decisive Argument against Manicheism

3. Deceived deceivers (4.11.16; 5.10.18), Manichees were loquacious mutes;[12] incessant talkers who were doctrinally dumb; ventilating

words barren of the Word of God, they vocalized sounds without meaning, akin to the grunts of a mute. Augustine recalls a decisive argument against the unintelligible verbosity of Manichees proposed by the unusually keen Nebridius (6.10.17). This negative valuation apparently contributed to Augustine's interior disaffection from Manicheism in Carthage in 382, some four years prior, around the time Faustus was tried and found pathetically wanting (5.6.11-3). Nebridius' apparently unassailable critique was based on the incorruptibility of God. If God is truly incorruptible, then the Manichean story of an invasion of the Kingdom of Light by forces of Darkness was unintelligible. Since God cannot be harmed or corrupted, such an assault would be futile; and if it occurred, God as unaffected would simply ignore it, without combating it. However, in fact, the Manichean narrative depicts God responding to the incursion, with the result that the human soul, an offspring of the divine substance, was contaminated by the agents of Darkness (Fort 1.7). As a consequence, the Word was missioned to purge the soul of corruption.[13] But this commission could not withstand close examen. The task assigned was impossible: the Word itself emanating from a corruptible divine substance has to be itself corruptible (Fort 1.3) since the Word has the same origin as the corruptible soul. Thus the Manichean account desecrates God, turning him into a corruptible thing that paradoxically needs healing and salvation himself. Nebridius' argument may be cast as a dilemma. Manichees believe either that God is incorruptible or corruptible. If God is incorruptible, Manicheism is incoherent, for its crucial battle between forces of Light and Darkness implies a corruptible God. If God is taken as corruptible, then Manichees are blasphemous. Their stance indirectly or directly entails the sacrilege of a corruptible God. In short, if Manichean salvation history is true, it is false, for it implies that the incorruptible God is corruptible.[14] The error was irreparable: this basic tenet could not be salvaged by clever dialectical ploys or ad hoc hermeneutic adjustments. From every angle Manicheism entrained the contention that the all-holy God was corruptible, a sacrilege so execrable that Nebridius' devastating criticism, when first heard, should have impelled him to regurgitate this poison; truth nourishes the mind while Manichean untruths or theoretical lies that disease the mind have to be violently expelled.[15]

Chapter 3: Free Will as Cause of Evil: a Problem

4. Proof that the creator is incorruptible left unresolved the problems of the whence and what of evil. Augustine could not explain evil; he could neither trace evil to its cause nor disentangle the main strands out of which to construct a definition. Shortly, he will specify the will as the cause of evil (7.3.5), then define it (7.16.22); only after precisely defining evil will he able to overcome obstacles in tracing evil to the will (7.16.22). The Manichean answer, which rendered God corruptible, was totally unacceptable. Were he to maintain this, he would be not an unriddler of the cause of evil but a cause of evil himself. In other words, to espouse a corruptible God is to commit blasphemy; in embracing the Manichean absurdity, he would be producing the evil that is sacrilege (7.2.3). In expositing the cause of evil, Manichees themselves were causing evil, that is, blaspheming God, implying that the divine substance was contaminated. Incongruously, while subjecting God to evil, they exculpated themselves from evildoing, for, according to Manichean teaching, not the person with his good nature but the evil, opposing nature within him is responsible for his evil acts. Surely a maliciously warped doctrine: the all-good God is tainted with evil while patently evil men are exonerated from all wrongdoing.

5. He was trying to explain ramifications of a truth gathered from Ambrose's sermons:[16] evil done flows from man's free will, and evil received is punishment inflicted for sins. But he could not set down exactly how free will is the cause of evil. His mind, plunged into a dark pit, hit on a seemingly illuminating idea, then again and again fell back into inky bafflement. The crux of his predicament was his misconception of evil. He could not discern the source of evil until he first understood the meaning of evil. At this juncture he held that evil was something positive, a thesis from which sprouted a number of difficulties. If the will is the cause of evil, it must be positively evil as well. First, to what cause are we to assign the evil of a bad will? Second, how are we to conceive the evil acts of the will as positively or quasi-substantially evil? Third, how can an all-good God contribute toward creation of an evil will? One fact, however, served as a rung on a ladder whereby he might ascend to full light: he was indubitably aware that he willed certain acts. It was as undeniable that he performed acts of will as that he was alive. The fact that he is

alive resists all solvents of doubt. He cannot be deceived about being
alive; the possibility that he is deceived about being alive entails the
impossibility of his being deceived about being alive: it is only
because he is alive that he can be deceived (T 15.12.21. CD 11.26). So
too he cannot be deceived about awareness of willing. To will evil
involves love of false goods; but unless the willing is not false but real,
he could not will false goods (CD 11.26). This was not a matter of
being deluded by misleading sensory phenomena, as Academic
skeptics alleged. Thus there dropped away one more barrier to
certitude that would lead to reasonably warranted faith. It was
unquestionably he who interiorly said yes or no to certain avenues of
action; and, as an inescapable corollary, he was absolutely certain
that he was the cause of his personal sins: beyond doubt, they were
his sins because he had chosen them. Furthermore, certain inward
and outward blows were suffered or received passively, any one of
which was not imputed as a fault but was due him as a punishment
for prior fault; a penalty justly inflicted because prescribed by the all-
just judge (CA 1.1.1).

The third problem blocking further understanding was the
apparent anomaly of a God not only good but goodness itself,
creating men who routinely will evil. If the will is the cause of evil,
how is the root of this production of evil implanted in the will? How
can his will have the seed of bitterness that is sin since it was wholly
fashioned by God who is absolutely sinless? God is the maker of the
whole being that is Augustine, yet he cannot be the cause of
Augustine's will that generates evil. The suggestion that the devil is
the cause of the evil will only restates the problem in an angelic
context. If the devil is a good angel become bad, the same difficulty
recurs: if the all-good God created the devil as a good angel, how did,
how could, his will become bad? Whether that of man or angel, a bad
will seems incompatible with an all-good God. Yet in his confusion he
had not plummeted to the bottom of hell, which symbolizes blindness
consequent upon pride (P 6.6); he had not tumbled into the
enormities of Manichees who degraded God to a helpless victim of
evil punished by the forces of Darkness, while insisting, in the teeth
of data manifest in man's own behavior, that man commits no moral
evil.

Chapter 4: Proof That God Is Incorruptible

6. Stymied in efforts to reconcile a will that causes evil with an all-good creator, he turned to other routes to uncover other truths. From the truth that the incorruptible is better than the corruptible, he argued to the truth that God, whatever his proper essence, has to be incorruptible. We cannot conceive a being better than God who is the highest good; every thing other than he is lower in goodness. God is the best; all other things are less than best. Since the incorruptible is better than the corruptible, and since God is the best, he has to be incorruptible. Negatively put, if God were not incorruptible, he would not be the best, the perfect good.[17] He notes parenthetically that the proof of God's incorruptibility holds the key to the perplexing problem of meshing God's goodness with man's evil will. Had he meditated more deeply, he would have discovered, as he later did, the source of evil, recognizing that since God is incorruptible, the source of evil must lie outside him; the corruption that is evil springs from a will deviating from God's incorruptible goodness (7.16.22).

Next, he elaborates a more detailed demonstration of divine incorruptibility.[18] Notice, this second line of reasoning is propounded from a later understanding of God; will and power are identified only in a spiritual God, attained through study of Neoplatonic writings (7.9.13;10.16). If God is corruptible, corruption can violate his being, according to an exhaustive division, by will or by necessity or by unforeseen chance. But it is impossible that he be corrupted by any of these three factors. First, will cannot corrupt him, for, as God, he is goodness himself who wills only what is good; thus he cannot will corruption (such willing would be nonsense, the equivalent of the suicide of God). Second, he is not compelled by necessity to do something against his will or beyond the control of his will. The necessary is what inescapably occurs, will or no, outside one's power to refuse. Men, for example, die by necessity; though unwilling, they are powerless in the face of death: every human being is necessarily destined to die (1.6.7). However, God is not subject to necessity, for his will is not superior to his power. In other words, God is not so subject since he is all-powerful as well as all-good. If God were forced to act against his will, his will would be greater than his power. For his power is his attribute of doing whatever he wills; but if he were compelled to act against his will, he would be willing more than whatever he wills: thus his will would be greater than his power. But this entails the absurdity that God as identical with his will is greater than God as identical with his power. It entails also that God is greater than the greatest and that God is better than the best. If God were subject to necessity, his will would be more perfect than an all-perfect will while his power remained simply all-perfect; this is of course impossible. Third, God cannot be harmed or corrupted by a chance event, which, as apparently incidental, as the undetermined intersection of two causal series, cannot be humanly foreknown. Augustine did not admit a radical indeterminacy in the cosmos. What is called a chance event is due to human ignorance; it is the outcome of determinate causation, whose lines of connection escape human knowledge. There is no chance as such in nature; like fortune, it is governed by a hidden order; chance is the name we assign to a causally produced occurrence whose explanation and cause lie outside human cognition (CA 1.1.1. R 1.1.2). God, however, knows all things in all their linkages, the humanly labeled incidental as well as the observably causal: hence nothing is unforeseen for his divine vision. Indeed no substance exists unless he knows it; his knowledge causes each substance in all its eventuations, causal or apparently incidental (CD 11.21). But, he remarks, this second, lengthier proof of God's incorruptibility is not strictly required. His earlier argument is sufficient: if God were corruptible, he would not be God; but God is indisputably God, the most perfect good, upon whose goodness not the slightest corruption can impinge. To hold that God is corruptible unGods God, effectively denying the very existence of a supreme being and all-perfect good.

Chapter 5: Attempts to Square God's Omnipotence with Evil

7. His unrelenting search for the origin of evil was thwarted because his mode of inquiry was itself evil, not sinful but mistaken in two of its preconceptions: that only the corporeal is real and that evil itself is a positive entity.

After briefly portraying under the figure of sunlight the universe as wholly physical, in which God is omnipresent (7.1.2), he now depicts the cosmos in more detail, with omnipresence symbolized by the ocean. Among visible objects are the earth, sea, air, and the stars (made of fire), representative of the elements, while above these on the cosmic scale are trees and mortal animals (including the irrational and rational or human). Things not accessible to sight include the firmament of heaven,[19] all angels, indeed all spiritual beings.[20] He imagined spirits in the line of phantasms as corporeal things, each ordered to its proper place as fire is directed upward or earth downward. The universe was a mass great in terms of ontic dignity, an ordered quasi-thing differentiated by various sorts of bodies. Outrunning his conception in ontic value was the actual universe that, he later learned, encompassed real spiritual beings such as angels, superior to bodies in nature. Consonant with his unshakable materialist outlook was his perception of the world as finite on all sides, penetrated through and through by God, who resembles a sea that permeates a huge sponge.[21] As ubiquitous, God fills the universe and, as infinite, overflows its boundaries. Earlier, sunlight that pervades air without displacing it metaphorically expressed the pneuma which constitutes things; here water symbolizes the constitutive pneuma filling every thing in the universe, as water saturates a sponge without dislocating the sponge.

At this point an almost insoluble enigma cropped up: the immensity of God seemed to cancel the possibility of evil. If everything is good because the universe is shot through with God's goodness, how did the tentacles of evil steal into this world? What is the root (cause) from which evil flowers forth, the seed (source) from which it grows? In wrestling with this redoubtable question, he ventures one solution after another, no one of them apparently tenable. (i) If everything is good, perhaps evil is an illusion, with simply no existence at all. Quick consideration punctures this suggestion; it seems unsatisfactory, for a sheer illusion does not continually evoke fear among normal men. Indeed even on the supposition that evil is an illusion, fear itself is an evil. And fear not evoked by an actual evil is worse, more evil, than ordinary fear arising from identifiable evil. Thus evil surely does exist: either it is evil that we fear or it is the fear that is evil. (ii) Yet the problem persists: if the supreme good and the whole of creation are proportionally good, how can evil enter in? Perhaps God created the universe out of matter, remnants of which are still evil, recalcitrant to his ordination, unconverted to good. But this hypothesis conflicts with omnipotence. If God is all-powerful, he should have been able to overcome any and all resistance in evil matter, turning it wholly into good entities. (iii) Further, if God is all-powerful, it would seem more reasonable that he simply annihilate the evil matter and not form anything good from it. (iv) Yet there remains the possibility that some primordial matter did exist contrary to the divine will: how square this counter-power with the all-powerful will of God? (v) Suppose, as some propose, that matter existed from eternity: why did God allow it to perdure through infinite periods of past time, then after so protracted a span decide to create a universe from matter? In other words, why did God let matter stay for so long only a bare matrix? Why did he not create a good universe much sooner? (vi) Perhaps an alternative is more intelligible. God should have utterly exterminated evil matter, leaving himself, the supreme good, alone in existence. (vii) Again, a more likely conjecture may be preferred. Perhaps it would be better if he communicated his goodness in creation; better if, after annihilating evil matter, God brought into existence good matter, out of which he could create a universe of good things. This last hypothesis, Augustine remarks, harmonizes more with God's omnipotence since it brings all things, including matter, under his total jurisdiction; the supposition of an evil matter somehow independent of God compromises, even subverts, his omnipotence. This final conjecture brings him full circle, with the initial question not solved but restated. The original puzzle still plagues his mind: how did evil emerge and perdure in a universe of good things hypothetically created out of good matter by a supremely good God? His dialectical turnings through a series of mazes led not to an exit but back to the point of entrance. In spite of the lucidity exercised, he was still stumbling in the dark, each fresh alternative that began with promise ending in a new impasse.

Wearied by an apparently fruitless inquiry, he felt perhaps more than a twinge of despair noted at the outset (7.1.1). His mind was also gnawed by the fear of death and inevitable judgment for countless sins of heart (6.16.26). Not a full-fledged Catholic, he entertained a belief short of fully formed faith. On a number of items he was uninformed or misinformed; earlier he had denied the virginal birth of Christ (5.10.20) and later considered Christ not the true God-man but only the most perfect divinely directed man (7.19.25). Though he vacillated, departing from the unchanging canon of right doctrine, nevertheless, despite incapacity to conceive of a spiritual being, despite misguided opinions about Christ, he cleaved loyally to Catholic teaching, apparently under the direction of Ambrose.

Chapter 6: Repudiation of Astrology

8. Probably because of its apparent scientific cachet and certainly because of astrologers' seeming success in making predictions, Augustine had turned a deaf ear to criticisms pressed against astrology (4.3.4). The discussion of his repudiation of astrology here is not a digression from the problem of evil but an immediate corollary of recognition that free will is the cause of evil and that God is neither the recipient nor the cause of evil. The astral determinism that locates each destiny in the stars abolishes freedom of will and its companion, moral responsibility (S 199.3.CD 5.1) and, worse, destroys God's all-goodness, for to God, who directs the movements of the stars, must be imputed all the sins of men controlled by the patterns of the stars that he himself ordains.

Left unspecified are the site and period (Carthage, 382-3, or Milan, 385-6) at which he came to expose these predictions as spurious, without scientific foundation, and impious, usurping the foreknowledge proper to God alone. Light from divine Fatherliness, so extensive yet so particularized that not even leaves fluttering on a wind-swept tree lie outside its power, healed Augustine of his adamant refusal to be swayed by the anti-astrological briefs of Vindicianus and Nebridius (4.3.5). Vindicianus vehemently inveighed against astrology as fakery while Nebridius, somewhat tentatively presenting his critique in sober rather than passionate style, repeatedly hammered home that astrology was essentially not art but lucky guesswork parading as applied science. ("Repeatedly" may indicate that he leveled his telling criticism over a considerable period of time, perhaps first in Carthage, then later in Milan, where Augustine had lengthy discussions with him and Alypius, after which he finally saw through the pretensions of astrology.) No doubt astrologers did sometimes hit the mark with an accurate forecast, but misses far outnumbered hits. The right predictions then could be ascribed to chance; they were the random outcome of guessing (guessing probably buttressed by confirmation disclosed by the corroboration of a client; too the predictions may have been at times completely vague). An encounter with Firminus led him to torpedo the claims of astrology. A frequenter of astrologers, Firminus asked Augustine to read his horoscope; Augustine's mathematical attainments enabled him to master astrological computations and acquire a certain skill in reading the stars (5.3.4).[22] After Augustine reluctantly agreed, while pointedly informing Firminus that he had lost confidence in astrology's scientific value—it now seemed nonsensical and worthless, Firminus narrated an event that, Augustine perceived, devastated astrological claims, yet one that did not shake Firminus' faith in this self-advertised science. Along with a close friend, his father had been an enthusiastic amateur practitioner, who scrupulously noted the exact moment, along with the position of its stellar correlate, in which dumb animals delivered offspring, thereby recording apparently scientific observations. The fact that his father and his friend were meticulous observers supplied veracity for their reporting of the co-temporal birth of Firminus and the infant boy of a female slave in his parents' household. Their simultaneous appearance under an identical constellation constrained his father and his friend to cast the same horoscope for both. Yet their destinies, contrary to astrological prognostications, proved to be radically dissimilar. Firminus, because highborn, traversed the more brilliant roads to success, i.e., became well-educated, gained more wealth, and was favored with positions of honor.[23] On the other hand, the child of the slave, ground down by servitude, was denied formal education and the opportunity to acquire wealth and higher status.

Augustine immediately recognized, as the less analytically adept Firminus did not, that the simultaneity of the births and the disparity in the children's lives shredded the credibility of astrology. Capitalizing on the data furnished by Firminus, Augustine tried to disabuse him of his serene trust in astrology. If Firminus had consulted him, he would have interpreted the constellation to warrant his high place, yet if the slave had sought his expertise, he would have read his horoscope along polar-opposite lines: the slave was fated to occupy the lowest social rung. Inspection of the same constellation would issue in radically diverse readings. However, if Augustine were to give the same reading for both individuals, his astrological predictions would be plainly false. In either case, whether different or identical forecasts are framed for widely different individuals, there is a substantial disparity between the course of the stars and the course of human lives; the link between the casting of horoscopes and individual destinies is not essential but only incidental.[24] When occasionally an astrologer devises a horoscope that turns out to be true, the reading is rendered right not by science but by chance; a chance event has no proximate determinate cause. An accurate casting of a horoscope is a lucky guess, a rationally inexplicable occurrence. A false reading cannot be blamed on incompetence but is a case of bad luck. In other words, astrological prediction is scientific sham, resting upon the irrational turnings of chance,[25] with its facade of skill facilitated by the suavity of the practitioner playing upon his credulous client.

10. Rejection of astrology resting on Firminus' testimony alone would be devoid of the demonstrative force required to undercut the claims of astrologers whose livelihood would be menaced by exposure of their pretentions—they were not detached scientists but hardworking vendors of horoscopes to deluded customers (QS 1.2.3). He was sensitive to the fact that astrologers might dismiss the basis of his critique as sheerly anecdotal, vulnerable to rebuttal because either Firminus or his father may have inaccurately reported or falsely embroidered the facts. This case was fundamentally historical; its conclusion, based on testimony eliciting natural faith (6.5.7), lacked the necessary nexus compelling scientific assent. It rested on a seemingly unique or very rare past event that was not repeatable. Further rumination, however, found that instances of twins were repeatable natural events scientifically ascertainable at any time. Twins such as Esau and Jacob were born by a kind of twin birth, the second emerging from the maternal nest immediately after the first with no astrologically significant or calculable interval of time differentiating their births; the difference would be almost infinitesimal—a slight fraction of the angle of a minute in the sun's course. Yet frequently twins born under the same constellation enact strikingly different careers. Augustine iterates the fatal objection to astral fatalism: its predictions are belied by empirical fact. Only by falsely reporting his reading could an astrologer adjust to factual divergences between an Esau and a Jacob; but lack of scientific rectitude would render his report valueless.[26] If, on the other hand, he concedes that the very same reading incoherently forecasts markedly diverse destinies, his science is inherently unreliable, not jibing with empirical data. So, he again concludes, it is by chance, not by scientific interpretation of astrological tables, that an astrologer hits

upon a true forecast.

In Carthage Vindicianus had insisted that astrologers' accuracy was
a matter of happy happenstance and, when pressed further, hypothesized that the lucky prediction was traceable to an inspiration from
a higher power (4.3.5). Here Augustine clarifies this from the vantage
point of a bishop in 397, not from that of the still searching inquirer
of 386. The higher power of the super-equitable governor of all things
infuses the secret inspiration for the correct astrological reading. The
immanent chance occurrence, the fortunate hitting of the mark, falls
under the transcendent ordering of God.[27] God works this inspiration
in view of the hidden merits of the souls involved, that is to say, the
inspiration enables them to grow in merits ordained for them. The
reason for this special inspiration operative in only certain souls lies
buried in the depths of divine wisdom. It is unreasonable to
querulously protest such predilection. Never forgetting that his
limited mind cannot remotely match and therefore should never
challenge unlimited divine justice, the religiously wise man, however
perplexed or pained, will bow down in resignation before the super-
wise One.

Chapter 7: Anguish over the Problem of Evil

11. As he fluctuated, essaying one solution to evil, then another, he
never wavered in his belief in basic religious truths; God exists
(1.14.19); his providence governs all persons (6.5.7); God will judge all
(6.16.26); Scripture, justified by Catholic authority (6.11.19), lays out
the way of human salvation, crowned in the life to come. In contrast
to these rock-solid certitudes was his endlessly pondered and always
unresolved pursuit of the cause of evil. In trying to give birth to the
meaning of evil, his spirit inwardly groaned in undergoing travail
analogous to the excruciating pains of a mother in labor. These and
subsequent lines may strike some as forced, effusions of a spirit that,
if not wholly posturing, has stooped to partial overdramatization. Yet
the sufferings he endured were authentic and realistically retailed in
this passage. Augustine, we must never forget, was a mastermind who
felt more piercingly than the common run of intellectuals the sting of
defeat in not bagging a long-pursued truth. If Nebridius was a
strenuous thinker (7.6.8), Augustine was a super-strenuous hunter
after the truth. A large problem was not a nuisance to be profes-

sionally wrestled with, then thrust aside. He carried a tantalizing problem with him day and night; he puzzled over it in the morning, analytically worried about it throughout the afternoon, then tussled with it till bedtime, so that during sleep it remained alive in his subconscious. If, in general, "The love of truth," as A.E. Housman somewhere shrewdly observed, "is the faintest of human passions," in Augustine it was the strongest of passions. Moreover, his search for the root of evil was passionate in the more customary acceptation; he was not discharging a totally disinterested academic task. Certainly he was withdrawn in the sense that he never let subjective concerns bias inquiry; never for one moment did he tolerate (to adapt a Scholastic formula) affectivity entering into the condition of the object. Always the painstakingly discriminating speculator, he was no sheer spectator insulated from the moral-practical domain. The answer to the question of evil would devour all his energies, demanding commitment and fidelity to a way of life.

Inability to track down the source of evil resulted in much more than intellectual frustration; he was lacerated in the very core of his spirit; the wound being unfulfilled desire for existential truth. So singular was his anguish that he could describe comparatively little of it to even his nearest confidants, words failing even this superb wordsmith. Only God above heard every sound of his inward agony that grieved over privation of spiritual goods; it was not a groaning of the flesh evoked by the death of a son or the ruin of a vineyard (P 37.13) but a prayer of the heart articulated in the loud outcries of silent sufferings (P 37.14). The light still not with him was God not yet present through faith and hope (P 37.15). Light lay within, in the nonspatial dimension of the spirit, while the eyes of his inner self were turned outward to material goods . Never discovering in material things a proper place fixing the term of restless movement, he was unable to tell himself, "This is sufficient," this is the proper place for fulfillment; nor could he say, "This place is good" since a material place could not be ultimately satisfying. Only in spiritual goods, only in a place not a place could his spirit find rest. Here he once more alludes to ancient physics, which, we saw, unlike the modern theory of gravitation, taught that each of the four elements, earth, water, air, and fire, had an ingrained inclination to its proper place. When a body reaches such a place, its movement comes to rest: its proper place is sufficient–it need move no more; its point of rest fulfills its natural appetite toward its good.

The triple concupiscence riveted on material things straitjacketed him; so possessed, he could not return to God, in whose abode he was ordained to realize sufficiency, fulfillment of desires in his proper good: God himself was his true place in which he was meant to rest (P 30[S.3].8). He could not rest in material things, for, as partly spiritual, he was higher in being: in lower natures a superior being cannot find fulfillment. As lower than God, he was oriented to God as his place of repose (1.1.1). Hence God is his true joy; in him alone can he achieve fulfillment and its corresponding delight. He is to rest in and enjoy God insofar as he lives by the sweet yoke of eternal law and insofar as he subjects material things to his spiritual good. This middle position is the right mean for man (1.1.1).[28] Whereas God is supreme, because immutable in space and time, man, recall, is on the middle level of reality because partly spiritual, his soul being immutable in space but mutable in time; things below the soul of man occupy the lowest plane because mutable in space and time (T 10.5.7). This right order is a paradigm for conduct engendering moral growth and fulfillment, a model first figuratively portrayed in the Garden of Eden. There the tree of life planted in the middle of paradise represented wisdom whereby the soul would understand that it was appointed to the middle level, below God to whom it is subject, above the bodily world subordinate to it, neither pretending to be Godlike on its own nor descending to the domain of beasts and matter. The tree of the knowledge of good and evil, which stood in the middle of paradise, also symbolized the soul's middle rank (GCM 2.9.12). Ruled by the true God above him, and ruling the material things beneath him, Augustine is to persevere in living according to the image of God; to attain sound self-knowledge he has to recognize that he is made in the divine image on his spiritual side, thereby becoming receptive to the light of truth inflowing from God and, renewed in his image through Christ, living according to the divine law of love (T 12.7.10).

Earlier he saw clearly that the immutable is always preferable to the mutable; yet his clarity was obscured by false images of a wholly material reality (7.1.1). Here he perceives that the path of the immutable God is superior to that of mutables, but his wayward cupidities had dug in so tenaciously that he could not translate into action the rule that mutables are to be subject to his partly immutable soul. His pride drove him to do battle with God's lights "with the thick neck of his shield,"; his thickheadedness served as a shield against mercy, deluded by self-confidence that he could repel the onslaught of his cupidities by his own power (AJ 15.26). Previously, materialist errors seemed like masses crushing him (5.11.21); now lower goods thrusting him down nearly suffocated his spirit. On every side images of sensual things, like wave after wave of assault troops, attacked him. Lower things that sneered at efforts to liberate himself flung in his face a contemptuous rebuke of his worthlessness signaled by his crawling along the ground in the image of beasts; a forfeiture of median rank so degraded that he could not renew congress with God.

Chapter 8: Healing out of Sorrow

12. The anger of the God who abides forever the same does not last forever. From the first making of man, marred by the primordial catastrophe, coursed mortality and sorrows prescribed by divine wrath; from the second making of man, through the descent of the Word among men, issued the promise of immortality and bliss due to mercy (P 84.7). Through his Son the Father bestowed mercy on an Augustine born of dust and ashes, choosing out of his benevolence to reform his deformed divine image. These three sentences, which explicate the first Latin sentence, encapsulate all that follows in Books 7 and 8 dealing with Augustine's intellectual and moral conversion. Never obliterated, the image of God in Augustine became worn; conformed to the threefold carnal cupidity, his mind became unrighteous (T 14.16.22). Since man who cannot make himself cannot remake himself (P 45.14), only God who formed the image could reform his deformity (S 43.3.4). The conversion that is taking on a new image is mediated through the Son, the perfect image of the Father (DQ 51.4). In Christ a new image is stamped as the old fades away, renewing the face of the soul in faith, hope, and charity (P 142.7). All this stems from the divine good pleasure, which signifies that God mysteriously delights in lavishing mercy on the miserable. All along, Augustine set his face hard as stone against mercy's influx, fighting off repeated attempts to free him from the darkness and chains of the flesh that tarnish the original image within (9.6.14; 10.27.38; 11.30.40; 12.16.13).

God used his distress to keep him disgusted, in an inward upheaval that would cease only when grace lit up the meaning of God and his plan of mercy. Meanwhile, without Augustine's awareness God's hand of pity was curing his tumor and, as his pride was deflating, murk smothering the gaze of his mind was being lifted by the stinging salve of sorrow. Once again God was garnering good out of evil; the torment functioned as a healing ointment that gradually cleansed his inner eyes, ointment, that he recognized later, stood for the humility of God, who, stripping himself of majesty, abased himself in the lowborn Christ: the humility of the Son as mediator healed the eyes of his mind become sightless through earthly attachments (J 2.16).[29]

Chapter 9: Neoplatonic Writings Compared with those of St. John and St. Paul

13. Whereas God resists the proud because the proud resist him, his mercy has shown men Jesus, the humble way to the Father, who is all humility: when the Word became flesh, God became humble. This is the lesson Augustine is to learn presently from St. Paul (7.18.24) as he achieves a religio-intellectual conversion by affirming belief in Christ as true God-man (7.21.28). But before understanding the meaning of Scripture, he will finally rise to a concept of spiritual being principally through Neoplatonic metaphysics.

Providentially, certain Neoplatonic writings (BV 1.4),[30] translated into Latin (8.2.3), fell into his hands through a glaringly proud intellectual, (whose identity, in spite of scholarly surmises, remains, and probably will remain, unknown),[31] who epitomized the peril of purely human wisdom like the arrogant natural philosophers whose mathematical skill helped him to pose objections, eventually mortal, to Manichean cosmology (5.3.5). This allusion, in addition to the repetition (7.9.14-5) of the charge of idolatry raised earlier (5.3.5), may suggest that this obscure figure with a philosophic proclivity was a pagan cut off from saving humility. While there is doubt about his religious affiliation, there can be no doubt that Augustine read these books, some from the *Enneads*, and others of Porphyrian provenance, through Christian eyes, under the guidance of perhaps Simplicianus,[32] Ambrose's teacher, who underlined the concordance between the opening of John's Gospel and Neoplatonic themes. The Plotinus that Augustine studied was partly baptized, interpreted in a Christian context, by a group of Christian Neoplatonists in Milan. In this atmosphere Augustine discovered, principally in Plotinus, concepts that, when reworked, could be applied to analyze Christian beliefs. What he found was not a verbatim rehearsal of St. John's Prologue[33] but the same meaning validated by a number of reasons. "In the beginning was the Word...and the Word was God": paralleling this text was the claim that the Intellect (Nous), the second hypostasis, the Word expressing the One, is begotten by the One as the eternal image of the One, that is always with God or the One.[34] "All things were made by him...": for Plotinus, all things derive from the Intellect; it produces all beings, all beauty of the Ideas, all the goods of the intelligible realm.[35] "In him was life,": on Plotinus' view, the Intellect contains all life, absolutely clear and perfect.[36] "...and the life was the light of men": for Plotinus, the Intellect is self-luminous, and its light enlightens the Soul by its rays, making it intelligent.[37] The soul of man,[38] "while it gives testimony of the light, is not itself the light": corresponding to these words is Plotinus' reflection that the Soul is an image of the Intellect and the activity whereby the Intellect pours out the life that brings other beings into existence.[39] "...and the world did not know him": according to Plotinus, the human soul, given to self-isolation and false independence, forgets its divine origin and ignores the influence of the divine.[40] Here Augustine registers the first discorrespondence with the Neoplatonic text: on those accepting him by faith the Son of God confers a participation in his divine sonship. This point of disanalogy, along with others, will be commented on after additional points of analogy are instanced in the next section.

14. "...The Word of God was born...of God": on Plotinus' reckoning, the Intellect or Word radiates from, is generated by, the One alone. The Son "did not think it robbery to be equal with God": in Plotinus' account, the Intellect images the One by possessing many of the features of the One, resembling the One as light resembles the sun, though, as complex, the Nous is unlike the One.[41] The only-begotten Son is coeternal with the Father: in Plotinus, the Intellect simply is, without past or future; it is eternally present.[42] "Of his fullness we all receive": according to Plotinus, the Soul turned toward Intellect receives beauty from Intellect so that the beauty of the Intellect becomes the Soul's own beauty.[43]

In the Christian Neoplatonic milieu in which Augustine first became acquainted with Neoplatonic writings, the *Enneads* were benignly read so as to yield a concept similar to the Word of St. John's Prologue. The second hypostasis or Intellect is so close to his begetter or the One, however distinguished from the One by his complexity. In the Intellect are contained the ideas, the intelligible patterns, of all things that come into existence. All life is in the Intelligence. The light that is the Soul (and individual souls) is communicated by the total light that is Intellect: the Soul is light looking on higher light. The presence of the light in this world passes unrecognized insofar as individual souls dissociate themselves from their intelligible-world progenitors, living for themselves and as prisoners of the body. Yet the Intellect remains the divine being proceeding from the One, coeternal with the Father; it is not the Good, the primary source of things. Individual souls denuded of self will share in the beauty and goodness of the Intellect.

Correlations between the Word and Plotinus' Intellect that rest upon an accommodated interpretation do not imply that Christian Neoplatonists were not well aware that the Intellect is a subordinate hypostasis whereas the Son is fully consubstantial with the Father. Nevertheless, they found it rewarding to accentuate affinities between the Word and the Intellect of the One, which helped clarify the meaning of the Word. Plotinus' metaphysics, purified of error, supplied analytical instruments for understanding the faith. This sort of selective interpretation is not uncommon in Christian thought. Church Fathers took Plato to be expounding a spiritual view of God and the universe that, at least in part, essentially accorded with revelation.[44] Much later St. Thomas' benign reading concluded that Aristotle had reached the concept of creation in the strict sense.[45] In this concordant style of understanding lofty-minded pagans, Christian interpreters, without diluting genuine doctrine, mustered all their energies to underscore the essential affiliations of the texts of gifted pagans with Catholic dogma, while putting divergences in brackets.

Yet the concordism that highlights the Christian Word and Plotinian Intellect construed in a Christian frame of references did not blind Augustine to the gulf that separated Christian and Neoplatonic versions of salvation. Very simply, Neoplatonism, he discerned, was totally devoid of reference to the humble God-man who laid down his life for the redemption of man. Consequently, Neoplatonic writings made no mention of the Son of God who, rebuffed by his own chosen people, was accepted on faith by many. Salvation does not come, as in Plotinus and his intellectual confreres, by metaphysically piercing through to the divine already present in oneself but by faith in Christ who transforms and in some qualified sense divinizes men, turning them by pure gift into sons of God.

Nor did Neoplatonism aver that the Word became flesh, an incarnation doubly absurd in a Neoplatonic perspective. First, flesh or matter is at the opposite pole from the divine. The Intellect taken as Word can no more fall from the heights of divinity than light can be vestured in semi-darkness. Plato's *soma-sema* theme that the body can be the prison of the soul, traces of which may implicitly linger in Plotinus, makes it unthinkable that the only-begotten God would be incarcerated in the body. Second, for Plotinus, as for every Neoplatonist, the body is an embarrassment, something to be ashamed of.[46] The one practical aim of Neoplatonic analysis and moral discipline is the subordination of the body to the soul. Hence for the Neoplatonist it is nonsensical for the Word to descend into the flesh to save man when the whole thrust of philosophical salvation is to enable the soul to transend the body so that it can ascend to the fully divine plane. The central dogma of Christianity appears self-crippling; its already transcendent savior inhabits a human body. Similarly, Neoplatonism carried not the slightest hint of Paul's teaching that the Son "emptied" himself of divinity by assuming human nature. Third, Neoplatonism deemed revolting the notion of a God dying on a cross: the all-powerful and all-holy was senselessly executed as an execrable criminal. Fourth, equally strange seemed the contention that the human Jesus gained sovereignty as Lord of all by undergoing a sacrificial death. Similar parallel texts bearing on the redemptive death of the Son were nowhere to be found in Neoplatonic discourse.

Certain Neoplatonists never subscribed to the doctrines of the incarnation and redemption because they had acquired on their own, they believed, the keys to salvation and redemption. By contrast, the lowly God-man disposes the hearts of disciples, not necessarily learned, to imitate him. Shouldering all the trials and tribulations to which life is heir, the humble savior sustains their yoke and lightens their burdens, freeing them from the crushing load of their sins, directing the meek in judgment in the sense that those who follow his way will not dread his judgment (P 24.9). However, the lowly cannot boast of their own righteousness. They are sinners forgiven not only earlier wickedness but, after faith, more recent misdoings committed under the influence of the evil empire that is the world (P 24.18). Christ's invitation is disdained by those very sharp minds puffed up in their skyey learning, who are ironically doomed to be abased, gaining nothing but scanty human knowledge. Their contracted wisdom is a wisdom of fools because it stems from the moral stupidity that is self-exaltation. True wisdom is founded on humility; the lowly sneered at as intellectual peons or dysfunctionals glow with the wisdom of the God-man.[47]

15. Therefore Rom 1 disclosed that some Neoplatonists succumbed to idolatry.[48] Because their unwisdom fathered by pride refused to bow down before the all-high, they degraded themselves by adoring images.[49] Though their traditions and language were Greek (perhaps this alludes to Porphyry), they copied the idolatry of Egyptians, who, unlike the Greeks who worshipped God in human form, stooped to the basest of idols;[50] their temples boasted not only figures of men but statues bearing the heads of dogs, bulls, vultures, and serpents (S 197.1).[51] The Jewish people had also sunk into Egyptian idolatry. Esau symbolizes the Jewish people, and the dish of lentils for which he sold his birthright stands for Egyptian idols on which the Israelites spiritually fed.[52] As Esau forfeited his inheritance by figurative Egyptian corruption, so the Jews lost their birthright by engaging in real Egyptian idolatry, specifically the worship of the golden calf (P 46.6), which was doubly perverse: a hay-eating beast was given worship due God; and man, whose mind is the image of God, homaged the image of a thing without a scintilla of intelligence. Though animal worship was commended in some Neoplatonic writings, as Augustine earlier resisted the idolatry of certain natural philosophers (5.3.5), so here he contemned the eating of Egyptian lentils that represented idolatrous practices, discerning that such mental food poisons the soul. God had assigned a higher status to Jacob the younger rather than to Esau the older son; analogously, he bestowed his birthright of full revelation on the Gentiles, younger or later in the line of revelation, in preference to the Esau-like Jewish people. Called as he was from among the Gentiles, Augustine sought the intellectual gold to be taken from the pagans, corresponding to the gold expropriated from the Egyptians by the chosen people. God could command this despoliation since the gold primarily belonged

to him as master, any man or any people being only stewards of their possessions. Since all property all over the world is absolutely owned by God, God could analogously enjoin Christians to carry off as their own from the pagans the intellectual wealth that consists of central philosophical ideas. Thus Paul, under God's direction, apparently employing a dictum of the Greeks when he spoke in the Areopagus, underscored God's administration of all things; in the universe it is from God we have all our life, all our movement, and the whole of our being[53]—everything men have belongs to God. The authors of the Neoplatonic writings were Athenians, that is, Greeks in the sense that they wrote in Greek and philosophized in the Greek tradition (figuratively they were Egyptians whose gold was to be expropriated). His eyes trained on the gold of the pagans, he averted his gaze from the idols of the Egyptians (taken figuratively); he repudiated the worship of idols shaped as animals which Porphyry tolerated among nonintellectuals. The idols of the Egyptians (here taken in the real, nonfigurative sense) were sometimes fashioned from gold, God's gold—a sacrilegious misuse of gold whereby the idolaters forfeited their right to the gold (DC 2.40.60), the gold given them by God being employed not for but against him. So Augustine declined to practice the idolatry of certain Neoplatonists, worship that turned the truth that God is the supreme being into the lie that God dwells within or dynamically exists in idols.

   In short, Augustine directs attention to three points: a connection between Neoplatonism and idolatry, his rejection of this false worship, and his appropriation of their intellectual wealth. First, he became aware that adherents of Neoplatonism were, in fact, disposed or at least not opposed to idolatry, which figuratively bore an Egyptian coloration. Associated with this is the consideration that in actually imitating the Egyptians, the Jews in the Sinai desert worshipped the golden calf, an idolatry symbolizing the loss of their divine legacy and their supersession by the Gentiles. Second, through admiring the nobility of the Neoplatonic outlook, he was revulsed by the idolatry that met with no disfavor among some Neoplatonists. Third, while shunning the dross of idolatry, he despoiled these Greeks of their religio-philosophical gold as the Jews once carried off the physical gold of their Egyptian captors; a permissible expropriation because the Lord owns all gold, which man only uses as steward, the truth of divine ownership being corroborated by

God's governance of the universe. Interwoven in these basic points are nuances that convolute this section. The idolatry that was Egyptian food or falsity is represented by the lentils for which Esau sold his birthright. Moreover, Esau symbolizes the Jewish people who were robbed of their birthright as the chosen people.

Chapter 10: Ascent to God Seen as Spiritual Light

16. The chief obstacle to Augustine's intellectual conversion to Catholic Christianity had been his incapability of thinking of God save as a vast body (5.10.19). At the start of this book Augustine relates how, after becoming certain that the corruptible and mutable are inferior to the incorruptible and immutable, he did not detect the incoherence of a God at once material and incorruptible. In his thoroughgoing materialism a nonmaterial thing was no more thinkable than an actually existing nothing (7.1.1). Once introduction to Neoplatonic writings opened his eyes, he could at last think of God as pure spirit. Under the tutelage of and in line with the example of the Neoplatonists, he did not simply come to know God abstractly, in the terms of strict ratiocination alone. At this stage he was convinced that he could intellectually experience God and attain in some measure a sort of vision (not the beatific vision) of God as light and truth even in this life. This chapter reports the first of his Neoplatonically inspired ascents to God.

The text breaks down into four parts: (i) understanding God as spiritual light; (ii) a prayerful excursus that exults in God as eternal truth; (iii) realization that the chasm dividing the divine from the human thwarts man's steadfast grasp of divine light; (iv) unshakable certitude based on vision that the immutable God is truth itself.

(i) Augustine is admonished by Neoplatonic writings to return to his inner self. Here admonition is employed in a technical sense to signify the arousal of the self to leave off the sensible world without and rise to the intelligible world within.[54] His ever-provident God was his guide, directing him to turn away from things outside and dwell in the inmost depths of his soul. He can accomplish this return to self only because God is his helper, help meaning grace; only because God endows him can he, so far as is within his power, come to honor God as God, as boundless spiritual light. Above his mind, the spiritual eye of the soul, he understood and somehow saw that God is immutable light or truth. This light, because purely spiritual, is totally dissimilar from ordinary sunlight that illuminates sensory objects and also, by implication, utterly different from the fantastic brilliance suffusing the Manichean Kingdom of Light (7.5.7. Fund 13.16). Physical light, even sunlight magnified innumerably many times in intensity, cannot match purely spiritual light (T 8.2.3). Unlike that of one element over another, this superiority is not spatially or physically measurable. Physical factors such as lightness and qualitative diversity determine that oil floats on water and that the heaven of fire be located far above the earth (S 242.3.5-4.6). The altitude of spiritual light, however, lies in the line of being. The light that is God is absolutely transcendent, simply not of this world, infinitely above physical light, just as the creator is infinitely beyond the creature. God alone truly exists while all creation exists only relatively, in total dependence on him (7.11.17). At this stage, as indicated earlier, he somehow saw God as immutable light. He was afforded a kind of vision, in this instance a short glimpse of the divine being. His seeing was intellectual; he had passed from the exterior and sensory to the interior and intellectual, in order to rise to an encounter with God. Yet his seeing was more than sheerly intellectual in the ordinary sense; it was a quasi-intuition of God as spiritual light. Perhaps his experience may be named an intellectual intuition. His understanding was operative, but at its highest level he intuited the divine light: above his mind, he says explicitly, he saw the unchangeable light that is God. While silent here about the affective resonances of the encounter, elsewhere perhaps he alludes to an affective note when he speaks of the "incredible blaze" (CA 2.2.5) inwardly ignited through meditation on the Neoplatonic works.

(ii) Immediately after relating his first ascent to God, he exults in the exaltation he experiences in communion with the God who is truth, eternity, and charity. This outpouring of ardent feeling is not the offshoot of his seeing of God but, rather, records his surge of religious fervor while he was setting down his *Confessions*. The three short sentences form a parenthesis to the first ascent, recounting his prayerful upwelling of joy as he momentarily mused on his text and rekindled the affective flame of his encounter with God in Milan. As in his ascent, so in his later contemplation, in which the Augustine of 386 relived in memory ceded place to the Augustine of 397 actually dictating his memoirs, the bishop of Hippo did not gaze admiringly on beauty bare or immutability depersonalized. Indeed his briefly expressed contemplation is pitched on a higher plane, that of a Christian proficient in the spirit. Through charity Augustine laid hold of the light as all-good, the object with deepest claims on his love. Through love a person cleaves to the highest good, conforming his conduct to accord with moral truth enshrined in the eternal law governing actions by the order of love. In other words, the soul possesses the light insofar as it is illumined by the light of God shining in his commandments or moral truth (ME10.18.GL12.21.59). Departing from his account of past experience, Augustine bursts forth in praise of the majestic but enchanting light. "O God," he cries out, in effect, "you are eternal truth, ever-abiding light that irradiates the dark spirit of man. You are true or absolute charity in which our charity shares, boundless love that incessantly heals. You are an eternity shot through with charity, not far removed but providentially applied to light up the temporal, dear and near to me as I pilgrim through time." Truth, charity, and eternity are not simply grand metaphysical objects but constitute Augustine's very own God. God as truth embraces him; God as charity is his friend and lover; God as eternity is an ever-abiding confidant. After exasperatingly futile years of labyrinthine errors Augustine now espouses the true God, continuing to thirst day and night for closer communing. He sighs or prays without respite amid a throng of engrossing episcopal duties because his ever-glowing desire itself is prayer (E 130.9.18).[55]

(iii) "You lifted me up": as through the light of grace he entered within himself, so through the power of grace he was raised up to a vision of God. The experience, however, was ambivalent: he was raised up to see what he might see but also to recognize that he lacked the spiritual stamina to sustain the vision. He was capable of attaining God but incapable of prolonging the vision. His elevation brought him to see in a vision the God who is light. Yet the vision was evanescent; he was pierced with a sense of his own incapacity to lay hold of God for a considerable span of time. Because the light was ravishingly fetching and awesome, his affective self throbbed with love for this light of lights, supreme in beauty and allure, while his mind trembled with reverential fear, abased in veneration in the face of this all-powerful light. But quick perception was succeeded by quicker loss of perception; so strong were its beams that his interior eye was forced in its weakness to turn its gaze aside; the enormous energy of the light repelled his weak vision.[56] After his fleeting awareness, he found himself once more *in regione dissimilitudinis,* rendered unlike God in three ways. First, an ontological gap yawned between the unchangeable God and his constantly altered mortal self.[57] Second, long submersion in the rut of Manichean materialism was one main reason why he could not unwaveringly fasten his gaze upon God as wholly nonspatial; corporeal images kept crowding in. Image-clouded thinking was the carnal or subintellectual obstacle blocking continual understanding of God.[58] Third, a carnal condition in the sense of moral waywardness helped undercut ongoing intellection of God. The manacles fashioned from lust of the eyes, lust of the flesh, and pride of life (1.5.10) shackled his mind and forced it downward, stifling a fixed intellectual union with God. This religio-philosophical insight explaining why he could not unwaveringly see God was an apparent interior locution; it was as if God spoke to him within. In other words, through rapid reflection he perceived somewhat more clearly the cognitive and moral components of his unlikeness that defeat an ongoing vision of God. From the supreme truth that is God he learned that, while he is a sort of spiritual, that is, a believer able to know God as spirit, he was not yet a full-blown spiritual. He still needed to grow, and he will do so, primarily by cognitive purification, by total emancipation from sense-controlled thinking, and secondarily by moral cleansing, by conquest of aberrant desires. God is the food, the intellectual nutriment of the fully developed. Only when he grows in cognitive-moral stature will he be strong enough to feed surely and securely upon the light and truth, the God who is spirit.[59] The food that his body digests and assimilates is changed into his own physical substance; the food of divine truth, on the contrary, will change Augustine into God.[60]

He expressly states that the moral factor, in addition to the cognitive component, was responsible for the weakness whereby he was repelled by the light. Because God chastens man for his weakness, his mind was humbled as punishment for his sins, a penalty that was, nevertheless, good insofar as it led to healing grace (P 38.17). God makes man shrivel up like a spider: press down lightly on a spider and it curls into a dead wisp. Pressed down by mortal flesh and equally death-prone, Augustine was driven down by his weakness; perception of the human condition drilled into him that any glory he might possess was owed to God; only by humbly acknowledging his infirmity can he wax strong (P 38.17). In fine, the power of God bore his mind up to contemplate the light while the weight of his weakness dragged him down. Still, in being pulled down, he was being readied to rise up once again: the heights of wisdom are won from the depths of humility.

Doubt about the reality of the spiritual, which had so long disconcerted him, surfaced once more, then was swiftly banished by an apparent divine locution, perhaps a thought prompted by God, heard speaking within from afar (the earlier close contact, recall, was only transitory), "I am who I am," the special name revealed to Moses (Ex 3.14). The God who is "I am who I am," who perdures unchangeably, must be spiritual. Were he material, he would be divisible and, as differentiated in parts, altered from segment to segment in space. His spatial presence would quantitatively vary according to the various magnitudes of delimiting places: more of him would be present in an elephant's than in a sparrow's body (7.1.2).

(iv) Now Augustine was irrefutably sure that God as truth is spiritual. So compelling was this certitude that he could have more easily questioned his own existence than the existence of God as truth. The fact that he was alive was unchallengeably evident, true beyond a shadow of doubt (T 15.12.21. CD 11.26); the existence of God as truth above the mind was even more indubitable. For Augustine, according to the human mode of knowing, his own existence is primarily certain. On the basis of this fact, which is known by direct intellectual inspection, he could argue to other certitudes. From this standpoint, the conclusion that God as truth exists analytically derives from the fact that Augustine exists. In the real order of things, however, the roles of primacy and derivation are reversed. The truth that Augustine exists depends on and descends from the existence of God as truth. All truths flow from and are measured by the primary ontological truth that is God. Hence, from the angle of the way things are, the existence of God as truth comes first, its certitude objectively more coercive than facts directly manifest to the human mind. If God does not exist, nothing can exist. Correspondingly, if God as truth does not exist, then no tributary truths can exist. In this sense the existence of God as truth struck Augustine as more certain than his own existence.

It might risk misunderstanding not to add that Augustine's close-knit reasoning draws support from his existential acquaintance with the divine by mental sight and interior hearing. He is more assured that God is the light than that he himself is alive because he has intuited the divine presence at the summit of his ascent. Again, he inwardly heard God name himself "I am who am," a locution existentially validating that God is immutable truth with a certitude more determinate than the bedrock empirical certitude that he is alive. Furthermore, it is arguable that the analytical frame of the reasoning that assigns greater certitude to God as truth than to this own existence is contextually subordinate to his interiorly visual and auditory contact, his undeniable glimpse of God and his hearing of God's self-disclosure as "I am who am." Because given by God in a kind of direct experience, the truths that this existential acquaintance communicates are more certain than the massively evident certitude of his own existence.

Whether this experience may be legitimately typed mystical still remains a disputed question.[61] Undoubtedly Augustine's upward movement to God is recounted within an analytical structure; yet it would seem that the analytical frame subserves the endeavor to reach God somehow beyond analysis.[62] Still, while the vision aimed at was not the simple upshot of rigorous reasoning, it appears hard to hold that the vision may be counted mystical in the strict sense now agreed upon among Catholic spiritual theologians. On their reckoning, mysticism is not the affective fruit of any experience of God but is restricted to infused contemplation, in all three degrees of which the soul is passive, lifted by special divine intervention to a level of union beyond active contemplation.[63] Augustine's ascent however, evinces no indicators of strict passivity. No doubt he does explicitly state that he was borne up by divine power; the same providence that led him within impelled him upward on his Godward climb. The turning to the interior and the ascension to the superior were initiated by grace, of which at that time he was unaware. But the grace, wondrous as it was, was a gift less than the strict passivity that characterizes infusion of special contemplation. In addition, it might appear well nigh impossible for even a zealous unbaptized seeker to be carried upward in a strictly mystical flight. Still, the language of the passage suggests that he was the beneficiary of a mystical encounter in the broad sense, along quasi-Plotinian lines. First, while intellectual, his encounter with the light was intuitive, an experimental contact by vision; his vision of God was founded upon understanding going beyond understanding. Second, this was an I-Thou encounter; God, after urging Augustine to grow so as to feed on the bread of the strong, utters his self-given name, initially revealed to Moses (a name which Augustine may have first come upon in one of Ambrose's sermons).[64] Disclosure of the divine name forestalled a lapse into incomprehension of things spiritual, but primarily in this locution God personally assures Augustine that, as pure being, he is immutable truth. Beyond his intellectual satisfaction Augustine was personally fulfilled by immediate union with the supreme light, a participation accompanied by affective joy. Third, his experience was inexpressible, describable but not definable, incommunicable in the sense that it cannot be gained by an analytic procedure such as the demonstrative steps leading to $a^2 + b^2 = c^2$, the Pythagorean theorem. We can know what an orange tastes like only by tasting an orange; we can envision God only by experiencing him in a vision. This encounter may be styled Plotinian because of its affinity with the ascent to God which Plotinus was privileged to receive four times and his disciple Porphyry once.[65] The qualifier, "quasi," must he added; it was quasi-Plotinian because Augustine's ascent diverges from Plotinus' on four scores. First, whereas the One is relatively transcendent, the summit within the universe, the God of Augustine is absolutely transcendent, utterly independent of the universe he freely created—he is wholly beyond this world. Second, Augustine recognizes the impulsion of grace inclining him within and upward, but in Plotinus' religious metaphysics the sage mounts the ladder of return on his own, unassisted by grace. Third, the goal of Plotinian ascent is the obscurely named One while the Christian ascent attains the God who personally reveals himself as "I am who am." Lastly, the union of Plotinus with the One appears less personal than that of union with the Christian God. The One does not speak to Plotinus while Augustine's encounter with the highest is an I-Thou commerce.

In closing this section, may we mention that the two sentences of the excursus parenthetically inserted by the bishop of 397 wear a notably different face, bespeaking a genuine Christian experience. The soul makes a swift transit from penetrating thought to prayer-filled feeling, from memorial reflection to ardent exultation. The outpouring of love is not subrational but grounded in reason; the flood of feeling is freighted with meaning. Description of his ascent detours into prayer or, perhaps better, the prayerful outcries are in a broad sense the affective fruit of the description. Augustine tastes and eats of divine light that is the food of the strong; the moment of nourishment is a moment of illumination; he affectively communes with the light, the path to which he has just retraced in memory. Still, however spiritually transfixing, his experience is not strictly mystical. While affectively carried upward in fervent praise and prayer, he was not carried out of himself; his eruption of ardor was not passively induced but actively produced.

Chapter 11: Creatures' Relative Existence Dependent upon God's Absolute Existence

17. After grasping that God is absolute being, he reflects on the relative existence of creatures, dependent upon the existence of God. They do not absolutely exist nor are they absolutely nonexistent. They surely exist because they receive existence from God, but in comparison to God they do not exist, for they lack true or absolute existence. God alone truly or fully exists because he alone is immutable, not only changeless but unable to change. God, the unchangeable "I am who am," wholly other from the things he made, always perdures in the same way while creatures are constantly changing and in that sense are tending to nonexistence, either whole or partial; hence creatures, measured against the absolute immutability of God, are said, relatively speaking, not to exist. Of course they definitely do exist; they are real, not shadows or mere appearances. But as mutable and finite, they are without full existence; in this sense they are said not to exist. As already pointed out, it would be a gross error to infer that, for Augustine, a creature is composed of being and nothing; as he was well aware, only by incoherence can a thing be said to be constituted of being and nothing; nonexistence simply cannot be a component of being. As his own existence, only God is absolutely existing, absolutely immutable. In the creator creatures live and move and have their being (7.9.15), which is derived from the immutable being of God, and, because derived and limited, because mutable, tending to nonexistence, they are relatively nonexistent.[66]

It is good for Augustine to cleave to God because if he did not remain in God, he would not abide in himself. If God withheld his sustaining power, he would not continue as a self or a substance—he would totally cease to exist (GL 4.12.23). The God who remains always unchanged ceaselessly renews all things (1.4.4); the developing universe is the outcome of his governance. Moreover, as his Lord, as lacking nothing, he needs none of the goods that Augustine might tender. God is good in the sense that he needs no goods from other beings. As he is existence itself, so he is goodness itself. He is the good of goods, the good in whose goodness all that is good shares. He is absolute existence; all other things relatively exist insofar as they receive being from him. Similarly, he is absolutely good; all other things are relatively good insofar as they partake of his immutable goodness. In short, as all-good, God is a giver rather than a receiver of goodness (P 134.4).

Chapter 12: Things Naturally Good. Evil a Privation of Good

18. The contact with Christian Neoplatonists was a crucial turning point that cannot be overestimated, all at once supplying conceptual instruments that discarded lingering remnants of Manicheism: he could think of God as spiritual, grasp the meaning of evil, and appreciate the ontic value of beings below God. He perceived that God is intelligible light, which, because immutable, subsists beyond space and time as purely spiritual (7.10.16). Thus things below God are not tainted with evil but are other than God, existing but only relatively, in dependence upon his absolute existence (7.11.17). Evil, he next discovered (7.12.18), is not a positive thing but a privation of good. So inferior things are not evil; the cosmos is a whole beautiful in the harmony of its parts, more beautiful than any one of its parts (7.13.19). All things, taken singularly and collectively, are true in virtue of the truth that is God; falsity resides in thoughts not corresponding to things. Moreover, despite Manichean caviling, God did not begin to create after a long stretch of time (7.15.21). Finally, after knowing the what of evil, he could lay hold of the whence of moral evil; the source of evil is the will: sin is the perversity of will turned away from God (7.16.22).

Earlier, when detailing his seduction by Manicheanism, he lamented that he had not realized that evil is a privation of good (3.7.12). Some thirteen years later that insight became pellucidly clear not by intuition but by dialectical analysis. Evil is the corruption of the good in things, specifically, the diminishing of natural measure, species, or order (NB 4). Corruption, the extermination, that is, the removal, of the good, can accrue in the line of species or form. Pain and illness are the corruption of health; sapping of energy, the corruption of vigor; ugliness, the corruption of beauty; a fracture or diminution, the corruption of integrity (CEF 35.39).[67] A child of five stricken with a fatal leukemia suffers corruption of measure or mode, deprivation of an ordinary life span. Since love is the weight of the soul (13.9.10), cupidity or disordered love is a corruption of weight or order; the soul is not properly placed or fulfilled and lacks the satisfaction or tranquillity of order called peace (CD 19.13). In brief, corruption supposes a good that is corruptible; or, all corruptible things are good. Supreme goods cannot be corrupted; otherwise they could not be supreme. Things in no way good are also not subject to corruption but for a much different reason: things that are totally without good have nothing within them to be corrupted. Where there is simply no good at all, there cannot be any corruption. Corruption supposes things able to be harmed or damaged; if there is no goodness to be lessened or diminished, there can be no corruption. A penniless man cannot be robbed of $1,000. Hence either corruption works no harm or corruption or evil is the deprivation of some good. It is impossible that corruption not cause harm, for by definition corruption is harmful—it removes some good. Thus the alternative is absolutely certain: corruption or evil is the lack of some good. Notice, evil is not the sheer absence of some good. Man's condition is not evil because he does not have the wings of a bird; a crocodile need not shed tears because it cannot talk. Evil is the absence of a *due* good; it is colon cancer in a man and blindness in a crocodile.[68]

Next, Augustine argues, it is impossible to conceive of something supremely or totally evil after the manner of Manichees, who contended that all the denizens of the Race of Darkness are inherently evil. For, a wholly evil entity would be totally devoid of goodness and therefore totally barren of being: a wholly evil thing would be wholly nonexistent. A totally evil substance is self-stultifying: it is both a nature and an anti-nature, both A and nonA. Further, if it could exist as substance, it would, as wholly evil, self-destruct: as evil, it would destroy its own nature (MM 2.2). Hence it is counter-natural to claim that a substance becomes better by loss of all its goodness. True, a being devoid of all goodness would be in some strained sense incorruptible; but this attribute is purchased at a frightful cost: such a being is already nothing, already totally corrupted. The body of a dead man is now incorruptible qua human body. Such a body, once corrupted, is henceforth oddly incorruptible. Death, the extinction of life, is the price paid for such dubious incorruptibility. It would be egregious sophistry to conclude that a dead man, who is no longer subject to death, is physically better off than a person who, because still living, remains subject to death. Contrary to the Manichean reification of evil, things cannot exist and be utterly without goodness; things deprived of goodness are nonthings, simply nothing at all. Hence goodness is correlative with existence; insofar as things exist, they are good; and, conversely, whatever is good has being. Good follows upon a thing's existence, and good implies the existence of a thing. Thus all things that exist are good. Evil, whose origin Augustine had pursued for so long, is not a substance, for it is privative rather than positive in character; it is not something but the lack of something. If it were a substance, it would be a good rather than a lack of good. If an entity is a substance, it is not evil; if an aspect of it is evil, that aspect is not a substance. A substance is either incorruptible or corruptible. If incorruptible, it is immune from corruption; as a being of the spiritual order, it is a great good, invulnerable to corruption. If corruptible, a substance has to be good because, if it were not good, it could not be corrupted or vulnerable to evil.

Things in the universe are various; diversity entrains that they be unequal. Things taken individually are good; in addition, things taken collectively, taken as parts of a graded diversity, as superior and inferior to one another in the order of the universe, are not just good but very good. Viewing the whole ensemble of his creation, God saw that it was very good (13.28.43). Each level of God's creation is beautiful; more beautiful still is the universe constituted of all these parts. Whereas an amputated hand seems defective (GCM 1.21.32), eyes, ears, and hands are individually beautiful in the human body; but the organism to which they contribute their beauty is even more beautiful. So the universe is more magnificent in the complexity and variety of its parts; the whole is greater in good than any one part: it is very good (13.28.43).

Ambiguous texts, we must iterate, should be read in terms of Augustine's view that evil has relative being. It is erroneous to infer, as some do, from the remark that it is God who shows him that evil is nothing (Sol 1.22), that Augustine goes so far as to deny the existence of evil. These words can be understood only within the framework of his constantly stressed view that evil is a privation of good; as a privation, it is not something but the lack of something; as a privation, it is a not-something or nothing. As a privation, evil of itself has no being; in terms of positive substance or accident, it is nothing. In and of itself, it is a lack of being, a lack of good. But its nonentitative status does not mean that it has no existence at all. It is absolutely nothing but relatively being; as lack of something, it is, loosely speaking, "situated" in being. Blindness is a condition in a man whose occipital lobe has been seriously damaged. As a defect of sight in this individual, the blindness has relative being. Put in another way, blindness has a fundament in reality. The physical fact of the damaged brain cells is the reason for the blindness. So with other types of evil; a person addicted to sex is thereby evil. The evil of sin is a privation, absolutely nothing; but it is relatively being: its fundament is the will's commitment to illicit sexual goods. The evil consists in the deordination of the will that covets illicit sexual goods whereas it should be ordered to sexual goods in conformity with the law of God. The evil consists in the gulf between what is and what should be; it is a deviation from the norm. In any case, it seems perilously misleading to simply assert that Augustine assigned no existence at all to evil; perilously so, for this risks countenancing Spinozism and Christian Science which with utter irrealism deny all existence to evil, a stance compared to which even Manicheism, for all its crudities, might seem in some sense preferable.[69]

Chapter 13: The Universe Is Good

19. For God, there is nothing absolutely or substantially evil, and in the universe taken as a whole there is no evil substance. However, for the Manichees, with whom Augustine is disagreeing here, the lower portion of the universe is a mixture of good and evil substances, so split because an outside agency, the Kingdom of Darkness, unexplainably besieged the Kingdom of Light, with the result that the earthly region is polluted with evil. The earth was fashioned from the flesh and filth of archons or demons, the mountains formed from their bones. Animals and vegetables as the products of the semen of male and female archons are contaminated with evil. Adam and Eve are the offspring of demons; the human race is the outcome of

demonized progenitors.[70] But, as already proved, purely evil
substances are absurd (7.12.18). Everything created is a naturally good
substance, and the system or ensemble of such substances is very
good (7.12.18). Yet there is some evil or privation of the good not only
in the single substances as such but in the universe as a whole. In
short, in the lower region a certain disharmony occurs. The bite of a
scorpion produces a painful swelling in the foot; men suffocate
underground, drown in water, and can be scarred or destroyed by
fire; on the other hand, air in which fish die sustains human life, water
is necessary for survival, and fire serves as a cauterizing agent. In fine,
these elements are not evil in themselves but only in relation to
certain entities (MM 8.11-3). In spite of relative or marginal conflict
order reigns throughout the earthly or lower realm of creation.
Without the ordered makeup and harmonious interplay of elements,
mixed bodies, plants, and animals, the lower world would rapidly
disintegrate, and human life would not last a single hour. It is true that
all nonrational creatures are transitory; some animals indeed are
devoured by predators (NB 8. CD 12.4). Because of man's mortal
condition, it is hard to grasp the meaning of the transitory in the
whole (CD 12.4); yet the transitory is necessary for the beauty of the
whole. If in listening to a polished discourse, an auditor concentrates
on each syllable, which, once pronounced, is gone, he denies himself
delight in the masterful speech. So if the mind attends to only the
transitory, it misses the beauty and order of even the lower world
(GCM 1.21.32).

Thus nonrational creatures fit nicely into the scheme of things in the
inferior part of the cosmos we name the earth, which has its own
heaven or sky, this inferior to the heaven of heaven or spiritual
heaven (12.12.15). Inferior though the earth may be, it is not evil; it
has parts consonant with one another; specifically, it has its cloudy
and windy heaven, congruous to its inhabitants; the air with its clouds
bears up birds; the clouds are formed by evaporation from land and
sea; the clouds drop down dew on plants (GCM 1.15.24).[71] Because
the superior is preferable to the inferior, he might want only the
better things, the more exalted beings of the upper world, to exist; but
even if only the lower region existed, he would be satisfied, for
therein he would be delighted in an intricate order mirroring the
beauty of its maker. Symbolically, all levels of lower creation,
mountains, trees, birds of the air, and cattle, proclaim their praise of

God (5.1.1); symbolically, because the voice of mute creation is man who alone perceives the God-crafted order and beauty in them and, struck with wonder, praises God in their name. It is the stunning beauty of all lower things, taken singly and collectively, which, seen and given utterance by man, cries out in praise of their all-beautiful creator(P 148.9).[72] Then the beings of the upper world join in the choruses of praise: the heaven that is the firmament with sun, moon, and stars (planets), the heaven of heaven that is angelic life, along with the Biblical waters above the firmament, cry out praise of the divine artisan in the name of all creation, upper as well as lower. After he dropped his desire for a universe restricted to beings of the highest grade, his judgment became more attuned to the total beauty of the universe. To be sure, things of the upper world are higher than and therefore preferable to the things of the inferior dominion. But a universe composed of both higher and lower domains, he saw, was superior to one limited to the higher alone.

Yet a certain obscurity beclouds the pain and travail in the lower world—such as the injuring and killing of men by dangerous animals; an obscurity, however, that is inevitable. Suppose that an unskilled man falls in a workshop and is hurt by a sharp instrument, inclining him to mistakenly infer that the workshop contains a number of harmful tools. Yet men who would not dare to voice criticism of an artisan whose workshop they know nothing about do not hesitate to complain about the divine artisan for his making and governing of a world far more complex than a workshop. They carp about occurrences whose causes lie beyond their ken, pretending to know what they do not know—the operations and instruments designed by an all-powerful artisan (GCM 1.16.26). Again, in harping on the imperfection of the lower world, many overlook the perfection of the whole universe. It is unreasonable to judge the beauty of a building by only one angle, or the rhetorical power of a speaker just by the movement of his fingers, or the course of the moon by only a phase of three days. The part may repel while the whole wins approval. A black spot viewed by itself seems ugly but, seen as part of the whole picture, contributes to the beauty of the whole painting (VR 40.76); correspondingly, imperfections of the lower world, when taken as parts of the whole universe, are envisaged as subserving the perfection of the entire universe.

Notice, this so-called aesthetic approach principally concerns the sphere of physical contingency and physical evil. However, Augustine's reconciliation of moral evil with order and ultimate good is in no way essentially aesthetic. Basing himself on Rom 8.20, "All things work together for the good of those who love God," Augustine argues that God brings good out of evil; as all-good, he desires the ultimate good of the universe: as all-powerful, he is able to work the miracle of bringing good out of evil (EN 3.10-1). Yet the miraculously generated good does not necessarily appear in this life. The wondrous outflowing of good from evil frequently fructifies in the next life: for those who love him, God bestows good in another world. Yet no doubt at times, as the *Confessions* attests, the providential derivation of good from evil can be discerned (5.8.15). In any case, the emergence of good from evil is accomplished by the transcendent wisdom of God. On the level of immanence good properly produces good, evil produces evil; figs cannot sprout from thistles. On the level of immanence, formally speaking, the evil remains evil; it is God's transcendence that orders it to the generation of good. It cannot be emphasized too much that evil as such is not turned into good. Some evil or, more precisely, evil men remain irredeemable because of their defiance of mercy. Thus, in contrast to the strict full-blown aesthetic explanation of evil, in which evil is reduced to nonmoral dissonance, Augustine does not explain away the moral dimension in evil; he refuses to collapse all discordance into apparently aesthetic harmony. For Augustine, evil is not abolished; in this life sinners leave a wake of disorder and destruction; in the next life certain angels and men remain forever blasted. The permanently evil do not elude the divine order; their punishment is the built-in redress for obstinacy in sin (LA 3.12.35. CD 11.23). In other words, in the divine order evil is not sublated or swallowed up in the good; the evil is still evil, an inexpungeable blotch forever darkening the pit of creation, its only beauty lying in this: the punishment entailed manifests the precious justice of God (LA 3.15.44).

Chapter 14: Review of Prior Errors about God

20. The Manichean theory that the lower regions contained evils, morally displeasing things, was a strain of spiritual illness afflicting Augustine for close to a decade. The motive for not ascribing to God the making of an evil physical world was a healthy one; it would be

blasphemous to call God the cause of evil. Thus there arose the opinion of the two substances; some entities are wholly good, others essentially evil. This theory is properly named an opinion, a vicious sort of belief in which the opinionated think they know what they actually do not know (UC 11.25). *Opinionator* neatly catches the younger Augustine, fierce proselyte for a strange sectarian mentality, whose intellect uncritically absorbed falsities and ennunciated alien things, namely, propositions alien from or other than the truth. After jettisoning the two-substances theory, he thought of God as materially infinite, occupying every nook and cranny of the universe (7.1.1). In worshipping this God as the almighty, he turned his inner self once again into a temple of an idol; once again, because earlier the Father of Greatness, material and, by implication, corruptible, had also been a false deity homaged in his interior sanctuary. Each spurious divinity was abhorrent because it usurped the throne of God, cheating him of due worship. However, the divine physician soothed his fevered brow, gently closing his eyes to the sight of untruth. Then his religio-philosophical "mental illness" or insanity of soul was lulled to sleep, tranquilizing his sick soul. When he awoke, his delirium of spirit was gone, healed by the divine touch; now he saw that God is infinite in a new mode, that is, spiritually; an insight originating not in the flesh, from sensory phenomena without, but in envisagement of immaterial truths within, grounded in the God who is truth itself (7.13.16). Significantly, he awoke in God, cognizant that his whole being derived from his maker present to his mind as truth itself (7.9.15).

Chapter 15: All Things Are True by God, Who Is Eternal

21. After understanding all things are good by the goodness of God (7.12.18), he recognized that all things are true by the truth that is God.

Augustine came to know that things other than himself receive their being from God. They are because he is, because he made them out of nothing. As Augustine is in God, so all other finite things are in God who is the super-vast container of all creatures not in a spatial but in a spiritual sense or through his governance. God is *omnitenens*; he maintains all things by the all-possessing hand of the truth that is his very own being. In him all things live and move and have being, that is, have truth. They have truth insofar as they have being; they are true inasmuch as they are; their truth, like their goodness, is the concomitant of their being. This is not propositional truth like 7+3=10 but truth identified with being, as when one says, "This is true gold" or "He is truly a physician": this true is distinguished from the existentially counterfeit. In this perspective falsity as such does not exist: everything that exists is true in the measure that it exists. So the Father of Greatness is false; but this false deity does not exist in some region of the universe; it is a phantasm invented by Manichees. Falsity does not exist in the real world; it occurs when a mind thinks that something exists which does not really exist. Falsity is then an error that ascribes reality to something that is not real at all. It is the lack of correspondence of the mind with reality, a privation of the true recognition of the real; it exists not in things themselves but in the mind. Thus the false gods of the Egyptians were real statues made of wood and stone, shaped in the images of a dog and serpent. The statues were real; but the falsity of the gods lay in the misrepresentation in the minds of their worshippers. So fool's gold or false gold is genuine or real pyrite; the pyrite is not false; gold is not false; the falsity occurs when someone holds that the pyrite is gold, thinking that it is what it is not.

As each thing has its proper place, according as its weight of heaviness or lightness predominates, so, he saw also, each thing has its proper time of existence.[73] In the beginning God created all things at once, but most things were created not actually but potentially in their seminal reasons and causal features. In the beginning the universe was pregnant with the causes of things destined to appear or be actualized later (T 3.9.16). Each plant, each animal, each physical thing that does not appear in full actuality in the beginning emerges at the proper time assigned for it according to the original plan of God. By its nature each thing is determined to a proper place; analogously, according to its nature each thing is predetermined to come into existence at a due time. Its appearance at a particular time is predetermined because prior to its actual existence it was present in an invisible manner, in its "hidden seed" or seminal cause (GL 5.23.45; 6.6.10) ordained to actual existence.

Augustine realized too that God as eternal transcends all time because he is the maker and measure of all time. In opposition to the Manichean contention that a creator-God would absurdly while away his days in time before creating the universe, he perceived that God did not start to create after eons of time had rolled by since, as creator of time, he was not subject to time (11.13.15). All the intervals of time, past or future, go and come only because God upholds them in existence (11.30.40). No time exists without God's creation: time cannot precede God, for it comes into existence only by his creative act that is identified with his immutable being. Time exists only because God who is eternal elected to create things that are temporal. No more than the infinite can be regulated by the finite he fashions can the eternal be subject to the time he creates.

Chapter 16: Not Things but Wills Are Evil

22. It is a commonplace that ordinarily delectable foods like bread are distasteful when one is ill and that sunlight usually lovely to normal eyes causes unhealthy eyes pain and distress. Bread and sunlight are good; maladies make them seem evil. Analogously, good things seem evil to minds spiritually diseased or wicked. These are the Manichees (5.2.2), who, because their spiritual eyes are infected by a blasphemous theory of God and creation, disapprove of the lower plane of nature, a level that an authentic religio-philosophical standpoint judges beautiful. So the justice of God displeases the sinful; here justice denotes God's just order in which a universe with higher and lower things exhibits more good than a universe containing no more than higher things (7.13.19). Not only were Manichees displeased with a lower range of things; they were even revolted by animals like the viper and the small worm. Animals arising out of the seed of demons were considered pure evil; but the viper, a venomous snake, and the small worm were held to be worse—they menace human life. However, these animals are good in themselves; they are fashioned according to a measure, number, and order manifesting the supreme measure, number, and order in God. Finely structured, with exquisitely crafted organs, they are suited to fit nicely into the lower order of creation. Though the roles they play may escape the mind, they have their ecological niches and functions appointed by the divine artisan (GCM 1.16.26).

Insofar as they are like God, Manichees themselves harmonize or are congruous with the lower level of creation; their wickedness, however, damages the image of God within.[74] This is of course ironic: Manichees who wrongly loathe the lower creation are loathsome in the eyes of God because their gaze is set on carnal things apart from

God. In misprizing the lower world rightly taken, they identified, in
their carnal vision, with the lower world taken evilly, taken in
aversion from God. In despising the lower world as degraded, they
became dissimilar from God, degraded in his eyes. However, they
would enter into harmony with the higher things of creation,
including the truly spiritual world, if they disencumbered themselves,
as did Augustine (7.10.16), of a materialistic outlook and embraced the
true God, a sharing in whose justice reforms deformed images,
making them once his more living likenesses. After probing the
inconsequences of Manichean iniquity, he raises a crucial question:
precisely what is iniquity? Since it is a species of evil, it cannot be a
substance; evil is not something but the lack of something (7.12.18). It
does not, cannot, come from the highest good (7.12.18); evil is not
from God but a turning away from God. Iniquity is a perversion of
the will, a lack or loss of proper order in the will (MM 6.8).[75] The
disorder consists of an inversion: the will, rather than "converting" to
God, perverts the right order by turning to lower things chosen
instead of and in defiance of God. Preference for one's own good
against the direction of God is radically an act of pride: the soul
becomes tumorous, swelling with pride, which rejects interior goods
in its preference for exterior things. The soul is intended to wax
morally in the light of God's inward presence (M 6.13.40). Thus a
proud sinner bends the knee before self rather than God; separation
from God is simply the expulsion of God inwardly present in moral
lights. The swelling concomitant with desertion of God and expulsion
of interior goods debases the soul to the disorder common to all sin:
the will "perverts to", turns to in warped fashion, lower goods
regarded as antagonistic to God.

Augustine's definition of sin successfully caps his search for the
answer to the question that had long vexed him: *unde malum*? whence
comes evil? Concern and anxiety for a quick solution impelled him
into Manicheism (LA 1.2.4). Now after grasping the what of evil, he
is equipped to enunciate its whence. In his definition of sin that
pinpoints the will as the whence of moral evil, Augustine fuses two
notions: sin as the product of a disordered will, and sin as rooted in
pride. First, each man or, more precisely, his will is the author of his
evil deeds. Sin is the privation of the will's movement to its proper
goods. It is due to a twisted will with its priorities upside down: lower
things are perversely preferred to the highest good. Second, his very

aversion from God springs from pride. Of itself each soul is nothing; it is causally dependent for its existence on God, whose presence enlivens its mind: this union with God is its interior good. But by divorcing the soul from God, pride expels this interior good, immersing the spirit in exterior goods. The soul affectively distances itself from God, sinking to a region of unlikeness, forfeiting its true self (M 6.13.40).

Chapter 17: Second Ascent of the Mind to God

23. Questing anew for a vision of God as truth, Augustine attempts a second ascent akin to the first. Against the background of Plotinian warranty there emerges a discursive search for God dispositive to an intellectual intuition recorded earlier (7.10.16). First, we will briefly explicate the text, then assess its meaning, and, after weighing its mystical value, finally examine the bearing of Augustine's pre-conversion status on the real possibility of a mystical experience.

(1) The text falls into five parts: (i) review of the prior ascent confirms that intuition of God as truth, while achievable, is slippery and transitory; (ii) many-splendored beauty with its unchangeable rules points to a supreme truth; (iii) a four-stage argument proves in greater detail that God is changeless truth; (iv) God as truth is that which is; (v) however fleeting the intellectual intuition, memory retains some fragrance of God.

(i) Reflection on his first ascent (7.10.16) sets him to wonder about—not to marvel at but to puzzle over—conflicting features.[76] He was perplexed by discordance between his success in loving the true God and his failure to possess him continually. Now his agonized search was essentially over, now he really loved a God who is infinite spirit rather than a phantom similar to the Manichean pseudo-God fabricated from misleading images, strictly material and therefore only illusorily infinite (7.1.2), but, oddly, his spirit could not secure its hold on God and go on delighting in him as its supreme good. Gliding upward to God, he had intellectually intuited and had been enveloped in the beauty of radiant truth. All too rapidly he had been wrenched from God and pulled earthward by his own condition, and momentary joy born of union with the truth had been displaced by sadness arising from engrossment in lower things. His *pondus* symbolized carnal habit. As the heaviness of a stone impels it earthward, so his customary immersion in sensory objects impelled his own mind downward. So ingrained is the force of thought habitually conjoined to sensorially perceived physical things that it seems almost necessary or compulsory.[77] Sense-bound as he was, he treasured in memory his first awareness of a kind of experiential contact with the truth that is God. Augustine was absolutely convinced that he was meant to adhere to this truth but also concretely certain that he was then incapable of cleaving to it, just as earlier he saw that there was divine truth to see, yet a truth that his mind could not steadily see (7.10.16). The mind is pushed back down into lower things because the soul operates through the body, which, while a gateway to the physical world, limits continual understanding of God. Hence, as a frequently cited text puts it, the still corruptible body weighs down the soul (Wis 9.15). His earthly habitation, the body encasing his soul, pressed down on his mind so that it scattered its attention to a multitude of passing physical things. After his wingbeat-brief understanding of the One that is God, the mind joined to a body was ordinarily enmeshed in the pursuit of the many, none of which is wholly satisfying because none is stable (VR 21.41).[78] Nonetheless, he remained unassailably certain with a certitude more coercive than the certitude of his own existence (7.10.16) that the truth which is God exists, accessible to intuition prepared for by scrutiny of the things of creation.

(ii) Augustine capsulizes his attainment of God in two steps. First, aesthetic appreciation of bodies on earth or in the heavens is grounded in rules of beauty, ultimately reducible to unity in his mind. Through these inner rules which exist *omnia simul,* all things all at once, in the divine mind, and are present to Augustine's mind (3.7.14), he can judge relative beauty or its lack in the cosmos (VR 22.43). On the one hand, sun, moon, and stars dazzle the mind (CD 22.43) and even lizards and spiders pouncing on prey disclose beauty (10.36.57); and two fighting cocks also display striking charm (O 1.8.25). In terms of these interior standards the mind pronounces its judgment: "These ought to be: they conform to the rules for beauty." On the other hand, various diseases, such as disfigurement, halting speech, and blindness offend aesthetic sensibilities or depart from the standard for bodily health. About each of these afflictions the mind judges, "This ought not to be." Second, he realized that these unchangeable rules could not arise from a mind changeable and subject to error. While the mind serves as a repository for perduring truths, its mutability bars it from serving as the residence of truth absolutely true and eternal; absolutely true, because totally immutable; eternal, because exempt from all transience: this eternal truth is God himself.

(iii) He next expands his earlier condensed account of the upward route to include all four stages: from the exterior to the interior, from the inferior to the superior (P 145.5).[79] First, the five exterior senses are superior to their respective objects, for they judge these objects; sight considers whether certain colors are sufficient or somewhat deficient while hearing evaluates the smoothness or harshness of voices (LA 2.5.12). Second, the external senses report their data to the interior sense, which is superior because it perceives their operations. This inner sense, not the eye itself, perceives that the eye sees, and, because it judges the eye's operation, the interior sense judges whether or not the ear is hearing properly (LA 2.5.12), (On the interior sense see Book 1, n. 28 supra.) Third, reason is superior to the senses, for, in turn, it judges them, distinguishing the external senses from the bodies perceived and recognizing that the interior sense is superior to the exterior senses (LA 2.6.13). Fourth, reason itself is inferior to immutable truths. The mind encounters mathematical truths such as $7+3=10$ and moral truths such as the rule of justice which prescribes that each one receive his due (LA 2.8.21; 10.28). We do not judge these truths; rather, in a sense they "judge" our mind. We cannot not assent to them; we are constrained to enunciate propositions in accord with them, for they are the standards or rules whereby mathematical and moral statements are measured. Only by a kind of logical arrogance could the mind aver, "These principles ought to be this way"; their discovery dictates their truth, compelling the mind to conform its particular judgments to them. Moreover, these truths are not equal to the human mind. The mind is mutable, truth immutable; the mind apprehends now more, again less, of the truth, but the mutability or more-or less-ness of its judgments does not affect the unalterable character of truth. Instead of sitting in judgment on truth, the mutable mind is judged in its immutable light. Thus since neither inferior to nor on the same level with human reason, immutable truth must be above it (LA 2.15.39).

(iv) A notch above reason is intelligence or understanding which focuses on intelligibles or notional realities beyond the compass of the senses. These intelligible realities, such as "definitions and rules and mathematical figures and numbers," are studied in all the liberal arts except astronomy (10.10.17-12.19). Understanding views truths within, grasped through illumination bestowed by God (P 32[S.2].22). On the higher plane of exact understanding, the mind is loosed from the fetters of habitual thinking linked to material images. These images did not faithfully represent reality but were only figments of unrestrained imagination with no objective correlates; they were, in particular, images of a material God to whom were assigned various dimensions and properties inconsonant with one another. A spatialized God cannot be infinite, yet an earlier Augustine paradox-ically visualized God as infinite and at the same time spatially circumscribed. He also imagined God as extended in space and existing everywhere—a self-defeating concept since a spatial God cannot be wholly everywhere.[80] In being lifted to the level of understanding, his mind was disenthralled from the usual mode of image-thinking, with its hordes of conflicting pictures. In understanding, his mind was bathed in light, assuring him impregnable certitude that the immutable is superior to the mutable and that the immutable being or God really exists as the source of immutable truths. Thus in one luminous moment, in one flickering but true glimpse, Augustine saw that God is that which is; he intellec-tually intuited pure existence, unqualified, immutable truth.

(v) Lacking the strength, which is analytical and spiritual maturity, to keep his intuition fixed on the pure existence that is God, he dropped back into his prior style of thinking, a hodge-podge interlacing thought with sensory impressions. Yet vestiges of his elevated intellectual experience lingered in an affective remembrance, a sharp recall with a penumbra of love. Allied with and fueled by this memory was the craving for a fresh intuition of God as pure existence. At this juncture the impression left by a fugitive glimpse could not be imprinted as a remembrance deep and solid. He had seized and therefore kept only a fragile, fleeting fragrance of full existence or total truth. Because discipline had not yet raised him to the full estate of those he later termed spirituals, those theoretically and morally strong, he could not continually feed on the food of truth that is wisdom.

(2) The first nine books of the *Confessions* retail Augustine's unstopping, intellectually passionate quest for truth, a truth that, he is confident, will basically assuage his spiritual hunger and lead to

fulfillment one with joy. Attainment of truth is the indispensable means to the end that is happiness. Analytical means tied to the service of a spiritual end is a conceptual hook-up sometimes difficult for contemporary man to appreciate in an epoch that tends to rigorously separate, at times to dichotomize, the analytical and spiritual. Thus, as in 7.10.16, Augustine's emphasis on an intellectual undergirding of an ascent is not surprising since spiritual-affective fulfillment is impossible without a foundation in analysis. Augustine is dispositionally engaged in rationally mounting up to God so that he may go on to intuit God as absolute truth or, from an existential perspective, as that which is, the perfect existent or absolute existence. Part (ii) in the passage summarizes the connection between beautiful things, which bear traces of God, and the laws of beauty, known interiorly, that shine as true in the light of truth itself. Similarly, part (iii) rehearses an argument for God's existence and nature, first formulated at greater length in 388 in LA 2.12.33-15.39; an argument based on his actual intellective-intuitive ascents at Milan in 386. A much shorter version of this argument was propounded previously (7.10.16). As in the first ascent, achievement of God as truth entrains an intellectual satisfaction and joy of the same caliber as, and no less heightened than, the joy of mind that exhilarated Evodius when his espousal of the truth issued in inexpressible joy at the terminus of Augustine's reasoning (LA 2.15.39). Augustine felt the thrill that spins off from any intellectual discovery: the mind exults in the fruition of its journey, here long and drawn-out, the road pockmarked with pitfalls, the right way many times lost in side paths, detours, and dead ends. But the analytical was not an end but a stage penultimate to a loftier height. After his reason rose a notch higher to understanding, understanding vaulted to an intuition of that which is, a very short glimpse of God as pure existence, which issued in a special spiritual-affective satisfaction. This spiritual-affective ingredient consequent upon intuition is the primary component in Augustine's joy; his intellectual satisfaction is the offshoot of his intuitionally begotten delight.[81]

(3) As with the first, the second ascent does not terminate in mystical union. The large part exercised by the ratiocinative does not preclude the mystical, for reasoning can act as a propaedeutic to mystical awareness.[82] Again, it is clear that Augustine's ascent consummates in an intellective intuition of God as truth and pure

existence, an experience accompanied by intellectual pleasure and affective satisfaction. Yet neither of these affective modes approximates full-flowered mystical experience. Significantly, the decisive factor of passivity is missing in the intimate, nonsensuous feeling. Augustine actively climbs step by step the scale whose highest point is God as truth, but at no stage is he borne out of himself or passively penetrated by the presence of God. Rational demonstration and mystical experience, to repeat, are not necessarily in tension with one another; the former functions as a dispositional condition, a springboard, to the latter. But apparently in the second ascent no mystical flight blossoms out of Augustine's analysis. His upward course comes to a halt in an intuition of God as pure truth, pure existence. His mind is unable to wing upward to a mystical apex. Instead, his spirit falls short of a mystical climax; a divine downrush does not invade the essentially passive soul to immerse it in his presence. So far as can be discerned, this text displays no signs, direct or indirect, of such uplifting seizure and absorption of the human by the divine.

4. An extrinsic indicator may furnish dialectical corroboration of the nonmystical content of this ascent, as well as that of its predecessor (7.10.16). It is hardly without moment that at this phase of his development Augustine had neither undergone conversion of will (8.12.28-30) nor received baptism from the hands of Ambrose (9.6.14). He was still substantially burdened by two of the three concupiscences. After he had repudiated astrology, a vehicle of curiosity or lust of the eyes, as a pseudo-science, he continued to be eaten up by a desire for worldly rank (7.7.8) and, more importantly, subjugated to love of the flesh, he was powerless to commit himself to total continence (7.7.17). True, Augustine later candidly portrays himself as struggling with temptations rooted in the triple concupiscence (10.30.41), but then he was writing as a zealous bishop, a proficient with a tender conscience concerned about walking the path toward perfection. While in c. 400 he was spiritually liberated, no longer under the thrall of the world and the flesh, in 386, prior to his moral conversion, he was certainly not even a rudimentary Christian, for he apparently lacked the systematic prayer life ordinarily required to dispose the soul to mystical ascent. In addition, because neither laved by baptism nor nourished by the Eucharist, he was not yet blessed with the sweet touches from God that enriched his

post-conversion days in Milan. To be sure, sacred history witnesses to the truth that no one can limit the exercise and timing of the *magnalia Dei* (Ac 2.11), the mighty works of divine mercy. No doubt God could have miraculously raised Augustine to a mystical level in his pre-conversion days. But nothing in the text can be adduced to lend empirical support to this possibility. Therein Augustine rises no higher than an actively pursued vision of God. The climax of his ascension is a self-wrought intuition of pure existence, not a mystical benison to which he is passively raised. He finally apprehended what Book 7 initially pictures him hungering for: an understanding of God as spiritual, an absolutely immutable existent, and, beyond that, an intellective intuition of pure existence; but neither the preparatory understanding nor the experience of God along with its intellectual affectivity comes close to a genuine mystical encounter.

Chapter 18: Christ the Way: Weakness the Font of Strength

24. Desire for continual union with God was frustrated because there were wanting intellectual sharpness and moral stamina to sustain seeing of God. Hence he started hunting for a means that would assure strength to enjoy God, that is, to go on envisioning and delighting in him even in this life. Still to be learned was that the one mediator is Jesus, whom he took to be a perfect man (7.19.25) rather than the God-man. Only later did he discern that he is the very wisdom of God, food to build up sinews of mind enabling him to continually see the light (7.10.16) or feed on divine wisdom (7.17.23). This wisdom of God that is food for man, he came to understand, was mingled with flesh, that is, the Word that is wisdom become flesh. Wisdom took on flesh as Christ so that nonspirituals, too weak to feed upon wisdom, might be nourished as religious infants, nursed with wisdom in the form of milk (P 130.11); the simple faithful are suckled at the breasts of the religious mother that is wisdom incarnate.

Meditating on the apparent paradox of weakness in strength, he recollects that he was not strong because he was not weak enough; he lacked wisdom because he was not lowly. Devoid of humility, he was helpless to grasp his God present in the one teacher whose weakness imparted the central lesson: man becomes great only by becoming small. The whole life of Jesus was a lesson in morality (VR 16.32), whose essential element is humility. As the very expression of God's mind, Jesus is super-eminent, far above all the highest creatures such as stars and angels, but in the divine plan he raises creatures, subject to him, up to the divine plane, not by lifting men tout court but by first abasing himself to the human plane. In the inferior region he carpentered for himself an earthly home, an abode of clay like that in which the children of Adam are housed, flesh made from the dust of the earth. Stripping himself in order to strip men of trust in themselves, he applied the surgical knife of his humility to the abscess of love-starved pride. Lying before their feet was a God weak because sharing in the garment woven out of skin that is our humanity (animal skins signify human mortality because taken from dead animals ([P 103(S.4).8]). Overcome by infirmity, men fall prone beside the fallen divinity, who, when he rises in weakness, raises them up. Jesus prostrate elevates man, Jesus weak strengthens man. Men become robust by acknowledging debility; procumbent beside Jesus flattened by fatigue, they are invigorated by the thews of the all-powerful Word.

Chapter 19: Erroneous Ideas about Christ

25. The foregoing paragraph by and large reflects Augustine's orthodox Christology at the time of writing in 397, but in 386 he was at first taken in by a mistaken view of Christ, one similar to that of Photinus, a fourth-century Arian bishop of Sirmium (d. 351), in whose opinion Christ was not God but a super-excellent man blessed with unparalleled wisdom and gifted with a unique vocation because miraculously born of a virgin. His entire life was a concrete teaching about how persons should supernaturally live (VR 16.32).[83] Birth from the virgin epitomized the superiority of the eternal to temporal concerns. As the exemplar of divine wisdom, Christ was to speak with the authority of God. One remark may give pause to some: Christ merited this great authority. According to Augustine's mature position, no human being can merit initial gifts and graces. Yet since he did not admit the priority of divine initiative until 395 in QS 1.2.2-3, it would seem likely that at this confused stage he held in some unexplained manner that Christ the man had truly earned his authority, perhaps by conduct habitually conformed to the divine will.[84]

Without proper catechesis and theological training he was not capable of articulating the proper meaning of the central Christian mystery, that the Word was made flesh. From the Gospels and some religious writers he had learned that Christ had a full human nature, equipped with both body and mind; he was alive, else he could not have eaten and drunk; sensory activity was registered in his experience of joy and sorrow; while his will directed bodily members, his preaching betokened the exercise of a rational mind. Uninstructed in theological niceties, Augustine could not fathom how Christ's full human nature, crystal clear in the Gospels, could be united as a single being with the Word. Early on, the notion that Jesus Christ was both true God and true man struck him as a self-contradictory claim that identified the immutable with the mutable. Certain that God could not be other than absolutely immutable, he was equally convinced that Christ's human nature was mutable in body and soul; he walked, then rested, felt joy, then sorrow, offered words of wisdom, then fell silent. If Christ were not changeable, the Gospels were purveying untruth and, if in error on this nuclear point, they could be dismissed as essentially worthless, their promise of salvation fraudulent. With the Gospels undermined, humankind would be dispossessed of traditional Christian faith and its tidings of healing.

One of the most misleading, one might say silliest, charges that some careless scholars continue to level at Augustine is that his Christian stance still harbors below-the-surface strains of Manicheism—this directed at a thinker who in book after book labored to devastate it. Yet it is reasonable to think that many times Augustine was still haunted by the specter of Manicheism and, in particular, to conjecture that in his first interpretation of the incarnation he felt the pressure of a possible Manichean critique. The slightest intimation that references to a changeable Christ were to be explained away might precipitate a fall into the Manichean trap. If Christ were unchangeable, the changes recorded in the New Testament would have to be put down as delusions, thus effectively vindicating the Manichean contestation against the reality of Christ: the Christ of Catholicism was either a ghost or an impostor. Hence Augustine accepted the Scriptures as literally true; the revealed Christ was wholly man, endowed with both soul and body. The Scriptures offered no support for either versions of the Apollinarist view; its main theory maintained that Christ had a soul which was the principle of his vegetative and sensitive life, with the office of the mind supplied by the Word; a broader version held that Christ had a body only, the Word substituting for his soul.[85] Yet he could not see how a wholly human individual could constitute one being with the wholly divine Word. He reverenced Christ as a preeminent man with the greatest sharing in divine wisdom, far more worthy of honor than other spirituals because of his miraculous birth from the Virgin Mary. His wisdom, however majestic, was no more than a participated wisdom. As this point he did not have access to analytical tools enabling him to think of Christ as the very person of truth, i.e., as essentially truth. Jesus as wisdom or truth is the divine wisdom or truth represented in human nature. To represent the person of truth is to evidence it in human flesh. Here "person" does not carry the still-to-come technical reference to the hypostatic union but signifies the concrete vehicle or the personage evincing the essential or nonparticipated wisdom of the Word.[86]

Alypius was also wide of the mark not about the humanity of Jesus but about Catholicism's position on Jesus' manhood.[87] Unlike Augustine, who along Photinian lines so accented the complete humanity of Christ that he suppressed his true divinity, Alypius maintained in nonApollinarist fashion that Christ was fully man without foreclosing the possibility of his being truly God. In spite of a persistent misinterpretation among some commentators, Alypius was not an Apollinarist.[88] Rather than being doctrinal, his error consisted in a miscontrual of Catholic teaching. Apparently under the influence of Apollinarists in Milan who promoted their heretical Christology as authentic Catholic doctrine, he falsely attributed to Catholicism the Apollinarist theory that Christ had no soul at all and that, in the absence of a human mind, his intellectual power was furnished by the Word.[89] Because the Gospels unquestionably portray Christ as man living through a soul and rational in virtue of a mind, he hesitated to assent to a Catholic doctrine on Christ wrongly identified with Apollinarism. Once further inquiry dispelled the Apollinarist misrepresentation, he embraced the Catholic stand. Only after Alypius had been freed from his error did Augustine learn, perhaps from Ambrose, that Jesus Christ was true God as well as complete man. As he said later, "The Word who created the whole man redeemed the whole man, assumed the whole man, delivered the whole man from sin" (S 237.4.4), words equivalent to those of Ambrose.[90] The stock soteriological formula, *Quod non est assumptum non est sanatum*, echoes Augustine's averral.[91] As a Manichee, he had denied that Christ was truly man; in his Photinian phase he denied that Christ was truly God; at last he saw that the Christ who was true man was God substantially equal to the Father (S 92.3).[92]

The rejection of heresies causes the soundness of orthodox teaching to stand out more boldly. Heresies are necessary not by direct divine ordination, since God directly wills only the good, but by necessity of fact, as the inevitable outcome of a skewered reading of Scriptures; a necessity falling under divine providence that draws good out of evil. God employs heretics to arouse spirituals to expound the truth more clearly, and to spur carnals to seek some understanding of the truth. Heresies bring to the fore approved Christians whose understanding enables them to recognize grave errors, thereby awakening fellow Christians from slumber in darkness (VR 8.15). Heretical errors, like thorns, sting Christians out of doctrinal inertia toward more meticulous scrutiny of Scriptures (P 7.15). Against the foil that is heresy the light that is truth shines forth in greater perspicuity so that truths misconstrued by heretics but reaffirmed by spirituals become evident to the weak who live and think in the flesh that connotes weakness (P 7.15; 9.20).

Chapter 20: Encounter with Neoplatonism Providentially prior to Grasp of Scriptures

26. He quickly recapitulates the immense profit gained from reading Neoplatonist writings, whereby he was admonished, bade to go inward so as to go upward to the invisibles of God through visibles made by God (7.10.16). After briefly seeing that God is truth itself, he was unable to hold his gaze steadily on the supreme light. One rapid glance, then he felt thrown back and downward (7.17.23). Nevertheless, he was absolutely certain that God exists, the truth on which hang all truths and all things, and that God was infinite according to his spiritual nature wholly present everywhere, unchangeable with respect to time and place and unalterable by any movement. Since God alone is absolute being, all other beings have relative being (7.11.17); mutable existents must derive from an immutable existent. While able to attain God as supreme existence and creator, pronounced debility of spirit debarred him experiencing the ongoing joy accompanying unbroken adherence to God. He was

afforded only a glimpse of the light (7.10.16), transitorily catching not the food that is truth but only its delicious odor (7.17.23); without a steady vision of the light he could not banquet upon divine wisdom. He had still to grow more acute and capacious and, on the moral side, his love needed further healing (T 4.11.15).

A skilled rhetorician heady with new Plotinian perspective, he gabbled as if advanced in wisdom, thereby slipping into the fallacy, not uncommon among academics, that voluble extolling of a virtue is equivalent to existential possession. His presumed wisdom was hardly even one-dimensional; had he not found Christ as the way to the Father, he would not have been skilled but killed (a play on the words *peritus* and *periturus*). Intellectually superior to lesser men, he craved the badge of higher learning of the spirit. The very sin of pulling the wool over his own eyes was its own punishment, cloaking him in self-delusion. He should have shed tears in repentance, but self-deception so blinded him that he was not conscious of wrongdoing. His knowledge bloated him with arrogance, yet he was not open to the charity building muscles of the spirit (1 Cor. 8.10), which constructs an interior edifice soaring to the very vision of God. The higher the structure, the deeper must be the foundation; the mansion of the soul rising to so high a pinnacle must rest on the foundation of humility (S 69. 2-3). Jesus Christ, the foundation of the Church, is also the foundation of divine life in each soul because, as wholly humble man and wholly humble God, he lived and died as the perfect model of humility (S 293.5; 304.3).

Members of the pagan Neoplatonic school exuded a hauteur that in every clime and culture seems inevitably associated with scholarly virtuosity. Augustine's state of mind, after studying Neoplatonic thought, attests to the large-scale temptation to pride latent in an understanding of religio-metaphysical truths in the absence of saving grace. The upshot of his reflections on Neoplatonism was a grand concept of God as the truth attainable by a mind honed by mental exercise and moral ascesis. However, the elation of resolving major intellectual cruxes was accompanied by the metastasis of pride. Even as he capitulated to intellectual triumphalism, the wounds of his spirit throbbed with pain. General and abstract knowledge of the shape of things left him morally hollow; a feeling of stultification of spirit mitigated only when he began to feed on the Scriptures, whose nourishment soothed soul and self. The divine physician's fingers lovingly applied ointment to sores of his spirit so that his eyes were opened to the fine, sometimes undiscerned, line between presumption that is pseudo-salvation and confession indispensable in genuine salvation.

One sort of presumption trusts so one-sidedly in mercy that it eliminates the justice of God; a sinner thinks that no matter how often and recklessly he wanders that divine pity will somehow rescue him. At issue here, however, is a second kind of presumption in which an individual relies solely on his own powers to keep the commands of God, confident that he will never seriously falter. Presumption of one's own righteousness is a form of self-glorification rebuked by God (P 31 [En. 2]. 11), for in a sense it wars against God, protecting itself with the thick neck of its shield. Once a man knows that of himself he is nothing, the weapons of his presumption are dismantled, his bellicose spirit subdued (P 45.13). Confession, recall, is twofold: when not well, a man confesses sins to the Lord; when well, he confesses, or offers praise, to God; in any event, he cannot spiritually thrive without confession (P 29 [En. 2]. 19). The primary grace granted man is the burning desire to confess the infirmity of sin. The spirit of confession transfixes an individual with awareness that whatever power he has is quickened by God. On the other hand, for all its excellence, Neoplatonism was vitiated by presumption and the pride in which it is rooted. The Neoplatonist who introduced Augustine to Neoplatonism was atypical only in the enormity of his self-exaltation; his superiority complex was typical of the purely philosophic tribe (to spare him from the ignominy of being stigmatized as the epitome of this revolting pride may be one reason why Augustine omits his name [7.9.13]). In rightly aspiring to a higher life untrammeled by material impulses, pagan sages wrongly believed that purely human strategies and ascetic techniques could disengage them from the dark of the lower self to rise to the luminous realm of divine union. Ironically, the more their philosophic vision was liberated, the more they were imprisoned by pride; victims of obstinate self-sufficiency in whom were verified to a degree words attributed to Edmund Burke: "Nothing can be conceived more hard than the heart of a thoroughbred metaphysician." Setting a granite face against lowliness, not one of the pagan Neoplatonists smugly cocooned in presumption could murmur one word of true confession pleading for mercy. Their principled approach to a higher life established them as

an intellectual aristocracy, which indirectly lorded over those not of
the elite. As they reached the summit of intellectual striving, they
became subtly corrupted with egoism. Augustine experienced this
suffocating egocentricity: the more apparently wise he became, the
more actually unwise he grew, consumed by overweening pride. The
very presumption that shut his eyes to his evildoing stopped him from
confessing his faults; he says explicitly, "I did not weep" for my sins.
He might admit blunders of the strictly intellectual order, but
protuberant presumption forestalled admission of moral violations of
God's law that required a higher power for remission.

In unveiling a superlative spectacle of man's union with the One,
Neoplatonists neglected to lay down the road to that glorious goal.
Portrayal of the distant end in abstract terms did not spell out the
concrete means. Further, it is notorious that academics of every era
can paint a stirring picture of the good life without bestirring
themselves to translate the account into their own lives. In himself, as
in others of Neoplatonic suasion, Augustine realized that his elevated
concept of union with God was concretely canceled by the near-total
absence of a map toward fruition. Perhaps bluntly put, all attainment
of this vision amounted in practice to cheap talk. In happy contrast,
Christians, who not only aspired to the end from afar but had a
hands-on grasp of the means to felicity, saw the way, which is Christ,
to their homeland that brings blessedness. Not only visualized, the
fatherland was also a land they would actually possess; their own
home country of the spirit was both intellectually seized and
affectively embraced.

Providence was also at work in his becoming acquainted with
Neoplatonic works before dwelling on the Scriptures. If he had first
reflectively prayed over the Scriptures prior to his encounter with
Neoplatonism, the purely philosophical works might have so
captivated him that he would have abandoned prayer inspired by
Scripture in preference for the austere thought of technical
philosophy. As he rated the style of Scriptures barbarous set over
against the eloquence of a Cicero (3.5.9), now, he suggests, he might
have put down the Scriptures as unscientific in comparison with the
analytical superiority of Neoplatonic writings. He would have
disdained the pious practices of Scripture as quasi-pictorial, partly
puerile methods, to be discarded as the mind trudged the upward
path to the One. The Scriptural approach might have been counted a

scaffolding, a dispensable stage toward a strictly rational communion with the immutable. In fine, he surmised that he might have fallen into a post-Manichean brand of rationalism, a more refined quasi-Gnostic posture that enthroned reason to the disparagement of faith. Augustine also suggests a second, less destructive but, perhaps for us, more puzzling possible outcome of having studied Scriptures before Neoplatonism. He might have kept his prayer and piety while erroneously thinking that he could have garnered equal salvific light and power from immersion in Neoplatonic doctrine alone. According to this second hypothetical scenario, reason is accorded a supernatural healing role parallel to that of faith. As mentioned earlier, prior to 395 Augustine vested an extravagant confidence in reason, opining that within the context of Christian belief the mind, once properly exercised in the liberal arts, with appetites pruned, could rise to an experiential vision of God in this life (7.10.16; 17.23). A more mature Augustine drastically curtailed the scope of reason operating somewhat independently of faith. Faith and understanding are coupled in the quest of spirituals for a sure knowledge and love of God. Yet faith remains fundamentally superior to and directive of reason; understanding analytically articulates the revelatory givens of faith. Only within the framework of faith can a soaring personal-experiential knowledge of God be won. Rationalism, whether the fantastic mutant of Manicheism or the sober species of Neoplatonism, is spiritually sterile, yielding no healing or kin spiritual fruits. Thus prior contact with Neoplatonism safeguarded Augustine from a fresh entrapment in a rationalism advertising itself as the open sesame to genuine purification and highest fulfillment. Neoplatonism, searching examen verified, was salvific promise without delivery, a program without actual fruits of the spirit. The requisite light and power would proceed only from faith to be sharpened by an ancillary reason in quest of understanding.

Chapter 21: Reading St. Paul: Healing Light and Power

27. Dividing the riches of the Neoplatonic ideal and the destitution of its means was a hiatus produced by exclusive self-reliance that knew nothing of the cry of mercy to an offended God for forgiveness of inner misery. Therefore Augustine turned, probably under the influence of Ambrose and Simplicianus, to the Scriptures, in

particular to St. Paul, for a way out of his existential quandary. Electric with enthusiasm, he did not consult the Apostle in a leisurely mood but abruptly snatched up the relevant epistle (CA 2.2.5)[93] with zeal and expectation, like a man with prostate cancer quickly seizing a medical journal that retails measures for a cure. Now he was capable of defusing charges lodged against the Catholic version of Paul, which, Manichees, borrowing from Marcion, alleged, had become Judaized through tampering and interpolation. First, the Catholic text, they contended, contained passages at loggerheads with one another; Rom 1.3, which asserts that the Son of God was born of the line of David according to the flesh, is rendered spurious because it contradicts the more spiritual passage in 2 Cor 5.16, according to which believers do not know Christ after the flesh. The Manichean error lay in running together two distinct senses of "flesh." "Flesh" in Rom 1.3 signifies Christ in his truly human body or material substance whereas "flesh" in 2 Cor 5.16 means the corruption of the flesh (CF 11.7). Second, Manichees berated Catholics for uncritically accepting the Old Testament and thereby yoking themselves under numerous cumbersome precepts while Paul's abolition of circumcision and kindred ceremonial practices is incompatible with submission to the Old Law. Augustine, however, distinguished two sorts of precepts of the Old Law: laws governing moral behavior, such as the ten commandments, which retain their force, and ceremonial directives, which no longer bind. Still, these latter functioned as prefigurations of the perfected religious dispensation of Christianity; circumcision, a sanctifying rite, is fulfilled in the sacrament of baptism. Exploiting the allegorical method, he was able to appreciate everything presented in the Old Testament, even many sections no longer obligatory; indeed not only their written words but the whole life of the Israelite people served as one great prophecy, foretelling Christ and his Church to come (CF 22.24). Thus part of the Law was abrogated, not because it was despised, but in order that it might be perfected. The Law promulgated through Moses reached fulfillment in the New Law of love conjoined to the grace and truth revealed through Christ. Elements of the Law still demanding obedience became concretely observable by individuals through power coursing from the merits of Jesus while requirements of ceremonial prescriptions law were subsumed in the full theoretical and practical religious life ordained by Christ for his Church (CF

6.2.3, 9; 19, 8, 9; 22.24). In spite of Manichean demurrals the Old and New Testament were not at dagger's point but formed one doctrinal countenance of lineaments knitted into one harmonious whole whose deliverances were chaste in the sense of holy, uncontaminated by the corrosion of deception (P 11.7). As he immersed himself in the beauties of Paul, whom he did not simply peruse but consumed with marked reverence (CA 2.2.5), he learned to exult with trembling; he eschewed a rash outburst of unbalanced ebullience; his joy was disciplined delight congruous with holiness (P 2.9).

He was struck by the fact that all truth in the basically sound Neoplatonic outlook was compassed by the Scriptures, but now transfigured, in a grace-filled perspective purged of boastful presumption (7.20.26). Not strutting on life's stage with bravado, the Christian, like Paul, continually puts to himself the probing question, "What have I that I have not received?" (1 Cor 4.7) (a text frequently used; quoted twenty-four times apiece in the *Sermons* and *Enarrations on the Psalms*). Behind and above all finite agencies, guiding and sustaining each and all is the providence of God from whom stems both the truth seen and the power to see. Indeed all without exception that man is and has is gift, forthstreaming from the immutable all. Neoplatonists bade seekers after wisdom to climb to a vision of the changeless One, but the exhortations and living examples of their teachers usually stopped short with sheer knowledge. Knowledge of what to do is not automatically enfleshed in the doing; the self-knowledge acclaimed remains cognition without resources of redemption, insights untranscribed into actual conduct. Scripture as the instrument of the Holy Spirit also admonishes, gently nudging the human spirit to withdraw from the outward so as to mount by an inward gradient to see the immutable; more, it cleanses the mind so that it not only catches a glimmer of changeless truth but may be empowered to retain some hold on the truth instead of almost immediately sliding back to nondivine rungs, as happened to a disappointed Augustine (7.10.16; 17.23). The sins of the individual far off, symbolized by the prodigal son, initially prevent him from seeing God; healing that is forgiveness of sin liberates him from the region of unlikeness (7.10.16), conducting him on the path that leads to vision and steadfast possession of God. Since learned and unlearned alike are called to citizenship in the religio-cultural democracy that is the body of Christ, those not afforded the opportunity to become lettered can walk the way to the truth, accessible to all of every class or talent (M 6.1.1). In any case, all Christians with or without academic credentials can aspire to holding fast to God as long as they live by faith operating through charity grounded in humility. The Neoplatonic pursuit of the vision of the One was restricted to a select few savants of high philosophical attainments, with its program of purification similarly circumscribed. However, from the vantage ground of revelation, contemplation, along with healing, is available to lettered and unlettered alike.

While dictating the *Confessions*, Augustine was of the opinion that Rom 7.22-5 applied only to those living under the Law, not yet dwelling in the realm of grace. Later, during the Pelagian controversy, he discerned that those under grace as well as those under the Law were prey to temptations upsurging from the lower self (CDEP 1.10.32). Healing is at bottom necessary for all, for since Adam all have fallen under the penalty of sin (S 125.2); hence the lines in Rom 7.22-3 from the mighty athlete of God (13.26.40) are addressed to all. However exteriorly tranquil, each man experiences an interior battle of flesh against the spirit (S 154A.2). Further, when man scorns the subjection to God that betokens spiritual freedom, he becomes the slave of things beneath him, the captive, Paul says, of the law of sin in his members. Proud man, in exalting himself, is cast down to the dust by the powerful weight of God's hand (P 31[En.2].14). In addition to enslavement to the subhuman, sinful man has been justly handed over to the devil: through Adam's first sin the devil acquired a certain de facto right over man. This is one more instance of the law of consequences, the nexus between moral causes and punitive effects; one outworking of man's sin is the dominion of the devil (LA 3.10.29). The rebellion of the devil was the very first sin, prior to that of Adam (S 124.15). Prince of all sin (LA 3.10.29), he is prince of this world inasmuch as he rules over that part of the universe that is the lowest and subject to death (LA 3.10.29); he is also prince of death, his seduction rooted in envy (P 50.9), for, in driving man from paradise, he exposed him to mortality. Moreover, he is "a murderer from the beginning" (Jn 8.44), who killed the life of grace in Adam and Eve by enticing them to sin (J 42.11). God made man in his own image; Satan, the ape of God, makes man in his likeness by goading him to duplicate his revolt against divine truth. Because hostile to God, some Jews were children of the devil; by imitating his enmity of God, they became his children in the line of will (J 42.10). As he gulled the first man, so Satan aims all the energies of his brilliant mind and crooked will at tricking each man to conform his will to his own *non serviam*, to become, like himself, a living lie. While the father of lies imprisoned man in the flesh, Jesus, the truth that frees (Jn 8.31-2), delivers him from the body of this death (body signifying the lower self oriented toward death that is sin), causing his love to reign over the flesh. Christ is incarnate peace that ends the hostilities between spirit and flesh. As the impeccable and sinless God-man, he could not be subject to the devil in the death caused by diabolical persuasion.

Though Christ could not be justly put to death, the devil killed Jesus. In overreaching himself, in unjustly extending his claims to include Christ, the devil forfeited his rights over man. Here Augustine is invoking one strand of his theology of redemption that accentuates Christ's ransoming of man from the devil, according to which Satan, in moving Adam to fall, gained a certain proprietary right over humankind. However, because Jesus was sinless, the prince of sin and death (LA 3.10.29) could not justly claim a right over him and could not rightfully have him put to death. In his hateful rage against God, the devil overstepped the bounds of his claims and had Christ crucified, thereby relinquishing his right of hegemony over man. Through the second Adam the handwriting or IOU owed him by man was canceled; man's debt to Satan was voided by Satan's unjustly induced crucifixion of the Lord. More precisely, Satan lost his right to subjugate men who gave their allegiance to Christ. Man then was freed from his just debt to Satan by Satan's infliction of an unjust death on the God-man (LA 3.10.31-2). A few lines from a later text concisely capture the substance of the ransom theory. "How was he [the devil] conquered? In this fashion: though he found in him [Christ] nothing deserving of death, nevertheless, he killed him. And it is indeed just that we whom he held as debtors should be freed of our debt insofar as we believe in him whom he killed without any debt" (T 13.14.18). It should not go unnoticed that the ransom theory never implies in the smallest measure an incongruous transaction between God and the devil in which Christ's death is the compensation directly paid by God to the devil for man's release from captivity to sin and death.[94]

However salubrious, the Neoplatonic writings were not salvific. Invaluable in helping to rid Augustine of misconceptions of God and evil, instrumental in smoothing the hierarchical ascent from visibles to invisibles, they were practically valueless because barren of concrete methods for liberating the spirit from toils of the flesh. Spectators of existence whose sole aspiration was union with the transcendent, Neoplatonists could prescribe no remedy for extricating ordinary individuals from the malaise consequent upon the tension-ridden disequilibrium of the cloven human condition. Their lucid pages nowhere illuminated the face of piety; they developed no genuine rites for purification disposing the soul for union with God. Their works were without piety because their authors were wholly ignorant of humility in profession and practice; not a single line proposes humility as a cardinal feature of spiritual wholeness (an omission conspicuous in practically all pagan moral treatises). Self-sufficiency was their deficiency; they judged themselves masters of their fates and captains of their souls, needing no gratuitous extra-human concourse from God. While they harvested natural wisdom to some extent from their admirable industry, their blinkered attitude toward grace foreclosed the possibility of feeding on the transforming food of divine wisdom (J 41.1), which contains at its core the lowly savior able to transform the proud into his own image that is a visible humility and invisible elevation (LA 3.10.30).

Neoplatonic writings enjoin no confession of sins to the point of tears bespeaking inward sorrow for the horror of malefactions; no hearkening to Ps 50.19 calling for a contrite and humble heart as an interior sacrifice to God in which pride rather than an animal is slain (P 10.21). Whereas an austere intellectualism never ventures beyond an ideal of individual self-deliverance, the New Covenant proclaims salvation to the new people of God, the body of Christ. More than a farflung organization, the Church is a supernatural organism, the whole Christ, in which Christ as head constitutes one body with his members. The Christ who healed, forgave sins, and fed five thousand with a few loaves lives on in the Church that is his body, daily working interior miracles of healing, absolution, and spiritual nourishment through the Eucharist in particular. Furthermore, the reward of this saved community is eternal espousal; the divine bridegroom marries his people as his bride in an everlasting wedding banquet. No supernatural union is more penetrating than that between God and his people recreated through Christ; the wholly spiritual nuptial union will be unendingly ecstatic, divine husband and redeemed spouse fused not into one body but into one spirit of supernatural fire. Even now the people of God enjoying a forestaste of the eternal nuptials welcome the pledge of the Spirit, the first installment of God's everlasting recompense in the world to come. Blessed with gift of the Holy Spirit (EJ 9.11), Christians already share to some degree in eternal peace, becoming meek and patient in God (S 9.6). The people of God are daily refreshed through the chalice of redemption, which mystically reenacts the salvific sacrifice of Christ on the cross (S 9.10. P 125.9. QH 1.3.57). Those maturing in and of Christ eat and drink of his body and blood so as to be healed of wounds and sinewed with his strength (10.43.69). This sacrifice of redemption (9.12.32) purchases release for detained souls, for it sacramentally sacrifices the holy victim through whom the decree against fallen man is expunged; the Eucharist celebrates the death of Jesus whose unjustly inflicted death blotted out the debt in which the devil held man bound (9.13.36).

Hence these pagan thinkers do not chant Ps 61.2-3, where the soul bends its knee before the God of mercy, under the shadow of whose wings it thrives in hope (P 61.2). Sufficient unto themselves, pagan savants are deaf to the call of the Lord promising to relieve pains and sweeten labors, the woes, of this life. Eaten up by pride stemming from self-attained assimilation of the highest human knowledge, they deem it senseless to accept the invitation of Jesus to interiorize the one great lesson he asks men to learn: to be, as is he, meek and humble of heart. Their worldly wise minds (Mt 11.25) are shut fast against the revelation that Jesus brings from the interior of the Father to souls lit up in faith. While the pagan philosophers trained their inner eyes on the goal, they were powerless to chart the means thereto (7.20.26). Furthermore, they wander far from the right road, besieged in their futile groping by apostate angels, fugitives who deserted the ranks of God's army to serve under their prince who is a fountainhead of terror and error; a roaring lion who incites violence to cause the deaths of martyrs; a dragon ever contriving by wile and guile to broadcast heresies (P 90[S.2].9). Natural scientists (5.3.5) and some sharp philosophical minds (7.9.15) left the door open to the worship of idols, manipulated by demons whose role in the malignity of the world is not to be underestimated. Christians, who follow the way protected by the power of their divine commander, need not fear attacks of these brigand-like demons. Indeed simply treading on that loathsome demon-infested road would be a horrible torment.

These truths entered deep within his conscious and subconscious, as he pondered on the civil war within man rivetingly described in Rom 7 by "the least of the Apostles," so self-styled because of his prior hatred of the Church. Not only did the self-deprecatory phrase convey a delicious irony, for the least turned out to be the greatest of the apostles, but it signalized the profound humility of the magnificent Paul, light-years higher than the self-elevation of pagan Neoplatonists. The truths were woven in his mind *miris modis*, in marvelous ways, a phrase employed before to indicate secret, inward workings of divine grace, in some instances of which God remarkably wrought good out of evil (4.4.7; 5.6.10; 5.7.13); here it underscores the surprisingly rapid grip the truths exercised on his soul. Only shortly before, he had been fumbling for a moral-salvific answer to mazy anxieties. Now almost immediately, as grace radiated in luminous truth, all became clear as daylight. The moral-existential key fitted perfectly into the lock and, as the portals swung wide, his inner eye feasted on the concrete design of salvation.

He was overcome by the splendor of the divine economy: weakness was a font of strength, lowliness catapulted souls to spiritual heights, and wisdom from the bosom of the all-high enlightened little ones. Spread before his gaze was the grand panorama of salvation; a new chosen people redeemed by Christ's sacrifice perpetuated in the offering of the chalice of redemption; a people as intimate with the infinite as bride with bridegroom; the earnest of the Holy Spirit that the redeemed will reign in divine peace; all these facets of the central truth that the universe is the mystery of God's mercy responding to humankind's and every man's misery: God is merciful to each as if each were all and all were but one (3.11.19). The plot of the drama of history, taken collectively and in all its particular actors, turned on wholly gratuitous mercy. The more he meditated, the more he was overwhelmed by surpassing majesty wedded to infinitely sensitive tenderness; the story of boundless mercy enrapt his soul in awe.

NOTES

1. The participial phrase, *nesciens unde et quomodo*, is elliptical and therefore ambiguous. It seems misguided to link it with Augustine's certain knowledge of the superiority of the incorruptible to the corruptible; rather than not knowing, he plainly knows by direct intellectual inspection the necessity of this superiority. However, he did not understand but only believed that God is incorruptible, for he lacked sufficient rational warrant for the predication, i.e., he did not know the whence, the rational ground of the divine perfections, and the how, the mode of their existence. The sentence under examination may be then paraphrased: I believed that God is incorruptible and so forth, not because I knew the whence and how of the attributes but because I knew with certitude that the incorruptible and so forth are superior to the corruptible and so forth.

2. DuRoy, 54

3. G. Madec, "La délivrance de l'espirit (*Confessiones VII*)," LASAP, Libri VI-IX, 53-4.

4. Ch. Baguette, "Une période stoïcienne dans l'évolution de la pensée de saint Augustin", REA 16, 1-2 (1970), 47-77, especially 73.

5. M. Colish, *The Stoic Tradition From Antiquity to the Middle Ages*, 1.25-6.

6. O'Daly, 66.

7. Colish, op. cit. 1.25.

8. Cited in D 2.396.

9. O'Daly, 81.

10. It is hard to nail down any one source for these Stoic ideas. O'Daly, 66, holds that the Stoic picture of God was transmitted through Varro. It does not appear improbable that Augustine proximately drew from Cicero the meaning of divine "inspiration" and indications concerning the intrinsic and extrinsic operation of God; on this see Ch. Baguette, n.4 supra. I have interpreted the intrinsic and extrinsic divine operation as an anticipation of GL 8.26.48, an adumbration that, once the materialist baggage is dropped, seems in essentials similar to the later account. According to GL 8.26.48, *ut... [Deus] naturas quas intrinsecus substituit, etiam administret,* "in order that God may also administer the substances that he intrinsically created."

11. On the Stoic nature of pneuma see A.A. Long, *Hellenistic Philosophy*, 159-60 and Colish, op. cit., 1.22-5; along with Starnes, 200, n. 12.

12. The oxymoron, "loquacious mutes," may bear a different import in 1.4.4 where, we saw, it may mean that all human utterance falls short of the infinite majesty of God; for when we say everything about God, we find we have said nothing worthy of God. J 13.5.

13. Resorting to religious formulas sure to appeal to Christians, Manichees, at least in the West, claimed to believe in a Word that was begotten from the creation of the world; it was this Word whom the Father of Greatness appointed to save and bring men into the Kingdom of Light. Fort 1.3.

14. Alfaric, 250, n.1, lists other places in which Augustine uses this argument: Fort 7. 23-6. CF 21.14; 22.22. Fel. 1.9; 2.8. C Sec. 20. P 140.11. S 182.4. D 2. 398-9 adds the following: O 2.17.46. Fort 1.36-7. C Adim 28.1. NB 43. CF 13.6.

15. Drawing on their impressive disputational virtuosity, some Manichees labored to maneuver out of the pincers of the dilemma but without success. (i) Some adopted the line that God did not resist the invaders to spare himself from harm but to impose a just and decent order on the fractious spirits of the invading forces. This response, a mere ad hoc device, is nowhere exposited in Manichean writings, which never fail to urge that God acted to protect himself. (ii) Yet even on the supposition that this reply is authentically Manichean, it cannot withstand counter-analysis. (a) God's alleged goodness to the Race of Darkness, unfortunately, works harm on his own subjects. (b) It seems odd also that while imposing order on the minions of Darkness, God neglected to protect his own subjects from every disorder. (iii) Other ingenious but logically defective Manichean partisans attempted to wiggle out of the dilemma by arguing that though the Kingdom of Light, because limited, was vulnerable to invasion, God himself could not be harmed. Nowhere, however, does Manichean sacred literature supply the slightest support for this claim. Further, it entails the inconsequence that it adds another substance to a dualistic outlook. Now there are three sort of substances: one subject to violation (the Kingdom of Light), another inviolable (God), and a third engaged in violation. MM 12.25-6.

16. According to BA 13, 148, Augustine absorbed from Ambrose the truth that free will is the cause of sin but lacked the cognitive apparatus, in particular, the understanding of a spiritual God and the meaning of evil, to explain this truth. Courcelle, 99-100, traces the Ambrosian influence to the sermons on the *Hexameron*, which, significantly, he notes, explicitly counter the Manichean denial of free will. Other sermons of Ambrose, *De Jacob*, 1.1.1 and 1.3.10, and *De Isaac*, 2.61, he suggests, left their impress on Augustine. He instances *Enn.* 3.2.10 and 6.8.6 as possible sources for Ambrose's justification of free will.

17. Some, e.g., G-M 171, n. 22, detect in Augustine's reasoning an adumbration of Anselm's so-called ontological argument in the *Proslogion* (a similar text is DC 1.7.7). However, Augustine is not proving the existence of God from the very concept of God alone. Rather, already knowing by faith and reason that God exists, he demonstrates that God must be incorruptible. As is well known, the *ratio Anselmi*, many hold, seems guilty of an illicit passage from the purely conceptual order to actual existence. Moreover, Anselm attempts to show that the existence of God needs no strict demonstration: it is self-evident, manifest in the necessary connection between the concept of God as perfect and existence. Once we truly think of God as perfect, he argues, we are compelled to admit that God exists. If we think of God as perfect but do not think of him existing, we are not truly thinking of God: he cannot be perfect if he lacks the attribute of existence (as just indicated, Anselm uses the word existence equivocally). But Augustine's proofs of God's incorruptibility are direct demonstrations, not sheer elucidations of what is self-evident. Each of the arguments is cast in the second figure of the Aristotelian syllogism. A

corruptible being is not the highest good; but God is the highest good; therefore God is incorruptible. Again, a corruptible being is a being that can be violated by its will or necessity or chance; but God cannot be so violated; therefore God is incorruptible.

18. According to BA 13, n.1, 589-90, Augustine's more extensive case for divine incorruptibility, based on God's perfect goodness, power, and knowledge, appears to carry echoes of passages in *Enn.* 6.8.8. However, Augustine's analysis seems to turn on God's incorruptibility while Plotinus principally deals with the freedom and will of the One.

19. The firmament of heaven with its stars (planets), including the sun and moon, was visible, but certain things lie so far up in the heavens that they are outside the reach of the senses. GL 5.18.36.

20. *Cuncta spiritalia* may embrace, beyond angels, a possible world soul, an organizing and integrating principle responsible for the harmonious co-working of all material things in the cosmos. In earlier writings Augustine seems inclined to make room for a cosmic soul: Imm 15.24. M 6.14.44. VR 10.18. GI 4.17. Later references evince a more circumspect stance; right to the end he reserved judgment, neither assenting to nor rejecting a world soul. R 1.11.14. V. Bourke, "The Problem of a World Soul," in *Wisdom from St. Augustine*, 78-90.

21. According to G-M 172, n.26, *Enn.* 4.3.9 uses the sponge analogy to illustrate the Soul's penetration of the world. However, since Augustine had yet to encounter Plotinus' work, it seems doubtful that the figure is adapted directly from Plotinus. Perhaps the metaphor was not uncommon in the doxographical literature from which Augustine culled formative ideas.

22. The fact that Firminus esteemed Augustine's proficiency in astrological practice confirms our earlier judgment that Augustine was no dabbler in matters of astrology. A caster of horoscopes had to have a basic knowledge of astronomy, from which, as an offshoot, the pseudo-science derived its apparent scientific respectability.

23. According to BA 13, 598, n.1, *dealbatiores vias*, which literally means "the more whitened roads," refers to newly repaired roads in which chalk or lime was inserted in the spaces between the stones to bind them. In the opinion of HC 118, n.11, the chalk was placed on the top layer, the effect of which is still noticeable on a Roman road in Tunisia or Algeria. G-M 176, n.11, prefers the general sense, "comparatively brilliant." In any case, however translated, the import is that Firminus traveled the well-marked roads leading to moneyed leisure, opportunity, and success.

24. Nigidius Figulus, a contemporary of Cicero, argued that to a small difference in an astrological reading there corresponds a large tract traversed in the heavens (since the heaven whirls with a great velocity in reference to the stationary earth), which great distance would account for the notable divergence of the later character and social status of twins at birth. The argument, Augustine counters, boomerangs. During the brief pulse of time intervening between the appearance of the second child following upon the first in a twin birth, no significant alteration is observable in astrological

phenomena. Such a change is mensurationally indeterminable or practically incalculable. Specifically, if the first of the twins is born in the zodiacal sign Gemini whose ruling planet is Mercury at a time when Mercury is in conjunction with, or possibly coincides with, another planet; the sign, the position of the ruling planet, and the planetary conjunction remain practically unchanged in the brief interval before the emergence of the second child. If all other astrological observations, that is, those apart from those dealing with twin births, were to try to cast horoscopes differentiated only in terms of minute pulses of time, such readings would also be mensurationally indeterminable or incalculable, for the planetary correspondences would stay the same during the brief interval separating the earthly events. In short, reliance on Niegidius' fictional hypothesis would render astrological forecasts incalculable or impossible. In fact, however, astrologers base their calculations in the case of ordinary births on longer time spans, not on the very small intervals of time between the moments of first and second arrivals in twin births (CD 5.3). Focusing in some detail on the fact of twin births, Augustine goes on to lay bare additional incoherences in astrological claims. Astrology cannot explain how twins fall sick at the same time since the tiny interval between their births should determine this situation as well the other events in their varied lives that, they hold, are differentiated because of the time difference at birth. If astrologers invoke the identical moment of conception, other paradoxes ensue; for, if astrologically determined by an identical conception, the twins should not be temporally differentiated at birth (CD 5.5). Other incongruities arise from a critical appraisal of astrological predictions as regards twins of a different sex (CD 5.6), and each choice of a wedding day and the choice of days for planting or sowing. CD 5.7. For overviews of astrology see, C. McIntosh, *The Astrologers and Their Creed: An Historical Outline.* J. Lindsay, *Origins of Astrology.*

25. As mentioned earlier (7.4.6), Augustine ascribes chance to human ignorance. The event is apparently causeless; the restricted scope prevents man from descrying the hidden causal mechanism at work issuing in the so-called casual occurrence. Elsewhere he provisionally lists, without endorsing, the opinion that a chance event lacks proper determinacy; it is causeless or, if it is assigned a "cause", it arises from an order without determinate factors or patterns. CD 5.1.

26. BA 13, 603, n.1, calls attention to QS 1.2.3, where prior to the *Confessions* Augustine instances the simultaneous birth of Esau and Jacob as proof that grace and salvation are not won by prior merits but are bestowed as the gift of God. St. Paul underscores simultaneity of their conception for a second reason, to puncture the pretensions of astrologers who sell to dupes their wares or predictions that, while advertised as scientific, are, when successful, only the result of fortuitous surmise. Later (CD 5.4) the story of Esau and Jacob is employed to concretely prove that astrology is devoid of empirical warrant and therefore scientifically valueless. Born at practically the same moment, they led markedly different lives.

27. GL 2.17.37 indicates that when a hidden inspiration that shapes an accurate reading of a horoscope is aimed at deceiving men, it is worked by evil spirits.

At times evil spirits can reliably predict the future because, under divine direction, good angels communicate to them what they have learned from God. It is God's hidden justice that ordains the disclosure of this knowledge by blessed angels to evil spirits. Moreover, the actions of evil spirits acting independently of the good spring from divine providence.

28.　On the soul's middle status see DuRoy, 476-8 along with Madec, "Diagramme augustinien," AUG 25 (1985), fasc. 1-2, 79-94, noted in Book 1, n.1 supra.

29.　See D 2.412.

30.　We need not try to retrace the terrain concerning "the books of Platonists," which has already been thoroughly covered by the considerable, even formidable, scholarship of a number of savants. Earlier P. Henry apparently leaned to the view that the books referred to were exclusively those of Plotinus, who is the lone Neoplatonist mentioned during the Cassiciacum period. The polar opposite of his view was preferred by W. Theiler, who maintained that Porphyry influenced Augustine (*Porphyrios und Augustin,* 1933). But today it seems safe to say that nearly all scholars concur in the opinion that works by both Plotinus and Porphyry were among what Augustine vaguely calls books of the Platonists. O'Meara, 134-55, holds that Porphyry exerted the more substantial, more abiding influence; Courcelle, 27-42, also assigns Porphyry a role of notable influence. Solignac, BA 13, 112, detects indications of the Porphyry's *Aphormai* or *Sententiae,* a work that may be considered a very short summary of the *Enneads.* It is well to bear in mind Solignac's cautionary comment, 111, that the input of Porphyry will never be finally settled since the large majority of his work is no longer extant, and much of what remains consists of unsystematic fragments. On this question see Du Roy, 70-2, with appropriate notes. See also TeSelle "Porphyry and Augustine," AS 5(1974), 113-47, and F. Van Fleteren, "Porphyry," AE 661-3. Not to be overlooked is the shrewd observation of G. Madec in LASAP, *Confessiones VII,* 60, that it is certain that while Augustine read writings of Plotinus, it is not certain in what guise they came into his hands. Perhaps, as P. Hadot remarks, he read extracts to which were joined commentaries by Porphyry. In any event, the question remains, and will probably remain, unresolved.

31.　In the opinion of Courcelle, 153-6, Mallius Theodorus, who was a Christian Platonist, was probably the prideful person who called Augustine's attention to Neoplatonic writings. But as O'Meara, 125-6, incisively argues, Augustine makes no mention of the presumed transmission of these key writings in BV 1.5, which is dedicated to Theodorus. O'Meara, 153, suggests that Augustine's reference was to Porphyry, who is usually designated as infected with pride. However, as Solignac notes, the very words of the text, *procurasti mihi* (you procured for me), apparently indicate a living intermediary who personally showed the relevant texts to Augustine; BA 13, 102, n. 3. As Solignac also remarks, there were a good number of nonChristian Neoplatonists with whom, because of his position, Augustine could have had no trouble becoming acquainted; BA 13, 103.

32.　According to Courcelle, 170-1, it was Simplicianus, who, during conversations with Augustine, pointed up the affinities of Neoplatonic thought with basic Christian truths about God and his Word (8.2.3).

33. The Scriptures upon which the Plotinian metaphysics of the Intellect or second hypostasis throw light are parts of the Prologue of St. John's Gospel and Phil 2.6. The Word is not only in the presence of God; he is God distinct from the Father. The Word is the source of all things created. In him is life, i.e., Godly existence. This life is the light of men; the Word communicates divine truths to the human spirit. Human beings bear witness to light they received from the Word, the only true light, the light of the invisible God. Unfortunately, those in the world, a world made through him, paid him little or no heed; he was rejected by self-centered men. Yet withal the Word was born of God, the only-begotten of the Father. Stated otherwise, the Word was in the form of the Father, perfectly God, consubstantial with the Father, absolutely coequal to him as God. The Word was not made in time: he is absolutely timeless, prior to all times, and supratemporal, i.e., eternal, as the Father is eternal. Yet the eternal Word communicates to men in time some of his inner riches to make them happy in the divine mode and shares with them his wisdom empowering them to live as new beings.

34. *Enn.* 5.1.6; 1.7.

35. *Enn.* 5.1.7

36. *Enn.* 7.3.16

37. *Enn.* 5.3.8.

38. CD 10.2 makes a similar point in greater detail about the parallel in teaching or illumination between Plotinus and the Prologue to St. John's Gospel. Like the rational or intellectual soul in Plotinus, the soul of John the Baptist is not the light but a sharer in the light, receiving a part of the fullness of light that is in or is God. For this text see D 2.425.

39. *Enn.* 5.1.3

40. *Enn.* 5.1.1

41. *Enn.* 5.1.7

42. *Enn.* 5.4.

43. *Enn.* 1.6.6. This correspondence of verses from the Johannine Prologue with texts from the *Enneads* is adapted from Solignac's admirable note in BA 13, n.25, 682-9. In his opinion, it is certain that Augustine read *Enn.* 1.8, 5.1, 5.2, 3.2, and 3.3; very probably 5.3, 6.6, and 6.9 came into his hands; and it is reasonable to believe that he was also acquainted with some tractates on the soul in *Enn.* 4; roughly ten tractates in all. DuRoy, 70, n.1, lists thirteen tractates that, he holds, Augustine was familiar with.

44. According to E. Gilson, *History of Christian Philosophy in the Middle Ages,* 93-4, the Fathers recognized a kinship with Plato's provident maker of the universe, intelligible world, and immortality of the soul, among other points of affinity. It would be misguided, however, to infer that the Fathers were thoroughgoing Platonists. While adapting Platonic concepts for theological analysis, they refused to assimilate the whole of the Platonic outlook.

45. *In phys.* 8.2.4, 5; 3.6. For Aristotle, God is "the principle of the whole of existence" (*principium totius esse*). Though he claimed that the world was eternal, he held that God is the cause not only of the motion but the very existence of the world itself.

46. The very first sentence of Porphyry's life of Plotinus mentions that the sage was ashamed to exist in a body. *Life of Plotinus* in A. Armstrong, *Plotinus*, 1.3.

47. In the view of Van der Meer, xxi-xxii, this decisive note of humility gave essential shape to the particular Christian configuration of the Augustine who practiced humility to "a heroic degree."

48. In "Connaissance de Dieu et action de grâces", RA, 2(1962), 223-309, which appraises the various citations of Rom 1.18-25 in Augustine, G. Madec establishes, by acute commentary on a wealth of sources, that this passage from Romans is a key text that thematizes the congruence and disparity between pagan Neoplatonists and Christian thinkers. The crucial passage points up the valuable scope but also underlines the decisive limits, including deficiencies, of nonbelieving Neoplatonists, who knew the *invisibilia Dei* but never attained inner healing and total salvation. They soared to a contemplation, an intellective intuition, of God in his invisible perfections but, instead of reposing on the heights, plummeted to the depths, some debasing their brilliant minds to the worship of mindless, senseless idols of stone. Philosophically exalted in knowing God, they became religiously degraded by adoration of false gods (a charge leveled, in particular, against Porphyry; CD 10.24). They were reduced to the religious bankruptcy and fraud that is idolatry because they turned their backs on the way of humility, the way that is the lowly Christ, whose wisdom is not revealed to the worldly wise but to little ones in spirit. Besides relevant parts of Book 7, Madec cites an impressive number of texts which include: 13.19.24. VR 4.7; 20.40; 25.47. T 4.7.11; 8.13; 15.20; 16.21-17.23. J 2.3-4. His essay may be taken as a nuancive commentary on 7.9.14 and what follows, reinforced by affiliated texts from other works, all combining to evidence that for Augustine, faith in Christ is "the stumbling stone of philosophies and the cornerstone of Christianity" (287).

49. Our interpretation of this complex section relies upon E. Gilson, "Egypt où Grèce," *Medieval Studies* 8 (1946), 43-52. A quite different interpretation is deftly proposed by TeSelle, 244-50, who argues that Egyptian food is a metaphor for phantasmata or mythological ideas. These imaginary notions are projected on God: in this figurative sense some Neoplatonists engaged in idolatry. Consequently, Augustine at this time was probably not acquainted with Porphyry, implicit reference to whom does not surface until Book 10.

50. P. Henry descries a possible permissive attitude to the mysteries of Isis in an illusion to them in *Enn.* 1.6, which deals with the ascent to the One. Ordinarily, however, it is Porphyry who is deemed more permissive of idol worship. According to Gilson, n. 49 supra, when Augustine mentioned idolatry, he may have had in mind Porphyry's *De abstinentia ab esu animalium*, an account of the worship of idols in animal form (the citations from Henry and Gilson are in DuRoy, 67, n.2). O'Meara, 134-55, rates the influence of Porphyry textually more pronounced, detecting a number of references to Porphyry that directly or indirectly endorse, and may suggest involvement in, idol worship. Porphyry is said to be under the dominion of demons in CD 10.24, which is paralleled by VR 4.7 and QA 33.76. E 118.5.33 retails the practice of magic by some thinkers in Plotinus' school at Rome; among the practitioners, it may be

implied, was Porphyry.

51. The idols of the Egyptians included Osiris as child (BA 14,15, n.2), Harpocrates, the child of Isis (Courcelle, 82-5; apparently referred to in CD 18.5), Anubis the barker, their dog-faced god (8.2.3), idols with faces of dogs and bulls (S 147.1), and images of a dog, serpent, and crocodile (S 241.33). Porphyry mentions vultures and rams. Apparently neither Plotinus nor Porphyry actually engaged in animal worship à la the Egyptians. But according to Courcelle, 88, both neglected to launch a strong attack against zoolatry and, if not initiates, both tolerantly described the mystery of Isis.

52. The *lenticula* that Esau ate were said to be the food of Egyptians since it is abundant in Egypt. P 4.6.6, cited in D 2.431.

53. According to UB 4.6, the saying that "in God we live, and move and have our being" derives from the truth which idolaters block or keep submerged in wickedness. All things live and move and are in God; they are all contained in him, all ruled and governed by him (T 14.12.16). This truth concerning God's sovereign control of the universe was grasped by certain pagan thinkers; but the truth was distorted and lost its force in idol-worship. P. Henry, *Plotin et l'Occident,* observes that the Pauline text in Ac 17.28 is echoed somewhat in *Enn.* 6.9.9; 7-11. In the opinion of Courcelle, 131, n.2, it was Ambrose who linked Ac 17.28 with a Plotinian text. As P. Henry also notes, the expression "as certain ones among the pagans said," is used in Acts to refer to the words that follow," for we are also his offspring." According to F. Chatillon, "*Quidam secundum eos:* note d'exégèse augustinienne," *Rev. Moyen Âge Latin* 1 (1945), 287-304, Augustine's handling of this text cannot be an oversight since he makes this apparently misguided linkage at least seven times in his works. BA 13, 614-5, n.1.

54. G. Madec, "Admonitio," AL 1. 96-7. The comments on 7.10.16, 7.16.23, 9.10.23-5, and 10.40.65 substantially derive from J.M. Quinn, "Mysticism in the *Confessiones,* Four Passages Reconsidered," 251-86, in *Augustine: Mystic and Mystagogue,* CollAug, (ed.) F. Van Fleteren and J. Schnaubelt.

55. For DuRoy, 74, n.5, the eternity-truth-charity triad is a Trinitarian schema explicitly reproduced in T 4.21-30 and (by emendation some fifteen years later) T 4 *Proem.* (*De trinitate* was begun around 399). Invocation of the trinity in this line would seem to buttress our view that this sentence is part of the short spiritual parenthesis recording the affective state not of the pre-baptism seeker in 386 but of the fervent bishop in 397.

56. His eyes are too weak to gaze steadily into the sun which symbolizes truth. The figure, common in the Platonic tradition, is traceable to Plato himself (*Rep.* 7.555C). For this and other possible sources of the blinding nature of light, see F. Van Fleteren, "Augustine's Ascent of the Soul in Book VII of the Confessions: A Reconsideration," AS 5 (1974), 46, n.69. See also F. Van Fleteren, "Ascent of the Soul," AE 63-7.

57. Though no longer a prodigal son far off from the Father (3.6.11), no longer a wasteland (2.10.18), Augustine, because a creature, was still a long distance from a steadfast grasp of God. He remains unable to bridge the gap between infinite and finite because he is radically unlike the infinite God. As spirit, his

soul is like God; as finite, he is unlike the infinite. His status or ontic space as creature constitutes his unlikeness; as created, he dwells in a region of unlikeness. See BA 13, 689-93.

58. The signification of carnal as sensory or sense-bound is fairly common in the *Confessions*. To instance only a few relevant texts, 9.10.24 speaks of *carnalium sensuum delectatio*, and 9.10.25, of *tumultus carnis* in reference to sensory perception of the physical world. Earlier, in the course of lamenting his seduction by Manicheism, Augustine explicitly contrasts the intellectual (here in the broad sense) and carnal conceptions of God:...*cum te [Deum] non secundum intellectum mentis...sed secundum sensum carnis quaererem* (3.6.14). As a Manichee, he was enjoined to cultivate a God who was outside and beneath him whereas the true God was intimior *intimo meo et superior summo meo*, "more inner than my innermost self and higher than my highest self" (3.6.11). The various ascents to God move from without to within and above the self. Van Fleteren, n. 56, 49-52 supra, proves that, contrary to opinions of leading commentators, *carnalis*, when implicitly or explicitly used in the ascents of Book 7, denotes a sense-biased knowledge that balks recognition of spiritual reality.

59. Augustine may be described as a sort of spiritual in two senses. First, ordinarily a spiritual was an intellectually and morally committed baptized Catholic; at the time of the first ascent in 386, he had still to undergo a moral conversion and hence had not yet been baptized. Second, he usually discriminates between an infant or child of the mind with simple faith, and a spiritual, an educated individual who achieves understanding of faith. Little ones in the line of faith, unable to spiritually understand the Scriptures, usually think of God in terms of sense-images, picturing him as circumscribed by a bodily figure; GCM 1.17.27. Here he apparently introduces a further nuance: in grasping God as a spirit, he is not strictly a child of faith but a spiritual; however, insofar as he needs further cognitive and moral refinement, he remains an immature spiritual, not yet a full-fledged spiritual. Recall, spirituals are full-grown Christians who participate in the gift of wisdom enabling them to feed directly on solid food of the Scriptures. The infants (1 Cor 3:1) or "carnal" individuals (1 Cor 2:14) are nourished only by milk. It is the spirituals who communicate to these the wisdom of the Scriptures (13.18.23). Later, J 98.2-4 again draws the line between spirituals and infants/carnals according to conception or lack of conception of spiritual reality.

60. In mentally feeding on God, Augustine's mind becomes like God. The forms of his thinking about God resemble God and thereby mold his mind after that of God. Put otherwise, in knowing God as truth, Augustine's mind shares in that truth and, in so sharing, becomes like God; becoming God, he is qualitatively transmuted into God. Elsewhere J 41.1 makes the same point: "Truth is bread; it refreshes minds without itself changing. It changes the mind feeding upon it while it is not changed into the mind nourished by it." The wise, who are comparatively few, are divinized in a specific mode: they become wise with the shared wisdom of God; T 12.14.23. According to some scholars, the insight that eating the food of truth changes Augustine into God bespeaks the Christian

Eucharist. So far as I know, nowhere does Augustine employ this expression in a Eucharistic sense. He frequently calls eating of the Eucharistic body of Christ a sign of incorporation into and unity within the mystical body of Christ. Reception of the one bread made from many grains of wheat symbolizes the unity of the many faithful within the one body that is the Church. The faithful are bade to become this one "bread" that is the mystical body; S 227; T 26. 13.15. Incorporation into the mystical body of Christ is hardly the same as transmutation into the divine food that is truth. The Eucharistic interpretation of this passage can be traced to at least the High Middle Ages. Albert the Great, (*Opera*, XXVI. 66, 48), Bonaventure (*Sent.* 4.8.1 *dubium*), and Aquinas (*S. th.* 3.73.3 ad 2) assign a Eucharistic sense to "*cibus grandium.*" See Courcelle, *Les Confessions de saint Augustin dans la tradition littéraire*, 309, 311, 314. Inevitably an accommodated reading backed by the prestige of such giants filtered into theological commentaries and manuals, from which it has been appropriated by spiritual writers and homilists down to our day.

61. C. Butler, *Western Mysticism*, pp.3,42, 61-2. Butler salutes Augustine as "the Prince of Mystics," 24. E. Underhill, *Mysticism*, 50, 250, apparently considers the contact with God in 7.10.16 a mystical experience. In *The Mystics of the Church*, 60, she calls Augustine "a natural mystic," whose mystical penchant was fulfilled through grace, a description apparently anticipating the later kin characterization of Augustine as a "natural-born mystic" ("un mystique né") by Henry, in *La vision d'Ostie*, cited in Solignac, BA 13, 144, n. 3, and Bonner, 98, n.6.

62. As F. Van Fleteren has shown in "The Cassiciacum Dialogues and Augustine's Ascents at Milan," *Mediaevalia* 4 (1978), 59-82, Augustine believed in 386 (and up until 394) that it was possible for the properly prepared mind to attain an understanding or vision of God in this life. Happiness consists in possession of the truth or wisdom that is God, a possession that becomes one with enjoyment of God.

63. For the traits of acquired and infused or mystical contemplation see A. Tanquerey, *The Spiritual Life*, 653-4, 666-95, and 737-40 and J. de Guibert, *The Theology of the Spiritual Life*, 202-8, 305-7, and 322-34. One scholar protested against imposing on Augustine categories foreign to his thought. However, since the word mysticism has been given diverse, even conflicting, meanings, it is necessary to set down constituents of a specific sense of mysticism. Moreover, such inquiry is not aprioristic but aims at empirically ascertaining whether such mystical features are within Augustine's experience. For other interpretations of mysticism see G. Bonner, "Augustine and Mysticism," 113-57, and F. Van Fleteren, "Mysticism in the *Confessiones*–A Controversy Revisited," in *Augustine: Mystic and Mystagogue*, (ed.) F. Van Fleteren and J. Schnaubelt 309-36.

64. Courcelle, 93-138, proved how Ambrose's sermons were a leading source for Augustine's instruction in crucial themes of Christian Neoplatonism such as the spirituality of God, the spiritual nature of the human soul, and the privative character of evil. Ambrose, in addition, opened Augustine's eyes to the profitable use of allegorical exegesis (6.4.6). Hence it seems permissible to

surmise that Augustine may have had his attention called to this divine name by a bishop who eloquently expounded key Scriptural texts with Neoplatonic concepts as his instruments.

65. Porphyry, *Life of Plotinus*, in Armstrong, *Plotinus* 1.71.

66. "What is said to exist in the supreme and greatest way is said to permanently exist in itself" (ME 6.8). Existence bespeaks continuance in existence. Whereas God as the supreme being continues to exist in and of himself, the continuance in existence of all other beings depends on the power of him who alone absolutely or truly exists. All other beings undoubtedly exist, but as subject in some way to the possibility of nonexistence, they do not truly or absolutely exist; theirs is only a relative existence.

67. In "Augustine on Mode, Form, and Natural Order", AS 31 (2000), 59-77, C. Schäffer clarifies Augustine's concept of privation, establishing that, taken specifically, it is not simply any negative alteration but a corruption affecting the mode, form, or order of a substance.

68. As Schäffer, art cit., 75-7, shows, though Augustine never formally uses the "due" or *debitum* formula, the concept is materially contained in his specification of evil in terms of corruption of mode, form, and order. The definition of evil as absence of a due good was apparently first explicitly coined by Anselm, then adopted by later scholastics.

69. In recent years the view that evil is a privation has come under considerable attack. In a penetrating article, "Augustine's Privation Account of Evil: a Defense," AS 20 (1989), 109-28, D. Cress critically examines current major animadversions against the privation theory, making it clear that, unlike M.B. Eddy's Christian Science view, evil, privatively taken, is not sheerly illusory. Were evil not in some sense real, the redemption would have been unnecessary. Second, the contention that analysis of evil as privation brings no consolation to sufferers ignores the fact that no metaphysical theory of any sort can be required to induce solace of soul. Rather, it is cultus, worship of God, that opens the soul to divine strength. Third, pain, it is urged, undermines the privative character of evil. No doubt pain is often felt as positively real, but it takes little analysis to establish that the pain occurs because of bodily disharmony. The pain from a fractured leg, pancreatic cancer, or simply a severe headache is a manifestation of disorder in the organism. Medicines or some forms of therapy aim at restoring bodily order. In other words, pain is felt privation of order in an organism. Fourth, the privation account, some hold, has no Biblical precedent. However as, J. Hick, *Evil and the God of Love*, 186, shows, the concept of privative evil is implied in the Biblical version of creation, for an infinitely good God cannot admit evil as a constituent in a good and very good universe. As we have already indicated, evil is indeed real but only relatively real. It is real as related to or connected with an entity that is absolutely being. It is not positively real; it exists only as a deficiency of the good or as a parasite on what is good. In the language of Aquinas (which is not used by Augustine) evil is a being of reason, which conceptually functions as if it were a fully real being. Perhaps some who demur at evil as privation fail to grasp the point and significance of beings of reason. Suppose a man is robbed

of $100. At present in the context of the robbery he has no money at all. He has nothing, i.e., he is currently deprived of his money. "Nothing" describes his deprivation; "nothing" signifies privation. Thus a privation realistically denotes the financial condition of the person robbed. Not that "nothing" is a positively real entity. Rather, "nothing" betokens his lack of the filched $100. His economic situation is evil insofar as he is deprived of the original $100. No reduction of evil to illusion here; no metaphysical sleight of hand: the evil that is nothing is the privation of the original $100. Correspondingly, every other evil taken as privation is not rendered illusory nor is it converted into a positively real entity. It is real, undoubtedly so, but it is relatively real, existing not in itself but as connected with an absolutely real entity.

In addition, further analysis shows that the privation theory is the only feasible explanation of evil. Both monism and dualism are fatally flawed. Monism effectively eliminates evil. For B. Spinoza, evil ceases to exist once it is viewed within the brilliance of eternal intuition. Taken transcendently, from the angle of God, evil reduces to an illusion, the outcome of a less-than-divine grasp of reality. On the other hand, dualistic systems such as Manicheism and the pessimism of A. Schopenhauer do not deny evil but positively existentialize anti-good factors. Consequently, the evil factor cannot be wholly evil. The Manichean Prince of Darkness or Schopenhauer's irrational will to live has to have a nature or ontic makeup that is good. In other words, the Prince of Darkness and the will to live are real beings, deprived of certain valuational features. Each is a basically good being with utterly warped tendencies. Similarly, every radical dualism implicitly justifies or implicitly falls back on the privation account of evil.

70. Coyle, 40-3.
71. Here Augustine may be alluding to the view held by some natural philosophers of old, left unidentified, that the lower world of incessant change is "ruled" by chance. The inconstancy and unpredictability of storms especially seem to point to a radical indeterminacy or chanciness in the lower regions. Ps 148, however, affirms that storms and winds, howbeit turbulent, plainly manifest order and beauty. The precise lines of such determination elude human analysis, it is true, but the order in various particular substances indicates that the whole of the lower regions is orderly. If all the parts of the lower regions are ordered, it is only reasonable to hold that the whole of the lower zone is the scene not of chance but of direction. Thus though the details of order involved in the turbulence of storms lie beyond our grasp, there has to be some basic order. In short, the underdeveloped state of the meteorology of his day did not debar Augustine from acknowledging a basic intelligibility in clouds and storms (P 148.7). It is the mind that is limited; it is not the things in nature that are wanting in structure and determinate actions: they are not unintelligible but orderly and patterned.
72. Lower things, mutable and corruptible, have their proper place and hence their proper order. According to their proper mode of being (pro modo suo), within the limits of their being, they complete the beauty of the universe and therefore praise God. See D 2.450.

73. God is governor of the proper times of things, especially in regard to their
     cessation. The lifetime of each specific thing is marked by boundaries fixed by
     its measure, number, and order (LA 3.15.43). Complaining about the
     transiency of things is self-stultifying, for the complaint consists of words made
     of sounds, each of us which has to pass away before the sentence or sentences
     can be completed. Moreover, as beauty is manifested in an eloquent oration
     made up of successive syllables, so in the material world the disappearance of
     the old and the appearance of the new lend beauty to the universe (NB 8). The
     whole beauty of the ages is woven out of things that pass away and come to be
     (GL 1.8.14); a theme also sounded in GL 4.23.51-2; 5.20.41; 5.23.46. P 144.13.
     CD 11.18; 22.24. The whole of the history of mankind is one long beautiful
     poem (11.28.38). Like a discourse, no poem can be declaimed without the
     lapsing and fresh pronunciation of different sounds (VR 22.43). The art of
     poetry rules the lines of poetry; so divine providence governs the "lines" of
     time (VR 22.43). As the rules of poetry are *omnia simul* (3.7.14), so the laws of
     providence are *omnia simul*. The remarkable beauty of the lower zone is hailed
     in CD 22.24.

74. As dissimilar from God, the wicked are suited to the lower world. The lower
     realm befits them as a dominion in which natural adversity becomes a source
     of punishment for sin. Therein they leave off dissimilarity and take on
     similarity to God through divine justice that by means of punishment exacts
     redress for sins. The path from a tarnished image to a purified image of God
     has to pass through punishment that is purgation for sin.

75. Undoubtedly Augustine owes a good deal to Plotinus' metaphysics, but
     Plotinus' influence on his view of evil has to be discriminatingly qualified.
     Augustine acquired the key definition of evil as *privatio boni* from St. Ambrose,
     to whose sermons *De Isaac* he listened in 386. Therein the Bishop of Milan
     defines evil as the lack of good, *indigentia boni*. It is from good things that evil
     things take their rise. The only evil things are those that are deprived of good;
     therefore lack (*indigentia*) of good is the root of evil (*malitiae*); *De Isaac*, 7.6;
     quoted verbatim in CJP 1.9.44. As C. Journet shows in *The Meaning of Evil*, 32-
     3, Courcelle, 107 and 124, fails to establish a parallel between this text and the
     Plotinian theory of evil. For his definition Ambrose probably drew upon Greek
     Fathers such as St. Basil and St. Gregory of Nyssa. Indeed Plotinus assigns a
     positive reality to evil; evil is identified with matter or nonbeing, the thing at
     the farthest remove from the One (*Enn.* 1.8.3-4) whereas for Augustine, evil as
     privation is absolutely nonbeing and relatively being. In addition, Plotinus, it
     seems, has good necessarily engendering evil (*Enn.* 1.8.7). However, it seems
     highly probable that some lines from *Enn.* 5.1.1., in which Plotinus avers that
     the beginning of evil consists in *tolma* or audacity, movement, and the desire to
     belong to themselves, features that dispose souls to pursue a course opposed to
     God, lie behind Augustine's designation of evil as the turning away from the
     highest substance in order to seek inferior goods (7.16.22). See BA 13, 106-7.

76. Worth mentioning also is that the correct translation of *mirabar* is "I was
     puzzled" rather than the rendering, "I marveled" or "I was astonished,"
     common in most translations True, in other passages *mirari* signifies "to

marvel," as in 9.10.24: *ascendebamus interius...mirando opera tua....* Here, however, the context demands the sense of puzzlement; Augustine cannot account for loving God while being incapable of maintaining his understanding of God. The wonderment or perplexity that he experienced is specifically identical in meaning with *admiratio* in 13.21.35: *...ignoratio mater admirationis,* "ignorance is the mother of wonder" or wondering why certain events occur. This pithily put insight originally derives from Aristotle, *Meta.* 1.983a 13-21, according to whom wonder or puzzlement is the beginning of science; puzzlement initiates inquiry into the reason why an event occurs. Science is the termination of wonder; once a conclusion has been demonstrated through a causal nexus, wonderment is evoked only by the self-defeating suggestion that the necessary conclusion can be otherwise.

77. As Van Fleteren, "Ascent" 49-52 (see n. 56 supra), shows, *pondus hoc consuetudo carnalis* echoes a parallel phrase in early works such as CA 3.6.13; 13.38. Imm 10.17, and QA 3.4, where *corporum consuetudo* or its equivalent is said to hamper, at times nullify, the conception of spiritual reality. Later, we may add, Augustine continued to refer to carnal habit, a bondage which serves as a characteristic setting apart the "animal" or carnal man, the unlettered "child" of faith, from the spiritual man, whose disparity is alluded to in 7.10.16. The carnal man wont to perceive God as material thinks of him with image-thinking (*imaginaria cogitatione*) whereas the spiritual man, repudiating concepts of God that are associated with a thought-style in terms of bodies (*ex corporum consuetudine*), understands God as a pure spirit; J 102.5.

78. According to Van Fleteren, "Ascent" 54, n. 103 (see n. 56 supra), in the Cassiciacum dialogues and by inference here, it is the body as such, the source of man's sense-conditioned knowing, that drives the mind downward, depriving it of sustained understanding of God. Later the accent shifts to the body as corruptible in the reign of sin due to man's fall from the One that is God (VR 21.41). T 8.2.3 also emphasizes that the moral or appetitive factor induces the relapse from understanding God. The weight that forces the mind to fall back down is a combination of wayward desire (depicted as birdlime) and false judgment due to man's still pilgriming in the body.

79. This section echoes or in part duplicates Augustine's proof for the existence of God in LA 2.3.7-15.39. In "Augustine's Argument for God's Existence *De Libero Arbitrio,* Book II," AS 14 (1983), 105-15, T. Kondoleon judges the argument generally convincing except for the Plotinian-inspired view that the mind can attain "light superior to itself." For R. Teske, in "The Aim of Augustine's Proof That God Truly Is," *Inter. Phil. Quart.* (1986), 253-68, the argument is valid in the special sense that it shows God as spiritual and truly immutable. In addition, Augustine compactly argued to the existence of God from efficient causation (10.6.9; 11.4.6). So impressed was he by the argument from universal consent that he held that except for a few of a depraved nature the whole of humankind recognized God as maker of the world (J106.41). Only those few who are afflicted with theoretical insanity assert that there is no God (S 69.2-3).

80. The concept of spatialized God is a vain idea or falsity that sullies the mind because it is the offspring of unclean images (7.1.1); it is blasphemy inasmuch

as it entails corruption in God. Hence this intellectual error is implicatively moral; it is an intellectual-moral component, a view both false and sinful. Perhaps the iniquity spoken of in 7.1.1, for which the mind suffers due punishment, is not a purely moral factor distinct from the cognitive element that pulls the mind earthward. If this be the case, earlier references have to be revised to designate only one factor, a moral factor that is the consequence of the image-ridden thought that blasphemes God, a moral factor that is effectively one with the emphasis on the body as such symbolized by the weight dragging down the mind.

81. Van Fleteren, "Ascent" 55-61(see n. 56 supra), proves that for Augustine at Cassiciacum and somewhat later man can rise even in this life to a continual understanding or intellectual vision of God that he equates with the blessed life. Moral purification of the eye of the soul and education in the liberal arts prepare the mind to climb and remain above sense-impregnated thinking so as to attain continual understanding of God; Sol 1.6-12-7.14. BV 2.14. Such a vision, Augustine came to realize, is more easily projected than possessed; hence his recognition that he was not yet capable of cleaving to the light (7.10.16); hence his perplexity about his simultaneous seeing of the light and his inability to sustain the vision (7.17.23). Yet he assured himself that once he conquered carnal habit or sense-oriented thinking, he would succeed in uninterruptedly seeing God. A few years later, for reasons listed in R 1.4.3, Augustine dropped this simplistic account of happiness. Man's sinful condition militates against perfect moral purification in this life, and not the soul alone but the body (as spiritualized) and soul are to rest in a deathless blessedness reserved for the life to come. Moreover, a constant vision of God is rendered illusory by the persistent pull, even if minor, of sin-prone appetites along with the proclivity to error in a nonspiritual body journeying to its homeland hereafter (T 8.2.3), a pilgrimage so fraught with labors and insecurity that endurance of the journey exercises a solid moral purification (DC 1.10.10). In any case, neither ascent in Book 7 climaxed in a strict mystical vision. Each terminated not in a vision in the sense of a seeing passively received it but in an act of understanding, a seeing that was the outcome of analysis.

82. The so-called vision at Ostia (to be appraised in 9.10.23-5), which may be regarded as mystical, is, in fact, preceded by a graded, upward movement of discursive thought. The spiritual experience in 10.40.65, analyzed below, while perhaps not indubitably mystical, arises out of prior reasoning. For Augustine, analysis and affective intimacy can go hand in hand; perhaps better put, the former can serve as a launching pad for the latter. Besides these analytic-affective linkages of 386, the affective parenthesis interpolated in 397 in the memorial reproduction of the first ascent in 7.10.16 broadly spins off from analysis.

83. Interestingly, in the early years of his Christian faith Augustine tended to stress Christ more as a teacher, as the way of light that led to the Father: Christ was the divine exemplar. Only as his thought ripened did he give proper emphasis to Christ as savior through his redemptive suffering and death. He first fully grasped Christ as wisdom, light, teacher of God; only later did he fully

understand Christ as savior, power, and suffering redeemer. See Garvey, *Augustine: Christian or Neo-Platonist?*, 230-1.

84. The assumption of the human nature of Christ by the Word is a sublime example of the gratuity of grace in the divine decree or predestination. No hypothetical action by the human nature of Christ could merit union with the Word. T 13.17. EN 11.56. PS 15.30-1.

85. According to Augustine, there are two sorts of Apollinarism; the main species held that the Word supplied the rational mind in Christ while a variant view maintained that the entire soul of Christ was furnished by the Word. DQ 80. 1-2. P 29 (En.2). 2-3. In accepting the Photinian theory, Augustine repudiated both strains of Apollinarism.

86. On the early Christology of Augustine see BA 13, 693-8. For Solignac's perceptive interpretation of *persona veritatis* with confirmation in AC 20.22, see 696-8. An equally perceptive reading is given by T. van Bavel, *Recherches sur la Christologie de saint Augustin*, who takes *persona* to mean the revelatory form of a thing. As the person of truth, Christ's human nature visibly manifests divine wisdom.

87. In Courcelle's opinion, 214, n.2, Apollinarists were actively disseminating their views in Milan in 385.

88. In spite of the cautionary remark in 1960 by J.K. Ryan (tr.), *The Confessions of St. Augustine*, 392, n.5, appended to 7.19.25, noting that the "Alypius foolishly attributed [Apollinarism] to orthodox believers," the opinion that Alypius had succumbed to Apollinarism persisted until R. O'Connell's clarification in REA 13 (1967), 209-10.

89. Alypius' misunderstanding of Catholic doctrine mistakenly attributed to Catholicism a sort of blending of the two strains of Apollinarism; the claim that the Word supplanted the whole soul of Christ had as its corrollary the replacement of the human mind by the Word.

90. *Ep.* 48.5

91. K. Adam, *The Christ of Faith*, 32. This negatively couched axiom reflects Augustine's positively expressed encapsulation: *totum suscepit, totum liberavit*, the Word "embraced the whole (of man), liberated the whole." S 237.4. See G. Madec, "Christus," AL 1. 845-908, especially 849-54, and B. Daley, "Christology", AE 164-9.

92. Elsewhere Augustine neatly contrasts three Christological observations. Photinians believe that Christ was solely man without being God; Manichees, maintaining the opposite, claim that Christ was God without being man; Apollinarians hold that Christ lacked a human soul, i.e., the rational soul that sets man apart from beasts; J 47.9. See Du Roy, 92, n.1. Interestingly, in this popular discourse Augustine lumps the two strains of Apollinarism.

93. J. O'Meara, "*Arripui, aperui, et legi*," AM 1.59-65.

94. See TeSelle, 166-76, who points up the decisive impact of Ambrosiaster on Augustine's formulation of the ransom theory. Ambrosiaster (pseudo-Ambrose) was the author of commentaries on the Pauline epistles that appeared between 363-84. See M. Mara, "Ambrosiaster," *Patrology IV*, 180-90, and D. Hunter, "Ambrosiaster," AE 19-20.

Book Eight
Witnesses, Struggle, Moral Conversion

In Book 7's search for the truth that is God and the way that is Christ, analysis predominated. Dialectical dissection showed Manichean tenets as inadequate, and a step-by-step conceptual climb up the scale of being brought Augustine to know God as the immutable One. Subsequent inquiry proved that evil was not positive but privative. Meditation on Paul established that Neoplatonism as such could not furnish concrete means for making the fractured moral self whole. As this book begins, Augustine is an intellectually assured Catholic not yet able to morally pledge himself to the rigors of continence. He has exhausted the arsenal of argumentative techniques strictly taken. Yet there remained room for a mode of discourse in the wide sense: witness or example, as etched in the lives of Victorinus (2.3-5), Antony (6.14), and monastically inclined associates of Ponticianus (6.15). A witness does not strictly expound but lives the truth, incarnating in choices the canons of the true and good. The cogency of a witness is not infrarational but rational in the line of practical reason, through which it is addressed to the will, the power of decision and action. Again, its appeal is existential; criteria for well-being are actually operative in personal actions. Moreover, the assent evoked is not a dispassionate yes to a speculative proposition like $7 + 3 = 10$ but is enunciated practically, in the line of choice. Unforgettably taught is the lesson that the victorious embodiment of values in this witness can be appropriated by action that imprints a similar pattern on one's character. A person admiring

423

such a performance is energized to imitate a witness (8.5.10), becoming not merely theoretically convinced but practically committed, motivated, as was the model, to override stumbling blocks and translate his life-plan into activity.

Longing for conversion was hampered by his vacillating will (8.19-20). The failure of the will to obey itself, he saw, arises from the fact that his will is not integral (9.21). Against the Manichean view he discerned that man has not two natures but one; that the one will harbors conflicting tendencies (10.22-4). To help him overcome lower drives the voice of continence seems to beckon (11.25-7). Finally, the voice of a child chanting "Take and read," suddenly triggers his moral conversion (12.28-30).

Chapter 1: Theoretical Certitude, Moral Hesitation

1. He recalls God's mercies, the gift of intellectual conversion, to be shortly followed by the grace of moral conversion (8.12.29); a remembrance, in effect, an outburst of praise for these blessings. His bones, which symbolize his whole being, are suffused with divine love, moving him to cry out, "O Lord, who is like you"? Nothing in the material universe matches his majesty, and dazzling invisibles such as the angels cannot qualify as peers, these brilliant with beauty only because they see him face to face (P 34[En.1.S.1].13). Indirectly spurning pseudo-deities, such as the absurd Father of Greatness and the materialistic divinity of the Stoics, he now recognizes the God of Christianity as creator and providential teacher and lover, alone worthy of worship. Not raw self-reliance of his own will but transfiguring divine power shattered his moral bonds so that, returning from his drifting, he is lovingly enshrined in God himself (P 115.7). Interiorly kneeling in grateful adoration, he offers to God as a sacrifice of praise this literary work, properly incensed with his eloquence (5.1.1). Book 8 will recount the denouement in the final act of the moral drama executed by the divine artist. Such narration plainly means that literary artifice will neither fabricate nor embroider the events of his conversion. Far from being a piece of fiction decked out with arcane literary allusions and semi-private symbols, his factual account will relate in exact detail how divine incursion broke his fetters to pieces, moving all who adore God as true Israelites without guile (P 75.2) to praise, along with Augustine,

the Lord of heaven and earth who still works marvels in individual hearts.

He intellectually embraced the key elements of the Christian view of God. The words of God, i.e., the teachings of Scripture, echoed incompletely by Neoplatonic thought, were implanted without the slightest doubt in his mind. He was analytically compelled to assent to the truths about God, by whom he was walled in, not locked in a prison of darkness, safeguarded in a citadel of light. Certain beyond all cavil of God's eternal life, that God is absolute being and therefore immutable truth, he apprehended this obscurely, as through a grossly imperfect ancient mirror, which, because fashioned of polished metal, afforded only a dim reflection. To his disconcertment he never reached the steady clarity of a habitual vision of God, which till 395 he believed was possible in this life to a mind purified of vice and refined by the arts. In any case, disburdened of Manichean errors, he knew God as the incorruptible creator of all good, who produces every substance in the universe (evil as parasitic of good is no substance). When ensnarled in materialism, he had been sorely perturbed because he could not properly grasp the divine nature. Now, after assimilating the essentials of the Christian God somewhat articulated through Neoplatonic concepts, he felt no immediate desire to perceive more sharply the nature of God. Prescinding for the moment from further speculative penetration of the divine nature, he aimed at fixing his will in God; in particular, his special moral bête noire being lust of the flesh, he wanted all sexual desire to be wholly governed by divine power. In 369-70, at the outset of adolescence, he had been spun about in the whirlpool of sex, wandering from the stability of God's changeless moral truths and rules, hurtling downward to a spiritual wasteland (2.10.18). A concubinage of some fifteen years (370-85) assuaged his voracious sexual appetite, but after severing his ties to his beloved concubine, his sexual desires once more flared up, appeasable only by a mistress (6.15.25). From on high streamed light bidding him to seek the counsel of Simplicianus, the Lord's good servant, upright in all the virtues, channeling grace through simplicity and ardor for the truth.[1] He was a long-faithful servant, a fervent Catholic since perhaps around twenty, and his advanced years now attested his qualifications to supply spiritual direction. His wisdom, not confined to books, was reaped from a rich spiritual experience in observing human character, a capital of hands-on sagacity from which Augustine felt he could profit. Simplicianus' prayer-illumined discernment would help unknot his problems and spell out means for following the way he should walk, for example, the particular vocation of celibacy he should follow. Evidently, like Ambrose, whom press of business apparently rendered largely inaccessible (6.3.5), Simplicianus was a spiritual, not only devout but theologically learned.

2. As a spiritual organism, the Church is full, containing many ministries, all subserving the unity and growth of a people of diverse callings; the greater majority work out their salvation in marriage while others are called to virginity (Cont 1.1). Previously Augustine had thirsted after status and money; now that the fires of ambition had cooled almost to ashes, his duties as public orator became well-nigh intolerable, a focus of pain instead of pleasure or psychic return; its promised goods, gewgaws in comparison with sweetness tasted in prayer, looked shabby in the light of the loveliness of the Church shining in its holy ones (P 25.12). Longing to live a celibate life, he still felt inextricably pulled by an insistent need to live with a woman. Paul, who did not forbid marriage, counseled his own path as the far better course. Yet prolonged indulgence in intercourse strangled his vague resolve, with the result that, in fact, he elected a less demanding lifestyle. Incapacity to forgo the married state implicitly obliged him to scramble for power and wealth. He had to exercise his professional rhetorical skills to earn income to maintain a wife and household in what we might label at least upper middle-class comfort (6.11.19). In opting for the apparently easier avenue, he was actually driven to trudge along the harder road. Since he could not forsake marriage, he had to go on being consumed by the thousand-and-one vexations of professional life. To support marriage he had to endure near-insupportable goods like position and affluence; in hankering after pleasures of body only marriage can bestow, he was forced to grab for station and income, which grieved his spirit.

Truth incarnate had taught that some make themselves eunuchs, that is, spiritually unmarriageable, for the sake of the kingdom of God, electing a life of virginity consecrated to God and lived only through his power. Since the tug toward marital union seemed irresistible, he would be kidding himself to deny that, candidly appraised, his situation offered little or no hope: he was the bondservant of overmastering sexual urges. He could, however, realistically hope for moral conversion from the all-caring God who had drawn him, by his intellectual turnaround, step by step closer. After being impressed for a short space by the scientific cachet of physical thinkers who analyzed the complexities of visibles but neglected to reason to the invisible God, he cast a critical eye on the vanity, the untruth, of this narrowly immanental explication (5.3.5). From a Neoplatonic vantage point he beheld contingent things as relativized, dependent upon, because coursing from, God and his Word, principles of all creation (7.11.17). He also succumbed briefly to another vanity, the falsity of knowledge-induced self-glorification which God's right hand punctured, directing him to pore over St. Paul, that threw in high relief the humble Savior as the way to salvation (7.21.27). As he ached for full moral reformation, piety, he realized, was wisdom: only unfailing religious practice that denudes the self of egoism harvests the wisdom that is conquest of the lower by higher strivings. There is indeed a wisdom of the philosophers, luminously exposited in Neoplatonic texts, yet salvifically exiguous, powerless to chart, let alone provide, healing of the whole self. To confuse this impractical brand of practical wisdom with the full-fledged wisdom of the Gospel is at bottom fatuous. Those who pretend that abstract categories applied by oneself alone can do duty as the concrete mode of wisdom relying on divine grace are fooling themselves. He had discovered the pearl of great price, Catholic wisdom that wholly saves, purchase of which demands divestiture of sexual desires and the choice of continence. He was experiencing, however, concrete moral doubt; faith-impregnated reason prodded him to say yes while the apparently irresistible attraction of appetite to marital union cried no; he was still remote from the sturdy resolution that surrenders self to celibacy.

Chapter 2: Simplicianus Relates the Conversion of Victorinus

3. So, shortly after reading St. Paul, probably in July, 386, he sought out Simplicianus, whose schooling in theology readied Ambrose for baptism prior to ordination as bishop of Milan (374); a spiritual father who helped instrumentally generate divine life in his soul. Augustine retailed the checkered course of past religio-philosophic misfortunes, described as circuits, wanderings about in a circle without entrance or exit, opposed to a straight-line path to the truth (CD 12.14). As a

member of the Milan Circle, Simplicianus considered Neoplatonist thought in many respects consonant with Christianity. Thinkers of other persuasions such as Stoics and Epicureans philosophize according to the elements of this world, centering almost exclusively on causes in the executive order of nature, the construction of methods for acquiring truth and the standards of moral conduct, whereas Neoplatonists direct primary attention to God as the cause of the universe, the source of truth, and the fount of happiness (CD 8.12), with implicit reference to the transcendent God figuring in all physical, logical, and moral analysis. Because of comparative indifference to God, the writings of more naturalistic thinkers were ridden with fallacies. On the other hand, not only God the Father but also the Word of God are inscribed in between the lines of Neoplatonic texts (7.19.13-4). One Neoplatonist of his acquaintance used to advocate that "In the beginning was the Word," along with the other opening lines of St. John's Prologue, should be written in gold and placed in the most prominent spot in every church (CD 10.29). Unlike pagan counterparts, who dismissed a God in human flesh as an appalling absurdity, Simplicianus was a fervent Catholic as well as a convinced Neoplatonist. Reference to Victorinus as the translator of Neoplatonic works encouraged him to tell the story of this Neoplatonist who humbly gave allegiance to the humble Christ.

Until his meeting with Simplicianus Augustine had tried to unriddle his problems by reading, reflection, and discussion that utilized the empirical test and analysis both a posteriori and a priori. He mustered the tools of dialectic to dismantle Manicheism and to exercise healthy skepticism about the Academics' skepticism. From time to time he had resorted in part to witness; reports of Mani's holiness first deterred him from totally discarding his sect's counter-scientific cosmology (5.5.9); and in the background hovered the ever-present model that was Monica. Here, however, as remarked earlier, witness takes center stage. Recourse to a moving example is only loosely a mode of discourse; loosely, taken objectively, since example dramatically actuates in a condensed fashion the usual types of reasoning; loosely, taken subjectively, since inquiry stimulated by a witness already acknowledges the truths he exemplifies. Its cognitive-appetitive approach, distinct from the inductive and deductive method, may be styled the conductive method; example spurs an existentially vacillating individual to strike out along a new line of conduct that creatively reproduces, without sedulously aping, the performance of the model. Overseeing this strategy was God to whom he owes praise for the grace given Victorinus, which duplicates the praise proclaimed throughout for his own conversion, this in essentials prefiguratively capsulized by the conversion of Victorinus, with the phrase, "great praise for your grace," replicating the opening line of his prose chant of praise, "Great are you, Lord, and greatly to be praised" (1.1.1). A thoroughpaced scholar and a thinker of no mean philosophical acumen, so revered by fellow nobles that he was secularly canonized by erection of his statue in the forum of Trajan,[2] Victorinus paid homage to Osiris[3] and foreign gods like Anubis the barking dog;[4] ironically, the gods that Rome had militarily conquered now religiously vanquished the Rome that pleaded for their subvention and intervention. His baritone voice boomed out his apologia for idolatry so thunderously that opponents quaked. Yet eventually this free citizen of Rome, brushing to one side disdain of former pagan colleagues, did not disdain to become a slave of Christ. The old pagan was renewed as a newborn infant in Christ, rejoicing in the opprobrium of the cross traced on his forehead at baptism.

4. The apostles, symbolized by the heavens that proclaim the glory of God worldwide, are inclined or humble, attributing their potency not to themselves but to the Lord so that his message may thrive in hearts. God touches the mountains that stand for the proud, causing them to emit smoke, that is, to confess their sins(P 143.12). By accommodation, to Simplicianus is deputed the role of an inclined quasi-apostle, disposing the mountain that was Victorinus to discharge smoke, to confess idolatry. The boundless power that drives the whole universe forward moved the mountain that was the aged rhetorician, gently enlightening his mind as he compared Christian texts with pagan writings. When he confided that he now believed, Simplicianus replied that he would reckon him a Christian only when he saw him inside a church, to which Victorinus wittily riposted that walls do not a Christian make; a shrewd rejoinder that traced a fine line between inward and outward observance; shrewd but only partly true, for fealty to the Church entrains worship inside a church. Right in assigning first place to inner belief, he was wrong in not manifesting faith by outer acceptance. Conscience, albeit undoubtedly primary, is a necessary, not a sufficient, condition; secondary, exterior observance is also necessary, a sign that a

Christian functions as a member of a community. Underlying the clever reply was dread of being mocked for enlisting in a low-class cult. Pagans then occupied a worldly peak of power, resplendent in the dignity of Babylon, which represented the kingdom of the devil and pride (2.3.8), demons being directly or indirectly involved in the worship of idols. Babylonians of the spirit were like the cedars of Lebanon, skyey trees to be toppled by the voice of the Lord that thrusts down the proud (P 28.5). In 386 idolatry still flourished but at the time of writing (397) the cedars had been felled; in 394 under Emperor Honorius pagan temples in Carthage were razed and their statues demolished (CD 18.54).

Along with meditating on Scripture, Victorinus went on longing or praying (holy desire is equivalent to prayer [S 80.7]), with the result that he feared God more than man, cognizant that it was not only illogical but immoral in terms of social sin, which is offensive to others (2.5.11), to feel shame about participating in the rites of a humble God, while experiencing no shame about defiling himself in demon-controlled rituals. He gladly suffered moral shame arising from fidelity to truth, a shame that was actually esteem; shame a good man feels from the scorn of the vicious that is a tribute to his virtue. Suddenly, to an overjoyed Simplicianus, Victorinus confided that he would enroll as a catechumen toward supernatural new birth. The bitter reaction of pagans was spiritually unproductive; such works wither away, like the flower planted in arid soil (P 111.8). Unswayed by erstwhile friends' derision, Victorinus renounced paganism as sacrilegious untruth and idolatry as religious nonsense.

5. The liturgy contained a custom peculiar to Rome, not prevalent in Milan or North Africa, which prescribed that the baptismal candidate mount to an elevated place, or platform, on which he recited the Apostles' Creed by heart.[5] Once he rose to profess his faith, any possible chagrin melted away in the fire of an enthusiastic congregation that, murmuring his name, spurred him to proclaim his profession with boundless confidence. His witty half-truth that walls do not a Christian make was irrefutably answered by the existential response of the people who embraced him not by outward but by inward hands, religiously hugging him with a Christian social love that joyed him with an ardor unthinkable in a frigid academic milieu or in the spiritually deadening atmosphere of idolatry.

Chapter 3: Reason for Special Joy over Conversion

6. It is perplexing that more joy is felt over the salvation of hardened sinners whose prospects of salvation look faint than over the salvation of someone whose return to grace seems bright. A like greater joy is excited by the salvation of an individual in greater spiritual peril, under siege from great temptations, than of another not so beleaguered. God himself rejoices more over one repentant sinner than over ninety-nine virtuous individuals. Men experience more abundant joy over the lost sheep recovered, the missing coin found, and the resurrection of the spiritually dead prodigal son. The poignancy of this last miracle of inward healing, which, when preached on, evokes tears in the congregation, moved Augustine to weep in joy, for it sketched in essentials his own conversion to his Father who, clasping him to his bosom, rained kisses on him (8.12.29). God's joy focuses on both sin-prone men and angels glorified by the vision of his face. God stays always the same, and his knowledge mirroring his unchangeable nature is not altered by the differentiation of objects known. Always in an unchanging fashion does he know creatures that do not always exist—only God is eternal while material beings come to be and pass away. Men, who do not live the same forever, spiritually fluctuate, now sinning, now being cleansed by saving grace.

7. Again raising the question, now slightly modified, he wonders why the soul itself (not as in the foregoing section, an observer of the soul) feels more delight in losing, then regaining, goods than in uneventfully retaining them. Instances in sectors other than the spiritual corroborate this fact, which will shortly yield a psychological pattern: a good is more appreciated when struggled for, when its loss is temporarily threatened, when it is actually lost before recovery. Victory tastes sweet to the general because he has fought the war; and the more menacing the danger, the more exultant the triumph.[6] Sailors who survive a storm-tossed episode prize their lives more than if they had crossed a calm sea. When a formerly gravely ill loved one is still not fully recuperated, friends rejoice more over his recovery than when he walked about well. At times some deliberately undergo prior discomfort to enhance the pleasure to come. As folk wisdom has it, hunger is the best sauce; after lengthy abstinence even bread and water savor of the nectar of the gods. So at times drunkards eat salty

foods that by, increasing thirst, maximize pleasure in drinking. In certain cultures it is customary for brides-to-be to delay the wedding date to ensure that fiancés will not rate their marital union cheaply.

8. The inductive method detects a general rule operative in a wide range of instances of achieving joy. In drunkards wallowing in their cups, in morally sanctioned delights of nuptial union, in the purest of friendships (in which absence makes the heart grow fonder), and in the prodigal son dead and resurrected, a universal law obtains: the greater the prior pain, the greater the ensuing joy. This oscillation has to be squared with the ever-the-same joy of God. God is his own everlasting joy in which angels in heaven unceasingly share, yet in the lower order there is no uninterrupted joy but an ongoing swing from decline to progress, from loss to gain, from pain to pleasure, a continuing alternation between confrontation and reconciliation, between conflict and harmony. In contradiction to Manichean theory, this shift from one pole to another does not prove that the lower region is an accursed realm subjugated by forces of the Prince of Darkness. The law of alternation between lack and satisfaction is actually good, expressing their mode of being, their limited determination as material things. Though different from beings in a higher order, they are not inherently warped. Not as steadfast as higher beings, they are nonetheless good, but good in their own way, according to the measure of their being. It is the one and the same all-providing God who guides every part of the universe, each in the mode appointed. In planning and execution he establishes in their proper places all types of good substances, along with their distinctive operations, everything from the heights of heaven to the depths of the earth, from highest angel to tiniest worm. Moreover, he superintends all times, from the beginning to the end of the world, directing every movement from the first to the last in the history of the universe, appointing the times of specific and individual operations, which include the beginning and the end of the life-span of individual things (the worm is outlived by man, and man, on his bodily side, by the never-dying angels). Earlier he put his finger on the law of succession governing material things: the beauty of material creation is wrought only through the birth, growth, and death of things. (4.10.15). Here he catches sight of a kin law, that of alternation between lack and satisfaction. Both laws spring from the special mode of being, the mutability of things rooted in matter. Lack, decline, death, and decay

are not substantially evil factors but features of a substantially good universe in which all things are exquisitely designed for his good by the all-wise One.

The all-enveloping sweep of the omnipresent God strikes him with awe and contrition. God, who is highest in the highest beings such as angels, is the deepest in the lowest things such as worms. His mind-staggering immanence also educes a twinge of sorrow. In his immanence God is always intimately present even in those who reject his presence. A solution of the apparent paradox, recall, distinguishes two species of presence (1.2.2-3.3). God is always present by nature, never leaving persons because his power sustains them in being, but in the line of grace those who resist his will split off from the ever-present One within. Turning his back on the God who by nature never leaves him, the obstinate sinner absents himself from the ever-present God.

Chapter 4: Reason for Greater Joy over the Conversion of a Famous Man

9. In a prayer not of the struggler toward conversion but of the autobiographer, Augustine beseeches the Lord to summon him back to his presence. God's grace precipitates man's love for him, first, by arousing the heart from its unspiritual slumber; second, by enkindling the first movement of responsive love; third, by bearing the soul up to his bosom, whose fragrance lures: ablaze with such love, the heart does not stroll but races into the heart of God.

At first blush, however, the general law of rejoicing–the greater the antecedent pain or displeasure, the greater the consequent joy–seems somewhat less than general, for apparently the law does not cover ordinary individuals less celebrated than Victorinus, whose prior spiritual malaise was much more grievous than his. Though their distress was greater, plainly the rejoicing that followed was less rather than more than that attending his conversion. Still, the general law of rejoicing, Augustine holds, remains intact, but the specific amount of joy exhibited by fellow Christians depends on the relative station and influence of the new convert. First, the conversion of a public figure kindles rejoicing in more individuals simply because he is more widely known. Second, the larger the group affected, the more intense the rejoicing. Size increases intensity, and intensity, in turn,

sets the group even more aglow, joy spreading like wildfire, inflaming
each and all. Third, a convert of high status will directly or indirectly
encourage the conversions of others; so those exultant over the
conversion of a Victorinus were also rejoicing in expectation of others
who would be persuaded to follow in his steps.

Another difficulty crops up. Stress on the value of prestigious
converts seems to lend countenance to so-called respect of persons,
assigning special place and privilege to the wealthy and highborn; a
strategy seemingly opposed to the makeup of the Church, which, as
Paul tells us, is drawn principally not from the ranks of the rich and
noble but from the downtrodden and disadvantaged. However, Paul
himself at the conversion of Sergius Paulus, proconsul or governor of
Cyprus, undercuts the charge of favoritism. When the court magician
tried to draw Paulus away, Paul, through the Holy Spirit, struck his
adversary blind, prompting Paulus, astonished by Paul's work and
word, to become a Christian, with the consequence that from this
time on, Acts names the Apostle Paul rather than Saul. Augustine
perceives not a coincidence but a causal nexus between Paulus'
conversion and the Apostle's change in name; since God had
wrought the submission of a dignitary like a Roman proconsul to the
humble Christ, Paul assumed a new name to signalize this spiritual
triumph in a spirit of humility, Paul signifying "little" (SL 7.12). In the
spiritual conquest of a high-ranking convert God wins a double
victory. Such conversion entails the overcoming of more swollen
pride presumably betokened by more elevated rank; the switch to
Christ of a man of status is likely to influence those of lesser authority.
Hence in its more abundant rejoicing the Church is not celebrating a
worldly notable as such but strictly his special conversion in which
the mighty brings himself low, identifying with a community
comprised of mostly baseborn nondescripts. Apart from historical
and geographical incidentals, the case of Victorinus is in essentials
similar to that of Paulus. His haughty mind an apparently unassailable
redoubt of the devil, he was caparisoned not with political but
immense rhetorical authority, whose eloquent tongue functioned as a
sword of Satan to slay many by enticing them into idolatry. Christian
hearts rang with more vibrant joy because the triumph was splendid
to behold: an apparently unconquerable fortress is captured by Jesus
the King who, binding the strong man, the devil,[7] takes possession of
the vessel of wrath named Victorinus. He purifies him into a vessel of

election (S 71.3), transforming the tongue that warred for darkness into a weapon for truth, so that the quasi-pastoral authority of a Victorinus prepared for every good work (S 137.11) would spread God's word unto his glory.

Perhaps prefigured here is a greater than Victorinus: unconsciously Augustine may have been prophesizing the worldwide impact of his own conversion. In 386 he possessed no high rank or celebration of literary prowess, yet embedded there was the potential to flower out and fructify. In 418 the sometimes acidulous Jerome hailed him as the second founder of the faith (E 195), a generous appreciation ratified by history; for some sixteen hundred years Western Christianity has revered him as the premier extra-Scriptural authority. Devil-induced pride overthrown, this mastermind, who had tricked many into Manicheism, was transformed into an arsenal for truth. The former vessel of wrath was elected for God's glory in a full pastoral way, for every good work, especially the analyses lighting up nearly every domain of theology. The extent of rejoicing over his conversion was severely limited (8.12.30), an initial sparseness more than compensated for by the ongoing joy over his conversion throughout the Christian era.

Chapter 5: Conflict between Higher and Lower Self

10. Augustine expresses the pith of the conductive method: he burned to imitate Victorinus. Precisely for this operational end, Simplicianus narrated Victorinus' conversion; the goal of a witness is not assent to a proposition but resolve for similar action. Furthermore, Victorinus had displayed self-denial and courage. When in 363 Julian the Apostate decreed that no Christian could teach literature or oratory, rather than desert his faith Victorinus bravely resigned his teaching post, electing the always efficacious Word of God rather than the often shallow word of man. His courage was rewarded by the blessing of God; no longer tied down to teaching, he was free to channel all his resources into writing and speaking in behalf of the Church. This happy turnabout, it seems suggested, may count as one more instance of the divine chemistry that confects good out of evil. While Augustine sighed or prayed to walk after Victorinus, he could not take a single practical step because he was shackled not by leg irons but by a will ironclad in lust.

Diabolical instigations had indirectly fashioned a chain from his will, which bound him tight. Notice, the will is not enchained; rather, here the will itself is the chain: his will was an instrument of slavery, crippling every good action. At the outset of activity the soul partly wounded by original sin is saddled with concupiscence or inordinate tendency. If concupiscence is not controlled, the soul caves in to libido or evil desire,[8] in particular, unchaste desire. Repeated submission to unchaste desires generates a habit of lust. Finally, ongoing capitulation to evil habit induces necessity. As an individual is naturally necessitated to seek food, drink, and sleep, so a person fettered by vice is inwardly driven to pursue an illicit good. A long-standing vice effectively balks any counter-tendency; a man steeped in vice can do no other. Thus four causally connected links constitute a vitiated will: concupiscence, warped desire, habit, and necessity. This is the pitiable lot of sin-dominated man: he is from sin, toward sin, for the sake of sin (P 57.4). From sin: as the heir of Adam, he comes from sin or is born in original sin; toward sin: concupiscence forges a bent toward evil; for the sake of sin: warped desire plunges him into sin, which, become entrenched in habit, is vice as imperiously demanding as necessity.[9]

So enchained, Augustine's spirit was condemned to a cruel slavery domineered by necessity, poles apart from the free servitude under the reign of charity got by grace (P 99.8). His fledgling new will was aiming to serve God unencumbered by self-interest that awards primacy to sexual pleasure or worldly honors; and through that loving service he was aiming at joy; God was to be his absolute source of delight, absolute, because the divine is immutable. Lamentably, his new desire could not eradicate his old will, affixed unshakably, apparently, in moral perversity. Conflict raged between the old or carnal will and the new or spiritual will, with the discord rivening his soul; civil war divided the one self into two warring camps. The intractability of habits is forcibly, perhaps a bit extravagantly, caught in the exclamation of the Duke of Wellington: "Habit a second nature? Habit is ten times nature." Habits are refractory to change because layer after layer is formed by a continual series of acts, each of which "in scientific literalness" is never wiped out.[10] Pathetic figures like hapless alcoholics and drug addicts of our own day illustrate that Augustine is not overstating the ironlike clamp in which a vicious will enchains the self, making it not master but bondservant of passions, as enslaved in the spiritual realm as on the physical plane were prisoners bound to forced labor in an ancient silver mine or in a Stalinist Gulag.

11. Here Augustine inductively verified what he had earlier read in Gal 5.17 but not in the Neoplatonists, the truth that flesh and spirit are locked in combat within the same personality. In one way the victim of this conflict, in a truer sense he was responsible for the battle of flesh against spirit.[11] Aspiring to rise higher, he was yanked downward by the dead weight of past sexual license. From one angle, he suffered sexual sins unwillingly, a marionette of passions-controlled habit. Passivity stemming from habit, however, was a secondary component, which did not absolve him from essential answerability. It was he who had actively willed to commit sins that bulked into the massive force of habit; it was he who was the protagonist in the drama of self-formation or, in this case, self-deformation. Through sexual encounters over roughly sixteen years he had constructed the gyves hobbling him. Only because of unrelenting willing of illicit goods had he reached this point of tension when his new will opposed these wrongful goods. Since his present character was of his own molding, he could not whine that he was a victim of injustice. The punishment for original sin is sin; the punishment for repeated sin is a sinful state, a quasi-automatic impulse to sin again and again. Nor could he, even in part, acquit himself of blame, as he had in the past, because he was without a sure hold on the truth. He vividly saw what he was obliged to do, while failing in the actual doing. Here, without explicitly adverting to it, Augustine is invoking the empirical test to abjure the so-called Socratic error, the opinion (widespread, we commented earlier, among some intelligentsia in the twentieth century) that knowledge is virtue, that once a person learns that a particular mode of conduct is right, he will inevitably choose it. His experience, which seems to be that of every man, contravenes the equation, knowledge = virtue. No matter how convincing the moral knowledge, the will can ignore the dictates of reason and elect otherwise. Practical knowledge and training in values, however precious, do not of themselves suffice for sound conduct; were moral education sufficient, the acquisition and retention of moral virtues would pose no more difficulty than mastering geometry, and, like Augustine, the vast majority of men would not have to struggle, futilely undergoing defeat after defeat in the quest for virtue. Certitude about God and the

way to him were not adequate to guarantee the discipline that would snap the chains of a servile self. He refused to be a soldier of God; he was not morally pledged to a virtuous mode of life dispositive to baptism, considered the moment of enlistment in the army of Christ. Freighted with earthly concerns that were like bulky military equipment, he was nevertheless loath to be relieved of what afforded so much sheer pleasure. While in God's army he would no longer be saddled with such paraphernalia, misgivings about being so loaded down were outbalanced by fear of forfeiting carnal delights indissociable from the baggage.

12. The weight retarding his progress is now designated *sarcina*, perhaps an analogous reference to the backpack weighing some sixty pounds (containing food, utensils, weapons, and so forth) that a Roman legionary carried on the march. In any event, whether or not specifically a backpack, the burden issued not in a grinding but a sweet pressure, comparable to the pleasant grip that continuance of slumber offers. His meditations on throwing off the burden were unstrenuous, like the half-hearted attempts of a slugabed cozily stealing a few extra winks. Absolutely sure that charity was superior to cupidity, he could not translate this abstract certitude into concrete resolution. His spiritual sloth was the opposite of the steeliness of will undergriding self-donation, which charity demands. Mere assent to general truth cannot overleap the gap separating it from particular choice opting for actual living of the law of divine love. Cherishing charity as an abstract ideal but morally reckless, he knuckled under, in fact, to wayward desire. The concrete yes of his will caved in to cupidity, eventually rendering him a prisoner of his lower self. Laziness of spirit muffled an active response of the sleeping soul to the call of Christ to wake from the dead. Such spiritual resurrection worked through righteousness due to grace is exemplified in the now sober ex-drunkard raised from the death of drunkenness to the risen life of sobriety (S 362.20.23 - 21.24). The call of Christ to a resurrected life of grace sounded fuzzy to his drowsy moral consciousness. Certain of the Catholic vision and modus vivendi, he could summon up only a feeble mumbling of intention to do good soon, in a little while; a gesture toward action virtually vacuous; "soon" never came and "a little while" stretched out interminably. The promise of definite action was a ruse of rationalization, a species of self-deception. The indecisiveness of the spiritually procrastinating

Augustine betrayed a pronounced will to fail: he simply did not want to abandon pleasures of the flesh. His morally fruitless state was the consequence of the law of sin that was the deep-seated power of habit. Long-standing habit is characterized by force that compels an individual to act contrary to his will. Whereas the violence of waves pounding a storm-battered ship can sweep a passenger overboard, an event for which he is not responsible, Augustine's actions were not totally involuntary. It was not unkind nature or perverse circumstances that swept him off his abstractly desired course; he was driven now to act against his will only because he had willed again and again to bow to warped desires (8.5.11). The punishment of violence was self-inflicted; he was the victim of his own moral folly. Manacled in irons of his own making, he existentially lived the bitter truth of Paul's cry for spiritual freedom. The light of the abstractly envisaged ideal of the interior self unbared the exterior man wasted away as a corpse by deadly sins.

Chapter 6: Ponticianus Relates a Monastic Conversion

13. Augustine was soon to arise spiritually from the dead through quickening by the Spirit (8.12.29). The path to his moral conversion was smoothed by the example of two imperial police officers who suddenly entered monastic life. His horizons were again expanded by witness, beckoning his soul to passionate, that is, intensely affective, commitment to life-altering conduct. Metaphysical truths and moral canons are not deprecated; their perplexities by and large resolved, they await the concrete application latent within their themes. This crux of existential determination demands not further analysis but spiritually bold action. Further philosophical musings at this juncture would be trivial or irrelevant, tantamount to spinning cobwebs or beating the air.

He praises God, whose redeeming grace was to incinerate the chains of desire for concubinage, indeed for all fleshly union, and, in addition, to dissolve longings for wealth and honor. Because primary, seemingly invincible bondage of the flesh receives most of the attention in the next seven chapters. Once he was released from slavery to sex, the cheating charm of the world also vapored off. Along with Alypius and Nebridius, he was still searching for practical wisdom, meditating in a church during times he could scrape from increasingly taxing official duties. Alypius, no longer an assessor, was hunting for clients in his law practice, to whom he might sell counsel as Augustine had formerly hawked the skill of speaking[12]–if indeed teaching can furnish an individual with the skill. Here Augustine may be alluding to his theory of education, according to which the human teacher does not strictly teach; rather, recall, it is the inner teacher, truth itself, that illumines the mind in the principles of an art (LA 2.2.4). On the other hand, perhaps he is simply recognizing that natural aptitude is a prerequisite; while the teacher can help develop this skill in the talented, the most sophisticated pedagogical techniques cannot beget the art in a student minus the proper assets. *Quod Deus non dat, Salmantica non praestat*: what God does not give, Salamanca (the university) does not bestow. No voice teacher can school a tone-deaf man to rise to lead tenor at the Metropolitan Opera. Correspondingly, as rhetoricians acknowledge, nature is essential in the shaping of an orator. It is practically impossible to communicate skill in speaking to an individual unhappily deficient in natural qualities of intelligence, memory, ear, and voice, a fact that did not escape Augustine's insight as he toiled at Carthage and Rome to make rhetorical silk purses out of sows' ears.

Nebridius, the third in the amical triumvirate, was hired by Verecundus (9.5.5) to assist in his secondary school for rhetoric and literature. Well-to-do in his own right, he could have easily secured a more advanced position for the exercise of his literary proficiency. Strictly self-disciplined with a remarkable force of character, he was generous to a fault, deferential and easygoing. As touched on before, his was a no-nonsense mind so singlemindedly dedicated to pursuit of truth that, by design, he avoided any waste of time that cultivation of influential Milanese might entail; economical of his free time, he spent every possible moment in the quest for wisdom.

14. When Ponticianus, a devout African Catholic attached to the imperial court, recounted the life of Antony (c. 250-356) (reputed to be the founder of monasticism), who had died only some thirty years before, a witness to the authentic Catholic faith, Augustine and Alypius were lost in wonderment over the incredible deeds worked in and through him. In a variant sense of wonderment, Ponticianus wondered why they wondered; he was puzzled that they were marveling over Antony for the first time; he could hit on no reason why these well-educated gentlemen were totally ignorant of the

widely circulated story.

15. Large numbers elected desert monasticism, where under a ascetic regimen they tasted sweetness of spirit. Through the inner rain of waters of the Spirit the desolate wilderness blossomed with divine virtues and gifts. Nor was monasticism confined to the East; on the outskirts of Milan there flourished a monastery under the jurisdiction of Ambrose. Indeed astonishing conversion stories were not unheard of in the West. Ponticianus told of an unexpected turn to the monastic way of *agentes in rebus,* government inspectors who sometimes functioned in part as a kind of secret police or collectors of inteligence but more frequently as members of a government communications apparatus.[13] Coming upon a small monastic community in Trier, their eyes were caught by a *Life of Antony.* One of them was at once so inflamed with longing for monastic holiness that his old life seemed squalid in comparison with the richness of monastic interiority. His new lifestyle, he warmly perceived, would guarantee him salvation as one of the friends of the heavenly king while his present occupation offered him hope for rank no higher than that of one of the "friends of the emperor," an inner circle of imperial advisers that had the monarch's ear[14] a select group that formed a kind of privy council. However, this lofty position was unstable; personal disgrace swiftly banished the privileged from the inner circle. By contrast, friendship with God is not restricted to a few but is available to all who faithfully obey the will of God (GCM 1.2.4). It is not attained by high-level interventions but is achieved immediately as long as man commits himself to God. Not a fragile position, easily lost through adverse publicity, it is relatively long lasting. The ardor of the first official then fired his companion to become one with him immediately in monastic life. In accord with the lesson of Lk 14.28 ff., they were ready to make the proper outlay, to renounce all, so as to erect the tower that represents the full life of faith of the complete disciple of the Lord (S 301A.2). Apprised of this radical vocational switch, Ponticianus and his companions, however, decided to forgo a monastic calling, returning to the palace as the new monks-to-be adapted to their primitive monastic cottage. Their hearts clung abjectly to earth while the hearts of the fledging religious soared upward, transported to things not of this world. The remarkable tale is idyllic to the very end; when the women to whom the officers had been engaged learned of their fiances' choice, they also consecrated

their virginity to the Lord, possibly joining a monastery of nuns.

Chapter 7: Inner Face Seen Deformed

16. Augustine experienced the truth of Ps 49.21: "I will set you before your face." He had been concealing his true self behind his back, out of sight of his inner self, but the real state of his soul was not behind but directly in front of conscience, the tribunal of his mind which functioned as judge of his wicked self (P 49.28). How hideous was his perverse self, chewed up by a sort of malodorous cancer that, mottling his complexion, left him pierced with running sores. While outwardly Ponticianus was dilating on the self-sacrifice of the imperial functionaries, inwardly God pressed his eyes open, forcing him to perceive himself as repulsive. Blinkered to his grisly inner face, he had, like many, imagined himself embodying his ideals, in this case, a well-heeled government official, renowned for oratorical brilliance, happily married to an affluent wife, a principled citizen conferring benisons on family and society. Now, however, this self-portrait looked fanciful in the light of divine truth, which flashed before his consciousness not his imaginary self but his actual disfigured countenance. Subconsciously somewhat cognizant of his befouled condition, he had deliberately suppressed gleams of self-knowledge. Now as he recoiled from his shocking sickness, every subterfuge was pitilessly stripped away.

17. His inner ugliness appeared all the more revolting when measured against the candent purity of the two officers; in the perspective of their renunciation, even the tiniest defilement stood out in bold relief; the more captivating their self-donation, the more abhorrent his twisted visage looked. The malformation did not take its rise the day before yesterday but was the gruesome outcome of a prolonged spiritual procrastination. The flow of time, which differs from never-changing eternity, may allude to the common measurement by water-clock (11.2.2). Significantly, the years are said to have flown with himself; his moral self, not yet stabilized in God, was still tossed about by passions centered on earthly objects, dominated by the moral time that betokens the disintegrated self (11.29.39).

He quickly reviews with regret his protracted will to fail. In 373, perhaps twelve years before (the figure may be actually thirteen or close to thirteen, for he made the acquaintance of Ponticianus in August, 386), *Hortensius* inflamed him with enthusiasm for wisdom (3.4.7). Even apart from secure possession the sheer search for wisdom is more precious than full satisfaction in the triple concupiscence. The amassing of treasures, hegemony over various nations, and indulgence in fornication at whim cannot match the intrinsic value of the very pursuit of wisdom. The felicity promised by worldly goods was effectively next to nothing, but he felt helpless to deny himself them for the sake of wisdom. Two lions, one moral, the other doctrinal, blocked the path from aspiration to actual possession of wisdom. The chief moral barrier was the wisdom, really the unwisdom, of the flesh, lust that yoked his higher self to the erotic impulses of the lower self (8.5.10). At the start of adolescence (373) he had begged divine assistance in the now well-known, all-too-human prayer expressive of the contending pulls in his sundered nature: "Lord give me chastity and continence–but not yet." However we may smile, this is an ambivalent prayer to which the experience of the ordinary Christian concretely relates, one that captures the simultaneous upward thrust and downward drive of the self. Abstractly, he longed to master his habitual proclivity for carnal union; concretely, he preferred that hot desires be satisfied in ongoing sexual encounters. Extinction in his guardedly nuanced assertion does not savor of the Stoic ideal commanding annihilation of passions; his higher self aimed not at eradication of the passion itself but total suppression of its aberrant exercise. The doctrinal obstruction to wisdom was the pseudo-wisdom of Manicheism, a phony rationalism that, railing against the credulity of orthodox Catholics, claimed to ground its teachings on reason alone yet, in fact, exacted from its followers belief in fables and astronomical incoherences (BV 1.4,5). A superstition barren of all reasonable support, it was sacrilegious, a quasi-idolatry that reverenced God as consubstantially present in fig trees and their fruit (3.10.18). He was not attracted toward but detested Catholicism because he had neglected to investigate its tenets with piety, in prayer-impregnated, honest inquiry. Deterred by arrogance from discovering the meaning of Catholicism from one of its educated adherents, he contented himself with understanding (which was nothing short of grossly misunderstanding) it through the distorting lens of Manichean apologetics. Instead of fairly querying Catholicism with an open

mind, he trashed it with savage polemics, resembling a barking dog
spewing out hate-filled prejudices (9.14.11).

18. After concluding that he could no longer hold incertitude liable
for inability to check wayward desire for carnal union (8.5.11), he
similarly recognized that incertitude is a lame excuse for not
overcoming worldly ambition.[15] After the witness of the imperial
agents shredded his moral defense mechanism, he was sure, as much
as they, that service of God was far superior to the summit of wordly
achievements. Nevertheless, his soul was obstinately balking at
conforming to the clear dictate of the mind. So before his inner eyes
his soul was divested of its dodges, in the penetrating light of the
example of the officials whose self-deprivation livingly refuted his
self-indulgence. Thus his conscience or inner moral self called him to
account: "Where is your tongue?" In other words, if this is the
affirmation of your will, what stops you from voicing an uncompromising yes to what you see you ought to do? The alibi that the
justification of God's service was less than certain was clearly
groundless. Abstractly, he perceived the fatuity of the fevered chase
after rank and honor. Simply one quiet, concrete yes to goods of the
higher self, and this taxing burden would drop from his shoulders.
The shuffling of his intransigent will, which kept him dragging along
in the dust of earthly ambition, looked odd over against the
immediate strength of will of those officers who did not wear
themselves to a frazzle by investigating every possible angle. Obeying
grace-illumined conscience, they took flight to upward life not by
lengthy disputation but by superterrestrial wings earned by freeing
themselves of wordly ambitions. While the figure of wings may be an
allusion to *Phaed.* 249[16] according to which the philosopher so
equipped can ascend more quickly to higher truths, more probably
he is touching on a point remarked before, that some who are
unskilled in the arts but aglow with the highest charity fly above
dialectical paths to lay hold of wisdom (M 6.1.1). The two wings
bearing the soul up to God are love of God and love of neighbor.
Unlike the irksome weight of ambition, their burden is light because
love from the Holy Spirit descends into the human spirit,
empowering it to lift upward in divine love (P 67.18; 54.8). It was
divine love, for which renunciation of status and prestige readied
them, that bewinged the imperial officers. The cross-questioning of
conscience biting into his carnal self released a terrible shame at the

spectacle of his morally absurd life: hearkening to the higher call was choked off by his lower self; men of little advanced education flew to the heights while worldly ambitions held his cultivated mind in thrall.

Once Ponticianus departed, Augustine's first or moral self faced down his second or carnal self. His moral self furiously berated his soul, the self tyrannized by ambition, scourging its carnal counterpart with stinging arguments, against which the lower self mounted a series of shoddy retorts. After the lower self had exhausted its counter-arguments, all of which were deftly confuted, its rebuttals ceded place to a fear that cringed at the prospect of forfeiture of ambition: removal of the worldly ambition that ensouled his status was tantamount to social death. A pall of anxiety enveloped him when he pictured himself suffering the disgrace of severe loss of income, if not penury, and reduction in class; existence empty of ambition would be the dreadful life of a social corpse, a life without a life. Control of the flux of habit, an instability stabilized only in God's law (4.11.16), apparently spelled social doom. Ironically, in drawing back from stability, he was reinforcing a habit causing his soul to wither to the point of spiritual destruction. Dread of social death precipitates decline into a denouement more dreadful—spiritual death; avoidance of a social tomb accelerates slippage into a spiritual grave.

Chapter 8: Inner Turmoil in the Garden

19. The emotional storm that was inwardly buffeting him burst out in the open. The fight his higher self was waging against his lower self, the rebel that commanded his conduct, flashed in full view to an astonished Alypius. In the past, however inwardly tormented, he had kept the even tenor of his ways, remaining outwardly composed. Now he was beside himself, his equipoise in tatters as he cried out his inner turmoil. He was chagrined that he and Alypius stayed submerged in the flesh while uneducated functionaries were taking heaven by violence (P 86.6).[17] Notice, he speaks of himself and Alypius "with our doctrines, without mind (*sine corde*)." Unhappily, one erudite Augustinologist translates the phrase as "heartless doctrines." However, since here *cor* means mind, Augustine is, somewhat elliptically, making the point: our learning lacked an adequate mind, meaning that the mind was not properly focused on

spiritual goods. No opposition could withstand the force of the resistless faith of the unlettered as they conquered the promised land. Far from it being a mortifying shame for the learned to imitate the unlearned, it would be ignominious if they did not walk in their footsteps. The tinge of scholarly elitism, which may color Augustine's exhortation to his friend, is partly explicable by his earlier overrating of the eudaemonistic value of learning. According to his opinion prior to 395, recall, cultivation of liberal arts functioned as one golden key dispositive to virtue and to wisdom capped by the vision of God somehow obtainable in this life. Hence the fact that the uneducated could rule lower desires more readily than the educated seemed to border on the paradoxical. His body language articulated his turbulence of soul more clearly than words. He was simply not himself; all his wonted calm was scattered into agitation, personal and professional equanimity giving way to fevered eruptions. His outer persona took on a drastically transmogrified appearance: his brow became furrowed, his cheeks reddened, his face flushed, his eyes darted nervously to and fro, his voice quavered, the trembling interlaced with anguished sobs. Alypius, thunderstruck, was speechless in the presence of a friend he had never before observed so gravely shaken. Though possessed of histrionic talents cleverly deployed in the oratory favored in his day, Augustine never let oratorical style obtrude upon ordinary conduct. Not only averse to stooping to self-dramatization, he rarely wore his heart on his sleeve. Hence, Alypius was keenly aware, Augustine's strange outcries and his fidgety expressions betrayed an extraordinary crisis tearing his heart apart.

To ensure privacy while soothing his troubled spirit, he retired to a small garden attached to the house, where no outsider would eavesdrop as he waged his fierce contest against his lower self. Alypius was not an intrusive presence but a second self voluntarily one with Augustine's soul, silently making his own Augustine's upheaval as he elsewhere shared his joys, so appropriating Augustine's solitude that Augustine did not cease to feel alone; a tower of strength tendering the support of love during Augustine's affective disequilibrium. Unbeknownst to Augustine, God was preparing his soul for a climactic point in which he would vault beyond the horizon of temporal goods. Thus his emotional madness was potentially a program of healing, his spiritual dying potentially a higher form of living, the evil he was throbbingly conscious of potentially the good in which he was soon to rejoice. Once again inimitable goodness and illimitable power were setting the stage for reaping good out of evil (as frequently noted, a persistent subtheme in the overriding theme of providence). Augustine's life incarnates one cardinal answer to the problem of evil: God permits evils in his life only in order to tap them for good. His biography portrays him as a kind of living spiritual miracle: evil is a continual fount of good because an all-bountiful God goes on working the naturally impossible; the bad tree of his life produces not only bad fruit but good fruit, some of which supernaturally springs from the bad fruit.

Angry with himself because he could not actually commit himself to God, all his bones, his whole spiritual self in terms of right relationship with God (P 34 [En.1.S.1].14), cried out that he should fully consent to the law in love. Yet he felt inwardly thwarted, like a man rendered mute by temporary paralysis, eager to say yes but unable to pronounce the clinching word. No vehicle bearing him over sea or land was necessary (1.18.28),[18] for the soul moves not by outer spatial transit but by interior affection. Notwithstanding enormous desire that needed no external apparatus, he could not utter a definitive yes. Augustine quickly points out the reason for the baffling indecisiveness that propelled him to seethe with indignation. His willing was not strong and whole; more precisely, his will was weak because it was not integral or whole. His will was split in two, semi-wounded, one part sound, the other sick, torn between the good toward which his higher self sped him and the lower goods toward which his lower self was dragged. His willing was not wholly trained on the higher good; because pulled in opposing directions, his will was weak. Further analysis arrives at the same conclusion below (8.9.21).

20. Reflecting on the problem afresh, he remarks the surprising divergence between the will's command of bodily movements and its inability at times to command itself. In his disgust over his irresolution, he struck his forehead or clasped his knees with locked fingers. The movement of members under the direction of the will seems almost automatic; performance straightway follows command, except when the movement is impossible or hampered, as in the case of amputees, prisoners with arms and legs in irons, or the seriously ill either deprived of energy or crippled by a stroke. In bodily

movements the willing (*velle*) is not the same as the power (*posse*) to move. As just mentioned, some defect in mobility could prevent the bodily members from heeding the dictate of the will. Yet so long as the members are healthy and unimpeded, the power of movement is the immediate upshot of his willing. In the will itself the willing and power to act are existentially or concretely identical. The desire of the will and the inward execution of the desire are aspects of one and the same will. It would seem then that the will's desire (*velle*) would be followed without fail by the power to act (*posse*). But, in fact, this is strangely not the case. Though the bodily members are distinct and separate from the will, the body can be relied on to obey the will more readily than the will to obey itself. Oddly, the will more easily commands the arm than it commands itself, i.e., it more readily commands outward execution than it commands the inward execution of its desire. The act of the will is called great, not because it cannot be badly used (LA 2.19.50) but because the will, while only an intermediate good, is a spiritual entity, superior to lower sensory powers or bodily agencies.

Chapter 9: Two Wills due to Diseased Will

21. Augustine initially characterizes the behavior of the will as monstrous, a phenomenon unnatural or counter-natural; in failing to carry out its own commands, the mind operates against its own nature. A mind that acts contrary to its own inclination is not self-commanding but self-crippling; a sort of freak, as unnatural as normal eyes that block seeing, healthy ears that foil hearing, or legs that not only do not walk but inhibit walking. Twice more he poses the question: whence or why this evil? What is the root reason for this unnatural phenomenon? Renewing his probing, he raises, then discards, the possibility that the darkness of mind that is the punitive legacy of Adam's sin foredooms the outcome of his inquiry. Perhaps implied here is the suggestion that the self-defeating mind itself, which is traceable to original sin (5.9.16), may be one of the riddlesome sorrows the flesh of Adam is heir to. After approaching the problem anew, he again points to the nub of the question. The body right away heeds the mind, with obedience so swift that dictate of will and execution by the body can be scarcely discriminated. A fortiori, we would expect, the mind should forthwith inwardly

execute the command of the mind. Yet frequently the opposite is the case. Mind mutinies against mind, obstinately refusing to carry out its own command. Through this absurd and unnatural move the mind apparently short-circuits its own activity. How, he repeats, can we account for naturally incoherent behavior in which the mind issues a command, then balks at compliance with its own dictate? Without engaging in further dialectical maneuvers, he simply supplies the key to the baffling anomaly, a solution already generally stated (8.8.19). The paradox is resolved by the insight that the willing of the will is not whole and entire; his will is a divided will. Since it does not totally will, it does not totally command. Insofar as it wills, it commands; the fault then lies in the will: the will, not some other will, commands; where there is resistance, the will itself, not some extrinsic agency, is to blame. Because it is split, because it does not wholly command, its command is not fulfilled but frustrated. If the will is whole and undivided, it does concretely command itself to perform an act; desire and execution are so existentially one in an undivided will that the desire is effectively identical with the inward execution of the desire; in an integral will desire and execution concretely fuse into one act.

Thus rejection by the will of its own command is not an unnatural event. Actually the will never stultifies itself nor negates its own act. Rather, the one will is pulled in diverse directions by opposing volitional tendencies. There is sharp operational disparity: the lower tendency is antagonistic to the tendency to higher goods; but there is no inherent aberration. In part, in terms of higher tendency, the will desires the higher goods of virtue, in this case, those of continence and chastity; yet in part also, in terms of inordinate tendency, it does not yearn for these goods of virtue. The mind then is ruptured, polarized (8.8.14), its affliction consisting in the clash of higher and lower tendencies. The core of the only apparently self-suppressive will lies in its dividedness or, more precisely, in the duality of its counteracting tendencies. The entitatively one will is operationally two, harboring two offsetting volitional inclinations. The ascendant aspiration of the morally light element is contravened by the descendant thrust of the morally heavy impulse.

Chapter 10: Not Two Natures but Two Opposed Desires

22. Next he explicitly censures the Manichean contention that two

natures or substances, one good, the other evil, underlie the willing of
good and evil in and by the one person. The vain talkers and seducers
of the mind are the Manichees, especially those whose fluent case for
vanity or untruth beguiles the unwary and religiously uneducated into
committing themselves to the twisted Manichean way. As was burned
into his memory, he was a religio-philosophically unknowledgeable
victim of their skillfully packaged apologetical legerdemain (3.6.10).
In praying that these glib proselytizers and their co-religionists, who
posit a distinct evil nature or will in man to explain evil behavior will
perish from the face of God (P 67.2), he again underscores that
obduracy in blasphemous superstition banishes Manichees from the
presence of God (P 67.2). Ironically, professing to act as spokesmen of
the good, they are themselves emissaries of evil. Only by disavowing
untruth and pledging fealty to truth, can they, like Augustine, pass
from darkness to light. In purposing to grow by light so as to enter the
Kingdom of Light, Manichees unhappily missed the true light that is
in and through grace diffused by the Lord. Trusting in themselves in
a kind of Pelagian spirit,[19] deeming their good nature or soul divinely
luminous, i.e., consubstantial with God, they strictly needed no
salvation; they had only to discern their divine substance and become
more enlightened by Manichean discipline. However, their error-
ridden pursuit of light transformed them not into light but denser
darkness. The radix of this more engulfing darkness was arrogance
that hardened them like stone in untruth, pride that, in proclaiming
that their blindness was sight, swept them further away from the true
light.

The Manichees were doubly arrogant, in the psychological and
theological sense. In their hauteur they ranked themselves as the
spiritual aristocracy among the scum, points of brilliant light
environed by filthy darkness, who treated disdainfully, or at best with
self-satisfied smiles, the barbarous breed without the pale. The
psychological stemmed from the doctrinal arrogance, whereby they
accredited to themselves a substantial, not an accidental, participation
in the very nature of the Father of Light; a tragically unrealistic
pretension that they were natural-born gods; a delusion experientially
refuted at every turn. He pauses to address salutary admonitions to
Manichees. (i) Realize that, in elevating man to a natural divine state,
you are degrading God to the human plane. (ii) Blush with shame;
shrink in dismay from your arrogance. (iii) Approaching Jesus, and

through him qualitatively sharing in the true light, your countenances, i.e., your souls, will not be ashamed; as with Jesus the light
who was not confounded during his passion, so with the truly
enlightened: affliction will not make them blush with shame (P 33
[S.1].10).

When he was deliberating about surrendering himself completely
to the Lord (8.9.21), it was one and the same self that was willing and
unwilling to take the step; willing according to the upward aspiration
of his higher self, unwilling according to the earth-oriented tug of his
carnal self. His irresolution betokened not a counter-natural disobedience by the will of its very own command but the lack of firm or
integral willing. A battle broke out, in which his higher self was
locked in conflict with his lower self. His will was not whole and one
but severed into two. Still, he was not directly responsible for the
bifurcation within. This involuntariness, we saw, did not spring from
some alien mind, a positively evil, intractable substance that was the
co-resident with and the antagonist of his good nature. The division
was indeed evil, but it was not due to an absurd evil of nature, nor
was it a sin; rather, it was the outcome of sin, the punishment of his
mind: the division, which he did not personally cause, was
bequeathed by the primordial sin of Adam. The sin that dwelt within
him was not an actual sin but a radical concupiscence, a basic
inordinate tendency to sin. Concupiscence was the price of his
solidarity in the human condition, part of his subsidence, his doleful
inheritance as a son of Adam. The division within was the offspring
of the sin of a freer Adam; freer, because created in a state of original
righteousness, in which he was wholly related to God, a state without
concupiscence. Provisionally unhampered by a built-in inclination to
sin, Adam could more easily shun sin, howbeit open to the real
possibility of disobedience rooted in pride, as his eating of the
forbidden fruit proved. In terms of spiritual light, Adam prior to the
Fall was freer than his descendants because he was able not to sin
(*posse non peccare*), while his sons without grace are not able not to sin
(*non posse non peccare*). Grace liberates fallen man; so fortified, his
freedom of choice (*liberum arbitrium*) is able to resist grave sins. The
life to come will endow the soul with a much greater liberty, that of
not being able to sin (*non posse peccare*) (CG 12.33). Tracing the
division back to Adam helps clarify a point raised earlier (8.9.21).
However initially obscure, the cleft in man's moral being is not totally

enshrouded in arcane mystery. Since his condition is not monstrous, it is historically explainable as one upshot of the Fall.

23. He next lays bare some incoherences latent in Manichean dualism. First, if a voluntary tendency opposed to the good is equivalent to an evil nature, the self will house more than one evil nature; there will be as many evil natures as inclinations contrary to the good. Suppose a Manichee is considering whether to go to a Manichean conventicle or to the theater. From a Catholic perspective, both courses of action are evil. Yet in the likely event that the Manichee will object to reproving attendance at his meeting as evil, suppose a Catholic is weighing the pros and cons of either going to church or to the theater. In a Manichean frame of reference, both choices are evil. This double censure, however, lands a Manichee in a dilemma. If he ventures the assertion that a good nature is operative, he is compelled to admit that attendance at a Catholic service is good—a consequent that makes shipwreck of Manichean faith. On the other hand, if he concedes that no good nature is operative but only two bad natures crossing swords, he is, by implication, discarding the standard Manichean contention that only a good and evil nature clash with each other. This disavowal of a eore Manichean theorem might well motivate a thoughtful Manichean to embrace Catholicism since this disclaimer nullifies Manichean denial of the fact that during deliberation the one and only one soul is pulled in opposite directions by contrary inclinations of the will.[20]

24. He multiplies examples confirming the irrationality of Manichean belief in two natures. If two diverse evil inclinations occur, there must be, on Manichean grounds, two evil natures. A murderer may ponder whether to poison or stab his victim; a thief may try to decide whether to steal one part or another of two sections of land; a worldling may debate within whether to indulge in sensuality or to hoard his money; another may have to choose between going to the circus or theater. The pluralism of conceivable bad natures can be extended beyond two.[21] The person undecided about the circus or the theater may also at the same time consider robbing a home or committing adultery; in this instance four evil natures would have to be posited. Indeed in other situations a greater number of evil objects could simultaneously contend for choice.[22] The Manichees do not explicitly pluralize evil substances within; yet this plurality is an embarrassing inconsequence inexorably proceeding

from the opinion that evil is positive and substantial.

Reflection on simultaneous good inclinations also saps the Manichean claim of two contrary substances, one good, the other evil. Suppose three Biblically based religious activities,[23] all good, beckon to the will in diverse directions, with a relative, not contrary, opposition among the inclinations; thus the will is a divided will solely with respect to the good. Diversity and opposition bespeak division without necessitating plurality of substances. The three tendencies are movements in the one soul of good will. To hold otherwise entails the untenable assertion that the three inclinations are at bottom actually three good substances. Truly divergent inclinations surely indicate division, but no less surely the relatively opposing tendencies cannot be substantialized as separate natures. Division vanishes once the will chooses one activity as best here and now. The divided will becomes one and whole by being weighted by its love toward one good. As with a will considering only good objects, so with a will deliberating between good and evil objects: there is no plurality of natures or substances. It is one and the same soul in which dwell diverse inclinations, one drawn by eternal goods above, the other conned by temporal goods below. Unlike the prior situation limited to a selection among goods alone, here the soul is torn between good and evil; morally unsettled and pained, its will is not whole but almost irredeemably divided. Moral truth, the eternal law, invites the soul to the higher way while deeply-ingrained habit, compelling it to stay fastened on lower goods, stops it from throwing off temporal pleasures.

Chapter 11: Victory over Lower Appetites Near but Still Unachieved

25. Augustine movingly portrays his tortured heart, fumblingly reaching toward a higher mode of life, yet continually incapable of grasping the prize. His depiction is scrupulously accurate, in no way flawed by rhetorically uninhibited embellishment. After demolishing the Manichean theory of two wills or natures within the soul, he returns to a description of inward distress that erupted in behavior so eccentric that it perturbed the ordinarily unflappable Alypius (8.8.19). He cuttingly denounced himself for his basically spineless lassitude, his inability to emancipate himself after the fashion of apparently less

gifted individuals. Still, he was not far from escaping bondage. His tormented inner self twisted and stretched itself, spun about and gyrated to loosen the links of the single chain that fettered him until the turning came close to snapping the chain. Some of his feeling of facing inevitable defeat faded in the soul's innermost chambers sealed to all except the inner teacher. He was oxymoronically blessed by God's harsh mercy; harsh, because he was doubly whipped, at once fearful and ashamed of possibly relapsing. This was trepidation contrary to that which seized him when he was appalled by the possible loss of senseless delights that his unshackling entrained (8.7.18). Now he shivered at the thought his loosened bonds would once again be fastened tight. Correlated with his fear was shame: he was aghast as he imagined himself once more in servitude at the bottom of the pit, a despicable slave rather than a partially free man. The whips were wielded by mercy because sternness assured partial success; he would not backslide. Raking up his courage, he steeled his will to more strenuous efforts by self-affirmation and self-stimulation: now is the time, he told himself; put aside pondering; choose right away. With all the psychic energy he could marshal he labored to climb up the incline but fell short, yet without forfeiting any ground. After regaining his breath, he struggled to move upward a second time, this attempt still leaving the goal beyond his compass, still shy of the clinching choice. His indecisiveness stayed him from dying to death, from sentencing to death the reign of inordinate desires; he thereby hesitated to live unto life, as a new man unto full supernatural life. Earlier as a bishop, in the state of grace, he prayed, "Let me die lest I die" (1.5.5), that is, let me continue to put the old self to death. Here he is seeking the death of the fleshly self in the primary sense, change from an evil to a virtuous life, dying to self so as to rise to life with God (S 231.3.). Pertinacious habit checked his desire to utter a liberating yes. The entrenched worse exercised more appeal than the unfamiliar better. The new life that looked charming became, under the pressure of habit, abhorrent. Instead of being pushed rearward in his striving, he was frozen in suspense, not the dialectical doubt of a pragmatic skepticism (6.4.6), but indecision, the affective suspense of a heart at once grasping for and backing away from transformation. Stuck at the crossroads, he could move neither backward nor forward; torn between elevated desire and redoubtable habit, he had no choice but no choice.

26. Crowding in were memories of the temptresses of the past; friends or mistresses, the vanity of those who acted vainly,[24] who were licentuously deceived or deceiving, enchanted him anew. Warmly stroking him, murmuring in honeyed tones not to banish them forever, the pleasure-companions of the spirit even boldly pictured him in lovely sordid practices. Significantly, the memorial images were not only visual but tactual. Touch, the basic sense of objectivity, is the fundamental earthy sense (2.5.10), through which the desires for food and sex are satisfied. Gestures of touch prepare for and precipitate coition, itself an act of deepest tactual intimacy. The memorial tactual phenomena served as agents of a kind of imaginative foreplay to beguile him into reaffirming dedication to sexual gratification. The employment of *in aeternum* in regard to sexual happiness seems telling. If he spurned the paradise of sexual bliss, his life would be turned into a terrestrial hell; without sexual bliss he would be damning himself to an unbearable wasteland of nongratification without end. *In aeternum* is clearly delusive; in fact, immediacy is a hallmark of sexual fulfillment; its heightened but contracted span of pleasure in no way savors of the everlasting. As he fought off the blandishments, susurrus after susurrus grew softer, and his temptresses no longer gazed at him full in the face. Their eyes no longer pools of fire invitingly magnetizing his, they enticingly stroked him from behind, pleading with him to recapture the most ravishing of sensuous delights. Shocked by the putrescence at the core of his wantonness, he, nevertheless, went on wavering, unable to bound upward. Although he now rated former delights the sleaziest of trifles, although he beat back new waves of temptation assaulting his conscience, the grip of habit, albeit more relaxed, made him helpless to live without things that his higher self could not live with. Augustine's unavailing struggle points up anew that while it is unreasonable to pour derision on reason, it is not unreasonable to specify its practical limitations. Of themselves, discernment and exhaustive introspection cannot suppress solicitations of a long-indulged sexual appetite. Contemporary man, with his prepossession for education as the all-potent medication for moral ills, may profitably meditate the lesson that straining for liberation drilled into Augustine. Whatever the light and vigor stiffening resolution to reform, a thousand images of memorially relived seductive pleasures rise up to entrance and even tenderly clasp the soul in the steely

embrace of old habit.

27. As the voice of habit stressing the impossibility of life without sex became fainter, before him suddenly appeared the engaging figure of continence,[25] wooing him in all purity toward a sex-free existence, poised to carry him to heights he could never attain, with blandishments other than coarse, with an embrace uplifting rather than degrading. Noble moral status is not reserved for a rare few; a large number from both sexes, of all ages, of all classes, including widows as well as lifelong virgins, had elected a lifestyle 180 degrees removed from a grim denial of nature. Virginity or continence, it has long been charged, is consecrated sterility; however, far from being sterile, continence is fecund, mother of the joys that are the issue begot through its divine spouse. The virginal union or spiritual marriage of the Lord linked to continence bears fruit in inexpressible spiritual transports. As God separates from the bitter sea of this world descendants of Abraham, made as numerous as the sand on the seashore, so his predilection lures special souls to continence, spiritually multiplying offspring of joy (P 112.8).

The chord is similar to that struck in Victorinus and the two converts to monasticism (8.2.3; 6.15): what these examples of flesh and blood accomplished Augustine can also achieve. It was impossible, the sirens had whispered, impossible to live without sex as without food and drink (8.11.25,26), but the unchallengeable empirical fact that numerous Christians surmounted sexual desires overrode the conclusions of his own constricted experience. Their success and his failure in dethroning the imperialism of concupiscence lay in their unceasing recourse to the influx of God. Sheerly personal exertions did not earn continence; it was God's gift in response to their beseechings. Because Augustine made the radical mistake of leaning on the weak reed of self, he faltered, then fell again and again. To sever the last links of his chain he had to cast himself on God. Flinging himself into the divine arms, supple to healing grace, he will dwell secure against sexual assaults. Only by abandoning himself to the God who will never abandon him would his inner torment be calmed. Unabashed, Augustine realized that even after these persuasive entreaties the old delights, however slender-seeming, went on tugging at his heart-strings, murmuring sweet nothings, freezing him in the indecision that was the affective analogue of analytical suspense (5.14.24). To break this affective stalemate, continence offers a sound moral-psychological stratagem, efficacious in vanquishing every sort of invitation to sin. The soul defeats temptation not by fight but by flight. Simply decamping, advancing by retreating, the soul shuns combat with temptation as a wise man runs away from a forest fire. Turning a deaf ear to carnal solicitations curtails a dangerous dialogue with wiles of the law of members, which, bewitching the mind with an outpouring of words, lights up only the surface and hides the deadly kernel of things carnal. God's law, on the other hand, delights not by words or appearances but by truth (P 118[S.20].5). While the scenes with the temptresses and continence were played in the theater of Augustine's mind, Alypius patiently waited for the climax of his friend's unprecedented agony of spirit.

Chapter 12: Take and Read: Moral Conversion

28. In the culmination of his search for total conversion God directly intervened to transfigure him. In a more low-keyed fashion the conversion of Alypius replicated that of Augustine. One influential scholarly opinion questioning the factual character of some details turns out to be, when critically probed, itself questionable. From start to finish this chapter vibrates with the supernatural, each of its five parts pulsing with grace: the spectacle of past iniquities provoking the outpouring of penitential tears; the child's chanting, "Take and read"; the reading of Rom 13.13-4; the like inner conversion of Alypius; and the exultation of Monica.

Augustine's profound consideration, his anguished prayer for deliverance, was at last fully answered. A tempest of tears welled up in his breast as he sorrowfully contemplated his wretchedness now and in the past. As Jesus weighed down in the garden of Gethsemane by the horrible mass of sins throughout history sweated blood in prolonged agony, so in his shorter agony in the garden of Milan Augustine was staggered by the sight of his own sins as rotten insults against God. Not on the natural level was he ready to weep, but apparently with the gift of tears, through a prompting of the Spirit that induces tears over the soul's corruption. Because the weeping to come was so intimate, he withdrew from Alypius' presence, a move that his empathetic friend understood: sobs were already making Augustine's speech husky; his voice was thickened with incipient tears. In

obedience to the directive of continence to cast himself on the Lord
in sheer trust (8.11.27), he flung himself under a fig tree, releasing the
reins of tears,[26] which burst forth in rivers, somewhat resembling the
river his mother shed for his salvation (5.8.15). This was an acceptable
sacrifice, that of a contrite and humble heart that God does not spurn
but welcomes because the most lowly are closest to the most high (P
50.21). In words similar to Ps 6.4, from the depths of his heart he cried
out, "How long must I wait?" He was impatient for healing, not
understanding at the moment that God ordinarily delays healing so
that the soul may become sharply aware of the gravity of its illness; a
quick cure is not likely to put the soul on the qui vive against
recurrence of the malady. Not out of cruelty but out of mercy does
God defer his reply; the soul has to learn to pray fully before God
satisfies its needs. Prayer of course does not inform God of man's
needs, which in his wisdom he knows, but is an agency that exercises
desire, disposing the soul for boons God is ready to bestow. Without
prayer the spirit is too puny to compass God's priceless gift; prayer
expands the capacity of the soul (E 130.8.17). Intensified prayer
illumines faith, buoys up hope, and enkindles love, opening the
trustful mind to hear the inward divine locution: "It is I who am with
you now as always." Still, no response was forthcoming; his prayers
seemed vacuous, the beating of sounds against a heaven of brass. His
whole past dragged him down with insufferable force, driving him to
wail for succor not tomorrow but now, the human present
compassing this hour.

29. Suddenly God did speak, not directly but through the now-
celebrated words: "Take and read," repeatedly chanted by a child
whose voice apparently emanated from a nearby house. He could not
determine whether the chanting came from a boy or girl, for an
almost identical high-pitched register causes young children of both
sexes to pipe in similar tones. However externally seeming an
inconsequential piece of happenstance, the chanting struck him as an
utterance of special import. His face underwent a change; the galling
stream of tears started to ebb. He began to intently explore the sense
and source of the words. He knew of no game in which children
chanted these words; never before had he even heard the expression.
As the tears dried up completely, his mind was illumined with the
insight that God was leading him to discover a clue to conversion in
Scripture, after the pattern of St. Antony, whose life was wholly

turned around by an apparently coincidental hearing of Mt 19.21. Snatching up the Epistle to the Romans near Alypius, he opened at random to Rom 13.13-4, which commanded him, in effect, to stop chasing women and the world, to stifle the clamor of the lower self and robe himself in the light of Christ.[27] At the moment he finished reading the lines, his soul was flooded with light, banishing all anxiety and bathing him in profound peace. The light dissipated all darkness and doubt, all travail and the gloom of spirit coupled with moral uncertainty, healing the paralysis (8.8.19) that benumbed his capacity to voice one definitive yes of the higher self to God's law.[28] When he related his inner transformation to Alypius, remarkably, he learned, Alypius had been graced with a like interior transmutation, applying to himself the following line, "But receive the man who is weak in faith" (Rom 14.1). In essentials like that of Augustine, the conversion of Alypius differed in secondary affective qualities; his decision occurred quickly, in line with his unbending adherence to the good, with neither disturbance nor delay.

30. An Augustine transformed begot a Monica transformed. Apprised of the details of his incredible conversion, this giant of prayer burst forth in exultation (6.1.1), outwardly radiant, inwardly jubilant. The labor pains forgotten, every fiber of her soul thrilled with the pleasure of a mother at the spiritual birth of her offspring (9.8.17). The trumpets of the victorious Church militant resounded throughout her heart, proclaiming triumph over the wickedness enslaving her dearest son. Borne aloft to a special spiritual delight she had so far not tasted, she never ceased for one instant to laud God over and over for doing immeasurably more than she had prayed for or could conceive. Not only did God draw good out of evil, but on this occasion he harvested a greater good out of evil. She had prayed only that a converted Augustine would live as a good Catholic husband and citizen. Her all-generous God granted her far more than she had asked for or dreamed of, a son dedicated to celibacy and dismissal of worldly ambition, the Lord repaying her absolute trust with extraordinary compensation: at last Augustine was firmly fixed on the Catholic rule of faith. as forecast in 373 (3.11.19), now standing tall with a higher vocation. Her protracted mourning was changed into a joy more precious and purer than she would have felt as a grandmother; more precious, because sprung from his nobler state; purer, because elicited by his voluntary chastity. Grandchildren

would have excited great pleasure; not having grandchildren favored
her with richer exuberance because his more prized status of
continence would prove to be an ever-fruitful mother of joys (8.11.27),
in which by anticipation she was already sharing in some measure.
Monica's spiritual elation would have shone more brightly had she
even glimpsed the unimaginably immense fruit that through her
prayers and tears God would reap after her death. Her son was to be
ordained priest, then bishop, then to become an outstanding
luminary of the Western Church in his own day, acclaimed, we noted
earlier, by an acute intellect not ordinarily lavish with compliments as
"the second founder of the faith" (E 195). Nearly sixteen centuries
after his death the son of Monica's flesh and heart (9.8.17) bestrides
the Western theological world like a colossus, his theses still re-
searched and rethought to this very day.

No one doubts that the experience in the garden of Milan was a
genuine grace-impelled leap forward in which Augustine gave
himself wholly to God. However, Courcelle, the eminent French
Augustinologist, whose many research-impregnated reflections have
let in daylight on many pages of the *Confessions*, argues that, while the
interior conversion was unquestionably factual, exterior details were
constructs of Augustine's literary imagination. The context, he holds,
abounds with such inventions. The metaphor of wings echoes
Plotinus (8.7.18); the conflicting prosopopoeias of the vanities and
continence (8.11.26-7) recall Hercules at the crossroads deliberating
whether to pursue pleasure or virtue; the tomorrow and tomorrow in
the garden (8.12.28) seem reminiscent of Persius. Thus it seems
appropriate to interpret the externals of the scene as fictive devices.
The fig tree symbolizes the shadow of death, the sinful condition of
man. Furthermore, the words, *Tolle, lege,* were not actually uttered by
a child; Augustine heard them interiorly in the same manner as he
heard continence speaking within. Again, Courcelle prefers a variant
reading, *de divina domo* (from a divine house) to the generally
accepted *de vicina domo* (from a nearby house) in order to shore up his
contention that the conversion was wholly interior: the voice was that
of God or a messenger of God. He also suggests that the conversion
of both Augustine and Alypius is a doublet of the dual conversion of
the imperial officers at Trier (8.6.15).[29]

(i) Unfortunately, Courcelle's analogies do not survive close
examen. Earlier texts explicitly indicate when Augustine is not

referring to exterior voices. In 7.10.16 he writes: it was "as if I heard your [God's] voice from on high…. And I heard these words in the manner one hears in the heart." Again, continence is clearly described as personified: it was as if she said the words, *quasi diceret* (8.11.27). But nowhere does the description of the garden scene remotely hint that the voice heard arose from a prosopopoeia source. Moreover, his inability to aver without question whether the voice was that of a boy or girl shows that the voice was not merely interior; if this were a point of literary imagination, the male or female origin of the voice would be plainly determined. The apparent singularity of the phrase, "Take and read," also confirms the unembroidered realism of his account; were a sheer literary device at work, the source of the phrase would have been at least implicitly identified.

(ii) The claim that the fig tree is symbolic apparently rests on a confusion of categories. In certain sermons, Courcelle shows,[30] Augustine does read the fig tree symbolically, as a sign of man's sin-streaked and death-prone situation. However, in Book 8, where he is not engaged in figurative exegesis of Scripture, instancing of the fig tree lies in an entirely different category, that of narrative, whose central thrust is to set down accurately the circumstances of an event. Furthermore, even in his homilies Augustine clearly distinguishes between the datum recounted in Scriptures and its figurative interpretation. It is a fact that Nathaniel was standing under a fig tree; according to Augustine, this symbolized man's condition shadowed by death (J 7.21). In Book 8 Augustine simply records the fact that he threw himself under a fig tree without appending any symbolic meaning. Some may think it profitable to draw a spiritual parallel between Nathaniel and Augustine; but Augustine neither explicitly nor implicitly intimates such a parallel. He is not sermonizing in terms of figurative interpretation; he is preoccupied not with homiletics but with narrative, intent on conscientiously recounting what his usually faithful memory recalls as fact. Indeed he is doing no more or no less than what John the evangelist does, without additional exegesis or comment; he simply reports what occurred under a fig tree.

(iii) As O'Meara maintains,[31] the suggestion that the scene in the garden doubles the conversion of the two men at Trier seems somewhat plausible. Yet, he shrewdly notes, the source of the connection might well be reversed: Augustine speaks of the two men at Trier because there are two in the garden. Nonetheless, the correspondence seems only accidental; if three rather than two officials became monks, Ponticianus' story would remain substantially unaltered. Again, Augustine is not interested in contriving a literary correlation; he is primarily concerned with strict narrative, with recording indubitable facts as his remarkable memory recollects them.

(iv) In his zeal for tracking down literary artifice, Courcelle misses the signal realism of the scene attested by Alypius, an eyewitness of Augustine's emotional storm who was also within earshot of the child's chanting. It was to Alypius that Augustine related all that had happened to him. If Augustine's conversion had been sheerly interior, with the external circumstances the fruit of literary invention, it is hard to believe that later on, after the *Confessions* came into his hands, that Alypius would not have been vexed, perhaps nonplused, and communicated his puzzlement to Augustine, mildly protesting the imaginative trimmings that were slipped in without alerting the reader. His straightforward, honest mind would have found it next to incomprehensible that Augustine would have fictionalized in part what is plainly reported as historical fact. Interestingly, it was Alypius, not Augustine, who apparently underwent a purely interior conversion, confiding to Augustine what had been transpiring within himself, without flinging himself on the ground or under a tree, without the stimulus of the casual utterance of a child.

(v) As already pointed out, Augustine gives no clue whatsoever that he is having recourse to literary constructs. He seems to be unequivocally stating the factual features and events in the decisive moments in his conversion. In other passages, where he introduces literary fictions, he is always scrupulously careful to call the reader's attention to such devices. In addition, it would seem odd to the point of verging on utter improbability for an individual to clothe in fictional garb the principal events in something so momentous as his sudden conversion. The intrusion of fictional ingredients would seem to obfuscate rather than illumine the crucial turn, serving to detract from the clarity and force of the presentation, diminishing rather than heightening its poignancy and power.

(vi) True, the chanting of *Tolle, lege* appears to be coincidental. Yet in other places Augustine remarks that coincidences are used by God to facilitate growth in grace toward total conversion. Hence it is not surprising that conversions of other holy persons hinged on fortuitous occurrences. Ignatius of Loyola was led to a close union with God through the chance reading of a volume of lives of the saints. Francis Liebermann's unexpected conversion to Catholicism was occasioned by his happening to wander into a Catholic church.

(vii) As C. Boyer notes,[32] application of such a loosely structured literary method might easily reduce to literary fiction many, perhaps most, of the unmistakably factual events and episodes in the *Confessions*. An ingenious literary sleuth could classify the death of Augustine's friend in Book 4, as wholly or partially fictional. The friend (for literary purposes left unnamed) might be analyzed as an imagined alter-ego of Augustine, intended to symbolize his eventual repudiation of Manicheism; meant also to reproduce the real possibility that he may have died as a young man in the darkness of Manicheism: the young man's illness was a partial presage of his own near-demise in Rome in 384. Furthermore, admission that the garden scene was largely invention might have evoked among Manichean adversaries suspicions about the historicity of other events, inclining them to discredit with ill-concealed glee their former adherent as himself a clever fabulist and teller of tall tales passed off as historical truth.

(viii) Courcelle's gloss seems vitiated by false analogy. Accidental associations in a prior chapter containing literary devices mislead him into reading literary embroidery into the conversion scene. Neglecting the emphatically factual character of Augustine's narration, he focuses on incidental and superficial resemblances that hardly suggest intentional literary construction. Ironically, it is not Augustine's text but Courcelle's misguided interpretation that is laced with literary inventions. However outstanding an Augustinologist, Courcelle is victimized by the occupational hazard of creative scholars constantly geared to ferreting out literary parallels and source-dependencies. A mind brimming with imaginative possibilities may at times be carried away by its own insufficiently validated guesses. In such an outlook novel theory at times overrides hard fact; unhappily, Courcelle's misreading of 8.12.29-30 unreasonably, albeit deftly, tortures the text to yield meanings in line not with the text but insupportable conjectures.

Interestingly, without totally surrendering the essentials of his thesis, under attack Courcelle beat a partial retreat. The scholarly acumen of C. Mohrmann forced him to acknowledge that *domus Dei* is common in Augustine while *divina domus* is rare.[33] In one place, falling back on a desperate argument, he claimed that though the correct reading was *vicina domus,* Augustine really meant *divina domus.*[34] If consistently pursued, such a tactic would undermine all textually grounded scholarship; the unreliable gloss would, by arbitrary scholarly fiat, displace the authentic reading. Moreover, he came around to conceding that there was not just a symbolic but a real tree in the garden, an acknowledgment seriously compromising his literary-symbolic interpretation. Furthermore, later he granted that the words, *Tolle, lege,* could have originated in a nearby house. However, no series of refutations issuing in fresh concessions could break the grip of the idée fixe that controlled Courcelle's thinking. "...the more Courcelle is countered, the more inventiveness he displays, and it would be impossible, not to say useless, to follow him through the maze of speculation" his rejoinders have spun.[35] As somewhere noted by the American philosopher Morris R. Cohen, there is, according to Cicero, no absurdity to which a philosopher will not resort to vindicate his position; to which Cohen added, there is no absurdity a thinker will not employ to escape a *reductio ad absurdum.* Correspondingly, there is no literary possibility, however farfetched, on which a scholar of Courcelle's virtuosity will not capitalize to prop up his faltering case.[36]

For those who consider L. Ferrari's supplementary support of Courcelle and Company somewhat persuasive, the matter is not entirely settled.[37] According to Ferrari,[38] the presence of Paul is doubly significant for the fictionalist claim. First, Paul's conversion is the model for that of Augustine. The garden scene evinces striking similarities to the turnabout on the road to Damascus. As with Paul, Augustine falls to the ground, his eyesight is affected, and he hears a divinely influenced voice. Moreover, to *Saule...Saule* corresponds the repetition, *tolle...tolle.* Whereas prior to 396 references to Paul's conversion are sparse, the six years around the time of the *Confessions* contain fourteen references. This concentration of references indicates that Paul's conversion served as a paradigm for fashioning the fictionalized garden scene. Unfortunately, this correlation does not pass scrutiny. The similarities are canceled out by more pronounced dissimilarities. Whereas Paul was stricken to the ground, Augustine fell prone on his own. Paul was blinded; Augustine's eyes were merely flooded with tears. The voice Paul heard descended directly from heaven while the child's chanting was only indirectly heaven-sent. Morever, the relevance of a repeated *tolle* with *Saule* seems no more than superficial. Most important of all, the text itself plainly confutes the parallel with Paul. The chanting of the child's voice reminded Augustine not of Paul but of Antony. Like him, he felt admonished to consult the Scriptures, and in line with a similar oracle or sign from heaven he was at once converted. This explicit textual pairing with Antony clearly undercuts any essential connection with Paul's conversion. Since not Paul but Antony is the conversional model, further textual analysis deriving from the faulty Paul hypothesis can only be fruitless.

Resort to Paul in a second case turns on Rom 13.13-4. One would expect that this key text would occur in citations from 386-401. Surprisingly, we are told, during this period this crucial quotation does not appear even a single time while texts similar in tone such as 1 Cor 15.53-4 (leave aside the perishable to put on the imperishable), Eph 5.8 (you are not darkness but light), and Col 3.10 (put off the old nature, put on the new) occur with some frequency. Thus the conclusion: Rom 13.13-4 did not actually play a part in the conversion scene but was a fictional embellishment. However, as an argument *ex silentio*, this approach is highly questionable. The fact that Augustine does not make a prior citation of the text in no way justifies the claim that he could not have had it in mind. Appeal to other instances of silence is questionable also. The silence at Ostia is not essentially similar to Ferrari's argument from silence; equally unconvincing is the comparison to the silence of a child heedless of his mother's call. Moreover, the force of the argument from silence is blunted by the fact that texts similar to Rom 13.13-4 were cited. The contrast between the perishable, darkness, and the imperishable, the light, and the new nature is echoed in the contrast in Rom 13.13-4 between fleshly and Christlike conduct. The thrust of Rom 13.13-4 was implicitly contained in texts with a similar theme. Furthermore, the use of the *absence* of prior or concurrent citations of Rom 13.13-4 as an argument for fictionalism is paradoxically juxtaposed with recourse to the *presence* of relevant texts to bolster the fictionalist hypothesis. An abundance of texts concerning Paul's conversion allegedly indicates that the conversion scene is essentially fictionalized. On the other hand, a total lack of texts citing Rom 13.13-4 purportedly confirms a radical fictionalism. It would seem that appeal to an abundance, followed by an absence, of texts for justifying fictionalism is self-stultifying. Thus despite the opinion of one renowned Augustinologist the case is apparently closed. The fictionalist hypothesis is no longer a live option.

NOTES

1. Born in Rome during the early part of the fourth century, possibly around 325, Simplicianus first exercised much of his priestly ministry in Rome (Amb., *Ep.* 65, 67), then was domiciled in Milan, where he baptized Ambrose in 374 (Ambrose had been appointed governor of Liguria and Aemilia in 373), and guided him in his theological education, later serving as a valuable consultant during his episcopacy (Amb., *Ep.* 37, 65). It is uncertain when he became a priest. Neither Ambrose nor Augustine refers to him as a priest. In 397 he succeeded Ambrose as bishop of Milan. *Senex sed sanctus*, Ambrose said three times in reply to the objection that Simplicianus' age was an impediment to his assuming the episcopal burden (Paulinus, *Vita*, 46), a description later repeated almost verbatim by Augustine, *sanctus senex* (CD 10.19). He served as bishop for roughly four years, between August 28, 397 and June, 401 at the latest, though he may have died as early as September, 400. At the time of his death he was perhaps in his seventies since he was active in Rome 350-60 in connection with Victorinus' conversion; on this reckoning, he was sixty-some years old in 386 when as an old man he met Augustine (8.1.1). Though learned and acute, he wrote practically nothing, contenting himself with playing the role of Socratic questioner (a number of his letters are no longer extant; F. Cayré, *Manual of Patrology*, 1. 605). Ambrose sent him four letters dealing with doctrinal issues (*Ep.* 37,38,61,67). Along with displaying a paternal affection for Augustine (E 37.1), he apparently helped school him in the essentials of orthodox Christology, with special attention to Christ's humility. Simplicianus followed the Master in humility by docilely sounding out his former pupil on vexing passages in Paul and the book of Kings. Augustine's analyses are elaborated in QS; Bk. 1 explains Paul's teaching on the law (Rom 7.7-25) and grace (Rom 9.10-29) while Bk. 2 deals with six problematic texts in Kings. See BA 14, 530-2 and Mc Namara, *Friends and Friendship for Augustine*, 87-9. Especially valuable is T.G. Ring, *An Simplicianus zwei Bücher über verscheidene Fragen*, 26-31. Helpful also are reflections on QS in an unpublished manuscript by a confrere, J. Schnaubelt.
2. BA 14, 15, n. 1.
3. Mention of the cult of Osiris rests on only a surmised interpretation of a corrupt text, a *locus desperatus* that has spawned over twenty distinct readings. BA 14, 536-7. D 3.17.
4. In Courcelle's opinion, the lines from the *Aeneid*, 8.698 ff., concerning monsters of every kind and Anubis the barking dog were also employed by Jerome, with the suggestion that the two drew from a common source. Cited in D 3.18-9.
5. On the baptismal custom singular in Rome, see S. Poque, "Au sujet d'une singularité romaine de la 'Redditio Symboli' ", AUG 25 (1985), 133-43.

    A word or two may be devoted to Victorinus, who was born in Africa probably around 290. He came to Rome around 350 to teach rhetoric and became so highly esteemed that his statue was erected in the Forum around 354. His conversion to the faith is put in 355. In 362, following Julian the

Apostle's edict that barred instruction by Christians, he relinquished his teaching post. The date of his death is unknown; in 386 Augustine assumes that he was deceased for some years. Prior to his conversion he authored commentaries and translations of ancient authors. It was his translations of the *libri Platonicorium* that came into Augustine's hands in spring, 386 (7. 9. 13). From 355-62 he wrote treatises defending the Catholic position on the Son against Arianism. After 362 he produced exegeses of the Pauline epistles, three of which, those on Ephesians, Galatians, and Philippians, remain extant. It seems probable that Victorinus' Pauline commentaries were read by Augustine prior to his baptism, traces of which readings can be detected in the early dialogues. See M. Simonetti, "Marius Victorinus," *Patrology IV*, 69-80, with bibliographies, and N. Cipriani, "Marius Victorinus," AE 533-5, with bibliography.

6. King Henry's words in Shakespeare's *King Henry V*, Act IV, Sc. III, catch the singular joy that vibrates through the frames of victors after a crucial battle won by scars later to be more prized than riches. "He that outlives this day, and comes safe home, / Will stand a tip-toe when this day is nam'd, / And rouse him at the name of Crispian. / He that shall live this day, and see old age, / Will yearly on the vigil feast his neighbours, / And say, 'To-morrow is Saint Crispian': / Then he will strip his sleeve and show his scars, / And say, 'These wounds I had on Crispin's day.' / Old men forget: yet all shall be forgot,/ But he'll remember with advantages / What feats he did that day. Then shall our names, / Familiar in his mouth as household words, / Harry the king, Bedford and Exeter, / Warwick and Talbot, Salisbury and Gloucester, / Be in their flowing cups freshly remember'd. / This story shall the good man teach his son; / And Crispin Crispian shall ne'er go by, / From this day to the ending of the world, / But we in it shall be remembered; / We few, we happy few, we band of brothers; / For he to-day that sheds his blood with me / Shall be my brother; be he ne'er so vile / This day shall gentle his condition: / And gentlemen in England, now a-bed / Shall think themselves accurs'd they were not here, / And hold their manhoods cheap whiles any speaks / That fought with us upon Saint Crispin's day."

7. "Christ bound the devil with spiritual fetters; ...we bound him by the mystery of his incarnation. Though nothing in him deserved death, nevertheless, the devil was permitted to kill him." P 67.16. Cited in D 3.29. This of course gives the pith of the ransom theory. See 7.21.27 supra.

8. (i) Taken generally in a pejorative fashion, libido means illicit desire or culpable cupidity, inordinate because it prefers temporal to eternal goods (LA 1.4.10). There are various types of libido or "lust", libido of vengeance (anger: 2.9.17), libido of possessing money (greed), and libido of glory (vainglory). Viewed specifically, libido commonly denotes illicit sexual desire (CD 14.15,16). See BA 14, 537-41. (ii) *Concupiscentia carnis* often corresponds to sexual libido. At times concupiscence refers to illicit desire that is not sexual (J 73.1). Occasionally, the word carries a morally good import, as in concupiscence for wisdom (Wis 6.21.); NC 2.30.52. See Bonner, 398-401, who also profitably canvasses the diverse usages of libido in Latin literature. (iii) *Consuetudo* or habit is a uniform pattern of conduct ingrained by repeated surrender to libido,

especially in the sexual sense. The inclination to sin is the fruit of original sin. Thus the sin that dwells within man results from the penalty of original sin and the penalty of habitual sin. Original sin and reenacted personal sin jointly constitute a reign of sin in fallen man. QS 1.1.10. See BA 14, 541-2. (iv) One powerful drift of current research, as noted earlier, indicates that it would be idle to try to square Augustine's view of libido with that of S. Freud. Psychologists of various hues have so battered Freud's outlook that it appears to be crumbling. The infantile sex theory and the Oedipus complex seem empirically baseless. Moreover, the so-called Freudian slip is radically vitiated by a confusion of associated source with the cause of the misstatement. Furthermore, the interpretation of dreams, which attempts to show the essential coherence of essentially incoherent dream material, is worked up by the imaginative ingenuity of the analyst. The most damaging evidence is the disclosure that Freud's clinical evidence is partially doctored; Freud imposed his own preconceptions on his data. See Book 4 , n. 23 above.

9. This is an accommodated reading. P 57.4 sees a causal chain of actual sins. A thief commits a second sin, the murder of a witness, to forestall detection. He then murders a second witness for the same reason. Finally, he consults an astrologer, haruspice, and magician to learn his probable fate. The theft is the sin; the murder of witnesses is from this sin; and consultation of the astrologer and associates is for the sake of sin.

10. See James 1. 120, 127, for these remarks on the tenacity of habit. On habit in general see A. Fitzgerald, "Habit (Consuetudo)," AE 409-11 and A. Zumkeller, "Consuetudo," AL 1.253-6.

11. In "L'exégèse augustinienne de Rom. 7, 7-25 entre 396 et 418," RA 16 (1981), 101-95, M.-F. Berrouard, engaging in a practically exhaustive examen of references to Rom 7. 7-25, establishes that the Augustine of 395-6 believed that the nineteen verses portrayed fallen man under the Law, as in QS 1.1.1-16. Not until NC 1.27,30,31, composed in the winter of 418-9, did he expressly recognize that the war of flesh against spirit was waged in the hearts of even Christians living under the dispensation of grace, including the great Paul himself. Berrouard nuances the gradual shift to his second position that jibes with Christian experience.

12. Here Augustine speaks deprecatingly of the teaching of rhetoric as the selling of words and legal activity as the selling of advice. As rooted in the liberal arts, rhetoric and law were rated culturally superior to commercial pursuits and mechanical arts. D 3.39.

13. HC 143, n.12.

14. This select group formed a kind of privy council. However, this lofty position was unstable; personal disgrace swiftly banished the priviledged from the imperial circle. By contrast, friendship with God is not restricted to a few but is available to all who faithfully obey the will of God (GCM 1.2.4). It is not attained by high-level interventions but is achieved immediately as long as a man commits himself to God. Not a fragile position, easily lost through adverse publicity, it is relatively long lasting. J. Lienhard, "Friendship with God, Friendship in God," 213-4, in *Augustine Mystic and Mystagogue*, CollAug, (ed.) F.

Van Fleteren and J. Schanubelt.

15. Augustine desired not more certitude about God but more stability in him (8.1.1.), which bespeaks the cessation of the flux due to habit. Stability means oneness of the self, patterned after the One that is God. Virtue restores order in the soul, integrating it into that unity from which it has flowed away into many temporal goods (11.29.40). The flow of bad habit is a species of moral time, the flowing away of the soul from oneness and integrity in God into the manyness of false temporal goods. Moral time is the prelude to the breakdown that terminates in spiritual death.

16. G-M 220, n.25.

17. Cited in D 3.47.

18. G-M 222, n. 10. BA 14, 49, n. 1, traces the affective movement to *Thaet.* 126a-14. See D 3.59.

19. Bonner, 174-5.

20. At times Augustine speaks of wills in the broad sense to signify voluntary tendencies or inclinations. Clearly *voluntates* is not taken in the strict sense; else he might lay himself open to the charge that he is indirectly conceding a Manichean dualism of natures or souls. May we note also that, according to R. Jolivet and M. Jourjon, BA 17, 42-3, Manichean doctrine seems to speak precisely of two natures rather than two souls. It appears reasonable to conjecture that in Augustine's day the use of two souls as interchangeable with two natures became commonly accepted. Surely Augustine was familiar with the shadings of Manichean terminology in his milieu, and undoubtedly is scrupulously faithful here as elsewhere in recording the import of these custom-sanctioned terms. In any case, however we rate the nicety of Augustine's language, his cardinal point stands: plurality is found only in diverse "wills" that are inclinations of the will. Underlying deliberation and persisting in the outcome of deliberation is the one soul, the one spiritual self. The main Manichean mistake consists in substantializing, "naturing," or reifying voluntary affections of the soul. Augustine's dialectical attack on this Manichean dualism lays bare one major inconsequence of such dualism, the multiplication of diverse natures ad infinitum.

21. Here and elsewhere (3.9.12; 7.6.8) *articulum temporis* denotes not the physical instant but a very basic span of time. Similarly, *punctum temporis* (8.11.25) signifies a short stretch of time rather than the indivisible point of time.

22. These instances are apropos since Manichees revered Paul while praying psalms close to the Christian version. L. Ferrari, "Isaiah and the Early Augustine," AUG (L) 41 (1991), 746.

23. Here *distendunt* betokens a volitional distension, which is distinct from the cognitive distension that constitutes psychic time (11.23.30). Because the will is attracted toward diverse goods that are not necessarily evil, its distension differs from the distension that is moral time, in which the soul is pulled apart and disintegrated by lower or temporal goods (11.29.39).

24. As later study of Scripture showed, the *vanitantium* of *vanitas vanitantium* is an imprecise rendering of Eccl 1.2, a misreading that crops up in other places, such as QA 33.26, ME 1.21.39, and P 4.3. Consultation of the Greek proved

that the correct translation was *vanitas vanitatum,* which the more reliable Latin texts contained. However, the basic import is the same: vanity is untruth afflicting the minds of deceived and deceivers. R 1.7.3.

25. Continence has various significations. In its broadest sense it means internal governance over desires so as to resist the three categories of vices that embrace all sins: carnal pleasures, pride, and curiosity (10.30.41). Less broadly taken, it signifies moderation of desire of food and drink (10.31.43-5). A third usage conveys the import of control of sexual desire (6.11.20). A fourth sense blends its meaning with virginal chastity, detachment from all sexual union (8.11.27), which Augustine strives for and attains in Book 8. A fifth acceptation denotes mastery of the triple concupiscence that entrains total self-giving of self to God; its spirit no longer divided, the wholly one soul gathers up its scattered desires and concentrates them on God alone (10.29.40). See Harvey, *Moral Theol.,* 55-7.

26. G-M 229.14, traces part of this line to *Aen.* 12. 499.

27. His cutting of the Bible, here the random opening, of Romans, was ventured in the context of Christian faith informed with practical wisdom; a casual dipping into a Scripture text, which imitated the conduct of Antony, whose coincidental hearing of Mt 19.21 he believed to be a divine admonition. As with Antony, Augustine's fortuitous selection of a text transpired in an atmosphere of prayerful searching for moral insight. Judicious recourse to chance cutting of passages from Scripture, however, does not countenance imprudent reliance on isolated Scriptural texts as nuggets supplying instant solutions to every sort of question. In E 55.20.37 (written in 400, three years after the composition of the first nine books of the *Confessions*) he cautions against cutting the Bible simply in order to reach answers to concerns of the world and passing vanities. While such random excerpting of Scripture is preferable to consulting demons, i.e., paying for guidance from horoscope casters or diviners, it runs counter to the import of divine oracles that speak essentially to the heart oriented to life not of this world. Implicit in Augustine's sanction of cutting the Bible is its restriction to seeking light on concrete moral decisions. It cannot be wielded as an artless technique for settling doctrinal questions or deemed an affidavit for sheer private interpretation. Martin Luther was apparently misguided in somewhere boldly averring that in interpretation of the Bible a plowboy in his field is as competent as the Pope in Rome. In the absence of proper doctrinal controls one individual reportedly cut open the Bible at Mt 16.19, from which he garnered the dubious assurance that God had given him, along with Peter, the keys of the kingdom of heaven. Even in moral matters casually culled texts cannot be counted infallible indices of proper choice. One parent, cutting the Bible to discover a divinely ordained name for his son, put his finger on the name Beelzebul. Another person given to random association came upon "Judas went out and hanged himself" (Mt 27.5); then, hunting for further guidance, his eyes fell upon Lk 10.37, "Go and do likewise," an imperative hardly to be ascribed to the Holy Spirit.

28. Contrary to some scholars, it would seem that Augustine's conversion did not fully replicate that of St. Paul. Augustine's conversion was not a Damascan

experience; he readied himself for the breakthrough step by step, through prayer, reading, and dialogue with friends. The crowning moment was indeed sudden and quasi-miraculous, but the ascent up the slope was gradual. On the other hand, the change of Saul into Paul was wholly unanticipated and unprepared for. On the road to Damascus the mind of the persecutor of the despised Jewish heretics was feverish with plans for arresting Christians, when suddenly he was engulfed in light and struck to the ground, becoming all at once converted to belief in Jesus as Lord, the very Christ he had condemned as a foe of the Israel of God (Ac 9.1-7). Augustine's conversion seems closer to that of Antony: both believed in Christ and were open to complete dedication to God by practicing the evangelical counsels. Of course at his conversion Antony was already a full-fledged, baptized Christian whereas Augustine, not yet baptized, was painfully fighting for mastery of libido that would be the gateway to baptism. Whatever further distinguishing details are detected, it seems reasonable to suggest that the conversions of all three share a common miraculous quasi-instantaneity, probably because to each was appointed an extraordinary mission, Saul transfigured into Paul was selected as the exceptional vessel of the Lord, destined to be the apostle to the Gentiles, perhaps the greatest missionary and mystic of all time. Antony was specially graced in view of his privileged role as father of monasticism, a way of life whose members unobtrusively but momentously mold the course of spiritual history through powerful works of constant prayer and penance. Augustine was gifted with a spectacular change of heart because God was grooming him to serve as a theologian of incalculable influence in Christian thought. After St. Paul no other single thinker has exerted so prodigious an impact on Christianity as Augustine. Through his singular conversion the Lord of history deputed him to be the intellectual apostle of the Gentiles. In August, 386, Augustine was probably rated by some as a brilliant rhetorician, perhaps a man of unusual promise. Only the Father who disposes all things sweetly knew that in an obscure garden in Milan his mercy converted a mastermind, whose super-genius and inexhaustible energy he would ordain for the ripening of Christian thoughtways, concepts and theories whose penetration and range still nourish minds.

29. Courcelle, 190-8.
30. J 7.21. S 69.3.4; 212.1.1. P 31.1 Cited in Courcelle, 193, n. 2.
31. O'Meara, 183-4.
32. C. Boyer, *Christianisme et néoplatonisme dans la formation philosophique de saint Augustin*, 112 ff., cited in Pellegrino, 118, n. 13.
33. Cited in O'Meara, 184.
34. O'Meara, 184.
35. O'Meara, 184.
36. Starnes, 241-2, n. 100, judges it strange or paradoxical that Courselle, whose main aim consists in "defending the historical accuracy of the text" of the *Confessions* de-historicizes or reduces to literary fiction crucial ingredients in the moral conversion. See the judicious comments on the phenomena of the Milan garden in BA 14, 546-9, n. 7.

37. According to G. Madec, "Conversio," AL 1. 1292, the debate initiated by Courcelle "is not yet finished." In "St. Augustine's Conversion Scene: the End of a Modern Debate?", *St. Patr.* 22 (1989), 235-50, L. Ferrari gives an overview of the problem of the historicity of the garden scene.

38. Ferrari's views have been exposited in several studies. "Paul at the Conversion of Augustine (*Conf.* VIII, 12, 29-30)," AS 11 (1980), 5-20. "St. Augustine on the Road to Damascus," AS 13 (1982), 151-70. "Ecce audio vocem de vicina domo (*Conf.* 8,12,29)", AUG (L) 33 (1983), 232-45. *The Conversions of St. Augustine* (1984), especially 59-70. "Beyond Augustine's Conversion Scene," in *Augustine: From Rhetor to Theologian*, (ed.) J. McWilliam (1994), 97-108.

Book Nine
Baptism.
Death of Monica

As one walks up the left side-aisle of the Villanova University chapel, the first full stained glass window that catches the eye contains panels of St. Rita, St. Augustine, and St. Monica. The center frame portrays Augustine prayerfully writing, eyes uplifted to heaven. To the right of his countenance is a small scroll bearing words in simple Latin: *In caelo sicut est Pater, talis est Filius. In terra sicut est mater, talis est filius* (In heaven as is the Father, so is the Son. On earth as is the mother, so is the son). Though apparently attributed to Augustine, these lines do not seem to be the genuine fruit of his hand. Whatever their provenance, however, they do summarize Augustine's special affiliation with Monica, his mother in a double sense, giving him birth to both temporal and eternal light (9.8.17). Under God, without her he would have been nothing in the natural and supernatural sense. In the line of nature Augustine was the progeny of the joint causality of Patricius and Monica; had they never met or married, Augustine would have never been born. In the line of grace Augustine was principally the issue of the supernatural mothering of Monica; had she not, under God's plan, been his mother, Augustine would not have been born in grace. As nuptial union inevitably assured the birth (after this particular conception) of Augustine, so then Monica's union with the heart of God infallibly assured his birth in Christ (5.9.17).

Books 1-9, whose primary theme is conversion, depict Augustine shaped at every turn by the strong and tender hand of God's providence. "Man proposes but God disposes,"[1] *The Imitation of Christ* incisively observes, yet we do not alter its thrust but may clarify its truth if we modify it to read," God disposes–through man." The divine disposition of drawing Augustine to conversion was channeled mainly through the prayers and sacrifices of his mother. The first eight books keep her decisive role largely in the background; then Book 9 brings her center stage with the majority of its lines bearing directly or indirectly on her. Previously accorded solid but apparently marginal attention, in Book 9 she is enwrapped in the full blaze of recognition. Emerging next to Augustine as the leading actor in his drama, she is lauded as mother, model, and mystic. She was mother of his natural life and life of grace; model of meekness, patience, and peace; mystic, whose long intimacy with God in Martha-like circumstances peaked in a vision at Ostia (9.10.23-6). Wholly self-giving, she was most chaste, living for God alone, who rewarded her self-donation with a giving of himself in the closest of unions. No doubt Augustine's faith was illumined by the ministry of Ambrose, God's preacher (1.1.1), but it was Monica's mountain-moving orisons that worked mightily to ready his spiritual eyes and ears to seize upon his discourses as vehicles of the word of God. The message was not lost on his spirit because Monica's beseechings had disposed him to the Spirit speaking through Ambrose.

The book breaks down into two clearly demarcated parts. Chs. 1-7 relate his remote and proximate preparation for baptism. After deciding to relinquish his professorship (2.2) and recording the conversions and deaths of Verecundus and Nebridius (3.5-6), he traveled to Cassiciacum for philosophical dialogues (4.7), where he meditated on Ps 4 (4.8-12). Back in Milan, after having resigned his teaching post (5.13), he was baptized on Easter eve (6.14). Then a hostile Justina failed to dislodge Catholics from the cathedral basilica (7.16). The second part, Chs. 8-13, is a filial tribute to Monica's virtues in life and death. Following an account of her childhood (8.17-8) is emphasis on her patience with the often errant Patricius (9.19-22). The vision at Ostia is depicted in some detail (10.23-5), shortly after which Monica died (16.27-8), plunging her son into profound grief (12.25-33). Confident of her salvation, he prayed for her soul along with that of Patricius (13.34-7).

Chapter 1: Praise and Thanksgiving for Liberation

1. Formerly the captive of sin, his freedom purchased at an

enormous price, he cries out gratitude in the words of the psalmist. Now the vassal of God, paying due service to the God who liberated him, he is the son of the handmaid that is the heavenly Jerusalem, the handmaid in the line of justice, the mother of all the healed, represented on earth by the Church (P 115.6). Since not he but God broke the chains of slavery to sin, he offers him not an exterior sacrifice but a sacrifice of praise, of inward self-giving. In his liberation he glories not in himself but in God who welcomes home again the prodigal son now bound by bonds of love and mercy (P 115.7), praising God with his whole being, heart and tongue and bones, i.e., the entire human frame, body and soul in all the their reaches. Who is like God? Nothing can be like the God who is inimitable infinite mercy; so he thanks him not because he has been benefited with some passing particular good but because the all-good has become his very own life (P 34[S.1].14). He begs God to pronounce the reassuring word that drowns out adversarial voices insisting that the God is not his salvation; an interior voice proclaims that God alone is his salvation: to live righteously he counts on no support beyond that of God (P 34[S.1].5).

In the existential-moral mode he poses the radical question of the meaning of self: what was my character then? Who am I now? In brief, he was a sinner trapped in vices; now, whatever minor remnants of sin persist, he lives as a new creation, translated from darkness to light by the healing of his merciful Father. After grave sinning rooted in his will turned his heart into an abyss of rottenness, God's right hand, his mercy-perfused power, resurrected his spirit from moral demise and decomposition. Simply expressed, new life and freedom consisted in this: his will is not as it was (8.5.10), morally dismembered, but integral, totally fixed on the will of God. The pith and marrow of his conversion come down to this: no longer willing what he used to dividedly will in subjugation to his lower self, now he totally wills in essentials what God wills.

During the long years in which he had wasted his spiritual substance on idols of the senses where was his free will: into what pit of the soul did it disappear? The apparent vanishing of his free will is a metaphorical indicator of complete subjection to sin. The freedom lost was not psychological freedom, which could not be aborted without erasure of all responsibility. What his vicious state effectively suppressed was moral freedom; in the grip of lower goods, his nominally free moral will was concretely impotent to choose higher goods. Though never dispossessed of ontic freedom or basic *liberum arbitrium* or free choice, he lacked *libertas* or freedom to choose to do good. As incapable of opting for higher goods, his will was existentially nonoperative, practically nonexistent: in this sense he was despoiled of freedom. The result not of sheer happenstance, his unfreedom was enforced by habits whose iron lines of his own contrivance imprisoned his soul in a moral dungeon. Even after analysis of the imperious nature of habit, a certain mystery envelops its potency, so crippling that it can make free will existentially unfree, so adamantine that not natural exertion but only grace could unfetter him. A certain obscurity also clings to his final conversion, moving him to wonder about the counter-force of grace from Christ, invoked as helper and redeemer[2] who, in place of the grinding yoke of sin, emancipated his will to shoulder the light burden of divine love.

Sensory goods having lost their allure, he relished the absence rather than the possession of pseudo-sweet honor and wealth, and delighted in deprivation of sexual delights. His transvaluation of values occurred because his will, no longer split, was anchored in divine sweetness, highest because immutable, and the only true, because absolutely unchanging, sweetness. In expelling inordinate desires for lower goods, the super-good Father did not simply empty Augustine but filled him with himself. Self-stripping was a self-opening; in divesting himself of lower goods, Augustine became fully hospitable to the all-good. Supplying for the loss of sexual intercourse, God proved to be more gratifying than every sexual delight; his spiritual pleasure surpassed that of flesh and blood, i.e., of carnal man. Again, God's light, compensating for the loss of the light of the Manichean Father of Greatness, was not outward but more inward than the hiddenmost chambers of the spirit.[3] Moreover, substituting for the discarded remuneration of worldly ambition, God was more exalted than any other honor, sharing in which is reserved not to those who magnify themselves but only to those who bend the neck to the abased savior. Curiosity, the third of the triple concupiscences, is passed over because prior to his conversion Augustine had largely curbed lust of the eyes. In fulfilling him, the super-good One healed him of *ambitio saeculi*, the near-uncontrollable impulse to get (6.9.9), which harrows the soul with anxiety, and also delivered him from his overheated urge for sexual union, here graphically depicted as rolling about in actual sensual passion. From another angle, sexual desire drives its slave to scratch the scab; unable to overthrow its despotic impurity, the soul feverishly goes on tearing at its manifold scabs.[1] Now, however, Augustine was joyed by the gift of informal prayer, in which he colloquied with God as friend, resting with childlike confidence on his bosom. God was his brightness, the true, nonManichean light; his wealth, infinitely more precious than earthly riches ambition pants after; his salvation, his true lover who makes entrance with intimate penetration of spirit.

Chapter 2: Decision to Abandon Teaching Rhetoric

2. Since less than three weeks separated his conversion, which occurred early in August, 386, from the vintage vacation, which ran from August 22 to October 15, he decided to stop teaching rhetoric on August 22 rather than provocatively resign immediately after conversion. Cessation from teaching would look normal, blending with the finish of the school term. Remembering the first flush of his new spiritual excitement, he deprecatingly puts down rhetoric; he would no longer be marketing glib fluency, in which, in contradistinction to religious thinkers who meditate on the eternal law and God's peace, young rhetoricians-to-be concentrate on manufacturing mendacious insanities, i.e., on constructing artfully deceptive defenses of what is morally wrong, and on peddling wares of the forum, i.e., on deploying debating techniques for rebutting opponents in courts of law and political assemblies. It would be anomalous for his soul bought by Christ's blood to continue to be sold for purely secular ends. He is of course not claiming that a Christian cannot be an accomplished rhetorician; his rhetorical skill in exposition and defense of the faith effectively argues otherwise. But at this time he felt called to quit an occupation entwined with worldly pursuits. Here he is not laying down a program for a Christian stance toward rhetoric but recounting post-conversion enthusiasm. The first fervor of a new convert explains, if it does not wholly justify, the extravagant devaluing of rhetoric as mean venality.

Wanting to forestall possible objections as long as possible, he let only God and intimate friends be privy to his resolution. He and his close associates were rising from the valley of tears, the breach between spirit and flesh to be mended by the grace of Christ (P 83.10-

1). The vale of tears also represents lowliness, in particular, the humility of Christ, whose suffering turned him into a valley of tears (P 119.1). In fine, the valley of tears symbolizes strife and oppression owing to sin, remedied by Christ who, becoming sin, became a valley of tears through his passion. In singing the canticle of the steps, the soul climbs the gradient of the heart, raised aloft through love to the heavenly Jerusalem (13.9.10). As he mounted upward, Augustine was blessed with two pieces of inward armor, sharp arrows and consuming coals, to shield him from dubious friends. Sharp arrows are the words of God that pierce the heart and ignite love; consuming coals are the examples of the martyrs and other saints who lived by the "impossible" commandments (P 119.5). The deceitful tongue is wielded by an advisor who, under the guise of proffering holy counsel, poisons the soul, its destructive love gobbling up the counselee as a trencherman pounces on food (P 119.3-4). Earlier Augustine had been bade to feed on truth that would spiritually change him into itself (7.10.16), but contact with cunningly appareled falsity threatened him with transmutation into death rather than life.

3. Setting his heart on fire with love of truth were perduring words of God proclaiming evangelical precepts that pierced his heart. Complementing the power of words was the force of witness. Though a misguided counselor might caution that a prior comfortable lifestyle ruled out austerity, Christian example countered carnal circumstances. If wealthy senators could forsake riches, if women could display strength, someone less well-off and naturally stronger than a woman could choose a life of self-denial. Concretely confuting the objection that holiness is barred to great sinners is the sinful woman forgiven much because she loved much (P 119.5). Numerous others were transformed from spirits pitch-black with sin into souls bright as small suns, corpses risen from the grave; witnesses who cauterized his sluggishness and slump in confidence (P 119.5). So intense was their fire that opposing gusts, instead of snuffing out the blaze, helped increase the ardor as bellows cause flames to grow hotter. Heart enkindled by fiery arrows and inspired by glowing coals, he did not shrink from disclosing that he was wholly committed to living the Catholic ideal. Nor did it escape him that his conversion would serve as a witness to others.[5] Spiritual Catholics would be stirred to praise God because of Augustine's vow to be baptized and the resolution of a rhetorician of prowess to undertake an ascetical life. Nevertheless,

prudence that was not calculation of self-interest but practical wisdom dictated that he not give up his teaching post forthwith. Since Christians of the strict observance insisted upon the apparent incompatibility between Christian allegiance and the professional teaching of rhetoric, for the first time Augustine felt called upon to justify himself to fellow Christians.[6] Postponement of withdrawal from teaching could not be blamed on compliance with dissembling counselors, probably pagan fellow-rhetoricians and officials in Milan; his Christian resolve stayed unshaken. Yet, he takes pains to point out, it would have been injudicious to announce suddenly, with fewer than three weeks left in the term, that he was forsaking professional rhetoric. A bolt-out-of-the-blue severance from his post might have set tongues wagging that his shift was contrived to center attention on himself as a very important person.

4. During the summer he was afflicted with an ailment of the lungs (CA 1.1.3. BV 1.4. O1.2.5) (perhaps asthma, bronchitis, or a prolonged influenza),[7] induced by overwork and stress, making it hard for him to breathe comfortably, with the result that his voice grew weaker. Naturally, at first he was apprehensive, for deterioration of voice might foreshadow the end of his career or at least force him into a prolonged leave of absence. But after his conversion he rejoiced in his malady because relinquishing his post would afford spiritual leisure to be still and know that God is Lord; be still: deliver his soul from the bustle accompanying secular occupations; know God is Lord: trust the One who alone can remake him because he alone made him (P 45.14). Deficiency of voice, though not his primary motive for resigning, constituted a sufficient reason in the eyes of affluent parents who would otherwise have protested his withdrawal from his almost unexampled expert training of their sons.

Delight over anticipation of spiritual leisure pervaded the short span remaining in the scholastic term, coupled with which, however, was exercise of fortitude. Prior to conversion, income and prestige had eased somewhat the drudgery of teaching. Fortunately, patience replaced worldly motives; else the onus would have nearly crushed him, for no longer did he garner earthly satisfaction from teaching, now rated not an inviting good but a barely tolerable evil. Perhaps some strict Christians might tax him for unwarranted procrastination; it seemed incongruous that total allegiance to truth did not result in straightway repudiation of untruth. With a tender, not to say scrupulous, conscience he grants that apparently prudent deferment of resignation may have strayed from the moral norm. In his humility he is consoled by mercy that forgave this possible fault along with many deadly, i.e., grave, sins when he was sanctified in the waters of baptism.

Chapter 3: Baptism and Death of Verecundus and Nebridius

5. Verecundus was eager to accept Catholicism but only along the path of perfection; a starry but unrealistic ideal, for he was already married to a practical Catholic: from his somewhat skewed standpoint the bond joining him to his spouse was a chain denying espousal of celibacy. He stubbornly persisted in refusing baptism that carried no guarantee of celibacy. In spite of disappointment he loaned his country home in Cassiciacum to Augustine and his friends for spiritual retreat and scholarly discussion; a generosity not to go unrequited in the life to come: providentially, he did accept baptism prior to his untimely death in 387-8, when Augustine was in Rome for a second time. Writing roughly a decade after Verecundus' demise, Augustine is confident that his soul is already perpetually happy with Christ, awaiting face-to-face vision of God after the resurrection. Had baptism not elevated Verecundus to the elect, the hearts of Augustine and his friends would have been unbearably tortured by the possibility of his perdition, suffering excruciatingly as would have Monica if Augustine had perished in his sin (5.9.7). The God who repays with even greater love is now recompensing Verecundus for his charity in putting his residence at the disposal of Augustine. His soul rests in a super-Cassiciacum, an eternally verdant paradise situated not among earthly mountains but on a mountain overflowing with unending happiness; the mountain that is Christ far above the valley of tears (P 119.1).[8]

6. As prior passages attest (4.3.6; 6.10.17), Augustine's bond of friendship with Nebridius was much stouter and deeper. Analytically sharper than Verecundus, he was equally overjoyed at news of Augustine's conversion. Earlier Nebridius had fallen into a variant of Docetism, believing that Jesus' body was a pure phantasm. Unlike other friends of Augustine, he never became entrapped in Manicheism, in which he detected a radical theological incoherence (an incorruptible God's kingdom cannot be invaded [7.2.3]). In 386,

while not baptized, he began to scrutinize Catholicism's claims with wonted seriousness. Perhaps in 387 or 388 he entered the Church and, after returning to his family estate in Carthage, brought all of the household into the faith. Never having married, probably when no more than thirty years of age, he died around 390, his correspondence ceasing in 389. Nebridius' spirit now resides, he feels sure, in the bosom of Abraham, a place of unending felicity in which the soul dwells in the presence of Christ as God. During this period and throughout most of his life Augustine distinguished two stages of blessedness; a first beatitude in the happiness-producing presence of Christ perceived in his divinity; a second, complete beatitude, subsequent to the resurrection, in which the blessed see the full Godhead face to face.[9] Still hesitant as late as 426, Augustine was unable to decide whether souls prior to the resurrection are as wholly glorified as angels already rejoicing in the beatific vision (R 1.13.3; 14.2). Fourteen years earlier he had stated, "The just enjoy the Word of God without reading; what is written for us in the pages [of Scripture], they see through the face of God" (P 119.6). His point, somewhat ambiguously phrased, would seem to be that the blessed see the import of Scripture through the face of Christ as God. In any event, Nebridius' soul enraptured by joy is now bathed in ineffable divine friendship as reward in part for cleaving to Augustine as a friend unwavering as a rock during his tormented wrestling with moral issues some months before actual conversion (6.7.11).

Released from servitude to sin at baptism, Nebridius now exults in the full freedom of baptismal life; not detained in purgatory, but, because of his Christlike self-donation, already everlastingly companioning with the God-man, his body dead and gone, his soul electric in with divine life. During his earthly sojourn Nebridius plied Augustine with many queries about the abode of the saints above. Apparently most of these were posed in personal conversation since their correspondence, while canvassing a number of philosophical issues interthreaded with religious motifs, hardly bears at all directly on the makeup of the supernal mansions. At that time, Augustine laments, he was analytically unequipped to cast much light on religio-philosophic matters.[10] An earthbound mind, he could at best sketch the geography of the heavenly country, but, in addition, and this is cardinal, Augustine was, he frankly admits, devoid of a wide and detailed knowledge of the truths of his new-found faith. He tended to focus on Christ as teacher and model, with little attention accorded the suffering redeemer; too his understanding of the role of the Holy Spirit was vague, and his early theory of the resurrected body left something to be desired.[11] Gifted with far more than an academic interest in the soul's communication with God, Nebridius cultivated interior prayer, his serenity in all circumstances betokening rootage in the divine (E 10.2-3).[12] This thirst for more intense union with God was the reason why he sought a holy eloquence of wisdom from Augustine (E 6.1). Now no longer hanging on Augustine's words, his spiritual mouth drinks fully from Christ, fountain of life and light of God (P 35.15). He is inebriated by the rich wine of God or the wine that is God; suffused with the inexpressible joy that is God, the soul, transcending normal human mentation, becomes divine (P 35.14). Whereas a drunkard in his cups ordinarily becomes oblivious even to nearest and dearest, the divinely intoxicated Nebridius, drinking the wisdom of the Christ ever mindful of Augustine, will always remember him.

Returning to the period prior to resignation, he implored Verecundus to understand that fidelity to spouse could be squared with fidelity to Christ to whom his soul would be wedded in faith and love, meanwhile looking forward to Nebridius' commitment, expected by the start of vacation (August 22). In recalling that the intervening three weeks struck him as a much longer extent of time, Augustine is remarking a common psychological experience: attention to the passage of time as such seems to prolong a span of time. Sheer waiting for a hoped-for event to transpire accents the emptiness of time, the hours and days apparently dragging on, sometimes interminably;[13] so holy impatience for refreshment in God magnified the delay by psychologically stretching the time-line. Prolonging his wait was a burning to seek the face of the Lord, i.e., to quest with eyes of the heart, not the body, for the light that is God (P 26[En. 2] .15).

Chapter 4: Cassiciacum: Teaching, Dialogue, Prayer

7. As noted above, the vintage vacation commenced around August 22, with official resignation from teaching duties effective around October 15, the beginning of the next term. Probably in November he trekked to Verecundus' villa in Cassiciacum,[14] where amid farm

work, private tutoring, and philosophical discussions, his hungry heart would pursue in the quiet time available more intense contemplation of God. Companions at the estate included Monica, his son Adeodatus, his brother Navigius, Alypius, two former students named Trygetius and Licentius, and his cousins or relatives Rusticus and Lastidianus. There he authored three works in dialogical format, *Against the Academics, The Happy Life,* and *Order,* to which is usually conjoined a fourth opus, the *Soliloquies,* which, as its title (a word coined by Augustine), evidences, was the fruit of solitary meditations in the divine presence. Dedicated to God, they were, nevertheless, tinctured with the school of pride, that is, modeled after the dialogues of Cicero. Furthermore, he still somewhat self-consciously performed as the master rhetorician, while still laboring under the misconception that the liberal arts constituted a ladder by which educated Christians, more favored than untutored brethren, could ascend to union with, even a vision of, God.

The little band stayed at Cassiciacum some eighteen weeks, from early November, 386, to nearly the middle of March, 387, departing before March 15.[15] Early in 387 Augustine dispatched two letters to Nebridius that broached only generally some of the topics more thoroughly ventilated by the dialogists. Despite Nebridius' kind comments he rates himself only relatively happy, still short of the absolute happiness springing from undiluted knowledge of intelligible realities. These, which connote riches, are like natural numbers, which can be infinitely increased but are not infinitely divisible. On the other hand, sensible objects, which imply poverty of mind, resemble continuous quantities that are physically limited and infinitely diminishable. The soul must be immortal; were it to die, truth, which resides in the soul, would perish—a nonsensical consequence (E 3.1-3). In progressing in knowledge of supersensible realities, he has become absolutely assured of their existence, (E 4.1-2).[16]

The passage of roughly a decade did not decrease gratitude for the blessings showered on him during his rustic retreat. In particular, he saw more keenly how shallow is the glitter of money and honor; here mountains and hills of his thought stand for vain aspirations for eminence (P 45.7). Prolonged prayer in solitude put these down as prettified delusions of a sham happiness, setting him on an even straighter course toward truth, so that he could no more deny the existence of eternal realities than he could deny his own existence. Alypius at first suggested that it would lessen their analytical thrust to interject Christ into philosophical dialogues purporting to establish certain truths by reason alone. Christian ideas, it seemed, were extrinsic to, and, if used, would intrude upon, strict rational discourse. Unpersuaded by this questionable rationalism, Augustine frankly appeals to religion in his dialogues; "Son of God" occurs in *The Happy Life* (4.34); "Christ" is mentioned once in *Against the Academics* (3.20.4) and five times in *Order* (thrice in 1.10.29 alone).[17] Alypius was uncritically enamored of the cedars of the schools, the apparently majestic rational claims, of a nonChristian mindset, which, Augustine implies, were perfused by the pride symbolized by the cedars (P 28.5), already felled by the humble Lord when he chose the weak to confound the strong.[18] After downing the cedars, Christ had devised medicinal herbs, his sacraments and prayers(9.4.8),[19] to immunize little ones against serpents, i.e., heretics like the Manichees and others, whose hardshelled error is hatched from the serpent who is the father of lies (P 57.15).

The stay at the villa of the always dynamic Augustine was hardly a period of carefree rest and relaxation. Besides orchestrating philosophical dialogues, teaching Virgil to Trygetius and Licentius and allotting extra hours to prayer, Augustine, along with his companions, shared in strenuous farm work. Not playing the country squire after the fashion of a Horace on a Sabine farm, he rose earlier than usual to lend a hand in chores (CA 2.4.10) and spent most of the day managing affairs of the farm (CA 1.5.15).[20] At the villa he was evincing an executive capacity to shift occupational gears, exercising on a small scale the rare adaptability of effortlessly combining speculative and practical pursuits, which ripened in his episcopal years when he labored as pastor all day and lucubrated as thinker all night.[21] The long arduous day at Cassiciacum administered with nearly inexhaustible energy portended the packed schedule of the later workhouse who bore without strain a prodigious load of diverse duties.

8. The psalms, which the *Confessions* quote or allude to nearly 400 times, ignited his heart and led him into more intimate prayer, making his own their song of love and cry for mercy, whose sacred language, he later saw, uttered the voice of Christ as head of his mystical body (P 64.7). Not yet a member of the Church, he

considered himself by and large uninitiated in the truth celebrated by the psalms. In his company, along with Alypius, a catechumen also, was Monica, outwardly womanly, inwardly virile in faith; grandmotherly in serene wisdom, motherly in spiritual élan; above all, through-and-through Christian in word and work. Charity radiating from the psalms sparked apostolic zeal to spread their pride-destroying love to the whole world, in consonance with the Church whose song of love in the psalms had been broadcast throughout the earth. The fire inspired by the Holy Spirit consumes the flesh that is grass and purifies gold with flames so devouring that no one can evade its heat (P 18[En.2].7); in particular, he longed to have Manichees burnt to a crisp, their souls transfigured by love. While biting indignation toward Manichean falsity stung him, he felt, loving the sinner, immense pity for spiritually sick men who, in their opposition to the Church's Spirit-filled prayers, brushed aside these spiritual medicines. Were it possible, he would have planned for Manichees nearby to be indirectly moved by the power of the psalms registered in the glow of his visage and fervor of his language.[22] Still, he would preferably be unaware of them; else they might accuse him of affecting a holier-than-thou attitude and, were he to advert to their presence, he would have been reserved. Yet even if they did detect his expressions of love, they would have missed the inward sweetness, perhaps disdaining them as run-of-the-mill formulas of piety. He has been renewed by the God of righteousness, who remade him righteous; who relieves his burden, not a tribulation of the heart, which disturbs sinners, but an exterior distress owed to outward circumstance. His heart has been so enlarged by the love of God that within he can dialogue with the Lord. Thereupon he iterates his plea for mercy; growth in spiritual union sprouts only from persistence (P 4.2).

9. Simultaneously, but without paradox, bestirred by fear and hope, he shivered with fear at the sight of his past sins and the severe punishment due them, and vibrated with hope centered on infinite mercy; a trembling and fervor evidenced in eye movements along with quavering and enthusiastic timbre of voice. While frightened by his unrighteousness, he exulted in God's mercy because he had confessed himself helpless to extricate his spirit from his wretchedness (P 30[En. 2.S.1].13). Not his own bad spirit, which spawned his perverse past (P 142.18), but the Holy Spirit conversed

with him in Ps 4, who, through the coming of incarnate truth, uplifts
the dull of heart. Until recently, Augustine had hankered after vanity
and lying. In one sense vanity consists in questing for the lowest and
last of goods as if they were the highest and first. Lying, which
includes self-deceit, arises when a vain seeker values as permanent
objects fast fading as shadows (P 4.3). The love of vanity may refer
particularly to his thirst for wealth, honor, and power (P
30[En.2.S.1].12). Again, his fall into Manicheism enmeshed him in
vanity in another sense, namely, lack of truth due to deprivation of
the light that is Christ: deceit may refer to espousal of Manichean
fallacies. After raising Jesus from the dead, God sent the Spirit of truth
to convert human hearts from love of this world (P 4.4). During his
Manichean darkness Augustine knew nothing of the true Holy Spirit,
for he believed the blasphemous doctrine that Mani was the Holy
Spirit (5.5.8). The prophet inspired by the Holy Spirit now cries out,
"Know you," certifying that the Lord is indeed speaking through the
vision he has received (P 4.4). Augustine shook with trepidation at the
prospect of God's wrath visited upon his froward allegiance to
Manichean absurdities. Whereas earlier he suggested that even if
Manichees had heard his exclamations, their depth would have
eluded them (9.4.8), now he ventures the hope that if some were
actually nearby, perhaps they might have been so revolted by pursuit
of phantoms as to disgorge their errors as the stomach regurgitates
poisonous food. The death of Jesus, he emphasizes, annuls the
contention that God could not assume human nature; Christ's bodily
nature was not sheer appearance nor was his death on the cross mere
seeming (E 23.6.2. CF 16.4). Contrary to all strains of Docetism,
Christ died in real, not apparent, flesh (P 37.26).

10. In line with "Be angry and do not sin," (Ps 4.5), he was already
doing penance for past wickedness to help eschew this in the future
(P 4.6). The directive can also be taken to mean: instead of consenting
to the first uprush of anger, control the impulse by reason and faith (P
4.6). Augustine's anger was justified; not some preposterous
Manichean evil nature within (8.10.24) but he was responsible for past
faults. Unhappily, Manichees who do not wax wroth over their sins,
which are, in their estimation, the behavioral progeny of the Race of
Darkness, are storing up anger that will inexorably smite them.
Augustine's true goods lay not without but within, to be beheld not
by the eye not of body but of mind. Those, who, like Augustine of

old, stoop to grab pleasure in external goods waste their substance on vanishing things of time, a discharge of the inner toward the outer betokening loss of self. Since only the true good nourishes the soul (E 1), inferior goods leave the soul starved, and hence Manichees, in pursuing corporeal goods, can do no more than lick images of earthly things with hungry cogitations. Licking apparently has a triple signification. First, those who lick the earth put their trust in pseudo-authority and therewith combat Scriptures that substantiate the claims of the Church (P 71.12), Augustine himself being such a hoodwinked licker for nearly ten years. Second, there may be insinuated an allusion related to Manichees as barkers (6.3.4), who, as worshipers of a false god, are somewhat akin to Gentiles, dogs that lick the stones of idols (S 154A.5). Third, licking suggests inability to swallow and digest. Since lower goods, only shadowy and insubstantial, cannot be eaten but simply licked, their cogitation leaves the soul essentially unfed, cheated of understanding of God and self. These famished spirits are mainly Manichees, who, while outwardly robust in propaganda, are inwardly emaciated from privation of the true and good. So they are bade heed the psalmist who, neither whining about present ills nor despairing about the life to come (P 4.8), seeks food from the God of all goods—the light of the Lord's face signed on the soul (P 4.6). On the spirit so sealed is stamped the image of God, one not entirely lost but blemished by sin; then restored to pristine beauty by graceful rebirth, the soul lies open to its eternal good. As a coin stamped with Caesar's image is rendered to Caesar, so the soul illumined by divine light is rendered to God, i.e., committed to him as its true good (P 94.2).

On Manichean reckoning, the elect especially are self-sustained lights; Christians, however, are not lights on their own but lamps borrowing illumination from the savior, becoming lights by participation in divine light. Augustine rejoiced in the light that is *internum/aeternum*; internal, in the highest part of the mind; eternal, originating in the everlasting light. To his dismay erstwhile Manichean colleagues, worshipers of the light sullied with the external and noneternal could make no sense of his luminous interior experiences. Within the chamber that is the heart he had grown angry at, i.e., repented for, his past (P 4.6). There his soul immolated itself on the altar of faith, consumed by the fire that is the Holy Spirit (P 4.7). There he savored sweetness flowing from Christ, the truth who indwells the cubicle of the praying heart (P 4.8), whose light enabled him to grasp inwardly words of the psalm read outwardly. The words, "In the time of wheat, wine, and oil they are multiplied," firmed his resolution not to be multiplied by things of earth, a proliferation issuing not in abundance but scantiness of fare. The soul chasing after countless passing phantasms is torn asunder; knowing no simplicity, no filling, no rest, it is divided, hungry, restless (P 4.9). No longer did he desire to devour times, i.e., to feed on unnourishing temporal goods. Nor did he want to be devoured by times: in pursuing temporals, the soul is gobbled up by times, becoming split and manifold like segments of time. In short, the soul that devours temporals is devoured by them, divided and multiplied like intervals of time. Now, however, he was pursuing not pluralized goods but the all-good whose eternal simplicity shares simplicity with the heart (P 4.9). Ordinarily divine simplicity means that God is what he has; not a substance in which accidents inhere, he is all and each of his attributes (T 15.13). Correspondingly, simplicity here signifies undividedness wholly without plurality, and therefore changelessness in duration. In communing with the eternally simple and unmultiplied, Augustine was spiritually unified, given abundance by spiritual wheat, wine, and oil; divine wheat is Jesus, the living bread come down from heaven (P 4.9); spiritual wine is the exuberance so intoxicating that the soul is insensible to the merely human (P 35.14); spiritual oil is divine delight that exults the mind (P 22.5). While earthly wheat, wine, and oil multiply and distend the soul, their divine counterparts cause it to more brightly image the very oneness of the One (11.29.39).

11. In saying not, "I sleep," but, "I will sleep," the psalmist shows that sovereign peace will reign only in the next life when the mortal frame will be robed in immortality. The resurrection from the dead fulfilling the psalmist's prophecy will, once for all, stop the mouths of foes, especially Manichean vilifiers of Catholicism. The stupendous fact of the resurrection, which will unanswerably silence the most savagely pertinacious decriers of the Christian way, will usher in a peace imperishable because it springs from union with *Idipsum*, the Selfsame. As simple, God is the One. As the Selfsame, God is being itself, pure existence. The term Selfsame philosophically expresses "He who is, " the Biblical name God gives himself (Ex 3.13 ff. 7.10.16. P 121.5). As the Selfsame, God "is the great Is" (P 101[S.2].10)],

absolute being, unmixed with limitation, accident, or change. Because God is being itself, he is immutable (CD 11.10), and so closely joined are his being and changelessness that existence or being (*esse*) is said to be the name of immutability (S 7.7). As immutable, he is exempt from every labor and suffering: he is all, and in that all lies total rest. So the soul one with the Selfsame does not simply long for the manifold of goods distinct from God but gains a measure of peace by centering its intuition on the One instead of being fragmented among the many. Hoping for full rest in the Selfsame, the soul is singularly established by God; singularly, in the sense that all its desires are braided into one single desire affixed on the One. God's holy children are sequestered from the throng of aborning and dying things of time, each a lover of eternity and unity so that even now, stabilized in hope, each can be fused, however distantly, with the wholly One (P 4.10).

Though his heart was aflame, he could not channel his light to former Manichean associates, deaf to every appeal and dead, barren of the life of God that is grace. Remorsefully he recalls how near-hopeless he had been as a proselytizing Manichee, a one-man epidemic, a barking dog bitterly maligning Catholic truth with misinformation and disinformation (3.7.12; 9.4.9). Sharply at variance with his bitterness, the Scriptures he misconstrued were overflowing with honey sweet to the spiritual palate (P 118 [S.22].7]), perfused with the very light that is God (P 118[S.23].1).[23] Blasphemous Manichean distortions of the honeyed and luminous Scriptures (P 138.27) sickened his heart to the point of hatred that was a perfect hate (5.12.22), directed not at their persons but at their malicious errors.

12. Also surfacing in memory was an instantaneous healing from a throbbing toothache, which was both a scourge of justice for sins and an occasion for an extraordinary sign of boundless mercy. So excruciating was the toothache that he could not even talk, allowing the surmise that his jaw was swollen from an abscess. As Thomas De Quincy in *Confessions of an English Opium Eater* observed from his own experience, if a toothache were less common, it would be counted among the most agonizing of pains.[24] Because speechless with agony, he requested on a wax tablet that his companions unite in prayer for healing. Power flashed down fast; no sooner had they knelt down than he was cured. Ever searching in the analytical mode, his mind

inquired into the reasons for the appearance and disappearance of the toothache. He was probably not unaware that the toothache was associated with tooth decay, but the limited medical science of his day left unexplained the particular mechanisms that induced the decay, which eventually irritates the nerves in the pulp chamber. His wonderment over the nature and cause of the pain arose from the underdeveloped state of a medical art incapable of clearly specifying the fundamental processes underlying caries.[25] Much more baffling was the almost immediate vanishing of the affliction plainly wrought by divine power in response to prayer of deep faith. Such a supernatural intervention is humanly inexplicable; precisely how and why God performs a particular miracle lies hidden in the depths of his wisdom and goodness.[26] Never before favored by such a singular visitation, he could not be other than overcome by awe over God's command of every fiber of human nature: one fiat of the divine physician, and his anguish was gone. His whole being uplifted in joy over the all-goodness of the Father who cares for each of his children as if each were the only one (3.11.19), he burst out in praise for his amazing cure. A now strong faith deferred a companion spiritual pleasure; he still could not believe with full certitude that he had been healed of all past sins; complete assurance would be his only when his forthcoming baptism washed away every least transgression.

Chapter 5: Resigns Teaching Post. Informs Ambrose of Desire for Baptism

13. At the end of the vacation period he notified his students' parents of his resignation as official rhetor, here belittlingly styled a vendor of words (as if teaching rhetoric were mainly a business, not a liberal art), adducing two reasons: a religious motive, his decision to give special service to God; a pragmatic consideration, the near-impossibility of teaching with labored breathing and a chronic chest pain.[27] When he asked Ambrose to designate a work of Scripture that might best ready him for reception of new life, the bishop proposed Isaiah because, Augustine believes from the vantage point of a mature Christian in 397, that this work clearly prophesies, more than those of other prophets, the Gospel and the call of the Gentiles. Isaiah foretold how beautiful would be the feet of those bringing good tidings of God's goodness (Is 53.7. CF 32.10), forecasting also that the Messiah

would sprout from a root of Jesse (Is 11.10), the anointed who would bear men's sins and suffer for them (Is 53.4-8.CALP 2.3. S 218.6). The Messianic kingdom will be a universal realm of grace, all nations streaming to the Lord's mountain (Is 2.2. EJ 1.13). God's law goes forth from Zion, but the Lord's word of the New Dispensation flows from Jerusalem (Is 2.3. S 218.6). In the new order God's salvific work and people extend to the ends of the earth (Is 48.6. S 199.1). As Is 65.2 prophesied, the Jews rejected the Messiah; hence the Lord revealed his word to the Gentiles who did not seek him (Rom 10.20-1); a like theme sounds in Is 6.9-10, quoted in Mt 13.14-5: the Gentiles acquired the heritage repudiated by the Jews (CF 13.11). Other texts may be cited; a virgin will bear a child (Is 7.14), the root of Jesse (Is 11.10 CF 13.3); the Christ foretold is the cornerstone of a new people (CR 23.43). Christ as a suffering servant rules the people of God (Is 52.13-54.5. CE 1.31.47); as head of the Church, Christ is king of the city of God (Is 52.13-54.5. CD 18.29).[28]

However, from a reading of the first section Augustine gleaned little or no insight probably because the book, the product of many hands, is so loosely organized that it is now labeled "a collection of collections." The unity of the first chapter, which he may have read, leaves much to be desired, ranging over diverse topics, including two sets of scattered sayings.[29] Understandably, a discouraged Augustine cast the codex aside, expecting to pick it up anew only after he had become more conversant with the conceptual style of divine writ. Ambrose's recommendation of a difficult book may have stemmed from thinking Augustine's stock of Christian learning was close to equivalent to his own Biblical erudition. Apparently he overestimated not Augustine's acumen but his fund of religious information; even a genius cannot go from the unknown to the unknown. We can only speculate about other reasons influencing Ambrose's suggestion.[30] Isaiah was his favorite Old Testament prophet, quoted 120 times, far more than any other prophet.[31] Moreover, at this time, 385/7, he was composing a commentary on Isaiah,[32] his mind brimming with the subject. Furthermore, aware of the Manichean contention that the Gospels and apostolic writings reject the law and prophets (R 1.22.1; 2.7.1),[33] he perceived that Isaiah's prophecy of the Gospel forged a link between Old and New Testament.[34]

Chapter 6: Baptized with Alypius and Adeodatus

14. Returning to Milan from Cassiciacum before March 15, 387, early in Lent, which began March 10,[35] Augustine enrolled as one of the competents or catechumens. Also a candidate was Alypius who had practiced a relatively severe form of asceticism to dominate the lower self, walking barefoot on the wintry-cold northern Italian ground; an especially mortifying abnegation for a resident of sultry North Africa, who was habituated to an urban professional lifestyle that had made him soft in comparison with peasants more inured to walking in harsh weather with slight or no footwear.[36] The mysteries to which Augustine refers were the three sacraments of the rite of Christian initiation.

Scheduled for baptism too was Adeodatus, the fruit of his illicit cohabitation with his unnamed concubine (4.2.2; 6.15.25), hence described as the child of his sin, his nonmatrimonial union. Born in 372, probably around the summer, in the spring of 387 he was nearly fifteen years old. Amazingly precocious, perhaps bordering on or actually a genius, he outshone many of the literati of Augustine's acquaintance. Modestly declining to take any credit for the young man's brilliance, his father deemed himself responsible only for the sin attached, the nonmarital union of which Adeodatus was the issue. Conferring a double goodness, the Lord who made Adeodatus' extraordinary intelligence is to remake his spirit in baptismal cleansing.

Adeodatus was an interlocutor with Augustine in *The Teacher*,[37] a work in the format of a dialogue, which occurred prior to the summer of 388 when Adeodatus was still in his sixteenth year, and probably prepared for publication in 389. Augustine takes care to underscore that the incisive comments accredited to Adeodatus were actually voiced by the young student. There was no need to play the proud father inflating his son's reputation; with genetic material the duplicate of his father's, Adeodatus was apparently a budding second Augustine. The father was astounded by other outstanding qualities, left unspecified. So superb did he rate him in all of the liberal arts in which he was instructing him that his awesome intellect led him to praise God for this young miracle, taken in the broad sense as signifying "anything difficult or unusual that exceeds the expectation and capacity of the person viewing it"(UC 16.34). A miracle in the strict sense is an event produced by God over and beyond the universal order of nature (J 24.1) that, as a sign, conveys to the senses a divine meaning (T 3.10.19): such was the instantaneous healing of his agonizing toothache (9.4.12). Adeodatus departed the earth in adolescence, apparently in 389 or 390, when only seventeen. Passing over in silence tears wrung by this untimely death, he feels certain of Adeodatus' eternal salvation, for he can recollect nothing reprehensible of which his son was guilty as boy and adolescent. As a boy, Adeodatus was never carried away by love of play, never thirsted to witness spectacles, never cheated at games, and never brazenly denied wrongdoings while bluffing hurt innocence (1.19.30). Unlike the adolescent Augustine, he did not at fifteen plunge into sexual dalliances (2.2.4; 3.7.8) or pilfer pears from a neighbor's orchard (2.4.9). Betraying no decided evil proclivities, he was, by African or any standards, unusually blessed with high moral stature. Though the father was more than twice as old as the son, in the line of grace Adeodatus was the same age as Augustine, both being potential *infantes*, about to be reborn in Christ. Yet as regards doctrine Augustine was superior; upon him devolved the duty of schooling his son in the creed and code of the Church.[38]

After seven weeks Augustine, along with Alypius and Adeodatus, was baptized by Ambrose (so named CJ01 6.21) at the Easter vigil service April 24/25, 387.[39] After entering the piscina naked to symbolize that they were to be born anew from the womb of holy mother Church, each was immersed in the flowing water three times in honor of the trinity. Along with baptism the new Christians received confirmation through the laying on of hands and anointing in the Holy Spirit, then fed upon the Holy Eucharist for the first time.[40] His carnal self dead and buried in baptismal waters, all lingering anxiety about remission of past sins (9.4.12) evaporated. In confirmation the same fire that fell on the disciples on the first Pentecost descended into his soul, purifying the spiritual self that is gold (S 227.P18 [S.2].7). In the Eucharistic liturgy he sacramentally ate of the power of the crucified body on the cross and drank of the blood dripping from Christ's side (P 33[S.1].S 228B.2). Fresh communing with God continued beyond the first absorption in the divine during Easter eve so that his heart was ever saturated but never sated with always-renewed delight. He tasted the depths of the wisdom and mercy in the salvific plan, rejoicing, in particular, in the momentous fact that on him had been visited healing with infinite care and love (3.11.19). Distinct from the tears of sorrow shed by Monica (3.12.21)

and the storm of contrition that erupted in the garden in Milan
(8.12.28), out of Augustine's heart now streamed tears of joy,
especially when excited by psalms and hymns of the Church,
liturgical chants expressing the sovereign confession that irrupted for
countless mercies that had lured the prodigal son home to a
celebration of renewed love. As the truth of the sacred songs that God
is an ever-tender Father flowed into his heart, he overflowed with
total self-donation, which released unstoppable tears begotten of piety
and praise: happiness was gladsome weeping.

Chapter 7: Antiphonal Singing. Discovery of Bodies of Sts. Gervasius and Protasius

15. Ambrose was a man of parts: skilled administrator, allegorical
exegete, judicious thinker, and accomplished homilist, he shone
perhaps mainly as a man of action, a bishop of indomitable character
in defending the rights of the Church against incursions of the state.
Of Arian persuasion,[41] the Empress Justina, ruling in place of the boy-
Emperor Valentinian II (born 371), around the start of Lent in 385
demanded the Portian Basilica outside the walls be ceded for use by
Arian clergy, a mandate Ambrose refused. Then just prior to Easter
she ordered him to relinquish the Basilica of Ambrose, the cathedral
church. Despite strong pressure, including the marshaling of troops,
Ambrose successfully withstood this second threatened intrusion on
his authority. In January, 386, after issuing an edict against Catholics,
Justina commanded the bishop to appear at the imperial court.
Ambrose stood firm, and in February, 386, to forestall arrest he took
refuge in the Ambrosian Basilica, there joined by many of the faithful.
For several days and nights the little band occupied the cathedral,
balking the attempt to seize it. Fortunately Arian Gothic troops
ringing the church desisted from storming it. Finally, acknowledging
defeat, the court rescinded the anti-Catholic edict.[42] Monica assumed
a leading part among the beleaguered Catholics, living on prayer day
and night, conceding scant attention to food and sleep. Not having
undergone moral or even full intellectual conversion, both of which
lay months away, Augustine kept coolly aloof from the heroism; still,
waves of turmoil sweeping through the city moved him.

During the crisis Ambrose introduced the custom, which originated
in Eastern churches, of congregational singing of psalms and hymns,

specifically adopting the Syrian style of antiphonal chanting, which is the singing of alternate verses by two choirs. Without this form of communal vocal prayer during the lengthy watch, the people might have been overcome by weariness of spirit and body. Their drooping frames reinvigorated, Ambrose's flock happily learned that hours absorbed in Christ did not drag but flew. Interestingly, the practice spread during the short space of the intervening eleven years (386-97) throughout nearly the whole of the Western Church. When Augustine was bishop of Hippo, antiphonal chanting was apparently practiced; certainly congregational singing was the established custom (P 18[S. 2].1).[43]

16. Directed by a vision, Ambrose discovered on June 17, 386, the bodies of Sts. Gervasius and Protasius in the church of Sts. Nabor and Felix, where they were entombed, and by June 19 had them translated to the Ambrosian Basilica.[44] Precisely how they lived and when they were martyred remained unknown, but miraculously, after apparently many years, their bodies were still incorrupt. So priceless were they in their triumphant self-immolation in death that the Lord preserved their bodies as a treasure, spared from inexorable disintegration. At the opportune moment God divulged their location; the supernaturally guided discovery and its consequences persuaded Justina that the hand of God was at work and, checking her imperial fury, dissuaded her from further persecution. When the exhumed bodies were transferred to the new basilica, spiritual and physical healings took place; a number of individuals were delivered from evil spirits as soon as the demons acknowledged the sacred remains, and Severus, a butcher blind for years (E 22.17), recovered his sight when a handkerchief touched to the bier was applied to his eyes.[45] The sacred remains, precious in God's eyes because the saints imitated the all-precious death of Jesus (P 115.5), were permeated with the healing power of Christ's crucifixion.

Augustine breaks out in thanksgiving for the mysterious manner in which God triggered his memory to praise him for events which he neglected to instance in prior chapters according to proper chronological sequence. During February and June, 386, he regretfully recalls, while impinged by the allure of God's affection represented by the odor of ointments, his heart, not yet being ignited, did not run after God; still unconverted, he was finecombing arguments instead of being caught up in Catholic devotion. Later, after baptism on April

24/5, 387, he wept with even more joy (9.6.14), mingled with sorrow to compensate for failure to join in the psalm-singing during the embattled days and nights of February, 386. In the past, before conversion, he had strained without success to capture God's fragrance; now, finally, as weeping redoubled delight, he could breathe the rich odor of divine ointments and race after his beloved within, insofar as such breath of loving response can manage free play in a house built of grass, an abode of flesh frail and fleeting as grass (Is 40.6).

Chapter 8: Preparation for Return to Africa. Monica's Childhood

17. The God who makes "men of one mind to live in a house" (Ps 67.7)[16] is wholly present in all creatures but spiritually inhabits graced individuals, who, of one mind in the line of community, constitute the Church that is the house of God (AC 4.32). In a special fashion he dwells in particular associations, holy sites in which men seek God in an organized horarium of regular prayer and sharing of goods (P 67.7), communities of a religious type like that Augustine proposed to form when he returned to North Africa.[17] One such member of the new monastic company was Evodius,[18] a fellow Thagastan, formerly a member of the imperial officers, who had been converted to Catholicism before Augustine, and now proposed to enlist in the legion of God, as a member of a monastic community in Thagaste, ministering as a servant of God rather than toiling as a servant of the world. After the long trip south from Milan to Rome, he and Augustine stayed at Ostia Antica, the seaport of Rome, from which they would embark for Africa. There the light of Augustine's life, Monica, was unexpectedly snuffed out.

Though he praises God in globo for numerous events of which pressure of time constrains him to skip notice, nothing can keep him from paying tribute to Monica, who mothered him both in the flesh, giving him the light of day, and in his heart, carrying him to the light of eternal day. His debt was total: she gave all to God and, in the power of the most high, all to him through her life of love. "To her merit I believe I owe all that I am," he wrote at Cassiciacum (BV 1.6). Without Monica there would have been no Augustine in the line of nature or grace. God implanted his gifts of virtue at work in her heart;

she endued herself with neither nature nor nurture of soul. It was God who created her with qualities of which her parents, her physical makers, had not the slightest inkling, and who were the primary agents of her rearing. Christian discipline, emblemized by the rod of Christ, raised her in holy fear; in the ancient world corporal punishment was routinely administered to children (1.9.14). Discipline points children toward virtue; virtues externalized out of fear of punishment are gradually internalized, so that fear leads to friendship with Christ (P 5.9), and the rod of the Lord, by restraining lower appetites, promotes spiritual growth and thereby becomes a consolation (P 22.4).

Because a layman at the time, Augustine could not deliver even the briefest eulogy at Monica's funeral liturgy. Now in these closing chapters of his autobiography proper, he offers an encomium of his loveliest friend, an accolade that does not extol her in the sometimes gauchely inflated language of a panegyric but simply delineates her beauty of spirit through her own words and actions, her life of holiness in bud and bloom being its own testimony of praise. After explicitly describing Adeodatus as a kind of miracle of mind (9.6.14), he limns Monica as a miracle of affectivity, a masterwork of the holiness of God. As the hound of heaven tirelessly hunted for the wandering Augustine, Monica served as a kind of surrogate-hound, a preeminent instrument applied, through never-ceasing prayer, to her son by the Father to bring her prodigal home. Whereas providential grace principally wrought Augustine's conversion, Monica's grace-filled presence throughout all nine books secondarily predominated in his supernatural shaping. If at every switch point God admonished Augustine which path to take, the subordinate source of that administration was the self-sacrificing Monica. Through prayer she pervaded the life of Augustine, implicitly "omnipresent" in every turning point on his road to healing. After earlier books depicting Monica as a model Christian mother, these final chapters portray her as child growing in virtue, exemplary wife, mystic, and Christian sage in the face of death. Most of Monica's moral education came not from her mother but from a nanny, an aged servant (actually a slave) who had cared for her father as an infant. Morally schooled in the stern but straight way of practical wisdom, the delegate-mother allowed the girls only moderate portions at table, forbidding food and drink between meals, even though at times in the heat of North Africa their throats seemed dry as dust. Strict discipline would flower into a habit of self-denial inclining them to take pleasure not in excess but in control of appetite, bridling any tendency toward overindulgence.

18. Receptive as she was to her moral tutor, Monica tumbled into a pattern against which her training was meant to arm her, becoming not a drunkard but a wine-bibber. When assigned to fetch wine from the cellar, in a youthful spirit of playful curiosity she innocently began to sample the wine, at first taking only a sip, gradually, however, imbibing nearly a cup at a time until she was addicted, "Habits are first cobwebs, then cables," goes a Spanish proverb. Yet her condition was not hapless. However, while parents and nanny were absent, God was always present, surgically healing Monica through a servant, whose insult he used as a scalpel to cut away diseased matter from her heart. Quarreling with Monica in the wine cellar, the maidservant silenced Monica with the sneer that she was nothing but a wine-bibber. Even as this stab panged her, the blade of the taunt pierced her conscience—she immediately made a clean break with her past. In verbally spearing Monica, the servant girl did not aim at correction; otherwise she would have driven her point home in public. A private quarrel may have sparked the private accusation; or perhaps the servant girl was simply waiting the opportunity to privately rebuke Monica, lest she herself be taxed for letting matters drift; in this second instance even apart from a verbal tiff she would have stung Monica rather than gently corrected her. Yet out of the ill-motivated act God drew Monica's amendment. Where flattery perverts, insult converts: God turned the cutting barb to the good of her soul. The ruler of the whole universe, who configures all to his lofty ends, turns to his good purpose the depths of the torrent, i.e., the deeps of the disorder that constitute evil. God fits within his divine plan the turbulent flow down through the centuries; from shifting currents that stand for evil actions, which deviate from the firmament of eternal law, God fashions his grand schemata of eternal justice and mercy. So in this singular event God extracted good from evil, disposing the unhealed passion of a servant to heal Monica. From the fact that the healing was ordained by God, Augustine draws a further lesson: not to a human being but to the Lord must be assigned ultimate credit for amending another even if one's fraternal correction is purposed toward such amendment.

Chapter 9: Monica Peacemaker and Servant

19. Born between November, 331, and November, 332, of Christian parents who instructed her in virtue under the close supervision of a jealous servant, she was pure in soul and comportment, self-controlled with a Christian common sense or prudence. In remarking that God made her subject to her parents instead of her parents making her subject to him, Augustine distinguishes between the divine plan itself and conformity to the plan. Clearly her parents trained her to obey God, but this moral education did not make her subject to God; it conformed to the subjection appointed by God. She was created to obey her parents and, through that subordination, made subject to God. In her teens she married Patricius, a pagan, to whom, as master of the household, she pledged obedience. From the start she aimed at conquering her lord for the Lord, evangelizing him not by word but example. Winning his respect were her spiritual charm and exceptional robustness of soul. Unhappily, he double-crossed her through adultery, a vice to which North Africans were distressingly prone. Pained by his repeated betrayals, she serenely tolerated his dalliances, never confronting him, always praying that God's mercy would render him fully faithful. Kindhearted as he was, Patricius erupted in Vesuvius-like outbursts of anger. Deliberately declining to battle back with a counter-tirade, Monica conquered him by meekness. Only when the storm had passed did she proffer an explanation for any action of hers that might have precipitated an explosion. Unfolding her strategy to other wives whose countenances had been routinely bruised and at times blackened by beatings of wrathful husbands, she half-jokingly but seriously reminded them that the terms of their marital contract committed them to be slaves of their husbands. When they became astonished that a spouse of Patricius' reputation for fury had not regularly pummeled her, she disclosed her policy: because it takes two to make a quarrel, gentleness effectively forestalls nasty conflicts. Wives who availed themselves of her virtuous program were no longer cuffed about while others continued to be physically abused.

20. When Monica's servants filled the ears of her mother-in-law with lies denigrating her, her unvarying response to her elder's irritation was gentleness that disarmed her misled critic, who, once undeceived, rounded upon the slanderers through Patricius, who had

the poison-tongued women whipped.

21. The Father of mercies, who, as his personal mercy, created him in the maternal nest of Monica (a nearly perpetual benediction [5.8.15]), channeled her love outside the home, molding her as a peacemaker par excellence. While attempting to repair enmities, she never repeated to her conferee blistering aspersions an adversary may have spewed upon her name but transmitted only words pregnant with hope toward rapprochment. Yet, as Augustine's pastoral experience informed him, such healing charity is exceptional. Many intermediaries are talebearers who not only relay to individuals ill-tempered abuse spat out by foes but cannot check the impulse to inflate it with fictive invective. Monica's loving words, however, quenched flames of anger verging on hatred, inspiriting enemies to bury their grievances. In knitting together hostile hearts in mutual forgiveness, she was not exhibiting dexterity in what is today labeled conflict resolution but practicing an art of peacemaking that was a "great gift" from God; she was what has been named a theodidact, tutored in concrete means of spiritual harmony by God himself. According to Augustine, every man is a theodidact in the general sense: the interior teacher teaches the standards of thinking, the rules of mathematics, the principles of aesthetics, the precepts of ethics, and the *lumina virtutum* or basic patterns of the virtues. Monica was, however, a theodidact in a special respect, a spirit instructed in the school of the Spirit, in which she was steeped in the science of the saints, the inner wisdom that God shares with his holy ones; a wisdom not elaborated by doctrinal analysis but ripened through ceaseless prayer and sacrifice. Impenetrated by God, she spoke and acted with the peace of God, submissive to the order within that constitutes the peace imaging to a high degree wisdom in the fullest; the serenity taught by her intimate teacher she communicated to others toward the healing of bitterness.[49]

22. Toward the end of Patricius' life, probably in 369-70 (he died in Augustine's seventeenth year, 370/1; 3.4.7), Monica's spiritual charm eventually lured him into the Catholic Church, with the result that, as she discerningly anticipated earlier (9.9.19), his newborn condition liberated him from his previously uncontrollable propensity to philander. She was a servant of the servants of God, exactingly and exquisitely attentive to their domestic needs. At Cassiciacum and Milan and for a short space in Rome, Augustine and his companions

banded together in a quasi-religious community to whose members he assigns the honored name *servi Dei*, servants of God (9.8.17). Later, in 388, first in Carthage, then in his paternal home in Thagaste, Augustine's spiritual associates will be bonded in a lay community pledged to an ascetical life according to the evangelical counsels.[50] Augustine's confreres reverenced Monica because her espousal with God radiated not only in mien and manner but especially in her daily life of prayer and duty consecrated to the Father. No doubt she continually enjoyed heart-to-heart union with God, an intimate presence manifest to those to whom she ministered. Incarnating the virtues of the model widow, she was married only once, lovingly providing for her parents in their old age, dedicating herself to good works that are the love of man manifesting the love of God. When her children went astray (here Augustine is thinking mainly of himself), she suffered birth-pangs, undergoing fresh travail of heart till they were once more formed in Christ (9.8.17). Already magnified, Monica's heart expanded the more to enfold the new community. She loved and looked after all as if mother of all, as if each were another Augustine; she served as if daughter of all, as if an inferior duty-bound to perform prosaic tasks indispensable for a community to survive and thrive, living the outwardly drudging but inwardly glorious life of a handmaid of the Lord, serving the Word by serving his servants in their quotidian wants.

Chapter 10: Contemplation at Ostia

23. Shortly before Monica's death, providential love enfolded Augustine and Monica in joint contemplative prayer, to which they were uplifted standing by a second-floor window that opened out on a courtyard garden in Ostia; a spiritual elevation captured in one famous painting by Ary Scheffer (1845), which takes the artistic license of picturing the two overlooking the Tiber. Augustine's account of the scene blends Plotinian and Christian language to convey what was, it is now generally admitted, lofty communion with God.[51] While practically all agree that their prayer rose to true contemplation, no consensus has been reached as regards the degree of the contemplation, some calling it active contemplation, others concluding that the pair were blessed with passive contemplation (true mystical prayer as defined in the modern sense), and still others

judging their mystical flight genuine ecstacy. After a gloss of sections 23-5, examination of key features of this remarkable experience apparently validates the claim that Monica and Augustine were favored with passive contemplation.

During a span of comparative leisure, after the taxing 400-plus miles trek south from Milan, while resting as they prepared to voyage to North Africa, mother and son entered into prayerful conversation, discoursing, in spiritually passionate accents redolent of the fragrance of the divine, about the heavenly city. In the words of Phil 3.13, they forgot things past and stretched toward those lying ahead, dialoguing in the light of the changeless truth about what will transpire in the eternal life of the saints. The language suggests a prayerful time-line, a past-present-future schema oriented toward eternity. Dropped from memory is the past, all that is freighted with the human and purely temporal; their present prayer is offered in the illumination of the ever-present eternal truth; they are extended futureward in a yearning for things eternal (P 89.5). Whereas an ordinary time-line is a psychic distension (11.26.32; 27.36), to which may be appended a moral connotation of dispersion (11.29.39), this supernaturalized time-line betokens an extension that is an upward tendency toward the eternal. As they discussed in plain but rich spiritual terms rather than in sophisticated theological parlance indescribable wonders of the life of the saints in and with God, as they colloquied in the presence of the truth, the Word of God, beseeching his light, they panted after heavenly waters streaming from the fountain of life that is Christ (P 35.15), which spring from the Spirit of Christ (P 14.8). They begged that the waters of the Spirit be sprinkled upon them, pleading for more wisdom so that they could plumb, as far as possible according to their potential degree of union with God, the meaning of the majestic life in the mysterious beyond.

24. Concluding that no sensory delight, however fetching, can match supernal joys—indeed such paltry delights seemed not even worthy of mention—they scaled the ladder of being from exterior to interior, from inferior to superior, to attain, hearts burning with holy desire, the Selfsame, the personal God who simply is (9.4.11). Step by step they rose, from earthly things up to the heaven itself, the abode of radiant sun, moon, and stars, finally standing agape with praiseful awe before all the stupefying works of the cosmos. Ascending to the next, supersensible stage, they beheld the rarer splendor of their own

souls. But quickly beyond that level they climbed, further rising to the supernatural, the realm of unending delight, where those in Abraham's bosom (9.3.6) feed on truth, the incorruptible bread of angels that is the Word of God (P 71.17), the changeless food that changes its consumers into itself (7.10.16). So transmuted, the blessed abound in the life that is the wisdom of the Word, the pattern for all things created in past, present, and future. But creative wisdom, by which things are created in time, is itself not created nor is it in time since it is eternal: the Word, its duration not subject to succession, simply is in an eternal present, without past or future. While meditating on wisdom, Augustine and his mother were suddenly rocketed up to its plane, actually touching it, faces of the soul pressed against it in a total élan of the spirit, which lasted *in ictu oculi*, only a short time.[52] There they left the first fruits of the spirit, all the issue of their fiery faith, hope, and love, expressed at the highest point of the soul.[53] Reluctantly, perforce they dropped back, down into the realm of time in which a word begins and ends, unlike the forever-changeless Word that in itself never grows old and, as creative wisdom, unceasingly makes all things new, perfectly imaging the Father who is *nunquam vetus, innovans omnia* (1.4.4). In this passage the two souls do not contact the allness of God as such but Christ as wisdom that beatifies souls before the final resurrection,[54] as the Word upon which contemplative souls can banquet, however briefly, even in this life.

Material things in their contingency must needs be grounded in a creator or, in the moving language of Augustine, cry out to the viewer: we did not make ourselves; he who unchangeably abides forever made us things of time (10.6.9). However, as Augustine and Monica mounted on high, all images and ideas became still; the Word alone spoke not through others but intimately to their spirits, and, in response, in a flash of mind they really touched in some measure eternal wisdom. Suppose all other inferior visions were blotted out; suppose this one vision went on and on forever; suppose the absorption in joy could be endlessly prolonged; then their moment of contemplation would fuse with everlasting beatitude. Their short span of rapture was a foretaste of an eternal intuition, an embryonic equivalent of the unutterable delight in the presence of the Lord that is Abraham's bosom or the happiness-conferring presence of Christ as God (9.3.6), now enjoyed by souls of the blessed awaiting the resurrection of the body when all will rise but not all will be changed.[55] At the crack of doom some men will still be dwelling on earth, but all, living and dead, gathered into heaven will be transformed, invested with glorified bodies, the mortal putting on immortality (S 351.8), with the result that humanity will be not only abide in the presence of the divine Christ but will see God face to face.

Only some sixteen months separate the two ascents analyzed above (7.10.16; 17.23) from the so-called vision at Ostia, but during that short stretch of calendar a spiritual era elapsed. In August, 386, Augustine's soul was inundated with divine lights, his spirit so transfigured that he instantly rived chains of unchastity and ambition which had shackled him for over fifteen years. After receiving baptism, confirmation, and the Eucharist on April 24, 387, he lived as a new creation singing the new song of freedom and love. The two experiences at Milan and their counterpart at Ostia transpired within a brief time span and on the same soil but under a vastly different spiritual sky. A state of profound inward renewal wrought by what a later age would call sacramental graces constituted a new mode of existence in which the celebrated interior event at Ostia occurred. This radical interior transmutation provides the framework for the essential disparity of the Ostia event from its predecessors. Whereas the earlier ascensions culminate not in mystic illumination but in a heightened lucid understanding of God or vision, only tenuously achieved, the Ostia event does not border on but is nothing less than a genuine mystical encounter.

Two main strands in Monica's and Augustine's post-experiential observations signalize the utterly superhuman configuration of their commerce with the divine. First, the crowning point of their contemplation did not intrinsically rely upon the preliminary upward movement to the heights. Human ratiocination functioned as an auxiliary, an external support so dispensable that God could have spoken to them without their initially hearing the words of changing temporals proclaiming that the unchanging eternal crafted them. If Monica and Augustine had not risen from the exterior to the interior to the superior and if images of earth and heaven had fallen silent, God could have spoken, as no doubt he did, to the prayerful pair. He could have manifested himself through his Word alone, without the mediation of other agencies. In fact, Monica and Augustine experienced God immediately, neither through intrinsic dependence on creatures betokening their creative cause nor through agencies disclosing the Word: they directly tasted wisdom itself. From one angle, they did not ascend to God; rather, he descended to and into them. God was essentially active, and they essentially passive, their hearts vessels into which was decanted the unmediated gift of closest communion with the all-high, their spiritual mouths drinking directly from the very fount of wisdom.

Second, assessment of their ravishing light assures Monica and Augustine of its supratemporal modality: if their union with God had been more than momentary, if it had gone on and on, it would have been substantially identical with the pre-resurrection beatitude of the blessed whose spirits feed on the wisdom that is the Word. At that moment they were enwrapped in a quasi-heavenly transport comparable to the supernal life of the blessed, beyond anything accessible to senses or understanding. Human effort, even if graced, cannot reap such quasi-beatific existence: it is the purest of gifts, an exceptionally gratuitous phenomenon. In short, mother and son were raised to passive contemplation, dowered with a spiritual sensitivity not of this world, indeed out of this world, enjoying a mode of cognition that departed, in a broad sense, only in degree of duration from the endless contemplation of wisdom enlightening the blessed. Moreover, Augustine's language carries an import of passive contemplation. He describes his and Monica's souls as caught up in a vision of God, as wholly taken out of themselves, so enclosed in the bosom of God that they were detached from all that was earthly. They were borne away from the bourn of the ordinary, enravished and sweetly buried in the plenitude of God from which blazes forth ineffable joy setting them on fire with exultation: their souls basked in light and delight unattainable by sheer striving in prayer.[56]

Two factors, one dispositive, the other collaborative, lend credence to the interpretation of the Ostia event as mystical. The first two ascents to God, we observed before, were markedly intellectual ventures that never reached steady vision, partly because they took place during a period when Augustine, barren of inclination to deep prayer, was still "cold, removed from the fire of the Spirit" (9.7.15). Following upon conversion, however, his heart, invaded by the Spirit, ate and drank insatiably of the sweetness of God while his soul was transformed by tears of delight (9.6.14). Thus, in contrast to the two previous ascents, at Ostia his soul was properly disposed, without being inevitably determined, toward the gift of mystical prayer. It was Monica who played the collaborative role or, more precisely, exercised, as a necessary condition of Augustine's elevation, a quasi-magisterial office in the school of Christ, the supreme teacher. Association with Monica helps explain the soaring of spirit with which Augustine was surprisingly favored less than six months after baptism. Monica was constantly imbued with the presence of God, her companionship with God within being so impressive that Augustine's fellow servants of God sensed godliness radiating from her (9.9.22). Because of intense immersion in God she was visited, we may conjecture, by penetrative caresses of the most intimate from the God who is all love. Prior to Ostia Monica was already proficient in existential wisdom (9.8.17) and exquisitely fluent in the language of God that is prayer. Probably, we may surmise, in earlier interior communing she had been transported into God and enrapt in his light in mystical trysts. Hence on this occasion Monica was the teacher and Augustine the student, she the master and he the apprentice.[57] Rising up in practiced flight to contemplation of the eternal that enveloped her, she bore the novice Augustine up on her eagle wings. Always the mother, Monica in a certain sense carried Augustine in her arms across the mystical threshold into the quasi-supernal region where, all veils of the natural and human dropping away, wisdom is tasted in itself, directly known and felt.

25. Because mother and son were carried out of themselves into the presence of God, the Ostia experience may be counted ecstatic in the broad sense. Nevertheless, it may fall shy of ecstasy in the strict sense in which there is a total suspension of sensory powers in every way. Moreover, ecstasy, according to some authorities, ordinarily lasts at least a short time whereas the Ostia union is characterized as only momentary or very fleeting.[58]

In resumé, the religiously charged atmosphere of the experience puts beyond the pale of doubt the claim that Monica and Augustine rose to the plane of active contemplation. Too it seems at least morally certain that they were lofted to the pitch of passive contemplation, their union with God purest gift, intrinsically independent of the rungs of their humanly initiated upward climb; at its consummatory point it was truly an extra-mundane communion with wisdom which, if protracted, would have become one with supernal beatitude.[59] Nonetheless, the experience does not qualify as strictly ecstatic according to the criteria set down by De Guibert, Tanquerey, and Poulain.

26. Augustine takes pains, however concise his statement, to stress that he is correctly recounting the essentials of their contemplation. Through unlettered, his mother was fully able to act as a compeer in their flight above because she was an outstanding example of the simple faithful firm in faith, strong in hope, vibrant with charity, who, mature in Christian wisdom, albeit without books, are doubly docile, pliable under the pressure of divine leading and teachable, self-opened to divine truth, specially illuminated by the teacher with whom they converse in accents of love.[60] Moreover, he points out, he is veraciously recording the substantial content of what he said at Ostia. However, he is now carefully paraphrasing; the words set down are not exactly the same as those spoken at Ostia nor did he then avail himself of some of the Plotinian conceptual language in which he now garbs description of his unforgettable encounter from on high.

In the perspective of eternal glory, all the delights of this world seem worthless or contemptible. In particular, Monica, full of God, saw no more reason for tarrying in this vale of tears. In long patience-testing, amid all the drudgery of ordinary existence, she had unwaveringly concentrated her energies to live for God alone, with complete trust beseeching only one object, the conversion of her son, a prayer answered superabundantly by the God who gives infinitely more than suppliants desire (8.12.29) since her son became not only a Christian but a servant of God, committed to live in community, forsaking wife and wealth for God. Her mission accomplished, no other motive obtained for staying on this mortal coil. In effect, Monica, masterful exemplar of prayer, was calling upon her Father to take her home.

Chapter 11: Final Thoughts, Death of Monica

27. When Monica was stricken with a fever roughly five days later, God signaled that he was fulfilling her implicit prayer to depart from the body. Employing supernatural discernment once more, she was certain that she would die in Rome. Renouncing concern about where her body was to be buried, she solicited one benefaction only,

this relevant to speedy attainment of beatitude of soul: "All I ask is that you always remember me at the altar of the Lord." In general, being present at the altar of God meant attendance at Mass (S 159.1), and remembrance at the altar of God betokened participation in Mass (CD 20.9). Her sole desire was that her sons always pray for her soul when they assisted at the sacrifice of the Mass, which she had never missed for one day (9.13.36). Though no longer in the body, dead Christians are still members of the kingdom of Christ that is the Church (CD 20.9), to whom Christians here below can extend assistance as fellow members of the communion of saints, the doctrinal foundation for remembrance of the dead, which was strongly characteristic of the African Church.[61] Present with Augustine on this sad occasion was his brother Navigius (so named BV 1.6).

28. Augustine thankfully reflects on the beyond-the-human gifts lavished by the invisible God, which are made visible in wonderful virtues of the faithful. Not sheerly external like fasting, prayer, and almsgiving in which Pharisees may excel, the works are principally interior, fruits of the Spirit so marked in Monica; love, joy, peace, patience, kindness, meekness, chastity (SDM 2.24.81). He further praises God for Monica's outstanding poverty of spirit evidenced in casting aside all that smacked in the least of the vain and temporal (SDM 1.1.3). Previously as a dutiful Christian wife, she had made every possible effort to guarantee that she be buried beside Patricius; sharing of a common earth by earthly remains witnessed that two who were one in life were fittingly one in death. This common plot, she believed, would enhance her happiness; she and her husband would be revered for oneness not only during but after life. Earlier, Augustine remarks, she was not able to grasp the divine plan, according to which the location of the body after death does not affect the felicity of the departed, for some martyrs' bodies were flung into rivers, never to be recovered, yet still assured resurrection on the last day (CM 8). It is fatuously this-worldly to be anxious about the condition of the body as surety for happiness in the afterlife. Howbeit true, these observations have to be somewhat qualified. He was sensitive to the reverence due mortal remains of dear ones; the vehicles of holy souls are not to be pitilessly disposed of as so much refuse. Loving loyalty to relatives demands that their bodies be accorded Christian burial (S 172.2.3). In a spirit of piety he does not

fault his mother for originally arranging to be interred beside her spouse. Moreover, admiring her poverty of spirit for sacrificing this legitimate desire in the face of death far from her homeland, he thanks God for her total abandonment to the divine will, self-denudation that was one more good given by infinite goodness.

Exactly when she was first released from her desire to be buried next to Patricius, Augustine cannot specify. At the window in Ostia she had implied a readiness to die before embarking for Africa. When at Ostia she spoke to his friends, as lovingly as a mother to children about the tawdriness of life and blessing of death, they were astounded by her divinely infused fortitude. She commented with a bit of humor that she had not the slightest fear that God would not be able to track down her body at the resurrection. The somewhat breezy touch to this grave statement also bespeaks power. Only the saintly like Thomas More, who joked as he lay his head on the block awaiting the headsman's ax, can front death in a lighthearted spirit. Roughly two weeks after the vision at Ostia, close to Augustine's thirty-third birthday, at the end of October or early in November, at the age of fifty-five her saintly soul took flight from her body to enter into the joy of her Lord not for a mystical moment but for the unbroken ecstacy of a changeless eternity.

Chapter 12: Augustine's Grief over the Death of his Mother

29. As he performed his filial act of piety, closing the eyes that had burned bright with such love, he experientially verified that a mother's death is much more distressing than its anticipation. Suddenly, with the exodus of the vigorous spirit, her body became limp, her ears deaf in death could no more hang on his words, her lips now dumb could not utter affection, her inert hands could no longer busy themselves in service (S 173.3). The terrible finality of his mother's death hit him with the force of a hammerblow—she was gone, never to be seen again on earth. Within, tidal waves of sorrow surged up, about to form a flood of tears, but a strenuous exertion of will checked the flow, the struggle to restrain tears interiorly panging him. Counting such weeping puerile, Augustine, technically a youth (youth obtained between twenty and forty) or mature man, felt obliged to suppress such outpouring. On the Christian attitude he then adopted (an outlook perhaps tinged somewhat with Stoic-

seeming insensitiveness), it appeared incongruous to give way to tears at the death of a loved one. Pagans without faith or hope generally gave vent to these exhibitions of sorrow because they rated death the worst of evils or because, bereft of belief in a life beyond, they reasoned that dissolution of the body entrained destruction of the soul as well: the deceased was blotted out forever, never again to be existentially known and loved. His mother, however, had not been paralyzed by fear in the face of death. Delivered from all anxiety, she had greeted death with open arms, not shrinking from it as the obliteration of all she held dear but welcoming it as the passageway to an unimaginably superabundant higher life (E 151.7). Instilled by her Catholic faith was confidence that her indestructible soul would survive the breakdown of her body. *Omnino moriebatur*: she did not altogether die; a phrase apparently echoing on the supernatural plane Horace's *non omnis moriar*[62] (a boast accurately forecasting literary immortality). Augustine was convinced that his mother's death would eventually usher her into a blessed afterlife. His certitude was grounded in his mother's godly fruits rooted in love (9.11.28) and her unfeigned or existentially true faith, unblemished by the bogus or hypocritical, a profession with which her practice of good works unfailingly squared.

His curbing of tears was not strictly Stoic since he did not advocate eradication of all feeling, but stressed–overstressed, some hold–stern self-command in encountering death, an austere resignation that discountenanced weeping as a compromise with lower nature. Repression of tears at Monica's death specifically arose from an astringently ascetical view of the subordination of family bonding to the demands of supernatural love. From a natural standpoint, human beings love one another as sons or wives or mothers, but Christians with eyes affixed on the eternal are bade transcend temporal affections. Each is to love himself not as a son but simply as a man redeemed in Christ. Correspondingly, each Christian is to love the other as himself, not as a mother or father but as a man. Though this severe teaching may seem inhumane, it is actually more inhumane to love another as your mother, in terms of what pertains to oneself than to love her as a human being, that is, in terms of what pertains to God. Had man remained obedient to God in the beginning, he would not be laden by such carnal necessities as sorrow and the tears it looses. At Monica's death the God who is truth apparently called Augustine to return to the vantage point of perfect human nature before the Fall, directing him to stifle the softness of merely human affection (9.12.31). The implication of this hard saying is plain. A disciplined Christian, aspiring to what is more human and more Christian, is bound not to weep for his dead mother. On fire with love for things eternal, he will not be tethered by temporal kinships. Rejoicing in Monica's happy death and the certitude of her eventual eternal felicity, he should not shed a single tear for the sundering of a bond woven by carnal custom out of fleshy linkages of this passing life (VR 46.88-91). Later this unbending posture was somewhat mitigated by meditation on 1 Thes 4.13 in a pastoral perspective, a change dealt with below (9.12.33).

30. The shattering of his life-long union with Monica broke his heart. During her last days she had gone out of her way to comfort him with endearing words, prodigally thanking him for all his selfless care, praising him as pious, as one endowed with love-motivated devotion to parents, and complimenting him, perhaps not without some exaggeration, for never stinging her with abusive speech. According to Aristotle, children can never strictly repay their parents, for they cannot become parents of their parents.[63] Any honor he paid his mother fell immeasurably far from repaying her for a life of consecration to him. His sacrifice of tears was only an infinitesimal token of her sacrifice of spirit: truest friend, she interiorly laid down her whole life for him. In losing his mother, he lost the woman who was his all (BV 1.6), the bedrock and lodestar of his life. This great light extinguished, he was frightfully lacerated by sorrow; her loss opened a gaping hole in his inward self. His whole life was torn in two, for their love had formed one life out of two. When his closest friend in Thagaste died, the desolate Augustine felt that his friend comprised one-half of his soul (4.6.12); much more so was Monica, his most cherished friend, the other half of his soul, for they had dwelt together for most of Augustine's nearly thirty-three years. In losing Monica, Augustine lost part of his self; he was one huge wound bleeding with grief.

31. As the whole household chanted Ps 100, he probably noticed that its verses appositely pertained to Monica's character. Her holy life had been a song praising God for divine mercy and judgment that family and friends now hymned. Dwelling in the presence of God, (9.9.22), innocent of heart, she would not companion with evildoers such as Manichees (3.11.19) nor associate with the slanderous, proud,

and grasping but communed with God's faithful, imploring him for the triumph of good and the uprooting of evil (9.7.15). Buoyed by the psalm-singing, the bereaved were further fortified by the charitable support of the local Christian community, many of whom flocked to console them. The women washed and clothed the body of Monica for viewing and interment, while probably also preparing meals for the distraught household. Whether the men who listened to Augustine were actually attuned to the intricacies of his mini-conference, their very presence as brothers in sharing his sorrow solaced him. Perhaps he dilated on the happiness death confers (9.12.29); in the light of divine truth death that seemingly reduces life to a farcical tragedy (4.4.9) turns into a gateway to a deathless glory.

Once more God's word braked a sudden uprush of tears, and despite inner surgings no trace of sorrow streaked his face. The tendency to sorrow and its concomitant weeping, he recognized, are governed by natural necessity and rooted in man's historical condition. Loss, grief, and tears are causally linked; bereavement spawns sorrow, with tears ordained as the outflow of deep grief. In the fallen state emotions are less easily controllable by the soul, for, as he often remarked, the earthly body weighs down the spirit. Yet in the perspective of God's word there was no reason for lamenting the death of his outstandingly graced mother, whose faith which had generated fruits of love guaranteed that her temporal end was the beginning of unending joy. Though Augustine lucidly understood the Christian meaning of death, to his keen displeasure he found himself incapable of aligning propensity to sorrow with supernatural truth; rebuke it as he would, his impulse to grieve proved refractory. Moreover, inability to turn principle into a working specific elicited a second mode of grief; sorrowful because he still felt driven to express sorrow over Monica's passing, he was now troubled by a double sadness.

32. Since a place of burial had to be obtained and a priest contacted to arrange for the time and place of the funeral liturgy, Monica was not buried till the morrow of her demise; most probably the following morning, for the mourners would be fasting before communion and Augustine refers to the period after the Mass as "throughout the whole day." In line with Roman custom her body was positioned at the grave site where there was celebrated the sacrifice of redemption through which God alleviates penalties of the faithful departed with

more mercy than their sins deserve, speeding their greater relief and
quicker release (S 172.2.2). While processing to the grave, during
Mass, then when returning, Augustine remained dry-eyed, yet all day
long a heavy load of inward grief so beset him that, as much as
possible, for it is hard, as saints attest, to pray when wracked by pain,
he begged for healing, prayer not answered at that moment but
presently (9.12.32, 33). No longer a victim of Manichean or pagan
misrepresentations, he had clearly grasped the Christian sense in
accord with which, after a swift initial sorrow, he should have become
holily indifferent, but the long-ingrained custom of surrendering to
sorrow internal and external repulsed efforts to throttle grief.

Next, he sought physical relief in the baths, believing according to
faulty etymology that *balneum* derives from the Greek *ballaneion,*
which means what drives away sorrow (in fact, the correct
etymological sense is "that which flows or drips").[64] Addressing the
Lord as Father of orphans, because, bereft of father and mother, he
was in some sense orphaned, he begs his God to do duty as both
parents, living in his heart as in his personal home (P 67.6-7). The
Roman being a kind of Turkish bath, his body perspired,[65] yet his
heart failed to sweat out its bitter sorrow, the drops of perspiration
symbolizing spiritual tears; still, the Father of orphans, he remained
confident, would ease his pains without a sweat bath. After awaking
from exhaustion-induced sleep, he mused, lying in bed, on
Ambrose's hymn, *Deus creator omnium*: sleep given by the God who
rules the heavens instills rest to soothe wearied hearts and becalm
anxious sorrows; besides throwing off fatigue and infusing fresh vigor,
it had pacified the turbulent waves of his heart.

33. He strained to disremember Monica except abstractly, but
inevitably the memory of the valiant woman who made and remade
him (9.8.7) rose to the surface, and he could no longer avert his
inward gaze from her loving countenance. More deeply did it sink in
that no longer would those eyes alive with God hug him in love;
succeeding her near-omnipresence was a chasm that became a
trauma within. So with a certain pleasure all the pent-up grief
discharged tears in the presence of God about her and for her, about
himself and for himself. About her: though her eventual glory was
beyond doubt, he cried over the loss of her body, the shrine of her
soul. For her: his tears were offered as a kind of prayer in the event
her soul might be languishing in purgatory. About himself: he felt

compunction for harrowing her by sexual excesses and thick-skulled allegiance to Manichean darkness. For himself: tears were released so unrestrainedly that they formed a mat on which his heart could lie, reposing, in God's presence, in a quasi-sleep that dissolved his anxious grief in line with Ambrose's hymn (9.12.32). A proud onlooker, however, might fault his weeping as subrational; "proud" suggests allusion to a pagan philosopher, in particular, Plotinus, according to whose Stoically tinged passionless standard, capitulation to tears even over a mother's death betrays submission to subintellectual drives.[66]

He begs the reader, presumably a Christian, probably a spiritual, to construe his outward mourning with eyes become benign, because alert to the poignant motives for his crying. It seems hardly unreasonable for Augustine to emit tears during a short spell for his mother dead only a short time since her spiritually dead son was the son of her tears (3.12.21), which, bedewing the ground wherever she prayed (3.11.19), were offered night and day as a sacrifice of her heart (5.7.13) for his full healing (5.9.17), multiplied the more as the hour of conversion drew closer (6.1.1). Given this context of motherly love and filial gratitude, a spiritual dedicated to the most exacting ideals, he trusts, will not be affronted by his weeping even if he categorizes it objectively sinful. Augustine requests that the spiritual Christian, supposing his heart capacious with charity, pray for him rather than look down on him, indeed mingling with his orisons tears for Augustine's failings in the presence of their common Father in whose family they are joined as spiritual brothers of Jesus who is the Christ of the Father.

Yet if grief is part and parcel of the human condition (9.12.31), why does Augustine tax himself for capitulating to it? Apparently as a servant of God constrained by a more austere norm, he was pledged to stamp out "human things," not only outward indices of grief but inward mourning as well. Since Monica's charity assured eventual eternal happiness, sorrow over departure would count as slippage from the canon of devotion to eternal truth. Aware that by finally weeping for Monica, he is not conforming to his ascetical paradigm, he confesses his sin to God, not to a "wise" reader of the Platonic school who delusively believes himself a self-made man, while appealing for compassionate understanding from fellow spirituals for briefly weeping for a mother who unstoppingly rained down tears for his total conversion.[67] Circumstances should also temper, without entirely neutralizing, animadversions of Augustine's seemingly extreme asceticism. Like every individual, a man of his time, he uncritically endorsed an excessive tough-souledness ashamed to soften into "tenderness of affection" (9.12.31). Moreover, whether or not ripe with the tolerance that is the fruit of charity, moderns might lament not Augustine's "sin" of weeping but current shortcomings spinning off a tilt toward a secular-humanistic perspective on life as well as death among the religious-minded. Perhaps in the divine balance Augustine's limited rigorism warrants less redress than a certain laxism of the modern era.[68]

Admirable as it may seem from the angle of strenuous self-discipline, the ascetical standard interdicting every brand of grief unfortunately bespeaks a partially distorted supernaturalism that borders on an anti-natural or unnatural posture.[69] It imposes an impracticable tension on the relation between faith and emotion by stifling signs of sorrow characteristic of every culture and particularly evident in the Old Testament, in accord with whose hallowed tradition weeping at the tomb of Lazarus was rightly interpreted as a legitimate token of intense love (Jn 11.35-6) (however, in J 49.21 Augustine does not explicitly advert to the natural and supernatural acceptability of weeping ratified by Jesus' tears). It is not surprising then that Augustine, the practiced pastor of experience lit by revelation, discarded the ideal of absolute restraint and made generous allowance for inward and outward grief, clearly recognizing mourning as an unsuppressible need of redeemed as well as natural man. He cautioned against a misreading of Paul that would advise Christians not to grieve, a misunderstanding that may have buttressed ascetics in their misguided zeal to transcend all sorrow (a misinterpretation, minus influence of a mistaken ascetical ideal, that has not wholly disappeared in our day). Paul does not forbid grief but instructs Christian to grieve in a Christian mode, "not to grieve as those who have no hope" (1 Thess 4.13). Where loss of a loved one plunges Christians into sadness, hope of reunion hereafter fructifies in consolation and, where grief enfeebles, faith strengthens, God's promise of resurrection healing sores of sorrow (S 272.1). Moreover, the concrete magnitude of the loss can hardly be overrated; because the invisible component, the soul, has made its exit, the visible remains release an outflow of grief, in time soothed, tears dried, by faith and hope in eternal life (S 273.3.3 E 263.3.). In sum, the supernatural does not squelch natural outpouring of sorrow but purifies and ennobles it through hope anchored in the world to come.

Though unmentioned by Augustine, disparallels between his reaction to his young friend's death and to that of Monica stand out in bold relief. In 375 in Thagaste he was gulled by an absurd Manichean belief system and a nearly unlivable value system; without faith (since he relied on a pseudo-reason that was actually credulous assent to nonsense); without hope (for the fantastic Father of Greatness could proffer no aid); without supernatural love (his friendship was rooted in the lower self). Twelve years later, when Monica died, Augustine accepted her death as ordained by the Father, securely hoping for her entrance into a deathless life, and through the communion of saints continued to embrace his truest friend. Severed in 375 from the true God and therefore devastated by his friend's sudden departure, he was begloomed by a kind of carnal dark night of the soul, rendering his whole existence blank, so drained not only of joy but capacity for joy that he was afflicted by displeasure in the presence of the pleasurable; so destitute of happiness that lovely goods looked abominable because shadowed over by death (4.4.9). Per contra, his mother's passing did not hurtle him into a slough of despond. Buoyed up by solaces of faith, rather than being swamped be dereliction, he controlled his sorrow through grace, which wove out of tears a mat on which his soul rested in God. Terribly wounded without being overwhelmed, he was not driven to color the universe an ebony smear, for he was heartened by the sacred fragrance of a woman unforgettable for vigor of piety (6.1.1), inwardly charming in the unfeigned faith (9.12.29) by which she lived (J 29.7. CDEP 3.3.5). When once queried by Henri Matisse why he kept on painting despite his excruciating arthritis, Auguste Renoir replied: "The pain passes, the beauty remains." Through all the pain of the loss of Monica, the beauty of her life remained sparkling in Augustine's memory and, with the healing time's physic affords (4.5.10), the pain would pass, and her inner beauty alone would continue not only in his memory but imperishably in the substance of her soul "ravished and absorbed and buried" in eternal wisdom (9.10.25).

Chapter 13: Everlasting Peace for Monica through the

Sacrifice of Redemption and Prayers of the Faithful

34. In 397, roughly ten years after Monica's death, Augustine pours out spiritual tears for Monica as, meditating on the human situation, he is perturbed by perils haunting the path of everyone who dies in Adam. Like all who spring from the one stock of the first sinner, Monica was conceived and born in original sin, with death as its punishment (S 90.7), but through baptismal faith operative in love she was so sanctified in Christ (S 90.7) that discerning spirituals like Ambrose (6.2.2) and Augustine's fellow servants of God (9.9.2) lauded the Lord for her flaming charity. It would be rash, however, to maintain that she was wholly sinless after baptism. Lingering in Augustine's sixteenth year on the fringes of the city of evil, she hesitated to recommend marriage to cool the fires of his lust, lest a wife hinder higher education (2.3.8). Apart from this failing, while later on ordinarily faultless perhaps in deed, she no doubt sinned at least in word; and even one word can warrant damnation, as with an angry man who, denouncing his brother under God as a fool, becomes liable to Gehenna (SDM 1.9.22). Far from insinuating that she verbally scourged her neighbor, Augustine is pressing the telling but easily forgettable point that if one word can deserve hell, then surely another, albeit not gravely sinful, does not go unpunished. Furthermore, the most purified of lives looks spotty if microscopically dissected by the all-penetrating eye of divine justice apart from balancing mercy. Happily, because God does not scrutinize infirmities with infinitesimally pitiless rigor, men resting trustful hands in his mercy can serenely hope for a mansion on high. Unquestionably men do merit heaven, for theirs are true merits, but merits due to grace, as mentioned previously, are free gifts of God. God is a debtor to man not intrinsically but extrinsically, not by contract but by generous promise (S 299A 19.2). Authentic merits sprout from works become supernaturally good only through infusion of faith and grace (EN 107). Infinitely wise goodness elects certain souls for glory; good works and merits are begotten of freely bestowed justification, election, faith, and grace (QS 1.2.2,3,6). Indeed the Paul who looks forward to "the crown of justice [from] the Lord, the just judge" (2 Tim 4.7-8), justly earns eternal life only because divine mercy originally justified him (S 218B 2.3.5). The heavenly crown is due only because God, without any debt due, graced the

Apostle; Paul terminally receives the crown as his due because God initially gave grace not his due. In crowning Paul, along with the glorified of every degree, God, we saw, crowns his own gifts (QS 1.2.4). Instead of posturing as self-redeeming gods, men should unblinkingly deem themselves absolutely dependent on God not only for the whole issue of salvation but for every atom of grace; potential monsters of iniquity, salvageable only by limitless divine mercy (J 25.16. S 136 A.2), whose treasure comes down from above as sheer gift of Christ (P 38.18; 93.15). A Christian made whole praises not himself but divine pity that molded a vessel of clay into a work of divine art (P 144.7).

35. The Lord God is his praise who through his own human praise lifts him up to the level of God (P 117.9), the true and supreme life (T 6.10.11), the life of life (3.6.10), quickening his soul as his soul gives life to the body and communicating not only natural life but also the life of grace with its wisdom and love (T 9.12.18). Fresh memory of his precious mother fills him with gratitude for her many-faceted spiritual diamonds, fruits of charity that is the gift of God (E 186.3.7). Momentarily prescinding, however, from her life of love, he fastens on prayer for her sins. Should she be detained in purgatory, he entreats the Father to purify her through Jesus, the medicine for the soul's ills; his humility cures pride, his patience anger, his charity lack of piety; his self-sacrifice shrinks all spiritual tumors to nothing, repairs lost parts, and wipes out all disease (AC 11.12), for he is the crucified pontiff always interceding for members of his body (S 75.2.3). Monica, Augustine attests, always forgave truly, from her heart, all who trespassed against her, in particular, remitting without rebuke the debt of Patricius' notorious adultery (9.9.19). Thus she surely deserved remission of her own faults, in line with the promise in the fifth petition of the Lord's prayer (SDM 2.8.28), sins of which she was guilty since baptism many years before, the sacramental waters having cleansed her of all prior failings (it seems implied that she was baptized not as an infant but probably as a young girl). He pleads that, strict justice suspended, she be assessed appropriate mercy since to a servant is due mercy instead of justice (P 142.6). Men who relieve the misery of helpless fellow men will be rewarded with liberation from their own miseries (SDM 1.2.7). When called to render accounts, the merciful will not squirm under the searchlight of an all-probing judge but will be warmed by the benediction of an all-

merciful Father, lovingly blessed in accord with the beatitude pledging mercy to the merciful (S 358A.11). Reborn by mercy as a child of God, Monica learned to work mercy through mercy gifting her with love, gladdening other human faces of God with the mercy God crowns as his own gift (9.13.34). Out of unfathomable generosity, God freely lavishes mercy on souls he has lovingly chosen to glorify, thereby stripping men of all pretense to self-salvation (EN 99), for divine mercy would not be the fruit of grace that is gratis were it not freely bestowed by infinite love (CG 7.13. E 186.6.16).

36. While dictating these memorial vignettes in 397, Augustine, in fact, believes that Monica's soul has been already loosed from purgatory. No longer beseeching eternal rest be accorded the sainted soul now reposing in the bosom of Abraham, his prayers are free offerings proffered by praise of charity, not by fear that rises from necessity (P 118[S.23].4), sacrifices of praise that, in effect, hymn the Father's glory for her exodus from purgatory. Deliverance from final purification is morally certain because self-renunciation beautified her heart, at death becoming detached from everything earthly, longing only for remembrance at the sacrifice of the Mass (9.11.27), in which she participated daily (5.9.17), convinced that on the altar the eternal priest who is sacramentally immolated for the remission of sins (S 228A 3.1-2) pleads as divine mediator (10.43.69) for the souls of the faithful departed (S 172.2.2).[70]

One cardinal feature of Augustine's doctrine of reconciliation is his theory of redemption in terms of ransom, discussed above (7.21.27), according to which Christ's death on the cross canceled the decree against sinful man, the handwriting that stands for the bodily death that is the penalty for Adam's sin. In tallying all the sins to be charged against human beings, the archenemy (P 40.4) abused his absolute right over sinful humankind (LA 3.10.31. T 4.13.17) when he had Christ condemned to death. Although Christ as God was naturally impeccable and, as a man born of the virgin, was exempt from original sin[71] and utterly sinless (J 79.2), the devil engineered the death of the sinless one with the result that unjust condemnation of the guiltless stripped him of dominion over guilty believers. By willing to be conquered in his body, Christ conquered Satan, and those who believe in him share in his conquest (T 4.13.17). The transaction is unilateral; it is impossible for man to repay his redeemer for delivering him from captivity. Since humankind is sinful, no guilty individual can restore to the sinless God-man his guiltless blood, even apart from the supposition, dubious at best, that such restoration is physically possible. Again, since no one can offer oneself as an all-pure oblation to the Father, no sinful person can recompense Christ for his ransoming blood, the infinitely valuable price of manumission from slavedom of spirit. The human Monica, in subjection to Satan by the bondage of guilt, escaped his thralldom by affixing her soul to the sacrament of redemption with bonds of faith.[72] Where guilt had chained her under Satan, liberating faith in Christ's ransom daily renewed as a sacramental sacrifice chained her in fetters of love. In praying that no one ever snap those chains of love-suffused faith shielding her from the evil one, Augustine imagines for a moment that her salvation is not yet determined; he entreats the Lord that her path not be blocked by Satan, symbolized by the roaring lion who persecutes Christians and by the serpent whose cunning tricks Christian into errors and heresy (P 39.1; 40.4; 69.2; 90[S.2].9). Should she, in this fictive scenario, confront the devil, her humble faith would throttle any proudful boast of freedom from sin and exemption from its debt. Were she to make the preposterous claim of self-sufficient innocence, she would lapse once more into servitude to the super-wily accuser. In such an encounter, robust in piety (6.1.1) and fruitful in faith (9.12.29), she would ardently chant the praises of God for blotting out debts through the death of his sinless Son. Significantly iterated is a point made a few lines back: neither Monica nor any other human being can reimburse Christ for the price paid for deliverance since the death of the innocent Lamb of God was undue, whereas the death of anyone lower than the savior is due, the penalty for sharing in the first sin of Adam.

Augustine's literary device, which considers Monica's destiny as yet unsettled (when, in fact, her soul had already been judged), was probably adapted from the liturgical style of prayers for the dead in which the ultimate outcome of the soul is depicted as if still in suspense. Similarly, in our own day God is beseeched "not to hand over it [the departed soul] into the hands of the enemy nor forever forget it [this soul]"(*ut non tradas eam in manus inimici, neque obliviscaris in finem*). Stanza after stanza in the *Dies irae*, which, as its title indicates, is concerned with the Last Judgment, begs for remission of sins prior to the Grand Assize, as if the particular judgment had not already definitively fixed the next-world lot of the departed soul.[73]

Such a liturgical *façon de parler*, perhaps an ingredient in the prayers for the dead of his time, probably influenced him to employ theological-literary license, to make a contrary-to-fact theological assumption that Monica's decisive particular judgment had not taken place and that her fate hangs on the judgment scheduled for the end of the world.

37. A richly affective closing prayer begs supplication for his beloved parents.[74] His consuming desire is that Monica and Patricius rest in peace by knowing the presence of Christ who is our peace, seeing the God who is peace himself (P 124.10), thereby enjoying a sovereign tranquility immune from all shocks and anxiety (P 4.9; 141.17); the peace that is their heritage in Christ (P 124.10), final benediction for living as lovingly believing sons of God. Monica, ever faithful, obeyed her husband as her master (9.9.19), exercising holy tolerance that is the offspring of charity, painfully enduring adulteries, offering her inner suffering of disesteem in order to garner the fruit of conversion for his pagan soul (9.9.22). Loving passivity triumphed over lustful activity; her weapons of the spirit captured him for Christ. Augustine entreats God to inspire, to effect by his Holy Spirit, prayerful succor for his dearest parents in fellow Christians who are servants of God and, as children or adopted sons of God, his brothers in the one family of their Father. Although governing them as their bishop, he addresses his flock as his masters, for he is a servant of these servants, ministering to them as pastor with heart (by raising them up in prayer), voice (through preaching), and pen (through writing). In particular, he begs readers to remember at the altar every time they participate in the Eucharist Monica and Patricius, without whom under God he would not exist, through whose marital union he entered this world, though the explanation of his incoming still eludes him. Augustine, recall, could never resolve, to his own satisfaction, the problem of the origin of the soul (R 1.1.3). He was unable to decide whether souls were somehow propagated by the souls of parents, a spiritual traducianism that easily accounts for the transmission of original sin, or were individually created at the formation of particular human bodies (GL 10.3.4-6; 6.9-11; 11.18-9).[75]

The prayers of fellow Catholics, he trusts, will thereby share his pious affection, filial love he owes his parents, who caused his existence in this time-suffused light, which contrasts with the eternal light that is God, his primary maker; progenitors who are, in another

JOHN M. QUINN, OSA

respect, his brethren, adopted son and daughter of the one Father, in their one mother that is the Catholic Church.[76] The whole Church is Christ's mother because she gives birth to each baptized infant (E 98.5) and indeed to all his members, no matter at what age they are reborn through grace (SV 5.5). Furthermore, his parents are to be his fellow citizens in the heavenly Jerusalem, the celestial "vision of peace" (P 124.10), where after the resurrection the angels will also be their fellow citizens (P 118[S.8].1) in the fatherland, for which the people of God hunger and thirst, after pilgriming in an exile of captivity and darkness that evokes groans (P 40.5; 147.5,6). Entry into the eternal Jerusalem is a coming home to peace in the house of God, where reigns liberation from toil and tears of the earthly journey (P 26[S.2].6,10;121.2;127.2). From another angle, the course to Jerusalem on high is exit and re-entrance, exodus and return. Man, first a citizen of paradise, then expelled by the sin of Adam, can in Christ reclaim a paradise super-sublime and everlasting (P 118[S.8].1).[77] Augustine expresses the hope that readers will never neglect to remember his mother at the sacrifice of the Mass, satisfying her end-of-life desire far more plentifully than she imagined, for readers of later generations were to add their many prayers, especially at Mass, not only for but to her.[78] The God able to do immeasurably more than we ask for, who richly hearkened to Monica's patient prayers for her son's conversion (8.12.28), is the same all-generous Father who superabundantly answered, through Augustine, Monica's request for remembrance, so that through more than sixteen centuries in a manner not even his farsighted genius foresaw she has been remembered at the altar of the Lord as a saint.[79]

NOTES

1. Thomas à Kempis, *The Imitation of Christ*, 1.19.
2. This is the only passage in the *Confessions* where Christ is directly addressed or prayed to. In two other places, 11.2.4 (twice) and 11.22.28, Augustine invokes God through Jesus Christ. G-M 233, n.2. In the Western Church liturgical prayer was customarily addressed not to Christ directly but to the Father through Jesus. K. Adam, *Christ Our Brother*, 38-76. See also T. Klauser, *A Short History of the Western Liturgy*, 30-2.
3. UC 1.3 remarks that Manichees ordinarily described apostates as individuals abandoned by the light: the light had passed through them; deserters from Manichean light were deserted by the light. Hence in gratitude Augustine addressed God as the true light, not the false Manichean brand; as supreme light, because spiritual and immutable in contrast to the material and mutable Manichean God of light. Courcelle, 239, n.3, cites UC 1.3 but not in reference to 9.1.1.
4. The scab may have been scabies, an irritating skin disorder. Habit impelled him to scratch the area, each attempt to relieve the itching making the condition worse. Analogously, so strongly was he under the spell of sexual impurity that every effort to ease his state inflamed the disorder more.
5. Augustine was aware, it seems reasonable to conjecture, that he was considered one of those witnesses transformed from pitch black to glowing white. However, very probably he had no inkling that his conversion from sinner to saint would be emblazoned in the history of the Church down through the centuries, even to this day when homilists dilate on the miraculous return to the Father of the prodigal son of Monica. For scholars and intelligentsia, especially in Europe, his writings function as "sharp arrows" transfixing minds and hearts. For the faithful with little opportunity and inclination to read his works, Augustine has continued to be an outstanding"consuming coal," a towering testimony to the mercy of God, sparking fresh hope in those disheartened by their own or their offspring's abject failure to respond to the challenge of the Gospel.
6. G-M 235, n.6.
7. Since the symptoms were organic, arising out of infirmity in organs sustaining vocalization, he may have suffered from a severe bronchitis or some recurring laryngitis. B. Legewie, "Die körperliche Konstitution und die Krankheiten Augustins," *Misc. Agost.*, 1931, 2.19-20; cited in BA 14,77, n.1.
8. The Alps visible from Cassiciacum symbolize the heights of heaven above the valley of tears. Specifically, the rich mountains (9.3.5) represent Jesus Christ, to whose peak all pilgrims are oriented to climb (P 119.1). From another standpoint, the highest mountain (Is 2.2), standing for Christ, is the mountain made of cheese, so formed for the benefit of tiny children to be nourished by grace as a kind of milk; an abundant mountain that enriches souls by its excelling gifts (P 67.22).
9. BA 14, 549-50.

10. As indicated above, Augustine's description of his theological learning as hobbled by ignorance and lack of breadth was not simply a gesture of self-abasement. At this point in time his faith was firm, his understanding hardly deep.

11. Garvey, *Christian or Neo-Platonist?*, 230-3.

12. Garvey, 211.

13. James 1.626.

14. Cassiciacum, from which high mountains are visible (E 26), has been identified with Cassago in the Brianza area, close to twenty miles north of Milan, and also Casciago, which is situated on the road from Varese to Gavirate, thirty-nine miles from Milan. The majority of scholars tend to favor Cassago di Brianza as the location of Verecundus' villa. BA 14, 79, n.2. Later scholarship seems to indicate that Cassago was indeed Cassiciacum. See G. O'Daly, "Cassiciacum," AL 1.772-4 and A. D. Berardino, "Cassiciacum," AE 135. According to O'Daly, "Cassiciacum," 777-9, while somewhat disputed, the historicity of the early dialogues seems firmly established. J. McWilliam, in "Cassiciacum Dialogues," AE 135-8, concludes that the dialogues are substantially historical.

15. Some hold that the Cassiciacum period ran from the beginning of November to the beginning of March.

16. In this time-bound existence, Augustine tells Nebridius, he is not absolutely but only relatively happy since he lives far distant from the wisdom in whose perfect grasp perfect happiness lies (E 3). He is marshalling his energies, he later reports, to wax in love of truth, to raise his mind to abiding objects of the intelligible world (E 4). Perhaps 9.3.6 alludes to these general reflections on happiness, which do not detail specifics of the nature of eternal life. In the opinion of some scholars, Augustine, while at Cassiciacum, probably wrote, in addition to E 3 and 4, other letters no longer extant.

17. Bourke, *Confessions*, 234, n.26.

18. BV 1.3 pictures pride as an obstacle blocking the way to wisdom; humility is a precondition for attaining truth.

19. As indicated in 9.4.8, the holy teachings of the Church, the sacred mysteries, are remedies for the ills of the soul.

20. Bourke, *Augustine's Quest Of Wisdom*, 70.

21. V, 24.10.

22. Manichees were strongly attached to their own psalms as a form of communal prayer, which bore resemblance, perhaps with some borrowings, to psalms of the Christian tradition. L. Ferrari, "Isaiah and the Early Augustine", AUG(L), 41, (1991), 745-6.

23. Honey symbolizes divine wisdom, holding primacy or the first place among foods of the heart (mind), a wisdom that flows from the rock that is Christ, the sweetness of which defies comprehension and description by words. Thus the honey of the Scriptures is heavenly wisdom (P 80.22). Elsewhere milk and honey are said to symbolize grace (S 25.1). Perhaps more exactly, it is milk that stands for grace; "it issues from the abundance within the mother's body, and with a joyful mercy is freely given to tiny children" (P 67.22).

24. Ryan, *Confessions*, 399, n.35.

25. Augustine does not report whether his tooth was repaired or whether the pain simply ceased even though the decay in the tooth, the source of the pain, still remained.

26. "Here if we seek a reason, there will be no miracle. If we require an example, the event will not be singular. Let us grant that God does something that we must admit we cannot investigate. In such events the whole reason for the miracle worked is the power of the one working the miracle (*tota ratio facti est potentia facientis*)" (E 137.2.8). In other words, a miracle is naturally inexplicable; no natural agencies can produce what is naturally impossible. Because dependent on the direct intervention of a supranatural cause, a miracle is unexampled and unpredictable, conforming to no verified established natural pattern. A miracle, however, is not a random or chance occurrence without a determinable cause. The divine power surpassing all nature is the whole and sole cause for an event outside the chain of natural causation.

27. See n.7 supra.

28. Ferrari, "Isaiah" 253-4.

29. McKenzie *Dictionary of the Bible*, 397.

30. Most of Ambrose's exegetical commentary is lost.

31. Ferrari, "Isaiah", 741, n.8.

32. Ferrari, "Isaiah", 741.

33. Ferrari, "Isaiah", 742.

34. Ferrari, "Isaiah", 742.

35. BA 14, 95, n.1.

36. Alypius' austere exposure to cold ground may have won his admiration because Augustine himself could not stand the cold, suffering from it most of his life. Van der Meer, 359.

37. As its title indicates, *De magistro* grapples with the vexing, at times seemingly irresolvable, problem of the nature of teaching. As Plato showed in *Meno*, teaching cannot be analyzed as a mechanical transfer from the teacher's to the student's mind. On Augustine's view, the teacher exercises an instrumental or auxiliary role by proffering words or signs of realities that prompt the student to inwardly pass judgment on their truth value. The student is the main agent in learning; yet derivatively so, capable of enunciating true judgments only because his mind is guided from above by the light of God that is truth itself. As eyes of the body see objects in the light of the sun, so the eye of the mind sees intelligible objects in the light of God's truth.

38. During the Lenten season when the *competentes* were instructed in the meaning of the Apostles Creed and the sacraments; not surprisingly, we may surmise, Augustine geared his capacious intellect to master the teaching of his catechists. *Fid et op* 6.9. Bourke, *Augustine's Quest Of Wisdom*, 81-2.

39. In blasting in 1967 for the Milan subway, workers came upon a remarkably preserved baptistery, now beneath the cathedral of Milan, which, scholars have since determined, was the actual holy pool in which Augustine and his companions were baptized some 1600 years before.

40. Van der Meer, 367-9.

41. Arianism, the most widespread heresy in the early Church, originated with

Arius (250-336), a priest of Alexandria, who maintained that the Logos or Word was not consubstantial with the Father but only similar to the Father. Hence he was not generated but created by the Father as the first creature, the highest son of God by the grace of adoption. Largely banished from Italy in the early fourth century, it was reintroduced into the Western Empire through the emigration of the Germanic tribes who had earlier assented to this essentially distorted view of Christ.

42. F.H. Dudden, *The Life and Times of St. Ambrose*, instances two separate persecutions. On April 4-5, 385, the Empress Justina asked that the New Basilica within the walls be turned over to the Arians, a request Ambrose refused. Next, on April 5 she commanded Ambrose to relinquish the Portiana or Old Basilica, an order Ambrose declined to comply with. Despite a military presence Ambrose occupied the Portian Basilica till April 10, Holy Thursday, when the soldiers withdrew. See 1.271-80. A second persecution occurred in 386. Defying an imperial edict, Ambrose remained in Milan, staying in the New Basilica, where he was joined by the faithful who engaged in antiphonal hymning (9.7.15). Once more Justina yielded to Ambrose, lifting the siege and effectively repealing the unjust edict. See 1.284-91.

43. Van der Meer, 326-7.

44. One scholar holds that Augustine and Paulinus of Nola, not Ambrose, claimed that a vision led to discovery of the relics. Moreover, he cautions against "the misleading impression" that the finding of the relics was causally connected with Ambrose's limited victory over Justina during Holy Week, 386, since a gap of two months separate the two events. May we be permitted to add that Augustine does not convey this misconception; he never maintains explicitly or implicitly that the discovery of the relics was linked to the solution of the crisis with Justina. Rather, on his reckoning, the relics pertain to the later behavior of Justina, restraining her from future harassment of Catholicism in Milan.

45. CD 22.8 recalls the miracle that Augustine did not witness but was observed by a large crowd of the faithful. In gratitude for his healing, the miraculously sighted man vowed service at the martyrs' shrine for the rest of his days (S 286.4).

46. *Qui habitare facis unanimes in domo* is a rendering that varies somewhat from the version of Ps 67.7 commented on around or in 392, roughly five years prior to the writing of the first nine books of the *Confessions*, whose pertinent passage reads, *Deus qui inhabitare facit unius modi in domo*. Augustine's exposition, however, immediately takes *unius modi* to mean *unanimes, unum sentientes*, of one mind, thinking along the same lines (P 67.7). Since his commentary on this line explicitly refers to the Greek text he has consulted, it does not seem unlikely that this version is a more precise rendering. If such be the case, the lines in the text would seem to be a partial paraphrase. Interestingly, *unanimes* seems to echo or indirectly refer to the first line in Ch. 1 of the *Rule: Primum, propter quod in unum estis congregati ut unamines habitetis in domo et sit vobis anima una et cor unum in Deum* ("First of all, the reason why you are joined together in community is that you may live with one mind in your house and that you may

be one mind and one heart focused on God"). The allusion to the *Rule* seems probable since the text deals with Evodius' joining their community as one of the *servi Dei*, members of a lay community in an elementarily monastic existence (see 9.9.22). In the judgment of G. Lawless, *Augustine of Hippo*, 43-4, who thoroughly scanned this passage, the words, *Qui habitare facis unanimes in domo*, clearly indicate that Augustine was embarking on some form of monastic life. May I mention that I came upon Lawless' authoritative analysis only after preparing a rough version of this note.

47. Lawless, 45-58, persuasively presents a solution of a still controverted question. At Thagaste, he claims, Augustine founded a community in which the four elements of monastic life were operative (50), where he was not simply a *servus Dei* in the sense of a lay ascetic but a monk united with fellow servants in community

48. The well-educated Evodius figures as interlocutor in two dialogues, LA (begun in Rome in 388) and QA (finished in Rome probably in 388). Earlier Evodius was at Cassiciacum. Like a number of other members of the later monastery at Hippo, Evodius was ordained bishop, probably occupying the see of Uzalis in 396. Four letters from Evodius to Augustine, nn. 158, 160-1, and 163, are extant. He died October 16, 424. See "Evodius," DTC 5.2, by P. Godet. *Agentes in rebus*, recall (8.6.15), functioned as couriers, commissariat officers, and a sort of secret police. *Cod. Iust.* 12.20-23. G-M 218, n.3. See also J. O'Donnell, "Evodius of Uzalis," AE 344.

49. It was the wisdom of the saints that taught her how to draw Patricius into the Catholic faith. Learned in the wisdom of the Spirit, she became, like the Master, a servant, self-abasingly looking after the needs of those attached to his household. Worth adding is that Monica, though largely uneducated and not given to study, was apparently endowed with a considerable measure of natural acumen. Her telling insights on the meaning of happiness and the nature of evil surprised and delighted her son at Cassiciacum (O 2.1, 1.32. BV 2.8, 10, 11, 4.27, 35). See J. Gavigan, "The Mother of Saint Augustine", *Amer. Eccl. Rev.* (119, no. 4), Oct., 1948, 271-3. According to J.K. Coyle, "In Praise of Monica: A Note on the Ostia Experience of *Confessions* IX", AS 13 (1982), 94-6, Augustine considers Monica a philosopher insofar as she loves the true wisdom revealed in Catholicism.

50. G. Folliet, "Aux origines de l'ascétisme et du cénobitisme africain", *Studia Anselmiana*, 46, 1961, 25-44; cited in Brown, 132, n.4.

51. According to P. Henry, *La vision d'Ostie*, 18-25, the account of the Ostia event is set in a Plotinian conceptual framework. The description of the ascent of the soul to God seems particularly dependent on "On the Three Principal Hypostases", *Enn.* 5.1, and on "On the Beautiful", *Enn.* 1.6.7. However, "...if the mentality is still Plotinian, the language expressing it is frequently Scriptural" (38). The analytical perspective of Plotinus is couched in the language of the Bible. The conceptual apparatus of Plotinus is an instrument utilized to communicate a Christian experience in which Scriptural features are primary. In the opinion of A. Mandouze, "Où en la question de la mystique augustinienne?," AM 3.113-4, the relation between Christian and Plotinian

factors in Henry's presentation is more complex. Three agencies are operative: the first, on the speculative level, derives from Plotinus (Henry, 88); the second, on the institutional level, concerns Scripture in an Ambrosian setting (Henry, 91); the third, in the mystical domain, is evidenced in Monica as a living symbol of full Christian living (Henry, 27). The mystical factor ensouls and activates the other two agencies. However, in another contribution to the same Augustinian Congress, "L'extase d'Ostie," AM 1.67-84, Mandouze cautions that an exhaustive analysis of textual parallels cannot exactly verify the impact of Scriptural sources. Though fourteen sources are traceable to Scripture and at least twenty-one to Plotinus, the texts cannot be explained in terms of sources alone. Moreover, verbal rapprochements are elusive; in general, identical words do not necessarily mean the same object. Furthermore, the influence of Ambrose has to be weighed in the use of Plotinian notions and the interpretation of Scripture. It must not be forgotten that Augustine creatively integrated pagan influences from a fundamentally Christian viewpoint.

52. *In atomo* means *in puncto temporis.* The *punctum* cannot be divided. *In ictu oculi* means with the greatest (*summa*) speed. E 205.4.

53. BA 14, 553-5.

54. As mentioned above (9.3.6), Augustine distinguished two states of blessedness, one before, the other after the resurrection on the last day.

55. While on the day of final reckoning those still alive on earth will die prior to the Last Judgment (CD 20.20), on the last day not all will be changed. Only the bodies of the just will be transformed into glorified bodies while those unhappily destined to the resurrection of judgment will have to perpetually suffer in corrupt bodies (E 205.4).

56. Solignac, BA 13,97, puts the mystical force of the verbs in bold: *haec una [visio]* RAPIAT et ABSORBEAT et RECONDAT *interna gaudia* (9.10.25); Monica and Augustine were ravished and absorbed and wholly lost in the interior joys flowing from and fused with this vision. In maintaining that the Ostia event was mystical, we have here chosen to put in brackets the problem of whether Augustine enjoyed mystical experiences on other occasions. In "In Praise of St. Monica," 87-52, J.K. Coyle judiciously surveys the views of scholars taking a pro or con stand on the matter. Opposed to or doubtful about genuine mystical strains at Ostia or elsewhere are G. Boissier, A. von Harnack, P. Alfaric, E. Hendrikx, J. Huby, J.-M. Le Blond, P. Courcelle, and J.J. Heitz. Those recognizing Augustine as an authentic mystic include C. Butler, F. Cayré, J. Maréchal, A. Mager, E. I. Watkin, W. Falkenhahn, A. Mandouze, C. Mohrmann, A. Solignac (cited earlier in this note), L. Eborowitz, V. Capánaga, and V. Zangara. Coyle's article evidently depends in part on A. Mandouze, "Où en la question de la mystique augustinienne?" AM 3, 103-163, which is a rich, highly condensed account of the status of mysticism in Augustine around 1950. Mandouze roughly divides approaches to Augustinian mysticism into three classes. A first approach, advocated by C. Butler, C. Boyer, J. Maréchal, and P. Henry, among others, holds that Augustine did reach the plane of infused contemplation at Ostia. A second group, which includes F, Cayré. E.I. Watkin, and F. van der Meer, recognizes Augustine as a mystic in a broad

sense. A third group, which includes E. Hendrikx and H. Meyer, considers him an intense religious thinker who was more of an intellectualist than a mystic. See also A. Mandouze, *Saint Augustin: L'aventure de la raison et la grâce.* More recently, the question has been addressed in articles in F. Van Fleteren, and J. Schnaubelt (eds.), *Augustine: Mystic and Mystagogue*, CollAug, F. Van Fleteren, "Mysticism in the *Confessions*–A Controversy Revisited," argues on the basis of texts in the *Confessions* and later works that Augustine did achieve a touching of God not only at Ostia but also at other junctures in his life, a contact of the eye of the heart that may be legitimately designated mystical. It would seem that, on his reckoning, Augustine was a mystic in the broad sense; the criterion of passivity is never invoked. In other words, Augustine could have been blessed with a lofty experience of God that did not reach the level of infused contemplation. However, the problem apparently remains insoluble, mainly because of a lack of consensus in the meaning of mysticism that involves specification of criteria for determining instances of mysticism.

57. An observation of E. Underhill, *The Mystics of the Church*, 66, which came into my hands only after I had written these lines, confirms the predominant role of Monica: "St. Monica was her son's first director in the contemplative life...[her soul] supported and led him on." The role of Monica as spiritual mentor would seem to dispose of some difficulties posed by other commentators. In "Ostia Reexamined: A Study in the Concept of Mystical Experience," *Internat. Journ. for Phil. of Rel.* 1(1970), 44, J. Mourant suggests that the experience, if it was mystical, should be ascribed to Monica alone. He is taking his cue from G. Bardy, *Saint Augustin, l' homme et l' oeuvre* (1940), 113, n. 2, who maintains that the so-called ecstasy was undergone not by Augustine but by Monica; cited in Coyle, "In Praise of Monica," 90, n. 22. Moreover, the problem raised by J.-M. Le Blond, *Les conversions de saint Augustin* (1950) concerning "extase à deux" would seem to be solved by the mentor-disciple relationship between Monica and her son; also cited in Coyle, 88, n. 13.

58. According to De Guibert, 354, in ecstasy properly taken the soul is so intensely concentrated on a spiritual object that sensory activity is practically suspended. A. Poulain, *The Graces of Interior Prayer*, 246, estimates that in most cases ecstasy lasts at least a half hour. Poulain illustrates, with a wealth of detail, ecstacy and other mystical phenomena. For Augustine, the attention of a mind in ecstasy is so removed from the physical senses that it does not advert to external sights and sounds (GL 12.17.2.5). The ecstatic soul, which is estranged from its bodily senses, afterward returns to normal activity in the body (S 52.6). In an exalted ecstasy or rapture the soul receives a foretaste of heaven, knowing God directly through a species (*per speciem*) that analogously resembles face-to-face knowledge of God (GL 12.26.54). Moses and Paul experienced the highest form of rapture. While still pilgrimming *in via*, they were gifted not with just a foretaste but an actual taste of heaven as they briefly saw God face to face in a strictly heavenly mode (GL 12.27.55; 28.56. E 147.13.32). C. Butler, who believes that the mystical encounter at Ostia included ecstasy, expounds Augustine's view of ecstasy in 71-8. In the judgment of Solignac, BA 13, 197, it may be noted, if the Ostia event was not unarguably ecstatic, it was marked by

fruits that were ecstatic.

59. The life beyond cannot be fully happy if it is not strictly eternal (CD 10.30). Only truly eternal duration can assure perfect knowledge and perfect love (DQ 35.2).

60. DC 1.39.43. Van der Meer, 433.

61. Augustine was acutely aware of Monica's unceasing care. If the souls of the dead communicated with their loved ones in dreams, his mother Monica would have so visited him every night, for on earth she pursued him over land and water to live with him (DCM 16.31). So later he sprang to her defense against the unfeelingly vicious attacks of Julian of Eclanum. Van der Meer, 244.

62. Ryan, *Confessions*, 401, n. 1, commenting on 9.12.1, suggests the connection. The famous line is from *Odes* 3.30.

63. *Nic. Eth.* 8.14.1163b 15-18.

64. G-M 266, n. 10.

65. F. Di Capua, *Vita Augustiniana* (1953), 9-12, cited in Pellegrino, 125, n. 16. Bonner, 102, n. 3.

66. *Enn.* 1.4.4. HC 176, n. 23.

67. Giving way to tears would indicate that he had not properly heeded the call of truth to live in the love of things eternal.

68. Later Augustine did yield to tears, which brought release and true, if passing, peace (9.12.33).

69. Augustine's earlier proscription of tears arose from a perhaps over-rigorous outlook that sacrifices everything earthly to the eternal. Prohibition of weeping is exacted of servants of God, especially those consecrated to truth and love in all their austere beauty. Later, as already mentioned, a more judicious Augustine sanctioned grief during bereavement. A pastoral approach nicely blends human and divine perspectives: Christians weeping over their beloved departed keep their inner eye fixed on the eternal homeland in which they will one day rejoice in union with loved ones. Christian ascetics after Augustine modified and somewhat more humanized his earlier over-severe program. Perhaps recalling Jesus himself weeping at the grave of Lazarus, they released feelings in tears without experiencing the slightest twinge of guilt. The wholly self-disciplined St. Francis de Sales wept at the death of his father; and when his mother died, his "heart nearly burst," pouring forth more tears than he had shed since entering the Church. H. Couannier, *St. Francis de Sales and His Friends*, 124, 243. After learning of Francis' death, St. Jane de Chantal, his spiritual daughter, wept nearly a whole night and day (392-3).

70. Christ's redemptive sacrifice is renewed at each Mass, each a repetition of the Last Supper (CJ 13.3.9). Christ is the only priest who immolated himself as the sacrifice (P 26[S.2].2). The Christ who in his passion was made the sacrifice restored in his resurrection life to what was slain, offering it as first fruits to God (P 129.3.7). The first fruits of the Spirit (9.10.24), the offering of the spiritual self at its highest, apparently imitates in some way Christ's definitive risen-life offering to the Father.

71. Christ's conception was exempt from the carnal concupiscence of parents because he was procreated without masculine semen by the Holy Spirit in the

womb of Mary. Not having contracted original sin by generation, he dissolved by regeneration original sin in others (CJ 6.22). Jesus was born of the Virgin Mary with absolutely no sin at all; he neither committed nor transmitted sin (E 164.7.19).

72. Etymologically, religion (*religare*) is what binds man to God (VR 55.113). Strong in piety of religion (6.1.1), Monica bound her soul in Christian faith to Christ's redemptive sacrifice (9.13.36).

73. See *Missae Defunctorum* (Teurs, 1962), 68, and *Dies irae*, 9-10. This practice remains current. *The Liturgy of the Hours*, 3, 1060, reads: "Be merciful to the faithful departed, keep them from the Evil One."

74. Monica is mentioned by name only at the end of Book 9. Perhaps stylistic constraints of Roman rhetoric dictated that references to parents and other family members be muted. Perhaps also Augustine never personally thought of his mother as Monica but spoke of her as simply mother or my mother. If a personal note is permissible, never did I interiorly or exteriorly refer to my own mother by her baptismal name. I never called her Rose but simply mother or (to others) my mother.

75. As noted above (Book 1, n. 23), early in his career Augustine suggested four live options for explaining the origin of the soul (LA 3.21.59), which he effectively reduced to two admissible hypotheses: creationism and generationism. In spite of its analytical appeal, creation of souls is apparently at loggerheads with the massive fact of original sin; direct creation seems to nullify any possibility of transmission of original sin, leaving the door open to Pelagianism (AO 1.16.13). According to Bellarmine, only the daunting problem of transmission of original sin prevented Augustine from accepting creationism (Portalié, 151); in fact, Augustine was never able to resolve this formidable crux. The excellent discussion of the question in Portalié, 148-51, has not been substantially improved upon by most later commentators.

76. Anointed by the Father, the Word made flesh took the name of Christ or the anointed one (CALP 2.3.11). Moreover, since the whole Christ is both head and body, all members of the Church are anointed or Christ-ed. Hence "all the brothers of your Christ" (9.12.33) has a dual signification: brothers of Jesus; and brothers within the one total Christ that is the Church (P 26 [S.2].2).

77. Exiled from paradise by disobedience, man is making a pilgrimage of return to a higher plane of human nature; one superior to what God provided before the Fall, a perfect life of graced nature possible only after death. Man's history in the line of grace is an exodus and return; an exodus into the valley of tears and, after a sojourn with hearts lifted up to the eternal hills, a return to an infinitely richer paradise (VR 46.88).

78. Early in the fifth century Anicius Aucherius Bassus, the consul in 431, prepared a metrical epitaph to be chiseled on Monica's tombstone, an inscription that has been preserved in at least ten manuscripts. In December, 1945, two boys at play in the courtyard of St. Aureas' church in Ostia accidentally came across a section of the original gravestone, broken into three pieces; part of the tombstone to which Augustine gave a last, loving look before sailing for Africa in autumn, 388. The epitaph may be rendered: "O Augustine, her offspring,

your most chaste mother, who gleamed as another facet of your merit, left her mortal remains here. As a priest [or bishop] upholding the heavenly laws of peace, you instruct by your character the people entrusted to you. Crowning both of you is glory greater than the praise of your deeds: O mother of virtues, O son even more blessed" (adapted from Gavigan, "The Mother of St. Augustine," 279; see also BA 14, 555-6).

79.   The *Confessions* remarks six deaths; three of immediate family: Patricius, (3.4.7) Adeodatus (9.6.14), and Monica (9.11.28); three of friends: his unnamed friend (4.4.7), Verecundus (9.3.5), and Nebridius (9.3.6).

Book Ten
Present State of Soul

The first nine books compactly chronicle disconcerting sidepaths and swampy detours in Augustine's analytical and affective journey to Catholicism. Plainly, however, his life did not stop in 387 during his thirty-third year. Probably because of unsettling conditions precipitated by the revolt of Maximus, he delayed return home, spending along with friends a year in Rome, after which, following the execution of Maximus in summer, 388 (CALP 3.25.30),[1] he sailed for North Africa in the autumn. Once in Thagaste, he joined with servants of God in the formation of a monastic community committed to observance of the evangelical counsels. Meanwhile, he pursued his literary apostolate, almost inevitably, one may say, since he was a kind of absolute thinking machine, his mind generating and orchestrating ideas as naturally as he breathed. As his reputation for learning quickly spread, he steered clear of dioceses hunting for a bishop, for fear in those days sans seminaries he might be pressed to accept ordination. When in 391 he visited Hippo to interview a prospect for his community, during his stay he attended Mass in the basilica celebrated by Valerius the bishop. Slowed down by his advanced years and acutely conscious that his fluency in Latin rhetoric was hardly the most desirable, Valerius had been keeping his eyes peeled for an educated layman whom he might ordain and groom as successor. When on that very day his sermon pointed up the need for such a candidate, the congregation in response, recognizing Augustine's potential, urged him forward, almost literally conscripting him into the service of the Gospel (S 355.2). A tearful Augustine submitted, little realizing at the time that God was going to work enormous good out of what his reluctant soul shrank from as a kind of apparent evil. A coincident was turned into a God-incident, fulfilling Monica's prayers beyond her wildest dreams (8.12.28).[2] In 395 he was ordained coadjutor bishop, taking the reins as ordinary in 396 after his elderly patron's death.

Augustine's surprising call to the priesthood was a vocation within his initial Christian vocation won by his conversion; a calling that radically altered his life, moving him to pray and think as a Catholic priest, then bishop, in the perspective of which he composes Book 10. Whereas the first nine books that portray his wrestling with God as he fumbled his way toward conversion were a confession of praise to God for healing past sins, Book 10 throws light on an Augustine no longer struggling to cast off the irons of grave sins; even in the state of grace he is searching for more of God as he battles the triple concupiscence: this is the confession of God's mercy for remedy of present sins as he strives to progress in living faith through the one mediator, Jesus Christ. No matter that the book was only appended later to the original nine; it meshes nicely with the prior autobiography as it sings God's inscrutable mercy for ongoing inward wonders. His past life was the story of superabounding grace; his present life is the tale of grace still victorious, hopefully on the march to further conquests in a drama of the spirit not to be ended this side of glory. In particular, some main points in the opening paragraph seem thematically continuous with the close of the prior book. Book 9 lifts eyes to the heavenly Jerusalem for which the footsore people of God sigh; Book 10 starts with a personal aspiration to attain face-to-face vision of God in his supernatural homeland in which he now rejoices in hope. Moreover, Book 9 pleads for remembrance of Monica (along with Patricius), for whom he at first problematically wept; Book 10 deplores extra tears in one instance, then recommends more in another. Again, while Book 9 terminates the confession of his past life, the outset of Book 10 signals that he will confess his present situation to God and man.

A first part (1.1-5, 10) supplies the reasons for his confession, which promises interior profit to both reader and author. A second part proves by efficient causality that God is the maker of the universe (6.8-9). The Lord who is also the life or his life (6.10) is cognizable not by sensory powers but by the mind alone (7.11). Third, since memory is the route to God, he explores this capacious power. Memory marvelously retains images of sensory data and intelligible objects, the former grasped a posteriori (8.12-5), the latter known a priori, such as the principles of the liberal arts (9.16-10, 17) and mathematical entities (12.19). The problem of forgetting seems theoretically baffling (16.24), though the fact of forgetting things and names is resolved by appeal to the original memorial unit 18.22-19.28. All men have an a priori desire for happiness that is satisfied only by true joy in God (20.29-25.36). Fourth, prayer begs God for the grace to fulfill his commands (26.37-29.40). Fifth, he scrutinizes his conscience to extripate any remnants of the triple concupiscence. Erotic dreams still persist (30.41-2), the intake of food and drink has to be properly moderated (31.43-7), the pleasure elicited by music requires control (33.49-50), and external beauties attractive to the eyes must be temperately received (34.48) while he allure of sense provokes little trouble. He has largely curbed idle curiosity though trivial objects continue to catch him unawares (35.54-7). Pride of life tempts him because of his status as a bishop, and as simply a member of society, he cannot escape need for social recognition, which may encourage love of praise (36.58-39.64). He is fortified by spiritual intimacies that at times mount to a quasi-supernal delight (40.65). Sixth, he seeks to reach God not by the false mediator that is Satan (42.67) but by Christ, the God-man, who, as Word, is one with God and, as man, is joined to the whole of humankind (43.68-70).

Chapter 1: Hope for Eternal Truth Inspires Truth in his Confessions

1. One day, he prays, he will see God face to face, knowing God as intuitively as God knows him (S 362.28.29; 337.5.5); the face of God signifies manifestation of his inner being to unmediated intuition (CD 22.1). The mind in *patria* will grasp God as directly as it is known, but proportionally so, since even in heaven the intellect can never exhaustively encompass the infinity of the God who exhaustively knows man (S 117.3.5). Divine strength, he hopes, will bolster his soul with fresh power, molding it to dovetail perfectly with divine being that is all love, so that God will wholly enfold his soul as a member of the Church, making it without spot and wrinkle, cleansed of all sin and resting in eternal life (S 342.11.13).[3] Only the heavenly Jerusalem is a Church holy in both its head and all its members (S 214.11),

completely without spot or wrinkle; when Christ its life appears in glory, it will become, like him, glorious and immaculate (R 1.19.9;2.18). The Church on earth is spotless in Christ its head and holy in its graced members, but the thorns intertwined with the lilies prevent it from being totally holy (S 293B). Eternal life subsists in a communal dimension; holiness here and glory hereafter can be attained only within the Church (S 4.11.11, UE 19.49): God is a common good possessed in a common vision (P 84.10) from which flows ineffable joy. Seeing God, the hearts of the blessed will rejoice (CD 21.1): beatitude consists in rejoicing for God, from God, and because of God (10.22.32). In the hope of the hereafter (one reason why he is dictating his *Confessions*), he rejoices insofar as the joy of a redeemed heart faintly prefigures the matchless delight to come.

Joyful hope in the eternal serves as a yardstick by which to measure the value of things temporal. Surely goods of this life are not to be eschewed, but it is an egregious blunder to equate their acquisition with full felicity, for possession is insecure, and the goods themselves unperduring (P 130.8; 143.18). Joy blossoming from hope in the supernal deems certain weeping excessive; yet it is rightly intermixed with sorrow in other cases. First, the more that idle tears are here expended on things, the less they deserve. The empire-builder whose grab for further power is blocked, the lustful individual unable to pull off sexual exploits, the miser prevented from heaping up more wealth—all experience sorrow; but the less sorrow over vain things the better. Second, the fewer tears shed over certain objects, the more they rightly deserve. A man may delight, as did Augustine, in obscene plays when he should spiritually sorrow over them (3.2.3). Theater-goers may weep over tragic scenes while unmoved to tears by their wallowing in lust, as was the case with a younger Augustine (3.2.4). Indeed the just man, who exults in the hope of the eternal, repeatedly lets fall true tears for fellow men who laugh foolishly or weep fruitlessly. He weeps over blinkered weepers and laughers, such as devotees of smutty comedies and drunks mirthful in their cups because weeping over the vain is useless, and laughing at the worthless hollow. A true Christian, more joyful in hope than the common run, spiritually cries more than others because he weeps over every instance of folly evident in wasted tears and empty-headed laughs (S 31.3.4).

While God dispenses mercy in forgiving sins, the truth he loves demands retribution (P 50.11). Unlike an individual who manufactures alibis for sins, the man who does the truth, which is the good work that is accusation of himself as a sinner, comes to the light that is Christ. In so doing the truth, he gladly welcomes for his sins the truth linked to punishment (J 12.13). In the presence of God Augustine aims at unsparingly stripping away all self-deceit. Even as he formulates this confession within, in colloquy with his God, he also purposes to publicize his sinfulness without, in the presence of many witnesses, Catholic brothers and sisters in Christ (10.4.5), mainly the spirituals.

Chapter 2: Why and How he Confesses to God

Augustine first discusses the meaning of confession to God, then in the two following chapters the import of confession to men.

2. Man's conscience is an abyss that can be plumbed by God alone. Conscience, we saw, is the capacity for discriminating between good and evil (S 12.4.4) in the light of the natural law inscribed on the heart (1.18.29; 2.4.9). In a second or analogous signification, it designates self-consciousness, in which the moral self scrutinizes actions to approve or rebuke them (S 7.18). Further extended, it denotes man's character or moral personality, the sum total of moral strengths and disabilities. In this last sense conscience resembles an inward canyon that seems unfathomable; indeed no abyss is deeper than that of the heart. An individual's words leave his most recessed thoughts and his heart itself undisclosed. So profound is it that a man himself cannot comprehend it. Deeper inclinations, harboring weakness, escaped Peter when he boasted that he would die with or for Jesus (P 41.13). Since hairs of the head are more easily numerable than affections within the deep that is the heart (4.14.22), abyssal conscience lies open only to the eyes of God, from whom nothing is veiled (P 41.13;134.16). Neither the greatest nor the least object or event is outside the purview of infinite knowledge, compassing past, present, and future (CD 11.21), of the God who sees all clearly because he sustains all. God is immanent in things through his knowledge; because he knows causatively (P 49.18), he is present in each thing, more interior than its innermost components (3.6.11).

Hence even if Augustine did not confess his sins, God as judge of his conscience (5.11.16) was aware of them in there least detail. Laid

out fully before the divine eyes is the story of each prodigal son: his
sitting down and rising up again, his squandering of his inheritance
with harlots, his hunger among pigs, his return to his father (P 138.5).[4]
Should Augustine try to conceal himself from God, he would be
concealing God from himself, not himself from God. Confession
unveils nothing new to God but is a form of self-revelation that bears
the heart into God's presence to partake of his light. As remarked
above (10.1.1), Augustine did the truth so as to come to the light that
is Christ (P 12.12), his inward groaning over spiritual misery testifying
that he was appalled by his sins. Indeed it was God's light that,
unmasking his sin, bared his repellent inner face. So God shines his
light on him: this first light bids him to do the truth, to acknowledge
himself as a sinner, impelling him not to forgive himself so that God
can forgive him. This pointing of finger of guilt at himself brings him
to a second light, to Christ, and, by finding his sin displeasing, he
finds God pleasing. By detesting his sin, he loves God; by despising
his old self, he longs for God. Stricken with compunction, he flings
aside his own self and interests, electing God alone as his good; a self-
renunciation in which he pleases neither God nor self save by God.
Positively put, God, the power of his soul (10.1.1) who purifies him
within, renders his soul attractive in both God's eyes and his own.[5] In
confessing to God, he fronts the ugly self whose perversions cry out
for divine cleansing. Thus he has shown why he confesses to God: not
to inform God since infinite knowledge probes every fiber of his
inward self; but, through God's first light, to inculpate himself and
sorrow over his sins. The fruit of confession is not expansion of divine
knowledge but growth in abasing self-knowledge. After putting his
finger on the why, he next focuses on the how of confession. He does
not employ exterior physical sounds like words and cries but interior
spiritual utterances and the fiery clamor of thought. A soul essentially
spiritual confesses to God interior words of contrition, movements of
spaceless thought pleading for spiritual healing. In himself he sharply
demarcates two features, man and sinner; God made him a man
whereas he made himself a sinner. In recognizing his sin, he is
censuring himself before confessing to God. In apprehending himself
as good, he attributes his goodness to God's light impelling him to
recoil from a soiled self. Man can make himself a sinner, but only the
maker can remake him as a new man, in right relationship with God
(S 12.13); a justification not merited by good works, for, like the Good

Thief, no sinner sunders the fetters of sin by his own strength (S 2.8.9). As fruit of justification, God blesses the just man with perduring grace, the indwelling of the divine in the soul as in a temple, an inhabitation distinct from his dynamic presence in all things (P 5.17).

His confession, because in the spiritual mòde, is made silently, yet from the aspect of interior utterance, his confession is not silent.[6] Silence: no vocalized sound is emitted, but no silence: interior phrasings cry out his sorrow. Though not vibrating through the air, spiritual speech is also enunciated, perhaps more really so than material locution. In any event, God's urging toward good is antecedent to spiritual utterance. Before Augustine even speaks good to men, God interiorly hears what is forthcoming, and indeed knows the utterance even before Augustine formulates it interiorly because his grace produces the goodness in the enunciation which Augustine first articulates within. Such prompting constitutes part of the blessing of the just: the good in his utterance is the fruit of sanctification of words and works that issue from justification (S 2.8.9; 10.3).

Chapter 3: Appeal to Believe him in Charity. Value of Past Confession

3. After noting earlier that he was baring his past to fellow men in order to bestir them to repentance (2.3.5), he narrows the range of readers to those prepared to believe him in charity.

He did not retail past sins to mere men in the hope that they would somehow cure his spiritual ills, for only the surgery of the divine physician can burn away sins (P 102.15). Recital of faults evokes from men in general not spiritual sympathy but a curiosity that bespeaks concupiscence of the eyes. For these, the Augustine of the past would be goggled at as a strange specimen, the tale of whose meanderings would be pored over simply for the pleasure that acquaintance with the odd excites (10.35.55). It is inconceivable that men who manifest little or no interest in learning from God what they are would turn to the *Confessions* to discover what he is. Living on the surface, they would be attracted only by the entertainment his misadventures promise, with scarcely a thought about prayerfully promoting his spiritual health. Deaf to divine admonitions to cry for help out of the depths (2.3.5), they could a fortiori gain nothing from testimony about his scramble from the pits to the heights through the mercy of God.

In addition, any and every sort of reader might question whether his self-portrait is veracious, for no one but he has private access to his own consciousness. Readers cannot peer into his mind to verify whether his *Confessions* harmonizes with his mind, no more than he can read their minds (S 217.2). If they garnered self-knowledge from God, they would be sure that God was speaking the truth to them and, if they knowingly lied, only they could inwardly certify their lying. No one other than the person who has experienced the events recounted can ascertain by direct evidence that his version is true. Since he cannot substantiate for others by direct inspection or ostensive demonstration that his account is veridical, he has to request readers to accept his words on human faith. Underpinning that faith of a restricted class of readers, actually fellow Catholics (10..4.5, 6), is their charity, which believes all things spoken by those whom it unites in Christian community (S 350.3). This salubrious chain binds Christians in one worldwide family, through a divine friendship (S 312.6.6) poured forth by the Holy Spirit (4.4.7), which nourishes faith in one another's word.

Frank airing of past sins harvests a double bounty; for Christians mired in vice, it arouses hope; for those in grace, it sparks joy in the triumph of mercy. Through his divine healer, for whose power and mercy no disease is incurable (P 102.5), his sins were covered up, i.e., abolished (P31[En.2].9); the deformed image scoured clean, his soul was reformed into a true image of God (T 14.16.22; 15.8.14). His conversion will fuel fresh confidence in baptized Christians sunk in their defects, who in the eyes of God look as disgusting as dogs who have returned to their own vomit (S 351.5.12), awakening them from their sleep of despair, sleep symbolizing the forgetfulness of God induced by slavery to vanities (P 62.4). His rise from spiritual rags to riches will help spur them to cry, as he did (2.3.5), out of the depths,[7] in contrition that readies a sinner for the influx of new sanctifying life (S 351.5.12).[8] As for graced Christians, the fruit of reading about his victory or, rather, about God's victory in him, is joy; not pleasure engendered by curiosity, which is fascinated by the spectacle of gross sins, but joy bursting from liberation from seemingly invincible iniquity.

There arises the second question: what is the spiritual value of his present confession to be articulated in Book 10? Sin still shadows his life as a bishop, as daily examen of conscience divulges, coupled with daily confession of wrongdoings, however minor. Prayer day by day imparts more peace from hope in the mercy of God unfailingly obtainable for reconciliation of spirit than does complacency in a fancied innocence; no man, however exalted his station in the Church, is immune to blemish of spirit.[9] About his present spiritual profile, many are piqued by a legitimate curiosity; inquirers include fellow bishops such as Alypius and Evodius, formerly members of his monastic community at Thagaste and later at Hippo, along with others not personally acquainted with him. Those who have heard from him are probably correspondents like Paulinus of Nola[10] while those who have heard about him are Catholics conversant with his writings.[11] In any case, no one interested in his current spiritual state can read his soul by external inspection. The configuration of his interior life, in its labyrinthine intricacies, is a closed book to the eyes of body and mind of another. His heart, where he is whatever he is, i.e., the locus of his character, cannot be cognized by direct evidence or inference. Obviously then, his inquirers are prepared to believe him, i.e., take his word as true: he is the sole reliable witness to his inner moral life. Charity, the root virtue that makes it supernaturally good (S 179A.5) and without which it is supernaturally nothing (S 209.3; 354.6), furnishes warranty that Augustine, their brother in faith and charity, would not lower himself to lying about the makeup of his spiritual self since he invokes God to attest to his veracity. Charity overrides every hesitation in assenting to the word of another. Where there is love, either there is no labor or the labor is loved (...*in eo quod amatur, aut non laboratur, aut et labor amatur* [Bon V 21.26]); any strain in believing is sublimated into love itself. Thus charity urges those rightly inquisitive to put their imprimatur on Augustine's testimony to his inward life, inaccessible, apart from his own conscience, to all save the all-seeing eye of God.[12]

Chapter 4: Value of Present Confession Addressed to Catholic Brethren

5. The fruit of the unbosoming of self is twofold because two faces of the moral self show themselves in the present Augustine as in every authentic Christian prior to full glory. In his graced dignity he communes with the Lord in prayer, but without being *simul justus et peccator* in the extreme sense, at once pillar of rectitude and whited

sepulcher; he is stung by awareness of inordinate drives that break
out in daily minor faults. In general, fellow Christians will bond with
him in praising God for any growth in virtue and will appeal for
further remedy when he is yanked downward and backward by his
own weight; the tendency to an object loved (4.14.2 and 15.27;
7.17.32), which here signifies custom-impregnated inclinations of the
carnal self, remnants of which stubbornly hang on after elevation to
the episcopate. While fire from the Holy Spirit has the potential to
carry him nearer to God (13.9.10), the earthiness of the old man, still
cumbered with vestiges of the triple concupiscence (10.30.41 - 38.63),
retards progress toward God. The harvest of self-disclosure may be
not slender but huge because many Catholic brethren will be
multiplying thanksgiving for God-bestowed virtues and petitioning
for relief from peskily persistent infirmities. Their beseechings will
bloom from a brotherly love receptive to divine illumination telling
them what is love-worthy in his conduct and what clamors for
amendment.

   This genuine love of brothers is shared by those inside the body of
Christ that is the family of God, not outsiders who, in feverishly
chasing after fleeting carnal goods, are heedless of Christians
witnessing to the truth (P 143.15). As their eyes light upon whatever
beauty shines from his soul, their souls will throb with wonder;
however, the sight of his shortcomings will induce them to breathe in
a different way, sighing now with hearts heavy with sadness.
Admiring spiritual strengths that are gifts from on high, they will
hymn God in thanksgiving; detecting disabilities, they will inwardly
grieve. The hearts of his brothers in Christ are censers holding the
burning incense, their thanksgiving and prayers arising as a fragrance
of sacrifice to the Lord, who will be delighted with the sweet odor
offered in his holy temple that is his Catholic Church, holy because
Christ sanctifies it (P 131.3;126.3).[13] As the sacred incense ascends
before the heavenly altar, mercy, he trusts, will cascade down as he
thirsts not for a trickle but for a downpour so abundant that he may
still re-experience compunction for deadly wounds he inflicted on
himself (P 50.6). His longing is anchored not in treacherous temporals
but in the changeless "I am who am" beyond the flux and reflux of
human existence (P 9.11). He begs the divine healer who supplies for
deficiencies to raise him up from the foothills of imperfection to a
peak of fulfillment, upgrading a beginner into ranks of the proficient

and, as far as possible, carrying him up to the realm of the wholly mature or perfect in spirit.

6. The inward fruit of his confession murmured in heart-to-heart converse with God is exultation and trembling; exultation, because the chains of death that are sin have been shattered, forbidding retreat to new discouragement over man's friable lot; trembling, because sound fear forestalls foolish outbursts of rashness and presumption (P 2.9). Additional inner fruit consists of sorrow for repeated lesser failings, along with remorse for past grave sins, both relying on measureless divine mercy (10.4.5). Fellow Catholics to whom he holds up the mirror of his soul will take spiritual pleasure in boons God has granted while lamenting banes that still trouble him. Companions of his joy, they outwardly delight in inward marvels of grace blessing him. Partakers of his mortal condition, they empathize with his struggles and sufferings; fellow citizens in the city of God, pilgriming to their homeland above, they are unceasingly consoled by hope that evokes praise of God (P 145.7). Expanding his horizons beyond his day, he embraces as fellow pilgrims not only those currently alive but Catholics who, like Monica and Patricius (9.13.37), in company with nameless others, have gone before as well as Catholics who will thrive in ages to come: his sweep engirdles the whole Church, past, present, and future, traveling toward the heavenly Jerusalem. The living are his brothers in the family of God, especially his flock in Hippo, along with others whom his works may reach, who are also his masters, he their servant.

Augustine deemed his episcopal rank not honor but onus, which grew more taxing as the years went on (S 339.2,4); a life of service that he initially assumed under duress (S 355.2). Not ruling as head of the household, he functions only as servant, an instrument applied to nourish his flock with the word from Jesus, the true head of the sheepfold. Prodigiously gifted speaker though he be, he esteems ministering the word a staggering burden. Though he would prefer to meditate and feed on the word in solitude (10.43.70), God commanded him to serve as a dispenser of the word to his people (S 339.4). If he turns his back on his commission, he will become unable to live with God, i.e., in accord with his will and in a communion of heart in prayer; and unable to live from him, i.e., cut off from grace. The words God speaks within are a treasure better distributed to others than hugged to his own bosom (S 339.4). In imitation of the

Word made flesh who acted as well as preached, his baring of soul concerns deeds as well. While confession can incite pride or serve to solicit praise (S 339.1), the divine wings with fortifications of charity and mercy (P 16.8) shield him from his weakness. He is only a tiny one; still, a lowly station lets in divine light refused the proud (S 67.9). He is borne up in the arms of the Selfsame, the everlasting Father who through his risen Son promises dust and ashes participation in his deathless life (P 102[S.2].14). The enveloping wings of the all-good and all-powerful Lord both protect and nurture his soul, watching over him as if he were the only one in existence (3.11.19). The Father is with him before Augustine is present with God; with him naturally through omnipresence before Augustine became aware of this; with him supernaturally because prevenient grace (13.1.1) disposed him to be with and one with God through divine life. To fellow Catholics whom he serves as bishop he will present his spiritual state. Only the God who appointed him to labor as a co-worker in the vineyard descries the secret intentions of his heart; not men, not Augustine himself, but God alone is his judge (S 49.2). Thus *sub specie divinitatis*, from the vantage point of God as ultimate arbiter, does he embark on his self-disclosure.

Chapter 5: Self-Knowledge Limited

7. No one but the Lord of his conscience (5.6.11) judges him because nothing of his mind lies outside the range of infinite wisdom (10.2.2), compared to which human knowledge of creatures resembles night (GL 4.23.45). Tracking down the causes of things is a tricky enterprise even for a consummate researcher (GL 4.32.49); yet the spirit of any thoughtful individual uncovers the secrets of his own inner life, veiled from others' gaze (10.3.3). Still, Augustine surely cannot know God now as God knows him. In the light of God's sinlessness, he, like Job (Jb 30.19), repentantly castigates himself as nothing but dust and ashes (CD 22.19). His prayer, which adapts the self-despising plea of an Abraham begging God to spare Sodom, betokens the posture of a penitent anguishing over past sins (P 147.24). Again, in this life the mind can understand God at best only in a blurred way, as in a mirror, i.e., indirectly, through creation, direct intuition being the glory of heaven. The God who is himself indescribable (P 85.12. DC 1.6.6) is grasped negatively, analogically, and eminently (1.4.4);

negatively: he is not temporal but eternal (11.13.16); analogically: creator of all that is good, he is all-good (T 8.3.4. P 134.3); eminently: he is super-good, unsurpassably wise, super-omnipotent (1.4.4. P 132.4; 109.12; 144.14. CD 21.7). In the night of this life Augustine perceives far more keenly his inner self than God's inner life. However, in one respect, that of vulnerability to attack, he apprehends more of God, ascertaining more about the inviolability of God than about his own violability. More precisely, he has adamantine certainty, in specific opposition to the implication of the Manichean war of Darkness against the Kingdom of Light, that God is inviolable: his being cannot be besieged (7.1.1). As a creature of flesh, Augustine is of course not exempt from assaults that are temptations, here not sallies of Satan from without but forays from within mounted by pride, lust, and curiosity, enemies encamped in the citadel of the self. Unlike his necessarily inviolable God, his spirit is inwardly violable due to his mortal, historical condition. Entertaining not the slightest doubt that he is violable, he remains unsure of exactly how strong are his forces of resistance. However, anxiety from incertitude is eased by certitude that God always tempers the wind to the shorn lamb. The divine artisan who through temptation burnishes the artwork that is the soul sets a limit to the quality and quantity of temptation a particular spirit has to undergo (P 94.9). The tester being also the helper, the heart upset by temptation does not have to flee for safety to a mountain of redoubt but need only prayerfully fly to its divine protector, a house of refuge to which Jesus the Good Samaritan leads it (P30[En.2.S.1].8), where he will confess whatever weaknesses God's illumination highlights. Because his soul is a vast deep (4.14.22), with layer upon layer of complex workings, many failings slip by examen. Yet he confesses these undiscovered tracts also, beseeching absolution of hidden faults (P18[En.2].13). Darkness stands for sin (P 7.19), which includes a second darkness that is ignorance of some sins. Only in the full blaze of glory symbolized by but brighter than any noonday sun will he know himself in the light streaming from the divine lover, in the secret of whose face the heart is ecstatically fulfilled (P 30[En.2.S.2].8).

Chapter 6: Creation Proclaims its Maker

8. Uneasy about his strength to ward off temptations, only partially

cognizant of the full splendor of divine being, he can, without pretense, avow that he loves all of God. Since his conversion he has lived as a servant of God, a monk pledged to common life and chastity, and, since 391 as priest, then bishop, has served his people out of love of God; a love not only affective but effective, not only spiritually impassioned but, more importantly, self-giving in the apostolate of incessant word and indefatigable work. His surety lies in the moral-affective line: his conscience, awareness of his moral self, certifies that he truly loves God. God impresses upon his heart the truth that is the divine word, shattering his deafness (10.27.38), opening his spiritual ears to listen to infinite love and respond with his own love engaged as well as intense.[11] Furthermore, all things in the universe proclaim God as creator, whose ravishing beauty captivating his heart bids him love God. Indeed the whole of creation never stops telling all men to know and love God. With the exception of a comparative few rightly dubbed fools, all of mankind admits that God is author of the universe (J 106.4. S 69.2.3). Natural philosophers who assign priority to creature over creator or who, while knowing God, pay him no homage or gratitude cannot be excused because of ignorance (5.3.3-5). But moral obtuseness indirectly blocking recognition of God is cleansed by grace, which is apportioned freely and more deeply in accord with divine knowledge that cannot be hailed before the tribunal of limited reason. "More deeply" underlines the unsearchable depths of wisdom that mysteriously distributes mercy, not deserved in justice, to those called (QS 1.2.12). Without healing of deafness-induced pride, men could not hear creation hymning praise of its creator. Heaven and earth praise God in the sense that man, discovering the dependence of their beauty on their creator, lends a surrogate voice to the praise of naturally dumb creatures (5.1.1). The language of natural things is their marvelous order, an intelligible structure manifest to the human intellect. Yet spiritual ears have to be disposed to listen so as to observe creature praising creator (P 144.13). Hence two sources nourish his love of God. The first arises from the experience of God in prayer; God touches his heart to hearken to words of love to which his own love answers. The second spins off from recognition of the beauty in creation pointing to its all-beautiful creator, whose infinite charm the heart cannot resist. This second theme branches off into emphasis on the transcendence of the creator (10.6.9), which, in turn, leads to an analysis of memory whereby man lays hold of God (10.8.12-25.36).

The meaning of God first flowers out of encounters in prayer that is love. As transcorporeal, the beauty of God seizing the heart is not sensorially accessible but channeled only, so to speak, through spiritual senses. God's beauty is not equivalent to the beauty, i.e., the order and harmony, in each material body. Nor is divine beauty the same as *decus temporis*, the glory of time that betokens the order of changes that include the alternation between day and night, the phases of the moon determining months, and the succession of the seasons marking the years; a pattern governed by the regular courses and revolutions of the heavenly bodies (Sol 1.1.4). Cosmic time that is regular and constant constitutes an engaging chant; the circuits of heavenly bodies harmonize in singing the song of the universe to a God above time (M 6.11.29). Again, God is not to be identified with brightness described as friendly to the eyes. The light that radiates from the eyes (10.6.9.S 277.10.10) is proportionate to and congruous with the light from the sun; as congruous, the two lights are, in some measure, quasi-equal and concordant. Since equality and concordance are attributes of friendship (4.4.7; 6.11;8.13. CA 3.6.13), exterior light is characterized as amicable to the eyes.[15] Moreover, God's beauty does not reside in sounds knitted together in every variety of enchanting songs; nor in olfactory objects like the fragrance of flowers and spices; nor in objects of taste like manna and honey; nor in the most pleasurable objects of touch such as limbs locked in nuptial union. All things evidence beauty because their order and harmony descend from their all-beautiful first principle. However immanently generative of all created beauty, the beauty of God remains formally distinct from that of his creation. To blur the lines between maker of beauty and beauty made, to collapse the efficient causality of God into essential identification with the creaturely, would annul his transcendence, rendering the ultimate meaning of beauty inexplicable.

Since God as spiritual is knowable only through the spirit, Augustine cannot love him as a five-faceted object captivating the senses. However, in the spiritual realm God's beauty is conveyed through light, sound, fragrance, food, and embrace that are supersensible. In an analogical mode of discourse implying the intimacy of divine lover with the soul, God satisfies the soul through spiritual impingings that, while somewhat resembling, far surpass, their sensory counterparts in enriching the soul. God's light is super-spatial; it is boundless, spiritually brighter than the most brilliant earthly light. Moreover, his interior locutions cannot be measured by a yardstick of time; the remorseless passage of time does not steal away their supratemporal beauty. Occasionally, time seems to stop when God's loving utterance lifts the soul out of itself, transporting it above passage (9.10.25). Again, the fragrance of the divine presence is not dissipated by a passing gust of air; its sweetness absorbed by the spirit continues delighting it. The food of God's presence, after filling the hungry, no matter how great the holy voracity, stays undiminished (S 28.3).[16] Finally, satiety cannot sunder the embrace of divine lover and soul-spouse; in any particular encounter the joy of union with the divine bridegroom goes on and on, with no slackening of spiritual pleasure.

9. What is this? In other words, what is the meaning of the God depicted with supersensory features perceived by five spiritual senses? Is the God who so communicates himself spiritual light and sound and the rest? "God is all of these because he is none of these. And he is none of these because he is creator of all of these" (S 28.2). The God who so entrances the soul that the overjoyed spirit murmurs its own love in return is not light and sound but essentially pure being, who out of his absolute existence creates beings with relative existence (7.11.17); he is, specifically, the creator of light and sound and everything else in the universe.

Turning next to consider things witnessing that God is their maker, he first canvasses material things, each of which fails to qualify as God since its order is not of its own making; as a work of art demands an artisan, so the order of things of nature requires a divine artist (P 26[En.2].22]). The earth and its bodies, nonliving and living, acknowledge that they are not God. So too the seas and their impenetrable deeps, along with creeping animals brought forth by the water (Gn 1.21), protest that their niches lie below the divine, exhorting the God-seeker to push inquiry higher. The air and its habitants, all flying creatures, deny that they are God. Air glosses its reply with a caution, "Anaximenes was wrong." At this juncture Augustine is following the lead of Cicero, who apparently reported that Anaximenes (fl. 550 B.C.) ascribed a divine character to air.[17] Cicero, however, was not an unimpeachable source, as a later modified statement (CD 8.2) indicates; for Anaximenes, air was not god but the basic substrate out of which the gods, along with other entities, are framed. Even heavenly bodies, the heaven or visible firmament, sun, moon, and stars (the planets), revered at times as gods, unhesitatingly aver that they are not the creator-God for whom he is searching. His next questions are addressed to the proper objects correlated with his sensory portals: light, sound, fragrance, savor, tactile features; secondary or accidental phenomena that are plainly not God. The things scrutinized figuratively speak, taking on a voice through the probing mind (5.1.1). Examination of this beauty serves as an interrogation. Augustine, notice, is not saying: my interrogation is my consideration; but the converse: my consideration is my interrogation. The insight that these material things cannot exist on their own is the voice whereby they confess their creator. Strictly, order bespeaks a maker as artwork bespeaks as artist; metaphorically, beauty speaks to the mind inspecting it: "The divine artist made me" (P 144.13).

After surveying corporeal beings, Augustine ponders himself: plainly he is not God but a man, a rational animal, a unit composed of body and soul, each with its special function and apparatus, the body being the exterior side of the one self, and the soul the interior man. Since the interior self, because constituted by reason, is superior to the body, the soul is the conduit through which he can grasp God. The body is passive in sensation, presenting the information to the soul to act upon; broadly defined, sensation is a passive condition of the body that does not escape the soul (QA 25.48). Since the body cannot act on the soul superior to it, it is not the body that senses but the soul by means of the body (M 6.5.10. GL 12.24.51).[18] The body acts as a kind of messenger delivering to the soul messages that are sense data from the external world (GL 12.24.51).[19] As mentioned earlier (Book 1, n.38), projected by the eyes outward to the objects viewed are beams of light also styled messengers, rays proceeding from the brain (GL 7.13.20; 16-32. T 9.3.3, S 227.10.10); this light is comparatively slight, for without outside light the soul through the eyes could perceive nothing (GL 1.16.31). Functioning as servants, special sensory messengers report to reason, which presides over the senses because only its operation can cognize the universe. Exercising its judicative role, reason, while distinguishing the senses from their special data, draws the line between itself and the senses, discerning that it not only receives but understands the data, while also aware that is understands itself in self-consciousness (LA 2.3.9). Reason that rules the senses, i.e., the ego or self taken interiorly, intelligizes deliverances of things in the universe, denying their identity with God and affirming creation by him. The universe as an ensemble, one great system that is a unity of order, also avows that it is not the absolute equal but the relative effect of God.

10. Although properly implemented animals sensorially encounter and pragmatically react to this order, adapting to it to satisfy individual and specific survival needs, they are devoid of the rational capacity to understand it. Though all men are cognitively organized to move from made to maker, some fail to rise rationally to a creator because they become subjugated to lower objects. A moral component enters to block the ascent of the mind. As remarked previously (1.12.16; 18.28), sin is the retribution for sin; the interior disfigurement that is sin is caused by actual sinning. As blindness in the strictly moral line is the penalty of disorder for disorder, so deafness in the line of cognition is interiorly inflicted for disorder; by turning aside to things inferior, the mind closes its ears to the voice of order in things proclaiming their creator. In searching for truth in things while neglecting inner truth, some thinkers who cannot hear the artwork of creation booming out that it is made mistakenly deem the entities comprising the universe to be both art and artist; a merger of God or immanent reason and the world characteristic of Stoics (VR 36.67). Out of this fusion of God and the universe are spawned various modes of idolatry; men who love the universe in preference to God wind up abjectly homaging creature rather than creator: some worship the soul, some the stars, others the air; still others, priding themselves on being most religious, worship the universe as a whole along with its world soul (VR 37.68). Rather than their minds commanding the senses, the sensory world rules their minds; divested of sovereignty, these minds effectively forfeit proper judgment. The objective order continues unaltered, its voices sounding in the same way to all, but subjectively disordered spirits become so fascinated with things which are true that they forsake the truth within that is their judicative standard. Others happily unburdened by this cognitive-moral disorder are attuned to voices of order demanding an orderer as they compare this order to the truth within. The inward yardstick of truth that is God is not to be reduced to things corporeal, whose quantitative character or mass nullifies equivalence with the

divine. One-half of a stone is in one place, the other half in another place, each part smaller than the whole stone; the whole stone is not present in half the stone, just as the whole stone is not equal to a part or a part, because smaller, equal to the whole stone (S 277.13.13). God, however, is spiritual, supremely because unchangeably so (7.11.17); uncircumscribed by place (5.2.2), unextended in space, always and everywhere present in his totality (CD 16.5.E 187.5.16).

Indeed the human soul itself, even in its basic animating or vegetative role, is superior to every material body, for no inanimate body can produce life in another inanimate. Only if it were already living could the body generate life, which generation is distinct from animation. Moreover, if a material body as such could animate another body, it would be a soul, with which, because a body is extended, it cannot be equated (Imm 16.25). At the vegetative level, which man shares with plants, the soul unifies the organism, proportionally distributes nourishment to members, and maintains the body's harmony and limits not only in terms of beauty but also in terms of growth and reproduction (QA 33.10). The soul is also higher than each body and the universe as a whole because it is nonspatial and unextended. Each body is a mass; mass is the body taken dimensionally or quantitatively.[20] As just mentioned, each extended part is less than the whole body; one soul, however, is not present in one part of the body, and another in another; the soul is *tota ubique*, totally present not only throughout the whole body but in each of its parts (QA 14.23). As vivifying the entire mass, the wholly present soul is present in every part because each and every part is alive. The whole soul is present, e.g., in the foot; otherwise it could not feel the pain there (Imm 16.25). In short, the wholeness in every part of the virtual quantity of the soul makes it superior to the part-outside-partness of dimensive quantity. Yet the life that is soul is neither entirely independent nor supreme. Only the creator is supreme life and the fount of all life (VR 11.21), sovereign and primordial life because he is his very life (T 6.10.11). God then is the life of life, the life that causes the life that is the soul (3.6.10; 10.20.29). Ontically, God is the life of every life that is soul, whether dead in sin or alive with grace. Morally, only the soul united to God by grace is quickened by the life of God that infuses wisdom, piety, and holiness (M 6.13.40. J 10.12;47.8).

Chapter 7: God Not Accessible through the Senses

11. Since, as life of his life, God is the cause of Augustine's soul, he must reside above the summit of the soul. This somewhat schematic statement requires further explication by the highest power in man's psychic structure, keyed to objects nonsensible and spiritual. It is impossible to grasp God by functions on the vegetative plane; otherwise, contrary to Scripture, horse and mule, enlivened by a fundamental factor in life, would be capable of laying hold of God. Higher than the life of nourishment and growth is that of sense perception, at which stage the soul not only vivifies but "sensifies" the body, presiding over the operation of the senses. According to divine design, knowable not by sense but by reason, if a man's eyes are open while his ears are plugged, he cannot visualize sounds (LA 2.3.9). To each of the senses is appointed proper receptor, function, and object. The eyes see, the ears hear, the sense of taste discriminates between bitter and sweet, the sense of odor distinguishes fragrant from foul, and the tactile sense demarcates hot and cold while the one soul actively attends to the diverse impresses various sensory objects stamp on the body. However, a matter-conditioned mode of operation debars sensory agencies from apprehending God; horse and mule that perceive sensory phenomena cannot know God. Since the light and voice of the life that is God accessible in intimate prayer (10.5.8) lie beyond the senses, Augustine has to transcend them to reach the divine.

Chapter 8: Memory of Objects Rooted in Sensory Experience

12. In pursuit of greater concretion, the question urges itself: in what precise sense can God, the life of his life, be called light, sound, and food for his spirit? Additional inquiry culminates in the inference: to embrace God who is truth the spiritual senses delight in the truth, made blissful to some degree by feeding upon the goodness that is God (10.22.32-26.37).

Before arriving at the conclusion that happiness consists in resting in God, Augustine undertakes an inquiry of memory, the route along which the self travels to inward knowledge of God. Employed not univocally but analogously, the term covers, first of all, its core meaning, the common signification of awareness of objects or events as past. It is then extended to denote cognition of basic notions and principles in the arts and sciences, including those of arithmetic and geometry. Further, memory also denotes recall of past affective and passional objects. After handling difficulties arising from forgetfulness, he widens memory to designate the way to happiness or union with the God who is truth, within `but above memory. In mounting step by step to his creator, he bypasses memory among animals. Memory, he was aware, operates even in fish observable at the fountain at Bulla Regia, southeast of Hippo, awaiting bits of food from passersby.[21] Higher animals more markedly evince memory; dogs run out to greet their returning masters, displaying their affection (H 7.49. CD 19.7), and lions perform in the amphitheater because they retain signs drilled into memory by a trainer (NG 47).

As later search indicates, Augustine is not unaware of primary memory in which the soul recalls items just gone or immediately past.[22] In singing or reciting the line *Deus creator omnium*, the soul, when pronouncing the last three syllables, retains in memory the first five syllables, all the syllables forming a continuous or psychic timeline in the soul (11.27.35). Here, however, in the section devoted to memory he confines himself to its nuclear signification, secondary memory,[23] in which a discernible interval of time divides the event and its recall. The reader may remember a witty phrase from a telephone conversation ten minutes before or unusual food he ate at breakfast one hour ago, examples that contain discontinuity, a cardinal component of secondary memory: a temporal break intervenes between present remembrance and objects recalled as past. From the secondary memory of objects sensorially experienced, the memorial scope broadens to compass mentally cognizable principles of the arts, the affective sphere, and the memory of self, which moves upward to the memory of God, the truth that joys the soul unto happiness: the God now more clearly specified, who resides above the *mens*, the topmost part of his soul (10.7.11).

Augustine marvels at the enormous breadth of memory which consists of not one field but fields, not of one huge palace but many. While the awesome extent of memory is verifiable in some measure in any normal mind, it seems safe to surmise that his gifts of memory, modestly described as "strong" (1.20.31), stimulated him to accent its range. His memory was so tenacious and prodigious that, in combination with his genius and unflagging labor, it qualifies him to be rated one of the folio editions of mankind.[24] Apparently the fact that he carried his filing cabinet in his head accounts for the facility with which he constantly quoted by heart verses of Scripture in extemporaneously delivered sermons.

Objects of all types originating in sensory experience are stored as memorial impresses, not simply passively resuscitated but actively cogitated or thought about, i.e., subsumed under the rightly judicative or pattern-discerning work of reason. Cogitation is an analogous term, which, in general, is not always employed with scientific precision. Though cogitation signifies fashioning of a figment of the imagination (Sol 2.20.34), a fantasizing brand evident in Manichean vanities (3.6.10), its most common acceptation designates thought or thinking. At certain points it carries the additional note of organization; it is thinking, correct because in line with rules of judgment, that sets in order objects in its purview. As linked to memorial images, cogitation is used in the general sense of true thinking in accord with proper judgment. Some sensory events are cogitated, i.e., synthesized, to afford a lesson. The pilfering of pears, re-thought, is expanded to explain sin as a bogus imitation of omnipotence (2.6.14). The encounter with the drunken bum in Milan is recalled in terms of the fatuity of panting after glitzy prizes of this world (6.6.9-10). Monica's dying is detailed to spotlight the beauty of detachment from all that passes away. Moreover, cogitation may abridge the memories retained. *Cartago* suggests *sartago*, a cauldron boiling with illicit love, a figure that catches in a smaller frame the picture of student days in Sin City (3.1.1). He pithily summarizes his role as rhetorician in a depreciative phrase: he was a vendor of words (9.5.13). Again, cogitation may modify remembrance. Recall of his weeping over the death of Dido is recorded with a touch of sadness over his puerile state of soul (1.13.21). The duping of his mother before sailing for Rome is remembered with inner pain and remorse (5.8.15). Moreover, in its ordering activity cogitation assures that memorized lines are grouped and retained as a meaningful whole; in recollection (10.8.12) it compares or measures the candidates against the item desired (say a particular color); its arranging is responsible for increased, diminished, or modified images (10.8.12,14). In a stronger, somewhat technical sense it is the detection of a common factor running through diverse data, operative in the construction of a definition from select images (10.11.18). Furthermore, other objects and occurrences go uncogitated, unglossed, so to speak, such as casual encounters in his hometown, routine daily events in classes over the years, and even the number of books in his earliest work, *De pulchro et apto* (4.13.20), items that, retained for a while, eventually fade into oblivion. Not all of this memorially lost material was originally scattered or unorganized; as a youth he memorized for class set pieces, some lengthy, from the poets, but, with the required recitation over and done with, he probably forgot many of the lines.[25]

Some of the easily accessible items lodged in memory emerge immediately. If he is searching for instances of pride, forthwith are flashed on the screen of consciousness arrogant instructors, misled Manichean co-religionists, puffed-up scientists, and the grossly proud individual who provided a copy of Neoplatonic writings. On other occasions, the mind has to rummage for an object desired, perhaps an apt line from Virgil or the appropriate text from Scripture. At times too items not exactly relevant surface, but since these are only approximate to and not identical with the memorial entity pursued, he has to re-deposit them in his memory-bank, then go on trying to track down the precise object wanted. In still other cases, in which the material has been learned by heart, as in the Lord's Prayer or a hymn or psalm, the association of words and verses in an organized fashion assures that enunciation of the first word or phrase will trigger the immediate appearance of the next unit, each link in the chain effort-lessly generating its successor. Here he differentiates three sorts of remembering. First, certain objects seem ready to hand; as soon as their stock is solicited, they make their appearance. He can memorially recapture without difficulty members of his first monastic community at Thagaste. Second, reliance on memory at times becomes a kind of recollection. The mind has to sift through prior experiences and memorial objects to hit on the entities desired. In a memory ample as Augustine's, possible candidates emerge in bunches, only to be brushed aside, as he goes on hunting for the right item. Third, recall can be smoothly sequential, as with remembrance of material learned by heart. The initial word or phrase furnishes the cue for its successor, and so on, in a memorial-causal chain till the piece is finished.

Augustine, we pointed out earlier (Book 1, n.78), lumps functions of the interior sense with what some Aristotelians label the estimative sense. Similarly, at this juncture he seems to subsume under the rubric of memory both memory proper (with specific reference to the past) and imagination (retention and reproduction of images). If memory is considered in the wide sense, i.e., as imagination, it contains two kinds of objects: those of productive or creative imagination, in which thought alters the original image, and those of simple reproductive imagination in which the original images remain unreconstructed by thought. In productive imagination, thought adds to the image; we can imagine not one but ten suns in the sky, or the sun traveling twice as fast in its daily circuit (11.23.30). The image can also be contracted or subtracted from; the sun can be pictured as a small disc in the sky. The image may be modified in other ways; parts of images can be combined as in mythical beasts like a centaur (man and horse) and griffin (eagle and lion), In the service of false religion free-wheeling cogitation can conjure up illusory phantasms. Flying Medea, along with other figures of pagan myth, issues from the misleading application of cogitation to images (3.6.10). Wild fancies of Manicheans such as buckets of light ascending to sun and moon, fig leaves that weep when plucked (3.10.18), and the five elements (3.6.10. CEF 19.28) are also fictions disguised as fact, delusive cogitations at wide variance from rules of judgment (Sol 2.20.35). Of course the majority of images are simply deposited in memory broadly understood, without undergoing cogitative recasting.

13. As the proper objects of the senses are perceived by distinct organs, so, once become images and consigned to memory, they are classified and psychically located in special sectors of memory.[26] The eye is sensitive to every sort of color, its proper object, along with the common sensible of shape (LA 2.3.81). Within its physiological capacity the ear hears every kind of sound. The olfactory sense receives odor through the nose, and the gustatory takes in tastes such as sweet and bitter through the mouth. What is today called the somesthetic sense, that of touch operative through the whole body, discriminates between stimuli involving texture (hard or soft, smooth or rough), temperature (hot or cold), and pressure (heavy or light). Most of these stimuli originate in the external environment, but at times they arise internally, from the state of the body itself, such as temperature associated with fever, and pressure due to a painful swelling. Obvious and routine as is memory or imagination, it is invested with a certain mystery—precisely how all these items are banked in memory lies beyond human ken (and this remains generally true today): all are accumulated in the huge, partly

sprawling, unknowable caverns of memory. Yet we do certainly know that each category of sense data enters by its special receptor; that not the sensory objects themselves but their images, their forms or representatives, reside in memory, awaiting the cogitation of the mind to recall them.

Although diverse data are undoubtedly funneled through their respective senses, we cannot specify in detail how the impresses within memory are fashioned; yet, introspection shows, the various particulars of memory are classified under their proper sensory headings.[27] At night too, when vision cannot make out colors, Augustine can discriminate between black and white or any couplets of colors he chooses for recall. When reviewing visual phenomena, he is not disturbed by the intrusion of sounds; each set of sense data exclusively transmitted through one sense is singled out for memorial revival. Should he so decide, he can evoke auditory phenomena, interiorly singing a psalm without recourse to the vocal apparatus. Replay of sound phenomena is, like that of visual recall, selective, undistracted by any other special-sensory remembrance; he can inwardly chant a verse of Ps 22 apart from memorial association with the green of the pasture. So with other senses: their data are selectively called up, without actual dependence on specific external senses. At will he can excerpt in memory the scent of lilies in isolation from that of violets, the sweet taste of honey in preference to the sharp savor of wine, and the feel of a smooth rather than that of a rough surface.

Fortunately working in the service of his outstanding mind was the remarkable breadth of his sensory acuity. Besides being an excellent visualizer, he was gifted with a refined auditory imagination, along with keen discrimination of olfactory, gustatory, and somesthetic images. Unlike Augustine, whose memory was both photographic and audiographic, educated persons are, not uncommonly, good visualizers but poor in auditory imagery or vice versa.[28] Furthermore, among some analytic and scientific types visual imagery tends to deteriorate with the passage of years because pronounced reliance on abstraction entrains infrequent use of imagination.[29] In addition, it seems probable that Augustine tested himself in reproducing various images. Sitting in the dark to establish the maximum of quiet and noninterference from external stimuli, he explicitly states that images occurred while he was in darkness and complete silence, presumably free from all sound. Moreover, since under ordinary circumstances men do not selectively observe memory images of each of the senses in isolation, Augustine's inductive truth, we may infer, was based on experiment or controlled observation at least in the broad sense.

14. In the immense room of memory, where inner eye fixes upon psychic duplicates of heaven and earth and sea and all their dwellers and denizens, he recalls, with memory proper, the location of each object labeled with the time in the past and the place he encountered it, along with his personal reactions, all of the contents being garnered by direct perception or on the word of another. Reading or conversation apprised him of objects accessible to human faith, historical facts impossible of personal verification, like Catiline's rebellion (2.5.11) and geographical data, verifiable but not conveniently so, like the lay-out of Trier (8.6.15). Under belief also fell information gained in exchanges with Monica's lapse into wine-bibbing and her peaceful conquest of Patricius' wrath and unfaithfulness (9.9.22) and Victorinus' public profession of divine faith (8.2.51). Not included under belief are the cosmological bizarreries of the Manichees he once puerilely accepted because he is attending to authentic copies of things or events, not weird concoctions mirroring not a grain of fact. Tying these representations to events in his personal history, he weaves the past into a schema with present and future. In mulling over the future emerging from the past as if future and its progenitive past were actually present, he anticipates features of his theory of time, according to which past and future actually exist only in present memory and present expectation: the time-line of past, present, and future is "presentialized" or known in a present interval by memory, attention, and expectation (11.20.26; 28.37-8). Deliberation culminates in decision by modeling its action in part on representations of past actions and objects drawn from the storehouse of memory. Perhaps once again the Lord's word pierced his heart (9.2.3), inflaming him to tread the path of some early saint, images of whose deeds or words he can straightway summon. On certain occasions, projects of deeds are presently pondered not in a future-oriented indicative mood but in the optative mood. Previewing an inviting possibility, the inner self says, "Would that this or that event occurred," or, if the prospect is undesirable, prayerfully murmurs, "May God forestall that." The two latter comments concerning the future seem to lie outside the control of decision-making. In the first

case, remembering the zeal of first-century Christians, he may hope for like intensity of fervor in his flock, and perhaps in the second instance, fearful of a barbarous oppression of the African Church, he shudderingly begs God to avert renewed persecution.

But whether geared to the future in indicative or optative mood, patterns for prospect sprout from images laid up in the past. Without the past that is the seedbed of the future Augustine could barely live in the present and hardly plan for the future. Deprived of memory, he is implicitly averring, a man's whole past would be swamped by darkness, leaving his future unilluminated save by the fugitive punctuated glow of a string of disconnected instants.[30] A blackout of the past entails a near-blind groping into the future. In terms of primary memory not even one syllable can be pronounced without remembrance; each syllable, however short, has beginning, middle, and end (M 6.8.21). Without ongoing retention of always fleeting fractions of experience man's consciousness would be almost insufferably barren. Moreover, where the past is a blank, the future becomes a desert; man can profit from the future only in virtue of capital from the past. Man without memory would be more hapless than animals so handicapped, which, if they lost memory, could fall back on instinct for survival. Unequipped with an elaborate instinctual apparatus, deprived of the memory that underpins learning for adaptation to environment, man would probably have quickly perished; to borrow part of Hobbes' well-known line, his life would have been "nasty, brutish, and short."[31]

15. So far-flung are memorial fields and palaces, apparently without discernible limit, that no one can sound the depths of his own memory or mind; memory being equivalent to the mind (*mens*) present to or aware of itself (T 14.11.14). Though belonging to him as man, it is unplumbable; he cannot grasp the whole breadth and depth of his own memory. The vast court (10.8.14) is also a cognitively limitless recess (10.8.13), defying probes to fully explore and map it. Clearly the unknown region cannot extend beyond the ambit of the mind; yet if this unfathomed sector is embraced by the mind, it seems incongruous that it eludes knowledge; how can any part of the self not be contained in the whole of the self, and, if so contained, how not known? Augustine is affected by two analogous sorts of wonder; the first consists of wonderment, perplexity over unexplained facts of nature and self; the second is amazement at the almost incredible

complexity of the mind. This second wonder harbors the answer to his question about the self's inability to encompass itself: memory is stupendously boundless and impenetrable. The interior self is undoubtedly the self, but certification of the mind itself does not entail cognitive self-containment. The wonder of the mind leaves unresolved the wonderment over its incapacity to reach an exhaustive knowledge of itself.[32]

Surprisingly, men who are awestruck by the wonders of the outer world regard with indifference the no less equally marvelous inner world. The magnificent wonder that is the conscious key to all other wonders strangely arouses no wonderment. Again, the inner world is, in its way, just as sweeping as the outer world. Within memory, situated in psychic resemblance, not in physical reality, are tall mountains, along with the great ocean taken on human faith (10.8.14). As the outer eye throws its light over things outer, so the inner eye of memory irradiates the inner contents of psychic space (M 6.8.21). Furthermore, he is captivated by the sheer representative power of human cognition. When his sight perceived mountains and sun, he did not absorb into consciousness the very things themselves but received and remembered them by replicates first imprinted on the senses. As mentioned earlier, in consciousness things without take on a second existence; they are invested with a new mode of being. Laws of nonliving and living things cannot explain the emergence of these indubitable psychic phenomena; however events in the brain may be correlated with knowledge, they cannot properly cause these transphysical objects. Still, these mental copies conform to specific physical realities; exactly how this correspondence is mediated remains a problem vexing, at least in part, to this very day.

Chapter 9: Strictly Intellectual Objects in Memory

16. Besides copies of sensory objects, this spacious receptacle carries purely intellectual objects achieved in the analysis of the liberal arts, which are more deeply recessed in a placeless place or immaterial region. Because immutable and necessary, the objects cannot be extracted from a sensory world that is changeable and contingent, and because not transmitted by the sensory world, they are not the images of things. Situated in the intellectual memory are the objects themselves, such as the definition of literature, the

definition of dialectic or the art of disputation, along with the determination of the three questions posed in dialectical inquiry or scientific analysis (10.10.17). The status of these intellectually remembered objects essentially departs from that of sensory-memorial deliverances, in which are gathered not the objects themselves but their copies like the sound of a friend's voice, the fragrance of a rose, and the taste of honey.

Chapter 10: Intellectual Truths Not Given through the Senses

17. In matters of inquiry, sometimes with disputative overtones, three questions have to be raised: (i) does the thing exist? (ii) what is it or how is it to be defined? (iii) what sort of thing is it? what is its ontic worth? where is it positioned on a scale of things?[33] Existence, whatness, and worth are verbalized with signs that pulsate in the air and pass away, but the objects meant are not sensorially perceivable nor are they imaged in memory, where there abide not proxies but the objects themselves. A quick check verifies that existence, definition, and worth are sensorially inaccessible, neither denoting nor connoting color, sound, or other proper sensibles. Not obtained or inferred from the senses, they are suprasensible objects, graspable only by some agency over and beyond the sensory. He cannot trace the source of these objects nor the path by which they entered memory. (Later he will argue that these truths derive from truth itself [10.26.37]). While aware that his memorial double of the sea originated in visualization of the Mediterranean, he never experienced how objects like definitions took up abode in his memory; yet by analysis and inference he can certify that they dwell in his mind. Granted, he gained these notions from a teacher but only in the sense that the words of the teacher prompted him to turn inward, to read, as it were, truths discernible within (Mag 14.45). A teacher does not transfer his knowledge of an art to a learner; otherwise, teaching would entail evacuation of the teacher's mind (Imm 4.5). Rather, he externally stimulates the learner to internally focus on the truth in his own mind. In learning, Augustine strictly took these objects to be true on the word of another, outwardly giving credence to the teacher, but inwardly measuring the teacher's assertions against the notions within, which function as a standard of truth. Recognizing these objects as veridical, he approved them, i.e.,

rationally judged them to be true; approbation is a positive judgment averring not just that something it is but that it must be so (LA 2.12.34).[34] More than mere matters of fact, objects internally cognized bespeak what cannot be otherwise; underlying the arts are notions and principles threaded with necessity. Going within to inspect them in their proper habitat that is intellectual memory, he apprehends them. Since intellectual memory is more withdrawn than the sensory, its contents have to be excavated by analysis initiated by admonition of a teacher, an exterior propaedeutic to interior insight.

Signs resolve the question whether something is; ostensive definition or pointing calls attention to a thing corresponding to a name. To a student wondering what *saraballae* means, a teacher points out or describes a particular headdress (Mag 10.33,35). Raising the question, does a thing exist?, however, is not achieved through sensory indicators; such existence can be laid hold of only in intellectual memory. In *Meno* Socrates elicits stepwise from an uneducated slave-boy the truth that the double of a square is obtained by drawing a diagonal on the original square.[35] To Plato it seemed plain that the untutored slave already knew some geometry, else Socrates could not have guided him to the conclusion. In short, learning is reminiscence: the slave-boy, under Socrates' direction, remembered a geometrical truth first acquired in a state preexisting this mortal life. Though he apparently leaned toward reminiscence quite early in his career, Augustine later dismissed the theory as counter-experiential. Simply stated, if men mastered geometry in prior life, all or most men in this life would be skilled in the science, but, in fact, geometers in this life are very rare. Augustine's confutation, however, is somewhat more convoluted. According to Plato, if all or nearly all were skilled in geometry in a previous existence, then all or almost all in this life are capable of learning geometry through the Socratic method. But, in fact, skilled geometers are few and far between. The factual denial of the consequent entails the denial of the antecedent: thus some in the prior life were not geometricians (T 12.15.24). Since Plato's assumption that all or nearly all in this life can learn geometric theorems through questioning is counter-factual, his inference of reminiscence is analytically untenable.

Yet while discarding reminiscence, Augustine continued to maintain that learning implies a kind of recall (10.13.20). Somehow stocked in the mind prior to actual sensory experience are intelligibles that include the principles of the liberal arts, rules or standards, spaceless and, in root, timeless, existing *omnia simul* (3.7.14). The basic constituents of grammar, dialectic, rhetoric, and poetry reside in the deepest level, the intellectual. The truths of mathematics are also lodged in the innermost region (10.12.19). Inscribed in intellectual memory, in addition, are the basic prescriptions of moral living (1.18.28), dictates of the natural law or true and interior justice (3.7.13), norms coextensive with the rules for the art of right living embodied in the moral virtues. Had he not been reminded by teaching, whether via lecture or book, Augustine would probably have never apprehended truths located in intellectual memory, which have to be laboriously dug out as a miner digs for a vein of gold. Distinct from theoretical truths that are grasped only insofar as they are explicated, moral truths such as the dictates of the natural law are vaguely and broadly known even by the illiterate; untutored thieves protest the stealing of their property (2.4.9). As remarked earlier, indispensable as is the teacher leading the learner to quarry truths in intellectual memory, his office is only conditional, not causal: the teacher is a sine qua non, not the essential agent in learning. While in the absence of a teacher individuals are ordinarily powerless to make explicit or intelligize strictly intelligible truths, it is the learner cued by the teacher who actively produces his own learning.

But how do these truths take up residence in the intellectual memory? As already noted, the early Augustine flirted with, then expressly repudiated, the theory of reminiscence; a prior godlike state cannot account for the truth within. Nor did he ever endorse the view that man's mind is godlike as such, the source of its own truths; broadly autodidactic, man cannot be auto-creative of the truth. Man is able, loosely speaking, to teach himself; he comes to understand only because instructed by the interior teacher, God or Christ, in whose light he sees strictly intelligible realities. This light streaming from God is not restricted to the line of grace but operates as well in the line of nature; the mind sees intelligible objects in an incorporeal light of a special sort, an envisagement similar to the way in which the bodily eye sees objects in corporeal light (T 12.15.24). It is gross error, pace N. Malebranche, to depute to the human mind the vision of the ideas of things in the divine mind.[36] Rather, God stamps basic truths on the human mind as the impression of a ring is stamped on wax while the original impression remains in the ring (T 14.15.21). To view intelligible objects in this incorporeal light is not to see God but to see the truths received from God who is truth. The mind so illumined sees not the divine mind as such but these truths as ultimately true in the incorporeal light, which, so to speak, furnishes the principles in which these truths are grounded. From another angle, the mind, when defining or analyzing, consults the truth presiding within the mind itself (Mag 11.38).

In the line of the existence of truth, immutable truths do not spring from a mutable mind but are grounded in truth itself, the absolutely immutable God (LA 2.12.34; 15.39).[37] In the line of knowledge of truth, the uncreated light that is God supplies man with participation in his light, a created light (CF 25.7), empowering the mind to "read" or intelligize notions and judgments inscribed in intellectual memory. To phrase it somewhat differently, the rules of judgment that express definitions are originatively written in the book of light called truth; these definitions are then transferred to the mind of man (T 14.15.21). This incorporeal light proper to the soul's natural operation is said to be sui generis (T 12.15.24), i.e., specific to man, for animals lack an illuminable mind and angels visualize objects in the mind of God (GL 4.24.41).

It seems instructive to briefly comment on similarities with the position of Aquinas. Though Augustine's theory of knowledge is not as empirical as Aquinas', vibrant chords of empirical realism resound throughout his analysis. Sensory impresses and sensio-intellectual objects duplicate their extramental originals. Purely intelligible objects, while not indirectly derived from sensory experience, are applicable to nature and man; corresponding to the intelligibles are their objective correlates, imperfectly realized, in the universe. Moreover, mathematical numbers, the numbers by which we formally count, are intelligible without images, yet sensible numbers in the physical things somehow accord with them (10.12.19). The mind, which knows without need of sensory check that $7 + 3 = 10$, ascertains that these formal numbers are exemplified in sensible numbers; it can truly judge, "Seven apples plus three apples equal ten apples." Furthermore, like Aquinas, Augustine is fundamentally an empirical-realist moralist who roots particular moral judgments in precepts of the natural law, concretely applied through conscience. The notion of justice lodged in the repository of moral intelligibles extends to particular individuals; a prudent mind can properly judge, "This man is just."[38]

Chapter 11: Process of Formulating Truths

18. Here he briefly shows how cogitation definitionally excavates or properly formulates notions latent within intellectual memory. Cogitation signifies a collation or arrangement of diverse mental items. A secretary collates in one folder correspondence on a similar subject, and a bricklayer arranges bricks to form a wall, but while both apply their minds to their tasks, neither arrangement is a cogitation since the objects gathered together are other than mental. Taken technically, cogitation denotes an activity in which the mind assembles mental features to constitute one mental object. As already mentioned (10.8.12), the term covers an analogical spectrum, referring diversely but similarly to a number of operations of the mind. Augustine's cogitation of Carthage, superior to that of Alexandria because gained by direct evidence (CF 20.7), is a complex cognition woven out of the images mirroring various experiences there as student and teacher. In its analytical acceptation cogitation cognizes intelligibles, not through psychic copies but in themselves, by organizing scattered features into a noetic pattern. In this respect, cogitation is a method of framing definitions or fashioning rules of judgment.[39] In some sense Plato exercised cogitation in dialogues that searched for a definition of courage, as in *Laches*, or probed the scales of being and knowledge, illustrated by the allegory of the cave in *The Republic*, or argued that all learning is reminiscence, as in *Meno*.[40] The inquiring mind, starting with a common-sense experience of the object sought, isolates significant factors, then builds them into a satisfactory definition, one neither too broad nor too narrow. Socrates, the first great master of definition, used the maieutic method; the midwife metaphor of course becomes misleading if we imagine that the definition pops out tout court; Socrates had to gradually formulate the definition from related aspects. Imitating Cicero, who resorted to cogitation toward a definition of friendship and in identifying virtue with happiness,[41] Augustine exploited cogitation, particularly in his earlier works, to establish that happiness consists in the possession of the truth that is wisdom. The meaning of happiness is a notion buried in intellectual memory, which has to be

unearthed (10.10.7), maieutically brought to light and explicated. Moreover, these definitions are fashioned; the parts are joined into a cogitative whole.

Once cogitated definitions and rules of judgment are arrived at, they are stored in memory, to which the mind can turn again and again, tapping them when necessary. Augustine's memory of course was packed with a large quantity of intelligized objects, including intelligibles that were the fruit of training in the various arts. But if certain intelligibles suffer desuetude, they sink into the more remote sections of memory, no longer ready to hand. However and whenever lost, they can be recovered in the way they were first discovered: the mind again assembles, perhaps with more ease than in its first cogitation, the dispersed parts of the definition or rule. It seems probable that the pressure of other obligations, especially the pastoral, may have caused many of the numerous laws of numbers (to be touched on in 10.12.19) to slip from facile recall. Leisure permitting, to regain them he would have had to re-cogitate their parts.

Chapter 12: Mathematical Objects in Intellectual Memory

19. As purely intelligible, objects of arithmetic and geometry are also located in intellectual memory. These include the rules and laws of numbers, or arithmetic, and dimensions, or geometry; the term dimensions, which signifies length, breadth, and depth, the three features of figures, may itself be taken to designate figures (QA 6.10). The term innumerable means practically countless or very numerous as in innumerable lies (1.19.20) and innumerable things accepted on natural faith (6.5.7) (In other texts also the word signifies what is not conveniently countable: 4.16.28; 6.10.16; 7.15.21; 9.8.17; 9.9.21; 10.7.12.) Certainly numbers, taken singly or in pairs, are innumerable in the sense they can go on to infinity or indefinitely (LA 2.8.23), but rules of arithmetic restrict or determine this indefiniteness (M 1.11.18). It would seem preferable not to translate *rationes* as principles since the principles of arithmetic and geometry are hardly innumerable. One and two are strictly not numbers but the principles of number; one is the starting point from which all numbers come, and two the source through which they come; three and four are the two fundamental numbers, odd and even (M 1.12.21). The principles of

geometry, which would appear to be the postulates, axioms, and basic definitions, are clearly not numerous. *Rationes* seems better rendered as rules, in accord with usage in parallel texts (M 1.12.20. LA 2.8.23). *Leges* adds the notes of certitude and immutability; every rule of arithmetic extends to all numbers according to a most certain and immutable law (LA 2.8.23). The rule that the double of any number lies precisely as far from that number as it does from the beginning of the series applies to all numbers with the force of immutable law; e.g., six, the double of three, is the third number after three; eight, the double of four, is the fourth number after four (LA 2.8.23). However, some rules of number do not include all numbers. Those named denumerates are measured only individually, by themselves, while others, called connumerates, are measured also in relation to other numbers. Some connumerates are complexes in which the smaller number is a fraction of the larger, as in the case of two and four and two and six: $2 + 4/2 = 4; 2 + 2(6/2) = 6$ (M 1.9.16).[42] Though limited in extent, such rules are also lawlike, absolutely certain and unchangeable.

Mathematical objects are inapprehensible by sense. Every two and triangle are devoid of all sense qualities by which they might be perceived by sight, hearing, taste, smell, or touch. We see two fingers but not two; two as such cannot be sensed but only intelligized. Again, a certain *ratio* or rule of numbers usually covers the whole series of numbers, which are innumerable, but no sense images can be stretched to embrace a series of innumerable numbers (LA 2.8.23). Moreover, every number is a multiple of unity; but no corporeal object is one—it is always spread out, always further divisible. Since the senses do not perceive unity that is the principle of number, no number can be grasped by the senses; each number is knowable by intellect alone (LA 2.8.22). No doubt men cannot avoid using conventional sounds or words to discuss mathematical entities, yet the words that are signs of these objects are not identified with the objects themselves. In the harmonious series that is the first four numerals there occurs the relationship (1:2 :: 2:4), a relationship named in Greek *analogia*, in Latin *proportio*. The relationship cannot be equated with either the Greek or Latin word; they are diverse sounds while the meaning of the relationship signified by both words remains the same. Because the relationship surpasses sense, it can serve as a common intelligible enabling the mind to translate from Greek into

Latin (M 1.12.23). The one-dimensional figure that is a line cannot be apprehended by sense but only by intellect. The most tenuous lines drawn by an artisan, lines as fine as those in a spider's web, are not one-dimensional; in spite of their initial appearance, they have width and depth or thickness as well as length. Mathematical lines, however, are sheerly one-dimensional. Thought apart from a corporeal setting, such lines are incorporeal, i.e., without normal physical associates such as width and depth (QA 6.10). They are de-physicalized; they exist as they are thought, in independence of the material world accessible to the senses. Nor are these lines the images of physical objects, like representations of the lines of a spider's web. Neither sensory receptor nor thought bearing on the physical world conveys these bodiless entities to the mind. Apprehended without intrinsic reliance on the senses or thought tied to sensory data, they are cognized interiorly by the intellect focused on what is purely intelligible. They have to be thought apart from sense because they can exist only apart from sense; no one-dimensional figures exist in the corporeal world.

Granted, we do sense numbers; we see two trees, hear two sounds, one after the other, taste successive sips of wine, smell a rose, then a lily, and touch two parts of the one surface. Still, we do not perceive numbers as such; we do not sense a two apart from corporeal objects. We sense not numbers as such but things numbered, numbered numbers, numbers imbedded in material objects. These numbered numbers are not the same as pure numbers, the numbers by which we number. Formal and immaterial numbers as such are not material or applied numbers but nonsensible numbers in virtue of which we number or count sensible objects.[43] Like other intelligibles, numbers as such, directly known by the intellect, do really exist; they are immaterially real, real in the stronger sense because not begotten of sensory objects nor represented in memory through images, real with a stable reality superior to that of corporeal things. The truth of an equation like $7 + 3 = 10$ is timeless and trans-spatial, always and everywhere the same (LA 2.8.21); this is why it cannot be proved or disproved by experiment or sensory inspection.[44] Admittedly, in teaching the basics of mathematics to younger students, sensory aids are highly effective. The five fingers of the hand employed in counting symbolize the number five, and a line drawn on a surface sensorially stands for the mathematical line. Perceptible and spatial, these auxiliaries point to, without truly representing, the nonperceptible and nonspatial mathematical objects that they help the mind fasten on in strict thought. Again, Augustine does not doubt for a moment that the psyche contains sensory images of five and a line. However, these images, only extrinsically correlated with the mathematical five and line, represent not the mathematical intelligibles but their corporeal embodiments as five and line, imaging these bodies qua quantified in a manner similar to the way an image of the sun represents the sun perceived.

Augustine had occasionally encountered individuals who could see sensible numbers in their five fingers and perceptible numbers in numerals standing for them, but could not bring themselves to grasp intelligible numbers as distinct from sensible numbers. If such a disputator laughs at him for his seemingly unsophisticated spinning of fictions, Augustine will weep over his laughing, in line with his earlier injunction (10.1.1): the less we weep over ridicule begotten of ineptitude, the more we should weep. Obtuseness evokes not reciprocal mockery but pity for a physically clearsighted critic who seems mentally blind to interior truths.

Chapter 13: Some Nuances in Cogitative Memory

20. Memorial recognition of intelligibles is marked with nuances. First, he remembers not only the truths attained but how they were attained, i.e., he recalls the dialectical strategy deployed for disclosing truths. These are the upshot of cogitation, a process in which truths are toilsomely mined from mind; a process in which various parts have to be grouped into the cognitive whole that is true definition or judgment (10.11.18). Second, dialectical technique does not speed the inquirer directly to the truth but exacts probing toward elimination of misleading suggestions or false solutions. Demonstration of the spiritual character of the soul implies consideration and refutation of materialist accounts (QA 6.10-15.22. GL 7.9.25-20.26). The first book of LA, which, some hold may aptly be entitled *Unde malum*, the cause of evil, after arguing that an action is not evil because forbidden by law or civilly punishable, proves that libido or perverse desire in a free will is the source of evil (LA 1.3.8). Again, learning in the common acceptation never occurs; all learning transpires within, through the interior seizure of truths in the light of truth: these are

insights, we saw, prepared for by the dismantling of the widespread opinion that teaching is a transaction in which an instructor quasi-mechanically transports knowledge from his to the student's mind. Reviewing these flawed positions adjudged fallacious by the inner standard of truth does not mire him in falsity; specification of the false as false presupposes union with truth. Too the fact that he remembers critiquing these stands, then labeling them false is true; he knows he has a true remembrance of the false. Third, he remembers drawing a fine line between the truths and their respectively opposing errors; he primarily remembered the truths, then secondarily the errors of their antagonists. Fourth, he is aware that he is now iterating that distinction, a cognitive act other than remembrance of frequent cogitation of that distinction in the past. With recall of his repeated prior recourse to the distinction, he couples the fact that he now cognizes the distinction, a present cogitation that will shortly depart, to be itself consigned to memory. Thus there is not only remembrance but remembrance of remembrance. Each time in the past that he exercised a re-cogitation of the truth vis-à-vis error, he remembered the original cogitation. Now, in addition, he remembers those successive re-cogitations. So if in the future he adverts to his present remembrance, he will be once more engaging in a remembrance of remembrance. Multiplicity of remembrances does not entail manifold memorative powers; one and the same memory operates through the many-layered remembrance. Complex and involuted as its objects and output are, the memory remains one power throughout.

Chapter 14: Memory of Affective States

21. This chapter deals with problems arising from recall of affections, variously rendered as affections, affective states, feelings, emotions, or passions, of which, as mentioned earlier, Augustine, relying upon Cicero[45] and the Stoics, lists four: desire, joy, fear, and sorrow (10.14.22).

Memory retains affective states in a manner strikingly different from the way in which the mind actually experienced these passions. The affective state as remembered is passionally cold, nonemotional in terms of bodily resonance. Without feeling joy, Augustine recalled the satisfaction that warmed him after his successful panegyric. In the absence of emotional overtones he resuscitated the sorrow that panged him when his concubine was torn from his side (6.15.25). Again, in remembering his fear of being beaten by the schoolmaster's rod (1.9.14), he did not reënact the original emotion of fear. Nor did passional stirrings recur when he remembered his first burning of sexual desire. Moreover, at times the memorial affective state ran counter to the original passion. On one occasion joy over his providential ordination accompanied reminiscence about past sorrow, evinced by tears shed when conscripted into the priesthood (E 21.2). At another time past joy evoked present memorial sorrow; he regretted the delight garnered from pagan plays (1.18.30; 3.2.2). An affective contrast between mind and body does not provoke a problem, for body and mind vary notably in makeup, from which stem distinct actual and memorial characteristics. In recalling with joy a past bodily pain, say his agonizing toothache that swift divine response to prayer healed (9.4.12), his mind, unlike his body, in that actual event was not sensorially influenced by remembrance of the excruciating toothache. Gripping pain is not the concomitant of remembrance of gripping pain. Puzzlement, however, is aroused by an apparent paradox: what is deposited in the mind is at odds with what is laid away in memory. The diversity and conflict of contents seem belied by the identity of mind and memory common in linguistic usage. Mind is equated with memory when memorization is described as keeping something in mind, and forgetfulness as slippage from mind. To repeat, if mind and memory are one and the same, why, in bearing on the same event, does the mind have joy and the memory sorrow? From this difficulty spins off a second problem: in possessing joy, the mind experiences joy while memory, in possessing sorrow, feels no sorrow. Surely we cannot put mind and memory at loggerheads with each other. They seem indissolubly joined; memory is part of, essentially linked to, mind.

He now takes up the second problem, the seemingly incongruous presence of an affective state in mind and its absence in memory. Perhaps, he conjectures, memory of sorrow carries no feeling of sorrow because memory functions in some respects as the stomach of the mind. Once lodged in the stomach, sweet and bitter food can no longer be tasted; similarly, once stored in the mental stomach that is memory, joy and sorrow can no longer be tasted or felt. Distinct from such passive memorial recall of, say, sorrow is the active reliving of the original sadness that is comparable to rumination of food in which the original taste is re-savored. On the anniversary of his mother's death a man may relive the experience of closing her eyes for the last time. Not merely memorially reporting the past scene, he reinstates it to the point that he again weeps, feeling or re-feeling, the sadness of the original scene; in effect, he memorially ruminates the original taste of passional bitterness that is sorrow. But when the original sorrowful event is simply deposited in memory and only reproduced for passive review rather than for active emotional re-engagement, no feeling of sorrow occurs. From one angle, a parallel between memory, a supracorporeal power, and the stomach, an organ of the body, may seem strained; yet, cautiously controlled, a comparison between the two is not entirely bootless; the analogy, judiciously deployed, can cast some light on the functioning of memory.

22. On the possibility that the passions as rationally understood may furnish some clue toward disposing of the second problem, he briefly elucidates the excogitation of the passions from intellectual memory. Since the passions belong to the supracorporeal soul, they reside in the intellectual memory, to be excerpted from there and cogitated, properly arranged and catalogued, by the strategy of dialectic, the logical art that exposits in a scientific way the rules for true definition, division, and distribution of parts (Sol 2.11.19,21). Each of the passions is classified according to genus and species. Generically, desire and joy bear on the good while fear and sorrow concern evil. Desire and joy are specifically distinct; desire is tendency toward the good, joy follows upon possession of the good. Fear and sorrow or sadness follow upon possession of an evil object. Notice, the dialectical or cogitative "disputation" or analysis of the passions occurs after the passions are drawn from intellectual memory. Augustine takes pains to indicate that this cogitative extraction from intellectual memory is quite different from an experience of the passions as actually felt. Two differences set apart passions situated in the pure intellect from passions released in concrete behavior. First, understanding joy or fear or sorrow does not precipitate the emotional reverberations associated with these passions. Proper classification of joy and fear does not make the cogitator joyful or fearful. Second, the notions of the passions are already located in memory prior to dialectical negotiation whereas the passions as emotional reactions are known only in actual

experiences. As he explicitly states, before he recalled and dialectically re-treated or categorized the passions as intelligibles, they
already lay in memory–that is why he could truly fetch them
therefrom.

Next hazarded is the conjecture that this process of recall and
cognition bears a resemblance to rumination in which food from the
stomach is re-tasted. Were this parallel true, the answer to the second
problem addressed above would be apparently reached: the passions
known in memory yield no experience of passions because they lie
there in memory. Perhaps when their notions are explicated in
cognition or dialectical analysis, they are intellectually ruminated
upon, issuing in some taste like that of passional experience.
However, a fatal objection negatives this correspondence. The
sweetness of joy and the bitterness of sorrow are not tasted in the
mouth of the cogitator, i.e., they are simply not experienced in the
mind of the dialectical classifier. On this radical point of dissimilarity
the hypothesized affinity breaks down. Indeed no one would initiate
dialectical discussion of sorrow and fear if he were convinced that
every time he named and analyzed these passions, he would be
ineluctably driven to feel real sorrow and fear. Yet unquestionably we
do possess notions of the passions, not conveyed through sense-
deliverance but excavated from intellectual memory. We could not
intellectually discourse about the passions unless, along with sense
memory of these as felt, we had also, and principally, notional
understanding of the passions. In sum, the words that name the
passions have a double signification, denoting both notions of the
passions and sensory images of emotional reactions.
Correspondingly, two functions of memory are operative: sense
memory retains images of the actual passional events, and intellectual
memory is a repository of notions of passions, domiciled there prior
to passional experience registered in sense memory. Without
explicitly disentangling the difficulties posed, Augustine implicitly
resolves his two problems. First, joy can be nonparadoxically joined
with the memory of sorrow because the joy is a spiritual joy,
analogously tied to the intelligible grasp of the passion of joy, a notion
on which he fixes attention. No radical incongruence splits spiritual
joy from memory of the sensorially rooted passion of sorrow. With a
spiritual joy springing from a right moral judgment on sufferings, the
Confessions praises God for the temporal reverses sustained.

Understood in their true structure and directedness, sufferings are instruments divinely applied toward healing. Second, the question of feeling his recall of feelings in sense memory is also implicitly decided. He is plainly aware of the distinction between a passionless remembrance of passion and an impassioned memorial reënactment of the original event. Even after writing his *Confessions*, he passionally relived in memory the warmth and joy he felt in first composing the work (R 2.6.1).

The fact that Augustine shifts the import of his terms somewhat does not blemish the coherence of his analysis. At the outset mind performs the office of actually attending to the passions while memory stores the passionless record of these passions. Next, mind is appointed a different role, wherein it views with joy a past sorrow in memory. In its first usage mind is followed by memory; in its second usage mind follows upon memory. Third, at the end of the chapter, once again mind carries out its function of attending to sensory or passional states while experience is deposited in sensio-intellectual memory.

Chapter 15: How Memory Is Known

23. Passions continue in sense-memory through images, and, prior to experience, abiding in intellectual memory, are apprehended directly without images. Now, he muses, is memory itself known without images? Obviously, things exterior to the self, like the sun and a stone, are memorially retained through images, without which surrogates he could not name the things. Even features within the self such as pain and health are likewise named because, after being experienced, they persist in memory through images. If Augustine had not felt, then remembered, pain via an image, he could not designate it in speech, for, bereft of the image, he could assign it no name. Were the existential referent not retained as an image, no name could signify it. The name points to the fact of existence; it is an index of an affirmative answer to the first dialectical question, whether a thing exists. Without an image certifying that pain exists, he could not dialectically determine what it is nor go on, through disputation, to distinguish it from pleasure. Similarly, naming health depends on an image of health. When Augustine is healthy, health is a quality of his bodily self, in virtue of which, without an image of health, he is aware

that health exists, and thus can name health. Still, an image has to be stamped on memory; otherwise, without this memorial trace, he could not recall what the name health means. In short, knowing what the word health denotes here and now needs only his state of health while recalling what the word signifies requires a mediator of recall, an image of health in memory. This distinction is verifiable in the chronically ill, who, confined to bed, unable to function normally, would think the word health meaningless did their memory not preserve an image of health.

As already indicated, intelligible objects such as numbers are recognized and named because they are present in themselves and not mediated through images (10.12.19). As regards the sun, he uses the word sun because his meaning betokens an image of the sun. However often he uses the word sun, recognition of its meaning relies on the original image, basically the same image since reiteration of recall does not depend on an image of an image (10.13.20). Too he knows what the word memory means; he is certain not only that it is but what it is. This provokes the question, is memory present in memory through an image or through itself, i.e., without an image? Or, in Augustine's formulation, is memory present to itself, i.e., aware of itself, through a memory image rather than through itself? Though here he leaves the matter expressly undetermined, an earlier treatment effectively intimates the answer: memory knows itself through itself, without memory images. A memory-image of memory would have had to gain entrance through the gateways of the senses; clearly memory is not perceived by any of the senses (10.10.17). Again, memory is a power of mind that belongs to his innermost psychic nature, a power inaccessible to sensory perception (10.8.5). Indeed the mind, which, because incorporeal, is not imaged in memory, is identified with memory (10.14.22). Thus memory is an intelligible object knowable directly, in itself, not indirectly, not through images. We are aware that memory exists through self-consciousness; through memory the self recalls itself and, in the very recalling, recognizes that memory exists. The act grounding knowledge that memory exists is a nonsensory experience: a psychic awareness of self in memory, and of memory in itself, wrought on the intellectual plane. What memory is in its various acceptations is dialectically discerned by reason; after discriminating between memory and external sensation, the mind differentiates the analogous significations of memory.

Not until the following chapter does Augustine explicitly resolve the problem concerning the mode of knowing memory: "When I remember memory, or the act of remembering, memory is present to itself through itself" (10.16.24). When remembering the sun, he is aware of the sun as remembered before; but he has no image of the act of remembering; his memory remembers its remembering through itself. He retains images of objects without having images of memory itself; he imagelessly knows that memory operates because of the images retained. Thus not only intellectual memory but sensio-intellectual memory is present to itself not through images but through itself. In the phrase, "remembrance of the sun," the signification of the word sun is mediated by an image of the sun while the denotation "remembrance" is transmitted through imageless thought, the outcome of the presence of memory to itself through itself.

Chapter 16: The Problem of Remembering Forgetfulness

24. Use of the word forgetfulness evidences ·that Augustine recognizes what the word signifies. If he forgot the object signified, he would be incapable of knowing the meaning of the sound; if he forgot the meaning of forgetfulness, "forgetfulness" would be a mere sound signifying no object. When he remembers memory, memory is present to memory through memory. However, when he remembers forgetfulness, both memory and forgetfulness are present. Forgetfulness is what he remembers, and memory, that by which he remembers; more simply, he remembers forgetfulness by means of memory. Since forgetfulness is the privation of memory, it seems paradoxical to speak of remembering forgetfulness. When present to the memory, forgetfulness is remembered; yet when forgetfulness is present, we cannot remember. Plainly forgetfulness is held in memory; otherwise the sound conveys no meaning. Nevertheless, the apparent paradox is not dislodged: because forgetfulness is present, we do not forget; yet because forgetfulness is present, we do forget. The very presence of forgetfulness in memory betokens the nonpresence of memory. Memory of forgetting seems to entail, self-stultfyingly, the forgetting of memory. Perhaps, he tentatively suggests, forgetfulness, unlike memory, is present in memory not through itself but through an image; a lead worth pursuing.

25. The Augustine who advised *Intellectum ama* (E 120.3.13) in reference to understanding of divine faith also valued understanding of things nonsacral, purchasable only by hard work. In cultivating the tough soil of memory, he exuded a heavy sweat (Gn 3.17-9). Profusion of perspiration that might be counted normal if he were spending hour after hour closely observing the zones of the heavens,[16] or determining the precise distances between the stars,or trying to calculate the forces keeping the earth in balance (*libramenta terrae*, obscure, may refer to the earth's equilibrium or the manner in which the earth hangs in space). It is not vexing that specification of the interconnections of faraway stars exacts strenuous labor, but what is perplexing is incapacity to grasp the self so close to hand, failure to comprehend the memory, without which he would dispossessed of self-consciousness since in the absence of memory his psychological "I" would vanish.

He restates the problem: absolutely certain that he remembers forgetfulness, he cannot reconcile this memory with the truth that forgetfulness is lack of memory. He is barred from maintaining that his remembrance of forgetfulness is not in his memory; this claim would be self-contradictory, tantamount to making remembrance equivalent to nonremembrance. Similarly, he cannot aver that forgetfulness is in memory to ensure that he does not forget; this assertion involves another self-contradiction, the effective identification of forgetfulness with nonforgetfulness. Discarding these self-refuting proposals, he takes up an aforementioned, a third alternative: forgetfulness is memorially recognized not in itself but through an image, an impression imprinted on memory by things originally perceived through the senses. Memorial duplicates of Carthage, the faces of his mother, father, and friends, and health and illness outlive the original experiences of events and persons: physically absent, they remain present in memory, to be revived and reconsidered. If forgetfulness is remembered through an image, it must have been present as itself in some way, so that memory can receive its psychic copy. But forgetfulness cannot write its image on memory since its very presence erases what is already known. Because it is counter-memorial, forgetfulness simply cannot engrave an image on memory; forgetfulness by definition is the deletion of memory. Thus the third alternative, forgetfulness as imaged, turns out to be absurd also: the image of forgetfulness is so imprinted on memory that it blots out imprints on memory. While it is unquestionable that he does truly remember not its image but forgetfulness itself in some manner, the precise what and why of the mode of remembrance remain unexplainable: lying athwart the road to an exact explanation is a formidable paradox: in remembering forgetfulness itself, he apparently obliterates remembrance.

In the opinion of some learned commentators, Augustine's bafflement arises from his neglect, surprising in view of his perspicacity, of certain distinctions, which, if not elementary, do not seem altogether subtle. Surely we do inscribe on memory a state of forgetting; every student not blessed with total recall regretfully remembers inability to reproduce items in examinations. Augustine, however, somehow fails to disassociate this state from the unfortunate personified[47] or reified[48] oblivion that renders his problem unanswerable. Moreover, he overlooks the distinction between forgetfulness itself (which remains a characteristic of the mind), particular cases of which can be remembered, and the data forgotten, which clearly cannot be remembered.[49] Again, he lays himself open to the charge that he does not draw the line between the capacity of memory and the act of remembering; nor does he distinguish between total oblivion and the forgetting of one particular item.[50] However, it would seem not only surprising but astonishing that a mind of Augustine's penetration, in overlooking such distinctions, should let solutions to his problem dribble through his fingers. But astonishment disappears when, taking second thought, we realize that he does indeed show a command of these distinctions, not in every detail in 10.16.25 but satisfactorily in other parts of his reflections. After sweating over the memorial status of forgetfulness, Augustine avows remembrance of forgetfulness; undoubtedly he recognizes a state of forgetfulness but is left in suspense about the mode of remembering forgetfulness (10.16.25). This avowal confirms his distinction, made earlier in passing, between contents of memory and forgotten items (10.18.14). Moreover, he signalizes the difference between forgetfulness itself and particular instances of forgetting when he explorers the method used by memory in recovering a lost coin (10.18.27), and the strategy deployed in searching for a forgotten name in the subconscious (10.19.28). Again, these same passages indirectly evince awareness of the distinction between the ability to remember and actual remembering. Furthermore, the latter section

(10.19.28) calls attention to the demarcation between total oblivion and partial forgetting. If memory of even one individual item is blotted out, recovery of the forgotten item is impossible; it is assumed a fortiori that if the whole of memory were effaced, then not one single item could be revived.

Forgetfulness becomes a *pons asinorum*, not because Augustine does not single out data concerning forgetfulness but because he cannot hit on a means of harmonizing the epistemic status of forgetfulness with that of memory. Having no image of memory, we conclude that memory exists from the fact that we recall objects; similarly, without an image of forgetfulness, we infer forgetfulness because we do recall acts of forgetting. Thus, like memory, forgetfulness must be apparently categorized as a purely intelligible object situated in intellectual memory. Memory and forgetfulness (10.16.24, 25) are not notions but notations (10.17.26) or forms of *notitia*, knowledge gained through supersensible experience. It is at this point that the problem becomes effectively irresolvable; he cannot coherently explain how forgetfulness can coexist as an intelligible object with memory. Memory, however, can contain forgetfulness as such only at the price of its own liquidation; as lack of memory, forgetfulness is counter-memorial or anti-memorial. Think of anti-memory lodged in memory: since forgetfulness is contrary to memory, it has to destroy memory as invading cancer cells crowd out and effectively destroy the normal cells that are their host. Or let memory be symbolized as 1 and forgetfulness as -1 (for forgetfulness is not the absence but the lack of memory); $1 + (-1) = 0$: the result of adding minus-memory to memory is zero—the abolition of memory. This anti-memorial status of forgetfulness would seem to deflect criticism that Augustine reifies forgetfulness, treating it as a positive reality that directly opposes memory. True, he twice refers to forgetfulness as a *res* (10.16.24), yet this *res* denotes what is signified as differentiated from the mere sound of the word. Too it is hard to lend credence to the contention that, in the very section in which he defines forgetfulness as privation, he would contradict his definition by designating forgetfulness a positive reality.

Augustine had no trouble in making proper distinctions apropos of various aspects of forgetting. What did nonplus him was that while undeniably remembering forgetfulness, he could not validate the mode of this remembrance, the way in which forgetfulness as an intelligible object can exist in, or coexist with, memory, without entraining the cessation of memory. He was stumped by this problem, genuine, from his perspective, because he did not fully understand the logico-epistemic tool named *ens rationis* or being of reason. A being of reason is a mental construct; it does not exercise existence in actual things but enjoys objective existence in the mind alone. Still, it is fashioned after the model of a real thing so that the mind enunciates judgments about it as if it had real existence.[51] Moreover, it is not a sheer fiction or piece of footloose creativity but has a foundation in reality. Beings of reason are hardly rare birds in our conceptual vocabulary. Nothing is an ontic being of reason, and evil, a metaphysical and moral being of reason. Genus and species, as logically ordered, are logical beings of reason. Zero and -1, along with their more complex offshoots, are mathematical constructs. The four-dimensional continuum serves as a physico-mathematical being of reason.[52] Augustine surely was not without some partial understanding of what was later called *ens rationis*. The word "nothing" does not signify some thing that is absurdly nothing but an *adfectio animi*, a state that occurs when the mind discerns that the thing it is looking for does not exist or is not there (Mag 2.3; 7.19). His discussion of this mental construct and, implicitly, of other beings of reason, is only sketchy, because only incompletely explored, as Adeodatus reminds his father (Mag 7.19). As far as I know, he never precisely specified how constructs or states of mind alone bear on real states of affairs; he never formulated the manner in which negations and privations are founded on real things. Clearly he regarded moral evil as a construct, a disorder of the will (7.16.22). However, unlike sin, which is a partial privation of the good of will, forgetfulness is considered not a partial but a total lack of memory.

But, the objection recurs, all this flies in the face of experience; the remembrance of forgetting simply does not blot out memory itself. Granted, Augustine admits that in some way or other he surely does remember forgetting without the liquidation of memory. Taken operationally, taken as a capacity with forgettable contents, memory is indeed compatible with forgetfulness. But Augustine locates the fatal marriage of memory with forgetfulness on the level of definition. Memory abides not through images but through itself, through an intelligible, and, like other affections of the mind, forgetfulness also is retained as an intelligible (10.17.26). When the notation that is memory remembers, or joins in its presence to itself, forgetfulness taken definitionally, this union wipes out memory. The definition of forgetfulness cancels the definition of memory; memory defined as capacity for retention is voided by its embrace of, or copresence with, privation of this capacity. The incapacity erases the capacity as total privation of life joined to life entrains the extinction of life. Augustine has not been spinning a web of words; he is mentally perspiring in an endeavor, unhappily less than successful, to reconcile the theory of intelligible definitions, according to which remembrance of forgetfulness entails the abolition of memory, with the indisputable fact that, operationally, there is no deadly encounter between memory and forgetfulness. Sharply conscious that his analysis limps, he cannot put his finger on reasons for its inadequacy. He has to leave the problem unsolved, deeming it virtually insoluble, because he cannot manage to break loose from a constricted epistemology descended from Neoplatonism.[53]

Chapter 17: Is God beyond Memory?

26. As before (10.8.12, 15), he is awestruck by the immensity of memory, capacious and deep enough to retain an indefinite multitude of objects. Not essentially spirit, to which the physical appendage that is the body is accidentally attached, man is a substantial unit composed of rational soul and material body. From the standpoint of consciousness, though, the mind is the self, and insofar as memory is equivalent to mind, memory is one with the self. While the whole self is comprised of soul and body, the psychological self operates in the inner world of notions, judgments, hopes, and fears, along with copies of events experienced before. In begging for light to answer the question, who am I?, he is not pursuing definition of specific human nature, of which he is already assured, but is hunting for the key that will unlock the signification of Augustine of Hippo. Because he is a vast deep (4.14.22) whose concrete individual nature is immeasurably diversified, the meaning of his inner I will always escape accurate explication. Teeming with innumerable types of things ("innumerable" occurs in three out of five words in one sentence), memory is concretely beyond the compass of full human reckoning. A review of the memorial objects lists bodies present through copies, the definitions in the liberal arts present in themselves, and the

notions of the passions (he skips over mathematical entities and
forgetfulness paradoxically copresent in memory). His mind's eye
can range rapidly, if somewhat unsystematically, over the whole
memorial landscape, trying to plumb, but always falling short of, the
abyss of memory. Memorial magnitude subserves an existence small
in span; memory is the power of life in man who, because his soul
animates a body, lives designed to die (1.6.7).

Alive in God, he aspires to vault above memory in some sense, so
as to enter into a divine region delicious to taste (10.6.8;34.52). He
aspires to rise above his mighty memory to almighty light, basking in
its richness, as capacity permits, in a union of sweetness unutterable
yet far from wholly satisfying here below, cleaving to unsurpassable
life with an embrace sustained not lastingly but fleetingly since the
bodily burden drags down the leaping spirit within (9.10.23-4. T 8.2-
3).

Higher animals and birds are endowed with sheer sense memory,
which functions as the repository of animal learning and, loosely
speaking, "custom" or "habit." Through memory that ensures their
deposit of practical experience, they recognize how to find food in
favorable spots visited earlier, or to respond to cues signaling the
approach of deadly enemies. Were they without memory, foxes could
never learn how to return to lairs, and birds would be unable to recall
either the route back to a nest or even the nest itself. A dog without
memory would be condemned to starting each day from scratch,
dispossessed of all but instinct to adapt to every routine situation,
powerless to even recognize its master. Where poverty and paucity
are the traits marking animal memory, man is memorially affluent;
his sensio-intellectual and intellectual memory set him apart from and
above other animals, undergirding his longing to dwell in a God who
is everlastingly stable. But where is he to discover God? If God can
be found only by going beyond memory, he will have no memory of
God, and, if he has no memory of God, he will not know him and,
not knowing him, will not find him. So another perplexity rears its
head. Since God as God plainly transcends memory, to find him he
must go beyond memory to find God, yet if he goes beyond memory,
he will not be able to know God. He is impaled on the horns of a
dilemma: if he does not go beyond memory, he will not find God; if
he does go beyond memory, he will not find God. God must be
somehow present in memory, so that, as he transcends memory to

reach God, he will recognize God in terms of his original memory. Thus he breaks out of the dilemma: he does not go wholly beyond memory; in virtue of his memory of God he recognizes God when he cleaves to him. Further inquiry clarifies this below. In virtue of knowledge or memory of happiness the mind recognizes God as its happiness (10.21.31-22.33); in virtue of knowledge or memory of truth the mind grasps God as truth beyond memory. From another angle, the distinction of two meanings, ontic and noetic, of "beyond memory" resolves the difficulty of finding God within. Ontically, God is beyond memory; as sovereign truth, he dwells above truth in the human mind. Noetically, in terms of knowing God, God is not beyond memory, for it is through memory that we know God as the transcendent source of truth, who is also the supreme good pouring in total satisfaction or happiness.

Chapter 18: Recovery of Objects through Memory Images

27. As we can find God only by somehow remembering him, on a humbler level we discover things lost by remembering them. Remembrance is the essential condition for recovery of lost objects. The woman in the parable who mislaid a drachma located it only because she recalled exactly what she was searching for. Had she no memory of the drachma, she would not have recognized it even if she came upon it. Occasionally, Augustine's razor-sharp memory proved treacherous as he mislaid perhaps a parchment or a writing instrument. His experience of regaining a lost item matched that of the woman in Luke; memorial retrieval was the standard against which he verified physical retrieval. Friends might ferret out similar items, which, his memory determined, did not meet specifications of the missing object. More precisely, it is the memorial copy that serves as the model for targeting the thing lost; the image of the object that lapses from sight stays ingrained in memory. Retention by image underlies recognition, and recognition underpins recovery.

Chapter 19: Vague Remembrance Necessary to Overcome Forgetting

28. The same rule obtains when the object is lost in memory; the object remains forgotten unless we somehow remember it. If we are searching for the name of an obscure historical figure now forgotten,

memory gropes to regain the unremembered item. During the hunt various names surface, then are discarded, till memory pinpoints the lost name. Again, the same law is at work: remembrance underpins recognition, and recognition underpins verification. Still, how square the remembrance of an object with its patent oblivion? If we did not forget, we would not have had to strive to remember; yet if we did not first remember, we could not put an end to forgetting. The conflict is settled by discerning that vague remembrance, which includes explicit forgetting, precedes attainment of explicit remembrance (with its attendant overcoming of forgetting). More precisely, the forgotten item is a part of a memorial whole. The whole is known explicitly save for the forgotten item, which is then vaguely remembered as a part, still unclarified or explicitly unrecognized, of this whole; it is a kind of missing link of an experiential whole. Augustine offers a kind of a Gestalt version of overcoming forgetting. The memorial whole lacks a part; the mind, following a law of closure, completes the whole by recovering a forgotten item. In short, a forgotten item is part of a complex whole, which is retrieved through its recollective hook-up with another part to form a whole. In Augustine's words, the memory, accustomed to having two items conjoined, is aware that the items are now memorially severed, one item having dropped out. The brokenness of its habitual account of the past causes the memory to limp;[54] not functioning with its normal facility, it casts about for the missing part.

Suppose he sees or thinks of an individual whose name eludes him. The man and his name are two parts of a memorial whole, with the name now forgotten. Though he cannot put his finger on the name, he recognizes, while rummaging through memory, that none of several names which parade by in review is the correct one. After disposing of these by trial and error, he gradually recollects the proper name, proper also in the sense that it is appropriate to this individual, fitting him as a complement to form an integrated memorial unit. Only memory that vaguely retained the name informs him that this is indeed the right name. If a friend, assisting in the search, mentions the desired name, it is still memory that certifies the name as exact. The name, which is not learned for the first time, is verified as accurate by memory within, the friend's role being that of facilitator. However, if the name were totally blotted out of memory, he would not remember it but would have to relearn it. Damage to the occipital lobe or visual center can wipe out much of the memorial data of an inveterate visualizer, who no longer remembers the faces of family members and professional associates, nor their names.[55] In the 1980's, while driving south, a Philadelphia-area priest was struck in a head-on collision by a northbound car that had jumped the median strip, with the result that he suffered considerable brain damage, which, even after therapy, left him with no remembrance of incidents prior to the accident. With the aid of friends who pointed to and described pictures from the past, he gradually recaptured some of his vanished experience, not by reviving mnemic traces but by step-by-step relearning. Ordinarily we do not totally forget what we remember; we retain a vague memory, an implicit trace, of the forgotten item that recollection arouses to vivid explicitness. But if, as occurs in exceptional instances, no faint semblance of the forgotten object persists, if all memory of it has been utterly uprooted, we cannot retrieve it; even if we come upon the correct item, we will not identify it, for we will have no vague remembrance against which to check it; then the only available cognitive route is not memorial recognition but re-cognition or relearning.

Interestingly, Augustine chooses an apt example of forgetting. Proper names more readily escape memory, apparently for the reason that they usually lack the large number of connections and threads of relevance that characterize common qualities and general names.[56] Ordinarily proper names of relatives and close friends do not drop rapidly out of memory because they are woven into the texture of affection bonding us to kith and kin and friends.

Chapter 20: Happiness Known in some way in Memory.

29. Even if tolerated as somewhat digressive, the discussion of forgetting contributed to the ideational drift by substantiating that, when searching for the forgotten, we preserve in memory, at least vaguely, some knowledge of what is sought. The search for God takes a similar course; correspondingly, as we seek him, memory holds some knowledge of him.

In seeking God, Augustine is seeking the happy life, and conversely, in seeking happiness, he is implicitly seeking God, who is the life of his life (10.6.10). What he is hungering for is life in which he will be perfected by the life of God (13.4.5), becoming one with the

happy life that is God himself. Not until the next life will he subjectively possess beatitude, knowing enough because satiated with God:
God will be his "enough." The Latin *sat* conveys the import of *satietas*
provided by the sovereign, because immutable, good: *satiabitur in
bonis desiderium ejus, bonis immutabilibus* (T 14.14.20); his desire will be
"enoughed" in changeless goods. Perfectly imaging God (T 12.14.22),
he will be filled with all the fullness of God; his desire satiated in the
immutable good, for any good that is perishable or alterable, the
plaything of fickle fortune, cannot produce the total satisfaction that
is beatitude (BV 2.11).

He pursues this happiness, first, through remembrance, in terms of
an object forgotten yet still known in some way; or second, through
fresh learning; or third, through relearning what has been erased
from memory. It seems clear that the second option is not tenable.
For all men desire happiness; it is impossible to be a man and not
desire happiness: the tendency is radicated in human nature.
Moreover, such a desire presupposes some knowledge of happiness
since no one can desire anything of which he has no knowledge
whatsoever (T 10.1.2). While each man indubitably possesses, i.e.,
knows, happiness, it remains hard to nail down how the mind primordially knows happiness. Men may be fully happy, partially happy, or
not happy at all. Those already feasting on the supreme good in the
next life are completely happy. Their compatriots marching to the
eternal city of God with hearts fastened on it in hope are partially
happy, still troubled by multiple ills. However, those despoiled of all
hope here below can boast of only a pseudo-happiness, really rank
misery, without a scrap of true happiness (S 158.8.CD 19.20). The
faithful in this life, with eyes fixed in hope, are more blessed than
individuals devoid of happiness in hope (*in spe*) as well as in actuality
(*in re*). Yet members of this third category must in some fashion know
or remember (in the broad sense) happiness; otherwise they could not
desire it. So certain is their desire that all men are constantly
motivated to act in view of happiness; they cannot not desire
happiness. But if members of the third class know happiness, the
question persists: how do they know or come to know it? Suppose, he
suggests, happiness lies in his memory taken strictly as a memorial
impress consequent upon an actual past experience of happiness.
Perhaps, he conjectures, every man in the past somehow felt
happiness he now recalls. Or perhaps a kind of race memory of the

happiness Adam enjoyed in the garden of paradise was bequeathed along with the sin and death transmitted to all descendants (CJ0I 2.163). Here Augustine is not formally exploring original sin but raising the question: do men now truly remember, in the strict sense of memory, a pristine state of happiness? Recall of primitive happiness is posited as a sheer possibility, a piece of speculation without grounding in basic principles or concrete fact. Because no historical annals recount the aboriginal human condition, it is divine faith that assures him of man's original justice and Fall, events handed down by the sacred writers (T 14.15.21). Faith also informs him that all men did not share a prior state of paradisal beatitude and that men now living evidence no race memory of Adam's pre-Fall state.

Because loved, happiness has to be first known. More than the sheer sound of the word delights the heart. An ordinary Greek is not attracted by *beatitudo*, the word for happiness in Latin, nor is a nonGreek-speaking Latin stirred to desire by *eudaimonia*, Greek for happiness. Latin speakers experience delight when they hear the Latin word just as Greeks take pleasure in hearing the Greek term. Latins and Greeks and indeed men of every language love not the word for happiness but the reality signified for which all men yearn. On the supposition that all men were asked in a common tongue whether they wanted to be happy, they would immediately respond that happiness was their single deepest desire. Yet they would be helpless to articulate this universal desire unless the reality itself, symbolized by the word for happiness, were not in some real way lodged in memory. In other words, the reality resides in every man's memory, not because of a past experience of happiness mysteriously transmitted as a racial inheritance, but because, as universally present in men everywhere, it is somehow impressed on memory prior to experience (exactly how is examined in the following chapter). Commonness inductively indicates that certain notions are impressed on memory. Common knowledge is a sign of the notional status of number; common cognitive accessibility establishes that wisdom is a notion; the fact that truth is not the private property of a particular individual but the common treasure of all proves that it is a notion; the commonly sought good is a notion (T 8.3.4). Since happiness is also a nonsensible common to and operative in every mind, it is a notion impressed on the memory whereby men are able to know and say firmly, without the slightest hesitation, that they want to be happy

(LA 2.8.24; 2.9.27; 2.12.33; 2.9.26).[57] The truth that all men desire happiness is not only evident but self-evident, not only factually but analytically universal. As rational soul and body are the necessary components of human substance, so the desire for happiness is a necessary ingredient of human volitional activity. It is a kind of first principle of human action; were it suspended or nullified, human action would come to a juddering halt. Men can opt for this or that means to happiness, but they cannot opt for happiness: the human mind is programmed to desire happiness. Pressed to explain why he wants a family, house, or occupation, an individual finally furnishes the root reason: he wants to be happy. But no one asks: why be happy? The desire for happiness is the reason for all striving, the necessary source of all the desires, these contingent, through whose mediation, it is hoped, happiness will be gained. All desire for happiness is universal, not only in fact but in virtue of rational necessity; a necessity ingrained in the mind or, in Augustine's conceptual language, a notion impressed on memory prior to all experience.

Chapter 21: Correspondence of Joy and Happiness

30. To specify how happiness is a notion, he first differentiates it from three other memorial impresses, then observes some kinship with happiness in knowledge of joy.

Happiness is not known as an image from the past or as notions of numbers and principles of a liberal art. Because notional, happiness is not stored in memory like his image of Carthage; manifesting no corporeal qualities, happiness is consequently not sensorially perceptible and retainable. Moreover, though notional, happiness is not memorially situated after the fashion of numbers. The mind that notionally knows $7 + 3 = 10$ is satisfied with this truth. It is otherwise with happiness: the mind knowing happiness is not content with initial knowledge and desire but longs to possess the object that will totally satisfy it. Moreover, no striving is implied in number; per contra, in virtue of a dynamic happiness, the mind is tendential, never fully at rest till it reaches its term, the happiness-bestowing object (1.1.1). Again, the notion of happiness is not consanguineous with the impress of a liberal art, in this instance rhetoric. Remembrance of eloquence coincides with the notion of happiness on three scores.

First, knowledge of the art can be sketchy while the science of numbers is more developed; a hearer can recognize eloquence without possessing it whereas arithmetic demands some science before facility with numbers. Second, there is a drive to mature acquisition; admiration of a masterful rhetorician bespeaks desire to imitate him. Third, the desire tends toward expertise in eloquence observed as a good accompanied by the affective tone that is delight: eloquence is viewed in the affective mode. However, one cardinal point divides the two. While eloquence embodied in a top rhetor can be sensorially perceived, happiness in others cannot be concretized for sensory inspection.

Next, Augustine canvasses a fourth alternative: knowledge of happiness may correspond to knowledge of joy. Significantly, after raising the possibility, he does not immediately demur. Perhaps, he muses, some admissible congruence without a grave disparallel may bind happiness and joy. First, as, when unhappy, he still recalls happiness, so, when sad, he recalls joy. In both cases opposites are concretely commingled. Second, diverging from the desire of eloquence, joy of the mind is not registered through deliverances of the external senses. The feeling of suprasensible joy transpires properly and exclusively in the mind; knowledge (*notitia*) of that experience is stamped in intellectual memory. Moreover, the converse of the first point above may occur: a past joyful event may be recalled with loathing; the theft of the pears that exulted him some thirty years ago (2.4.9) he now abhors. Furthermore, past joy that welled up from morally good situations and honorable goods (*honesta*), intrinsic goods or goods pursued for their own sake, are remembered with a longing that they be actually repossessed. However, spiritually pleasurable encounters with Monica are no longer possible nor will he ever again be stirred by the beauty of the discourses of Ambrose. Since death barred access to these rich moral goods, a certain sadness tinges memory of these joyful events. Joy, it will shortly become clear, is intertwined with the achievement of the desire for happiness: happiness is rejoicing in the truth. While happiness primitively known is a notion impressed on the mind prior to experience, the actual attainment of happiness is not a notion but a notation, experientially arrived at when the mind possesses its fulfilling spiritual good. Subjectively, joy is the accompaniment of that actual possession or, succinctly stated, happiness is the very joy in the possession. As the next paragraph puts it, men strive to be happy; objectively, to possess the good in order to be joyful; subjectively, to experience satisfaction in possession of the fulfilling good.

31. Happiness shows two cognitive countenances; it exists in the mind as a notion, an innate impress antecedent to experience (10.20.29); it is also apprehended as a notation, intellectual knowledge subsequent to experience, involving concrete awareness of desire for happiness. As a notation, happiness resembles joy in two ways: the present state may affectively differ from its past counterpart; and both are suprasensible. To these two are joined a third component, one of closest similarity. In which situation and at what moment in the past has he so experienced happiness that he can concretely recall desiring it? The upshot of the inquiry is that his quest for and acquisition of happiness are in some measure a pursuit of and attainment of joy. Not he singly or a handful of others but all men without exception desire happiness. This desire can be absolutely certain only if the knowledge of irrefragable happiness is assured. The knowledge is, first of all, an innate notion infixed within, which is as determined as the mind itself. But the certitude and universality of this notion are verified in actual experience, which blends with a concrete knowledge (*notitia*). The question, what is this?, signifies: what does certitude of knowledge and volition of happiness concretely mean or entail? What are the where and when of its concrete recognition? Suppose John comsiders life as a soldier a means to happiness while his brother Joseph turns to a calling other than military service as a path to happiness. John is aiming at satisfaction in one occupation, his sibling, joy in a different line. The divergence of means geared toward a common end is characteristic not only of John and Joseph but of all men. However varied the occupations, each and every man is looking for an unvarying happiness through his work. However sundry and heterogeneous particular pursuits, they share in one common pursuit: all desire happiness, all seek joy. In fact, they identify joy with happiness: happiness is joy in the possession of the good initially sought. No matter how manifold the lifestyles, each individual traverses a different route to reach one and the same satisfaction; search for and attainment of joy are undeniably registered in everyone's experience. In sum, happiness consignifies the joy that from previous experiences is embedded in memory. Since happiness, a primitive notion

inscribed in the mind a priori, means procurement of happiness equivalent to possession of joy, joy is also a notion, one implicated in the notion of happiness. Experience attests to the nexus between happiness and joy; all men are observed to desire happiness in the sense that they desire satisfaction or joy. This concrete experience yields particular knowledge (*notitia*) of happiness and joy, in which they are so indissociably linked that the word happiness carries the concomitant import of joy retained in memory.

Chapter 22: True Happiness Centered on God

32. The claim that happiness consists in joy has to be modified. Not any joy at all entirely satisfies the heart; the impious, who are irreligious in belief and conduct, do not possess the happiness that is true joy. Only those who worship God gratis affix mind and will on God who is joy itself. Sharply at odds with authentic worshippers are individuals who worship God for the sake of a created good, e.g., idolaters of money who exploit God as a means for amassing more wealth (CD 11.25). God is joy itself, everlasting joy, the happiness that makes men happy, the joy that joys them (Sol 1.1.3. S 117.3.5). Properly taken, the happy life consists in rejoicing to God, from God, and for the sake of God. To God: the pursuit of joy is oriented toward him as the end of the seeking. God made man *ad te* (1.1.1); the weight of the soul that is love bears the soul upward toward God as its term (13.9.10), which, taken subjectively, is the peace that is tranquillity of order (CD 19.13). Correspondingly, quest for joy is *ad Deum*, directed to God as the terminus or rest-point, which, taken subjectively, is joy, fruition in the supreme good. Subjectively, the happiness that is peace consequent upon reaching God who is the soul's proper place is effectively one with the happiness that is full delight in the highest good. From God: the joy of man irrupts from the joy that is God; divine joy being the principle of human joy, man becomes joyful by touching God in his heart and thereby participating in his everlasting joy (S 117.3.5). For the sake of God: God is sought for God alone, delighted in for no other reason than God: lesser goods are enjoyed or, more properly, the joys accompanying their possession are subordinated to joy in the supreme joy. As moral tumult in every age witnesses, it is no secret that every day, indeed every hour, men chase after lesser joys as if they were the top joy, but, none of these being

God, none is joy unalloyed, the fruit of resting in him who is weight without weight (GL 4.4.8). Yet while hankering after satisfactions other than true joy, men undoubtedly feel joy, like that Augustine experienced in winning first place in class declamation (1.17.27) and in greater measure like that which thrilled him when he delivered a masterly panegyric for the emperor in Milan in November, 385. Entertained rightly, subordinated to true joy, lower-level joys partake of the highest joy. Cultivated misleadingly, lesser joys deflect the mind from the supreme joy. Yet at core those misdirectedly pursued participate in some fashion in the highest joy. Strip away the egoism, extirpate traces of the fleshly self, straighten out the deordination: the purified article that remains is an authentic indicator of true joy. An image of each experience of joy, he significantly remarks, is deposited in memory. Serving as an eventual portal to genuine joy is the memorial representation, albeit partly blemished, in virtue of which the heart is not wholly diverted from laying hold of true joy; or, positively put, through an image of partly disordered joy the heart stays hospitable to attraction to authentic joy. As a notation, joy is suprasensibly grasped, but since the event is recalled in a sensio-intellectual manner, the joy accompanying possession of the good is remembered with a sensory fringe; hence the word image designates the memorial impress.

Chapter 23: Even in Evil Men Basic Desire for Happiness Remains

33. The fact that many men, in not seeking joy from God, do not actually desire happiness may throw doubt upon the proposition that all men desire happiness. The doubt is dissolved by the distinction between the fundamental inherent drive for happiness in general and the choice of particular means to realize this basic directedness. Not pure spirits, nor spiritually integrated so as to adhere only to the good, men are inwardly divided; within, a kind of civil war rages, flesh and spirit battling against each other (S 25.4.4). Often the outcome is the defeat of the spirit; spiritual in intention, many are actually carnal in resolution and execution. After repeated failures drive home the lesson that they cannot resolutionally opt for the spiritual, they drift into carnal lives, convinced they cannot walk the way of the spirit (S 30.3.4.). Yet even individuals who because,

weighed down by the flesh, do not concretely quest for God, do elect, when queried, to draw joy from truth rather than falsity. As they avow without question a desire for happiness, so they unhesitantly express preference for garnering joy from truth. Hence in some remote fashion, however hard to explicate with crystal-clear analysis, they do pine for true happiness that is joy from the truth, for they desire joy springing from the truth. In holding that simultaneously men do and do not desire true happiness, Augustine is not trafficking in higher doublethink. The very same men aspire to happiness but do not desire happiness, yet without absurdity, for the desire and its negation are willed in different respects. Vaguely, in the line of end, they desire true happiness; concretely, in the line of means, dominated by the downward pull of the flesh, they choose goods other than those leading to true happiness. Indeed since rejoicing in truth is rejoicing in God, Augustine pauses for a moment to joyfully invoke God as light and salvation of his inner self. Without God: darkness and debility of fleshy life; with God: light and strength of spirit-ruled life (P 26[En.2].3). Unfortunately, darkness engulfing some men obscures the God Augustine is hungering for. Three times over he stresses the inescapable orientation of all to happiness: all men desire happiness; this is the only true happiness; it is a happiness that is joy produced by feeding upon truth.

As a rhetorician, Augustine was acquainted with colleagues adept in subtle, even outright mendacity, deceivers aplenty, but not one who wanted to be deceived. The affirmative side of this coin reads: all men desire to know the truth. Knowledge of truth is knowledge of happiness: both truth and happiness are notions engraved on the mind prior to experience. All not only know but love the truth; a sign of this is the fact that they have no desire to be told untruth. Universal knowledge of truth, we saw, carries with it universal knowledge of happiness. Conversely, from another perspective, love of happiness that is joy from truth includes love of truth. Thus knowledge and love of truth reciprocally imply knowledge and love of happiness. Notionally, in terms of innate knowledge, and notationally, in terms of cognition arising from experience, knowledge of truth and knowledge of happiness as joy from truth also mutually entrain one another. Yet the problem recurs: if all know truth, why do they not all rejoice in the truth that is fulfilling? Why are many, in fact, unhappy rather than happy? As mentioned earlier, the answer turns on the

distinction between aim and choice; generally all men desire
happiness, but executively many immerse themselves in goods that
objectively conduce to unhappiness. While good men who elect to
live according to the virtues obtain happiness, their evil fellows
express a velleity for happiness but miss or misapply the concrete
means to happiness. Allied with a wish for a happiness is neglect of
its concrete concomitant and necessary condition, which is right
moral living. Without directly willing unhappiness, evil men, by
choosing carnal ways, inexorably visit upon themselves the
unhappiness that is the penalty necessarily ingredient in sin. It is
notorious that men are more forcibly seized by delights of temporal
goods than of a comparatively dim high ideals. Yet faint as it is, there
remains a glimmer underlying the wish for happiness that undyingly
perdures. May the all-merciful God, he prays, spare from everlasting
night those seduced by meretricious temporals, gracing them to draw
near to the light, fanning the minuscule spark within to flame into a
rebirth that is to expand into full awareness of truth (J 52.13).

34. The dictum that all men love truth seems belied by the
experience distilled in Terence's biting line, "Truth begets hate."[58] If
love of truth is exceptionless, why do some individuals hate truth with
a passion? Even Jesus, who radiated light and love, was reviled by
enemies who, because he proclaimed the truth, engineered his death
as the final solution. However, particular instances of hatred do not
undercut universal love of truth since hatred of truth compasses, in a
skewed way, love of truth. More precisely, men abhor the real truth
because they love a pseudo-truth. The Pharisees who sneered at the
truth of Jesus were enamored of the bogus truth of pride in their
preeminent religious status and their inwardly corrupt lives. In line
with La Rochefoucauld's well-known epigram, "Hypocrisy is the
homage vice pays to virtue," their hypocritical posture was the tribute
that hatred of truth renders to love of real truth. Haters of real truth,
by loving the sham as if it were genuine, satisfy their desire not to be
or appear deceived. Joined to their misguided desire not to be
deceived, their fierce love of pseudo-truth blinds them to the
troubling fact that the "truth" which exacts their allegiance is
spurious. Ironically, a misconstrued desire not to be deceived keeps
them deceived. Relatively speaking, on the condition that it may be
made consonant with their lifestyle, they love the real truth; but,
absolutely speaking, since their vicious ways deviate from the real

truth, they abominate it. The real truth, which is abstractly loved truth insofar as it diffuses light, is concretely despised because it sheds light rebuking their weakness. Not wanting to be deceived, they abstractly love the truth as a source of light or nondeception; but wanting to stay in the darkness or deception that is evil, they concretely scorn the truth. Relatively, they love the truth because it reveals a broad sketch of desirable conduct; absolutely, they loathe the real truth because its austere light lays bare their fraudulence. Set over against the real truth that is constitutive of moral law, their characters look, as they are, shockingly disfigured: truth tells them they are living lies. Contrary-to-desire compensation penalizes their desire that their diseased condition be concealed but that truth itself be revealed. The mirror of real truth reveals their hideous condition. But the real truth, though revealing the malformed mind, remains concealed; minds loaded down with vices are morally sightless and crippled, incapable of concretely grasping the real truth. Still, in the unhappiness that a retributive law of contraries levels, the wayward mind never ceases hungering for authentic happiness, preferring to rejoice in the true rather than the false good. Even while it clings to and is sullied by pseudo-truth, its desire for real truth never halts. As in the sinner a deformed image of God persists, so in the lover of pseudo-truth a radical desire, however disordered, remains open to the real possibility of reform begot by conforming to real truth. Once disburdened of dark ways, the mind will delight in the real truth, drawing all its joy principally from God, the truth alone in which all other truths participate.

It does not appear unlikely that these few lines recount, in a dry and detached vein, Augustine's tormented trek from counterfeit to genuine truth. For nearly a decade he was beguiled by Manichean pseudo-truth, which perversely satisfied his hunger for truth and deceptively assuaged his appetite not to be deceived. Outbalancing abstract love of the real truth was his concrete hatred of it; he contemned Catholicism as a blasphemous fabrication riddled with irrationalities. Once the relentless critic of Catholicism turned self-critical, once his mind awakened to the dawning light that it was he who might be deceived, he realized step by step that it was Manicheism that was a cunningly disguised tissue of absurdities offensive to God and repugnant to the mind. Even when he was immured in Manichean night, there remained the slim potential for growth to fruition in actual joy in the God who is the one and only full truth revealing himself in errorless plentitude in Catholicism. Stated in the past instead of the future tense, the last sentence of this chapter sums up his journey from Manicheism to Catholicism, from unhappiness to happiness, however attenuated here below, nourished by the healing truth that is God himself.[59]

Chapter 24: God Not beyond but in Memory in virtue of Truth

35. Here he starts to unriddle the apparent dilemma posed earlier (10.17.16): as supreme, God has to be beyond memory, yet, if beyond memory, he cannot be known. Distinguishing two senses of "beyond memory" resolves the problem: ontically, God as unchangeable is beyond or above memory (10.25.36) but, noetically, is not beyond memory. In some way God is always present in memory, not explicitly but implicitly, not as God but as effect of his Godness, present not as supreme truth but as shared truth because descending from the very truth that is God. Augustine has traveled the length and breadth of memory in search of God, discovering him not outside but within memory, in which he first acquired cognition of God that never left him. Specifying how God stays unforgettably present, he argues that wherever he learned truth, he found his God who is truth itself. Truth is a notion, an a priori cognitive element implanted in the mind by divine light. Once he uttered any correct judgment in the light of truth, he reached experiential knowledge or a notation of truth. In apprehending that truth, howbeit simple and homely, he implicitly knew the truth itself, as the cause imbedded in knowledge of effect, as ground implicitly grasped in consequent. From the first moment he implicitly learned of the truth itself through knowledge of derivative truth, God always dwelled in his memory; there he still finds God: reflection on truth inferentially elicits the presence of truth itself. In remembering God, he delights in him, i.e., experiences happiness, which is joy in the truth. The delights, which surpass the merely human plane, are holy, streaming from and coruscating with the very holiness of God. Moreover, they are not recompense due in justice for good works but freely given out of mercy responding to his misery, in which he was fettered by mortality and corruptible flesh (P 68[S.2].18). God casts eyes of pity on the dreadful destitution of Augustine (P 68[S.2].18), who prostrates himself before the Lord as a

beggar pleading for the inner riches of the divine heart (S 61.7.P 68[S.2].15).

Chapter 25: God Present as Lord of Memory

36. God's habitation in memory which is of his, not man's, making, is a kind of private dwelling in which God is at home and rests, a sacred abode because a temple of the divine. God is not present in bodily images, psychic data available even to animals, nor accessible in affections of the mind (broadly taken to include affective states and their remembrance), nor in the throne of the mind, where self-consciousness reigns. He is lord of the mind, superior to bodily images, psychic affects, and self-awareness as he is to all other lower things because, while they unceasingly change, he remains unchangeable. Transcendent to all creatures, he generously condescends to take up residence in memory, where Augustine initially becomes acquainted with his presence. Strictly the purest of spirits, he does not lodge in any place, yet just as certainly does he dwell in memory—a certitude grounded in a twofold experience: in memory Augustine first came to cognize God, and there too does Augustine once more recognize him when he recalls his presence.

Chapter 26: Ontically God above Memory

37. This chapter, though raising a question verbally the same as the last, alters the frame of reference. Above, posed in a noetic framework, the inquiry, "Where is God?", issues in a noetic response: God is learned in memory. Here the question is transposed into an ontic context: where was God prior to memorial cognition? God's *esse* is not *memorari*; not a memorial *percipi*, not wholly dependent on memory, God exists prior to human memory. Ontically, he discovers God in God above his memory. In God: as maker not contained by the work of his hands, God exists in himself. Above Augustine: he is supreme truth infinitely higher than mind (7.10.16. LA 2.15.39. VR 31.57).[60] Without being spread out in space or circumscribed in place, the immutable God is operatively immanent in all things, and equally responsive, as seated in consciences, to all praying for light (P 45.9). Not all clearly hear the clear answer divinely proffered. Prayers are not always satisfied in tune with the desires of those praying; in one sense their prayers go unanswered. But strictly, no prayer goes

unheard; any lapse is imputable not to God but to the listener who
fails to accept God's answer. The best servant of the Lord is open not
to hearing what he wants but to wanting what he hears. Though the
sole food of Jesus was to do the will of the Father (Jn 4.34), here the
best servant strictly designates the Christian patterning himself after
the savior perfectly surrendered to the Father. Implicitly inscribed
within every true prayer is the petition, "Thy will be done." The best
servant trusts that compliance with God's will assures partial
happiness which adumbrates the matchless splendor promised in
eternity (E 130.8.15). To adapt the definition of the happy life
(10.22.32), prayer of the best is toward God alone, from him (inspired
by his Spirit) and for his sake (in perfect accord with his plan of love).
Prayer perseveringly offered with purity of heart is guaranteed an
affirmative reply. God had to work Augustine's conversion because
Monica's prayers complied with all the conditions to which the all-
high had bound himself (5.9.17). It was he who laid out the road to
conversion; Monica's beseechings that her son not voyage alone went
unheeded that he might travel to Milan to learn Christ at the feet of
Ambrose. In general, all prayers for spiritual goods are substantially
answered. On the other hand, it is painfully plain that not all prayers
for particular temporal goods, such as health of body and mind and
material necessities are accorded successful issue. However, in such
instances God answers the petitioner rather that the petition; while
the object sought is unchanged, the subject praying is changed. The
cup of suffering did not pass, but Jesus' prayer of self-surrender in
Gethsemane signaled that his human will had been transformed (E
130.14.26). His repeated prayers for physical healing unfulfilled, Paul
was blessed with grace sufficient to endure the thorn in his flesh (E
130.14.25) Furthermore, at times God delays his response so as to
expand the heart into a channel of divine energy, ensuring that in it
God's will is to be done (E 132.8.17). A man need not be as super-
bright as Augustine to cull from experience that it is not at all easy to
translate into action conformity to God's will; mastery of the triple
concupiscence exacts nothing short of the battle of a lifetime.

Chapter 27: Memory of his Conversion

38. A lovely lyrical passage recapitulates flight from God capped by
life-transfiguring conversion. He had come to love God compara-

tively late in life. At the time of writing (c. 400) he was roughly forty-
six years old and, since his conversion occurred in his thirty-second
year (386), he had wasted close to seventy percent of his life cut off
from the beauty of all beauties (3.6.10). God's beauty is absolute, that
of all others relative: beautiful as they are, measured against his
beauty, they are not beautiful (11.4.6). In a human perspective, God
is ever ancient, ever new; older than the universe yet, as
indestructible, always young. Because the day of this most ancient is
eternal (11.13.16), he seems born afresh every day. A mournful chord
is struck in this "late"–so many tears squandered on false loves,
indeed on the love of false love itself (2.2.2).[61] In his first three decades
he had turned his back on this "most beautiful of all beings" (2.6.12)
as he feverishly scrambled for the beautiful in objects without while
God was tabernacled within (3.6.11). Things that enchained his mind
were really beautiful, for the God that is all beauty shared his beauty
with them (3.6.10); in, by, and through him are all creatures beautiful
(Sol 1.3). Sadly, his unbeautiful will was twistedly opting for fugitive
temporal beauties (2.2.3), so that, forsaking the eternal One, he threw
himself downward into multiplicity, to be drowned in the torrent of
earthly things without that made him morally earthy within. While
God was with him, divine immanence maintaining him in existence,
he was not with God; perversity of spirit prompted him to consort
with lower beauties (4.13.20) rather than with supreme beauty. Pursuit
of sexual pleasures, riches, and honors distanced him from the God
in whom these things were, i.e., the God who contained them. God
was in him, and the things wrongly pined for were in God, yet God,
so near by immanent governance, was morally and supernaturally
driven far off by his deformed love of the inferior in preference to the
highest good. Then all at once through the childish chant, "Take and
read," God shouted so loudly that the reverberating sounds shattered
his spiritual deafness. Here, shifting from the usual relation of spiritual
senses to their objects (10.6.8), the objects wondrously re-energize the
dysfunctional spiritual senses. His spiritual ear did not first hear the
divine voice; rather, God's mighty cry released his ears. So enslaved
had been his spiritual senses that they were inoperative; he was
spiritually deaf and blind to God. God who is light itself shone with
such splendor upon his unseeing eyes that his blindness was healed.
God's delightful fragrance restored his sense of smell, activating it to
pant after the ravishing aroma that is God. The divine honey (10.6.8)

revived his sense of taste, making him ravenously hungry for the food
that is divine life. Finally, God's touch resuscitated his lapsed sense of
touch; inflamed by the Spirit, he burned to be clasped to the divine
bosom in peace without end (13.9.10).[62] The impact of divine force
upon spiritual senses is the exact contrary of what ensues when
stimuli that are too powerful impinge on physical senses. Whereas
continual exposure to very loud sounds may induce deafness, God's
booming cry undeafens spiritual ears. While too intense physical light
can blind, God's spiritual light unblinds eyes. So prodigious is the
divine action that it does not stop at partial repair but fully restores
the failed spiritual faculty to normal acuity.

Chapter 28: Life a Continuous Trial

39. Intense desire for peace will be consummated only when all of
self in indivorcibly wedded to the God who is peace; wholly one with
the God who is all joy, no longer will he suffer. Then his life will be
not be mixed with un-life; life that is a living death (1.6.7) will be
transfigured into deathless life because surcharged with the purest life
that is God. Now, not wholly afire with divine life but still partially
earth, he cannot stay his earthbound self from driving his spirit
downward. The burden, in particular, involves tension between good
and evil tendencies that can be both rejoiced in and sorrowed over.
Even after conversion the fight between flesh and spirit rages without
cease; no man can totally observe the injunction, "Be perfect as your
heavenly Father is perfect" (P 130.44). In his less-than-perfect
condition he is torn by the conflict of joys he should sorrow over and
of sorrows that he should rejoice in. Lamentable joys include
indulgence in curiosity and giving way to love of praise; beneficial
sorrows probably cover remorse for capitulating to lust of the flesh
and pride of life. Conversely, his inner self is also the battleground
where evil sorrows and good joys clash. Evil sorrows designate
complaints about the grind wearying body and spirit. Good joys
betoken delights in the self-denial exacted by virtue, out of which
blossom satisfaction of heart. Day by day the two sorts of combat go
on, their outcome ever undecided, with no warranty that good
sorrows and joys will overmaster their evil counterparts. Fatigued by
the strain of affective undercurrents whose conflict remains
unresolved, he holds out his wounds, which are his sins, self-inflicted,

principally through pride (AC 12), to the Father, through the wounds of whose Son they are to be healed (T 3.3). The man who makes himself ill cannot make himself well; healing being dispensed only by the divine physician (S 156.2.2), he begs for mercy that is infinite love applied to the misery of man (E 210.1).

Significantly, Job did not say that there are trials here, but that the whole of life is a trial (S 351.3). Since men ordinarily tend to eschew rather than pursue hardships, God commands tolerance of difficulties. While most show little desire for evils that demand endurance, they do covet strength to endure. Though they experience joy in conquering evils by enduring them, they would prefer to have no evils to front. Even Job, the "great athlete of God," when stricken with wounds from head to foot, voiced not the slightest desire for a single one of his sores (S 359A.6). Like that of every man, Augustine's life is cyclical, moving from prosperity to adversity, then to new prosperity. When plagued by adversity, he longs for prosperity and, when smiled on by prosperity, fears fresh adversity. So far the history of the human adventure has not discovered a kind of quasi-paradisal El Dorado in between prosperity and adversity, in which man neither yearns for the one nor dreads the other. In this middle sphere, where psychological equilibrium would reign, and with it uninterrupted contentment, no goods would be lacking, no fear of loss would haunt their possession. However, life on earth exempt from deprivation or dread of loss is utopian delusion; no one can be fully and lastingly happy outside heaven (S 359A.6). Prosperity of this world, carrying no guarantee of happiness, is twice overshadowed by unhappiness; fear of loss clouds satisfaction; then delight in a worldly lifestyle unable to rein in appetites leads to a vicious darkening of the soul. Adversity is also infected, thrice indeed, with unhappiness: first, desire for prosperity connotes a certain dissatisfaction; second, adversity itself obviously can be unrelievedly grim; third, if adversity proves to be so harsh as to be unbearable, endurance falters, then collapses under the rain of hammerblows. Since both prosperity and adversity are ineluctably charged with potential or actual tribulations, all of life is truly a trial that perdures unabatedly. In a this-world perspective, the sorrow-soaked tale of man's earthly span constitutes a tragedy that is depressing, at times close to ghastly. Tribulations, however, need not be unmitigated evils; in a divine frame of reference they are convertible into blessings if they point the mind Godward. Moreover, God in his mercy withholds certain goods, no matter how appealing from a shortsighted, timebound outlook because from his eternal vantage point he sees that they will work harm. Nor is prosperity, properly designed by providence, a necessarily evil factor; both prosperity and adversity spring from an all-wise mercy. Prosperity as gift consoles while the gift that is adversity admonishes man (E 210.1).

Chapter 29: Grace Makes the Soul Continent

40. All, not simply a slice, of his hope for virtue hangs on measureless mercy, which is applied with the suppleness of wisdom and boundless power (S 335K.6). This is enunciated in the now-celebrated formula: "Give what you command, and command what you will." Let God order any spiritual work at all, even seemingly impossible, but let him also supply light and power to execute the command, and Augustine will do the undoable. What God commands for all is continence, taken in the broadest sense as self-control or mastery of all disorderly appetites. As remarked earlier (8.11.27), continence, less broadly viewed, signifies control of the triple concupiscence (10.30.41). In its strict acceptation it denotes restraint of sexual desires, either within marriage or apart from the marital bond, the latter involving total abstinence from sexual union (Cont 1.1). According to Wis 8.21, only God can bestow continence or restraint from illicit intercourse in marriage; by extension, every sort of continence is divine gift (Cont 1.1). However closely connected with it, continence is not identical with chastity; rather, it is the indispensable means or necessary condition for its practice; through continence, which harnesses sexual cupidity, chastity is ensured. So with all the other virtues cooperating in the triumph of spirit over flesh: through continence wayward desires are curbed; the good of continence vanquishes the evil of concupiscence that is malordered inclination (Cont 3.7). Its lower tendencies subdued and works of flesh checked by continence, the heart is able to engender fruits of the Spirit such as love, joy, and peace (Cont 3.9).

Thus liberated from lower impulses, the soul lives integral and self-controlled, riveted on the good of the spirit (8.9.21). Its discordant appetites put in harmony with the spiritual law of vitality, it is no longer tugged here and there by multiple lower goods. As One, God contains the world; in containing its "world" of desires, the soul becomes one after the model of the One. By nature God is eternal and One, man, changeable and weighted toward the manifold; but by grace man sharing in the stability of divine life becomes one like the One; so made one, the soul is said to be returned to the One. Specifically, it is in virtue of continence that the human spirit becomes one, its oneness imaging the One. Continence fuses the soul's diverse parts into unity: thus one, the soul is carried upward by the fiery force that is divine love to the One, from which it fell away through sin. Sin rips asunder the soul, which surrenders to the many temporal goods. More explicitly, sin passes through three stages: the soul departing from the One is divided; no longer solid, it streams downward; finally, it is submerged in temporal multitude. On the other hand, the soul reformed in the image of God grows through three contrasting phases: under the aegis of continence it resists the pull of the many upon disordered desires; regulated by divine law, it gathers together diverse tendencies into unity; so unified, the soul turns back to the One deserted through sin.

In general, no one in this life is confirmed in perfect love that loves all things for the sake of God alone in all circumstances. Like all other individuals, the Mother of God excepted (NG 36.42), Augustine finds that his conduct attests only a lesser love since at times he loves creatures not for the sake of God alone nor in God (T 9.8.13) but for themselves, for his own use and enjoyment. The chapters that follow (30-41) portray Augustine grappling with temptations concerning lust of the flesh, lust of eyes, and pride of life: indulgence in food and drink, curiosity, and the pride that is worldly ambition; in effect, examen of conscience convicts him of inablility to avoid all minor failings and imperfections. To be fully integrated he requires divine love that burns away infirmities and turns the soul into a being of fire to be returned to the One that is inextinguishable love. "My God," he cries out, "set me on fire with your fire." Let his God who commands continence enkindle him with his very own love to wholly observe this, and God may command whatever he will.

Chapter 30: Problem of Erotic Dreams

41. Along with continence in a lesser sense that controls the triple concupiscence, there is prescribed the strict brand, abstinence from

relations outside marriage. Specifically, God forbids concubinage, a state in which he had lived for some fifteen years. Though Roman law permitted the practice, and while he and his beloved partner remained admirably faithful, their extra-marital cohabitation had to be judged habitually sinful. However, not commanded but only counseled is consecrated celibacy, today called vowed chastity. Marriage at conversion would have been licit, but God drew his servant to a total celibacy, a state superior to that of matrimony since it sacrifices marriage for the sake of service to God (SV 10.9;18.18). Certainly the state is higher; yet superiority of state, carries no certain guarantee that every celibate is holier than every married Christian; the life of Monica existentially refutes such a contention. Because graced, he was able to live out the divine ordinance of chastity, to which he committed himself from the moment of his quasi-miraculous conversion (8.12.30) in 386, prior to priestly ordination in 391, which deputed him to be a dispenser of the sacrament of God; sacrament refers collectively to all the sacraments and principally to the Eucharist; the priest baptizes, reconciles sinners, and by consecration of the species invites others to banquet on the body of the Lord (E 28.8).

In daily dedicating himself to celibacy, to his dismay he discovers in memory embers still alive, unextinguished traces of prior sexual excesses. When awake, he can resist the solicitation of these images, which have happily lost most of their potency. Still, on occasion while asleep, he feels not only excitation, an internal pleasure attracting him to an illicit sex object, but a kind of dormitive quasi-acquiescence, entraining at times emission of seed. Indeed in a way sexual enticingness is at times more forceful during sleep; illusory images, fantasized in sleep, prove more alluring than real objects in the waking state. Yet in spite of similarities and the fact that the self remains unchanged in changing from one state to another, notable differences set the two states apart. In the waking state his reason stands firm against temptation, fending off without disturbance the appeal of actual sex objects. During sleep the eyes of the mind close along with the eyes of sense, and the operation of reason, like that of the senses, is generally discontinued. True, during initial dozing when sleep is gradually overcoming the body, the mind is vaguely alert, capable of refusing assent. On other occasions, when the restraint of reason is fully suspended, the dormitive imagination gives way to sexual gratification, yet without sin, for reason and volition have been rendered inoperative. During the ensuing wakefulness he experiences not remorse but peace of conscience because he was not responsible for the pleasure. The action was nonvoluntary: he did not will it; and involuntary: he expresses regret, which is congruent with his constant displeasure with such temptations in the waking state. The action was done not by but in him, outside the governance of reason.[63]

42. He intensely desires continence, the extirpation of all impulses of concupiscence, however involuntary, to be wrought through a richer inpouring of grace: thus will be snuffed out the tiniest cinders of sexuality during sleep. Rescued from the bird-lime of concupiscence, his soul will correspond to the waking-state desires of the interior man. Extra graces will quell the insurrection of the sleeping-state soul against the wakeful interior self, with the result that not only acts of pollution will cease but appearance of consent as well. Total suppression of such excitations would be appropriately solacing during the prime of life, even before the onset of old age when sexual fires are presumably banked. This is not wildly wishful thinking, not an impossible dream, for the Father's mercy can do immeasurably more than man can pray for or even conceive—significantly, the very text, Eph 3.20, that Monica recalled when she learned of his conversion not just to the ordinary Christian way but to a vocation of celibacy (8.12.30). The God who lavished the extraordinary grace to be continent, he trusts, could infuse continence of even involuntary sexual incitements during sleep.

In unveiling his state, chaste but still prey to nocturnal pollution, he is humbly de-privatizing himself for the inspection of others; humbly, because while such manifestation of conscience would be exceptional in a layman, public exposure of the private self is all the more remarkable in an officially esteemed bishop. Rejoicing over the continence divinely cultivated within is mingled with trembling, i.e., with circumspection lest hardihood stifle holiness of the spirit that the Lord gives (P 2.6). Intermingled with joy is sorrow over the fact that his continence and chastity do not yet fully suppress dormitive impulses of concupiscence, inclining him to hope that mercy will seal him in total continence, regnant in both waking and sleeping states. Such perfect order of a continent soul will be oriented toward the plenitude above, which partakes of the peace that is God, a peace in which interior and exterior self, spirit and flesh, will delight. After the final resurrection, when death is wholly conquered, there will be no more warring of flesh against spirit but only peace in each, perfect harmony between the glorified spirit and the glorified flesh that is the spiritualized body after 1 Cor 15.44 (GL 9.3.6; 10.17).

Chapter 31: Temptations in the line of Taste

Flesh that lusts against spirit has its roots not only in touch, so closely hooked up with sexual excess, but in the other four senses, temptations to which he attends in this and following chapters (10.31.43-34.53). Unless we envisage Augustine as monk and bishop, we may mistakenly discount his minute examination of conscience in these areas, especially that concerning food and drink, as too stern, bordering on rigorism. In probing his character, he is not laying down minimal moral-theological prescriptions for run-of-the-mill layfolk; rather, as a monk, living under a *Rule* he himself authored, he is measuring himself by ascetical ideals. As regards food and drink, he strove to obey his own practical ordinance of mortification: "Subdue the flesh, so far as your health permits, by fasting and abstinence from food and drink."[64] As a bishop, he was expected to live as exemplary, not only for the *continentes* vowed to chastity and committed to an austere regimen marked by constant fasting, but also for the faithful whom he had to exhort to observe the Church's rules for fasting which, by our contemporary practice, were severe. Generally, during Lent no meat was eaten, with no food at all consumed till the one meal at sunset; in addition, besides ordinary fasting on the vigils of great feasts, many took it upon themselves to fast every Wednesday and Friday (S 163B.6).[65]

43. The inexorable necessity of eating and drinking in order to survive is styled an evil only in the loose sense, a burden of man's mortal condition, to be tolerated in faith and hope of blessedness in the beyond (S 351.4). It is not strictly penal, as he maintained before (SDM 2.56), because prior to the Fall Adam and Eve ate in Eden (R 1.19.9). Ideally, if not always in fact, each day should satisfy his necessity, without anxiety about the morrow. Here is shrewdly enunciated a common-sense truth validated in detail by modern science: food is required to build up the body, to replace parts that have ceased to exist and to repair daily deterioration. Once man is wholly satiated with God, his spiritualized body will be food-

independent and incorruptible. This transformation will suspend the physical law that no engine can produce more work at one place than is put into it at another; a law that is special case of the law of conservation of energy, according to which energy can neither be created nor destroyed. A human body cannot normally operate without an influx of energy that is food and drink; no living body is a perpetual motion machine. In the next life, however, through divine power output will exceed input; the body will work as a perpetuum mobile, expending energy without compensatory intake of fuel indispensable here below for replacing sloughed-off parts. Then his will not be a dying life (1.6.7) but a divinized existence exempt from iron laws of natural necessity.

Hand in hand with this necessity, when sated, goes pleasure, which is not without its pitfalls; if unwary, the consecrated Christian may be beguiled by its allure. As indicated above, Augustine disciplined his body by daily fasting, a strategy deployed in the ongoing battle of spirit against flesh. Well-nigh inexhaustible, he was not gifted with a strong constitution, yet he fasted every day, ordinarily eating only one meal, this around 3:00 P.M., for in the monastery only invalids and the ill were allowed an earlier meal, usually at noon. The meal itself, plain even by standards of the simpler economy of late antiquity, was generally frugal and sparse, consisting of vegetables; only occasionally was meat served to guests or the more infirm brethren.[66] He customarily drank some wine, in accord with Paul's advice, confirmed by modern science, that a little wine is good for the stomach, i.e., aids digestion.[67] Like a fever, hunger and thirst burn; under the pitiless African sun a throat parched by thirst seems on fire. Like a fever, they can kill: lack of food drains the body of strength, and deprivation of water entrains certain death within less than two weeks. Food and drink, whose pleasure replaces the pain of hunger and thirst, function as a medicine that heals their "fever." From the divine hand pour out manifold sources of food; the earth abounds with crops and animals, the water or sea is thronged with fish, and the sky furnishes edible birds and rain water, bounty that consoles the body, i.e., eases or dispels distress of hunger and thirst. So ready to hand are food and drink that the very debility may be designated delightful; in other words, hunger and thirst that invite enjoyable eating and drinking are so quickly assuaged that the line between hunger and satiety seems blurred, the lack itself appearing to blend with the appetite's satisfaction and concomitant pleasure.

44. Counting food a nutritive medicine to relieve pangs of hunger, he cannot stipulate exactly how much food he needs to restore energy. Transition from relative emptiness to satisfaction always induces pleasure; the very transition is pleasure in the sense that pleasure is a sign of satiety. The whip of necessity drives him along the path involving pleasure that, in fact, may ensnare him in concupiscence. While ostensibly he eats for the sake of health, with pleasure relegated to the status of lackey, pleasure proves precarious when it arrogates to itself the primary role; frequently, self-examen catches him eating primarily for pleasure and only secondarily for reasons of health. The measures of satisfaction of health and pleasure do not coincide; food sufficient for health seems all too meager fare for pleasure. Often he cannot ascertain whether he is taking more food because of the need of body or because of the clamor of pleasure; in eating more rather than less, he cannot detect whether he is obeying reason or surrendering to pleasure. At times he pulls the wool over his eyes; health is only a pretext to disguise craving for more sensory delight. Not a day passes in which he is not bent on unmasking covert pseudo-justification of excessive pleasure of palate. Calling on God's right hand, which symbolizes strength, to lay down a clear prudential guideline, he entrusts his anxieties to the Lord: as yet he has not discerned a concrete rule that draws a bifurcating line between food necessary for health and that indulged in primarily for pleasure.

45. Light and power to reach the right decision so as to steadily deny himself without impairing health will descend from on high to his vacillating nature. He can command his desire in accord with God's command only because the God who issues the ordinance also infuses the power to dominate his appetites (10.29.40), eschewing both drunkenness and the slightest tendency to overeating. Happily untroubled by drunkenness, he prays that mercy which has kept him sober will defeat insobriety. Overeating, or a touch of gluttony, is another matter; as astutely noted, it steals in, camouflaged as a support for health (10.31.44). Mercy will repress both brands of intemperance; mercy is all: upon it totally hangs continence of every sort. Prior to praying, men are endowed with many blessings, all owed to grace; graces begged for are also divinely conferred; indeed the very insight that everything men have is gift is a light of grace.

Every good a man possesses, whether he be, like Augustine, a teetotaler, or a reformed drunkard, is wrought by ever-operative mercy. Excessive boozing was not uncommon at martyrs' shrines, but habitual drunkenness was apparently not widespread among African Catholics, though, he conjectured, as many as ten percent of Rogatists were chronic topers (S 252.4; E 22.2-3; 93.48-9).[68] To liberation from drunkenness are concretely applied the threefold action of grace: it protects individuals, like Augustine, from wallowing in their cups; it burns away the shackles of drunkenness; it illumines minds to realize that, whether or not former drunkards, to God's power is due suppression of demon wine.

God speaking to him through Scripture has further underlined the primacy and ultimacy of grace in self-conquest. First, Eccl 18.30 bids him avoid pleasure-seeking as such. Second, 1 Cor 8.8, glossed in an accommodated sense, assures him that food as such is not the font of happiness; abundance will not enrich nor lack impoverish his spirit. Third, another Pauline text reaffirms the key to satisfaction: self-sufficiency in regard to food emanates from grace. From divine assistance comes, first, the command to rule the appetites; from it arises, second, the perception that inner contentment does not hinge on food; by it is initiated, third, the crucial light that strength of self-mastery is guaranteed by God. These are the ringing words of Paul, peerless warrior in the heavenly army whose king is Christ. Measured against this outstanding soldier of God, Augustine appears to be nothing but an earthbound clod. Yet God breathes soul into dust: man is inspirited dust; moreover, like the prodigal son, he has been drawn home to the Father–Augustine recalls his conversion: a Christian is transfigured dust, bearing the now refurbished image of God within. So the chasm between the Apostle and Augustine narrows; like Paul, he is also redeemed, and, like him, Paul was originally only dust, so that Augustine can claim as his very own a line of Paul he loves with a holy passion, for it promises investiture with the might of God: "I can do all things in him who strengthens me"; a verse that his earlier insight reformulates: "Give what you command and command what you will" (10.29.40). Let the truth within teach him how to accredit, as did Paul, all gifts to divine strength; let him existentially boast that he boasts of nothing save the Lord of mercy; then will he wax strong not by self-reliance but the God-reliance of Paul prefiguratively confirmed by Sirach (Ecclus

23.6.) who begs God to break his enchainment in gluttony. As the word of God repeatedly evidences, only because the holy One who calls to holiness infuses power do frail creatures execute his holy commands.

46. Once more he spears the Manichean dogma that some things in nature are essentially infected with evil. First, a general truth obtains; for the good-willed and clean of heart all things are good and clean. Second, eating certain foods may be evil, not because the food is unclean but because such eating may cause scandal, offending charity and disrupting the peace of the community. A third quotation furnishes the reason why all food is good: it is the gift of the all-good God, to be welcomed with praise and gratitude. Fourth, though food is per se good, its eating does not render the eater per se good or worthy in the eyes of God. Fifth, since dietary laws are now abolished, Christians cannot be put down by nonChristians still yoked by food regulations now void of force. Sixth, nor should food be a bone of contention among Christians themselves. Those moderate in mortification should not tax the apparently over-austere as scrupulous, and, conversely, the stringently abstemious should not deprecate less ascetical brethren as laxist. Though Manichean darkness concerning uncleanness of food no longer arouses fear, he continues to spiritually fear impurity latent in the disordered desire that is gluttony. Scripture witnesses to the goodness of food and the evil of inordinate desire not only in words but in persons and works. Noah had access to flesh meat, Elijah ate meat, and even John the Baptist, a champion in the line of abstinence, consumed meat in the guise of locusts. Meat as such is not evil, but cupidity for fare less luxurious than meat lies at the heart of evil. Esau sold his birthright for a mess of pottage and lentils; David, king of the Jews, confessed that he had sinned in craving water from a cistern near Bethlehem; and Jesus, king of the new Israel, was tempted, after a forty-days fast, to cupidity not by meat but bread. Granted, the Israelites in the desert, fed by, then fed up with, manna, hankered after meat, but it was contumacy, not craving for meat, that unleashed God's just rebuke.

47. Not a single day passes during which he is not thrust into the thicket of temptations to gluttony. It is otherwise with difficulties related to sexual union; fortunately walled off by his monastic lifestyle from occasions of fornication, he had by and large vanquished

wayward sexual desires. But every summons to the table compels him to apply the golden mean, consuming no more and no less than necessary, neither caving in to indulgence nor stiffening into scrupulosity. A rare achievement indeed such exact and exacting temperance: hardly anyone can consistently avoid taking more food than health requires. An individual with such exquisite self-control is great and, as *magnus*, properly disposed to magnify the name of the Lord. Feeling spiritually stunted, however, he makes Peter's confession his own: "Lord, I am a sinful man." Howbeit dwarfish, he is entitled to magnify the power of God because Jesus, his mediator, elected him to be a member, still infirm, of his body. The prince of the apostles, blustering with bravado prior to the suffering of his master, warmed himself by the fire during the passion but was so frozen with fright that he thrice denied Christ—a denial that would have been quite prolonged had the questioning not ceased (S 135.7.8). The cocksure Peter fell ignominiously, his boasting exposed as bluff, because he presumed on his own strength. Like Peter, Augustine, priest by the will of God, labels himself imperfect; with his flock he, a sinner, strikes his breast, begging pardon from God (S 135.6.7). Again, like Peter, he can boldly hope for more grace, every day affording opportunity for more intimate absorption in the heart of the One who is love (P 138.21).

Chapter 32: Temptations from Scents

48. When pleasant odors are missing, he feels no desire for them, and, when available, he does not self-denyingly spurn them, yet this estimate of apparent indifference to scent-allurement, which stems from surface-consciousness, could be askew. Within the intricately complex mind may lurk pockets of potential darkness, undescried by his usual examen of conscience; the secrets of evil subconscious tendencies show their faces only in actual experience. If tested, he might betray subservience to fragrances; it would be folly for his unproved soul to rest complacent in the conviction that it was free of fault. In a life that is an ongoing trial (10.28.39), in which temptations unendingly assail the spirit, fragile human nature that rises can easily relapse. The old man is never wholly subdued; an insurrectionist crouches beneath, ready to overthrow the higher self. Drummed in by horrendous failings is one central truth of ongoing regeneration:

he cannot lean on the reed of fickle humanity; his unconditionally guaranteed one and only hope is the mercy of God.

Chapter 33: Temptations concerning Church Music

49. Musical sounds, unlike scents, raise some moral problems. In pre-conversion days he had been smitten by the pleasures of music till grace broke their sensuous yoke. At present when a well-trained precentor leads responsorial singing, he takes some delight in music since it is ensouled by the divinely composed psalms; yet he is not enthralled by the singing as such. Because melodies are enlivened by Spirit-inspired psalms, they deserve a place of reverence, becoming quasi-sacred also, with the result that in the ascription of honor he fears to sin more by defect than by excess.[69] Still, at times he apparently esteems these melodies too highly. No doubt the psalms, when artistically sung, set the heart aglow with more fervor than when simply recited.[70] Again, affective states are attuned to certain melodies.[71] Some melodies lend themselves to mourning, others warm to joy and exultation, others rouse a surge of triumph, still others convey impressions of the noble and sublime. The impassioned figures of music resonate with the feelings of the soul. Unhappily, he often became too absorbed in the melody as such; the music, instead of elevating the religious spirit, produced a lapse into a kind of musical intemperance. The melody insinuated itself as the principal source of delight; sense outstripping reason that grasps the words, the secular accompaniment usurped the primary focus proper to the sacred text. At the time he was caught up in the beauty of the singing, he was unaware that he was assigning precedence to the inviting chant, and only afterward, upon self-scrutiny, did he discern he had allotted priority to the sheerly aesthetic component; so he sorrowed over the minor fault.

On other occasions when, erring in the opposite direction, he acquiesced in the temptation of overseverity for fear of being seduced by sensuous delight, he nurtured the hope that all chanting would be banned in church services. He thereby found himself in company with the apparently spiritually safer course of St. Athanasius (295-373), the famous anti-Arian bishop of Alexandria, who enjoined the reader to sing the psalms *recto tono*, with little or no variation in melody, the singing prescribed being more recitation than chant.

Chant, on the other hand, cannot be discounted as a forcible instrument in moving the spirit. After baptism in Milan in 387, the antiphonal singing of the psalms and Ambrosian hymns impelled his leaping and bounding spirit to release of tears of joy mingled with gratitude and peace (9.6.14). Now, some thirteen years later, he still vibrates to the chanting, primarily uplifted not by the human melody but by the divine message. Clear and true singing acts as an affectively stimulating foil, religiously valuable because it musically highlights the inner wealth of the sacred psalms. He oscillates, sensitive to both claims, the one discarding music because of the peril of pleasure, the other ratifying chant because he himself has fed on its spiritual energy. Without adopting an irrevocable stance, since it is a contingent matter variously modified by local customs, he prudentially opts for the chanting of psalms in church; among the less devout the charm of the music heightens perception of the loveliness of the word of God. Yet if the chant touches him more than the sacred content, he has fallen into minor sin, not without its due penalty; and were he to foresee and so forestall such a fault, he would prefer to hear the psalms recited rather than sung.

Again, he divests himself of every appearance of finished sanctity. However skyey his aspirations as a shepherd of souls one with his flock in struggling for hegemony over appetites, he self-abasingly divulges a self far from confirmed in grace. He implores fortifying prayers from co-religionists who, having fought the good fight against the blandishments of music, empathize with his anxiety. Weep with me, he exhorts: share my sorrow over misuse of musical delight; weep for me: pray that I may tear off the mask of self-deception in regard to church music. So he calls on mercy to heal him of decline into misdirected joy in chant. At the core of this difficulty is the problem that is himself in the sense that execution does not always jibe with intention; desire to master beguilement is not always existentially elected. Failure to square execution with intention bespeaks a breach in his spirit that is a kind of malady. Augustine is surely not laboring to make a moral mountain out of a molehill. Whatever the quality of his actual virtue, his spiritual ideals are more elevated than the norms by which the mediocre Christian evaluates himself. Not content with half-measures, he brooks no compromise in what is nowadays called the pursuit of perfection. The problem that is himself along with its concomitant infirmity would have probably been treated as a peccadillo by ordinary fellow Catholics. However, while not in the least wrapping himself in a holier-than-thou mantle, he was enrolled as a monk in the hard school of sanctity practicing unremitting self-renunciation, purposing to become holy as God is holy, toiling to uproot every misguided inclination and its kindred spiritual sickness.

Chapter 34: Temptations Arising from Sight

51. Reversing the order of dignity by starting with touch, lowest of the senses, he ends with difficulties arising from sight, the noblest (10.35.54). Consoled that fellow Catholics in God's temple that is the Church will welcome his confession in a brotherly spirit, he once again remarks the disparity between woe here and joy hereafter, which he ingeminates under the blows of temptations, while sighing to be clothed in a heavenly body never to be ravaged by the wracks of time. His refined sensibility throbbed to many charming patterns vested in dazzling colors. Still, he cannot permit this gorgeous spectacle to distract him from primary focus on the sovereign good that is truly his personal good. The beautiful objects on which his eyes banquet are indeed very good since they form a complex, an order or universe of goods (13.28.43), but should they eclipse vision of the all-good, he will drift back into evil. On every side bewitching colors enchanted his eyes; the first fingers of dawn, then the emerging sunrise, the awakening of a day whose curtain-fall is portended by the rich crimson of the sunset; all day long life unfolded under the canopy of a pure blue sky; after a storm nature fanned out its spectrum of colors in a shimmering rainbow.

Moreover, numerous forms and figures win attention and elicit pleasure. A fight between two aggressive cocks accents the beauty of their wings, heads, and combs, along with their grace and dexterity (O 1.8.25;2.4.12). Again, compared to a man, an ape may at first blush look ugly, but, in fact, a simian is beautiful, with its own measure, equality, proportion, harmony, and unity: its body has its own limit or proper size and symmetry of parts constituting one whole organism (NB 14). Also fascinating is the lowly worm that exhibits a brightness of color with a congruence of parts; its skin shines in the light, its shape is nicely rounded, symmetrically arranged front and back parts harmonize, all for the purpose of maintaining the unity of the whole (VR 41.77). Unlike those of sound, delights of visual beauty clamor for recognition every waking hour; while at times he hears no singing, and less frequently all sounds cease in his environs, light suffuses him all day long. White is "the queen of colors," labeled primary because without it no colors can be seen. Light manifests itself constantly throughout the day, altering somewhat from morning to high noon to late afternoon, but, even when not directly observed, its intensity and brightness are always enticing. When it suddenly disappears, say, when he enters a cave-like cubicle, he longs for its return. So enfolded by light is he that lengthy isolation from it sorrows his heart. Love of light is an inescapable lineament of his physical and psychological ambience; an earth animal, he is necessarily also a light animal; light is his natural milieu, without which he feels disaffected.

52. Beyond and above the physical lies divine light that is truth, an inner wisdom by dint of which Old Testament leaders and patriarchs, although wholly blind or weak-sighted, descried paths of virtue decreed by prudence. Light illumined Tobit to instruct his son by word in the ten commandments and by example to illustrate the way of charity. Eyesight failing while seeing the inward light, Isaac did not bless his sons because he recognized them; rather, he recognized them as first-born and second-born by first blessing Jacob, then Esau. Out of reverence for the patriarchs, be it noted, Augustine declined to count Jacob's deception of his father Isaac a genuine lie; Jacob or Israel could not prevaricate since a true Israelite is without guile (S 89.5. CD 16.37). The apparent deception, a figure in the sense that lamb or lion is predicated of Christ, was not a lie but a mystery or sign: the skin of a kid goat that Jacob wore signified the sins of men borne by the Jesus whose saving death for sin won for man the blessing of the Father. Furthermore, the primogeniture belonged by right to Jacob because Esau had sold it to him for bread and lentil stew; and Isaac confirmed the exchange by bestowing his benediction on Jacob (S 4.15-6,22-3). Jacob in his old age, also afflicted with defective vision, was gifted by the light of God to predict the courses of the tribes headed by his twelve sons. His nearly sightless eyes could not project rays of light, but, lit up by divine light, his inner eyes radiated beams foretelling the lot of his sons' tribes. Too he mystically, i. e., by sacred sign, prefigured that the power of the descendants of Ephraim, the younger, would be greater than that of

Manasseh, the first-born of Joseph. While Joseph, depending simply on natural vision, urged Jacob to place his right hand on Manasseh's head and his left on Ephraim, the divinely enlightened Jacob insisted on the reverse, resting his right hand of blessing on Ephraim and his left on Manasseh.

Since this light is identified with God, who is supremely One, it is super-brilliantly one. Moreover, everyone who contemplates this light in prayer and loves it, i.e., bends his will to its norms, becomes one, spiritually and morally integrated (8.10.24), cured of disparate yet tyrannous pulls of lower desires. Again, all who become individually one in the One, it seems implied, become socially one, united by and in love with one another.

Whereas physically blind or near-blind lovers of divine light charting a path of charity marvelously read the present and forecast the future, spiritually blind lovers of the light of this world are swept down dangerous byways by the sweetness of corporeal-light pleasures. Physical light itself is not to be faulted; Christians praise God for its diurnal appearance and cessation, capitalizing on it in the manner melodiously recorded in Ambrose's *Deus creator omnium.* Rather than a temptation, it serves as a means of lauding God for exquisitely robing daytime (9.12.32); and at night light cannot play on eyes shut in sleep that soothes labor-wearied limbs. This mastery of light he thirsts for: to chant God's praises for light during the day, to be spared by sleep from its allure during the night. Thus upraised on wings of praise of God for light, day by day he works to fend off enticements that would slacken spiritual progress. In prayer his invisible eyes are blessedly unable to fasten on things of earth; he fears no earthly perils, for the light to whom he pleadingly looks upward will snatch his feet from the snare (P 24.15). Disengagement does not occur once for all but has to be renewed, for he often gets caught, at least superficially, in traps everywhere around, light and its charms being almost ubiquitous during every waking hour (10.34.51). Unfailingly ready for rescue is the divine guardian of Israel who, unlike man, never sleeps. Israel, which means "one who sees with God" (today its etymology and meaning are considered uncertain), symbolizes the Christian who, seeing God by faith, believes that Jesus died and rose from the dead and, sharing in that resurrection, will be, like Christ, spiritually sleepless or deathless (P 120.6).

53. Even diehard critics may be hard put to build a brief for the

contention that Augustine was feelingless toward art, casting a cold eye on art in every form. Lapses into faults of the eyes commented on in foregoing paragraphs were plainly occasioned by the various works of art on whose moral import he now reflects. His artistically sensitive spirit was stimulated, then led somewhat morally astray, not by artifacts as such, in which he analytically apprehended the hand of the human imitating the divine artist, but by excessive elaboration squandered on such works: too splendid apparel, shoes crafted out of the finest material, golden vessels shining with delicately cut figures on the cups, lavish paintings, and ornate statuary. No devotee of art for art's sake, he held that all art, including what we distinguish as liberal from mechanical art, is ordained to the human good, this, in turn, ordered to the divine good. Pointed toward a purpose beyond its own goal, art, as not grossly but properly utilitarian, is a means geared to moral ends. Indiscriminate refinement of functional objects transgresses the moral limitations due an artifact; it goes beyond the proper measure appointed by moral reason. Even artifacts shaped to honor departed parents and other family members, such as structures adorning grave sites, may be too ostentatious (P 48 [S.1]. 15). Makers of such works, going outward to inferior things, abandoned the interior man and thereby forsook the maker of these things in their pristine goodness. Moreover, by constructing what is immoderately ornamental, these artisans partially corrupted the naturally good things created by God. Contrary to some interpreters, Augustine is not arguing that misguided artists annihilated or utterly destroyed things made by God; rather, extermination here means corruption in the sense of adulteration or perversion. Objects like wool, silk, leather, gold, and stone are good in themselves and through human processing, but the luxurious artifacts into which they are fashioned are, as objectively immoderate, partial corruptions of the original good. Nevertheless, whatever animadversions one may lodge against his stance, it would seem wide of the mark to stigmatize it as Puritanical,[72] for the Puritans were infamous for their fanatical execration of any connection between art and religion—all pictures and statues, abominated as the recrudescence of idol-worship, were to be ruthlessly smashed; church after church in England and Scotland was reduced to rubble by these cultural savages. Yet while Augustine pronounced what is may be today deemed a sterner moral judgment on certain art-objects, criticism of his apparently too severe repudiation of the needlessly ornamental in functional objects might well be softened by closer attention to the context: he was censuring these seeming excrescences from the standpoint of an ascetic striving for perfect custody of the artistic eye. Moreover, it is not without moment that he lived in a scarcity economy, a sphere bereft of thousands of technical devices that today lend themselves easily to prolific artistic ornamentation. Hence, however questionable it may appear in accidentals, his basic provision remains sound: artistic beauty must be governed by a moral good that lays down limits to expressions of beauty in concrete functional objects like shoes and clothing. Nor has the point that artistically dazzling extravagance is ethically wrong been lost sight of in modern times. With the rise of new Croesuses in the nineteenth and twentieth centuries there flourished, especially prior to World War I, the morally repulsive phenomenon labeled conspicuous consumption, in accord with which the exorbitantly wealthy built huge estates cluttered with artistic bric-a-brac as a form of exhibitionism of monetary grandeur. Artistically remarkable no doubt, these constructions were condemned as horribly wasteful, far exceeding, in Augustine's idiom, the boundaries appointed by necessary use and moderation. Modern critics without the slightest tincture of the Puritanical deplore such artistic-economic works as grossly extravagant and morally questionable. Analogously, from an ascetic-aesthetic vantage point, Augustine reckoned certain artistic-functional objects of his day excessive in their needlessly glittering detail and showy intricacies.

God he hails as loveliest beauty of all in a hymn that serves as a sacrifice of praise, in which, offering himself to the Father, he commits himself to God alone. This sacrifice partially compensates for God's sacrifice for him, this enacted through the sacrifice of Jesus, whereby Augustine the prodigal son, returned to the Father (P 115.7). From another angle, Christ, the perfect priest, was the sacrificer, offering himself as the perfect victim so as to make man one with the Father as he, the Christ, is one with him (13.43.69. T 4.14.19). Able to lift up his *sacrifice* of praise because ransomed by divine sacrifice, he offers it as a sacrifice of *praise* because he sees that all beauty, including that of his hymn, descends from on high; all beauty is channeled through the artistic soul into dexterous hands that weave clothing, shape pottery, fashion goblets, and make shoes. This duplicates, however skimpily, divine beauty, for which he pines without respite, his sacrificial hymn of praise bodying forth never-failing longing for the breath-taking splendor that is his very own God.

God who is all beauty contains, ultimately, the standards by which beautiful artifacts are crafted and appraised. The rules of each art exist *omnia simul*, altogether all at once, transcending space and time, rooted in divine wisdom (3.7.14). Whether explicitly cognizant of these or not, artisans and admirers of artifacts rate them as beautiful in terms of an invisible standard that originates in the supreme beauty (VR 32.59-60; 33.62-3). Unfortunately, some, submerging themselves in external beauties, do not conform their moral behavior to the proper measure for using external beauties, which subordinates them to interior and transcendent beauty. Like the rules for numbers, rules of moral wisdom are unchangeable and commonly accessible to all (LA 2.10.29), but men bewitched by external beauties avert their gaze from these rules by fixing attention on externals. Bound in the execution of polished artifacts to obey the measure of beauty, they are, because not morally free, not constrained to conform to the norm of wisdom. Whereas earlier he viewed the beautiful as one with the moral good (2.5.10-1), here he differentiates the two: a creative artisan can be aesthetically superb but morally depraved; indeed the works themselves can be technically excellent but, if extravagantly textured, morally disordered (10.34.52).

If lovers of external artifacts were enlightened by prudence (LA 2.10.29), they would go no further, i.e., not immerse themselves in externals, but, assaying them from the perspective of the interior man, would husband their strength for God alone; as nothing but sinners, they would, through him, direct all toward him. Affixed by pure prayer and sound living on the One whose unity is a source of all true beauty, they would not un-one themselves and forfeit interior beauty by scattering themselves upon the manifold of external beauties, which are only passingly pleasing, the most savory soon seeming insipid, the most electrifying dull, the most ravishing disgusting (P 58[S.2].1). Although cleaving to the God to whom grace inextricably joins him, from time to time he is tripped up by beauties without merits, an ensnarement from which he is always set free not by merits but by mercy; mercy always before eyes that do not angle for outward approval but inwardly seek the blessing of the One who sees within (P 25[En.2].8). Not infrequently (10.34.52) he is caught by prepossessing artifacts and wonders of nature radiant in North African light, yet without fail mercy looses him: his fall is so slight that entrapment is imperceptible; on other occasions lapses seem spiritually stabbing because he is enamored of a beguiling sight from which grace alone can disentangle him.

Chapter 35: Concupiscence of the Eyes: Curiosity

54. The eyes also figure, even more prominently, in the second type of the triple concupiscence. While lust of the flesh, when channeled through the eyes, is fascinated by the lovely and bright in beautiful forms, lust of the eyes as such is triggered not by pleasurable objects but by the desire for personal experience usually bearing on strange phenomena. Curiosity, which, as the ape of science (2.6.13), parades as search for genuine knowledge, misguidedly craves knowledge not in order to learn but simply in order to be gain affective satisfaction; carnal in the sense that the curiosity-seeker pursues not truth as such but the feeling that certain objects arouse. It is called concupiscence of the eyes not restrictively but analogously; seeing proper to the eyes, called the principal agent among the senses because the most powerful, is broadly extended to other sensory functions. While it sounds gauche to say, "Hear how this shines" or "Taste how it glows," convention legitimizes the expressions, "See how this tastes" or "See how hard this is." Common usage betokens a similar role in seeing relevant to concupiscence of the eyes; concupiscence that is curiosity can be elicited in any one of the senses, but its appellation is confined to sight because seeing occupies the top rung among senses and is analogously applied to the operations of the other four. Strictures on curiosity do not entail devaluation of serious search for knowledge. Indeed, as we saw, curiosity is a kind of ersatz-studiousness. The curious man, avid about garnering information, attends to idle points, of no marked concern to him. His counterpart, the authentic knowledge-seeker, does focus on what concerns him, with this decisive qualification, to the extent that such knowledge will feed his soul and thereby enrich his cultural outlook, a posture sharply divergent from that of the curious who pounces on glittering scraps calculated "to turn him on."[73]

55. Unlike an earlier passage (2.6.13) setting curiosity over against proper zeal for knowledge, this section discriminates between ocular

concupiscence of the flesh and concupiscence of the eyes that is curiosity.[74] The curious gather satisfaction by fastening on objects from which pleasure-seekers would recoil in disgust. While victims of lust of the flesh chase after attractive objects in all five senses, those bitten by curiosity frequently, if not always, are attracted to the exact opposite of what is pleasant, hunting for the sensorially degrading not to inflict discomfort upon themselves but in order to relish the thrill of staring at the shockingly abnormal. A mutilated corpse from which men ordinarily shrink somehow captivates the curious, who endure the initial revulsion for the pleasure of feasting on the unusual. Oddly, in the dreams of the curious the allure of what is revolting fades, ceding place to a quiver of horror in the presence of a repellent image. Incongruously, the curious are frightened by a gruesome dream image over which they have no control, yet freely, with psychological but no moral self-control, they hurry to snatch a glimpse of a bloodstained, partially dismembered body.

Limitations of time induced by pressures of the apostolate dictate that he skip instances peculiar to the other senses. Diseased hankering after the strange send men flocking to theaters to giggle at freaks and stand open-mouthed before sword-swallowers and tightrope walkers (P 39.9.E 9.3; 120.5). In addition, certain individuals hunger after perverse pseudo-scientific data. Ostensibly bent on penetrating the causes of things beyond the pale of human investigation, they want knowledge for the sake of knowledge only in a skewed way since their primary interest is the personal satisfaction such unveiling of the inscrutable affords. More precisely, curiosity that is a simulacrum of science departs from genuine science on three scores. First, the curious person lays hold of objects simply for the pleasure he can squeeze from the cognition, always panting after a novel cognitive kick. Second, the mind in this vise is continually prowling for bizarre facts, the more sensational the better. Third, the spirit so devoured expects to reap knowledge without tears, by sheer inspection of events, the actual result being mere fragmentary information. On the contrary, authentic knowing for the sake of knowing is, first of all, objective, directed simply at uncovering the truth. Naturally, search that fructifies in discovery is accompanied by a sense of accomplishment; however heady, this affective compensation is secondary. Second, an authentic scientific mentality restricts itself to sober inquiry into the reasons that explicate puzzling data, with no

cultivation at all of the out-of-the-ordinary. Third, *studiosi*, realizing
that a royal road to knowledge is fantasy, devote long hours to
relative mastery of a province of learning, then labor to advance its
frontiers in theory and practice.

Hence underlying Augustine's avoidance of illicit curiosity was
pronounced esteem for authentic knowledge in all its reaches.
Though the bodily condition hampers acquisition of truth, man's
partial knowledge, he was confident, can achieve certitude (CD
19.18), with some opinions, however, never progressing beyond the
probable (GL 2.18.38). As noted earlier, he always retained a lively
inquisitiveness about natural phenomena, especially those related to
man. Medical men, so-called anatomists, examined by dissection the
limbs, veins, nerves, and other parts of the human body (AO 4.2.3).
He was abreast of the views of his day on central localization, the
three ventricles of the brain, and the sensation, movement, and
memory that they organically mediate (GL 7.18.24). Moreover,
monkeys and even lowly worms serve as apt subjects of scientific
inquiry (VR 41.77. NB 14). Again, as indicated above, knowledge of
the universe is transcendentally valuable because its workings reveal,
albeit faintly, traces of the face of the author of nature (CF 21.6. GL
5.16.34).

Given Augustine's respect for and cultivation of the scientific
outlook, it would seem inaccurate to read an anti-scientific tenor into
his caveat concerning the futility of scrutinizing natural occurrences
beyond the scope of human knowledge. Viewed contextually, this
thrusts not at genuine scientific inquiry but at the wildly speculative
posture that raises, in a flighty and perhaps fantasizing temper,
questions unanswerable according to the contracted knowledge not
only of late antiquity but of any period. Whatever the particular
questions, the style departs notably from the strategy of genuine
investigations; for the curiosity-ridden, tracking down knowledge is a
kind of game to be played offhandedly, whose main purpose lies in
stuffing a voracious appetite with the strange and, where perceivable,
the weird.

Akin to scurrying after disordered knowledge is lust of knowledge
for its own sake through magical arts such as necromancy, which
purports to unlock secrets of the life beyond; spiritism, which
communicates with demons to discern hidden personality traits; and
augury, in which demon-assisted adepts decode entrails of birds for

portents of the future (DC 2.24.37). Such techniques stripping away the veils shrouding past, present, and future enable the curious to be privy to truth off-limits to normal rational inquiries. Knowledge, usually pseudo-knowledge, promised by astrologers also victimizes the curious (DC 2.23.35-6); yet the information read out of horoscopes is not for perversely theoretical ends but for almost exclusively pragmatic purposes; only when the stars are propitious will businessmen travel or launch fresh enterprises (S 298.2). The distorting influence of curiosity impinges on even religion, or, rather, pseudo-religion, when individuals demand from God signs not to fortify faith or validate the mission of an apostle but simply in order to appease an insatiable appetite for the spectacular. God is summoned in a command performance to act as a celestial virtuoso who empties his bag of tricks solely for the squeals of delight of childish humans. Significantly, at the outset of his public career the God-man was externally exposed to and resisted curiosity that is a temptation of God. When Satan urged him to fling himself down from the pinnacle of the temple, so as to test divine power to bear him up, Jesus spurned the suggestion as an attempt to manipulate God into pulling off a miracle to evoke the oh's and ah's of onlookers (P 90 [S.2].7).[75] In accord with his wisdom God does of course work miracles not to feed human curiosity but to witness to the truth. Christ's miracles authenticated his claim to be the Son of God; belief in his divinity was irrefutably founded on divine signs he wrought. Since men can see a man but not God, God became man so that there would coexist in one and the same person what they see and what they believe (UC 16.34. S 126.4.5). Because Christ is still present in his body, the Church, the age of miracles has not ended; now less abundant, these divine wonders, especially through the intercession of martyrs and other saints, go on blessing the Christian community toward the further upbuilding of faith (CD 22.8).

56. His past life resembles a journey through a great forest, this symbolizing the darkness pictured earlier as a mass of thick leaves and branches blocking out the light (2.1.1). Happily, grace has felled many of these trees whose leaves hide dangerous traps or vices. Since his conversion the Lord strengthened him to cast off much darkness, in particular, to cut down many proclivities to curiosity. Here God is the God of his salvation not in the initial but terminal sense; as redeemed and restored, he hopes for the salvation to be bestowed

from on high, when all the elect from the beginning to the end of the world will each be rewarded with the precious denarius that stands for the rest of the everlasting sabbath (P 17.47; 37.28).

It would be foolish to aver that he had suppressed every inclination to idle curiosity—a noisy throng of such objects daily crowd around him. Still, he has uprooted the major sources of curiosity. He is no longer enslaved by theatrical spectacles, the quasi-childish games which adults play (1.10.16), and, after resistance to Vindicianus' and Nebridius' critiques (4.3.4-6), his encounter with Firminus finally convinced him that astrology was a sham science and therefore a bogus art, so much charlatanry that its callous professionals put no stock in its astral determinism (7.8.8-10). Deluded by astrology, he never fell prey to necromancy (broadly referred to in 10.35.55); no doubt at Saul's bidding a necromancer summoned Samuel's shade from the beyond, which predicted Saul's downfall and death (1 Sm 28.14-20), yet such practices are abhorred as sacrilegious (DC 2.23.35) because, along with spiritism and even astrology, these rites, as perverse sacraments of the overlords of the spiritual underworld, are orchestrated by demons (4.2.3).[76]

No longer vulnerable to dabbling in diabolically-rooted arts, he does experience temptations to request special signs from God, suggestions he accredits to Satan, because they are so subtly textured that they cleverly counterfeit impulses of the Spirit. Through the light and power of the king who governs the Church and his soul, through the vision of the fatherland of glory (P 37.28) chaste with the holiness of God, he beseeches the vigor to rebuff such temptations, driving even further away lust for special signs. However, these last lines may admit a somewhat different interpretation. Invocation of Jesus his king and the new Jerusalem to help distance himself from craving for physical miracles lays primary stress on the divine physician who produces eternal wholeness. The Jesus who assumes a body oriented to death in order to put to death eternal death prosecuted all his physical miracles to assure healing that will not pass away. Through visible temporals that are miracles was ignited and confirmed faith in invisible eternals. Augustine appeals to the heavenly homeland because healings accomplished in time are not stamped with timeless duration; death finally closed the eyes of the blind whose sight Jesus restored, and Lazarus raised from the dead was entombed a second time (S 88.1). After the ascension physical miracles were not worked in the same abundance. Still, although the dead do not rise, or the blind commonly see, or the deaf often hear, souls dead in sin are supernaturally revivified, and spiritual eyes and ears miraculously opened to the word of the Lord (S 88.3). While it may be temerarious to pester God for physical miracles, it is fitting to pray for the resurrection of the spiritually dead and the restoration of spiritual vision and hearing in the stone-blind and stone-deaf. Understanding that God will achieve what he wills in accord with his wisdom and love, he trusts that God has given, does give, and will give him light and power to align his with the divine will. An inflow of divine life urges prayer for others' spiritual healing; the upshot he commits to God's hands, confident that almighty love will work nothing less than the best.

This section describes Christ as king in three modes. First, as king triumphing over the temptation to hurl himself down from the pinnacle of the temple, he serves as a model for rejection of curiosity. Second, as priestly king (P 26[En.2].2), he underwent salvific death (P 115.3) which furnishes the grace to balk the lure of curiosity. Third, Augustine begs Christ his king for wisdom and power (P 26[En.2].2) to repel curiosity, regression into which may weigh in his disfavor when the King of kings comes to determine who will enter the kingdom that is the new Jerusalem.

57. Curiosity insinuates itself daily in countless petty events. While listening out of charity to an individual retailing unusual aspects of his neighbors' behavior or odd occurrences, he catches himself lapping up pleasure from the stream of trivia. Again, when, traveling by horseback, he is perhaps mentally composing a letter on some doctrinal question, his train of thought is broken by the sight of a dog panting after a rabbit–an incident akin to curiosity eliciting events in the circus he has routinely denounced in sermons. At times divine light leads him to vault from the beauty of beasts to praise of divine beauty. On other occasions he simply dismisses such a scene as a silly distraction, brushing it off as he might a pesky gnat. Where these two avenues are closed, however, he may let his guard drop and become diverted, losing his interior recollection, and, in faltering, it is his mind, not his horse, that is deflected from its proper course. Again, at home his attention is solicited by the dexterity of a lizard or spider capturing flies. The comparatively diminutive size of these predators does not diminish one whit the stimulus to curiosity. The exquisite

coordination of lizard and spider in snaring hapless prey turns his mind to God who wonderfully makes and administers the universe; natural events betokening laws of nature partially lift the veil from the all-beautiful face of the maker and director of nature (O 1.8.25; 2.4.12). The book of nature is written in the language of beauty; patterns point to the author of nature (S 68.6). Unhappily, he is not initially inclined to discern the hand of God in the workings of remarkably designed dogs, rabbits, lizards, spiders, and flies. Rather, at first his mind, swept away from religious reflection, is seized by vagrant curiosity. Certainly speedy rebound ensues upon beguilement; yet more preferable is staunch opposition from the start that forestalls the least tint of curiosity.

The allure of the curious, he frankly acknowledges, never stops chafing him. Nothing but divine understanding and forgiveness can avail in the teeth of the swarm of impressions that continually make incursions into consciousness. The enormous repository that is memory reluctantly houses numerous bootless thoughts, wellsprings of almost inevitable interruptions that short-circuit meditation. His intention in prayer is unwaveringly sound: to pour love into the always-open ears of his ever-understanding God; yet even while basking in his presence, curiosity-tinged trivialities crowd in, blunting concentration and effectively severing union with God.

Chapter 36: Dangers of Vainglory

58. Recognition of a fresh fault need not discourage, for mercy that unshackled him in the past can further liberate him in present and future. Praise goes up, first of all, for deliverance from self-justification, which is tantamount to self-glorification or pride, with its affiliated deficiencies, vainglory and *ambitio saeculi*. His parents, impressed by his precocity, pushed him to develop his astonishing potential, though his education strained their budget. However, as is not uncommon even among the less prodigiously endowed, legitimate aspiration for the outflowering of native capacities with its attendant self-esteem became gradually twisted into passion for self-exaltation. The flush of triumph upon winning a classroom contest is dramatic oratory was only one sign. Throughout his career self-love spurred him to outstrip colleagues. Roaming about for new fields of conquest for self-centeredness, he angled for the post of public orator

at Milan in which he officially lauded imperial figures like Bauto and the young Emperor Valentinian II in panegyrics that not only verged on but crossed the border of lying; these extravaganzas of praise were virtual instruments of self-praise, vouching that not God but self was number one. The miraculous rain of grace in the garden of Milan not only snapped self-forged chains of impurity but extinguished lust for earthly renown, which sprouted from love of self. Eradication of pride in the guise of self-justification disposed him toward the healing of secondary vices.

It was God who cured all his dread spiritual infirmities; once the saving death of Jesus ransomed him from corruption, his crown or glory became the infinite mercy of God. Charmed by interior delights in place of pleasures of flesh and eye and worldly ambition, he feasted on the God who was his sweetness, his brightness, his riches (9.1.1). Fear of just punishment had partly reined in his pride; indeed many times he had tasted the dust and ashes that are the eventual wages of pride. God had tamed his neck to the divine yoke, neck symbolizing a froward spirit; accepting the yoke or cross of obedience molded him into a spirit meek and humble; God literally made his neck meek by his yoke. In accord with Christ's promise (Mt 11.30), he is gratified that the yoke is not galling but gentle, as actually it always had been, but in his protracted ignorance, allied with his grotesque misrepresentation of Catholic truth and divine mercy, he had demurred at bending his neck to the yoke of God's loving command curbing the triple concupiscence.

59. Only the Lord does not fall victim to the lust to dominate that distorts a licit office of dominion into illicit domineering because he alone is *Dominus*, supreme and therefore not subject to a higher lord. One basal occupational hazard of a human lord is vainglory, self-glorification in a high station, which arises from love of the plaudits of men. So concretely entwined in the power of governance is the egoism of authority which is vainglory that Augustine worries whether he will be nettled by it his whole life long. Clearly vainglory is not without its delights, but the joy peculiar to it is ungraced, incommensurate with God's design, and therefore a zero joy. Vainglory harvests only pseudo-happiness that is actually wretchedness since it shuts out the God who is happiness itself. All outward glamour aside, greed for applause that is inwardly repulsive is one reason why men deny proper love and holy fear to God. By

abandoning God, the vainglorious are abandoned by God, who of necessity refuses grace to those whose arrogance flies in his face. God thunders, releases his wrath upon those infected with worldly ambition, causing the bases of the mountains, i.e., the hopes of the vainglorious exercising worldly power, to tremble (P 17.8).

Figures of authority, like bishops and civil officers, garner love and respect because of their dignity and service, and incite fear because of punishment levied for transgressing ordinances. While necessary, love and fear that ensue upon authority can be a source of danger because they may be treasured for one's own glory instead of being oriented to the Lord who alone is loved and feared for his own sake. Apparently sincere praises of men that ring in Augustine's ears may contrive traps of vainglory, deceitfully mimicking words of approbation to faithful servants. Bowled over by adulation, a bishop may easily slip into vainglory, craving satisfaction not in God's way of glory but in the cheating flattery of men, welcoming love and fear not for God but for self in usurpation of God. In this respect a vainglorious bishop images not God, likeness to whom a communal concord of charity conduces, but the devil, with whom he contracts a perverse fellowship in the punishment due vainglory. In his pride the devil ambitioned to make himself like or equal to the most high, striving to enthrone himself as Lord of lords (Is 14.13-4). His grab for absolute power repelled, he was unseated from his angelic perch and flung into the pit, where out of envy he schemes without respite to drag down with him men who will worship him as a surrogate deity. Whereas God requires service by obedience to his commands, the devil exacts obedience that is disobedience, imitation of his refusal to serve that encapsulates his revolt against God. Pride-infected and vainglorious, tools of Satan wander frozen in the dark, poles asunder from servants of God warmed and lit up by the fire of divine love.

The love and fear accorded authority issue in diverse social outcomes: either concord in charity or, by contrast, a consortium of punishment due uncharity. Ensouled, as it were, by the unholy spirit that is the adversary, the synagogue of Satan generates pride and the progeny of vices it mothers, whose prosecution is accompanied by a surface delight, which is actual punishment compounded of anxiety and unjoy.

Praying that the divine mantle will shield him from the Evil One, he identifies the whole Church, not the small band of disciples, as

God's little flock (Lk 12.32), little not in quantity but in humility: the people of God are spiritual toddlers (Mt 11.25) absolutely dependent on God's mercy. Helpless in themselves, they are clasped close as the personal family of the mother-Lord under whose wings tiny ones flee for safety from Satanic wiles. Not self but God being their boast, self-glory will be superseded by true glory. Any love enkindled among his flock toward Augustine the shepherd, he trusts, will be forthwith transmitted to God; in short, in loving Augustine, his people will love God. Any fear he may be compelled to evoke stems not from his human rank but from the Scripture, the foundation of his authority; the word that as bishop he is primarily commissioned to proclaim, explain, and, where necessary, lovingly enforce by sanctions of the Church.

At times a sinner praised for evil deeds is delighted by human approval instead of being fearful of divine reproval; tongues of flatterers bind sinners in the chains of their sins (P 9.21). However, pleasure in false praise is short-lived, counting for nothing before the divine tribunal, where it will be powerless to mount a defense against the negative verdict that banishes the person praised to punishment without praise. In a quite different setting an individual deploying authority, when lauded for his gift, may become more satisfied with the praise than with his God-dowered talent that arouses admiration, with the result that a less gifted praiser is more praiseworthy in the eyes of God than a vainglorious recipient of praise. The praiser rejoices in the work of God while the praised exults in the praise that is the human gift rather than in the divine gift eliciting praise. Apparently Augustine is recalling special marks of appreciation tendered by his people, murmurs of admiration along with clapping that an eloquent homily excited in their largely untutored hearts.[77] In these instances, as the praised vulnerable to the temptation of vainglory, he runs the risk of being less praiseworthy than the praiser. When vainglory creeps in, the less gifted praiser is blessed with more of the gift that is grace than the outwardly gifted recipient of praise.

Chapter 37: Difficulty in Detecting Love of Praise

60. Because he constantly preached and ministered to his flock, he was besieged by temptations to vainglory as his clients heaped praise upon him for his expenditure of himself. The tongues of praisers

functioned as a furnace purging his virtue of the dross of self-praise. Earlier he prayed for divine power enabling him to fulfill the stringent command of continence (10.29.40) and to reject lust of the eyes (10.31.45); here he begs for a richer outpouring of God's strength to conquer *ambitio saeculi*. His groaning is not that of flesh bewailing a temporal loss like the theft of a farm animal but a mournful cry induced by a wound of the heart (P 37.13); yet in private he has outwardly wept over the inward distress due to unrelenting pressure to savor self-praise. So meticulously does he pore over his conscience that he can usually specify without difficulty how far he is healed of this disease; still, perhaps concealed from his gaze are secret defects perceived by God alone. Stated simply, his problem lies in his inability to apply to love of praise the test that verifies the presence or absence of attachment to the pleasures of the flesh, curiosity, or love of riches. The criterion is this: men are certain they possess a thing without love when they relinquish it without sorrow. Deprivation of an object from which the mind claims detachment probes character; perturbation at loss proves that the presumed detachment was only illusory (VR 47.92). The measure of freedom from pleasures of the flesh and curiosity is the degree of equanimity maintained at their loss or absence, whether voluntary or nonvoluntary. Also calculable is the magnitude of the grip of riches, which are means for satisfying one or the triad of concupiscences. Wealth capacitates its possessor to gratify his penchant for luxurious living and easy sex; to travel far and wide in search of curiosities, or, in the absence of wanderlust, to fund an amphitheater at home, to buy political influence, and, when conspicuously displayed, purchase honor. Because wealth facilitates, not structures, worldly ambition, its hold on moral personality can be ascertained: voluntary renunciation of riches in whole or part enables one to discern whether he is master rather than slave of money. Unfortunately, no such test can determine whether love of praise is one's ruling passion since it is existentially impossible to survive, without psychological damage, wholly deprived of praise. Only unspeakably loathsome behavior warrants total absence of praise; a personification of iniquity is effectively ostracized by all. But this course of action is morally insane; a more stupid strategy seems hardly conceivable. Augustine is then required to live a virtuous life that entrains, as one unavoidable concomitant, human praise. Because it is practically absurd to live without praise, he cannot invoke the criterion of privation of praise to indicate whether he can function equably or forbearingly without it. Praise being concretely inescapable for the good man, he is without a concrete test for certifying that he is disengaged from praise. Augustine's hypothesis of social exclusion as a penalty for a notoriously vicious life is not an ivory-tower supposition of academic imagination but is verifiable in the abhorrence of certain communities for paroled pedophiles responsible for grisly rape-murders. The detestation directed at such beasts is a punishment of the severest sort. "No more fiendish punishment could be devised than that one should be turned loose in society and remain absolutely unnoticed by all the members thereof."[78] Collective revulsion in a small community toward a social menace is physically practicable; a monster denied all praise is not only cold-shouldered as a social zero but, the target of explicit dispraise, is also condemned as a social leper. Since existence barren of praise or life environed in dispraise is existentially unlivable, praise, whatever the moral problems it may cause or occasion, is an indispensable ingredient for surviving as well as thriving in society.

61. While acknowledging that praise unquestionably delights him, he believes that it is truth per se rather than praise itself that engenders this joy. From the truth he exposits primarily arises his joy; praise as such is only a secondary spring. Suppose two alternatives lie before him; one, a life of analytical madness that is radical error replete with praise; the other, a life of constant devotion to unshakable truth that is vituperated rather than lauded. Without hesitation he would opt for truth empty of praise rather than for untruth full of praise. Furthermore, were it possible, he would forgo all joy that arises from praise, yet, as a matter of fact grounded in ineradicable psychological law, praise does inevitably produce greater joy, and dispraise lesser joy.

Still, his conscience goes on nagging. Does this increase in joy consequent upon praise signal that subconsciously he is actually taking pleasure in praise as such? While reflection finds a plausible explanation for this upsurge in joy, it is not clear whether the justification proposed is a solid reason or a subtle rationalization. God has commanded continence and justice, both in the broad acceptation; continence whereby we withhold love from certain objects, and justice whereby we apportion love to certain persons. Strictly, justice inclines us to give another his due (LA 2.10.28); loosely, it moves us to give others the twofold love due them, enjoining love of neighbor in virtue of love of God. Like St. Paul, Augustine can aim at pleasing his neighbor for the other's spiritual profit, in view of his growth in salvific love (1 Cor 10.32-3); in particular, he can accept, without pining for, praise that implies his neighbor's progress. When a fellow Christian rightly praises a spiritual good in Augustine, the praiser rather than the praised develops spiritually. Praise enlarges Augustine's joy because the praise inductively proves that his fellow Christian is exhibiting spiritual advancement. What adds to his joy is not appreciation of his talent but recognition by a fellow Christian of the spiritual value of truth that he took pains to expound. Similarly, his joy decreases or some sadness steals in, not because he is deprecated by a fellow Christian but because his querulous neighbor reproves a truth he has misconstrued or mistakenly labels as bad what is, in fact, good. Further vindication of his averral that he is not fishing for praise is furnished by the fact that some praise pains rather than pleases. Misguided praise provokes a certain sorrow when it responds to personal qualities he rates unsatisfying or displeasing, or when marginal features are enthusiastically applauded out of all proportion to their actual worth.

Despite data marshaled in support of detachment, the matter remains inconclusive. Three possible misreadings of his own motives fuel doubt. Perhaps subjective self-satisfaction instead of objective truth serves as the crucial reason why the opinions of some please while the praise of others displeases him; the ground for his increase of joy may be not his fellow Christian's spiritual progress but the congruence of the praiser's view of Augustine's own opinion. Moreover, perhaps the basis of sadness or diminution of joy is not his neighbor's crude intellectual or moral misconception but the fact that the belief on which his groundless dispraise rests clashes with Augustine's own view. Again, perhaps an undetected self-centeredness underlies misgivings over ill-founded praise; he may be disconcerted because he himself is despoiled of praise when praised for the wrong reason. Turning a searchlight on motives that may be at bottom selfish leaves him uncertain; he cannot determine whether joy in rightly ordered praise and displeasure with misdirected praise are grounded in an authentic desire to objectively serve the truth in the spiritual enrichment of his neighbor or whether these are subjectively self-regarding, begotten by covert love of praise and disguised vainglory.

62. In one respect he knows less about self than God or, obversely, in one narrow area he knows more about God than self. More about God: he plainly grasps God's command to welcome the glory of God and the good of neighbor. Less of self: he cannot descry whether such joy in praise shows him self-seeking or self-denying. His apprehension of God is general and uninfluenced by affective strains whereas his cognition of self bears on contingent particulars of conscience hard to nail down with precision; his self-cognition may fuse with self-deceit spun off from pride which inclines him to believe he is rendering glory to God when, in fact, he is enwebbed in fine cords of vainglory. Furthermore, this tough-grained inquiry raises further questions about possible bad faith. If, in accepting praise, he is objectively concerned first and foremost about his neighbor's spiritual profit, why is he not as acutely stung by an unjust accusation against his neighbor as when a like charge is leveled against himself? In other words, an apparently ineliminable element of subjectivity colors and perhaps vitiates his value judgments. When a fellow Christian is wrongly inculpated, Augustine does not feel the same aching sense of hurt as when such a slander is hurled at himself. Conversely, when he himself is falsely maligned, he is torn with grief; when a fellow Catholic is so maltreated, he experiences no such pangs. Is his problem also a matter of ignorance, i.e., is it impossible for him to ascertain whether what he deems slander against his neighbor is equally malicious as that against himself? Rather, he next suggests, the subjectivity of his much stronger affective reaction to the slander against himself may set in relief a near-unpalatable truth: in believing that he draws delight from praise because this spiritually benefits the praiser, he is actually cocooned in refined self-glorification. A terrible thought strikes him: in purportedly unbaring his soul, he is not revealing but concealing the truth about himself; mind and tongue pressed into the service of the untruth are distorted into tools of self-deception. He begs his God to evict from his heart the moral madness that is self-deceit so that his own mouth not be "the oil of the sinner to fatten his head," the oil symbolizing false praise or flattery; that he be delivered from conning himself into the deceit that such praise is beneficial when it is really an astute brand of destructive self-praise. Far better were the wise virgins, representing the witness of a good or nondeceiving conscience (P 140.13).

Although Augustine leaves explicitly unanswered the question of his disguised self-praise, it seems safe to infer that his microscopic inspection of motivation certifies that his repeated efforts to stifle it were by and large free of infection by vainglory. Dogged labors to track down and exterminate the last remnant of self-deception would seem to existentially substantiate that for the most part he had dissipated the vicious cloud of unknowing that is self-delusion. Individuals sunk in self-deceit, and their number may be legion, pay only the scantiest, if any, attention to this moral crux, for they usually assume, without daily examen of conscience, that they are spared of this infirmity. Certainly no self-probing, however minute, and no vigilance, however tireless, will ferret out every last speck of self-delusion. According to a shrewd insight attributed to St. Francis de Sales, "Self-deceit will not wholly die till fifteen minutes after we die." In spite of Augustine's near-heroic striving to expel all that is carnal, one tiny tincture of vainglory may have soiled some of his apparently purely motivated actions. Slender filaments of vainglory that may have unobtrusively sneaked in, we may estimate, were comparatively minor, almost negligible in their impact on character. Moreover, it cannot be too much emphasized that Augustine is not scrupulous in the technical moral-theological sense. He is not huffing and puffing to inflate minor shortcomings into major faults, nor labeling innocent actions small sins. Far from canonizing the trivial, his strenuous, at times agonizing, self-scrutiny is enacted in an ascetic frame of reference keyed to holiness. He is endeavoring, with all the sensitivity of a tender conscience, to sincerely practice what he preached so often; he is bent on becoming a saint. While necessarily falling shy of the ideal of being perfect as is the Father (P 83.4), he is resolved to leave no stone unturned in his quest to obliterate every scrap of self-approbation, be it ever so oblique or buried deep beneath the surface of consciousness.

Chapter 38: Vainglorious Reproval of Vainglory

63. Renewed scrutiny trains the spotlight on his indigence: he looks spiritually impoverished and infirm. It would have been carnally painless to brush aside any real possibility of vainglory, but it turned out to be more enriching to undergo displeasure marked by groaning for healing. If he is lacerated by vainglory, his plea for mercy will win

medicine to close the wound, gladdening him with a tranquility after anxiety that the eye, i.e., the mind, of the arrogant knows nothing of. Sealed in the armor of self-importance, the proud man is untouched by a sense of insolvency of spirit; self-satisfied, he is encased in the illusory peace of his imaginary eminence. Augustine cannot relax his guard; the words and actions of public figures command such attention that they always incur the peril of temptation to vainglory, in which an individual values his private good as most excellent, instead of serving the common good, which is God, or that of the God who alone is supremely unexcelled. In his privatized pride a vainglorious individual homages the puny one that is self in place of and in defiance of the One that is God (3.8.16). So famished for renown is the vainglorious man that his quest for emblems of praise ironically demeans him; he wanders around like a beggar, bowing and scraping in order to amass honeyed compliments that are really no more than gossamer pittances of flattery.

The temptation to vainglory cowers even beneath resistance to vainglory. In rejecting vainglory, Augustine remains vulnerable, with apparent paradox, by the very fact he has rejected it. Often, not just rarely, the very scorn for the vainglorious renders a man more vainglorious. As one familiar saying has it, a man may become proud of his humility; correspondingly, an individual may wax vainglorious over his dismissal of vainglory. Admission that he is vainglorious about his seeming reproval of vainglory implies that, all along, his contempt for vainglory was no more than specious; glorying in contempt for vainglory evidences that his despisal was only pseudo-contempt. A man vainglorious about lack of vainglory really does not lack vainglory, just as an individual proud of his humility can hardly be esteemed a paragon of radical humility.[79] Once more Augustine is unable to unequivocally draw a fine line between the presence and absence of vainglory. So infinitely insidious is man's capacity for self-deceit that he can vainly glory in freedom from vainglory; glorying in his super-virtue converts victory over vainglory into a vehicle for vainglory.

While Augustine does not establish beyond all doubt that he is not kidding himself into believing himself unvainglorious, his austere conscientiousness is one valid indicator, to repeat, that he was essentially liberated from vainglory and unvictimized by essential self-deception. Without question, marginal vestiges of this bete noire may have lingered on in his reception of praise, without adulterating his essential emancipation. It is impossible to pinpoint how humble and by extension how free of vainglory one is; at a certain juncture the matter must be simply left in the hands of God; excessive analysis may subtly mislead the self-scrutinizer into becoming proud of his progress in humility.[80] Perhaps slight tinges of the Pharisee persist in even great saints; the inclination to thank God that one is not like the rest of the men dies a very slow death, and, along with this propensity to pride, its twin, the virus of self-deceit, may cling to life. In sum, Augustine's unsparing frank investigation of the likelihood of self-delusion persuasively establishes, without strictly demonstrating, that he had largely overcome self-deceit. Such tenacity of spirit absolutely trusting in cleansing mercy could hardly be cankered with dishonesty or near-totally duped by vainglory.

Chapter 39: Peril of Self-Complacency

64. A vice bearing affinity to vainglory is self-complacency. While, like the victim of vainglory, the spiritually smug individual is gratified with himself, he differs from his vainglorious kin in one notable respect: he is not at all interested in accumulating tokens of praise. Wrongheadedly self-pleased, the complacent individual displeases God in one or more of five ways. First, he may feel contented with an evil quality he mistakenly esteems good; e.g., he may credit himself with judicious firmness when, in fact, he is ferociously obstinate. Second, he may congratulate himself for, in effect, gifting himself with what is actually bestowed by God. Third, should he trace his virtues to an ultimate source, he appreciates them as the outflowering of his own merits. Fourth, granting that his virtues are effected by God, he does not socially rejoice in these grace-dependent strengths; somehow he internally appropriates or privatizes his virtues: they are his and no one else's, unique to himself. Fifth, as a consequence, disconcerted by like virtues operative in others, he becomes envious because they are approximating riches that constitute prosperity of his spirit (3.8.16). With a realism learned in the school of hard knocks that involve daily struggles against multiple outbreaks of pride of life, Augustine expects to buckle again and again yet stays sure that the Father of mercy will be ever at his side cleansing his sores.

Chapter 40: After Brief Recapitulation Intimate Union in Prayer

65. After rapidly reviewing some features of his memorial search for God, he reflects on special loving touches of the divine presence. Walking with him as his ever-present companion is God, the truth whose luminous counsel teaches what to avoid (objects of triple concupiscence) and what to seek (sensory things pointing to their maker). He first addressed questions to the material world, each denizen of which disclaimed divineness; turning inward, he verified that his soul neither as animator nor as source of sensation can be identified with God (10.7.11). Next, adventuring in the profusion of memorial contents exciting awe (10.8.12-5), he saw that without God, the life quickening his life and the light of his mind whose rays of truth instruct him (10.24.35), his memory could not have differentiated these objects, each of which was causally derived from God, none of which was ontically one with him (10.25.36-26.37).

Dialectical probing (10.10.17) defined objects peopling his inner terrain, rating them according to their ontic standing: material objects occupying a lower rung, passional appetites, and numbers, along with other notions. Within he interrogated, i.e., dialectically examined, impressions of material objects to determine their makeup; in other words, his inner self or mind distinguished the specific objects of the sensory powers (10.7.11) Above, when attending to the various excellences of things, he is simply recognizing the scalar diversity of sensory powers: the eye is superior to other senses (10.6.8). Augustine's self was intertwined with these objects insofar as he distinguished them within, sheerly by memory; without actually smelling, he marked off the fragrance of a lily from that of a violet (10.8.13). Moreover, he recalled the sensory ambience of certain past actions (10.8.14). In the continent of memory he marvelled at mountains and seas and stars (10.8.15); other things he stored away for future pondering (10.8.14); still other objects, not sensorially available, he dug out of the recesses of memory—definitions in the liberal arts and numbers (10.10.17-12.19). However enormous its power engirdling so much and so many, his memory is not commensurate with the mind of God, for, unlike his mutable and fallible self, God perdures changelessly in sovereign identity. Moreover, he is the light in virtue which Augustine's memory operates, the radiance through whose shining he can grasp objects, the truth deputing him to judge whether things exist, to fix their definitions, and to appoint them higher or lower ontic worth: superior to existence is life, and to life, sensation, and to sensation, reason, and to reason, the light or truth guiding all judgment (10.10.17).

As often as he can, Augustine, faithful to his own counsel, meditatively listens to his Lord teaching what paths lead to union and what he commands as a means to union (10.29.40), a fusion of hearts that bursts into the rejoicing in truth that is happiness (10.23.32). Contemplative in temper, a lover of solitude (10.43.70), he was enwrapped in pleasure when he joined his soul to God, special insofar as it afforded a kind of short-spaced spiritual vacation from the overwhelming load of episcopal duties, with its inescapable hourly round and daily grind of never-stopping demands. Such uninterrupted colloquy in which God's direction bathes him in serenity is a priceless garden of holy leisure. There all the dispersed fragments of self are magnetically drawn into unity by the One (11.29.39); there he adheres undistractedly to God, the whole of his being intensely centered on the rest that gives him rest; there limited but real, muting busyness and restlessness, is a haven wherein divisions are knitted into harmony. This touch of God's calm through recollection was a regular, apparently a daily, occurrence in Augustine's prayer life. Very frequently, breaking away from pressures of office, he would retire within to repose in the divine arms, delighting in the inward peace that insulated him from the incessant clamor of particular appointments (P 41.9). At times, however infrequently, ordinary union was elevated into extraordinary union; when God introduced him into an extra-special communion, nourishing him with a sweetness so far beyond the usual that he is at a loss to describe it. If this experience of super-union and super-joy were perfected in him, i.e., if this super-communion became constant and normal, he would be interiorly living a life that would not be this life; in other words, were the experience protracted and continuously operative, he would be living a life not of this world: his existence would be quasi-heavenly.

At first glance this passage appears to harbor mystical chords or overtones. The portrayal of heightened spiritual experience seems to reproduce in smaller space the apparently mystical flight in the vision of Ostia (9.10.23-6), iterating the claim that if the moment of illumination could be indefinitely extended, it would merge with the sempiternal intuition of the divine enjoyed by the blessed. Such intimacy of union, fully developed and ripened, would be utterly outside this world, and, in effect, quasi-celestial. Here may be an intimation of a touch of the Lord that is consanguineous with the clasp of the soul by God reserved for heaven. According to one judicious commentator,[81] these few compact lines are strictly mystical in character. The contemplation is infused because, not growing from ordinary recollection, it irrupts from direct divine intervention betokened by the words, "at times you make me enter," into a higher state. Second, its passive feature is evident in the expression, "a most extraordinary affective experience in the core of [his] being", accompanied by an ineffable far-above-the-human sweetness. Nevertheless, because Augustine's comments are so abridged, it is hard to precisely specify whether these elevations of spirit were strictly mystical. The description of the Ostia vision seems to unmistakably join his transient intuition and the abiding heavenly intuition: indefinitely prolonged, that love-packed moment would in essentials become one with the beatifying vision of wisdom (9.10.25). However, this passage only vaguely states the nexus between divine union here and sempiternal absorption hereafter. If his affective experience and its attendant joy were perfected, he says, they would properly pertain to the next life. Since Augustine does not explicitly and unequivocally declare that he was raised to the summit in his life, his report may be reasonably taken to mean only that the richness of his union and its affiliated delight distantly foreshadowed their supernal counterparts. Surely, frequent seeking of God is not uncommonly rewarded with foretastes of heaven like lights and touches of delight from above that fall below the mystical plane. Moreover, the words, "you make me enter into an extraordinary affective experience," do not necessarily carry a mystical connotation. It is God, the all-generous giver of all gifts, Augustine stresses, who lifts him up to an astonishingly exalted union of delight-penetrated love. Similarly, an extraordinary affective experience need not be categorized as mystical; here the indispensable note of passivity does not seem undeniably present. Warmth of spirit kindled by soothing inward kisses from the divine spouse has been showered on spiritually advanced souls who have yet to cross the border into infused contemplation. Granted, it is possible that here Augustine is recording a genuine mystical experience; yet since his key phrases may be read as no more than allusive, no incontestable reason demands that his lines be assigned a strictly mystical tenor. In a word, the data for a mystical occurrence seem somewhat soft and tenuous rather than hard and solid, thus excluding any real possibility of incontrovertibly detecting a mystical encounter.

At any rate Augustine was unquestionably blessed, from time to time, throughout his life with touches of intimate communication that bespeak prayer of a higher order, whether or not codified as strictly mystical. However, the uplifted state of prayer lasts for no more than a short spell, and he sinks back to earth, engrossed in material concerns. Though implicitly oriented toward the heavenly, his heart is pulled downward by weights of matter, i.e., objects of this-world interest (P 41.10). Once again he is submerged in routine episcopal affairs, so yoked to these that he often weeps over his condition. Yet tears effect no inner release; the freer the tears, the tighter the vise clamping him to the earthly. His office high in dignity weighs him down with cares low in dignity. Here below he lives but does not want to; there above he wants to live but cannot. In each instance he is unhappy: here below actual life without the desire fulfilled; there above actual desire without the life desired.

Chapter 41: The Triple Concupiscence a Barrier to Contemplation of God

66. Following the brief digression on the heights of prayer to which he has been intermittently raised, he concludes his quick summary of his analysis of his spiritual state. He probed into soul-diseases by considering the difficulties of totally overcoming the threefold concupiscence: lust of the flesh, including temptations from all the five senses (10.20.41-34.53); lust of the eyes or curiosity (10.35.54-7), the pride of life, here in the specific form of vainglory (10.36.58-38.63) and complacency (10.39.64). Crying out for healing, he invokes God's right hand, the grace that is strength (P 17.36), to reinvigorate him. Next, he shifts to the period preceding his spectacular conversion, when he was endeavoring to mount even in this life to some vision of God but, lacking spiritual purity, could not obtain sustained union. While still subjugated by two concupiscences—he simply could not practice continence and was gnawed by

worldly ambition—he was capable of climbing intellectually to the perception that God was the light above his mind, whose brilliance filled him with awe, but since he languished in the region of darkness, he could not spiritually maintain his grasp of "I am who I am" (7.10.16; 17.23). His venture at vision frustrated, he was thrust back, so that his soul was tremulous with fear like that of Peter who, after initial hope, became frightened and sank into the water. Augustine too, in his dread of perishing, plaintively besought divine help. With all his infirmities, he was not the blind slave of pitiless pride; feeling empty because of indigence, pained by tribulations, he pleaded for release from the two concupiscences (P 30 [En.2.S.3].10). Prior to his conversion, Augustine was pinned down by lust of worldly ambition because, paying no heed to the supreme truth illumining seekers of his counsel, he was dominated by avarice in the broad sense, prideful greed eager for its own private good, a craving for all which ironically hazards losing all (3.8.16). Yet his avarice was oddly mitigated; while his arrogant attitude of grab set his paltry one in opposition to the One that is God, he also longed for communion with the truth ruling all things. In short, intellectually, by rational ascent, he could reach God as truth, but morally, in terms of prideful greed, which lay at the root of his capitulation to two of the concupiscences, he could not conform himself to God's truth synonymous with fruitful living. He never ceased trying to possess God, but on his own terms, wanting to retain, along with God, a lie. In this broad acceptation a lie signifies a mode of living which fails to comport with the standard ordained by the sovereign truth, a respect in which every sin is a lie, for the sinner wills to live contrary to the truth of the divine will. Every sin wears a lying countenance also because the happiness promised is a fraud (CD 14.4). Moreover, a sinner patterns himself not after God but the devil, the father of lies, becoming like his model, a grotesque mimicker of God, each of whose sins perversely images an attribute of God (2.613).[82]

Hence, in ambivalently opting to see the truth that is God and live a life that is a lie, he severed contact with God in the moral dimension because God cannot demean himself to be possessed simultaneously with a lie. In other words, he might ache to reach God by rational ascent, but, as a living lie, he could not become contemplatively one with the God who is truth. Not that God icily withdraws; rather, it is impossible for the truth to coexist with a lie; God can no more wed truth to a lie than square the circle or, perhaps more aptly, delight in the father of lies.

Chapter 42: Demons: False Mediators.

67. Augustine continues to recall the circumstances prior to this moral conversion when he agonized over the problem of overcoming alienation from God. Some in his predicament cultivated demons by engaging in rites that were part and parcel of magical arts (P 96.12). Indeed many, apparently genuinely aspiring to strip off their sordid garb of sinfulness and candidly conscious of spiritual helplessness, were drawn to prophesying and magical rituals that were actually manipulated by demons. Deliberately hankering after visions, they besought illumination from pagan prophets reportedly gifted with prodigious insight into personal destinies. Because these visionaries were counseled by evil spirits, the curiosity of the seekers exposed them to illusions fashioned by demons. In this case an illusion is not simply an error based on a mistaken reading of a phenomenon; it consists also in being made the butt of deceivers. Earlier Augustine had been gulled by illusions manufactured by Manicheans out of their fraudulent claims of austerely rational certitude (6.4.5). Here Neoplatonic thinkers and their epigoni are reduced to playthings of demons who concoct a fantastic brew of truth and untruth.[83] In the pedigree of Porphyry[84] they permitted theurgy as a means of gaining access to the succor of demons. By and large highly refined, they considered their minds the key to fulfillment, simply esteeming themselves already substantially healed. Like demons, radically self-seeking (CD 14.4), these proud minds bear a resemblance to the hearts of demons. Each is assimilated to the object it loves; as a man submerged in sensual pleasures takes on the likeness of a cattle (T 12.11.16), so a person craving his own private good as supreme wears the twisted likeness of a petty false god. Analogously, rebellious angels are even more deformed; created to be God's highest images, they chose to become his horrible parodies. Similarity in self-adulation bonds the proud and demonic as kindred spirits in a sort of society of the proud; self-exaltation is the common factor fusing them into a vicious friendship (CA 3.11.16), joining them in a concord of discord, a communion of anti-saints.

Demons, it was believed, inhabited the atmosphere and therefore were designated powers or princes of the air (T 13.12.16). Worshippers of demons implored purification, freedom from spiritual misery, by means of these super-earthly powers placated through the potency of diverse magical practices. They were searching for an intermediary that would couple a divinity exempt from imperfection with their fault-stained selves. Unfortunately, the pathetic truth was that they were homaging only a pseudo-mediator, Satan, who, as the moral essence of duplicity, hoodwinked his disciples by transforming himself into an angel of light (S 301A.2). Always the caricature of the divine, Satan accomplished for the propagation of the lie what Jesus worked for the fortifying of true faith: he was transfigured, but his vesture of light was a bespangled costume camouflaging the prince of darkness. As a fake angel of light, he mockingly copied the true mediator who is the light of the world. Now, a true mediator, an in-between reconciling God and man, must be, like God, deathless and sinless, and must be, like man, mortal, and, if sinless, identified with man's sinful condition. If simply man, a mediator would be far beneath God and, if simply God, infinitely remote from man; in neither case could he act as mediator. The devil, however, was an impostor who, pretending to be the authentic mediator, played the role of a pseudo-God-man. As a monstrous sinner, he shared the sinfulness of man. As an angel untrammeled by physical flesh, he was a superhuman being, deceptively Godlike because not clothed in a body programmed to die. As sinful, he resembled man; as immortal, he counterfeited resemblance to God. Although physically deathless, he was not spiritually deathless; although naturally superhuman, in the line of the supernatural his sin warranted the penalty of the unending death of self. Whereas those who tread the path of the humble savior are quickened by his divine life, those who share in the pride of the devil are destined to eternal death.

Chapter 43: Christ Jesus the True Mediator

68. While many of its analytically argued tenets were compelling, Neoplatonism proved ultimately disappointing because its limited conceptual apparatus and existential aids could not assure attainment of its end, blissful union with the One (7.21.27). Its theoretical agenda was excellent: emigration from the exterior to the interior, then ascent to, capped by union with, the One. However, its inviting

scheme did not work in practice. After broadly describing the region
of divine peace, it failed to furnish a detailed map for actually arriving
at this goal. At the root of the Neoplatonists' inadequacy lay not
exercise of reason but reliance on reason alone. From trust in the self-
sufficiency of the human germinated a self-exaltation to the
quasi-divine, an arrogation to the self of power beyond its reach.
Augustine amended the radically rationalist and salvifically ineffi-
cacious posture of Neoplatonism by averring dependence upon
supra-philosophic authority and by committing his mind to supra-
rational faith in divine revelation in which, after the example of
Christ, humility supersedes pride. Thus did he discover a concrete
route to climb and cleave to the divine: Christ is the way to the
Father, the undeceivable truth that cannot deceive men (J 22.8). The
foregoing remarks about the Neoplatonists' nonpractical approach
have to be qualified; some did recognize the need of, and actively
pursue, extra-human support, but, unhappily, through magical rites
that are perverted sacraments (10.42.67). For Augustine, Christ was
the way from which course light and life, in particular, through prayer
and the sacraments, especially the Eucharist, which mystically represents the salvific death on the cross. Appropriately, in response to
a resurgence of interest in or practice of magical invocation of
demons stimulated in part by Porphyry's writings, Augustine re-
emphasizes the pivotal role of Christ as the one true mediator. In his
mercy, called secret because hidden in the depths of transcendent
wisdom, God commissioned Christ to mediate between God and
man, teaching by lived-out lowliness that the way to the Father is one
of humility. He is the true mediator because he alone is truly both
man and God. With man he shared mortality, human weakness, and
possibility of death, but sans all vestige of sin; Jesus came in the flesh,
i.e., in the likeness of sinful flesh (T 12.10.17), but not in sinful flesh
since he was utterly immune to all sin (J 41.5). With God he shared
righteousness, absolute sinlessness, and, on his divine side,
immortality. The true mediator was sent to dispense life and peace; as
mediator, he earned the wages of justice that is godly life and peace.
Consequently, through justice streaming from God he put death to
death, wiping out all the inward death of sinners whom his healing
restored to righteousness. He nullified the eternal death due sin, with
the guarantee that temporal death following upon the first sin would
also be robbed of its victory. He killed death by laying down his life:

proneness to death was a condition *in forma servi* (S 279.8), which, as mediator, he held in common with men. Saints of the Old Dispensation were blessed with a real faith, though only vaguely formulated through prophecy, in the passion of Jesus by which he would reconcile man with God. Ps 109 plainly alludes, it seems, to the torrent of sorrows from which Christ of the passion will drink: "he will drink from the torrent on the way" (P 123.7); and Isaiah foretold the passion when he wrote that Christ was led like a lamb to sacrifice (J 50.2). It is not simply as God that Christ is mediator, for, on par with the impeccable God infinitely removed from man, he cannot be grasped by man (P 134.5). In order that man ascend to God, God must first descend to man; before man can be divinized, God must be humanized. Neither as God nor as man but as God made man does Christ redeem man, the mediator reuniting alienated man to the Father (En 33.10). As mediator, Christ is God with the Father and man with men (S 47.21).

In another perspective, the doctrine of salvific mediation emerges from contrast of the old and new Adam. The old Adam ushered in the reign of death, in which man, veering off on crooked paths, was plunged into darkness. The new Adam is the wellspring of new life, in which the redeemed abundantly thrive, walking the way that is Christ, and illuminated by the light of truth that is Christ (E 190.2,8). As God, the Word is the former, creator, and maker of man; as God-man or mediator, he is the reformer, recreator, and remaker of man (J 38.8), reforming the old Adam's tarnished image, recreating man in truth, remaking him in new life.[85] This implies that Jesus does not only provide the way, the truth, and life; he is the way, the truth, and the life: the mediator "does not simply build the bridge" to God but "is himself the bridge."[86] Not merely pointing out the way, he is the way, not just stipulating prerequisites for new life, he is the life; not simply propounding the truth, he is the truth.[87]

69. However towering its vista of the transcendent and delicately nuanced its argument, the Neoplatonic account of God is affectively and existentially truncated. There is not a single fiber of genuine love in the God of Plotinus. Although eminently good, the One from which all else emanates is not the God of love. No greater praise of love than this can be discovered in all the other pages of Scripture (EJ 7.4), and, from an affective standpoint, no greater praise of God is conceivable: he alone is infinite love. The love of God is a triune love,

Father loving his Son in the Holy Spirit, the Son loving the Father in the Spirit, and the Holy Spirit loving Father and Son; the three-personed total possession of the divine nature is a communion of love (EJ 7.6). It is God who first loved man; out of love he fashioned man, out of love he re-fashions man. So prodigal was the Father's love, (which Augustine signalizes by addressing him as "good Father," for love is rooted in goodness) that he did not spare his only Son but handed him over for sinners; this done out of charity whereas Judas handed him over out of perfidy (EJ 7.7). Christ enshrined in his own life the hallmark of love he stresses: "No man has greater love than this that he lay down one's life for one's friends" (EJ 7.7). As simply equal to God, the Word could not be mediator; so from the heights of the Godhead he came down to the inferior region of matter, took on flesh, and *in forma servi* became obedient to death on the cross. Canceling by his blood the debt-laden charge against man, he bonded together man and God (P 103.8). Christ was free among the dead; free, because living among sinners in the likeness of sinful flesh, he alone was utterly immune to sin; among the dead, because slaves of sin are spiritual corpses. It is the ransoming love of the free Son of man that frees men from their sins (Jn 8.36). Divinely alive and free, he dwelt among the dead because, alone among the dead, he had the power of laying down his life and taking it up again. Free among the dead, he freely laid down a life that no one could take from him, and he could revivify, where and as he freely willed, his flesh that was destroyed as a temple by his enemies (P 47.5).[88]

In and by his death he was both victor and victim. As victim, he freely offered himself as a sacrificial offering (T 4.14.19). His self-immolation effaced the debt formerly held by the devil against men. Exteriorly conquered by death, he interiorly conquered evil; his death as victim made him victor over sin and the devil; thus he was victor because victim.[89] His gruesome death was a glorious triumph for and liberation of man (PMR 2.30.49). Moreover, as the mediator reconciling man to God through his sacrifice of peace, he was both priest, the offerer of sacrifice, and the sacrifice, the victim offered. As mediator, he remained one with the God to whom the sacrifice was offered, and he made one in himself the men for whom the sacrifice was offered (T 4.14.19). He was priest because sacrifice: since he freely offered his body as the flesh of sacrifice, he acted as a priest. The immolation was analytically prior: first, he freely offered himself as victim, as body for sacrifice; then, since it was he who made the offering, he functioned as priest. Christ's triumphant abjection transmuted men from slaves of sin into adopted sons, a liberation he accomplished as mediator: as God, he was born of the Father; as man, he assumed the form of a slave, surrendering his life as ransom for many. Never for one moment forfeiting the divine nature possessed as the only-begotten Son, he fully shared in lowly human nature, going down as God so that man might go up to God (E 104.4.10). He who was God became man in order to make those who were men God (S 192.1); or, in a formula commonly attributed to Augustine, God became man so that man might become God; *Factus est Deus homo ut homo fieret Deus.*[90]

So Augustine's hope is fortified by Christ who as mediator is priest and sacrifice. Christ's universally salvific death can banish all the diseases, all the remnants of his vices, for Christ's wounds continuously plead with the Father for the healing of Augustine's wounds. Later he capsulized his existential spiritual theology: "Christ is my origin, Christ is my root, Christ is my head" (CALP 1.7.8). Christ is his origin, the primal source of his deified life as a Christian; his root, the principle of the vital sap or grace that supernaturalizes his actions; his head, the light and directive power of his shared divine existence. Without this origin, root, and head, he would have been denuded of all realistic hope, flung into a pit of unending enchainment to vice. But with and through Christ all his intransigent infirmities, especially those of the triple concupiscence, can be cured, for the power of the medicine that Christ channels to men produces, because divine, the humanly unproducible; pride, avarice, wrath, and impiety can all be definitively healed by the humility, poverty, patience, and charity of the Son of God made man (AC 11.12). Had there been no incarnation, Augustine might have plausibly deemed it inconceivable that the Word infinitely far off could be united with man; such an apparent impossibility would have induced hopelessness over the impossibility of breaking out of his sin-suffused malaise. However, divine love enfleshed in Jesus and enunciated in his freely offered immolation supplies the humanly unthinkable medicine for all ills of soul. His death was doubly ineffable, at once the holy instrument of exacting divine justice and the epiphany of infinite mercy. Only in the mystery of the God who is love does Augustine reach a partial answer to the death of Jesus in love that saved the universe from being a living hell peopled by slaves buried in desolation and desperation due their depravity.[91]

70. When terrified by his sins and overwhelmed with a sense of wretchedness, he seriously debated within whether to forgo active ministry and consecrate himself to God in solitude.[92] Perhaps too the relentless pressure of daily work that constituted such a taxing load, along with inward and outward trials, especially vicious attacks of enemies within and without the Church, strongly urged him to take wings like a dove and companion with other solitaries in the desert (P 54.8).[93] Such an attraction is not unparalleled in the history of the Church. His compeer, St. Jerome, opted for a life of solitude for a while in the Holy Land. Some 1400 years after Augustine St. John Vianney (1786-1859) embarked on four aborted efforts at withdrawal form his apostolate as curé of Ars to a life of near-total silence and prayer, the first attempt at flight occurring around forty.[94] As the final decision of John Vianney to prefer the active to the contemplative life was no doubt the fruit of intense prayer, so it was with Augustine centuries before. Through divine light he perceived that, however grinding his exertions, they were necessary for the sustenance and growth of the Church. Were there no workers travailing to bring forth children in the Church, contemplatives themselves would never have been born to sempiternal life (E 48.2). Moreover, solitude is hardly exempt from all dangers. Solitaries seem particularly susceptible to temptations of idleness; in any case, no matter how elevated the ecclesial vocation, the devil is always roaming about trying to set traps (E 48.2). Again, lights from prayer along with experience with refractory human nature in all its guises had hammered home that no earthly community, however noble its rule, verged on an earthly paradise, so that to those living in solitude the well-known lines are also pertinent: "To live with the saints above, / Ah, that's eternal glory. / To live with the saints below, Oh, / that's another story." Specifically, it was not lost on him that some members of a contemplative community exercise others in patience, for in every association some bad brethren are unavoidably present (P 54.9). Furthermore, trenchant insights into the mystical body convinced him that because he was a member of the one body under the one head, he partook of the rest of the solitaries just as they shared in the fruits of his ministry; they were engaged in apostolic activity with him while he enjoyed the oasis of solitude in them (E 48.1).

The force of 2 Cor 5.15 ignited a renewed confidence and steady influx of energy to persevere in his active ministry, so inwardly transforming him that he might live not for himself but for Christ (P 59.2). Aware through painstaking self-scrutiny of woeful debits, he casts his care not upon a mere man, not even a mighty soldier of Christ like Paul, but upon the Lord alone. His declaration of dependence signifies that he counts himself a tiny one, trusting that despite storms his Lord will carry his soul to safe harbor (P 54.24). Eyes wide open through lightsome power, he will contemplate the wonders of divine law, especially the law decreeing payment of good for evil; nothing is more demanding than the command to love one's enemies (S 90.9); relying totally on the Lord, his soul will mature to accomplish the humanly impossible, to forgive his enemies, in particular, bitterly hostile heretics like Manichees and Donatists. God, who intuits his two chief privations, ignorance and sinfulness, will provide for his lack of knowledge and heal his debility of will, illumining his mind with greater sharing in the wisdom and knowledge hidden in Christ, and making him whole through the sacramental outpouring of the blood of Christ. Thus in Mass he daily eats and drinks the Eucharist that is the Son of God (S 228B.3), feeding upon the body of Christ offered as a sacrifice of praise (CALP 1.20.39), and drinking the precious blood shed for the remission of sins (QH 3.57). As bishop, he distributes the sacramental body and blood of Christ to his people, his flock who are also his fellow Christians and co-disciples (S 261.2: 270.1; 278.11). As a poor man in Christ, he is empty and therefore able to be sated with the Lord who is the riches of the poor (P 21[S.2]27) whereas the rich cannot be filled since, already full of self, they are not hungry for God. So Peter, James and John, unlettered fishermen, relatively empty of self, were satiated. But in partaking of Christ's supper, they were called upon to share in the passion signified by his supper, to the point that they might live wholly for Christ (S 194.1) so as to draw others to him (P 55.14). Though never coerced to shed his blood, Augustine was tested not only by ongoing attacks on the faith by Manicheans and Donatists but was also assaulted by slings and arrows of outrageous slanders. The sacramental sacrificial banquet infuses into Augustine's heart the steel and fire of the heart of Jesus operative during his passion; in communing in the body and blood of Christ, he is made intimately one with his suffering, partaking of the very patience of the God-man.

NOTES

1. According to Dudden, *Life and Times of St. Ambrose*, Maximus, who overthrew the Emperor Gratian in 383 (1.219), was vanquished by the eastern Emperor Theodosius in June, 388, then executed in July, 388 (1.553-5). See also Bonner, 105-6.
2. As is well known, St. Therese of Lisieux, before her death in 1897, prophesied that she would spend her heaven doing good upon earth. Monica, we may surmise, spent the first part of her heaven doing good in North Africa; God used her intercessory prayer in the communion of saints to call her son to the priesthood.
3. Perhaps quoting from memory from a *vetus Latina* text, Augustine here describes the Church as without spot *and* wrinkle. Elsewhere his phrasing is in line with that of the Vulgate, *sine macula aut ruga*; R 1.17.26; 3.18.23. R 1.19.9; 2.18. See Grabowski, *Church*, 453-60, 590-6.
4. A person sunk in sin should not despair but cry to the Lord out of the depths, as did the people of Nineveh whose penitential cries propitiated God. A baptized sinner, who has become a dog horrible in God's eyes, should fly to the mercy of God by repentance. Always can sinners, on the model of David and Peter, fly from a severe to a kind God who is certain to pardon. S 351. 5.12.
5. Augustine says not just, "when I am good," but, "when I am pious," piety being the worship of God that is rooted in charity (E 167.3.11). This is the first time that he ascribes to himself piety in the religious sense; now he is a bishop of the Church unified by charity, imaging in some measure his holy mother who was *fortis pietate* (6.1.1), robust in piety through worship of God at daily Mass and constant prayers, welling up from a heart of charity.
6. Each is emboldened to call God my God, because he believes in and loves God; with confident affection each one say, "you are my God." However, the God who is truly his own good is not his exclusive possession. God is a common good to be enjoyed by all, as the one light from the sun belongs to each and all without being the private property of any one. Hence Zaccheus' possession of God does not diminish or take away from Peter's. The possession is bilateral: he possesses us, we possess him; he possesses us so that he may cultivate (*colat*) us, and we possess him so that we may worship (*colamus*) him. S 47.16.30. P 145.11.
7. Both David, the anointed of the Lord, and Peter, the chief of apostles, repented; the pardon of lesser souls who cry out of depths is no less assured. S 351.5.12.
8. Proportionally, the empowering grace that was lavished on the martyrs in their weakness is available to all Christians conscious of their fragility. *Sic moriar ne de hoc permoriar*, says the martyr (S 335D.5): "Let me die at your hands so that I may not die forever because of denial of faith."
9. According to Possidius, V, *Praef.*, 5-6, Augustine wrote the *Confessions* to humble himself, to glorify God, and to beg the prayers of his brethren. Though Augustine does not explicitly instance this, to publicly manifest one's conscience requires a special humility from a bishop whose ecclesiastical rank

might incline him to back away from retailing his sins. Moreover, glorifying God in the grandeur of his mercy is one reason for ventilating failings. Again, support by prayers of fellow Catholics is a strong motive, one that lasted to the very end of his life (E 231.6, written around the beginning of 430); Pellegrino, 8-9. Edification also counts as a motive (R 2.6).

10. Cardinal Baronius suggested that Paulinus of Nola occasioned the writing of the *Confessions*, but Pellegrino, 7-8, thinks this has not been verified. We have dealt with this matter in more detail in the Introduction, n. 1, and Book 6, n. 28

11. Some know about him *ex se*, from his writings; others, *de se*, from an evaluation of his writings given by readers.

12. In Book 8 the witness of St. Antony, the two nameless imperial functionaries who became monks, and Victorinus spurred Augustine to imitation. Here he self-deprecatingly offers himself as a witness to fellow Christians. The conductive method can envelop them in a like peace of soul.

13. Through the resurrection God changed the evening sacrifice of Jesus on the cross into a morning gift. Therefore when the heart of a faithful Christian is raised up in prayer that is pure, i.e., wholly directed to God, the prayer rises like incense from a holy altar, its fragrance indicating that believers are to become fragrant with the sweetness of the Lord. P 140.5.

14. The spiritual word from God struck the ear of his heart just as sound strikes the air and touches the ear. S 28.4. The sound that is God or his word brings gladness that beckons the soul to a corresponding love. S 28.2.

15. Friendship is "benevolent and charitable agreement about things human and divine" (CA 3.6.13), which derives from Cicero, *De am.* 6.20. Thus light is friendly to the eyes in two senses: (i) it is the object of visual perception; (ii) more appropriately, since the eyes radiate light outward, there is a mutual sympathy between the eyes and physical light.

16. The food is that of the interior man, which is not decreased by being consumed. S 28.3. S 28 was delivered in May-June, 397, probably after the compilation of Books 1-9 and prior to the composition of Book 10.

17. *De nat. deor.* 1.10.2.

18. *Enn.* 3.6.1.

19. The metaphor, but not the theory of sensation, is drawn from Cicero, *De leg.* 1.9.26 and *De nat. deor.* 2.56.140. Taylor, *Literal Meaning*, 2.247.35.

20. *Moles* signifies bodily magnitude. QA 14.24. Although it would not be irrational or wholly inappropriate, he wittily suggests, to call bodily magnitude *tumor* (a swelling), yet even massive elephants cannot be named wise simply in virtue of their bulk. QA 14.24.

21. Pope, 243.

22. On the meaning of memory, see Solignac's nuanced commentary in BA 14, 557-67. O'Daly, 131-51, 202-16, provides an excellent analysis of memory, indicating that memorial images are not spontaneously formed but depend on the direction of the will (T 1.1.5). Too he stresses that experiential self-knowledge in *Conf.* 10 is not confused with self-reflection of mind (T 10.5.16). In "Remembering and Forgetting in Augustine, *Confessions* X," in *Memoria–Vergessen und Erinnern*, (eds.) A. Haverkamp, R. Lachmann, and R. Herzog, 31-

46, O'Daly offers a more thorough and systematic inquiry into Augustinian memory, grappling more seriously than most with the problem of forgetting. See also N. Cipriani, "Memory," AE 553-5. Worth consulting for one contemporary (1996) analysis is D. Schacter, *Searching for Memory*. Though it devotes only an epigraph to Augustine, the work further develops with scientific sophistication the empirical account of Augustine.

23. The terms primary and secondary memory derive from James 1.642-3 and 1. 648.

24. This vivid metaphor originates with James 1.660.

25. See James 1. 685.

26. In 10.8.13 Augustine considers imagination or memory broadly taken, in which there is no explicit or implicit reference to the past as such.

27. Interestingly, modern physiology of the brain confirms Augustine's comments on the selective recall of specific sense data. Various parts of the brain furnish a specialized organic substrate for the psychic functioning of the five senses. Visual sensitivity is centered in the occipital lobe, and the auditory in the temporal lobe, while olfactory and gustatory sensations are mediated through an area just beneath the temporal lobe; the somesthetic sense is localized in the parietal lobe.

28. See examples in James 2.56-61. James himself confesses that he possessed a weak visual but a stronger auditory imagination, with practically no images of taste or smell (2.64,65n.).

29. This according to F. Galton, *Inquiries into Human Faculty*, 83-114, as quoted in James 2.51-6.

30. James 1.606.

31. T. Hobbes, *Leviathan*, I.13; 82 in M. Oakeshott's edition (Blackwell, 1946). In the state of nature, without political law, "the life of man [is] solitary, poor, nasty, brutish, and short."

32. The problem of the mind's failure to grasp all of itself is a genuine one. If the spirit attends to each sensory object, it would seem initially plausible that it cognitively control all of its contents. But, in fact, and regrettably so (otherwise learning would be less laborious), data acquired slip from immediate awareness and cognitive mastery, and a good bit are lost in forgetfulness. According to Thomistic theory, only a pure spirit, in perfect possession of all its mental forms, absolutely retains all of its contents. Not received from without, the mental forms are given with angelic nature. An angel's mental contents are always actually known; its ideas are not just objectively intelligible but subjectively intelligized. Human representations, because received from outside the mind, are not constantly intelligized. Aquinas, *S. th.* 1.57.2. Moreover, refinement in theory of the acquisition of knowledge has not wholly accounted for the meaning of knowledge. Some mystery persists; at a certain point we simply accept the fact that cognition of the world is mediated by likenesses of the things themselves.

33. According to A. Schindler, *Wort und Analogie in Augustins Trinitätslehre* (Tübingen: J.B.C. Mohr, 1965), 56-60, this triad is found, with inessential variation, in Cicero, *Or.* 15.45, Quintilian, *Inst. orat.* 3.6.80, and Martianus

Capella, *De nupt. philol. et Merc.* 5.444. Du Roy, 384-5, n.6. It is applied in the treatise on time; see infra 11.14.17.

34. BA 14, 170-1, n.1.

35. *Meno* 82b-85b.

36. According to the theory of illumination, God supplies incorporeal light for the grasp of intelligible objects as the sun furnishes light for the perception of physical entities (Sol 1.8.15). Divine illumination is required for the mind to lay hold of immutable ideas since the mind is in itself mutable (LA 2.13.35; T 14.15.21). As participating in the light of God (T 4.2.4), the created light, which functions in the natural mode (GL 12.31.59), is distinct from the uncreated light (CF 20.7). However, the precise nature and scope of this illumination are not entirely clear. An earlier claim that this light was substantially similar to the active intellect in Thomistic theory of knowledge (S.Th. 1.84) has now been generally discarded. According to E. Gilson, *The Christian Philosophy of St. Augustine.* 87-8, 91, a view to which F. Copleston, *A History of Philosophy: Augustine to Scotus*, II, 61-2, ascribes, Augustine invoked illumination not to account for the content of concepts but to explain the certainty and necessity of judgments. In *The Light of the Mind*, 102-11, R. Nash offers an alternative interpretation that makes room for content as well as formal factors in cognition. Divine illumination conveys to the mind basic a priori forms in the light of whose content the mind understands sensory precepts and images. In her survey of the views of German scholars in the first half of the twentieth century, *The German Controversy on Saint Augustine's Illumination Theory*, 77-8, C. Schützinger concurs with Nash's insistence that not only the formal aspect but the material aspect involving content are produced by illumination. In any case, as she remarks, 30-8, Augustine's account does not lapse into twentieth-century versions of ontologism akin to that of N. Malebranche in *Recherche de la vérité*, (ed.) G. Rodis-Lewis (Vrin, 1964), t. III, *Eclaircissements*, 127-43, according to whom because the divine mind is universal reason that contains immutable truths, the human mind sees these in God. For Malebranche, who counts himself a disciple of Augustine, 12.25.34 justifies the universality of reason (129) and LA 2.8.20-12.33 establishes the existence of immutable truths in the divine mind (130).

37. Whereas the created light is mutable (CF 20.7), passing from oblivion to remembrance, the divine light perdures by an immutable will, truth, and eternity. Thus it is the principle of existence, the *ratio* of knowing, and the law of loving. Here *ratio* signifies the archetype; the general patten written in the book of light to be impressed on the intellect (CF 20.7). As truth, God is the source of knowing; man's intellect shares in his truth by a created light that partakes of uncreated light. As immutable will, God is the law or standard of love.

38. In one and the same concrete act man envisages objects on three levels of cognition. In the reading of the precept, "You shall love your neighbor as yourself," three sorts of vision are simultaneously operative: sensory, in which the eyes read the letters; sensio-intellectual, in which one's absent neighbor is thought about; and purely intellectual, in virtue of which the meaning of love,

carrying no penumbra of sensory images (GL 12.3.6), is understood by pure intellection. GL 12.6.15. T 10.10.14.

39.   Cogitation may be a species of *ratiocinatio*, which is "the search of reason, i.e., the movement or process of the sight of mind over those things that are to be viewed or inspected." QA 27.53. *Ratio* connects one item with another; it is the job of reason to distinguish and connect things being learned. O 2.11.30. An earlier section (10.8.12) examined the various senses of cogitation. In "Cogitation," AL 1.1046-51, G. Watson, after noting the linkage of cogitation to imagination, specifies cogitation-thinking as "the bringing to consciousness of various kinds of latent knowledge (*notitia*)...for application in thinking and acting."

40.   *Laches* 198d-199e. *Rep.* 514a-518d. *Meno* 85c-86e.

41.   Cicero, *De am.* 6.20,18.15. *Tusc. disp.* 4.37-38a.

42.   Jackson-Knight, *St. Augustine's De Musica*, 14-7. Ladner, 216.

43.   To forestall the objection that his definition of time as number mathematicizes time, Aristotle, in *Phys.* 4.11.219b5-9, distinguishes between physical number or numbered number, and mathematical number or the number by which we number. As in and of motion, time is physical number. Surely this discrimination between arithmetical and physical number is reiterated in Augustine. Although he was not acquainted with this text, there can be little doubt that an approximation of the Aristotelian distinction was incorporated in doxographical literature that later fell under his eyes. According to Solignac, BA 14, 174-5, n.3, who notes its presence in CA 2.11.25, O 2.14.41, LA 2.8.20, and M 6.6.16, the distinction between sensible and intelligible number probably originates with the Pythagoreans. It occurs also in *Enn.* 5.5.4-5; 6.6.16; 6.6.15-6.

44.   Mathematical number must be distinguished from ontological number, the metaphysical equivalent of species or form. More precisely, ontic number is the principle of form, that whereby a thing is formed or unified; it is part of the Scriptural triad of measure, number, and weight (Wis 11.21), which, philosophically interpreted, Augustine makes the parallel of mode, species, and order (LA 2.11.31 GCM 1.16.26. GL 4.3.2-4.8).

45.   *De fin.* 3.10.35. *Tusc. disp.* 4.6.110.

46.   Cicero, *De div.* 2.30. Ennius, Fr. 277V. G-M 292.7.

47.   G-M 293.1.

48.   BA 14, 564.

49.   J. Mourant, *St. Augustine on Memory*, 19.

50.   Bourke, *Confessions*, 284, n. 52.

51.   Aquinas elaborated a sophisticated notion of *ens rationis*. Beings of reason are rational structures that owe their objectivity to works of the mind (*In meta.*4.4., n.574, ed. Cathala-Spiazzi). When some states of affairs are inexpressible, the mind has to devise concepts whose objectivity begins and ends in the mind (*De potentia* 7.11). Beings of reason divide into two broad groups: negations and relations of reason (*De veritate* 21.1). Negations include conceptual objects that involve lack of some entity: zero, evil, the state of forgetting (cognitive being of reason). Relations of reason subdivide into logical relations such as genus and

species and relations bearing on nature (*De potentia* 7.10,11).

52. As will be mentioned in more detail in Book 11, n.45, the space-time continuum is not an actual physical reality but a mathematical-physical construct. Space and time are not fused; for explanatory purposes the physicist thinks of them as fused.

53. Lest we succumb to a condescending attitude toward limitations of the ancients, it seems worth noting that some contemporary outlooks are bedeviled by unsolvable conundrums. Denied knowledge of the concept of being of reason by an impoverished understanding of the history of logic, the logistical school of mathematics defines zero as a null set, a class without members; unfortunately, this is a self-defeating idea since a class without members is as senseless as a house without parts. Other problems, while strictly not connected to omission of beings of reason, stem from a faulty material logic and inadequate philosophy of nature. Moreover, induction is a notorious crux for empiricists, who, unable to propose a principle of uniformity, cannot validate with scientific surety that the future will repeat or resemble the past. Some analytic efforts to establish uniformity in nature on empiricistic grounds lapse into vicious circularity; a general natural pattern is implicitly invoked to justify a particular natural pattern, then the particular pattern is used to substantiate universal uniformity in nature. Furthermore, the verification of hypotheses entrenched in philosophical journals as well as most logic textbooks is technically invalid because it relies on affirming the consequent: if the law of falling bodies is true, the argument runs, this mass will fall 144 feet in three seconds; it does so; therefore the law is verified. A defective material logic or logico-epistemic theory of science keeps some contemporary philosophers of science trapped in this flawed HD (hypothetico-deductive) model.

54. The figure of *claudicans* does not indicate that the breaking of the connection between the parts fractures the leg of memory, inducing it to limp. Rather, the import is this: once a part is broken off from a complex whole (the name separated from the face), the memory limps: it cannot quickly stride to remembrance of the name but must fumble for it, perhaps first recalling a syllable or another name with the same initial letter. Ordinary recall is swift, direct and easy; once a part is forgotten, it becomes slow, indirect (through clues), and laborious.

55. James 2.58-60.

56. James 1.683.

57. The dictum, "All men desire to be happy," which derives from Plato's *Euthydemus* 278E and Aristotle's *Protrep.* Fr. 3 and 4, first came to Augustine's attention during his felicitous encounter with *Hortensius*, Fr. 36, a point on which he explicitly comments in T 13.4.7. He quotes or paraphrases this self-evident first principle of action in numerous texts: BV 2.10. CA 1.2.5. ME 1.3.4. T 13.4.7. CD 10.1. P 32 (S.2).14. S 53.1.1, and eight times in the *Confession*, thrice in 10.20.29, four times in 10.21.31, once in 10.23.32. On happiness see Gilson, *The Christian Philosophy of St. Augustine*, especially 3-10. R. Holte, *Béatitude et sagesse*, in particular 193-300. W. Beierwaltes, *Regio Beatitudinis*. H. Galvão, *Beatitudo*, AL 1. 624-38. J. Bussanich, "Happiness, Eudaimonism," AE 413-4.

58. Terence, *Andria* 1.68. BA 14, 202. n.7.
59. Augustine searches for the truth through dialectical method, which is effectively the strategy of interrogation and response. Sol 2.7.14. Dialectical questioning leads to truth, then moves from the truth to another truth. C. Cresc. 1.16.20. Not only here but in the preceding chapters Augustine employs his dialectical procedure; again and again he poses questions as a device for exposing faulty or inadequate alternatives prior to determining the truth. See J. Pépin, *Saint Augustin et la dialectique*, 196-7.
60. Only because ontically above memory is God discovered noetically in memory. Only because he is absolutely transcendent, higher than the highest point of the mind, is he noetically immanent, present in the throne of the mind, more inward than the most inward portion of the knowing self, to adapt the expression of transcendence-immanence in 3.6.11.
61. Courcelle, along with discussing the *sero* motif in pagan and Christian thinkers prior to Augustine, notes its accents in works prior to the *Confessions*, then tracks echoes in posterity, from Paulinus of Nola and St. Patrick in the fifth century down to its surprising word-for-word reproduction in the well-known *Prayer at the Acropolis* addressed to Athena, the goddess of wisdom, by the nineteenth-century ex-seminarian rationalist Ernest Renan. See "Le thème du regret: 'Sero te amavi, pulchritudo'...," in Appendix VIII, 441-78. Courcelle's essay is cited in BA 14, 209, n.1, which also calls attention to I. Perez, "Sobre la hora en que San Agustin comienza a amar la Verdad", *Estudios Filosoficos* 4 (1955), 353-66, which suggests a nexus between "Late have I loved you" and the conversion scene in Milan.
62. In other accounts of the senses, Augustine always lists eyesight first, followed by hearing and the rest. Here he appoints primacy to hearing, probably because words that God uttered through the child (8.12.29) precipitated his conversion experience. It may be named first also because the context is one of prayer. Throughout his dialogue with God he urges God to press his mouth close to his inward ear so as to unmistakably communicate the truth he is begging for.
63. According to GL 12.15.31, though during waking hours we can think and speak about sexual union without being carnally excited, during sleep images of sexual union that arouse the soul can induce pollution. While awake, we can discuss sexual intercourse but without sin because reason bridles movements of concupiscence. While asleep, we may desire sexual intercourse but without sin because, when its operation is suspended by cessation of sensory activity, reason cannot control carnal movements toward images that appear as tempting as real bodies. Interestingly, Aquinas' discussion of nocturnal pollution in *S. th.* 2. 2. 154.5 bases its key conclusion on the analysis in GL 12.15.31.
64. *Rule* 3.14.
65. Those who fasted ordinarily did not eat until the *cena*, which occurred at 3:00 PM. Thus they skipped the *prandium* or midday meal (*Rule* 3.14). In Augustine's day the Church observed the forty-day Lenten fast. In addition, outside Paschal Time Wednesday and Friday were considered fast days. His *Rule* does not

require special days of fasting beyond the prescriptions of the Church. However, a number of monks and nuns kept a perpetual fast except for Saturdays and Sundays. See A. Zumkeller, *Augustine's Ideal of Life*, tr. E. Colledge, 68-9, and L. Verheijen, *Nouvelle Approche de la Règle de saint Augustin* (Abbaye de Bellefontaine, 1980), 306.

66. A. Zumkeller, *Augustine's Rule: A Commentary*, 69. Sr. Agatha Mary, *The Rule of Saint Augustine*, 119-20.

67. V 22.2.

68. Van der Meer, 131, 518-9.

69. Singing, though not a matter of faith but of liturgical practice, is Scripturally supported by the example and precepts of the Lord and his apostles. Moreover, it causes hearts to resound with greater love of God. Donatists, he notes, reprove Catholics for their listless singing—"the law of liturgical inertia" notorious among modern Catholics was already operative (Van der Meer, 327); nontheless, the Catholic service provides ample opportunity for singing, except when the bishop prays aloud and when the deacon's voice leads the common prayer. E 55. 18.34.

70. Augustine, not reserved but enthusiastic about singing accompanied by instruments in ennobling the word of God, warmly comments on the zither and psaltery, mentions the ministries of precentor and choir, and lauds the singing of the amen and the protracted singing of the alleluia during the Easter liturgy. P 87.1 J 41.3 229, 229B. Van der Meer, 334-5. In the ancient world, and for centuries thereafter, musical instruments were generally employed only to accompany song. Langer, *Philosophy in a New Key*, 252-3, in dependence on W. Wallace, *The Threshold of Music*, 35-42.

71. Augustine seems to lean toward the view, originating with Pythagoras, endorsed by Plato and embraced, with modifications, by Aristotle, that music, by becalming emotions, influences formation of character. M. Beardsley, *Aesthetics from Classical Greece to the Present* (Macmillan, 1966), 46, 49-50, 60, 64-5, 72.

72. Van der Meer, 317-8.

73. In spite of the opinion of R. Joly, "Curiositas," *L'antique classique* 30 (Louvain, 1961), 40, "curious" is at times employed as a synonym for "studious." Two passages in the *Confessions* accord the term a eulogistic sense that makes it a synonym of *studium*: a free curiosity, i.e., a spirit of study freely embraced, is a more powerful force in learning language than fear-laden constraint (1.14.23); astronomers mathematically chart the stars and their courses through a curious skill, a habit of mind gained and sustained by a zeal for study (5.3.4). In twenty-eight other places curiosity is assigned its more common acceptation as a branch of the threefold concupiscence.

74. The early Augustine tended to identify curiosity with Manichean espousal of a materialist view of the world. Manicheans were infected with all three concupiscences; they arrogantly asserted that God and the soul had the same nature or substance; lust of the flesh ensnared them in the opinion that guilt for whatever impurities they committed was to be imputed to the Race of Darkness rather than to themselves; as curious, they narrowed their vision to

earthly things alone, seeking realities with a purely earthly eye. GCM 2.26.40.

75. UC 16.34 mentions flying as a miraculous occurrence that might well stimulate wonder but fails to foster belief in God. D.D. Home, (1833-86), was observed apparently flying out one window and in another over a courtyard (see n. 76 below). Simon Magus, it is reported, died trying to carry out his boast that he could fly through the air. W. Barclay, *The Gospel of Matthew*, 1.62. Exhibitionism that tends to nourish curiosity rather than faith is sensation-mongering for which a ready appetite is never wanting.

76. D.D. Home was a remarkable spirtualist who was apparently in contact with spirits beyond this world. Occasionally while in a trance, he floated in and out of windows, but more frequently he caused phenomena such as the repeated playing of the accordion without use of his hands or fingers, levitation, and endurance of the fire ordeal. For descriptions of these data see F. Podmore, *Mediums of the Nineteenth Century* (first published, 1902; reprinted, 1963), 23, 253-6, 262-3. E. J. Dingwall's 1963 Introduction, xviii-xxii, faults Podmore for his tenuously based skepticism about these phenomena, for there can be little doubt that at times Home was engaged in activities inexplicable by human agencies. H. Thurston, a perceptive observer and critic, cautions against an unhealthy skepticism that totally dismisses all spiritualistic events as fraudulent. Such a sweeping incredulity that repudiates the veracity of judicious witnesses undercuts the value of all human testimony for the miracles worked by Christ. A more prudent strategy would admit the veridical character of some spiritualistic phenomena prior to analyzing the extra-human sources of the phenomena. See *The Church and Spiritualism*, 167-87, 162, 168. Thurston argues that spiritualistic marvels are to be traced to evil spirits; his analysis of the veracity of some of the extraordinary phenomena and their origin in evil spirits substantially jibes with the position of Augustine.

77. The applause of his congregation is explicitly mentioned in S 128.8; 301A.9; 229E.4. See M. Pellegrino, *The True Priest*, 83.

78. James 1.292.

79. Shakespeare's line seems apposite here: "I thank God for my humility" (*Richard III*, Act 2, sc. 1, l.72).

80. Pascal, *Pensées*, 377: "Discourses on humility are a source of pride to the vain and of humility to the humble." Assured by the highest authority that is himself that he has reached the pinnacle of virtue, the proud man praises himself for being humble; the blindness of self-deceit inspires him to thank God that he is not like the rest of men, haughty and enamored of their own excellence.

81. BA 13, 199-200.

82. In contrast to God, who proclaims, "I am the truth" (Jn 14.6), the devil declares implicitly, in his rebellious choice of self, "I am the lie," with this qualification: the devil is not the Manichean Prince of Darkness. Not pure evil, he is an adamantine privation of the truth, a living lie (CD 14.4). All who live the lie of sin and thereby imitate the devil instead of God are his moral progeny (Jn 8.44.CD 14.3), In departing from the truth, a sinner tarnishes the image of God within and, insofar as a lie is the disimage of truth, becomes unlike God and loosely assumes the image of Satan. In imaging Christ, the perfect image of the

Father, a Christian becomes another Christ, a son of God; in imitating the devil, the most hideous disimage of God, a sinner turns into a kind of mini-devil, an offspring of the Evil One.

83. Bochet, *Saint Augustin et le désir de Dieu*, 100, n. 1.

84. Here, rather than in 7.9.15, we may justifiably detect the figure of Porphyry in the background. Whereas nowhere in the prior passage did Augustine advert directly to the work of demons, here, presumably after encountering a work of Porphyry or selections from his writings, he explicitly focuses on the problem of magical rites and demon-worship, neither practiced but both permitted by Porphyry (CD.10.27). In effect, Porphyry endorses theurgy, advocating veneration or worship of demons, the fruit of which is purportedly union with the divine (CD 10.29).

85. "None of the Church Fathers or early Christian theologians emphasized the mediating significance of Christ's humanity as decisively as St. Augustine. It is the heart of his theology." K. Adam, *The Christ of Faith*, 300. See the whole of the rich, measured treatment, 300-2 upon which our discussion draws. May we be permitted the observation that this Adam, faithful Catholic priest as well as scientific theologian, is evidently more the offspring of the new Adam than of the old. See also, G. Madec, "Christus," AL 1. 845-907, especially 869-70, 886-90, with bibliography. Also, B. Daley, "Christology," AE 164-9, especially 168-9, with bibliography.

86. Adam, *The Christ of Faith*, 301.

87. Adam, *The Christ of Faith*, 301.

88. Reconciliation presupposes prior enmity. Men became enemies of God not by nature but by sin, which in time turned its perpetrators into its slaves. In God's eyes freedom and enmity are incompatible; the liberating death of Christ won reconciliation that terminated enmity and ushered in freedom. J 41.5.

89. In other passages Augustine does not specify the sacrifice as analytically prior to the priest. "...the whole redeemed...society of the saints is offered to God as a universal sacrifice through the great priest who also offered himself for us in his passion...according to the form of a servant. For it was this form he offered, in this form he is priest, in this form he is sacrifice." CD 10.6. Interestingly, in this text the offerer precedes the offered, the priest is mentioned before the sacrifice, though Augustine declines to equate this verbal priority with analytical priority.

90. The line appears in S 13 *de tempore*, PL 1098, selected for the *Liturgy of Hours* I (Advent Season, Christmas Season), New York: Catholic Book, 1973), 541; this liturgical accreditation does not nullify the current judgment that the sermon is spurious. In other texts Augustine plainly speaks of graced Christians as deified or as Gods. The very act of justifiction produces sons of God; they become Gods. However, the deification is not substantial but accidental. The only-begotten Son of God is born of the substance of God, receiving the fullness of the divine nature from the generator or Father. Redeemed Christians, on the other hand, are deified by grace, not born of the divine substance; they are Gods by grace of the Father adopting them, not in virtue of generation of the full divine nature by the Father. In brief, only the Word is totally God by

generation; Christians adoptively participate in Godness by grace. P 49.2. See V. Capánaga, *Agustin de Hipona*, 114-61, along with G. Bonner, "The Spirituality of St. Augustine", *Sobernost*, N.J., 4 (1982), especially 157-9, reprinted in *God's Decree and Man's Destiny*.

91.   Man's death-bound body is the upshot of original sin. PMR 2.30.49. Jesus the mediator spiritually heals the sick and raises the dead to life, i.e., bestows justice on the impious. NG 26.29. Jesus as mortal and blessed entered human history in order to abolish mortality and confer immortality on those who were dead. CD 9.15.

92.   Augustine does not specify the exact time of his desire to pursue a life of greater solitude. According to BA 14, 267,n.1, De Labriolle suggests that Augustine experienced this urge to flee to the desert shortly after his conversion; *Conf.* 2.292, n.2. However, it seems probable, as Pellegrino, 218, n. 25 (a note added to the French translation) following Cayré, holds that Augustine's strong desire to abandon the active life surfaced after his ordination as priest (391) or bishop (395). In the opinion of Pintard, the impulse to solitary life gained force between 395 and 398, evoked by distress over savage Donatist calumnies. According to Augustine, his vocational crisis arose from a contemplative penchant for holy leisure (CD 1.19) and from fear of the severe accounting he would have to render for discharge of the heavy burdens of the episcopate. E 21.4; 95.2-3; 193.13. S 334.4; 340.1. A letter to Evodius (E 95.2-3) indicates that the vocational problem had been solved by 398. F. Cayré, *L'Année théologique augustinienne*, 1951, 256-7. J. Pintard, *La sacerdoce selon saint Augustin*, Paris, 1961, 327 ff.

93.   One particular calumny may have fueled Augustine's inclination to enjoy the fruits of solitude. Prior to his ordination to the bishopic in 395, Megalius, the bishop of Calama and honorary primate of Numidia, circulated a story that Augustine had given a love potion to a woman, so potent that it moved her to commit adultery. In light of this accusation Megalius was prepared to block Augustine's ascension to the episcopate. Happily, an episcopal commission's investigation proved the charge to be false – Augustine had handed the woman nothing more than an unconsecrated loaf of bread. Not surprisingly, this vicious falsehood was picked up and accorded wide dissemination by the Donatists; see Bonner, 120-1. It is not unlikely that this was one of the principal calumnies to which 10.43.70 refers. His anguish may have prompted him to meditate at length on the real possibility of abandonment of active life. Such a calumny was a portion of the passion of Christ, a sort of thorn piercing his mind, received in communing with the Lord in the Eucharist.

94.   H. Ghéon, *The Secret of the Cure d'Ars*, in a one-volume edition of four of Ghéon's works entitled *Secrets of the Saints*, 103-6.

Book Eleven
Reflections On Scripture: Creation, Eternity, Time

As indicated in the general Introduction, the inclusion of the last three books remains a puzzle that apparently lies beyond complete solution. Though 11.1.1 explicitly connects the concluding part with the opening chapter of Book 1, a marked dissimilarity divides the last part from the first ten books. Simply put, the last three books are in no way substantially autobiographical. Succeeding phenomenology and analysis of the self is exegesis; personal history and soul-searching give way to a detached probing of the meanings of Genesis. As noted earlier, it seems plausible to see a correlation between Books 10 and 11. Both recognize a combination of illumination and lingering darkness. Book 10 focuses on the moral plane while the last three books grapple with problems on the theoretical level. Specifically, Books 1-3 try to resolve some of the exegetical difficulties raised by Manichees. In Books 3-6 Augustine struggles to extricate himself from the toils of Manichean error. Book 7 records his transcendence of Manichean-rooted materialism while Book 8 recounts his moral conversion through conquest of concupiscence. Manicheism hovers in the background of his post-conversion spiritual experience of Book 9. The ascetical canons by which he measures his episcopal conduct in Book 10 are sharply at variance with their misguided Manichean counterparts. Thus in some sense a doctrinal and moral response to Manichean distortions very broadly links the last three books with the prior ten. Still, this does not furnish a tidy unity to the *Confessions*; the earlier and later books are thematically connected only in a quite loose sense.[1]

After an introduction in which he renews the confessional theme (1.1) and prays for understanding of Scriptures (2.2-4), Book 11 divides into four parts.[2]

1) Creation of heaven and earth (3.5-9.11).
2) Creation and eternity (10.12-13.16).
3) Definition of psychological time (14.17-28.38) and moral time (29.39).
4) Reprise of difficulties (30.40-31.41). An Excursus on the kinds of time is appended.

Chapter 1: Renewal of Theme: Confession to God for his Mercy

1. God knows all things, for the very existence of things present speaks to him, things past are wholly manifest, and future events are not hidden from his wisdom. Indeed whatever has passed, is occurring, or will come to be is permanently present to his wisdom (SDM 2.3.12). Yet if God already knows outside and above time what Augustine is going to write, there would seem to be no point in narration of his life and exploration of his mind; God cannot learn piecemeal from Augustine's writing in time what divine wisdom wholly possesses in eternity. Not Augustine but God is the teacher who spurs him to rekindle his love of God, which, in turn, stirs up fresh love in his readers, bidding them to unite with him in loving God so as to praise him in accord with the opening line (1.1.1): the great Lord is greatly to be praised. So magnificent is God that no sacrifice of praise, no matter how fragrant, coursing from however masterly the mind and eloquent the tongue, can proffer the measureless praise due God (P 95.4). Also reiterated is the grace-impelled motive for writing: he is authoring his *Confessions* by love of God's love (2.2.2), a human-divine love which, as far as possible, is disinterested, aiming neither at plaudits nor self-satisfaction, a testimony of praise and gratitude dedicated to God alone. The love of God is expanded by confessional reflections developed in an atmosphere of prayer. Since the Father already knows the needs of persons before they ask, his meditations do not inform God but help further reform his spirit. The gaze of the simple heart is sharpened to bear, then rest in, the light of God with joy not of this world, which,

while it connotes, strictly crowns, happiness (10.22.32-23.33).

Thus in voicing love, he is imploring increase of love; in confessing mercy, he is beseeching total healing. He has traveled miles from the excesses of his sixteenth year, over thirty years before, yet, as his searching self-examen in Book 10 detailed, his journey is far from finished. Plainly less miserable than before his conversion, even as a bishop he is still not fully imaged after God, not yet completely happy. Nonetheless, God is calling him to felicity through the directives to happiness termed the beatitudes. The seven sanctifying gifts of the Holy Spirit (Is 11.2-3, Septuagint) lead him to live the happiness-causing life prescribed by the beatitudes. Only seven of these are instanced because the eighth, which hails those who suffer persecution for righteousness's sake, manifests the happiness promised in the first seven. Too once an advanced Christian is purified in wisdom through the first seven beatitudes, he is sinewed to withstand and even suffer joyfully all assaults from without. The gifts of the Spirit that fructify in the seven beatitudes arm a Christian robust enough to endure the persecution that is the inevitable lot of the godly in this world (CD 18.51). It would seem other than accurate to hold, as do some scholars, that here and in SDM the eight beatitudes are reduced to seven. Rather, Augustine retains all eight, while claiming that only the first seven parallel the seven gifts; the eighth remains but, because not correlated with a gift, performs a different function (SDM 1.4.11).

The narration retailing numerous events and features of his inner and outer life was prosecuted only because divine willing graced him with the will and power to write. Then he expresses in the most succinct fashion the reason why man praises God: God is good. In other words, man alive with God praises God because God is God. Goodness that is God is displayed not only in returning evil for evil, in apportioning just penalty for sin, but supremely in returning good for evil, in showering on sin-laden man mercy to last forever (P 117.2).

Chapter 2: Prayer for Guidance in Understanding Scripture

2. He longs to praise God for all the light sustaining him in his priestly vocation, in particular, for exhortations in Scripture: Augustine must be consecrated to serving the people of God (S 304A.2-3); for warnings: the scandalous pastor invites dire retribution

(E 208. 3-4), a potential fate that moved him to weep when drafted into the priesthood, sensitive even then to its perils (E 21.1-2); and, not to be slighted, for countless consolations: uplifting touches soothe his labor-worn spirit (10.40.65). Moreover, divine direction blessed him with practical insight in decision after decision in episcopal affairs and especially in all his writings and discourses elucidating Scriptural cruxes and related theological and philosophical issues. Absolute trust in divine providence undergirds his ceaseless begging for divine illumination toward the unraveling of knotty problems.[3] Time permitting, he would hope to articulate point by point praise of the God who specially chose him for his priestly apostolate. Each drop of time in the water clock is precious, not a single moment of which he dare waste. However, at this juncture the clamor of his packed schedule obliges him to postpone this praise till S 399 and S 340 (whose dates remain undetermined) wherein is elaborated the confession focusing on his priestly life.[4]

Intent almost from ordination (391) on penetrating the Scriptures, he authored several commentaries on Genesis, two of which, GCM (388-390) and GI (393), precede this passage, and two of which, GL (401-415) and CD 11-12 (416), postdate it.[5] While confessing God for progress in understanding, he praises him also for deficiency in perspicacity, this without paradox since it implicitly includes a petition for further lights to decipher perplexing places. Already the beneficiary of God, he hopes that all patches of darkness will be banished. Much of his day is budgeted for necessary tasks: repair of the body through at least minimal food and sleep – even his untiring frame craved some slumber; reflection and reading in preparation for his books; indispensable refection of soul in prayer; preaching, celebrating Mass, and administering the sacraments; arbitration of matters of litigation along with pastoral counseling. Not a single segment of time is to be let flow away in idleness and frivolous recreation; every fleeting but invaluable drop is to be expended on delving into Scripture.

3. No deskbound theologian, he is on fire to expound Scripture not simply for his own understanding but, more importantly, for the illumination of his flock. His deeper grasp wears the livery of fraternal charity; light from high is given first to the preacher of truth who is to minister radiance to the earth (P 75.7). In accord with the thrust of ecclesiastical charity, Books 10 and 11 offer the service of his thought

and tongue as a sacrifice of praise (4.1.1; 5.1.1; 8.1.1; 9.1.1; 12.14.33).[6] Echoing in part the earlier " Give what you command" (10.29.40; 31.45;32.60), he pleads for understanding to offer oblations of expository power exercised upon the Scriptures. Unsparing in pitiless perception of his lacks, he declares his indigence; not like the hollow Pharisee, stuffed with egoism, so splendid in his self-generated merits that he brags of his excellences, he is a wretched publican who confesses his sins (P 85.2), relying wholly on God who heaps virtues on all who cry out humbly. In diametrical opposition to earthly abundance that fades like flowers of the field, divine wealth endures forever (P 53.2); super-rich in peace, wholly without care, God tirelessly cares for men (3.6.9). The Lord, he hopes, will purify his lips, both interior (his mind) and exterior (his mode of expression) of all rashness, i.e., precipitous, slipshod misreadings of hard passages, and of lying, deliberately sophistical interpretations, thus assuring that his toilsome analysis will be transmuted into a labor of love, a fount of chaste delights, these counterpoised to unholy pleasures in which flesh luxuriates. Holy boldness prompts an extraordinary petition; he begs the gift of understanding Scriptures errorlessly and transmitting without error their meaning to his flock; an infallibility that would be an exceptional participation in the truth of the God who can neither deceive nor be deceived.

His confidence anchors him in the mercy of the Lord who is the light of the blind and strength of the weak. A certain moral blindness, recall, is woven into vices (1.18.29), sometimes so delusive that sinners boast of their very blindness (3.3.6). While not entirely excluding every bit of this privation of sight, here he is mainly concerned with a sort of quasi-theoretical blindness, which during his Manichean captivity sealed his eyes to Catholic dogma and moral values (3.7.14: 6.4.5; 9.4.11). As with Victorinus, light from on high released him from a pit of blindness, recreating him into a son of God (8.4.9; 10.27.38). No doubt the physically blind or near-blind, Tobit, Isaac, and Jacob, were interiorly illumined (10.34.52), yet very probably he is not referring to this uncommon sense of "light of the blind." Moreover, God is the strength of the weak; in the garden in Milan (8.12.29) divine power shattered incontinence. In addition, God can radiate further light, whose beams unlock puzzles in Scripture. Correspondingly, God further upbuilds him with patience that will not be disheartened by obstacles; else brilliant understanding will be short-circuited by a spiritual failure of nerve. In other words, God who is super-strong (1.4.4) has already conferred on him a portion of his vigor, confounding the worldly mighty by infusion of his spiritual force into the feeble (8.4.9). Feeding on the food of the strong (7.10.11), he will become not simply more luminous but more thewed with religious stamina, thereby more nearly imitating his mother strong in piety (6.1.1).

Now vibrant with the life of Jesus, he no longer cries out from the depths of sin in the strict sense (P 129.2), though, broadly speaking, his prayer goes on rising from the abyss of his mortal condition that, however lit up and vigorous, depends on ever-fresh light and power. Fortunately, filling the whole world from heights to depths (P 138.10) is the spirit of the Lord whose acute ears are attentive even in the depths, whose sonorous voice is poised to utter, within, forcible words of assurance (12.10.10). Members of the Church belong to the Lord day and night in the moral-spiritual sense. God addresses spirituals symbolized by the day, Christians advanced in religious understanding, enlightening them with immutable wisdom. But he speaks to carnals, symbolized by the night, Christians of rudimentary religious knowledge, by manifesting his Word in the flesh (P 73.19). However, here Augustine probably glosses Ps 73.16 in the nonfigurative sense patent in the text: as eternal, God is maker and administrator of all times and seasons. At his creative command the moments of time past fleet by; hence man who cannot prevent one syllable from succeeding another cannot retain a day or hour as standing changeless. From these moments, swift departing though they be, he implores God to weave an expanse of time sturdy enough for him to continue knocking on divine law, and complete his prayerful reflections on the Scriptures, secret because, as the word of God, they bear principally on the God who is strictly incomprehensible (S 52.16).[7] Moreover, God conceals his treasures not out of envy but in order to ensure that readers will appreciate their value, experiencing delight upon decoding an obscure passage (VR 17.33.E 137.5.18; S 60A.1; 352.6) in an arcane work (12.10.10). Certainly God has not made his word so dense that it is studied in vain; perservering inquiry, with the aid of the Holy Spirit (S 152.1), releases glimmers of light in Scriptures that can never be exhaustively understood (J 63.1). The forests, the darksome Scriptures, can be inhabited by harts (one of whose company Augustine seeks to be) who repair to divine letters that bathe the eyes of the mind and soothe the whole spirit of man (J 35.6), their many medicines healing all ills of the soul (S 32.1). The harts, fully restored, walk about in tranquillity and feed upon the energizing word of God (P 141.1.S. 95.1; 57.7). They lie down, i.e., repose, in contemplation of the word, which, lodged in the stomach of memory, is cognitively ruminated or re-thought (P 141.1). This bread which is truth, recall, "refects" rather than "defects" the soul, changing not food into eater but eater into food (7.10.11. J 41.1).[8] The Lord's voice will grant perfection as he drives away poisonous tongues, i.e, false ideas, in the way harts repel poisonous snakes (P 28.9); a perfection that unveils the fullness of truth.[9] The voice of the Lord results in joy, which, linked to truth, defines happiness. Any discovery of truth excites a certain delight, but because the slightest gain in divine knowledge outstrips any advances in lesser brands of knowledge (CEF 1.2), the truth the divine voice communicates conveys delights richer than a profusion of lesser pleasures. Moreover, since his desire for full meaning is pure benefaction, the Lord, he hopes, will not abort the gift of yearning for understanding, which, like grass or fledgling herb, thirsts for divine rain that is truth to nourish growth in wisdom (P 98.15). Spiritual ears alert to catch the voice of God's praise, he recognizes that everything good is a benediction from God. Correspondingly, he abhors self-praise: any fresh disclosure of the good of the mind that is truth should elicit praise not of self but of God, for his good originates not in himself but in God (P 25[En.2].11). As a parched herb, he wants to drink in the truth and wisdom substantially identified with God (P 62.6). So refreshed, he will plumb the wonders of God's law, which here signifies the salvific design of salvation, eternal law governing the whole of salvation history that runs from the creation of the world until the triumphant entrance into the heavenly Jerusalem at the end of time when the elect will reign in everlasting ecstasy with God (CD 22.1); a plan essentially one of love since every page of Scripture bespeaks love (S 350 A.1) or, in the economy of redemption, the plot of the saga of mercy in which good is miraculously rendered for evil (P 118 [S.6].4).

4. Asking only to be bathed by more light bearing on Scripture (P 26[En.2].16), he wants nothing for himself; no goods linked to worldly ambition: no wealth in the guise of money, no insignia of wealth like splendid apparel; no socio-psychological goods associated with

vainglory like high position. Since liberation in the garden in Milan (8.12.29) he has mastered his inclination to fleshly pleasure. Indispensable goods such as food, drink, clothing, and shelter he cannot forgo, but these are pursued as mere means to minister to the primary end that is the kingdom of truth and justice. In sum, he does not seek truth to eat but eats to seek truth. Food and its kin are infrastructural basics for the service of the kingdom, yet, however necessary, they remain only useful goods, secondary for the soldier of Christ in a life that is both battle and journey (SDM 2.16.53-4). While delight may imply attractively garbed false teaching (P 118 [S.20].5), here the word simply means pleasure associated with the pride of life and concupiscence of the flesh. Not acquisition of worldly pleasures but insight into Scripture for closer union with God is the sole reason why he hungers to unriddle its secrets. His spiritually grounded desire warranted in God's eyes, he will be quickened with grace in the form of light and power (11.2.3); light to descry the "interior parts," i.e., the meaning lying within, below the surface of the text. He knocks instead of asking and seeking because he searches for understanding, as full as possible here below, of the truth (11.2.3).

This fresh life will flow into him, as does all grace, through Jesus in virtue of whose example and power he can love God as God, as sovereign good rather than the finites partaking of his goodness (P 29.18). Christ is the one mediator between God and man (10.43.68). Through Christ who is God with the Father and man with men (S 47.12.21) the Father sought out fallen man, who, distanced by his sinful condition, could not seek God, in order than man might seek the Father. The Father sent his Son to inspire the prodigal son that is sin-stricken humankind to return. Jesus Christ is the Word through whom all were made; the redeemer through whom those called to be adopted sons of God, were remade, not simply as isolated individuals but as members of the supernatural community that is the Church or body of Christ (P 138.2). Moreover, in Christ, who, enthroned beside the Father, goes on interceding for redeemed man, are stored all wisdom and knowledge, more of which treasures will help throw floodlights dispelling obscurities in Scriptures. With such cognitive riches he can enter the mind of Moses who, Jesus apparently believed, composed the Pentateuch wherein Moses wrote about Christ; a statement seemingly beyond challenge since Christ, who is the truth, so averred. Everything set down in the Old Testament can be interpreted as signifying future events of the New (P 47.1). In particular, the Old Testament foretells the coming of Christ in two ways. First, as Mt 13.17 indicates, Old Testament spiritual leaders vaguely longed for the future redeemer; things as well as personages obscurely suggested lineaments of the expected Messiah. So, in his authoring the Pentateuch, Moses roughed out features of Christ; the account of the creation of light, for example, predicted the rising of the light that is Christ at the resurrection; a perspective in which Christians understand that God spiritually made the light when Christ rose from the dead (P 47.1). At times slightly clearer lines of a portrait of Christ emerge from a discerning gloss of figures like Noah, the patriarchs, Samson, the prophets, Moses, Joshua, David, and the earlier Solomon (DC 4.31.45. J 15.32; 24.7. S 78. 1-3; 352.4. P 51.1,3; 80.8,11; 126.2).[10] Second, some texts more boldly depict characteristics of Christ. David, in sparing Saul, betokens the gentleness of the savior to come (P 131.2) while David's mourning over Absalom foreshadows Christ's rebuke of Judas (P 3.1; 142.1-4). Moreover, Isaiah's description of an individual wounded from the sole of his feet to the crown of his head designates the suffering Christ (P 142.1-4).[11]

His prayer that Christ flood his mind with wisdom desires the Lord operative in both subject and object of knowledge; the light of Christ aglow within penetrates Christ present in Scripture.

Chapter 3: Inner Truth Source of Understanding Scripture

5. In interpreting "In the beginning God made heaven and earth," Book 11 restricts itself to an analysis of making or creation and definitions of eternity and time implied in "In the beginning", with an explanation of the meaning of heaven and earth deferred until Book 12. He obviously cannot query the long-dead Moses, the deliverer and promulgator of the Law, who has gone from God to God, from partial presence and intimacy on earth to union and bliss with God at least in the bosom of Abraham (9.3.6). Were he to encounter Moses, Augustine would implore him to explicate through God's light the meaning of Gn 1.1. If in the more likely case Moses spoke in Hebrew, the sounds striking his ears would leave his mind uninformed, for though he had a marginal knowledge of Hebrew via Punic, he lacked an elementary grasp of the language of the Jews (QH 7).[12] However, if Moses' answer were couched in Latin he would undoubtedly

understand him. Still, the explanation tendered would not be self-authenticating. For even if Moses related the ground in truth for his exposition, Augustine could not verify this simply from his outer witness. Only in virtue of the truth consulted within could Augustine assert with certitude, "Moses is speaking the truth," while also assuring Moses that he was indeed veracious. Truth is not the private preserve of any one individual nor the particular possession of any special ethnic strain or language group. Resident in its natural home, the mind, above the flux of the senses, it is the common object of every man's understanding (LA 2.12.33) and is not limited to Hebrew, Greek, Latin, or any barbarian (here neither Greek nor Latin) tongue. The truth about the veracity of Moses is verified in the supersensible mode, without the organs of mouth and tongue that subserve speech. In accord with the truth within and above his mind, he can truly certify that Moses is speaking the truth. Since Moses, long ago gathered to his fathers and now dwelling in the Father's house, cannot interpret Gn 1.1, he calls on the truth[13] who divulged these truths to gift him with godly acuity to divine their meaning, in preparation for which God will spare, i.e., forgive, his sins, further cleansing his inner eye.

Chapter 4: Heaven and Earth Created by God

6. As in a previous passage (10.6.9), voice metaphorically designates limitation in being or simply basic makeup and mode. In particular, heaven and earth and all things in them are changeable; their mutability, the radical characteristic of all things made, is the voice or bedrock reason why they cry out that they are made, showing themselves as made. An unmade being is immutable; it neither gains increment nor suffers loss during any conceivable span of duration. What it is or has now is exactly the same as what it was or had before, and, by implication, will continue to be and have afterward. Change, however, bespeaks dependence on another; change in being bespeaks dependence in being. Things in the universe rely for their very existence and ontic structure on another being: they are made. Their makeup or fundamental character evinces that they are not self-made. It is impossible that plainly contingent things, which are not responsible for their own making, be other than made since, to be other than made, mutables would have to be immutable. It is also

impossible that they make themselves; to be self-makers or causes of their own existence, they would have to preexist their own existence. Since a generative cause must existentially precede its effect, a self-caused thing would have to exist before bringing itself into existence. If it already existed at time t_1, there would be no need of producing its existence at time t_2. Conversely, if it came into existence at time t_2, it could not have been in existence at time t_1. If nonexistent at the moment of production, it could not have functioned as cause of its own existence. The voice of things that are made figuratively refers to the evidence of their intelligible nature: by its very makeup no thing can make itself.

Not self-made, heaven and earth have to be made by God alone. According to their mode of actual existence, things are beautiful because God is beautiful. But following the human procedure of knowing, Augustine argues that we know that God is beautiful because things made are beautiful; correspondingly, he is good, the mind concludes, because what he has made is good; and he exists, it is certain, because the things he made exist. Things, in fact, derive their beauty, goodness, and being from God. God and things made are similar: we know that he exists and is good from analyses of the beings and goods he made; and the existence and goodness of things made copy in some measure the existence and goodness of God. But in terms of mode of possession of these attributes, a radical dissimilarity splits off God from things made. Things evidently beautiful, good, and existent are not such in the same manner as their creator possesses these attributes. In comparison with the beauty and goodness of immutable being, only unchangeable being is true being or being in the fullest sense; mutable beings cease to be what they were and begin to be what they were not (S 7.7). Uncompared to God, creatures exist because they derive being from him, but compared to God, they do not exist, i.e., they do not have true or unchangeable being, which God alone is (P 134.4). In other words, only the creator[11] exists in the absolute sense; all creatures exist only relatively. As Augustine phrased it earlier, creatures do not wholly exist nor do they wholly not exist. They exist because they draw being from God; they do not exist because they are not what God is, not immutable, not endowed with true or fullest being (7.11.17).

Augustine praises God for this nuanced cognition of creator and creature. Yet set over against the wholly unchangeable knowledge of the immutable being, human knowledge is ignorance or nonknowledge because, like all that is created, it is striated with mutability. Insofar as human knowledge arises from and mirrors divine knowledge, it is indeed, relatively speaking, knowledge. But matched against transcendent divine knowledge, it is nonknowledge because it is not what God is, unchangeable, knowledge in the absolute sense.

Chapter 5: Human Art Distinct from that of the Creator

7. Art, recall, is an organized disposition (M 6.12.35), a practical science or know-how in making things (M 1.2.2), the skill consisting of certain rules of practical principles of operation, in line with which according to a particular plan the artisan imprints a form on the natural object that is his raw material (Imm 4.5. GCM 1.8.13). In distinguishing the human from the divine artisan, at the outset he raises the possibility that the creator made the world after the fashion of a prodigious quasi-human artisan: what type of gigantic contrivance, he muses, did God apply in his construction of the universe? Some lines below, this possibility is dropped as a piece of woolly thinking; God produced the world without dependence on huge machinery or the least particle of matter.

An artisan exercises his craft by deciding to fashion an artwork according to a pre-thought design or form in his mind, which is impressed on already existing material such as earth, stone, wood, and gold, to issue in pottery, a statue, a stool, or a crown. Not spontaneously executed, the finished product is the outcome of the ministry of members of the body painstakingly stamping the form on the raw material. The artistic movement goes not simply from mind to matter, but also from matter back again to mind, as the artisan checks and rechecks to validate that his artifact, when rounded out, conforms in every key detail to the original plan. In short, the artwork does not spring fullblown from the wedding of art-pattern and matter; it has to be edited, so to speak, modified and refined. Undoubtedly a human craftsman, whose artistry sets him apart from and above the other animals, is a limited maker. God, the supreme artisan, shaped all the causal factors operative in the process: the mind that invented artistic models and superintends bodily members; the special aptitude for cultivating a particular art; the senses of the body that mediate between mind and matter, channeling mental directives to matter; then transmitting the state of the artifact back to the mind till the final reworking of the roughly hewn work. The conscientious artisan measures his actual product against an inner yardstick, the truth within that is or articulates the rules of his metier. The particular rules derive from more general rules that exist *omnia simul,* altogether at once, in a changeless, timeless, and spaceless manner (3.7.14), which for workmanship of any sort requires unity, equality, and proportion of parts. Denied advanced educational opportunities and/or deficient in analytical ability, an ordinary artisan cannot set down precisely why certain arches are beautiful or properly ordered, though, in employing particular rules for his art, he is implicitly invoking the why and wherefore ingredient in more general rules. The truth embracing general rules that reside in the mind originates in God who is truth presiding above the mind, which is the unchangeable law of all arts, the art of the omnipotent artist (VR 30.55-33.59).

All subrational creatures praise God as their creator through man, their voice being their beauty, which, observed and reflected upon, moves his heart to praise the Lord in their stead as their surrogate, as priest of all creation (5.1.1). But exactly how does God create things? First, he cannot create heaven and earth in heaven and earth since the whole cannot be contained in the part. If heaven and earth already contain either heaven or earth, they cannot be made or contained in heaven or earth. A fortiori, heaven and earth cannot be made in air or in water since the whole cannot be contained in lesser parts. If air and water are contained in heaven and earth, heaven and earth cannot be contained in them. In short, the greater cannot be in the lesser nor the whole in a part nor the container in the contained. Second, the whole world was not made in the whole world because there was no place in the universe in which it could be made prior to its coming into being. All possible places for its making were places in the world; no places were available outside the universe. In other words, the whole world could be made in the whole world only if the place of making were not in the world. To make the whole world in the whole world would require an out-of-this-world place, which is absurd. Because a whole world includes all physically possible places, a place outside the whole world is physically impossible. Third, unlike a human artisan, the creator cannot count on a matter preexistent to his making heaven and earth. A preexisting matter would have to be produced by a cause independent of God. On that supposition, however, the matter would acquire existence apart from God. But if it were prior in existence to God's creative activity, God would not be creator of all things, a consequence disproved by the argument that all things mutable must be made by an immutable being (11.4.6). Everything that exists in the universe exists only because God exists. Anything that exists, including the hypothetical matter, has to derive existence from God. To put it otherwise, the hypothesis of matter preexisting creation, a matter independent of God, a matter on which God is dependent, is an impossible supposition. This is not to say that a primordial unformed matter is inconceivable; in fact, Augustine reasons that the structured universe was fashioned out of unformed matter, itself created by God (12.6.6). Unformed matter has existence, and therefore has to be created by the God who exists without qualification, whose creative art imprints on beings a share in his existence, goodness, and beauty. Absolutely self-sufficient, needing no resources outside his fecundity, God created all things through his fiat, indeed through his eternal Word.

It seems very probable that in this passage Augustine is vaguely dismissing, as elsewhere he specifically targets, the Manichees' thesis that God, while omnipotent, cannot produce the world except with dependence on preexisting matter (GCM 1.6.10. FS 2.2). As late as 421 Manichees insisted that the world was fashioned from some nature or matter eternal with God (CALP 1.1.1). Based upon a false analogy with human making, Manichean belief that God cannot create without matter anthropomorphizes divine activity. Moreover, it is paradoxical to link omnipotence to preexisting matter since an all-powerful artisan has to make all things, not only forms but things unformed or formable as well. Furthermore, the Manichean notion of matter seems inconsistent; presumably passive, it is also an active constructor of bodies. Manichean matter is misnamed; their *hyle* is not pure subject but identified with the Race of Darkness, which encompasses corporeal forms and a productive mind (CF 20.14). In addition, to Primal Man is ascribed the formation of visible creation such as sky, earth, and mountains (CF 6.8); however, the Living Spirit is also described as a builder of the visible world (CF 20.9). The confusion probably lies not in Augustine but in diverse interpretations by teachers of Manicheism, in which analytical clarity and coherence are often conspicuous largely by their absence not only in regard to the concept of matter but throughout their bizarre world picture.

Augustine was acquainted with a more precise sort of matter, of which the active Manichean type is an illegitimate offspring, what the ancients or Greeks named *hyle*, a formless subject denuded in itself of all form but capable of receiving all corporeal forms, which, not knowable in itself, is known through the changing forms or qualities impressed on it (CF 20.14). The counterpart in ordinary experience of wholly formless matter is also called *hyle*; just as wood is the matter for chairs, tables and stools, so matter is the substrate for natural corporeal forms (NB 18). According to some pagans, primitive matter coeval or coeternal with God was not divinely created, though corporeal forms imprinted on matter emerged from his creation (CF 20.14). It is not easy to name the ancients or Greeks to whom Augustine attributes a theory of matter independent of God but formable by divine action into actual substances. Prior to Aristotle, thinkers such as Anaximentes, Thales, Parmenides, and Empedocles considered respectively air, water, a combination of fire and earth, and a mixture of all four elements as the basic quasi-substantial matter out of which all beings of nature are constructed.[15] Consistent with their materialistic monism, none of these philosophical physicists posited a divine being to cause forms organizing eternal matter. In the view of one scholar,[16] the Greek opinion mentioned in NB 18 is expressly that of Plotinus, with some connection to that of Plato and Aristotle. However, CF 20.14, which echoes NB 18, explicitly speaks of a matter not derived from God whereas the matter of Plotinus somehow emanates from the One.[17] It seems permissible then to suggest that Augustine was reporting the theory of Plato or a faithful descendant, according to which the demiurge or divine artisan frames causally, if not temporally, an ordered natural universe out of the receptacle or preexisting matter after the model of ideal forms.[18] The foundational truth of creationist philosophy, that creation is not *de Deo* but *de nihilo*, which Augustine later underscores (12.7.7), is implicitly stated here. Since God needs no matter, he must create without dependence on a subject, out of nothing whatsoever. Plainly creatures are not *de Deo*; otherwise, like the Son, they would be generated within the divine substance. Creatures are neither begotten nor fashioned from uncreated matter but produced from nothing, *de nihilo* (CD 12.5). Elsewhere the phrase *ex nihilo* is used (Oros 1.3). From the side of the efficient cause things are made by the creator: created goods flow from him (*a quo*, NB 3); and creatures originate *ex Deo* as from their producer (VR 18.35). Augustine's position is succinctly resumed in the line: "For when it is said, 'God produced from nothing (*ex nihilo*) this means nothing other than this: there was nothing from which he made the universe, and, nevertheless, because he is so willed, he produced (*fecit*) the universe" (Oros 1.31).[19] This text captures the absolute transcendence of God. Independent of any subject from without, not necessitated from within to generate creatures, he freely created the universe from nothing.

Given a benign reading, the incoherent Manichean Father of Light was at best relatively transcendent. Moreover, however more analytically powerful and logically cohesive, the concepts of God in Plato, Aristotle, and Plotinus yielded only a relatively transcendent deity. They are unquestionably transcendent because the Good, Self-Thinking Thought, and the One are supreme in the universe, far superior to lesser entities. Yet only relatively so; situated at the peak of the universe, they remain part of the world, unthinkable as existing apart from the universe. But the creator-God is absolutely transcendent; in the medieval phrase, *non de hoc mundo*, not of this world, not a part of the universe. Infinite in his own being, existing totally apart from the universe, in no way does he need the universe, which is the outcome of superabundant goodness, the universe coming into being not in virtue of inward necessity but out of generosity, from goodness-diffusing freedom. Prior to the world's beginning in time God dwelt in his eternal mode of existence, utterly without dependence on a world, whereas for its beginning in time the world is dependent upon God. In the perspective of relative transcendence, God is the capstone of the universe; the world is inconceivable without God, its highest cause, yet God is also inconceivable apart from the world: God and the world continually coexist, albeit on planes far from one another. An absolutely transcendent God, however, is so thinkable apart from the world that he is unthinkable dependent on the world since prior to creation he was serenely God, and, had there been no creation, his existence would have perdured for all eternity. Without a created world God would exist in infinitely perfect life while without the creation and conservation of God the world would simply not exist. Ontically, not spatially, an infinite gap separates infinite creator and finite creature:

God unqualifiedly transcends his creation. The ontic divide, we saw earlier, is bridged by creative action, consequent upon which God is causally present in everything created. He is omnipresently immanent; because absolutely transcendent, he is everywhere immanent; because wholly other, totally not of this world, causally he is totally everywhere, *totus ubique.*

Chapter 6: The Creative Act Not Expressed in Words

8. Divine transcendence is first vindicated in utter independence from matter. Needing no goods prior to creation nor after creation as well (GL 4.16.27), his divine making does not, indeed cannot, rely on an intermediate factor or instrument (CD 12.25). Not God plus a creature but God alone made the entire universe (P 135.5). This first attestation leads to a second warranty of God's transcendence: his creative act is articulated not in words but through the Word.

If God spoke a command initiating creation, Augustine hypothesizes that God might have vocalized his fiat after the fashion of his utterance at the baptism of Jesus. Bearing the features of time, such a pronouncement began, then ended, with its parts not fixed, one syllable succeeding the other till the sentence was terminated. Coming to be and passing away with a span of successive parts signalize time. The sound was emitted in accord with the true eternal will, but the succession of sounds was unquestionably temporal. The outer ear, functioning as sensory messenger,[20] carried the words to the prudent mind, whose interior power of hearing consulted the eternal Word that is truth. The mind is characterized as prudent in the analytical, not the moral, sense; as moral prudence distinguishes between moral right and wrong, so theoretical prudence or acumen marks the difference between theoretical right and wrong (5.10.19). Scrutiny discerns a gulf between temporal words and the eternal Word. Because evanescent, these words do not absolutely exist; compared to absolute existence, they do not exist. The Word, on the contrary, is fixed and deathless, abiding forever outside time beyond the human mind. Audible and transient words cannot serve as an instrument of God's creative act. First, if such words were spoken, they would have to be uttered in terms of sound, which is the corporeal vehicle or body of a word's meaning which is, as it were, its soul (QA 37.66); a body, in effect, prior to heaven and earth.

However, according to Scripture, no body preceded heaven and earth. Second, even granting, without conceding, that there existed a body prior to heaven and earth, it would have been made by God without utilizing a transient voice. As eternal, he cannot voice a sentence whose syllables are pronounced successively, for example, in time, and whose bodily apparatus is sound consisting of temporal movements following one after another. Were God to resort to a passing voice, he would be de-eternalized and reduced to subjection to change, simply ceasing to be God. Third, even if on the assumption that somehow preexisting heaven and earth there was a sound (the corporeal container of the meaning or "soul" of a word), which serves as a material basis or vehicle of such a voice, it would have null being; it would not exist at all unless given existence by God's creative act. Next, continuing to assume that a sound (along with the air required) may have antedated the making of heaven and earth, Augustine asks: how did God initiate the making of the body or sound from which words are formed? Which spiritual out-of-time word did God utter to make the sound out of which temporal words such as "Let there be heaven on earth" are made?

Chapter 7: God Speaks in Time through his Eternal Word.

9. This chapter solves the problem raised at the end of the foregoing chapter. Speaking by a word but not by a word or words freighted with time, God spoke his creative fiat by his coeternal Word, always one with him in nature, however differentiated in person. God calls Augustine, be it remarked, to perceive the truth in response to the divine call involved in justification; here a specific call to understand, to apprehend the meaning of his teaching beyond simple faith. The Word is eternally uttered by God; a Word or Son not made but begotten by the Father. Always with God, he was or is prior to all time because eternally generated from the very substance of God. It is through and in the eternal Word that the Father eternally utters things that are noneternal (S 135.3.4). Unlike the word of time, the Word is not uttered successively but wholly all at once, and, since its enunciation is nonsuccessive, without passage of parts, it is eternal. Succession and passage bespeak time and change[21] (change connoting corruption and extinction), neither of which is admissible and constitutive of or accidental to the divine nature. The Word interiorly

spoken by God has to be truly eternal, totally immune from the least tincture of time; and truly immortal or deathless, wholly exempt from any intrinsic nexus with the change that portends dissolution.

Along with other spirituals, Augustine not only believes but understands, albeit without comprehending or exhaustively understanding, that the Word which God speaks and by which he speaks his creative command is fully eternal. Temporal words conditioned by time die;[22] no longer what they once were, they cease to be; and they come to be: they are now what they once were not.[23] The Word that is God because of God does not cede place to one word or follow upon another word; it neither ceases nor begins to be. It is truly changeless and deathless; it is absolutely timeless and eternal. Since the Word is eternal, the creative decree that God utters is not pronounced in time but in eternity through his eternal Word. Moreover, whatever God orders to be made is simply made; his command is creative: in virtue of his simple fiat, the thing is instantaneously made. No hiatus intervenes between directive and actual making; the very ordaining utterance is the production of the thing. Still, a caveat must be entered. The modes of making and the made are not one and the same. Creative utterance is simultaneous, without succession of syllables, and eternal, without before or after. But the things made, which issue from a simultaneous and eternal fiat, are not made simultaneously and eternally; they come to be successively and in the line of mutation and time. In brief, the act of creation is simultaneous and eternal, but the things created exist successively in the order of time. Since God is immutable, his creative act entails no change in himself; his duration remains immutable or eternal. Since God cannot create another God, things made have to exist in a nondivine mode; they are bound to be subject to mutation and time.

Chapter 8: In Christ the Beginning Man Learns the Truth.

10. The solution apparently generates a paradox: how can the Word be eternal and the creatures he makes temporal? how can the creative fiat be simultaneous and semipiternal and its creaturely outcome successive and temporal? Unable to completely understand the problem, he can explicate it in some measure. Whatever begins and ceases to be is programmed to be temporal according to a timeless type or pattern. In God, who exists eternally before there was a

temporal "before," stand or reside the stable or fixed causes of unstable or transient things; the multiple eternal reasons or types of temporals are located in the one eternal reason, the mind or thought of God that is the eternal Word. This Word is the beginning, he remarks elliptically, because he also speaks to us. Stated less compactly, we believe that the Word is the beginning (Jn 8.25) because he has spoken to us in the flesh. Since the Word as purely intelligible, as second Person, was cognizable by intellect alone, he could not have been believed save through words, evidence accessible to the senses (J 38.11). The beginning signifies what absolutely exists, i.e., what is completely immutable, and from this changeless principle, which makes all things new, originates the changing things of time. In revealing himself as the beginning, the principle, Christ adapted himself to the human condition, employing human speech to impart his unique divine character. To the senses were transmitted the outward sound, but it was the inward mind that judged it, verifying it in the ever-abiding truth, which is the eternal Word, whose rays illumine the mind. Christ the interior teacher, source of the light within that evidences and clarifies the truth, is, recall, the only teacher in the sense that human teachers are instrumental factors, whose words admonish the listener to turn inward to learn from the Christ presiding within (Mag 11.38; 12.40; 14.45). In the line of natural knowledge all men consult him to learn the truth; but in the sphere of revealed knowledge bad will can block the influx of light (Mag 11.38).

Within, Augustine learns the inner locution of God since Christ, the one teacher one with the Father, speaks the truth. Here speaking is identified with teaching; hence, he argues, the so-called human teacher speaks externally, but since he does not strictly, i.e., inwardly, teach, he is not really speaking. Like his teaching, his speaking as sheerly exterior is no more than appearance, for it does not convey the truth. Only immutable truth can communicate truths that are immutable; the human mind, varying in its opinions, always prey to error, cannot be the ultimate source of the fixity and stability at the core of truth. Whereas mutable fellow men engage in external seeming-teaching that consists of specific acts and reminders, proffering proper signs that dispose persons inward, without bestowing truth (EJ 3.13), individuals learn the truth by standing in the truth, which signifies remaining fixed in grace (J 14.2). Satan courted disaster, it may be noted, because he refused to stand in the truth that is Christ (J 42.11). (Indeed the devil is the father of lies; as the Father begot his Son or truth, so the devil begot falsehood as a kind of son [J 42.1].) Standing or remaining stable in this grace like John the Baptist, we rejoice not because we hear the voice of Christ the truth, the bridegroom espoused to souls, but because we are illumined by Christ the light, because the inner ear hearkens to the Word uttering the truth; all the while standing and not falling because our spirit is based on the solid ground of humility (J 13.12). Christ as truth teaches a doctrinal truth that is personal and existential as well, engendering happiness (Mag 12.40; 14.46); so we rejoice in hearing the voice of our redeemer-bridegroom, who shed his sacred blood as the price of our redemption (J 13.13). Appropriately, God originally made man in the Word, the perfect image of God (GI 16.60-1), and through the death of the Word made man remakes man (P 44.14). Hence joy over the voice of the bridegroom is delight in the healing truth that is Christ, through whom as Word we come from God, through whom as Word made man we are restored to the source of our being.

Were the Word not the principle or immutable being, did he not remain always the same, then when we wandered astray in the moral error that is sin, we could never return to him, for he would have altered his ontic position, having become other, no longer absolute but unfixed truth, no more available than a boat that has slipped its moorings. Happily, the principle that is the Word is stable,[24] blessing us with certitude rather than with sheer surmise that we have genuinely come back home; stable knowledge radiated from stable truth, the Word within, who alone can teach because he is the immutable principle.

Chapter 9: The Beginning Is Christ, the Healing Wisdom

11. So super-wondrous is creation in the beginning, through the Word who is the power and wisdom of the Father, and, as wisdom, the truth of God, that it is beyond comprehension, beyond total understanding, ineffable, leaving Augustine, master of eloquence, helpless to do it full justice. In contrast to physical light whose brilliance may blind, this spiritual light overpowering in its splendor does not damage his intellectual vision in the least. Currently graced

but prone to and haunted by venial sin, a propensity meditated on in Book 10, he is both repelled and attracted by divine light. In the line of the spirit, if not in one sector of modern physics, unlikes mutually repulse while likes are drawn to one another. Insofar as he still falls into sin, he is unlike God; even minor instances of earthiness impel him to recoil in a kind of horror, unholiness rendering him repugnant to the light of the all-holy. On the other hand, as similar to God, his spirit alive with Christ-grace yearns for greater intimacy with the divine truth.[25] The wisdom that is Christ the truth suffuses the fibers of his spirit, piercing through the dark clouds that symbolize his still-sinful state. Guilty of daily faults, he is beset by a twofold evil: the darkness of the cloud that is sin covering him and the penalties inevitably due his sins. His moral vigor falters under the dark weight of punishment; his stamina is sapped in destitution of spirit, so marked that he cannot support his proper good, which is the good of all goods (P 102.8). Although he is bent down by the load of retribution, God unfailingly dispenses forgiveness for sicknesses of soul. So definitive is healing of heart by the divine physician, superior to uncertain and short-lived healing of body by human hands, that the spirit, to some degree, delights in the stinging cauterizing and painful cutting that make his soul sound (P 102.5).[26] God redeems man from corruption through Christ whose blood on the cross made the exchange for human ransom (P 102.6). He is promised the crown of glory not out of earthly justice but in virtue of the mercy of God. After the battle comes the crown; after the crown, the total consummation of all desires, union with the infinite good, (P 102.8); no less than full satisfaction because he will live on eternally, wholly possessing the good of goods without change or diminution, without intrusion of possible loss or pain or evil in a resurrected body (P 102.9). So revitalized, he will feed on the super-solid, the living bread that is Christ, the three loaves of the Gospel that represent the triple divine food of Father, Son, and Holy Spirit (P 102.10).

But the boundless plenty in which sons of God shall be like him lies in the future. There he shall actually see God as he is, the "Is"[27] who does not increase because perfect, who does not decrease because eternal (EJ 4.5); he shall actually become like God, as eternal and deathless as he. Now, not yet resting *in re*, he sojourns *in spe*; there above is the reality, here below the hope. Saved through hope, raising up his heart to the life to come (S 395.1), he waits with patience[28] that, upbuilding his spirit (S 3336.5), sharpens longing for the heavenly kingdom (EJ 4.6). Spirituals adroit enough to move beyond simple faith to understanding of the revealed text[29] are bade to hearken to wisdom[30] within transmitting the meaning of "In the beginning." Through the light interiorly bathing his mind, he cries out exteriorly, making his own the line of God's oracle, the psalmist who channels divine communication; words that praisefully echo the first verse of Genesis: super-magnificent is the universe that God created in the wisdom that is Christ (P 103 [S.3].25). Overawed and yet uplifted, he exults in the beauty of the universe fashioned in the wisdom that is Christ; this wisdom is the beginning and, he notes summarily, in the beginning that is wisdom or the Word God made the universe.

Chapter 10: Objections to the Christian View of Creation

12. The principal opponents of the Judeo-Christian view of creation are Manichees (GCM 1.2.3-4), ostensibly religious but actually "full of old-agedness." Old age, a symbol of carnality (S 267.2), a state not due to necessity of nature (for men do not choose to be born or grow old) but to free choice (EJ 3.1), is a condition proper to those living in accord with the exterior man, slaves of things temporal (P 131.1).[31] Spiritual growth not renewed, the weakness-causing beaks of these aged eagles are not struck and shortened on the rock that is Christ (P 66.10).[32] Since they denounce the crucified savior as an impostor, their old man within is not crucified with Christ (S 336.5). Frozen in spiritual decrepitude, Manichees cannot recognize that Christ is eternal wisdom, the beginning in and through whom God created the universe.

Though apparently trivial and superficially formulated at the outset, strictures against creation turn out to be forceful and, in one respect, formidable.[33] First, creation in time seems inexplicable. No sound reason is advanced to account for an eternal God's forsaking his solitary bliss, unencumbered by activity ad extra, to construct a world independent of himself.[34] Simply informed that God created the world in time, we are left in the dark as to why he abandoned his workless existence in order to venture the creation of the universe. Why did an eternal God not remain forever a noncreative God? Creationists' lips are silent, unable to tender an explanation. Second, creation by an eternal God seems self-stultifying. Creation entails a new movement, a fresh act of will decreeing a creature never before made. But this novelty of will is apparently at loggerheads with the immutable duration of God. If God is truly eternal, his will never changes, whereas creation implies a change in the divine will. Prior to creation his will was immutable, but the activity of willing creation introduces a change in his will. Nor can it be contended that his will is accidental to God, so that a change of will does not affect the unchangeable core that is substance; since the will of God belongs to his very substance, the divine nature admits of no distinction between substance and accident. Because God's will is one with his substance, a new election of will would entrain a change in his very substance. Thus creation that betokens a novel will-act undercuts the immutability of God. A creator-God, because altered by his creative act, cannot be truly eternal; God is either truly eternal or really creative; only at peril of absurdity can he be both. Third, since an eternal God who creates through a new act of the will is inconceivable, the will of God to create must not be new but always present and one with his substance. His will to create must be as eternal as the very substance. If his will to create is eternal, then the created universe must be inescapably necessary. If creation is eternally necessary, then the universe created is necessarily eternal.

None of these objections is explicitly confronted and effectively nullified at this stage. Perhaps he believes that he has implicitly confuted them by underlining, in reply to a fourth objection (11.12.14), that eternity, properly understood, so totally transcends time that God acts immutably, according to his changeless substance, in creating mutable beings. In short, any change in creation is registered in the effect, not in the changeless cause. It is in CD that Augustine expressly grapples with and resolves these spiny problems, which, however, are not listed in the manner of 11.10.12. Though creation itself is naturally knowable, clinging to the mode of creation are indissoluble mists of obscurity. Unlike its partially intelligible meaning, its mode resists anything close to satisfactory explanation. Since the depth of God's creative wisdom is, in the last analysis, unfathomable, at a certain juncture the mind is brought up short, balked from further sounding of the eternal fiat commanding creation. God created newly existent things not by a sudden act of will but in accord with his changeless and eternal decree (CD 12.15). Nevertheless, Augustine does formulate telling responses to the three objections. In reply to the first, since no man thinks and acts in the eternal mode, it is impossible to set down in concrete detail primarily why God, as the objection puts it, forsook leisure and produced a universe. The implication that prior to creation God was relaxing in a sort of blissful idleness is misleading. Even before creation God at rest was wholly active since his rest is, internally, infinitely intense activity (CD 12.18). What motivated God to create, we may say, was "gratuitous goodness" (CD 12.18). Absolutely happy in his perfect goodness, he could profit nothing from making beings of lesser goodness. His creation then is simply an outpouring from which he does not expect a return; his felicity stays always perfect; he would have exulted in infinite happiness if he had never made a single thing: thus not creator but creature benefits from creation. Thus too his will to create is not groundless: the creative act is rooted in goodness that can give all while receiving no intrinsic compensation; more precisely, it is a goodness that gives a share in the all that is his goodness. In other words, God, while necessarily existing, is not necessitated to create. Lacking nothing, he can earn nothing from creation. The motive for creation lies in the goodness to be given, not in any gain to be received.[35] Hence the nonnecessitating reason for his creation is a gratuituous goodness. Needing nothing outside himself, God had no need to create. As Augustine succinctly argues: "A being without need is nonnecessitated; a being without defect is without need; but God is a being without defect; therefore, God is not necessitated" (DQ 83). Yet, it must be stressed, the creative act, while not necessitated, was not impulsively spontaneous; it was not an capricious eruption without rhyme or reason. An all-sufficient God created for a nonnecessitating but sufficing reason, out of disinterested goodness, out of nonself-seeking love. Still, because the depths upon depths of the workings of an infinite mind remain impenetrably obscure, the precise reasons for this particular creation slip through the meshes of limited concepts.

The second objection is by far the most potent, its paradoxical core seemingly insurmountable. A creative act apparently implies a new act of will in God. Because not previously existent, this fresh volition apparently entails a change in God. Yet God's will as volition is entirely one with, immutably joined to, his eternal substance. If a new volition is introduced into God, making his will mutable, the divine substance one with his will ceases to be immutable or eternal. For

Augustine, two roads lie open, one terminating in strict paradox, the other arriving at a slim but real intelligibility shrouded in mystery. The first alternative would concede that creation demands a change in God. This route, however, is internally incongruous: a mutable God is self-contradictory; a mutable God is no longer God but a nonGod posing as God. In order to bypass this inconsistency, Augustine retains a God who remains absolutely immutable. The work of creation and things created is new, yet the decree is not new but changelessly eternal. In God a later will-act did not alter or supersede a prior will-act; rather, in virtue of one and the same immutable will things were created. The divine will that determined things stay uncreated when not in existence was the same will that caused them to begin to exist (CD 12.18). Hard as it is to conceive, the eternal character of the divine decision to create is rendered more elusive still because of the all-too common tendency to anthropomorphize divine volition, gauging divine willing by mutable and narrow human willing. Faced with fresh problems, inherently changeable men venture new decisions. Unable to understand God's willing, they erect their own mode of willing as a paradigm by which to account for the divine decree. Neglecting to judge God's willing by his eternal mode, they measure his will according to a sheer human standard. Not letting God be God, they distortedly trim his time-transcending volition down to a temporal context (CD 12.18).[36]

According to the third objection, granted that God eternally willed the existence of creation, creatures have to exist from all eternity. Since the decision to create is eternal, creatures must be coeternal with God. Put otherwise, since God's will to create is eternally necessary, creatures must emanate from him with inexorable necessity from all eternity. Augustine counters this necessitarian brief with two arguments. (i) Since, as indicated earlier, God cannot reap any boons from lower-order things, he is not constrained to act by necessity. Nothing within his absolute independence coerces him to create. Indeed because he is wholly self-sufficient, it is self-defeating to claim that he is ineluctably moved to create. (ii) Since God cannot create other Gods, created entities cannot be eternal, for eternity bespeaks immutable duration (CD 12.16). Viewed from another angle, Augustine judges this third line of anti-creationist attack radically incoherent because it conflicts with the divine nature; it ungods God by stripping him of essential attributes of immutability and eternity. Where there is no lack, we saw, there is no necessity. Conversely, when there is necessity, there is lack: only a mutable God is intrinsically determined to create. Moreover, if created beings are coeternal with God, he is coeternal with them only in the loose sense of endlessly successive duration; not strictly changeless, his diluted eternity is no longer absolutely time-transcending.

Chapter 11: Time-Bound Minds Cannot Grasp Differences between Time and Eternity

13. Minds wholly immersed in process and time cannot grasp eternity. Here without directly dissolving the nettlesome objections (11.10.12), he works to undermine them by proving that they are founded upon a confusion of eternity with time. The objectors do not understand the Word or wisdom of God because they fail to apprehend his eternal mode of operation; they do not properly conceptualize how creation occurs, that it proceeds from an eternal source or in the eternal mode. Creatures are made through the Word, who fashions all things with form (measure), organization (number), and concordance of parts (weight and order) (J 1.13). All things are made in wisdom in the sense that things created exist after the pattern of divine art in the Word, in which are situated all the *rationes* or types of creatures (J 1.17). However strenuous, efforts of anti-creationists to lay hold of eternals miscarry because their minds fluctuate, i.e., are made mutable or fall into error. Moments and time-intervals speed away (P 38.7), and minds attuned only to the temporal mentally imitate the fleetingness of future time never-stoppingly succeeding past time. Their thoughts become unstable, wanting in truth and certitude since thinking of the temporomorphic stripe has to be vain or barren of truth (P 5.11). Such minds need to be loosed from entrapment in time; halted in their flight, gradually detemporalized, then stabilized, they are made capable of seizing the splendor of an always standing eternity. Once fastened on its true meaning, formerly temporalized minds recognize that eternity is incomparable, utterly incommensurate with time. Not a higher species of time, eternity is strictly out-of-time, totally supratemporal, ontically separate from and superior to time: it is the timeless dimension of duration. Three major differences divide eternity from time. (i) Eternity is ever-standing, always unchangeable duration, whereas time is never-standing,

always proceeding from one interval to another. (ii) Eternity is *totum praesens*, a whole that is only present, a present that is an indivisible whole. As a whole, it has no parts and, as simply present, it includes neither past nor future. Time, per contra, is not an all-at-once whole. Each segment of time consists of many already past intervals. Because time is successive, one part following the other, time is not a whole or stable present but comprised of past and future extents, every past segment being forced out of existence, made past by an incoming future interval or, from another angle, by every future interval following upon a past interval. (iii) All past and future intervals derive from and depend on the ever-present eternity. Created by the eternal, they take their origin from an eternity that has no origin; the nonsuccesive eternal sets and sustains them on their successive path.

Can anyone liberate a time-constricted human mind from temporomorphic constraints? Can anyone, staying its evanescence, hold it firm so as to see that eternity is fluxless and unalterable, a wholly present duration without future or past intervals, which, through the Word, shapes future and past times? Perhaps, he modestly hopes, his hand, standing for the hand of his mouth, i.e., the power of logical acumen, may help time-imprisoned spirits detemporalize themselves, becoming hospitable to the meaning of eternity. A veteran of dialectical battles on several fronts, he is far from being naively unaware that his words garbing his arguments seem mean over against the magnitude of the labor of moving biased minds to understand eternity. As the history of philosophy attests, it is a somber fact that not infrequently it is very hard, if not impossible, to bend the minds of analytical adversaries toward the truth. However egregiously erroneous, an intellectual outlook tends to become entrenched rock-solid in the mind, clung to uncompromisingly in the teeth of relentlessly impinging fact and cogent critique. In contemporary sectors dwelling in a dark age of naturalism, true-believing empiricists, while self-refutingly invoking free will in practice, deny free will in theory and, while effectively admitting lawlike behavior in science and medicine, reject, after the sensism of D. Hume (1711-76), necessary connection in causation–temporal sequence, not causal consequence, accounts for a nail being hammered into wood;[37] yet they resist the most powerful appeals to jettison their irrationalism. Here Augustine is apparently recalling a similar stiffedneckness of erstwhile Manichean colleagues, who simply ignored numerous criticisms launched against their rickety pseudo-system in the years following his conversion.

Chapter 12: Fourth Objection. First Response: No Creation before a Creator.

14. A fourth objection to creation, this, like the first (11.10.12), raised by Manichees, holds it unthinkable that God was not active prior to creation: what was God doing before he created heaven and earth?[38] This difficulty, at least as formulated, hardly seems overpowering, yet it is not without force. Hence in a spirit of irenic exchange he declines to evasively brush it off with a comic riposte, as did the Christian who laughingly rejoined that during that span God was readying a furnace in hell for reckless inquirers. His intellectual integrity would choose to confess ignorance rather than mask it by mockery. Oddly, some mindlessly heap ignoring-the-issue ridicule on such objectors, while shallowly lauding fellow Christians who, however well-intentioned, try to blunt the objection with a pointless answer. Such levity bespeaks a lightweight mind, incapable of deflecting a serious objection, so feeble that it cannot perceive the flimsiness of a fellow Christian's reply. Apologias for Christian teaching are ill served by question-dodging flippancy and infirmity of logical temper.[39] He tenders an initial response that lays stress on the meaning of creature, but this cautiously, because probing into the sublime workings of the eternal mind may savor of a certain audacity: prior to making the universe that consists of heaven and earth, God did not make anything at all. If God did create something before he created heaven and earth, clearly what he created was a creature. Wherever we posit the beginning of the created world, creation always bespeaks a creature; the terms are reciprocally implicative. Thus prior to creation there was no creation and, correspondingly, prior to creation there was no creator as such, God being denominated creator only in virtue of actual creating. Prior to a creature that was made there was no creature that was made. No creature was made before a creature was made because a creature made prior to the making of a creature would be a noncreature. It is self-evident that a noncreature cannot be a creature, and vice versa.

Chapter 13. Second Response: No "before" or "then" before
Creation. Third Response: the Timeless Transcends Time

15. Once more (11.11.13) he characterizes the mind of the objector
as temporalized; whirled about in the flux, incapable of cognitively
standing still to fasten on the stable truth, it topples into error. Not
directed straight toward the goal of truth, the mind meanders among
the images of past times that provoke pseudo-questions. As all-
powerful, God is the master-architect of heaven and earth;
all-creating, because he actually made the whole universe; all-
sustaining, because he administratively conserves all in the universe.
A time-bound mind, trapped in a temporomorphic framework,
however, raises a false problem: why did a creator-God let age after
age go by before making the universe? Such a questioner is
somnolent, i.e, in darkness or error, his puzzlement fallaciously
grounded; he is pondering a question absolutely irresolvable because
its assumption-structure is temporalized, because one of its key
suppositions concerning God vis-à-vis time crudely distorts divine
duration. The fundamental misconception is the contention that God
is in time or subject to time whereas God is actually, and cannot be
other than, eternal. First, it is false to picture innumerable ages
hurrying by while God prepared himself to create since ages began to
exist only with the beginning of the created universe with which the
beginning of time is concomitant. A second argument makes the
same point, with emphasis now not on prior countless ages but on
any tracts of time. No extents of time could preexist creation since
they began to exist only by being entrained in the creation of the
universe. A third line of reasoning situates the incongruity in the
passing away of what does not exist. As things not alive cannot die,
so time-intervals that never existed cannot cease to exist. Before
becoming past, a time-interval has to be first present or exist; yet it
cannot be present or exist unless it is created. Fourth, according to Gn
2.3, God rested after his work of creation. Since Scripture significantly
does not say that God rested before his work, it is clearly implied that
God was not unoccupied in some period of time prior to creation. To
repeat, no tract of time enjoyed antecedence to creation; God created
time, and thus God could not have been behaving as a gentleman of
leisure before creation. It is profitless therefore to become entangled
in image-clouded vexation about what God was doing then, in a span

of time prior to creation. For, before time was created, there could be no time, there could no "then", there could be no "before" (taking "before" in the strict acceptation of an earlier period of time).

16. God was before time but not before time in the strict temporal sense of "before." His priority to creation was not priority in time. If he had been prior to created times in a temporal sense, he could not have preceded all times; as temporalized or subject to time, as a being of and in time, he would coexist with tracts of time, a coexistence that therefore would cancel precedence of all times. Incapable without absurdity of existing before time in a temporal sense, a creator-God, however, does precede all times in his eternity. As eternal, he is above all times and therefore before all times. Eternity, as already mentioned (11.11.13), is a whole, totally indivisible without successive parts; as immutable, it is always the same, always one and the same present without past and future. Thus God is before all past intervals, not in time but in the unsurpassable peak of an always-present eternity. While eternity is always and simply present, past intervals do not exist always: once existent, they no longer exist. Past intervals are simply not present; once present, they have ceased to be present. Moreover, unlike eternity, future intervals are neither always nor simply present. They do not always exist, for, as future, they do not yet exist; nor are they present: they will become present, only to cease to be and become past. Differentiated from creatures, God perdures as the Selfsame, the "I am who am," the changeless "Is" (P 121.5), whose duration is unchangeable or, in Biblical idiom, whose years do not fail. The years of the wholly and always present eternal do not pass away and come into existence. On the contrary, human years disappear into the past and come to be, the future incessantly succeeding the past. Human days go and come so that all may come, i.e., so that human life is over and done with.[40] Once all of man's days have come, they no longer come; his days are ended, his life finished in death. All of God's years, however, stand all at once; his duration, figuratively expressed by years, remains fixed and changeless. In the indivisibly one divine duration there is no departure of years into the past nor incoming into the present of previously future years. Human years, he iterates, are utterly different: only when all are no more will all be; the span of human life is achieved only at the point that life ceases to be. Temporal fullness is engraved with an ultimate seal of mutability: human life stops changing only when it stops. God's years

are, as Scripture has it, one day, not an ordinary day preceded by one and followed by another; his is a day that is only today, simply present, without similar day before or after, a changeless today without yesterday or tomorrow.[41] In the today that is ever-present duration the Father says to his coeternal Son, "This day [an eternal today] I have begotten you"(Ps 2.7): within the eternal divine nature the Father eternally generates the Son.

The final sentence recapitulates sections 15 and 16 and their common conclusion. (i) Because God created all intervals of time, it is inadmissible to speak of a strictly temporal "then" prior to the creation of time. (ii) God is before all intervals of time, past, or future, not on the plane of time, not according to a strictly temporal "before", but on the plane of eternity, as perduring above time in a *totum praesens* prior both in origin and in cause to all time. God's transcendent eternity is the reason why there was no temporal "then" or "before" in relation to creation. (iii) Since the creator of time exists before time only in terms of his eternity, no time existed prior to the creation of time. To maintain otherwise entails the self-contradictory position that there was time when there was no time. Plainly time cannot simultaneously exist and not exist prior to the creation or beginning of time. Time cannot exist before time: as a creature cannot preexist its own existence (11.12.14), so time cannot preexist its own existence.

It seems appropriate to close this section with remarks on the precise meaning of eternity.[42] Nowhere does Augustine develop a formal exposition of eternity comparable to his treatise on time. Yet it seems possible to piece together a tenable definition from his condensed reflections. Because God is supreme life, he is immutable and, from the side of duration, eternal (1.7.10). Indeed, it may be added, eternity is the substance of God (P 101(5.2)10). As mutability is the root of time (12.6.6), so immutability is the root of eternity. As spiritual and immutable, eternity is one individual whole, without parts; without past, present, and future components. It is a *totum praesens*, a whole-present, a present and nothing more (1.11.13). It is *totum* that is *simul*, an all-at-once duration (11.13.15), which is, in other words, without beginning or end (a point explicitly stated in T 15.5.7). Furthermore, since the divine present that is eternity is the transtemporal analogue of the strict physical present, which is the extentless instant (11.15.20), eternity, it is suggested, is a standing instant (11.11.13, 15.20) or, in the language of some medievals, a *nunc stans.* Ordinarily Augustine speaks of the present as a *totum* and a *simul* standing fixed, without expressly averring that eternity is a standing instant. Augustine's formulation essentially anticipates, without necessarily directly influencing, Boethius' celebrated definition of eternity, a classic *authenticum dictum* in the Middle Ages, *interminabilis vitae tota simul et perfecta possesio* (the wholly all-at-once perfect possession of unending life),[43] lies in between the lines of Augustine's analysis: eternity is the wholly present and all-at-once life (T 6.10.11) that is without beginning or end (P 134.6), complete in itself, needing no temporal augmentation (S 225.2).[44]

The sovereignty of eternity does not sever every linkage with time. Ontically transcendent, eternity is causally immanent in time. Eternity is the container and governor of the time. The days of men pass through the eternal day or eternal present. The standing present that is eternity causally intersects with time by fixing the boundaries for the passage of beings of time.

At this juncture Augustine begins his compact treatise on psychological time. Since his analysis has suffered misinterpretation, it seems worthwhile to outline the main factors in his reasoning.

Introduction: The perplexity and the problem (14.17). The perplexity: common knowledge of time leaves us analytically ignorant of what time is. The problem: how can past, present, and future exist if they are either nonexistent or unknowable?

Part I: Real Time as Present Time (15.18-21.27).
1. Whereas the physical present is pointlike, the present that we sensibly observe can be measured (16.21).
2. Past and future exist (17.22) but only insofar as they are known as present (18.23-4).
3. Though incapable of explaining how men prophesy (19.25), we can see that all three times, past, present and future, are in some way present time (20.26).
4. One difficulty remains unresolved: how can we truly measure the present interval if the extentless present has no interval (21.27)?

First Interlude: Prayer for More Light (22.28).

Part II: Time Not Dependent on Motion (23.29-24.31).
    1. Time is not identical with the motions of celestial bodies
       (23.29).
    2. Nor is it dependent on the motion of the sun (23.30).
    3. It is not dependent on any bodily motion (24.31). Positively
       put, time is an independent distension or measure of motion.

Second Interlude: Another Prayer for Light (25.32).

Part III: Time as Distension of the Soul (26.33-27.36).
    1. We cannot measure times in their very passing (26.33, 27.34).
    2. Inductive analysis of *Deus creator omnium* proves that time is
    a distension of the soul (27.35).
    3. Measurement of silent intervals establishes the same point
       (27.36).
    4. Silent rehearsal before speaking also proves that time is a
       psychic distension (27.36).

These inductions solve the initial perplexity in 14.17.

Resolution of the Problem (28.37-8).
    1. Future, past, and present exist in the soul by virtue of
       expectation, memory, and attention (28.37). This insight
       solves the initial problem stated in 14.17.
    2. The distension in the soul during the recitation of a psalm
       exemplifies shorter intervals of time and longer spans like the
       life of a man and the history of man (28.38).

Chapter 14: Perplexity and Problem

17. Two points expose the specious character of the claim that God
was strangely idle prior to creation. First, this is a reprise of a retort
offered earlier (11.13.16); there was simply no time prior to creation.
Since time began only with creation, it is lapsing into pseudo-thinking
to imagine God enjoying a lordly idleness in a time before creation.
It is incoherent to portray God in time before there was time. Second,
the third objection (11.10.12), that an eternal God is bound to make a
coeternal creature, is untenable. Time cannot be coeternal because
God's duration is changeless, whereas so necessarily does time imply

change that time can be changeless or eternal only by ceasing to be time.

Scientific inquiry poses these questions about its object: (i) does the entity exist? (ii) what is it? (iii) what is its ontic value? (10.10.17). Augustine deals briefly with the existence of time. After a short dialectical investigation (11.14.17) he recognizes that it is an illusion of irrationality to consider time illusory or unreal; an ingredient evident in every man's experience, time undeniably exists (11.15.18). Earlier discussion which established that eternity as unchanging and stable ranks ontically higher than time (11.11.13) implicitly answers the third question: time as a mode of duration is inferior to eternity. Thus most attention is directed to a solution of the second question, to specification of the what of time by dialectical and inductive strategies.

The perplexity of time arises from the contrast between common-sense and analytical or definitional cognition of time. Nothing is more familiar and well-known in conversation than time, exchanges in which we are well aware what we and associates are talking about. Human speech is laced with references to time, such as hours and days, long and short syllables, events of the past, prospects for the future. Our very speech is laid out in temporal past, present, and future tenses. Moreover, life is marked by a secure orientation in time, normal men knowing when it is early in the morning or late at night. Yet sure common-sense apprehension of time is not paralleled by analytical certitude. If no one asks what time is, we know what it is: we have a speculatively vague and practical grasp of time. If, however, we attempt to reply to a questioner, we do not know: we cannot easily and exactly state what time is. While we broadly and operatively lay hold of time, the exact formulation of its definition may elude us.[45] Augustine will eventually pinpoint the meaning of time, but the road to the definition will not be dialectically straight and the route not short—it will consume fifteen chapters of analysis.

Nevertheless, at the outset he is analytically certain that the parts of time, past, future, and present, exist. Not mere opinion, his view is intellectually grounded: things do pass away, and their transition and past times are mutually implicative. More clearly expressed, his reasoning runs: if and only if nothing is passing, there are no past times. Because antecedent and consequent are reciprocally related, their positions can be switched, so that the conditional proposition reads: if there is no past time, then nothing is passing away. The denial of either antecedent or consequent entails the affirmative of the other proposition. Things do pass away: so plainly past time does exist. Similarly, if there is no future time, nothing is coming into existence; but plainly things come to be: hence the future exists. Again, if there is no present, nothing exists; but it is evident that things, we among them, exist: therefore present time exists.

However, dialectical inquiry raises doubts about the existence of past, future, and present, thus posing the key problem. Whereas perplexity stems from difficulty in stating exactly what time is, the problem of time lies in explaining precisely how past, future, and present exist. For, as just intimated, although common-sense experience or phenomenological reports apparently certify the existence of time's triadic parts, critical examen initially seems to establish the opposite: none of the three possesses actual physical existence. By definition the past is bereft of actual existence; the past means what no longer exists. Similarly, the future as future is void of actual existence, signifying what is yet to be. The existential status of the present is also suspect, this for a somewhat different reason: the present exists only in order not to exist. If the present always remained the same, never flowing into or becoming past, it would not be a temporal but an eternal present (11.13.16), eternity rather than a feature of time. But the present of time or simply present time occurs nonpermanently, eventuating in order to make its passage into the past. Its reason for being is to immediately not to be, existing so as not to exist. Beginning to exist in order to cease to exist, its existence is ordained to straightway nonexistence. The present exists only in a tendentially nonexistent fashion.[46] Thus the three times betray a counter-existential or nonexistential makeup. neither the past, which no longer exists, nor the future, which does not yet exist, can lay claim to actual existence while the present's actuality seems negated by its orientation to immediate nonexistence.

Part I

Chapter 15: No Long or Short Past or Future or Physical Present (Instant) Is Measured

18. Augustine does not directly and immediately wrestle with the conundrum of the apparently nonexistential character of time. Along

with most thinkers before and after him, he is convinced of the reality of time. Language that bespeaks our life is so suffused with time (11.14.17) that unless man is a victim of radical delusion, time, including past and future, must in some coherent sense be undeniably real. We do reasonably speak of a long and short past and future, even though these are physically nonexistent. The problem then is the reconciliation of two facts; the fact that past and future do not actually exist, and the fact that we do realistically and intelligibly describe them as long and short. A first step of constructive dialectic discloses that past as such and future as such cannot be long or short. Clearly we speak of a hundred years in the past or a hundred years in the future as a long time while, compared to a century, ten days is regarded as a short past or future time. Still, the nagging difficulty of existential status recurs. Since we cannot predicate long or short of what does not exist, we cannot say that past or future is long. Perhaps, he conjectures, the past was and the future will be long. Discarding this wobbly conjecture, he sees that he cannot strictly say that his past was long since the past as past does not exist; a nonexistent cannot have attributes like long or short. Rather, we should say that a span of time, when present, was long; only when existent could it have the attribute "long" predicated of it.

19. Yet this alternative proves unfruitful, for neither one hundred years nor one year nor one month can be deemed totally present. A century cannot be perceived or measured all at once. Prior to the third year are two past years no longer in existence, and lying ahead are ninety-seven future years not yet in existence. Similarly, one year fails to pass the test of presentiality. For the whole year occurs not all at once but month by month. When the second month is occurring, the first is past, and the other ten future: eleven months are nonexistent from the perspective of the purportedly present one month. Moreover, one month cannot exist as a present whole, for it consists of days, which do not simultaneously coexist with one another. Whether the first, the last, or an in-between day is designated as present, all the other days are past and/or future, i.e. nonexistent.

20. However, not even one day is present in its totality. As with the parts of a century, a year, and a month, its parts, in this case, twenty-four hours, do not exist all together. When any one hour exists, the other twenty-three are either past or future. Correspondingly, one hour does not exist all are once, for it consists of fugitive smaller parts,

some departed or past, others yet to come or future.

Since each extent of time is further divisible and, as further divisible, able to be divided into past and future, the strict physical present has to be the instant.[17] The instant is the partless point of time, which is absolutely indivisible, in contrast to the apparently tiniest parts of time that are always divisible into tinier subparts. The instant speeds so rapidly from future to past that it occupies no extent; it has no "space" or magnitude. The physical present is punctiform and indivisible, so fast-flying that it does not exhibit, because it does not have, length or magnitude. If the instant were extended, it would no longer be simply and solely the physical present; as extended in the most infinitesimal way, it would be divisible into past and future parts. The specification of the instant as the physical present, however, does not immediately provide warrant for intelligibly predicating "long" of time. As noted above, we claim not that a future time is long but that it will be long or, more precisely, that, when present, it will be long. The future enters into existence when it begins to be present; then we may truly say, "This time exists and it is long." Yet the only physical present is the instant, which, as extentless, can have no magnitude, neither long nor short. Thus the mind is brought to a halt by an apparent dead end as regards predication of "long" of time. We cannot say that past time was long in the sense that this present time was long nor that the future time was long in the sense that present time will be long since the physical present itself cannot be long: pointlike, without magnitude, without parts to be counted as subsegments of a time-segment, it cannot be long. At this juncture Augustine has made some advance, however slight, beyond the earlier negative-dialectical impasse (11.14.17). While nonexistent, past and future, he claims, can be known as long in terms of present time. Unhappily, the present turns out to be not a stepping stone but a stone of stumbling. The strictly physical present, utterly without parts, is lengthless and therefore cannot be said to be long or have length. Still, Augustine accepts the present as truly existing, fleeting from future into past. He suspends or effectively drops the earlier charge that the instant, because immediately tending to nonexistence, is ingrainedly nonexistential. Here, in contrast to 11.14.17, he accents the physical reality of the instant as indivisible into past and future, with unstoppable fluency into the past reduced to a secondary role, a penumbra that does not dim the corona of its primary reality.

Chapter 16: The Present Perceived Not as Instantaneous but as Passing

21. Nevertheless, in spite of dialectical criticism deeming it impossible, we undoubtedly do measure time-intervals. Two sentences register three inductive truths: (i) we sense and know time-intervals; (ii) we compare one time-segment with another; (iii) we sharpen the comparison, specifying precisely how much longer one time-interval is than another. The familiar *Deus creator omnium* contains eight syllables that break down into four iambs, each iamb having a short and long syllable, with the long twice the length of the short (11.27.35.M 6.2.2). This third induction is premissed upon, or has packed into it, the two prior, simpler inductions. To restate it, even an untutored person is aware that each of the words in the line involves a time-interval: its utterance occupies a temporal extent or "space." Then, with instruction, he realizes that one syllable is longer than another. After schooling in Latin versification, he recognizes that the second syllable or iamb is twice as long as the first and that short syllables of different iambs are of the same length.

Worth remarking is the fact that the instant is not sensed or perceived. We measure time in its actual transit, the present in its passage, or the passage as present, the passage that is the present. We measure times; the educated ear of the rhetorician estimates the length of each syllable. We measure an interval by perceiving it; in other words, the perception of the interval involves a measurement, either implicit, as with the untrained observer, or explicit, as with the educated ear. We measure by perceiving the interval; in perceiving what is present, we measure what is present.[48] Furthermore, we perceive and therefore measure the present as an interval, not as an extentless, indivisible instant.[49] The physical present is not perceived; its intellection is the fruit of analysis concluding that past and future are distinguished by an indivisible (11.15.20). One dialectical obstacle removed or circumvented, others persist. While the present is perceivable and measurable, past and future apparently defy measurement; only a foolhardy inquirer would defend the position, bordering on nonsense, that we actually measure the nonexistent past and future. Surely we can and do observe and measure time in its passing, but surely also we do not, because we cannot, measure time as past since it no longer exists.

Chapter 17: Prophecy and History Prove that Future and Past
Exist

22. Aware that his mind is still engaged in dialectical testing, he
expressly states: I am involved in posing questions and shaping
answers that are only tentative and therefore subject to revision. He
has just ventured the suggestions that past and future do not exist
(11.15.20) and that we measure the passing present (11.16.21),
opinions that will be altered and reworked through more exact
analysis here and later (11.20.26; 27.35). If at this stage he were setting
down hard-and-fast conclusions, he would be laying himself open to
the charge that in the chapters ahead he was shifting from one stance
to another.

His early education in grammar showed him how to distinguish the
three basic tenses, past, present, and future, three times for expressing
verbs. Indeed he himself instructed his students in these tenses
bearing grammatical witness to the existence of past and future.
Educational recourse to these tenses/times provides dialectical
suasion for the existence of more than present time. Yet if past and
future exist, in what sense do they exist? Perhaps, he muses, the
present emerges from some secret existential source in which the
future is hidden, then departs into some existential recess that is the
habitat for the past. He forthwith discards this surmise because it
mythologically reifies parts of time; then, postponing the question of
the manner the existence of past and future, he focuses on rehabili-
tating the real status of past and future. Portions of sacred and secular
literature, specifically prophecy and history, testify to the existence of
future and past. If the future does not exist, then prophets could not
have foretold things to come. More generally, if a thing does not exist,
it cannot be perceived—but future events are somehow prophetically
viewed or previewed. Similarly, if no past exists, historians could not
narrate the past; but since in their minds they evidently do accurately,
if not exhaustively, record the past, the past somehow exists. It is
impossible that future and past be at once nonexistent and known. If
nonexistent, they are not known; a consequent at loggerheads with
the incontestable data afforded by prophecy and history. Conversely,
if they are known, future and past have to exist in some fashion;
veridical knowledge of a thing is a sign of its existence. Fresh resort
to *modus tollens* substantiates the reality of past and future; it is evident

that past and future do somehow exist. As evident, the past cannot be strictly demonstrated, but its evidential character can be validated by indirect demonstration, by displaying the absurdity entrained by the denial of the past. Such reasoning ordinarily turns on denial of the consequent that carries with it the denial of the antecedent, which is equivalent to re-affirmation of the evident. If future and past do not exist, then prophecy is fraudulent and history does not convey truth;[50] hence it is not the case that future and past do not exist: they undoubtedly do exist. Otherwise put, the line of argument runs: if past and future do not exist, they are not knowable; but they are knowable; therefore they do exist. In this perspective the fact that they are known establishes that they exist. This rational route, it may be remarked, is not a twin of G. Berkeley's erroneous *esse est percipi*, which, in effect, means that existence is constituted by perception. Whereas Berkeley oddly holds that existence is causally dependent on perception, for Augustine, knowledge of past and future is a sign of their existence: here, as with other entities and events, our knowledge causally depends upon the objects cognized.

Chapter 18: Past and Future Grounded in the Present

Past and future exist insofar as they are related to or grounded in the present. Specifically, the past is alive in present memory, and the future exists, in human affairs, in current prospects and, in nature, in foresigns or predetermining causes.

23. His desire to know exactly where or in what fashion future and past exist, remains at this stage unfulfilled, the puzzle undeciphered. Yet he is convinced that wherever they may be, they cannot exist simply as future or past but as present, for the very definitions of past, the already gone, and of the future, the not-yet, betoken nonexistence. Definitionally nonexistent, they can have existential anchorage only in the nonfuture and nonpast that is the present. Past events are re-viewed and relived in present memory. A true chronicle of the past, however, does not reinstate prior events in their physical currency. Not the events themselves but their images, registered on memory when the events actually occurred, are grasped in present cognition. The images, fixed remains of events in flux, serve as the footprints or traces engraved by the events when they coursed through the senses to be recorded in memory. Narration of past

JOHN M. QUINN, OSA

events consists of words conceived from images; description of one's past life is an intellectual verbal report based on or generated from the images of past events. Narration of the past is the verbalized conception or offspring of memorial images. Augustine's boyhood, which is physically irrecoverable, physically induplicable, can be, as Book 1 attests, revivified in memory-images, which psychically reproduce physically enacted boyhood episodes. He recaptures his boyhood by "intuiting" or seeing it in the present memorial image. The past can recur, can be resurrected, not physically but memorially, living on in present memory. At the moment he cannot determine with certitude whether a cause similar to that of memory is operative in forecasting future events, in particular, whether a prospective image of future events functions like a retrospective image of the past. The answer will be forthcoming from analysis, but, in any event, he is absolutely sure that present project makes straight the way for future action. For the most part mature individuals plan ahead, designing beforehand a course of action. So the remarkable executive mind of Augustine scheduled his horarium: the hours for common prayer, Mass and sermon, arbitration of litigants' disputes, along with blocks of time for formal treatises. Foredained actions, once they take place, are no longer future but present.

24. While foresight at first blush may seem somewhat opaque, however we explain foredetermination, the future can be foreseen only in virtue of seeing in the present. Foreseeing rests upon present seeing or upon seeing what is present. It is impossible to see future events in themselves, in their very futurity, since they do not yet exist; rather, we see things to come in present causes or signs. Thus the future does not exist but preexists in its causes or signs or, perhaps more exactly, is known as preexistent in its causes and signs. The mind forms conceptions of the future that causatively or significatively link present events to future events. The future as such is cognized not as existent but as the outcome of a causal or significative nexus. Not the future event but the conception of the causal or significative connection is present: the future is predicted as the upshot of a presently conceived hook-up. Foreconception of the future based on foresignication or causal preordination is a present conception. A large number of examples are ready to hand.[51] In the line of causation the seed is harbinger of the full-grown wheat stalk, and the present constellation of stars inexorably necessitates a future

eclipse of sun or moon (5.3.4). In the line of sign Jesus appeals to the signposts of the future: red sky at night, sailors' delight, red sky in the morning, sailors, take warning, while the fig tree's fructification is a pointer that summer is nigh (Lk 21.30). Passing over such illustrations, Augustine opts for a familiar sign heralding the future; break of day announces the rising of the sun.[52] The dawn is present, the sunrise foretold is future; not the sun, which already exists, but the sunrise is forecast. Without an image of the sunrise-to-be he could not predict the sunrise to come. Neither the dawn nor the sunrise constitutes the sunrise to come. They are co-present in the mind, one seen, the other imagined; their co-presence is a correlation, one viewed as sign, the other as signified, dawn and sunrise-to-be. In conceiving the nexus between sign and signified, the mind foreknows the sunrise to come. The conception of the relation between dawn as sign and sunrise as signified underlies and mediates the foreknowledge; dawn and sunrise are intelligized as co-present, one following from the other.

Thus he settles the question raised earlier (11.18.23): does prediction function, as does memory, simply through present images? Memory of the past and foreknowledge of the future are similar in this respect: like things of the past, things of the future cannot be known in themselves, as actually existing here and now. In practical activity and in observation of nature we foresee in present knowledge the future that is in the making. But prediction is sharply distinct from memorial retrodiction. Whereas a present memorial image duplicates past events, no single image pre-visions the future. In forecasting, the mind has to conceive the relation between two images, the percept of the present dawn and the image of the sunrise to come; the nexus between relata joined as sign and signified. The dawn is not simply perceived but is conceived as a sign; correspondingly, the sunrise is not simply pre-seen in a present image but conceived as signified, as the referent of a sign. In addition, the capacity to grasp the signified relation that is a conceived pattern derives from past experience. Regularity of sequence (as with dawn as a prelude to the sunrise) or, in a situation not explicitated by Augustine, regularity of consequence or causal connection (as with the present stellar constellation that is prior cause of a future eclipse) supposes a prior observation of specific factors as causal precursors of certain events.

Chapter 19: Mode of Sacred Prophecy Obscure

25. After showing the basic symmetry, along with a secondary disparity, between memorial review and conceptual preview, he devotes special attention to sacred foretelling that is marked by exceptional characteristics. Divinely infused prophecy illumines the prophet to predict with absolute certitude future contingencies, radically indeterminate events that cannot be forecast by strategies relying on causal predetermination. No doubt God, sovereign of creation, comprehends in one intuition the past, present, and future of the universe; no doubt too he teaches prophets future events, yet the precise mode of this extraordinary enlightenment is at this point opaque. Certainly God does foresee the future; strictly, he sees all in his eternal present. Certainly also, in whatever medium it is transmitted, the divine communication must foretell the future in terms of the present, for the future as future is nonexistent and what is nonexistent is incommunicable or unteachable. The concrete features of the illumination escape Augustine.[53] Its meaning lies far above his mental gaze, too strong in the sense that his vision is too infirm, just as human eyes are too weak to stare directly at the sun. Grace alone can infuse new strength into his hidden eyes, the eyes of the mind (J 13.3).

Chapter 20: Each Time Properly a Present Time

26. Employing as a minor premise the self-evident proposition that past and future as such do not exist (11.16.21), he reasons: real or proper times exist (1116.21), but past and future as such do not exist; therefore, it clearly follows, past and future are not real or proper times. Built upon this syllogism is a second argument: only the present exists or whatever exists is present time (11.16.21); but past and future exist not as such but in present knowledge (in present memory and foreconception; 11.18.23-4); therefore (along with the ordinarily styled present) past and future are present times or, perhaps, properly speaking, there are three presents, the present of past things, the present of present things, and the present of future things. The time we know as existing is always present time: time as present, time as re-present, time as pre-present. This analysis solves the earlier query posed somewhat crudely (11.1.22): where are past and future? Along with the present, past and future reside in the soul,

and nowhere else. Three acts of the soul subserve the three-faceted present: memory is the source of the present of the past; direct preception is centered on the present of the present; expectation contains the present of the future.[54] However odd-sounding the claim, he affirms or positively concludes that there are three present times.[55] Common usage referring to past, present, and future times is technically inexact, but such expressions bother him not one whit; he feels no inclination to stifle such usage, so long as such phrases are counted popular ways of speaking, *façons de parler*, so long as we do not seriously think of past and future as existing independently of the present, implicitly endorsing the balanced policy of prudent Greeks: think with the wise but speak with the common. A necessary strategy indeed because men ordinarily use proper language, analytically refined terminology, of the purest precision only in learned scientific writings and discussions. For the most part, even the highly educated have recourse to loose terminology that does not square with the highest exactitude, ordinarily without generating any misunderstanding; their listeners or readers are not misled about their meaning, however clothed in less-than-scientific garb.[56]

Chapter 21: Restatement of Difficulty of Measuring an Extentless Present

27. At the close of this first stage of inquiry he restates the apparent impossibility of measuring the punctiform present (11.15.20). As previously ascertained, we measure time-intervals in their very passing;[57] for instance, we report that one time-segment is twice as long as its companion syllable, and another interval equal in length to its associate syllable. The warrant for our knowing passing durations is evidence and self-evidence. Evidence: we do measure passing intervals regarded as durationally present–such measurement is verified in direct experience. Self-evidence: we measure only present durations since past and future of their very nature do not, because they cannot, physically exist as present.

Yet evidential and self-evidential truth rooted in fact seems to conflict with the meaning of the strict present. While measuring the present as passing, we cannot measure the actual physical or strict present as passing. The time we measure courses from the not-yet existing future through the extensionless present into the no-longer existing past. He continues to emphasize that an extentless time is measureless. In describing one syllable or word as the double or triple or equal of another interval, we are speaking of temporal extents or magnitudes, one of which is laid against or compared with another. Measurement always supposes an extent able to be measured. This extent, to repeat, cannot numerically specify the length of the punctiform present that has no length; an extentless time is measureless.

Augustine is unable to break out of the impasse: experience of a passing present is paradoxically coupled with the impossibility of measuring an extentless present. Still, this crux does not invalidate earlier empirically won truths: the induction that we apparently measure the passing present we observe and the empirically based conclusion that all three times are in diverse fashion present times.

First Interlude

Chapter 22: Prayer for More Light

28. Signaling a transition in inquiry, he appeals for additional light on the riddle of time. Standing before an impassable wall, with divine energy he will leap over the barrier into God's sanctuary to share his light, ending his toil in grasp of the truth (P 72.22-3). He prays through Christ, whose human nature personally joined to the Word enjoys the most sublime sanctity possible for a created being, surpassed only by the holiness of the divine nature alone (CM 2.25.T 15.26.46). In the name of the super-saintly redeemer he begs that his quest not be muffled by objectors who decry his as a fool's errand, a futile enterprise to ground time in the mind when to all appearances time insistently presses upon us as purely extramental (a point reiterated in 11.27.36). Indicating the religious context, in the words of the psalmist he speaks out in a full-fledged profession of faith before the angels of God (P 115.2). Though his investigation is strictly philosophical, its inspiration and broader format are theological, so that, in undertaking the very analysis of time that occurs in time, he hopes not only for a resolution here and now but also the eternal reward for confession of Christ in time, in which his inner eyes will feast on the divine face in a day of everlasting light (P 26[S.2].8).

Meditation on the hope of the timeless is cut short by realization that he is still in time grappling with time. As he hungers for days that never grow old, he analytically perceives that God made his days grow old (P 38.9); the years fleet by, without his understanding how, for he has not yet nailed down the mode of transiency rooted in the meaning of time. He is not reflecting on transiency in a theological vein; he is convinced that while the outer man ages and breaks down, the inner man is renewed and rejuvenated, partially here, fully hereafter (P 38.9). Nor is he dealing with biological time; aging is a presumptive necessity, an inexorable law for all. Rather, he is posing again the question: what is time? He cannot explain the passingness of the years until he analytically fathoms time. He returns to the initial perplexity, the apparent paradox of common-sense cognition and analytical noncognition of time. Augustine, like his fellows, constantly speaks of time and times. He routinely refers to time when asking at which time in the past he so acted and at what time he actually observed an event. He also discusses times, measuring one time in terms of another, the second syllable of an iamb being twice as long as its companion. The time and times at the center of these exchanges are totally clear, yet the definition of time escapes analytical grasp (11.14.17). Plain in ordinary usage, time, analytically taken, remains an enigma masked in the clearest and commoness of utterances. He is not trying to discover all over again the "wheel" that is the existence of time but striving to definitionally explain, to theoretically "invent", the meaning of time. The spur toward that "invention" urges him to make a fresh start in the second part of his dialectical examen.

Part II

This second part shifts from a consideration of the past-present-future frame to an inquiry into a tenable basis for measuring time in celestial and terrestrial movements. If time as measure lies outside the soul, it must reside in the general movements of heavenly bodies or in the movement of one particular body. Dialectical critique and empirical tests, it is argued, certify that we cannot identify time with any physical movement. Time as measure is neither dependent on nor constituted by any particular physical movement.

Chapter 23: Time Not Identical with Celestial Movement
Nor Dependent on Solar Movement

29. In the opinion of an unnamed savant time consists of movements of the sun and moon and stars.[58] But on the assumption that time is constituted by physical movement, any movement can serve to constitute time. In any case, it seems certain that celestial movement is not the privileged movement constituting time. Suppose that the movements of the heavenly bodies came to a halt while a potter's wheel kept turning. The cessation of the course of the heavens would not stop time, for we would go on measuring the wheeling, the times of the turnings, as equal to or longer and shorter than others. Moreover, the very verbalizing of this objection lays bare the mortal weakness of the claim since the words uttered occupy intervals of time; and some syllables are counted longer, others shorter, that is to say, the time-interval of one is longer or shorter than another: time is measured independently of heavenly movements.

Interior eyes opened, men will see the meaning of a common notion[59] like time evident in comparatively minuscule events like the turning of a potter's wheel and the diverse words expressing the import of the turning. The common notion of time or, rather, the time that the common notion signifies, is manifest both in small movements such as the turning of a potter's wheel and large movements such as the paths of the heavenly bodies. No doubt, as Scripture informs us, the movements of the heavenly bodies serve to demarcate divisions of times like days and years, and therefore in some sense time is associated or concomitant with these movements. However, if we experience time also in the humbler spinning of a potter's wheel, it is misguided to insist that the wheel's turning involves no time. It would be a mistake for Augustine to assert that the turning of a little potter's wheel constitutes one day; yet it is no less erroneous to maintain that only the movements of heavenly bodies, however large, constitute the whole of time.

30. Pursuing the import of the common notion that is time, his mind will not rest satisfied till he cognitively specifies its power or nature, i.e. apprehends the exact signification, the *ratio* or pattern of the time whereby we measure bodily movements. Here the unequivocal averral that he is hunting for the nature or definition of time would seem to cast mortal doubt on the contention of some

scholars that he never aimed or arrived at such a definition. As mentioned in the section above, it is false to contend that a wheel's turning constitutes a day. Now, he will argue, it is also wide of the mark to maintain that the movement of one heavenly body, the sun, constitutes a day. Celestial movements, we saw, do not constitute the whole of time; now, we will see, one celestial movement does not constitute even a part of time. Augustine takes day to mean not day as distinguished from night, but an entire day, including day and night, marked by the complete circuit of the sun from east to east. This full day may signify one of three factors: (i) the sun's movement; (ii) the twenty-four-hour period ordinarily occupied by this movement; (iii) both movement and period together. (i) Let day mean one complete circuit. On the hypothesis that the sun travels twenty-four times faster than its given rate, a day would occur in one hour, not in twenty-four hours. This first supposition entails, in effect, the inconsequence that one hour equals twenty-four hours. (ii) Let a day mean a twenty-four-hour period. On the same hypothesis that the sun moves twenty-four times faster than usual, the sun would require twenty-four trips to complete one day. This second supposition is also burdened with an embarrassing implication: twenty-four days are equal to one day. (iii) Let day mean jointly movement and period. On this hypothesis, if the sun completed its circuit in one hour, there would no longer be a day meaning a period of twenty-four hours. Again, if the sun stood still, a day, the time equivalent to twenty-four hours, could pass: there would be a day without solar movement. This supposition then leads to a double anomaly: there would be solar movement without a day or a day without solar movement. Thus all three alternatives render incomprehensible the claim that solar movement constitutes a day. (i) If a day means the sun's movement, it follows that there can be a day (one hour long) without a twenty-four-hour period. Insistence that a stepped-up velocity does not alter the situation amounts to holding that one hour equals one day. (ii) If the period constitutes a day, there can be a twenty-four-hour period with one day. This is, to repeat, tantamount to maintaining that twenty-four days equal one day. (iii) If both movement and period are taken together to mean a day, there can be movement without a day or a day without movement. Repudiation of these inconsequences entrains not escape from but entrapment in absurdities: one hour is made equal to a day; or, if the sun's movement ceases, time preposterously stops and keeps going in the same respect.[60]

The truth of the matter is the other way round. As just demonstrated, rather than movement measuring time, it is time that measures solar movement. If the sun's present velocity were doubled, we would use time in relating the usual or former rate to the new. Suppose that the sun makes one round trip constituting a day, d_1, in twelve hours. The present circuit, d_2, plainly takes twice as long as d_1, or, conversely, d_1 completes the circuit in one-half the time taken by d_2. Notice, we are comparing a day occupying a single or twelve-hour circuit with one occupying a double or twenty-four hour circuit by reference to a common standard independent of both movements. This common measure whereby we measure comparative quantities is time. Again, according to Jos 10.12.ff., the sun stood still, not hypothetically but really, during Joshua's battle, a fact that corroborates the hypothetically based arguments for the independence of time from solar movement. The battle took place during a length of time, but since the sun was motionless, its movement could not constitute time. The battle occupied a length of time sufficient for its successful outcome, a time-segment not hinging on solar movement.[61]

As an inductive reading of common experience indicates, it is by time that we measure bodily movements; we commonly observe that movement m_2 is twice the length of movement m_1. From this induction issues a simple but important demonstrative conclusion: time is a measuring stick or distension. Set out explicitly, the argument runs: that whose office is to measure is a measuring-stick or distension; but time is that whose office is to measure; therefore time is a distension. But what kind of distension? That must remain unclarified till the third part (11.27.35-6). Unable to specify the precise character of this distension, he can proffer no more than a conjecture. Until he ascertains the special makeup of time's distensiveness, he cannot be sure that this insight is valid or other than a questionable hypothesis.

Chapter 24: Time Not any Bodily Movement

31. Next confronted is the question raised in the previous chapter (11.23.29): why not hold that time consists of the motion of any and every body? Two arguments establish that time is not the movement

of a body: (i) movement is measured in time by time; (ii) lack of movement is measured by time. First, although time ordinarily coexists with movement, and no movement eventuates outside time, time is not constituted by bodily movement. As with the sun, so with any particular body: its motion in time is measured by time. The end of the last chapter (11.23.30) concluded that time is a distension, a temporal extension, a kind of ruler that measures motion as a meter-stick measures space or magnitude. In spatial measurement we determine how long a segment is by fixing one place as the starting point and another as the terminus. So in temporal measurement we determine how long it took a body to traverse a path from its place of departure to its terminal place. Perception of the movement may tell that the movement is long, but only by comparison with another movement can we exactly determine how long this movement took, i.e., show that its time is equal to or twice that of the other. In certain instances, as in the turning of a lathe, we measure not the movement of the whole body from initial to terminal place, but the parts of the rod of wood or metal that are being turned in the lathe, noting the time that it takes for a part that has been chiseled or sheared to return to its original position.[62] Whether a body is moved from one place to another or its parts are turned in one place, as in a lathe, we measure the movement not by itself but by another movement: we measure movement by time. Time, as the measure whereby we assign each movement a time-length, has to be distinct from each and every individual movement. Second, again as with the sun, so with any body: its lack of movement in time is measured by time. We reckon an amount of time for a body's period of rest correlated with its period of movement, judging that it was at rest as long as, or twice or thrice as long as, it was moving. Other exact rates may be registered, along with rough, more-or-less estimates. In any case, because a motionless body does not become timeless, time cannot be equated with the movement of any particular body.

The main thrust of arguments in this second part has been logically negative: to submit to a dialectical test and to reject candidates from physical movement as unfit to serve as the constituent and defining core of time. Time is not the movement of the heavenly bodies; time is not the movement of the sun; time is not the movement of any one body. This extrusion is primarily precursive, making the way straight for positive induction that unveils the proper definition of time. Yet a second positive conclusion was garnered from this second part: time is a distension or temporal extension whereby we measure every bodily movement. But precisely what kind of distension? The third and final part will inspect fresh data to specify the makeup of the distension that defines time, directly and via corollary resolving difficulties that proved baffling in the first part.

Second Interlude

Chapter 25: New Prayers for Light

32. Augustine again confesses that he is still snarled in the apparent paradox of not knowing what time is while being aware of the fact and features of time. Clearly he has some grasp of time; he is conscious of time in time—it is time that measures his speaking[63] as long, yet oddly, it seems, the meaning of time still resists understanding. Perhaps, he muses, the problem is simply semantic or linguistic, a matter of deftly coining felicitous expressions articulating cognition of time. Not only does he not know what time is, but, sadly, he does not even know what he does not know; so ignorant is he that he cannot fix the scope and limits of his ignorance. God knows that he is not stooping to intellectual posturing, pretending to be stumbling in the dark when, in fact, he has the solution neatly tucked up his sleeve. Still wrestling with a riddle that seems naggingly intractable, once more he pleads for light to dissipate the opacity shrouding the meaning of time.[64]

Part III
Time as a Distension of the Mind

Chapter 26: Tentative Grasp of the Meaning of Time

This and the following chapter solve his perplexity. He first conjectures, then inductively validates, that time is a distension of the mind.

33. As already substantiated (11.24.31), we measure physical movement in and by time, an operation requiring a measure of time also, for we cannot set down precisely the length of the movement

measured without in some way first determining the length of the measure, in this case time. The argument hinges on the analogical resemblance of time to space. We measure distension or temporal extension in a manner analogous to the way we measure spatial extension. We measure a rod as, say, two cubits long by a measuring stick one cubit long.[65] We measure a poem in terms of verses according to the distension or temporal measuring-stick that is one verse. As we measure a rod by counting the number of times that a cubit, our measuring-stick, is moved across its magnitude or length, so we measure a poem by counting the number of times that one verse, our distension or temporal measuring-stick, is moved across the full extent of the poem. Correspondingly, a foot, syllable, or short syllable can serve as a measurational unit in temporal extension. We name a verse or line long or short according to the number of its feet; we assign length to a foot according to its syllables; and we measure or count the length of a long syllable set over against a short syllable. Two points of disanalogy qualify this correspondence of temporal and spatial extension. First, words written on pages remained fixed in place whereas spoken words, like all extents of time, pass away. This first difference gives rise to a second disparity. Lack of natural fixity leaves the measuring-units of temporal extension open to variation. An ordinarily short syllable does not always function as a definite measure of a long syllable. On occasion we may alter the length of long and short syllables by rapidly snapping out the long syllable and protractedly drawling the short syllable. Similarly, we can modify the customary length of foot, verse or line, or whole poem so that offices of measure and measured are interchanged.

Here he catches the first glimmering of the truth: time is a distension of the mind. Neither the instant nor any particular bodily movement, we observed earlier, can serve as a defensible foundation for a definition of time. More recent exploration argued that physical time-lengths are transient and alterable measures. To a time without a ground in the physical world, the mind, it seems, is the only habitat whereon to stand. Since time is not outside the mind, it would be wondrous, he muses, if time were anywhere save in the mind. His hesitancy cautions that his conclusion still wants empirical verification. He still has to furnish hard data that will turn a suasive conjecture into the positive induction that time is a distension of the mind. The measuring-stick that is time cannot measure the future that does not yet exist, nor a past that no longer exists, nor the physical present, the instant, which, because dimensionless, is physically measureless. Apparently, as already maintained (11.16.21; 21.27), he does measure the passing present, time passing but not yet past; but this claim will be corrected and refined in the ensuing chapter.

Chapter 27: Inductive Conclusion: Time is Distension of Mind

34. The truth adawning,[66] residual patches of darkness start to lift as he comes to realize that we do not measure time in its very passing (11.16.21; 21.27). The elimination of this final feature of the physical given as a basis for time-measurement opens the door to warranted recognition that time is psychic distension. Before, it only seemed likely that time is a distension of the mind; now, the last physical prop disposed of, we can verify that time is indeed psychic distension.

Submitting it to more searching scrutiny, he clarifies the prior observation that we measure time in its passage. Ordinarily, it seems, we do measure the ongoing passage of time. When someone utters a sound, the sound begins, goes on sounding, then comes to a stop, followed by silence. Before being sounded, the sound as future or not yet existing cannot be measured. After being sounded, the sound now past, no longer in existence, cannot be measured. When actually sounding, the sound apparently can be measured, for it does exist, though its existence is fugitive and vanishing. In contrast to the extentless and therefore measureless physical present, the passing present stretches over an extent or segment of time, whose length is measurable. A second example, however, negates the conclusion of the first: time as passing is not measurable. Suppose that someone utters a single sound, say a long "a," then continues to utter the sound without break, without stopping. As indicated earlier (11.24.31; 26.33), to measure a length of time means to mark its outer boundaries, both beginning and end. The sounding of the one unbroken note has an observable beginning, but inasmuch as it has not ended, we cannot designate its end-point. The incontestable empirical fact that it is still passing rules out its having passed. While perceiving the ongoing sound, we cannot strictly measure it. We cannot determine how long or short it is; nor can we say exactly whether its length equals that of another sound, or whether, taken proportionally, its length is single or double in comparison with that of another sound. True, we ascertain its terminus when the sound ceases, but then the sound is over and gone, no longer a passing present but an unchanging past. Plainly we can measure times because we do, but plainly also we do not measure times as physically passing because we cannot. An extended sound cannot perdure through an instant whose unextendedness puts it outside the pale of measurement. Passing sounds or times, because deprived of an observable terminus, elude measurement.

Notice, as just mentioned, that while unable to *measure* time as passing, we do *perceive* time as passing: this perception of the passing present will be underscored shortly (11.28.37). Thus while forgoing his earlier claim that we measure the passing present (11.16.21; 21.27), he continues to insist that we do undoubtedly observe or attend to the present in its very passage.[67]

35. The full sunrise of truth heralded by the dawn (11.18.24; 27.35) now blazes on the horizon. Three empirical proofs, the first in this section, the latter two in the following section, let in the daylight of certitude on the view that times measured are distensions held in psychic existence.

The first induction seizes the meaning of time latent in the voicing of the eight syllables of St. Ambrose's line, *Deus creator omnium* (9.12.31), "O God, Creator of All Things." The Latin verse contains four iambs, each iamb consisting of a short and long syllable (u-). Augustine's practiced ear is unmistakably sure that in comparing short to long syllables, each long is twice the length of its short companion.[68] He declaims the syllables, i.e., says them aloud, and in so voicing them, he proclaims or vocally evidences that the long is double the length of the short.[69] It is sensorially clear, beyond all doubt, that he measures the long syllable by the short, applying the short to the long as one applies a ruler or meter-stick to an object to determine its length. However, reason seems to militate against the report of the senses. Solid sense-evidence witnesses that we do lay the short against the long syllable, counting it double the length of the short.[70] But reason apparently contends that we cannot so measure the long by the short syllable since, to be measured, both have to have become past; and what is not existent is definitely not measurable. Neither short nor long syllable so lasts that the short may be applied to the long. The short one has to be completed or past before the long is sounded. Furthermore, the long cannot be measured in its very passage (11.27.34) but only when its terminal point is reached, only when it is not present but past. At first glance analysis apparently proves that time is not measurable. The short cannot serve as measure since it does not physically coexist with the long syllable. The long cannot be measured; the long is so designated only by being terminated or ceasing to exist: what ceases to exist is apparently not measurable. Both sounds, long as well and as short, speed by to become past; no time can be measured when both measure and measured are nonexistent. Yet the attestation of sensory report, which is as reliable as any empirical evidence, remains unchallengeable; we do match short against long syllable, recognizing that the long is double the length of the short. However, Augustine sees, he can incontestably measure the short by the long syllable only after both have ceased to physically exist, only after both have become past. Thus does he break the deadlock of measuring apparently nonexistent syllables: the syllables are truly measured because they really exist, not in their original physical sounds but in their psychic representations or duplicates. They truly exist and coexist not in their physical occurrence but in their images retained, fixed in memory. The conflict between reason and sense is resolved through more penetrating empirical inspection that assures for perceived temporal phenomena the existential status necessary, according to reason, if they are measured. A more nuanced sensory examen discloses that the time-intervals, both measure and measured, enjoy a psychic existence.

36. After continuing to emphasize that time-intervals are measured in the mind, he proposes two additional inductions for the psychic residence of measured time.

He counsels his mind itself to desist from protestations that time as measured possesses physical existence as the passing present.[71] Earlier he had gleaned as the yield of sensory experience that he not only perceived but measured time in its passing (11.16.21; 21.27). As with a delimited movement, so with measured time: it seems to be physically present with its initial and terminal boundaries. This habitual way of considering measured time physically existent clamors against his more exact empirical inquiry proving that only in its psychic existence can time be measured. The ingrained posture is pictured as crowds of prior impressions, because throughout his preceding life he had collected a stock of sense-data that accumulatively seemed to indicate that time as measured is physically existent. In departing from his prior average intelligent misunderstanding of the existential residence of measured time, he insists, in accord with the witness of sharper empirical analysis, that it is strictly in his mind that he measures intervals. He measures not the physical sounds now past but their psychic impresses still present; not physical intervals that pass away but what they mentally produce, the upshot that is psychic images presently retained; not the evanescent physical sounds but their memorial vicars. Clinching his point is an exhaustive disjunction: "Either these very [psychic impresses] are the time-intervals [measured] or I do not measure time-intervals." Either time is a distension of the mind or our sense of time anchored in natural experience is a hopelessly inexplicable illusion. But since basic time-awareness is not radically or even superficially treacherous, time is a psychic distension.[72]

A second induction bolsters this conclusion. As Augustine measures times in which bodies are at rest (11.24.31), so he describes periods of silence as long or short, "A ten-second pause for station identification" exemplifies this sort of measurement.[73] But what Augustine is mainly focusing on as measure is not the exterior visible movement of a clock hand across a dial but an interior auditory interval that is applied to and measures the pause. Although no sound is emitted, the span of silence, he determines, occupies the same interval as a spoken verse or psalm. In making this comparison, he "extends his cogitation," mentally forming an unspoken time-line as an interior distension equivalent to a time-line of actually spoken syllables. This unspoken time-line or distension enables him to measure the duration of a period of silence. Reviewing a distension previously heard, he runs over in imagination and thought a poem, a verse, or any potentially vocalized segment, or indeed any measurable movement (perhaps a sound or succession of notes from a musical instrument such as the lyre or psaltery). He sounds out within his mind a whole sequence of syllables of a verse or poem, then lays their temporal measuring-stick against the interval of silence to mentally compute its length. He legitimately predicates long or short of stretches of silence, setting the length of one pause against another, only because he imaginatively puts a time or time-length of sound alongside the pauses to be measured; only because at root time is a distension of the mind. Not simply a buttress of the first induction, this second induction more cogently establishes that time is a psychic distension, for no exterior movement occurs, no exterior measure can appear to occur: the measure, the imagined length of a verse or poem, is wholly within, to be applied to the measured, which is not exterior movement but the absence of exterior movement.

A third induction also relies on silence, now taken prior to speaking. Not only does the mind retain sounds uttered; not only does a distension of sound measure a period silent interval without; but also a silent interval of inner preparation measures, fixing beforehand the length of the speaking to follow. Before voicing a long-sounding single syllable, a speaker may rehearse interiorly and silently the utterance yet to come and thus measure its time-length within the mind. Whereas according to the second induction, a distension of sound measures a period of silence after the period has passed, in this third induction a period of silence spent in interiorly rehearsing a prolonged sound measures a duration of sound before it is spoken. The sound as vocalized, as forming an exteriorized successive continuum, lasts the length of the time measured, for it is measured by an interior distension unfolded in silence. Traversing the temporal course of the sound charted by forethought and committed to memory, a speaker starts to utter the prolonged note that sounds until it reaches the foredesigned terminal point. More precisely, not only present but past and future are involved; once begun, the departed segments of the sound have sounded, have become past, and those yet to come will sound, flowing in from the future. A speaker gradually utters the earlier parts of his prolonged sound, so that what were future parts become past. His onward passage changes still later parts, formerly future, into past. Steady present attention to the utterance of the sound transfers the future parts into past parts, the past increasing with the decrease of the future. Finally, at the end of his speaking, the whole of what was originally projected as future has become wholly past: there is completed another extent of time, another distension, whose measure lies within the mind.[74]

Chapter 28: Resolution of the Problem: Acts of the Mind Furnish Psychic Distensions of Past, Present, Future.

37. The definition of time as a distension of the mind dissolves the paradox of knowing while not knowing time (11.14.17): he now grasps

with analytical precision the what of time that he has always known in a vaguely speculative and practical manner. The unknotting of the initial perplexity ushers in the resolution of the original problem: how can time exist if past, present, and future do not exist? (11.14.17). The future can decrease and be consumed, and the past increase only in terms of acts of the mind that subserve distensions of the mind. Consequently, not future and past themselves but expectation and memory are said to be long.

Since time measured is a distension of the mind, physically nonexistent times exist and coexist in the mind. Future, extended present, and past owe their continuity and continuance in existence to acts of the mind. The mind expects the future, attends to the present, and remembers the past; thus the mind confers psychic existence and fixity on the extents of movement to be measured, so that what the mind expects (future) passes through what the mind attends to (present) into what the mind remembers (past). In each particular distension or time-line expectation projects the psychic extent of what is to come; memory stably duplicates events already gone; attention abides to perceive the passing present. The physical present lacks extent or duration since it passes away in point-like fashion. As temporally dimensionless, the physical present is sensorially unattainable; an unceasingly alternating physical present cannot be directly attended to and grasped. In one respect the time-line is centered in attention. Attention endures and lays down, as it were, an expanse in the mind, the pivotal strand that binds future and past, serving as a bridge linking the two: "...attention perdures and, throughout, that which will be present passes on its way to being no longer present."

This analysis confirms and amplifies the earlier insight that past and future can exist only as two of the three present times: the present of the past, the present of the present, and the present of the future, each of which is the outcome of an act of the soul, in particular, of memory, perception, and expectation (11.20.26). The exact character of their residence in the mind or soul is furnished by the conclusion that time is psychic distension. Moreover, this solution of the initial problem carries with it the key to a corollary difficulty: how can we ascribe the attribute long to nonexistent past and future? (11.15.18-20). Long is predicated of future extents of time presently expected and past extents recently remembered, A long future is a long expectation of the future, a long past, a long memory of the past. The acts themselves need not be prolonged. Expectation or memory may take only a short time, perhaps less than a minute, but, rummaging through a store of imagined distensions, we can intellectually recapitulate the last one hundred years or conjecturally prognosticate a whole century ahead, tracing in imagination a line that stands for the strictly unimaginable but thinkable length of one hundred years. The line drawn in memory and the cogitation that it represents are the subjects or noetic recipients of the predicate long. Similarly, when we imaginatively depict a line drawn from present into future, this projected line or distension and the conceptualized span that it illustrates are properly said to be long.

38. The mind is triply active during recitation of a psalm. At the outset, when expectation embraces the whole psalm, the time-line symbolically stretches futureward. Once we actually start reciting, the duration is distended in two directions: memory takes in the parts now spoken, and expectation includes the verses yet unspoken, while attention fastens on the phrase being spoken. The more the recitation goes on, the longer the memory becomes and the shorter the expectation, until expectation is exhausted and what was first wholly expected is at last wholly remembered. Thus we experience roughly three sorts of time-line; the distension may be a segment entirely oriented toward the future; it may arise from confluent acts of expectation, attention, and memory; it may issue from memory alone.[75]

The triple psychic activity results in a threefold time-line on a smaller scale in every verse and every syllable of the psalm. What occurs in the psalm holds true also for a longer prayer or service of which the psalm itself may occupy but a small portion. Miniaturized or magnified, the time-line is first a distension of expectation alone; then a linking of future and past across the present of attention; finally, a distension pointed toward the past alone. The amplitude of duration of the threefold schema can be broadened to comprise also the life story of a man or the history of man. First, Augustine can imagine the life of a newborn child, about to be baptized, as stretching forward for the next fifty years. Second, he can reflect on his own present condition, memorally surveying his past of roughly forty-six years while vaguely estimating the road ahead. Third, he can range over in one memorial span alone the fifty-six years of his mother Monica. Furthermore, situated on the plane of universal history, he can plant himself at the dawn of man, whence to draw a line to the end of history. Again, from the vantage point of 400 A.D., he can summarily recollect man's past and dimly peer into the distension of years till the Day of the Lord. Finally, he can picture himself at the Last Judgment, encompassing in one sweep the vasty distension extending from the instant of the creation of Adam down to the last stroke of doom.

Chapter 29: Moral Time: Distraction, Disorder in the Soul

39. In this short moral postscript to the theoretical analysis of time the word distension undergoes a radical alteration in meaning; used equivocally, it denotes distraction and, by corollary, disruption and disorder.[76]

God's mercy is better than our lives, for his mercy points all hearts, multiple and diverse in desires, to the one life of grace and glory. Some are businessmen, others farmers, still others bankers or soldiers, but by mercy, not men's merits, on all God bestows holiness, divine life higher than human lives (P 62.12). Still dwelling in the body, Augustine's life is a distension, not in the sense of a lived span of past, present, and future activity (11.28.38), but in the sense of distraction, in which the time-line is broken into various, even opposing, segments. Whereas theoretical distension is one time-line composed of past, present, and future parts that are conjoined and concordant, moral distension is not one but split into diverging segments, the moral self being pulled in different directions and, as disoriented, the victim of disorder.

In the past during his gravely sinful pre-conversion submersion in the carnal, his moral personality was a distension sundering and dissipating his unity of self among manifold earthly goods. He had devoured times, i.e., temporal things, and, as a consequence, had been devoured by times (9.4.10); becoming morally temporalized, his inner being was disfigured by evil, his soul fused with the moral disorder that is moral time. Happily, the right hand or power of God released him from slavery to time through Christ, Son of God and son of man, the one mediator between the eternal One and temporally multiform man. Through and in Christ the multiplicity of moral time is healed by the One of eternity. Unlike God, individuals are many and various, their ontic manyness a sign of their moral manyness; their divided hearts are dispersed, seeking many various goods through many diverse desires. Through healing grace during conversion he was grasped, taken possession of, by Christ, so that he might grasp the goal, union with the One, which was the reason why Christ lovingly captured his soul. Through Christ, the One in the flesh, the parts of his soul strewn about "by the days of the old man," the life of sin, are gathered into unity so that, redeemed from malign temporality, the Augustine made new might wholly surrender himself to pursuit of the eternal One. Appropriating Phil. 3. 12-4, he aspires to rise above things of time; to forget, to take no delight in, things past; to quest for things to come, not transitory future goods but imperishable riches of eternity. In reaching toward the eternal goods that lie before, the soul is not distended, not morally temporalized, not multiplied and scattered among temporals; rather, it is unitively stretched out in one harmonious desire for the eternal One, an extension that will fructify in the actual joy of fullest union with the One (P 39.3). Not according to distension, not according to fragmentation among morally temporal goods, but according to intention, according to unwaveringly concentrated attention of heart on the One above, his whole being equivalent to one holy desire (EJ 4.6), he presses on to the prize of his heavenly calling, the pearl of great price that is the One. There, in consummated nuptial union of spirit with the One, he will contemplate the God whose boundless delight admits of no injury or loss, no slightest possibility of pain or insecurity (P 26 [En. 2].9); an ecstatic rejoicing wholly unstreaked by time, suffering neither coming from the future nor departure into the past. Yet sojourning in the body, he is far from being enfolded in inexpressible bliss but is afflicted with all the ills that sinful flesh is heir to. While extended to the eternal, his soul is bowed down by labors and moral failings, his noneternal duration pockmarked with sighs and groanings (P 66.10). Still, through the travails of time his eternal Father abides, solacing his sorrowful temporal lot.

The adolescent Augustine hurled himself down from the divine firmament or eternal law, to be dashed to pieces on the rocks below; disruption in the manyness of moral time spun off from spurning of the eternal One (2.4.9). Now, even while no more than venially culpable, he broadcasts himself among times, becoming in some measure morally temporal, the parts of his moral time-line are severed one from another, with the result that he does not know the order of moral time. As psychological temporal disorientation betrays mental deterioration, so moral temporal disorientation signalizes the moral breakdown that is sin. Disorder that breeds disorder in the soul (1.12.19) deforms the inner self, producing the disarray that specifies moral time. As a sinner, he becomes morally disoriented, and since sin is disorder, he does not, because he cannot, know the order of dispersed moral times, for, as disorganized, they have no order.

When sinning, even in a minor way, his thoughts, which shape his moral personality, are torn apart. Moral time betokens tumultuous diversity and variation, with sin distending his soul, rending it asunder. This disorder, which fragments the spiritual self through the meretricious seduction of the moral-temporal manifold, never stops so long as the body lasts. Only entrance into eternity will seal total liberation from moral time; only then will his soul be melted into pure liquid by the fire of God's love given by the Holy Spirit (13.9.10). So cleansed, his soul will stream into God. As fire melts and liquefies gold, letting the dross go free, so the love poured forth by the Holy Spirit (13.9.10), will burn away all vestiges of moral time, enabling the purified soul to flow into the bosom of the eternal One. Therein he will be cast into pure gold, purged of all impurities, molded into his true form of moral fulfillment as determined by his true plan (11.30.40); the form that is the individual *ratio* or pattern ordained by God's truth that is creative wisdom.

Worth stressing once more is the salient truth that the spirit leading him on high remains always the Spirit of Jesus. Because the eternal Word was born in time as Jesus Christ, Augustine, as is the case with all others, is gifted with an eternal vocation (P 101[S.2] .10). Through the divine-human intermediary between eternity and time his soul is empowered to let the One extend him, i.e., to yield to grace energizing him to wholly aspire for the One, repelling the allure of the many that divorces it from the One (S 255.6.6). As mediator, the eternal Word becomes a being of time to make beings of time eternal (EJ 2.10), liberating man from moral time and stabilizing him in eternity, utterly exempt from the turmoil of time (J 31.5).

Chapter 30: Reprise: God Eternal Creator of Time

40. The first part of the opening sentence iterates and completes the

insight at the end of the prior chapter. After the fire of the Holy Spirit
(13.9.10) burning away debris of moral time causes his inner self to
flow as pure gold, his spirit will be cast into the mold planned by the
One who is Father. So shaped in eternity, he will stand absolutely
firm, no longer whirled about in the flux of time. In the life beyond,
for which he hungers with utmost extendedness or maximum desire,
he will be made solid in his form, his deepest yearning for the One
fully consummated. Form, deputed to symbolize the mold for pure
gold, properly means an ideal pattern in the divine mind according
to which each type and each individual exists and is distinguished
from others (DQ 46.2). In this life through grace he is constantly
extended toward his ideal form, the paradigm of fullness of being or
goodness. In the next life the archetype of self will be wholly
actualized through final divine union, fixed forever in his formed
destiny. Still short of full realization of form, he has to suffer the
misguided questions of adversaries, probably Manichees, who are
stricken with a sort of malaria of the soul, one sign of which is an
unappeasable thirst for truth about creation that their minds cannot
attain or retain; a malady that is the punishment consequent upon
their materialism and spiritual darkness. Their thirst for the water of
truth goes unsatisfied in the sense that their naturalism, cramping the
universe into categories of matter and time, is too stunted to account
for the spiritual and timeless, indeed the strictly eternal. In their eyes
creation is ridiculous because they are imprisoned within a shrunken
temporalized framework. Inability to conceive the eternal debars
them from understanding a creation conceivable only in terms of an
eternal creator.

He repeats earlier objections, partially disposed of in foregoing
chapters (11.13.15-6; 14.17). The first reproduces almost verbatim a
prior objection (11.10.12) that coarsely overlays eternity with
temporal features: what was God doing before he created? The
second objection, in part a rephrasing of the first, also raises again the
staggering problem of a possible change in the changeless divine will:
if the cosmic artisan had never before created, how did he change his
mind so as to suddenly create? As before (11.13.15), Augustine makes
quick work of the misuse of temporal language. If Manichean
complainants rethink the import of their language, they will notice
that the word "never" always bespeaks a time and is therefore
inapplicable to or unpredicable of what is above and outside time.

More simply, "never" means "in no time"; the reference to time is direct and inescapable. To associate God with time in this wise implies that time preexisted its own existence. Time began only with creation, and, if God operated in time prior to creating time, time would preexist its own existence: surely a self-defeating inconsequence. If his objectors' minds are extended toward the meaning of eternity, i.e., emancipated from their strangulating temporalism, they will stop venting a crude falsehood that in this instance is nothing short of nonsense. So instructed, they will recognize that, as eternal creator of all times, God is prior to all times; as an artisan is prior to his artifact, so God is prior to the times he creates. Because eternity is immutable all-at-onceness, times, which are rooted in mutability and concomitant with movements, cannot be coeternal with God. If times were coeternal, God, made subject to time, would be incoherently de-eternalized, or, conversely, times, rendered fixed and abiding, would be incoherently eternalized; collapsed into the eternal mode, times would effectively vanish. A final nuance specifies that a creature may be above time or timeless without being eternal; such a supertemporal yet noneternal creature is the heaven of heaven, immune to all variation and free from all subjection to time (12.2.2).

Chapter 31: Mystery of Eternity: God Changeless in Act of Creation

41. However colossal, a super-intelligence that apprehended the whole history of the universe according to a past-present-future schema cannot be equated with the eternal mind of God. Mystery enters as Augustine contemplates a creator who remains immutable while eternally thinking about what to create and eternally deciding to create. With God's light he has been able to negotiate a partial intelligibility, a contracted but real hold on the meaning of eternity. But because it is impossible to comprehend God and his attributes, much of eternity is conceptually inaccessible. The bosom of God, in which the Word dwells, seems opaque, fold upon fold of it making it unfathomably deep, almost humanly impenetrable. Not only does the impoverished range of the mind balk sallies at understanding eternity, but the consequences of personal failings such as darkness and a certain blindness put understanding further out of reach. His eyes cleansed of these obstacles, he will bathe in God's light, radiating

in some measure the happiness that consists in rejoicing in the truth
(10.22.32).

He wonders whether the eternal mind is identical with a super-
mind that, employing a past-present-future frame, understands on an
immense scale what his mind grasps only in miniature fashion. As
Augustine, while singing a psalm, knows by memory, attention, and
expectation the incoming and outgoing parts of the psalm, so a super-
intelligence would be maestro of the whole song of the universe,
remembering its past, attending to its present notes, and looking
forward to future musical passages. The entire history of the cosmos,
the whole tale of angels and men, would lie open to its threefold
temporalized cognition. No part would be veiled from the sweep of
its super-schema, no more than a part of the psalm Augustine is
singing lies outside memory, attention, and expectation. Such a super-
prodigious intellect, whose enormous knowledge and foreknowledge
dwarf the stretch of the human mind, excites awe, even a tremor of
fear.[77] No matter how exalted this super-intelligence, however
unerringly exact its knowledge of all the particulars of time that are
notes of the Cosmic Song, it falls infinitely short of the divine mind
operating in the eternal mode.[78] However magnificent, such a super-
mind is created and therefore finite, one creature superior to other
created beings. God, maker of souls as well as bodies, causes all things
to exist by his knowledge. Unlike even a created super-mind, he does
not know times because they exist; rather, times exist because he
knows them. His causal knowledge makes him more inwardly
present to the substance or inward core of a thing than the substance
itself (3.11.16). Substances, their movements, and their times proceed
from his causal or creative cognition. His intelligence, higher than the
highest of created minds, compasses future and past with a creative or
causal knowledge that makes them exist while a super-intelligence is
confined to knowing them only insofar as they actuate knowledge.
Since his is an uncreated mind, he knows things and times according
to his creator-intelligence, in a manner infinitely more penetrating
than that of a sheerly created mind, whose perception of a whole of
time is always mediated by a psychic distension formed by impresses
begotten from expectation and memory.[79]

Moreover, divine duration admits of neither variation nor
distension. As absolutely existing, God is absolutely immutable and
therefore unchangeably eternal, truly eternal, "truly" certifying that

he undergoes not the slightest alteration. The heaven of heaven, though exempt from variation and timeless, is not truly or absolutely eternal; its timelessness is that of a created entity subject to the influence of the creator (11.30.40). In terms of the triadic schema, God simply is: in his being there is no "was" because this signifies what no longer exists; nor is there "will be," for this means what does not yet exist; in him there is simply and solely unchangeable present existence (P 101.10). Existing only presently, he knows events only presentially. Not tethered to the passage of things in terms of a timeline or distension, he does not cognize a changing universe retrospectively or prospectively but presentially. He does not "retrosee" or foresee but simply sees all times in an infinite intuition that encompasses in one eternal present all humanly discerned past, present, and future. Though the events caused and seen are changing, his eternal vision remains changeless (CD 11.21). In sum, God's eternity is true or immutable because he simply is, without past or future, existing in an eternal present; and because he knows nondistensively, without past or future, he comprehends the whole course of creation in eternally present cognition.

Augustine next confronts the second, more baffling part of the second objection posed above (11.30.40): how did it enter the divine mind to initiate the creation that was a novel idea? This question, which restates a previous difficulty, the second and most troublesome objection raised earlier (11.10.12), consists of three sub-questions. (i) Why did God suddenly create in time? Is it not more reasonable to think that an eternal creator would produce an eternal world? (ii) Why did an inactive God suddenly become active? (iii) Does not an innovating idea of creation that implies a novel decision to create entail a change in God incompatible with changelessness? Augustine's response is succinct: when the eternal God created the universe in the beginning, which was the first moment of time, his eternal will and action were altered not in the slightest. Packed in this summary reply are answers to the three subquestions. (i) God did not suddenly or capriciously change his mind. His decree to create was eternal, but since he was not bound to create, since he created out of his gratuitous goodness or outstreaming love (CD 12.17), he was not necessitated to create an eternal world. Whereas his decree to create and to determine that the world begin at a certain moment in time was eternal, the effect, the actual creation of the universe, transpired in time. (ii) God did not abruptly switch to activity. As eternal life, he is always active, always the same in his activity. Not his incessant action but the result of this eternal activity, a universe created in time irrupts into existence without prior existence. (iii) God's eternal knowledge and eternal will always remain the same. Throughout the universe things change because God wills changes, but his will stays immutable, changelessly willing the changes of things. The origin of the world is similar. When God willed to create, to change things by bringing the nonexistent into existence, his will did not change. His creative will willed change, but it was the nonexistent world that was changed, so to speak, into an existent universe (CALP 2.11.37). In short, God is eternal, wholly independent of and absolutely sovereign to time, utterly unaffected and unimpacted by time. Transcendent to all variation and succession, he eternally causes the times rooted in variation and succession. Thus his creative act eternally decreed in his lovingly fecund wisdom is eternal also, wholly unconstrained by time. His eternal knowledge and will to create are eternally decreed once for all, irrevocably, without shadow of alteration; God cannot remain God unless he remains immutable in every way.

But harmonizing this eternal decree with the apparent novelty in creation is a super-challenging enterprise. At a certain juncture the mind is brought up short, unable to take one step further, conceding that the enigma, while partially decipherable, ultimately lies cloaked in densest obscurity. Along with those who understand to some degree how God creates in his eternal mode, less endowed spirits, who cannot mesh in any manner God's immutable decree with the seemingly innovating choice of creation, are also bade to laud the Lord of wisdom. Even the perspicacious catch no more than a glimmer of understanding, for the concrete mode of eternal operation is lost in dark, swirling mists enwrapping the majestic peak of divine life, inspiring Augustine to burst out in praise of matchless supremacy: "Lord, how sublime you are!" While those who exalt themselves repulse God's light, the super-exalted One stoops down to the humble, unveiling the secrets of the kingdom (P 50.21.S 68.7), residing in the lowly as in his special abode, where is imprinted an image of God modeled after the perfect image, the Christ who humbled himself to death on the cross (S 304.3). God raises up to his eminence those who are cast down (P 144.18), and, insofar as they are lowly, they remain lofty, not falling but continually elevated, because God himself is their elevation, sharing his grandeur with them. The hearts of the humble are the very home of God, and, in turn, the heart of God becomes the very home of the humble who, hospitable to his wooing, are exalted in his exaltation (P 44.7). Strictly speaking, it is through charity that the soul abides in the God who is love (CALP 3.5.6. J8.14). It is through humility as conjoined to love as its foundation, (7.20.26) that the soul is lifted to live in the very home of God or that God lives in the soul as his home (E 187.5.16; 10.32. P 98.3).

Humility is one indispensable key to the existential moral truth that is salvation. Without the strength of God he is feeble and infirm (4.16.31); to be and stay healed he must recognize that only mercy can cure his wounds (10.28.39). In brief, he is no more than a man, powerless to pull himself up out of a deep cistern (4.1.1). Humility, moreover, plays a crucial role in acquisition of speculative truth linked to salvation. Earlier, pride cutting him off from God so swelled his spiritual countenance that his eyes were closed (7.7.11). Pride ensnared Manichees in religious darkness, duping them into giving their imprimatur to the grossest physical absurdities (5.3.3-5). Again, the smug self-sufficiency of Neoplatonic thinkers who sketched the goal of man denied them recognition of the means of humility exemplified and mediated by Christ (7.9.13; 21.22). The polar opposite of pride, whose punishment is sightlessness (1.18.29), humility authentically opens the mind, disposing it toward clear reception of truth presiding within (10.26.37). Wedded to charity, it is enabled to see the truth (7.10.16). In seeing the truth, the humble inquirer sees that not all of the truth concerning God vis-à-vis his creation is perfectly seeable on this side. With a mind severely limited in purview and depth, he is constrained to let God be God, to bow down before the unsearchable features of the act of creation. Not a creator of the mind but a mind created, he cannot understand in the smallest measure exactly how an eternal mind concretely operates. Raised up by lowliness to the height that is God, his mind dwells in some sense in the secret folds of the divine bosom, there docilely assenting to the inscrutable character of creation. It is true that God is immutable, and it is no less true that, while not necessitated to create, God, in inaugurating creation, remains immutable in will. Full reconciliation of these two truths enveloped in mystery, it is submission to the elusive nature of the eternal that preserves Augustine from tumbling into falsity, from either forfeiting divine immutability or relinquishing the nonnecessary or gratuitous production of the universe. Were he tumorous with self-exaltation, he would run the risk of toppling from the divine elevation where truth, partly enfolded in darkness, resides. Lowly union with truth on high saves him from plunging into errors that are the offspring of pride blinded to the impassable chasm between a narrowly restricted intellect and the heights of divine truth.

Excursus: Four Kinds of Time

It seems appropriate to append some remarks on the four faces or kinds of time in Augustine: psychological, physical, moral, and historical.[79]

On Augustine's reckoning, we saw, time is first of all psychological, a distension of the mind which embraces the whole of the time-line that emerges from experience. Regrettably his account has been branded extravagantly subjective or subjectivistic. According to St. Albert the Great, Augustine's analysis eliminates physical time; there simply cannot be any time outside the soul.[80] To counteract this psychologism, Albert arrives at a wholly physicalized time, turning the blind eye to the undeniable fact that time is a successive continuum, whose lapsing parts have to be psychologically retained to complete the time-line. Like motion, of which it is the concomitant, time is known in its totality by psychological assistance. In the opinion of B. Russell, Augustine's theory is "one of the most extreme forms of...subjectivism."[81] Quite the opposite: Augustine's time is basically connected with the world outside the subject. The psychologically retained time-line is outward-oriented. *Deus creator omnium*, psychologically held within, duplicates the succession of sounds without that were first physically heard. Occasionally, misleading comparisons with other thinkers are suggested. For one scholar, Augustine's view anticipates the transcendental consciousness of time in Kant.[82] As such consciousness synthesizes a number of extents of time, so in Augustine memory serves as a unifying power for successive time-intervals. Per contra, a parallel text shows not a trace of Kantian subjectivity. Just as light rays from the eyes help us to grasp spatial extents, so the light of memory enables us to grasp intervals of time (M 6. 8. 21). Time-intervals are objectively present and objectively observed in a way similar to the perception of spatial extents. Others have detected striking similarities between Augustine's view and the lived time of H. Bergson.[83] Nevertheless, the apparent points of agreements are outbalanced by essential dissimilarities. The self of Bergson is incongruously subjectless; without an enduring subject the successive eventuations of the ego cannot be linked. Again, *la durée*, unbroken, continuous duration that is purely qualitative and nonquantitative, is a construct unverifiable in concrete experience. The intervals of time in the flow are always measurable, always quantitatively determinable (11.27.34)

Physical time, measured succession which occurs in nature independently of the mind, is the measurable concomitant of successive phases of motion (12.8.8.CD 12.16). As far as I know, no scholar identifies physical with psychological time.

Unlike psychological and physical time, moral time does not prescind from but is interwoven with human change and the weal of man. Thus it is only equivocally related to the theoretical time that is psychological and physical. Unfortunately, some commentators confuse moral with psychological time. According to one moralizing interpretation, the instability and insecurity with which time is freighted can be mastered by a conquest of time that paves the way to eternity. However, grasping time as a distension does not necessarily lead to an awareness of the eternal nor does time as distension bear, within, a vertical thrust toward the eternal.[84] Another opinion also lumps the psychological with a moral stance, arguing that the mind is both temporalizing and temporalized.[85] It temporalizes, i.e., surmounts time in virtue of intention or attention, while it is temporalized by distension: so time is both distended intention and intentionalized distension. However, since the text contains no indication whatsoever of polarity, this must be deemed a misreading of Augustine's psychological time. G. O'Daly also accents the moral connotation. Though recognizing that distension can mean extension, he emphasizes the distraction and disturbance distension brings to the spirit.[86] Man finds fulfillment not in distension but in the upward tendency *secundum intentionem* of Phil 3:12-14 whereby the mind is fixed on the God above. Thus the theoretical sense of distension as psychic extension is effectively swallowed up in its equivocal counterpart, distension as depression and distress. In a somewhat different vein, N. Fischer maintains that time is a distension of the mind in the special sense that distension is divided into times of expectation, attention, and remembrance, leaving the human spirit unfulfilled. Psychic distension symbolizes time's transitoriness that can be overcome only in the hoped-for eternity of God.[87] Fischer misses the equivocal switch in 11.29.39, where Augustine shifts from theoretical to moral time. The difficulty of theoretical time is resolved in 11.28.38, but the existential distension of moral time remains unresolved until the spirit is fully united with the eternal. Moralistic interpretation wears theological garb in the analysis of R. Teske.[88]

Time is fleeting and death-laden. The Word of God beyond time entered time to free man from time (S 340A.5), to disenthrall him from the distension of past, present, and future. True, yet this leaves intact the psychological definition of time as the distension of time (J 31.5), a theoretical category that cannot be broadened without equivocation to include Christian liberation from time.

Historical time is human time in the specific sense that it sees man in his past as a member of a nation or a body politic. The confusion of psychological time with historical time, which is rather infrequent, occurs in C. Dawson's claim that Augustine's "novel concept of psychic time issues in a fresh concept of historical time". Because man is master of time, history becomes a creative process.[89] Unhappily, the theoretical definition of time has no per se nexus with the time of history.

A number of strictures have targeted Augustine's psychological theory, but spatial constraints here bar any serious attempt to examine such critiques in a rejoinder that might run to a small-book length.

NOTES

1. In "L'Antimanicheismo nelle Confessioni di sant' Augustino," GM 20 (1965, 1-2), 91-120, A. Vecchi finds anti-Manichean themes operative, sometimes implicitly, in the first nine books. Book 10 and 11 stress the transcendence of God while the last two books focus on a spiritual mode of Scriptural exegesis.

2. This outline is partially adapted from N. Fischer, "Distentio Animi: Ein Symbol der Entfluchtigung des Zeitlichen," CAH, 545-6

3. See Pellegrino, *The True Priest*, 105-9. L. Verheijen, *St. Augustine: Monk Priest Bishop*, 28-31.

4. BA 14, 272, n.11.

5. In *Cing Études d'Augustin sur le début de la Génèse* G. Pelland fully explores the interpretations of the first four verses of Genesis. GCM (388-90) uses both literal and figurative interpretation. GI (396) attempted a literal commentary, this abandoned at 1.26, though Augustine appended material while writing R. The *Confessions* ventures a literal interpretation in Books 11 and 12, then offers a mostly figurative reading in Book 13. The masterly GL (399-415) presents a strictly literal commentary. CD 11 (417) accords special attention to the nature and role of the angels. See Taylor, *Literal Meaning*, 1. 1-4, and R. Teske, "Genesis Accounts of Creation," AE 379-81.

6. BA 14, 273, n. 2.

7. On the secrets of Scripture see Pontet, 119-48.

8. Pontet, 39.

9. BA 14, 247-5, nn. 1-2.

10. Pontet, 316-20.

11. Pontet, 319.

12. Bourke, *Confessions* 331, n. 29.

13. J 54.8 distinguishes between the Father, *verax*, and the Son, *veritas* or truth; it is *verax* who begot *veritas*. Yet 11.2.4 and 11.8.10 speak of Christ as the truth while 11.3.5, toward the end, identifies truth with God as such. However, ordinarily when accounting for truth in the mind, he refers to God, not the Word, as the truth from whom truths derive.

14. This chapter calls God the *conditor* of things. The word *condere* more precisely expresses *creator* than *creare* because in Augustine's day *creare* was used at times to signify *gignere*, to beget or generate. Yet, in fact, Augustine frequently refers to God as *creator omnium*. C. O'Toole, *The Philosophy of Creation in the Writings of St. Augustine*, 3.

15. *Phys.* 2.1.1. 93a21-8. See W.D. Ross, *Aristotle's Physics*, 503.

16. R. Jolivet, *Essai sur les rapports entre la pensée greque et la pensée chrétienne*, 12.

17. *Enn.* 8.7; 2. 3.17; 3.4.1.

18. *Tim.* 30 a 3-4, 30b1-c1, 49a5-6.

19. O'Toole, 3-4.

20. A dubious etymology prevalent during Augustine's schooling derived *verbum* (word) from *verbero* (to strike) because a pronounced word strikes the ear; Mag 5.12. According to more recent scholarship, the word apparently has an Indo-

European root: wer, linked to which is the word *epéw* (epw), "I shall say." See the translation, *The Greatness of the Soul and The Teacher*, by J. Colleran, 228, n. 23.

21. Though physical time is rooted in mutability (12.6.6), this chapter speaks of time and change rather than, as one might expect, of change and time. Here he is stressing that the Word is eternal and consequently immortal; creaturely counterparts are temporal and changeable, with change connoting passing away or death in both broad and strict senses.

22. Here death is broadly taken to signify the cessation of any state. "Walking is dead in the body of a person standing still, speech is dead on the lips of a silent man" (J 38.10). So too Augustine's infancy is long dead (1.6.9) and in 384-5, in his thirty-first year, Augustine's adolescence was dead (7.1.1). As mentioned above, such cessation justifies the description of human existence as a dying life (1.6.7).

23. Instead of speaking of things of time as aborning, then dying, Augustine depicts them as dying, from which something new has its origin. The shift is owed to his stress on the unceasing nature of the divine Word in opposition to the inevitable cessation of human words in a sentence; only as one word is spoken or dies away is its successor able to be born or take its rise. In the human word utterance occurs only through the dying of prior vocables ceding place to the birth of new vocables. But the Word spoken by the Father, the Word through whom all creatures are made, is eternal: since spoken eternally, he does not cease to exist. Because uttered by the eternal God through his eternal Word, the creative fiat is uttered all at once, not successively, not with lapsing and aborning words, but eternally, unchangeably.

24. "Stable" signifies immutable. BA 14, 289, n. 2.

25. Men are similar to the light because children or adopted sons of God, recreated in his image after the perfect image that is Christ (EJ 4.5), but dissimilar insofar they deviate from the life of charity.

26. The Latin for Ps 102.5 in the text differs somewhat from that used in P 102.5, which is very close to the Vulgate.

27. God is Is: he truly is, immutable, always abiding, not corrupted in any part (EJ 4.5).

28. Desire remains firm and constant. Christians are to abide in hope as God abides (*manet*) in reality, perservering in walking as pilgrims to reach their homeland, because the good or heavenly Jerusalem does not "migrate" or change its location (EJ 4.7). Throughout (11.8.10) it is God who abides so that men can find a fixed point of return.

29. As simple ones, first nourished by the humble Christ, we are strengthened to feed on solid food, knowledge that Christ is equal to the Father. To touch by mind, i.e., to know, Jesus spiritually is to know that he is equal to the Father. Not the simple but only the spirituals (EJ 3.1) spiritually touch Christ, understanding that he is one with the Father (EJ 3.2).

30. Wisdom is indeed a polyvalent term in Augustine. F. Cayré, "La notion de sagesse chez saint Augustin" *L'Anné théologique augustiniene* 4 (1943), 433-56, instances thirty-one senses and Marrou, 564-9, some thirteen meanings. See V.

Bourke, *Wisdom from Saint Augustine,* 60. n.7.

31. Since in their sinless condition our first parents could not be changed by age (GL 11.32-42), their years would have increased without their growing old. However, the state of sin connotes old age. In lapsing into sin, we arrive at old age (P 124.1). Man grows old through sin but is made new through grace (P 6.9). Days according to Adam are days according to old age that is putrefaction (P 114.3). The old man also bespeaks degenerative moral time, fast-flying time and successive "ages" (P 38.9), in which every advance is a decline (S 38.5, P 127.15), in which newborn children say to their parents: "Alas, think of departing the scene. Now let us play our role" (P 127.15).

32. The description of Manichees as "full of oldness" suggests itself because, until he had been undeceived, his youth could not be spiritually renewed like the eagle's (11.9.11). In the version of the ancient legend received by Augustine, an eagle can be rejuvenated. Aging causes the upper part of an eagle's beak to grow so long that is cannot open its mouth to grasp food. Thus old age inflicts a double burden: natural decline of vigor plus additional disability consequent upon inability to eat. Happily, an eagle recovers its youth by striking its beak against a rock in order to cut off the extra offending length (P 102.9). Analogously, Christ is the rock upon which spiritual youth is renewed (P 66.10). Manichees are full of oldness because their view is wholly carnal or materialistic and because their world picture is hopelessly muddled, ridden with opinions that run counter to scientific fact, along with others that are self-refuting.

33. According to BA 14, 581, n. 18, Augustine has in mind two views counter to Christian creation, the Manichean and the Neoplatonic. Manichees contend that the universe, while without a beginning in time, was not strictly created by God; the universe emanates from God as its transcendent source but it cannot be created from nothing. God is not absolutely transcendent; he cannot exist without a universe which has no beginning or end and necessarily takes its rise from him. Pride is the ruling passion or dominant vice of Neoplatonists (7.9.13; 21.27). The God who never ages leads the proud into spiritual old age (1.4.4). However soaring their wisdom, it is devoid of humility and results in spiritual decrepitude. Though superior to Manichean materialism, Neoplatonic recognition of spiritual realities and cultivation of interiority are vitiated by pride. In the broad sense of disassociation from the true creator-God, their posture is carnal and therefore dodders with the ills of old age.

34. Both objections are ascribed to Manichees. What motivated God, they ask, to suddenly do what he had not done through eternal times? GCM 1.2.1; 11.10.12; first objection. Too what was God doing before he made heaven and earth? GCM 1.2.1; 11.12.14; fourth objection. In this place he considers these as two distinct objections. GCM 1.2.1.

35. According to A. Lovejoy, *The Great Chain of Being,* 348, n. 24, Augustine (CD 13.14-7), in spite of painful wrestling with the problem of immutability vis-à-vis creation, is enmeshed "in an amazing tangle of formal contradictions." Similarly, Lovejoy puts down the usual replies to difficulties as evasions or downright inconsistencies; for an immutable God who is perfectly self-

contained, "a created world is a *groundless* superfluity"; 156-7. As our foregoing text and related notes indicate, creation is not groundless; God creates out of his infinite generosity or gratuitous goodness. Lovejoy's mistake lies in his assumption that God must have an absolutely necessary motive for creating; as pointed out earlier, the reason for creation is not an absolutely necessary but a sufficing reason, the desire to share divine goodness. Analogously, the free decision to choose one business position rather than another is not absolutely necessitated—otherwise it would not be free. But if undertaken with proper deliberation, the choice, far from being groundless, is based on a sufficing reason.

36. Reconciliation of volition with immutability in the creative act is one of the most vexing enigmas in philosophical theology. Augustine insists on two points that safeguard the sovereignty, the very Godness, of God. (i) God realizes no profit from creation. No aspiration for an extrinsic good motivated him to make the universe. Still, his creative act is not a sheerly arbitrary upshot of reasonless spontaneity; he creates out of gratuitous goodness. (ii) Since God's decision to create is one and the same with his immutable will, creation inserts no novelty or change in God; not the creator but the creature is new and "changed." Interestingly, St. Thomas espouses, with perhaps somewhat more conceptual sophistication, the essentials of these two positions. (i) As supremely perfect, the divine artisan needs no one object for the exercise of its power. That God is not dependent on extrinsic goods entrains not a defect in the divine will but a lack in the created good. In short, without creation God would have continued perfectly good, whereas without creation creatures would not have been good at all. *S. th.* 1.19.3 ad 4. *C. Gen.* 1.82. (ii) God wills his own good by absolute necessity: by his very nature he has to will his own goodness and beatitude. However, God wills things other than himself by a suppositional necessity, a necessity that stems from the antecedent but is in the consequent: if Socrates is sitting down, he is necessarily sitting down; correspondingly, on the supposition that God wills something other than self, he necessarily wills it. If he wills this universe, he must will it; he cannot not will it—otherwise his will would not be immutable. *S. th.* 1.19.3. *C. Gen.* 1.83. Over the centuries much exquisite subtlety and acuity have been expended on this exceptionally tortuous and arcane riddle, but in the end, after some partial intelligibility has been thrown on some facets, a core stumbling block seems irremovably shrouded in mystery: how can God stay immutable while deciding to create this particular universe? For a balanced, thoughtful survey of various Scholastic opinions, see E. Gisquière, *Deus Dominus*, 2. 91-8.

37. D. Hume, *A Treatise of Human Nature*, 1.iii.14, (ed.) L.A. Selby-Biggs, 165-6, 168-9.

38. According to GCM 1.2.4, the will of God is sovereignly distant from its human counterpart, which is motivated or caused by a good on which it depends. It is incongruous to demand a dependence-inducing cause of God's will to create when the divine will is the very cause of all things that exist ad extra. Such a stipulation implies the impossibility that some cause preceded the divine will. Why did God make heaven and earth? Simply because he willed it: we cannot

find anything greater in reason or power than his will. Later Augustine more specifically argues that God was moved to create by his disinterested goodness to share himself with other beings. Things are good only because their maker is good. E 166.5.15; CD 11.21-2. The words, "God saw that it was good" (Gn 1.4), clearly attest that God did not create by necessity or for the satisfaction of some inner deficiency but out of sheer goodness alone. CD 11.24. In short, as DC 1.32.35 concisely phrases it, "Because he [God], is good, we exist; and insofar as we exist, we are good."

39.   As noted by W. Christian, "The Creation of the World," in Battenhouse, *Companion to St. Augustine*, 319 and 339, n. 12, Calvin, in *Institutes* 1.14.1, endorsed the mocking reply Augustine repudiated as intellectually barren and affectively coarse.

40.   Usually we speak of coming and going, with the past viewed moving into the future. Augustine, however, ordinarily speaks of going and coming; the past is made outgoing by the future.

41.   As immutable, God is ageless; never new, never old (1.4.4). From another angle, in transcending decrepitude due to time, he is beauty ever ancient, ever new (10.27.38); by human reckoning, ancient, far older than the universe, but, in virtue of his timeless duration, ever new, changelessly youthful, immutably beautiful.

42.   On eternity see J. Guitton, especially 147-77, *Le temps et l'éternité chez Plotin et saint Augustin* (Paris 1959); W. Gundersdorf von Jess, "Divine Eternity in the Doctrine of St. Augustine," AS 6 (1975), 75-96; E.P. Meijering, *Augustin über Schöpfung, Ewigkeit und Zeit. Das Elfte Buch der Bekenntnisse.* Solignac, BA 14, 573-7.

43.   *Cons. phil.* 5.6.

44.   As related in A. Bower, "Boethius," AE 108. H. Chadwick considers Boethius "deeply Augustinian." However, in the opinion of T. McTighe, there is little evidence that Augustine's concept of eternity affected Boethius.

45.   The gap between familiar awareness and analytical precision is not a problem peculiar to time. Even educated minds, who know in a realistic, practical way other common sensio-intellectual items of experience such as motion, place, and space, are initially rendered analytically mute or stammering when challenged to set down proper definitions. Oddly, contrary to clear textual evidence some claim that Augustine was not seeking a definition but engaging in phenomenological musings. Again, in "Time as *Distentio* and St. Augustine's Excursus of Philippeans 3, 12-14", REA 23 (1977), 265-71, O'Daly argues that, while Augustine proposed to define time, he never succeeded in reaching a definition because he relied on distension in a metaphorical sense. However, as n.76 below indicates, distension is used analogously, as a legitimate psychic kin of physical distension. O'Daly runs together the distension that is psychological time with its equivocal counterpart that is moral time (11. 29. 39). According to HC 230.19, Augustine, after raising the question of definition, claims it unanswerable in the face of seeming historical chaos and the apparent meaninglessness of past and future. However, K. Flasch, *Was ist Zeit?*, 332-41, strongly affirms that Augustine undoubtedly set out to really define time.

It may be mentioned here also that, as indicated in Book 10, n. 54, relativity theory has no essential influence on the meaning of basic physical time (and, by extension, psychological time). The special theory of relativity does not provide a new meaning of time but a new way of measuring time. In relativistic transformation equations time enters as a fourth or quasi-spatial dimension. Whereas Galilean transformation equations specify differences only in the three spatial coordinates(with time identical in different frames of reference), relativistic equations give the time as well as the spatial position in each frame of reference. Time is not the same in two frames of reference, i.e., the clocks in the two frames of reference are not identical. However, this mathematical-physical mode of measuring space and time does not actually fuse space and time. Though treated as a fourth coordinate, physical time remains distinct from space. One telling indicator of the distinction is the fact that passage along the time-line is irreversible while passage in space can be reversed. In other words, the physical universe is not actually a four-dimensional continuum; the so-called spatiotemporal continuum is a mathematical-physical construct or being of reason that measures the physical world in which space and time remain physically distinct. In short, Augustine's general natural-psychological definition of time remains unaffected by new constructs bearing on the measurement of time in specialized physical science.

46. The dialectical dissolution of time, because composed of a nonexistent past and future, may be traced at least to Aristotle, *Phys.* 4.10.218 a3-7, where, however, the actual now or instant is not considered a part of time since time cannot be composed of instants. In Augustine's dialectical treatment the instant is an actual feature of time that seems paradoxically programmed to be immediately nonactual.

47. Augustine does not designate the indivisible present as the instant or now but calls it *quid temporis*, something of time, a feature or factor of time. Significantly, he does not term it a time or time-interval, which betokens magnitude and divisibility. Nor does he name it a part of time, for a part can be directly perceived or understood. The instant is not grasped by sensory or intellectual perception but is the outcome of analysis. Without the indivisible divisor of past and future we could not distinguish past from future in physical events. A moment, a short interval of time, does not name or connote the indivisible of time; unfortunately, one otherwise admirable rendering mistranslates *minutissimas partes* as tiny parcels of instants; a moment is divisible whereas in current usage the instant is indivisible.

48. This initial induction, that we perceive and measure time-intervals in their very passing, is modified and amended in 11.27.34. It is unquestionably true that we do perceive not the instant or physical present but a temporal extent. We perceive each moment or submoment of a syllable, but we do not measure the whole temporal extent apart from immediate memory, whereby the foregoing parts of the interval are held or retained as an impress in the mind duplicating spread in its passing. We can know the interval is long only by knowing the whole interval, but the whole interval can exist as a whole only as retained in immediate memory. Take the Latin verb *est* (it is or he is). A word of three

letters, its vocalization occupies only a single moment, yet in that very moment or beat we cannot reach the second letter until the first is finished: the third letter will not sound or be pronounced unless the sound of the second has passed (P 38.7); quoted in BA 14, 305. n 1, although Solignac links the text, inadvertently, in my opinion, with Augustine's conclusion that the instant is extentless or durationless (11.15.20). In other words, a single syllable pronounced in a moment involves submoments: only when the three subsyllables or letters are pronounced, do we directly perceive the word *est*, but, in truth, the first and second subsyllables or letters are held within to be completed by the third subsyllable or letter: we know the full word as mentally retained. Yet it remains true that we do *perceive* each sounding of the passing letters, but we do not *measure* the length of the word or sound until all letters are pronounced.

49.   The brief time-interval that we directly perceive seems similar to what was later termed the specious present (James 1.609). The present is qualified as specious or seeming to distinguish it from the real or strictly physical present, the instant. The present we actually perceive "is no knife-edge, but a saddle back...with a certain breadth of its own...." This initially perceived present is specious in a second sense: it embraces at its margins, at its waning and waxing borders, an immediate or second past and an on-the-threshold future. For example, first, we grasp *Deus* as one word, as a presentational unit, as an appreciable span; we do not perceive an indivisible or even infinitesimal cut between past and future. Second, *Deus*, because it has parts, is heard partitively: the first syllable is becoming past as the second syllable is pronounced. However, the perceived present may vary in amplitude or duration. A short sentence is grasped as a durational whole: "Please give me the book" or "This table is really smooth." Again, we say: "Just now [as a perceived present] I heard the thunder" or "At the moment light suddenly flashed through the room, the painting fell from the wall." Probably because he lacked a sound philosophy of nature, it may be mentioned, James' account of the specious present tends to overstress the interior cognition of time, for the sense of time does not primordially originate within but is begot by physical transiency (12.6.6).

50.   As noted earlier (6.5.7), historical truths are strictly believed rather than evidentially or demonstratively known. We accept historical events as true on faith, on the reliable word of another. Though never attaining ironclad certitude, many historical documents are practically warranted, verging as close to strict certitude as possible. Thus it was eminently reasonable for Augustine to believe, though he could never demonstrate, that Cicero (2.5.10) once really existed.

51.   Hewing to the pedagogical rule of proceeding from the more familiar to the less known, the discussion begins with an example of foreseeing the future from ordinary experience, according to observation and science. Passing over the cause-effect linkage in, say, eclipses as somewhat recondite, he illustrates natural prediction of the future in terms of an easily recognized sign-signified relation.

52.   Examples of harbingers of the future are abundant. In the line of causation

mating portends birth of offspring, puberty is augured in a boy, and successful surgery supplies prognosis for full recovery. In the line of sign thick, dark clouds indicate rain; a fever with a coma foreshadows death; a sunset is the precursor of twilight.

53. In CE 1.34.37 (composed a little while after 400, i.e., close to the time of the last three books) Augustine proposes two conjectures concerning the mode in which God infused prophetic light. First, God may have dispatched to the prophets angels who imparted a picture of the future through appropriate sensory objects. Second, through the Holy Spirit their minds may have been elevated to the level of the angels themselves, empowering them to see the future with the insight proper to angels, i.e., in one of the *rationes* or types in the Word (GL 4.23.41). In any case, prophecy is a charism, an extraordinary gift of the Spirit whereby through the ministry, direct of indirect, of angels prophets perceive future events as if present, whether through sensory figures or in the very presentiality of an eternally present *ratio* or divine idea. In "Saint Augustine on History, Prophecy, and Inspiration," AUGS 12 (1967), 271-280, especially 276-8, R. Markus distinguishes prophecy, taken broadly, that understands the meaning of experience, from prophecy, strictly taken, that includes visions of events and their understanding, a category that embraces foresight of future events. See GL 12.9.20.

54. The conclusion that there are three present times mediated by memory, observation, and expectation adumbrates the solution to the the problem of time (11.28.37).

55. Augustine seems to speak tentatively about the conclusion that there are three present times. The "perhaps" and his request for permission to so express his point bear not on the content of his claim but on the apparent awkwardness of the formulation. However cognitively precise, his phraseology, he suggests, may strike some as gauche.

56. Augustine can hardly be said to wholly eschew less proper or technically inexact language. God repents and becomes angry (1.3.3). Time is described as vacationless, an ever-active agent that provides healing for sorrows (4.8.13). Though there is only one teacher, Christ (Mag 14.46), without hesitation he names his instructors teachers (1.13.20). Nor would he cavil over popular parlance suggesting that the bodily senses actively know, even though, according to his theory, the soul senses through the bodily activity. In our own day we unabashedly list the times of sunrise and sunset while scientifically certain that the earth rotates on its axis about the sun. We also depict death as the Grim Reaper, refer to darkness overcoming daylight, talk of witty remarks stimulating the brain, and picture evil as a sort of positive force of malevolence. Popular expressions comprise an indispensable part of the *lingua franca* that joins individuals of diverse background and education in a common linguistic culture.

57. As mentioned above, Augustine later qualifies or modifies the claim that we measure present time as passing. In truth, we do not measure a time as passing but as immediately past, where it forms a single temporal unit, a fixed whole with initial and terminal points (11.27.34-5). Moreover, through perduring

attention we do observe or experience, without strictly measuring, passing spans of time (11.28.37).

58. It seems close to impossible to identify the learned man from whom Augustine became acquainted with the theory that celestial movements constitute time. G-M 353, n. 10, suggests that the source was Eratosthenes and Hestiaeus of Perinthus, quoted in Stobaeus, *Ecl. phys.* 1.8.40. J. Callahan traces the view to the Arian bishop Eunomius, criticized by Basil of Caesarea in *Adv. Eunom.*; see "Basil of Caesarea. A New Source for St. Augustine's Theory of Time," *Harvard Studies in Class. Philol.* 63 (1958), 437-54. After listing these sources, then tentatively proposing Chrysippus, Solignac, BA 14, 586, shrewdly remarks that this opinion is syncretic, the outcome of a mix of Platonic, Aristotelian, and Stoic ideas. Augustine, apparently familiar with the treatise on eternity and time, may have come upon this theory in *Enn.* 3.7.7. The position that makes time one with celestial movements apparently goes back to Plato; see Aristotle, *Phys.* 4.10.218b33, with probable reference to *Tim.* 39c5-d2 (Ross, *Aristotle's Physics,* 59-61).

59. Unlike purely intelligible notions like numbers (10.12.19), common notions emerge in some manner from sensory experience. They are common in two senses: common ideas that bear on common or general aspects of the universe; the common property of all normal men, known at least pre-reflectively by all minds. Motion, space, place, and time would seem to fall under the rubric of common notions. The apparent paradox of knowing and not knowing what time is alludes to time as a common notion (11.14.17); commonly found in experience and conversation, it is pre-analytically common to all. Inductive proof preceded by dialectical inquiry verifies the analytical meaning of the common notion of time. The term derives from the Stoics. Max Pohlenz, *Die Stoa,* Gottingen, Vanderhoek v. Ruprecht, 1948, 56; cited in BA 14, 319, n. 2. See also O'Daly, 184.

60. In exploring the connection between time and celestial movements, then between time and sun, Augustine capitalizes on a dialectical-empirical technique today generally labeled thought-experiment. The grounds of these arguments and variations in solar velocity could but never do occur through natural agencies. The method is empirical insofar as the hypothetical experiments conducted in the imagination establish that the suggested dependence of time on solar and other celestial movements is not verifiable in natural events.

61. Augustine makes room for a physical time that is the numerable and measurable aspect of movement. More specifically, while not constituting time, celestial movements are conventional and also proper or quasi-natural means of measuring time. We employ such movements to measure time in the universe, but as proved below (11.27.35-7), the distension by which we apply these cosmic measures resides in the mind.

62. A lathe is a device that uses a cutting tool to chip away material so as to gradually make round the rod (turning on the lathe) to which the cutting tool is applied. Thus at any one juncture a part of the turning rod is made round. From another angle, the rod is successively, part by part, made round. In any

case, the turning rod remains strictly in the same *place*: as it turns, its *position* is altered, and the different points are cut over a certain period of time.

63. Augustine's explicit remark that he had been speaking of time for a long time furnishes internal evidence of dictation of the *Confessions.*

64. It seems probable that at this transitional point Augustine broke off from composing the remainder of the treatise on time. How long or short was the cessation of dictation, it is hard to say. But some period in which to tussle further with and decipher the meaning of time must have intervened prior to additional composition. Otherwise his confession of genuine puzzlement would be rendered questionable. Perhaps his pause for additional rumination lasted a day or two or only a few hours. Whatever the length of the hiatus, hard concentration had to clear the way for flawless analysis of his solution in the third part.

65. A cubit, the length of a forearm, between seventeen and twenty-one inches long, is usually designated eighteen inches.

66. Some detect an allusion to *Aen.* 4.586, in the reference to the dawning of the truth. Bourke, *Confessions,* 368, n. 99.

67. Time as measured involves or is an interval or continuum bounded by initial and terminal points, by a before or starting point and an after or end point. For Aristotle, we move from the before-point into the future after-point. The now becomes successively present, leaving the past in its wake as it moves toward the future. For Augustine, time moves from the not-yet of the future into the present, then into the past. The difference is one of perspective. From the angle of local motion, the now moves forward to a future position on the time-line while, from the angle of speaking, the sound not yet uttered is future; as being spoken, it is present; and once spoken, it is past. Yet on occasion, we may view a verse as a time-line, the initial sound pointing toward the last syllable of the verse as future: "We measure the very interval from some beginning up to some end" (11.27.34). Later (12.11.14; 12.15) Augustine will describe the before and after of time in terms of physical motion.

68. "Simple" is an attribute of a foot; a short foot is so characterized in relation to a long foot, being specifically one-half the length of a long foot (11.27.35).

69. Professional declamation of the line proclaims that the long is twice the length of the short syllable; BA 14, 331. n. 1. Skilled vocalizing of the syllable convincingly evidences that he is indeed measuring time-intervals.

70. In remarking his confidence in the veridical character of his sensorially registered measurement of time, Augustine is not, as some suggest, displaying latent distrust of the senses. In fact, he is acknowledging an explicit trust in the senses, arguing, in effect, that no other sensory evidence could be more coercive. As far as it is possible as regards sensory deliverances, he stays unshakably sure that his measurement of time is not illusory but revelatory of the real. Of course sense judgment itself is subject to the judgment and control of reason (CA 2.3.9;6.13).

71. The first part of this section, which expands upon and confirms the conclusion of a 11.27.35, seems logically and therefore organizationally misplaced. The import of its argument would seem to require its location not at the beginning of Ch. 36 but at the end of Ch. 35. The gifted, hardworking editor responsible

for the demanding task of arranging and enumerating chapters was apparently not wholly attuned to the drift of Augustine's reasoning at this juncture.

72. Some scholars dispute the meaning of *quod est* in the second sentence. Some translate it simply as "that it [time] is" or "that is to say" while others render it, "But it [time] does exist", meaning that time objectively exists. This last interpretation, however, does not square with text and context. For Augustine, no deep-seated groove of thinking protests that time is indeed objective, for the troubling subject-object dichotomy began only as the dreadful legacy of Carteisian dualism. Augustine's prior, unreflective style of thinking about the status of time, a stance held by most men, maintained that time as measured seemed to enjoy physical existence as undeniable as that of movement. It is then not the objective existence that is at issue. Through empirical analysis he concludes that time as measured has psychic existence, a real existence, an objective existence, a true existence in the mind.

73. The distension within the psychic duplicate of sound or silence is the analogue of distension without, which in musical instruments subserves physical sounds. Diverse tension issues in diverse sounds; in the lyre the strings are distended (S 243.4); in a drum the skin or drumhead is stretched (*extenditur*); in a psaltery the strings are stretched; the greater the extension of the strings, the sharper they sound (the higher the pitch or note) (P 149.8). A drum beat occupies a certain interval, and the strumming of the strings of the lyre and psaltery occupies other intervals—measurable movements arising from physical distensions.

74. Here and elsewhere Augustine analogously employs the term memory. First, the word denotes elementary present retention or primary memory of sense data, a function that realistic psychologists strictly assign to imagination. The word *Deus* is so memorially imaged prior to one's hearing *creator*. The memory that makes possible primitive knowledge of a succession of sounds is named primary or immediate memory in James, I.634-48. See also P. Fraisse, *The Psychology of Time*, 81-9. In this broad acceptation of memory no distance, no intervening gap, severs the connection between earlier and later events. What is primarily remembered has been just perceived, and forms with the posterior data an unbroken perceptual whole or continuous distension. Second, memory signifies a sensory recall of the absent past as such; so Augustine, while not experiencing joy, recalls a past time when he was joyful (10.14.21). Third, the word may mean intellectual memory, as in the judgment, "A hundred years is a long time." While we cannot sensorially recollect one hundred years in one image, we can intellectually review a century in compact thought. As Augustine establishes, convincingly it would seem, primary memory or imagination-memory is primordial in cognition of time. All three inductions verifying that time is psychic distension hinge on a quasi-perceived, imagined succession of sounds. Distensions due to recall-memory and intellectual memory bear on what is presently perceived.

75. The three ways of forming time-lines seem to jibe roughly with the three kinds of inductive data in 11.27.35-6. The speaker silently rehearsing a piece beforehand, which provides raw material for the third induction, projects a

distension of expectation. Utterance of *Deus creator omnium*, treated in the first induction, evidences a distension jointly wrought by expectation, attention, and memory. In the second induction an observer reckons the length of a pause by laying it against a verse recalled from memory.

76. Distension primarily signifies spatial extension, as indicated in expressions such as the distension of spatial extent of air (P 45.4), the distension of mass (T 5.1.2), and spreadoutness by distension (E 187.41). As mentioned in n. 68 above, musical instruments are linked to such distension also; strings of a lyre are distended, different distensions producing different sounds (S 243.4). Unlike physical entities, the heaven of heaven does not undergo change or physical distension in time (12.11.12). It is in a secondary or analogous sense that distension is used to denote the psychic time-line. Distension of mind is the psychic equivalent of physical-temporal distension. Contrary to the opinions of Gilson, *The Christian Philosophy of St. Augustine*, 194, Callahan, *Four Views*, 176, and O'Daly, "Time as *Distentio* and Augustine's Exegesis of Philippians 3, 12-14," REA 23 (1977), 265-71, distension in the psychic sense is not a metaphor. Acquiescence in a sheerly metaphorical psychic distension would defeat resolve to track down "the meaning and nature of time" (11.23.30). Recourse to the merely figurative would seem to amount to tacit admission that the mind had failed to track down its prey. Distension is essentially no more metaphorical than stock terms like deliberation and discourse, which initially referred to weighing and running. Original physical denotation does not prevent distension from being employed in the definition of time any more than the original sense of quantity meaning magnitude bars the mind from speaking precisely of a spiritual quantity or power manifested by the soul (QA 32.69). Furthermore, the theory of illumination rests upon a nonmetaphorical or analogical extension of the term light. In addition, other objects of the senses such as embraces and food can be analogically said of inner touches and spiritual nourishment lavished on the spirit by God (10.6.8). However, in its third sense, distension taken as distractedness of mind and dispersion of spirit is related not analogously but equivocally to the first two senses. Distension now bespeaks not one unified time but a fragmented time-line; not a continuum but a discontinuum; not a ordered scheme of parts but dispersion, indeed disintegration. Scattered into various times, the soul is helpless to discern any order. The disorder tumbling out from the diversity of times blinds the mind to any objective pattern in the pell-mell shifting of times. The disparity between physical and moral distension is so pronounced that they share only a common name with diverse and unrelated significations. Similarly, psychological time, which belongs to the theoretical order, is also related equivocally to moral time, which is situated in the ethical sphere, a time that our contemporaries ordinarily term temporality.

77. In the nineteenth century P. Laplace hypothesized the existence of a super-mind that would derive from a single formula all the future states of the universe, including human actions (*A Philosophical Essay on Probabilities*, 4). While grasping, as does Augustine's super-mind, the whole future course of the universe, that of Laplace diverges from Augustine's super-intelligence in two

notable respects. First, the Laplacean mastermind is a super-mathematical-physicist who knows in one mathematical formula all past and future physical states. Augustine's super-intelligence, however, knows past, present, and future in a musical mode, a later phase of the song of the universe following upon anterior parts. Second, Laplace's universe is a rigidly determined complex, all of whose events occur with ironclad necessity. With every least event subsumed under the reign of law, there is nothing that is not absolutely controlled by its antecedent causes. By way of corollary every event is necessarily connected with every other event. The fact that a writer is typing a page in Philadelphia is inexorably linked to the contemporaneous fact that at the same time a worshipper is kneeling in prayer in St. Peter's Basilica in Rome. Into one massive tissue of necessity is every event interlaced with every other event, whether prior, collaterally contemporaneous, or posterior. In contrast to this closed system of inflexible determinism, Augustine, while recognizing a universal rule of law governing natural phenomena, admits a certain immanent contingency that includes accidental vicissitudes. Furthermore, he situates humanly free action outside the chain of natural causation. The realm of human life is the kingdom of freedom in which human beings make contingent human choices that help configure their moral personalities and fix in some measure their destinies. Human life is not simply the stringently programmed outflow of effects from higher-level causes. Each human career is in the main a drama whose bewilderingly tangled plot is contingently woven from countless strands of free or actively indeterminate choices.

78. In "Distentio Animi", CAH, 407-8, K. Flasch maintains that this super-mind surveying the whole history of man and cosmos is identical with God. However, Augustine cautions, God does not know the unfolding of the universe according to a past-present-future scheme but in his distensionless eternal mode. In the opinion of R. Teske, *Paradoxes of Time in St. Augustine*, 55, the mind of 11.31.41 has to be "the universal soul with which each individual soul is one." Unfortunately, there is no evidence that Augustine ever accepted a Plotinian universal soul. Texts such as J 18.4 establish only that devout Christians become *anima una et cor unum* not in a substantial sense but in a qualitative and affective mode. The citation from J. Rist, *Augustine*, 126, does nothing to buttress this shaky analogy. In addition, Teske is compelled to confront one of the paradoxes that bedeviled O'Connell's now largely discredited hypothesis of the fall of the soul: if the soul's fall into time occurs at its creation, the soul is apparently created in original sin; 58.

79. See J.M. Quinn, "Four Faces of Time in St. Augustine," RA 26 (1992), 181-231, for a more extensive, annotated account of this view.

80. *Physica* 4.3.3 See "Faces of Time" (n. 79), 183-4.

81. B Russell, *Human Knowledge*, 212, and *A History of Western Philosophy*, 354. See "Faces of Time" (n. 79), 183.

82. P. Lachièze-Rey, "Saint Augustin précurseur de Kant dans la théorie de la perception," AM 1. 425 -8.

83. Detailed references to Bergson's works are available in J.M. Quinn, *The Concept of Time in St. Augustine*, Studia Ephemeridis Augustinianum, no. 5, Patristic Institute, Rome, 1965. In *The Christian*

Philosophy of St. Augustine, 339, n.33, Gilson notes the obvious analogies linking Bergson's thought to Augustine's psychology of perception. K. Flasch, *Was ist Zeit?*, 26-36, detects resemblance between Bergson and Augustine. According to Guitton, *Le temps et l'éternité*, 15, Bergson informed him that similarities between his and Augustine's images were not due to any direct influence.

84. Ladner, 209-12.
85. BA 14, 590.
86. O'Daly, loc cit. (n.76 above).
87. N. Fischer, loc.cit. (n.2 above).
88. R. Teske, "Vocans Temporales, Faciens Aeternos: St. Augustine on Liberation from Time," *Traditio*, 41 (1983), 32.
89. C. Dawson, "St. Augustine and His Age," in *A Monument to St. Augustine*, 20-1.

Book Twelve
Understanding Genesis 1.1-2

Chapter 1: Confidence in Divine Light to Resolve Difficulties

1. Continuing endeavors to elucidate Genesis make him more sensitive to his ineptitude. For the most part destitution of understanding is dressed in a wealth of language; the outflow of words is spawned by a near-infecundity of thought, especially in speculative worrying over exegesis. More utterance is expressed in seeking than in finding, where seeking connotes dialectical inquiry, and finding, discovery, instanced in the search for the definition of time that generated more discussion than the formulation of the definition itself; and to be illustrated perhaps more appositely in sifting through the multiple interpretations proposed for Gn 1.1 alone (12.13.16-20). Ordinarily an individual pleading his case for an office musters many more words than does the authority petitioned. Moreover, it takes more time and energy to knock on than to open a door. Yet in commerce with God the seeker-asker-knocker is infallibly assured of a loving answer, the promise unbreakable because made by the omni-veracious God. Engraved on the hearts of the martyrs was the word that steeled them to unflinching resolve in the face of horrific tortures: "If God be for us, who is against us?" Similarly, if God is for Augustine, neither sweat nor tears wrung by interpretive deadlocks can deter him from decoding the cipher of Genesis (S 334.1).

After an introduction renewing confidence in God's direction (1.1), Book 12 divides into two parts that examine and review alternative interpretations while a resumé urges pursuit of truth in love. 1) Heaven signifies the heaven of heaven (2.2), and earth means formless matter (3.3-6.6), both created from nothing (2.7). Since neither is measurable by time (9.9.; 12.15), no days are mentioned in Gn 1.1-2. 2) While in agreement about certitudes, believers may reach different interpretations (14.17 15.18-22; 17.24-6). Loving tolerance should govern divergences of opinion (18.27; 23.32; 17.34) since Moses would have countenanced all true views (36.26). Various interpretations (28.38) bearing on "At first" in Gn 1 prompt distinctions of four kinds of priority (29.40). A conclusion (32.43) once more sounds the need for joint inquiry rooted in charity (30.41) in line with the insight that Moses intended a diversity of meanings (31.42).

Chapter 2: The Meanings of Heaven and Earth

2. Heaven and earth signify the physical objects so ordinarily designated, heaven meaning the visible firmament, the locus of sun, moon, and stars, including planets, and earth meaning the planet that is man's natural habitation, the home on which he walks about. Earth is also the primary source of the element, earth, marked by heaviness, that naturally tends downward. Since Augustine's body, while composed also of water and some ingredients of fire, contains earth as its dominant element, it is fixed to the earth instead of floating about in air. Earthiness is found primarily in the planet called earth; a human body like his secondarily shares in the primordial earthiness of the planet: his earth is derived from the earth.[1]

However, heaven and earth are assigned broader senses. Heaven also signifies the heaven of heaven, a spiritual heaven, variously described as the abode of intelligences (12.9.9), the house of God (12.11.12), the heavenly Jerusalem (12.11.12), and created wisdom (12.15.20).[2] It belongs to the Lord because he raised up minds wholly to his plane, there to be taught not by men but by God himself (P 113[S.2].11). Compared to this invisible heaven, the whole of visible creation, embracing both the visible firmament and earth, may be basically called earth. Whereas earth, properly speaking, means the lowest region of the visible world, its broad acceptation denotes the entire cosmos, viewed in relation to the inexpressibly beautiful realm that is the heaven of heaven. The visible universe that is a corporeal whole is not everywhere whole; in the cosmos parts are divided and set over against one another.[3] Again forestalling Manichean disparagement of matter, he does not neglect to add that the visible world, though inferior, is enrobed in its proper form and beauty, even the earth, its basest part, making an irreplaceable contribution to the variegated material ensemble of the universe (LA 3.9.24). Hence the earth, broadly designated, is given to the children of men for reflection so that minds can hail God as its creator (P 113[S.2].11).

Chapter 3: Matter without Form

3. Gn 1.2 also describes the earth as unformed: "the earth was invisible and unorganized, and darkness was over the abyss." In its first stage the earth was formless, without organization or order, a totally dark deep, lacking light because lacking all forms. As silence is the absence of sound, so darkness is the absence of light. God's interior light disclosed to Augustine what he now confesses to him; confession, which means more than praise or admission or confession of sins, here means profession or expression of truth. Before God built forms into formless matter and, through these forms, distinguished things from one another, only formless matter existed, wholly without determination. Because the matter was totally unformed, there was no definite thing or substance with special characteristics, no three-dimensional body and, consequently, no accidental features like shape and color, nor was there a spirit animating a body. Yet this primordial matter was not synonymous with absolute nothing; not simply nonbeing, it had a certain modicum of being, however tenuous. Its being was its formlessness; its being was its being without all form. As will be explicitated below, matter is the capacity for form (12.6.6);[4] its formlessness that constitutes its being is its capacity for form. Because it is capacity for form, it has being, but because it has no form, it borders on nonbeing.

Chapter 4: Common Terms Express Matter

4. God used common terms to convey his meaning to minds whose lack of aptitude or schooling leaves them ill-disposed to understand unformed matter. "Earth" and "deep" are suitable terms for formless matter because, occupying the lowest rungs in the physical universe, they most approximate unformed matter. They are less beautiful and

more grossly formed than superior entities such as the sun and stars, radiant with and reflective of light. Augustine recognizes familiar language as a pedagogical device to adapt Scriptoral contents to minds unable to make sense out of more sophisticated terminology. The common expression, "the earth invisible and unorganized," is accommodated to the less educated, so as to inform them of the formlessness of matter, matter made without form or beauty, out of which the formed and beautiful cosmos was made.

Chapter 5: Matter Defined by way of Negation

5. Matter cannot be apprehended by the usual process of cogitation, in which the inquiring mind assembles pertinent features into a definitional whole (10.11.18). The what or definition of matter eludes ascription of positive attributes; the mind can say not what it is but only what it is not. It is not an intelligible form such as life,[5] for life involves a soul, which is without physical dimension; nor is it similar to justice, a nonmaterial virtue of the soul, since matter is the matrix out of which bodies are made. Nor is matter a sensible form, for what is invisible cannot be seen and what is unorganized cannot be sensorially perceived; color and sound impinge on the senses as Gestalts or patterns. Thus cogitation aiming at the usual positively constructed definition is brought to a halt. The mind knows matter by not knowing it; it negatively knows matter by not knowing it positively. The verbally paradoxical coinage makes the nonparadoxical point that the mind knows matter in the negative mode: it is neither an intelligible nor a sensible form; it has no form, no quality, no measure, no number, no weight, no order, no distinction (CEF 1.29). Matter is formlessness, the utter absence of form that makes it capacity for all forms. Its quiddity is a nonquiddity in the line of form; knowing it as bereft of all form, the mind does not know it as formed. In fine, matter is defined as a nonformal something; close to nothing because nonformal; yet something because it is capacity for form.

Chapter 6: Difficulties in Understanding Matter: More Precise Definition

6. The notion of primordial or formless matter cannot be easily pinned down. When he first became acquainted with the name matter, he and fellow discussants were stumped by an object whose

essential characteristic is having no characteristic. A first attempt at proper cogitation turned out to be fruitless, for he was working toward a definition without precise components. His mind was immersed in imaginative representations, picturing matter as a semi-shapeless mélange of "forms," so hideous that it would shock normal perception. This version of formless was only relatively formless, an ugly mishmash seemingly formless in comparison with intricately designed forms. Further reflection established that properly conceiving the strictly formless requires removal of every least trace of form. Though so persuaded by true reason, i.e., reason emancipated from imagination, he could not initially bring himself to intelligize an entity bare of all form, for a being deprived of all form appeared to be equivalent to no more than nonbeing; total absence of form seemed tantamount to total absence of being. At the outset it seemed paradoxical to speak of a formless being lying between form and nothing; something that was neither form nor nothing, a formless being that verged on without collapsing into nothing.

He broke out of this impasse by hewing to true reason, by total disengagement from images. Up to this point he had been dialoguing with his spirit,[6] here signifying imagination, in pursuit of data from which to articulate a sound conception of formless matter. Forgoing his imagination-based exploration, he fixed rational attention on bodies outside imagination, scrutinizing physical process to discover factors that subserve change. Things come to be and pass away; or, in Augustine's phrasing, things cease to be what they were and begin to be what they are not. Grass consumed by a sheep ceases to be by becoming part of animal tissue. This passage from one form to another, from plant to animal life, is not grounded in absolute nothingness. Not utterly destroyed or annihilated, the grass does not wholly vanish into nonbeing but becomes part of the sheep. Similarly, new tissue in the sheep does not arise out of absolute nonbeing; clearly it emerges from digestion and ingestion of grass. Physical process is inexplicable without a common ground or continuous substrate that links diverse forms. Yet such process is unexplainable also if nothingness is hypothesized as the ground. Nothingness cannot ground anything; nothingness undercuts rather than underlies passage from one form to another. Were nothingness the substrate, there would be no transition, no continuity, but simply the abrupt annihilation of the old form unaccountably followed by the abrupt emergence of the new form. Thus the substrate or ultimate subject has to be an unformed being; as a being, other than nothing; as unformed, other than a form or formed being, since a form or formed being cannot be the common subject underlying passage from one form to another. If formed being were the substrate, all changes would be accidental variations in the one monistically conceived formed being. From another angle, formed being cannot serve as substrate, for, as formed, it would have to be grounded in an unformed being.

   Though his source[7] of this analysis may have considered the conclusion certain, Augustine rates it no more than conjectural,[8] not achieving a rigorous proof because the argument does not clearly yield the character of this formless something, a lacuna to be shortly disposed of. Refusing to be satisfied by any answer less than scientific, he went on probing till the Lord's illumination enabled him to disentangle countless knots. While not spelling out details leading up to his adequate determination, he will not stop praising God for numerous precious lights guiding his anfractuous course. Finally, he sets down briefly the certain upshot, the true knowledge harvested from his protracted inquiry. Formless matter is the very mutability of mutable things in the physical world. As the real possibility of becoming other, as the capacity for all forms into which changeable things are changed, it is the root of all process in the cosmos.[9] As radical capacity for change, it grounds all the changes in the physical universe. As subject, it is the reason why all changes occur; as substrate lacking all formal raison d'être, it is the raison d'être of all change. Still, some shadows cling to a notion without formal what or quiddity. Matter is not mind, it is not body, nor is it a mind or body of a special sort. If it were possible, it might be called a nothing-something and an is-is-not, a that-which-is that is a that-which-is-not. But such expressions savor of the self-refuting, for a thing cannot be a combination of being and nothing. Less rhetorically but more analytically stated, formless matter is in no way nothing, for it has to exist in some manner, however slightly, in order to be capable of receiving, or being the substrate of, visible and organized forms. It is simply sheer capacity for all forms.[10] It is not a form; but if it were not formless, no dynamism, no change, would exist in the physical universe. It is not a form, but it is the pure changeability that makes it possible for one form to pass into or emerge from another form.[11]

Chapter 7: Creation from Nothing

7. Whatever difficulties becloud determination of its nature, there is no problem about the origin of unformed matter. However we clarify its mode of being, the totality of its existence is owed to God's creative power. An enormous difference gulfs between God and his creatures, God being more distant insofar as creatures are variously dissimilar from him. Spiritual beings and formed material beings are nearer in likeness, and a formless entity like unformed matter marks the furthest departure from the divine. The distance between God and creatures is measured not in terms of physical place but of ontic makeup: God is not situated far above material things as the sun lies above the earth, for, as purely spiritual, he has no place at all (9.4.11). Not only locatively unalterable, not moving from place to place, God is unqualifiedly immutable, the Selfsame (7.10.16), whose sacred name is "I am who am." The term Selfsame is twice repeated to underscore that God is unchangeably one and three, one in nature, three in persons, signalized in the threefold chant of "holy" in adoration and praise (Is 6.3. Rev 4.8). The Selfsame fashions the total being of things in the beginning, this signifying his eternal Word, the wisdom which perfectly images, because begotten of, his own divine substance. Unlike the Word eternally generated from God, the world produced in or through the Word is not generated from God, for such generation would raise it to an ontic dignity the equal of the Word; the world would be effectively a second Son, begotten, like the Word, from the Father and, if equal to the Son, equal to the Father also. This is of course an embarrassing inconsequence: God cannot produce another God because if there are two Gods, neither is God, neither uniquely absolute existence; and because another God, an effect dependent on cause, has to be less than God. It is not just that anything not generated from God's very own substance be reckoned the equal of God. Justice here is not a moral but an ontic rightness; as it is morally unjust to give another more than his due, so it is ontically inequitable, false, to give a produced world more than its due by assigning it a status equal to God's.

Since there was originally no being other than or outside the God who is both one trinity and threefold unity, God created out of nothing a universe consisting of the magnificent heaven of heaven and the tiny earth, unformed matter scanty in being. As all-powerful,

God gives being to all made out of nothing; as all-good, he confers ontic value on all, both the majestic heaven of heaven and the entitatively baser earth. Prior to creation only God, who is absolute being, existed; out of absolute nonbeing or nothing were created the heaven of heaven and earth. The heaven of heaven, because spiritual and immutable, most closely resembled God; hence it is nearest to him. The earth, on the other hand, was unformed matter; neither spiritual nor formed, it has the slenderest of being, existing at the verge of nothing. As matter, it is not nothing; as formless, it is next to nothing, lying at the farthest frontier of real being. Only God as absolutely immutable is superior to the heaven of heaven; at the other end of, and outside, the hierarchical scale of being, only nothing is inferior to unformed matter, for nothing, which is matterless as well as formless, is an ontic zero.

Chapter 8: Visible Earth Formed from Invisible Earth

8. The pristine stuff that is initial Biblical earth was unformed, without organization of parts or quantity, barren of sensory qualities, an abyss enclosed in darkness; hence the words, "darkness was over the deep" (Gn 1.2). This line may also be taken to mean that the darkness above the abyss was denser than that within the abyss; an interpretation resting on an analogy with present observation of the fact that the deep or the sea contains less light than the extra-marine atmosphere, yet a light strong enough for fish to navigate in the water and for other marine species to crawl on the ocean floor. In any case, this abyss, as remarked earlier (12.6.6.), was next to nothing because wholly devoid of form. Though formless, it was not absolutely nothing; stamped with a measure of being, it was the matrix out of which formed things are fashioned. Made out of nothing, formless matter is that out of which all things are made. Out of what is thinnest in being are shaped the massive entities that set the mind agog (10.8.15). The starry heaven above, sublime in its order and beauty, especially excites wonder and awe. This firmament, made on the second day, lies between the Biblically evidenced waters above it and the atmosphere beneath it. The earth and sea were produced on the third day. As explicitly reported in Gn 1.1, both the heaven of heaven and unformed matter were created prior to the first day, on which light was made.

The ever-changing world about us is comprised of these entities formed out of formless matter, manifesting constancy insofar as formed, lacking constancy insofar as formed out of formless matter, which invests things with never-ceasing change. As formed, things are stable; as made of the formless, they are unstable, tending to become other; rooted in changeability, they incessantly tend to change. Because mutable, things are temporalized or measurable by time. As mentioned in Book 11, Excursus, concomitant with change is physical time: time numbers or measures movements according to the variation and succession of forms. It took, we say, three months for the plant to grow for harvest; the movement toward the new form is measured by the 29-30-day cycle of the moon. Here firmament signifies the sidereal heaven, located between water and water, between water above the heaven and seas contiguous with dry land. As the sky or firmament in the broad sense is positioned between the vaporous atmosphere and liquid water adjacent to land, so the sidereal heaven lies between super-celestial waters and the earthly water of the seas. No doubt water is ordinarily heavier than the pure fire constituting the heaven, but the water of the super-celestial region may be conceived as divided into particles so infinitesimal that they become less heavy than pure fire (GL 2.4. 7-8). Moreover, the coldness of Saturn, whose rapid daily movement should make it extremely hot, may be accounted for by the cooling action of the waters above the heaven (GL 2.5.8).

Chapter 9: Neither Heaven nor Earth Measurable by Time

9. Gn 1.1 does not refer to any segment of time and, in particular, makes no mention of a day: heaven and earth were created before the first day. The heaven of heaven is not governed by time because in our signification it embraces the whole community of good angels, beatified after a probational test, failing which the devil and his demons hurled themselves into hell. While clearly not coeternal with the trinity—otherwise they would be self-stultifyingly rendered equals of God—they participate in the divine eternity, in some respect supernaturally dwelling in the all-at-once, nonsuccessive divine duration. So eternalized, they are immovably enrapt by a vision of God face to face, a transport liberating them from thralldom to mutability and nullifying essential subjection to time. In brief, sharing

in the divine immutability liberates them from mutability, so that indefectibly cleaving, after their probation, to the eternal God, they transcend the unrolling of the time-line.

The heaven of heaven lies outside time because of its superior order and form. At the bottom of the spectrum of being unformed matter does not fall under time proper because, bereft of order and form, it cannot undergo change. Physical time measures roughly the succession of forms in mutable things; where there is no succession, there is no change, and, where no change, no time. Thus Gn 1 does not list its creation as occurring in any day or days, for, as formless and changeless, its making is dayless, prior to all days. While formless matter is mutability and the matrix of changing things measurable by time, it is itself changeless and therefore not measurable by days or any segment of time. Whereas the heaven of heaven is supertemporal, unformed matter in a certain sense seems subtemporal; as unformed, it is situated beneath formed mutables measurable by time.

Chapter 10: Prayer for More Light

10. In the past he flung himself outward and downward, in wild pursuit of darkness or untruth: feeding on darkness, he became darkness. Still, he somehow faintly loved God; even when hankering after pseudo-happiness, he was hungering for the delight-conferring truth that is God. During his wandering like a lost sheep, patiently searched after by the Good Shepherd (P 118[S.32].7), he vaguely remembered God, in the sense that he was obscurely conscious of truth reigning within; in assenting to ersatz brands, he was dimly fumbling toward authentic truth. The voice of the Lord, nudging him to return to the Father's house, fell somewhat indistinctly on his ears, because bitter animadversions were spat against the Church and Scriptures by Manichees especially (12.14.17; 15.8). Now back in the household of God, he is on fire to drink from the fount of God's light that is life, concretely realizing God as the life of his life. In the past he was death to himself, his old self snuffing out every pulsation of his godly inner being. As he more and more relives his life in the Lord, he beseeches God to continue unveiling Scripture. Truth bore him up from the darkness of the flesh to the light of faith. The Scriptures, however, are not without their own species of darkness, not darkness

consanguineous with falsity but darkness arising from the double wonder of awe and bafflement before the profundities of revelation.

Chapter 11: Review of Four Truths

11. (1) God is eternal, immutable in duration, unaffected by any sort of change, substantial or accidental, physical or spiritual. Even in his single creative act his sovereign will stays absolutely unchangeable, always trained on his own divine good, never shifting from one option to another. As he judges this truth according to divine standards, he trusts that under God's wings, through his luminous superintendence, he will remain immutable in adherence and commitment to the basic doctrine of immutable creator of mutable creatures.

(2) Equally certain is that God created all natures (here nature means substance) other than himself, which, unlike God, do not absolutely exist yet actually exist, i.e., relatively: what is absolutely nothing does not come from God. Nor is social or personal sin, each of which is in a way relatively nothing, made by God. Sin is not a movement from God but a perversity of the will twisted away from him (7.16.22). As aversion from the higher goods and conversion to the lower, sin embraces what is less than God, and, by choosing the lesser, a sinner turns into the lesser and deficient (S 142.33.3). Sin is relatively nothing in the sense that if the deficiency were carried to the limit, nothing would remain (C Sec 8. EJ 1.13). Earlier he became convinced that, in contradistinction to Manichean opinion recounting a mythical war of minions of Darkness inflicting violence on the divine kingdom, God cannot be harmed (7.4.6). Nor does sin upset the balanced running of the universe, an order inviolable on its highest and lowest planes. As alluded to above (12.7.7), the primary or highest refers to the heaven of heaven, which, unlike the Manichean Kingdom of Light, is invulnerable to disruption such as an invasion by evil agencies, while the lowest denotes unformed matter, which, as the polar opposite of Manichean matter that is the principle of evil (CF 20.2, 14), is in itself good because created by God. As permitted, sin is integrated into the divine order by being punished according to flawless justice; and from evil God's goodness and power miraculously harvest good.

12. (3) The heaven of heavens, an intellectual creature or

community of spirits, however it partakes of eternity, cannot be
coeternal with God. It feeds on the divine good in continual chastity,
i.e., holiness, so that its radical creaturely mutability is in this wise
nowhere and never, i.e., is not exercised in changes of place or time.
Living only in a shared eternal present, it experiences neither future
by expectation nor past by memory, and therefore its inner duration
is basically not a scheme of past-present-future. It perdures not along
but above the time-line, in the transcendent never-varying divine
present. The heaven of heaven is a community unfailingly contemplating the one sovereign good, here named God's delight, in
love-impregnated knowledge wholly concentrated on the God it sees
face to face. The heaven of heaven rejoices as a single collective pure
mind, concordantly one to the highest degree, unified in the perfect
harmony of the super-peace of the sanctified spiritual beings who
reign as citizens of the city of God.

13. His thirsting in time, he prays, will be satisfied in an eternal
drinking at the fount of life. The tears he sheds are sweet, bread that
the more often he eats it, the more fiercely he will thirst for water of
the life of soul that is God himself, which is everlasting (P 41.5-6).
God's years do not cease; his days do not succeed one another; his
day is the one eternal day (1.6.10), a today on which no sun sets (P 26
[En. 2].7). Hopefully, each spiritual will cognize how ontically higher
than all times is the eternal; an infinite divide separates the succession
of times from the all-at-once duration that is the eternal life of God.
The heaven of heaven that is the house of God is not a tent for
wayfaring pilgrims (P 26 [En.2].6) but a supernal abode that is quasi-
unchangeable, quasi-eternalized. Adhering to the eternal presence, it
continues unceasingly, without change in place or any sort of
alteration, suffering no succession in time, a supratemporal
habitation, causally no more affected or measured by time than the
very being of the eternal God.

14. (4) An unformed factor or formless matter (called "I know not
what" because, devoid of form, it escapes strict definition) subserves
changes in the elements or basic units of nature, termed the last and
lowest parts of the cosmos. Earlier (12.8.8; 9.9) he proved that
unformed matter cannot be measured by time. An image-tyrannized
mind that is temporalized, not stabilized by truth, wanders aimlessly
and, somewhat like time, rolls successively, from one image to
another, puppet of phantasmal association rather than analyst of

unformed matter. We are bade think of every form stripped away, consumed to the vanishing point, leaving nothing but sheer formlessness, the radical substrate underpinning all change, the mutability in virtue of which things are converted from one form to another. It is simply impossible for such formlessness to evidence or be measured by successive intervals of time. Physical time is an indissociable companion of motion; without a diversity of phases of motion there are no time-intervals; unformed matter cannot exhibit diversity of phases of motion because, as purely formless, it contains in itself no forms at all. A Goclenian sorites mirrors the actual thread of discourse: whatever has no motion has no time; whatever has no diversity has no motion; whatever has no form has no diversity; unformed matter has no form; therefore unformed matter has no time.

Chapter 12: Heaven of Heaven and Unformed Matter Independent of Time

15. Mercifully responding to his knocking that is prayer (12.1.1), God has directed his inward eyes to discern that both the highest and lowest in creatures are not measured by time, though neither is coeternal with God. The first, the heaven of heaven, is positively timeless, liberated from time because, as changeless, it is superior to time. Wholly concentrated on God, its gaze neither wavers nor falters in the least; no span of change intervenes between contemplation and its lack. As a creature, the heaven of heaven is radically mutable, with an inbuilt tendency to become other, yet it undergoes no change because the inclination to change is supernaturally suspended by participation in divine eternity. The second time-free factor, unformed matter, is negatively timeless; unformed matter is without time not because specially formed but because void of all form. Barren of form and therefore incapable of movement, it does not fall under the sway of time. But as subsequent verses of Genesis attest, God did not simply create primordial matter and leave it unformed; it is made from nothing to serve as the matrix out of which all formed substances are to be fashioned. The notion of a formlessness that somehow exists is far from easy to apprehend, less so for the unlettered. So that the uneducated might lay hold of this elusive idea step by step, Gn 1.2 describes the earth as invisible and darkness lying

over the waters. The more familiar verbal garb of earth and water enables the unlettered to gain a rudimentary hold on something that, while totally deprived of form, is not equivalent to nothing at all. Earth and water suggest raw material disposed to be shaped into an organized object by an artisan (GCM 17.12. GL 1.15.30). Out of this formlessness, described as invisible earth and darkness-engulfed water, were crafted another heaven, i.e., the firmament distinct from the heaven in Gn 1.1, and another earth, distinct from the unformed matter that Gn. 1.1 names earth, along with the formed water[12] of the seas differentiated from the unformed water of Gn 1.2, and everything else that was made. Unlike the unformed matter mentioned in Gn 1.1,2, these formed entities are fashioned on certain days, the term days bespeaking time; as formed, these things underwent the alteration of form that is movement, which is measurable by physical time. The succession of time-intervals occurs because there is movement from one form to another, movement that is ordered or according to laws of nature. The passage of time, described in Gn 1 as days, measures the passage of movement of which it is the concomitant.

Chapter 13: No Days Mentioned in Gn 1.1,2

16. At this point he takes the heaven of Gn 1.1 to mean an intellectual heaven of spirits, which knows God not in part but wholly: not blurrily as in a mirror but by immediate vision, not by a succession of thoughts or variation in cognitive times but in a single enduring instant. The earth that is unformed matter, deprived of all form and order, is also not measurable by time since what is formless admits of no distinction between one form and another: it is an undifferentiated, featureless stuff. While succession of physical times implies passage from one state or quality to another, absence of formed differences entails absence of times. Pristinely, the heaven of Gn 1.1 is formed, and the earth completely unformed. The heaven of heaven and unformed matter being without time, Scripture significantly does not specify that they were made on a certain day; as timeless, their production is dayless. The timeless character of the original heaven and earth is validated in ensuing verses; Gn 1.2 qualifies the earth as formless and implicitly timeless, and Gn 1.8 recounts that God made the firmament, a heaven in a second sense,

on the second day, a temporal reference that intimates that the creation of the heaven in the first sense occurred timelessly, marked by no day at all.

Chapter 14: Opposing Faithful Interpreters Distinguished from Enemies of Scripture

At this juncture he makes a transition to the second part of Book 12, whose Chapters 14-32 are exercised by the problem of gauging interpretations that part company with his own views.

17. If even its surface meaning attracts little ones, uneducated Christians, much more soul-enriching must be inner treasures to be tapped by prayerful study of Scripture, which excites spiritual feelings analogous to those elicited by the divine presence itself: like their author, Scripture is at once inviting and staggering. As God truly known evokes awe, so meditation on his words also begets awe. With a reverential fear born of love, the faithful mind trembles before Scripture as it would if it personally encountered the almighty himself, quavering at the magnitude of the task of plumbing the depths that unveil the mystery of God's being and design for man. Moreover, he hates the enemies of Scripture with a passion. These are mainly Manichees, who reject creation in the beginning as incoherent since it leaves inexplicable what God was doing before creation (11.10.12;13.15. GCM 1.2.3); a creation which blasphemously contaminates the Father of Light by turning him into the maker of matter which is evil (CF 22.4). Indeed they abominate the whole of the Old Testament as a devil-authored document (3.7.12; 5.14.22. CF 8.1; 12.1. H 46). His is, however, a hatred truly spiritual: hating the sin, he loves the sinner (5.12.22.P138.28). With this perfect, because love-animated, hatred he begs that enemies of the word of God be converted into friends of God; that God slay them with his two-edged sword, the dual revelation of himself in the Old and New Testament (P 149.12), one promising earthly goods, the other, eternal, putting to death the darkness of errors of the old self through the puissant light of his word. With hatred that is actually love of enemies imitating divine redemptive love, he pleads that God dispatch them as regards themselves, killing the old or exterior man, so that they may live in terms of the new, interior man lit up by the divine. His prayer for Manichees substantially replicates his earlier prayer for himself: let

me die to self lest I die an eternal death, in order that I may live for God unto eternal life (1.5.5). So here: let Manicheans be slain to self, lest they be eternally slain, so as to live for God. Essentially different from Manichean foes are certain fellow Catholics who criticize not Genesis but Augustine; reverence for the revealed word notwithstanding, they are not inclined to endorse his exegesis.

Chapter 15: Agreement of Opponents with Basic Truths concerning Creation

Though certain Christians disagree with his doctrinal or theological interpretations of the opening lines of Genesis, they acknowledge the validity of his basic theses on creation. God's creative act is immutable and eternal (18); God created unformed matter and the heaven of heaven (19); the wisdom that is the heaven of heaven is not the same as the wisdom that is the Word (20); God, as immutable, is wholly other than the radically mutable heaven of heaven (21); neither the heaven of heaven nor unformed matter is subject to time (22).

18. No doubt his critical brothers in the Lord concur on the eternal substance of God and his immutable will in the act of creation. His substance remains absolutely invariable, in no way under the empire of time, and absolutely changeless also is his will one with his substance. The attributes and powers of God are not accidents; he does not have them but simply is what they are. God's willing is a once-for-all act embracing all created things, which remains forever the same. Its simultaneity sets it apart from human decisions again and again renewed. Covering all things at once, it differs from successive acts of the will desiring this object at one point, then another good at another stage. God's will-act is unchangeable, whereas men change their minds, either choosing later what they once did not want or no longer choosing what was willed earlier. A human will that chooses diverse goods and cancels previous choices is mutable; as mutable, it is measurable by time; because not eternal, it cannot be equated with the will of God. In short, Augustine argues in the Aristotelian second figure: a being with a mutable will is not eternal; God is eternal; therefore his is not a mutable will. He deploys the same pattern of reasoning to infer that God's knowledge is eternal. In human thinking the time-line consists of future, present,

and past. Expectation of the future yields to perception in the present, and the present, when it ceases, becomes past deposited in memory. Thought that varies along the time-line is mutable and, as mutable, is not eternal; but God's thought is eternal; therefore God's thought is not mutable. In conclusion, he joins under the common concept of immutability the divine will and knowledge in regard to creation. God did not create the universe by a novel will-act, an operation other than and distinct from his immutable substance; in willing creation, something new, God's will does not become new but stays changelessly one with his substance (11.31.41). Similarly, in creation God's knowledge does not suffer any change; before and after creation his knowledge of his creatures is the same.

19. Catholics disputing his Scripture-based interpretation also concede that God created matter and the heaven of heaven. God created every formed substance and all matter capable of being formed; because he is good, both formed and unformed are good, their relative existence deriving from sovereign existence that is absolute. God also created the heaven of heaven, the highest creation bonded to God in chaste, i.e., holy, love, so close in its cleaving to the eternal that it partakes of his eternity. Not God but fused with God through love, quasi-eternal or supertemporal, it does not split off from God and sink into lower, fluent things; hence it is not swept along in the variety and succession that mark the time-line. The heaven of heaven rests or is terminally stabilized in the truest or highest contemplation of God alone, rest signifying not peace but the proper terminus of movement; having reached its goal, it need not progress further. Because the heaven of heaven totally loves God by obeying his commands, he reveals himself to it as the sovereign good that is all-sufficient; absorbed in this delight, it does not forsake him nor lapse into self-idolatry. A community wherein God dwells and rules, it is not a heavenly body such as the sun but a habitation that, like God, is eternal, participatively so, never suffering deficiency, which Ps 148.6, adaptively read, confirms: God has established the heaven forever according to his unalterable decree. The heaven of heaven will go on forever but not as coeternal; it is not beginningless, owing its beginning in being to the eternal One.

20. The heaven of heaven is wisdom that was created before all things, created indeed before time itself. There is however, a vast disparity between this wisdom and uncreated wisdom begotten of the

Father and therefore coeternal with God. It is truly wisdom but, as created, it shares in uncreated wisdom. An intellectual, a purely spiritual, entity, it is light not of itself but by participation, becoming light only by turning toward and contemplating uncreated light. An infinite distance sets apart creative light that confers light and created light that receives light, the first being cause and source, the second effect and sharer. A like relation obtains between uncreated wisdom (the Word) and created wisdom (the heaven of heaven), and also between the divine justice given and the human justice received that is justification. As redeemed in Christ, who mediated justifying grace, men are truly the justice of God, i.e., divine justice not of themselves but partakers of God's justice. This created wisdom is the community of blessed on high, enwrapped in the glory that is the fruit of justification, the holy city of God, free of all sin and its consequences, an eternal city whose citizens' principal work is praise of God (P 148.4). Created prior to time, the heaven of heaven is not measured by time, yet it is not absolutely first; prior to it is the eternity of the creator. Its beginning lies not in the line of time but in the line of being; its very creation is its beginning.

21. Though intemporal, the heaven of heaven cannot be equated with God, who alone is the Selfsame, unqualifiedly immutable existence. Not only before all time, the heaven of heaven is not contained under time because it is always turned toward the divine face. By divine gift it undergoes not the slightest change, though, as creature, as programmed with a built-in propensity to be other, it is radically mutable. Apart from God's special dispensation it would become dark and grow cold, bereft of the light and warmth of God who continuously shines like a sun at an eternal high noon, setting aglow the heaven of heaven. However, as a pilgrim, Augustine travels through and in time, here taken in its moral acceptation, to mean night and frigidity compared to the light and fire of eternity. Earlier in his sojourn he strayed off the Catholic way like a dumb sheep; after being pulled free from Manichean thickets, he is now carried forward on the shoulders of the builder of the house of God. Hopefully, the Good Shepherd will go on bearing his still struggling self upward to possess the home in which the Father will possess him.

22. While at loggerheads on particulars of the exegesis, his opponents are, as Catholics, bonded in agreement on fundamentals of the faith, recognizing Moses as the true servant of God who (it was

held in his day) veraciously wrote Genesis, and also believing that the books he composed, Genesis, along with the other four works of the Pentateuch, originated in the Holy Spirit, the principal author of Scripture; works of the Bible being Spirit-oracles, responses from the divine Spirit to the human spirit. As participatively eternal, this heaven transcends the distension characteristic of time; time is a line whereas eternity is immaterially instantaneous. As unchangingly all-at-once, the house of God is rapt in God, eternally adhering to its highest good (P 72.34). Matter also is nontemporal, not supertemporal like the heaven of heaven, but in way subtemporal, outside time not in virtue of excellence but due to a certain deficiency. Because aboriginal matter is formless, it has no order, no disposition of parts.[13] Where there is no differentiation of types, no diversity of parts, one thing cannot become other; where all is totally blank, without any distinction at all, change, the passage from one to a different state, is impossible. Further, where there is no movement, there can be no time measuring change; or, succinctly put: no change, no time. Though formless and orderless, matter does exist: though next to nothing, it has real being. As not nothing, it derives from God, the source of every creature, however meager its budget of being.

Chapter 16: Openness to Discussion of other Interpretations of Believers

23. According to divine arbitrament, he will dialogue with fellow believers who, while in accord concerning fundamental truths (12.15.18-22), contest particular readings of Gn 1.1-2. While God speaks the truth within, Manichees bark their untruths without, a pack whose canine cries affect no one but fellow curs. Regrettably, he will have to leave them outside, bending their snouts to earth, stirring up in voluble protests a storm that increases not clarity but obscurity: fierce blowing into the ground causes the swirling dust to rise and cover their own eyes, their earthbound arguments serving only to further blind their minds. For his part, he will rest in the private chamber that is his inmost heart, its door closed against the fleshly, there to pray in secret (SDM 2.3.11), there to sing inward hymns hailing his redemption, songs of the new man in the New Covenant (S 34.1.1). Since these are not sempeiternal hymns (P 148.17), he is still groaning with unutterable groanings (P 149.5) under the impulse of

the Holy Spirit, his love charged with hunger for the life to come (Ex R 54). He ponders Jerusalem on high, lifting up his heart,[14] i.e., dwelling in heaven by aspiration (P 132.13), living not by distension among temporals but by intention of heart extended out in hope toward the heavenly city (11.29.39); a celestial homeland that is his mother, the Church, now the heavenly body of Christ, that gave him birth and nourished him into eternal life (P 9.12; 149.5. SV 5.5). He also stretches his spirit in longing for the King of Jerusalem, the light of whose face illuminates the saints, its shield forestalling all evil, Father of his fatherland, spouse of the bride, the Church; the font of inexpressible delights, all simultaneously present in his eternal good. He will not be averted from but remain converted toward his highest good, persevering, he trusts, till he reaches the city wherein lie the first fruits of his spirit. The spirit is the high point of the inner self; the first fruits[15] signify the proper disposition toward eternal life through sacrifice of self in faith, hope, and love, through his whole being concentrated on the celestial community, so that, toiling in time, he lives in eternity by a hope affording a foretaste of eternal peace (9.10.24). The heavenly Jerusalem is the source whence these things, i.e. all celestial goods enjoyed all at once, are in his eyes *certa*, unchanging and stable.[16] Shaping his deformity into a uniformity with a plan that designs a practical form for Augustine and knits the dispersed strings of his tattered self into a conformity, which is a solid whole invulnerable to breakdown, is an artisan who is not simply a detached mastermind but a lover whom he calls my very own God, my personal mercy.

He opts to dialogue not with Manichees who impugn the Old Testament but with Catholic believers who, howbeit dissenting on particulars of interpretation, make common cause with him in reverencing Scripture as the holy peak of authority in Christian doctrine.

Chapter 17: Four Alternative Interpretations of Gn 1.1-2

Four other interpretations of the first two verses are listed. The first two take heaven to designate the visible heaven while the latter two understand it to signify a spiritual or invisible entity. Along with Augustine, all four recognize a formless stuff out of which the universe was constructed.

24. (1) According to the first theory, "heaven and earth" generally and succinctly denotes the whole visible world, the creation of whose particular parts is narrated in the six days. No reference is made to a spiritual creation because the Holy Spirit realized that the largely untutored members of a nomadic people would be incapable of understanding spiritual entities. However, proponents of this view do not regard it as unreasonable to maintain that the unformed earth and dark abyss out of which the ordered material universe was molded might be well taken to mean the formless matter of Augustine's exegesis.

25. (2) A second theory lumps heaven and earth with formless matter; out of this are formed all the substances that we count as visibly existing in heaven and earth in the customary sense.

(3) On a third reading, heaven signifies things of an invisible spiritual nature while earth denotes substances of a visible, corporeal nature. Because not begotten of God but created from nothing, both heaven and earth are radically mutable. The heaven of heaven, the eternal house of God, as fully attached to God, is, in fact, changeless, yet, as created, it remains mutable in principle whereas man's soul and body are mutable both in principle and fact. Such mutability is resident in or identified with a common unformed matter. The "invisible and formless earth" designates formless matter that underlies visible entities; this is corporeal matter before being qualified or shaped by form. The "darkness over the abyss" signifies the matter which is the substrate of things spiritual; this is spiritual matter before it was stamped with its mode that delimited its mode-free state of indetermination, i.e., lack of spiritual solidity or firmness. This also expresses spiritual matter prior to its supernatural determination, its conversion to and steady illumination by the light that is divine wisdom.

26. (4) Just as the second theory collapses the visible heaven and earth into formless matter, so the fourth opinion, denuding the invisible heaven and the visible earth of all form, fuses them with a common formless matter, a matrix void of all formal and qualitative differentiations.[17] Out of this unformed matter, which is the unformed heaven and earth, are produced the heaven that is spiritual creation and the earth that is corporeal creation. Out of the formless stuff called heaven and earth in Gn 1.1 are formed the spiritual and corporeal creatures that we now usually style heaven and earth.

Chapter 18: Loving Tolerance of Others' Interpretations

27. He and the other interpreters jointly believe that God created all things, heaven and earth, out of nothing. Hence while there is only one literal interpretation, there can be a variety of doctrinal readings according to diverse Catholic theological positions. He refuses to engage in a wrangle over words, an acrid debate over secondary questions, which would be ultimately profitless, for it would treat subordinate concerns as if primary; a heated imbroglio that might boil over into ruinous acrimony, corroding, if not doctrinal faith, the charity that binds all Christians. As with the Law, discussion in secondary matters ought to contribute to the upbuilding in love of the members of the body of Christ; the aim of exchanges should be charity that bespeaks a heart unsullied by ill-will. Within the divinely appointed context of the commandments of love of God and love of neighbor on which all moral precepts and doctrine hinge, Augustine is to sift through conflicting interpretations, without suffering an offense in charity from readings negativing his position. The fundamental exegetical imperative is: do not rashly declare that what Moses wrote is in any way false. Spinning off from this is a second directive: though there is only one literal meaning, graciously make allowance for a plurality of doctrinal interpretations. Here he implicitly invokes a triple formula for handling theological disputes, which, though sometimes ascribed to him, because reflective of his irenic approach, is nowhere explicitly laid down in his works. *In certis unitas*, in matters that are certain, unity: all should assent to the literal truth of Genesis. *In dubiis libertas*, in doubtful matters freedom; in doctrinal interpretation a plurality of answers may be proposed. *In omnibus caritas*: in all things charity: all disputation should be leavened by a spirit of never-ceasing charity and ever-patient tolerance.[18]

Chapter 19: Basic Certitudes Catholic Interpreters Hold in Common

28. Augustine sets down ten truths that he and Catholic disputants deem indisputable. First, God created heaven and earth. Second, "beginning" signifies the wisdom or Word in which God created all things. Third, the two great parts of the visible universe are heaven and earth, which summarily include all created substances. Fourth, every mutable implies a certain formlessness, which is capacity for

form, the dynamic principle underlying all change. Fifth, because it adheres to an immutable form, the top spiritual creature, although radically mutable, undergoes no change and is therefore not measured by time. Sixth, formlessness, a real being closest to nothing, is so undifferentiated that it cannot admit succession in time. Seventh, capacity for form can be assigned, by analogy, the same name as the thing that is formed from it; the formlessness out of which heaven and earth are formed can be termed heaven and earth. Eighth, as formlessness is nearest nothing, so earth and the abyss, formed beings, are closest to formlessness. Ninth, God created not only all formed things but also the formable matter out of which formed things are built.[19] Tenth, a formed thing is first unformed, then formed out of matter. As will be explained below (12.29.40), unformed comes before formed matter not in the line of time but according to origin; it is not temporally but subjectively prior.

Chapter 20: Various Interpretations of "In the Beginning"

29. For Augustine, "the beginning" signifies the Word of God in which God created heaven, a spiritual creature, and earth, a corporeal creature. Four other interpretations, however, diverge from his gloss. (i) In his coeternal Word God made heaven and earth, i.e., the whole physical world, including all its observable substances. (ii) In his coeternal Word God created formless matter out of which were formed heaven, the spiritual creature, and earth, corporeal creation. (iii) In his coeternal Word God created unformed matter, out of which emerged the whole physical world of heaven and earth; heaven and earth, first present confusedly, later exhibited in their distinctive properties. (iv) At the outset God made unformed matter, in which were latent in an indistinct manner heaven and earth; at a subsequent stage these, along with all beings they contain, were properly formed.

These alternative interpretations mirror in whole or part those reported in 12.17.24-6. Interpretation (i) duplicates in essentials earlier interpretation (1). Interpretation (ii) echoes interpretation (3). Interpretation (iii) resembles interpretation (2). Interpretation (iv) is a kin of interpretation (4), generally taken.

Chapter 21: Diverse Interpretations of "Invisible Earth" and "Abyss"

30. Once more he first restates his own view: the invisible and unorganized earth and the abyss signify unformed matter, which, as unorganized and dark, is devoid of order and light. As in 12.17.24-6 and 20.29, he next sets forth opinions at odds with his reading. (a) The formless earth and the darkness denote the heaven and earth as formless and darksome matter; out of this matter are produced the visible heaven and earth, along with all their sensorially observable entities. (b) The key words of Gn 1.2 refer to heaven and earth as formless matter; out of this matrix are formed the intelligible or spiritual heaven, i.e., the heaven of heaven, and the earth, which embraces the whole cosmos, including the material heaven. (c) The heaven and earth of Gn 1.1 designate spiritual and corporeal creation. Only the words of Gn 1.2 denote the primitive unformed matter, out of which God later made the aforementioned heaven and earth. (d) Gn 1.2 describes the original formlessness out of which God formed the entire physical universe, whose two greatest parts are the heaven, the higher region, and the lower region; in each of these regions are fashioned now-familiar entities such as the sun, planets, trees, and animals.

These opinions carry resonances of previous interpretations expressed in 12.17.24-6 and 20.29. Interpretation (a) by and large resembles interpretations (1) and (i). Interpretation (b) is apparently similar to interpretations (3) and (ii). Interpretation (c) roughly parallels interpretations (3) and (ii). Interpretation (d) corresponds to interpretation (1) or (2) and interpretation (i) or (ii). It is difficult to map the precise lines of division separating the various views, some of which apparently overlap.[20]

Chapter 22: Response to Objection to Formless Matter

31. Since Catholic critics concur in essentials with his stance (12.15.18-22), he is content to withhold a counter-critique of particular divergences from his posture. So long as "contradictors" subscribe to primary and fundamental tenets, there is no pressing need to level strictures on opposing theses dealing with less-than-essential points. In an irenic temper he defends the last two views of 12.21.30 insofar as they harmonize with his own version of formless matter as the first

stage in creation, which is not to be identified with heaven and earth. In declining, along with these two opinions, to merge unformed matter with heaven and earth, he is implicitly justifying his own position by recourse to a nonpolemical strategy that expressly confutes criticism not in defense of his own theory but of that of fellow Catholics repudiating the opinion which fuses formless matter with heaven and earth. His approach is not a sheerly humanistic rhetorical contrivance to assuage disputants but part of a policy of Christian tolerance that is the offshoot of charity. Love is the fulfillment and end not only of the Law but of the whole of Scripture. Scripture is searched first of all for analytical understanding, then meditated for agapistic understanding that consists in the upholding of love of God and neighbor, the twofold charity for the sake of which the Scriptures were written (12.25.35).

The Scriptural ground for a formless matter strictly distinct from heaven and earth, the objection runs, seems dubious. To deny that heaven and earth signify formless matter entails positing an entity somehow not made by God. If heaven and earth do not include formless matter, then God did not create all things; some formless matter lay outside his creative agency. Significantly, Scripture entirely omits mention of such independent formless matter. Hence formless matter must be signified by heaven and earth, either by both terms or by earth alone. The earth without order of Gn 1.2 repeats, with more detail, the signification of formless matter included in heaven and earth, which is set down in Gn 1.1. Writing in the name of the proponents of the last two opinions, Augustine first replies that this position does not imply a matter prior to and outside the range of creation. A being that is created, i.e., fully fashioned and formed, has more ontic value than a formless being, an entity that is only creatable, i.e., capable of being ordered and formable; though less in value, the formable is not entirely without being and value. Again, absence of explicit reference to formless matter does not prove that it was not independently created. The creation narrative does not list cherubim and seraphim or other angelic ranks like thrones and dominations, yet Scripture later unmistakably records the existence of these angels undoubtedly created by God (Gn 3.24.Is 6.2; 37.16. Col 1.16). Moreover, if earth means formless matter, it is not easy to explain how the waters over which the Spirit moved can be thought formless since the waters are beautiful, i.e., formed or ordered.

Furthermore, if earth means formless matter, then we must incongruously hold that the firmament, the heaven, was fashioned out of this earth or formless matter. In addition, if earth is equated with formless matter, it seems odd that the waters are not reported as being made from the earth. Still, even if the so-called gathering of the waters is taken to mean the formation of the waters under the firmament, there remains an intractable problem in regard to waters above the firmament. As remarked earlier (10.8.8), Augustine insisted, mainly on the authority of Scripture, that, however tough to justify on natural-philosophical grounds, water lay above the firmament or heaven of the stars (GL 2.4.8;5.9). Clearly this elevated locus of the waters above even the naturally eminent sidereal heaven rules out as impossible any contention that they are formless. As with formless matter, so with super-sidereal waters: lack of explicit reference to their creation cannot be used to argue that they were not created. Again, it would be unreasonable to claim that since their existence is not ascribed to creation, they have to be coeternal with God. Put simply and positively, though their creation goes unreported, the waters above the firmament were formed, created by God, and therefore are not coeternal with him. Correspondingly, it seems equally reasonable to maintain that, while Scripture does not indicate the exact moment when formless matter, termed the unorganized earth and darksome abyss, was made, there is no doubt that it was created by God and hence is not coeternal with him.

In short, countering the objection that Scripture nowhere relates the making of formless matter, Augustine responds that entities other than formless matter which were unquestionably created are accorded no Scriptural evidence of their creation: various ranks of angels, perhaps subatmospheric waters, and certainly the waters above the firmament. Thus it can be convincingly held that God created formless matter though Scripture does not specify the moment of its creation.

Chapter 23: Two Kinds of Disagreement

32. Exegetical questions arise in two quite distinct provinces. The first concerns the truth of things: the correct theological or doctrinal interpretation of key factors in creation. The second bears on the meaning intended to be conveyed to hearer and reader by Moses,

lauded as an outstanding servant of the household of faith, subordinate to Jesus who rules the house. Augustine dissociates himself from erroneous commentators in both sectors, those whose theological analyses are blemished with falsities and those who temerariously allege that Moses' writings are marred by untruths. By contrast, he unites in harmony of mind and will with fellow Catholics to validate the truth not in the narrowness of self-seeking, which engenders distrust and bitter squabbling, but in the spaciousness of spirit that is the hallmark or fruit of charity.[21] In attaining any truth, he will not appropriate it as a sheer individual but share in the pleasure consequent upon its collective attainment, a joy in the common truth and good that is God. He invites fellow Catholics to join in a common enterprise of love, becoming co-exegetes in discovering the meaning God communicated through Moses who, as steward of the house of God, dispensed food that is God's truth.

Chapter 24: Easier to Attain Theological Certitude Than to Determine What Moses Had in Mind

33. As a son of the handmaid that is the Church, set apart from heresy-mongers outside the Church (P 115.6), he proclaims the truth. Prior parts of his *Confessions* and, in particular, his present exegetical searchings represent a vowed sacrifice of praise that offers not holocausts but his entire self, in a self-donation in line with the Lord's words, " Render to God the things that are God." As the coin bearing Caesar's image is paid to Caesar, so the self bearing God's inward image renewed in Christ is to be paid to God (P 115.8). Because all along he has prayerfully consulted the truth concerning the theological meaning of the opening verses, he confidently articulated his own theological reading: "In the beginning", in his immutable Word, God made heaven and earth, i.e., all things invisible and visible. But he is far from sure what Moses had precisely this in mind when he wrote Gn 1.1. Certain that his own theological interpretation is true in the light of the truth of God, he cannot attain a like certitude concerning exactly what Moses purposed in composing Gn 1.1. Theological certitude is not paralleled by literal certitude of Moses' meaning.

Moses could have intended the meaning that Augustine's theological interpretation described, yet he might well have enunciated an alternative meaning. "In the beginning", according to his conception, might have meant, "At the very first moment of God's creative activity," and "heaven and earth," on his view, might have denoted not any substance, whether spiritual or bodily, fully formed and complete in all its parts, but something only inchoatively spiritual or corporeal, as yet unformed. Augustine does not doubt that if Moses had wanted to express either of the two meanings, that preferred by himself or an alternative, either one could have been Moses' true meaning. But he does doubt whether either of these interpretations or any other interpretations duplicate Moses' authentic meaning. In any case, though unsure about what Moses intended, whether it was either of the two meanings explicated or some other left unremarked, he is absolutely certain that, in writing Gn 1.1, Moses inwardly perceived a meaning that was true and expressed the truth aptly, i.e., in language properly imparting the truth in a manner adapted to his readers.

Chapter 25: Common Truth To Be Pursued not by Individual Pride but by Mutual Charity

34. In response to opponents who rashly identify their particular theological interpretation with the genuine literal meaning of Moses' words, he follows the line of argument already laid down, with the proviso that if the inquirer proves unbending, he would amplify his case with subsidiary arguments. Apparently one and the same opponent makes two inconsistent claims: first, that his own interpretation, not that of Augustine, is the only reliable reading of Moses; second, each interpretation is true. After the first contention intolerantly excludes any truth in Augustine's interpretation, the second flatly contradicts the first claim. The God who is invulnerable to incoherence, he trusts, will rain down meekness, softening his heart to keep ire in check, gently overcoming evil with good (SDM 1.2.4) and lovingly withstanding self-contradictory adversaries stiff with a kind of rigor mortis in their blunders (P 31 [En. 2].20; 54.8).

Underlying this obstinacy is pride, self-magnification of the self-made intellectually wealthy (SDM 1.1.3. P 71.14, 15) who implicitly make a pretense of being gifted with insight into Moses' meaning originally inspired by the divine Spirit. While unable to grasp Moses' meaning, they are enamored of their own opinion not because it is true but solely because it is theirs, ranked as infallible because proceeding from self, *numero uno*, the highest being in the universe. A sure index of self-adulation is the fact that they dismiss out of hand any view that does not totally coincide with theirs. Hence they fail to see that a proposition they enunciate is true˙ not because it is theirs; rather, it is theirs because it is true. Stated generally, truth is morally as well as noetically common. Noetically common: as the eyes of different individuals attend to a common object, say the green of the grass, so different minds grasp a common nonmaterial object, say 7 + 3= 10; not subjectively constructed by any one mind, truth is not mine or yours but the common focus of intelligence (LA 2.12.33). Morally common: a good of the mind is not the singular preserve of one person but a boon commonly available to each and all. In brushing aside Augustine's view, they are acting boldly, not with the boldness of an explorer who opens up a new frontier of knowledge, but with the audacity of a narrow-minded inquirer precipitously firing off reckless judgments on others' opinions. Their denigration of Augustine's account is fathered not by perspicacity but by pride, whose offshoot of temerity calls down upon its victims fearsome divine judgment. This spirit of private-possessiveness, is, we saw, akin to *privata superbia* (3.8.16), in which an individual chooses his own private good apart from and in defiance of the common good that is God. Here the privatized pride is more restricted in scope, bearing on the realm of morally common truth. Each of Augustine's over-possessive opponents pounces on the truth as *his* truth, the "his" devouring the truth. Exclusive appropriation amounts to expropriation; he usurps what is not wholly his. His exercise in intellectual avarice proves to be self-defeating. In confiscating all of the truth, he is left with none; in grabbing all, he gets nothing; privati-zation of truth becomes deprivation of truth. Furthermore, he effectively becomes a liar. The man who "speaks a lie speaks from his own" (Jn 8.44); Augustine takes the converse as equally true: the man who speaks from his own is a liar. In rebelling against God, Satan trumpeted, in effect, "I am my own truth," his horrible punishment being that, severed from God who is truth, he turned into untruth, a living lie. Analogously but less frighteningly, the man who hoards the truth for himself alone loses it. He is also transmogrified into a liar because, in repulsing God's plan for the moral commonness of truth, in robbing others of truth, in a diminished sense he is twisted into a living lie, propelled into untruth because a sin intrinsically generates its own punishment.

35. Adopting a fresh approach, he shifts from a framework of fear to one of charity; from warnings about penalties built into privatizing truth to stress on the love-impenetrated joint quest for truth in the common light descending from God; from stern injunction to a mild appeal vested in brotherly love that issues in peace and harmony. Briefly stated, his argument addressed to opponents within the context of charity is structured along a fortiori lines: if we both admit that we know the truth in the light of immutable truth, all the more should we be noncontentious about the derived light in which each of us know his truth; or if we both accept the underived light as the source of truth, all the more should we accept the derived light of fellow men who are closer to us than God. One important qualification has to be appended: while each one sees the truth within himself in the immutable light, he cannot see but only believe the truth within his fellow Catholic. Lacking immediate inspection of another's mind, he accepts the presence of truth within the other on his testimony. Even if Moses personally voiced his prophetic message, Augustine would be limited to believing him, for he would be barred from direct access to Moses' inward self. Augustine of course assumes that the belief is reasonable, recognizing that another's interpretation squares with epistemic canons of evidence and consistency, in addition to harmonizing with Church doctrine. Since the dialogue is not a formal dialectical exchange but a personal encounter with a fellow member of the body of Christ, trust enters in to buttress a favorable judgment on the integrity of the other and the credibility of his claim. Trust arises not from boastful self-preoccupation but from lowliness of heart, itself grounded in love. The interpreter who loves his neighbor as himself, with a love branching from love of God (J 65.2), bestows on another's interpretation the same disinterested yet committed love he accords his own.

Reference to the twofold law of charity in Scriptural interpretation is not accidental and marginal but essential and primary, for love controls the provenance and goal of Scriptures. The God who is love poured love into the sacred writers to impel them to author various parts of the Bible. Moreover, the sovereign and core content in divine teaching is love of God and love of neighbor. Furthermore, not only the New Testament but everything in Scripture was proclaimed to inflame hearts with love of God and fellow man. Moses, who knew this universal and invariable imperative (3.8.15), wrote Genesis under the sweet pressure of love to move readers and interpreters to love of God and neighbor. Anyone who interprets Moses in a spirit of uncharity, branding erroneous any interpretation other than his own, makes the Lord a liar. The foundation for this denunciatory charge is an extended reading of 1 Jn 5.10: "Whoever does not believe in the Son makes a liar of God because he does not believe in the testimony that God has given about his Son." Augustine apparently applies the text in an accommodated sense to signify: "Whoever does not believe in Moses, the prophet of his Son, makes a liar of God, for he imposes on Moses a meaning other than that inspired, and implicitly attested, by God." It is intellectual obtuseness then to insist that Moses made room for only one meaning when his text easily yields a number of basically compatible theological meanings. Further, it is spiritual folly to bicker, in a spirit of uncharity, over the one exclusive sense of a passage that was written for the sovereign purpose of engendering charity. It is morally self-stultifying to quarrel uncharitably over the interpretation of words intended to foster charity in interpreters.

Interestingly, according to Augustine, Moses recognized the two great commandments of love (Dt 6.5. Lk 19.18) and was motivated by charity to compose Genesis.[22] Indeed the patriarchs and prophets, including Moses, were made new by Christ's new commandment of love (J 65.1), for they were members of the Church, taken in the broad sense, that extends from Abel down to the last redeemed soul before the crack of doom (J 45.9); rendered righteous by sharing beforehand in the merits of the passion of Christ whom they believed to be the redeemer to come (10.43.69). So illumined was Moses by the living faith that works through love that he observed the peak precept of charity which is forgiveness of enemies, loving the sinner while hating the sin (P 138.28). Still, the awareness of twofold charity in Moses was neither as clear nor as centrally enunciated as the love revealed in the New Dispensation, which found its focus and fulfillment in the God-man. Infinitely intimate with the Father, in whose bosom he dwells, the Word made flesh brings all the hidden treasures of wisdom and knowledge of God to man: he is the one and only true mediator (10.43.68. P 134.5). By matchless self-giving evinced in his crucifixion, Jesus is the perfect model of charity. Further, from his death wells a ceaseless stream of divine life, supplying the power to practice the humanly impossible divine commandments, in particular, the seemingly irrational directive to forgive one's enemies again and again (10.43.69), healing love being the chief medication dispensed by the crucified physician (J 3.3). Although, in Augustine's judgment, at times Moses was blessed with a face-to-face vision of God, he did not and could not enjoy the unbroken union of Christ with the Father. Moses was one of a number, perhaps the greatest, of Old Testament intermediaries chosen by God, yet, as one of many, he could not be the absolutely one mediator between God and man. No doubt this promulgator of the Law obeyed the Law with outstanding virtue, yet shortcomings inevitable in even the most spiritual ruled out the possibility of his being admired as a perfect exemplar of conduct. Moreover, giant though he was, no redemptive power coursed from his limited individuality to heal fellow Israelites.

Chapter 26: Had he Been Moses, he Would Have Aimed at Including All True Views

36. The sovereign Lord is the rest of the lowly in a double sense; the final good in whom his work will terminate; and the refuge in which inward repose soothes his heart apart from demanding duties (10.40.65). Omnipotent mercy forgivingly hearkens to his confession of lapses into intolerance (12.25.34). Since he is bound to love Moses as much as himself, he would not want Moses to be less supernaturally talented than himself if he had been appointed to Moses' grand office as an inspired channel of truths propagated universally in time, unbrokenly down all centuries, and universally in space, to all nations throughout the whole world, the overtopping authority of whose salvific doctrine would grind to powder all the skewed claims of the proud. Surely then God favored Moses with gifts he would not have withheld from Augustine, had Augustine been assigned an identical revelatory mission.

Forestalling a possible accusation of overweening ambition sired by pride, he emphasizes that Moses himself was only a man. As any sin that any one man commits, we saw, any other can commit (S 99.6.6), so any gift that any one man receives from God any other man can receive. Wrought from the common clay[23] that Moses and he share, Augustine could have been shaped for a like ministry: each man is precious only because the all-generous Father elects him as the beneficiary of wholly gratuitous love. If deputed to write Genesis, he would have wanted two literary gifts; eloquence, the power of lucid and moving expression, and the skill of adapting his message so as to appeal to both rustic and lettered. Incapable of articulating precisely how creation occurs, children of faith would assent to the bare fact of creation while spirituals, whose acumen delineates in some measure a sort of fundamental metaphysics of creation, would discern in the terse language of Scripture a validation of whatever true interpretations they espoused. Conceivably still another spiritual might propose yet another reading under the aegis of the truth that is God, distinct from those already discussed; an alternative reading that would also mesh with the text.

In brief, since Moses could not have been less insightful than Augustine himself in the same role, Moses' prose was clear and forcible, flexible enough to win the belief of the unlettered and to implicitly engird diverse doctrinal interpretations of spirituals.

Chapter 27: God's Word Rich in Fertility Simple Enough for the Simple

This and the following chapter elaborate the reflections toward the close of the preceding chapter. The words of Genesis, minute in compass yet vast in consequences, are apprehensible by the simple of faith and variously interpretable by spirituals; this latter claim is expounded in general in the next chapter, with particular nuances reserved for the concluding chapters.

37. Smaller than a stream flowing from it, a spring, as the source of numerous streams, is more abundant in its effects than any one of the streams taking rise from it. Out of the tiny flow of words in the spring that was Genesis poured mighty rivers of limpid truth, from which various individuals drew, according to talent and training, various truths, these enunciated not in a few but many words that were the outcome of sinuous discourse, i.e., of the winding of analysis analogous to the course of a river.

Whereas the uneducated are fundamentally accurate in affirmation of the fact of creation, they tend to think of the mode of creation in terms of material images, incapable, as was Augustine early in 386 (7.1.2), of precisely conceiving a spiritual entity. They depict God as some sort of a supergigantic man or an extra-human force resident in an enormous body. He is not considered immutable since the decision to create entrains a sudden change in will. Correspondingly, his creative act is regarded as outside himself, a mutable action distinct from his permanent self. Again, however massive, he is situated in space; his creative act occurred in a region distant from the universe, which basically comprises the heaven and earth containing all creatures. Moreover, God is represented as time-bound as well as space-bound; the words, "Let this be made," were successive transient sounds measured by time. These and perhaps similar image-ridden ideas stem from the customary style of speaking in the flesh, i.e., from a sensory fashion of discourse among the common run of unlettered Christians, whose views are opinions, which, in contrast to true knowledge or belief, are erroneous; opinion-mongers delusively believe that they know what they do not know (UC 11.25). It was these errors that his analysis of Gn 1.1 explicitly took pains to circumvent so as to attain a God who is absolutely immaterial; immutable, his will always unchangeably one with his changeless substance; immense, with no circumscription in space; and eternal, his creation of the world enacted in the beginning that is his Word; in addition, the heaven is glossed to mean the heaven of heaven, and earth unformed matter (11.6.8-12.14). Dominated by sensory associations, the analytically disadvantaged are like toddlers[24] who, not strong enough in intellection to navigate by themselves, have to be carried in the arms of mother Church.[25] While their understanding is feeble, their basic faith is strong, a salubrious quality indicated in their unwavering assent to the fact of creation, the truth that God alone produced all substances in the stupendously intricate universe. For proper interpretation, understanding begotten of and flowering out of faith is necessary. Yet most Christians are not spirituals but children in the line of mind. Still, faith minus understanding suffices for development in love, provided little ones remain receptive to growth in understanding.

A third alternative, however, is undesirable and reprehensible: the case in which understanding, in fact pseudo-understanding, is pitted against faith so as to sap and destroy it. Cankered with this spurious rationalism that condemns the teachings as a superstition,[26] a simple Christian jettisons faith, and, though unable to fly or use understanding, leaps out of the nurselings' nest symbolizing the

Church, and, because featherless, plunges to the ground. Lord, rain down your mercy on this dumb birdling, Augustine cries out; otherwise passersby will tread upon and crush the life out of the unplumed nestling; send some angel, some minister of your healing grace, to restore it to the nest of simple faith until it learns to fly, i.e., unfurl its wings in understanding. Far from inventing a plausible example, Augustine is alluding to his own anguished entrapment in which, hoodwinked by the Manichean boast to propound doctrine and chart life in virtue of reason alone, he despised the path of faith as puerile and the teachings of Genesis as blasphemous, because depicting God with nostrils, fingernails, and other less prepossessing human features (3.7.12). Delusively pretending to be full of understanding, he forsook the nest of faith but, since featherless, plummeted earthward. Happily, God in his mercy dispatched an angel, principally symbolizing Ambrose (6.1.1), to save him from being trampled to death by returning him to the nest (S 51.5.6).

Chapter 28: Spirituals' Interpretation of Gn 1.1.

38. Unlike featherless little ones, spirituals are full-fledged birds not confined to the nest that stands for Scripture attainable by bare faith, but, as they fly freely about in shady thickets that symbolize the more ample and textured region that is Scripture accessible to understanding, their analytical prowess enables them to observe the fruits, the doctrinal meanings, of Scripture, hidden from the purview of sheer faith. They wing their way joyfully, in anticipation of feeding upon the fruits that are truths, chattering or chirping, i.e., canvassing the plausible senses of Gn 1.1. After weighing the veridical merits or truth-values of the fruits, each bird or spiritual plucks a different fruit as its true interpretation.

Spirituals lay bare meanings wrested from the tyranny of sense-impressions befogging the account of the unlettered. God is not crudely portrayed as a superman residing in a far-above-the-heavens region, variable in volition and subject to time, but conceived as an unchangeable spirit, not only timeless but transcending all times, with a *tota simul* duration, all of his being existing all at once, while things under the dominion of time perdure successively. Without being enmeshed in time, the eternal God has crafted every creature, which, because inscribed within it is the possibility of change, is radically temporal. Though things created newly exist, subject to change, the creative act introduces no novelty in the will of God. In some profound, perhaps unfathomable, mode his decree to create this universe remains immutably one with the immutable divine substance (11.6.8-12.14).

Whereas God generates out of his own substance the Word, his perfect likeness that is the form of all things (VR 36.66), he creates out of nothing the unformed unlikeness that is formless matter. By recurring to the One, formless matter is formed into a being, spiritual or material, through the perfect likeness of God that is the Word.[27] Each thing is formed by the One through the form of all things according to its specific type ordained by God in the ensemble that is the universe. All specific things are good, but, as parts organized into a multi-leveled universe, they are very good (13.2.2;34.49). The highest of these comprise the heaven of heaven, spirits formed by being so illuminated that they intuit the light that is the form of all things (13.2-3; 3-4), a choir continuously praising God as they surround his throne. Below the realm of endlessly happy angels lies the cosmos, descending in scalar fashion from the top grade of the heaven of fire with its sun, moon, and stars (VR 29.52; 37.68) to the earthly level of men, animals, plants, and nonliving beings. Material status exhibited in spatial and temporal limitations bespeaks a proportionate decline in unity. Bodies possess less unity because their parts are divided into segments (VR 31.60), and, since the parts of their history, so to speak, do not exist all at once, they exist in time (VR 22.42). Yet spatial extension and temporal distension do betoken traces of the unity that is the root of beauty and, as an intricately organized whole, each body is one and therefore beautiful (VR 30.59). Granted, bodily beauty is most inferior, yet succession assures an epiphany of fresh temporal forms that, together, constitute a whole that is a unified beauty. If the material universe were static, possible new forms would not emerge; the universe is like a poem: without successive syllables and verses there cannot exist the whole of a poem that is beautiful (VR 22.42-3). Moreover, all spatial extension and all temporal distension are deemed beautiful not in virtue of spatial segments or temporal intervals, however large, but in terms of engagement in the harmonious whole that is the natural world (VR 43.80). This holistic beauty is the reason why physical things enact or undergo alterations in accord with the categories of action and passion (4.16.28), variations, like the shifting colors of flowers and the sea (CD 22.42), so charming that they excite delight in the eye of the beholder. Spirituals take pleasure in the hidden fruits in the light of the truth that is the Word, tasting, in the slight measure possible here below, the happiness that is joy in truth (10.22.32).

39. Augustine restates a few of the opinions concerning Gn 1.1 by and large already set down in 12.20.29 and 12.17.24-6.

(1) According to one view, basically his own, "In the beginning" signifies "in the wisdom" that is the coeternal Word (11.9.11). (2) Another exegete[28] takes "In the beginning" to mean "in the commencement," assigning the first words the sense, "At first he made" (12.20.29). Spirituals who hold position (1) that "beginning" denotes wisdom diverge on the meaning of heaven and earth. (i) One opinion maintains that both heaven and earth signify the matter out of which they are to be created (12.17.25; 20.29). (ii) According to another interpretation, these terms mean substances already furnished with forms and therefore distinct from one another (12.17.24; 20.29). (iii) A third opinion holds that heaven is the name of a fully formed spiritual being, and that earth denotes an unformed thing in the line of bodily matter; this view is not explicitly listed in foregoing texts.

Interpreters are further divided on the specific senses of suppositions (i) and (ii) above. According to (i), we saw, heaven and earth signify formless matter. Two specific views part company on the import of the heaven and earth formed out of matter. (a) One view has it that matter is the matrix from which intelligible (spiritual) and sensible (corporeal) creatures are perfected, that is, completely formed according to their types (12.17.25). (b) According to a second opinion, out of matter comes only corporeal creation, the physical universe, described, in effect, as mother nature, whose bosom is so broad that it embraces all perceptible substances in their stunning diversity; this view also is apparently not set down in earlier texts.

Disagreement arises also concerning the precise interpretation of subposition (ii), which contends that heaven and earth designate already formed and organized things. (a) A first opinion maintains that heaven and earth denote respectively invisible and visible creation (12.17.25). (b) An alternative view holds that the words signify only the visible universe, with heaven referring to the brilliant zone of fire, and its stars and earth denoting the comparatively dark terrestrial sphere with its multitude of less noble entities (12.17.25). The earthly region is termed dark because of itself it has no light, being illuminated from without by luminous or light-containing heavenly bodies like the sun and perhaps the moon (Gn 1.15-7). (Scientific evidence for the moon's illumination by the sun was not decisive in Augustine's day [GL 2.15.31].)

Chapter 29: Four Kinds of Priority

40. An exegete who, following position (2) mentioned above (12.28.38), takes "In the beginning" to mean "At first" is bound to maintain as a consequence that "heaven and earth" signify the matter out of which heaven and earth customarily designated, both spiritual and bodily things, are made. For, were a proponent of position (2) to insist that heaven and earth meant the universe as fully formed once for all, he would not be able to explain the further making of things on the days of creation. He would be barred from answering, without self-contradiction, the question: "What does `At first' mean if there is no `after' in creation?" If God made everything at ·the start, there could be no afterward, there could be no further steps in creation; but the consequent is plainly refuted by subsequent verses detailing later stages of creation. If, however, such an exegete holds that God at first made unformed matter, then afterward, and out of it, formed matter, the absurdity of speaking of a wholly formed universe created at the first stage that is followed by further stages of creation is forestalled. First, the unformed; afterward, the formed.

But this claim can be justified only if the mind determines the relevant sort of priority, discriminating the four kinds of priority which obtain in the line of eternity, time, choice, and origin. In the line of eternity God is prior to the universe created. In time the flower as a necessary precondition precedes the emergence of the fruit. By choice, however, the reverse is the case; the fruit precedes the flower. Finally, by subjective but not temporal priority or origin a sound is antecedent to the song that shapes it.

The second and third kinds of priority do not provoke much trouble. Empirical observation shows that the flower comes before the fruit, in some sense predisposing the occurrence of the fruit. Again, choice is grasped with comparative ease: the planning of the fruit, the end, precedes the planting of the seed and the flowering of the plant. Whereas in the executive order of nature and temporal development the seed and flower are antecedent to the fruit, in the line of end determining means the fruit is prior to the flower and the planting of seed. But the first and fourth types of priority are nettlesome, even somewhat baffling. As earlier chapters testify, it is a rare, because demanding, achievement to mount to a proper understanding of eternity or the eternal God who creates novel changeable things without himself undergoing change in substance or novelty in will; all the powers of mind have to operate at full stretch to compass how without paradox eternity remains immutable while from it and "after" it are created mutable temporals. However sharp his understanding, an inquirer soon arrives at a resignation point: the depths of the nexus between immutable cause and mutable effect are enfolded in the darkest of clouds.

Less slippery than the priority of eternity, priority of origin, exemplified in the priority of sound to song, is, nevertheless, not at all simple to exposit. It is hard to see that a song is formed sound in the sense that the sound serves as the matrix formed by song. The sound does exist as something unformed; as real, it is distinct from what does not exist at all and therefore cannot be formed. As sound is prior to song, so matter is prior to what is formed from it. Matter is not causally prior to what is formed from it; no more than the sound produces the song does matter actuate what is formed. Rather, like the song, it itself is produced as sound and song are jointly produced by a singer. Moreover, the sound is not temporally prior; a singer does not first emit unmusical sounds, then after an interval harmonize the sounds into a song. The art of singing differs in this respect from the arts of carpenter and silversmith, whose wood and silver are materials prior in time to the chest and vessel shaped from them. The sound is not temporally antecedent to the song; both sound and song are voiced simultaneously. Indeed because of its fluency the sound cannot function as stable material out of which to fashion a song. While wood remains substantially unchanged before being crafted into a chest, sound occurs consecutively, one part ceasing as its successor emerges, so that a singer cannot first utter a sound, then weave its parts into a song. All the parts successively vanish, all being physically irrecoverable. It is impossible to identify the parts that no longer physically exist; and since they are no longer there and are not observable, they cannot be recaptured and fused again so as to provide material to be organized into song. The song requires the sound as its matter; where there is no sound, there is no song. Moreover, the song requires form also: it is formed sound. As already noted, the matter that is sound, prior to the form of the song, is not prior as cause is prior to effect–a priority implying temporal priority. The sound does not produce the song as a singer voices a song or a carpenter makes a chest. Rather, the sound is caused by the body, in particular, by the voice-box (with the aid of the diaphragm and other organs) to serve as a substrate to be artistically shaped by the art of the singer. As mentioned above, it is not prior in time as such, for sound and song are voiced simultaneously. Furthermore, sound is not prior to song in the line of choice, for the song is not sung for the sake of the sound; the sound is not the end fixing the song as its means. The nonbeautiful exists for the sake of the beautiful; but the song, not the sound, is beautiful. Not prior in an end-means connection, the sound is prior in origin, as matter that exists to be formed by the song. The end-means relationship is really the other way round: the sound is the means, the song the end. A song is not formed in order that sound may exist; sound is formed in order that the song may exist.

The apt example of the priority of sound to song facilitates understanding of the elusive priority of the matter of heaven and earth to the fully formed heaven and earth of ordinary experience. The matter is prior not in time but in origin. It cannot be prior in time because intervals of time measure the movements of organized, i.e., formed, things. Time is concurrent with the motion of formed things; where there is only matter, there are no forms and hence no time. As the sound does not precede the song in time, but both occur together at the same time, so matter does not first occur, to be temporally followed by forms, but both occur together at the same time. Though distinct from form, matter cannot be thought of as actually existing in time separate from the form that it underlies. While we cannot conceive of matter as prior in time, we do speak successively of matter and of form, succession in speech seeming to betoken a succession in time, a temporal priority of matter to form. Though matter and form are distinct but not actually separated, our limited mode of speech requires that we speak of them separately, matter first, then form. Simply put, in dealing with matter and form, we have to speak of matter as if it were prior in time. Precision in thinking that never loses sight of the conceptual and subjective priority of matter corrects and refines this possibly misleading *façon de parler*. Matter is conceptually prior in the sense that we cannot think of form without conceiving it as subjectified in matter; the formed presupposes the subjectively prior state of the unformed. Matter, however, is not ontically prior because matter is ordered to form; God makes the matter exist for the sake of the superior factor that is form. Subjectively, matter is prior to form; the formed thing is made out of matter. Ontically, form is prior to matter; matter is subordinate to form, to which it is ordained.

In accord with the method of speculative inquiry touched on earlier (10.40.65), Augustine determined that matter exists and what it is. Now, addressing the third dialectical question, the worth of matter, he explicitly states that its value is the least, for formed things are more valuable than the formless that is matter, which exists only at the lowest end of the scale, not as nothing but as next-to-nothing. It is situated on the lowest rung of existence; nothing can be lower than matter or, from another angle, only nothing is lower than matter. Subjectively prior in origin to form, matter itself is preceded by eternity. God is prior to matter not in time but in eternity, prior in the line of eternal cause as regards temporal effect, so that the matter out of which formed things are made is itself made out of nothing.

It seems appropriate to devote a word or two to the references to causation in this section. As noted earlier, Augustine, who had no direct or indirect acquaintance with Aristotle's *Physics* or *Metaphysics*, does not expressly invoke the Aristotelian fourfold framework of causality.[29] Only to the efficient cause does he assign the name cause (DQ 28). Without listing it previously, Augustine implicitly introduces the priority of the efficient cause; the singer is prior to the song he sings. In this context such causal priority is counted a species of priority in time. Not all priority in time is causal (failure to observe this rule leads to lapse into the *post hoc, propter hoc* type of the false-cause fallacy), but all priority in causation is prior in time, as the carpenter preexists the wooden chest he constructs. When conjoined, Aristotelian matter and form constitute physical entities, but Augustine never capitalizes on form as the principle of life or defines soul as the first act or intrinsic pattern of a living entity. Again, though weight and order bespeak finality, he never specifies the good as a final cause and therefore does not rank the final cause as the top reason-why within the cosmos and the universe at large for the ordination of individuals and events. It is not surprising then that he illustrates the means-end relationship of flower and a fruit in terms of art rather than nature; the fruit is said to be prior not by end but by the choice of the farmer intending the flower to appear first in time so as to usher in the fruit, which is primary by choice. In every art the end intended is first elected by the artisan, all of whose work is designed in view of the primarily intended end. In the Aristotelian frame of reference the end is first in intention, last in execution, with art imitating nature in the sense that art adaptively duplicates causal processes operative in the physical world. Furthermore, a finalistic chord is struck in the claim that the sound exists in order that the song may exist. As the flower is intended for the sake of the fruit, as the sound is for the sake of the song, so matter exists for the sake of the formed thing. From the perspective of creation, the divine artist makes, or chooses to make, the matter for the sake of formed things.

Chapter 30: Charity Necessary in Common Search for Truth.

41. Since all true statements are by and large from the one truth, hopefully the one truth that is God will beget unanimity of hearts out of the many minds that advocate conflicting but true views. Peace from mercy that the divine husbandman rains down on the soil of the mind will induce disputants to control exchanges through charity refined of self-seeking and intolerance. Whatever the literal meaning of Gn 1.1, various doctrinal interpretations are admissible. However, the anthropomorphic picture entertained by carnals in the thrall of image-thinking can in no way be accorded acceptance (12.27.37). Nevertheless, firm hope of tiny ones who long for satisfaction in the world to come cancels any fear of Scripture into whose words, sublime in their lowly linguistic garb, is packed a cornucopia of lights.[30]

Whatever their doctrinal views, all Catholic interpreters owe reverence to Moses, ministrant of truth through the Holy Spirit, who proffered the best in speculative truth illuminating the mind and the finest in "fruit of utility," virtues centered in love of God and neighbor. As the light is the truth, so the fruit is the useful, this being mainly charity, which the vine communicates to the branches. The fruit that is pure charity sums up all the commandments and regulates all the other virtues. Lovingly prayed over, Scripture itself germinates the fruit of charity that should animate all interpreters proposing divergent views (J 87.1). The fruit is designated useful because it is the supreme means for reaching the highest end that is happiness, which consists in cleaving to God or, finally, being caught up in his ecstasy-inducing embrace (CD 11.2).

Chapter 31: Moses Intended a Diversity of Meanings

42. Rather than argue that one particular interpretation is precisely what Moses had in mind, it is more judicious to claim that in his one global literal meaning Moses generally intended several doctrinal interpretations, each of which is true.[31] Indeed it was God himself who through Moses shaped the literal sense to accommodate various doctrinal readings. This more expansive exegesis is preferable because more religious, i.e., more charitable, for by religion we bind the self to God by love or we re-elect God by tending toward him by virtue of love; radically true religion is love of God (VR 55.111.CD 10.3). (R 2.13.10 rates more acceptable the former derivation that has religion binding man to God.) Were he, like Moses, commissioned to write words sealed with the highest authority, i.e., that of Scripture, he would prefer to frame a literal meaning hospitable to a diversity of true doctrinal interpretations rather than formulate one meaning excluding all others. Far from indulging in a pipe-dream about being a vessel of extraordinary predilection, Augustine did not think it a flourish of audacity to imagine himself donning the mantle of a Moses, but he would judge it temerarious to deny to Moses the more charitable attitude that he ascribes to himself. To put it mildly, surely Moses was no less worthy than Augustine would have been, no less deserving in the loose acceptance of merit, i.e., in the sense that God fittingly but not necessarily graced him with the requisite charity. Fully understanding the width and depth of what he wrote, Moses perfectly conceived whatever his words conveyed, including both whatever Augustine and co-exegetes have dug out of the text and whatever they are not capable, or not yet capable, of quarrying from it, assuming that such veins are really latent within Moses' words.

Supplementing and expanding Solignac's above-mentioned distinction between the literal sense and multiple doctrinal meanings is the approach of De Margerie, according to whom a unipluralism governs Augustine's theory of interpretation; one: a single literal sense was intended by the author; pluralistic: not being exclusive, the one literal meaning is open to a plurality of objective secondary senses.[32] A Scriptural text may be pregnant with secondary meanings; it is, if not actually, potentially polysemous, bearing, within, the seeds of a number of secondary objective senses. The meaning of the Scriptural text is both one and plural under the direction of the God who authors it. By uniting his will with that of God, the inspired writer implicitly anticipated all the veridical interpretations to be reached later. While aiming at implicitly encompassing all potential interpretations, Moses principally specified only one meaning that was the object of his primary intention. Clearly unipluralism does not invite anyone at all to engage in a free-wheeling interpretation, similar to the strictly taken private interpretation favored by the original Reformers, which devastates doctrinal unity, fissioning the one Church into ever-multiplying sectarian fragments. An interpreter qualifies as discerning only if he passes the muster of definite criteria. As a spiritual, he must situate his views within an ecclesial dimension, never proposing a reading at odds with the teachings of the *Catholica* (GL 1.21.41). Moreover, any interpretation proposed has to harmonize with Scripture.[33] Furthermore, a spiritual has to search the meaning of the word of God by conscientious reflection permeated with a spirit of prayer akin to that of Augustine, asking, seeking, knocking for illumination from above.[34]

Chapter 32: Appeal for Guidance by the Holy Spirit

43. No matter how narrow and single a meaning Moses may have purposed, Augustine can uncover additional doctrinal shades. Withal, Moses, no more than human, may not have laid hold of a plurality of meanings. God, however, who is not a mere man, is able and willing to divulge the multitude of texts imbedded in the single literal sense. His Spirit who, as good, leads, or has led, Augustine into the region of righteousness (the contrary of the region of unlikeness), the state of sanctifying grace (P 142.8), can be relied on to open up concealed treasures that stimulate growth in grace. What Moses may have missed seeing can be laid bare by the Spirit that compressed the various truths in Moses' lines. Most desirable of all would be disclosure of the acme of possible meanings, the very sense Moses envisaged. Failing that, God in his good pleasure or particular

generosity will manifest another true meaning secreted therein. In any event, whether Augustine learns the very meaning Moses enunciated or some other doctrinal theme hidden in the original, he will be consoled by assurance that God is nourishing him with truth and that, negatively, blunders like those of the Manichees no longer beguile his mind.

Suddenly struck by the prolixity of his outpourings on seventeen words, seven in the first verse, ten in the second in his Latin version, he implicitly begs to be dispensed from a commensurate expenditure of energy on the whole of Scripture–a stamina over enormous extents of time so staggering as to beggar belief. So he will essay a much shorter confession or commentary, selecting as one tactic of brevity only one doctrinal interpretation. Hopefully God will infuse this one meaning, which will be doctrinally true, congruent with the literal meaning; certain, invulnerable to alteration; and good, energizing the practical fruit of virtue. In opting for only one interpretation, he is aware of other tenable glosses, having already confessed his belief in a legitimate plurality of doctrinal readings (12.30.41).[35] Ideally he would want to fashion an interpretation identical with what Moses had in mind, a meaning right and best; right, true for the mind and morally correct for the will; best, most excellent in reaping the fruit that is charity (12.30.41). Should he not achieve this goal of duplicating Moses' meaning, he remains confident that his interpretation will be doctrinally true because deriving from the truth one with God. The commonly accessible divine truth, which willed that Moses enunciate revealed meanings, can evidence to Augustine the exact sense Moses intended or, this beyond reach, a meaning that, albeit of lesser value, is nonetheless true, nicely jibing with Moses' meaning.

NOTES

1. The rhetoric of 9.11.28, this passage reminds us, is not a piece of extravagant word play but has a solid physical basis. A conjoined earth, it was hoped, would cover the earth of the two conjoined as spouses. The two "earths" or bodies of Monica and Patricias that were one when alive were meant to remain, when dead, one in a common earth.

2. The heaven of heaven is a multi-faceted concept. (i) It is the residence of intelligences, principally the angels who are in glory (12.12.15). As at once individual and collective, it is a Christian adaptation of the Nous of Plotinus, a society of spirits united in a common contemplation. (ii) It is the house of God not in the sense that it is a place but in the sense that it constitutes a family one in and with God. (iii) It is the heavenly Jerusalem for earthly pilgrims, toward which they stretch with every fiber of their being (12.16.23). (iv) It is wisdom that is not uncreated but created, sharing in the wisdom of the Word. The heaven of heaven is an intellectual nature or substance (12.15.20) that finds its fulfillment in its wisdom: in the line of being, it is an intellectual creature; in the line of end, it is created wisdom. In the later GL the heaven of heaven is proposed only as an hypothesis (GL 1.9.15, 17; 17.32). After Book 12 the angelic nature is designated by the light of the first day of creation (13.2.3; 3.4). See Solignac's illuminating treatment in BA 14, n. 19, 542-8, and in "Exégèse et Métaphysique Genèse 1, 1-3 chez saint Augustin," in In Principio, especially 158-60.

3. The contrast between the part-like character of the physical things and the whole-like constitution of the world of spirits is apparently derived from Enn. 3.2.1,2. BA 14, 598, n. 20.

4. Materies, a synonym for materia, seems to connote matter as disposed to be formed. As wood is materies to be formed by a carpenter into a chair, so unformed matter is materies to be formed into an element by the creator. For similar usage: 7.5.6; 12.8.8. See F. Van Fleteren, "Matter", AE 747-9.

5. Though animal life is specifically characterized by sense organs, life as such is not sensed since it does not fall among objects perceivable by the external senses or the interior sense. Like existence, life is an intelligible form, accessible to reason alone.

6. Spiritus, a term to which various meanings are deputed, may signify the human soul (T 9.2.2), the mens (T 14.16.22), or imagination (GL 12.9.20). Here the term denotes the imagination, the repository of the strange images.

7. In the opinion of BA 14, 351, n. 1, the individuals who brought the term and notion of an underlying formless matter to Augustine's attention were Manichees. According to Simplicius, the Manichean Prince of Darkness possessed four animal structures such as a lion's head, eagle's shoulders, and so forth, along with feet of a demon; a fantastic combination from which Augustine's grotesque forms may have derived (HC 248, n.1). Some, however, may be inclined to demur at ascribing to Manichees Augustine's introduction to matter because Manichean matter is a wholly evil substance or quasi-substance rather than an unformed object that, though close to nonbeing, does

exist and is therefore presumably good. Moreover, it was a bizarre admixture of diverse forms, not a single freakish entity, that Augustine at first equated with formless being.

8. Aristotle proved the existence of primary matter by *demonstratio quia*, demonstration in terms of reasoned fact. His reasoning may be compactly, somewhat roughly, expressed in a syllogism: a process involving privation and form (first observed in accidental or qualified change) requires a common subject; but substantial or unqualified change involves privation and form; therefore substantial change requires a common subject (that is primary matter). *Phys.* 1.6-7. 189a11-191a 20. *Meta.* 8.1. 1042a 33-67. For Plotinus, however, induction discloses the existence of unformed matter (*Enn.* 2.4.6); a logically odd claim, since his analysis, a compressed restatement of Aristotle's argument, is, in fact, not an induction but a *demonsratio quia*. Augustine's appreciation of the probative force of the analysis is more restrained; it generates not certainty but logical suspicion or high probability. His hesitation may arise from the apparent failure of the argument to exactly specify the character of unformed matter. The proof then is a dialectical rung on the ladder mounting to the later developed certitude that unformed matter is the ground of the mutability of physical mutable substances; the very capacity for all physical forms.

9. Augustine's empirically based validation of unformed matter, a mode of reasoning he initially regards as only conjectural, stems from *Enn.* 2.4.6, where the argument, basically taken over from Aristotle, is set forth more explicitly. Though indebted to the Plotinian notion of matter, he never identifies, as does Plotinus, matter with privation (*Enn.* 2.4.14-6), nor does he regard it, after Plotinus, as evil and a principle of evil (*Enn.* 2.4.16). His quasi-definition of matter as capacity for all forms and as the radical mutability of all mutables, besides bypassing the confusions of Plotinus, seems to further clarify the elusive notion. Plotinus' recourse to Aristotelian analysis to demonstrate the existence of an undifferentiated matter would seem to be an eclectic importation, for his outlook is strictly metaphysical—everything below God is deduced or established in an priori fashion as emanating from the One. Augustine's use of the argument to prove matter does not seem as cumbersome. Augustinian matter is reached in the perspective of a philosophy of nature that, in the absence of wholly sophisticated logical and natural-philosophical concepts, leaves the notion of matter without a satisfactory nexus to substance, nature, form, and finality, fundamentally Aristotelian themes somewhat unsystemized in Augustine.

10. According to St. Thomas, Augustine's unformed matter is equivalent to a totally unformed primary matter; *De pot.* 4.2 and *S. th.* 1.66.1; a reading that seems benign. To be sure, Augustinian matter is barren of all forms, yet Augustine, though apparently approximating the insight, never conceived matter as pure potency. Significantly, he never capitalized on pure potency to solve the dark puzzle of the substantial union of soul and body. So baffled was Augustine by this crux, the joining of the soul, one spiritual substance, with the body, one material substance, to compose a substantially one human being,

that he deemed it less problematic to justify the union of two natures in the incarnate Word than to explain the union of two substances, spiritual and material, in man (E 137.3.11). If he had held that matter is pure potency, it seems reasonable to think that he would have accounted for the union of human soul and body as a special case of the reciprocal causation of matter and form. Lacking a full array of natural-philosophical conceptual tools, Augustine attained a totally unformed matter that falls short of pure potency; a matter that is capacity for all forms but never functions precisely as a material cause. In Augustine's natural philosophy, material substances have natures, *rationes* or patterns, implanted by God, consisting of measure and number (a sort of formal cause) and weight or tendential determination (a sort of final cause). While verifying matter as capacity for form, Augustine never comes to conceive it as an intrinsic cause of nature that, along with form, constitutes a hylemorphic composite. While claiming that matter as mutability is responsible for change and contingency in the cosmos, he never arrives at matter as a principle of nature, the potential principle whose actual correlate is form. Though, in contrast to Plotinus' view, matter does not intrusively enter in an eclectic, incongruous manner, Augustine's notion is left somewhat vague, too unnuanced to adequately explain natural process in material substances. Hence in Augustine's eyes the union of soul and body is a mystery, partially intelligible but incomprehensible by human reason. "There is another manner by which spirits are joined to bodies and thereby become living things. This manner of union is utterly marvelous, one that cannot be comprehended by man; and the being formed by this union is man himself" (CD 21.10). The crucial difficulty is this: two substances join to constitute one substance. Man is not an accidental conjunction or mixture of two independent substances but one substance somehow composed of two substances. Consonant with Neoplatonic tradition, in particular that of Porphyry, Augustine maintained that soul and body were joined to compose one substance in an ontic mixture analogous to the union of light and air in which the entities are combined without being irreversibly mixed together (E 137. 3. 11). This union is an "inexpressible mixture" (GL 3. 16.25), that, as not properly definable, resists comprehension. E. Fortin, "Saint Augustin et la doctrine néoplatonicienne de l'âme," AM 3. 371-80, was the first to verify this signification of the soul. See also O'Daly, 42-73, and "Anima, Animus," AL 1.331-2.

11. VR 18.35 raises the possibility that unformed matter may have some form: "if it has some modicum of form, howbeit exiguous, howbeit inchoate, it is not nothing." The possible assignment of some meager form to unformed matter, it turns out, is no more than surmise, for the next paragraph (VR 18.36) describes unformed matter as capacity for form: matter is what can be formed. This last statement may seem to carry a slight hint of potency or potential existence, but Augustine, for whom the ruling Aristotelian concepts were inaccessible, apparently never attained the notion of pure potency.

12. *Aqua speciosa*, almost invariably translated "beautiful water," seems more aptly rendered as "formed water", for here Augustine is attending to the difference between the formless earth and water of Gn 1.2 and their subsequent formed

counterparts.

13. At present Augustine is still exposed to vanity which betokens subjection to moral time that includes the dispersion and disaggregation of the self (11.29.39. P 143.11). This life is a shadow, a dark night, an icy span of tribulation, during which by works of love a Christian struggles toward the eternal daylight of joy.

14. Frequently used in sermons; Morin, *Misc. 1*, Index. As Bourke, *Confessions*, 385.1, following Skutella, 308.22, notes, *Sursum cor* was used to introduce the preface of the Mass. Also Van der Meer, 400 and 641, nn. 39 and 42.

15. See the excellent analysis of first fruits in BA 14. pp. 553-5, already annotated above in Book 9, n. 53.

16. Though rendered by some as certitudes, in this context *certa* would seem to refer to the *bona* of heaven, which are fixed or stable. For Augustine (*mihi*), these are invariable goods to which in his present variable state he can anchor himself in hope.

17. As BA 14, 383, n. 2, remarks, this view suggests a resemblance to the theory of Anaxagoras, according to which at the beginning all things were confusedly mingled together, later to be distinguished. Aristotle, *Meta*, 23, 7.1072a20, refers to Anaxagoras' opinion.

18. The attribution of this triple formula to St. Augustine appeared in 1830 on the shield of the Catholic Theological Faculty of the University of Giessen. However, further research discovered that the expression was actually coined in the first quarter of the seventeenth century by Peter Meidenlein, a theologian affiliated with the *Augustin Konfession* branch of the Lutheran church. It has been traced also to Richard Baxter, a dissident Anglican theologian, who employed it in 1651. This information is owed to F. Van Fleteren.

19. In stating the ninth truth, the creation of what is formable as well as what is formed, he characterizes matter as *creabile atque formabile*, creatable and formable, plainly employing creatable in a broad sense, as equivalent to formable. In the strict sense matter is not thus creatable; according to priority of origin it is created before it is formed; once matter is created, it is formable.

20. For a more thorough treatment of the interconnections see BA 14, 607-9.

21. Through sin men are death-bound, carrying fragile vessels of clay, which cause them to rub against one another. But if vessels of clay produce friction, the spaces of charity are expanded; where cupidity is narrow and constricted, charity is spacious and all-embracing. *Si angustiantur vasa carnis, dilatentur spatia caritatis.* S 69.1.1.

22. These reflections depend on B.de Margerie, S.J., *An Introduction to the History of Exegesis III: Saint Augustine*, 20-35, with accompanying notes. De Margerie hypothesizes that Moses may have received his sure grasp of the twofold law of love in his vision of God or in a special infusion of wisdom. In addition, he suggests that Augustine's uncompromising anti-Manichean posture may have inclined him to enlarge the scope of Old Testament revelation, while noting also his shift from his earlier claim (C Adim 3.4) that all the doctrines and precepts of the New Testament were operative in the Old Testament to the more circumspect judgment that almost all were contained in the Old Dispensation (R 1.22.2).

23. Though translating *massa* not as clay but as *masse* (mass), BA 14, 404-5, n.1, does not detect any reference or alllusion to *massa peccati* (QS 1. 2. 16) that implies man's fallen condition. *Massa* appears in a favorable sense in P 51.62; D 3. 335.

24. The babes are Christians who, accepting by faith only elementary truths formulated in the creed and the Lord's Prayer, are limited to drinking milk while solid food is reserved for the spirituals whose mature understanding can analyze truths of faith. Little ones are called carnal because their ideas of God and other spiritual objects are by and large tainted with sensory connections that are received carnally, tied to the senses seated in the body or flesh (J 98.2-6).

25. *Animalis homo* is the "soulish" man, since *animalis* bespeaks *anima* (soul) as *carnalis* bespeaks *caro* (flesh), the *animalis* being a little one who has not yet attained the maturity of a spiritual. According to J 98.3, commenting on 1 Cor 2.14, little ones mistakenly opine that the cross of Christ is proposed only as an example to be imitated, failing to grasp that Christ crucified as the power of God arms them with the strength of Christ in order to fight for the truth unto death. In brief, little ones shortsightedly see the cross solely as an exemplary, not as an efficient, cause of salvation.

26. The description of the spurner of faith as one who accords its dicta no value (*quasi utilitatem dictorum aspernatus*) echoes the defense of the value of faith critiquing the Manichees in UC (a portion of which is summarized in 6.5.7-8) as guilty of the worst sort of opinion; claiming to know what they did not know, they stubbornly closed their minds to true belief and knowledge. Ironically, these contemners of faith exacted the utmost credulity from their followers (6.4.5. CF 32.19). Their fantastic cosmogony and cosmology were chockablock with logical and physical absurdities. So irrational was this vaunted scientific yet actually pseudo-scientific version of religion that, instead of requiring a reasonable faith, it extorted from members mindless submission to a *Weltanschauung* that was, broadly, mumbo-jumbo, a religio-scientific hoax.

27. The trinitarian context of the likeness theme is expounded at the very end of VR 55.113. The Father is the One, the source of all; all things made by the One tend to be the One, yearning to be like him. The Son is the truth, the supreme likeness of the Father, perfectly mirroring him in one substance. As spirituals recognize, he is the model of all things, the form through which all things are made. As perfect likeness of the One, he alone perfectly fulfills likeness to the One to which all creatures aspire. The Holy Spirit is the gift of God in the line of goodness. The Father as One is the principle to which we return; the Son is the grace by which we conform ourselves to reach the One; the Spirit is the grace by which we are reconciled to the One. The Father is the One who creates us; the Son, the likeness of the One through which we are formed to unity; the Spirit, the peace by which we cleave to unity. The Father said, "Let the world be"; through the Word all things were made; the Spirit is the gift of benignity reconciling all to the Father. The Father is the One, the creator by which we live; the Son is the form through whom we are reformed so as to live wisely; the Spirit is the person whom we lovingly enjoy and thereby live in happiness.

28. Ambrose, *In Hexam.* 1.8.28.

29. On causality see Bourke, *Augustine's View of Reality*, 125-34. As HC 269, n. 27, observes, it seems likely that the principal source of Augustine's types of priority is the five kinds of priority distinguished in the *Cat.* 12.42a26-42b22, a work he thoroughly understood (4.16.28). His second kind of priority, that of time, coincides with Aristotle's third and, from another angle, seems broadly reducible to Aristotle's fifth. Eternity, Augustine's first kind, cannot be correlated with any of Aristotle's kinds because the *Categories* deals with the logical structure of physical entities whereas God and eternity are considered metaphysical objects, knowable in the light of being as being or being common to both material and immaterial entities. *Meta.* 5.11.1018b9 ff., inaccessible to Augustine, contains a more sophisticated discussion of various priorities without commenting on the priority of eternity.

30. Scripture does not make little ones tremble; its grand ideas wear the simple garb that is the language of the ordinary man; its abundance is condensed into comparatively few words whereas lengthy exposition would dishearten the unlettered. Basic Scriptural truths constitute an unshakable foundation for confidently expecting happiness incomparably superior to all earthly goods in this vale of tears.

31. BA 14, 611.

32. De Margerie, 59-66.

33. DC 2.12.18 restricts the sense of Scripture to the sense intended by the writer; a position that is of course modified here, in which to the sense of the author is added the legitimate sense detected by the discerning reader. Augustine apparently softens his first claim that Moses made room for the other meanings (12.31.42) when he writes that even if Moses did not forsee other meanings, the Holy Spirit would provide a plurality of interpretations (12.32.43). In any case, if Moses did not include all other interpretations, he did not exclude them. DC 3.27.38, without mentioning Moses, confirms this pluralistic approach.

34. Augustine's uniplurality thesis has not always enjoyed widespread acceptance. While basically concerned with Augustine's view, Pontet, 147-88, nn. 164-5, rejects the interpretations of Père Assouad in *Polysema sunt Sacra Biblica. Disputatio, Pars Altera. Pars Tertia et ultima* (n.d.) and J. Llamas, "San Augustin y la multiplicidad de sentidos literales en la Escritura," *San Augustin XV centenario de su muerte, Estudios varios*, 238-74. For these references see Carol Harrison, " 'Not Words But Things': Harmonious Diversity in the Four Gospels," in F. Van Fleteren and J. Schnaubelt (ed.), CollAug, *Augustine: Biblical Exegesis*, 172, n. 34. Not wholly in agreement with Augustine, according to De Margerie, 56-8, have been more recent scholars such as F. Talon in "S. Augustin a-t-il enseigné reéllement la pluralité des sens litéraux dans l' Écriture?", *Rev. sc. rel.* (1921) 1-28, and C. Basevi, *San Augustin, la interpretacion del Nuevo Testamento*, 141-62. Still, De Margerie, 84, n. 20, notes, Dominican scholars have indicated that St. Thomas effectively endorsed Augustinian uniplurality in *Sent.* 4. 21.1 ad 3; *De pot.* 4 . 1; *S. th.* 1. 1. 10; *Quodl* 7. 15 and 16; and *Ad Gal.* 4. 7. Moreover, the development of contemporary hermeneutics has placed fresh emphasis on the uniplurism or polysemy advocated by Augustine. L. Lavelle, H. Gadamer, and

P. Ricoeur have thrown light on the polyvalent character of language. See De Margerie, 47-88.

35. At times the phrase, *a fide confessionis meae*, is translated erroneously or ambiguously; erroneously, when rendered as "according to the belief that divine truth will speak to him concerning Moses' meaning"; ambiguously, when rendered as "by the understanding of this, my confession." It would seem better rendered: "by [or in accord with] the belief expressed in my confession" made earlier (12.30.41), the confession that Genesis admits of a number of doctrinal interpretations.

Book Thirteen
Allegorical Interpretation of Genesis 1.2-31: The Structure of the Church

Chapter 1: Mercy Made and Remade Him

1. Mercy called Augustine from oblivion of God to a life of grace in which he calls upon God (1.2.2). Prior to conversion he was gratuitously drawn out of nothing into being in order to be blessed with goodness of being. On the plane of grace God is his salvation and strength, these grounded in faith, hope, and charity, while from mercy also blossom all goods of nature such as existence, temperament, and lifestyle (P 58[S.2].11). Boundless pity made, then remade him. Dwelling first on the second point, he looks forward to fresh grace in meditations on Genesis because during his miserable past when not crying out for help, God was unwearyingly luring him to conversion by multiple -accented voices; through indices without, such as punishment at school, psychic blindness toward Manichean delusions, Monica's admonitions, the concepts of the spiritual in Ambrose and Neoplatonic books, the encouragement of Continence, all of these external graces directly or indirectly readying him for intellectual and moral conversion. At first the prodigal son languished in a region of indigence (2.10.18) and unlikeness (7.10.16) where first fuzzily, then more distinctly he caught God's call, slowly turning his mind to the only Church in which he could fully invoke the Lord who had long wooed him and was still inviting him to closer intimacy.

Transformed, he became a new creation, new in two senses; his past sins were blotted out, with the punishment owed canceled, the retribution due not being imputed to his will; then was also hallowed a faculty to perform good works (*merita*) deserving of reward.[1] This power arose from, or was, grace that is prevenient,[2] prior to and causative of human action, supernaturally awakening accomplishments and principally responsible for his merit, with the result that, in recompensing him, God is primarily giving glory to his own hands, the divine power that, before remaking, made Augustine: when God crowns man's merits, we saw, he crowns nothing but his own gifts (E 94.5.19).

Next elaborated is his first point, that God made him. Augustine had no ontic right to existence. Though not necessitated to exist, Augustine exults in the marvelous fact of his actuality, pure gift from an infinitely good God. It was not his foreseen goodness that motivated God to give him being; rather, it was God's goodness that causatively preceded his existence. He exists not because he is good but because God is good (DC 1.32.25). God's goodness was the prior ground of all that God made him and of all from which God made him:[3] "all that God made" refers to his formed being, soul and body, while "that from which God made him" denotes formless matter. Since God is the good that totally helps Augustine, help signifying grace in the supernatural line and qualities in the natural line, Augustine does not supply energy to keep God from tiring in his far-flung operations. In the cosmic enterprise Augustine is not a joint owner, without whose cooperation the master of the economy becomes fatigued or without whose input the universe runs less efficiently. The relation is asymmetrical: Augustine needs God, but God does not need Augustine.[4] The divine husbandman cultivates Augustine, who is like soil that, unless worked, remains unfruitful. But the reverse is not true; Augustine's cultivation does not move God to bring forth fruit. Instead, he serves God by cultivation that is cultus or worship of praise and prayer, from which not God but Augustine profits (2.3.5). By cultivation he is cultivated by the divine husbandman who nourishes his soul thirsty for more mercy (EN 66.1). Thus Augustine cultivates God that he may retain not only *esse* but enjoy *bene esse*, that he not only be but be good, with the well-being that is especially the life of grace, ultimately peaking in the life of glory.[5] First made to be so as to be made good (1.20.31), Augustine did not merit to be; else he would have existed before he existed. Correspondingly, he did not merit to be good; else he would have been good before he was made good. By the gift of God he is; nor by the gift of another than God is he good; otherwise this second giver would be intrinsically better than God, for morally fulfilled being is more precious than being alone. But because no one is more generous than God, it is from God that he was endued with both being and goodness (P 58 [S.2].11). The chapter ends with the insight with which it begins: for no other reason than his goodness God exercises mercy in both creating and recreating Augustine, benefiting him with both being and supernatural well-being or goodness.

Following the foregoing introduction, this book is made up of four parts.[6] First examined is why God created (2.2-11.12). (i) According to literal exegesis, "Let there be light" indicates a spiritual illumination (3.4), and divine goodness is the reason for creation and beatification of angels (4.5). (ii) Literal - figurative exegesis establishes that the Spirit's eminence lies in charity,(2.8). Spirit-fire lifts the soul stepwise up to God (9.10). Father, Son, and Spirit are imaged in being, knowing, and willing (11.12). 2) This is an allegorical version of the six days (12.13-30.45). (i) First day (12.13-14.15). The pilgrim Church is illuminated by Christ (12.13) with light that preludes eternal light (13.14), toward whose fullness Christians are borne by hope (14.15). (ii) Second day (15.16-16.19). The firmament symbolizes Scripture (15.16) while the waters above the firmament are a figure of supercelestial angels (15.18). Clouds stand for preachers (15.18). (iii) Third day (17.20-1). The sea serves as a figure of evil men (17.20) while the dry land stands for the community of the good men (17.21). (iv) Fourth day (18.22-19.25). Lights in heaven symbolize good works prompted by the Spirit (18.22). The lights of Gn 1.14-7 signify gifts of the Spirit in 1 Cor. 12.4-11 through which Christ enlightens the world (18.23). Spirituals, gifted with wisdom, demarcate the light of mature Christians from the darkness of little ones (19.25). (v) Fifth day (20.26-8). Fish symbolize the sacraments (20.26). Birds and sea monsters are allegorized respectively as evangelizers and miracles. Creeping things of the sea are correlated with baptisms (20.26). (vi) Sixth day (21.29-30.45). (a) Creation of animals (21.29-31). The creation of living souls who are mature Christians is due to evangelists (21.29). (b) Creation of man (22.32-27.42). It is principally the spiritual who is made in the image of God (22.32). Though gifted with judgment, spirituals cannot adjudicate distribution of the gifts (23.34) nor can they distinguish the saved and lost (23.33-4). The directive, "Increase and multiply", is allegorized (24.35-7). Seed-bearing plants symbolize material assistance to ministers of the word (25.38) meant to bear spiritual fruit (26.39-41-27.42). (c) Universe as very good (28.43-30.45). In contrast to Manichean rejection of creation (30.45), the universe as a whole is very good (28.43) 3) Summary of exegesis (31.46-34.49). (i) Literal exegesis (32.47-33.48). (ii) Allegorical exegesis (34.49). 4) The seventh day (35.50-38.53). Man achieves final rest in the peace of everlasting beatitude bestowed by God who is all rest and all activity.

It is hard to put one's finger on a single overiding theme running through the first and second parts. The outset of part one continues Book 12, explaining "Let there be light" (3.4) and grounding creation and beatification of angels in the divine goodness (4.5). Reference to the Spirit in Gn 1.2 assures him a more pronounced place than in prior books. The claim of some scholars that the Spirit is the leading figure in Book 13 as the Father predominates in Book 11 and the Son in Book 12 is unsupported by textual evidence. Book 11, recall, deals mainly with eternity and time, with eternal as an attribute of the whole Godhead. Book 12 concerns various interpretations of heaven and earth, without assigning a central function to the Word. The part occupied by the Spirit, notable as it may be, is not paramount. Moreover, if the Spirit's operation were preponderant, one would expect mention of the Spirit as the soul of the Church. True, the charisims of 1 Cor. 12.4-11 are discussed yet without stress on the fact that these are ministry gifts of the Spirit (18.23).

It would seem that the makeup of the Church is the principal theme of part two. The life of the Church is hierarchical, a point implied in the account of the functions of the spiritual, whose chief representative is the bishop. The Church is also sacramental, bestowing baptism (20.26) and the Fish symbolic of the Eucharist (21.28), indicators of all the sacraments. Furthermore, the Church exercises the ministry of the word, its preachers acting as the posterity of the first evangelizers (21.29-30). Or to use Eph. 4.5 in an accommodated sense, the Church consists of one Lord manifest in the hierarchy; one faith preached by evangelists; one baptism representative of one sacramental system.

From another angle the Church supplies the answer to three basic questions.[7] What we are to believe: under the guidance of the firmament that is a figure of Scripture taught by the Church, Christians grow through the teaching of evangelists. What we are to do: Christians made in the image and likeness of God strive to live as spirituals who are mature Christians (22.32). What we are to hope for: Christians find everlasting rest in the fullness of divine peace (35.50-38.53). Whereas Genesis presents a literal version of creation, Augustine's commentary ventures a figurative interpretation of the recreation of man in the Church of Christ. This symbolic reading is not attained without a certain inevitable stretching of ideas and images. The adjustment of the structure of the Church to the text of Genesis is not altogether smooth and neat. One comment specifically directed at the treatment of spirituals and carnals seems applicable to much of the figurative exegesis of this second part: the manifest coherence and clarity may be more the product of free meditative play in the presence of God than of a tightly knit logical exposition.[8]

Chapter 2: Creation and Formation Gifts of God's Goodness

2. Like its predecessor, 13.2.2 sounds the creationist theme that from God alone emerge all being and goodness in the universe. God does not create goods for his own fulfillment; nor does any created thing proceed from God as the Word is generated from the Father; such a creature would be essentially divine—an unthinkable position. Not indispensable to God, the universe is given existence out of sheer goodness able to be variously shared without loss to God. God is not good because the universe is; rather, the universe is good because God is. With no existence prior to creation, no created thing is good of itself; with no goodness on its own, it cannot deserve a creation that arises from gratuitous goodness. Not only every spiritual and corporeal substance but also heaven and earth, the formless antecedents out of which they came forth, cannot establish a right to existence. In the wisdom of God are produced formless entities of two general sorts, spiritual and material, that commonly tend away from mode and likeness to God, that is, are inclined toward lack of mode or definite specific limit (as formless, they have no delimited boundaries) and, according to type, an unlikeness furthest from God. As formless, an inchoate spiritual thing is most remote from God in the spiritual realm, but, as spiritual, it outranks in ontic value a formed body; and an unformed corporeal thing has higher status than

if it were pure nothing. Indeed all of creation would have stayed formless in divine wisdom if through the Word they had not been recalled to the One, sharing in the One through the form received through the Word. Things are returned to the One from whom they originated through formation of their formless matter; on each is conferred its proper form by the Word in which the forms of all creatures reside. Created things are not jumbled in a loose collection but organized into a universe, which God sees as very good (13.28.43), an intricately ordered variety whose oneness resembles, because caused by, divine oneness, and whose very goodness images divine goodness. A universe one and very good can participate in, without matching, a God immeasurably one and good. Even as formless, possessing only the flimsiest being, things cannot claim existence on their own; their slim possibility of being has to be created.

3. Neither corporeal nor spiritual formlessness holds a de jure title to existence. Corporeal matter cannot merit this since to do so it would have to exist before it existed–which is of course impossible. So corporeal matter exists because God made it for no reason other than that he is plenarily good. Correspondingly, without a preexistent existence the initial state of spiritual creation cannot deserve existence. In its formless origin spiritual creation was spun about, its flux not yet stabilized by form imprinting species and limit. Darksome like the abyss, unlike the light that is God, it would have remained fluid and lightless if it had not been converted to the Word. Made through the Word, it is remade by conversion, causing it to be formed according to its proper form or eternal reason in the Word. The formation is specifically an illumination. Through the light that is the Word the spiritual creation is illumined, becoming light in a participated sense. Unlike the form that is the Word which perfectly imitates the originative One, the spiritual creation conforms in a limited fashion to the form equal to the Father; it joins itself to, and is fulfilled by union with, its proper form within the perfect form of the Father and thereby attains the One. As through the Word it is shared form conformed to the form that is the Word, so through the Word it is illuminated to become shared light conformed to the light that is the Word. In short, illumination converts the formless state to the light whereby it is formed.

In the beginning of creation angels, all created in grace, were gifted with the power to intuit all created things in the eternal patterns of things in the Light of Light (GL 4.24.41). However, the devil and his subordinates, averting their minds from the light (CD 12.6), lost the illumination whereby they contemplated the eternal causes of temporal events, forcing them to speculate about the future from indicators in the universe itself (CD 9.22). These features of angelology may help dispel shadows obscuring Augustine's seemingly cryptic observation that living and living wisely are distinct in created spirits. All angels live the life of spirits, but only good angels live wisely or super-live in endless union with the divine light. Regrettably, malevolent spirits, delighting more in themselves than in God (GL 4.24.41), destroyed all prospect of living a life of everlasting wisdom. It is good for a created spirit to adhere to God, a beatitude grounded in resolute cleaving to God won by initial obedience. It remains abstractly, though not concretely, possible for radically mutable good angels to fall away from the light. Were good angels somehow to revolt against, and thereby forfeit, the light gained by conversion, they would suffer a kind of relapse into a life similar to abyssal darkness. Still, this second darksomeness, since it is the state of a formed spirit, albeit morally deformed, differs from the first lightlessness characteristic of an unformed spirit. Through irreparable disobedience fallen angels lose original illumination and, as punishment, are restricted to a knowledge of things tantamount to a sort of darkness. Hate snarled in the face of the Father strips them of daylight knowledge of eternal reasons of things, reducing them to evening knowledge of things in themselves, which, compared to brilliant cognition in the Word, resembles night (GL 4.23.40).

Through his soul, which is spiritual, man originally images God and, in addition, resembles an angel; so in man, in Augustine in particular, the motif of the opposition of darkness and light is reenacted. The Manichean Augustine was darkness; he opined that his soul was essentially, however partially, identical with the substance of God, arrogantly insisting that his soul was light on its own when it was really bereft of the true light (8.10.22). The true light that enlightens all in the world expelled the inner darkness that was sinful error, nourishing his spirit in light internal and eternal; internal, at the highest point of the mind; eternal, because derived from the eternal light that is God; totally other than Manichean pseudo-light urging him to crave goods external and noneternal (9.4.10). His darkness, though earthly and therefore remediable, was not altogether dissimilar from that of the fallen angels. Indiscipline manifest in conceiving God as spatial entailed the blasphemy of imputing corruption to God (7.2.3), and, as a consequence, his spirit was flung into flux, feverishly grabbing for fleeting temporals until, invaded by the miracle of grace, his mind was cleansed by light so as to focus on the One rather than the many.

Nevertheless, while walking as a new creation, he was far from wholly illuminated and, as a pilgrim, went on struggling with remnants of darkness. Even a fervent spiritual cannot steadfastly set his inner vision on God and cannot quickly pierce the meaning of Scripture. So long as he is weighed down by the body, sense-bound thinking and engrossment in temporal duties block gazing upon God that is uninterrupted understanding of the One (7.10.16; 17.23;10.40.65). A moral downdrag due to original sin also short-circuits ceaseless understanding of God; like birdlime, wayward desires, even of a minor grade, keep the mind stuck in temporal concerns (T 8.2.3). He will effectively shake off remaining vestiges of darkness only when he becomes the justice of God, rising in stature, like the mountains of God, in and through Christ. As redeemed, he has fundamentally become the justice of God, healed from unright-eousness to adopted sonship by grace mediated through the incarnate Word. Now he aspires to a higher Christian estate, that of the mountains of God,[9] eminently holy preachers who proclaim the truth from on high both by the force of their words and the eloquence of their lives bright with goodness (P 71.5). Whether prophets, precursor, apostles, or evangelists, they are one and all humble, exalted only because they recognize that divine light courses not from but through them (P 35.9; 39.6). The light of justice, he trusts, will so irradiate his mind that, understanding the Scripture, he can minister its truths to others, while also winging perhaps to an uninterrupted understanding of God (P 5.9. J 2.3). In any event, he is no longer the judgment of God, like a great abyss that symbolizes the depth of sins into which detestation of divine truth cast him; because of Manichean pride God delivered him over to concupiscence of the mind, i.e., to evil actions. Happily, through restorative grace he is no longer an abyss, and, though not yet a mountain, with fresh influx of light he can raise his eyes above the mountains to call upon the God whose light is communicated through them (P 35.10).

Chapter 3: Let there Be Light: Spiritual Illumination

4. It is not improper[10] to refer the creation of light to the illumination of spiritual creation. Because created by God from nothing, the formless spirit could merit its existence, recall, only by existing before it existed, which is patently absurd. Similarly, its illumination is not a wage it earns from God; its unformed state provides no basis for merit. An unformed spirit, because unorganized, and therefore not prepossessing,[11] cannot move God, or win the merit, to be illumined. Unformed creation became lovely only by being formed—an illumination unmerited, owed solely to divine generosity. Not light in its aboriginal state, unformed creation became light by directly seeing the fontal light, on which it continuously fastens its gaze.[12] Both its life of original unformed state and its illuminated life are the fruit of grace, here broadly meaning any pure gift or gratuitous benefit: both life and the life of beatitude are gifts from God, the first natural, the second supernatural. Under the influence of grace the spiritual creature is converted through a better change, transmutation into what is higher; changed for the better by being illumined by the being that cannot be changed into better or worse, than whom, as changelessly sovereign, there is no better. In God no gulf divides life and the life of beatitude. Because he exists simply,[13] he is what he has (T 5.57-8); because he is supreme goodness, he does not strive to acquire beatitude: he is his beatitude. Of himself, of his very nature, he adheres to and rejoices in the highest good that is himself. Wholly good in himself, he is wholly his own happiness.

Chapter 4: God's Goodness the Reason for Creation and Beatification of Angels

5. Because simple, God is not impelled by a nisus to increase his store of happiness. He is his own good for himself alone, exulting in a beatitude not magnified by the goods that are creatures. If no creatures existed or if, once made, formless entities were left without form, his beatitude would be wholly unaffected. Not out of the most minuscule exigency but out of his infinite goodness, God planned things first as formless, then, turning flux into fixity, formed them according to their form. His joy, the satisfaction consequent upon possessing what is good, did not reach fullness through formed things; rather, already full, he fulfilled unformed things out of the plenitude

of his beatitude. It is the formless, not God, who are imperfect, but it is God who, by impressing form, perfects their being. Gaining nothing for himself from formation, he makes them perfect without being made perfect by their perfection.

This point of the independence of God and the dependence of things formed is expressed in Gn 1.2: the good "Spirit was borne over the waters." The Spirit is called good because he pours out goodness of form upon the spiritually formless. The Spirit does not rest on things locally, as oil lies upon water. Instead of things upholding the Spirit, the Spirit supports them, who rest in him in terms of dependence: the formless symbolized by waters comes to rest in him, being formed by him.[14] In other words, the will of God, as unchangeable, does not rest in or is not dependent on the life that it forms into a complete spirit; the whole good of this self-sufficient will lies within itself.[15] As simply living, the spiritual creature is like waters in flux, not stabilized, enclosed in darkness. The spiritual creature is ordained to live a life of beatitude by a conversion to its creator, and, so formed, rejoices in the beatitude that consists in everlastingly drinking at the fount of life, in having its thirst quenched by the vision of God (13.16.19) or Christ (P 35.15). In God's light empowering its mind to see, the spiritual creature intuits the light that is God, in which it is perfected, the addition of form fashioning it into a complete being; illumined as a participated light imitating perfect light; and beatified, enjoying the beatitude of God by becoming a shared light. The beatitude is essentially permanent, but since God is inexhaustible in goodness, spirits blessed by his presence experience an insatiable satiety (S 362.28,29); a true satiety yet insatiable in the sense that more and more of God can be enjoyed.

Chapter 5: Signs of the trinity

6. The first two lines suggest a sketch of the trinity. The Father is called maker of heaven and earth, the Son is the Beginning, the wisdom begotten of and coeternal with the Father. The Son converts invisible and unorganized matter into formed bodies (13.2.2) and shapes the heaven of heaven out of the spiritually formless, whose undetermined state, like meandering waters, drifts aimlessly. By conversion to the Father through illumination from the Word the spiritually formless becomes light (13.2.2), fully organized life: this is

the heaven of heaven which, as spiritual, is distinct from the heaven or firmament positioned between supercelestial waters and the earthly atmosphere, the heaven which, as physical, was created later (Gn 1.6). The spiritual heaven is as far above the physical heaven as the physical heaven is superior to the earth (GL 1.9.15. P 113.11); in comparison, the whole created universe, including the physical heaven, may be denominated earth in the broad sense (12.2.2). If Gn 1.1 names Father and Son, Gn 1.2 is bound to explicitly designate the Spirit. Thus for works ad extra the whole trinity is responsible; the triune God operating as one agent created the universe (12.7.7), diverse aspects of which are attributed to each of the three persons.

Chapter 6: Why No Mention of the Spirit until Gn 1.2

7. He begs for more insight through mother charity that gives birth to supernatural children, which originates in the Holy Spirit (P 147.14); a charity that will hopefully nourish him, now no longer an infant but a spiritual hungering to ascertain why the Spirit that is divine is mentioned, apparently incongruously, only after the lowest ingredients in the universe. If the Spirit were to be so portrayed, Augustine then realized, the things over which he was to be borne had to be recounted first. Obviously he could not be forthwith linked with the Father and Son; it would be nonsensical to have him borne over divine persons. Plainly too it would be absurd to infer that he was borne over nothing at all. Hence it was necessary to state first the things to be borne over, then to specify the Spirit's function, which is to be borne over the spiritually formless.

Chapter 7: Supereminence of the Spirit Is Charity

8. The theme of mother charity (13.6.7) is expanded; the Spirit is source and term of charity. Relevant to the role of the Spirit is Paul's discernment that love within flows down from the Holy Spirit (Rom 5.5, a text Augustine cites over 150 times); so charity is hailed as the supereminent way, "more excellent" than all the ministry gifts. Displaying the profundity of his solicitude, Paul departs from the Jewish practice of praying with hands upright and kneels or prostates himself to implore the Father to teach his flock the superlatively elevated knowledge of charity, breathing into their minds the very charity ablaze in the heart of Christ. This is the very reason why the

Spirit is depicted as borne over the waters, a figure symbolizing his supereminence: it is the mission of the Spirit to communicate super-sublime charity so that minds can rise from the waters, which signify the earthbound and sinful, to his divine pinnacle.

To spirituals he will exposit the psychic movements of cupidity[16] and charity not metaphorically but by proper analogy, a ladder on which the mind mounts from physical to superphysical objects. Cupidity is like an earthy, downward-tending weight that drives the mind into the deep dark and distant from God (13.2.3). Charity, on the other hand, resembles an element like fire that naturally tends upward through the power of the supereminent Spirit that is person-alized charity, a force that impels the mind toward the supereminence borne over the waters. Clearly psychic places are not the same as physical places, such as a body of water in which we bathe and, cleansed, out of which we emerge. Yet the analogy between physical and psychic place is fundamentally sound: a psychic movement to an affectively desired place does resemble the naturally propelled downward movement of an earthy object to its proper place on the surface of the earth.[17] The disanalogous component, however, cannot be neglected. Psychic movements are far from being wholly of the same character as physical movements. Physical movements are strictly determinate and intrinsically unalterable while psychic movements such as desires subject to free judgment and therefore alterable are indeterminate, open to choice. Freighted with cupidity, the human spirit becomes befouled because its false love inclines it downward, to things that sully it insofar as they are craved in separation from God. Goods hankered after become anxieties, depressing the spirit that clutches them. Since a possessor of earthbound goods is possessed by them (P 123.9), a miser's hoard enslaves his spirit, cramping his delight with worry. The holiness of the Spirit, on the other hand, raises the human spirit to goods on high, by sharing with the soul his upward-tending charity. This love, because divine in origin, liberates man from his sinful condition; divine truth whose goods it seeks sets it free. Accompanying and undergirding this liberty is freedom from care, in which the spirit possesses goods such as the virtues and God, the source of virtues, which cannot be forfeited against the will (LA 1.11.22). There is security too because God is a common good, an affective whole embraceable by all without envy or division (LA 2.13.37-14. 38. P

33[S.2].6).[18] Under the impulsion of Spirit-diffused love Augustine, adapting the familiar formula of the liturgy (S 25.7), lifts up his heart to the super-loftiness of the Spirit. Even now he can abide by faith and love in the supereminence of the Spirit; a present union making straight the way for a final ecstatic embrace, a rest forever in divine supereminence after his soul will have passed through and beyond the waters without substance, i. e., waters that are sinful, since sin precisely as a privation lacks substance or reality (P 123.9). This comment probably alludes to his prior wretchedness, when, like the prodigal son, he squandered his whole substance on waters without substance, seduced by prostitute-like lower goods, these submerged in sin-polluted waters, which were worthless, equivalent to nothing real, a privation without exact objective correlate (P 123.9).

Chapter 8: Man Can Rise to Light after Fall into Darkness

9. The fall of the apostate angels and the fall of the human soul[19] into original sin analogously manifest the darkness of spiritual creation prior to formation and illumination by the Word. Their deprivation, after reception, of light furnishes actual clues to the lightless state of spiritual creation before God's formative and illuminative fiat. After their defection prideful angels and human souls were transmogrified into blackened spirits, aimlessly roaming in lightless pits due their self-elevation. Without God's light-creating command the brilliant heaven of heaven itself would have stayed unformed, without one gleam of radiance. Darkness due to moral deformity after illumination indirectly evidences the elusive darkness due to ontic nonformation before illumination; a sad truth markedly illustrated in the declension of angels who, after being first formed partially, were subsequently defrocked of their pristine vesture of light. Their original lightsomeness was shy of perfection; else they could not have fallen away. Their self-adoring breakaway from the light primarily exposed their own darkness and, secondarily and analogously, afforded some inkling of the prior formlessness of spiritual creation. Spiritual creation became wholly fulfilled in two stages. First, angels passed from formlessness to formation and structure of being; fused with this ontic formation was an initial moral formation through supernatural illumination; angels were simultaneously formed in nature and grace. Second, the initial fulfillment being provisional,

only obedient intelligences won terminal beatitude that was complete and everlasting.[20] Whatever the concrete character of the test, some angels revolted against a divine ordinance and, sundered from the light, effectively became darkness, irredeemably maimed spirits doomed to wander endlessly apart from God and, because their destiny is irreversibly blighted, totally miserable.

Unlike inferior things, a rational creature does not reach fulfillment from a good proper to its nature. Sensory and intellectual powers and even moral virtues that man may acquire are dogged by multiple evils. Man's highest good, which engenders happiness, resides above man, beyond this life, in God who alone bestows beatific satisfaction (CD 19.4). Analogously, no proper angelic good but only the divine good wholly fulfills an angelic spirit; not even its magnificent self, because radically open to variation and restlessness, can confer rest that is supernatural blessedness. Thus eudaemonistic orientation to God significantly attests the grandeur of a rational entity. In their fall the angels' moral being was ruined, their garments of light torn to shreds, hopelessly beyond repair. Happily, it is otherwise with the human spirit, which, however black the abyss, always remains illuminable on this side. Even after restoration to a supernatural state, the Christian still dwells in partial darkness, not yet wholly purified; so God will continue to cleanse residual patches of small sins and imperfections. The God who at the start robes Christians in light will in the end, in the state of glory, erase all vestigial spots or, in the words of Isaiah, will make all darkness like noonday: in the blaze of his countenance all defects will be forever consumed (10.5.7;12.15.21). To program him for entrance into that eternal noon, his already authentic love of God will hopefully grow more intense, though he cannot calculate how much more grace he requires until successive embraces[21] dispose him to be hidden in the recesses of the divine face, a figure of paradise or the bosom of God. God is the home above of those who are his home below: wholly healed, they enter into the infinitely brilliant mansion that is God (P 30[En.2.S.3].8). Withal, Augustine is absolutely certain that apart from God he is entangled in evil. Lower things outside cannot substitute for God, and inner life cultivated independently of God entrains self-deification (7.9.13). Without God his intellectual attainments, even his moral virtues, are effectively valueless; everything not centered in God is destitution. Without the all that is

God his abundance is nothing; he is empty-handed, his heart a wasteland (2.10.18). Allusion to his protracted separation from God as a starving prodigal son is not a piece of armchair religious analysis; he has actually suffered through the hapless lot of an abject indigent who crazily deserted God. (P 18 [En. 2].3).

Chapter 9: Fire from the Spirit Bears Souls Up to Rest in God

10. Neither Father nor Son but the Spirit alone is described as borne above the waters, the movement being only symbolic, not strictly physical, for otherwise it could not be predicated of the Spirit, who lives untrammeled by all physical movement and local circum-scription. Superiority to the waters metaphorically depicts the supereminence of the unchangeable creator above mutable creatures. Yet such elevation pertains not just to the Spirit but to all three persons; all works ad extra, outside the Godhead itself, are produced by the one God whose one nature and one will are responsible for all things made (C s arr 3-4. C Max.2.10.2. Sym ad cat 2.3). Within the trinity, relatively to one another, the Father is the principle of the Son, and both Father and Son are the common principle of the Holy Spirit, but as regards creatures outside the trinity, all three persons in one divine nature are the joint cause of the whole of creation (T 5.13.14;14.15). Still, if all three are eminent, why is the Spirit alone singled out as moving above the waters? In particular, if a symbolic place is appointed to the Spirit called the gift of God (Ac 2.38), a more specific question arises: what is the connection between a spiritual place and the gift of God?

The soul is oriented to terminate its movement in God, its proper place, arriving at its rest in the gift of God that is Spirit. From the Father the soul comes forth, through the Son makes its return to the One, and in the Holy Spirit is blessed with the permanence by which it adheres to unity. From another perspective, the soul is recalled to the One that is the Father by being formed and illuminated by the Word so as to attain rest in cleaving to God by the Spirit that is charity (VR 55.113. LA 3.16.33). It is in virtue of the Spirit that the soul attains its fruition in or enjoyment of God because, as the gift of God, the Spirit pours forth charity that culminates in enjoyment of God (VR 13.24). So, Augustine says explicitly, the rest of the soul is its place, which is figuratively ascribed to the Spirit who is the gift of

God, because the Spirit infuses the charity whereby the soul
terminates its movement to its foredestined place, God himself. The
movement of charity, because upward, lifts the soul to the eminent
place of rest that is God, the charity proceeding from the Spirit who
is called good because he is the gift of benignity or goodness whereby
a soul is reconciled unto peace with the Father (VR 55.113). Through
the outpouring of charity the Spirit raises the soul enmired in goods
earthly and temporal up to things heavenly and eternal, emancipating
the heart from the gates of death, a symbol of perverse cupidity that
is a gateway to delights inducing spiritual death (P 9.14). The upward
impetus of charity from the Spirit counteracts and reverses the
downward pull of cupidity due to the flesh (13.7.8), conferring a peace
of soul that consists in a good will; the spirit is rendered good by the
good Spirit who communicates divine love that rightly points the face
of the soul toward God. Thus well-ordered, the good-willed soul
possesses peace, the tranquility of order (CD 19.13), outflowing from
and sharing in the peace that is the Holy Spirit whereby the soul
clings to the One that is the Father (VR 55.113).

More detail clarifies how the gift of God that is the Spirit is coupled
with place, the soul's proper site of rest. As mentioned earlier,
according to ancient physics, each of the four elements, fire, air,
water, and earth, is naturally inclined to move either upward (most
marked in fire) or downward (most marked in earth). Fire is naturally
light, earth naturally heavy, and in virtue of lightness or heaviness
each is drawn to its natural place above or below. Mixed or complex
bodies, which are composed of various elements, move upward or
downward according to the inclination of the dominant element in
their nature. Thus, Augustine writes, in virtue of its weight every
body, whether elemental or composite, tends to its proper place. The
word weight usually bespeaks a heavy mass; but, scientifically
speaking, every body, even the most tenuous, has weight. So, he
cautions, it is inaccurate to think that weight necessarily involves
heaviness, that it inevitably bears a body downward, to the lowest
point; rather, weight impels a body to move to its proper place,
whether above or below. Fire, the element with the greatest lightness,
tends upward while a stone, a mixed body that is dominantly earthy,
naturally tends downward, each impelled to its proper place by its
proper weight. Similarly, oil and water are moved to their proper
places. Though poured under water, oil is drawn by its proper weight,

its greater lightness, above water. On the other hand, water, though poured on top of oil, sinks beneath the oil since it is carried to a lower place by this lesser lightness. Like all other bodies in the universe, they are impelled by their respective weights to aspire to their proper places. When bodies are not properly ordered and are therefore prevented from pursuing their tendencies, a certain physical turbulence occurs. Inadequately ordered, bodies are restless, misdirected, because not targeted toward proper goals. However, bodies properly directed reach their places: they are at rest.

Analogously, psychic or spiritual entities are governed by psychic laws of movement upward and downward, toward and away from proper psychic places through affective inclinations, variously specified by goods toward which they have a nisus. As the celebrated line states it, "My love is my weight."[22] According to his love or psychic inclination, Augustine's spirit is carried toward a specific good. The heart, unlike physical entities, is indeterminate; it is not inevitably driven down one track or up another to a fixed goal but opts for one course of action over another. The mind is borne about by its love, but its freedom entails a certain dominion over the love that impels it to a good. Deluded by carnal appetites, it is borne downward to earthly goods, the counterpart of earthly places, and because love assimilates the lover to the object loved, the heart, carried by earthly desire to the earthly, becomes morally earthly (EJ 2.14). But the Holy Spirit, the gift of God who grants the gift that is purifying grace, turns around the soul's downward plunge, and with the fire that is divine love burns away elemental earthiness, pointing the soul toward the eternal One. Thus is Pentecost daily renewed, as the Spirit who came down on the disciples in the upper room under the sign of tongues of fire enkindles the soul with spiritual fire, symbolizing charity, which, like its physical analogue, raises its possessor aloft. A spirit open to the Spirit is inflamed, permeated with love, becomes fire through whose impulse it goes forward and upward, ascending not by physical steps but by affective movements within (P 121.6). So the soul sings the song of the steps upraising it to God because in the ardor of holy love the new man energized by the Spirit-fire has to sing the new song of love (S 34.1.1). The upward climb is not tension-free but evolves from the struggle between the interior man and the downward-tending of his members (P 83.6). The steps betoken a gradual ascension, a development beginning with the gift of fear of the Lord and culminating in the gift of wisdom, a climb not uncommonly troubled by suffering inflicted by slanders and bitter adversaries (P 119.1, 2). Not by his own fire but that of God does his heart become ablaze. "Your fire, your good fire, sets me on fire," a reiteration serving to highlight the theme of salvific life: not by his own merit but through the good fire, grace distributed by the good Spirit, does man mount to God; only through the gift bestowed by the gift that is Spirit can he abound in new life pregnant with eternal life (P 60.8; 83.6).[23]

Aflame with Spirit-fire, the heart rises up to the peace of Jerusalem, the heavenly city, the everlasting peace in which rest ensues. The peace that is the tranquility of order (CD 19.13) means here calm that fructifies from well-ordered love, the Spirit-given fire that is charity, resting at last in its proper place that is eternity. The heart singing as it climbs is overwhelmed with delight because it is ascending to its own home, the very home of God that is God. All its restlessness will be finally stilled because it wills only one good, God himself, thereby sharing forever in the permanence of God, a stable terminal good (LA 3.11.33) attained through the Spirit. Ordinarily eternity is not reached by a sudden rocket-like upthrust but issues from unglamourous, day-by-day trudging ever higher, headway often made only inch by inch, at times in the teeth of tensions within and adversaries without (P 60.10).[24]

Chapter 10: Spiritual Creature Given Eternal Beatitude by the Spirit

11. The good angels never tramped through a protracted restlessness to enter their everlasting mansion. From the first instant, without an interval of time between formless and formed estate, through the gift that is grace from the gift that is Spirit, they were borne upward to the light in which they were made light, stabilized in their vocation as shared light in the symbolic enunciation, "Let light be made." The formless state came before, the formed after, the priority lying not in the line of time but in that of order, as the sound precedes, by underlying, the song (12.29.40). The case of man is otherwise. After creation in grace, through original sin man dwells first of all in actual darkness, then, after a time, becomes light through the redeeming light that is Christ. Though the prior state of darkness

of the heaven of heaven was formless, the Scriptural account of dark abyss imparts at first blush the impression that the prior darkness was truly actual. This quasi-actual note is accented to drive home that the formation of the spiritual creature, whereby it is enrapt in everlasting happiness, was the upshot of a special work: it was transformed into light by a conversion to inextinguishable light. If in spite of acumen and schooling some spirituals cannot make sense out of his interpretation, prayerful meditation should seek the answer not from Augustine who only can nudge a learner forward but from Christ himself, the only teacher (12.18.27), shepherding minds to perception of various truths;[25] the light that especially lit up John the Baptist and John the Evangelist harbors truths accessible to all minds made in the image of God (J 1.18).

Chapter 11: Being, Knowing, Willing: an Image of the trinity.

12. Few can properly understand the trinity, described as omnipotent because in creation the holy three jointly exercise divine power one with their immutable will (7.4.6; 12.15.18. T 4.21.30);[26] and fewer can articulate the doctrine without falling into error or perhaps material heresy (E 169.1). Most Christians of course do speak of the trinity when they rehearse the fundamentals of the creed and recall that they were baptized in the name of Father, Son, and Holy Spirit (13.12.13). Still, the faith shown in invoking the trinity is not often duplicated by proper understanding. Catholics speak and do not speak of the trinity, words attesting faith but not understanding. Belief is incontestably firm, but, with most, understanding is inadequate, neither talent nor training favoring them with analytical instruments to fashion the right distinctions. Moreover, some Christiana wrangle over the doctrine in a combative style that defeats unwavering focus on its complexities, thus wrecking the peace of heart that is one of the necessary moral preconditions for envisaging the trinity, for contemplating, or steadily knowing and enjoying, the inner truth about God (T 14.12.15).[27]

Nevertheless, the trinity, incomprehensible and unprovable by reason, can be understood in part as intimated in the triple activity of the soul.[28] While probing leads the mind to realize the enormous divide between the triple activity of man and the threefold life of God, the disanalogy is not total: the triad in the soul does shadowily depict the triple distinction within the one Godhead.[29] Clearly observable in man is the triad, existing, knowing, and willing; each one can indubitably claim, I am and I know and I will.[30] Each of these affirmations is an evident truth,[31] known not by demonstration or strict proof but by direct inspection, here intellectual, of the object, which is bolstered by dialectical vindication. *Si enim fallor, sum.* Even if I am mistaken, I exist. Expanded in a dialectical scheme, this becomes: if I do not exist, I am not mistaken; but I am mistaken; therefore I exist. Similar dialectical arguments may be constructed to indirectly prove the evident propositions, "I know" and "I will" (CD 11.26). Furthermore, the activities are mutually interconnected; operationally, they co-implicate one another, so that each individual can say: I am a knowing and willing being, and I know that I am and I will, and I will that I am and I know. Operationally, these modes of activity are co-inclusive, distinct in aspect but so intermeshed that they are three in one, three co-activities in the one being; three modes evincing the one concretely inseparable life; triply expressing the one life that is also one mind and one essence or substance. The three modes of life are inseparable yet distinct; inseparable, because they do not concretely exist or operate apart from one another: one ordinarily does not exist without knowing and willing one's own existence; yet distinct, for existing differs from knowing and both from willing; otherwise the terms would be synonyms, without varying objective referents. The spiritual or educated Christian, upon reflection, can recognize this three-in-one and one-in-three psychological state; surely one is aware of oneself, and surely, after remarking one's inward workings, one verifies what Augustine reports of himself. He is indivisibly one life, one mind, and one essence[32] or substance.[33] But, Augustine cautions, the trinity in human life cannot be erected as a perfect model of the trinity in the Godhead. Similarity between the trinity in man and God is outbalanced by greater dissimilarity. It would be a blunder of the first magnitude to infer that seeing the trinity of being-knowing-willing furnishes the key essentially unlocking understanding of the holy trinity. The human triad is no more than a dim clue to the threeness in God that, even after lengthy analysis, remains veiled in unfathomable mystery since the inner life of the immutable absolutely transcends all that is mutable. As unchangeable, God's existence is super-existence, his knowing super-knowing, his willing super-willing.

In groping to set down precisely how the triad of being, knowing, and willing coexist in God, we can first take the three features broadly, each constitutive of a person, with being signifying the Father, knowing the Son, and willing the Holy Spirit. Second, we can properly think of these acts as common to all three; since each is God, each of the three immutably exists, knows, and wills. Third, we can combine the first and second perspectives. God is simple and multiple; multiple according to the number of his attributes such as life, knowledge, and power; simple, because, being whatever he has, he is his life, knowledge, and power. The second approach underlines the simplicity of God, the unity of acts in the one divine nature: being, knowing, and willing are conjointly exercised by the holy three. The first approach, on the other hand, highlights multiplicity. The three acts[34] of being, knowing and willing, looked at broadly, are appropriated respectively to Father, Son, and Holy Spirit. In this wide sense being, knowing, and willing relatively denote the holy three. The Father is conceived as relationally constituted by being, the Son by knowing, and the Spirit by willing. But the multiplicity, while real, is only relative: each person[35] is God, each totally possesses the divine nature. The Father is as much God as all three together; Father and Son, taken together, are no more God than the Spirit alone. "Each of the three is in each of the others, and all three are in each one, and each one in all three, and all three in all three, and all three are one" (T 6.10.12). This blending of simplicity and multiplicity involves limits, each of which is in itself and for itself, each of which is infinite.

The limits are the discriminations or determinations within the triune God. In terms of divine essence or nature alone, without reference to the trinity, God is both simple and multiple; simple in that he is absolutely one supreme existence and therefore unchangeable (CD 11.10); multiple in that his infinite being includes all perfections, such as wisdom, goodness, justice, and beauty. God is one in being, manifold in his perfections, each of which he does not have but is. In terms of the trinity God is simple and personally multiple; simple: he is supremely one; multiple: his essence contains three relatively distinct persons. Father, Son, and Holy Spirit are the limits, points of distinction within God; though each is and all three are God, the Father is neither the Son nor the Spirit, and so conversely. They are "mutually determined to one another" (T 6.10.12), relatively differentiated and so co-inhering that they constitute the one Godhead. But these relative distinctions do not introduce finite limitations within God: each of the holy three persons is, and all together are, infinite (T 6.10.12). Each distinction is an infinite limit in God and for God. The distinction is in the Selfsame (9.10.24.); it is not a finitizing limitation from the outside, whose consequent division would entrain imperfection. The distinction is for the Selfsame; it does not arise out of dependence upon or need of an extra-divine good or being. In other words, distinction does not necessitate a de-deifying finiteness because each of the distinct three persons is infinite, each commonly and totally possessing the one divine essence or substance. According to this triple interior limit or discrimination, God exists (this representing the Father), knows himself (this signifying the Son), and fully satisfies himself, i.e., wills himself as his own supreme good (this denoting the Holy Spirit). All three acts are immutable; their distinction does not insert change into the unchangeable God. God remains the Selfsame, absolutely one in his abundant greatness, in the infinite richness of his many perfections, each supreme, each radiating his simplicity. No mind can swiftly penetrate the core of this mystery; no one can capture its meaning in words—an elliptical line whose import is: no words can adequately express the trinity.

Chapter 12: The Pilgrim Church Enlightened by Christ

13. While praying the triple "Holy" (Is 6.3) in adoration of the trinity, he recognizes that he sacramentally affirms the doctrine: baptized in the name of the holy three, as a bishop he continues to so lave new Christians. Baptismal regeneration with its instreaming of spiritual light is allegorically portrayed in Gn 1.2-3. Through the grace of the one mediator (10.43.68) God made heaven and earth in his Church.[36] From one angle, heaven symbolizes the just, whose souls, bearing God within, even now are joined to Christ in heaven by faith, hope, and charity (P 10.7;18[En.2].2,3;26[En.2].11) while earth stands for sinners, members of the Church who resist grace (P 10.7). But since Augustine seems to parallel the spiritual and the carnal with heaven and earth, heaven functions also as a figure for the spiritual, who understands Scripture in a conceptual mode, with earth representing the carnal, who accepts Catholic truths largely by faith alone, with hardly a smattering of understanding. In any case, as the

community that is the heaven of heaven was formed out of the unstable flux and illuminated by the wisdom that is the light of Christ, so the Church was formed out of the darkness that is ignorance which blankets the earth (symbolizing the human condition) by the teaching of Christ, which encompasses both theoretical and moral truths, demanding not faith alone but faith that works through charity. To correct iniquity, God applied both penalty and grace, punishment manifesting the sinner's lowliness, divine initiative moving him to turn to God for reform (P 38.17). Divine judgments are a huge abyss, which figuratively signifies the depths of sins, into which pride causes spirits to be snared by fleshly concupiscences. Glorying in, rather than confessing, their wickedness, they protest their innocence, perversely honoring what the word of God condemns: such is the abyss (P 35.10).

Happily, the fire of the Spirit transmuted hearts into fire that carried them upward (13.9.10). In other words, the mercy of the Father channeled through the Spirit of Christ healed the wounds of fallen man. Apparently in between these lines runs the story of Augustine's own conversion by healing light. His soul had been anguished, staking all hope on his fragile self (P 41.12). Then training his sight on the lowly Christ, he recalled Jordan, signifying descent, which spurred him to be humbled so as to be uplifted by and in grace. He remembered from the little hill; through acceptance of his littleness he could become great by grace, following Christ, the little hill, who, as Word, is a mountain equal to the Father and, as Word made flesh, became little for the sake of man: no one was more exalted than the Christ than whom none was more abased. With Christ as his model, he wept in the garden over his rottenness, a cataract of tears without and bitterest contrition within (8.12.28-9), transfigured when light banished every least shadow of moral indecision. While explicitly depicting the switch point from darkness to light of numerous Christians, he is implicitly revivifying images of his own miraculous transition to life, the high moment of whose illumination was preluded by the ragged wretchedness of the prodigal son, who, confessing himself unworthy darkness, proved himself worthy of light (P 18 [En.2].3).

Chapter 13: In Faith and Hope Christians Yearn
for Fullness of Light

14. Only partially enlightened, Christians hold God not in super-thrilling actuality but in hope anchored in divine veracity and mercy to secure eternal union of light with light. If the wayfarer were deprived of the fortifying hope of arriving at the reality, his zest would be sapped by the futility of his traveling (S 158.8.8). Yet aspiration is heightened as abyss calls upon abyss, here a figure of the mind, *grande profundum*, (4.14.21), whose inner workings in all their concretion escape full explication. Spirit-filled preachers, each an abyss, call out to fellow abysses by laying before them truth ordained to eternal life (P 41.13). Guiding the voice of the preacher is the voice of God's floodgates; originating in the Spirit are waters channeled through preachers to sanctify hearts (P 45.8). As Paul, also living in God not by sight but by faith, instructed carnals, some of whom he would lead to become spirituals, this superbly spiritual teacher, fearful of missing supernal fulfillment, focused not on the bygone but on the world to come, projecting all his powers to seize life without end that transcends past and future. Sighing under the load of the corruptible body, which only after death will be clothed in glory (S 359A.8), in this life short of satiety (S 359A.8), thirsting to contemplate forever the delights of the Lord (P 41.3), he panted like a hart for the fountain of waters never drying up, for light never extinguished (P 41.2). He trusted that when death peeled off his tunic of flesh, he might stand before the son of man garmented with the breastplate of faith (S 344.4). Hence the groaning; the whole of this life is one long trial marked by abjection, an ongoing penance, so that the most magnificent of saints were constantly stabbed by sorrow, mourning because still sojourning (S 351.3.3). Moved by the Spirit, Paul entreated his flock to transform their outlook, no longer to conform to a fleshy soul-style but to be reformed[37] after the image of Christ, such a remaking being equivalent to gaining the new mind of the new man. Paul directed Christians to lance the tumor of pride and become like little ones, childlike in the sense of innocent of malice, not, however, childish in mind but mature in religious understanding (S 340A). Unfortunately, some Galatians became spiritually infantile when, misled by Judaizers, they valued circumcision as efficacious, thereby substituting a dead rite for the sacrament of life. The obtuse

Galileans represent all Christians who, surrendering to fleshly modes of thought, sink back into their old death; who, forsaking eternal truth for temporal turpitude, commit fornication against God (S 10.2.2). But Paul's voice, not exclusively or primarily his own, rings with the authority of the Father, whose Son ascended on high to make captivity captive, to liberate men from sin (P 67.26). Through Jesus the Father missioned the Holy Spirit[38] to distribute gifts to Christians in the body of Christ that is the Church. Otherwise expressed, through the Spirit of Jesus the Church is inundated with heavenly waters, so that out of its members so quickened flow rivers of divine life, all arising from the one source, with whose streams many are filled; streams sanctifying souls and exciting joy in the whole city of God (P 45.8).

Like John the Baptist, Paul was a friend of the bridegroom who yearned for lasting transfiguration of heart. The patriarchs, prophets, the apostles, and the pastors who are their successors fall under rubric of friend of the bridegroom (P 128.12). As a pastor called to be a friend of the bridegroom, Augustine extols Paul as his model. Standing in Christ (P 131.14), listening to him in humility (S 288.2), Paul is jealous not about his own concerns but only about the good of the bridegroom. Invoking the other abyss, he speaks not in his own voice but in the voice of Christ. He is the intermediary between Christ and the ordinary faithful (J 13.17).[39]

Already enriched with the first fruits of the Spirit (9.10.24; 12.16.23), upraised on occasion to the highest fusion of heart with God in this life, he was not only vested with the charism of mountain-moving faith but was energized by an unflagging spirit of self-sacrifice, with the result that his soul fully dwelt in God by faith, hope, and charity as Christ dwells in his body that is the Church by divinity, goodness, and unity (P 26[En.2].11). While the indwelling Christ (S 158.8.8) activated his concrete aspiration in his race forward, Paul was, nevertheless, weighed down by his corruptible frame. Though he contemned his sufferings as trifles (S 158.8.8), without sinning he bemoaned in part the burden of a pilgrimage remote from the heights. As a member of the bride of Christ, he longed for consummatory spiritual union with the beloved bridegroom. As friend of the bridegroom, he was jealous not for himself since to him was appointed the demanding responsibility to protect the chastity or sanctity of his bride. As mentioned above, his voice was Spiritimpregnated; a vehicle through which was uttered the voice of God's floodgates, the voice of the Spirit, symbolized by waters pouring out graces. Vocally prompted by the Spirit, Paul, one abyss that is a holy preacher, called upon, by communicating eternal truth, the lower abyss made up of souls who first need basic formation, then further elucidation. Apprehensive that the bride might become unchaste, he alerted Christians to the danger of forfeiting innocence through the cunning of Satan. Comparatively few women and men live virginal lives, but the whole Church is called a virgin because its members can preserve virginity of mind through an integral faith, unwavering hope, and unalloyed charity (J 13.12); without these, sheer membership in the Church does not guarantee continuance in the chastity that is holiness nor warrant felicity hereafter. That glory consists of the light of the super-beautiful face of God which beggars description; then all veils withdrawn, the elect will be transported with illumination that blazes more brilliantly than a billion suns.[40] Then, along with other blessed, Augustine will hopefully no longer shed sweet rather than bitter tears, sweet since here below he feeds upon them as bread. The more nourished by these tears, the more he thirsted for the fountain of life, his thirst for the heavenly waters even in favorable days never being slaked, for fast-flying lower goods are more deceptive than delectable. Once he contemplates the very face of God, he will no longer be compelled to refute pagans who challenge him to show them his God, to prove that God is invisible, transcending the soul as creator and governor of all things: wholly enrapt, the glorified eyes of his spirit will banquet on the invisible God seen face to face (P 41.61).

Chapter 14: Amid Mixture of Light and Darkness Hope for Eternal Light

15. Translated into his own experience, the challenge at the close of the last chapter, "Where is your God?", becomes, "Where are you, my personal God?" He discovers his very own God within and above his soul. Meditating on the God above his soul who draws him to and into the divine (P 41.10), he feasts in joy upon the divine presence, whose praises resound in the soul (P 41.10). Yet he sorrows also because his cupidities have yet to be wholly mastered; the devil sleeplessly sets traps for him and others, and sadly too evils never

stop flourishing in the world (P 41.10). His innermost spirit counsels his self to hope in the Lord, whose word, principally contained in Scripture, is a lamp, a light participating in light, to guide his steps in the environing darkness (P 118[S.23].1). As yet without fullness of light, he must never surrender to discouragement, always sticking to the narrow path until night is swallowed up in everlasting light. He does possess the shared light of God, over against which worldly illumination seems like night, yet in comparison with the maximum to come, his present portion seems like night. Now the universe is partially mantled by the night that is the mother of wickedness, symbolizing man's fallen condition, from which are bred countless sins. When the night vanishes, the visitation of the Lord's retribution upon the wicked will pass away also. Augustine himself was once one of the children of wrath threatened by just punishment. Disenthralled from darkness, he has ingrained in his fleshly self unholy relics of his past, ineradicable tendencies to sin that still persist in his lower man that was once a spiritual corpse, patches of darkness destined to persist till the never-ending day of eternity scatters the last shadows of this life.

Of course the present yields only hope, containing the germ of the world to come. At the everlasting daybreak, having cracked through the hard shell of mortality, he will stand before God, delighting in his face; upright because he has not been wrenched downward into the flux of sensual pleasure. In other words, God does not desire iniquity; for, if by some moral grotesquerie, God willed it, he would be seen by the iniquitous, who do not stand but wallow in the shifting muck of sensory pleasures (P 5.5). Standing before and in God, he will praise him because the God-man suffered man's wounds so as to heal his wounds (CJ 3.3.19), God opening his eyes wide to see his salvation in the endless morning that is eternity (P 42.7). No doubt mortal bodies are inexorably fated to die, but God will breathe a resurrection-life into these death-oriented entities, immortalizing them in virtue of the Spirit of Christ abiding within, spiritualizing them with life in the Spirit that, beginning in time, fully fructifies in eternity. The Spirit, whose outpouring of charity (13.2.8) was a movement of mercy, transformed Augustine's sin-blackened inner self into light. Still en route, he has received only a pledge, a kind of first installment of the complete compensation of light and love. At present he is only partial light, living in initial salvation, pointed by hope toward terminal salvation, counted among the children of light ransomed from darkness by the light that is Christ. Precisely who are members of the children of light and the children of darkness it is impossible for constricted human understanding to establish. Even the most sagacious may reasonably guess but never unerringly determine which individuals are to be grouped in the two kingdoms. Only God, who gauges hearts according to conformity to his law, reading with flawless accuracy the most arcane motives, can discern the innermost configuration that stamps one man as a child of light and his neighbor as a child of darkness. Only God, who named light day and called darkness night, can equitably draw the line between the spiritually lightsome and the darksome because his mercy invests persons with light. As physical light emanates from his creation, so spiritual light springs from his recreation. Since man, physically made, receives light from God and, spiritually remade, receives light from God through Christ, he can claim neither physical nor spiritual light as his right: both are gifts of God. The justified as well as the sinful are fashioned from the identical lump or originally sinful mass of humanity. According to his unsearchable wisdom and justice of predestination (13.34.49), God's mercy molds some into vessels of honor while his justice shapes others into vessels of dishonor. Because his eternal decree marks off the children of light from those in darkness, he alone sees with infallible certainty which individuals fall into each category (QS 1.2.16).

Chapter 15: Firmament Figure of Scripture. Waters above the Firmament Figure of Angels.

16. After their fall from grace Adam and Eve dressed in the simple garb of animal skins, which, because adapted from dead animals, represent the death-prone condition of fallen man (GCM 2.21.32). To disseminate his divine words, God chose prophets and apostles, frail men whose writings have outlasted their mortal spans. Scripture is like a skin that, resembling the firmament, perdures on high. Messages confined in some instances to Judea alone, in all cases to particular localities, spread after the deaths of the Spirit-inspired writers to all peoples and climes. Thus was the heaven stretched worldwide like a skin; the writers' renown was everywhere extended, their names becoming household words throughout the whole world

(P 103 [S.1].8). The harmony of their words may allude to the concordance and coherence of Old and New Testament; in the Old Testament Christ is latent in the seed of the patriarchs while in the New he comes to full flower and fruit (P 72.1).[41]

17. Aspiring to see the heavens, i.e., the Old and New Testament, produced, through the Spirit's inbreathing, by the fingers of God who are the divinely elected ministers of the word (P 8.7), he asks God to dissipate the cloud, here symbolizing the obscurity of Scripture (12.14.17) (shortly clouds will be figuratively modified to depict preachers of the word [13.15.18]). The wisdom of the word is revealed to tiny ones rather than to the worldly wise whose cleverness is a pseudo-wisdom since it repudiates Christ's salvific light. Simple faith alone insufficient, he prays that God perfect his praise, raising it to understanding, which blossoms only from faith grounded in humility. Scripture, which pictures man hollowed out by sin, crying out for mercy, appeals to humility, which deflates the self-centeredness of enemies, self-styled defenders of the faith, who block reconciliation; a pride that is a spiritual defense mechanism inducing them to blindly deny their pride. The foes of Scripture (12.14.17) are mainly Manichees, who scorn faith as puerile, while slickly promising belief-free rational knowledge as the sole road to salvation (6.5.7). Bumptious persistence in errors is an apologia not for Christianity but for their own sins because their conception of God as corruptible is blasphemous (P 8.6). Whereas Scripture, exposing the emperor without his clothes, portrays man powerless to climb out of the pit, the Manichee exculpates himself by blaming his sins on a wholly evil nature over whose aberrant impulses he exerts no control. The defense of wisdom in some pagan philosophers is also at bottom dubious and bootless since their participation in or at least approval of superstitious practices involving worship of idols is inimical to true wisdom (P 8.6). So holy and pure, moreover, are the works composed by sacred writers for the sake of truth, without the slightest tincture of personal advantage (P 11.7), that, holding the mirror up to his own woeful condition, they arouse sorrow for sins; next move him to bend his neck to the mild yoke of the Lord, to yield to the way of life rooted in divine love (9.1.1); then lead him to worship God simply out of love of God alone. So he longs to be firmed in word and work by richer understanding of the Scriptural firmament.

18. Allegorically interpreted, waters above the firmament are

supercelestial angels, deathless and exempt from deleterious change or loss, which are organized into various orders, each a community, the office of one and all being praise of God. Because already in glory, they do not, unlike pilgriming men, have to pray and labor to understand Scripture but see within God himself the design of mercy and justice decreed by his eternal will, reading all at once in one timeless intuition of the divine will, without need of successive syllables retained in a distension of time; an instantaneous insight that goes on for ever since the pattern they read remains ever immune to decay. They wholly read God's plan by an irrevocable choice that is obedience crowned by changeless love of the supreme good. The unchangingness of their acts of will meshes with, empowering them to see, God's changeless decree. The codex is never closed, the book, here meaning scroll, never rolled up: for supercelestials, God lies forever open as codex and book. The firmament that is Scripture was made firm, a source of strength, bespeaking healing for the infirmity of men, subangelic peoples of numerous communities, uncivilized as well as civilized, distributed through time and space. These subcelestial peoples lift up eyes and hearts to the firmament that is Scripture, cherishing the plot of mercy unfolding in time, spelled out in the temporal language of Scripture, originating in the eternal will of the maker of all times.

The truth about heavenly mercy is communicated by clouds, preachers of the word of God, principally prophets in the Old Testament (P 10.10) and apostles under the New Dispensation (P 35.8) and, by extension, all preachers whose saving words water souls. Death snatches away successive preachers, but the heaven that is Scripture lasts till the end of time, its message of salvific mercy lightsomely stretched out to compass peoples of the whole earth. Moreover, the whole cosmos, heaven and earth as we know it, will be destroyed, but the design of God's changeless self will not pass away. At the end of history the skin or book that is Scripture, no longer necessary, will be rolled up and put away; and the grass figurative of mortal human life will, despite its glory, wither, with the result that only the word of God, the immutable plan one with his immutable being, will perdure forever (P 91.8). On this side brilliant clouds or preachers, because limited, cannot fully proclaim the whole truth in all its concretion; hence darkness clings to the most lucid of clouds. Scripture itself, albeit the word of God, is a partially obscure mirror, whose revelation is so overlaid with mystery that even Christians, beloved brothers of the Son, must wait for full clarity in the life beyond. Now the Son loves his beloved as a spouse. Garbed in our very own flesh, he murmurs tender words of endearment in accents of affection that enkindle hearts, alluring them, Augustine especially, to hurry after his fragrant presence, not just walking but running after the intimate clasp of the all-lovely God-man. In the next life Augustine's mind, become Godlike, will see God not through the heaven that is Scripture but as he is, in his very Godness, an all-consuming vision toward which he now vaults in faith, hope, and charity. Again, the now and then are in tension; or rather, the now that is a not-yet will flower out into the then, in which seeing will be a seeing-as-it-is;[12] the seer made Godlike will coincide with the God seen, lover and beloved fused in one globe of fire.

Chapter 16: Only the Wholly Immutable Can Wholly Know the Wholly Immutable

19. He quickly appends a caveat lest the unwary leap to the faulty conclusion that the glorified mind exhaustively sees God as he is or knows God as absolutely as God knows himself. Only the God who absolutely exists absolutely knows himself. God absolutely exists because he is utterly immutable, immutable as essence or highest existing being, immutable in his knowing, immutable in his willing, which are concretely interwoven as one in his indivisible life. So his existing being knows and wills immutably; his knowing exists and wills immutably; his willing exists and knows immutably. It is analytically unjust to make unequal and equal the same, asserting, say, that $0=1$ or $1=100$. Similarly, it would be analytically unjust for God to appoint a mutable creature, below and unequal to God, to contemplate God in exactly the same measure as the wholly immutable God contemplates himself. Indeed it would be impossible; the mutable creature would have to be incongruously raised to an estate the equivalent of God's—an absurdity since there cannot be two equally supreme beings. Thus the mutable creature is converted into participated light by the immutable creator who is unparticipated light. The glorified mind sees God as he is not in the absolutely immutable manner in which God sees himself, not in an infinite but in a finite mode, by means of light radiating from God. In relation to

God his soul is like parched earth, thirsting to drink water not from itself but from the living God if it is to bear the good fruit of virtue (P 142.11).[43] A mutable deriving its being from the immutable, his soul of itself cannot furnish water for its growth; of itself it cannot bathe itself in light; of itself it cannot fulfill itself. The soul's thirst is satisfied by ceaseless streams; its light is always borrowed light in which it everlastingly sees the changeless light that is God (P 35.13). Total quenching of thirst from the fountain of life; endless enlightenment from God who is light; as in this life, so in the next, Paul's words, often cited by Augustine, ring forever true: man has nothing that he has not received (1 Cor 4.7).

Chapter 17: Bitter Sea Symbolizes Evil Men, Dry Land the Good

20. The sea as bitter with salt is allegorized as the lovers of this world, embittered by evil concerns, all those who unbendingly aim at one end only, happiness in time and on earth. Like the sea, they fluctuate, unstable hearts tossed in innumerable directions, according to varying personal and social interests, yet all riveted on a common goal, felicity here and now that is the overriding motivator in all actions. From another angle, they resemble fish rapaciously devouring one another, the little gobbled up by the big, and the big by the bigger still (P 64.9). In a certain sense, because they pursue a common goal, these misguided persons constitute a common society or community of the evil. The sea as such, however, is good, formed by the mixture of waters, assigned extent and limits according to God's command, the lines between sea and land sharply drawn while at certain junctures the waves break upon themselves, perhaps a reference to the ebb and flow of the tides (Jb 38.10-1). Fixation of the waters' boundaries metaphorically means the restraints on malevolent cupidities; however wild, evil appetites will be reined in, their uninhibited passions balked from inundating the dry land representing good persons.

21. The dry land stands for the community of good persons evident to the all-discerning eye of God that unerringly discriminates light from darkness (13.14.15).[44] These are distinguished from the society of evil persons because, setting their desires on the highest end, they love God first and foremost as well as gratis.[45] God himself waters the

land from the fountain of life, the source of grace that is secret, originating in his transcendent mind, and sweet, issuing in waters free of salt, pure of imperfections, potable and absorbable by the ground, which symbolizes righteous souls thirsting for divine life. Earth made fertile by fresh water figuratively signifies souls that drink the waters of grace disposing them to engender fruit that is virtue. As the earth brings forth edible plants of various types, so the grace-invigorated soul produces various works of mercy according to its, i. e., in accord with the, human condition confronted with human exigencies and privations. The soul is also seed-bearing according to its kind; moved by divine pity, it reaches out to succor others; showering charity on its fellow man deprived of necessities, feeding the hungry, clothing the unclad, visiting and nursing the sick. The soul is seed-bearing according to its likeness also; conscious of its own infirmity in the light of the Golden Rule, the soul envisages itself in similar distressful circumstances, compassionating its neighbor as if it itself were crying out to be compassionated in destitution. As God ordained large fruit-bearing trees, so he commands that some souls function as major protectors of those who fall afoul of, and suffer injustice at the hands of, weighty social authorities. The just judgment of this massive social tree checks and overcomes harm inflicted on the socially feeble and helpless. Here Augustine may be alluding to his role as a fifth-century bishop who daily arbitrated cases, some of which involved shielding members of his flock against the predacity of highly placed figures.[46] On certain occasions he excoriated public officials for their exploitation of the poor, in particular, a certain Romulus who had doubled the taxes he was exacting from *coloni*, the free but grindingly impoverished tillers of the soil under his jurisdiction (E 274.1-4).[47] It was not unlikely that also in his subconscious there bulked the forceful personage of Ambrose who resisted the attempt of the Empress Justina in 386 to expropriate for Arian use a Catholic basilica in Milan (9.7.15); a tower of strength who, never squeamish about admonishing emperors that they were not above but under the law of Christ, personally excommunicated Theodosius because of his wanton slaughter in Thessalonica.[48]

Chapter 18: Lights in Heaven Symbolize Good Works
Produced through Gifts of Spirit

22. God who bestows special powers or gifts along with delight in
fruits borne by gifts, he trusts, will cause truth to arise from the earth,
precipitating virtues that are moral truths in action that sprout in
hearts. Justice, looking down from heaven, justifies human persons in
and through works of mercy since it is mercy that, by imaging divine
pity, wins redemptive mercy covering a multitude of sins (P 95.15).
Mercy to the needy, paid in recompense for mercy God lavishes on
our need, extinguishes sin (S 389.5). Deeds of compassion dispose the
soul to be a light in the firmament or heaven. Feeding the hungry,
sheltering the homeless, and clothing the naked constitute doing the
truth; emergence of the fruit that is good (Gn 1.12) displays the justice
of God reigning in the hearts of persons. Such charity with its fruit of
action on earth readies the soul for the joys of contemplation of the
Scriptural word of life in heaven; the delights, indicated above,
inevitably coursing from the power for doing and contemplating the
truth. As the soul adheres through understanding to the firmament of
Scripture, it becomes a light in the firmament, a light in the world for
a lifetime, to be capped by becoming a light in the timeless "lifetime"
of God.

In trying to unpack Scripture, the spiritual person who is such a
light engages in lovingly irenic discussion with God or, as Augustine
phrases it, God converses with him, God being the truth itself to
whom the inquirer puts questions, toward fathoming messages of
God's Spirit, as in the inquiry prosecuted in Book 12. With God
solving questions posed in prayer, the spiritual person detects the
difference between day and night, between intelligible objects arrived
at by analysis and sensory objects obtained in a sensio-intellectual
mode, and between spirituals, with capacity to expound Scripture,
and carnals whose sense-laden thinking defeats proper conceptu-
alizing of truth. Prior to creation of the firmament God in the
inaccessible recesses of his eternal judgment divided light from
darkness, allegorized as a distinction between elect and lost, between
children of light and darkness (13.14.15). Analogously imitating God,
the spiritual person situated as a light in the firmament distinguishes
light from darkness, yet in a different sense, day and night now
symbolizing the spiritual and carnal man. The spiritual man makes

his entrance only in the New Dispensation, the last act in the history of the world, when grace, no longer restricted to Jews alone, expands in its worldwide epiphany. Lights shining allegorically in the heaven that discriminate between spirituals and carnals, spiritual men also demarcate the times or spiritual seasons, principally Old and New Testament periods.[49] Spirituals understand that, ages of the past gone, they are now new creatures under the New Covenant with its new song and new commandment of love (S 34.1). Spirituals further realize that the age of the New Testament is transitory so that they are nearer to terminal salvation and the general resurrection; the long night of this life drawing to a close is the prologue to everlasting day. Again, God, spirituals perceive, appoints sowers and reapers for the two main eras of salvation, the Old and New Testament. Patriarchs and prophets sowed the seed whose fruit the apostles reaped and, responding to the prayers of his new people, God commissions fresh laborers for the harvest, the apostles and all preachers of the truth who broadcast abroad the seed that is the word of life. The first harvest into which the apostles entered was prepared by Jewish saints of old, who gathered what they sowed. A second sowing still proceeds, to go on until Lord dispatches angels for the final harvest, separating wheat from weeds (P 64.17. J 15.32). Thus the Lord will bless the crown of the year of his mercy, the end of the year standing for the end of time when God's mercy will crown with his victory the elect who are the fruit for harvest of apostolic laborers (P 64.6), thereby answering the prayer that laborers be sent into the harvest. God blesses with fulfilling fruits or virtues the lifetime of the just man, who lives by faith quickened by charity. The "I am who am" unaffected by the erosion of time (P 101[S.2].12), God constructs a granary in which are stored the merits of the fruits or virtues of the years that pass away, the departing years signifying the transient life-spans of the just. Laid up in the granary that is the treasury of heaven are their fruits, works of mercy benefiting needy members with whom Christ is one (S 18.4). God's decree, albeit eternal, is operative in time so that in accord with his wise economy he dispenses heavenly goods, graces that generate fruits of the earth. Bountiful fruits are the outcome of God's abundant gifts; in rewarding merits, God, we noted, is crowning his own gifts (S 299A .19.2; 299B .23.5). Merits deposited in the heavenly granary fructify from generous giving of self that is in a real sense a restoration to God of his own gifts; the storehouse of fruits is a repayment for gifts distributed from the storehouse of divine grace (P 95.15).

23. Taken allegorically, the lights of Gen 1.14-7 signify the gifts of the Holy Spirit listed in 1 Cor 12.4-11. The sun, the greater light that rules the day,[50] represents the word of wisdom, the gift enabling the mind to delight in truth as transparent, contemplated as eternal and immutable (T 12.15.25). The comparatively few vestured in wisdom gaze on the patterns of things laid up in the mind of God, while striving for a vision or intellectual-affective contact with God. Corresponding to the moon, the lesser light, is the word or gift of knowledge, which, unlike wisdom, attends to sensible and temporal objects dealing with action, the application of rational cognition to manage things necessary for maintenance of individual and social life (T 12.12.17). Stars that dot the night sky, including the planets such as Venus, symbolize the other gifts: mountain-moving faith, healing, the power of performing miracles, prophecy, discernment of spirits, and the gift of speaking in tongues.[51] Augustine omits the ninth gift instanced, the interpretation of languages, which is implicit in, because coupled with, glossolalia.[52] Diverse in operations and effects, all of the gifts are worked by the one Holy Spirit for the upbuilding of the body he ensouls (1 Cor 12.7).[53] Whereas 1 Cor 12.7, as usually glossed, holds that all of the charisms are granted for the good of the Church, Augustine considers only the gifts related to the stars (the six latter gifts, beginning with faith) as contributing to its common welfare; probably because each of these is a display of the divine demonstrating in a quasi-ocular manner even to the uneducated the presence of the Spirit in the Church and thereby buttressing the faith of believers and gripping the attention, hopefully dispositive toward conversion, of nonbelievers.   The word of knowledge contains all mysteries or sacraments that vary with time. The sacraments of the Old Law have been superseded by those of the New, which are fewer, more easily administered, more sanctifying, more fruitful, and more conducive to eternal happiness. While Old Testament rites were enacted according to the promise of a savior, the main New Testament sacraments flow from and are principally confected by the savior himself. The commandments, however, remain unaltered because they explicitate man's continuing obligations to serve God (P 73.2). The basic mysteries of the faith, which transcend fluctuations of time, do not undergo change.[54] Knowledge varies like its symbol, that

which waxes and wanes (GL 2.15.32), while the sun, representing wisdom, remains constant. The other six gifts are called *notitiae,* forms of "knowledge" akin to the gift of knowledge. Unlike the word of wisdom and like the word of knowledge, these knowledges vary with time, and pertain to night insofar as their lights only faintly resemble the full brightness of wisdom symbolized by the sun, in which the day rejoices, that is, in which the wise, who attain the full light of truth, delight. So sun or wisdom emerges at the beginning of day; so the moon and stars appear at the beginning of night.[55]

The gift of wisdom is reserved for spirituals, intellectually accoutred for understanding the faith and morally purified. Knowledge and its cognates fall within the ken of carnals, whose thinking is interlaced with and enervated by sensory images, and who, infantlike, can be nourished only by milk since they are not sturdy enough to feed on the solid food accessible to understanding. The distinction between spirituals and carnals was formulated by the Apostle blessed with all the charisms, designated most prudent[56] because, aglow with the Spirit (Rom 12.11), he possessed in the highest degree wisdom, both theoretical and practical, to draw the line between the moral and immoral and, among moral goods, to differentiate the means of growth among spirituals and carnals (ME1.15.25.ExR 49). Though carnals cannot visualize the sun that symbolizes truth[57] and are incapable of contemplating eternal truths that make up the realm of wisdom, they can remain satisfied with the lesser illumination afforded by the moon and stars that stand for the word of knowledge and associated gifts. As Augustine was engaged in a wondrous contemplation (contemplation, because geared to eternal truths; wondrous, because divinely germinated), his inner vision caught the spiritual nuances just commented on, seizing all the eternal truths lying below the surface, yet with an understanding of things eternal under temporal conditions, in a soul and body still trekking through time, marked by celestial signs that specify seasons, days, and years. In the next life he will, along with the angels, see with light given by the One eternal truths not in a temporal but in an eternal mode (13.15.18).

Chapter 19: Exhortation to Detachment and to Living as Lights of the World

24. In the adapted words of Isaiah Augustine urges a three-step program for acquiring wisdom. First, the soul is to purge itself of serious sin and empty itself of worldly desires; this cleansing suppresses the bitter sea so that the dry land, the foundation of virtue, can be formed, then become hospitable to God's action. Second, the seeker of God should expend mercy on the needy, deprived of goods and bereft of family; thus does the land bring forth plants and the fruit-bearing tree. Third, inwardly healed and outwardly compassionate, the pursuer of wisdom is motivated to prayerfully unravel the obscurities of Scripture; contemplating God in God's word, he becomes a light in the firmament, a luminary radiating the light of God to others.

Unhappily, the rich young man let slip through his fingers a golden opportunity to enrich himself when he turned down the invitation to become perfect, a Christian mature in wisdom. Christ demurred at being called good because the young man deemed him a great prophet no more than human; and because his human nature, while good, was only secondarily and instrumentally good, owing its goodness to the Father who, as absolutely immutable, is utterly perfect. All creatures, including the divinized humanity of Jesus, are derivatively good, recipients of the goodness effected by God (S 15.5.5). Christ taught the young inquirer that conquest of eternal life demanded, first, repudiation of sins proscribed by the commandments, a purgation begetting the dry land divided from the bitter sea of malice, and, second, reverence for parents and love of neighbor, these latter exemplifying fruits of mercy. Addiction to wealth, however, restrained him from taking a third crucial step that would unlock the door to wisdom. Though he strictly observed the commandments, his yield of fruit was only short-lived; clusters of thorn bushes in his heart, representing avarice, threatened to rob the ground of nourishment and choke virtue. Christ counseled him to tear up the avarice by the roots, the upshot being not loss but gain (S 389.4), for in exchange for fleeting temporal baubles he would amass eternal wealth, assured of elevation to the perfection that is wisdom. Like the Lord, he would, with a participated wisdom, judge spiritually, differentiating spirituals from carnals, precisely understanding the various gifts of the Spirit shining in the firmament that is Scripture. But to develop in wisdom he would have to set his heart on treasures enshrined in eternal truths rather than in earthly holdings. Unfortunately, so impoverished was he by riches, so tenaciously possessed by possessions, that even the magnetic allure of Christ's appeal was nullified. Fertile only with infertility, the earth that was his heart collapsed into sadness; from fetters of riches were woven thorns that strangled any further advance in virtue, effectively killing the seed that was the word of the Lord.

It hardly seems irrelevant to suggest that the failure of one rich young man may lend additional sparkle to the success of another, who, under the irresistible force of Monica's prayers (5.9.17), finally heeded the teacher's invitation to sell all and follow him. Not actually but potentially affluent in this world's goods, he exhibited a wealth of character in triumphing over the triple concupiscence. He was unbelievably rich also in a sense to which, early on, even his subconscious afforded few clues; a Croesus of intellect working with nearly inexhaustible energy that would effortlessly execute ideas; the many veins ramifying from his lode have been and are still tapped to supply capital for the Christian theological economy.

25. Members of the body of Christ are a "chosen race" that yearns for full union with God in Christ (P 118[S.20].1); a people that, including poor as well as opulent, are, like the first disciples, feeble as was Jesus in the eyes of the world (S 281.1); a Church initially comprised not of emperors but fishermen that still boasts of the lowly in its ranks (S 250.1). Specifically incited to increased apostolic zeal are spirituals, who, emulating the first disciples, have forsaken all so that, weak in self but strong in Christ, they may confound the mighty with otherworldly prowess. The material possessions abandoned were trivial, but the inner riches with which they gained sway over cupidity have to be estimated enormous (S 301A.2). The bearers of the word are the beautiful feet of the Lord, mainly the apostles, but derivatively all evangelizers (P 90[S.2].8). Moreover, allegorically regarded, the heavens are the apostles who proclaim God's redemptive glory that abides in Christ, communicated through grace gratuitously given; *quia gratis, ideo gratia* (P 18[En.2].2). Apparently preachers also function as heavens that blaze abroad the glory of God's mercy.

Spirituals, to whose height of wisdom it is appointed to judge, differentiate the light of the spiritually mature, who are only relatively perfect,[58] from the darkness of little ones, only relative because lit by faith, a darkness wholly distinct from that of nonbelievers barren of hope in eternal life (S 172.1.1). Both day and night illuminate the earth, the daylight diffusing the word of wisdom, the light of moon and stars conveying the word of knowledge. The night light of knowledge is a practical wisdom segregating Christians from the darkness, invigorating them to live in union with God amid a perverse people that constitutes this world (P 135.8). As night does not extinguish stars, so night that is wickedness does not quench lights that are the faithful cleaving to the firmament of Scripture (P 93.29). Unseduced, Christians with knowledge emit exemplary truth in the world, illumining it according to night's capacity to accept and not fend off the light (P 146.9).

In creating lights in the heavens, God, according to one theory, shaped fires or units of fire. Advocates of the opinion that the firmament or heaven is pure fire hypothecate that the stars and lights, or heavenly bodies, are composed of fiery light, molded and distributed in the forms of fire observable in the firmament (GL 2.3.6).[59] Allegorically interpreted, in putting lights in the firmament, God was, in effect, fashioning tongues of fire that settled on Christians, thereby making them units of fire who steadfastly witness to the Scriptural word of salvific life in the teeth of a degenerate world. Hence these are holy fires because sanctified by the Holy Spirit's gift; beautiful, because they are to enkindle in hearts the kerygma of order unto peace, the reconciling message of forgiving love. Modeled after Christ whose Spirit inflames them, they are to be fires casting more fire on the earth (Lk 12.49), running like wild fire among their fellows with an ardor that will set ablaze with truth and love even the hearts of enemies (P 96.7). Hearts may be closed to the iron sword, but none are hardened against souls of fire who fight with fire (P 95.2). Kindled by the Spirit, each Christian is designed to shine publicly; a light to be lifted high by Christ the light exalted in his glory. Here the term "word" undergoes a shift; it is Christ the Word of life whom Christians who are holy fires hold fast unwaveringly as stars maintain their courses. As evils never force stars to deviate from their regular procession, so evils are powerless to cause religious luminaries to compromise resolute devotion. But this word or Word is not simply to be hugged to their bosom; in a missionary spirit they are to spread it to all peoples, their lights begetting other lights, their fires setting others on fire, and these, in turn, igniting still others into fresh fires.

This section, notice, does not address its appeal for evangelization exclusively to spirituals. The carnals or little ones beam knowledge in the night that is a world awash in sin, and, while to apostles and preachers is assigned the principal work in disseminating the Gospel, lesser lights of knowledge practically proclaim the word of life by livingly witnessing to the truth. Though with less intensity than apostles and preachers, they are conglomerates of fire whose heavenly incandescence penetrates the darkness of earthly night.

Chapter 20: Symbols of Sacraments, Miracles, and Evangelizers

26. Tying his comments to the lights in the last chapter, he briefly directs remarks to the spiritually wise: signaling the superiority of the living creature or soul to fish and birds, they have divided the precious (the living soul enlivened by grace) from the vile (beings lower than man, which stand for those incapable of being graced) and have undertaken a prophetic task, not a foretelling but a forth-telling-of-the-truth mission similar to that of Jeremiah (Jer 15.19). At this stage there emanate from the sea not living souls but fish and birds.

Fish symbolize the sacraments, in particular, baptism, that sanctify the people of God. Through the apostolic zeal of lights of the world, who in their holiness administer baptism, baptisms swim among the temptations or waves of evil in the world to supernaturally cleanse all nations in its Spirit-filled waters. In other words, all nations are swept along in the waves or flux of passions in the sea that is the world; the fish, standing for baptisms administered, weave through the menacing sea, saving peoples from destruction by their laving regeneration. Correlated with and supporting the birth of new Christians through baptism were *magnalia mirabilia*, super-prodigious marvels, perhaps suggesting *magnalia Dei* (Ac 2.11); miracles symbolized by sea monsters, which confirmed the presence and power of the true God in the sacramental enactment. Proclaiming the New Covenant were the voices of messengers, the apostles and first disciples, pictured as birds of the air, who were mandated to teach the new revelation everywhere, along or under (not in) the firmament standing for the Scriptures,[60] the authority at whose behest and with whose warranty they were charged to fly over the whole earth, there being no language in which the messengers of God have not communicated the divine word. From the moment that under the Pentecostal prompting of the Spirit the apostles spoke in the tongues of all peoples present, the Good News has never stopped sounding from Jerusalem to all over the globe (P18[En.2].5). God so blessed the office of preachers that, by a kind of spiritual law of reproduction, through a divine call to special service, evangelizers have increased and multiplied throughout the centuries, members of a celibate priesthood proving remarkably fecund in spiritual posterity.

The symbolic liaison between creeping creatures of the sea and baptism, which may seem somewhat contrived, apparently arises from a conflation of Ac 2.1-12, 38-41 and Mk 16.15-8, whose import is applied to an allegorical account of Gn 1.20-1.[61] After invoking the Pentecost event as a source of the lights of wisdom and knowledge (13.19.25), Augustine allegorically exposits the following verses in Genesis, considering the operation of the charisms as a means for expanding the Church through baptism of new members (Ac 2.38-41. Mk 16.15). Prior to baptism evangelizers expound truth sealed with the authority of the Scripture (Ac 2.4, 14-36. Mk 16.15), the divine origin of their preaching and of the sacrament of rebirth authenticated by miracles bearing the signature of God (Ac 2.11. Mk 16.17-8). The living things emerging from the sea function as symbols of the preaching, sacraments, and miracles. While the allegorical kinship of birds and sea monsters with evangelizers and miracles seems permissively apt, the comparison of creeping things of the sea with baptisms may not appear altogether felicitous; perhaps this unusual parallel inevitably results from the narrow constraints of the logic of his allegorical interpretation.

27. In case an unintended one-sided stress on variance in foregoing sections may disconcert, by misleading, some readers, Augustine hastens to add that he is not lying, not watering down the invariance of Catholic doctrine by mixing changeless truths with changing ingredients.[62] By calling attention to the sharp line between lights in the firmament and the corporeal actions under the firmament, he makes it clear that unchanging truths above are not rendered mutable by physical actions in the fluctuating sea that is the world below the firmament. The objects on which wisdom and knowledge[63] focus are

fixed, not subject to flux, and determined, needing no further refinements that might be appended by successive generations. These notions, eternal truths in the case of wisdom, firm commandments to be applied to conduct in the case of knowledge, are changeless; in themselves they undergo no growth; in themselves they are unalterably true, like 7+3=10 or the definition of justice (LA 2.10.28; 12.34). However, physical actions such as sacramental rites have been manifold and variable.[64] As noted earlier, sacraments of the Old Law were replaced by those of the New; circumcision gave way to baptism, and the rite of the Passover lamb prefigured, and was fulfilled in, the spiritual reality that is the sacramental sacrifice of the Lamb of God (CF 19.11). Through divine blessing the sacraments increased and multiplied,[65] and the sacraments of the New Testament were "reproduced by", developed out of, the sacraments of the Old. Moreover, in the New Testament there are many sacraments, differentially designed to meet multiple needs and various stages and vocations in the human pilgrimage. God constructs the sacraments to adapt his unchanging notations or truths to the changing sensory condition of man. Through the sacraments God eases the tedium of sensory knowledge which, bound to particulars, is slowly acquired in a drawn-out process. Divine consolation re-energizes the sagging self by employing sensible signs to register supersensible truth: physical movements that in diverse ways concretely symbolize one notation expressing one spiritual reality. Unlike rites connected with a pagan cult, these are not false but true sacraments. In fact, stemming from the word of God and propagated in revelation mediated through Christ, they are necessary because aliens traveling in sensory conditions remote from their homeland in which abides eternal truth are constrained to rely on sensory indicators of truth; and because an aboriginal malady afflicts the human race: the sensible signs that are sacramental rites emerged from the waters to heal the bitter legacy, the fallen situation of man.

28. The whole universe and its tiniest unit are perfectly ordered and harmonious because crafted by the hands of the divine artist. Their beauty is only a feeble finite flickering of their maker's infinite beauty, so inexpressible that all thought falters, all speech stammers, in groping to articulate its super-ravishing splendor.

If Adam had not sinned, he and Eve would have enjoyed fecundity and fertility, procreating offspring not ordained to die (R 1.13.8).[66] In fact, prior to the Fall they did not engage in nuptial union, either because the interval between their creation and first sin was short or because they were awaiting a direct command from God (GL 9.4.8). Unhappily, Adam did fall, and in his fall all human beings fell. His disobedience rooted in pride was the original sin, the loss of original justice that is endemic in the race. Original sin as historically intrinsic to man's present condition is universal and all- pervasive. The state of original sin is the bitter saltiness of the sea coursing from the bosom, literally the womb, of Adam.[67] Among its acrid consequences is a radical susceptibility to the triple concupiscence: curiosity that is an abyss, a region of darkness for those hankering after the sensually spectacular or pseudo-scientific (such as gulls of Manicheism and astrology); the storminess that is pride, so pictured because pride that is swollen erupts in discord; the uncontrolled flow of the passions, especially the libidinal bespeaking lust of the flesh, its inconstancy resembling the ceaseless to-and-fro of ocean waves. Apart from the Fall there would have ensued no triple concupiscence that called for healing through mystical, i. e., supernatural, work and word, through sacraments (principally baptism, fundamental in Christian initiation) and preaching, administered by servants of God. As humans, dispensers of these healing agencies carry out their office along corporeal lines, in a sensory medium, since they are active in the manifold waters, the human milieu of a physical world. Creeping things and birds stand for the sacrament of baptism and authority-sanctioned preachers (13.20.26). But baptism and initial instruction, however indispensable and valuable, designate only the outset of Christian life. Submission to corporeal rites is intended to ripen into a more abundant life on the plane of the spirituals. The baptized person should hunger for further growth, setting his sights on consummatory Christian living, Christian maturity achieved by spirituals who are theoretically and affectively wise; wise in understanding Christian truths and wise in harnessing affections under the aegis of love.[68] Ideally such a ripened Christian exemplifies the living soul exposited in the following chapter.

Chapter 21: Living Soul Symbol of Mature Christian

29. Because of this, that is, in view of the Christian growth to adulthood ordained in the divine plan, the earth set apart from the

bitter sea engendered a living soul that symbolizes the relatively perfect or full-fledged Christian. Creeping things and fowl from the sea were required for the first propagation of Christian truth preparatory to baptism of unbelievers. Baptism that was necessary in the beginning to wash the soul clean of the bitterness of the sea, the sinful lot bequeathed by the Fall, is the basic means for entering the kingdom of heaven from the time when Christ so instituted it (S 71.12). Prior to his advent, when of course baptism was not prescribed, some vehicle for healing infants from original sin, probably some sacrament, was available for those in the state of nature who had faith in the mediator who was to come in the flesh (CJ 5.11.45); and under the Old Law circumcision had the efficacy to purify infants of original sin, functioning for pre-Christian saints in place of baptism (NC 2.11.24. E 187.11.34). At first *magnalia Dei* (Ac 2.11) mighty marvels, were necessary to solidly implant the new way, but now in a Church on firm footing the living soul does not reckon on prodigies nor does its assent hinge on frequent outpouring of signs and wonders. Though miracles continue, they are not proportionally as numerous and varied as the marvels Christ wrought in his brief public career. The living soul believes the word of Christ in spite of the comparative paucity of signs and is therefore blessed because, not seeing, it believes. Since the Church has sunk its roots deep and far, a copious proliferation of pristine signs and wonders is not requisite to help spark faith. Now that the Church is flourishing, a gift like Spirit-inspired speaking in foreign languages is no longer operative in official Church worship. The gift of tongues that amazed the first converts at Pentecost, a charism so pronounced in the Corinthian assembly, disappeared from official usage in later centuries. The passage of time definitively verified Paul's words; tongues is a sign to attract unbelievers at the beginning; but once the Church grows vigorous, the faith of believers no longer depends on such a pointer. Specifically, the gift of tongues presaged that all tongues would believe in Christ; now that the sign has been fulfilled in the reality, the universal spread of the Church, this wondrous charism ceased to play a part in regular worship (P 130.5). Once the earth was raised above the sea, once the Church was supernaturally stabilized above the world, the first apostles and evangelists, symbolized by winged creatures produced from the waters, were no longer needed. The time set for a profusion of awesome phenomena passed; so the trailblazing workers of miracles finished their appointed mission.

When death silenced the voices of these first messengers (13.20.26), the office of preaching the word, now directed toward formation of living souls, fell to new generations of messengers. Augustine may recount the evangelical works of these successors as if they were primarily theirs, but they are ministers, vessels of God's potency, quasi-apostles commissioned in his name and with his power; it is God who works in them to preach and to accomplish their call. Insofar as the message is channeled through the mediator, Christ speaks through the latter-day disciples; the faithful hearing those sent hear his voice (J 47.5). Surely since they labor in the vineyard, the living soul or mature Christian is the outcome of their work, but only secondarily; the primary artisan applies them as his instruments; the principal producer of the living soul is God and, in mediatorial union with the Father, Christ. Like the sea, which is the matrix out of which creeping things and the first birds (the sacraments and apostolic preachers and wonder-workers) thrust up, so from the earth, the Church as institutionalized with baptized members, emerges the living soul. As just remarked, once firmly founded, the Church does not require a recurring exhibition of spectacular phenomena. Yet in one sense it is still fed by nutrition from the sea: the living soul, the mature Christian, daily consumes the Fish that is the Eucharist; in Greek the acrostic for Jesus Christ as Son and Savior (*Iesous Xpeistus Theou Uios Soter*) is IXTHUS or fish (CD 18.23). The Christ raised up out of the deep that is the human condition, the Christ who is exalted in humbling himself unto death for sin, is brought to the table of believers, prepared for the mature who, no longer drinking milk of infants, eat the food of wisdom on which spirituals feed, adult food for strength in spiritual combat (P 22.5). In being lifted high on the cross, Jesus was exalted in glory, so that his saving life might be the food of spirituals on the earth. Similarly, birds, which took their rise from the sea, increase and multiply on earth to sanctify not by sacrament but by word. Expressed otherwise, the first evangelists originated from the sea that was the world to preach repentance leading to baptism, then multiplied, counting on spiritual descendants, later generations of evangelists, through whose sermonizing, since it is grounded on the New Testament, the first evangelists still exhort, i. e., practically apply truths to the faithful, for the successors expound truths packed in the original evangelists' discourses. The later evangelists, because supernaturally increased and multiplied, bless the faithful. Since it is first at Gn 1.22, then at Gn 1.28, that God is said to bless birds and men respectively with the imperative, "Increase and multiply," the highest and proper sense of blessing is enshrined in multiplication; the main meaning and efficacy of benediction are evidenced in multiplication (P 66.9). In Christ God has blessed man through multiplying his adopted sons and, after the model of the first evangelists, has blessed Christians by multiplying later evangelists whose preaching lights up and inflames minds. The blessings that recur not yearly or seasonally but daily rain down from day to day in another sense, from the day of time to the day of eternity, invigorating the faithful who daily feed on Gospel-centered preachments to persevere unto the end that assures eternal salvation (P 60.10). Each of the faithful so blessedly exhorted is a living soul, or spiritual, that rises not from the sea or infidelity but from the earth, a Christian not only converted and baptized but consecrated to a life of the charity and piety[69] that ideally typify the adult Christian. Before, the soul was immersed in delights, inordinate desires shared with cattle, indulgence in pleasures like gluttony, drunkenness, and fornication, fatal because they severed the soul from the life that is God. Now, curbing aberrant affections by continence, the soul lives according to piety, according to charity toward God and neighbor, (S 229V.1). In fine, the living soul wholly devoted to the all-good, joy in whom bestows not death but true superabounding life, is hallowed with a pure heart, simple or single in focus and object (SDM 1.2.8).

30. Because embarked on the momentous mission of converting individuals all over the world swirled about in the bitter sea of unbelief, the first dispensers of the Good News were provided with extraordinary Spirit-prompted means to engender conversion, often performing miracles, manifesting sacred signs, and resorting to mystical words, that is, Spirit-gifted utterance in foreign languages, to promote and validate the divine message proclaimed. Ignorance is the mother of wonder, an adage possibly coined by Augustine or perhaps borrowed from a Latin writer, which echoes a line from Aristotle, that science begins in wonder or puzzlement about the reason for specific facts or configurations, the mind probing why solstices occur and why the diagonal of a square is incommensurable with the side.[70] Wonder is the beginning of science, science the end of wonder. As natural events arouse wonder, moving the scientist to

hunt for specific causes of the regular run of things, so supernatural phenomena such as miracles and glossolalia capture the attention of and excite wonder in the ordinary person who is basically a religious animal. After being rendered fearful or awestruck by these unusual occurrences, his puzzlement ends not in science but in faith; he believes the kerygma because it is sealed with the divine warranty of stupendous miracles and speaking in tongues. Prior to Christ people shrouded in unbelief were children of Adam, like Adam after the Fall hiding from God because of their sin. Evil ways drove them away from God, blotting him out of memory. Thus did they turn into an abyss, tossed about by the whirlpools of lower goods. Happily, these prisoners of darkness (unbelief) or flux (carnal conduct) were intrigued by astounding signs, which transformed wonderment born of ignorance into convinced faith.

Unlike pioneering ministers of the word, preachers in post-apostolic times mainly marshal their efforts not to attract unbelievers to conversion but to shepherd little ones up to the advanced level of Christian maturity. Though not extraordinarily gifted by the Spirit, they must be, like their ancestors, proficient in wisdom and charity, serving as models through lived-out love of God, a concrete vision that fuels admiration that is imitation. Hearing the word that is to be translated into action is stimulated by a living word whose voice trumpets the word loudly but whose actions enfleshing his message boom out the word even more loudly. So do little ones grasp the truth: "Seek God, and your soul shall live"; perceiving in their morally strapping preachers exemplary God-seekers, they nourish themselves on the Lord who is the living bread whereby their souls grow toward maturity (P 68[S.2].17).

A preacher retains virtue by repelling enticements of the world, in particular, by conquering the triple concupiscence. The preacher is bade to first practice continence in the most general sense, restraining his heart from enamourment of this world, which is spiritually deadly (13.21.29); rejection of the world leads to life, misguided love to death. The beasts, cattle, and serpents of Gn 1.24-5 are allegorized in terms of the triple concupiscence; the living soul is urged to exercise continence in a more specialized sense, controlling lust of the flesh, lust of the eyes, and pride of life (10.30.41. P 8.13).[71] Wild beasts vividly betoken the enormous ferocity of pride, which here connotes lust for domination and its attendant cruelty, so notorious among some brutal Roman emperors (2.6.13). Cattle geared exclusively to animal pleasures stand for self-absorption in total sensuality. Serpents represent false curiosity that is ersatz knowledge, observation of odd objects like monsters, or knowledge evoked by bloody spectacles, or insight into the inscrutable future peddled by the scientific quacks called astrologers; all sought not for truth but for sheerly subjective pleasure (10.35.54-5). First, the wild beasts become meek; pride cedes place to humility, which, in turn, gives birth to meekness, the opposite of the will to power, the meek being ambitionless, content to rest in their proper station. Instead of trampling upon others in ruthless pursuit of power, the meek overcome evil with good; at peace with the eternal God, they refuse to battle over temporal concerns (SDM 1.2.4). Second, cattle are domesticated; carnal appetites are tamed for the good of the soul. Third, continence renders the serpents harmless; the sting of false curiosity is extracted, opening the mind to healthy curiosity. Impulses like desires for food and drink and pleasurable objects, along with the tendency to know, are movements of the soul, which, when governed by right reason, are good; only when they slip free of the bridle of reason illumined by faith are these inclinations debased into domineering pride, pleasure-enslaved cupidity, and poisonous curiosity. Such warped desires are the movements of a dead soul; not of course psychologically dead—otherwise there could be no movement whatsoever—but morally dead, empty of the life of God because strangulated by delights of the flesh (13.21.29). Quitting the life of its life, the soul is swept up, through its skewed impulses, in temporal currents, capitulating to the world. In contradistinction to disaggregating inclinations that tyrannize the soul, continence integrates the soul's desires, making them one in the One that is God (10.29.40).

31. Unlike seductive words that bewitch the soul downward into the flux, the word of God gushes forth from a fountain of everlasting life and therefore does not pass away. Released from trammels of this world, the soul can become a living soul through the font of life that is grace or, in the idiom of Genesis, the earth produces a living soul, victorious over the triple concupisence. Vitalized through evangelists' preaching and practice, the soul casts itself in a Christ-mold by duplicating the Christlike virtues in his mirror-images that are his preachers. As cattle and serpents physically reproduce according to their kind, so living souls morally reproduce by imitation, according

to their kind. Since brothers and sisters in the body of Christ are broadly spiritual friends in the Lord, living souls are begotten according to the mode of friendship; a friend strives to copy character traits of his friend (GLI 16.59). Thus did Paul entreat his Galatian converts: become like me, as I have imitated Christ by conforming my life to him and his Gospel. Actually Paul is pleading with his converts not to be mature Christians but to become wholly nonJudaic in ritual, adjuring them not to reintroduce the obsolete rite of circumcision. Adaptively read, Paul is making the point: follow me in religious belief and conduct as I have followed you in social identity. Underlying his appeal is his friendship with the Galatians; bonded as we are as friends, he reasons, we should imitate one another, making your own my Christian (nonJewish) word and deed as I have made my own your Gentile (nonJewish) class.

Conformity of the wrong sort, it may be remarked in extenso, can be suffocating. Slavish imitation of an immoral model demeans, even degrades, a personality. But through authentic conformity the soul bursts out of the straitjacket of the old man, liberating its heart from the dictatorship of the lower passions, and thereby releases its true ego, the form planned by God. Because individually differentiated, imitation does not issue in sheer cloning or stereotypical replication of the original. Each imitator of Christ images him in a unique, inimitable way. As G.K. Chesterton somewhere observed, saints are more diverse in kind than murderers. Correspondingly, each imitation singularly reenacts the life of Christ, its inner countenance shining with a unique lineament of the holy face. Each Christian configures himself after the incarnate Son of God not by being reduced to a replaceable carbon copy but by ripening into a fully free saint with a small s, in some measure holy as Christ is holy. An outstanding imitator of Christ, the great Paul, bearing in his body the signs of the crucified, unflinchingly endured hunger, thirst, shipwreck, persecution, every sort of suffering within and without, in total love of God and consecration to Christ, in self-sacrificing love of neighbor that made him all things to all (S 16A.10). Though plainly not every preacher can aspire to be as wholly self-spending, one should be thoroughly good in work as well as word, not only proclaiming but loving and living peace (S 101.11). The faithful are to reproduce actions of only the sincere while, as regards unfortunate preachers who do not self-denyingly live out the word, they should heed the Lord's injunction, doing what they say rather than what they do (S 101.10-1).

Union with and radical imitation of Christ imply conquest of wayward drives; properly regulated, passional tendencies become structural components of the character of the living soul. Disciplined, the raging beast of domination grounded in pride is converted into a dynamic force of meekness rooted in humility. Again, self-control in the guise of temperance changes cattle or sensual drives into sound desires, the appetite for pleasures so firmly checked that the proper amount of food is eaten for bodily sustenance and energy for work. To bolster his point, Augustine adapts a line from Paul on the morally objective use of food earlier offered to idols. As the consumer of such food gains no special benefit and the nonconsumer suffers no loss, so the temperate do not grow morally better by eating or morally worse by not eating since food as such is not a strict moral good.[72] By the standard of temperance food is a lower-order or instrumental good to be utilized for proper care of a body in the service of a soul subordinate to God. The person of intemperance, whose indulgence in food and sex is malordered, effectively values these as intrinsic goods, to be sought for their own sake since for the sensual person eating fetches superabounding bliss, with deprivation of food a pit of misery. Governance of right reason also transmutes bad into good serpents, by replacing false with commendable curiosity, which, far from corrupting thirst for knowledge with a toxic fever for the sensational, aims at decoding the makeup of the temporal universe. This wholesome strain is serpentine-wise; as the astute serpent sheds its old skin, the God-seeker is enjoined to strip himself of the old man, thereby disposing self toward development in moral perspicacity (P 57.10). Religiously astute, genuine curiosity circumspectly steers clear of a search for causes of temporal phenomena that lured some pagan astronomers to avert their eyes from God and, in some cases, slip into idolatry (5.3.5). It explores temporal natures or physical substances subject to time, determining their patterns and workings so as to trace their nexus with eternal causes. The three modes of desire depicted by beasts, cattle, and serpents are so rectified by reason that they are restrained from hurtling down tracks that spell moral death, and, so spared, spiritually adorn the living soul.

Chapter 22: Man Made in God's Image, Principally the Spiritual Man

32. An individual becomes a living soul in two stages. First, as set forth in the preceding chapter, a person turning his back on meretricious delights that spiritually kill the soul curbs passions by continence, resisting the specious pulls of the triple temptation, in line with Paul's injunction to renounce conformity to the world. The second stage, ordained in Gn 1.26, calls for the complement of aversion from the world: total reformation, radical remaking of heart.[73] Significantly, the text does not state, as did Gn 1.25, "according to his kind." The soul that is living is not transmuted by imitation of mere man, whether this model be an older individual revered because of his years or a contemporary, superior not in age but in virtue.[74] Unquestionably the latter's moral excellence commands respect and elicits emulation, but in God's plan the Christian is not to fashion himself after a man sheerly as man. Rather, he is enjoined to image God either through Christ the mediator or through a saintly Christian who authentically reflects Christ. So the import of the text is: let us make man according to our divine image and likeness, not according to a pure human likeness. Transformed into divine life, Christians are equipped to prove, i.e., to test and experientially ascertain, what God prescribes, verifying the moral-spiritual pathways of goodness and perfection God lays down for them. In short, renovated into godlike beings and hospitable to grace, Christians will become spirituals. Paul spiritually fathered converts as his Gospel children; as an apostle of Mother Church, he also mothered fledgling Christians, nursing these tiny ones with milk (P 49.27). But his overriding purpose was to foster their growth into spirituals, adult enough to determine on their own, without dependence on substitutional guidance, indicators of the will of God.

Because capital, the point is reiterated that for Genesis man is made not according to kind but according to God's image since man is specially bonded to and oriented toward his maker.[75] Undoubtedly man is shaped after his proper type, being neither angel nor ape but a rational animal that occupies a median station in creation.(1.1.1). However, man is destined for a higher estate, called to be qualitatively deified. Allegorically interpreted, "to our image and likeness" means that man, particularly the spiritual, is remade after the pattern of divine fulfillment. Since he is divinely alive, he is excepted from human guidance, such as, we saw, would stem from a predecessor or a compeer distinguished for virtue. The spiritual trains his gaze on truth, and because God, his teacher, inwardly leads him, he can discern the authentic will of God working in concrete personalties and events. Mentally and morally refined, the spiritual has the capacity, as the carnal does not, to be tutored by God, understanding to some degree the trinity of unity, that there are three relations in the one divine nature, and the unity of the trinity, that the one divine nature is common to Father, Son, and Holy Spirit. The plural "us" (Gn 1.26) connotatively hints at the trinity while the singular "God" (Gn 1.27) indicates the unity. Similarly, "to our image" (v.26) bespeaks the trinity whereas "to the image of God" betokens unity. With his intellection of the triune God the spiritual catches adumbrations of the holy three, foreshadowings that in an allegorical setting, albeit vaguely, spiritually point to the trinity in the very first book of Scripture. Moreover, renewal authorizes him to judge all things not absolutely but relatively, such as all objects that fall within his constricted ambit. Furthermore, as already touched on, the spiritual, divinely directed, not made or remade according to humankind, is not subject to the judgment of mere man.

Accent on the independence of spirituals, grounded in their illuminated subjectivity, should not be misconstrued. The claim that the spiritual, detached from need of man, turns to God alone for light that certifies understanding of divine truth may carry, for some, a ring of anti-institutionalism, apparently portending elements of the peculiar inner-light doctrine propagated over twelve centuries later by George Fox (1624-91), the founder of the Quakers.[76] However, the context dispels suspicion of a shallow illuminism. Members of the Church, (13.12.13; 23.33), spirituals are gifted with the word of wisdom and carnals with the word of knowledge, both charisms bestowed for the general welfare of the Church (13.18.23). Moreover, the distinction between spiritual and carnal is explicitly adopted from St. Paul, who codifies the two as stages of growth in apprehending Church doctrine. Again, texts outside the *Confessions* confirm the ecclesial mise-en-scène; spirituals rest on the rock-solid pronouncements of the mountains that are the apostles (P 103 [S.3].5). Moreover, the author of these lines was a committed bishop, hardly liable to subvert an institution in whose hierarchy he serves. True,

God instructs the spiritual within, by special illumination streaming from infinite light; this is the epistemic mode of learning, or development in understanding, to which Augustine appeals frequently in Books 10 and 12, without the slightest suggestion of deconstructing the Church. The indispensable Church is one with the total Christ, the treasury of divine life and doctrine. Outward presentation of doctrine, prior to inward illumination, presupposes the Church that is the body of Christ. Per contra, the inner-light thesis of George Fox and his followers was one logical consequence of the abolition of the visible Church by the Reformers. If the visible Church disappears, with Scripture relegated to a secondary role, sacramental rites and ministers can also be discarded, so that each believer draws enlightenment and infallible doctrinal authority for his judgments and actions directly and immediately from God himself.

In sum, messengers of God's word, spirituals are sent to carnals as angels from heaven to earth (13.12.13); and "aglow with the Spirit" (Rom 12.11), are living fires like Stephen; instruments through which is imparted the Spirit of Jesus, who came to cast fire on the earth (Lk 12.49) and now dispatches ministers full of fire to spread this love (13.19.25. P 103[S.1].16). Moreover, spirituals resemble birds flying in the free air, who enjoy the serenity of heaven but rest and feed on the mountains,[77] whose rocks symbolize the firmament of precepts, all dependent on the one rock that is Christ; mountains that also stand for the apostles and all preachers of truth. Furthermore, as they judge all, they dwell in peace, not divided as are carnals between Peter and Paul. Finally, imitating the imitators of Christ, spirituals participate in the authority of the saints, with no subjection to sheer human authority (P 103[S.3].5). It goes without saying that spirituals, who are ordinarily not confirmed in grace, are not ipso facto candidates for canonization; should they relapse, they have to be born and nursed anew in the faith (P 49.27).

Chapter 23: Limits and Scope of a Spiritual's Judgment

33. Higher than other animals not in virtue of unsurpassed sensory activity but in virtue of mind, man is lord of the earth, a steward charged to exercise dominion over lower animals. Happily, a spiritual, concentrating graced understanding on spiritual features of the new creation, is geared to observe lineaments proper to the Spirit

of God. On the other hand, man made in God's image to rule beasts may morally slump to the level of beasts. Tossed about in the transitory, obsessed with memorializing, after death, his name in marble monuments, he lives and dies, in effect, with no more apprehension of the supersensible and timeless than animals locked in the hard shell of the senses (P 48[S.1].16;[S.2].11). Like every redeemed individual, every spiritual is the handiwork of God, formed by creation, then, after human deformation, reformed by recreation, his fruition caused by the all-good Spirit active in and through him. So pervasive is grace unto good works that not only Church authorities such as bishops and priests but also subjects of authority such as the unordained may wield the judgment deputed to spirituals. Church governance being hierarchical, only a small number can rule, but, the activity of spiritual judgment being quasi-democratic, the grace proper to a spiritual is comparatively unrestricted, inspiriting souls in every organ of the Church, lowly artisan as well as bishop, mother making a home as well as priest dispensing sacraments. Both male and female are one in the one man who is head of the whole Christ, all acting virilely, i. e., with full power, in Christ Jesus. When functioning as spirituals, they remain male and female in grace, yet spiritually the distinction that connoted the superiority of the male is nullified or transcended. In Christ a woman can be the spiritual equal, or equal as a spiritual; and some women are called to be spirituals while many men are not so favored. As the inequality between man and woman is spiritually repealed, so the religious difference implying superiority of Jew to Greek is surmounted and the social gap between free man and slave spiritually bridged.

The range of spirituals' adjudicative power does not encompass the whole of the Church or all of its actual or potential members. First, spirituals cannot pass judgment on various gifts of cognition such as wisdom, knowledge, prophecy, discernment of spirits, and so forth, for these are distributed according to a will that cannot fall under the arbitrament of even spiritual persons. Spirituals are clearly not entitled to sit in judgment on the operations of the Holy Spirit whose judgment enacted these gifts and whose grace in Christ makes them spirituals (13.18.23). Located in the spiritual firmament, the authority of such gifts is sublime, and is therefore the source, not the subject, of spirituals' judgment; it is an authority whose own source is super-sublime, the Holy Spirit himself.[78] Second, Scripture, because God's

book, lies beyond the jurisdiction of spirituals. As God's word, all that
it expresses has to be true, shining light into the mind, and right,
prescribing the eternal law for human conduct. To be sure, parts of
Scripture are not altogether limpid; certain passages apparently
withstand facile explanation. Nonetheless, recognizing that it contains
truths authored by supreme truth, spirituals must bow to its authority.
However renewed in knowledge, a spiritual submits to rather than
judges Scripture, acting as "a doer of the law," one who, espousing its
teachings, squares one's behavior with its standards. Third, the
spiritual cannot sit in judgment on God's differentiation of Christians
into spirituals and carnals, who were secretly selected, assigned their
special vocations, by God prior to the making of the firmament.
Pushed to its embarrassing consequence, in order to serve as such a
judge, a spiritual would have to absurdly preexist his own existence.
True, at present Augustine, along with other spirituals, can detect by
their fruits which Christians are spirituals, which carnals. However,
invincibly ignorant of the future, he cannot forecast who will be
spirituals and carnals in the centuries ahead. Fourth, just as he lacks
clues bearing on apportionment of spirituals and carnals in ages to
come, the spiritual cannot predict who in the bitter sea, the stormy
world, will be gathered into the fold of Christ, at long last tasting the
sweet grace of salvation, finally parting company with the miserable
feeding on acrid fruits of impiety that is life in separation from God.
The spiritual person cannot arrogate to himself the power to specify
which individuals will be assembled with the sheep, which with the
goats, at the Grand Assize: God alone will reign as perfect judge at
the Last Judgment.

34. In short, the spiritual exercises no dominion over the lights of
the heavens that stand for gifts of the Spirit; nor over the hidden
heaven, the invisible heaven of heaven; nor over day and night that
symbolize those living in the light of Christ and those submerged in
the dark of sin and ignorance; nor over the bitter turbulence
representing sin-soaked humankind, for it was out of this ebony flux
that Christ's power rescued him. The spiritual person, however, can
pronounce judgment on fish, fowl, beasts, all the earth, and creeping
creatures. The waters are the point of provenance of salvation
through baptism. The fish symbolize the Fish that is the Holy
Eucharist; the fowl, preachers whose expositions lie open to examen;
the earth, land made fruitful through good works; beasts, prideful and

sensual appetites to be curbed; serpents, impulses to false curiosity that must be controlled, then reoriented.

The spiritual may legitimately pass judgment, approving or disapproving, on particular administrations of baptism and particular celebrations of the Fish (the Eucharist) that nourishes the devout of the pious earth (the Church). The spiritual, however, cannot adjudge these sacraments, which he embraces on faith as instituted by Christ, nor can he elaborate the rituals to be employed in dispensing the sacraments, prescriptions reserved to Church authority; yet he need not hesitate to voice evaluation, positive or negative, concerning the manner a minister confers baptism or celebrates Mass. A sacrament confected reverently evokes praise; one enacted without due propriety, disapproval. The spiritual may justifiably criticize sacramental administration once the human element, a peccable strain unavoidably ingredient in every period of Christendom, obtrudes itself. Moreover, while submitting mind and will to truths and ordinances of Scripture, the spiritual is competent to endorse or raise questions about exegesis of fowl (preachers). If qualified, he can propose his own interpretation, while irenically differing with the opinions of others. Furthermore, he approves of blessings excerpted from Scripture and prayers originating in Biblical passages, to which the people respond "Amen", meaning "That is true", but the spiritual may entertain reservations about some of the glosses proferred.[79]

This outflow of words to explicate and illustrate the word of God is demanded by the human condition, the abyssal darkness in which the sense-enslaved inner eye is uncleansed to the point of blindness that is incapacity to spiritually understand:[80] first, blurring, then total obscuration, of inner vision. Were inward sight utterly purified, people would be able to pellucidly grasp the sense of Scripture without the analyses of preachers, or, conversely, since, in fact, the eyes are sightless, meanings have to make entrance through the ears. Thus while fowl (preachers) increase and multiply over the earth (members of the Church), they arise from the waters, the bitter sea inducing blindness; were this sightlessness wholly healed, no preachers would be needed to transmit truths through the ears.

The spiritual rates fellow Christians in terms of virtuous acts and conquest of the triple concupiscence, Christlike character observable in works of mercy, fruit borne by the earth (13.25.38), notably exhibited in almsgiving, which ensures glory for the giver because the indigent is Christ in disguise (P 48 [S.1].12). Almsgiving is rooted first of all in justice. God alone has dominion over the earth's goods; all gold and silver absolutely belong to him (7.9.15.S 50.1.2). Since earthly goods are to be used for the benefit of man, which means all men, an owner retains possessions as God's steward, bound to allot excess property to the poor. From this angle, the rich person who refuses to distribute superfluous holdings is defrauding the poor of what God provides for the needy (S 206.2). Besides aiding the almsgiver to do reparation for past misdeeds, almsgiving in a way opens the door to more personal knowledge of Christ, for the almoner is not just a hearer but a doer of the word (QE 2.51).[81] Moreover, the spiritual counts estimable the living soul who substantially bridles the threefold concupiscence. First, chastity, here purity of soul that lives for God alone, turns the raging beast of pride into a docile creature (13.21.31). Second, fasting domesticates the cattle symbolizing lust of the flesh. The lower self is a beast of burden whose recalcitrance to walking the way that is Christ is subdued by fasting (UJ 3); through fasting fascinations of the senses are resisted (E 55.15.28), and the spirit, disburdened of nether-tending tugs, surges to delights on a higher level (UJ 2.2). Third, unhealthy curiosity is sublimated by holy contemplation of sensory objects that bear the mind up to God. The spiritual, declining to lazily watch for his own satisfaction the movements of a lizard or spider (10.35.57), pores over the harmony of the animal, stirred to marvel at its exquisite beauty, then to praise the matchless super-beauty of its maker (P 148.15).

Thus does the spiritual preside in judgment over all ecclesial matters in a relative sense, i.e., over sectors he can legitimately, nonarrogantly, amend or rectify.

Chapter 24: Allegorical Meaning of "Increase and Multiply"

35. To resolve a certain mystery that clings to "Increase and multiply," he proposes to answer two questions: first, what is the specific problem raised by these words? (handled in this section); second, what is its value?, is it worthwhile laboring to untie the knot of a perhaps niggling point? (settled in the following section).[82]

It seems odd that God instructed humankind to reproduce but withheld this benediction from the light named day, the firmament, the stars, earth, and sea. One plausible reply, that such a blessing is reserved for man because he is specially formed in the image and likeness of God, is nullified by the observation that God also blessed fish and birds in this wise. An alternative response, that such a blessing properly pertains to all living things which naturally reproduce from seed, unfortunately can cite no basis in Scripture. No herbs, trees, beasts, and serpents are blessed with "Increase and multiply", even though, proliferating by generation, they assure preservation of their species.

36. He dismisses the suggestion that the problem of the imperative is a near-valueless quibble, without substantial point or purpose. Were he, a ministrant of the word, to put down an inspired injunction as inconsequential, he would be violating piety, the proper spirit of religion, effectively heaping irreverence on a sacred text. If its meaning evades him, he remains confident that the utterance is meaningful; a mystery to be untangled by minds sharper because so gifted by God. Should his acumen be of lower caliber, hopefully the Father will look kindly on his confession of belief that God would not darken revelation with an expression practically empty of import. Moreover, he will not hesitate to expound the fruit of meditation on a text originating with the Spirit of truth, who does not toss off random deliverances of next-to-no significance. For a reason furnished below (13.24.37), he believes it admissible to posit an allegorical interpretation, or, as he guardedly states it, apparently therein lies nothing unreasonable, no analytical lion blocking his path.

The explicit blessings accorded offspring of the sea and progeny of men are allegorized thus.[83] One mental judgment may be signified by a number of bodily signs;[84] this is the allegorical meaning of the multiplication of denizens of the sea. Conversely, what is signified in one way by the body, or one bodily sign, may be understood by various mental judgments; this is the allegorical sense of the proliferation of human offspring. First, the one mental judgment generating or being signified by multiple bodily signs is exemplified in the fundamental, all-embracing understanding of love of God and neighbor. Taken compactly, as the fusion into one of the two principal commandments, the *intelligentia* that is love is simple or incomplex, though it virtually harbors all the other commandments. Yet this one intellection is signified by a large number of bodily signs, sacral and profane. Simple love of God and neighbor is manifoldly signified by sacraments or sacred signs. "A sacrifice is a visible sacrament, that is, a sacred sign, of an invisible sacrifice" (CD 10.5). In the Old Law the sacrifices of many kinds that were divinely commanded were fashioned to express love of God and neighbor, the two precepts on which depend the whole law and prophets (CD 10.5). The modes of Jewish sacrifice were many. Besides cereal offerings, animal sacrifices, whole burnt and partly burnt, there were celebrated, along with partly burnt-offerings that included covenant offerings, family feasts, the sacrifice of the Passover lamb, peace offerings (with three subtypes), and atonement sacrifices.[85] The Eucharist is the supreme sacrament or sacrifice, whose victim-priest eliminates, by transcending, the sacrifices of the ancient covenant that prefigured the consummatory sacrifice of the God-man. Jesus' death on the cross, with its reenactment in the Eucharist, sovereignly proclaims the love of God and neighbor that is the invisible sacrifice outwardly signified. Since Christ is the principal agent in sacramental action, the other sacraments also signify, albeit nonsacrificially, the one understanding that is love of God and neighbor. Moreover, in the nonsacral sphere languages beyond numbering employ different words or verbal signs to denote this love, and in each particular tongue countless terms variously mean love of God and neighbor. Second, whereas the one understanding that is expressed in many bodily signs is symbolized by the increase of marine offspring, the reverse is the case in interpretation of Gn 1.28. The one bodily sign gives birth to many mental "signs" or judgments. The single line, "In the beginning God made heaven and earth", can be legitimately understood by many interpretations; legitimately, since variety does not necessarily imply error, Scripture being receptive to a diversity of intellectual renderings. Earlier (12.20.29-22.31) he took pains to list a number of readings of key words that diverge from his own exegesis, contending that a Scriptural text is susceptible of various interpretations, all of which can, without incongruity, lay claim to be true.

37. In its literal acceptation "Increase and multiply" properly betokens the built-in tendency to generate offspring that is characteristic of living things. According to their natures or intrinsic patterns of activity, living things are substances that beget offspring by seed. Gn 1, however, confined that blessing to marine animals and men (along with birds, as recorded in 13.24.35). This inclusion of only some of the living under the blessing, and its corollary, the exclusion

of other living things, indicate that it is preferable to construe the law of multiplication in an allegorical fashion, a reading the sacred author himself very probably intended first of all.[86] Scripture limited the imperative to a selection of living things to point up that its rule of reproduction is applicable not only in all living things but in all creatures mentioned in Gn 1.1. 1) Hence spiritual creatures and corporeal things, respectively symbolized by heaven and earth, increase and multiply in ways proper to them; spirits are multiplied by creation while new complex bodies arise during a ceaseless coming to be and passing away. 2) Light and darkness, standing for good and evil persons, also increase and multiply according to the laws of moral-social psychology. 3) Writers of Scripture were broadly multiplied as ministers of the dictates of God's law summed up in the one commandment to love God and neighbor; members of the one spiritual species reproduced until public revelation stopped with the book of Revelation, all functioning as authors in the firmament that stands for Scripture. 4) Unjust and just persons are again regarded as symbolically multiplying respectively in the community of evil, the society of those polluted by sin, figuratively abiding in and of the turbulent sea that is the world, and in the community of the devout represented by the dry land whose words and deeds of piety give birth to other dedicated souls. 5) Offspring symbolized by the ongoing reproduction among seed-bearing trees are manifold and multifarious; plants and trees are works of mercy accomplished during the course of life on earth or dry land. 6) Gifts of the Spirit manifested for general ecclesial welfare are still multiplied; spirituals dowered with wisdom and carnals favored with knowledge continue to "be born", to blossom in the Church. Two of the gifts, tongues and their interpretation, are no longer exercised in official Church assemblies, but the remaining seven are deployed, though only among a small minority, in every generation. 7) Perhaps somewhat elliptically, Augustine remarks that affective movements regulated by temperance in living souls also increase and multiply. Less compactly stated, souls ripening into spirituals by conformity to God's law that is virtue multiply by emulating apostles, contemporary preachers, and other spirituals. Affectivity molded according to temperance evokes Rom 12.1-2. To become a living soul a Christian must discipline his body, placing its members at the service of God, which is the pith of Paul's exhortation to offer one's body as a living victim, a sacrificial gift, to God. As the body governed by temperance is a sacrifice, so the soul, electing to be reformed according to the unchangeable form of divine good, is also a sacrifice, in obedience to Paul's directive not to be conformed to this world but to be reformed in newness of mind (CD 10.6). Moreover, affections so renovated to multiply in the sense that spirituals grow in numbers by imitating the pattern of virtue in other spirituals, notably Paul and other prominent saints, form a paradigm realized to a lesser degree yet impressively in preachers, relatives, and friends, whose moral persons are configured, albeit imperfectly, in the likeness of Christ (13.21.30-1).

Allegorically running through all seven instances, three of which are pairs, is the theme of multiplication and fruitful issue. Yet only in the two cases considered prior to these is the schema of the one generative of the many operative (13.24.36), in which intellection is manifoldly embodied and, conversely, one bodily sign multifariously intelligized; in which are generated, on the one hand, a large family of bodily signs and, on the other hand, a harvest of ratiocinative fruits. First, a multitude of corporeal signs is indispensable for human education in divine truths because in man's present *carnalis profunditas* flesh blinds the heart whirled about in the abyss of this world (13.23.34). Reproduction of bodily signs is fittingly symbolized by the generations in the waters, for the waters represent the lapsed state of man prior to the call to repentance and baptism (13.17.20; 20.26). As the waters or man's abyssal carnality required preaching for perception of Gospel truths, so engrossment in the flesh necessitated bodily signs, sacred and nonsacred, for transmitting core Scriptural truths like love of God and neighbor. Second, human generations ordained by "Increase and multiply" congruously represent the multitude of interpretations constructed by various intellectual exegeses since human reason is fecund. From one man are engendered many offspring because the human body is physically fertile; correspondingly, from one Scriptural line are generated numerous exegetical progeny because human reason, distributed in diverse interpreters, is analytically fertile. Parallel to the mode of human generation, many offspring from one progenitor, is the mode of exegetical generation, many interpretive offspring from one progenitive human reason. Thus immersion in the flesh and fecundity of the mind are the reasons why God blessed marine animals and men with the capacity to multiply (13.24.361). The power of begetting in marine animals stands for the manifold declaration of bodily signs of one mental conception while the human inclination to reproduce represents the manifold of mental conceptions of one Scriptural text that is bodily articulated. The marine animals filling the waters symbolize countless bodily signs, sacred and nonsacred. In a related but diverse manner of multiplication the earth becomes filled with the human progeny representing divergent intellections of the one bodily enunciated passage. Furthermore, the dryness of the earth,[87] which separates it from the sea, is attested by studious probing and judicious dissection that interpreters expend upon a perplexing text. Hence reason, because fecund, reigns in the domain of dry land, entitled to primacy because analytical power makes it the progenitor collectively responsible for the generation of various interpretations.

Chapter 25: Seed-Bearing Plants a Figure of Material Assistance Owed to Ministers of the Word.

38. God alone being the truth, any truth Augustine expresses originates in God; what he conveys is principally not his but God's. A sheerly human teacher is inherently a purveyor of falsity since every one, with an infinite capacity for error, is a liar, speaking from within, from one's own fallible spirit (P 115.3). As the father of lies begot falsity from within his own disordered nature, so fallen man under Satan's sway is a kind of natural-born liar, habitually inclined to utter untruths (J 42.13). Whoever speaks the truth speaks from God; the contrary of this is: whoever does not speak the truth does not speak from God; in other words whoever tells a lie speaks from himself. So Augustine speaks the truth only by welcoming truth from truth, only by opening his mind in prayer to be lit by the light of God (P 91.6).

God who is truth will help him discern the spiritual sense of Gn 1.28-9, in which God provides every seed-bearing plant and all fruit-bearing trees as food for man and also for birds, beasts, and serpents. Allegorized, fruits of the earth are works of mercy performed by the faithful for the living soul or spiritual symbolized by man, for spiritual preachers represented by birds, and for those who have overcome pride by meekness, those who are continent, and those who descry God in the universe, symbolized respectively by tame beasts, docile cattle (by implication), and harmless serpents (13.21.31). Actually beasts, cattle, and serpents are varying pictures of the morally disciplined living soul. Fish and sea monsters are accorded no food, apparently because the uninstructed or nonbelievers to whom they are related lack genuine linkage to fruits that are deeds of mercy (13.27.42).

Previously Augustine described the earth bearing fruit as a symbol of the good Christian, whose faith is tangibly executed in works of mercy imaging and amplifying the mercy of God (13.17.21). Now, with the symbolism made more specific, the earth stands for the faithful Christian who is carnal bade to extend mercy to spiritual teachers and models. A salient example of such fruitfulness was Onesiphorus, pious in the sense of prayerfully self-giving, on whose family God lavished mercy in recompense for his mercy to Paul. When Onesiphorus, who had consistently dispatched material assistance to Paul in Ephesus, learned the apostle was incarcerated in Rome, he risked the sea voyage to the capital, to visit him not once but frequently, always carrying food and articles along with the cheer of friendship and the sustenance of spiritual companionship; not for one moment ashamed of associating with a man in chains. Undoubtedly some Christians shunned Paul, fearing that they would forfeit social approval, tremulous too that their hardihood, fomenting the displeasure of Roman authorities, might expose themselves to a like durance vile (2 Tim 1.16). Again, brethren from Philippi in Macedonia provided material succor to Paul when he labored in Corinth (it being his practice not to be subsidized by the local community to whom he was currently ministering), producing, like Onesiphorus, fruits that were works of mercy (2 Cor 11.9). Sadly, not every convert assisted Paul, and out of trepidation some of these trees, with the potential to bear fruit due Paul in justice and charity, neglected to champion him in his hour of want. Prior to being jailed, in Rome Paul was haled before the magistrate for a preliminary hearing; during those trying moments not a single one of his brothers in the faith rallied to his cause. Every one deserted the apostle, anxious lest he be disgraced, perhaps even branded a secret enemy of Caesar, possibly tagged a criminal through guilt by association because of overt backing of a suspect headed for prison (2 Tim 4.16). Fruits rich in mercy are owed in charity not only to Paul but to all dispensers of the Gospel designated ministers of rational doctrine; rational not in the sense that Christian truths are apprehended by pure reason but in the sense that reason explicates its truths in conjunction with and subordination to faith, yielding understanding of divine mysteries. Reason claims dominion (13.24.37) only as the instrument and servant of faith, in the light of which spirituals' analysis of the Christian message formulates rational doctrine that later centuries will classify as supernatural theology.

Three motives prompt the faithful to tender means of subsistence to spirituals. First, social justice demands that superfluous goods be distributed to fellow men in destitution, especially members of the Christian family that is the Church. Second, material help must be granted them because they are models of complete continence, this signifying mastery of the three major concupiscences (10.31.41). Imitators of Christ are flesh-and-blood patterns of the subduing of passions portrayed as wild beasts, cattle, and serpents (13.21.30-1). Living souls personify total continence, leading the faithful to be transformed in newness of mind, thus to progress from the carnal to the spiritual level (13.22.32). Third, relief of their need is due ministers of the Gospel, for they inherit the office of exhortation from the first evangelists, not by miracles, which were performed to arrest the attention of unbelievers, so drawing them out of the bitter waters (13.21.30), but by Spirit-filled preaching of inward renewal of virtues to which their practice livingly witnesses, energizing carnals to develop into spirituals. God's blessing is demonstrated in the multiplication of proclaimers of the word, spiritual descendants of the apostles, so that, as with them, the sound of their heart-transfiguring message is broadcast worldwide, for they preach in the *Catholica*, the geographically universal Church (13.20.26;21.29-30).

Chapter 26: Fruit Depends on Good Will

39. Not subjugated by concupiscence of the flesh, Paul received with open arms material donations from the Philippians because his converts, having undergone a second conversion, were once more engaged in works of mercy. He was not of that company of unfortunate Christians whose God is their belly, who live to eat rather than eat to live, whose *summum bonum* consists in gorging themselves with food and drink at banquets, acting like cattle at the feeding-trough (S 51.24), oxymoronic Christian Epicureans, dedicated to eating and drinking, oblivious to an afterlife (S 150.5.6), not using

food, as did Paul, to replenish energy for service of God (S 51.24). Worshippers of the belly cannot rejoice in the fruits of mercy since their sole pleasure lies in satisfying fleshly desires. Only the continent, like Paul, maintain the spiritual outlook directing them to delight in food as the outcome of a work of mercy. No doubt grateful for food the Philippians sent through Epaphroditus, Paul was spiritually nourished by and rejoiced in not the food as such but the spiritual fruit that was their work of mercy, in the fruit not of the right field but of the loving heart.[88] Apparently his flock had been afflicted with weariness in doing good, the sap in these trees having dried up, with some of the branches close to withering. The food contributed was a sign that their charity had revived. Not the supplies as such but the fresh fructification within was what fed and joyed his soul.[89] He did not consider himself needy, for absolute dependence on his all-providing Father ensured inner contentment. Prayer-illumined experience had schooled him to find felicity in penury as well as plenty, in each and every circumstance acting with vigor always inflowing from the strength of God.

40. Paul is hailed as great,[90] the towering stature of his inner self the opposite of exterior features. Reputedly short with a name etymologically meaning small, he was ennobled with a skyey sanctity. Humbly deprecating himself as the least and last of the apostles (1 Cor 15.9), he proved himself to be *facile princeps*, the first and foremost of missionaries. One of the loftiest exemplars of the living soul, who in his self-donation without stint was splendidly renewed in the image of God, he reached a near-perfect self-mastery coupled with deepest intimacy with the Father. He was one of the original birds of the air, the farthest-traveled and most prolific of letter writers, whose tongue winged across the world "speaking mysteries," that is, ministering rational doctrine, in which faith flowers into understanding (13.26.39). *Loquens mysteria* is broadly attributed to Paul as proclaimer and explainer of the word; strictly, the phrase denotes a glossolaliac who utters mysteries in the Spirit in strange tongues intelligible not to man but to God (1 Cor 14.2). The cause of Paul's delight is not material assistance but spiritual action, his followers' works of mercy, a delicious fruit inducing joy upon which his soul feeds. Not food to appease hunger but just and charitable self-giving underlay his rejoicing, works of mercy that simultaneously nourished and pleased his spirit.[91] Paul, was, in effect, praying Ps 4.2, "When I was in distress,

you enlarged me." Initially he was constricted by physical and psychological anguish consequent upon destitution. In answering his pleas, God expanded his heart not by sparing him from all material exigency but by filling him with total detachment from all material concerns. The narrowness of his distress was superseded by the dilation of his spirit through the inpouring of the power of the Holy Spirit; (P 4.2), enabling him to do all things in God who strengthens him (Ph 4.13);[92] making him satisfied in all circumstances, gratefully welcoming abundance and peacefully enduring privation, with a self-sufficiency descended from on high:[93] this is why the Philippians whose earlier generosity alone relieved his material need after he departed Macedonia once more lovingly responded to his want in a reviviscence of gladdening active mercy. Their souls, which had lain fallow, were now, fecundity restored, bursting forth with new fruit (S 46.7.4).[94]

41. Further evidence that Paul's joy was initiated not by material assistance but by the fruit that was the Philippians' regained active mercy is adduced in his claim to seek not the gift but the fruit. While the gift is the material covering basic necessities, the fruit is the good will, the right intention, of the giver, a will good because yoked to the will of God, an intention right because rectified by the law of God.[95] As Jesus teaches, the Christian is blessed not for showing hospitality to a prophet or just man or tendering a cup of cold water to a disciple but for acting for a holy purpose, for which he is infallibly promised no less than their reward, precisely because he aims at succoring a prophet or just person or disciple as such. The sheer gift is the material aid that is lodging or drink; the fruit is the supernatural motive for bestowing the gift. It is the graced right motive that transmutes gift into fruit, hallowing it into an offering whose fragrance ascends to please God. In comparison with opulent benefactions, the gift itself may look paltry indeed. Housing among most early Christians was hardly splendid, usually in the lowest scarcity-economy class, and practically nothing seems cheaper than a cup of cold water, even less valuable than water warmed over firewood. However, it is the fruit, the pure intention that God ordains as the price to be paid for the assured grand reward. The hands of the donor may be far from overbrimming, but, so long as the fervent heart lying at the center of the giving is full, the fruit purchases recompense rich beyond comprehension (S 105A; 107A). The widow who fed Elijah

because he was a man of God granted not just a gift but a fruit spurring the inner self to rejoice, whereas food from the raven, obviously not influenced by the right motive, was no more than a gift nourishing only the outer man. From the standpoint of moral-economic realism, however, the gift, albeit not fruit, that the raven transmitted was not to be deprecated, opportunely arriving at a critical moment of extreme necessity, a gift without which the prophet might have starved to death.

Chapter 27: Good Will Lacking in Unbelievers

42. The "therefore" opening the passage alerts the reader that what follows extends the line of argument in 13.26.41 and, in particular, perhaps notifies that he is picking up one thread of analysis left unfinished before, when Augustine averred, without explanation, that fish and sea monsters are excluded from reception of fruits (13.25.38).

Fish and sea monsters are figures respectively of the initial sacraments and astonishing feats of God that are miracles (13.20.26). The miracles worked by Peter, Paul, and other apostles excited wonderment in unbelievers, (13.21.30), disposing them for catechesis, after which the sacraments of initiation apportioned them a share in the Church's life of grace. When unbelievers, whether or not they later become Christians, contribute food or other material aid to apostles or their successors, without recognizing what ought to be done (that the little ones [96] or apostles have a right to such support) and what purpose it serves (that the subsidy is offered to sustain an apostle as such), their benefactions, however naturally commendable for their commiseration, can be rated no higher than gifts. Their actions not being fruits, the apostles do not joyfully relish the sight of their giving (13.26.40). Nor are the donors themselves fed, i.e., endued with more divine life, since they are bereft of supernatural motivation, the correct intention to assist the apostles precisely as apostles. Not incorporated in the holy life of the Church, and therefore devoid of a holy will, they cannot eat so as to grow in grace and toward meriting a divine reward. The little ones whom these gifts aim at satisfying are not nourished by joy because they are disappointed in being supplied with a gift but no fruit. Iterated for emphasis, on the contrary, is the apposite point that the very visualization of fruit as a work of mercy evokes nourishment that is joy

(13.26.40).

Hence it becomes clear why fish and sea monsters do not receive fruit. The theater of missionary endeavor of spiritual ministers is confined to the sea, the domain of unbelievers who can proffer no more than gifts; it is only the dry land or Church that brings forth fruits that feed the ministers of God. At this juncture there occurs, unremarked in the text, an analogical alteration, in the allegorical meaning of fish and sea monsters. Whereas in the first line these stand for, as before (13.20.26), sacraments administered and miracles performed, in the last line fish and sea monsters symbolize not events caused but potential beneficiaries of the events, namely, the unbelievers for whose sake miracles are worked and to whom sacraments of initiation are to be dispensed. It is in this latter transferred sense of unbelievers that fish and sea monsters are not spiritually fed by fruits of the earth in Gn 1.29 (13.27.38). Still resident in the sea, unbelievers are denied access to food germinating on the dry land or Church. As separated from the Church, they can neither nourish nor be nourished by spirituals.

Chapter 28: The Universe Very Good

43. A simple scheme controls the narration of each stage of creation: first, God decrees that things be made; second, the things are actually made; third, he pronounces them good. Seven sorts of creation are recorded: light; the firmament, the dry land called earth and the assemblage of waters named the sea; plants and trees; sun and moon; creeping things, sea monsters and birds with respect to the sea; beasts, cattle, and serpents on the earth; and seven times God deems his work good (Gn 1.4, 8, 10, 12, 18, 21, 25). At the conclusion of his manifold making God prized the whole ensemble of creation as very good (Gn 1.31). Each part of creation, precisely as distinct part, is good, but the totality, the entire universe, is not only good but very good, with a goodness higher in kind than that of the particularly good. A material thing composed of beautiful parts is far more beautiful than any one of its members; in the line of being a whole is self-evidently greater than any one of its parts; in the line of goodness and beauty a whole is far better and more beautiful than any one of its parts. So, analogously, the universe, a whole that is not an organism but an ordered whole of distinct things, is superior in

beauty and in goodness to any one of its parts. To be sure, each of the parts in a body is ordered into a unity that bespeaks beauty, but the arrangement into a whole is most ordered, to the highest degree in that genre, because the ordering culminates in a perfectly formed thing. A part qua part is ordered but always incompletely; it is devised to be fitted into other parts to constitute a whole. As with a whole body, so with the entire universe; its parts, taken singly, exhibit beauty, but the whole, because it harmonizes and joins together the ordered or beautiful parts, is most ordered, most beautiful: it is very good. Because ruled by measure, number, and order, each part of a human body is beautiful: eyes, nose, cheek, head, hands, feet, and so forth. If each of these is singly beautiful, the whole body composed of these beautiful members is plainly much more beautiful: it is very good (GCM 1.21.32).

While six bespeaks perfection because it is the first number whose fractional parts $1 + 2 + 3$ add up to six (CD 11.30), seven symbolizes the perfect sense of the unlimited; the seventh day on which God rested prefigures the unending day of eternity (CD 11.31). Eight, it may be added, is significant because the Lord rose from the dead on the eighth day, one that foreshadows the everlasting today of indefatigable activity that is rest in God (S 260A.4; 260C.2.3).[97]

Here the reasoning that the universe is very good rests on the principle, "The whole is more beautiful than any one of its parts;" a whole made up of good parts is not only good but greater than good: very good. Prior chapters (7.12.18; 13.19) took another tack to reach the conclusion that the universe is very good, arguing that diversity and variety with many levels of being and value result in a complete universe superior to a possible world in which only superior entities exist. Only a universe containing the lower in addition to the higher domain engirdles all things, and only in such a universe can all things be praised as very good. Put more succinctly, if things were equal, not all things would exist; but all so exist; therefore they are not equal. Because equality was not the criterion for creation, there are various grades running from first to least (DQ 41). Inequality betokening differentiation and diversity of types from highest to lowest constitutes a universe more beautiful than one including only the topmost species (LA 3.9.24). The principle of the greater good and beauty of variety is also operative in the arts and the human organism. Isolated from the whole painting, a black color may seem repulsive, but, considered as a part of the picture, it contributes to the beauty of the whole (VR 40.76). Again, viewed in themselves, individual syllables or letters may exhibit no grace, but, integrated with the oration, they are parts of a polished piece of rhetoric. Moreover, the hand justly regarded as beautiful within the body forfeits its beauty when amputated, and, in virtue of that loss, other parts look disfigured. Conversely, a detached hand that is offensive looks beautiful when united to a beautiful body (GCM 1.21.32).

Chapter 29: What Man Sees and Says in Time God Sees and Says in Eternity

44. Reconciliation of the temporal character of the enumeration of Scriptural passages with the supratemporal vision of the author of Scripture defeats easy understanding.[98] On the one hand, the very counting of the number of verses in which God describes his works as good implies times or time. Because each number carries a specific valuational import, Augustine took pains to reach the exact number of times. So not offhandedly does he say, "seven or eight times;" from the perspective of the special parts of creation God said, "It is good," seven times; and in terms of the whole universe he vocalized his pleasure an eighth time (13.28.43). On the other hand, God is *esse* or *ipsum esse* (S 7.7), absolute existence, so transcendent to vicissitudes of time that, were he temporalized, he would cease to be God. Hence in the vision that is eternal Augustine could not discover times that would furnish lucent understanding of the number of times that the divine mind perceived his creation good. God is Augustine's own God;[99] thus the divine response to his prayerful inquiry is couched not in a soft but a high-powered voice, a deliverance not of ordinary amplitude but a cry so loud that it punctures his deafness, shattering the callus around the inner ear that was blocking admission of sound. As in 10.27.38, the energy of the sound metaphorically signifies the irresistible force of God's reply, disintegrating encasement in doubt. As the potency of the shout broke through a sound barrier, so the compelling texture of divine logic broke down his incapacity to grasp truth.[100]

Scripture has recourse to a temporal mode of discourse, the words of God being numbered in time, but God's word is not ruled by the empire of time.[101] Whatever he knows and pronounces lies within his eternity; as he exists eternally, so he knows and speaks eternally within himself (13.16.19). Time does not impinge on his word because his word is commensurate with his eternity; what the eternal God utters is eternal in a mode equivalent to his eternal existence. Moreover, the word emitted within God enjoys a duration equally eternal as divine existence because the Scriptural word is verbalized through the Word, the Second Person whom the Father eternally generates by thought. Through his coeternal Word the Father speaks all at once and eternally his creative words, paramount among which is the word of Scripture. In brief, through the Word coeternal with God is spoken within the Godhead a Scriptural word coeternal with God (11.6.8; 7.9).

Since only the Holy Spirit penetrates the things of God, it is only through his Spirit that persons lay hold of the things of God revealed in Scripture. Similarly, only in virtue of his Spirit are persons activated to tell or preach the things of God in Scripture. Furthermore, what persons see and say through his Spirit, God truly sees and says, a somewhat tricky point to be explored in 13.31.46. While man sees the things of God in an unabatedly transitional time, one thing coming before or after the other in a past-present-future frame, God's intuition comprehends all at once in a transcendent changeless present the past, present, and future time-line (CD 11.21). Similarly, while persons speak the Scriptural things of God in time, verbalizing the present verse after the past verse and before the future verse, God utters these things of God in eternity, within himself, through his Word in whom are contained all the eternal reasons, preeminent among which are the things of God that are words of Scripture. The sapiential voicing of Scriptural words in the eternal Word causes the existence in time of these words; the cause is eternal, the effect temporal. Words pronounced in time come to be and pass away, but words of God spoken through his eternal Word, which are one with eternal knowledge, everlastingly perdure (T 5.10.11).

Chapter 30: Manichean Denial of Creation

45. Augustine's inner mouth sucked in one sweet drop from God's truth, learning once again that while he saw in time, God saw in eternity; sweet because the response sated his hungry mind; no more than a single drop because he had posed only one question. Drop

alludes to the measurement of time through successive drops in a water-clock (11.2.2); the solution occupied only one drop of time, in which he savored one truth with its provenance in one eternity.

Reaffirmation of the truth that God created all things making one and all good stimulates remembrance of a main ideological adversary, the Manichean dualism that, repudiating total creation by God, argues that a purely evil intelligence, the Principle of Darkness, is responsible for inherently evil ingredients in the universe. Augustine briefly iterates three Manichean anti-creationist contentions. (i) God did not freely create but was compelled by events outside his control to construct the heavens and give the stars their special composition. (ii) God did not strictly create but manufactured the cosmos from preexistent materials.[102] Like a superhuman artisan, he organized materials at hand to build the earth, so as to forestall any renewed assault of the forces of evil against the realm of the good. (iii) The frames of large animals, tiny animals, and vegetables were not even designed by God but were caused, indirectly, by the Principle of Evil. An elaboration of these points, even at the risk of repetition, seems permissible.

(i) When his kingdom was invaded by minions of Darkness, the Father of Light had to counter them. Unfortunately, the warriors of light were defeated in the opening battle, with the result that the light-elements were commingled with components of darkness. Since the particles trapped in darkness were parts of his divine light, the Father of Light felt constrained to deliver them from captivity. His principal purpose was to preserve the light-elements, the necessary means to that end being the construction of the universe (VR 9.16. MM 12.25. CD11.22. H46) In accord with his command an angel fashioned ten heavens and eight earths, among them our visible heaven and earth (CF 32.19). Chief among the agents in the visible celestial machinery were the moon and sun. Light-particles liberated from captivity were carried up for deposit in the moon, from which, after roughly fifteen days, they were transferred to the sun; in turn, the sun transported them to the Kingdom of Light (H 46). The crucial point is that the Father of Light was necessitated to create the visible cosmos. As established earlier (7.4.6), necessity from outside God derogates from his incorruptibility. Since divine will and power are identical, if God were forced to create, his will would be greater than his power. For, we saw, his power is his attribute of doing whatever he wills; but if he were compelled to create, he would be willing more than whatever he wills: thus his will would be greater than his power. But this entails the absurdity that God as identical with his will is greater than God as identical with his power. If we intelligize God as more or less than God, we are self-stultifyingly maintaining that God is not God.

(ii) The Manichean God did not strictly create the heaven and its luminaries; it did not make them out of nothing nor create things from his very own (*de tuo* in the second person).[103] Rather, he molded actual preexisting matter into variously patterned entities. The sun and moon were fabricated out of pure light, the stars from light-elements still slightly contaminated by elements of darkness. The earth was also shaped from preexisting materials. When sexually aroused, captured demons released, along with light-elements, some evil seed (abortions of she-devils) that fell to earth and resulted in five species of good trees and five species of evil trees (CF 6.8. NB 44). The remnants of light in the demons were extracted by Primal Man and utilized to construct the earth.[104] The sky was fashioned from their flayed skins, the earth from their excrement, the mountains from their bones (CF 6.8. NB 44), plants from their hair, and wine from their gall (MM 16.49. H 46).[105] Capitalizing on his enemies to block any further incursion, the Manichean God framed components of the visible world out of parts of their bodies to erect ramparts impregnable against any future penetration. Unhappily, all these assertions are barren of experiential warrant, totally inconsonant with the observationally grounded astronomy and earth science of Augustine's day. Manichean cosmogony consists not of the outgrowth of scrupulously checked facts and tested hypotheses but of the outpourings of a fantasizing imagination.[106]

(iii) Some vegetation, animals, and tiny animals are neither created nor constructed out of preexisting matter. When sexually excited, captured demons, discharged, along with releasing light-elements, some evil seed that dropped to the earth and in dry form issued in five species of evil trees, from which sprang the vegetable domain (CF 6.8. NB 44). Under the influence of the rapidly rotating heaven certain pregnant female demons gave birth to abortions. After abortions of both sexes fell to the earth, they thrived, sexually united, and produced progeny. Hence all the animals on the earth and in the air and sea are the offspring of demonic union (CF 6.8). Tiny insects, such as lice, bugs, and fleas, are spontaneously generated from the dirt and filth of human bodies (MM 17.63). A Principle of Evil or Darkness, which is not created by God, is the polar opposite of the good God and hence is not only an utterly different substance but also a mind at enmity with God, its hostility displayed in the demonic generation of plants and animals in the lower regions of the cosmos, namely, the earth, its atmosphere, and the sea. The Principle of Evil caused these things indirectly, mainly through emissions and copulations of demons.

Their worldly scientific theses prove the Manichees deranged, not psychopathologically so but in the line of intelligibility; religiously insane: in being forced to create, their God is stripped of incorruptibility and sovereignty; philosophically insane: they press the self-defeating claim that the evil is a real substance, with some things purely evil; scientifically insane: their mythically contrived formation of heaven, earth, plants, and animals is an incoherent patchwork, far-fetched, without foundation in empirical fact and analysis. Deluded Manichees promulgate this nonsense because, deprived of the light of faith and the direction of the Spirit (13.31.46), they fail to recognize the all-good creator of all things that are good because they reflect his goodness.

Chapter 31: Through his Spirit God Sees in Man his Works as Good

46. Meditating on God's creative expenditure, Augustine came to understand that the Spirit enlightening spirituals to esteem creation also directly sees creatures through spirituals as his vehicles. Through the Spirit spirituals awed by wonders of creation are gifted to discern that God's works are good. Yet the perspective may switch from that of effect to that of cause. Whereas spirituals contemplate the goodness of creation because of the Spirit, the Spirit envisages creation's goodness in the spirituals, applying them as his conduits of vision and appreciation.[107] Spirituals see creation's goodness through the Spirit; conversely, the Spirit sees this goodness through or in spirituals, the converse being a rich vein mined from 1 Cor 2.11-2. Only the spirit of an individual is privy to his intimate thoughts; analogously, only the Spirit of God fathoms the innermost secrets of God. Thus it is not through his own spirit but through the Spirit that a spiritual understands the gifts of God. A further step draws out the implication

of direct divine seeing. If only the Spirit can cognize things of God, without the Spirit spirituals can know nothing of the things of God. Yet there is more: it is the Spirit himself in spirituals who perceives the things of God. Through God spirituals see the good gifts of God but, since the seeing is caused by God, it is the indwelling God in spirituals who sees his own marvelous gifts.

Christ promised his followers that during persecution not they but the Spirit would speak in them. During the near-unbearable rending of the body the spirit of a martyr trembles and falters: it is then that the Spirit speaks in him. Wanting in spirit, he becomes full of the Spirit, who speaks in him the truth to his persecutors (P 141.5). While the flesh without is agonizing under torture, the Spirit within is proclaiming the truth (S 75.1;227A.2). From the viewpoint of truth, each martyr as human was, like every human being, a liar and therefore unable to be truthful, but insofar as the Spirit aflame in him spoke, he expressed the truth, the Spirit within employing him as his instrument (S 335E.5). The operation of the Spirit in martyrs extends also to spirituals who prize God's gifts in the Spirit; at work within is God who sees that all this is good. It is in a supernatural context that God furnishes what is lacking. In the line of natural activity God's power conserves things and concursively works in actions of creatures, applying them as intermediate causes to produce proper effects(GL8.23.44). Operatively present in creaturely activities, he does not act in them in the sense that he grows in a tree or barks in a dog, for neither tree nor dog is inherently deficient; each is organically structured to engage in its specific activities. Moreover, such contortion would seem to savor of pantheism; a God growing in a tree suffers the loss of transcendence, reduced to a world-soul immanent in his creation. Moreover, in the line of natural activity God does not see in man that $7+3=10$ (LA 2.12.34); illumined by standards of truth grounded in truth, a person naturally enunciates this judgment. However, it is otherwise in the cases of a martyr speaking the truth and a spiritual valuing creation as good. Both are supernaturally exigent; on one's own neither can pronounce this supernaturally based judgment (S 333.6). Each can speak the truth only through the Spirit, or, from the standpoint of cause, the Spirit, or God through his Spirit, speaks in him.

Regrettably, not everyone looks at creation with spiritual or divine eyes. Manichees disdain portions of creation like plants and animals

as contaminated with evil, incongruously viewing good as evil
(13.30.48). Another group of noncreationists consider the universe
good, but in their absorption in the world they directly or indirectly
exclude the creator. In lieu of parallel texts, one can do no more than
conjecture with whom this indeterminate category is peopled.
Perhaps this class includes astronomers (5.3.4-5) and other scientists
who, tracking down the intricacies of the universe, turned the blind
eye to its maker; for physical thinkers with acute minds and pride-
bloated egos, nature was a closed executive order (S 283.3.3). Again,
poets may sing of beauties of flora and fauna and the splendor of the
starry sky without hailing their creator. Indeed individuals with no
skill in science and no talent for art may relish the sight and utility of
sun, wind, water, and fertile land, all along blind to the maker and
sustainer of all things great and small. Stunting this genre of men is
destitution of a religious sense, the piety that trains the eyes on the
goodness of God luminous in his creation. When through his Spirit
spirituals see creation as good, God in them envisages the divinely
bestowed goodness, impelling them not to delight in creation alone
but to hunger to see more intensely the face of the loving artist
mirrored in his physical masterpiece.

Not on their own do spirituals love God, but the love of God is
poured forth in their hearts through the Holy Spirit (Rom 5.5). Only
from God is God loved; a spiritual loves God with the very love God
implants in his heart (S 169.11.14;34.2.3). The inpouring of this love
is appropriated to the Holy Spirit, the personalized love of Father and
Son (T 8.10.14); this love is the proper, the greatest, gift of the Spirit,
its singular font (EJ 7.6), who dwells within the soul (E 187.13.38).[108]
The fire of love blazing forth from the Spirit (13.9.10) bears the mind,
rung by rung, up the ladder of being, from exterior to interior, from
inferior to superior, until it lays hold of the creator of all good things
(10.6.8-7.11). Through grace, a supernatural good given by the gift of
God that is the Spirit (T 8.17.29), spirituals perceive as good the *bona*,
natural good things, of creation, cherishing them as flowing from the
all-good: "from you, O God," Augustine prays, "all good things
come" (*ex te omnia bona, Deus*, 1.6.7).[109] For them, unlike Manichees,
whatever exists in any way is good: every being as such is good; no
per se evil does or can exist. Every created thing, which exists in some
limited way is good because made by God who, as absolutely
existing, is absolutely good. God, recall, is existence itself, *ipsum esse*,

being without limitation, absolute being (P 134.4). God is not a being
of a circumscribed type, restricted to some special mode. His measure
being measureless, he is the "is" (*est est*), unqualified being. "He is the
'is' just as he is the good, the good of all goods" (P 134.4). As the "is,"
as absolute existence, he is the super-being in which all other beings
share; as absolute goodness, he is the super-good from whom flow all
other goods.

Since Augustine's outlook is not acosmic, God does not act
immediately in the exercise of multiform activities.[110] Were he to act
immediately in all operations, the existence of things would be
hollowed out, effectively diluted to illusion, their proper operations
mere seeming, leaving, in effect, God the only real being and cause at
work in the production of all effects. God's activity is mediate,
accomplishing effects he ordains through intermediate beings, which
act under his administration and in accord with his direction. In the
order of nature rain falls, fertilizing the soil so that grass grows, in
order that, in turn, cows dine on the grass. From the vantage point of
principal causality, God applies the rain to fall, the grass to grow, and
cows to munch on grass. God acts through created causes to execute
their specific effects: through the rain he waters the soil, through the
grown grass he nourishes cows. Monica and his nurses fed the infant
Augustine with their milk, but from the angle of primary causality, it
was God who fed him through them; in line with the physiology of
maternal milk-production he devised, the milk came not from them
but from God through them (1.6.7). Yet the metaphysically
circumspect Augustine never hazards the fatal suggestion that God
grows in the grass and feeds on the grass in cows. The claim that God
directly acts in the human agent, a position glossing St. Paul, is
restricted to the supernatural sphere, in which, because the human
spirit, while *capax Dei*, inherently lacks divine seeing and divine love,
the Spirit, or God through his Spirit, sees and loves in man the
goodness of his creation.

Chapter 32: Gratitude for Creation Taken Literally

47. Through the Spirit Augustine sees, as God sees, each particular
thing radiating goodness, and the magnificent ensemble as very good.
The goodness of each phase of creation, here understood literally,
excites thanksgiving. While a grateful man gives to God what he did

not receive (P 44.7), gratitude, which is rooted in charity or good will (P 36[S.2].13; 72.1.S 236.1.1), is not a gratuitous gesture but the payment of a debt in recognition of countless boons (P 36[S.2].13). More specifically, perception of the goodness of creation stokes love of the creator, which issues in praise that is partially couched in thanksgiving. Whereas love of self leads to dispraise of God, love of God triggers praise appareled in thanksgiving (P 44.9). Praise and thanksgiving are distinct; praise is focused on God simply as God, as all-good, while thanksgiving is directed to God as the giver of goods. Concretely, however, they are frequently intermingled, praise manifesting itself in or effectively fused with thanksgiving. Thus the sacrifice of praise, which is offered on the altar of conscience, consists of thanking God for blessing us with any and every good we possess (P 49.21).

Through the impulse of the Spirit (13.31.41) he reviews nine portions of creation, taken literally, each re-seeing companioned by love and praise-in-thanksgiving of their super-good maker. First, heaven and earth (Gn 1.1) can signify respectively either the celestial firmament and the regions below it or the realm of spirits or angels and the physical universe.[111] Second, light was created to illuminate the world, whether taken to mean the physical universe or the whole of creation, including angels (Gn 1.3-4). Third, the firmament was created, with waters above and beneath it. Firmament may denote the heaven, called the primary body in the universe because it is qualitatively highest, containing pure fire and exercising a primary causal efficacy. Positioned above it are spiritual waters,[112] and below lie the familiar corporeal waters of the sea. Heaven may also designate the atmosphere or region of air in which birds fly about. Above the body of air are lighter waters comprised of vapor or clouds, which fall to the earth as dew on clear nights;[113] below are waters that, because heavier, settle on and flow over the earth (Gn 1.6-8). Fourth, the mind's eye envisages the beautiful, i.e., the formed, waters of the sea, and the dry land, whether bare (unformed matter) or the formed earth capable of bearing vegetation, poetically depicted as mother of plants and trees (Gn 1.9-10). Fifth, luminaries in heaven provoke admiration, the sun appointed for the day, and moon and stars whose dimmer beams afford a kind of consolation, which is relief for misery (P 85.25), for the grief of the sunless period that is night (Gn 1.14-8). The sensorily apparent rotation and orbiting of the

sun constitute day and year, and the periodic revolution of the moon
about the earth delimits a month. Sixth, the wet or humid quality is
present in sky and sea, every part of which contains fish, sea-
monsters, and birds. The density of the air, high enough to support
birds in their flight, is thickened by the evaporation of water from the
sea (Gn 1.20-2).[114] Seventh, animals adorn the earth (Gn 1.24-5).
Eighth, man, in virtue of his spiritual soul, is made in the image and
likeness of God. As rational, he is lord of creation, in particular,
master of animals devoid of reason (Gen 1.29). Man's taming of
beasts, and not vice versa, is an empirical proof evident to any and all
that man is specifically superior to the other animals (DQ 13). Ninth,
as companion to the first man, a male (Gn 2.7), a woman is formed
from his side (Gn 2.22).[115] The woman is strictly rational, with an
intelligence of the same order as that of the male, and therefore fully
equal to the first man in the line of mind. But in the line of body, in
terms of her sex, the woman is functionally subordinate, subject to the
reason of man as the tendency to action is subject to reason, to be
directed by skill in acting in accord with right reason. Reason rules
the lower appetite of the soul through whose help it exercises the
members of the body; so the male should govern the female, his
helpmeet in the economy of the home (GCM 2.11.15).

Augustine's assessment of the status of women was unquestionably
influenced by the lower position assigned to women in Roman
society. In the political sphere, in business affairs, and social concerns
women occupied a stratum beneath that of men. Various data
apparently lend support to the view that the female is not the equal
of the male. Men are generally taller, more muscular, quicker, faster,
and stronger than women. Physiologically, a woman's monthly cycle
is a social handicap as well as a physical discomfort. Psychologically,
women seem to be endowed with more aptitude for word fluency
than for acuity of analysis; and a woman's proneness to weep in
difficulties may insinuate a measure of emotional oscillation. Not
unaware of these or similar data, Augustine believed that the
feminine is the weaker sex (AdC 2.20.21). In not elaborating a more
nuanced interpretation of the data, Augustine was, as is every
individual, a man of his time, enriched by its cultural heritage but
hamstrung by its inevitable deficiencies. It was sociologically
impossible that his outlook not be affected by prevailing cultural
patterns. Still, while the mores of Roman society only conditioned his

mind, it was the Christian religion grounded in Scripture that decisively shaped his posture. God created woman principally for the sake of childbearing. Besides being more qualified to share field labor, another man would have served also as more apt friend than a woman (GL 9.5.9). However elementary, practical medicine of his day attested that a woman's physique and physiology are designed for childbearing. Moreover, as the history of most cultures substantiates, woman's psychology and social role seem to dovetail with her role as childbearer; she is structured by nature to be nurturer and homemaker. Yet Paul seems to consign woman to an ontically inferior position; man is the image and glory of God while woman is the glory of man (1 Cor 11.7), with the result that the function of man is to deliberate and plan, that of woman to obey and prosecute the action prescribed. Still, this diversity of function, because figuratively expressed and secondary, does not derogate from woman's essential dignity. In the line of *mens* woman is the image of God and the equal of man, no less capable of being rewarded in the spirit of her mind. In short, as a human being and as a Christian, woman is fully equal to man, and only in the line of body, in terms of sex, does differentiation of social function arise (GL 3.22.34. T 12.7.10).

In practice, even in a Christian society notably molded by Roman customs, a homemaker was not demeaned as a subordinate in a dyslogistic sense; she was in no way a slave to her master. Granted, Monica counseled other wives to deem themselves slaves of their husbands, yet, Augustine significantly remarks, she offered this advice jokingly (9.9.19). True also, she willingly served Patricius "as her lord" (9.9.19, in dependence on Eph 5.2). The lordship, however, was a spiritual one in which the husband ideally loves his wife as Christ loves his Church. Not simply a legal contract with a division of economic responsibilities, their marital union was essentially a spiritual covenant of love that was, in practice, an association of friendship; a social bonding woven out of ongoing dialogue in which the wife, albeit theoretically subordinate, proffered suggestions, raised questions, and diplomatically and gently pressed her case, ideally, as demonstrated in Monica's example, without becoming embroiled in angry shouting matches (9.9.19). The woman in the home wields power not by authority of position but by suasion in an affectively delicate and socially sensitive idiom of which women are masters; not by a direct but by an indirect strategy that merits a hearing because of long, love-infused commitment. In addition, as impressively illustrated in the self-spending of Monica, a woman could become a spiritual in the Church, elevated by grace-filled understanding above male associates and companions (13.23.33). It was she who converted the two males closest to her, Patricius prior to his death (9.9.22), and Augustine prior to her death (8.12.30). Expert in mystical union, she led Augustine up to absorption in God in the vision at Ostia (9.10.23-5). Second place in supernatural organization that is the means does not debar women from outstripping men in the end, in rising to the one thing necessary, primacy in holiness. Church history glows with other such spiritual superstars like the astounding Catherine of Siena (1347-80) who towered over male contemporaries.

The charge of misogyny has been leveled at Augustine, unfortunately so, since in his relationship with women of every social level, he never failed to respect their dignity as sisters in Jesus favored with a call to the highest sanctity.[116] Augustine has also been denounced for committing the new "sin" of sexism, which imprisons woman in a servile, lowest-caste station.[117] His accusers are apparently ignorant of the fact that, far from putting down women, he exalted them as images of God, not to be systematically exploited and victimized but appointed to cooperate in an irreplaceable way in the work of redemption. By contrast, one crusader against sexism, best left unnamed, sneers at the vocation of motherhood as the reduction of woman to "a baby-making machine." Furthermore, after we modify or put in brackets Augustine's comparison of man to reason and woman to desire for action, the massive fact of social differentiation between man and woman in the family and the Church remains undeniable. The conclusions of Catholic thinkers and experimental studies verify key physical, physiological, and psychological differences between men and women present in practically all cultures, indicating that the core of Augustine's position is sound and that a suppression of differences between man and woman tends to lead not to the liberation of most women but to their devaluation and immoral, however subtly imposed, subjection to men in a secular-humanist culture.[118]

Chapter 33: Praise of Basic Features of Material Creation

48. The mindless and voiceless agencies of material creation are vested with mind and voice through man. When man discerns the

beauty of material things, he praises God at work in them. In noting their beauty, in lifting his praise to God, man acts as a priest of creation, a mediator through whose spirit and tongue all creation sings its song of praise to its maker (5.1.1. P 144.13).[119] Because praise of God in his works is purposed for love, a praiser of God inevitably becomes, because intended to be, a lover of God; in singing God's praises man pours out the affection of a lover (P 77.1). Conversely, man loves God for the purpose of praising him. Here there is no strict *circulus in probando*; the appearance of vicious circularity is only appearance, for the relationship of the terms is altered when their positions are changed. In the convertend, praise is strictly ordered to love as the lesser to the highest form of worship. In the converse, love is not strictly ordered to praise. Man loves God with the result that he further praises God. Fructifying in an increase in the spirit of praise, love ignites fresh articulation of praise. Or, as love-knowledge, it descries other, more delicate ingredients worthy of praise.[120] In love-knowledge affection enters into the condition of the object in the loose sense that intensity of love makes the beloved more entrancing. The "blindness" of love moves the lover to ignore or significantly prescind from blemishes, making the beloved more praiseworthy. Analogously, love of God inspirits the Christian to see his works as even more attractive.

As created, material things are rooted in mutability; they are inherently subject to change. As mutable, they are temporal; their changes are measured by time. Unlike immaterial things, material things are mortal: they exist so as not to exist. As material things are out of or from material mutability, so they are out of or from time: like mutability, material time may be likened to a sort of "stuff" out of which their contingent careers are figuratively fashioned. They are out of or from time in the sense that time bears with it both initiation and extinction; they come to be and eventually cease to be at definite points of time. Each is a tiny sun that rises, then forever sets; each progresses, then declines and dies; each is marked by form, then by privation that is the loss of form; existing successively, they appear in the morning, then disappear in the evening of existence. In one respect their coming and going are partly patent; the coming to be and passing of species are clearly observable; life and death in the broad acceptation are realities, daily noticed and confronted by ordinary persons. Other features of physical entrance and exit, however, are not so crystal clear. First, determination of particular modes of change needs exploration; second, grasp of the reason why the universe includes material mutables is the outcome of ratiocination; third, the ultimate reason for change has to be sought in the creation of mutables. First, the acquisition and loss of being are hidden in the sense that the particular agencies and mechanisms operative in various sorts of generation and corruption do not easily unveil their secrets even to patient probers. There is no royal road to a specialized science of the rise and fall of corporeals. Second, a universe without decline and death might seem abstractly preferable to one in which destruction is intertwined in the fabric of the material universe. Yet concretely, cessation of the old is the price paid for the emergence of the new in a frame of reference in which the whole can be beautiful only through lapsing parts, as a poem can be recited only if prior words cease so as to make room for succeeding words till the whole poem is declaimed. Again, as argued before (7.12.18;13.19), because of its differentiation and variety, a universe with spiritual and material mutables is superior to one with spiritual mutables alone. "If all things were equal, all things would not exist" (DQ 41). Elimination of inequality entails nullification of multiplicity and diversity of things; equal is at odds with all: if all were equal, there would be no all.

Third, material mutables tend to dissolution. Because created with relative being, they are mutable; because material, destructible. As mutable, material things derive from the absolutely immutable One; created by God from nothing, without dependence on any factor co-equal or coeval with him, they are made *a Deo*, not *de Deo*; else they would be consubstantial with God, a self-destructive consequence since an infinite spirit cannot parcel out its substance to material things. In departure from Manichean cosmogony, the world is not fashioned from matter that is not God's, namely, a matter that consists of parts of bodies of demons originally alien to and at war with the divine realm (13.30.45). Nor is the cosmos constructed out of preexisting matter like that posited by Neoplatonists. The world is indeed made out of matter, which is unformed matter; not an uncreated but a concreated matter, concreated in the sense that it was created simultaneously with form, no interval of time separating the creation of formless matter and its organization by form. The matter of heaven and earth, first created, precedes the form, created second, not in time but in origin; not temporally but subjectively is matter prior to form (12.29.40). In this respect matter was made wholly out of nothing while the form of heaven and earth, i.e., the world as formed, was made out of unformed matter. Before and after in origin, matter and form were created at one and the same time.

Chapter 34: Summary of Allegorical Interpretation of Creation

49. Broadly recapitulated are allegorical exegeses of periods of creation and their description in 13.4.5-28.43. Through the Spirit of God he saw at the end of Gn 1 that, appreciated as particular individuals and types, created things are good, and, prized as parts of the more treasured whole, very good(13.28.43). Participating in the goodness of an all-good creator, all creatures are good. Again, on the level of immanence they are, as existents, good, and they exist because made "in the beginning", in and through the Word containing all the eternal reasons of things (DQ 23. T 4.3). Earlier Augustine reached a literal reading of Gn 1: heaven denotes the unformed spiritual realm; earth, unformed matter (12.11.11-14); "in the beginning," in the wisdom or Word of God (12.19.28; 20.29). Without dropping the literal interpretation of "in the beginning," for the first time he probes an allegorical gloss of heaven and earth, a parenthetical addendum to a rehearsal of prior allegorization.

"Heaven and earth" symbolize the head and body of the Church, the Church as predestined, the Church outside and before time, seen from an eternal perspective; the Church without morning or evening, as everlasting, without divisions or succession in time.[120] The terms Church, Church as heaven, and predestination would seem to invite brief comment.[121] (i) Church refers analogously to the external, the internal, and the eternal Church. (a) The external Church is the visible Church on earth, the body of Christ, whose head in heaven comprises one supernatural organism with its members on earth. Head and members constitute one body that is the plenitude of Christ (J 21.8), the members so one with their head that they can with absolute veracity claim, "We are Christ himself" (S 133.8. J 111.5). The Church on earth is not a community of the elect or unfailingly virtuous but compasses sinners as well as saints, all who are at least juridically bonded to the Church. According to divine preordination, many sheep are outside, many wolves within, the flock (J 45.12). (b) The internal Church consists of only those alive in Christ, free from mortal sin. Yet neither is this a community of the saved, for some now vibrant with grace will fall away, choked by self-indulgence or darkened by error that precipitates apostasy. (c) The eternal Church is the heavenly Jerusalem, no longer plagued by hypocrites, i.e., sinners (DC3.32.45), but embracing only those who have departed this valley of tears graced with charity (CG 7.16). It is the consummation of the Church on earth, an unimaginably resplendent everlasting city of God (EN 57,58) in which the devout are no longer physically intermixed with sinners. (ii) Heaven represents Christ, the head of his body that is the Church because at every stage the God-man is in heaven. When Christ walked the earth, his "I" or divine person dwelt with the Father; significantly, in Jn 3.13 Jesus avers not that he will be but that he is in heaven (S 263A.1). After his ascension Jesus became corporeally present with the Father (S 265C.2), remaining spiritually present in his body on earth through divinity, power, and love (S 263A.1). As predestined, the God-man abides uninterruptedly with the Father, eternally present in his decree prior to the incarnation. He is, prior to creation, already foreseen in glory, as the head of the Church, for the formation and triumph of which the universe has been fashioned. (iii) The predestined are so sanctified by grace that they are assured of final deliverance (DP 14.35). Specifically, they are called, justified, and glorified (J 45.12) through incorporation in the body of Christ (S 96.7.8), their total sanctification being wrought through the one perfect mediator (PJH 21.44.CJ 3.18.35) since incorporation in the Church is incorporation in Christ; those who are one in the Church are one in Christ (DP 7.7). Perseverance in Christ to the end, it follows, is also the outworking of predestination (DP 1.1). The *Catholica* is broadly universal in time, extending to all the just prior to Christ. Because salvation is in Christ (J 5.31), the saints of old before the incarnation were redeemed by faith in the Christ to come (CD 18.47). Thus the head and body of the Church, symbolized by heaven and earth, are identical with the total Christ, the Church of the predestined redeemed by the predestined humanity of Christ; it is the body of Christ divinely envisioned before all time, prior to the making of the universe. In eternity, a changeless existence without the succession of morning and evening, God foresees as already matured to full stature the body of Christ as it will reign in glory. Prior to creation God's joy is overbrimming; already he exults in predestining members of the body of Christ (J 83.1).

The glorified Church, the goal of all creation, is the reason why the allegorically understood universe was made; its features are means that subserve the fulfillment of the end that is the head and body of Christ in glory. The stages in creation are short chapters in a compendiously recounted salvation history, the graced life of the Church on the many times rocky and zigzag road to everlasting life. As described in Gn 1, God begins to execute in time what was predestined in eternity, supernatural factors that would activate the Church to live and thrive as an instrument of redemption toward the world to come. Thus are revealed secret matters, details of the salvific plan previously buried in divine wisdom. Disclosure of the redemptive mystery entrains liberation from sin, an implanting of order in disordered hearts. Prior to deliverance their lives not in right relationship with God, they panted after lower goods, with the result, this an intrinsic punishment, that they became inwardly disorganized, barren of virtue, their souls in the line of morality resembling disorganized, formless matter in the line of the bodily (12.3.3). As form organizes formless matter, so the form of virtue, charity in particular, organizes souls into spiritual wholes (12.8.8;13.9.10). People's sins were upon them (Ez 33.101); they were living in grievous sin (13.8.9); in near-desperation they were driven to learn existentially that they can survive only by healing mercy (S 339.2-3). Prodigal sons, they wandered away from the Father and, disoriented, plummeted into the dark abyss; the flux represented the dominating swirl of their passions, the dark, their spiritual blindness and deprivation of light (13.8.9). The Holy Spirit was borne over the waters, over unstable and night-begloomed spirits (13.10.11), to spur them to repentance, to beam light into them (13.12.13), and to inflame their hearts with love whose upward impetus lofts them toward their proper place that is God (13.9.10). The Spirit pours forth the new life at an opportune time also; opportune as favorable with the grace that is divine life, opportune also as the due, the best, time, the hour appointed by loving wisdom. After calling them (S 158.4.4), God justifies the impious; not by their own enervated "strength" but by God's power are they invested with justice, snatched from darkness into light and given a share in the life of God through Christ (P 44[En.2].3.S 144.1). The just are liberated from the people of the bitter sea, members of the earthly city, and are shaped into dry land capable of germinating fruits that are works of mercy (13.17.20,21).

Ruling the community of the just is the firmament of Scripture, to whose authority leaders of the Church and ministers of the word submit, an authority that appoints them to preach the word and instruct the simple faithful occupying lower stations in the structure of the Church (13.20.26;21.29). At odds, even at dagger's point, with the society of the just, which is the Church in its purest mode, is the earthly society, the community of nonbelievers bonded by aspiration for evil. One common motif interlinks their variegated concerns: love and worship of self, incessant cravings for self-satisfaction that turns its back on God. Their devouring selfishness acts as a foil to set off the bright unselfishness of the people of God that produces fruits that are works of mercy, self-givingly handing over earthly riches to the poor so as to amass treasures neither rust nor moth consume (13.17.21).

Moreover, through the Spirit are enkindled lights of the spiritual firmament, starry globes of fire, holy men commissioned to be lights of the world, preachers schooled in the word so as to spread it to others (13.19.25). Endued with the great light, the ministry gift that is the word of wisdom (13.18.23), they shine brightly over the whole world, as heavens proclaiming the glory of God, as lights in the firmament of the Church brilliant with sublime authority. Next are made out of corporeal matter the sacraments, which use water, oil, and bread in their confection, validated with the imprimatur of miracles ultimately workable only by the hand of God. Propounding the meaning and value of these sacred rites and wonders are potent words of the messengers of God, apostles and evangelists, whose preaching is genuine because exercised in alignment with the firmament, the authority of Scripture. This first evangelization aims at turning nonbelievers into Christians and at instructing the converted (13.20.26). The faithful are also blessed by evangelical teachings, for their holy doctrines are still preached by progeny of the apostles and first evangelists (13.21.29,30). Subsequently, God forms living souls, spiritual persons, through the activity of evangelists, themselves living souls: in becoming living souls, these faithful pattern themselves after the imitators of Christ who are the evangelists. Continence in the broad sense regulates appetites of the living soul, affording mastery over the triple concupiscence (13.21.30,31). Next, the living soul or spiritual created in the image of God is supernaturally transformed, becoming, as Christlike, more distinctly the image of God. Hence the spiritual bypasses sheer human authority for progress in understanding and virtue. Made and remade after the image of God, the living soul images not his own humankind but waxes through spiritual insights from the truth within and above his mind (13.22.32). Furthermore, God fashions rational action, conduct according to right reason subject to the understanding that is superior to reason, as woman is subordinate to man (13.32.47). At this juncture Augustine transposes the order of the terms in the analogy introduced two chapters back (13.32.47). There the comparison is stated: as the desire for action is governed by right reason, so woman is subordinate to man. Here the relata transfer positions: as woman is subordinate, so rational action is subject to understanding. Note too, the alteration in the designation of the interior factors pertinent to action. While in the first case desire for action is controlled by right reason, in the second case action covered by right reason is subject to understanding that, because superior, commands reason. Contemplation of moral truths presides over the application of these standards to action by right reason. Unless persons understand moral canons, they cannot apply them to direct action by *sollertia* (13.32.47) or right reason. In the first instance, it may be remarked also, woman is likened to the appetite for action, which becomes rational through subjection to right reason; but in the second instance woman is compared to rational action itself, now subordinate to a higher understanding. Understanding, which speculatively grasps notional realities like numbers and dimensions, also contemplates definitions of the virtues, thereby fixing the gaze of the mind on moral truths. A kind of cognitive-illuminative causal chain is formally operative: moral truths enlighten understanding; understanding shares this light with reason; reason applies the light to the appetite for action, assuring right or reasonable action.[122] Finally, the faithful to whom priests and bishops minister are to provide temporal goods to dispensers of the word of life. As ministers of God feed the faithful with spiritual nourishment necessary for preservation of and growth in faith, the faithful, in turn, are bound to supply goods required for priests' temporal nourishment. In distributing temporal fruits that are works of mercy, they are begetting within their spirits fruits of love to last for eternal glory (13.25.38;26.39-41). Through his Spirit God sees in the spiritual that each part is precious and the universe very good in order that through the love cascading down from the Spirit the spiritual may see and love the divine artisan in all of his awesome creation.

Although this may not be exactly the proper venue, it seems allowable to append a few remarks on the confounding problem of predestination whose proponents have to essay the reconciliation, which may seem unachievable, between divine foreordination and human freedom. Free will is surely evident and justifiable by reason. Divine foreordination, while not initially evident, would seem to be analytically indispensable also; it is inconceivable that at the Last Judgment the Lord will be surprised by the particular composition and number or the sheep and goats (S 47.15). Both divine sovereignty and human freedom must be retained, neither sacrificed to the overreaching claims of the other. Tipping the scales in favor of God's sovereignty may lead to theological determinism that guts freedom while one-sided emphasis on freedom may entrain diminution, equivalent to deletion, of the role of grace. For Augustine, Pelagianism effectively eliminated the need of grace for salvation: a self-disciplined man works out his own salvation. To confute this quasi-naturalism, Augustine proffered a Scripturally based concept of predestination, defined as "the foreknowledge and preparation of the benefits of God whereby they who are freed are most certainly freed" (DP 14.35). All is grace: for those who are called and justified so as to be glorified by the divine decree, every supernatural action from the first act of faith until the last prayer-filled breath before death is energized by foreordained grace. Yet freedom remains intact. "Grace does not suppress it" (E 157.2.10). Moreover, to scotch a misconception that persists to this day, it should be mentioned that Augustine did not strictly teach double predestination, meaning predestination to reprobation as well as to glory. Only in a few instances when employing the expression in a loose sense does he refer to those predestined to damnation (J 3.18.5.EN 100. PMR 2.17.26. CD 22.24). Again, not once does he slip into a harsh determinism resembling that of Calvin, for whom the supralapsarian decree positively foreordains the lost to damnation and positively ordains the sins of the nonelect; acting with only freedom from external coercion, the foredoomed are paradoxically programmed to be evil by a just deity. However, it would be be misleading not to mention that at times Augustine's preaching modifies and tones down the apparent severity of his theoretical stance. Many of his sermons unmistakably insist on human freedom and cooperation with grace. While never neglecting the primacy of grace (God, recall, crowns not man's merits but his own gifts [P 102.7]), he accents active openness to divine life: "If you so will, you shall obtain this salvation" (P 102.6). Commenting on Ps 146.4, "God calls all the stars by name," he observes, "We have certain names with God; in order that God may know our names, we ought to desire this, busy ourselves with this, preoccupy ourselves with this as much as we can" (P 146.10). Again: "If you so desire, the blood of Christ was given for you; if you do not desire this, it is not given for you" (S 344.4).[123]

Augustine's view, however, compelled him to endorse consequences with which later ages were to demur. Unable to accept on its face "God wills all men to be saved (1 Tim 2.4), he qualified "all" to mean the many actually predestined or all classes and types of men (PS 8.14.CG 14.44) or those whom God wills to be saved (E 217.6.19.EN 22.103). Moreover, unbaptized children are condemned, though undergoing only the mildest of punishment (E 166.4.10; 186.8.30). Furthermore, it would seem that all pagans warrant perdition because they do not belong to the Church (CJ 4.17). While treasuring the essentials of Augustine's invaluable contribution, the Roman Catholic Church has distanced itself from questionable corollaries. Distinguishing, along with Aquinas,[124] between the antecedent and consequent will of God, the Church unqualifiedly declares that God wills all men to be saved. Moreover, it recognizes that pagans of good will outside the Church can be saved by the all-just and all-merciful Father. Moreover, according to the *Catechism of the Catholic Church* (1992), which omits all reference to limbo, the Church "can only entrust" unbaptized children "to the mercy of God," hoping that God has ordained "a way of salvation" for them.[125]

Like all profound mysteries of faith, predestination defies definitive resolution in the analytic line. No doubt partially intelligible, it is no less undeniably incomprehensible. Every explication is dogged and shadowed over by predicaments. Neither the Thomistic physical-premotion theory nor the Molinists' *scientia media* approach seems invulnerable to an indictment of implicit determinism. The Arminian alternative to Calvinism, in preserving foreknowledge but discarding foreordination, bypasses the pitfall of determinism. However, this strategy, which appeals to some contemporary Christians, is purchased by the emasculation and, effectively, the destruction of divine sovereignty; a God whose causative arms are paralyzed is no longer Lord of history. Probably every solution, no matter how subtly framed, to this mystery will be plagued by impasses because divine knowledge and foreknowledge transpire in an ineffable mode (QS 2.2.2). Time-bound human intelligence cannot concretely, experientially, grasp a mode of operation that intuitively cognizes all events in one eternal present. At some stage analysis grinds to a halt, to be superseded by prayer.[126] After pressing understanding to the resignation point, a believer, imitating Paul and Augustine (11.31.41), can only fall to his knees, to adore and praise the God of wisdom and mercy whose judgments are inscrutable, whose ways unfathomable (Rom 11.33).

Chapter 35: Prayer for Peace of the Sabbath without Evening

50. The three final chapters meditate on the partly literal, partly symbolic meaning of Gn 2.2-3. The peace besought is not human but divine; a daring request perhaps, but audacity is dynamized by confidence in his very own Lord whose prodigality has nearly emptied the coffers of his pity, to dispose his soul for super-calm. It is a peace of rest; as rest terminates natural bodily movement, so the rest that is God is the all-satisfying term of his supernatural aspiration, which echoes the celebrated words: "O Lord, you have made us for yourself and our heart is restless till it rests in you" (1.1.1). When the heart oriented toward God arrives at its resting place, it is finally located where it should be, properly ordered in its fulfillment; the experience of that fulfilling order is the tranquility that is the peace of rest. Not only the culminating point of a graced pilgrimage, the rest will also be repose and refreshment of spirit. Burdens that pressed down unrelentingly on the spirit will vanish; gone will be toil, sweat, tears, pain of body, anxieties of heart; all tribulations will evaporate in the sunlight of repose. Moreover, it will be the peace of the Sabbath, participating in the rest God enjoyed after finishing his work; a peace without end (a theme that recurs in the following chapter).

The stupendously beautiful world will eventually pass away, for it is shot through with contingency; its material mutability seals its death warrant. The sublime ensemble is very good (13.28.43); here, analogously, the things in the world order are styled very good: the framework of the universe will crumble to bits once things have reached their modes. A mode, recall, is a specific limit of being; by extension the end of a thing's existence is also named its mode. When all things have arrived at their existential terms, all ceasing to exist, the orderly system binding them will disintegrate. The grand finale of parts and whole is appointed by God; the world will not decline and decompose but will be obliterated by direct divine intervention, in particular, by a universal conflagration consuming heaven and earth (CD 20.18). Morning and evening of creation betoken a morning and evening of the universe itself, a dawning and final darkness, a first and last moment in cosmic time.

Chapter 36: Eternal Sabbath

51. Overpassing the universe of the first six days whose things emerge, then dissolve, in days delimited by morning and evening, the world to come, that of the seventh day, is marked by a morning without evening, a sunrise without sunset, a beginning without ending. The seventh day is endless because God has made it holy as he is holy, one with the everlastingness in which he shares his sempiternal peace with all the redeemed. After producing the very good works of the six days, God rested on the seventh; since God is always at rest, he rested in the sense that after six days the production of new things stopped (GL 4.12.22). Correspondingly, after their very good works, fruits produced in this life, good by the goodness of the God who recompenses men's merits that are his own gifts (S 299A.2; 299B.5), the redeemed, as promised in Scripture, will rest in God in an eternal Sabbath. The seventh day was sanctified to excite the heart to long for this rest with every fiber of its being (GL 4.16.27). Image-laden mentation that bedeviled Manichees should not befog analysis of divine rest. It is self-stultifying to imagine God fatigued by his work of creation. His effortless intellectual utterance immediately effected the mighty making of things; creation was accomplished with no labor at all, with the greatest ease (GL 4.8.15-6). Again, God's rest is equivalent to his beatitude. He is strictly at rest in the sense that he is his own beatitude. Happiness is not a good that he has to strive to rest in; as infinite happiness, he is infinite rest; as always happy, he is always at rest. Fulfilled in himself, he is independent of all goods exterior and therefore inferior to himself, (GL 4.16.27). The

redeemed will rest in God insofar as they participate in the divine rest
that is infinite happiness, attaining perfect felicity only in the good
that is God (GL 4.17.27). Similarly, they will not find rest in their
works, which are limited, derived, and transitory, but in the
illimitable, all-fulfilling good (GL 4.17.29); the reward of a good work
that passes away is rest that remains forever one with God's rest (T
1.10.20).

Furthermore, this peace will be perfect because it is grounded not
in a precarious but in an absolutely unchangeable good. While on
earth the Christian is able but does not will to be here, he wills but is
not able to be there [in heaven] (10.40.65). On the seventh day the
glorified Christian wills and is able to be there; his glorified body will
be miraculously endowed with such agility that he will be wherever
he wills to be, without being apart from God for one moment. Perfect
peace will be his since he will always be with the God who beatifies
him by sharing his infinite peace (S 242.8.11).

Chapter 37: The Way in which God Rests and Acts in Man

52. Augustine draws a parallel between the rest of God in man and
his work in man now. God will rest in man: this means not that God
finds rest or happiness in man but that God will cause man to
eternally rest in God (GL 4.9.17). This causation of rest corresponds
to God's present operation in man. God works even until now in the
sense that after creation he continues to sustain things in existence,
men in particular, according to their proper natures (GL 4.12.23).
Moreover, this eternal rest will belong to each man because it will be
God's rest through men who are at rest. Rooted in love, the rest of
God will be intimate, related to each man one on one or one in one,
for God says: "My rest. I rest there" (P 131.22), with the soul
responding, it is implied, "I also rest there because he rests in me." As
source of the rest, eternal rest in men is God's rest present through
men. Insofar as men receive it, the rest is theirs and, insofar as God
gives it, the rest is his, indeed primarily his, since receivers rest only
in the measure that God enfolds them in rest: the divine rest attained
through men dovetails with the divine action accomplished through
persons. The fruits that are virtues, all offspring of the one main fruit
that is love, are engendered by the power and mercy of God. From
the angle of divine giving, these fruits are his, achieved through men

because he applies human beings as instruments for the germination of these virtues. Unquestionably these are the virtues of men actuating them, yet only secondarily; primarily these are God's inasmuch as grace from his mercy executes them through men.

God's ongoing causation upholds things in existence. Were the governance proceeding from his power withdrawn, the universe would disappear in the twinkling of an eye (GL 4.17.27). Taking "live" in a broad acceptation, in God all things live and are moved and exist (Ac 17.28). God unstoppingly works in things, supporting their existence, impelling them to be moved and to exercise activities in accord with natural tendencies. Wisdom governs all things mightily, maintaining them by divine power, and disposes all things sweetly, sustaining each being in its proper mode of movement (GL 4.12.27). On the other hand, God is always at rest, his rest being his beatitude. He is not compelled to strain for happiness he always possesses; rather, he is everlastingly his own supreme good.

The operation and the ever-present rest of God are ceaseless because he is eternal. It would be anthropomorphic to picture God acting, as people do, in time, Unlike man, God does not see or plan for a time nor is he moved for a time; nor does he rest during an interval of time. Yet by eternal power he wills that things exist in time, causing temporal envisagements in which things are seen and planned in time. Such temporal vision is triadic: memory of the past, attention to the present, and expectation of the future (11.28.37). By fashioning human mentality, God causes the vision of time, the psychic distension that is the interior measuring-stick of passage. God also makes times themselves, the extents of movement distinguished according to before and after or, concretely put, the days, months, and years ordinarily distinguished according to the movements of heavenly bodies (GL 2.14.29). Again, God produces the rest that is the terminus of natural movement measured according to physical time. The rest is said to be *ex tempore*, after or resulting from time; it is the outcome of the completion of movement of which time is the concomitant insofar as time measures movement.

Chapter 38: God Immutable and Eternal in Knowledge and Goodness

53. This final paragraph continues the relative opposition, at the

end of Chapter 37, between man's temporal and God's eternal mode of knowledge and action. Though God does not know or operate or rest in time, he eternally causes such temporal behavior. Hence in transcending the temporal framework of human living, God causally knows things, viewing them within himself, in his eternal reasons. So too he immutably does good; independent of all other goods, he is his eternal rest. (i) Men know created things because they exist; human knowledge, which follows upon their existence, is caused by them. But God's knowledge as eternal and independent causes things to exist; he eternally knows them as things to be made; his knowing them as existent makes them actually exist. (ii) Men see outside themselves; they rely on sensory and intellectual data to grasp things as existing. Verification that things exist is not garnered by consulting inner rules of necessary truth but by direct observation of things outside the perceiving subject. It is otherwise with judgments bearing on the goodness of things, for the good is not sensorily-existentially verifiable. Men cognize that things are good within, in terms of inner rules of goodness whereby they apprehend things as good, ranking them according to their degree of goodness. However, God saw things constituted in existence through his eternal power; he saw them made: his knowledge caused them to exist. In one eternal intuition he viewed them in his eternal reasons as about to be made, then, after creation, as actually existing. Implicit is the companion point that in his eternal knowledge God sees things to be made as good, and things made as actually good. (iii) Human adherence to the good varies through time. When the Holy Spirit pours forth his love in one's heart, a person is moved to produce acts of virtue; the offspring that is good action is conceived not by the spirit but by the Spirit. At an earlier time the same individual, because he rebuffed God, was driven by the downward propulsion of lower appetites to commit evil (4.11.16;12.18). But God is supremely good, who, because unchangeable, does not oscillate between good and evil. It is unthinkable that he do other than the good; as absolute goodness, he has to unceasingly do good. Only a God less than immutably good, only a God less than God, or a pseudo-God, could do evil. (iv) When people perform good works, these are truly their own works but rendered good by grace infused by the Holy Spirit. However set ablaze in holiness by the fire of the Spirit, these good works bear the imprint of time, fast fading, not abiding, transient rather than enduring. Even the superb fruits of Paul flourished in superabundance only in his lifetime, but the merits of his works, along with those of other persevering, if less heroic, Christians, win endless beatitude in God's "great sanctification", that is, in the seventh day that his unsurpassable sanctity has made holy as the eternal day of rest for his faithful ones. Still, the God who shares his rest or beatitude on the holy day that is "an end without end" (CD 22.30) does not himself come to rest; dependent on no good outside himself, he is always at rest because he is his rest.

God's eternal mode of being, his eternal knowledge, his eternal activity, his eternal rest–all this eludes comprehension, the total understanding, of angel as well as man. No mere human intellect can comprehend God and transmit this comprehension to another mind (S 117.3.5). Even the super-capacious intellects of angels fall infinitely short of comprehension of the mysterious eternity of God. Though angels cognitively encompass all creation in the Word in whom reside the eternal reasons of things (GL 4.22.39; 24.41), the enormous sweep of their cognition does not comprehensively capture the very eternity of God. Hence no angel can communicate total understanding of the eternal God to another angel or the human mind. Trusting in the divine promise to answer all prayers pursuing spiritual goods, the heart must ask, seek, knock (S 105.3.4), praying constantly, persistently beseeching, seeking, pounding on the door (S 61.5.6). Only through persevering prayer that releases fresh divine lights will the mind receive, find, have opened to it ever new, ever deeper understanding of eternity, even though it can neither realize nor even aspire to comprehension.

Fittingly the *Confessions* finishes on an explicitly prayerful note, for running between the lines of narration, analysis, and exegesis throughout this dialogue with God have been prayer and praise. The last chapters on eternal peace marginally indicate that the restlessness of the human heart (1.1.1) can be utterly quieted only in the life to come. Man is pointed by grace toward the blessedness of God one with divine peace, the repose in whose sharing the heart can reach the rest that is the fulfillment of all its strivings. This note of fulfillment, however, is peripheral, at best secondary in the end of Book 13, whose closing lines round out not the whole work but only the last three books, reiterating the prayers for light and direction from truth in the exegesis and theological understanding of Gn 1 that preoccupy

Augustine. It would seem then misguided to suggest that the final chapters of Book 13 show a systematic linkage of Books 1-9 and Book 10 with Books 11-3. Since Augustine is questing not for peace of soul but for light on wisdom and knowledge in Scripture, in particular Gn 1, Book 13 terminates in renewed prayer for illumination as the mind ponders, partially understanding but never comprehending, the mystery of the eternity of a God always at work and always at rest. It is delusion to claim comprehension of God, for the God so comprehended is un-Goded, cut down to fit narrow human categories (S 52.6.16). But it is not delusion but robust Christian realism to pray without ceasing for even miniscule shafts of understanding that, albeit always light years distant from strict comprehension, further enrich the spirit with treasures not of this world.

Concluding Remarks

Writing finis to the *Confessions* did not mark the finish of Augustine's life. Roughly thirty years, around seventy percent of his full-fledged Christian career, lay ahead, to be self-sacrificingly expended in the service of God in his Church. Within, engaged in incessant prayer, the desire to pray being equivalent to prayer (E 130.9.18. EJ 4.6), and unflagging in work consecrated to the Lord, which counts as the prayer of action (P 32 [S.2].16), his spirit ripened to a rich peace of conscience, the sabbath of the heart (P 91.2) consequent upon the relative triumph of the spiritual over the carnal self, which heralds the inexpressible peace on high (P 137.16). Since he was called not to the strictly contemplative sphere (10.43.70) but to a contemplative-active life, charity impelled him to forgo holy leisure so as to succor the body of Christ (CD 19.19). He became immersed in quotidian duties foreign to the sequestered scholar, toiling as both quasi-magistrate and *magister*, arbitrating legal disputes and unstintingly feeding his people with the word of God in a steady stream of sermons, only a fraction of which have come down to us. However, acquisition of inward peace did not exempt him from outward combat for the protection of the flock (P 137.16), especially against errors that threatened to undermine and wreck the Church. He was forced to confront the Donatist schism and to muster all his powers to confute the Pelagian heresy, which persisted in troubling him down to his later years, one of his last opera being an *Incomplete Work Against Julian*

(428-30), a second response to Julian of Eclanum whose acidulous tongue as well as dialectical dexterity had been enlisted in the Pelagian cause. Numerous other works drained his time and stamina, notably *De trinitate* (399-419), perhaps his most systematic work, and *The City of God* (413-26), *magnum opus et arduum* (CD *Praef.*), his outstanding masterpiece, whose composition was squeezed into intervals in his tight schedule. It is no extravagance to aver that his whole ecclesial life was one great and arduous work–in plain English, he was a willing workhorse; laboring all day and lubricating all night, we saw, he never stopped ministering to the faithful and shaping ideas for the upbuilding of the Church.

The foundation of his tireless dedication as servant of God and man was his profound humility (S 69.2). The counsel he proferred to Dioscorus as the way to truth he daily applied in every pursuit of analytical and existential truth: the first way is humility, the second, humility, the third, humility (E 118.22). His self-nothinging (P 70.1) was nourished by meditation on the law of the Lord day and night, which supplied the energy not only to teach but to do the truth of the kingdom (Mt 5.19).

Through and through spiritual, saintly, he daily disposed himself for death, his self-abasement and affective union with the Lord detaching him from the earthly so that toward the end he could appropriate in a Christian sense the then well-known words of Plotinus, "He is not a great man who thinks it is a great matter that wood and stones fall and that mortals die."[127] During the third month of the Vandals' siege of Hippo, Augustine, stricken with a fever, lay dying, his last ten days prior to death on August 28, 430, absorbed by constant concentration of heart on the penitential psalms attached to the wall opposite his bed. He spent his final brief span prayerfully continuing to live the leitmotif of the *Confessions*: in a spirit of faith he confessed his sins, begging mercy while implicitly praising the boundless goodness of his all-forgiving God. Thus he drew near to the region of imperturbable life (4.11.16) long asked, sought, and knocked for, eager to drink of the fountain of everlasting wisdom (9.3.6;19.23), to joy forever in the truth (10.23.33), to rest without end in the "peace of the heavenly city, the perfectly ordered and harmonious society whose members rejoice in God and in one another in God" (CD 19.13).

NOTES

1. *Merita* seems better translated as meritorious deeds, which entail either punishment or reward.
2. *Praeveniens,* used here three times in some form, stresses the priority and the supreme autonomy of divine initiative. Because sovereign, God's action is always prevenient in the line of the natural and supernatural.
3. The passage in which *unde me fecisti* occurs, "that out of which you made me," may be expansively rendered: "out of your goodness you preveniently produced this whole that you made (a whole completed by formation) and that out of which you made me."
4. Augustine offers no clues concerning the provenance of the God who is dependent on human service for no slackening of stamina and no shrinkage of power. Certainly he cannot be leveling strictures on a God in the Platonic tradition, for which the topmost being is unquestionably immutable and independent of lower beings for the force and scope of its activity. He may have had in mind some Roman gods, that, borrowed largely from Greek mythology and therefore made in the image of man, were supported by mortal servants, in the absence of whom they became tired and their power contracted. Lineaments of these anthropomorphic deities may have been sketched in *De nat. deor.* Interestingly, Augustine's critique of a God dependent on man contains elements of a realistic refutation of nineteenth- and twentieth-century finite-God theories, especially those prominent in the process philosophy of A.N. Whitehead and C. Hartshorne, according to which the relation between God and man is reciprocal and real: the God whom man needs also needs man. See A. N. Whitehead, *Process and Reality,* and C. Hartshorne, *The Divine Relativity.* For a critique of a process God see J. M. Quinn, "Triune Self Giving: One Key to The Problem of Suffering", *The Thomist,* 44(April, 1980), 173-218.
5. *Bene esse,* which signifies human existence made good by mercy, is grace-filled living short of glory. It would not seem to be identical with *sapienter vivere* of 13.2.3., which is equivalent to *beate vivere* or complete beatitude attainable only in the next life. For another opinion see BA 14, 426, n. 1.
6. This outline basically derives from that in D 3.343.
7. This threefold division depends on BA 14, 627-9. On the overall theme of Book 13 see F. Cayré, "Le livre XIII des *Confessions*", REA 2 (1956), 146-61.
8. See BA 14, 632.
9. Not all mountains, which symbolize great minds, are good; imposing figures like Arius ventilate untruth and disorder (P 35.9). While the mountains of God do not pertain to the next life, rest on God's holy mountain (in the singular) may signify the everlasting domicile, and, in particular, mountain may be taken to mean the super-eminence of Christ in eternal life. The mountain of God stands for Christ in eternity; the mountains of God symbolize outstanding ministers of God's word in this life (P 14.1).
10. He is not speaking improperly (*non incongruenter*) in asserting that the light

means the illumination of the spiritual creature. This cautious phrasing, however, does not indicate that he rates his view no more than an opinion. Earlier (CF 22.10[397-8]) he is hesitant, leaving it unsettled whether the light is spiritual or corporeal. The somewhat later GL 1.3.7; 9.15 (401) plainly avers that the light signifies spiritual illumination. In the still later CD 9.19 (415) a circumspect chord is again sounded: there is nothing absurd in contending that the production of the first light means the creation of the angels. Here, it seems clear, Augustine is saying, in effect: my position is one doctrinal truth that can be extracted from the text. His wary language serves to deflect any charge that an ipse-dixitism is dictating that his is the only doctrinally sound interpretation. Diverse true doctrinal interpretations can be achieved by meditation on the one literal meaning (12.31.42). His claim then is not improper; it is true in the sense that it is not the only possible true interpretation. In 12.11.12 he speaks conjecturally of the beatitude of the heaven of heaven: "O blessed creature, if there is any such being." Later discussion, however, removes the dialectical hesitancy. In short, *non incongruenter* conveys the import not of mere opinion but of the limitations of his own truth-claim.

11. The formless is displeasing because to a perfect being, what is imperfect is displeasing; lacking order, it lacks beauty; lacking beauty, it is displeasing.

12. Angels are called light because they participate in the light. CD 11.9.

13. He is simple because he is not other than what he has (E. 69.2.7), and called simple because he is what he has (CD 1.10). In divine simplicity to be wise is not other than to exist; his wisdom is his being (*esse*) (T 15.3).

14. It is the Spirit who causally supports things, which garner form and goodness from him, not he from them. Moreover, they rest in the Spirit, reaching their terminus or place of rest in his goodness (BA 14,579, n.5), becoming fully good or beatified only by participating in his goodness. Hence the Spirit over the waters is identified with the will of God decreeing that the formless become formed and beatified, resting in the goodness that is the Holy Spirit. Whereas 13.2.3 underscores the light coursing from the Word, this chapter emphasizes the will directing the formless to formation one with beatitude whose goodness shares in the goodness of the Spirit: they rest in his goodness.

15. According to Du Roy, 425, n.4, to the Holy Spirit is appointed a role in creation itself, in the sense that the *reditus* or return of the spiritual creature is the culmination of creation and illumination. His opinion explicitly diverges from that of BA 14,579-81.

16. In LA 1.4.9-10 *cupiditas* that generally means the desire of any good cannot be taxed as blameworthy. Culpable cupidity is called *libido* (LA 1.4.10; 11.12.13), this derived from *Tusc. disp.* 3.11.24. Later *cupiditas*, specially taken, signifies evil desire: "As cupidity is the root of all evils, so charity is the root of all goods" (P 90[S.1].8). Cupidity loves things inferior to God apart from God and against God. ME 1.22.41. Du Roy, 305, n.1. BA 14,437,n.1. Under cupidity is subsumed pride in addition to illicit desire of lower things.

17. The compact *Quid similius et quid dissimilus?* may be recast and expanded: no relata are more similar yet more dissimilar than physical movements toward places and psychic inclinations toward goals. This claim, of course, sacrifices

analytical precision somewhat to the rhetorical force of seeming paradox, for plainly physical movements and places are not most like and not most unlike their psychic counterparts. Still, this minor literary extravagance points up parallel features while equally underlining the factor of disanalogy, the gap between physical and psychic phenomena. Yet, as noted earlier, weight, connoting psychic tendency, exercises not a merely figurative but a properly analogical function. If we discourse analogically on the magnitude of the soul and define time as the distension of the mind, it is not surprising that analogical extension may legitimately ascribe weight to psychological entities.

18. G. Madec, BA 6 (1976), 344, n. 35.

19. Augustine refers not to the Fall of man but to the fall of the soul because he is paralleling man's forsaking of God with that of the angels.

20. The text implies that the destiny of both good and bad angels was determined in the first instant of creation, a view that GL 11.26.33 guardedly endorses. However, CD 11.11-5 leaves the question unsettled. Later, in 426-7, in CG 10.27 Augustine leans to the opinion that for a time prior to their apostasy the bad angels were blessed with a partial happiness, incomplete because they were not assured that their happiness would be endless. See Taylor, *Literal Meaning*, 2.294, n. 87, and BA 49, n. 2, 546-51.

21. A Christian is said to enjoy the embraces of God since the heart cleaves to God by successive modes of union; where there is growth, each fresh embrace pulsates with richer light and love.

22. Occasionally scholars characterize *Pondus meum amor meus* as a spiritual law of gravity; this well-intentioned attempt at updating unhappily lapses into anachronism. According to the Newton's inverse square law of gravitation, all particles of matter are attracted to one another directly according to the product of their respective masses, and inversely according to the square of the distance between them. Contrary to ancient physics, certain bodies do not have a principle of heaviness and others a principle of levity; each and every body has a fundamentally identical gravitational component. In other words, Newtonian gravitation departs from ancient theory on three counts. First, gravitational pull or attraction is universal; each particle of matter has the basically same gravitational ingredient. Second, each body exerts a pull on the other; however negligible its influence, a gnat exercises a pull on the earth. Third, there are no privileged zones of pure fire or pure air.

23. The famous line, *Pondus meum amor meus*, throws light on the more famous line, *inquietum cor nostrum donec requiescat in te* (1.1.1). Each human mind is so ordered to God as to its proper place that apart from its divine domicile, it is unterminated, without rest, and, because restless, without final peace and security. Man has a built-in tendency toward God, but ascent to God in his fullness is beyond natural powers. Great as a rational creature is (13.8.9), his mind can be satisfied not by a specific finite good but by the infinite God alone. But since only God can unite man with God, man needs grace or the fire of the Spirit to be lifted Godward. Even now some measure of rest and peace is attainable; faith and love join the mind to the eternal. Strictly, only after death and completely after the resurrection will the whole man achieve rest in his

proper place that is God, an everlasting stability overflowing with delights beyond comprehension, in a consummated love of the fulfilled God-seeker with God.

24. This ascent to God echoes in part the escape from moral time accentuated earlier (11.29.39). The heart transposed into fire by the Spirit flies upward to the eternal One, urged now not *secundum distensionem*, not according to the distraction and division that is moral time, but *secundum intentionem*, according to the concentration of the fiery vertical impulse of the heart moved by the Spirit.

25. BA 14, 442, n. 1.

26. Since he accords primacy to the divine unity, trinity in Augustine's usage principally signifies the holy three not personally but essentially, as a unity of substance. So he speaks of "God as creator, the omnipotent trinity" (T 4.21.30). BA 15, 25.

27. Cogitation on the trinity cannot be profitably pursued in a noisy environment punctuated by sharp dissension with little prospect of resolution of differences. Only within, only in the inner chamber of conscience, can the interior self docilely assimilate words from the light that brings understanding (S 52.9.22).

28. Earlier 13.5.6 dealt with the trinity in reference to the opening lines of Genesis: the Father is named God, the Son the Beginning or wisdom, and the Holy Spirit the Spirit borne over the waters. The triad in 13.11.12, however, is the first to function as an image of the trinity in the interior man.

29. Over twenty triadic traces and images of the trinity occur in Augustine. Portalié, 134-5, lists twenty-two; Moriones, *Enchiridion* 140-1, twenty-five.

30. This triad is anticipated somewhat in Sol 2.1.11 (Du Roy, 174, n. 31), while adumbrating the *meminisse-intelligere-velle* of T 10.11.17 (Du Roy, 175, n.6).

31. An evident truth may be attained by sensory inspection. Senses bearing on their proper objects yield certitude; this appears white, that tastes sweet (CA 3.11.26). Bypassing wrangles arising from tricks of the senses and illusions of the imagination, Augustine achieves unchallengeable certitude by appeal to self-consciousness (CD 11.26). May we remark, in addition, that an evident truth should not be confused, as not infrequently occurs, with a self-evident truth. The latter consists of a proposition whose subject and predicate co-implicate each other, as in the enunciation, "A whole is greater than any one of its parts" or "A cannot be at one and the same time nonA." "I exist" is an evident truth, but it is not a self-evident truth since there is no necessary connection, discernible simply by inspection of the terms, between "I" and "existing thing."

32. As GCM 412,n.8, comments, the third item in "one life and one mind and one essence" or substance seems somewhat incongruous. One would have expected *una voluntas* so that this trio of subjects would correspond to the triad of being, knowing, and willing. However, as far as is known, no manuscript contains *voluntas* as a variant. If we dismiss the remote possibility that Augustine was guilty of a slip of the tongue, it seems that he is emphasizing the unity of the subject of the three acts of being, knowing, and willing. Still, he accords this subjective unity a conceptual threeness by listing three concretely

identical but aspectually differing designations of the one subject. The one subject itself is conceptually triadic. In other words, each of the three, life, mind, and essence, is taken with respect to itself, substantially or nonrelatively, whereas each of the *esse-nosse-velle* triad is taken with respect to another or relatively (T 10.11.18). Augustine employs the triplet, *vita-mens-essentia*, allusively and elliptically; allusively, because he subconsciously iterates earlier somewhat cognate formulations as in the being, life, and thought of him (Imm 1.1, possibly derived from *Enn.* 1.6.7 and other passages; Du Roy, 176,n.4, relying on P. Hadot); elliptically, because he does not expressly specify, as he does in T 10.11.18, that *vita-mens-essentia*, are to be understood substantially, in contradistinction to the triplet of relative terms, *esse-nosse-velle.*

33. Augustine distinguishes between *substantia* and *essentia*, both of which mean "that which is". Because it implies a subject "standing under" or determined by accidents, substance cannot be properly said of God without compromising his simplicity. *Essentia*, he holds, is preferably predicated of God since it carries no suggestion of accidental inherence. Still, substance may be said of God if it is stripped of all reference to the accidental. In this case God's existence (*esse*) is identical with his *subsistere*: his substance is pure *essentia*, immune to the least admixture of the accidental. We have coupled substance with essence because for many contemporary thinkers, especially Thomists, essence denotes not that which is but the whatness or pattern of a thing, that by which it is what it is. To posit Augustinian *essentia* without its close kinship with substance might be misleading. Indeed one outstanding historian of medieval philosophy unfortunately lumped Augustine's *essentia* with whatness or quiddity, inducing him to falsely tax Augustine with essentialism.

34. For want of a better common term I have named being, knowing, and willing three acts. Clearly *esse* is an act only in the wide sense since *esse* betokens the substantial existence in *essentia* or that which is.

35. Augustine does not refer to the holy three as persons, probably because at that time the term person conveyed a substantial rather than a relative import. Person ordinarily bespeaks a substance or essence, a that-which-is, rather than a relation (T 7.6.11). However, he does come around to accepting the term but only reluctantly since it does not precisely signify relativity. Instead of vaguely designating the holy three as three somethings, it seems preferable to name them three persons (T 5.9.10). See C. Richardson, "The Enigma of the Trinity", 246-7, in Battenhouse *Companion to St. Augustine*, and BA 15 (*La Trinité*), 49-50. See E. Hill, *The Mystery of the Trinity*, 58-60, 100-7. Also W. O'Connor, "The Concept of Person in St. Augustine's *De Trinitate*," AS 13 (1982) 133-45.

36. Corresponding to heaven and earth, are spiritual and carnal members of the Church (13.12.13), carnals being deficient in understanding. This usage departs from the opposition of spiritual and carnal outlooks in terms of orientation to or rejection of God. To live according to the spirit is to live a life for God, governed by love of God. To live according to the flesh is live a life blemished by vices not only of body but also of mind; a life that is earthly because it clings to temporal goods in defiance of God (CD 14.2).

37. Reformation bespeaks a purification of the image of God in the soul distorted

by sin. Through grace poured forth by the Spirit of Christ man is renewed in the spirit of his mind, i.e., in his mind (Eph 4.23).

38. By appropriation the term grace may be predicated of the Holy Spirit. Grace is the gift of God, and since the Spirit is the greatest gift of God, he may be called grace (S 144.1). Charity is also appropriated to the Holy Spirit (T 15.19.37).

39. M. Sherwin, " 'The friend of the bridegroom stands and listens.' An Analysis of the Term Amicus Sponsi," AUG 38 (June, 1998), 197-215. He remarks also that Donatists can be configured to Christ in baptisim without becoming living members of his mystical body. Because not quickened by the Spirit, they possess only outward form.

40. In the life beyond, the human mind will see God just as he is because man, already through grace God by participation, will through glory fully share in Godness. The person who, by loving God, becomes God qualitatively in this life will become God by greater participation in the next life. Then while remaining ontically human, the mind, divinized by participation, sees God as he is because, having become more like God, it sees him with a more divinized understanding. At the outset of 10.1.1 Augustine prayed that he would know God, his knower, as God knows him. Now God knows him with divine understanding; then sharing in divine understanding, he will know God as God knows him; seeing God with participatively the same eyes with which God sees him.

41. Pontet, 311.

42. G-M 420, n. 3.

43. Souls thirsting for God appear before God's eyes in a manner interiorly consonant with the exterior appearance of the dry land (Gn 1.9).

44. The distinction between the bitter sea and the dry land adumbrates the later celebrated division between the terrestrial city and the city of God central in Augustine's interpretation of history. The anticipation is only vague, for the key roles of love of God and pride as demarcating the two societies (CD 14.28) are left unspecified, and historical ramifications of this world-encompassing polarity within humankind have still to be developed.

45. Down to the end of the world God knows all the people of God, the wheat apart from the chaff. Although the bishop as superintendent vigilantly watches over those entering and leaving the Church, he cannot discern what they are actually thinking in their hearts, for only the Lord knows those who are his own. Again and again is underscored the crucial truth that Christ is the one and only teacher, whose chair is in heaven, under whom, while faithfully exercising his office as bishop, Augustine is one of he sheep along with his flock, so that he discourses to his congregation not as a teacher but a minister of the word; not to disciples but to co-disciples, not to servants but to co-servants (S 292.1.1). As co-sheep, co-disciple, co-servant, he could not penetrate, as does God, the secret intentions within that divide the good from the evil. For texts on *condiscipuli* see Madec, BA 6, n.7 545-8.

46. Van der Meer, 259.

47. Van der Meer, 262.

48. C. Dawson, *The Making of Europe*, 56, 248.

49. Elsewhere the spiritual light that is Augustine more concretely details the seasons of sacred history. Corresponding to the six days of creation are six ages of historical time. The first runs from Adam to Noah; the second, from Noah to Abraham; the third, from Abraham to David; the fourth, from David to the Babylonian captivity; the fifth, from the captivity in Babylon to the coming of Christ; the sixth, from the incarnation until the end of the world (GCM 1.23. 35-40. DQ 58.2. P 92.1). The sixfold division is paralleled by the classical six stages of individual life: infancy, boyhood, young manhood, manhood, later manhood, and senescence (GCM 1.23. 35-40. VR 26.48.). The seventh and eighth days are transhistorical, symbolizing two periods of one and the same age of eternal happiness (CD 22, 30). A. Luneau, *L'histoire du salut chez les Pères de l'Église*, 291-2.

50. In rendering *in principio diei* and its companion, *in principio noctis* as "to rule the day" and "to rule the night", however, some translators do not seem aware that Augustine is using a slight variation of the Old Latin text: *inchoationem diei...et...noctis*. Yet elsewhere he recognizes that the *arché* of the Septaugint may be translated *principatus*, dominion or rule (GL 2.15.32), an identical point made in P 135.8, which speaks of the sun with power over the day, *in potestatem diei*, and the moon with power over the night.

51. Later Catholic theologians distinguish the seven sanctifying gifts from the nine ministry gifts of 1 Cor 12.4-11. Quickening the first set is *gratia gratum faciens* or grace sanctifying the soul while each of the latter group is *gratia gratis data*, a special gift for ministering to the body of Christ, which does not necessarily render its recipient holy or presuppose minimum holiness for its exercise. Without employing this terminology, Augustine, there can be no doubt, was alert to the disparity between the two species of gifts. The examples of Saul and Balaam testify that in 1 Cor 12.4-11 Paul was not constructing a purely hypothetical case but averring that some evil men gifted with prophecy actually lack charity, a truth that will be terrifyingly confirmed when at the Last Judgment the Lord banishes from his sight those who, though prophesizing in his name, had cold hearts devoid of charity. QS 2.8-9. J 65.3. Here, however, Augustine regards the ministry gifts as essentially linked to grace. The power to shine during the day or night symbolizes the spiritual gifts, each of which confers the power to become sons of God (P 135.8). Through the descent of the Holy Spirit these lights or fires are intended to set the whole world on fire with the Gospel of love (13.19.25). On the sanctifying gifts see C. Van Lierde, "The Teaching of St. Augustine on the Gifts of the Holy Spirit from the Text of Isaiah 11.2-3", updated for publication in *Augustine: Mystic and Mystagogue*, CollAug., 5-110

52. QS 2.8 also omits explicit mention of the ninth gift, *interpretatio linguarum*, which is, however, listed in P 135.8.

53. Not all of the gifts in 1 Cor 12.7-11 have been continuously deployed throughout the history of the Church. During the fourth and fifth centuries, and probably a century or two prior, speaking in tongues and interpretation of tongues dropped out of the community liturgy or official Church worship. Yet, according to Augustine, the gift of tongues is still analogously operative since,

as universal, the Church speaks in all languages. Indeed, he holds, along with every Catholic, he can boldly but truthfully claim to speak all languages, Greek, Syriac, Hebrew, and the others: as a member of the *Catholica*, the body of Christ that utters its truths in all tongues, as one with all peoples, he speaks in all languages (P 147.19).

54. Earlier Augustine had been inclined to maintain that miracles were by and large limited to the apostolic age. At first miracles were required to raise minds from visible to invisible realities; now that the faith has been preached and accepted all over the world, they need no longer be performed. If they did frequently, even routinely, occur, their familiarity would breed, if not contempt, general indifference since only novel and unusual events excite wonderment (VR 25.47. UC 16.34). Later, pastoral experience opened his eyes to the undeniable fact of ongoing miracles, not as magnificent and striking as some New Testament predecessors, but miracles nonetheless, such as the healing of the blind man in Milan through the intercessions of Saints Protasius and Gervasius (9.7.15. R 1.13.7; 14.5). In CD 22.8 he records twenty-five miracles, with some of which he was personally acquainted. According to Possidius, one sick man was healed by the laying on of Augustine's hands (V 29). Notice, we are taking miracles in the broad sense to include healings whereas in 1 Cor 12.4-11 Paul distinguishes the charisms of the working of miracles and healings. The rise in the U.S.A. in 1967 of Catholic charismatic renewal, a movement that has since spread worldwide, remarkably evidenced that the charisms operative in Augustine's day are still being exercised not only among the saintly but among ordinary Christians as well. Unfortunately, incautiously adopting modern Pentecostalist theology, some Catholic charismatics tend to confuse praying in tongues, which is Scripturally baseless, with the speaking in tongues of 1 Cor 12.10. For a critical appraisal of praying in tongues see J.M. Quinn, "Praise in St. Augustine: Some Reflections", in *Searching For God*, 57-91, especially 57-63.

55. Those with lesser gifts can be content, for even the wise are far from fulfilled in this valley of tears. Maximum contentment occurs only above, when the soul is insatiably sated with the God who is all goodness.

56. In the moral line prudence is the virtue whereby a person readily distinguishes things to be desired and things to be avoided (ME 24.45). However, broadly considered, it signifies the power to cognize, e.g. the connection of the specific parts of the physical world to the whole that is the universe (GCM 1.21.32). Hailed as *prudentissimus* in this sense, Paul is not only practically but theoretically wise, sharply discriminating spirituals and carnals. A masterly teacher, Paul had the finesse to adapt his teaching to spirituals and carnals, feeding the former with solid food, the latter with milk.

57. As noted above (7.10.16), the figure of eyes too weak to gaze goes back to Plato, *Rep.* 7.55 C.

58. Not only carnals but also spirituals are not to be piqued if they obtain less than the maximum here and now. The spiritually perfect in this life still struggle with imperfections that do not mar the blessed above. The Son assumed the form of a servant to reform men in the likeness of God, thereby readying them to see

the form of God. Like God, of the same form as the Son, the soul will see his form, and, seeing him as he is, will be filled with the treasures of wisdom and knowledge, wholly assuaged by the fountain of life (S 194.3-4).

59. The opinion that the firmament consists of pure fire apparently descends from Heraclitus and Parmenides (Diels, DG 340b5-6). The hypothesis that stars are conglomerates of fiery light was generally held, Aristotle being the most notable dissenter (*Meteor* 1.342b5ff.) Augustine probably gleaned this information from handbooks of astronomy or from Celsus' *Opiniones omnium philosophorum.* BA 48, 595, n. 2.

60. It seems inaccurate to translate, as some do, *volantes super terram juxta firmamentum* as "flying over the earth in the firmament" since birds, unable to reach the firmament, fly in the atmosphere below; hence the text reads not *in firmamento caeli* but *juxta firmamentum,* near (but under) the firmament (GL 3.7.10).

61. On the probable influence of Mk 16.15-18 see BA 14, 627, n.1.

62. Mixture (*mixtio*) in 13.20.27 is analogous to the mixture of two liquids in which each loses its identity. However, *mixtio* is used in a quite different sense to mean the union, without confusion, of soul and body to constitute one human person (E137.3.11).

63. Augustine views wisdom and knowledge as special cases of *notiones.*

64. Not truths of faith but the sacramental rites of Old and New Testament vary. BA 14,467,n.1. See 13.18.23. For Augustine sacrament has a broad and strict sense. Taken broadly, a sacrament is a sacred sign that betokens or reveals an invisible reality. In the Old Testament there are numerous sacraments such as circumcision, temple sacrifices, altars, priesthood, and unleavened bread. In the New Testament the word is applied to the sign of the cross, exorcism, penance, penitential garments, prayer, the Lord's Prayer, reconciliation, and hymns. However, in the strict sense there are only a few sacraments administered by the Church, special sacred signs through which grace is bestowed on the recipient, six of which are enumerated: baptism, the Eucharist, chrismation (confirmation), penance, holy orders, and matrimony. Nowhere in his writings is found a reference to extreme unction or anointing of the sick; Portalié, 247, and Moriones, *Enchiridion,* 556-7. See E. Cutrone, "Sacraments", AE 741-7, with bibliography. See also Van der Meer, 279-82.

65. "Increase and multiply" is a directive that, figuratively read, applies to more than sacraments and preachers of truth. Among other factors, it prescribes the multiplication of works of mercy and diverse interpretations of Scripture (13.24.36-7).

66. In GCM 1.19.30 Augustine maintained that the ordinance, "Increase and multiply," had a strictly spiritual acceptation prior to the Fall. Had Adam not sinned, he and Eve would have abstained from nuptial union and, instead of giving birth to children, would have engendered spiritual offspring of supersensible and immortal joys. VR 46.88 proposes a similar view, contending that had there been no Fall, men would not have been bonded by temporal relationships in the flesh. Rejecting this account, R 1.13.8 holds that if there had been no sin or death, kinships stemming from marriage would exist.

The omission of explicit reference in 13.20.28 to the opinion espoused in GCM and VR and reproved in R would seem to suggest that Augustine had already discarded it.

67. G-M 428,n.9, comments that *ex utero eius* is "a remarkable example of catachresis", an apparent misuse of the term "womb" in reference to a male, justifiable here because it betokens Adam as the point of origin of all other human beings. From Adam issued the whole human race, including Eve; after Eve all except Christ were of the seed of Adam. But since Eve was not from the seed but from the side of Adam, Augustine assigns a uterus to Adam to designate the common matrix of humanity. We sometimes speak metaphorically of all events emerging from the womb of time; less metaphorically but still figuratively Augustine describes all men as born from the womb of Adam taken in a generic or asexual sense.

68. Augustine is generally regarded as the main architect of the sacramental system. The richness of his sacramental concept may seem somewhat devalued here by his straining to adapt sacraments to an exegesis that is at times not markedly deft. It would be unjust, however, to claim that his allegorical method serves as a kind of Procrustean bed. While the extent and nuances of his sacramental theology are clearly reduced, at no juncture are any of its main limbs lopped off.

69. Piety distinguishes Catholic Christians from Donatists. The form of the sacrament, available to Donatists, is the visible sacrament of baptism while the *virtus* of the sacrament, an invisible power that is piety or charity, enriches only Catholics united through the Holy Spirit in the one body of Christ. Only Catholics can grow into living souls, mature Christians energized by the power of the sacrament (S 229U). Baptism outside the Church is objectively valid but subjectively ineffective or fruitless since those outside the unity of the Church lack the Holy Spirit who confers grace (S 268.2). As a severed hand has form but no life, so a recipient of baptism cut off from the Church obtains the form but not the life of grace of the sacrament (S 268.12). Once a baptized person returns to the Church, he is vivified by the charity poured forth by the Holy Spirit (S 71.19.32). In particular, the baptism of Donatists, collectively regarded as in bad faith, is valid but unfruitful. Still, an individual born of heretical or schismatic parents must not be judged at fault as long as he is open to the whole truth (E 43.1.1). Again, separated brethren not yet sharing in the fullness of light must be treated with a generous tolerance rooted in love. Catholics who are enjoined, "Love men, slay errors," are to claim the truth without pride and to fight for the truth without harshness (CALP 3.1.29). See K. Adam, *The Spirit of Catholicism*, 197-8, 204-5. Grabowski, *Church*, 236-7.

70. Aristotle, *Meta.* 1.2.983a13-22. See Book 7,n.76 above.

71. In GCM 1.23.40, a work, its title shows, targeted at Manicheism, cattle symbolize carnal appetites, and serpents, dark curiosity, but birds of the air are symbols of pride. Manichean pride consists in identifying the substance of God and man; free abandon is given to lust of the flesh because the coercive evil nature or soul forces them to sin without responsibility; curiosity, hugging the earth like serpents, relishes earthly things and futilely attempts to understand

spiritual objects with merely earthly eyes (GCM 2.26.40).

72. After granting in 1 Cor 8.8 that in terms of moral object there is nothing wrong in availing oneself of meat that had been sacrificed to idols, Paul stipulates that such eating is circumstantially wrong for a clear-minded Christian if his eating confuses or scandalizes a fellow Christian, a former idol-worshipper whose conscience is not certainly formed on the issue. Augustine's decontextualized, accommodated recourse to the passage need not take into account Paul's nuancive comments.

73. The clean of heart, who overcome the world as Christ did, will see him who made the world. After putting on the new man created in justice and holiness of truth (S 163.4.4), the Christian sings a new song (S 216.2.2), imitating the new-born child who found the world old when he came to the old man Simeon (S 163.4.4).

74. "*Praecedentem proximum*" (the neighbor who precedes us), considered precisely as no more than human, cannot qualify as an ideal to be imitated according to the supernatural criteria of Rom 12.2 and Gn 1.26. Still, in a less restricted sense such a neighbor, if graced, even if not a paragon, certainly helps mold behavior. So taken, the term covers forebears, familial or socio-political, whose personality and character remain precious in memory, social progenitors to whom the living owe gratitude, to whom admiration pays the tribute of emulation, posterity tending to imitate its fathers, whether good or evil (P 48[S.2].11).

75. As other citations showed, man is made in the image of God not in the line of body but in the line of mind (GL 3.20.30). The rational soul, after a first ontic, not temporal, stage as an unformed creature, is formed or fully made by being illumined or converted toward its creator (GL 3.10.30). Prior to the Fall, man as an intellectual creature knew the Word, through whom it was created, but after original sin made him spiritually decrepit, through Christ he is "renewed in the knowledge of God according to the image of its creator" (Col 3.10) (GL 3.10.31-32), a full renewal achieved in the spiritual person.

76. R. Knox, *Enthusiasm*, 152.

77. In commenting on Ez 34.16, Augustine takes the mountains of Israel as a symbol of the authors of the Scriptures, from which descend the streams of evangelical preachings. S 46.24.

78. The spiritual is unable to judge matters over which God alone has jurisdiction. BA 14,n.30, 632.

79. In listing instances within the scope of spirituals' judgment, Augustine apparently restricts himself to the functions of the spiritual bishop, whose role is *sacrificare, praedicare, et benedicere*: administration of the sacraments of initiation along with celebration of the Eucharist, preaching the word, and blessing and praying over the people. Spirituals whom providence did not appoint to the hierarchy participate in the Eucharist, are instructed and moved by sermons, and profit from blessings and prayer. BA 14,n.30, 632. As mentioned in our text, a spiritual can also assess the enactment of the liturgy, administration of the sacraments, and the doctrinal and moral caliber of sermons. Prior to conscription into the priesthood, Augustine as head of a lay

monastic community no doubt perceptively noticed, perhaps at times with less than 100% approbation, the conduct of liturgical celebrations and the content and delivery of sermons.

80. The lamentable *abyssus saeculi* and *caecitas carnis* (13.23.34) are a portion of the punishment paid for the Fall. In paradise man, his mind focused on God, lived as he willed so long as he willed what God commanded, his existence being one of knowledge and fruition of God, in virtue of whose good he was made good. His body was ordered to his soul, and his soul to God, with the result that his soul was wholly tranquil. Because there was no sin, there was no abyss of this world (CD 14.26), and because the body was fully controlled, no sense-dominated image-thinking that obscured knowledge of God and defeated understanding of objects of thought.

81. In the framework of justice mercy is a certain compassion in the heart whereby men are obliged to help, as far as possible, another in his misery. This affection of the soul conforms to reason when mercy is tendered in a way that preserves justice, either by giving an alms to someone needy or by forgiving a repentant individual (CD 9.5).

82. The *quid* and *quale* are the second and third aspects of an object under inquiry (10.10.17;40.65). *An sit* is not asked, for the problem is plain: "Increase and multiply" seems unexplicably omitted in certain passages of Gn 1.

83. He skips reference to the allegorical sense of the multiplication of birds (Gn 1.22), which has already been treated above (13.21.29-30). The first birds stand for the earliest apostles and evangelists, whose offspring are succeeding generations of ministers of the word, usually spirituals, whose preaching brings down ongoing blessings on the faithful.

84. Earlier 13.20.27 remarked the one-conception-many-bodily-operations motif in reference to wisdom and knowledge; the bodily workings are no doubt signs such as words.

85. McKenzie, *Dictionary of the Bible,* 254-8.

86. BA 14.495, n. 2.

87. Previously (13.17.20,21) Augustine speaks of the thirst of the dry land, but in this context the question of thirst does not arise. The accent is put on the fecundity of reason whose fruits or multiple interpretations are reaped by the sweat of the mind's brow.

88. As noted in BA 14,501,n.1, Augustine's Latin version of Ph 4.10 differs somewhat from the Vulgate. Augustine uses *repullulastis* where the Vulgate has *refloruistis,* and *taedium habuistis* where the Vulgate, in conformity with the Greek, reads *occupati eratis.* Again, his translation of Phil 4.10-3 differs from the Vulgate. He puts *minus habere* where Jerome translates *humiliari.* However, his *in omnibus et in omni,* with the phrases transposed, more faithfully renders the Greek than the Vulgate's *ubique et in omnibus.*

89. As a bishop, a Christian preacher bent on imitating Paul as Paul imitated Christ, Augustine put his finger on the principal reason why Paul rejoiced in material aid donated by the Christian community in Philippi. Surely whatever offerings the faithful in Hippo brought to the altar aroused similar joy, effected not by material gifts but by the wholly supernaturally motivated ardor of

donors

90. Great also as a mountain, Paul was eminent in sanctity (P 72.5), outstanding in massive solidity of doctrine and character (P 39.6), with a mind supernaturally brilliant because superbly illumined by divine justice (P 39.6).

91. In holding that joy was Paul's food, Augustine seems at first blush to be telescoping cause (the fruit of mercy that Paul feeds upon) and effect (the joy that ensues). However, from another angle, cause and effect are not rhetorically blended. As sight of food for the body excites delight, so, Augustine apparently maintains, recognition of the fruit that is active mercy produces the nourishment of the heart that is Christian joy.

92. Before journeying to Thessalonica, Paul, Silas, and Luke evangelized Philippi, a main city in Macedonia, where they converted the wealthy Lydia and her household and a clairvoyant slave girl, before he and Silas were put in stocks for a time (Ac 16.11-40).

93. However deprived of material goods, Paul was always affluent in goods of the Spirit; any quite modest material abundance he occasionally enjoyed was far distant from the luxury that for an avaricious man becomes a lifestyle and a snare (S 177.7).

94. The trees that are the faithful drink in the rain, grace from above, without which they cannot bear fruit (S 47.14.25).

95. An act with right intention is directed by grace to the one and only end, the *summum bonum* that is God. Hence acts and virtues of˙ pagans, properly performed but deprived of the proper intention, are, like gifts, sterile; not strictly good, which is impossible, but simply without fruit. CJ 4.3.21,22. Moreover, so necessary is grace that if we dispense with it, we are compelled to accept as virtuous the avaricious who exercise carnal prudence, fortitude, temperance, and justice; they cleverly figure out strategies for amassing wealth, in the hunt for which they bravely endure hardship while avoiding a luxurious lifestyle and observing laws for just transactions. From another angle, apart from right intention that ensouls true virtues, the infamous Catiline would have to be absurdly credited with justice, fortitude, and patience. CJ 4.3.19. See E. Gilson, *The Spirit of Medieval Philosophy*, 477-8, n.12.

96. *Pueros tuos* means your little ones in the spirit. Boy signifies a little one who has been denuded of pride through the discipline of suffering (P 68 [S.2].2); thus *pueri* is a synonym for *minimi* and *discipuli* (13.26.41). As G-M 441, n.5, notes, servants is the sense of the Septaugint and Hebrew equivalents of *pueri.* Augustine, however, seems to take the word in the acceptation of little one or child, one of the least or tiny ones. This interpretation jibes with the *ex minimis meis* of 13.26.41, which echoes *ex his minimis* of Mt 25.40 and also indirectly refers to Paul, styled in his own words *minimum apostolorum* (7.21.27; 8.4.9, after 1 Cor 15.9), applauded as a gigantic living soul, paradigm of apostolic spirituals entitled to live by the Gospel, deserving of much more than a plain cup of cold water.

97. Pontet, 291-8.

98. Though Book 11 substantially solved the problem of the connection between eternity and time, Augustine raises it again in a new setting. The relationship

between eternity and time remains knotty, in some respects baffling, whose further elucidation requires renewed scrutiny and ongoing reconsideration.

99.   To God who is sovereign over all, only a Christian can, along with Augustine, say with holy boldness, "my God"; a Christian who loves God is convinced that he can claim as his own the Lord who owns him, an approbation God himself loves. A Christian murmurs this aspiration with affection and assurance because what he claims is true. Each Christian, however, tells God, "You are mine," in a way that does not bar God from belonging to others. God is the personal possession of each but the private property of none. He is the whole in all and the whole in each, a good for one and all to enjoy. As the same sermon is heard by all, as the one light from the sun shines on all, so the common good that is God is possessed by all (S 47.30).

100. No doubt God's truth spoke into Augustine's inner ear, yet it is not altogether doubtless that Augustine was accorded an interior locution. After praying over the difficulty, the key was intellectually enunciated in his mind; this rational answer to his question, supplied by divine assistance, he seems to describe rhetorically as a direct locution from God.

101. More than a few translators of no mean competence take *verbum* (*verbo...meo tempus non accedit*) to refer to the Word instead of the word of God. Since this passage partially rehearses analysis of the distinction between eternity and time (11.6.8-7.9), according to which it is the Word, coeternal with the Father, whom the Father utters eternally and in whom all things are uttered eternally, it seems understandable that a translator be inclined to favor Word as the correct equivalent of *verbum.* Granted the plausibility of such a rendering, it seems preferable, however, because the context demands it, to translate it as word: the passage deals expressly with the import, varying in eternity and time, of the word of Scripture, a word whose eternity within God equals that of God since it is spoken by the Word, the coeternal wisdom.

102. For Manichees, "not God but the Race of Darkness created grains and plants and all roots and shrubs" (CF 24.2). Augustine takes care not to say that the Principle of Darkness *generated* animals and plants.

103. The phrase *de tuo,* may at first strike some as vague to the point of ambiguity. It may be rendered "of what is yours" or "of what is subject to your power." It cannot bear on the very substance of God; for only the Word is begotten *de te* or *de Deo,* no creature being equal to God (12.7.7). Heaven and earth are not *de ipso,* of God, but are *ex ipso,* from God (NB 27). However, in 13.30.45 Augustine employs *de tuo* rather than *ex tuo.* The phrase may convey the import of *de nihilo,* as in the proposition, "God made heaven and earth *de nihilo*" (13.7.7), yet it seems gauche to imply that *nihil* is God's own. It seems reasonable then to infer that the phrase refers to the only remaining semantic candidate: formless matter. God made the world of formless matter, *de materia informi,* the next-to-nothing made out of nothing (12.8.8). In opposition to the Christian God who made the heavens from his very own (in the Augustine's dialogical format, *de tuo*), the Manichean deity, under the whip of necessity, made the heavens not of formless matter but of already fully formed things. This interpretation is confirmed by the summary comments in 13.33.48. Things were made by God

not *de te*, from himself, but *de nihilo*, from nothing, not from something that was not God's (*non de aliqua non tua*) or which (as Manichees contended) was already actually existing before creation. It was from matter made by God (matter that was *de tuo or de tua*) that material things were formed; a matter concreated with form (13.33.48); prior not in time but in origin to form (12.29.40); prior in mode of being, as subject to form.

104. In CF 6.8 Primal Man builds the world by means of Princes of Darkness. According to CF 20.9, however, it is the *spiritus potens* who shapes the world from the captured bodies of the Race of Darkness.

105. We may touch on a few nuances of the Manichean version of the origin of the world. (i) After defeating the Archons, the Living Spirit constructs the universe from the parts of their bodies, and the heaven from their skins. (ii) The universe consists of ten firmaments and eight earths borne up by Atlas (CF 20.9). (iii) There are three regions of light. (a) From pure light is made sun and moon. (b) Out of slightly contaminated light are formed stars. (c) The Third Envoy is evoked to organize the world into machinery for freeing light, the wheels of which are Wind, Water, and Fire. Collected particles of light are carried to the moon, whence they are shipped to the sun. See Bonner, 160-9; Coyle, 32-42.

106. Some odd physical explanations may be singled out. (i) As mentioned in n. 101, Atlas supports ten firmaments and eight earths (CF 20.9). (ii) The powers in the sun manifest themselves to the fiery demons; their sudden appearance causes lightning (NB 44). Thunder occurs when the demons explode with anger at the sight of light escaping their grasp (CF 21.12). (iii) The sight of miserable souls still trapped in matter moves Primal Man to veil his face for a time, a frequently repeated gesture that is the source of eclipses. CF 22.12. Similarly, according to Simplicius, *In Epict. Enchiridion*, 27 (cited in Lieu, *Manicheism in Mesopotamia and the Roman East*, 171-2), when the movements of evil archons produce disorder, light particles within them fashion a kind of evil to mask their excitement, with eclipses resulting from the evil. Their God covers himself with a veil so as not to see his followers plundered by the enemy (CF 18.7); refusing to look at his works as good, he covers his face (CF 22.12).

107. See BA 14, 510-1, n.2.

108. Concerning the Holy Spirit and charity see Grabowski, *Church*, 272-5, 354-5.

109. Creation is good in itself, signalizing its creator, reflecting his glory, and moving man to delight in God. Things of creation are intended to be used and enjoyed. The uses of fire are manifold, and even the simplest of foods tastes sweet to the palate of the lowliest of the *plebs*. But criteria of human convenience and inconvenience can function only as secondary measures for assessing the goodness of creation. The primary reason for deeming creation good is that it was made by God, who is to be understood and loved in his handiwork as the *bonum bonorum*, the supreme good from whom all other goods derive. It is an intellectual disorder to rate the secondary standard primary, to the exclusion of knowledge and love of God (CD 12.4).

110. The beings that God intrinsically created he also extrinsically administers (GL 8.26.48). This brief proposition summarily expresses three points. First, in his intrinsic operation God, as underived existence, creates from nothing the

limited beings of creatures. Second, he creates not quasi-nonentities, not phantoms, but things pulsating with their proper mode of being, their specific makeup, and an ordination to inner harmony (CD 12.5). Because God is all-powerful, he makes not a tissue of appearances but an actual cosmos of relatively autonomous beings. Third, in his extrinsic operation God is causally immanent in his creation, conserving the being and concurring in the action of things made. The Father is at work even till now, sustaining his creation (GL 4.12.23.J.2.10). While their existence totally derives from God, creatures enjoy a being other than his and, similarly, while their continuance in existence hinges on God's administration, they prosecute activities in accord with their natures (CD 7.30). On creative causation see Grabowski, *All-Present God*, 135-88.

111. The opinions that heaven and earth may signify either all visible creation or the spiritual and corporeal realms of creation were listed earlier (12.17.24,25) as acceptable alternatives to Augustine's exegesis.

112. R 2.6.2 repudiates the surmise about spiritual waters above the firmament, a suggestion proposed without adequate analytical and empirical support. To justify the Scriptural text Augustine later advances the hypothesis that material waters are located above the firmament. Though water is heavier than air and fire, drops of water that are infinitesimally tiny can be present above the heaven (GL 2.4.8-5-9). However, because of the paucity of hard empirical data, the matter evades exact verification.

113. Accepting the received scientific theory of his day, Augustine subscribed to the opinion that dew dropped from the heaven or atmosphere on clear nights. Surely a prima facie plausible view: if rain falls from clouds, the moisture called dew, it would appear, also falls from the atmosphere. Not until the nineteenth century did further investigation prove this plausible account untenable. Dew occurs, we now know, when warm air comes in contact with a cold object; for example, on a hot day small drops of water condense on a pitcher of ice water. When warmer air contacts leaves and grass, which radiate or lose heat at night, drops of water appear on their cooler surfaces. The dew point or saturation point of water in air becomes lower as the temperature drops. When air particles touching cold surfaces become colder, they release condensation, the drops of moisture named dew. In short, dew does not fall to objects on the ground.

114. (i) The puzzling reference to birds emerging from the waters is perhaps explainable by the fact that the air close to the earth is moist, a datum verified by the apparent fall of dew on clear nights. Water may signify this moist air of the clouds, the sort in which birds fly. In the region of higher and purer air birds cannot fly, for its thinness or slight density cannot support their flight (GLI 14.44). (ii) Birds fly beneath the firmament that is the region from the clouds to the starry heaven (GLI 14.45). (iii) Air becomes thicker or denser when mixed with water, leading to the formation of clouds (GL 3.2.3). (iv) On Augustine's reckoning, which jibed with that of scientists of his time, air when not rarefied but somewhat mingled with moisture, is dense enough to uphold the small-and-light-boned bodies of birds in flight. However, as modern science

demonstrates, factors other than comparative weight underlie aerial flight. In actively flying with wings flapping, a bird maintains its lift by the downward motion of its wings, the reaction to which is an upthrust of air. During passive flying or gliding, lift is sustained by the increased pressure under the wings, which is explained by the Bernouilli effect, an extension to air of the Bernouilli principle. According to this principle, in an ideal fluid the total mechanical energy of the unit volume remains constant. Applied to air, this means that pressure and velocity in moving air are inversely related; when velocity increases, pressure decreases. Air passing over the nearly motionless wings of a bird in flight has a slightly greater surface to cover; so it travels faster. The increase in velocity over the wings is accompanied by a decrease in pressure on the upper side of the wings. Thus the pressure from the under side becomes greater than that on the upper side of the wings; this greater pressure from below supplies lift and keeps a gliding bird aloft. The Bernouilli effect also furnishes the basic reason why airplanes gain lift and maintain altitude in flight. A. Kolin, *Physics*, 155-8.

115. The distinction between male and female is recorded in Gn 2, to which Augustine accorded no explicit attention, all his prior comments being deliberately confined to Gn 1.1-31. The reflections on the lines from Gn 2 seem to be parenthetically inserted by way of corollary or quasi-footnote, duplicating in different words observations set down in the earlier GCM 2.11.15.

116. For a detailed convincing refutation of the indictment of misogynism see F.E. Weaver and J. Laporte, "Augustine and Women: Relationships and Teachings," AS. 12 (1981), 115-31. In "Augustine's View on Women" AUG(L) 39, 1989, 5-53, a delicately nuanced and thoroughly documented study, T. van Bavel shows that on Augustine's reckoning, women are basically the intellectual equivalent of men; in practice they behaved as the moral superior of men; women are by nature, not only by grace, the image of God (even though functionally, due to social inferiority, somewhat lower than men); and women will retain their sex after the resurrection, some points of which were denied by previous writers, all the while recognizing that cultural deficiencies kept Augustine from achieving a modern appreciation of women. Interestingly, he indicates, one contemporary radical feminist, attempting to make Augustine square with her preconceptions, misses the very fact that in her *mens* woman is the image of God and also misconstrues the post-resurrection state of a woman's body, claiming (against the textual evidence) that the female sex organs will be mysteriously transformed, i.e., effectively disappear. In partial accord with van Bavel, K. Børrensen, in "In Defence of Augustine: How *Femina* is *Homo*", AUG (L) 40 (1990), CollAug, *Mélanges T.J. van Bavel*, t. 1, 411-28, maintains that Augustine's general intention is sound though spoiled by his doctrinal content, while noting that Augustine was the first of the Church Fathers to hold that woman also is created in God's image. It should no go unremarked, however, that Augustine's views have been subject to criticism by feninist theologians, not all of whom ground their dontentions in reliable scholarship. One of the best known, R. Ruether, who is commonly called a radical feminist, argues that Augustine's partriarchal anthropology implies

hierarchy, which entails subordination and inevitable oppression. Still, it is hardly clear that dismantling of its heirarchy will leave the Roman Church continuous with its rich past. See E. Ann Matter, "Women", AE 887-92, with bibliography.

117. Orania Papazoglou, "Despising Our Mothers, Despising Ourselves," *First Things*, January, 1992, 11-9, incisively critiques this anti-natural radical feminism. In the name of liberation a small clique of socio-economic elitists pretending to speak for all women have laid siege to the shrine of motherhood, the very meaning and glory of womanhood. In striving to elevate women by dehumanizing them, they have destroyed their value and trashed their self-esteem. "You cannot devalue motherhood without devaluing everything else women do. You cannot train a whole generation in contempt for their mothers without training them in contempt for themselves" (19).

118. For solidly descriptive and experimental-scientific data tellingly establishing the differences between men and women see S. Clark, *Man and Woman in Christ*, 377-410.

119. For more detailed reflections on praise see J.M. Quinn, *Praise in St. Augustine*, which interweaves analytical and devotional motifs.

120. Earlier heaven and earth are said to symbolize spiritual and carnal members of the Church (13.12.13). Here, however, heaven and earth are assigned a new figurative import, with no reference made to the prior allegorical meaning.

121. The discussion of the Church and the Church as heaven depends on Grabowski, *Church*, 582-99.

122. It is wisdom through which men are formed in the knowledge of God. It is continence through which men are not conformed to this world but formed in the knowledge of God (BV 15.2.21). Continence or rational action is subordinated to understanding of moral truths known by illumination.

123. For these and other texts see Pontet, 511-4, who draws upon O. Rottmanner, *Geistesfrüchte aus der Klosterzelle* in *Gesammelte Aufsatze*, 30-2. According to Rottmanner, 30, "For Augustine, in theory only a few were predestined, in practice all were predestined" (30). It would seem more accurate to aver that while, according to his theory, only a few were predestined, in practice he exhorted his congregation to act as if predestined, exploiting all the means available to dispose their souls for predestination. In a like vein, in "The Person and Work of Christ", Battenhouse, *Companion to St. Augustine*, 359-60, A. Outler calls attention to Augustine's "homiletical mood" displayed within the Christian community at variance with the "polemical mood" predominant in attacking Pelagian errors.

124. *S. th.* 1.19.6 ad 3;23.3.

125. Para. 1261.

126. In commenting on *S. th.* 1.22.4, *Opera Omnia* (Leonine) 4, 269-70, Cajetan (1469-1534), regarded by many Dominicans as the greatest Thomistic commentator, concludes that the problem of accounting for free will in divine predestination is insoluble. While God clearly provides for necessary and contingent events, it is hard to harmonize the indeterminate character of free actions with infallible providence. The crux lies in reconciling the compossi-

bility of events that are providentially inevitable with actions that are evidently freely or avoidably chosen. *Secundum quid,* the event is avoidable, but, absolutely, all things considered, the event is inevitable. The event is not only de facto inevitable from the divine perspective but from the human standpoint as well. However, it is not inconceivable that the supereminent divine word can arrange that something higher than inevitability or avoidability flow from the providential decree; in such a case neither the inevitable nor the avoidable would necessarily issue from passive providence. Such an alternative would not stem from analytically coercive truth; it would appeal to the unattainable peak of divine wisdom concealed from human eyes. In short, here, as with the trinity, when the matter is inexplicable, the mind falls back on faith alone, which is surely sufficient. While freedom of will is evident and rationally validated, the reconciliation of freedom with the inevitability of providentially ordained events escapes analysis by a limited intellect. Grabowski, *Church,* 605-49, contains a solid treatment, with a wide-ranging bibliography. Bonner, especially 386-95, offers a judicious assessment. Also valuable is the appraisal of TeSelle, 320-38. See the excellent discussion in A. Trapè, "St. Augustine", *Patrology IV,* 441-5, with bibliography. See also M. Lamberight, "Predestination," AE 677-9, with bibliography.

127. *Enn.* 1.4.7. As Pellegrino notes in V, 28, n. 12, Plotinus' dictum expresses a notion commonplace in antiquity, similar sayings being employed by Cicero, Seneca, and Ambrose.

Select Bibliography

Adam, K., *The Spirit of Catholicism*, (tr.) J McCann, New York, 1929.

—— *Christ Our Brother*, (tr.) J McCann, London, 1931.

—— *The Christ of Faith*, (tr.) J Crick, New York, 1957.

Agaësse, P./Solignac, A., *La Génèse au sens littéral*, BA 48-9, Paris, 1982.

—— and J. Moignet, *La Trinité VIII-XV*, BA 16, Paris, 1999.

Agatha, Mary, S.P.D., *The Rule of St Augustine*, Villanova, 1992.

Alfaric, P., *L'évolution intellectuelle de saint Augustin*, 1, Paris, 1918.

Allers, R., *The Successful Error*, New York, 1940.

Angus, S., *The Sources of the first ten books of St. Augustine's* De Civitate Dei, Princeton, 1906.

Aristotle, *Categories, Physics, De Anima, Metaphysics Nicomachean Ethics*, in the *Basic Works of Aristotle*, (ed.) R. Mckeon, New York, 1941.

Ayres, L., and Boros, M., "God", AE 384-90.

Ayres, L., "Measure Number, and Weight", AE 550-2.

Baguette, Ch., "Un période stoïcienne dans l'évolution of la pensée de saint Augustin," REA 16, 1-2 (1970), 47-77.

Balter, M., "Academia", AL 1. 40-6.

Battenhouse, R.(ed.), *A Companion to the Study of St. Augustine*, New York, 1955.

Bauerschmidt, J., "Abortion", AE 1.

Beardsley, M., *Aesthetics from Classical Greece to the Present*, New York, 1966.

Beare, J., *Greek Theories of Elementry Cognition from Alcmaeon to Aristotle*, Oxford, 1906.

Beierwaltes, W., *Regio Beatitudinis*, Villanova, PA, 1981.

Berrouard, M. F., "L'exégèse augustinienne de Rom. 7,7-25 entre 396 et 418," RA 16 (1981), 101-95.

Bettetini, M., "Augustinus in Karthago. Gleich einem Roman", CAH, 133-64.

Blaiklock, E. (tr.), *The Confessions of St. Augustine*, New York, 1983.

Blanshard, B., *The Nature of Thought*, 2 vols., New York, 1939.

——— *Reason and Goodness*, New York, 1961.

Bochet I., *Saint Augustin et le désir de Dieu*, Paris, 1982.

Boethius, *The Consolation of Philosophy*, (tr.) J. Stewart, London, 1920.

Böhmer, H., *Die Lobpreisungen des Augustins, Studien zur Kirchegeschichte*, Munich, 1974.

Boissou, G., "Le Style des Confessions", BA 13, 207-35.

Bonner, G., *St. Augustine of Hippo: Life and Controversies*, 2nd ed., Philadelphia, 1986.

——— *God's Decree and Man's Destiny*, London, 1987.

Boros, L., "Les catégories de la temporalité chez saint Augustin", *Archives de philosophie*, July, 1958.

Børresen, K., *Subordination and Equivalence: The Nature and Role of Woman in Augustine and Thomas Aquinas*, Washington, D.C., 1981.

——— "In Defence of Augustine: How *Femina* Is *Homo*," AUG(L) 40 (1990), *Mélanges T. J. van Bavel* 1, 411-28

Bourke, V., *Augustine's Quest of Wisdom*, Milwaukee, WI, 1945

——— (tr.), *The Confessions of St. Augustine*, New York, 1953.

——— *Augustine's View of Reality*, Villanova, PA, 1964.

——— *Wisdom From St. Augustine*, Houston, TX, 1984.

C. Boyer, *Christianisme et néoplatonisme dans la formation de saint Augustin*, Paris, 1920.

Brown, P., *Augustine of Hippo*, Los Angeles, 1967.

B. Bruning, "De l'astrologie á la grâce", AUG(L) 41 (1991), *Mélanges T. J. van Bavel* 2, 575-643.

Burkitt, F., *The Religion of the Manichees*, Cambridge, 1925.

Burt, D., *Augustine's World*, Lanham, MD, 1996.

―― *Friendship and Society: an Introduction to Augustine's Practical Philosophy*, Grand Rapids, MI, 1999.
Butler, C., *Western Mysticism*, London, 1922.

Cajetan, T., *Commentarium S. th. Sancti Thomae, Opera Omnia*, 4 (Leonine), Rome, 1882.

Callahan, J., *Four Views of Time in Ancient Philosophy*, Cambridge, MA, 1948.

―― "A New Source for St. Augustine's Theory of Time", *Harvard Studies in Class. Philol.*, 63(1958), 437-54

Campbell, C. and McGuire, M., *The Confessions of St. Augustine*, New York, 1931.

Capánaga, V., *Agustin de Hipona*, Madrid, 1974.

Carey, P. "Academics", AE 4-5.

―― "Skeptics, Skepticism", AE 802-3.

Cayré, F., "La notion de sagesse chez saint Augustin", *L'Anné théologique augustinienne*, 4(1943), 433-56

―― "Le sens et. l'unité des Confessions", *L'Année théologigue augustinienne* 13 (1953), 13-32.

―― "Le livre XIII des *Confessions*," REA, 2 (1956), 146-61.

Chadwick, H., *Augustine*, Oxford, 1986.

―― (tr.), *Saint Augustine Confessions*, Oxford, 1991

Chatillon, F., "*Quidam secundum nos*: note d'exégèse augustinienue", *Rev. Moyen Âge latin* 1(1945), 287-304.

Christian, W., "The Creation of the World", in Battenhouse, *A Companion to the Study of St. Augustine*, 315-42.

Choron, J., *Death and Modern Man*, New York, 1964.

Cicero, *M. Tullii Ciceronis Opera*, (ed.) J. Orelli, J. Baiter and C. Halm, Zurich, 1845-61.

Cipriani, N., "Memoria", AE 553-5.

——— "Marius Victorinus", AE 533-5.

Clark, E., "Adam's Only Companion. Augustine and the Early Christian Debate on Marriage", RA 17 (1986).

Clark, M.T., *Augustine Philosopher of Freedom*, New York, 1959.

——— *Augustine*, Washington D.C., 1994

——— "Augustine's Christian Humanism", *University of Dayton Review*, 22, n.3(1994) 309-28.

——— "Spirituality", AE 813-5

Clark, S., *Man and Woman in Christ*, Ann Arbor, MI, 1980.

Colish, M. *The Stoic Tradition From Antiquity to the Middle Ages*, 2 vols., Leiden, 1985.

Colleran, J. (tr.), St. Augustine: *The Greatness of the Soul, The Teacher*, Wesminster, MD, 1950.

Collinge, W., "Hortensius", AE 37.

Collins, J., *The Mind of Kierkegaard*, Chicago, 1953.

Combès, G., *La doctrine politique de saint Augustin*, Paris, 1927.

Copleston, F.A., *History of Philosophy II*, New York, 1962.

Couannier, H., *St. Francis de Sales and His Friends*, (tr.) V. Morrow, New York, 1964.

Courcelle, P., *Recherches sur les Confessions de saint Augustin*, 2nd ed., Paris, 1968.

——— *Les Confessions de saint Augustin dans la tradition littéraire*, Paris, 1963.

Coyle, J.K., *Augustine's De Moribus Ecclesiae Catholicae*, Fribourg, 1978.

——— "In Praise of St. Monica; A Note on the Ostia Experience of *Confessions IX*," AS 13(1982), 87-96.

——— "Mani, Manicheism," AE 820-5.

Cress, D., "Hierius and Augustine's Account of the Lost *De pulchro et apto*, "AS 7 (1976). 153-63.

——— "Augustine's Privation Account of Evil: A Defense", AS 20 (1989), 109-28.

Cutrone, E., "Sacraments", AE 741-7.

Daley, B., "Christology", AE 164-9.

Dassmann, E., "Ambrosius", AL 1.269-86

Dawson, C., *Progress and Religion*, New York, 1930.

——— "St. Augustine and His Age", in *A Monument to St. Augustine*, New York, 1930, 11-77.

——— *The Making of Europe*, New York, 1932.

Deane, H., *The Political and Social Ideas of St. Augustine*, New York, 1963.

De La Peza, E., *El significado de "cor" en san Agustin*, Paris, 1962.

Decret, F., *Aspects du Manichéisme dans l'Afrique romaine*, Paris, 1970.

De Margerie, B., *An Introduction to the History of Exegesis III: St. Augustine*, Petersham, MA, 1991.

De Simone, R., "Modern Research on the Sources of St. Augustine's Doctrine of Original Sin", AS 11 (1980), 205-27.

Di Berardino, A.(ed.), *Patrology IV*, (tr.) P. Solari, Westminister, MD, 1986.

——— "Cassiciacum", AE 135.

Dill, S., *Roman Society from Nero to Marcus Aurelius*, New York, 1956.

Dodaro, R., "Church and State", AE 176-84.

Donnelly, D., *De Civitate Dei: An Annotated Bibliography of Modern Criticism*, New York, 1991

Dudden, F., H., *The Life and Times of Saint Ambrose*, 2 vols, Oxford, 1935.

Dulaey, M., *Le rêve dans la vie et la pensée de saint Augustin*, Paris, 1973.

Durant, W., *Caesar and Christ*, New York, 1944.

Du Roy, O., *L'intelligence de la foi en la Trinité selon saint Augustin*, Paris, 1966.

Engels, F., *Herr Dühring's Revolution in Science*, (tr.) E Burns, New York, 1935.

Esterson, A., *Seductive Mirage*, Chicago, 1993.

Evans, G., *Augustine on Evil*, Cambridge, 1982.

Feldmann, E., "Confessiones", AL 1. 1134-93.

——— "Das literarische Genus und das Gesamtkoncept der *Confessiones*", CAH, 11-59.

Ferrari, L., "The Pear-Theft in Augustine's 'Confessions' ", REA 16(1970), 234-42.

——— "Symbols of Sinfulness in Book II of Augustine's Confessions", AS 2(1971), 93-104.
——— "Monica on the Wooden Ruler", AS 6(1975), 193-205.

——— "Augustine's 'Nine Years' as a Manichee", AUG(L) 36 (1975) 210-216

——— "The Theme of the Prodigal Son in Augustine's Confessions", RA 12(1977),105-18.

——— "The Dreams of Monica in Augustine's *Confessions*", AS 10(1979), 3-17.

——— "Paul at the Conversion of Augustine (*Conf. VIII*, 12, 29-30)", AS 11(1980), 5-20.

——— "St. Augustine on the Road to Damascus", AS 13(1982), 151-70.

——— "Ecce audio vocem de vicina domo (Conf 8.12,29)," AUG(L) 33 (1983), 232-45.

——— *The Conversions of St. Augustine*, Villanova, 1984.

——— "Beyond Augustine's Conversion Scene", in J. McWilliam (ed.), *Augustine: From Rhetor to Theologian*, 1994, 97-108.

——— "Isaiah and the Early Augustine", AUG(L) 41(1991), *Melanges T. J. van Bavel* 2, 539-36.

N. Fischer and C. Mayer (ed.), *Die Confessiones des Augustinus von Hippo*, Freiburg, 1998.

Flasch, K., *Was Ist Zeit?*, Frankfurt, 1993.

Forbes, R., *Studies in Ancient Technology*, Leiden, 1955.

Fortin, E., "Saint Augustin et la doctirne néoplatonicenne de l'âme", AM 3, 371-80

———"The Political Implications of St. Augustine's Theory of Conscience", AS 1(1970), 133-52.

——— "Augustine, Thomas Aquinas, and the Problem of Natural Law", *Mediaevalia 4* (1978), 179-208. Reprinted as Ch. 10 in E. Fortin, *Classical Christianity and the Political Order*, Lanham, MD, 1996, 199-222.

——— "The Political Thought of St. Augustine", in *History of Political Philosophy*, (ed.) L. Strauss and J. Cropsey, Chicago, 1987, 176–205. Reprinted as Ch. 1 in E. Fortin, *Classical Christianity and the Political Order*, Lanham, MD., 1996, 1-27.

Fraisse, P., *The Psychology of Time*, (tr.) J. Leith, New York, 1963.

Gabillon, A., "Romanianus, Alias Cornelius", REA 24(1978), 58-70.

Galvão, H., *Beatitudo*, AL 1. 624-38.

Gannon, A., "The Active Theory of Sensation in St. Augustine," NS 30 (1956) 154-80.

Garvey, M. P., *St. Augustine: Christian or Neo-Platonist?*, Milwaukee, 1939.

——— *St. Augustine Against the Academicians*, Milwaukee, 1943.

Gavigan, J., "The Mother of St. Augustine", *Am. Eccl. Rev.*, 119, no. 4 (Oct. 1948), 254-80.

Ghéon, H., *Secrets of the Saints*, (tr.) F. Sheed and D. Atwater, Garden City, NY, 1963.

Gibb, J. and Montgomery, W. (eds.), *The Confessions of St. Augustine*, Cambridge, 1927.

Gilson, E., *The Spirit of Medieval Philosophy*, (tr.) A. Downes, New York, 1936.

——— *The Unity of Philosophical Experience*, New York, 1937.

——— *History of Christian Philosophy in the Middle Ages*, New York, 1954.

——— *The Christian Philosophy of St. Augustine*, (tr.) L. Lynch, New York, 1960.

——— "Égypt où Grèce", *Medieval Studies* 8 (1946), 43-52.

Ginsberg M., *On the Diversity of Morals*, London, 1953.

Gisquière, E., *Deus Dominus*, t. 2, Paris, 1950.

Grabowski, S., *The All-Present God*, St. Louis, 1954.

—— *The Church*, St. Louis, 1957.

Green, W., *Initium omnis peccati superbia: Augustine on Pride as the First Sin*, Univ. of Cal. Publications in Class. Philol. 13, Berkely, 1949, 407-31.

Grotz, K., *Die Einheit der "Confessiones". Warum bringt Augustinus in letzen drei Büchern seiner "Confessiones" eine Auslegung der Genesis?*, Tübingen, 1970.

Guibert, J. de, *The Theology of the Spiritual Life*, (tr.) P Barrett, London, 1954.

Guitton, J., *Le temps et l'éternité selon Plotin et saint Augustin*, Paris, 1933.

Gwynn, A., *Roman Education from Cicero to Quintilian*, Oxford, 1926.

Hagendahl, H., *Augustine and the Latin Classics*, 2 vols., Göteberg, 1967.

Harrison, C., *Beauty and Revelation in the Thought of St. Augustine*, Oxford, 1992.

—— "Not Words but Things. Harmonious Diversity in the Four Gospels", in *Augustine: Biblical Exegete*, CollAug, (ed.) F. Van Fleteren and J. Schnaubelt, New York, 1999, 169-201.

Hartshorne, C., *The Divine Relativity*, New Haven, 1948.

Harvey, J., *Moral Theology of the Confessions of St. Augustine*, Washington, D.C., 1951

Hebgin, S. and Corrigan, F., *St. Augustine on the Psalms*, (trans. and notes), Ps 1-29, 30-7, 2 vols., New York, 1960-1.

Hendriks, E., *Augustins Verhaltnis Zur Mystik*, Würzburg, 1936.

—— "Introduction", *La trinité 1*, BA 15, Paris, 1997.

Henry, P., *Plotin et l'Occident*, Louvain, 1934.

—— *La vision d' Ostie*, Paris, 1938.

Hick, J., *Evil and the God of Love*, London, 1977.

Holte, R., *Béatitude et sagesse*, Paris 1962.

Jackson, B.D., "The Theory of Signs in St. Augustine's *De Doctrina Christiana*", in R. Markus (ed.), *Augustine: A Collection of Critical Essays*, Garden City, NY, 1972, 92-147.

James, W., *The Principles of Psychology*, 2 vols., Boston, 1890.

Johnson, P., *Modern Times*, New York, 1984.

—— *Intellectuals*, New York, 1988.

Jolivet, R., and M. Jourjon, *Six traités anti-manichéens*, BA 17, Paris,1961.

Joly, R., "Curiositas", *L'antique classique*, 30 (Louvain, 1961).

Journet, C., *The Meaning of Evil*, (tr.) M. Barry, New York, 1963.

Kant, I., *Kritik der reinen Vernunft*, Leipzig, 1922.

Kato, T., "Melodia interior: sur le traité *De pulchro et apto*", REA 12 (1966), 229-40.

Kavanagh, D., *Answer to Skeptics (Contra Academicos)*, New York 1943.

Kevane, E., *Augustine the Educator*, Westminster, MD, 1964.

Kienzler, K., "Die unbegreifliche Wirklichkeit der menschilchen Sehnsuch nach Gott", CAH, 61-105.

Klauser, T., *A Short History of the Western Liturgy*, (tr.) J. Halliburton, New York 1979.

Knauer, G., *Psalmenzitäte in Augustins Konfessionem*, Gottingen, 1955.

—— *"Peregrinatio animae"*, *Hermes 85* (1957), 216-48.

Knight, W. Jackson, *St. Augustine's De Musica A Synopsis*, London 1949.

Knox, R., *Enthusiasm*, Oxford, 1950.

Kolin. A., *Physics*, New York, 1950.

Kondoleon, T., "Augustine's Argument for God's Existence *De Libero Arbitrio*, Book II," AS 14(1983), 105-15.

La Bonnardière, A., "En marge de la 'Biblia Augustiniana': une 'retractatio'", REA 10 (1964), 305-7.

Labriolle, P. de, *Saint Augustine. Confessions*, (ed. and trans.), Paris, 1925.

Lactantius, *De ira Dei*, ML 7.121A.

Ladner, G., *The Idea of Reform*, Cambridge, MA, 1959.

Landsberg, P., "La conversion de saint Augustin", Supplément à *La vie spirituelle*, 1936, 31-6.

Langer, S., *Philosophy in a New Key*, 3rd ed., Cambridge, MA 1959.

Laplace, P., *A Philosophical Essays on Probabilities*, (tr.) F. Truscott and F. Emory, New York, 1902.

Lawless, G., "Interior Peace in the Confessions of S. Augustine", REA 26 (1980), 45-61.

––––– *Augustine of Hippo and His Monastic Rule*, Oxford, 1987.

––––– "St. Augustine and His Critics", in *Augustine Presbyter Factus Sum*, CollAug, (ed.) J. Lienhard, E. Mullen, and R. Teske, New York, 1993, 3-28.

Le Blond, J.-M., *Les conversions de saint Augustin*, Paris 1950.

Legewie, B., "Die körperliche Konstitution und die Krankheiten des Augustins," *Miscellanea Agostiniana*, 2, Rome, 1931, 5-21.

Lienhard, J., "Friendship with God, Friendship in God", in Augustine, *Mystic and Mystagogue*, CollAug, (ed.) F. Van Fleteren and J. Schnaubelt, New York 1994, 207-29.

––––– "Ministry", AE 567-9.

Lieu, S., *Manicheism*, Dover, NH, 1985.

––––– *Manicheism in Mesopotamia and the Roman East*, New York 1994.

Lindsay, J., *Origins of Astrology*, Barnes and Noble reprint, New York, 1971.

Long, A., *Hellenistic Philosophy*, London 1974.

Lovejoy, A., *The Great Chain of Being*, Cambridge MA, 1936.

Luis, P. de, *Las Confesiones de San Agustin Commentadas* (Libros 1-10), Valladolid, 1994.

Luneau, A., *L'histoire du salut chez les Pères de l'Église*, Paris 1964.

Madec, G., "Connaisance de Dieu et action de grâces", RA 2 (1968), 233-309.

––––– "La déliverance de l'esprit (*Confessions VII*)", LASAP Libri VI-IX, 45-69.

––––– "Diagramme augustinien", AUG 25 (August, 1985), 79-94.

—— *Dialogues Philosophiques III*, BAC, Paris, 1976

—— "Adeodatus", AL 1. 87-90.

——"Christus," AL 1. 845-907.

Mager, C., "Conscientia", AL 1.1218-28.

Malebranche, N., *Recherche de la vérité*, (ed.) G. Rodin-Lewis, Paris, 1964.

Mallard,W., "The Incarnation in Augustine's Conversion", RA 15(1980), 80-98.

Mandouze, A., *Prosopographie de l' Afrique chrétienne* (303-353), Paris, 1982.

—— "Où en la question de la mystique Augustinienne?", AM 3.103-63.

—— "L'extase d'Ostie", AM 1.67-84.

—— *Saint Augustin: L'aventure de la raison et la grâce*, Paris, 1968.

—— "Le Livre V des Confessions de Saint Augustin", LASAP, Libri III-V,39-55.

Mara, M., "St. Ambrose of Milan", *Patrology IV*, 144-80.

Markus, R., "St. Augustine on Signs", in *Augustine A Collection of Critical Essays*, (ed.) R. Markus, Garden City, NY, 1972 61-91.

Marrou, H-I., *Saint Augustin et la fin de la culture antique*, Paris, 1938, and "*Retractatio*", Paris 1949.

—— *A History of Education in Antiquity*, (tr.) G. Lamb, London, 1956.

—— *L'ambivalence du temps du histoire chez saint Augustin*, Montreal, 1950.

—— *Théologie de l'histoire*, Paris, 1968.

Matter, E., "Women", AE 887-92.

Maxsein, A., "Philosophia cordis bei Augustinus", AM 1.357-71.

—— "Das Herz in der Erkenntnis bei hl. Augustinus", AUGUS 3, (1958), 323-30.

McEvoy, J., "*Anima una et cor unum*. Friendship and Spiritual Unity in Augustine," *Recherches de théologie ancienne et mediévale*, 53 (1986), 40-92.

McIntosh C., *The Astrologers and Their Creed: An Historical Outline*, London, 1960.

McKenzie, J., *A Dictionary of the Bible*, Milwaukee, 1965.

McNamara, M., *Friends and Friendship for Saint Augustine*, New York, 1964.

McWilliam, J., *Augustine: From Rhetor to Theologian*, Waterloo, Ontario, 1992.

——— "Academicos Contra", AE 2-4.
——— "Cassiciacum Dialogues", AE 135-8.

Meijering, E., *Augustin über Schöpfung, Ewigkeit und Zeit. Das Elfte Buch der Bekenntnisse*, Leiden, 1979.

Mellet, M. and Camelot, J. *La Trinité*, I-VIII, BA 15, Paris, 1997.

Moriones, F. (ed.), *Enchiridion Theologicum Sancti Augustini*, Madrid, 1961.

Mosher, D., "The Argument of St. Augustine's *Contra Academicos*", AS 12(1981), 89-113.

Mourant, J., "St. Augustine and the Academics", RA 4(1966), 67-96.

——— *Immortality in St. Augustine*, Villanova, PA, 1969.

——— "Ostia Reexamined: A Study of the Concept of Mystical Experience", *Intern. Journ. for Phil. of Religion*, 1(1970), 34-45.

——— *St. Augustine on Memory*, Villanova, PA, 1980.

Nash, R., *The Light of the Mind*, Lexington, KY, 1969.

——— "Some Philosophical Sources of Augustine's Illumination Theory", AS 2(1971), 47-66.

Nietzsche, F., "Brief an Franz Overbeck in Basel vom 31 Marz 1885," *Samtliche Briefe, Kritische Studienausgabe*, Band 7, 33-5, (ed.) G. Colli and M. Mortinari, Berlin, 1986.

O'Connell, R., *St. Augustine's Early Theory of Man, A.D. 386-391*, Cambridge MA, 1968.

——— *St. Augustine's Confessions: The Odyssey of Soul*, Cambridge MA, 1968.

——— *Art and the Christian Intelligence in St. Augustine*, Cambridge, MA, 1968.

O'Daly, G., "Did St. Augustine Ever Believe in the Soul's Preexistence?," AS 5(1974), 227-35.

—— "Time as *distentio* and St. Augustine's Exegesis of Philippians 3, 12-14", REA 23(1977), 265-71.

—— "Augustine on the Measurement of Time: Some Comparisons with Aristotelian and Stoic Texts", *Neoplatonism and Early Christian Thought*, (ed.) H. Blumenthal and R. Markus, London, 1981, 171-9.
—— *Augustine's Philosophy of Mind*, Berkeley, CA, 1987.

—— "Anima, Animus", AL 1.316.

—— "Cassiciacum", AL 1.272-4.

—— "Remembering and Forgetting in Augustine, *Confessions X*," *Memoria-Vergessen und Erinnern*, (ed.) A. Hauerkamp, R. Lachmana, and R. Herzog, Munich, 1993, 31-46.

O'Donnell, J., *Augustine*, Boston, 1977.

—— "Augustine's Classical Readings", RA 15 (1980), 144-75.

—— *Augustine Confessions*, 3 vols. (text and commmentary), Oxford, 1992.

——"Evodius of Uzalis", AE 344.

O'Donovan, O., *The Problem of Self-Love in St. Augustine*, New Haven 1980.

O'Meara, J., "*Arripui, aperui, et legi*", AM 1.59-65.

—— *St. Augustine Against the Academics*, New York, 1951.

—— *The Young Augustine*, New York, 1954, 1980 (2nd ed.).

—— "Augustine and Neoplatonism", RA 1(1958), 91-111.

—— "Research Techniques in Augustinian Studies", AS 1(1970), 277-84.

—— "The Neoplatonism of St. Augustine", in *Neoplatonism and Christian Thought*, (ed.) D. O'Meara, New York, 1982, 34-41, 233-4.

—— "Augustine's Confessions: Elements of Fiction", in *Augustine: From Rhetor to Theologian*, (ed.) J. McWilliam, 77-95.

O'Toole, C., *The Philosophy of Creation in the Writings of St. Augustine*, Washington, D.C., 1944.

Outler, A., "The Person and Work of Christ", in Battenhouse, *A Companion to the Study of St. Augustine*, 343-70.

Pelland, C., *Cinq études de saint Augustin sur le début de Génèse*, Paris, 1972.

Pellegrino, M., *Le 'Confessioni' di Sant' Agostino*, Rome, 1956.

―――― *The True Priest*, (tr.) A. Gibson, Villanova, PA, 1988.

Pépin, J., *Saint Augustin et la dialectique*, Villanova, PA, 1976.

Perkins, R. (ed.), *Kierkegaard's Fear and Trembling: Critical Essays*, University, Alabama, 1987.

Perler, O., *Les voyages de saint Augustin*, Paris, 1969.

Peters, E., "Aenigma Salomonis: Manichean Anti-Genesis Polemics and the Vitium Curiositatis in Confessions III", AUG(L) 38 (1986), 48-64.

Plato, *Collected Works*, (tr.) B. Jowett, Oxford, 1892.

Pfligersdorfer, G., "Augustins 'Confessiones' und die Arten der Confessio" in *Augustino Praeceptori*, Salzburg, 1987, 59-77.

Plotinus, *Enneads*, (tr.) A. Armstrong, 7 vols., Cambridge, MA, 1966-1988.

Pontet, M., *L'éxegèse de s. Augustin prédicateur*, Paris (n.d.).

Popazoglou, O., "Despising Our Mothers, Despising Ourselves," *First Things*, January, 1992, 11-9.

Podmore, F. *Mediums of the Nineteenth Century*, London, 1902.

Pope, H. *St. Augustine of Hippo*, London, 1937.

Poque, S., "Au sujet d'une singularité romaine de la 'Redditio Symboli'", AUG 25 (1985), 133-43.

Portalié, E., *A Guide to the Thought of St. Augustine*, (tr.) R. Bastian, Westport, CT., 1975.

Possidio, *Vita di S. Agostino*, (tr.) M. Pellegrino, Alba, Ediz. Paoline, 1955.

Poulain, A., *The Graces of Interior Prayer*, 6th ed., (tr.) L. Smith, London, 1911.

Puech, H., *Le Manichéisme: son fondateur, sa doctrine*, Paris, 1949.

Quinn, J. M., *The Concept of Time in St. Augustine,* Studia Ephemeridis Augustinianium, no. 5, Patristic Institute, Rome, 1965.

—— "Some Reflections on Praise in St. Augustine", in *Searching for God, Rome,* 1985, 57-91.

—— *Praise in St. Augustine: Readings and Reflections,* Norwell, MA., 1987.

—— "Anti-Manichean and Other Moral Precisions in *Confessions* 3.7.12-9.17", AS 19(1988), 165-94.

—— "Four Faces of Time in St. Augustine", RA 26(1992), 181-231.

—— "Triune Self-Giving: One Key to the Problem of Suffering", *The Thomist,* 44(April, 1980), 173-218.

Ramirez, J., "The Priority of Reason over Faith in St. Augustine", AS 13(1982), 123-31.

Ramsey, P., *Deeds and Rules in Christian Ethics,* New York, 1965.

Raphael, B., *The Anatomy of Bereavement,* New York, 1984

Ratzinger, J., "Originalität und Überlieferung in Augusins Begriff der 'confessio'", REA 3(1957), 385-92.

Reta Oroz, J., "Conversion", AE 239-42.

Richardson, C., "The Enigma of the Trinity", in Battenhouse, *A Companion to the Study of St. Augustine,* 235-56.

Ries, J., "Saint Augustin et le Manichéisme à la lumière du Livre III des *Confessions*", LASAP, Libri III-V, 7-26.

Rigby, P., *Original Sin in Augustine's Confessions,* Ottawa, 1987.

Rinetti, P., "Sant' Agustino e *l'Ecclesia Mater,*" AM 2.691-201.

Ring, T., *An Simplicianus zwei Bücher über verscheidene Fragen,* Würzburg, 1996.

Rist, J., *Augustine,* New York, 1994.

Roche, W., "Measure, Number, and Weight in Saint Augustine", NS 15(1941) 350-76.

Rodriguez, D. , "El libro VI de *Las Confesiones,* LASAP, Libri VI-IX, 9-44.

Rondet, H., "Le Symbolisme de la mer chez saint Augustin", AM 2.827-34.

Ross, W., *Aristotle's Physics*, Oxford, 1936.

Russell, B., *A History of Western Philosophy*, New York, 1945.

Russell, R., "Two Book Reviews," *Thought*, 44(1969). n. 173, 303-5.

—— *The Rule of Our Holy Father St. Augustine*, Villanova, PA, 1976.

—— "Man's Search for God in the *Confessions* of Saint Augustine", *Second Annual Course on Augustinian Spirituality*, Rome, 1976, 24-46.

——"The Role of Neoplatonism in St. Augustine's *De civitate Dei*," in Blumenthal, H., and Markus, R. (ed.), *Neoplatonism and Early Christian Thought*, London, 1981, 160-70.

Ryan, J.K., *The Confessions of St. Augustine*, (trans. with notes), Garden City, NY, 1960.

Sage, A., "Péché original: naissance d'un dogme", REA 13(1967), 11-46.

—— "Le péché original dans la pénsée de saint Augustin de 412 à 430", REA 15(1969), 75-112.

Salvian, *De gubernatione Dei*, 7. 13-8, *Salviani Presbyteri Massiliensis Opera quae supersunt*, (ed.) F. Pauly, CSEL, 8, Vienna, 1883.

Salway, P., *Roman Britain*, Cambridge, 1965.

Schacter, D., *Searching for Memory*, New York, 1996.

Schäffer, C., "Augustine on Mode, Form, and Natural Order", AS 31 (2000), 59-77.

Schilpp, P. (ed.), *The Philosophy of George Santayana*, LaSalle, Ill.., 1940.

Schindler, A., *Wort und Analogie in Augustins Trinitätslehre*, Tübingen, 1995.

Schumacher, W., *Spiritus and Spiritualis: A Study in the Sermons of St. Augustine*, Mundelein, IL, 1957.

Schützinger, C., *The German Controversy on Augustine's Illumination Theory*, New York, 1960.

Sherwin, M., " 'The friends of the bridegroom stand and listen'. An Analysis of the Term Amicus Sponsi", AUG 38 (June, 1998), 197-215.

Solignac, A., "Doxographies et manuels dans la formation philosophique de saint Augustin", RA 1(1958), 113-48.

——— *Les Confessions*, BA 13-4, Paris, 1962.

——— "Exégèse et Métaphysique Génèse 1, 1-3," *In Principio*, Paris, 1973, 153-71.

Sorabji, R., *Time, Creation and the Continuum*, Ithaca., NY., 1983.

Starnes, C., *Augustine's Conversion*, Waterloo, Ontario, 1990.

Steinhauer, K., "The Literary Unity of the Confessions," in J. McWilliam, (ed.) *Augustine: From Rhetor to Theologian*, 15-20.

Svoboda, K., *L'esthétique de saint Augustin et ses sources*, Brno, 1933.

Tanquerey, A., *The Spiritual Life*, 2nd ed., Tournai, 1930.

Taylor, J., *The Literal Meaning of Genesis*, (trans. with notes), 2 vols., New York, 1982.

TeSelle, E., *Augustine the Theologian*, New York, 1970.

——— "Porphyry and Augustine", AS 5 (1974), 113-47.

——— *Augustine's Strategy as an Apologist*, Villanova, PA, 1974.

Teske, R., "The World-Soul and Time in St. Augustine", AS 14(1983), 75-92.

——— "*Vocans Temporales, Faciens Aeternos:* St. Augustine on Liberation from Time", *Traditio 41* (1985), 29-47.

——— "The Aim of Augustine's Proof 'That God Truly Is' ", *Intern. Phil. Quar.* 26(1986), 253-68.

——— *Paradoxes of Time in Saint Augustine*, Milwaukee, 1996.

——— "Genesis Accounts of Creation", AE 329-81.

Testard, M., *Saint Augustin et Cicéron*, 2 vols., Paris, 1958.

Tester, J., *A History of Western Astrology*, Suffolk, 1987.

Thurston, H., *The Church and Spiritualism*, Milwaukee, 1933.

Trapé, A., "St. Augustine", *Patrology IV*, 342-462.

Thomas Aquinas, St., *Summa theologiae*, Madrid, 1961.

—— *In Octo Libros Physicorum Aristotelis Expositio*, (ed.) P. Maggiolo, Rome, 1954.

Underhill, E., *Mysticism*, 12th ed., New York, 1930.

—— *The Mystics of the Church*, London, 1925.

van Bavel, T., *Recherches sur la Christologie de saint Augustin*, Fribourg, 1954.

—— "L'humanité du Christ comme lac parvulorum et comme via dans la spiritualité de saint Augustin", AUG(L) 7(1957), 248-81.

—— "God inbetween Affirmation and Negation according to Augustine", *Augustine Presbyter Factus Sum*, CollAug., 1993, 75-97.

—— "Augustine's View on Women", AUG(L), 39 (1989), 5-53.

—— "The Creator and the Integrity of Creation in the Fathers of the Church, especially in St. Augustine", AS 21(1990), 1-34.

—— "Discipline", AE 273-6.

—— "Love" AE 509-16.

Van der Meer, F., *Augustine the Bishop*, (tr.) B. Battershaw and G. Lamb, New York, 1961.

Van Fleteren, F., "Ascent of the Soul in Book VII of the Confessions: A Reconsideration", AS 5(1974), 29-72.

—— "The Cassiciacum Dialogues and Augustine's Ascents at Milan", *Medeaevalia* 1978, 59-82.

—— "Mysticism in the Confessions–A Controversy Revisited", *Mystic and Mystagogue*, 309-86.

—— "Angels", AE 20-2.

—— "Confessiones" AE 227-32.

—— "Matter" AE 747-9.

Van Lierde, C., "The Teachings of St. Augustine on the Gifts of the Holy Spirit from the Text of Isaiah 11.2-3," *Mystic and Mystagogue*, CollAug, (ed.) F. Van Fleteren and J. Schnaubelt, New York, 1994, 6-110.

Vecchi, A.,"L'Antimanicheismo nelle Confessioni di sant' Agustino", GM 20(1965), 94-120.

Verheijen, L., *St. Augustine: Monk Priest Bishop*, Villanova, PA, 1987.

——— *Nouvelle Approche de la Régle de saint Augustin*, Abbaye de Bellefontaine, 1980.

Vega, A. C., *Confessiones*, Madrid, 1946.

Vivas, E., *The Moral Life and the Ethical Life*, Chicago, 1951.

Von Jess, W. G., "Divine Eternity in the Doctrine of St. Augustine", AS 6(1975), 75-96.

Voss, B., "Academicis(De)", AL 1.45-51.

Weaver, F., and Laporte J., "Augustine and Woman: Relationships and Teachings", AS 12(1981), 112-52.

Weismann, W,. "Amphitheatrum", AL 1. 300-3.

Whale, J., *Christian Doctrine*, Cambridge, 1941

Wermingler, O., "Abortus", AL 1. 6-10.

Whitehead, A. N., *Process and Reality*, New York, 1929.

Wild, J., *Plato's Theory of Man*, Boston, 1974.

Wills, G., *Saint Augustine*, New York, 1999.

Williams, R., "Creation", AE 251-4.

——— " 'Good for Nothing?' Augustine on Creation", AS 25(1994), 9-24.

Zumkeller, A., *Augustine's Ideal of the Religious Life*, (tr.) E. Colledge, New York, 1986.

——— *Augustine's Rule: A Commentary*, (tr.) M. O'Connell, Villanova, PA., 1987.

——— "Consuetudo", AL 1.253-6.

Index

Ayres, L., 63 n. 12, 70 n. 30

Babylon, 90-1

Baguette, Ch., 407 n. 4

Balter, M., 289 n. 23

Baptism
    deferred, 41;
    of friend, 209;
    symbolized by creeping creatures
    of sea, 833

Barbarism, 53-4

Barclay, W., 185 n. 38

Bardy, G., 531 n. 57

Barnes, M., 63 n. 12

Baronius Card., 653 n. 10

Basevi, C., 801, n. 34

Basil, St., 419 n. 75

Bassus, A., 533 n. 78

Beardsley, M., 659 n. 71

Beare, J., 118 n. 11

Beatitude, 665

Beautiful and Fitting, The, 225-7

Beautiful, overlaps with good, 94

Beauty, 99-100;
    rules of, 621

Beierwaltes, W., 657 n. 57

Beings of reason, 656-7 n. 51

Bellarmine, R., 533 n. 75

Bergson, H., 733, 748-9 n. 83

Berrouard, M-F., 469 n. 11

Bertrand, L., 336 n. 56

Bible, Churchly, 307

Birds,
    figures of apostles, 843;
    flight of, explained by Bernouilli
    effect, 917-8 n. 114

Bishop,
    role of, 177-8, 191 n. 67;
    rank of, not honor but onus, 545

Blaiklock, E., 13 n. 36

Blanshard, B., 184 n. 34, 247 n. 23

Blessedness, two stages of, 483

Blindness,
    moral, 667;
    Manichean, 667

Bochet, I., 75 n. 52, 661 n. 83

Böhmer, H., 2, 10 n. 7

Boissier, G., 7, 11 n. 21, 13 n. 34, 36

Bonner, G., 74 n. 49, 245 n. 7, 252
    n. 59, 416 n. 61, 468 n. 8, 652 n.
    1, 662 n. 93, 916 n. 105, 920 n.
    126

Bossanich, J., 657 n. 57

Bourke, V., 70 n. 30, 182 n.21, 409
    n. 20, 526 n. 17, 527 n. 38, 656 n.
    50, 736 n. 12, 745 n. 66

Deification of man, qualitative, 854-5

De Margerie, B.,793-4, 799 n. 22,
801 n. 32

Descartes, R., 302, 331 n.14

Devil, 402, 403;
false mediator, 645;
a kind of living lie, 660 n. 82

Dew, does not fall from
atmosphere, 917 n. 113

Dewey, J., 242

Di Berardino, A., 526 n. 14

Di Capua, F., 532 n. 65

Dialectic, method of, 658 n. 59

Dido, false compassion for, 44-5

Difficulty in determining proper
amount of food, 610;
difficult to live without praise,
631-2;
difficulty of bishop's work, 333 n.
34

Disagreement, two kinds of, 776-7

Discipline, 499

Dishonor in honorable studies, 129

Distension,
equivocal term, 723;
as distraction and disorder, 723;
various meanings, 746 n. 73;
volitional, 470 n. 23

Divine art, 250 n. 50

Divine light, source of human light,

233-4

DNA, 65-6 n. 21

Docetism, 194

Drunkenness, moral, 315

Du Roy, O., 186 n. 45, 413 n. 50,
414 n. 55

Dudden, F., 528 n. 42, 652 n. 1

Duns Scotus, 12 n. 32

Earth,
various meanings, 752-3;
as formless matter,753;
visible formed from invisible,
758-9

Eborowitz,C., 530 n. 56

Eclipses foretold, 257-8

Eddy, M. B., 417 n. 69

Egyptians, exploitation of, 169-70,
364-6

Elpidius, 279, 285

Empedocles, 677

Enneads, 360, 361

Eno, R., 332 n. 21

Envy, 105

Epaphroditus, 868

Epicurus, 328-30;

Epoché,
suspense of judgment, 275;